Microsoft® Office Excel® Functions

Function	Description
AVERAGE	Returns the arithmetic mean of a range its arguments.
BINOM.DIST	Returns the individual term binomial distribution probability.
CHISQ.DIST	Returns a probability from the chi-squared distribution.
CHISQ.DIST.RT	Returns the one-tailed probability of the chi-squared distribution.
CHISQ.INV	Returns the inverse of the left-tailed probability of the chi-squared distribution.
CHISQ.TEST	Returns the value from the chi-squared distribution for the statistic and the degrees of freedom.
CONFIDENCE.NORM	Returns the confidence interval for a population mean using the normal distribution.
CORREL	Returns the correlation coefficient between two data sets.
COUNT	Returns the number of cells in the range that contain numbers.
COUNTA	Returns the number of non-blank cells in the range.
COUNTIF	Returns the number of cells in a range that meet the specified criterion.
COVARIANCE.S	Returns the sample covariance.
EXPON.DIST	Returns a probability from the exponential distribution.
F.DIST.RT	Returns the right-tailed probability from the F distribution.
GEOMEAN	Returns the geometric mean of a range of cells.
HYPGEOM.DIST	Returns a probability from the hypergeometric distribution.
MAX	Returns the maximum value of the values in a range of cells.
MMEDIAN	Returns the median value of the values in a range of cells.
MIN	Returns the minimum value of the values in a range of cells.
MODE.SNGL	Returns the most-frequently occurring value in a range of cells.
NORM.S.DIST	Returns a probability from a standard normal distribution.
NORM.S.INV	Inverse of the standard normal distribution.
PERCENTILE.EXC	Returns the specified percentile of the values in a range of cells.
POISSON.DIST	Returns a probability from the poisson distribution.
POWER	Returns the result of a number raised to a power.
QUARTILE.EXC	Returns the specified quartile of the values in a range of cells.
RAND	Returns a real number from the uniform distribution between 0 and 1.
SQRT	Returns the positive square root of its argument.
STDEV.S	Returns the sample standard deviation of the values in a range of cells.
SUM	Returns the sum of the values in a range of cells.
SUMPRODUCT	Returns the sum of the products of the paired elements of the values in two ranges of cells.
T.DIST	Returns a left-tailed probability of the t distribution.
T.INV.2T	Returns the two-tailed inverse of the student's t-distribution.
VAR.S	Returns the sample variance of the values in a range of cells.

Essentials of Modern Business Statistics ^{7e}

with Microsoft® Office Excel®

David R. Anderson
University of Cincinnati

Dennis J. Sweeney
University of Cincinnati

Thomas A. Williams
**Rochester Institute
of Technology**

Jeffrey D. Camm
Wake Forest University

James J. Cochran
University of Alabama

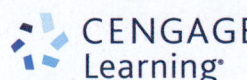

CENGAGE
Learning®

Australia • Brazil • Mexico • Singapore • United Kingdom • United States

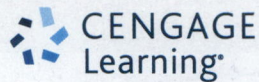

Essentials of Modern Business Statistics, Seventh Edition
David R. Anderson, Dennis J. Sweeney, Thomas A. Williams, Jeffrey D. Camm, James J. Cochran

Senior Vice President, General Manager, Social Science, Business and Humanities: Erin Joyner

Product Director: Michael Schenk

Product Team Manager: Joe Sabatino

Sr. Product Manager: Aaron Arnsparger

Content Developer: Anne Merrill

Product Assistant: Renee Schnee

Digital Content Designer: Brandon Foltz

Sr. Marketing Manager: Nathan Anderson

Sr. Content Project Manager: Colleen Farmer

Manufacturing Planner: Ron Montgomery

Production Service: MPS Limited

Sr. Art Director: Michelle Kunkler

Internal Designer: Beckmeyer Design

Cover Designer: Beckmeyer Design

Cover Image: Spectral-Design/ Shutterstock.com

Intellectual Property:
Analyst: Brittani Morgan
Project Manager: Nicholas Barrows

For product information and technology assistance, contact us at **Cengage Learning Customer & Sales Support, 1-800-354-9706**

For permission to use material from this text or product, submit all requests online at **www.cengage.com/permissions**
Further permissions questions can be emailed to **permissionrequest@cengage.com**

Microsoft Excel® is a registered trademark of Microsoft Corporation. © 2016 Microsoft.

Unless otherwise noted, all items © Cengage Learning.

Library of Congress Control Number: 2017930365

Package ISBN: 978-1-337-29829-2

Book only ISBN: 978-1-337-29835-3

Cengage Learning
20 Channel Center Street
Boston, MA 02210
USA

Cengage Learning is a leading provider of customized learning solutions with employees residing in nearly 40 different countries and sales in more than 125 countries around the world. Find your local representative at **www.cengage.com**.

Cengage Learning products are represented in Canada by Nelson Education, Ltd.

To learn more about Cengage Learning Solutions, visit **www.cengage.com**

Purchase any of our products at your local college store or at our preferred online store **www.cengagebrain.com**

Printed in the United States of America
Print Number: 01   Print Year: 2017

Brief Contents

Contents

Chapter 2 Descriptive Statistics: Tabular and Graphical Displays 35

Chapter 3 Descriptive Statistics: Numerical Measures 108

Chapter 4   Introduction to Probability   180

Chapter 5   Discrete Probability Distributions   228

Chapter 6   Continuous Probability Distributions   285

Chapter 8   Interval Estimation   363

Chapter 9   Hypothesis Tests   405

Chapter 10   Inference About Means and Proportions with Two Populations   455

This text is the seventh edition of *Essentials of Modern Business Statistics with Microsoft® Office Excel®*. With this edition we welcome two eminent scholars to our author team: Jeffrey D. Camm of Wake Forest University and James J. Cochran of the University of Alabama. Both Jeff and Jim are accomplished teachers, researchers, and practitioners in the fields of statistics and business analytics. Jim is a fellow of the American Statistical Association. You can read more about their accomplishments in the About the Authors section that follows this preface. We believe that the addition of Jeff and Jim as our coauthors will both maintain and improve the effectiveness of *Essentials of Modern Business Statistics with Microsoft Office Excel*.

The purpose of *Essentials of Modern Business Statistics with Microsoft® Office Excel®* is to give students, primarily those in the fields of business administration and economics, a conceptual introduction to the field of statistics and its many applications. The text is applications oriented and written with the needs of the nonmathematician in mind; the mathematical prerequisite is knowledge of algebra.

Applications of data analysis and statistical methodology are an integral part of the organization and presentation of the text material. The discussion and development of each technique is presented in an applications setting, with the statistical results providing insights for decision making and solutions to applied problems.

Although the book is applications oriented, we have taken care to provide sound methodological development and to use notation that is generally accepted for the topic being covered. Hence, students will find that this text provides good preparation for the study of more advanced statistical material. A bibliography to guide further study is included as an appendix.

Use of Microsoft Excel for Statistical Analysis

Essentials of Modern Business Statistics with Microsoft® Office Excel® is first and foremost a statistics textbook that emphasizes statistical concepts and applications. But since most practical problems are too large to be solved using hand calculations, some type of statistical software package is required to solve these problems. There are several excellent statistical packages available today; however, because most students and potential employers value spreadsheet experience, many schools now use a spreadsheet package in their statistics courses. Microsoft Excel is the most widely used spreadsheet package in business as well as in colleges and universities. We have written *Essentials of Modern Business Statistics with Microsoft® Office Excel®* especially for statistics courses in which Microsoft Excel is used as the software package.

Excel has been integrated within each of the chapters and plays an integral part in providing an application orientation. Although we assume that readers using this text are familiar with Excel basics such as selecting cells, entering formulas, copying, and so on, we do not assume that readers are familiar with Excel 2016 or Excel's tools for statistical analysis. As a result, we have included Appendix E, which provides an introduction to Excel 2016 and tools for statistical analysis.

Throughout the text the discussion of using Excel to perform a statistical procedure appears in a subsection immediately following the discussion of the statistical procedure. We believe that this style enables us to fully integrate the use of Excel throughout the text, but still maintain the primary emphasis on the statistical methodology being discussed. In each of these subsections, we provide a standard format for using Excel for statistical analysis. There are four primary tasks: Enter/Access Data, Enter Functions and Formulas, Apply Tools, and Editing Options. The Editing Options task is new with this edition. It primarily involves how to edit Excel output so that it is more suitable for presentations to users. We believe a consistent framework for applying Excel helps users to focus on the statistical methodology without getting bogged down in the details of using Excel.

In presenting worksheet figures, we often use a nested approach in which the worksheet shown in the background of the figure displays the formulas and the worksheet shown in the foreground shows the values computed using the formulas. Different colors and shades of colors are used to differentiate worksheet cells containing data, highlight cells containing Excel functions and formulas, and highlight material printed by Excel as a result of using one or more data analysis tools.

Changes in the Seventh Edition

We appreciate the acceptance and positive response to the previous editions of *Essentials of Modern Business Statistics with Microsoft® Office Excel®*. Accordingly, in making modifications for this new edition, we have maintained the presentation style and readability of those editions. The significant changes in the new edition are summarized here.

Users of the previous edition will notice that the chapters offered and topics covered in this edition differ from previous editions. While the topical coverage of the first nine chapters remains the same, the organization and coverage in some of the later chapters have expanded. We have eliminated the coverage of the advanced topic of Time Series and Quality Control in favor of the expanded coverage in Chapters 10, 11, 12 and 13. Chapter 10 now provides coverage of inferences of means and proportions for two populations, and chapter 11 is focused on inferences about population variances. Chapter 12 is a discussion of comparing multiple proportions, tests of independence and goodness of fit and chapter 13 covers experimental design and ANOVA. We believe you will find the expanded coverage in these chapters useful in your classes. Coverage of regression is now in chapters 14 and 15. These two chapters are revisions of the regression chapters from the 6th edition. In additions to these changes, we made the following revisions:

- **Microsoft Excel 2016.** Step-by-step instructions and screen captures show how to use the latest version of Excel to implement statistical procedures.
- **Data and Statistics—Chapter 1.** We have expanded our section on data mining to include a discussion of big data. We have added a new section on analytics. We have also placed greater emphasis on the distinction between observed and experimental data.
- **Descriptive Statistics: Tabular and Graphical Displays—Chapter 2.** Microsoft Excel now has the capability of creating box plots and comparative box plots. We have added to this chapter instruction on how to use this very useful new feature.
- **Interval Estimation—Chapter 8.** We have added a new section on the implications of big data (large data sets) on the interpretation of confidence intervals and importantly, the difference between statistical and practical significance.
- **Hypothesis Tests—Chapter 9.** Similar to our addition to Chapter 8, we have added a new section on the implications of big data (large data sets) on the interpretation of hypothesis tests and the difference between statistical and practical significance.
- **Simple Linear Regression—Chapter 14.** Similar to our addition to Chapter 8, we have added a new section on the implications of big data (large data sets) on

the interpretation of hypothesis tests in simple linear regression and the difference between statistical and practical significance.

- **New Case Problems.** We have added thirteen new case problems to this edition. The new case problems appear in the chapters on descriptive statistics and regression analysis. The case problems in the text provide students with the opportunity to analyze somewhat larger data sets and prepare managerial reports based on the results of their analysis.

- **New Examples and Exercises Based on Real Data.** We have added approximately 126 new examples and exercises based on real data and recently referenced sources of statistical information. Using data obtained from various data collection organizations, websites, and other sources such as *The Wall Street Journal*, *USA Today*, *Fortune*, and *Barron's*, we have drawn upon actual studies to develop explanations and to create exercises that demonstrate many uses of statistics in business and economics. We believe the use of real data helps generate more student interest in the material and enables the student to learn about both the statistical methodology and its application.

- **Updated and Improved End-of-Chapter Solutions and Solutions Manual.** Partnering with accomplished instructor Dawn Bulriss at Maricopa Community Colleges, we took a deep audit of the solutions manual. Every question and solution was reviewed and reworked, as necessary. The solutions now contain additional detail: improved rounding instructions; expanded explanations with a student-focus; and alternative answers using Excel and a statistical calculator. We believe this thorough review will enhance both the instructor and student learning experience in this digital age.

Features and Pedagogy

Authors Anderson, Sweeney, Williams, Camm, and Cochran have continued many of the features that appeared in previous editions.

Methods Exercises and Applications Exercises

The end-of-section exercises are split into two parts, Methods and Applications. The Methods exercises require students to use the formulas and make the necessary computations. The Applications exercises require students to use the chapter material in real-world situations. Thus, students first focus on the computational "nuts and bolts" and then move on to the subtleties of statistical application and interpretation.

Self-Test Exercises

Certain exercises are identified as self-test exercises. Completely worked-out solutions for those exercises are provided in Appendix D in the Student Resources online. Students can attempt the self-test exercises and immediately check the solution to evaluate their understanding of the concepts presented in the chapter.

Margin Annotations and Notes and Comments

Margin annotations that highlight key points and provide additional insights for the students are a key feature of this text. These annotations are designed to provide emphasis and enhance understanding of the terms and concepts being presented in the text.

At the end of many sections, we provide Notes and Comments designed to give the student additional insights about the statistical methodology and its application. Notes and Comments include warnings about or limitations of the methodology, recommendations for application, brief descriptions of additional technical considerations, and other matters.

Data Files Accompany the Text

Approximately 220 data files are available on the website that accompanies this text. The data sets are available in Excel 2016 format. DATAfile logos are used in the text to identify the data sets that are available on the website. Data sets for all case problems as well as data sets for larger exercises are included.

MindTap

MindTap, featuring all new Excel Online integration powered by Microsoft, is a complete digital solution for the business statistics course. It has enhancements that take students from learning basic statistical concepts to actively engaging in critical thinking applications, while learning valuable software skills for their future careers.

MindTap is a customizable digital course solution that includes an interactive eBook, autograded, algorithmic exercises from the textbook, Adaptive Test Prep, as well as interactive visualizations. All of these materials offer students better access to understand the materials within the course. For more information on MindTap, please contact your Cengage representative.

For Students

Online resources are available to help the student work more efficiently. The resources can be accessed through **www.cengagebrain.com**.

For Instructors

Instructor resources are available to adopters on the Instructor Companion Site, which can be found and accessed at **www.cengage.com**, including:

- **Solutions Manual:** The Solutions Manual, prepared by the authors, includes solutions for all problems in the text. It is available online as well as print.
- **Solutions to Case Problems:** These are also prepared by the authors and contain solutions to all case problems presented in the text.
- **PowerPoint Presentation Slides:** The presentation slides contain a teaching outline that incorporates figures to complement instructor lectures.
- **Test Bank:** Cengage Learning Testing Powered by Cognero is a flexible, online system that allows you to:
  - author, edit, and manage test bank content from multiple Cengage Learning solutions,
  - create multiple test versions in an instant, and
  - deliver tests from your LMS, your classroom, or wherever you want. The Test Bank is also available in Microsoft Word.

Acknowledgments

A special thanks goes to our associates from business and industry who supplied the Statistics in Practice features. We recognize them individually by a credit line in each of the articles. We are also indebted to our product manager, Aaron Arnsparger; our content developer, Anne Merrill; our content project manager, Colleen Farmer; our project manager at MPS Limited, Gaurav Prabhu; digital content designer, Brandon Foltz; and others at Cengage for their editorial counsel and support during the preparation of this text.

We would like to acknowledge the work of our reviewers, who provided comments and suggestions of ways to continue to improve our text. Thanks to:

James Bang, Virginia Military Institute
Robert J. Banis, University of Missouri–St. Louis
Timothy M. Bergquist, Northwest Christian College
Gary Black, University of Southern Indiana
William Bleuel, Pepperdine University
Derrick Boone, Wake Forest University
Lawrence J. Bos, Cornerstone University
Dawn Bulriss, Maricopa Community Colleges
Joseph Cavanaugh, Wright State University–Lake Campus
Sheng-Kai Chang, Wayne State University
Robert Christopherson, SUNY-Plattsburgh
Michael Clark, University of Baltimore
Robert D. Collins, Marquette University
Ivona Contardo, Stellenbosch University
Sean Eom, Southeast Missouri State University
Samo Ghosh, Albright College
Philip A. Gibbs, Washington & Lee University
Daniel L. Gilbert, Tennessee Wesleyan College
Michael Gorman, University of Dayton
Erick Hofacker, University of Wisconsin, River Falls
David Juriga, St. Louis Community College
William Kasperski, Madonna University
Kuldeep Kumar, Bond Business School
Tenpao Lee, Niagara University
Ying Liao, Meredith College
Daniel Light, Northwest State College
Ralph Maliszewski, Waynesburg University
Saverio Manago, Salem State University
Patricia A. Mullins, University of Wisconsin–Madison
Jack Muryn, Cardinal Stritch University
Anthony Narsing, Macon State College
Robert M. Nauss, University of Missouri–St. Louis
Elizabeth L. Rankin, Centenary College of Louisiana
Surekha Rao, Indiana University, Northwest
Jim Robison, Sonoma State University
Farhad Saboori, Albright College
Susan Sandblom, Scottsdale Community College
Ahmad Saranjam, Bridgewater State University
Jeff Sarbaum, University of North Carolina at Greensboro
Robert Scott, Monmouth University

Toni Somers, Wayne State University
Jordan H. Stein, University of Arizona
Bruce Thompson, Milwaukee School of Engineering
Ahmad Vessal, California State University, Northridge
Dave Vinson, Pellissippi State
Daniel B. Widdis, Naval Postgraduate School
Peter G. Wagner, University of Dayton
Sheng-Ping Yang, Black Hills State University

We would like to recognize the following individuals, who have helped us in the past and continue to influence our writing.

Glen Archibald, University of Mississippi
Darl Bien, University of Denver
Thomas W. Bolland, Ohio University
Mike Bourke, Houston Baptist University
Peter Bryant, University of Colorado
Terri L. Byczkowski, University of Cincinnati
Robert Carver, Stonehill College
Ying Chien, University of Scranton
Robert Cochran, University of Wyoming
Murray Côté, University of Florida
David W. Cravens, Texas Christian University
Eddine Dahel, Monterey Institute of International Studies
Tom Dahlstrom, Eastern College
Terry Dielman, Texas Christian University
Joan Donohue, University of South Carolina
Jianjun Du, University of Houston–Victoria
Thomas J. Dudley, Pepperdine University
Swarna Dutt, University of West Georgia
Ronald Ehresman, Baldwin-Wallace College
Mohammed A. El-Saidi, Ferris State University
Robert Escudero, Pepperdine University
Stacy Everly, Delaware County Community College
Soheila Kahkashan Fardanesh, Towson University
Nicholas Farnum, California State University–Fullerton
Abe Feinberg, California State University, Northridge
Michael Ford, Rochester Institute of Technology
Phil Fry, Boise State University
V. Daniel Guide, Duquesne University
Paul Guy, California State University–Chico
Charles Harrington, University of Southern Indiana
Carl H. Hess, Marymount University
Woodrow W. Hughes, Jr., Converse College
Alan Humphrey, University of Rhode Island
Ann Hussein, Philadelphia College of Textiles and Science
Ben Isselhardt, Rochester Institute of Technology
Jeffery Jarrett, University of Rhode Island
Barry Kadets, Bryant College
Homayoun Khamooshi, George Washington University
Kenneth Klassen, California State University Northridge
David Krueger, St. Cloud State University
June Lapidus, Roosevelt University

xxiii

Martin S. Levy, University of Cincinnati
Daniel M. Light, Northwest State College
Ka-sing Man, Georgetown University
Don Marx, University of Alaska, Anchorage
Tom McCullough, University of California–Berkeley
Timothy McDaniel, Buena Vista University
Mario Miranda, The Ohio State University
Barry J. Monk, Macon State College
Mitchell Muesham, Sam Houston State University
Richard O'Connell, Miami University of Ohio
Alan Olinsky, Bryant College
Lynne Pastor, Carnegie Mellon University
Von Roderick Plessner, Northwest State University
Robert D. Potter, University of Central Florida
Tom Pray, Rochester Institute of Technology
Harold Rahmlow, St. Joseph's University
Derrick Reagle, Fordham University
Avuthu Rami Reddy, University of Wisconsin–Platteville
Tom Ryan, Case Western Reserve University
Ahmad Saranjam, Bridgewater State College
Bill Seaver, University of Tennessee
Alan Smith, Robert Morris College
William Struning, Seton Hall University
Ahmad Syamil, Arkansas State University
David Tufte, University of New Orleans
Jack Vaughn, University of Texas–El Paso
Elizabeth Wark, Springfield College
Ari Wijetunga, Morehead State University
Nancy A. Williams, Loyola College in Maryland
J. E. Willis, Louisiana State University
Larry Woodward, University of Mary Hardin–Baylor
Mustafa Yilmaz, Northeastern University

David R. Anderson
Dennis J. Sweeney
Thomas A. Williams
Jeffrey D. Camm
James J. Cochran

CHAPTER 1

Data and Statistics

STATISTICS *in* PRACTICE

BLOOMBERG BUSINESSWEEK*
NEW YORK, NEW YORK

With a global circulation of more than 1 million, *Bloomberg Businessweek* is one of the most widely read business magazines in the world. Bloomberg's 1700 reporters in 145 service bureaus around the world enable *Bloomberg Businessweek* to deliver a variety of articles of interest to the global business and economic community. Along with feature articles on current topics, the magazine contains articles on international business, economic analysis, information processing, and science and technology. Information in the feature articles and the regular sections helps readers stay abreast of current developments and assess the impact of those developments on business and economic conditions.

Most issues of *Bloomberg Businessweek,* formerly *BusinessWeek,* provide an in-depth report on a topic of current interest. Often, the in-depth reports contain statistical facts and summaries that help the reader understand the business and economic information. Examples of articles and reports include the impact of businesses moving important work to cloud computing, the crisis facing the U.S. Postal Service, and why the debt crisis is even worse than we think. In addition, *Bloomberg Businessweek* provides a variety of statistics about the state of the economy, including production indexes, stock prices, mutual funds, and interest rates.

Bloomberg Businessweek also uses statistics and statistical information in managing its own business. For example, an annual survey of subscribers helps the company learn about subscriber demographics, reading habits, likely purchases, lifestyles, and so on. *Bloomberg Businessweek* managers use statistical summaries from the survey to provide better services to subscribers and advertisers. One recent North American subscriber

Bloomberg Businessweek uses statistical facts and summaries in many of its articles.

AP Photos/Weng lei - Imaginechina

survey indicated that 90% of *Bloomberg Businessweek* subscribers use a personal computer at home and that 64% of *Bloomberg Businessweek* subscribers are involved with computer purchases at work. Such statistics alert *Bloomberg Businessweek* managers to subscriber interest in articles about new developments in computers. The results of the subscriber survey are also made available to potential advertisers. The high percentage of subscribers using personal computers at home and the high percentage of subscribers involved with computer purchases at work would be an incentive for a computer manufacturer to consider advertising in *Bloomberg Businessweek.*

In this chapter, we discuss the types of data available for statistical analysis and describe how the data are obtained. We introduce descriptive statistics and statistical inference as ways of converting data into meaningful and easily interpreted statistical information.

*The authors are indebted to Charlene Trentham, Research Manager, for providing this Statistics in Practice.

Frequently, we see the following types of statements in newspapers and magazines:

- Uber Technologies Inc. is turning to the leveraged-loan market for the first time to raise as much as $2 billion, a sign of the popular ride-sharing network's hunger for cash as it expands around the world (*The Wall Street Journal*, June 14, 2016).
- Against the U.S. dollar, the euro has lost nearly 30% of its value in the last year; the Australian dollar lost almost 20% (*The Economist*, April 25th–May 1st, 2015).

- VW Group's U.S. sales continue to slide, with total sales off by 13% from last January, to 36,930 vehicles (*Panorama*, March 2014).
- A poll of 1320 corporate recruiters indicated that 68% of the recruiters ranked communication skills as one of the top five most important skills for new hires (*Bloomberg Businessweek* April 13–April 19, 2015).
- Green Mountain sold 18 billion coffee pods in two years (*Harvard Business Review*, January-February, 2016).
- Most homeowners spend between about $10,000 and roughly $27,000 converting a basement, depending on the size of the space, according to estimates from HomeAdvisor, a website that connects homeowners with prescreened service professionals (*Consumer Reports*, February 9, 2016).
- A full 88% of consumers say they buy private label, primarily because of price, according to Market Track (*USA Today*, May 17, 2016).

The numerical facts in the preceding statements—$2 billion, 30%, 20%, 13%, 36,930, 1320, 68%, 18 billion, $10,000, $27,000 and 88%—are called **statistics**. In this usage, the term statistics refers to numerical facts such as averages, medians, percentages, and maximums that help us understand a variety of business and economic situations. However, as you will see, the field, or subject, of statistics involves much more than numerical facts. In a broader sense, statistics is the art and science of collecting, analyzing, presenting, and interpreting data. Particularly in business and economics, the information provided by collecting, analyzing, presenting, and interpreting data gives managers and decision makers a better understanding of the business and economic environment and thus enables them to make more informed and better decisions. In this text, we emphasize the use of statistics for business and economic decision making.

Chapter 1 begins with some illustrations of the applications of statistics in business and economics. In Section 1.2 we define the term *data* and introduce the concept of a data set. This section also introduces key terms such as *variables* and *observations,* discusses the difference between quantitative and categorical data, and illustrates the uses of crosssectional and time series data. Section 1.3 discusses how data can be obtained from existing sources or through survey and experimental studies designed to obtain new data. The important role that the Internet now plays in obtaining data is also highlighted. The uses of data in developing descriptive statistics and in making statistical inferences are described in Sections 1.4 and 1.5. The last four sections of Chapter 1 provide the role of the computer in statistical analysis, an introduction to business analytics and the role statistics plays in it, an introduction to big data and data mining, and a discussion of ethical guidelines for statistical practice.

1.1 Applications in Business and Economics

In today's global business and economic environment, anyone can access vast amounts of statistical information. The most successful managers and decision makers understand the information and know how to use it effectively. In this section, we provide examples that illustrate some of the uses of statistics in business and economics.

Accounting

Public accounting firms use statistical sampling procedures when conducting audits for their clients. For instance, suppose an accounting firm wants to determine whether the amount of accounts receivable shown on a client's balance sheet fairly represents the actual amount of accounts receivable. Usually the large number of individual accounts receivable makes reviewing and validating every account too time-consuming and expensive. As common practice in such situations, the audit staff selects a subset of the accounts called a sample. After reviewing the accuracy of the sampled accounts, the auditors draw a conclusion as to whether the accounts receivable amount shown on the client's balance sheet is acceptable.

Finance

Financial analysts use a variety of statistical information to guide their investment recommendations. In the case of stocks, analysts review financial data such as price/earnings ratios and dividend yields. By comparing the information for an individual stock with information about the stock market averages, an analyst can begin to draw a conclusion as to whether the stock is a good investment. For example, *The Wall Street Journal* (February 27, 2016) reported that the average dividend yield for the S&P 500 companies was 2.3%. Microsoft showed a dividend yield of 2.61%. In this case, the statistical information on dividend yield indicates a higher dividend yield for Microsoft than the average dividend yield for the S&P 500 companies. This and other information about Microsoft would help the analyst make an informed buy, sell, or hold recommendation for Microsoft stock.

Marketing

Electronic scanners at retail checkout counters collect data for a variety of marketing research applications. For example, data suppliers such as ACNielsen and Information Resources, Inc. purchase point-of-sale scanner data from grocery stores, process the data, and then sell statistical summaries of the data to manufacturers. Manufacturers spend hundreds of thousands of dollars per product category to obtain this type of scanner data. Manufacturers also purchase data and statistical summaries on promotional activities such as special pricing and the use of in-store displays. Brand managers can review the scanner statistics and the promotional activity statistics to gain a better understanding of the relationship between promotional activities and sales. Such analyses often prove helpful in establishing future marketing strategies for the various products.

Production

Today's emphasis on quality makes quality control an important application of statistics in production. A variety of statistical quality control charts are used to monitor the output of a production process. In particular, an x-bar chart can be used to monitor the average output. Suppose, for example, that a machine fills containers with 12 ounces of a soft drink. Periodically, a production worker selects a sample of containers and computes the average number of ounces in the sample. This average, or x-bar value, is plotted on an x-bar chart. A plotted value above the chart's upper control limit indicates overfilling, and a plotted value below the chart's lower control limit indicates underfilling. The process is termed "in control" and allowed to continue as long as the plotted x-bar values fall between the chart's upper and lower control limits. Properly interpreted, an x-bar chart can help determine when adjustments are necessary to correct a production process.

Economics

Economists frequently provide forecasts about the future of the economy or some aspect of it. They use a variety of statistical information in making such forecasts. For instance, in forecasting inflation rates, economists use statistical information on such indicators as the Producer Price Index, the unemployment rate, and manufacturing capacity utilization. Often these statistical indicators are entered into computerized forecasting models that predict inflation rates.

Information Systems

Information systems administrators are responsible for the day-to-day operation of an organization's computer networks. A variety of statistical information helps administrators assess the performance of computer networks, including local area networks (LANs), wide area networks (WANs), network segments, intranets, and other data communication systems. Statistics such as the mean number of users on the system, the proportion of time any component of the system is down, and the proportion of bandwidth utilized at various times of the day are examples of statistical information that help the system administrator better understand and manage the computer network.

Applications of statistics such as those described in this section are an integral part of this text. Such examples provide an overview of the breadth of statistical applications. To supplement these examples, practitioners in the fields of business and economics provided chapter-opening Statistics in Practice articles that introduce the material covered in each chapter. The Statistics in Practice applications show the importance of statistics in a wide variety of business and economic situations.

Data

Data are the facts and figures collected, analyzed, and summarized for presentation and interpretation. All the data collected in a particular study are referred to as the **data set** for the study. Table 1.1 shows a data set containing information for 60 nations that participate in the World Trade Organization (WTO). The WTO encourages the free flow of international trade and provides a forum for resolving trade disputes.

Elements, Variables, and Observations

Elements are the entities on which data are collected. Each nation listed in Table 1.1 is an element with the nation or element name shown in the first column. With 60 nations, the data set contains 60 elements.

A **variable** is a characteristic of interest for the elements. The data set in Table 1.1 includes the following five variables:

- WTO Status: The nation's membership status in the World Trade Organization; this can be either as a member or an observer.
- Per Capita GDP ($): The total market value ($) of all goods and services produced by the nation divided by the number of people in the nation; this is commonly used to compare economic productivity of the nations.
- Trade Deficit ($1000s): The difference between the total dollar value of the nation's imports and the total dollar value of the nation's exports.
- Fitch Rating: The nation's sovereign credit rating as appraised by the Fitch Group[1]; the credit ratings range from a high of AAA to a low of F and can be modified by + or −.
- Fitch Outlook: An indication of the direction the credit rating is likely to move over the upcoming two years; the outlook can be negative, stable, or positive.

Measurements collected on each variable for every element in a study provide the data. The set of measurements obtained for a particular element is called an **observation**. Referring to Table 1.1, we see that the first observation contains the following measurements: Member,

---

[1]The Fitch Group is one of three nationally recognized statistical rating organizations designated by the U.S. Securities and Exchange Commission. The other two are Standard and Poor's and Moody's investor service.

TABLE 1.1 DATA SET FOR 60 NATIONS IN THE WORLD TRADE ORGANIZATION

Nations

Data sets such as Nations are available on the companion site for this title.

Nation	WTO Status	Per Capita GDP ($)	Trade Deficit ($1000s)	Fitch Rating	Fitch Outlook
Armenia	Member	5,400	2,673,359	BB−	Stable
Australia	Member	40,800	−33,304,157	AAA	Stable
Austria	Member	41,700	12,796,558	AAA	Stable
Azerbaijan	Observer	5,400	−16,747,320	BBB−	Positive
Bahrain	Member	27,300	3,102,665	BBB	Stable
Belgium	Member	37,600	−14,930,833	AA+	Negative
Brazil	Member	11,600	−29,796,166	BBB	Stable
Bulgaria	Member	13,500	4,049,237	BBB−	Positive
Canada	Member	40,300	−1,611,380	AAA	Stable
Cape Verde	Member	4,000	874,459	B+	Stable
Chile	Member	16,100	−14,558,218	A+	Stable
China	Member	8,400	−156,705,311	A+	Stable
Colombia	Member	10,100	−1,561,199	BBB−	Stable
Costa Rica	Member	11,500	5,807,509	BB+	Stable
Croatia	Member	18,300	8,108,103	BBB−	Negative
Cyprus	Member	29,100	6,623,337	BBB	Negative
Czech Republic	Member	25,900	−10,749,467	A+	Positive
Denmark	Member	40,200	−15,057,343	AAA	Stable
Ecuador	Member	8,300	1,993,819	B−	Stable
Egypt	Member	6,500	28,486,933	BB	Negative
El Salvador	Member	7,600	5,019,363	BB	Stable
Estonia	Member	20,200	802,234	A+	Stable
France	Member	35,000	118,841,542	AAA	Stable
Georgia	Member	5,400	4,398,153	B+	Positive
Germany	Member	37,900	−213,367,685	AAA	Stable
Hungary	Member	19,600	−9,421,301	BBB−	Negative
Iceland	Member	38,000	−504,939	BB+	Stable
Ireland	Member	39,500	−59,093,323	BBB+	Negative
Israel	Member	31,000	6,722,291	A	Stable
Italy	Member	30,100	33,568,668	A+	Negative
Japan	Member	34,300	31,675,424	AA	Negative
Kazakhstan	Observer	13,000	−33,220,437	BBB	Positive
Kenya	Member	1,700	9,174,198	B+	Stable
Latvia	Member	15,400	2,448,053	BBB−	Positive
Lebanon	Observer	15,600	13,715,550	B	Stable
Lithuania	Member	18,700	3,359,641	BBB	Positive
Malaysia	Member	15,600	−39,420,064	A−	Stable
Mexico	Member	15,100	1,288,112	BBB	Stable
Peru	Member	10,000	−7,888,993	BBB	Stable
Philippines	Member	4,100	15,667,209	BB+	Stable
Poland	Member	20,100	19,552,976	A−	Stable
Portugal	Member	23,200	21,060,508	BBB−	Negative
South Korea	Member	31,700	−37,509,141	A+	Stable
Romania	Member	12,300	13,323,709	BBB−	Stable
Russia	Observer	16,700	−151,400,000	BBB	Positive
Rwanda	Member	1,300	939,222	B	Stable
Serbia	Observer	10,700	8,275,693	BB−	Stable
Seychelles	Observer	24,700	666,026	B	Stable
Singapore	Member	59,900	−27,110,421	AAA	Stable
Slovakia	Member	23,400	−2,110,626	A+	Stable

Slovenia	Member	29,100	2,310,617	AA−	Negative
South Africa	Member	11,000	3,321,801	BBB+	Stable
Sweden	Member	40,600	−10,903,251	AAA	Stable
Switzerland	Member	43,400	−27,197,873	AAA	Stable
Thailand	Member	9,700	2,049,669	BBB	Stable
Turkey	Member	14,600	71,612,947	BB+	Positive
UK	Member	35,900	162,316,831	AAA	Negative
Uruguay	Member	15,400	2,662,628	BB	Positive
USA	Member	48,100	784,438,559	AAA	Stable
Zambia	Member	1,600	−1,805,198	B+	Stable

5400, 2,673,359, BB−, and Stable. The second observation contains the following measurements: Member, 40,800, −33,304,157, AAA, Stable, and so on. A data set with 60 elements contains 60 observations.

Scales of Measurement

Data collection requires one of the following scales of measurement: nominal, ordinal, interval, or ratio. The scale of measurement determines the amount of information contained in the data and indicates the most appropriate data summarization and statistical analyses.

When the data for a variable consist of labels or names used to identify an attribute of the element, the scale of measurement is considered a **nominal scale**. For example, referring to the data in Table 1.1, the scale of measurement for the WTO Status variable is nominal because the data "member" and "observer" are labels used to identify the status category for the nation. In cases where the scale of measurement is nominal, a numerical code as well as a nonnumerical label may be used. For example, to facilitate data collection and to prepare the data for entry into a computer database, we might use a numerical code for the WTO Status variable by letting 1 denote a member nation in the World Trade Organization and 2 denote an observer nation. The scale of measurement is nominal even though the data appear as numerical values.

The scale of measurement for a variable is considered an **ordinal scale** if the data exhibit the properties of nominal data and in addition, the order or rank of the data is meaningful. For example, referring to the data in Table 1.1, the scale of measurement for the Fitch Rating is ordinal because the rating labels which range from AAA to F can be rank ordered from best credit rating AAA to poorest credit rating F. The rating letters provide the labels similar to nominal data, but in addition, the data can also be ranked or ordered based on the credit rating, which makes the measurement scale ordinal. Ordinal data can also be recorded by a numerical code, for example, your class rank in school.

The scale of measurement for a variable is an **interval scale** if the data have all the properties of ordinal data and the interval between values is expressed in terms of a fixed unit of measure. Interval data are always numeric. College admission SAT scores are an example of interval-scaled data. For example, three students with SAT math scores of 620, 550, and 470 can be ranked or ordered in terms of best performance to poorest performance in math. In addition, the differences between the scores are meaningful. For instance, student 1 scored $620 - 550 = 70$ points more than student 2, while student 2 scored $550 - 470 = 80$ points more than student 3.

The scale of measurement for a variable is a **ratio scale** if the data have all the properties of interval data and the ratio of two values is meaningful. Variables such as distance, height, weight, and time use the ratio scale of measurement. This scale requires that a zero value be included to indicate that nothing exists for the variable at the zero point. For example, consider the cost of an automobile. A zero value for the cost would indicate that the automobile has no cost and is free. In addition, if we compare the cost of $30,000 for one automobile to the cost of $15,000 for a second automobile, the ratio property shows that the first automobile is $30,000/$15,000 = 2 times, or twice, the cost of the second automobile.

Categorical and Quantitative Data

Data can be classified as either categorical or quantitative. Data that can be grouped by specific categories are referred to as **categorical data**. Categorical data use either the nominal or ordinal scale of measurement. Data that use numeric values to indicate how much or how many are referred to as **quantitative data**. Quantitative data are obtained using either the interval or ratio scale of measurement.

The statistical method appropriate for summarizing data depends upon whether the data are categorical or quantitative.

A **categorical variable** is a variable with categorical data, and a **quantitative variable** is a variable with quantitative data. The statistical analysis appropriate for a particular variable depends upon whether the variable is categorical or quantitative. If the variable is categorical, the statistical analysis is limited. We can summarize categorical data by counting the number of observations in each category or by computing the proportion of the observations in each category. However, even when the categorical data are identified by a numerical code, arithmetic operations such as addition, subtraction, multiplication, and division do not provide meaningful results. Section 2.1 discusses ways of summarizing categorical data.

Arithmetic operations provide meaningful results for quantitative variables. For example, quantitative data may be added and then divided by the number of observations to compute the average value. This average is usually meaningful and easily interpreted. In general, more alternatives for statistical analysis are possible when data are quantitative. Section 2.2 and Chapter 3 provide ways of summarizing quantitative data.

Cross-Sectional and Time Series Data

For purposes of statistical analysis, distinguishing between cross-sectional data and time series data is important. **Cross-sectional data** are data collected at the same or approximately the same point in time. The data in Table 1.1 are cross-sectional because they describe the five variables for the 60 World Trade Organization nations at the same point in time. **Time series data** are data collected over several time periods. For example, the time series in Figure 1.1 shows the U.S. average price per gallon of conventional regular gasoline between 2010 and 2015. Note that gasoline prices peaked in May 2011. Between June 2014 and January 2015, the average price per gallon dropped dramatically. In August 2015, the average price per gallon was $2.52.

Graphs of time series data are frequently found in business and economic publications. Such graphs help analysts understand what happened in the past, identify any trends over time, and project future values for the time series. The graphs of time series data can take on a variety of forms, as shown in Figure 1.2. With a little study, these graphs are usually easy to understand and interpret. For example, Panel (A) in Figure 1.2 is a graph that shows the Dow Jones Industrial Average Index from 2005 to 2015. In September 2005, the popular stock market index was near 10,400. Over the next two years the index rose to almost 14,000 in October 2007. However, notice the sharp decline in the time series after the high in 2007. By March 2009, poor economic conditions had caused the Dow Jones Industrial Average Index to return to the 7000 level. This was a scary and discouraging period for investors. However, by late 2009, the index was showing a recovery by reaching 10,000 and rising to a high of over 18,000 in May 2015. By October 2015, the index had dropped substantially to just under 16,300.

FIGURE 1.1 U.S. AVERAGE PRICE PER GALLON FOR CONVENTIONAL REGULAR GASOLINE

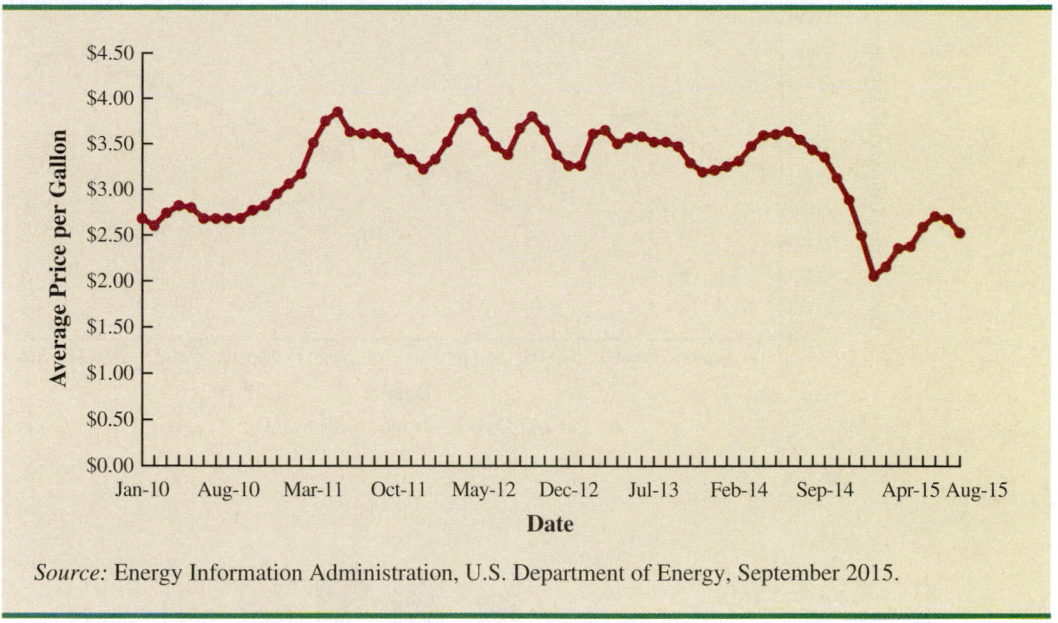

Source: Energy Information Administration, U.S. Department of Energy, September 2015.

The graph in Panel (B) shows the net income of McDonald's Inc. from 2007 to 2015. The declining economic conditions in 2008 and 2009 were actually beneficial to McDonald's as the company's net income rose to all-time highs. The growth in McDonald's net income showed that the company was thriving during the economic downturn as people were cutting back on the more expensive sit-down restaurants and seeking less expensive alternatives offered by McDonald's. McDonald's net income continued to new all-time highs in 2010 and 2011, remained at about 5.5 billion from 2011 to 2013, decreased substantially in 2014, and dropped again in 2015. Analysts suspect that the drop in net income was due to loss of customers to newer competition such as Chipotle.

Panel (C) shows the time series for the occupancy rate of hotels in South Florida over a one-year period. The highest occupancy rates, 95% and 98%, occur during the months of February and March when the climate of South Florida is attractive to tourists. In fact, January to April of each year is typically the high-occupancy season for South Florida hotels. On the other hand, note the low occupancy rates during the months of August to October, with the lowest occupancy rate of 50% occurring in September. High temperatures and the hurricane season are the primary reasons for the drop in hotel occupancy during this period.

NOTES AND COMMENTS

1. An observation is the set of measurements obtained for each element in a data set. Hence, the number of observations is always the same as the number of elements. The number of measurements obtained for each element equals the number of variables. Hence, the total number of data items can be determined by multiplying the number of observations by the number of variables.

2. Quantitative data may be discrete or continuous. Quantitative data that measure how many (e.g., number of calls received in 5 minutes) are discrete. Quantitative data that measure how much (e.g., weight or time) are continuous because no separation occurs between the possible data values.

FIGURE 1.2   A VARIETY OF GRAPHS OF TIME SERIES DATA

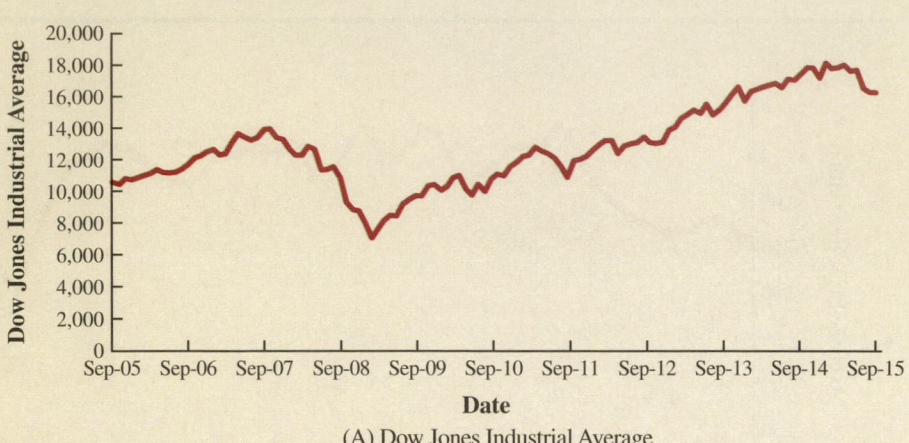

(A) Dow Jones Industrial Average

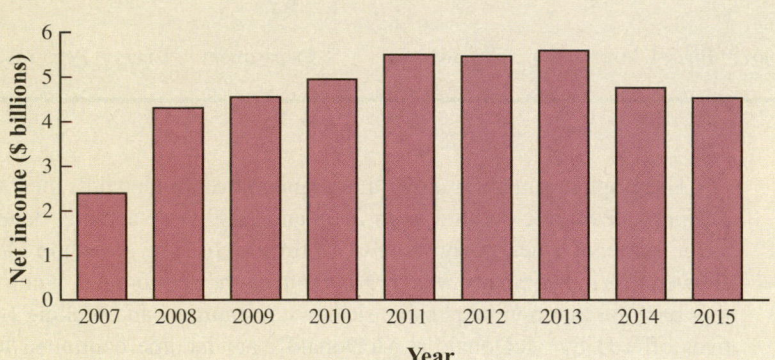

(B) Net Income for McDonald's Inc.

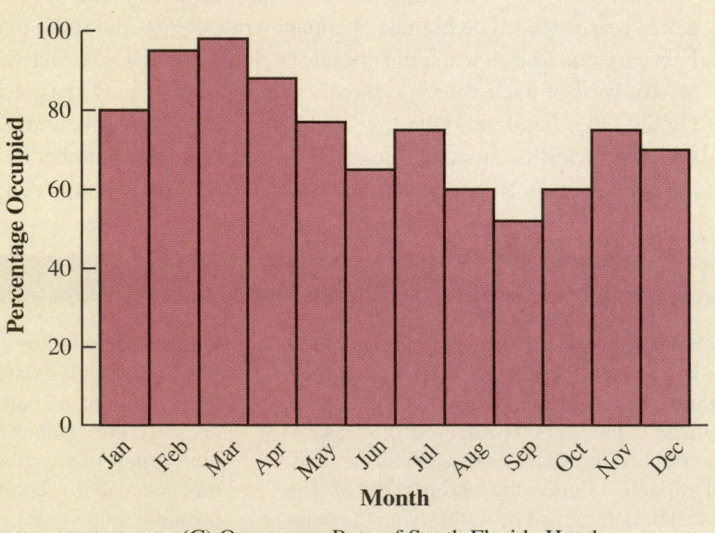

(C) Occupancy Rate of South Florida Hotels

1.3 Data Sources

Data can be obtained from existing sources, by conducting an observational study, or by conducting an experiment.

Existing Sources

In some cases, data needed for a particular application already exist. Companies maintain a variety of databases about their employees, customers, and business operations. Data on employee salaries, ages, and years of experience can usually be obtained from internal personnel records. Other internal records contain data on sales, advertising expenditures, distribution costs, inventory levels, and production quantities. Most companies also maintain detailed data about their customers. Table 1.2 shows some of the data commonly available from internal company records.

Organizations that specialize in collecting and maintaining data make available substantial amounts of business and economic data. Companies access these external data sources through leasing arrangements or by purchase. Dun & Bradstreet, Bloomberg, and Dow Jones & Company are three firms that provide extensive business database services to clients. ACNielsen and Information Resources, Inc. built successful businesses collecting and processing data that they sell to advertisers and product manufacturers.

Data are also available from a variety of industry associations and special interest organizations. The Travel Industry Association of America maintains travel-related information such as the number of tourists and travel expenditures by states. Such data would be of interest to firms and individuals in the travel industry. The Graduate Management Admission Council maintains data on test scores, student characteristics, and graduate management education programs. Most of the data from these types of sources are available to qualified users at a modest cost.

The Internet is an important source of data and statistical information. Almost all companies maintain websites that provide general information about the company as well as data on sales, number of employees, number of products, product prices, and product specifications. In addition, a number of companies now specialize in making information available over the Internet. As a result, one can obtain access to stock quotes, meal prices at restaurants, salary data, and an almost infinite variety of information.

Government agencies are another important source of existing data. For instance, the U.S. Department of Labor maintains considerable data on employment rates, wage

TABLE 1.2 EXAMPLES OF DATA AVAILABLE FROM INTERNAL COMPANY RECORDS

Source	Some of the Data Typically Available
Employee records	Name, address, social security number, salary, number of vacation days, number of sick days, and bonus
Production records	Part or product number, quantity produced, direct labor cost, and materials cost
Inventory records	Part or product number, number of units on hand, reorder level, economic order quantity, and discount schedule
Sales records	Product number, sales volume, sales volume by region, and sales volume by customer type
Credit records	Customer name, address, phone number, credit limit, and accounts receivable balance
Customer profile	Age, gender, income level, household size, address, and preferences

TABLE 1.3   EXAMPLES OF DATA AVAILABLE FROM SELECTED GOVERNMENT AGENCIES

Government Agency	Some of the Data Available
Census Bureau	Population data, number of households, and household income
Federal Reserve Board	Data on the money supply, installment credit, exchange rates, and discount rates
Office of Management and Budget	Data on revenue, expenditures, and debt of the federal government
Department of Commerce	Data on business activity, value of shipments by industry, level of profits by industry, and growing and declining industries
Bureau of Labor Statistics	Consumer spending, hourly earnings, unemployment rate, safety records, and international statistics

rates, size of the labor force, and union membership. Table 1.3 lists selected governmental agencies and some of the data they provide. Most government agencies that collect and process data also make the results available through a website. Figure 1.3 shows the homepage for the U.S. Bureau of Labor Statistics website.

Observational Study

In an *observational study* we simply observe what is happening in a particular situation, record data on one or more variables of interest, and conduct a statistical analysis of the resulting data. For example, researchers might observe a randomly selected group of

FIGURE 1.3   U.S. BUREAU OF LABOR STATISTICS HOMEPAGE

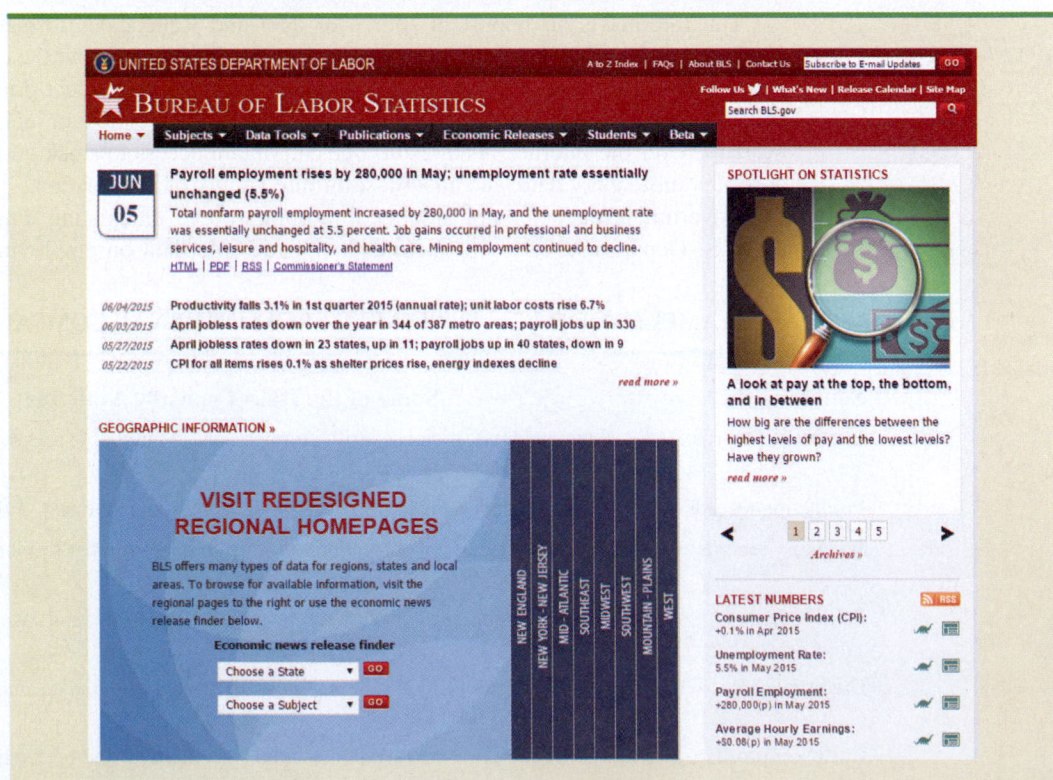

Studies of smokers and nonsmokers are observational studies because researchers do not determine or control who will smoke and who will not smoke.

customers that enter a Walmart supercenter to collect data on variables such as the length of time the customer spends shopping, the gender of the customer, the amount spent, and so on. Statistical analysis of the data may help management determine how factors such as the length of time shopping and the gender of the customer affect the amount spent.

As another example of an observational study, suppose that researchers were interested in investigating the relationship between the gender of the CEO for a *Fortune* 500 company and the performance of the company as measured by the return on equity (ROE). To obtain data, the researchers selected a sample of companies and recorded the gender of the CEO and the ROE for each company. Statistical analysis of the data can help determine the relationship between performance of the company and the gender of the CEO. This example is an observational study because the researchers had no control over the gender of the CEO or the ROE at each of the companies that were sampled.

Surveys and public opinion polls are two other examples of commonly used observational studies. The data provided by these types of studies simply enable us to observe opinions of the respondents. For example, the New York State legislature commissioned a telephone survey in which residents were asked if they would support or oppose an increase in the state gasoline tax in order to provide funding for bridge and highway repairs. Statistical analysis of the survey results will assist the state legislature in determining if it should introduce a bill to increase gasoline taxes.

Experiment

The largest experimental statistical study ever conducted is believed to be the 1954 Public Health Service experiment for the Salk polio vaccine. Nearly 2 million children in grades 1, 2, and 3 were selected from throughout the United States.

The key difference between an observational study and an experiment is that an experiment is conducted under controlled conditions. As a result, the data obtained from a well-designed experiment can often provide more information as compared to the data obtained from existing sources or by conducting an observational study. For example, suppose a pharmaceutical company would like to learn about how a new drug it has developed affects blood pressure. To obtain data about how the new drug affects blood pressure, researchers selected a sample of individuals. Different groups of individuals are given different dosage levels of the new drug, and before and after data on blood pressure are collected for each group. Statistical analysis of the data can help determine how the new drug affects blood pressure.

The types of experiments we deal with in statistics often begin with the identification of a particular variable of interest. Then one or more other variables are identified and controlled so that data can be obtained about how the other variables influence the primary variable of interest. In Chapter 13 we discuss statistical methods appropriate for analyzing the data from an experiment.

Time and Cost Issues

Anyone wanting to use data and statistical analysis as aids to decision making must be aware of the time and cost required to obtain the data. The use of existing data sources is desirable when data must be obtained in a relatively short period of time. If important data are not readily available from an existing source, the additional time and cost involved in obtaining the data must be taken into account. In all cases, the decision maker should consider the contribution of the statistical analysis to the decision-making process. The cost of data acquisition and the subsequent statistical analysis should not exceed the savings generated by using the information to make a better decision.

Data Acquisition Errors

Managers should always be aware of the possibility of data errors in statistical studies. Using erroneous data can be worse than not using any data at all. An error in data acquisition occurs whenever the data value obtained is not equal to the true or actual value that would be obtained with a correct procedure. Such errors can occur in a number of ways. For example, an interviewer might make a recording error, such as a transposition in writing the age of a 24-year-old person as 42, or the person answering an interview question might misinterpret the question and provide an incorrect response.

Experienced data analysts take great care in collecting and recording data to ensure that errors are not made. Special procedures can be used to check for internal consistency of the data. For instance, such procedures would indicate that the analyst should review the accuracy of data for a respondent shown to be 22 years of age but reporting 20 years of work experience. Data analysts also review data with unusually large and small values, called outliers, which are candidates for possible data errors. In Chapter 3 we present some of the methods statisticians use to identify outliers.

Errors often occur during data acquisition. Blindly using any data that happen to be available or using data that were acquired with little care can result in misleading information and bad decisions. Thus, taking steps to acquire accurate data can help ensure reliable and valuable decision-making information.

1.4 Descriptive Statistics

Most of the statistical information in newspapers, magazines, company reports, and other publications consists of data that are summarized and presented in a form that is easy for the reader to understand. Such summaries of data, which may be tabular, graphical, or numerical, are referred to as **descriptive statistics**.

Refer to the data set in Table 1.1 showing data for 60 nations that participate in the World Trade Organization. Methods of descriptive statistics can be used to summarize these data. For example, consider the variable Fitch Outlook, which indicates the direction the nation's credit rating is likely to move over the next two years. The Fitch Outlook is recorded as being negative, stable, or positive. A tabular summary of the data showing the number of nations with each of the Fitch Outlook ratings is shown in Table 1.4. A graphical summary of the same data, called a bar chart, is shown in Figure 1.4. These types of summaries make the data easier to interpret. Referring to Table 1.4 and Figure 1.4, we can see that the majority of Fitch Outlook credit ratings are stable, with 65% of the nations having this rating. Negative and positive outlook credit ratings are similar, with slightly more nations having a negative outlook (18.3%) than a positive outlook (16.7%).

A graphical summary of the data for quantitative variable Per Capita GDP in Table 1.1, called a histogram, is provided in Figure 1.5. Using the histogram, it is easy to see that Per Capita GDP for the 60 nations ranges from $0 to $60,000, with the highest concentration between $10,000 and $20,000. Only one nation had a Per Capita GDP exceeding $50,000.

TABLE 1.4 FREQUENCIES AND PERCENT FREQUENCIES FOR THE FITCH CREDIT RATING OUTLOOK OF 60 NATIONS

Fitch Outlook	Frequency	Percent Frequency (%)
Positive	10	16.7
Stable	39	65.0
Negative	11	18.3

FIGURE 1.4   BAR CHART FOR THE FITCH CREDIT RATING OUTLOOK FOR 60 NATIONS

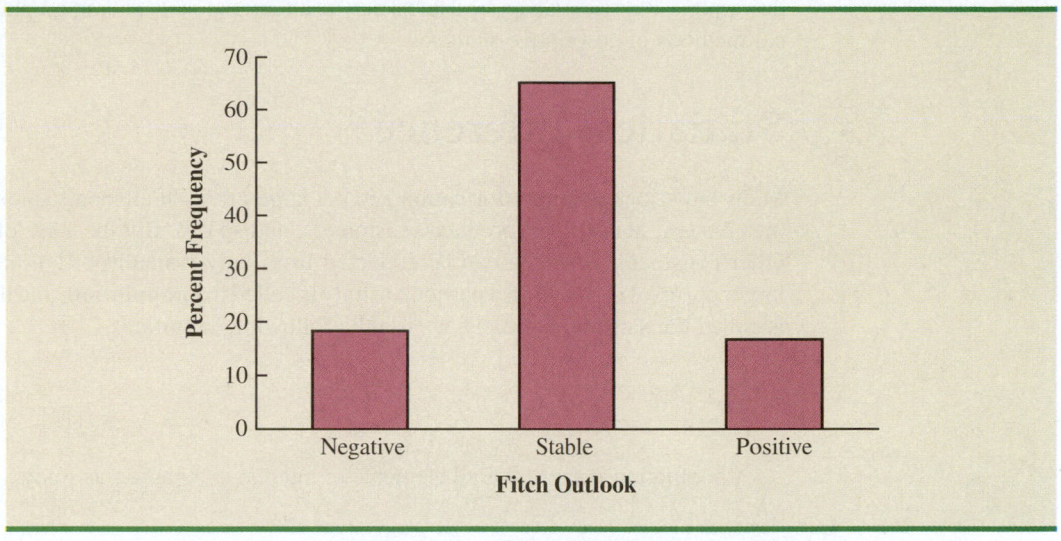

In addition to tabular and graphical displays, numerical descriptive statistics are used to summarize data. The most common numerical measure is the average, or mean. Using the data on Per Capita GDP for the 60 nations in Table 1.1, we can compute the average by adding Per Capita GDP for all 60 nations and dividing the total by 60. Doing so provides an average Per Capita GDP of $21,387. This average provides a measure of the central tendency, or central location of the data.

FIGURE 1.5   HISTOGRAM OF PER CAPITA GDP FOR 60 NATIONS

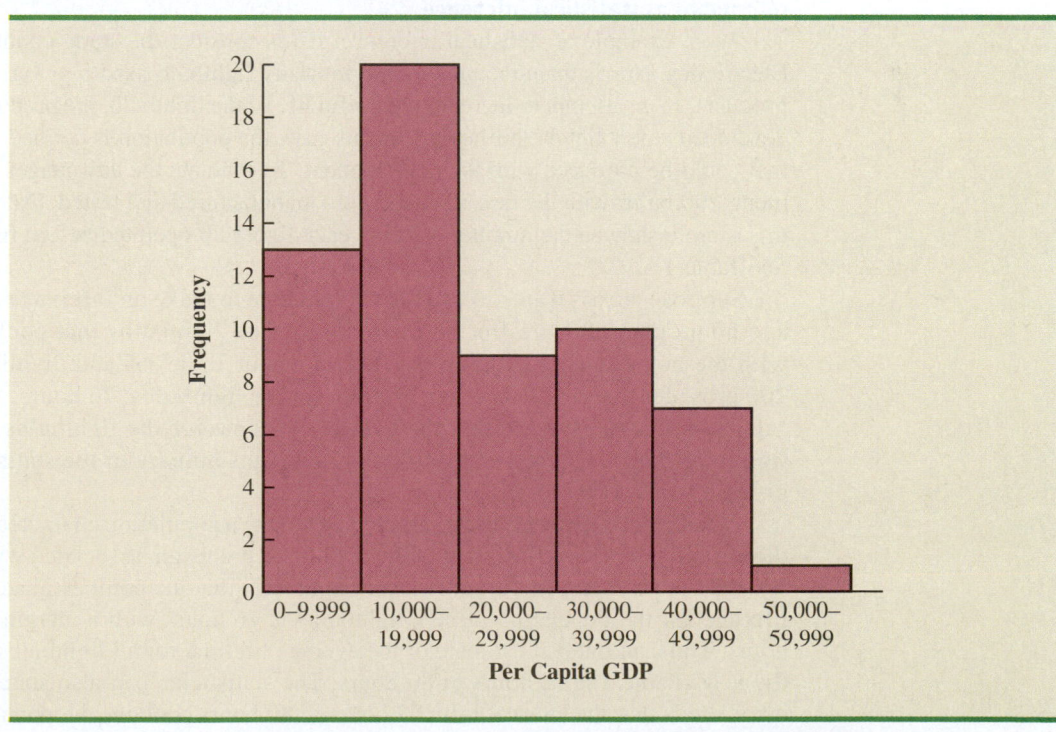

There is a great deal of interest in effective methods for developing and presenting descriptive statistics. Chapters 2 and 3 devote attention to the tabular, graphical, and numerical methods of descriptive statistics.

1.5   Statistical Inference

Many situations require information about a large group of elements (individuals, companies, voters, households, products, customers, and so on). But, because of time, cost, and other considerations, data can be collected from only a small portion of the group. The larger group of elements in a particular study is called the **population**, and the smaller group is called the **sample**. Formally, we use the following definitions.

> **POPULATION**
>
> A population is the set of all elements of interest in a particular study.

> **SAMPLE**
>
> A sample is a subset of the population.

The U.S. government conducts a census every 10 years. Market research firms conduct sample surveys every day.

The process of conducting a survey to collect data for the entire population is called a **census**. The process of conducting a survey to collect data for a sample is called a **sample survey**. As one of its major contributions, statistics uses data from a sample to make estimates and test hypotheses about the characteristics of a population through a process referred to as **statistical inference**.

As an example of statistical inference, let us consider the study conducted by Norris Electronics. Norris manufactures a high-intensity lightbulb used in a variety of electrical products. In an attempt to increase the useful life of the lightbulb, the product design group developed a new lightbulb filament. In this case, the population is defined as all lightbulbs that could be produced with the new filament. To evaluate the advantages of the new filament, 200 bulbs with the new filament were manufactured and tested. Data collected from this sample showed the number of hours each lightbulb operated before filament burnout. See Table 1.5.

Suppose Norris wants to use the sample data to make an inference about the average hours of useful life for the population of all lightbulbs that could be produced with the new filament. Adding the 200 values in Table 1.5 and dividing the total by 200 provides the sample average lifetime for the lightbulbs: 76 hours. We can use this sample result to estimate that the average lifetime for the lightbulbs in the population is 76 hours. Figure 1.6 provides a graphical summary of the statistical inference process for Norris Electronics.

Whenever statisticians use a sample to estimate a population characteristic of interest, they usually provide a statement of the quality, or precision, associated with the estimate. For the Norris example, the statistician might state that the point estimate of the average lifetime for the population of new lightbulbs is 76 hours with a margin of error of ± 4 hours. Thus, an interval estimate of the average lifetime for all lightbulbs produced with the new filament is 72 hours to 80 hours. The statistician can also state how confident he or she is that the interval from 72 hours to 80 hours contains the population average.

TABLE 1.5   HOURS UNTIL BURNOUT FOR A SAMPLE OF 200 LIGHTBULBS
FOR THE NORRIS ELECTRONICS EXAMPLE

Norris

107	73	68	97	76	79	94	59	98	57
54	65	71	70	84	88	62	61	79	98
66	62	79	86	68	74	61	82	65	98
62	116	65	88	64	79	78	79	77	86
74	85	73	80	68	78	89	72	58	69
92	78	88	77	103	88	63	68	88	81
75	90	62	89	71	71	74	70	74	70
65	81	75	62	94	71	85	84	83	63
81	62	79	83	93	61	65	62	92	65
83	70	70	81	77	72	84	67	59	58
78	66	66	94	77	63	66	75	68	76
90	78	71	101	78	43	59	67	61	71
96	75	64	76	72	77	74	65	82	86
66	86	96	89	81	71	85	99	59	92
68	72	77	60	87	84	75	77	51	45
85	67	87	80	84	93	69	76	89	75
83	68	72	67	92	89	82	96	77	102
74	91	76	83	66	68	61	73	72	76
73	77	79	94	63	59	62	71	81	65
73	63	63	89	82	64	85	92	64	73

FIGURE 1.6   THE PROCESS OF STATISTICAL INFERENCE FOR THE NORRIS
ELECTRONICS EXAMPLE

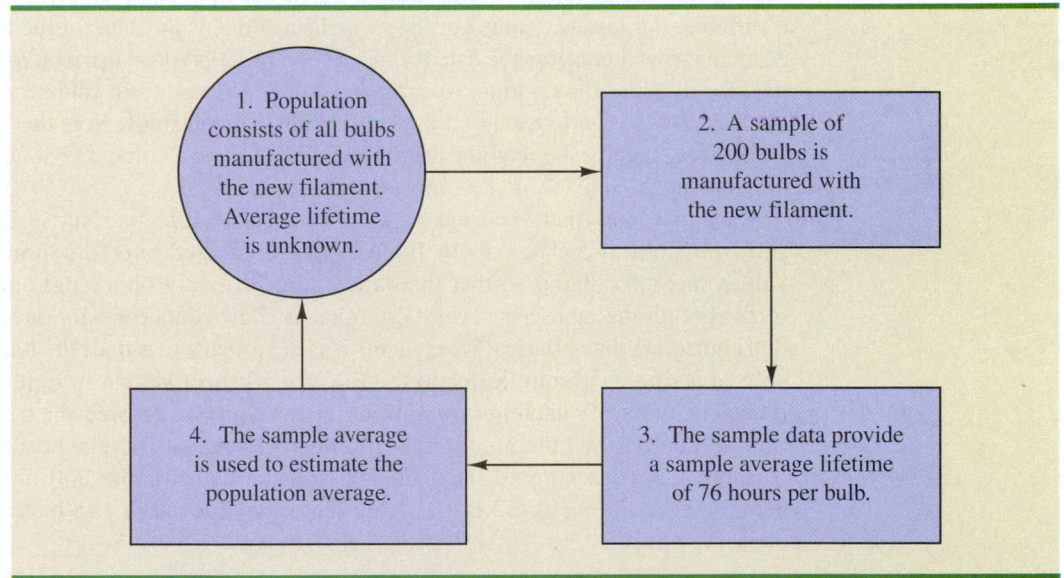

1.6   Statistical Analysis Using Microsoft Excel

Because statistical analysis typically involves working with large amounts of data, computer software is frequently used to conduct the analysis. In this book we show how statistical analysis can be performed using Microsoft Excel.

We want to emphasize that this book is about statistics; it is not a book about spreadsheets. Our focus is on showing the appropriate statistical procedures for collecting, analyzing, presenting, and interpreting data. Because Excel is widely available in business organizations, you can expect to put the knowledge gained here to use in the setting where you currently, or soon will, work. If, in the process of studying this material, you become more proficient with Excel, so much the better.

We begin most sections with an application scenario in which a statistical procedure is useful. After showing what the statistical procedure is and how it is used, we turn to showing how to implement the procedure using Excel. Thus, you should gain an understanding of what the procedure is, the situation in which it is useful, and how to implement it using the capabilities of Excel.

Data Sets and Excel Worksheets

To hide rows 15 through 54 of the Excel worksheet, first select rows 15 through 54. Then, right-click and choose the Hide option. To redisplay rows 15 through 54, just select rows 14 through 55, right-click, and select the Unhide option.

Data sets are organized in Excel worksheets in much the same way as the data set for the 60 nations that participate in the World Trade Organization that appears in Table 1.1 is organized. Figure 1.7 shows an Excel worksheet for that data set. Note that row 1 and column A contain labels. Cells B1:F1 contain the variable names; cells A2:A61 contain the observation names; and cells B2:F61 contain the data that were collected. A purple fill color is used to highlight the cells that contain the data. Displaying a worksheet with this many rows on a single page of a textbook is not practical. In such cases we will hide selected rows to conserve space. In the Excel worksheet shown in Figure 1.7 we have hidden rows 15 through 54 (observations 14 through 53) to conserve space.

The data are the focus of the statistical analysis. Except for the headings in row 1, each row of the worksheet corresponds to an observation and each column corresponds to a variable. For instance, row 2 of the worksheet contains the data for the first observation, Armenia; row 3 contains the data for the second observation, Australia; row 3 contains the data for the third observation, Austria; and so on. The names in column A provide a convenient way to refer to each of the 60 observations in the study. Note that column B of the worksheet contains the data for the variable WTO Status, column C contains the data for the Per Capita GDP ($), and so on.

Suppose now that we want to use Excel to analyze the Norris Electronics data shown in Table 1.5. The data in Table 1.5 are organized into 10 columns with 20 data values in each column so that the data would fit nicely on a single page of the text. Even though the table has several columns, it shows data for only one variable (hours until burnout). In statistical worksheets it is customary to put all the data for each variable in a single column. Refer to the Excel worksheet shown in Figure 1.8. To make it easier to identify each observation in the data set, we entered the heading Observation into cell A1 and the numbers 1–200 into cells A2:A201. The heading Hours Until Burnout has been entered into cell B1, and the data for the 200 observations have been entered into cells B2:B201. Note that rows 7 through 195 have been hidden to conserve space.

Using Excel for Statistical Analysis

To separate the discussion of a statistical procedure from the discussion of using Excel to implement the procedure, the material that discusses the use of Excel will usually be set apart in sections with headings such as Using Excel to Construct a Bar Chart and a Pie

FIGURE 1.7 EXCEL WORKSHEET FOR THE 60 NATIONS THAT PARTICIPATE IN THE WORLD TRADE ORGANIZATION

Note: Rows 15–54 are hidden.

	A	B	C	D	E	F	G
1	**Nation**	**WTO Status**	**Per Capita GDP ($)**	**Trade Deficit ($1000s)**	**Fitch Rating**	**Fitch Outlook**	
2	Armenia	Member	5,400	2,673,359	BB-	Stable	
3	Australia	Member	40,800	-33,304,157	AAA	Stable	
4	Austria	Member	41,700	12,796,558	AAA	Stable	
5	Azerbaijan	Observer	5,400	-16,747,320	BBB-	Positive	
6	Bahrain	Member	27,300	3,102,665	BBB	Stable	
7	Belgium	Member	37,600	-14,930,833	AA+	Negative	
8	Brazil	Member	11,600	-29,796,166	BBB	Stable	
9	Bulgaria	Member	13,500	4,049,237	BBB-	Positive	
10	Canada	Member	40,300	-1,611,380	AAA	Stable	
11	Cape Verde	Member	4,000	874,459	B+	Stable	
12	Chile	Member	16,100	-14,558,218	A+	Stable	
13	China	Member	8,400	-156,705,311	A+	Stable	
14	Colombia	Member	10,100	-1,561,199	BBB-	Stable	
55	Switzerland	Member	43,400	-27,197,873	AAA	Stable	
56	Thailand	Member	9,700	2,049,669	BBB	Stable	
57	Turkey	Member	14,600	71,612,947	BB+	Positive	
58	UK	Member	35,900	162,316,831	AAA	Negative	
59	Uruguay	Member	15,400	2,662,628	BB	Positive	
60	USA	Member	48,100	784,438,559	AAA	Stable	
61	Zambia	Member	1,600	-1,805,198	B+	Stable	
62							

FIGURE 1.8 EXCEL WORKSHEET FOR THE NORRIS ELECTRONICS DATA SET

Note: Rows 7–195 are hidden

	A	B	C
1	**Observation**	**Hours Until Burnout**	
2	1	107	
3	2	54	
4	3	66	
5	4	62	
6	5	74	
196	195	45	
197	196	75	
198	197	102	
199	198	76	
200	199	65	
201	200	73	
202			
203			

Chart, Using Excel to Construct a Frequency Distribution, and so on. In using Excel for statistical analysis, four tasks may be needed: Enter/Access Data; Enter Functions and Formulas; Apply Tools; and Editing Options.

Enter/Access Data: Select cell locations for the data and enter the data along with appropriate labels; or open an existing Excel file such as one of the DATAfiles that accompany the text.

Enter Functions and Formulas: Select cell locations, enter Excel functions and formulas, and provide descriptive labels to identify the results.

Apply Tools: Use Excel's tools for data analysis and presentation.

Editing Options: Edit the results to better identify the output or to create a different type of presentation. For example, when using Excel's chart tools, we can edit the chart that is created by adding, removing, or changing chart elements such as the title, legend, data labels, and so on.

Our approach will be to describe how these tasks are performed each time we use Excel to implement a statistical procedure. It will always be necessary to enter data or open an existing Excel file. But, depending on the complexity of the statistical analysis, only one of the second or third tasks may be needed.

To illustrate how the discussion of Excel will appear throughout the book, we will show how to use Excel's AVERAGE function to compute the average lifetime for the 200 burnout times in Table 1.5. Refer to Figure 1.9 as we describe the tasks involved. The worksheet shown in the foreground of Figure 1.9 displays the data for the problem and shows the results of the analysis. It is called the *value worksheet*. The worksheet shown in the

FIGURE 1.9   COMPUTING THE AVERAGE LIFETIME OF LIGHTBULBS FOR NORRIS ELECTRONICS USING EXCEL'S AVERAGE FUNCTION

background displays the Excel formula used to compute the average lifetime and is called the *formula worksheet*. A purple fill color is used to highlight the cells that contain the data in both worksheets. In addition, a green fill color is used to highlight the cells containing the functions and formulas in the formula worksheet and the corresponding results in the value worksheet.

Enter/Access Data: Open the DATAfile named *Norris*. The data are in cells B2:B201 and labels are in column A and cell B1.

Enter Functions and Formulas: Excel's AVERAGE function can be used to compute the mean by entering the following formula into cell E2:

$$=AVERAGE(B2:201)$$

Similarly, the formulas =MEDIAN(B2:B201) and =MODE.SNGL(B2:B201) are entered into cells E3 and E4, respectively, to compute the median and the mode.

To identify the result, the label Average Lifetime is entered into cell D2. Note that for this illustration the Apply Tools and Editing Options tasks were not required. The value worksheet shows that the value computed using the AVERAGE function is 76 hours.

1.7 Analytics

Because of the dramatic increase in available data, more cost-effective data storage, faster computer processing, and recognition by managers that data can be extremely valuable for understanding customers and business operations, there has been a dramatic increase in data-driven decision making. The broad range of techniques that may be used to support data-driven decisions comprise what has become known as analytics.

Analytics is the scientific process of transforming data into insight for making better decisions. Analytics is used for data-driven or fact-based decision making, which is often seen as more objective than alternative approaches to decision making. The tools of analytics can aid decision making by creating insights from data, improving our ability to more accurately forecast for planning, helping us quantify risk, and yielding better alternatives through analysis.

We adopt the definition of analytics developed by the Institute for Operations Research and the Management Sciences (INFORMS).

Analytics can involve a variety of techniques from simple reports to the most advanced optimization techniques (algorithms for finding the best course of action). Analytics is now generally thought to comprise three broad categories of techniques. These categories are descriptive analytics, predictive analytics, and prescriptive analytics.

Descriptive analytics encompasses the set of analytical techniques that describe what has happened in the past. Examples of these types of techniques are data queries, reports, descriptive statistics, data visualization, data dash boards, and basic what-if spreadsheet models.

Predictive analytics consists of analytical techniques that use models constructed from past data to predict the future or to assess the impact of one variable on another. For example, past data on sales of a product may be used to construct a mathematical model that predicts future sales. Such a model can account for factors such as the growth trajectory and seasonality of the product's sales based on past growth and seasonal patterns. Point-of-sale scanner data from retail outlets may be used by a packaged food manufacturer to help estimate the lift in unit sales associated with coupons or sales events. Survey data and past purchase behavior may be used to help predict the market share of a new product. Each of these is an example of predictive analytics. Linear regression, time series analysis, and forecasting models fall into the category of predictive analytics; these techniques are discussed later in this text. Simulation, which is the use of probability and statistical computer models to better understand risk, also falls under the category of predictive analytics.

Prescriptive analytics differs greatly from descriptive or predictive analytics. What distinguishes prescriptive analytics is that prescriptive models yield a best course of action to take. That is, the output of a prescriptive model is a best decision. Hence, **prescriptive analytics** is the set of analytical techniques that yield a course of action. Optimization models, which generate solutions that maximize or minimize some objective subject to a set of constraints, fall into the category of prescriptive models. The airline industry's use of revenue management is an example of a prescriptive model. The airline industry uses past purchasing data as inputs into a model that recommends the pricing strategy across all flights that will maximize revenue for the company.

How does the study of statistics relate to analytics? Most of the techniques in descriptive and predictive analytics come from probability and statistics. These include descriptive statistics, data visualization, probability and probability distributions, sampling, and predictive modeling, including regression analysis and time series forecasting. Each of these techniques is discussed in this text. The increased use of analytics for data-driven decision making makes it more important than ever for analysts and managers to understand statistics and data analysis. Companies are increasingly seeking data savvy managers who know how to use descriptive and predictive models to make data-driven decisions.

At the beginning of this section, we mentioned the increased availability of data as one of the drivers of the interest in analytics. In the next section we discuss this explosion in available data and how it relates to the study of statistics.

1.8   Big Data and Data Mining

With the aid of magnetic card readers, bar code scanners, and point-of-sale terminals, most organizations obtain large amounts of data on a daily basis. And, even for a small local restaurant that uses touch screen monitors to enter orders and handle billing, the amount of data collected can be substantial. For large retail companies, the sheer volume of data collected is hard to conceptualize, and figuring out how to effectively use these data to improve profitability is a challenge. Mass retailers such as Walmart capture data on 20 to 30 million transactions every day, telecommunication companies such as France Telecom and AT&T generate over 300 million call records per day, and Visa processes 6800 payment transactions per second or approximately 600 million transactions per day.

In addition to the sheer volume and speed with which companies now collect data, more complicated types of data are now available and are proving to be of great value to businesses. Text data are collected by monitoring what is being said about a company's products or services on social media such as Twitter. Audio data are collected from service calls (on a service call, you will often hear "this call may be monitored for quality control"). Video data are collected by in-store video cameras to analyze shopping behavior. Analyzing information generated by these nontraditional sources is more complicated because of the complex process of transforming the information into data that can be analyzed.

Larger and more complex data sets are now often referred to as **big data**. Although there does not seem to be a universally accepted definition of *big data*, many think if it as a set of data that cannot be managed, processed, or analyzed with commonly available software in a reasonable amount of time. Many data analysts define *big data* by referring to the three v's of data: volume, velocity, and variety. *Volume* refers to the amount of available data (the typical unit of measure for data is now a terabyte, which is 10^{12} bytes); *velocity* refers to the speed at which data is collected and processed; and *variety* refers to the different data types.

The term *data warehousing* is used to refer to the process of capturing, storing, and maintaining the data. Computing power and data collection tools have reached the point where it is now feasible to store and retrieve extremely large quantities of data in seconds. Analysis of the data in the warehouse may result in decisions that will lead to new strategies and higher profits for the organization. For example, General Electric (GE) captures a large amount of data from sensors on its aircraft engines each time a plane takes off or lands. Capturing these data allows GE to offer an important service to its customers; GE monitors the engine performance and can alert its customer when service is needed or a problem is likely to occur.

The subject of **data mining** deals with methods for developing useful decision-making information from large databases. Using a combination of procedures from statistics, mathematics, and computer science, analysts "mine the data" in the warehouse to convert it into useful information, hence the name *data mining*. Dr. Kurt Thearling, a leading practitioner in the field, defines data mining as "the automated extraction of predictive information from (large) databases." The two key words in Dr. Thearling's definition are "automated" and "predictive." Data mining systems that are the most effective use automated procedures to extract information from the data using only the most general or even vague queries by the user. And data mining software automates the process of uncovering hidden predictive information that in the past required hands-on analysis.

The major applications of data mining have been made by companies with a strong consumer focus, such as retail businesses, financial organizations, and communication companies. Data mining has been successfully used to help retailers such as Amazon and Barnes & Noble determine one or more related products that customers who have already purchased a specific product are also likely to purchase. Then, when a customer logs on to the company's website and purchases a product, the website uses pop-ups to alert the customer about additional products that the customer is likely to purchase. In another application, data mining may be used to identify customers who are likely to spend more than $20 on a particular shopping trip. These customers may then be identified as the ones to receive special e-mail or regular mail discount offers to encourage them to make their next shopping trip before the discount termination date.

Statistical methods play an important role in data mining, both in terms of discovering relationships in the data and predicting future outcomes. However, a thorough coverage of data mining and the use of statistics in data mining is outside the scope of this text.

Data mining is a technology that relies heavily on statistical methodology such as multiple regression, logistic regression, and correlation. But it takes a creative integration of all these methods and computer science technologies involving artificial intelligence and machine learning to make data mining effective. A substantial investment in time and money is required to implement commercial data mining software packages developed by firms such as Oracle, Teradata, and SAS. The statistical concepts introduced in this text will be helpful in understanding the statistical methodology used by data mining software packages and enable you to better understand the statistical information that is developed.

Because statistical models play an important role in developing predictive models in data mining, many of the concerns that statisticians deal with in developing statistical models are also applicable. For instance, a concern in any statistical study involves the issue of model reliability. Finding a statistical model that works well for a particular sample of data does not necessarily mean that it can be reliably applied to other data. One of the common statistical approaches to evaluating model reliability is to divide the sample data set into two parts: a training data set and a test data set. If the model developed using the training data is able to accurately predict values in the test data, we say that the model is reliable. One advantage that data mining has over classical statistics is that the enormous amount of data available allows the data mining software to partition the data set so that a model developed for the training data set may be tested for reliability on other data. In this sense, the partitioning of the data set allows data mining to develop models and relationships and then quickly observe if they are repeatable and valid with new and different data. On the other hand, a warning for data mining applications is that with so much data available, there is a danger of overfitting the model to the point that misleading associations and cause/effect conclusions appear to exist. Careful interpretation of data mining results and additional testing will help avoid this pitfall.

1.9 Ethical Guidelines for Statistical Practice

Ethical behavior is something we should strive for in all that we do. Ethical issues arise in statistics because of the important role statistics plays in the collection, analysis, presentation, and interpretation of data. In a statistical study, unethical behavior can take a variety of forms including improper sampling, inappropriate analysis of the data, development of misleading graphs, use of inappropriate summary statistics, and/or a biased interpretation of the statistical results.

As you begin to do your own statistical work, we encourage you to be fair, thorough, objective, and neutral as you collect data, conduct analyses, make oral presentations, and present written reports containing information developed. As a consumer of statistics, you should also be aware of the possibility of unethical statistical behavior by others. When you see statistics in newspapers, on television, on the Internet, and so on, it is a good idea to view the information with some skepticism, always being aware of the source as well as the purpose and objectivity of the statistics provided.

The American Statistical Association, the nation's leading professional organization for statistics and statisticians, developed the report "Ethical Guidelines for Statistical Practice"[2] to help statistical practitioners make and communicate ethical decisions and assist students in learning how to perform statistical work responsibly. The report contains 67 guidelines organized into eight topic areas: Professionalism; Responsibilities to Funders, Clients, and Employers; Responsibilities in Publications and Testimony; Responsibilities to Research Subjects; Responsibilities to Research Team Colleagues; Responsibilities to Other Statisticians or Statistical Practitioners; Responsibilities Regarding Allegations of Misconduct; and Responsibilities of Employers Including Organizations, Individuals, Attorneys, or Other Clients Employing Statistical Practitioners.

One of the ethical guidelines in the professionalism area addresses the issue of running multiple tests until a desired result is obtained. Let us consider an example. In Section 1.5 we discussed a statistical study conducted by Norris Electronics involving a sample of 200 high-intensity lightbulbs manufactured with a new filament. The average lifetime for the sample, 76 hours, provided an estimate of the average lifetime for all lightbulbs produced with the new filament. However, consider this. Because Norris selected a sample of bulbs, it is reasonable to assume that another sample would have provided a different average lifetime.

Suppose Norris's management had hoped the sample results would enable them to claim that the average lifetime for the new lightbulbs was 80 hours or more. Suppose further that Norris's management decides to continue the study by manufacturing and testing repeated samples of 200 lightbulbs with the new filament until a sample mean of 80 hours or more is obtained. If the study is repeated enough times, a sample may eventually be obtained—by chance alone—that would provide the desired result and enable Norris to make such a claim. In this case, consumers would be misled into thinking the new product is better than it actually is. Clearly, this type of behavior is unethical and represents a gross misuse of statistics in practice.

Several ethical guidelines in the responsibilities and publications and testimony area deal with issues involving the handling of data. For instance, a statistician must account for

---

[2]American Statistical Association, "Ethical Guidelines for Statistical Practice," 1999.

all data considered in a study and explain the sample(s) actually used. In the Norris Electronics study the average lifetime for the 200 bulbs in the original sample is 76 hours; this is considerably less than the 80 hours or more that management hoped to obtain. Suppose now that after reviewing the results showing a 76-hour average lifetime, Norris discards all the observations with 70 or fewer hours until burnout, allegedly because these bulbs contain imperfections caused by startup problems in the manufacturing process. After these lightbulbs are discarded, the average lifetime for the remaining lightbulbs in the sample turns out to be 82 hours. Would you be suspicious of Norris's claim that the lifetime for their lightbulbs is 82 hours?

If the Norris lightbulbs showing 70 or fewer hours until burnout were discarded simply to provide an average lifetime of 82 hours, there is no question that discarding the lightbulbs with 70 or fewer hours until burnout is unethical. But, even if the discarded lightbulbs contain imperfections due to startup problems in the manufacturing process—and, as a result, should not have been included in the analysis—the statistician who conducted the study must account for all the data that were considered and explain how the sample actually used was obtained. To do otherwise is potentially misleading and would constitute unethical behavior on the part of both the company and the statistician.

A guideline in the shared values section of the American Statistical Association report states that statistical practitioners should avoid any tendency to slant statistical work toward predetermined outcomes. This type of unethical practice is often observed when unrepresentative samples are used to make claims. For instance, in many areas of the country smoking is not permitted in restaurants. Suppose, however, a lobbyist for the tobacco industry interviews people in restaurants where smoking is permitted in order to estimate the percentage of people who are in favor of allowing smoking in restaurants. The sample results show that 90% of the people interviewed are in favor of allowing smoking in restaurants. Based upon these sample results, the lobbyist claims that 90% of all people who eat in restaurants are in favor of permitting smoking in restaurants. In this case we would argue that sampling only persons eating in restaurants that allow smoking has biased the results. If only the final results of such a study are reported, readers unfamiliar with the details of the study (i.e., that the sample was collected only in restaurants allowing smoking) can be misled.

The scope of the American Statistical Association's report is broad and includes ethical guidelines that are appropriate not only for a statistician, but also for consumers of statistical information. We encourage you to read the report to obtain a better perspective of ethical issues as you continue your study of statistics and to gain the background for determining how to ensure that ethical standards are met when you start to use statistics in practice.

Summary

Statistics is the art and science of collecting, analyzing, presenting, and interpreting data. Nearly every college student majoring in business or economics is required to take a course in statistics. We began the chapter by describing typical statistical applications for business and economics.

Data consist of the facts and figures that are collected and analyzed. The four scales of measurement used to obtain data on a particular variable are nominal, ordinal, interval, and ratio. The scale of measurement for a variable is nominal when the data are labels or names used to identify an attribute of an element. The scale is ordinal if the data demonstrate the properties of nominal data and the order or rank of the data is meaningful. The scale is interval if the data demonstrate the properties of ordinal data and the interval between values is expressed in terms of a fixed unit of measure. Finally, the scale of measurement is ratio if the data show all the properties of interval data and the ratio of two values is meaningful.

For purposes of statistical analysis, data can be classified as categorical or quantitative. Categorical data use labels or names to identify an attribute of each element. Categorical data use either the nominal or ordinal scale of measurement and may be nonnumeric or numeric. Quantitative data are numeric values that indicate how much or how many. Quantitative data use either the interval or ratio scale of measurement. Ordinary arithmetic operations are meaningful only if the data are quantitative. Therefore, statistical computations used for quantitative data are not always appropriate for categorical data.

In Sections 1.4 and 1.5 we introduced the topics of descriptive statistics and statistical inference. Descriptive statistics are the tabular, graphical, and numerical methods used to summarize data. The process of statistical inference uses data obtained from a sample to make estimates or test hypotheses about the characteristics of a population. The last four sections of the chapter provide information on the role of computers in statistical analysis, an introduction to the relatively new fields of analytics, data mining, and big data, and a summary of ethical guidelines for statistical practice.

Glossary

Analytics The scientific process of transforming data into insight for making better decisions.

Big data A set of data that cannot be managed, processed, or analyzed with commonly available software in a reasonable amount of time. Big data are characterized by great volume (a large amount of data), high velocity (fast collection and processing), or wide variety (could include nontraditional data such as video, audio, and text).

Categorical data Labels or names used to identify an attribute of each element. Categorical data use either the nominal or ordinal scale of measurement and may be nonnumeric or numeric.

Categorical variable A variable with categorical data.

Census A survey to collect data on the entire population.

Cross-sectional data Data collected at the same or approximately the same point in time.

Data The facts and figures collected, analyzed, and summarized for presentation and interpretation.

Data mining The process of using procedures from statistics and computer science to extract useful information from extremely large databases.

Data set All the data collected in a particular study.

Descriptive analytics Analytical techniques that describe what has happened in the past.

Descriptive statistics Tabular, graphical, and numerical summaries of data.

Elements The entities on which data are collected.

Interval scale The scale of measurement for a variable if the data demonstrate the properties of ordinal data and the interval between values is expressed in terms of a fixed unit of measure. Interval data are always numeric.

Nominal scale The scale of measurement for a variable when the data are labels or names used to identify an attribute of an element. Nominal data may be nonnumeric or numeric.

Observation The set of measurements obtained for a particular element.

Ordinal scale The scale of measurement for a variable if the data exhibit the properties of nominal data and the order or rank of the data is meaningful. Ordinal data may be nonnumeric or numeric.

Population The set of all elements of interest in a particular study.

Predictive analytics Analytical techniques that use models constructed from past data to predict the future or assess the impact of one variable on another.

Prescriptive analytics Analytical techniques that yield a course of action.

Quantitative data Numeric values that indicate how much or how many of something. Quantitative data are obtained using either the interval or ratio scale of measurement.

Quantitative variable A variable with quantitative data.

Ratio scale The scale of measurement for a variable if the data demonstrate all the properties of interval data and the ratio of two values is meaningful. Ratio data are always numeric.

Sample A subset of the population.

Sample survey A survey to collect data on a sample.

Statistical inference The process of using data obtained from a sample to make estimates or test hypotheses about the characteristics of a population.

Statistics The art and science of collecting, analyzing, presenting, and interpreting data.

Time series data Data collected over several time periods.

Variable A characteristic of interest for the elements.

Supplementary Exercises

1. Discuss the differences between statistics as numerical facts and statistics as a discipline or field of study.

2. Tablet PC Comparison provides a wide variety of information about tablet computers. Their website enables consumers to easily compare different tablets using factors such as cost, type of operating system, display size, battery life, and CPU manufacturer. A sample of 10 tablet computers is shown in Table 1.6 (Tablet PC Comparison website, February 28, 2013).
   a. How many elements are in this data set?
   b. How many variables are in this data set?
   c. Which variables are categorical and which variables are quantitative?
   d. What type of measurement scale is used for each of the variables?

3. Refer to Table 1.6.
   a. What is the average cost for the tablets?
   b. Compare the average cost of tablets with a Windows operating system to the average cost of tablets with an Android operating system.
   c. What percentage of tablets use a CPU manufactured by TI OMAP?
   d. What percentage of tablets use an Android operating system?

4. Table 1.7 shows data for eight cordless telephones (*Consumer Reports*, November 2012). The Overall Score, a measure of the overall quality for the cordless telephone, ranges from 0 to 100. Voice Quality has possible ratings of poor, fair, good, very good, and excellent. Talk Time is the manufacturer's claim of how long the handset can be used when it is fully charged.

TABLE 1.6 PRODUCT INFORMATION FOR 10 TABLET COMPUTERS

Tablet	Cost ($)	Operating System	Display Size (inches)	Battery Life (hours)	CPU Manufacturer
Acer Iconia W510	599	Windows	10.1	8.5	Intel
Amazon Kindle Fire HD	299	Android	8.9	9	TI OMAP
Apple iPad 4	499	iOS	9.7	11	Apple
HP Envy X2	860	Windows	11.6	8	Intel
Lenovo ThinkPad Tablet	668	Windows	10.1	10.5	Intel
Microsoft Surface Pro	899	Windows	10.6	4	Intel
Motorola Droid XYboard	530	Android	10.1	9	TI OMAP
Samsung Ativ Smart PC	590	Windows	11.6	7	Intel
Samsung Galaxy Tab	525	Android	10.1	10	Nvidia
Sony Tablet S	360	Android	9.4	8	Nvidia

TABLE 1.7　DATA FOR EIGHT CORDLESS TELEPHONES

Brand	Model	Price ($)	Overall Score	Voice Quality	Handset on Base	Talk Time (Hours)
AT&T	CL84100	60	73	Excellent	Yes	7
AT&T	TL92271	80	70	Very Good	No	7
Panasonic	4773B	100	78	Very Good	Yes	13
Panasonic	6592T	70	72	Very Good	No	13
Uniden	D2997	45	70	Very Good	No	10
Uniden	D1788	80	73	Very Good	Yes	7
Vtech	DS6521	60	72	Excellent	No	7
Vtech	CS6649	50	72	Very Good	Yes	7

   a.　How many elements are in this data set?

   b.　For the variables Price, Overall Score, Voice Quality, Handset on Base, and Talk Time, which variables are categorical and which variables are quantitative?

   c.　What scale of measurement is used for each variable?

5.　Refer to the data set in Table 1.7.

   a.　What is the average price for the cordless telephones?

   b.　What is the average talk time for the cordless telephones?

   c.　What percentage of the cordless telephones have a voice quality of excellent?

   d.　What percentage of the cordless telephones have a handset on the base?

6.　J.D. Power and Associates surveys new automobile owners to learn about the quality of recently purchased vehicles. The following questions were asked in the J.D. Power Initial Quality Survey, May 2012.

   a.　Did you purchase or lease the vehicle?

   b.　What price did you pay?

   c.　What is the overall attractiveness of your vehicle's exterior? (Unacceptable, Average, Outstanding, or Truly Exceptional)

   d.　What is your average number of miles per gallon?

   e.　What is your overall rating of your new vehicle? (1- to 10-point scale with 1 Unacceptable and 10 Truly Exceptional)

Comment on whether each question provides categorical or quantitative data.

7.　The Kroger Company is one of the largest grocery retailers in the United States, with over 2000 grocery stores across the country. Kroger uses an online customer opinion questionnaire to obtain performance data about its products and services and learn about what motivates its customers (Kroger website, April 2012). In the survey, Kroger customers were asked if they would be willing to pay more for products that had each of the following four characteristics. The four questions were as follows:

Would you pay more for

   products that have a brand name?
   products that are environmentally friendly?
   products that are organic?
   products that have been recommended by others?

For each question, the customers had the option of responding Yes if they would pay more or No if they would not pay more.

   a.　Are the data collected by Kroger in this example categorical or quantitative?

   b.　What measurement scale is used?

8.　*The Tennessean*, an online newspaper located in Nashville, Tennessee, conducts a daily poll to obtain reader opinions on a variety of current issues. In a recent poll, 762 readers responded to the following question: "If a constitutional amendment to ban a state income tax is placed on the ballot in Tennessee, would you want it to pass?" Possible responses were Yes, No, or Not Sure (*The Tennessean* website, February 15, 2013).

a. What was the sample size for this poll?

b. Are the data categorical or quantitative?

c. Would it make more sense to use averages or percentages as a summary of the data for this question?

d. Of the respondents, 67% said Yes, they would want it to pass. How many individuals provided this response?

9. The Commerce Department reported receiving the following applications for the Malcolm Baldrige National Quality Award: 23 from large manufacturing firms, 18 from large service firms, and 30 from small businesses.

a. Is type of business a categorical or quantitative variable?

b. What percentage of the applications came from small businesses?

10. The Bureau of Transportation Statistics Omnibus Household Survey is conducted annually and serves as an information source for the U.S. Department of Transportation. In one part of the survey the person being interviewed was asked to respond to the following statement: "Drivers of motor vehicles should be allowed to talk on a hand-held cell phone while driving." Possible responses were strongly agree, somewhat agree, somewhat disagree, and strongly disagree. Forty-four respondents said that they strongly agree with this statement, 130 said that they somewhat agree, 165 said they somewhat disagree, and 741 said they strongly disagree with this statement.

a. Do the responses for this statement provide categorical or quantitative data?

b. Would it make more sense to use averages or percentages as a summary of the responses for this statement?

c. What percentage of respondents strongly agree with allowing drivers of motor vehicles to talk on a hand-held cell phone while driving?

d. Do the results indicate general support for or against allowing drivers of motor vehicles to talk on a hand-held cell phone while driving?

11. In a Gallup telephone survey conducted on April 9–10, 2013, each person being interviewed was asked if they would vote for a law in their state that would increase the gas tax by up to 20 cents a gallon, with the new gas tax money going to improve roads and bridges and build more mass transportation in their state. Possible responses were vote for, vote against, and no opinion. Two hundred and ninety-five respondents said they would vote for the law, 672 said they would vote against the law, and 51 said they had no opinion (Gallup website, June 14, 2013).

a. Do the responses for this question provide categorical or quantitative data?

b. What was the sample size for this Gallup poll?

c. What percentage of respondents would vote for a law increasing the gas tax?

d. Do the results indicate general support for or against increasing the gas tax to improve roads and bridges and build more mass transportation?

12. The Hawaii Visitors Bureau collects data on visitors to Hawaii. The following questions were among 16 asked in a questionnaire handed out to passengers during incoming airline flights.

- This trip to Hawaii is my: 1st, 2nd, 3rd, 4th, etc.
- The primary reason for this trip is: (10 categories, including vacation, convention, honeymoon)
- Where I plan to stay: (11 categories, including hotel, apartment, relatives, camping)
- Total days in Hawaii

a. What is the population being studied?

b. Is the use of a questionnaire a good way to reach the population of passengers on incoming airline flights?

c. Comment on each of the four questions in terms of whether it will provide categorical or quantitative data.

FIGURE 1.10   GOOGLE REVENUE

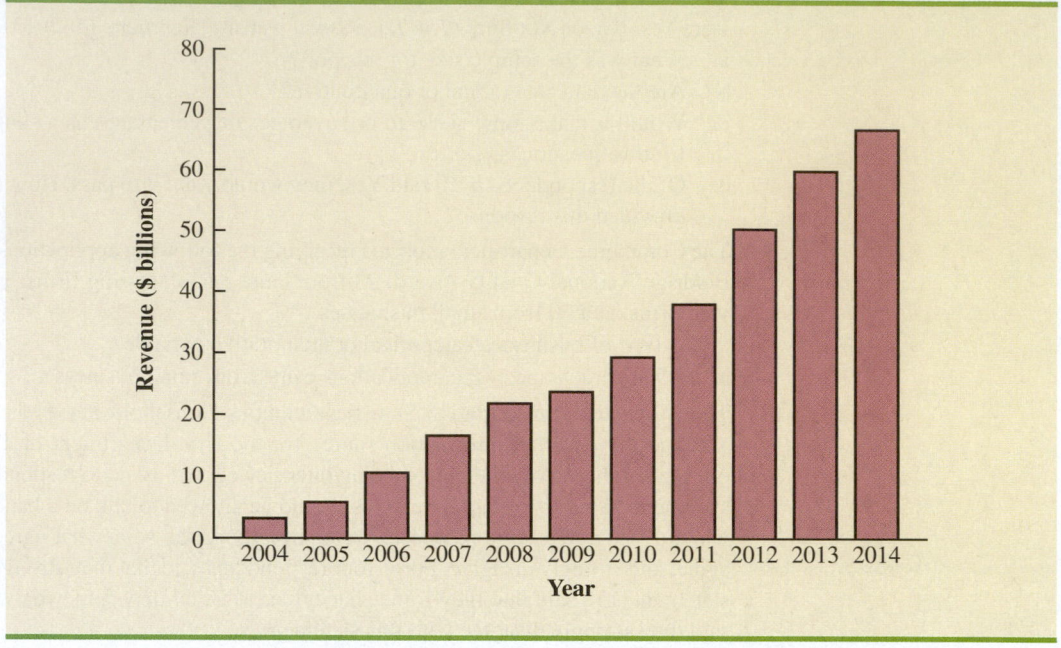

 **SELF***test*

13. Figure 1.10 provides a bar chart showing the annual revenue for Google from 2004 to 2014. (*The Wall Street Journal,* August 19, 2014).
   a. What is the variable of interest?
   b. Are the data categorical or quantitative?
   c. Are the data time series or cross-sectional?
   d. Comment on the trend in Google revenue over time.

14. The following data show the number of rental cars in service for three rental car companies: Hertz, Avis, and Dollar, over a four-year period.

Company	Cars in Service (1000s)			
	Year 1	**Year 2**	**Year 3**	**Year 4**
Hertz	327	311	286	290
Dollar	167	140	106	108
Avis	204	220	300	270

   a. Construct a time series graph for the years 1 to 4 showing the number of rental cars in service for each company. Show the time series for all three companies on the same graph.
   b. Comment on who appears to be the market share leader and how the market shares are changing over time.
   c. Construct a bar chart showing rental cars in service for Year 4. Is this chart based on cross-sectional or time series data?

15. The U.S. Census Bureau tracks sales per month for various products and services through its Monthly Retail Trade Survey. Figure 1.11 shows monthly bookstore sales in millions of dollars for 2014.
   a. Are the data quantitative or categorical?
   b. Are the data cross-sectional or time series?
   c. Which month has the highest sales?

FIGURE 1.11   MONTHLY BOOKSTORE SALES FOR 2014

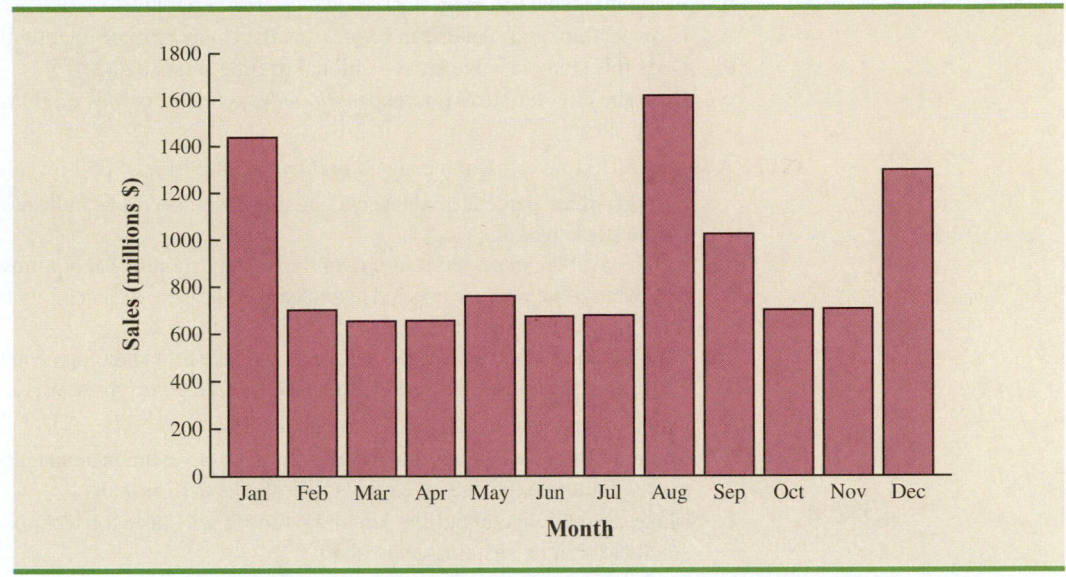

d. Which month has the second highest sales?

e. Why do you think the answers to parts (c) and (d) might be the two highest months? Explain.

16. The Energy Information Administration of the U.S. Department of Energy provided time series data for the U.S. average price per gallon of conventional regular gasoline between January 2007 and March 2012 (Energy Information Administration website, April 2012). Use the Internet to obtain the average price per gallon of conventional regular gasoline since March 2012.

    a. Extend the graph of the time series shown in Figure 1.1.

    b. What interpretations can you make about the average price per gallon of conventional regular gasoline since March 2012?

    c. Does the time series continue to show a summer increase in the average price per gallon? Explain.

17. A manager of a large corporation recommends a $10,000 raise be given to keep a valued subordinate from moving to another company. What internal and external sources of data might be used to decide whether such a salary increase is appropriate?

18. A random telephone survey of 1021 adults (aged 18 and older) was conducted by Opinion Research Corporation on behalf of CompleteTax, an online tax preparation and e-filing service. The survey results showed that 684 of those surveyed planned to file their taxes electronically.

    a. Develop a descriptive statistic that can be used to estimate the percentage of all taxpayers who file electronically.

    b. The survey reported that the most frequently used method for preparing the tax return was to hire an accountant or professional tax preparer. If 60% of the people surveyed had their tax return prepared this way, how many people used an accountant or professional tax preparer?

    c. Other methods that the person filing the return often used include manual preparation, use of an online tax service, and use of a software tax program. Would the data for the method for preparing the tax return be considered categorical or quantitative?

19. A *Bloomberg Businessweek* North American subscriber study collected data from a sample of 2861 subscribers. Fifty-nine percent of the respondents indicated an annual income of $75,000 or more, and 50% reported having an American Express credit card.

a. What is the population of interest in this study?

b. Is annual income a categorical or quantitative variable?

c. Is ownership of an American Express card a categorical or quantitative variable?

d. Does this study involve cross-sectional or time series data?

e. Describe any statistical inferences *Bloomberg Businessweek* might make on the basis of the survey.

20. A survey of 131 investment managers in *Barron's* Big Money poll revealed the following:

    • Forty-three percent of managers classified themselves as bullish or very bullish on the stock market.

    • The average expected return over the next 12 months for equities was 11.2%.

    • Twenty-one percent selected health care as the sector most likely to lead the market in the next 12 months.

    • When asked to estimate how long it would take for technology and telecom stocks to resume sustainable growth, the managers' average response was 2.5 years.

    a. Cite two descriptive statistics.

    b. Make an inference about the population of all investment managers concerning the average return expected on equities over the next 12 months.

    c. Make an inference about the length of time it will take for technology and telecom stocks to resume sustainable growth.

21. A seven-year medical research study reported that women whose mothers took the drug DES during pregnancy were twice as likely to develop tissue abnormalities that might lead to cancer as were women whose mothers did not take the drug.

    a. This study compared two populations. What were the populations?

    b. Do you suppose the data were obtained in a survey or an experiment?

    c. For the population of women whose mothers took the drug DES during pregnancy, a sample of 3980 women showed that 63 developed tissue abnormalities that might lead to cancer. Provide a descriptive statistic that could be used to estimate the number of women out of 1000 in this population who have tissue abnormalities.

    d. For the population of women whose mothers did not take the drug DES during pregnancy, what is the estimate of the number of women out of 1000 who would be expected to have tissue abnormalities?

    e. Medical studies often use a relatively large sample (in this case, 3980). Why?

22. A survey conducted by Better Homes and Gardens Real Estate LLC showed that one in five U.S. homeowners have either moved from their home or would like to move because their neighborhood or community isn't ideal for their lifestyle (Better Homes and Gardens Real Estate website, September 26, 2013). The top lifestyle priorities of respondents when searching for their next home include ease of commuting by car, access to health and safety services, family-friendly neighborhood, availability of retail stores, access to cultural activities, public transportation access, and nightlife and restaurant access. Suppose a real estate agency in Denver, Colorado, hired you to conduct a similar study to determine the top lifestyle priorities for clients that currently have a home listed for sale with the agency or have hired the agency to help them locate a new home.

    a. What is the population for the survey you will be conducting?

    b. How would you collect the data for this study?

23. Pew Research Center is a nonpartisan polling organization that provides information about issues, attitudes, and trends shaping America. In a poll, Pew researchers found that 73% of teens aged 13–17 have a smartphone, 15% have a basic phone and 12% have no phone. The study also asked the respondents how they communicated with their closest friend. Of those with a smartphone, 58% responded texting, 17% social media and 10% phone calls. Of those with no smartphone, 25% responded texting, 29% social media and 21% phone calls. (Pew Research Center website, October 2015).

a. One statistic (58%) concerned the use of texting to contact his/her closest friend, if the teen owns a smartphone. To what population is that applicable?

b. Another statistic (25%) concerned the use of texting by those who do not own a smartphone. To what population is that applicable?

c. Do you think the Pew researchers conducted a census or a sample survey to obtain their results? Why?

24. A sample of midterm grades for five students showed the following results: 72, 65, 82, 90, 76. Which of the following statements are correct, and which should be challenged as being too generalized?

a. The average midterm grade for the sample of five students is 77.

b. The average midterm grade for all students who took the exam is 77.

c. An estimate of the average midterm grade for all students who took the exam is 77.

d. More than half of the students who take this exam will score between 70 and 85.

e. If five other students are included in the sample, their grades will be between 65 and 90.

25. Table 1.8 shows a data set containing information for 25 of the shadow stocks tracked by the American Association of Individual Investors. Shadow stocks are common stocks of smaller companies that are not closely followed by Wall Street analysts. The data set is also on the website that accompanies the text in the DATAfile named *Shadow02*.

TABLE 1.8   DATA SET FOR 25 SHADOW STOCKS

Shadow02

Company	Exchange	Ticker Symbol	Market Cap ($ millions)	Price/ Earnings Ratio	Gross Profit Margin (%)
DeWolfe Companies	AMEX	DWL	36.4	8.4	36.7
North Coast Energy	OTC	NCEB	52.5	6.2	59.3
Hansen Natural Corp.	OTC	HANS	41.1	14.6	44.8
MarineMax, Inc.	NYSE	HZO	111.5	7.2	23.8
Nanometrics Incorporated	OTC	NANO	228.6	38.0	53.3
TeamStaff, Inc.	OTC	TSTF	92.1	33.5	4.1
Environmental Tectonics	AMEX	ETC	51.1	35.8	35.9
Measurement Specialties	AMEX	MSS	101.8	26.8	37.6
SEMCO Energy, Inc.	NYSE	SEN	193.4	18.7	23.6
Party City Corporation	OTC	PCTY	97.2	15.9	36.4
Embrex, Inc.	OTC	EMBX	136.5	18.9	59.5
Tech/Ops Sevcon, Inc.	AMEX	TO	23.2	20.7	35.7
ARCADIS NV	OTC	ARCAF	173.4	8.8	9.6
Qiao Xing Universal Tele.	OTC	XING	64.3	22.1	30.8
Energy West Incorporated	OTC	EWST	29.1	9.7	16.3
Barnwell Industries, Inc.	AMEX	BRN	27.3	7.4	73.4
Innodata Corporation	OTC	INOD	66.1	11.0	29.6
Medical Action Industries	OTC	MDCI	137.1	26.9	30.6
Instrumentarium Corp.	OTC	INMRY	240.9	3.6	52.1
Petroleum Development	OTC	PETD	95.9	6.1	19.4
Drexler Technology Corp.	OTC	DRXR	233.6	45.6	53.6
Gerber Childrenswear Inc.	NYSE	GCW	126.9	7.9	25.8
Gaiam, Inc.	OTC	GAIA	295.5	68.2	60.7
Artesian Resources Corp.	OTC	ARTNA	62.8	20.5	45.5
York Water Company	OTC	YORW	92.2	22.9	74.2

a. How many variables are in the data set?

b. Which of the variables are categorical and which are quantitative?

c. For the Exchange variable, show the frequency and the percent frequency for AMEX, NYSE, and OTC. Construct a bar graph similar to Figure 1.4 for the Exchange variable.

d. Show the frequency distribution for the Gross Profit Margin using the five intervals: 0–14.9, 15–29.9, 30–44.9, 45–59.9, and 60–74.9. Construct a histogram similar to Figure 1.5.

e. What is the average price/earnings ratio?

CHAPTER 2

Descriptive Statistics: Tabular and Graphical Displays

CONTENTS

STATISTICS IN PRACTICE:
COLGATE-PALMOLIVE COMPANY

STATISTICS *in* PRACTICE

COLGATE-PALMOLIVE COMPANY*
NEW YORK, NEW YORK

The Colgate-Palmolive Company started as a small soap and candle shop in New York City in 1806. Today, Colgate-Palmolive employs more than 38,000 people working in more than 200 countries and territories around the world. Although best known for its brand names of Colgate, Palmolive, and Fabuloso, the company also markets Irish Spring, Hill's Science Diet, and Ajax products.

The Colgate-Palmolive Company uses statistics in its quality assurance program for home laundry detergent products. One concern is customer satisfaction with the quantity of detergent in a carton. Every carton in each size category is filled with the same amount of detergent by weight, but the volume of detergent is affected by the density of the detergent powder. For instance, if the powder density is on the heavy side, a smaller volume of detergent is needed to reach the carton's specified weight. As a result, the carton may appear to be underfilled when opened by the consumer.

To control the problem of heavy detergent powder, limits are placed on the acceptable range of powder density. Statistical samples are taken periodically, and the density of each powder sample is measured. Data summaries are then provided for operating personnel so that corrective action can be taken if necessary to keep the density within the desired quality specifications.

A frequency distribution for the densities of 150 samples taken over a one-week period and a histogram are shown in the accompanying table and figure. Density levels above .40 are unacceptably high. The frequency distribution and histogram show that the operation is meeting its quality guidelines with all of the densities less than or equal to .40. Managers viewing these statistical summaries would be pleased with the quality of the detergent production process.

In this chapter, you will learn about tabular and graphical methods of descriptive statistics such as frequency distributions, bar charts, histograms, stem-and-leaf displays, crosstabulations, and others. The goal of

The Colgate-Palmolive Company uses statistical summaries to help maintain the quality of its products.

these methods is to summarize data so that the data can be easily understood and interpreted.

Frequency Distribution of Density Data

Density	Frequency
.29–.30	30
.31–.32	75
.33–.34	32
.35–.36	9
.37–.38	3
.39–.40	1
Total	150

Histogram of Density Data

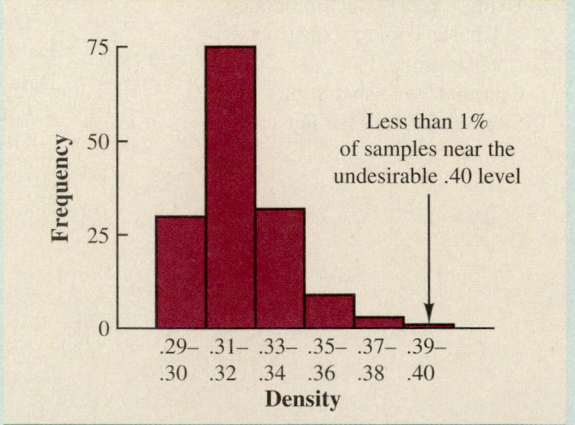

*The authors are indebted to William R. Fowle, Manager of Quality Assurance, Colgate-Palmolive Company, for providing this Statistics in Practice.

As indicated in Chapter 1, data can be classified as either categorical or quantitative. **Categorical data** use labels or names to identify categories of like items, and **quantitative data** are numerical values that indicate how much or how many. This chapter introduces the use of tabular and graphical displays for summarizing both categorical and quantitative data. Tabular and graphical displays can be found in annual reports, newspaper articles, and research studies. Everyone is exposed to these types of presentations. Hence, it is important to understand how they are constructed and how they should be interpreted.

We begin with a discussion of the use of tablular and graphical displays to summarize the data for a single variable. This is followed by a discussion of the use of tabular and graphical displays to summarize the data for two variables in a way that reveals the relationship between the two variables. **Data visualization** is a term often used to describe the use of graphical displays to summarize and present information about a data set. The last section of this chapter provides an introduction to data visualization and provides guidelines for creating effective graphical displays.

2.1 Summarizing Data for a Categorical Variable

Frequency Distribution

We begin the discussion of how tabular and graphical displays can be used to summarize categorical data with the definition of a **frequency distribution**.

> **FREQUENCY DISTRIBUTION**
>
> A frequency distribution is a tabular summary of data showing the number (frequency) of observations in each of several nonoverlapping categories or classes.

Let us use the following example to demonstrate the construction and interpretation of a frequency distribution for categorical data. Coca-Cola, Diet Coke, Dr. Pepper, Pepsi, and Sprite are five popular soft drinks. Assume that the data in Table 2.1 show the soft drink selected in a sample of 50 soft drink purchases.

TABLE 2.1 DATA FROM A SAMPLE OF 50 SOFT DRINK PURCHASES

SoftDrink

Coca-Cola	Coca-Cola	Coca-Cola	Sprite	Coca-Cola
Diet Coke	Dr. Pepper	Diet Coke	Dr. Pepper	Diet Coke
Pepsi	Sprite	Coca-Cola	Pepsi	Pepsi
Diet Coke	Coca-Cola	Sprite	Diet Coke	Pepsi
Coca-Cola	Diet Coke	Pepsi	Pepsi	Pepsi
Coca-Cola	Coca-Cola	Coca-Cola	Coca-Cola	Pepsi
Dr. Pepper	Coca-Cola	Coca-Cola	Coca-Cola	Coca-Cola
Diet Coke	Sprite	Coca-Cola	Coca-Cola	Dr. Pepper
Pepsi	Coca-Cola	Pepsi	Pepsi	Pepsi
Pepsi	Diet Coke	Coca-Cola	Dr. Pepper	Sprite

TABLE 2.2

FREQUENCY
DISTRIBUTION
OF SOFT DRINK
PURCHASES

Soft Drink	Frequency
Coca-Cola	19
Diet Coke	8
Dr. Pepper	5
Pepsi	13
Sprite	5
Total	50

To develop a frequency distribution for these data, we count the number of times each soft drink appears in Table 2.1. Coca-Cola appears 19 times, Diet Coke appears 8 times, Dr. Pepper appears 5 times, Pepsi appears 13 times, and Sprite appears 5 times. These counts are summarized in the frequency distribution in Table 2.2.

This frequency distribution provides a summary of how the 50 soft drink purchases are distributed across the five soft drinks. This summary offers more insight than the original data shown in Table 2.1. Viewing the frequency distribution, we see that Coca-Cola is the leader, Pepsi is second, Diet Coke is third, and Sprite and Dr. Pepper are tied for fourth. The frequency distribution summarizes information about the popularity of the five soft drinks.

Relative Frequency and Percent Frequency Distributions

A frequency distribution shows the number (frequency) of observations in each of several nonoverlapping classes. However, we are often interested in the proportion, or percentage, of observations in each class. The *relative frequency* of a class equals the fraction or proportion of observations belonging to a class. For a data set with n observations, the relative frequency of each class can be determined as follows:

RELATIVE FREQUENCY

$$\text{Relative frequency of a class} = \frac{\text{Frequency of the class}}{n} \tag{2.1}$$

The *percent frequency* of a class is the relative frequency multiplied by 100.

A **relative frequency distribution** gives a tabular summary of data showing the relative frequency for each class. A **percent frequency distribution** summarizes the percent frequency of the data for each class. Table 2.3 shows a relative frequency distribution and a percent frequency distribution for the soft drink data. In Table 2.3 we see that the relative frequency for Coca-Cola is 19/50 = .38, the relative frequency for Diet Coke is 8/50 = .16, and so on. From the percent frequency distribution, we see that 38% of the purchases were Coca-Cola, 16% of the purchases were Diet Coke, and so on. We can also note that 38% + 26% + 16% = 80% of the purchases were for the top three soft drinks.

TABLE 2.3   RELATIVE FREQUENCY AND PERCENT FREQUENCY DISTRIBUTIONS
OF SOFT DRINK PURCHASES

Soft Drink	Relative Frequency	Percent Frequency
Coca-Cola	.38	38
Diet Coke	.16	16
Dr. Pepper	.10	10
Pepsi	.26	26
Sprite	.10	10
Total	1.00	100

Using Excel to Construct a Frequency Distribution, a Relative Frequency Distribution, and a Percent Frequency Distribution

We can use Excel's Recommended PivotTables tool to construct a frequency distribution for the sample of 50 soft drink purchases. Two tasks are involved: Enter/Access Data and Apply Tools.

Enter/Access Data: Open the DATAfile named *SoftDrink*. The data are in cells A2:A51 and a label is in cell A1.

Apply Tools: The following steps describe how to use Excel's Recommended PivotTables tool to construct a frequency distribution for the sample of 50 soft drink purchases.

Step 1. Select any cell in the data set (cells A1:A51)
Step 2. Click **Insert** on the Ribbon
Step 3. In the **Tables** group click **Recommended PivotTables**; a preview showing the frequency distribution appears
Step 4. Click **OK**; the frequency distribution will appear in a new worksheet

The worksheet in Figure 2.1 shows the frequency distribution for the 50 soft drink purchases created using these steps. Also shown is the PivotTable Fields dialog box, a key component of every PivotTable report. We will discuss the use of the PivotTable Fields dialog box later in the chapter.

FIGURE 2.1 FREQUENCY DISTRIBUTION OF SOFT DRINK PURCHASES CONSTRUCTED USING EXCEL'S RECOMMENDED PIVOTTABLES TOOL

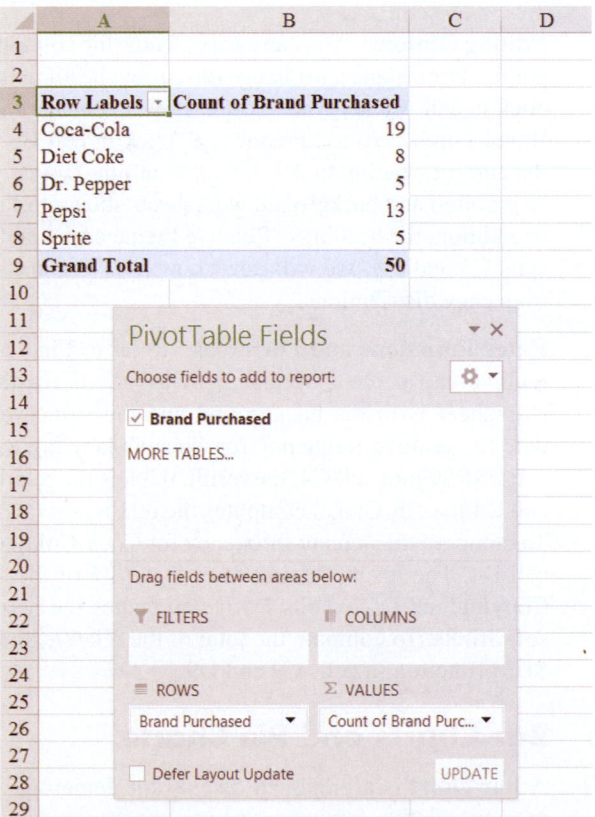

FIGURE 2.2   RELATIVE FREQUENCY AND PERCENT FREQUENCY DISTRIBUTIONS OF SOFT DRINK PURCHASES CONSTRUCTED USING EXCEL'S RECOMMENDED PIVOTTABLES TOOL

	A	B	C	D	E
1					
2					
3	Soft Drink ▼	Frequency	Relative Frequency	Percent Frequency	
4	Coca-Cola	19	=B4/$B$9	=C4*100	
5	Diet Coke	8	=B5/$B$9	=C5*100	
6	Dr. Pepper	5	=B6/$B$9	=C6*100	
7	Pepsi	13	=B7/$B$9	=C7*100	
8	Sprite	5	=B8/$B$9	=C8*100	
9	Total	50	=SUM(C4:C8)	=SUM(D4:D8)	
10					
11					

	A	B	C	D	E
1					
2					
3	Soft Drink ▼	Frequency	Relative Frequency	Percent Frequency	
4	Coca-Cola	19	0.38	38	
5	Diet Coke	8	0.16	16	
6	Dr. Pepper	5	0.1	10	
7	Pepsi	13	0.26	26	
8	Sprite	5	0.1	10	
9	Total	50	1	100	
10					

Editing Options: You can easily change the column headings in the frequency distribution output. For instance, to change the current heading in cell A3 (Row Labels) to "Soft Drink," click in cell A3 and type "Soft Drink"; to change the current heading in cell B3 (Count of Brand Purchased) to "Frequency," click in cell B3 and type "Frequency"; and to change the current heading in A9 (Grand Total) to "Total," click in cell A9 and type "Total." The foreground and background worksheets shown in Figure 2.2 contain the revised headings; in addition, the headings "Relative Frequency" and "Percent Frequency" were entered into cells C3 and D3. We will now show how to construct the relative frequency and percent frequency distributions.

Enter Functions and Formulas: Refer to Figure 2.2 as we describe how to create the relative and percent frequency distributions for the soft drink purchases. The formula worksheet is in the background and the value worksheet in the foreground. To compute the relative frequency for Coca-Cola using equation (2.1), we entered the formula =B4/$B$9 into cell C4; the result, 0.38, is the relative frequency for Coca-Cola. Copying cell C4 to cells C5:C8 computes the relative frequencies for each of the other soft drinks. To compute the percent frequency for Coca-Cola, we entered the formula = C4*100 into cell D4. The result, 38, indicates that 38% of the soft drink purchases were Coca-Cola. Copying cell D4 to cells D5:D8 computes the percent frequencies for each of the other soft drinks. To compute the total of the relative and percent frequencies we used Excel's SUM function in cells C9 and D9.

Bar Charts and Pie Charts

A **bar chart** is a graphical display for depicting categorical data summarized in a frequency, relative frequency, or percent frequency distribution. On one axis of the graph we specify the labels that are used for the classes (categories). A frequency, relative

FIGURE 2.3   BAR CHART OF SOFT DRINK PURCHASES

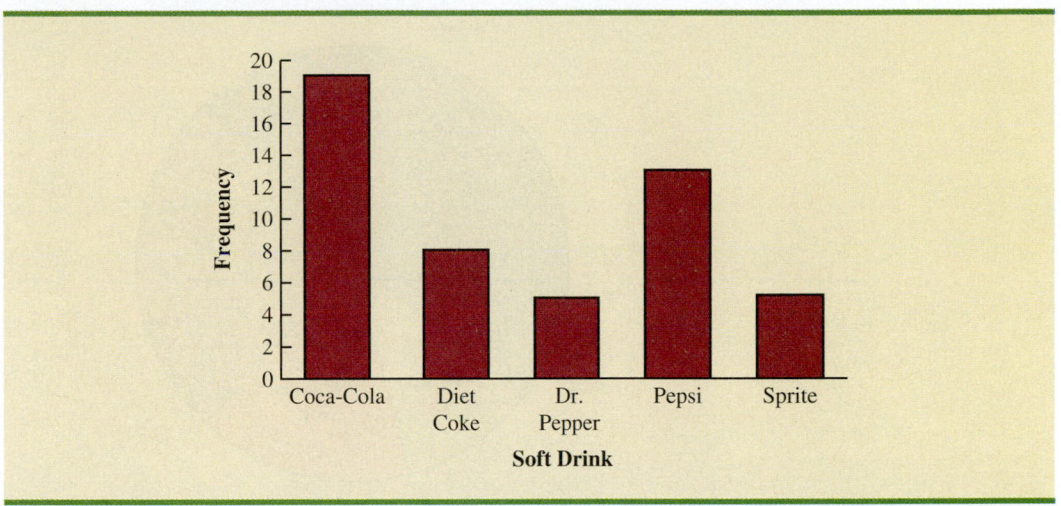

In quality control applications, bar charts are used to identify the most important causes of problems. When the bars are arranged in descending order of height from left to right with the most frequently occurring cause appearing first, the bar chart is called a Pareto diagram. *This diagram is named for its founder, Vilfredo Pareto, an Italian economist.*

frequency, or percent frequency scale can be used for the other axis of the chart. Then, using a bar of fixed width drawn above or next to each class label, we extend the length of the bar until we reach the frequency, relative frequency, or percent frequency of the class. For categorical data, the bars should be separated to emphasize the fact that each class is separate. Figure 2.3 shows a bar chart of the frequency distribution for the 50 soft drink purchases. Note how the graphical presentation shows Coca-Cola, Pepsi, and Diet Coke to be the most preferred brands.

In Figure 2.3 the horizontal axis was used to specify the labels for the categories; thus, the bars of the chart appear vertically in the display. In Excel, this type of display is referred to as a *column chart*. We could also display the bars for the chart horizontally by using the vertical axis to display the labels; Excel refers to this type of display as a *bar chart*. The choice of whether to display the bars vertically or horizontally depends upon what you want the final chart to look like. Throughout the text we will refer to either type of display as a bar chart.

The **pie chart** provides another graphical display for presenting relative frequency and percent frequency distributions for categorical data. To construct a pie chart, we first draw a circle to represent all the data. Then we use the relative frequencies to subdivide the circle into sectors, or parts, that correspond to the relative frequency for each class. For example, because a circle contains 360 degrees and Coca-Cola shows a relative frequency of .38, the sector of the pie chart labeled Coca-Cola consists of .38(360) = 136.8 degrees. The sector of the pie chart labeled Diet Coke consists of .16(360) = 57.6 degrees. Similar calculations for the other classes yield the pie chart in Figure 2.4. The numerical values shown for each sector can be frequencies, relative frequencies, or percent frequencies.

Numerous options involving the use of colors, shading, legends, text font, and three-dimensional perspectives are available to enhance the visual appearance of bar and pie charts. When used carefully, such options can provide a more effective display. But this is not always the case. For instance, consider the three-dimensional pie chart for the soft drink data shown in Figure 2.5. Compare it to the simpler presentation shown in Figure 2.4. The three-dimensional perspective adds no new understanding. In fact, because you have to view the three-dimensional pie chart in Figure 2.5 at an angle rather than from straight overhead, it can be more difficult to visualize. The use of a legend in Figure 2.5 also forces your eyes to shift back and forth between the key and the chart. The simpler

FIGURE 2.4 PIE CHART OF SOFT DRINK PURCHASES

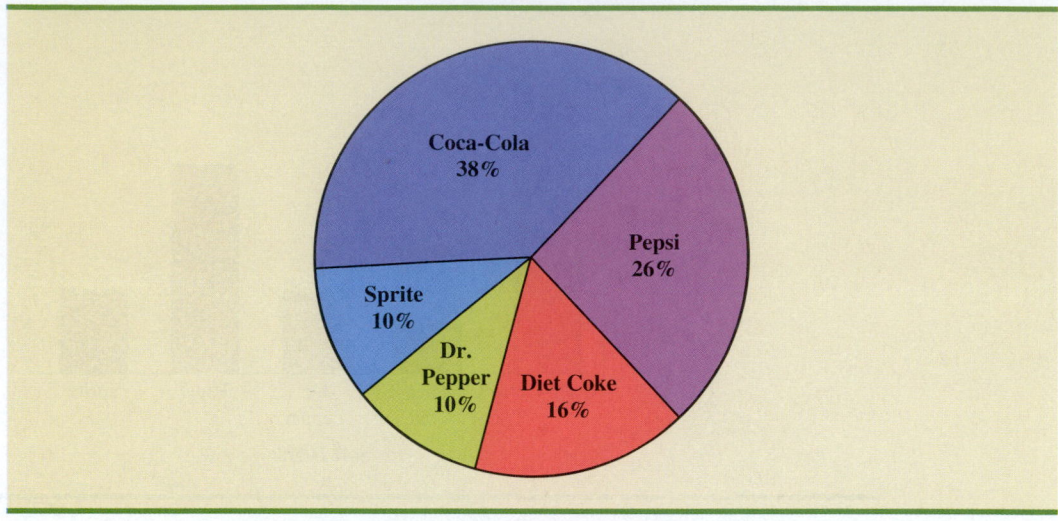

FIGURE 2.5 THREE-DIMENSIONAL PIE CHART OF SOFT DRINK PURCHASES

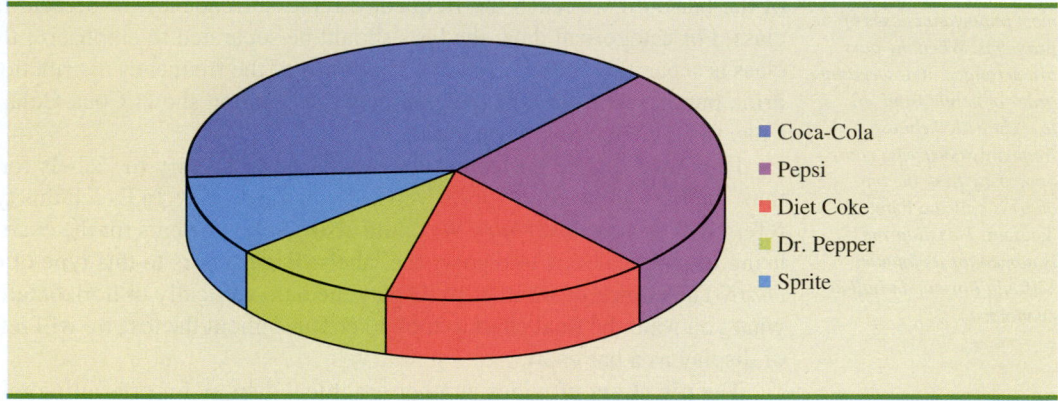

chart shown in Figure 2.4, which shows the percentages and classes directly on the pie, is more effective.

In general, pie charts are not the best way to present percentages for comparison. Research has shown that people are much better at accurately judging differences in length rather than differences in angles (or slices). When making such comparisons, we recommend you use a bar chart similar to Figure 2.3. In Section 2.5 we provide additional guidelines for creating effective visual displays.

Using Excel to Construct a Bar Chart and a Pie Chart

We can use Excel's Recommended Charts tool to construct a bar chart and a pie chart for the sample of 50 soft drink purchases. Two tasks are involved: Enter/Access Data and Apply Tools.

Enter/Access Data: Open the DATAfile named *SoftDrink*. The data are in cell A2:A51 and a label is in cell A1.

FIGURE 2.6   BAR CHART OF SOFT DRINK PURCHASES CONSTRUCTED USING EXCEL'S RECOMMENDED CHARTS TOOL

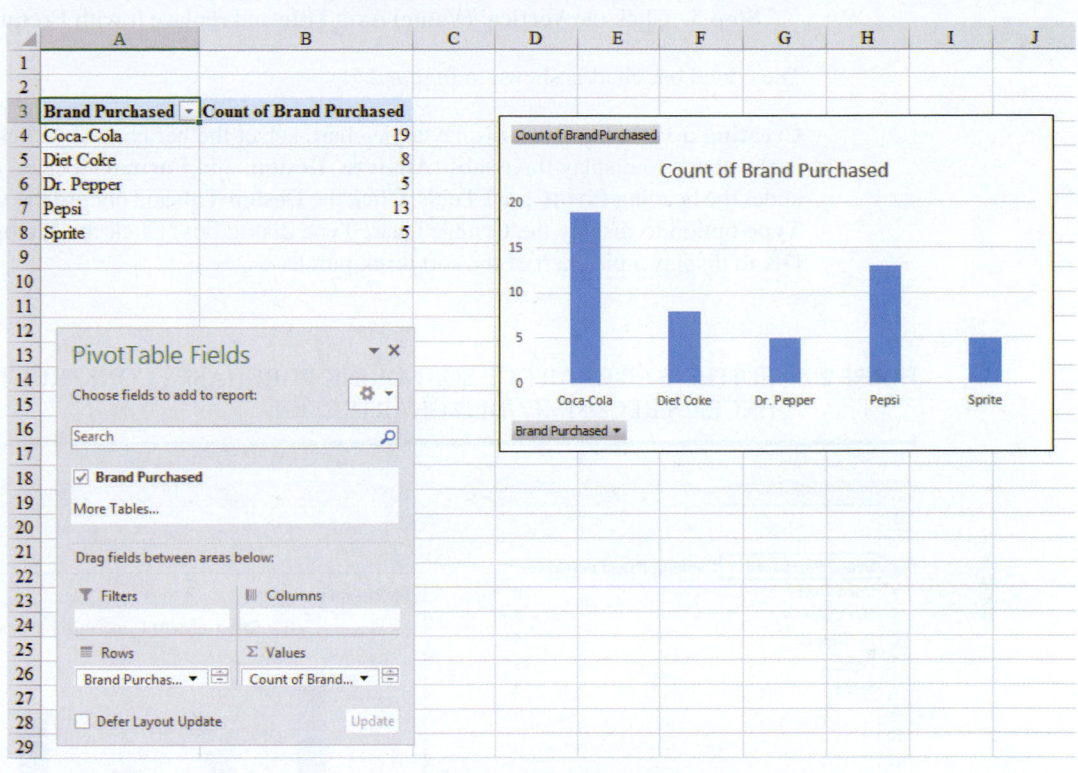

Apply Tools: The following steps describe how to use Excel's Recommended Charts tool to construct a bar chart for the sample of 50 soft drink purchases.

> **Step 1.** Select any cell in the data set (cells A1:A51)
> **Step 2.** Click **Insert** on the Ribbon
> **Step 3.** In the **Charts** group click **Recommended Charts**; a preview showing the bar chart appears
> **Step 4.** Click OK; the bar chart will appear in a new worksheet

Excel refers to the bar chart in Figure 2.6 as a Clustered Column chart.

The worksheet in Figure 2.6 shows the bar chart for the 50 soft drink purchases created using these steps. Also shown are the frequency distribution and PivotTable Fields dialog box that were created by Excel in order to construct the bar chart. Thus, using Excel's Recommended Charts tool you can construct a bar chart and a frequency distribution at the same time.

Editing Options: You can easily edit the bar chart to display a different chart title and add axis titles. For instance, suppose you would like to use "Bar Chart of Soft Drink Purchases" as the chart title and insert "Soft Drink" for the horizontal axis title and "Frequency" for the vertical axis title.

> **Step 1.** Click the **Chart Title** and replace it with **Bar Chart of Soft Drink Purchases**
> **Step 2.** Click the **Chart Elements** button ⊞ (located next to the top right corner of the chart)

Step 3. When the list of chart elements appears:
>   Click **Axis Titles** (creates placeholders for the axis titles)

Step 4. Click the **Horizontal (Category) Axis Title** and replace it with **Soft Drink**

Step 5. Click the **Vertical (Value) Axis Title** and replace it with **Frequency**

The edited bar chart is shown in Figure 2.7.

Creating a Pie Chart: To display a pie chart, select the bar chart (by clicking anywhere in the chart) to display three tabs (**Analyze**, **Design**, and **Format**) located on the Ribbon under the heading **PivotChart Tools**. Click the **Design Tab** and choose the **Change Chart Type** option to display the Change Chart Type dialog box. Click the **Pie** option and then **OK** to display a pie chart of the soft drink purchases.

FIGURE 2.7   EDITED BAR CHART OF SOFT DRINK PURCHASES CONSTRUCTED USING EXCEL'S RECOMMENDED CHARTS TOOL

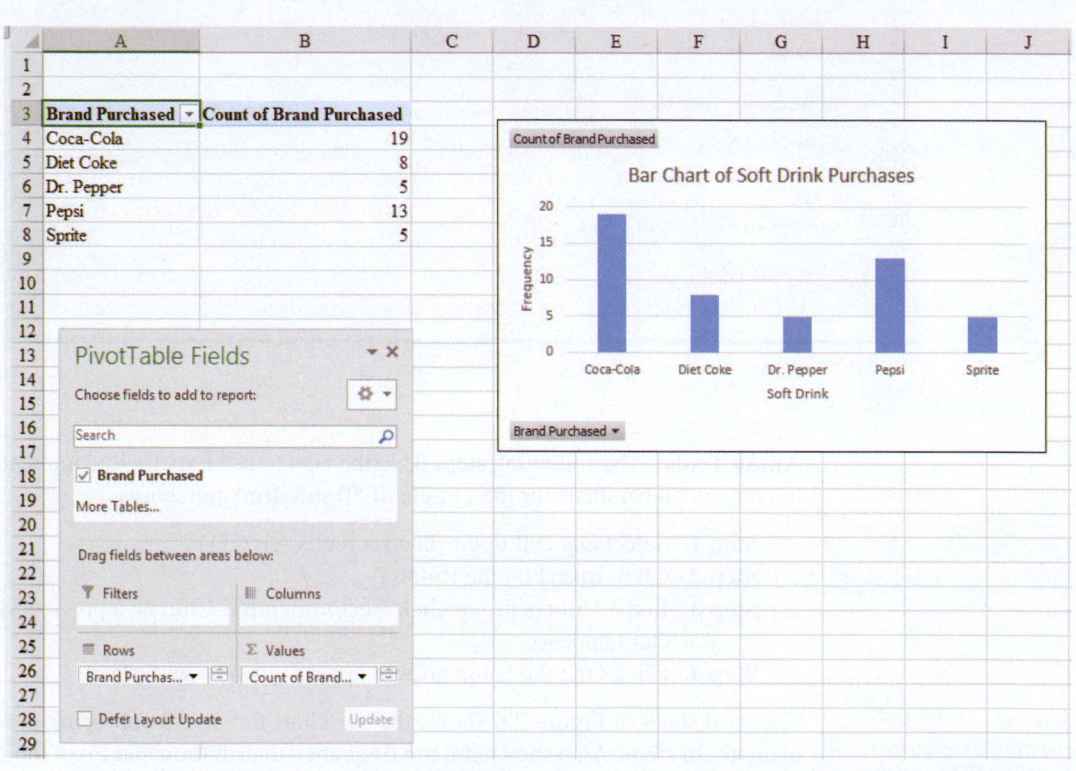

Exercises

Methods

1. The response to a question has three alternatives: A, B, and C. A sample of 120 responses provides 60 A, 24 B, and 36 C. Show the frequency and relative frequency distributions.

2. A partial relative frequency distribution is given.

Class	Relative Frequency
A	.22
B	.18
C	.40
D	

a. What is the relative frequency of class D?
b. The total sample size is 200. What is the frequency of class D?
c. Show the frequency distribution.
d. Show the percent frequency distribution.

SELFtest

3. A questionnaire provides 58 Yes, 42 No, and 20 No-Opinion answers.
a. In the construction of a pie chart, how many degrees would be in the section of the pie showing the Yes answers?
b. How many degrees would be in the section of the pie showing the No answers?
c. Construct a pie chart.
d. Construct a bar chart.

Applications

DATA *file*

Syndicated

4. For the 2010–2011 viewing season, the top five syndicated programs were *Wheel of Fortune* (WoF), *Two and Half Men* (THM), *Jeopardy* (Jep), *Judge Judy* (JJ), and the *Oprah Winfrey Show* (OWS) (Nielsen Media Research website, April 16, 2012). Data indicating the preferred shows for a sample of 50 viewers follow.

WoF	Jep	JJ	Jep	THM
THM	WoF	OWS	Jep	THM
Jep	OWS	WoF	WoF	WoF
WoF	THM	OWS	THM	WoF
THM	JJ	JJ	Jep	THM
OWS	OWS	JJ	JJ	Jep
JJ	WoF	THM	WoF	WoF
THM	THM	WoF	JJ	JJ
Jep	THM	WoF	Jep	Jep
WoF	THM	OWS	OWS	Jep

a. Are these data categorical or quantitative?
b. Provide frequency and percent frequency distributions.
c. Construct a bar chart and a pie chart.
d. On the basis of the sample, which television show has the largest viewing audience? Which one is second?

5. In alphabetical order, the six most common last names in the United States are Brown, Johnson, Jones, Miller, Smith, and Williams (*The World Almanac,* 2012). Assume that a sample of 50 individuals with one of these last names provided the following data.

DATA *file*

2012Names

Brown	Williams	Williams	Williams	Brown
Smith	Jones	Smith	Johnson	Smith
Miller	Smith	Brown	Williams	Johnson
Johnson	Smith	Smith	Johnson	Brown
Williams	Miller	Johnson	Williams	Johnson
Williams	Johnson	Jones	Smith	Brown
Johnson	Smith	Smith	Brown	Jones
Jones	Jones	Smith	Smith	Miller
Miller	Jones	Williams	Miller	Smith
Jones	Johnson	Brown	Johnson	Miller

Summarize the data by constructing the following:

a.   Relative and percent frequency distributions
b.   A bar chart
c.   A pie chart
d.   Based on these data, what are the three most common last names?

6.   Nielsen Media Research provided the list of the 25 top-rated single shows in television history. The following data show the television network that produced each of these 25 top-rated shows.

DATA *file*
Networks

CBS	CBS	NBC	FOX	CBS
CBS	NBC	NBC	NBC	ABC
ABC	NBC	ABC	ABC	NBC
CBS	NBC	CBS	ABC	NBC
NBC	CBS	CBS	ABC	CBS

a.   Construct a frequency distribution, percent frequency distribution, and bar chart for the data.
b.   Which network or networks have done the best in terms of presenting top-rated television shows? Compare the performance of ABC, CBS, and NBC.

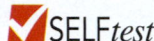

SELF*test*

7.   The Canmark Research Center Airport Customer Satisfaction Survey uses an online questionnaire to provide airlines and airports with customer satisfaction ratings for all aspects of the customers' flight experience (airportsurvey website, July 2012). After completing a flight, customers receive an e-mail asking them to go to the website and rate a variety of factors, including the reservation process, the check-in process, luggage policy, cleanliness of gate area, service by flight attendants, food/beverage selection, on-time arrival, and so on. A five-point scale, with Excellent (E), Very Good (V), Good (G), Fair (F), and Poor (P), is used to record customer ratings. Assume that passengers on a Delta Airlines flight from Myrtle Beach, South Carolina to Atlanta, Georgia provided the following ratings for the question "Please rate the airline based on your overall experience with this flight." The sample ratings are shown below.

DATA *file*
AirSurvey

E	E	G	V	V	E	V	V	V	E
E	G	V	E	E	V	E	E	E	V
V	V	V	F	V	E	V	E	G	E
G	E	V	E	V	E	V	V	V	V
E	E	V	V	E	P	E	V	P	V

a.   Use a percent frequency distribution and a bar chart to summarize these data. What do these summaries indicate about the overall customer satisfaction with the Delta flight?
b.   The online survey questionnaire enabled respondents to explain any aspect of the flight that failed to meet expectations. Would this be helpful information to a manager looking for ways to improve the overall customer satisfaction on Delta flights? Explain.

8.   Data for a sample of 55 members of the Baseball Hall of Fame in Cooperstown, New York are shown here. Each observation indicates the primary position played by the Hall of Famers: pitcher (P), catcher (H), first base (1), second base (2), third base (3), shortstop (S), left field (L), center field (C), and right field (R).

DATA *file*
BaseballHall

L	P	C	H	2	P	R	1	S	S	1	L	P	R	P
P	P	P	R	C	S	L	R	P	C	C	P	P	R	P
2	3	P	H	L	P	1	C	P	P	P	S	1	L	R
R	1	2	H	S	3	H	2	L	P					

a.   Construct frequency and relative frequency distributions to summarize the data.
b.   What position provides the most Hall of Famers?

    c.   What position provides the fewest Hall of Famers?

    d.   What outfield position (L, C, or R) provides the most Hall of Famers?

    e.   Compare infielders (1, 2, 3, and S) to outfielders (L, C, and R).

9.   Nearly 1.8 million bachelor's degrees and over 750,000 master's degrees are awarded annually by U.S. postsecondary institutions (National Center for Education Statistics website, November 2014). The Department of Education tracks the field of study for these graduates in the following categories: Business (B), Computer Sciences and Engineering (CSE), Education (E), Humanities (H), Natural Sciences and Mathematics (NSM), Social and Behavioral Sciences (SBS), and Other (O). Consider the following samples of 100 graduates:

Bachelor's Degree Field of Study

Majors

SBS	H	H	H	E	B	O	SBS	NSM	CSE
O	B	B	O	O	H	B	O	SBS	O
H	CSE	CSE	O	CSE	B	H	O	O	SBS
SBS	SBS	B	H	NSM	B	B	O	SBS	SBS
B	H	SBS	O	B	B	O	O	B	O
O	H	SBS	H	CSE	CSE	B	E	CSE	SBS
SBS	NSM	NSM	CSE	H	H	E	E	SBS	CSE
NSM	NSM	SBS	O	H	H	B	SBS	SBS	NSM
H	B	B	O	O	O	NSM	H	E	B
E	B	O	B	B	B	O	O	O	O

Master's Degree Field of Study

O	O	B	O	B	E	B	H	E	B
O	E	SBS	B	CSE	H	B	E	E	O
O	B	B	O	E	CSE	NSM	O	B	E
H	H	B	E	SBS	E	E	B	O	E
SBS	B	B	CSE	H	B	B	CSE	SBS	B
CSE	B	E	CSE	B	E	CSE	O	E	O
B	O	E	O	B	NSM	H	E	B	E
B	E	B	O	E	E	H	O	O	O
CSE	O	O	H	B	O	B	E	CSE	O
E	O	SBS	E	E	O	SBS	B	B	O

    a.   Provide a percent frequency distribution of field of study for each degree.

    b.   Construct a bar chart for field of study for each degree.

    c.   What is the lowest percentage field of study for each degree?

    d.   What is the highest percentage field of study for each degree?

    e.   Which field of study has the largest increase in percentage from bachelor's to masters'?

HotelRatings

10.   VirtualTourist provides ratings for hotels throughout the world. Ratings provided by 649 guests at the Sheraton Anaheim Hotel, located near the Disneyland Resort in Anaheim, California, can be found in the DATAfile named *HotelRatings* (VirtualTourist website, February 25, 2013). Possible responses were Excellent, Very Good, Average, Poor, and Terrible.

    a.   Construct a frequency distribution.

    b.   Construct a percent frequency distribution.

    c.   Construct a bar chart for the percent frequency distribution.

    d.   Comment on how guests rate their stay at the Sheraton Anaheim Hotel.

    e.   Results for 1679 guests who stayed at Disney's Grand Californian provided the following frequency distribution.

Rating	Frequency
Excellent	807
Very Good	521
Average	200
Poor	107
Terrible	44

Compare the ratings for Disney's Grand Californian with the results obtained for the Sheraton Anaheim Hotel.

2.2 Summarizing Data for a Quantitative Variable

Frequency Distribution

TABLE 2.4

YEAR-END AUDIT TIMES (IN DAYS)

12	14	19	18
15	15	18	17
20	27	22	23
22	21	33	28
14	18	16	13

Audit

As defined in Section 2.1, a frequency distribution is a tabular summary of data showing the number (frequency) of observations in each of several nonoverlapping categories or classes. This definition holds for quantitative as well as categorical data. However, with quantitative data we must be more careful in defining the nonoverlapping classes to be used in the frequency distribution.

For example, consider the quantitative data in Table 2.4. These data show the time in days required to complete year-end audits for a sample of 20 clients of Sanderson and Clifford, a small public accounting firm. The three steps necessary to define the classes for a frequency distribution with quantitative data are as follows:

1. Determine the number of nonoverlapping classes.
2. Determine the width of each class.
3. Determine the class limits.

Let us demonstrate these steps by developing a frequency distribution for the audit time data in Table 2.4.

Number of classes Classes are formed by specifying ranges that will be used to group the data. As a general guideline, we recommend using between 5 and 20 classes. For a small number of data items, as few as 5 or 6 classes may be used to summarize the data. For a larger number of data items, a larger number of classes is usually required. The goal is to use enough classes to show the variation in the data, but not so many classes that some contain only a few data items. Because the number of data items in Table 2.4 is relatively small ($n = 20$), we chose to develop a frequency distribution with five classes.

Making the classes the same width reduces the chance of inappropriate interpretations by the user.

Width of the classes The second step in constructing a frequency distribution for quantitative data is to choose a width for the classes. As a general guideline, we recommend that the width be the same for each class. Thus the choices of the number of classes and the width of classes are not independent decisions. A larger number of classes means a smaller class width, and vice versa. To determine an approximate class width, we begin by identifying the largest and smallest data values. Then, with the desired number of classes specified, we can use the following expression to determine the approximate class width.

$$\text{Approximate class width} = \frac{\text{Largest data value} - \text{Smallest data value}}{\text{Number of classes}} \qquad \textbf{(2.2)}$$

The approximate class width given by equation (2.2) can be rounded to a more convenient value based on the preference of the person developing the frequency distribution. For example, an approximate class width of 9.28 might be rounded to 10 simply because 10 is a more convenient class width to use in presenting a frequency distribution.

For the data involving the year-end audit times, the largest data value is 33 and the smallest data value is 12. Because we decided to summarize the data with five classes, using equation (2.2) provides an approximate class width of $(33 - 12)/5 = 4.2$. We therefore decided to round up and use a class width of five days in the frequency distribution.

No single frequency distribution is best for a data set. Different people may construct different, but equally acceptable, frequency distributions. The goal is to reveal the natural grouping and variation in the data.

In practice, the number of classes and the appropriate class width are determined by trial and error. Once a possible number of classes is chosen, equation (2.2) is used to find the approximate class width. The process can be repeated for a different number of classes. Ultimately, the analyst uses judgment to determine the combination of the number of classes and class width that provides the best frequency distribution for summarizing the data.

For the audit time data in Table 2.4, after deciding to use five classes, each with a width of five days, the next task is to specify the class limits for each of the classes.

Class limits   Class limits must be chosen so that each data item belongs to one and only one class. The *lower class limit* identifies the smallest possible data value assigned to the class. The *upper class limit* identifies the largest possible data value assigned to the class. In developing frequency distributions for categorical data, we did not need to specify class limits because each data item naturally fell into a separate class. But with quantitative data, such as the audit times in Table 2.4, class limits are necessary to determine where each data value belongs.

TABLE 2.5

FREQUENCY DISTRIBUTION FOR THE AUDIT TIME DATA

Audit Time (days)	Frequency
10–14	4
15–19	8
20–24	5
25–29	2
30–34	1
Total	20

Using the audit time data in Table 2.4, we selected 10 days as the lower class limit and 14 days as the upper class limit for the first class. This class is denoted 10–14 in Table 2.5. The smallest data value, 12, is included in the 10–14 class. We then selected 15 days as the lower class limit and 19 days as the upper class limit of the next class. We continued defining the lower and upper class limits to obtain a total of five classes: 10–14, 15–19, 20–24, 25–29, and 30–34. The largest data value, 33, is included in the 30–34 class. The difference between the lower class limits of adjacent classes is the class width. Using the first two lower class limits of 10 and 15, we see that the class width is $15 - 10 = 5$.

With the number of classes, class width, and class limits determined, a frequency distribution can be obtained by counting the number of data values belonging to each class. For example, the data in Table 2.4 show that four values—12, 14, 14, and 13—belong to the 10–14 class. Thus, the frequency for the 10–14 class is 4. Continuing this counting process for the 15–19, 20–24, 25–29, and 30–34 classes provides the frequency distribution in Table 2.5. Using this frequency distribution, we can observe the following:

1. The most frequently occurring audit times are in the class of 15–19 days. Eight of the 20 audit times belong to this class.
2. Only one audit required 30 or more days.

Other conclusions are possible, depending on the interests of the person viewing the frequency distribution. The value of a frequency distribution is that it provides insights about the data that are not easily obtained by viewing the data in their original unorganized form.

Class midpoint   In some applications, we want to know the midpoints of the classes in a frequency distribution for quantitative data. The **class midpoint** is the value halfway between the lower and upper class limits. For the audit time data, the five class midpoints are 12, 17, 22, 27, and 32.

Relative Frequency and Percent Frequency Distributions

We define the relative frequency and percent frequency distributions for quantitative data in the same manner as for categorical data. First, recall that the relative frequency is the proportion of the observations belonging to a class. With n observations,

$$\text{Relative frequency of class} = \frac{\text{Frequency of the class}}{n}$$

The percent frequency of a class is the relative frequency multiplied by 100.

Based on the class frequencies in Table 2.5 and with $n = 20$, Table 2.6 shows the relative frequency distribution and percent frequency distribution for the audit time data. Note that .40 of the audits, or 40%, required from 15 to 19 days. Only .05 of the audits, or 5%, required 30 or more days. Again, additional interpretations and insights can be obtained by using Table 2.6.

Using Excel to Construct a Frequency Distribution

We can use Excel's PivotTable tool to construct a frequency distribution for the audit time data. Two tasks are involved: Enter/Access Data and Apply Tools.

Enter/Access Data: Open the DATAfile named *Audit*. The data are in cells A2:A21 and a label is in cell A1.

Apply Tools: The following steps describe how to use Excel's PivotTable tool to construct a frequency distribution for the audit time data. When using Excel's PivotTable tool, each column of data is referred to as a *field*. Thus, for the audit time example, the data appearing in cells A2:A21 and the label in cell A1 are referred to as the Audit Time field.

Step 1. Select any cell in the data set (cells A1:A21)
Step 2. Click **Insert** on the Ribbon
Step 3. In the **Tables** group click **PivotTable**
Step 4. When the Create PivotTable dialog box appears:
        Click **OK**; a **PivotTable** and **PivotTable Fields** dialog box will appear in a new worksheet
Step 5. In the **PivotTable Fields** dialog box:
        Drag **Audit Time** to the **Rows** area
        Drag **Audit Time** to the **Values** area
Step 6. Click on **Sum of Audit Time** in the **Values** area
Step 7. Click **Value Field Settings** from the list of options that appears

TABLE 2.6   RELATIVE FREQUENCY AND PERCENT FREQUENCY DISTRIBUTIONS FOR THE AUDIT TIME DATA

Audit Time (days)	Relative Frequency	Percent Frequency
10–14	.20	20
15–19	.40	40
20–24	.25	25
25–29	.10	10
30–34	.05	5
Total	1.00	100

Step 8. When the Value Field Settings dialog box appears:
   Under **Summarize value field by**, choose **Count**
   Click **OK**

Figure 2.8 shows the resulting PivotTable Fields Dialog and the corresponding PivotTable. To construct the frequency distribution shown in Table 2.5, we must group the rows containing the audit times. The following steps accomplish this.

Step 1. Right-click cell A4 in the PivotTable or any other cell containing an audit time.
Step 2. Choose **Group** from the list of options that appears
Step 3. When the Grouping dialog box appears:
   Enter 10 in the **Starting at** box
   Enter 34 in the **Ending at** box
   Enter 5 in the **By** box
   Click **OK**

Figure 2.9 shows the completed PivotTable Fields dialog box and the corresponding Pivot-Table. We see that with the exception of the column headings, the PivotTable provides the same information as the frequency distribution shown in Table 2.5.

The same Excel procedures we followed in the previous section can now be used to develop relative and percent frequency distributions if desired.

Editing Options: You can easily change the labels in the PivotTable to match the labels in Table 2.5. For instance, to change the current heading in cell A3 (Row Labels) to "Audit Time (days)," click in cell A3 and type "Audit Time (days)"; to change the current heading in cell B3 (Count of Audit Time) to "Frequency," click in cell B3 and type

FIGURE 2.8   PIVOTTABLE FIELDS DIALOG BOX AND INITIAL PIVOTTABLE USED TO CONSTRUCT A FREQUENCY DISTRIBUTION FOR THE AUDIT TIME DATA

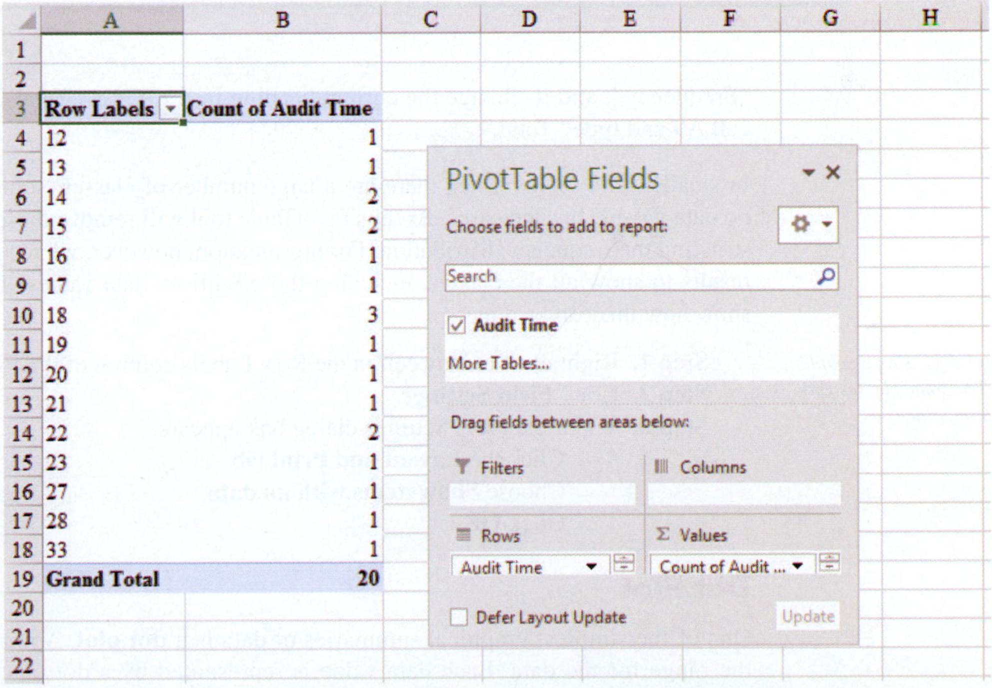

FIGURE 2.9   FREQUENCY DISTRIBUTION FOR THE AUDIT TIME DATA
CONSTRUCTED USING EXCEL'S PIVOTTABLE TOOL

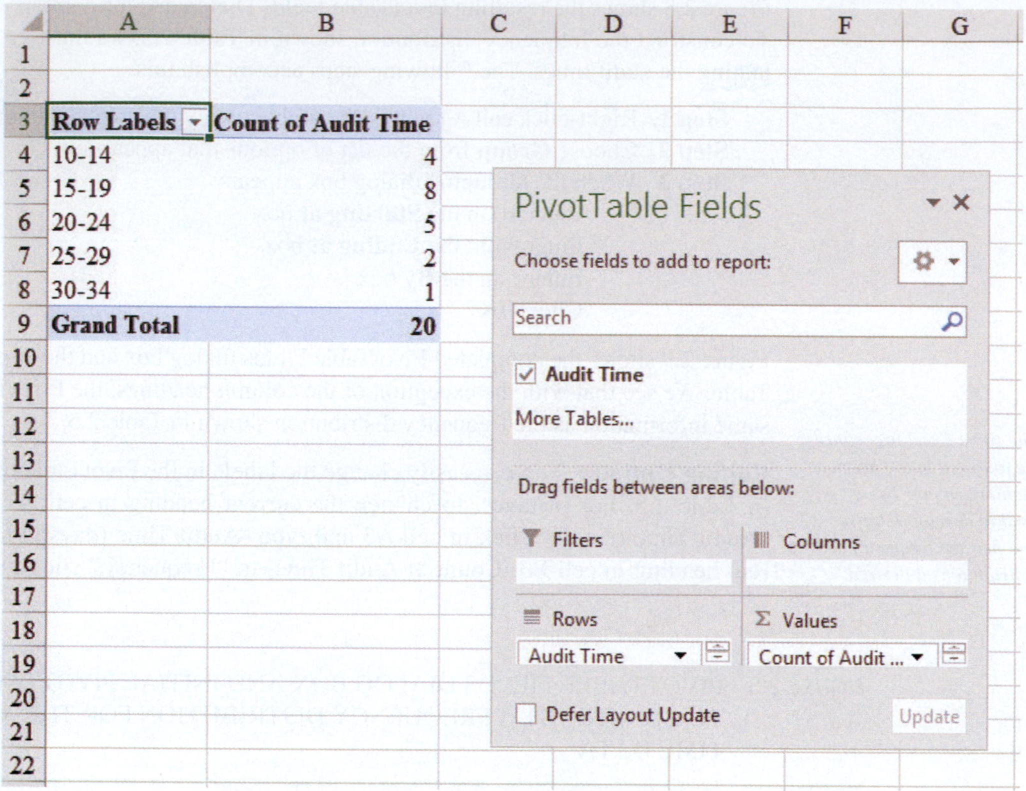

"Frequency"; and to change the current heading in A9 (Grand Total) to "Total," click in cell A9 and type "Total."

In smaller data sets or when there are a large number of classes, some classes may have no data values. In such cases, Excel's PivotTable tool will remove these classes when constructing the frequency distribution. For presentation, however, we recommend editing the results to show all the classes, including those with no data values. The following steps show how this can be done.

Exercise 21 is an example that has some classes with no data values.

Step 1. Right click on any cell in the Row Labels column of the PivotTable
Step 2. Click **Field Settings**
Step 3. When the Field Settings dialog box appears:
Click the **Layout and Print** tab
Choose **Show items with no data**
Click **OK**

Dot Plot

One of the simplest graphical summaries of data is a **dot plot**. A horizontal axis shows the range for the data. Each data value is represented by a dot placed above the axis. Figure 2.10 is the dot plot for the audit time data in Table 2.4. The three dots located above 18 on the horizontal axis indicate that an audit time of 18 days occurred three

FIGURE 2.10   DOT PLOT FOR THE AUDIT TIME DATA

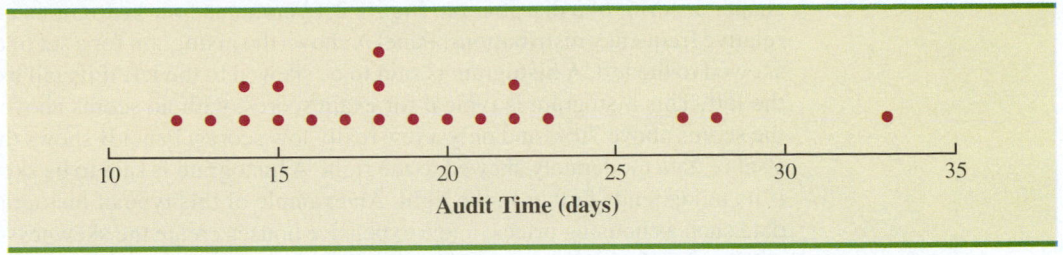

times. Dot plots show the details of the data and are useful for comparing the distribution of the data for two or more variables.

Histogram

A common graphical display of quantitative data is a **histogram**. This graphical display can be prepared for data previously summarized in either a frequency, relative frequency, or percent frequency distribution. A histogram is constructed by placing the variable of interest on the horizontal axis and the frequency, relative frequency, or percent frequency on the vertical axis. The frequency, relative frequency, or percent frequency of each class is shown by drawing a rectangle whose base is determined by the class limits on the horizontal axis and whose height is the corresponding frequency, relative frequency, or percent frequency.

Figure 2.11 is a histogram for the audit time data. Note that the class with the greatest frequency is shown by the rectangle appearing above the class of 15–19 days. The height of the rectangle shows that the frequency of this class is 8. A histogram for the relative or percent frequency distribution of these data would look the same as the histogram in Figure 2.11 with the exception that the vertical axis would be labeled with relative or percent frequency values.

As Figure 2.11 shows, the adjacent rectangles of a histogram touch one another. Unlike a bar chart, a histogram contains no natural separation between the rectangles of adjacent classes. This format is the usual convention for histograms. Because the classes for the audit time data are stated as 10–14, 15–19, 20–24, 25–29, and 30–34, one-unit spaces of 14 to 15, 19 to 20, 24 to 25, and 29 to 30 would seem to be needed between the classes. These spaces are eliminated when constructing a histogram. Eliminating the spaces between classes in a histogram for the audit time data helps show that all values between the lower limit of the first class and the upper limit of the last class are possible.

FIGURE 2.11   HISTOGRAM FOR THE AUDIT TIME DATA

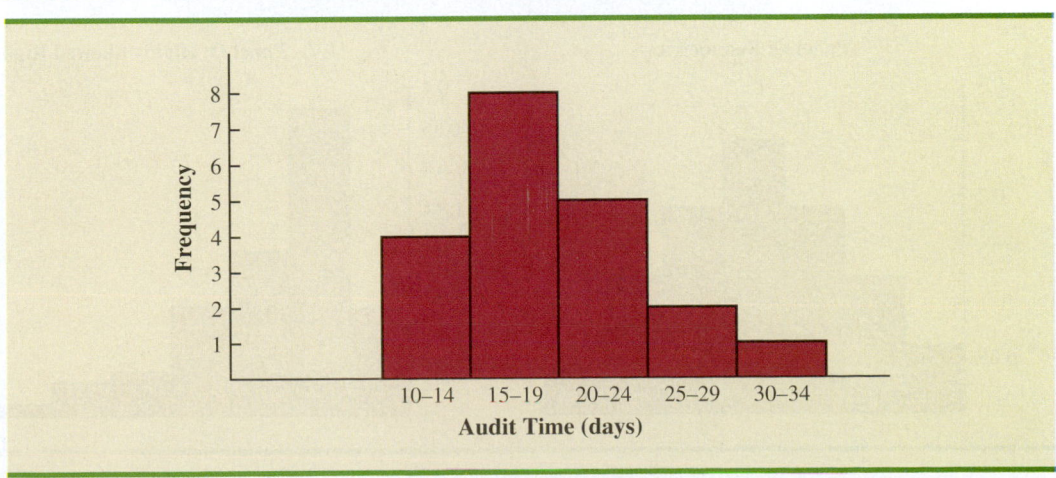

One of the most important uses of a histogram is to provide information about the shape, or form, of a distribution. Figure 2.12 contains four histograms constructed from relative frequency distributions. Panel A shows the histogram for a set of data moderately skewed to the left. A histogram is said to be skewed to the left if its tail extends farther to the left. This histogram is typical for exam scores, with no scores above 100%, most of the scores above 70%, and only a few really low scores. Panel B shows the histogram for a set of data moderately skewed to the right. A histogram is said to be skewed to the right if its tail extends farther to the right. An example of this type of histogram would be for data such as housing prices; a few expensive houses create the skewness in the right tail.

Panel C shows a symmetric histogram. In a symmetric histogram, the left tail mirrors the shape of the right tail. Histograms for data found in applications are never perfectly symmetric, but the histogram for many applications may be roughly symmetric. Data for SAT scores, heights and weights of people, and so on lead to histograms that are roughly symmetric. Panel D shows a histogram highly skewed to the right. This histogram was constructed from data on the dollar amount of customer purchases over one day at a women's apparel store. Data from applications in business and economics often lead to histograms that are skewed to the right. For instance, data on housing prices, salaries, purchase amounts, and so on often result in histograms skewed to the right.

FIGURE 2.12   HISTOGRAMS SHOWING DIFFERING LEVELS OF SKEWNESS

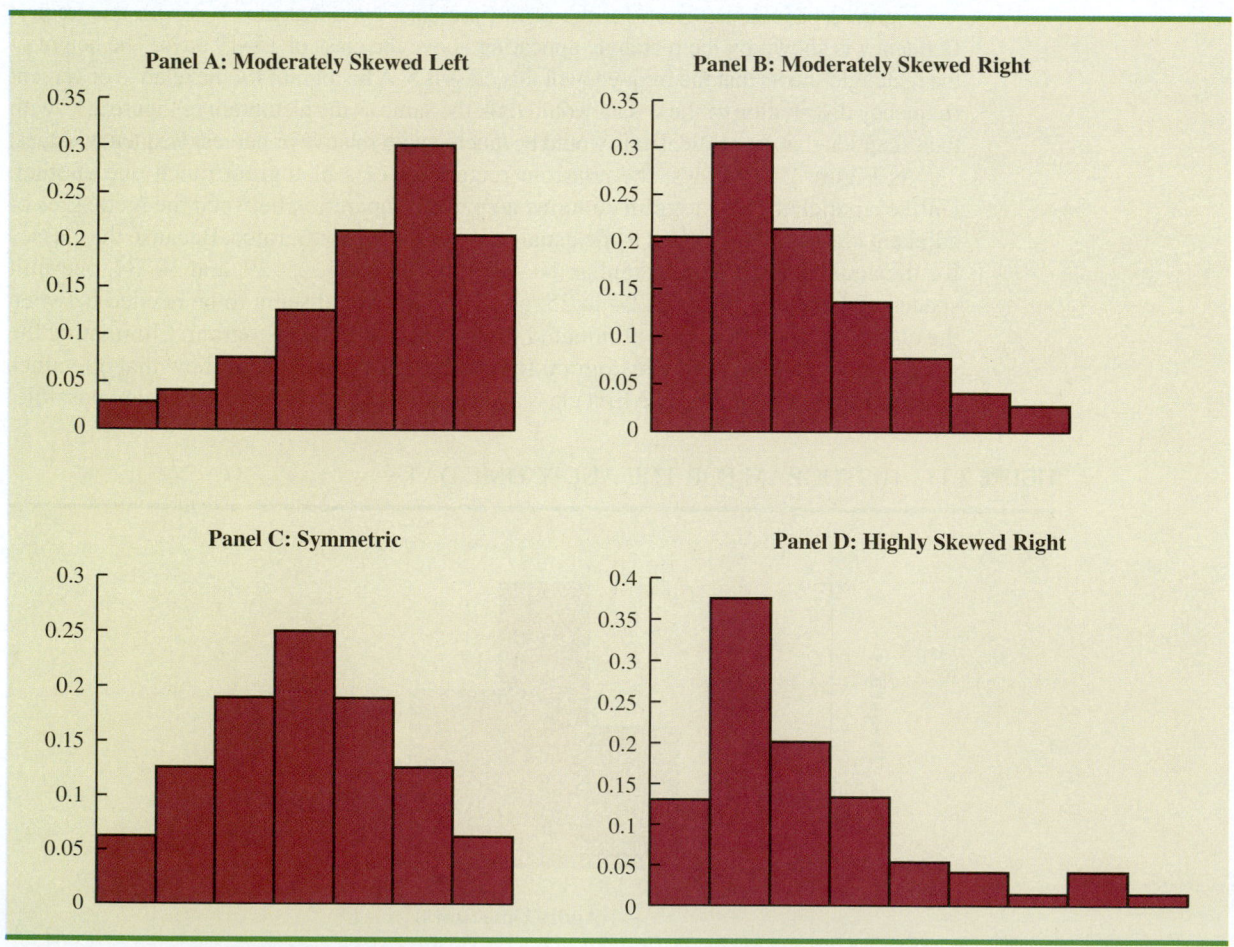

Using Excel's Recommended Charts Tool to Construct a Histogram

In Figure 2.9 we showed the results of using Excel's PivotTable tool to construct a frequency distribution for the audit time data. We will use these results to illustrate how Excel's Recommended Charts tool can be used to construct a histogram for depicting quantitative data summarized in a frequency distribution. Refer to Figure 2.13 as we describe the steps involved.

Apply Tools: The following steps describe how to use Excel's Recommended Charts tool to construct a histogram for the audit time data.

Step 1. Select any cell in the PivotTable report (cells A3:B9)
Step 2. Click **Insert** on the Ribbon
Step 3. In the **Charts** group click **Recommended Charts**; a preview showing the recommended chart appears
Step 4. Click **OK**

The worksheet in Figure 2.13 shows the chart for the audit time data created using these steps. With the exception of the gaps separating the bars, this resembles the histogram for the audit time data shown in Figure 2.11. We can easily edit this chart to remove the gaps between the bars and enter more descriptive axis labels and a chart heading.

FIGURE 2.13   INITIAL CHART USED TO CONSTRUCT A HISTOGRAM FOR THE AUDIT TIME DATA

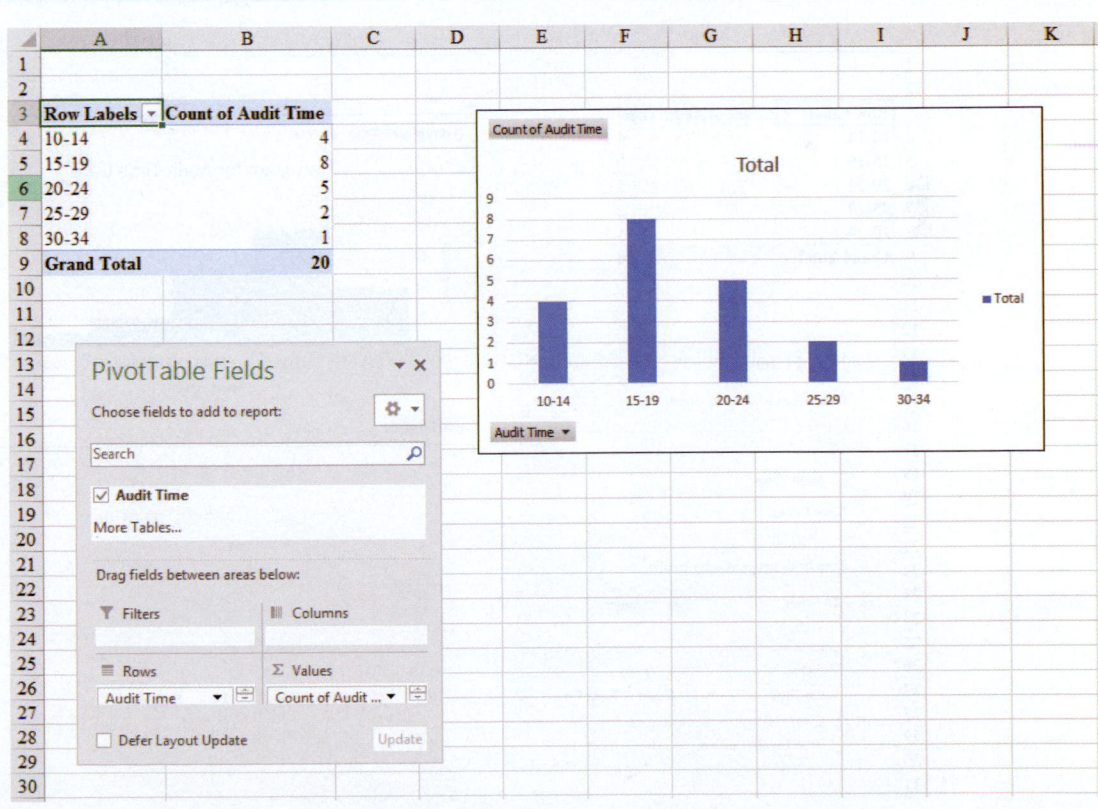

Editing Options: In addition to removing the gaps between the bars, suppose you would like to use "Histogram for Audit Time Data" as the chart title and insert "Audit Time (days)" for the horizontal axis title and "Frequency" for the vertical axis title.

Step 1. Right-click any bar in the chart and choose **Format Data Series** from the list of options that appears

Step 2. When the Format Data Series dialog box appears:

Go to the **Series Options** section

Set the **Gap Width** to 0

Click the **Close** button ✖ at the top right of the dialog box

Step 3. Click the **Chart Title** and replace it with **Histogram for Audit Time Data**

Step 4. Click the **Chart Elements** button ➕ (located next to the top right corner of the chart)

Step 5. When the list of chart elements appears:

Click **Axis Titles** (creates placeholders for the axis titles)

Click **Legend** to remove the check in the Legend box

Step 6. Click the **Horizontal (Category) Axis Title** and replace it with **Audit Time (days)**

Step 7. Click the **Vertical (Value) Axis Title** and replace it with **Frequency**

The edited histogram for the audit time is shown in Figure 2.14.

FIGURE 2.14   HISTOGRAM FOR THE AUDIT TIME DATA CREATED USING EXCEL'S RECOMMENDED CHARTS TOOL

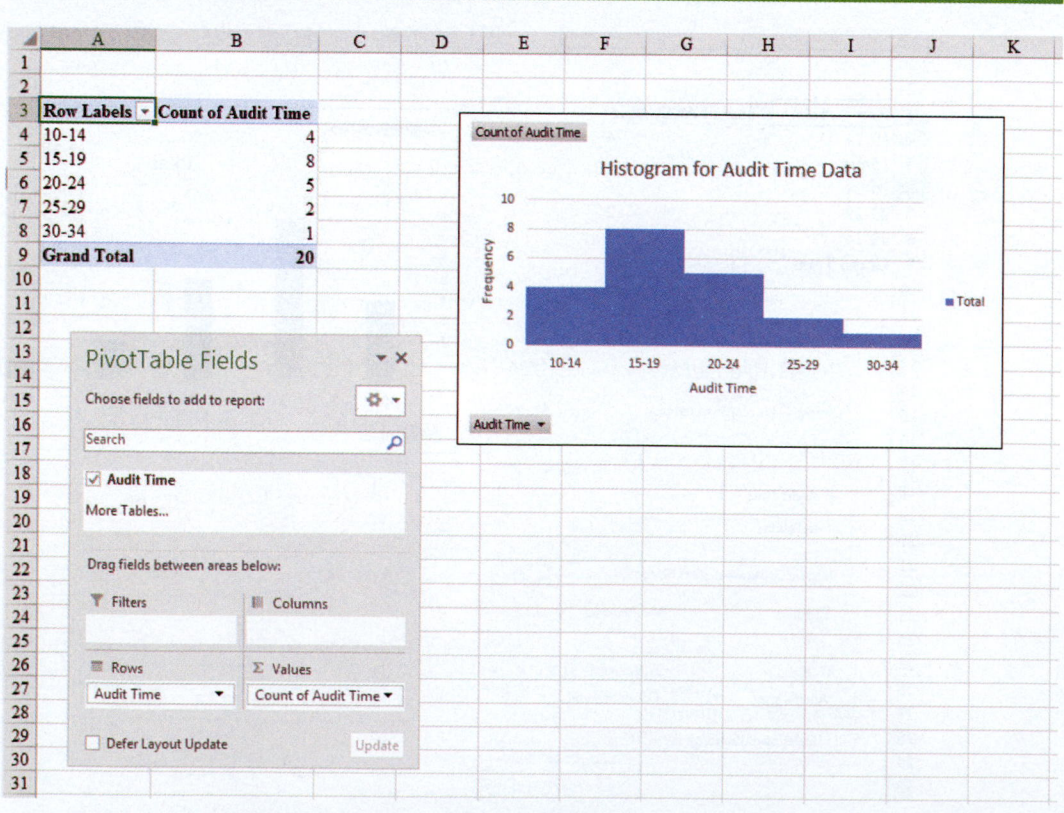

In smaller data sets or when there are a large number of classes, some classes may have no data values. In such cases, Excel's PivotTable tool will automatically remove these classes when constructing the frequency distribution, and the histogram created using Excel's Recommended Charts tool will not show the classes with no data values. For presentation, however, we recommend editing the results to show all the classes, including those with no data values. The following steps show how this can be done by editing the PivotTable tool output before constructing the histogram.

Step 1. Right click on any cell in the Row Labels column of the PivotTable
Step 2. Click **Field Settings**
Step 3. When the Field Settings dialog box appears:
 Click the **Layout & Print** tab
 Choose **Show items with no data**
 Click **OK**

Exercise 21 is an example that has some classes with no data values.

After performing steps 1–3, the PivotTable will display all classes, including those with no data values. Using the Recommended Charts tool will then create a bar chart that displays all classes.

Cumulative Distributions

A variation of the frequency distribution that provides another tabular summary of quantitative data is the **cumulative frequency distribution**. The cumulative frequency distribution uses the number of classes, class widths, and class limits developed for the frequency distribution. However, rather than showing the frequency of each class, the cumulative frequency distribution shows the number of data items with values *less than or equal to the upper class limit* of each class. The first two columns of Table 2.7 provide the cumulative frequency distribution for the audit time data.

To understand how the cumulative frequencies are determined, consider the class with the description "less than or equal to 24." The cumulative frequency for this class is simply the sum of the frequencies for all classes with data values less than or equal to 24. For the frequency distribution in Table 2.5, the sum of the frequencies for classes 10–14, 15–19, and 20–24 indicates that $4 + 8 + 5 = 17$ data values are less than or equal to 24. Hence, the cumulative frequency for this class is 17. In addition, the cumulative frequency distribution in Table 2.7 shows that four audits were completed in 14 days or less and 19 audits were completed in 29 days or less.

As a final point, we note that a **cumulative relative frequency distribution** shows the proportion of data items, and a **cumulative percent frequency distribution** shows the percentage of data items with values less than or equal to the upper limit of each class.

TABLE 2.7   CUMULATIVE FREQUENCY, CUMULATIVE RELATIVE FREQUENCY, AND CUMULATIVE PERCENT FREQUENCY DISTRIBUTIONS FOR THE AUDIT TIME DATA

Audit Time (days)	Cumulative Frequency	Cumulative Relative Frequency	Cumulative Percent Frequency
Less than or equal to 14	4	.20	20
Less than or equal to 19	12	.60	60
Less than or equal to 24	17	.85	85
Less than or equal to 29	19	.95	95
Less than or equal to 34	20	1.00	100

The cumulative relative frequency distribution can be computed either by summing the relative frequencies in the relative frequency distribution or by dividing the cumulative frequencies by the total number of items. Using the latter approach, we found the cumulative relative frequencies in column 3 of Table 2.7 by dividing the cumulative frequencies in column 2 by the total number of items ($n = 20$). The cumulative percent frequencies were again computed by multiplying the relative frequencies by 100. The cumulative relative and percent frequency distributions show that .85 of the audits, or 85%, were completed in 24 days or less, .95 of the audits, or 95%, were completed in 29 days or less, and so on.

Stem-and-Leaf Display

A **stem-and-leaf display** is a graphical display used to show simultaneously the rank order and shape of a distribution of data. To illustrate the use of a stem-and-leaf display, consider the data in Table 2.8. These data result from a 150-question aptitude test given to 50 individuals recently interviewed for a position at Haskens Manufacturing. The data indicate the number of questions answered correctly.

To develop a stem-and-leaf display, we first arrange the leading digits of each data value to the left of a vertical line. To the right of the vertical line, we record the last digit for each data value. Based on the top row of data in Table 2.8 (112, 72, 69, 97, and 107), the first five entries in constructing a stem-and-leaf display would be as follows:

```
 6 | 9
 7 | 2
 8 |
 9 | 7
10 | 7
11 | 2
12 |
13 |
14 |
```

For example, the data value 112 shows the leading digits 11 to the left of the line and the last digit 2 to the right of the line. Similarly, the data value 72 shows the leading digit 7 to the left of the line and last digit 2 to the right of the line. Continuing to place the last digit of each data value on the line corresponding to its leading digit(s) provides the following:

TABLE 2.8   NUMBER OF QUESTIONS ANSWERED CORRECTLY
ON AN APTITUDE TEST

112	72	69	97	107
73	92	76	86	73
126	128	118	127	124
82	104	132	134	83
92	108	96	100	92
115	76	91	102	81
95	141	81	80	106
84	119	113	98	75
68	98	115	106	95
100	85	94	106	119

DATA *file*

ApTest

```
 6 | 9  8
 7 | 2  3  6  3  6  5
 8 | 6  2  3  1  1  0  4  5
 9 | 7  2  2  6  2  1  5  8  8  5  4
10 | 7  4  8  0  2  6  6  0  6
11 | 2  8  5  9  3  5  9
12 | 6  8  7  4
13 | 2  4
14 | 1
```

With this organization of the data, sorting the digits on each line into rank order is simple. Doing so provides the stem-and-leaf display shown here.

```
 6 | 8  9
 7 | 2  3  3  5  6  6
 8 | 0  1  1  2  3  4  5  6
 9 | 1  2  2  2  4  5  5  6  7  8  8
10 | 0  0  2  4  6  6  6  7  8
11 | 2  3  5  5  8  9  9
12 | 4  6  7  8
13 | 2  4
14 | 1
```

The numbers to the left of the vertical line (6, 7, 8, 9, 10, 11, 12, 13, and 14) form the *stem*, and each digit to the right of the vertical line is a *leaf*. For example, consider the first row with a stem value of 6 and leaves of 8 and 9.

```
6 | 8  9
```

This row indicates that two data values have a first digit of six. The leaves show that the data values are 68 and 69. Similarly, the second row

```
7 | 2  3  3  5  6  6
```

indicates that six data values have a first digit of seven. The leaves show that the data values are 72, 73, 73, 75, 76, and 76.

To focus on the shape indicated by the stem-and-leaf display, let us use a rectangle to contain the leaves of each stem. Doing so, we obtain the following:

```
 6 | 8  9
 7 | 2  3  3  5  6  6
 8 | 0  1  1  2  3  4  5  6
 9 | 1  2  2  2  4  5  5  6  7  8  8
10 | 0  0  2  4  6  6  6  7  8
11 | 2  3  5  5  8  9  9
12 | 4  6  7  8
13 | 2  4
14 | 1
```

Rotating this page counterclockwise onto its side provides a picture of the data that is similar to a histogram with classes of 60–69, 70–79, 80–89, and so on.

Although the stem-and-leaf display may appear to offer the same information as a histogram, it has two primary advantages.

1. The stem-and-leaf display is easier to construct by hand.
2. Within a class interval, the stem-and-leaf display provides more information than the histogram because the stem-and-leaf shows the actual data.

Just as a frequency distribution or histogram has no absolute number of classes, neither does a stem-and-leaf display have an absolute number of rows or stems. If we believe that our original stem-and-leaf display condensed the data too much, we can easily stretch the display by using two or more stems for each leading digit. For example, to use two stems for each leading digit, we would place all data values ending in 0, 1, 2, 3, and 4 in one row and all values ending in 5, 6, 7, 8, and 9 in a second row. The following stretched stem-and-leaf display illustrates this approach.

In a stretched stem-and-leaf display, whenever a stem value is stated twice, the first value corresponds to leaf values of 0–4, and the second value corresponds to leaf values of 5–9.

```
 6 | 8  9
 7 | 2  3  3
 7 | 5  6  6
 8 | 0  1  1  2  3  4
 8 | 5  6
 9 | 1  2  2  2  4
 9 | 5  5  6  7  8  8
10 | 0  0  2  4
10 | 6  6  6  7  8
11 | 2  3
11 | 5  5  8  9  9
12 | 4
12 | 6  7  8
13 | 2  4
13 |
14 | 1
```

Note that values 72, 73, and 73 have leaves in the 0–4 range and are shown with the first stem value of 7. The values 75, 76, and 76 have leaves in the 5–9 range and are shown with the second stem value of 7. This stretched stem-and-leaf display is similar to a frequency distribution with intervals of 65–69, 70–74, 75–79, and so on.

The preceding example showed a stem-and-leaf display for data with as many as three digits. Stem-and-leaf displays for data with more than three digits are possible. For example, consider the following data on the number of hamburgers sold by a fast-food restaurant for each of 15 weeks.

1565	1852	1644	1766	1888	1912	2044	1812
1790	1679	2008	1852	1967	1954	1733	

A stem-and-leaf display of these data follows.

Leaf unit = 10

```
15 | 6
16 | 4  7
17 | 3  6  9
18 | 1  5  5  8
19 | 1  5  6
20 | 0  4
```

A single digit is used to define each leaf in a stem-and-leaf display. The leaf unit indicates how to multiply the stem-and-leaf numbers in order to approximate the original data. Leaf units may be 100, 10, 1, 0.1, and so on.

Note that a single digit is used to define each leaf and that only the first three digits of each data value have been used to construct the display. At the top of the display we have specified Leaf unit = 10. To illustrate how to interpret the values in the display, consider the first stem, 15, and its associated leaf, 6. Combining these numbers, we obtain 156. To reconstruct an approximation of the original data value, we must multiply this number by 10, the value of the *leaf unit*. Thus, 156 × 10 = 1560 is an approximation of the original data value used to construct the stem-and-leaf display. Although it is not possible to reconstruct the exact data value from this stem-and-leaf display, the convention of using a single digit for each leaf enables stem-and-leaf displays to be constructed for data having a large number of digits. For stem-and-leaf displays where the leaf unit is not shown, the leaf unit is assumed to equal 1.

NOTES AND COMMENTS

1. A bar chart and a histogram are essentially the same thing; both are graphical presentations of the data in a frequency distribution. A histogram is just a bar chart with no separation between bars. For some discrete quantitative data, a separation between bars is also appropriate. Consider, for example, the number of classes in which a college student is enrolled. The data may only assume integer values. Intermediate values such as 1.5, 2.73, and so on are not possible. With continuous quantitative data, however, such as the audit times in Table 2.4, a separation between bars is not appropriate.

2. The appropriate values for the class limits with quantitative data depend on the level of accuracy of the data. For instance, with the audit time data of Table 2.4 the limits used were integer values. If the data were rounded to the nearest tenth of a day (e.g., 12.3, 14.4, and so on), then the limits would be stated in tenths of days. For instance, the first class would be 10.0–14.9. If the data were recorded to the nearest hundredth

of a day (e.g., 12.34, 14.45, and so on), the limits would be stated in hundredths of days. For instance, the first class would be 10.00–14.99.

3. An *open-end* class requires only a lower class limit or an upper class limit. For example, in the audit time data of Table 2.4, suppose two of the audits had taken 58 and 65 days. Rather than continue with the classes of width 5 with classes 35–39, 40–44, 45–49, and so on, we could simplify the frequency distribution to show an open-end class of "35 or more." This class would have a frequency of 2. Most often the open-end class appears at the upper end of the distribution. Sometimes an open-end class appears at the lower end of the distribution, and occasionally such classes appear at both ends.

4. The last entry in a cumulative frequency distribution always equals the total number of observations. The last entry in a cumulative relative frequency distribution always equals 1.00 and the last entry in a cumulative percent frequency distribution always equals 100.

Exercises

Methods

11.   Consider the following data.

Frequency

14	21	23	21	16
19	22	25	16	16
24	24	25	19	16
19	18	19	21	12
16	17	18	23	25
20	23	16	20	19
24	26	15	22	24
20	22	24	22	20

a.   Develop a frequency distribution using classes of 12–14, 15–17, 18–20, 21–23, and 24–26.
b.   Develop a relative frequency distribution and a percent frequency distribution using the classes in part (a).

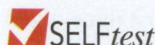SELF*test*

12. Consider the following frequency distribution.

Class	Frequency
10–19	10
20–29	14
30–39	17
40–49	7
50–59	2

Construct a cumulative frequency distribution and a cumulative relative frequency distribution.

13. Construct a histogram for the data in exercise 12.

14. Consider the following data.

8.9	10.2	11.5	7.8	10.0	12.2	13.5	14.1	10.0	12.2
6.8	9.5	11.5	11.2	14.9	7.5	10.0	6.0	15.8	11.5

a. Construct a dot plot.
b. Construct a frequency distribution.
c. Construct a percent frequency distribution.

SELF*test*

15. Construct a stem-and-leaf display for the following data.

11.3	9.6	10.4	7.5	8.3	10.5	10.0
9.3	8.1	7.7	7.5	8.4	6.3	8.8

16. Construct a stem-and-leaf display for the following data. Use a leaf unit of 10.

1161	1206	1478	1300	1604	1725	1361	1422
1221	1378	1623	1426	1557	1730	1706	1689

Applications

SELF*test*

17. A doctor's office staff studied the waiting times for patients who arrive at the office with a request for emergency service. The following data with waiting times in minutes were collected over a one-month period.

2   5   10   12   4   4   5   17   11   8   9   8   12   21   6   8   7   13   18   3

Use classes of 0–4, 5–9, and so on in the following:
a. Show the frequency distribution.
b. Show the relative frequency distribution.
c. Show the cumulative frequency distribution.
d. Show the cumulative relative frequency distribution.
e. What proportion of patients needing emergency service wait 9 minutes or less?

18. CBSSports.com developed the Total Player Ratings system to rate players in the National Basketball Association (NBA) based upon various offensive and defensive statistics. The following data show the average number of points scored per game (PPG) for 50 players with the highest ratings for a portion of the 2012–2013 NBA season (CBSSports.com website, February 25, 2013).

DATA *file*

NBAPlayerPts

27.0	28.8	26.4	27.1	22.9	28.4	19.2	21.0	20.8	17.6
21.1	19.2	21.2	15.5	17.2	16.7	17.6	18.5	18.3	18.3
23.3	16.4	18.9	16.5	17.0	11.7	15.7	18.0	17.7	14.6
15.7	17.2	18.2	17.5	13.6	16.3	16.2	13.6	17.1	16.7
17.0	17.3	17.5	14.0	16.9	16.3	15.1	12.3	18.7	14.6

Use classes starting at 10 and ending at 30 in increments of 2 for PPG in the following.
  a.   Show the frequency distribution.
  b.   Show the relative frequency distribution.
  c.   Show the cumulative percent frequency distribution.
  d.   Develop a histogram for the average number of points scored per game.
  e.   Do the data appear to be skewed? Explain.
  f.   What percentage of the players averaged at least 20 points per game?

19.   Based on the tons handled in a year, the ports listed below are the 25 busiest ports in the United States (*The 2013 World Almanac*).

DATA *file*

Ports

Port	Tons Handled (Millions)	Port	Tons Handled (Millions)
Baltimore	39.6	Norfolk Harbor	41.6
Baton Rouge	55.5	Pascagoula	37.3
Beaumont	77.0	Philadelphia	34.0
Corpus Christi	73.7	Pittsburgh	33.8
Duluth-Superior	36.6	Plaquemines	55.8
Houston	227.1	Port Arthur	30.2
Huntington	61.5	Savannah	34.7
Lake Charles	54.6	South Louisiana	236.3
Long Beach	75.4	St. Louis	30.8
Los Angeles	62.4	Tampa	34.2
Mobile	55.7	Texas City	56.6
New Orleans	72.4	Valdez	31.9
New York	139.2		

  a.   What is the largest number of tons handled? What is the smallest number of tons handled?
  b.   Using a class width of 25, develop a frequency distribution of the data starting with 25–49.9, 50–74.9, 75–99.9, and so on.
  c.   Prepare a histogram. Interpret the histogram.

20.   The London School of Economics and the Harvard Business School conducted a study of how chief executive officers (CEOs) spend their day. The study found that CEOs spend on average about 18 hours per week in meetings, not including conference calls, business meals, and public events (*The Wall Street Journal,* February 14, 2012). Shown below is the time spent per week in meetings (hours) for a sample of 25 CEOs.

DATA *file*

CEOTime

14	15	18	23	15
19	20	13	15	23
23	21	15	20	21
16	15	18	18	19
19	22	23	21	12

  a.   What is the lowest amount of time spent per week on meetings? The highest?
  b.   Use a class width of two hours to prepare a frequency distribution and a percent frequency distribution for the data.
  c.   Prepare a histogram and comment on the shape of the distribution.

21.   *Quantcast.com* provides the number of people from the United States who visit a given website. The list below shows the number of U.S. visitors for the 50 most highly visited websites (*Quantcast.com* website, December 2015).

DATA *file*

WebVisitors

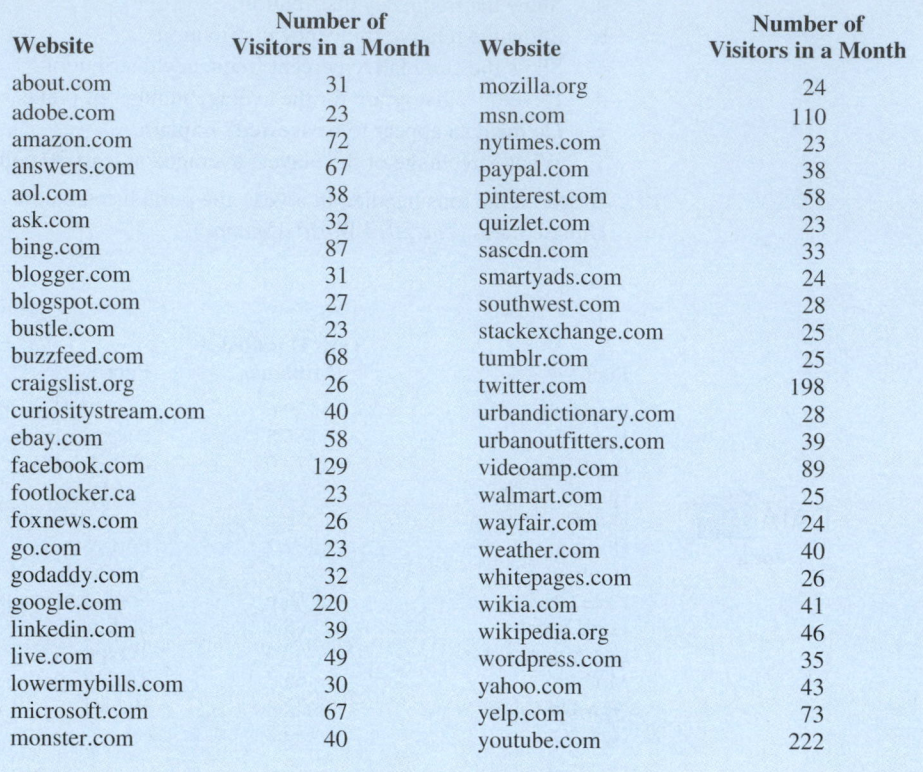

Website	Number of Visitors in a Month	Website	Number of Visitors in a Month
about.com	31	mozilla.org	24
adobe.com	23	msn.com	110
amazon.com	72	nytimes.com	23
answers.com	67	paypal.com	38
aol.com	38	pinterest.com	58
ask.com	32	quizlet.com	23
bing.com	87	sascdn.com	33
blogger.com	31	smartyads.com	24
blogspot.com	27	southwest.com	28
bustle.com	23	stackexchange.com	25
buzzfeed.com	68	tumblr.com	25
craigslist.org	26	twitter.com	198
curiositystream.com	40	urbandictionary.com	28
ebay.com	58	urbanoutfitters.com	39
facebook.com	129	videoamp.com	89
footlocker.ca	23	walmart.com	25
foxnews.com	26	wayfair.com	24
go.com	23	weather.com	40
godaddy.com	32	whitepages.com	26
google.com	220	wikia.com	41
linkedin.com	39	wikipedia.org	46
live.com	49	wordpress.com	35
lowermybills.com	30	yahoo.com	43
microsoft.com	67	yelp.com	73
monster.com	40	youtube.com	222

Summarize the data by constructing the following:
a.   A frequency distribution (classes in millions: 20–29.999, 30–30.999, and so on).
b.   A relative frequency distribution.
c.   A cumulative distribution.
d.   A cumulative relative frequency distribution.
e.   Show a histogram. Comment on the shape of the distribution.
f.   What is the website with the most U.S. visitors? How many people from the U.S. visited the site?

22.   *Entrepreneur* magazine ranks franchises using performance measures such as growth rate, number of locations, startup costs, and financial stability. The number of locations for the top 20 U.S. franchises follow (*The World Almanac,* 2012).

DATA *file*

Franchise

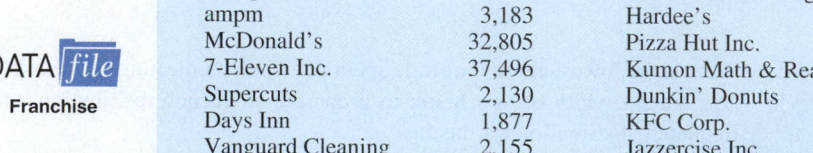

Franchise	No. U.S. Locations	Franchise	No. U.S. Locations
Hampton Inn	1,864	Jan-Pro Franchising Intl. Inc.	12,394
ampm	3,183	Hardee's	1,901
McDonald's	32,805	Pizza Hut Inc.	13,281
7-Eleven Inc.	37,496	Kumon Math & Reading Centers	25,199
Supercuts	2,130	Dunkin' Donuts	9,947
Days Inn	1,877	KFC Corp.	16,224
Vanguard Cleaning Systems	2,155	Jazzercise Inc.	7,683
		Anytime Fitness	1,618
Servpro	1,572	Matco Tools	1,431
Subway	34,871	Stratus Building Solutions	5,018
Denny's Inc.	1,668		

Use classes 0–4999, 5000–9999, 10,000–14,999, and so forth to answer the following questions.

   a. Construct a frequency distribution and a percent frequency distribution of the number of U.S. locations for these top-ranked franchises.

   b. Construct a histogram of these data.

   c. Comment on the shape of the distribution.

23. The following data show the year-to-date percent change (YTD % Change) for 30 stock-market indexes from around the word (*The Wall Street Journal*, August 26, 2013).

MarketIndexes

Country	Index	YTD % Change
Australia	S&P/ASX200	10.2
Belgium	Bel-20	12.6
Brazil	São Paulo Bovespa	−14.4
Canada	S&P/TSX Comp	2.6
Chile	Santiago IPSA	−16.3
China	Shanghai Composite	−9.3
Eurozone	EURO Stoxx	10.0
France	CAC 40	11.8
Germany	DAX	10.6
Hong Kong	Hang Seng	−3.5
India	S&P BSE Sensex	−4.7
Israel	Tel Aviv	1.3
Italy	FTSE MIB	6.6
Japan	Nikkei	31.4
Mexico	IPC All-Share	−6.4
Netherlands	AEX	9.3
Singapore	Straits Times	−2.5
South Korea	Kospi	−6.4
Spain	IBEX 35	6.4
Sweden	SX All Share	13.8
Switzerland	Swiss Market	17.4
Taiwan	Weighted	2.3
U.K.	FTSE 100	10.1
U.S.	S&P 500	16.6
U.S.	DJIA	14.5
U.S.	Dow Jones Utility	6.6
U.S.	Nasdaq 100	17.4
U.S.	Nasdaq Composite	21.1
World	DJ Global ex U.S.	4.2
World	DJ Global Index	9.9

   a. What index has the largest positive YTD % Change?

   b. Using a class width of 5 beginning with −20 and going to 40, develop a frequency distribution for the data.

   c. Prepare a histogram. Interpret the histogram, including a discussion of the general shape of the histogram.

   d. Use *The Wall Street Journal* or another media source to find the current percent changes for these stock market indexes in the current year. Which index has had the largest percent increase? Which index has had the smallest percent decrease? Prepare a summary of the data.

EngineeringSalary

24. The DATAfile *EngineeringSalary* contains the median starting salary and median mid-career salary (measured 10 years after graduation) for graduates from 19 engineering schools (*The Wall Street Journal* website, November 2014). Develop a stem-and-leaf display for both the median starting salary and the median mid-career salary. Comment on any differences you observe.

25. Each year America.EDU ranks the best paying college degrees in America. The following data show the median starting salary, the mid-career salary, and the percentage increase from starting salary to mid-career salary for the 20 college degrees with the highest mid-career salary (America.EDU website, August 29, 2013).

Degree	Starting Salary	Mid-Career Salary	% Increase
Aerospace engineering	59,400	108,000	82
Applied mathematics	56,400	101,000	79
Biomedical engineering	54,800	101,000	84
Chemical engineering	64,800	108,000	67
Civil engineering	53,500	93,400	75
Computer engineering	61,200	87,700	43
Computer science	56,200	97,700	74
Construction management	50,400	87,000	73
Economics	48,800	97,800	100
Electrical engineering	60,800	104,000	71
Finance	47,500	91,500	93
Government	41,500	88,300	113
Information systems	49,300	87,100	77
Management info. systems	50,900	90,300	77
Mathematics	46,400	88,300	90
Nuclear engineering	63,900	104,000	63
Petroleum engineering	93,000	157,000	69
Physics	50,700	99,600	96
Software engineering	56,700	91,300	61
Statistics	50,000	93,400	87

DATA *file*
BestPayingDegrees

a. Using a class width of 10, construct a histogram for the percentage increase in the starting salary.
b. Comment on the shape of the distribution.
c. Develop a stem-and-leaf display for the percentage increase in the starting salary.
d. What are the primary advantages of the stem-and-leaf display as compared to the histogram?

26. The Flying Pig Half-Marathon (13.1 miles) had 10,897 finishers. The following data show the ages for a sample of 40 half-marathoners.

DATA *file*
Marathon

49	33	40	37	56
44	46	57	55	32
50	52	43	64	40
46	24	30	37	43
31	43	50	36	61
27	44	35	31	43
52	43	66	31	50
72	26	59	21	47

a. Construct a stretched stem-and-leaf display.
b. What age group had the largest number of runners?
c. What age occurred most frequently?

2.3 # Summarizing Data for Two Variables Using Tables

Thus far in this chapter, we have focused on using tabular and graphical displays to summarize the data for a single categorical or quantitative variable. Often a manager or decision maker needs to summarize the data for two variables in order to reveal the relationship—if any—between the variables. In this section, we show how to construct a tabular summary of the data for two variables.

TABLE 2.9   QUALITY RATING AND MEAL PRICE DATA FOR 300 LOS ANGELES RESTAURANTS

DATA *file*

Restaurant

Restaurant	Quality Rating	Meal Price ($)
1	Good	18
2	Very Good	22
3	Good	28
4	Excellent	38
5	Very Good	33
6	Good	28
7	Very Good	19
8	Very Good	11
9	Very Good	23
10	Good	13
.	.	.
.	.	.
.	.	.

Crosstabulation

A **crosstabulation** is a tabular summary of data for two variables. Although both variables can be either categorical or quantitative, crosstabulations in which one variable is categorical and the other variable is quantitative are just as common. We will illustrate this latter case by considering the following application based on data from Zagat's Restaurant Review. Data showing the quality rating and the typical meal price were collected for a sample of 300 restaurants in the Los Angeles area. Table 2.9 shows the data for the first 10 restaurants. Quality rating is a categorical variable with rating categories of Good, Very Good, and Excellent. Meal Price is a quantitative variable that ranges from $10 to $49.

A crosstabulation of the data for this application is shown in Table 2.10. The labels shown in the margins of the table define the categories (classes) for the two variables. In the left margin, the row labels (Good, Very Good, and Excellent) correspond to the three rating categories for the quality rating variable. In the top margin, the column labels ($10–19, $20–29, $30–39, and $40–49) show that the Meal Price data have been grouped into four classes. Because each restaurant in the sample provides a quality rating and a meal price, each restaurant is associated with a cell appearing in one of the rows and one of the columns of the crosstabulation. For example, Table 2.9 shows restaurant 5 as having a Very Good quality rating and a Meal Price of $33. This restaurant belongs to the cell in row 2 and column 3 of the crosstabulation shown in Table 2.10. In constructing a crosstabulation, we simply count the number of restaurants that belong to each of the cells.

Grouping the data for a quantitative variable enables us to treat the quantitative variable as if it were a categorical variable when creating a crosstabulation.

TABLE 2.10   CROSSTABULATION OF QUALITY RATING AND MEAL PRICE DATA FOR 300 LOS ANGELES RESTAURANTS

Quality Rating	Meal Price				Total
	$10–19	**$20–29**	**$30–39**	**$40–49**	
Good	42	40	2	0	84
Very Good	34	64	46	6	150
Excellent	2	14	28	22	66
Total	78	118	76	28	300

Although four classes of the Meal Price variable were used to construct the crosstabulation shown in Table 2.10, the crosstabulation of quality rating and meal price could have been developed using fewer or more classes for the meal price variable. The issues involved in deciding how to group the data for a quantitative variable in a crosstabulation are similar to the issues involved in deciding the number of classes to use when constructing a frequency distribution for a quantitative variable. For this application, four classes of meal price was considered a reasonable number of classes to reveal any relationship between quality rating and meal price.

In reviewing Table 2.10, we see that the greatest number of restaurants in the sample (64) have a very good rating and a meal price in the $20–29 range. Only two restaurants have an excellent rating and a meal price in the $10–19 range. Similar interpretations of the other frequencies can be made. In addition, note that the right and bottom margins of the crosstabulation provide the frequency distributions for quality rating and meal price separately. From the frequency distribution in the right margin, we see that data on quality ratings show 84 restaurants with a good quality rating, 150 restaurants with a very good quality rating, and 66 restaurants with an excellent quality rating. Similarly, the bottom margin shows the frequency distribution for the meal price variable.

Dividing the totals in the right margin of the crosstabulation by the total for that column provides a relative and percent frequency distribution for the quality rating variable.

Quality Rating	Relative Frequency	Percent Frequency
Good	.28	28
Very Good	.50	50
Excellent	.22	22
Total	1.00	100

From the percent frequency distribution we see that 28% of the restaurants were rated good, 50% were rated very good, and 22% were rated excellent.

Dividing the totals in the bottom row of the crosstabulation by the total for that row provides a relative and percent frequency distribution for the meal price variable.

Meal Price	Relative Frequency	Percent Frequency
$10–19	.26	26
$20–29	.39	39
$30–39	.25	25
$40–49	.09	9
Total	1.00	100

Note that the sum of the values in the relative frequency column does not add exactly to 1.00 and the sum of the values in the percent frequency distribution does not add exactly to 100; the reason is that the values being summed are rounded. From the percent frequency distribution we see that 26% of the meal prices are in the lowest price class ($10–19), 39% are in the next higher class, and so on.

The frequency and relative frequency distributions constructed from the margins of a crosstabulation provide information about each of the variables individually, but they do not shed any light on the relationship between the variables. The primary value of a crosstabulation lies in the insight it offers about the relationship between the variables. A review of

TABLE 2.11 ROW PERCENTAGES FOR EACH QUALITY RATING CATEGORY

	Meal Price				
Quality Rating	$10–19	$20–29	$30–39	$40–49	Total
Good	50.0	47.6	2.4	0.0	100
Very Good	22.7	42.7	30.6	4.0	100
Excellent	3.0	21.2	42.4	33.4	100

the crosstabulation in Table 2.10 reveals that restaurants with higher meal prices received higher quality ratings than restaurants with lower meal prices.

Converting the entries in a crosstabulation into row percentages or column percentages can provide more insight into the relationship between the two variables. For row percentages, the results of dividing each frequency in Table 2.10 by its corresponding row total are shown in Table 2.11. Each row of Table 2.11 is a percent frequency distribution of meal price for one of the quality rating categories. Of the restaurants with the lowest quality rating (good), we see that the greatest percentages are for the less expensive restaurants (50% have $10–19 meal prices and 47.6% have $20–29 meal prices). Of the restaurants with the highest quality rating (excellent), we see that the greatest percentages are for the more expensive restaurants (42.4% have $30–39 meal prices and 33.4% have $40–49 meal prices). Thus, we continue to see that restaurants with higher meal prices received higher quality ratings.

Crosstabulations are widely used to investigate the relationship between two variables. In practice, the final reports for many statistical studies include a large number of crosstabulations. In the Los Angeles restaurant survey, the crosstabulation is based on one categorical variable (Quality Rating) and one quantitative variable (Meal Price). Crosstabulations can also be developed when both variables are categorical and when both variables are quantitative. When quantitative variables are used, however, we must first create classes for the values of the variable. For instance, in the restaurant example we grouped the meal prices into four classes ($10–19, $20–29, $30–39, and $40–49).

Using Excel's PivotTable Tool to Construct a Crosstabulation

Excel's PivotTable tool can be used to summarize the data for two or more variables simultaneously. We will illustrate the use of Excel's PivotTable tool by showing how to develop a crosstabulation of quality ratings and meal prices for the sample of 300 restaurants located in the Los Angeles area.

Enter/Access Data: Open the DATAfile named *Restaurant*. The data are in cells B2:C301 and labels are in column A and cells B1:C1.

Apply Tools: Each of the three columns in the Restaurant data set [labeled Restaurant, Quality Rating, and Meal Price ($)] is considered a field by Excel. Fields may be chosen to represent rows, columns, or values in the PivotTable. The following steps describe how to use Excel's PivotTable tool to construct a crosstabulation of quality ratings and meal prices.

Step 1. Select cell A1 or any cell in the data set
Step 2. Click **Insert** on the Ribbon
Step 3. In the **Tables** group click **PivotTable**
Step 4. When the Create PivotTable dialog box appears:
  Click **OK**; a **PivotTable** and **PivotTable Fields** dialog box will appear in a new worksheet

Step 5. In the **PivotTable Fields** dialog box:

Drag **Quality Rating** to the **Rows** area
Drag **Meal Price** to the **Columns** area
Drag **Restaurant** to the **Values** area

Step 6. Click on **Sum of Restaurant** in the **Values** area

Step 7. Click **Value Field Settings** from the list of options that appears

Step 8. When the Value Field Settings dialog box appears:

Under **Summarize value field by**, choose **Count**
Click **OK**

Figure 2.15 shows the PivotTable Fields dialog box and the corresponding PivotTable created following the above steps. For readability, columns H:AC have been hidden.

Editing Options: To complete the PivotTable we need to group the rows containing the meal prices and place the rows for quality rating in the proper order. The following steps accomplish this.

Step 1. Right-click cell B4 in the PivotTable or any other cell containing meal prices.

Step 2. Choose **Group** from the list of options that appears

Step 3. When the Grouping dialog box appears:

Enter 10 in the **Starting at** box
Enter 49 in the **Ending at** box
Enter 10 in the **By** box
Click **OK**

Step 4. Right-click on **Excellent** in cell A5

Step 5. Choose Move and click Move "Excellent" to End

The final PivotTable is shown in Figure 2.16. Note that it provides the same information as the crosstabulation shown in Table 2.10.

FIGURE 2.15 INITIAL PIVOTTABLE FIELDS DIALOG BOX AND PIVOTTABLE FOR THE RESTAURANT DATA

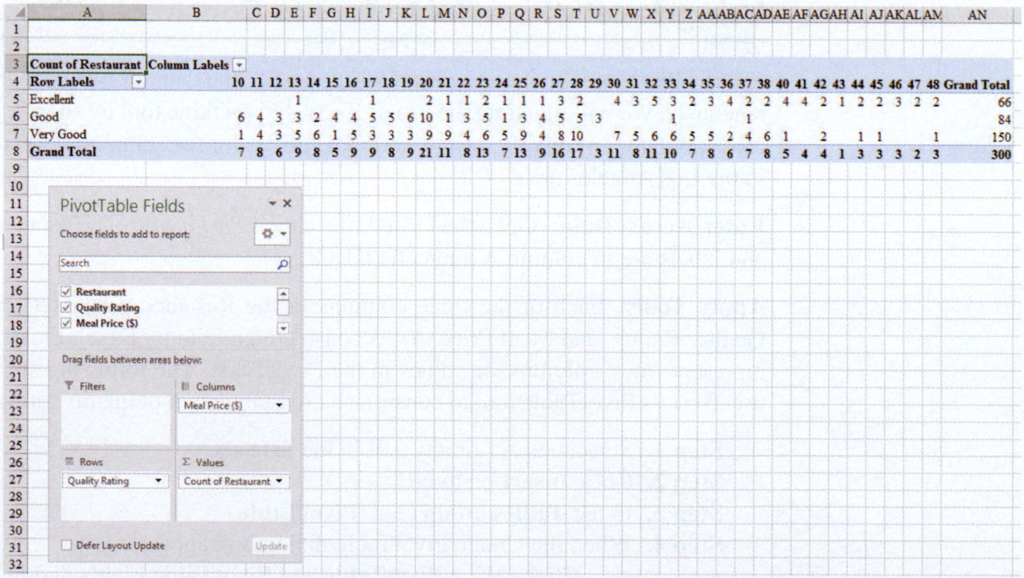

Count of Restaurant	Column Labels																			
Row Labels	10	11	12	13	14	15	16	17	18	19	20	21	22	23	24	25	26	27	28	29
Excellent				1				1			2	1	1	2	1	1	1	3	2	
Good	6	4	3	3	2	4	4	5	5	6	10	1	3	5	1	3	4	5	5	3
Very Good	1	4	3	5	6	1	5	3	3	3	9	9	4	6	5	9	4	8	10	
Grand Total	7	8	6	9	8	5	9	9	8	9	21	11	8	13	7	13	9	16	17	3

Row Labels	30	31	32	33	34	35	36	37	38	40	41	42	43	44	45	46	47	48	Grand Total
Excellent	4	3	5	3	2	3	4	2	2	4	4	2	1	2	2	3	2	2	66
Good				1				1											84
Very Good	7	5	6	6	5	5	2	4	6	1		2		1	1			1	150
Grand Total	11	8	11	10	7	8	6	7	8	5	4	4	1	3	3	3	2	3	300

Simpson's Paradox

The data in two or more crosstabulations are often combined or aggregated to produce a summary crosstabulation showing how two variables are related. In such cases, conclusions drawn from two or more separate crosstabulations can be reversed when the data are aggregated into a single crosstabulation. The reversal of conclusions based on aggregate and unaggregated data is called **Simpson's paradox**. To provide an illustration of Simpson's paradox we consider an example involving the analysis of verdicts for two judges in two different courts.

Judges Ron Luckett and Dennis Kendall presided over cases in Common Pleas Court and Municipal Court during the past three years. Some of the verdicts they rendered were appealed. In most of these cases the appeals court upheld the original verdicts, but in some

FIGURE 2.16 FINAL PIVOTTABLE FOR THE RESTAURANT DATA

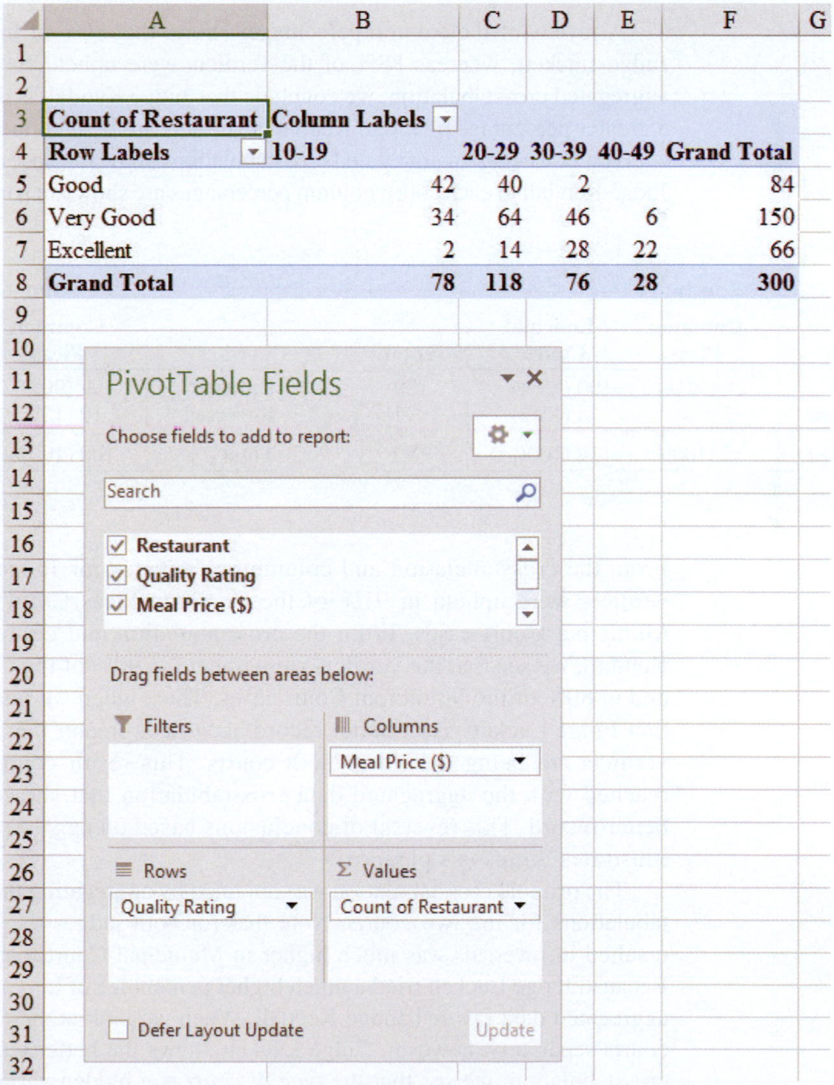

	A	B	C	D	E	F	G
1							
2							
3	Count of Restaurant	Column Labels ▼					
4	Row Labels ▼	10-19	20-29	30-39	40-49	Grand Total	
5	Good		42	40	2		84
6	Very Good		34	64	46	6	150
7	Excellent		2	14	28	22	66
8	Grand Total		78	118	76	28	300
9							
10							

PivotTable Fields ▼ ✕

Choose fields to add to report: ⚙ ▼

Search 🔍

☑ **Restaurant** ▲
☑ **Quality Rating**
☑ **Meal Price ($)** ▼

Drag fields between areas below:

▼ Filters | ▥ Columns
| | Meal Price ($) ▼

≡ Rows | Σ Values
Quality Rating ▼ | Count of Restaurant ▼

☐ Defer Layout Update | Update

cases those verdicts were reversed. For each judge a crosstabulation was developed based upon two variables: Verdict (upheld or reversed) and Type of Court (Common Pleas and Municipal). Suppose that the two crosstabulations were then combined by aggregating the type of court data. The resulting aggregated crosstabulation contains two variables: Verdict (upheld or reversed) and Judge (Luckett or Kendall). This crosstabulation shows the number of appeals in which the verdict was upheld and the number in which the verdict was reversed for both judges. The following crosstabulation shows these results along with the column percentages in parentheses next to each value.

	Judge		
Verdict	**Luckett**	**Kendall**	**Total**
Upheld	129 (86%)	110 (88%)	239
Reversed	21 (14%)	15 (12%)	36
Total (%)	150 (100%)	125 (100%)	275

A review of the column percentages shows that 86% of the verdicts were upheld for Judge Luckett, whereas 88% of the verdicts were upheld for Judge Kendall. From this aggregated crosstabulation, we conclude that Judge Kendall is doing the better job because a greater percentage of Judge Kendall's verdicts are being upheld.

The following unaggregated crosstabulations show the cases tried by Judge Luckett and Judge Kendall in each court; column percentages are shown in parentheses next to each value.

	Judge Luckett					Judge Kendall		
Verdict	**Common Pleas**	**Municipal Court**	**Total**		**Verdict**	**Common Pleas**	**Municipal Court**	**Total**
Upheld	29 (91%)	100 (85%)	129		**Upheld**	90 (90%)	20 (80%)	110
Reversed	3 (9%)	18 (15%)	21		**Reversed**	10 (10%)	5 (20%)	15
Total (%)	32 (100%)	118 (100%)	150		**Total (%)**	100 (100%)	25 (100%)	125

From the crosstabulation and column percentages for Judge Luckett, we see that the verdicts were upheld in 91% of the Common Pleas Court cases and in 85% of the Municipal Court cases. From the crosstabulation and column percentages for Judge Kendall, we see that the verdicts were upheld in 90% of the Common Pleas Court cases and in 80% of the Municipal Court cases. Thus, when we unaggregate the data, we see that Judge Luckett has a better record because a greater percentage of Judge Luckett's verdicts are being upheld in both courts. This result contradicts the conclusion we reached with the aggregated data crosstabulation that showed Judge Kendall had the better record. This reversal of conclusions based on aggregated and unaggregated data illustrates Simpson's paradox.

The original crosstabulation was obtained by aggregating the data in the separate crosstabulations for the two courts. Note that for both judges the percentage of appeals that resulted in reversals was much higher in Municipal Court than in Common Pleas Court. Because Judge Luckett tried a much higher percentage of his cases in Municipal Court, the aggregated data favored Judge Kendall. When we look at the crosstabulations for the two courts separately, however, Judge Luckett shows the better record. Thus, for the original crosstabulation, we see that the *type of court* is a hidden variable that cannot be ignored when evaluating the records of the two judges.

Because of the possibility of Simpson's paradox, realize that the conclusion or interpretation may be reversed depending upon whether you are viewing unaggregated or aggregate crosstabulation data. Before drawing a conclusion, you may want to investigate whether the aggregate or unaggregate form of the crosstabulation provides the better insight and conclusion. Especially when the crosstabulation involves aggregated data, you should investigate whether a hidden variable could affect the results such that separate or unaggregated crosstabulations provide a different and possibly better insight and conclusion.

Exercises

Methods

27. The following data are for 30 observations involving two categorical variables, x and y. The categories for x are A, B, and C; the categories for y are 1 and 2.

Crosstab

Observation	x	y	Observation	x	y
1	A	1	16	B	2
2	B	1	17	C	1
3	B	1	18	B	1
4	C	2	19	C	1
5	B	1	20	B	1
6	C	2	21	C	2
7	B	1	22	B	1
8	C	2	23	C	2
9	A	1	24	A	1
10	B	1	25	B	1
11	A	1	26	C	2
12	B	1	27	C	2
13	C	2	28	A	1
14	C	2	29	B	1
15	C	2	30	B	2

    a. Develop a crosstabulation for the data, with x as the row variable and y as the column variable.

    b. Compute the row percentages.

    c. Compute the column percentages.

    d. What is the relationship, if any, between x and y?

28. The following observations are for two quantitative variables, x and y.

Crosstab2

Observation	x	y	Observation	x	y
1	28	72	11	13	98
2	17	99	12	84	21
3	52	58	13	59	32
4	79	34	14	17	81
5	37	60	15	70	34
6	71	22	16	47	64
7	37	77	17	35	68
8	27	85	18	62	67
9	64	45	19	30	39
10	53	47	20	43	28

a. Develop a crosstabulation for the data, with *x* as the row variable and *y* as the column variable. For *x* use classes of 10–29, 30–49, and so on; for *y* use classes of 40–59, 60–79, and so on.
b. Compute the row percentages.
c. Compute the column percentages.
d. What is the relationship, if any, between *x* and *y*?

Applications

29. The Daytona 500 is a 500-mile automobile race held annually at the Daytona International Speedway in Daytona Beach, Florida. The following crosstabulation shows the automobile make by average speed of the 25 winners from 1988 to 2012 (*The 2013 World Almanac*).

| | Average Speed in Miles per Hour | | | | | |
Make	130–139.9	140–149.9	150–159.9	160–169.9	170–179.9	Total
Buick	1					1
Chevrolet	3	5	4	3	1	16
Dodge		2				2
Ford	2	1	2	1		6
Total	6	8	6	4	1	25

a. Compute the row percentages.
b. What percentage of winners driving a Chevrolet won with an average speed of at least 150 miles per hour?
c. Compute the column percentages.
d. What percentage of winning average speeds 160–169.9 miles per hour were Chevrolets?

30. The following crosstabulation shows the average speed of the 25 winners by year of the Daytona 500 automobile race (*The 2013 World Almanac*).

| | Year | | | | | |
Average Speed	1988–1992	1993–1997	1998–2002	2003–2007	2008–2012	Total
130–139.9	1			2	3	6
140–149.9	2	2	1	2	1	8
150–159.9		3	1	1	1	6
160–169.9	2		2			4
170–179.9			1			1
Total	5	5	5	5	5	25

a. Calculate the row percentages.
b. What is the apparent relationship between average winning speed and year? What might be the cause of this apparent relationship?

31. Recently, management at Oak Tree Golf Course received a few complaints about the condition of the greens. Several players complained that the greens are too fast. Rather than react to the comments of just a few, the Golf Association conducted a survey of 100 male and 100 female golfers. The survey results are summarized here.

Male Golfers

	Greens Condition	
Handicap	**Too Fast**	**Fine**
Under 15	10	40
15 or more	25	25

Female Golfers

	Greens Condition	
Handicap	**Too Fast**	**Fine**
Under 15	1	9
15 or more	39	51

a. Combine these two crosstabulations into one with Male and Female as the row labels and Too Fast and Fine as the column labels. Which group shows the highest percentage saying that the greens are too fast?

b. Refer to the initial crosstabulations. For those players with low handicaps (better players), which group (male or female) shows the highest percentage saying the greens are too fast?

c. Refer to the initial crosstabulations. For those players with higher handicaps, which group (male or female) shows the highest percentage saying the greens are too fast?

d. What conclusions can you draw about the preferences of men and women concerning the speed of the greens? Are the conclusions you draw from part (a) as compared with parts (b) and (c) consistent? Explain any apparent inconsistencies.

32. The following crosstabulation shows the number of households (1000s) in each of the four regions of the United States and the number of households at each income level (U.S. Census Bureau website, August 2013).

	Income Level of Household							Number of
Region	**Under $15,000**	**$15,000 to $24,999**	**$25,000 to $34,999**	**$35,000 to $49,999**	**$50,000 to $74,999**	**$75,000 to $99,999**	**$100,000 and over**	**Households (1000s)**
Northeast	2,733	2,244	2,264	2,807	3,699	2,486	5,246	21,479
Midwest	3,273	3,326	3,056	3,767	5,044	3,183	4,742	26,391
South	6,235	5,657	5,038	6,476	7,730	4,813	7,660	43,609
West	3,086	2,796	2,644	3,557	4,804	3,066	6,104	26,057
Total	15,327	14,023	13,002	16,607	21,277	13,548	23,752	117,536

a. Compute the row percentages and identify the percent frequency distributions of income for households in each region.

b. What percentage of households in the West region have an income level of $50,000 or more? What percentage of households in the South region have an income level of $50,000 or more?

c. Construct percent frequency histograms for each region of households. Do any relationships between regions and income level appear to be evident in your findings?

d.   Compute the column percentages. What information do the column percentages provide?

e.   What percent of households with a household income of $100,000 and over are from the South region? What percentage of households from the South region have a household income of $100,000 and over? Why are these two percentages different?

33.   Each year Forbes ranks the world's most valuable brands. A portion of the data for 82 of the brands in the 2013 Forbes list is shown in Table 2.12 (Forbes website, February 2014). The data set includes the following variables:

Brand: The name of the brand.

Industry: The type of industry associated with the brand, labeled Automotive & Luxury, Consumer Packaged Goods, Financial Services, Other, Technology.

Brand Value ($ billions):   A measure of the brand's value in billions of dollars developed by Forbes based on a variety of financial information about the brand.

1-Yr Value Change (%):   The percentage change in the value of the brand over the previous year.

Brand Revenue ($ billions):   The total revenue in billions of dollars for the brand.

a.   Prepare a crosstabulation of the data on Industry (rows) and Brand Value ($ billions). Use classes of 0–10, 10–20, 20–30, 30–40, 40–50, and 50–60 for Brand Value ($ billions).

b.   Prepare a frequency distribution for the data on Industry.

c.   Prepare a frequency distribution for the data on Brand Value ($ billions).

d.   How has the crosstabulation helped in preparing the frequency distributions in parts (b) and (c)?

e.   What conclusions can you draw about the type of industry and the brand value?

34.   Refer to Table 2.12.

a.   Prepare a crosstabulation of the data on Industry (rows) and Brand Revenue ($ billions). Use class intervals of 25 starting at 0 for Brand Revenue ($ billions).

b.   Prepare a frequency distribution for the data on Brand Revenue ($ billions).

TABLE 2.12   DATA FOR 82 OF THE MOST VALUABLE BRANDS

DATA *file*

BrandValue

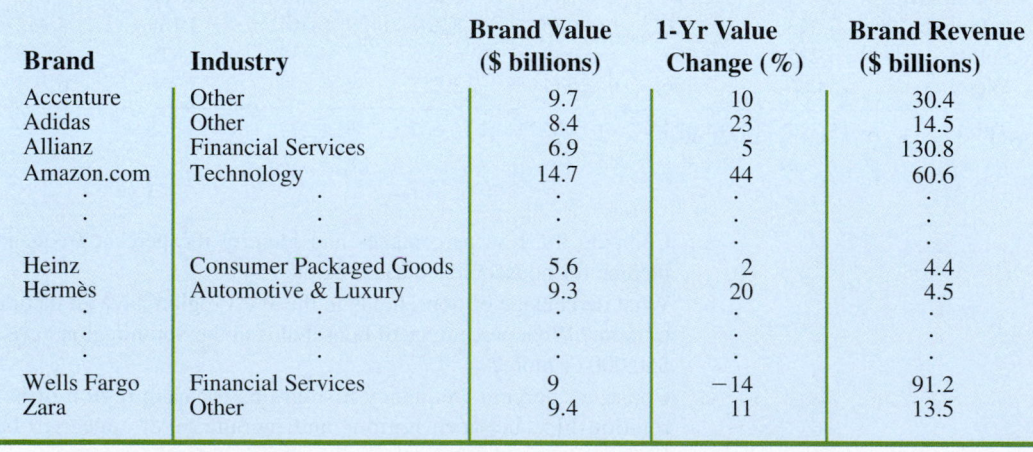

Brand	Industry	Brand Value ($ billions)	1-Yr Value Change (%)	Brand Revenue ($ billions)
Accenture	Other	9.7	10	30.4
Adidas	Other	8.4	23	14.5
Allianz	Financial Services	6.9	5	130.8
Amazon.com	Technology	14.7	44	60.6
.	.	.	.	.
.	.	.	.	.
.	.	.	.	.
Heinz	Consumer Packaged Goods	5.6	2	4.4
Hermès	Automotive & Luxury	9.3	20	4.5
.	.	.	.	.
.	.	.	.	.
Wells Fargo	Financial Services	9	−14	91.2
Zara	Other	9.4	11	13.5

Source: Data from Forbes, 2014.

c. What conclusions can you draw about the type of industry and the brand revenue?

d. Prepare a crosstabulation of the data on Industry (rows) and the 1-Yr Value Change (%). Use class intervals of 20 starting at −60 for 1-Yr Value Change (%).

e. Prepare a frequency distribution for the data on 1-Yr Value Change (%).

f. What conclusions can you draw about the type of industry and the 1-year change in value?

35. The U.S. Department of Energy's Fuel Economy Guide provides fuel efficiency data for cars and trucks (Fuel Economy website, September 8, 2012). A portion of the data for 149 compact, midsize, and large cars is shown in Table 2.13. The data set contains the following variables:

Size: Compact, Midsize, and Large

Displacement: Engine size in liters

Cylinders: Number of cylinders in the engine

Drive: All wheel (A), front wheel (F), and rear wheel (R)

Fuel Type: Premium (P) or regular (R) fuel

City MPG: Fuel efficiency rating for city driving in terms of miles per gallon

Hwy MPG: Fuel efficiency rating for highway driving in terms of miles per gallon

The complete data set is contained in the DATAfile named *FuelData2012*.

a. Prepare a crosstabulation of the data on Size (rows) and Hwy MPG (columns). Use classes of 15–19, 20–24, 25–29, 30–34, 35–39, and 40–44 for Hwy MPG.

b. Comment on the relationship beween Size and Hwy MPG.

c. Prepare a crosstabulation of the data on Drive (rows) and City MPG (columns). Use classes of 10–14, 15–19, 20–24, 25–29, 30–34, and 35–39, and 40–44 for City MPG.

d. Comment on the relationship between Drive and City MPG.

e. Prepare a crosstabulation of the data on Fuel Type (rows) and City MPG (columns). Use classes of 10–14, 15–19, 20–24, 25–29, 30–34, 35–39, and 40–44 for City MPG.

f. Comment on the relationship between Fuel Type and City MPG.

TABLE 2.13 FUEL EFFICIENCY DATA

DATA *file*

FuelData2012

Car	Size	Displacement	Cylinders	Drive	Fuel Type	City MPG	Hwy MPG
1	Compact	2.0	4	F	P	22	30
2	Compact	2.0	4	A	P	21	29
3	Compact	2.0	4	A	P	21	31
.	.	.	.	.	.	.	.
.	.	.	.	.	.	.	.
.	.	.	.	.	.	.	.
94	Midsize	3.5	6	A	R	17	25
95	Midsize	2.5	4	F	R	23	33
.	.	.	.	.	.	.	.
.	.	.	.	.	.	.	.
.	.	.	.	.	.	.	.
148	Large	6.7	12	R	P	11	18
149	Large	6.7	12	R	P	11	18

2.4 Summarizing Data for Two Variables Using Graphical Displays

In the previous section we showed how a crosstabulation can be used to summarize the data for two variables and help reveal the relationship between the variables. In most cases, a graphical display is more useful for recognizing patterns and trends in the data.

In this section, we introduce a variety of graphical displays for exploring the relationships between two variables. Displaying data in creative ways can lead to powerful insights and allow us to make "common-sense inferences" based on our ability to visually compare, contrast, and recognize patterns. We begin with a discussion of scatter diagrams and trendlines.

Scatter Diagram and Trendline

A **scatter diagram** is a graphical display of the relationship between two quantitative variables, and a **trendline** is a line that provides an approximation of the relationship. As an illustration, consider the advertising/sales relationship for a stereo and sound equipment store in San Francisco. On 10 occasions during the past three months, the store used weekend television commercials to promote sales at its stores. The managers want to investigate whether a relationship exists between the number of commercials shown and sales at the store during the following week. Sample data for the 10 weeks with sales in hundreds of dollars are shown in Table 2.14.

Figure 2.17 shows the scatter diagram and the trendline[1] for the data in Table 2.14. The number of commercials (x) is shown on the horizontal axis and the sales (y) are shown on the vertical axis. For week 1, $x = 2$ and $y = 50$. A point with those coordinates is plotted on the scatter diagram. Similar points are plotted for the other nine weeks. Note that during two of the weeks one commercial was shown, during two of the weeks two commercials were shown, and so on.

The scatter diagram in Figure 2.17 indicates a positive relationship between the number of commercials and sales. Higher sales are associated with a higher number of commercials. The relationship is not perfect in that all points are not on a straight line. However, the general pattern of the points and the trendline suggest that the overall relationship is positive.

Some general scatter diagram patterns and the types of relationships they suggest are shown in Figure 2.18. The top left panel depicts a positive relationship similar to the one for

TABLE 2.14   SAMPLE DATA FOR THE STEREO AND SOUND EQUIPMENT STORE

DATA *file*

Stereo

Week	Number of Commercials x	Sales ($100s) y
1	2	50
2	5	57
3	1	41
4	3	54
5	4	54
6	1	38
7	5	63
8	3	48
9	4	59
10	2	46

---

[1]The equation of the trendline is $y = 36.15 + 4.95x$. The slope of the trendline is 4.95 and the y-intercept (the point where the trendline intersects the y-axis) is 36.15. We will discuss in detail the interpretation of the slope and y-intercept for a linear trendline in Chapter 14 when we study simple linear regression.

FIGURE 2.17   SCATTER DIAGRAM AND TRENDLINE FOR THE STEREO AND SOUND EQUIPMENT STORE

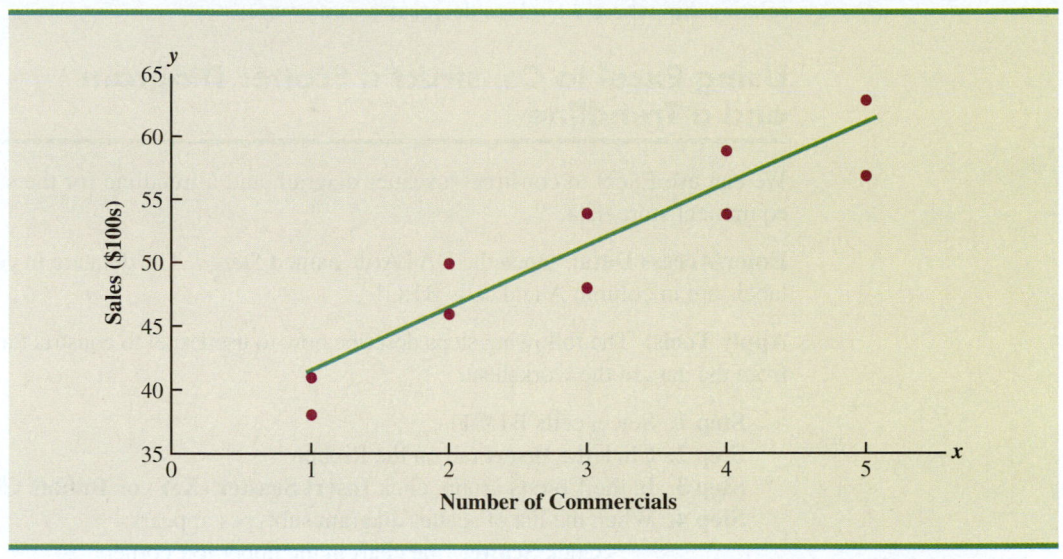

FIGURE 2.18   TYPES OF RELATIONSHIPS DEPICTED BY SCATTER DIAGRAMS

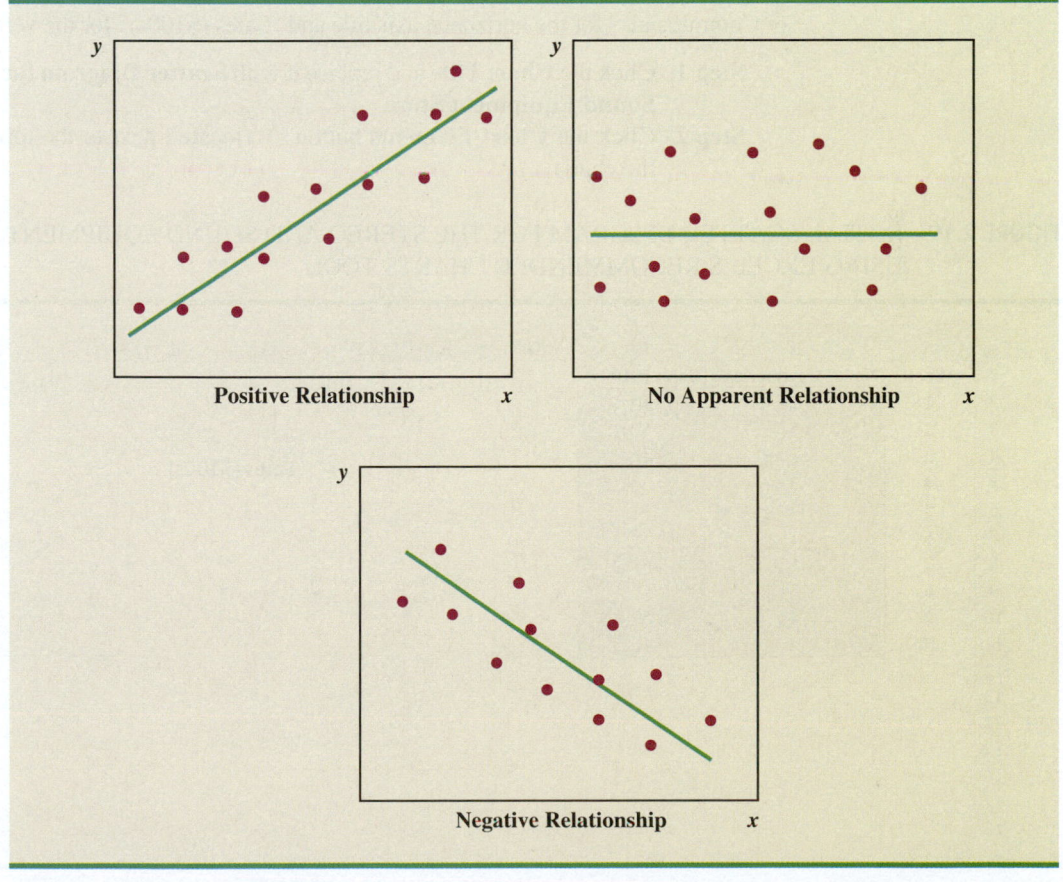

the number of commercials and sales example. In the top right panel, the scatter diagram shows no apparent relationship between the variables. The bottom panel depicts a negative relationship where *y* tends to decrease as *x* increases.

Using Excel to Construct a Scatter Diagram and a Trendline

We can use Excel to construct a scatter diagram and a trendline for the stereo and sound equipment store data.

Enter/Access Data: Open the DATAfile named *Stereo*. The data are in cells B2:C11 and labels are in column A and cells B1:C1.

Apply Tools: The following steps describe how to use Excel to construct a scatter diagram from the data in the worksheet.

> **Step 1.** Select cells B1:C11
> **Step 2.** Click the **Insert** tab on the Ribbon
> **Step 3.** In the **Charts** group, click **Insert Scatter (X,Y) or Bubble Chart**
> **Step 4.** When the list of scatter diagram subtypes appears:
>   Click **Scatter** (the chart in the upper left corner)

The worksheet in Figure 2.19 shows the scatter diagram produced using these steps.

Editing Options: You can easily edit the scatter diagram to display a different chart title, add axis titles, and display the trendline. For instance, suppose you would like to use "Scatter Diagram for the Stereo and Sound Equipment Store" as the chart title and insert "Number of Commercials" for the horizontal axis title and "Sales ($100s)" for the vertical axis title.

> **Step 1.** Click the **Chart Title** and replace it with **Scatter Diagram for the Stereo and Sound Equipment Store**
> **Step 2.** Click the **Chart Elements** button ⊞ (located next to the top right corner of the chart)

FIGURE 2.19   INITIAL SCATTER DIAGRAM FOR THE STEREO AND SOUND EQUIPMENT STORE USING EXCEL'S RECOMMENDED CHARTS TOOL

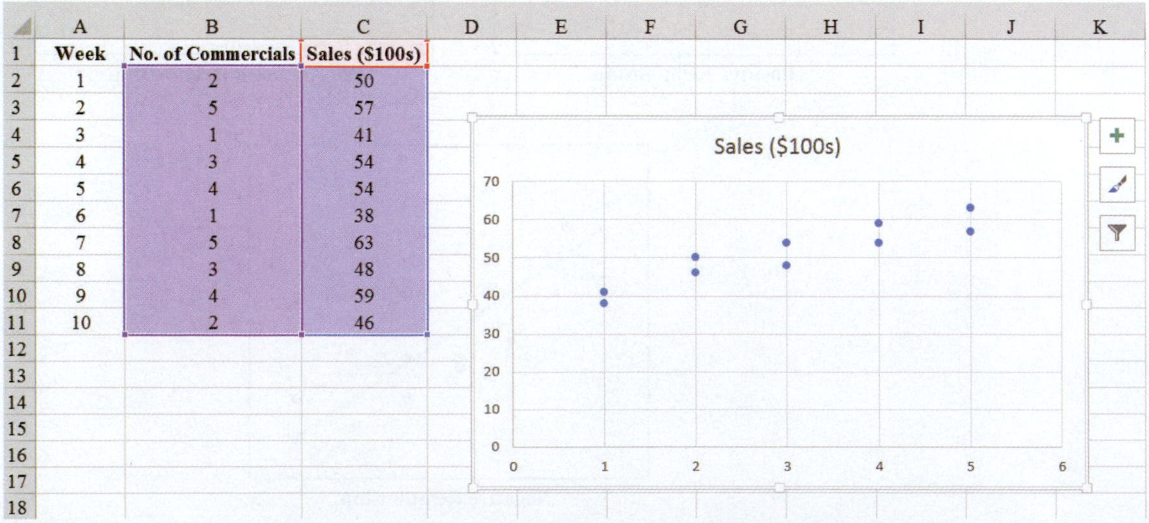

Step 3. When the list of chart elements appears:
Click **Axis Titles** (creates placeholders for the axis titles)
Click **Gridlines** (to deselect the Gridlines option)
Click **Trendline**

Step 4. Click the **Horizontal (Value) Axis Title** and replace it with **Number of Commercials**

Step 5. Click the **Vertical (Value) Axis Title** and replace it with **Sales ($100s)**

Step 6. To change the trendline from a dashed line to a solid line, right-click on the trendline and choose the **Format Trendline** option

Step 7. When the Format Trendline dialog box appears:
Select the **Fill & Line** option
In the **Dash type** box, select **Solid**
Close the Format Trendline dialog box

The edited scatter diagram and trendline are shown in Figure 2.20.

Side-by-Side and Stacked Bar Charts

In Section 2.1 we said that a bar chart is a graphical display for depicting categorical data summarized in a frequency, relative frequency, or percent frequency distribution. Side-by-side bar charts and stacked bar charts are extensions of basic bar charts that are used to display and compare two variables. By displaying two variables on the same chart, we may better understand the relationship between the variables.

A **side-by-side bar chart** is a graphical display for depicting multiple bar charts on the same display. To illustrate the construction of a side-by-side chart, recall the application involving the quality rating and meal price data for a sample of 300 restaurants located in the Los Angeles area. Quality rating is a categorical variable with rating categories of Good, Very Good, and Excellent. Meal Price is a quantitative variable that ranges from $10 to $49. The crosstabulation displayed in Table 2.10 shows that the data for meal price were

FIGURE 2.20 EDITED SCATTER DIAGRAM AND TRENDLINE FOR THE STEREO AND SOUND EQUIPMENT STORE USING EXCEL'S RECOMMENDED CHARTS TOOL

	A	B	C
1	Week	No. of Commercials	Sales ($100s)
2	1	2	50
3	2	5	57
4	3	1	41
5	4	3	54
6	5	4	54
7	6	1	38
8	7	5	63
9	8	3	48
10	9	4	59
11	10	2	46

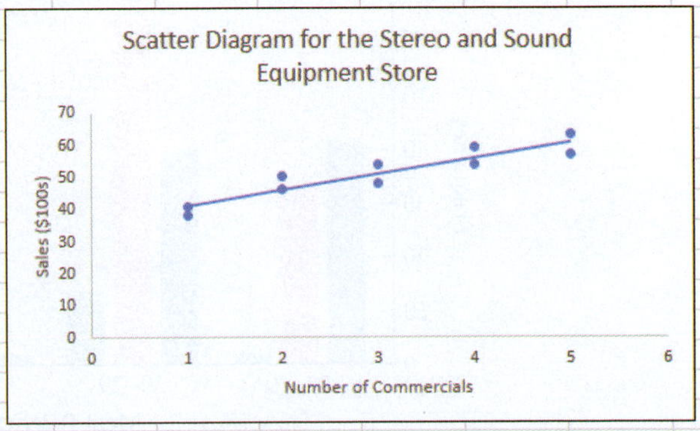

grouped into four classes: $10–19, $20–29, $30–39, and $40–49. We will use these classes to construct a side-by-side bar chart.

Figure 2.21 shows a side-by-side chart for the restaurant data. The color of each bar indicates the quality rating (blue = good, red = very good, and green = excellent). Each bar is constructed by extending the bar to the point on the vertical axis that represents the frequency with which that quality rating occurred for each of the meal price categories. Placing each meal price category's quality rating frequency adjacent to one another allows us to quickly determine how a particular meal price category is rated. We see that the lowest meal price category ($10–$19) received mostly good and very good ratings, but very few excellent ratings. The highest price category ($40–49), however, shows a much different result. This meal price category received mostly excellent ratings, some very good ratings, but no good ratings.

Figure 2.21 also provides a good sense of the relationship between meal price and quality rating. Notice that as the price increases (left to right), the height of the blue bars decreases and the height of the green bars generally increases. This indicates that as price increases, the quality rating tends to be better. The very good rating, as expected, tends to be more prominent in the middle price categories as indicated by the dominance of the red bars in the middle of the chart.

Stacked bar charts are another way to display and compare two variables on the same display. A **stacked bar chart** is a bar chart in which each bar is broken into rectangular segments of a different color showing the relative frequency of each class in a manner similar to a pie chart. To illustrate a stacked bar chart we will use the quality rating and meal price data summarized in the crosstabulation shown in Table 2.10.

We can convert the frequency data in Table 2.10 into column percentages by dividing each element in a particular column by the total for that column. For instance, 42 of the 78 restaurants with a meal price in the $10–19 range had a good quality rating. In other words, (42/78)100 or 53.8% of the 78 restaurants had a good rating. Table 2.15 shows the column percentages for each meal price category. Using the data in Table 2.15 we constructed the stacked bar chart shown in Figure 2.22. Because the stacked bar chart is based on percentages, Figure 2.22 shows even more clearly than Figure 2.21 the relationship between the variables. As we move from the low price category ($10–19) to the high price category ($40–49), the length of the blue bars decreases and the length of the green bars increases.

FIGURE 2.21   SIDE-BY-SIDE BAR CHART FOR THE QUALITY AND MEAL PRICE DATA

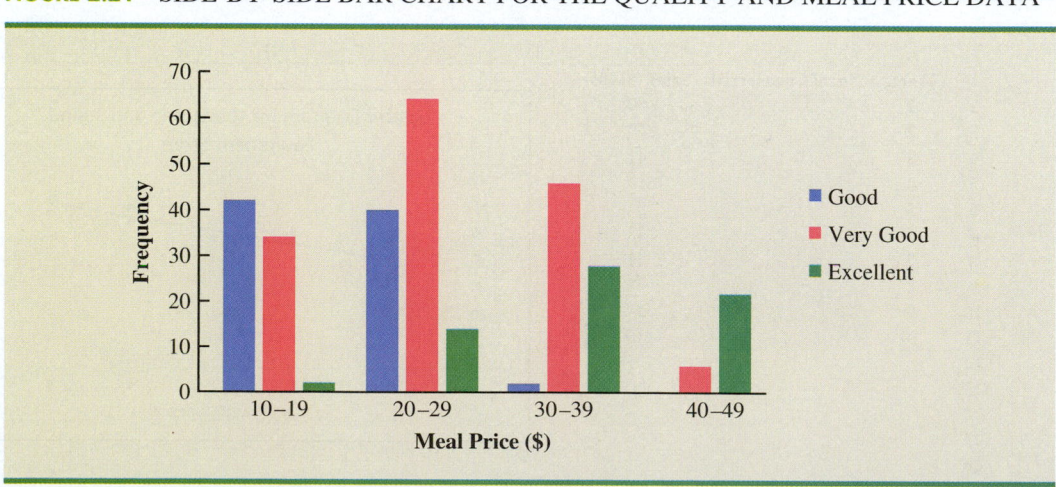

TABLE 2.15 COLUMN PERCENTAGES FOR EACH MEAL PRICE CATEGORY

Quality Rating	Meal Price			
	$10–19	**$20–29**	**$30–39**	**$40–49**
Good	53.8%	33.9%	2.6%	0.0%
Very Good	43.6	54.2	60.5	21.4
Excellent	2.6	11.9	36.8	78.6
Total	100.0%	100.0%	100.0%	100.0%

FIGURE 2.22 STACKED BAR CHART FOR THE QUALITY RATING AND MEAL
PRICE DATA

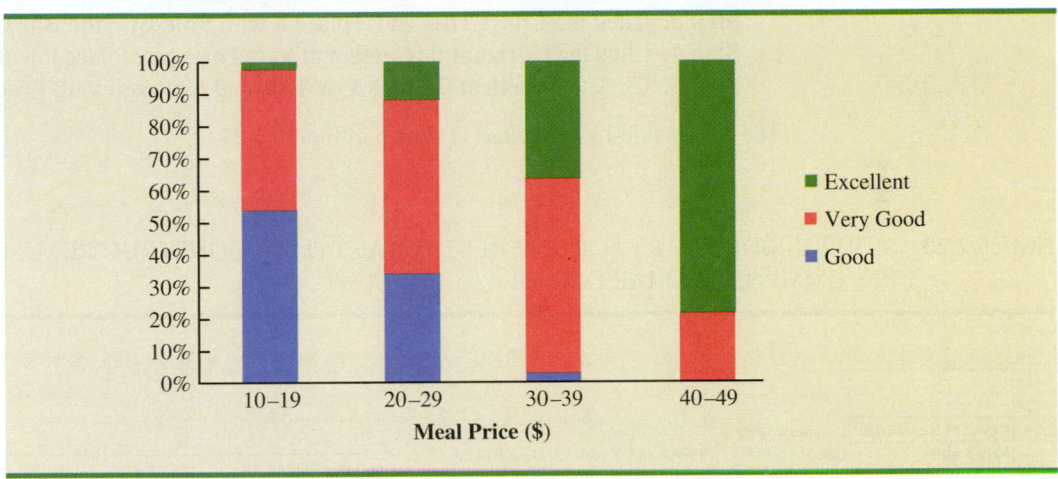

Using Excel's Recommended Charts Tool to Construct Side-by-Side and Stacked Bar Charts

In Figure 2.16 we showed the results of using Excel's PivotTable tool to construct a frequency distribution for the sample of 300 restaurants in the Los Angeles area. We will use these results to illustrate how Excel's Recommended Charts tool can be used to construct side-by-side and stacked bar charts for the restaurant data using the PivotTable output.

Apply Tools: The following steps describe how to use Excel's Recommended Charts tool to construct a side-by-side bar chart for the restaurant data using the PivotTable tool output shown in Figure 2.16.

Step 1. Select any cell in the PivotTable report (cells A3:F8)
Step 2. Click **Insert** on the Ribbon.
Step 3. In the **Charts** group click **Recommended Charts**; a preview showing a bar chart with quality rating on the horizontal axis appears
Step 4. Click **OK**

Step 5. Click **Design** on the Ribbon (located below the **Pivotchart Tools** heading)

Step 6. In the **Data** group click **Switch Row/Column**; a side-by-side bar chart with meal price on the horizontal axis appears

Excel refers to the bar chart in Figure 2.23 as a Clustered Column chart.

The worksheet in Figure 2.23 shows the side-by-side chart for the restaurant data created using these steps.

Editing Options: We can easily edit the side-by-side bar chart to enter a chart heading and axis labels. Suppose you would like to use "Side-by-Side Bar Chart" as the chart title, insert "Meal Price ($)" for the horizontal axis title, and insert "Frequency" for the vertical axis title.

Step 1. Click the **Chart Elements** button ⊞ (located next to the top right corner of the chart)

Step 2. When the list of chart elements appears:
   Click **Chart title** (creates placeholder for the chart title)
   Click **Axis Titles** (creates placeholder for the axis titles)

Step 3. Click the **Chart Title** and replace it with **Side-by-Side Bar Chart**

Step 4. Click the **Horizontal (Category) Axis Title** and replace it with **Meal Price ($)**

Step 5. Click the **Vertical (Value) Axis Title** and replace it with **Frequency**

The edited side-by-side chart is shown in Figure 2.24.

FIGURE 2.23   SIDE-BY-SIDE CHART FOR THE RESTAURANT DATA CONSTRUCTED USING EXCEL'S RECOMMENDED CHARTS TOOL

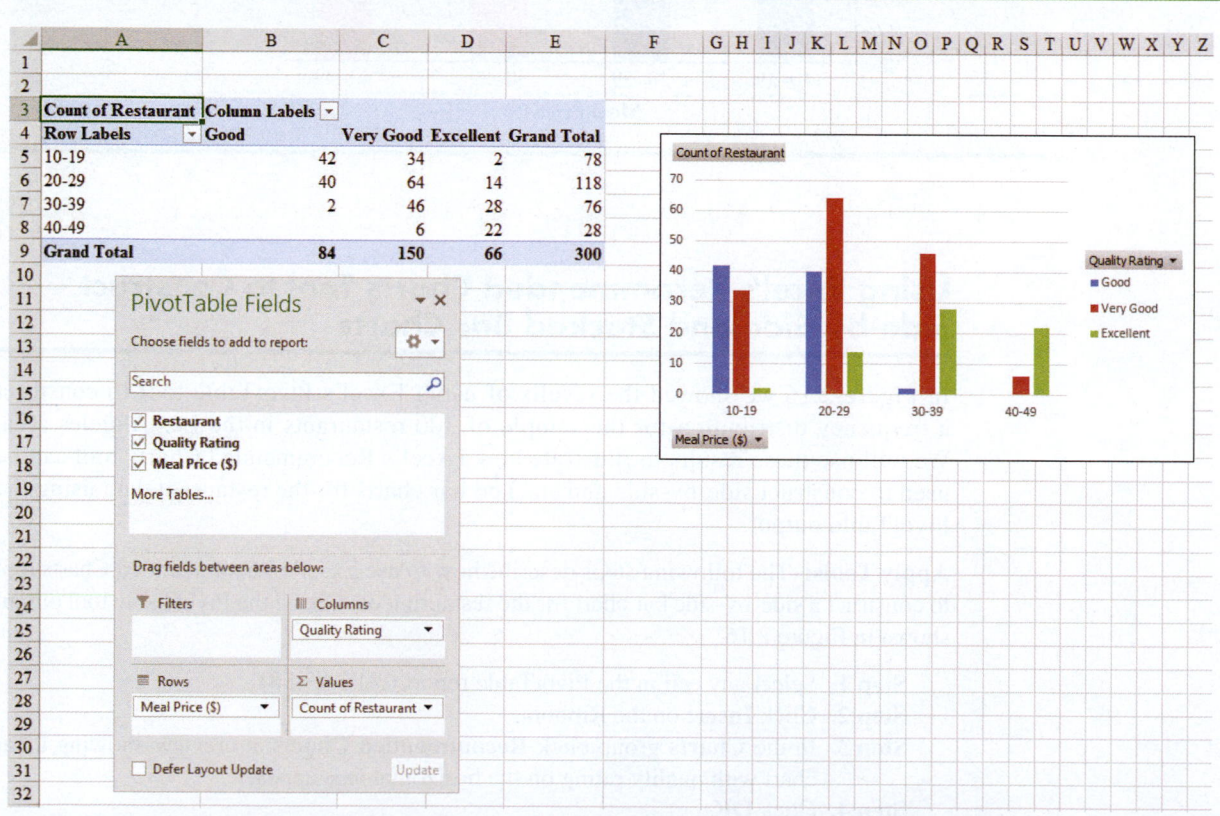

FIGURE 2.24   EDITED SIDE-BY-SIDE CHART FOR THE RESTAURANT DATA CONSTRUCTED USING EXCEL'S RECOMMENDED CHARTS TOOL

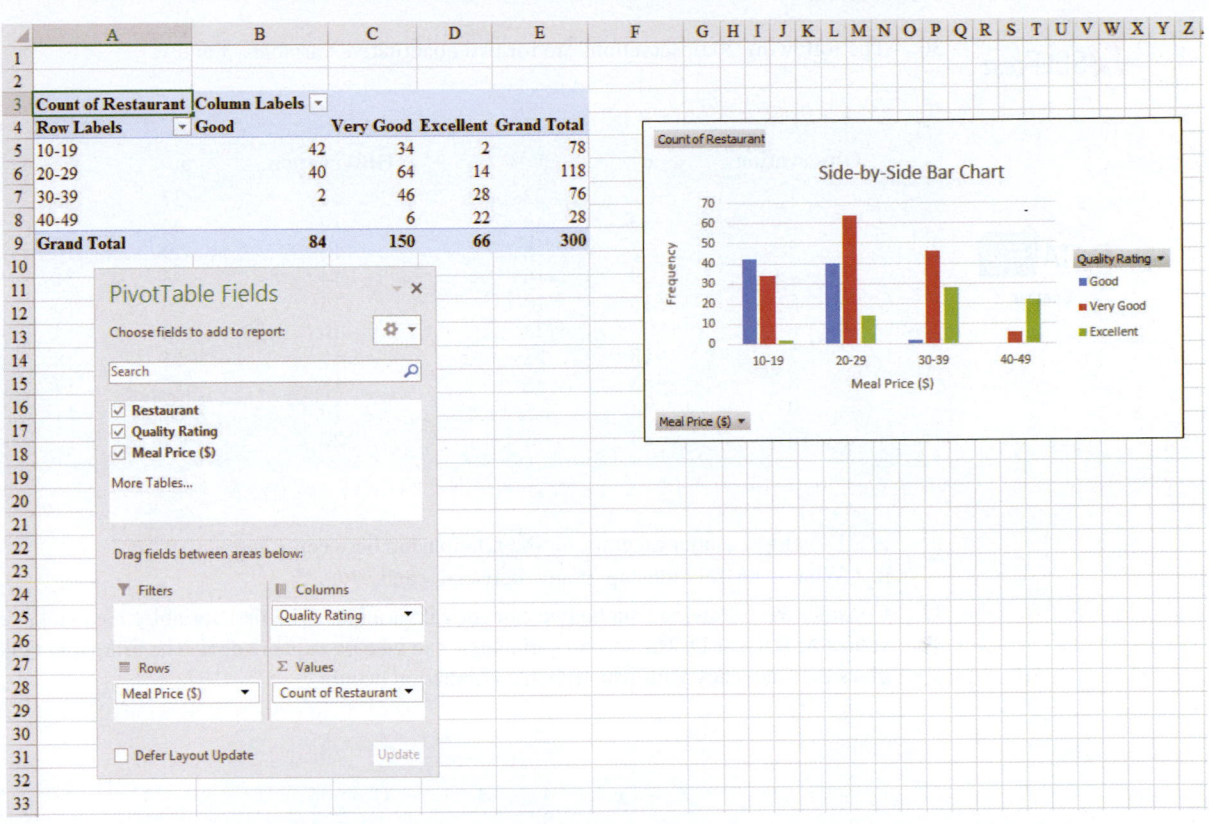

You can easily change the side-by-side bar chart to a stacked bar chart using the following steps.

Step 6. In the **Type** group click **Change Chart Type**
Step 7. When the Change Chart Type dialog box appears:
       Select the **Stacked Columns** option
       Click **OK**

Once you have created a side-by-side bar chart or a stacked bar chart, you can easily switch back and forth between the two chart types by reapplying steps 6 and 7.

NOTES AND COMMENTS

1. A time series is a sequence of observations on a variable measured at successive points in time or over successive periods of time. A scatter diagram in which the value of time is shown on the horizontal axis and the time series values are shown on the vertical axis is referred to in time series analysis as a time series plot.

2. A stacked bar chart can also be used to display frequencies rather than percentage frequencies. In this case, the different color segments of each bar represent the contribution to the total for that bar, rather than the percentage contribution.

Exercises

Methods

36. The following 20 observations are for two quantitative variables, x and y.

Scatter

Observation	x	y	Observation	x	y
1	−22	22	11	−37	48
2	−33	49	12	34	−29
3	2	8	13	9	−18
4	29	−16	14	−33	31
5	−13	10	15	20	−16
6	21	−28	16	−3	14
7	−13	27	17	−15	18
8	−23	35	18	12	17
9	14	−5	19	−20	−11
10	3	−3	20	−7	−22

a. Develop a scatter diagram for the relationship between x and y.

b. What is the relationship, if any, between x and y?

37. Consider the following data on two categorical variables. The first variable, x, can take on values A, B, C, or D. The second variable, y, can take on values I or II. The following table gives the frequency with which each combination occurs.

	y	
x	I	II
A	143	857
B	200	800
C	321	679
D	420	580

a. Construct a side-by-side bar chart with x on the horizontal axis.

b. Comment on the relationship between x and y.

38. The following crosstabulation summarizes the data for two categorical variables, x and y. The variable x can take on values Low, Medium, or High and the variable y can take on values Yes or No.

	y		
x	Yes	No	Total
Low	20	10	30
Medium	15	35	50
High	20	5	25
Total	55	50	105

a. Compute the row percentages.

b. Construct a stacked percent frequency bar chart with x on the horizontal axis.

Applications

39. A study on driving speed (miles per hour) and fuel efficiency (miles per gallon) for midsize automobiles resulted in the following data:

MPG

Driving Speed	30	50	40	55	30	25	60	25	50	55
Fuel Efficiency	28	25	25	23	30	32	21	35	26	25

  a. Construct a scatter diagram with driving speed on the horizontal axis and fuel efficiency on the vertical axis.
  b. Comment on any apparent relationship between these two variables.

40. The DATAfile *Snow* contains average annual snowfall (inches) for 51 major U.S. cities over 30 years. For example, the average low temperature for Columbus, Ohio is 44 degrees and the average annual snowfall is 27.5 inches.

Snow

  a. Construct a scatter diagram with the average annual low temperature on the horizontal axis and the average annual snowfall on the vertical axis.
  b. Does there appear to be any relationship between these two variables?
  c. Based on the scatter diagram, comment on any data points that seem unusual.

41. People often wait until middle age to worry about having a healthy heart. However, recent studies have shown that earlier monitoring of risk factors such as blood pressure can be very beneficial (*The Wall Street Journal,* January 10, 2012). Having higher than normal blood pressure, a condition known as hypertension, is a major risk factor for heart disease. Suppose a large sample of male and female individuals of various ages was selected and that each individual's blood pressure was measured to determine if they have hypertension. For the sample data, the following table shows the percentage of individuals with hypertension.

Hypertension

Age	Male	Female
20–34	11.00%	9.00%
35–44	24.00%	19.00%
45–54	39.00%	37.00%
55–64	57.00%	56.00%
65–74	62.00%	64.00%
75+	73.30%	79.00%

  a. Develop a side-by-side bar chart with age on the horizontal axis, the percentage of individuals with hypertension on the vertical axis, and side-by-side bars based on gender.
  b. What does the display you developed in part (a), indicate about hypertension and age?
  c. Comment on differences by gender.

42. Smartphones are mobile phones with Internet, photo, music, and video capability. The following survey results show smartphone ownership by age.

Smartphones

Age Category	Smartphone (%)	Other Cell Phone (%)	No Cell Phone (%)
18–24	49	46	5
25–34	58	35	7
35–44	44	45	11
45–54	28	58	14
55–64	22	59	19
65+	11	45	44

a. Construct a stacked bar chart to display the above survey data on type of mobile phone ownership. Use age category as the variable on the horizontal axis.

b. Comment on the relationship between age and smartphone ownership.

c. How would you expect the results of this survey to be different if conducted in 2021?

43. The Northwest regional manager of an outdoor equipment retailer conducted a study to determine how managers at three store locations are using their time. A summary of the results is shown in the following table.

DATA *file*

ManagerTime

| Store Location | Percentage of Manager's Work Week Spent on | | | |
	Meetings	Reports	Customers	Idle
Bend	18	11	52	19
Portland	52	11	24	13
Seattle	32	17	37	14

a. Create a stacked bar chart with store location on the horizontal axis and percentage of time spent on each task on the vertical axis.

b. Create a side-by-side bar chart with store location on the horizontal axis and side-by-side bars of the percentage of time spent on each task.

c. Which type of bar chart (stacked or side-by-side) do you prefer for these data? Why?

2.5 Data Visualization: Best Practices in Creating Effective Graphical Displays

Data visualization is a term used to describe the use of graphical displays to summarize and present information about a data set. The goal of data visualization is to communicate as effectively and clearly as possible the key information about the data. In this section, we provide guidelines for creating an effective graphical display, discuss how to select an appropriate type of display given the purpose of the study, illustrate the use of data dashboards, and show how the Cincinnati Zoo and Botanical Garden uses data visualization techniques to improve decision making.

Creating Effective Graphical Displays

The data presented in Table 2.16 show the forecasted or planned value of sales ($1000s) and the actual value of sales ($1000s) by sales region in the United States for Gustin Chemical for the past year. Note that there are two quantitative variables (planned sales and actual sales) and one categorical variable (sales region). Suppose we would like to develop a graphical display that would enable management of Gustin Chemical to visualize how each sales region did relative to planned sales and simultaneously enable management to visualize sales performance across regions.

Figure 2.25 shows a side-by-side bar chart of the planned versus actual sales data. Note how this bar chart makes it very easy to compare the planned versus actual sales in a region, as well as across regions. This graphical display is simple, contains a title, is well labeled, and uses distinct colors to represent the two types of sales. Note also that the scale of the vertical axis begins at zero. The four sales regions are separated by space so that it is clear that they are distinct, whereas the planned versus actual sales values are side by side for easy comparison within each region. The side-by-side bar chart in Figure 2.25 makes it easy to see that the Southwest region is the lowest in both planned and actual sales and that the Northwest region slightly exceeded its planned sales.

TABLE 2.16   PLANNED AND ACTUAL SALES BY SALES REGION ($1000s)

Sales Region	Planned Sales ($1000s)	Actual Sales ($1000s)
Northeast	540	447
Northwest	420	447
Southeast	575	556
Southwest	360	341

Creating an effective graphical display is as much art as it is science. By following the general guidelines listed below you can increase the likelihood that your display will effectively convey the key information in the data.

- Give the display a clear and concise title.
- Keep the display simple. Do not use three dimensions when two dimensions are sufficient.
- Clearly label each axis and provide the units of measure.
- If color is used to distinguish categories, make sure the colors are distinct.
- If multiple colors or line types are used, use a legend to define how they are used and place the legend close to the representation of the data.

Choosing the Type of Graphical Display

In this chapter we discussed a variety of graphical displays, including bar charts, pie charts, dot plots, histograms, stem-and-leaf plots, scatter diagrams, side-by-side bar charts, and stacked bar charts. Each of these types of displays was developed for a specific purpose. In order to provide guidelines for choosing the appropriate type of graphical display, we now provide a summary of the types of graphical displays categorized by their purpose. We note that some types of graphical displays may be used effectively for multiple purposes.

Displays Used to Show the Distribution of Data

- Bar Chart—Used to show the frequency distribution and relative frequency distribution for categorical data

FIGURE 2.25   SIDE-BY-SIDE BAR CHART FOR PLANNED VERSUS ACTUAL SALES

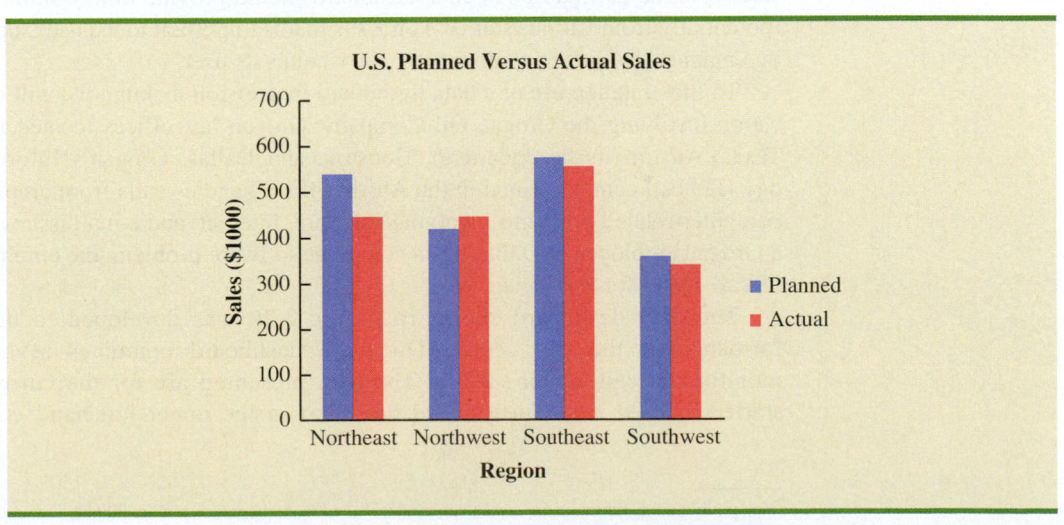

- Pie Chart—Used to show the relative frequency and percent frequency for categorical data
- Dot Plot—Used to show the distribution for quantitative data over the entire range of the data
- Histogram—Used to show the frequency distribution for quantitative data over a set of class intervals
- Stem-and-Leaf Display—Used to show both the rank order and shape of the distribution for quantitative data

Displays Used to Make Comparisons

- Side-by-Side Bar Chart—Used to compare two variables
- Stacked Bar Charts—Used to compare the relative frequency or percent frequency of two categorical variables

Displays Used to Show Relationships

- Scatter Diagram—Used to show the relationship between two quantitative variables
- Trendline—Used to approximate the relationship of data in a scatter diagram

Data Dashboards

Data dashboards are also referred to as digital dashboards.

One of the most widely used data visualization tools is a **data dashboard**. If you drive a car, you are already familiar with the concept of a data dashboard. In an automobile, the car's dashboard contains gauges and other visual displays that provide the key information that is important when operating the vehicle. For example, the gauges used to display the car's speed, fuel level, engine temperature, and oil level are critical to ensure safe and efficient operation of the automobile. In some vehicles, this information is even displayed visually on the windshield to provide an even more effective display for the driver. Data dashboards play a similar role for managerial decision making.

A data dashboard is a set of visual displays that organizes and presents information that is used to monitor the performance of a company or organization in a manner that is easy to read, understand, and interpret. Just as a car's speed, fuel level, engine temperature, and oil level are important information to monitor in a car, every business has key performance indicators (KPIs)[2] that need to be monitored to assess how a company is performing. Examples of KPIs are inventory on hand, daily sales, percentage of on-time deliveries, and sales revenue per quarter. A data dashboard should provide timely summary information (potentially from various sources) on KPIs that is important to the user, and it should do so in a manner that informs rather than overwhelms its user.

To illustrate the use of a data dashboard in decision making, we will discuss an application involving the Grogan Oil Company. Grogan has offices located in three cities in Texas: Austin (its headquarters), Houston, and Dallas. Grogan's Information Technology (IT) call center, located in the Austin office, handles calls from employees regarding computer-related problems involving software, Internet, and e-mail issues. For example, if a Grogan employee in Dallas has a computer software problem, the employee can call the IT call center for assistance.

The data dashboard shown in Figure 2.26 was developed to monitor the performance of the call center. This data dashboard combines several displays to monitor the call center's KPIs. The data presented are for the current shift, which started at 8:00 A.M. The stacked bar chart in the upper left-hand corner shows the

---

[2] Key performance indicators are sometimes referred to as Key Performance Metrics (KPMs).

FIGURE 2.26   GROGAN OIL INFORMATION TECHNOLOGY CALL CENTER DATA DASHBOARD

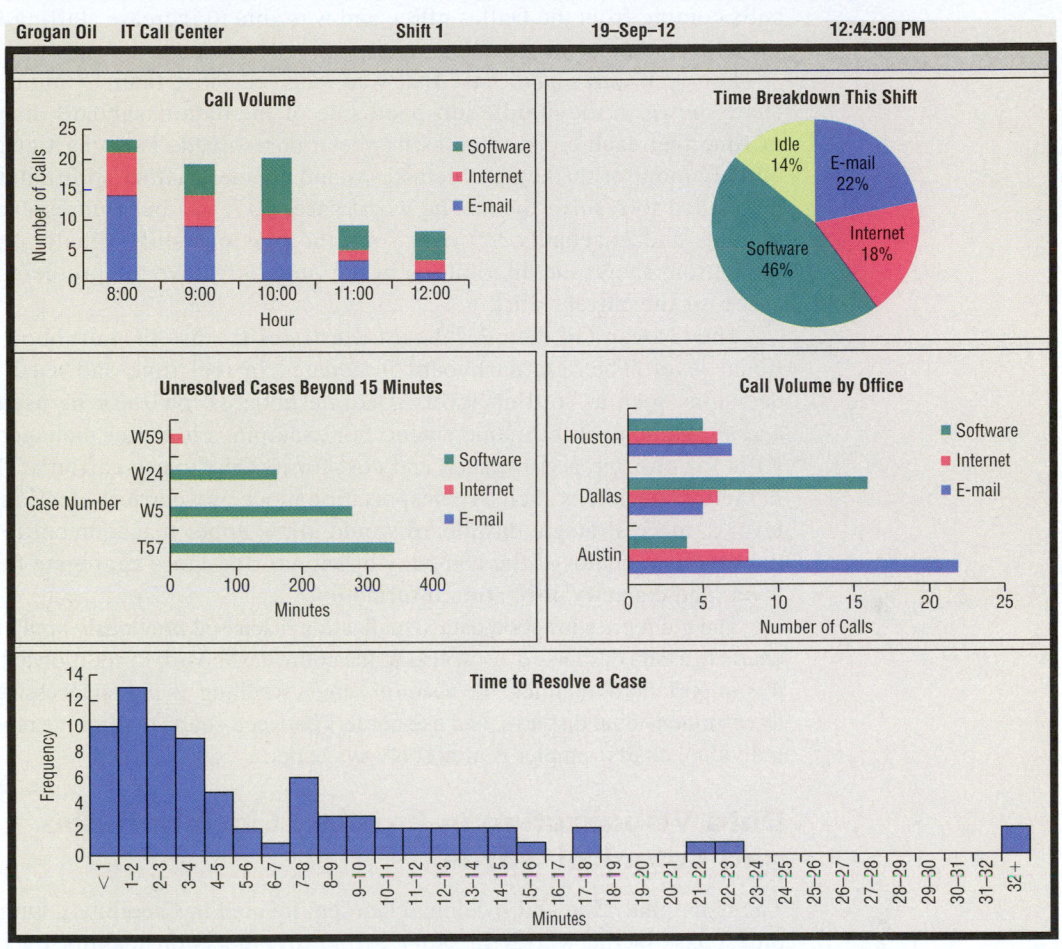

call volume for each type of problem (software, Internet, or e-mail) over time. This chart shows that call volume is heavier during the first few hours of the shift, calls concerning e-mail issues appear to decrease over time, and volume of calls regarding software issues are highest at midmorning. The pie chart in the upper right-hand corner of the dashboard shows the percentage of time that call center employees spent on each type of problem or not working on a call (idle). Both of these charts are helpful in determining optimal staffing levels. For instance, knowing the call mix and how stressed the system is—as measured by percentage of idle time—can help the IT manager make sure there are enough call center employees available with the right level of expertise.

The side-by-side bar chart below the pie chart shows the call volume by type of problem for each of Grogan's offices. This allows the IT manager to quickly identify if there is a particular type of problem by location. For example, it appears that the office in Austin is reporting a relatively high number of issues with e-mail. If the source of the problem can be identified quickly, then the problem for many might be resolved quickly. Also, note that a relatively high number of software problems are coming from the Dallas office. The higher call volume in this case was simply due to the fact that the Dallas office is currently installing new software, and this has resulted in more calls to the IT call center. Because the IT manager was alerted to this by the Dallas office last week, the IT manager knew there would be an increase in calls coming from the Dallas office and was able to increase staffing levels to handle the expected increase in calls.

For each unresolved case that was received more than 15 minutes ago, the bar chart shown in the middle left-hand side of the data dashboard displays the length of time that each of these cases has been unresolved. This chart enables Grogan to quickly monitor the key problem cases and decide whether additional resources may be needed to resolve them. The worst case, T57, has been unresolved for over 300 minutes and is actually left over from the previous shift. Finally, the histogram at the bottom shows the distribution of the time to resolve the problem for all resolved cases for the current shift.

The Grogan Oil data dashboard illustrates the use of a dashboard at the operational level. The data dashboard is updated in real time and used for operational decisions such as staffing levels. Data dashboards may also be used at the tactical and strategic levels of management. For example, a logistics manager might monitor KPIs for on-time performance and cost for its third-party carriers. This could assist in tactical decisions such as transportation mode and carrier selection. At the highest level, a more strategic dashboard would allow upper management to quickly assess the financial health of the company by monitoring more aggregate financial, service level, and capacity utilization information.

The guidelines for good data visualization discussed previously apply to the individual charts in a data dashboard, as well as to the entire dashboard. In addition to those guidelines, it is important to minimize the need for screen scrolling, avoid unnecessary use of color or three-dimensional displays, and use borders between charts to improve readability. As with individual charts, simpler is almost always better.

Data Visualization in Practice: Cincinnati Zoo and Botanical Garden[3]

The Cincinnati Zoo and Botanical Garden, located in Cincinnati, Ohio, is the second oldest zoo in the world. In order to improve decision making by becoming more data-driven, management decided they needed to link together the different facets of their business and provide nontechnical managers and executives with an intuitive way to better understand their data. A complicating factor is that when the zoo is busy, managers are expected to be on the grounds interacting with guests, checking on operations, and anticipating issues as they arise or before they become an issue. Therefore, being able to monitor what is happening on a real-time basis was a key factor in deciding what to do. Zoo management concluded that a data visualization strategy was needed to address the problem.

Because of its ease of use, real-time updating capability, and iPad compatibility, the Cincinnati Zoo decided to implement its data visualization strategy using IBM's Cognos advanced data visualization software. Using this software, the Cincinnati Zoo developed the data dashboard shown in Figure 2.27 to enable zoo management to track the following key performance indicators:

- Item Analysis (sales volumes and sales dollars by location within the zoo)
- Geoanalytics (using maps and displays of where the day's visitors are spending their time at the zoo)

---

[3] The authors are indebted to John Lucas of the Cincinnati Zoo and Botanical Garden for providing this application.

FIGURE 2.27   DATA DASHBOARD FOR THE CINCINNATI ZOO

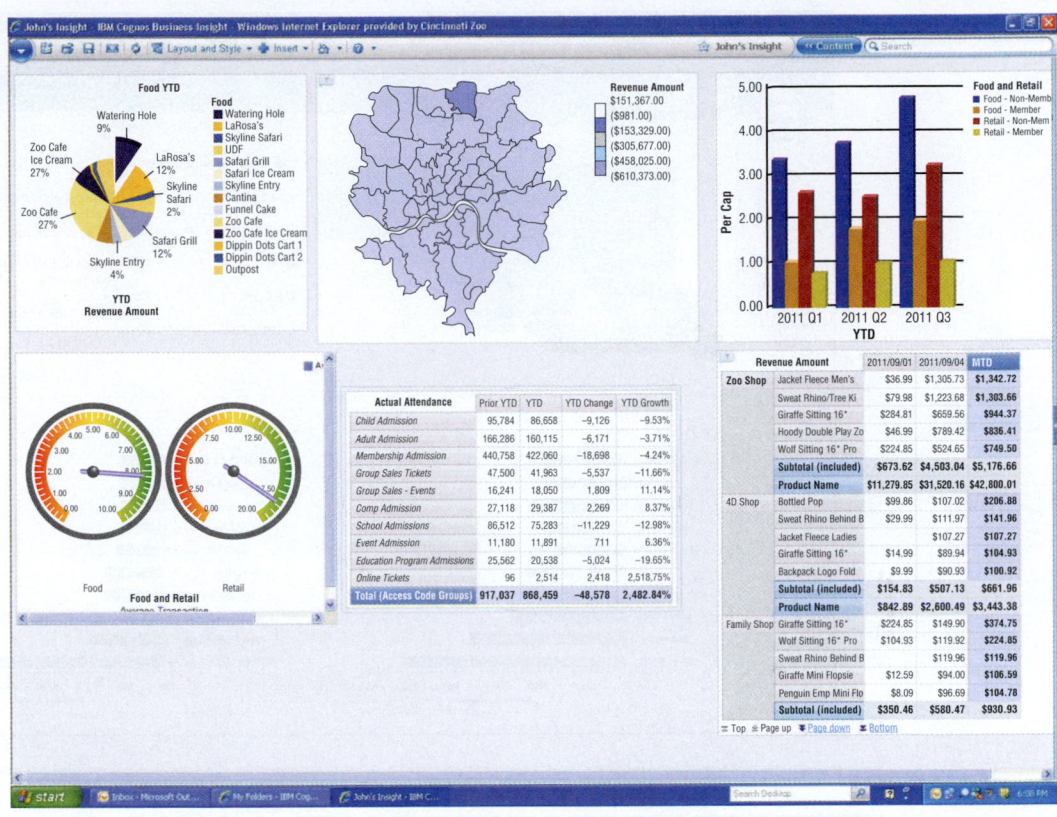

- Customer Spending
- Cashier Sales Performance
- Sales and Attendance Data Versus Weather Patterns
- Performance of the Zoo's Loyalty Rewards Program

An iPad mobile application was also developed to enable the zoo's managers to be out on the grounds and still see and anticipate what is occurring on a real-time basis. The Cincinnati Zoo's iPad data dashboard, shown in Figure 2.28, provides managers with access to the following information:

- Real-time attendance data, including what types of guests are coming to the zoo
- Real-time analysis showing which items are selling the fastest inside the zoo
- Real-time geographical representation of where the zoo's visitors live

Having access to the data shown in Figures 2.27 and 2.28 allows the zoo managers to make better decisions on staffing levels within the zoo, which items to stock based upon weather and other conditions, and how to better target its advertising based on geodemographics.

The impact that data visualization has had on the zoo has been substantial. Within the first year of use, the system has been directly responsible for revenue growth of over $500,000, increased visitation to the zoo, enhanced customer service, and reduced marketing costs.

FIGURE 2.28   THE CINCINNATI ZOO iPAD DATA DASHBOARD

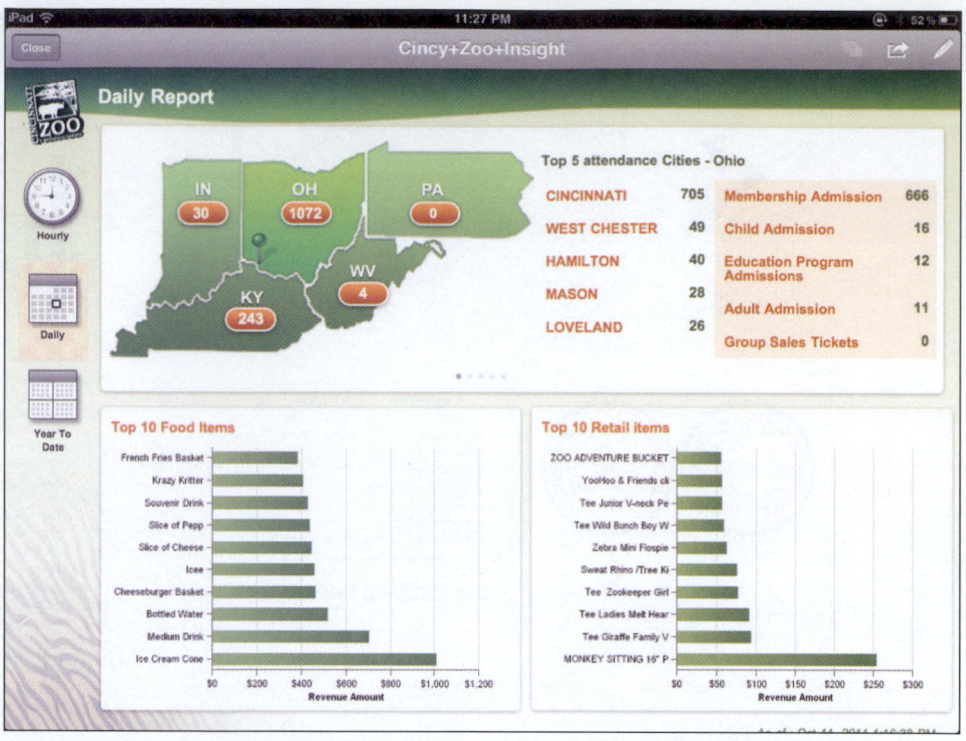

1. A variety of software is available for data visualization. Among the more popular packages are Cognos, JMP, Spotfire, and Tableau.

2. Radar charts and bubble charts are two other commonly used charts for displaying relationships among multiple variables. However, many experts in data visualization recommend against using these charts because they can be overcomplicated. Instead, the use of simpler displays such as bar charts and scatter diagrams is recommended.

3. A very powerful tool for visualizing geographic data is a Geographic Information System (GIS).

A GIS uses color, symbols, and text on a map to help you understand how variables are distributed geographically. For example, a company interested in trying to locate a new distribution center might wish to better understand how the demand for its product varies throughout the United States. A GIS can be used to map the demand, with red regions indicating high demand, blue lower demand, and no color indicating regions where the product is not sold. Locations closer to red high-demand regions might be good candidate sites for further consideration.

Summary

A set of data, even if modest in size, is often difficult to interpret directly in the form in which it is gathered. Tabular and graphical displays can be used to summarize and present data so that patterns are revealed and the data are more easily interpreted. Frequency distributions, relative frequency distributions, percent frequency distributions, bar charts, and pie charts were presented as tabular and graphical displays for summarizing the data for a single categorical variable. Frequency distributions, relative frequency distributions, percent

FIGURE 2.29 TABULAR AND GRAPHICAL DISPLAYS FOR SUMMARIZING DATA

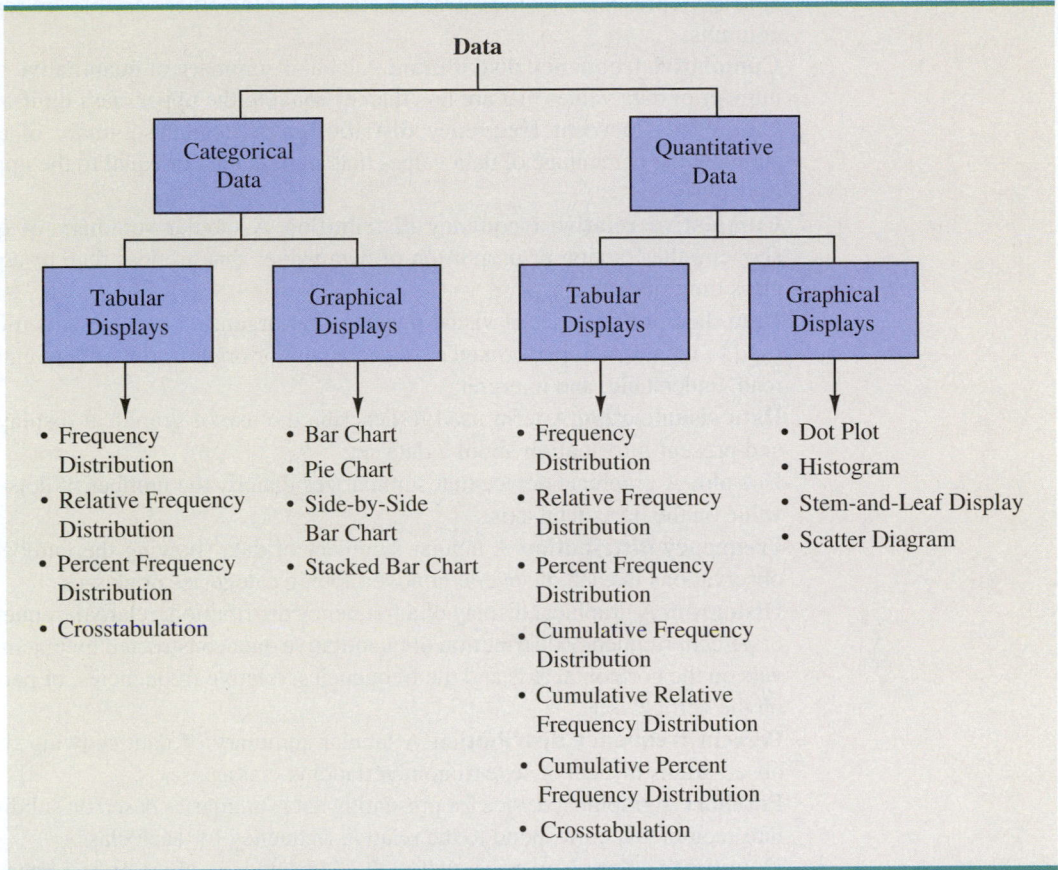

frequency distributions, histograms, cumulative frequency distributions, cumulative relative frequency distributions, cumulative percent frequency distributions, and stem-and-leaf displays were presented as ways of summarizing the data for a single quantitative variable.

A crosstabulation was presented as a tabular display for summarizing the data for two variables, and a scatter diagram was introduced as a graphical display for summarizing the data for two quantitative variables. We also showed that side-by-side bar charts and stacked bar charts are just extensions of basic bar charts that can be used to display and compare two categorical variables. Guidelines for creating effective graphical displays and how to choose the most appropriate type of display were discussed. Data dashboards were introduced to illustrate how a set of visual displays can be developed that organizes and presents information that is used to monitor a company's performance in a manner that is easy to read, understand, and interpret. Figure 2.29 provides a summary of the tabular and graphical methods presented in this chapter.

Glossary

Bar chart A graphical device for depicting categorical data that have been summarized in a frequency, relative frequency, or percent frequency distribution.

Categorical data Labels or names used to identify categories of like items.

Class midpoint The value halfway between the lower and upper class limits.

Crosstabulation A tabular summary of data for two variables. The classes for one variable are represented by the rows; the classes for the other variable are represented by the columns.

Cumulative frequency distribution A tabular summary of quantitative data showing the number of data values that are less than or equal to the upper class limit of each class.

Cumulative percent frequency distribution A tabular summary of quantitative data showing the percentage of data values that are less than or equal to the upper class limit of each class.

Cumulative relative frequency distribution A tabular summary of quantitative data showing the fraction or proportion of data values that are less than or equal to the upper class limit of each class.

Data dashboard A set of visual displays that organizes and presents information that is used to monitor the performance of a company or organization in a manner that is easy to read, understand, and interpret.

Data visualization A term used to describe the use of graphical displays to summarize and present information about a data set.

Dot plot A graphical device that summarizes data by the number of dots above each data value on the horizontal axis.

Frequency distribution A tabular summary of data showing the number (frequency) of observations in each of several nonoverlapping categories or classes.

Histogram A graphical display of a frequency distribution, relative frequency distribution, or percent frequency distribution of quantitative data constructed by placing the class intervals on the horizontal axis and the frequencies, relative frequencies, or percent frequencies on the vertical axis.

Percent frequency distribution A tabular summary of data showing the percentage of observations in each of several nonoverlapping classes.

Pie chart A graphical device for presenting data summaries based on subdivision of a circle into sectors that correspond to the relative frequency for each class.

Quantitative data Numerical values that indicate how much or how many.

Relative frequency distribution A tabular summary of data showing the fraction or proportion of observations in each of several nonoverlapping categories or classes.

Scatter diagram A graphical display of the relationship between two quantitative variables. One variable is shown on the horizontal axis and the other variable is shown on the vertical axis.

Side-by-side bar chart A graphical display for depicting multiple bar charts on the same display.

Simpson's paradox Conclusions drawn from two or more separate crosstabulations that can be reversed when the data are aggregated into a single crosstabulation.

Stacked bar chart A bar chart in which each bar is broken into rectangular segments of a different color showing the relative frequency of each class in a manner similar to a pie chart.

Stem-and-leaf display A graphical display used to show simultaneously the rank order and shape of a distribution of data.

Trendline A line that provides an approximation of the relationship between two variables.

Key Formulas

Relative Frequency

$$\frac{\text{Frequency of the class}}{n} \tag{2.1}$$

Approximate Class Width

$$\frac{\text{Largest data value} - \text{Smallest data value}}{\text{Number of classes}} \qquad \textbf{(2.2)}$$

Supplementary Exercises

NewSAT

44. Approximately 1.5 million high school students take the SAT each year and nearly 80% of colleges and universities without open admissions policies use SAT scores in making admission decisions. The current version of the SAT includes three parts: reading comprehension, mathematics, and writing. A perfect combined score for all three parts is 2400. A sample of SAT scores for the combined three-part SAT is as follows.

1665	1525	1355	1645	1780
1275	2135	1280	1060	1585
1650	1560	1150	1485	1990
1590	1880	1420	1755	1375
1475	1680	1440	1260	1730
1490	1560	940	1390	1175

   a. Show a frequency distribution and histogram. Begin with the first class starting at 800 and use a class width of 200.
   b. Comment on the shape of the distribution.
   c. What other observations can be made about the SAT scores based on the tabular and graphical summaries?

MedianHousehold

45. The DATAfile *MedianHousehold* contains the median household income for a family with two earners for each of the fifty states (American Community Survey, 2013).
   a. Construct a frequency and a percent frequency distribution of median household income. Begin the first class at 65.0 and use a class width of 5.
   b. Construct a histogram.
   c. Comment on the shape of the distribution.
   d. Which state has the highest median income for two-earner households?
   e. Which state has the lowest median income for two-earner households?

46. Data showing the population by state in millions of people follow (*The World Almanac*, 2012).

2012Population

State	Population	State	Population	State	Population
Alabama	4.8	Louisiana	4.5	Ohio	11.5
Alaska	0.7	Maine	1.3	Oklahoma	3.8
Arizona	6.4	Maryland	5.8	Oregon	4.3
Arkansas	2.9	Massachusetts	6.5	Pennsylvania	12.7
California	37.3	Michigan	9.9	Rhode Island	1.0
Colorado	5.0	Minnesota	5.3	South Carolina	4.6
Connecticut	3.6	Mississippi	3.0	South Dakota	0.8
Delaware	0.9	Missouri	6.0	Tennessee	6.3
Florida	18.8	Montana	0.9	Texas	25.1
Georgia	9.7	Nebraska	1.8	Utah	2.8
Hawaii	1.4	Nevada	2.7	Vermont	0.6
Idaho	1.6	New Hampshire	1.3	Virginia	8.0
Illinois	12.8	New Jersey	8.8	Washington	6.7
Indiana	6.5	New Mexico	2.0	West Virginia	1.9
Iowa	3.0	New York	19.4	Wisconsin	5.7
Kansas	2.9	North Carolina	9.5	Wyoming	0.6
Kentucky	4.3	North Dakota	0.7		

a. Develop a frequency distribution, a percent frequency distribution, and a histogram. Use a class width of 2.5 million.

b. Does there appear to be any skewness in the distribution? Explain.

c. What observations can you make about the population of the 50 states?

47. A startup company's ability to gain funding is a key to success. The funds raised (in millions of dollars) by 50 startup companies follow (*The Wall Street Journal,* March 10, 2011).

StartUps

81	61	103	166	168
80	51	130	77	78
69	119	81	60	20
73	50	110	21	60
192	18	54	49	63
91	272	58	54	40
47	24	57	78	78
154	72	38	131	52
48	118	40	49	55
54	112	129	156	31

a. Construct a stem-and-leaf display.

b. Comment on the display.

BBB

48. Consumer complaints are frequently reported to the Better Business Bureau. In 2011, the industries with the most complaints to the Better Business Bureau were banks, cable and satellite television companies, collection agencies, cellular phone providers, and new car dealerships (*USA Today,* April 16, 2012). The results for a sample of 200 complaints are contained in the DATAfile named *BBB*.

a. Show the frequency and percent frequency of complaints by industry.

b. Construct a bar chart of the percent frequency distribution.

c. Which industry had the highest number of complaints?

d. Comment on the percentage frequency distribution for complaints.

49. The term *Beta* refers to a measure of a stock's price volatility relative to the stock market as a whole. A Beta of 1 means the stock's price moves exactly with the market. A Beta of 1.6 means the stock's price would increase by 1.6% for an increase of 1% in the stock market. A larger Beta means the stock price is more volatile. The Betas for the stocks of the companies that make up the Dow Jones Industrial Average are shown in Table 2.17 (*Yahoo Finance*, November 2014).

TABLE 2.17   BETAS FOR DOW JONES INDUSTRIAL AVERAGE COMPANIES

DJIABeta

Company	Beta	Company	Beta
American Express Company	1.24	McDonald's Corp.	0.62
The Boeing Company	0.99	3M Company	1.23
Caterpillar Inc.	1.2	Merck & Co. Inc.	0.56
Cisco Systems, Inc.	1.36	Microsoft Corporation	0.69
Chevron Corporation	1.11	Nike, Inc.	0.47
E. I. du Pont de Nemours and Company	1.36	Pfizer Inc.	0.72
The Walt Disney Company	0.97	The Procter & Gamble Company	0.73
General Electric Company	1.19	AT&T, Inc.	0.18
The Goldman Sachs Group, Inc.	1.79	The Travelers Companies, Inc.	0.86
The Home Depot, Inc.	1.22	UnitedHealth Group Incorporated	0.88
International Business Machines Corporation	0.92	United Technologies Corporation	1.22
Intel Corporation	0.9	Visa Inc.	0.82
Johnson & Johnson	0.84	Verizon Communications Inc.	0.04
JPMorgan Chase & Co.	1.84	Walmart Stores Inc.	0.26
The Coca-Cola Company	0.68	Exxon Mobil Corporation	1.1

a. Construct a frequency distribution and percent frequency distribution.
b. Construct a histogram.
c. Comment on the shape of the distribution.
d. Which stock has the highest Beta? Which has the lowest Beta?

50. The U.S. Census Bureau serves as the leading source of quantitative data about the nation's people and economy. The following crosstabulation shows the number of households (1000s) and the household income by the level of education for heads of household having received a high school degree or more education (U.S. Census Bureau website, 2013).

Level of Education	Household Income				
	Under $25,000	$25,000 to $49,999	$50,000 to $99,999	$100,000 and Over	Total
High school graduate	9,880	9,970	9,441	3,482	32,773
Bachelor's degree	2,484	4,164	7,666	7,817	22,131
Master's degree	685	1,205	3,019	4,094	9,003
Doctoral degree	79	160	422	1,076	1,737
Total	13,128	15,499	20,548	16,469	65,644

a. Construct a percent frequency distribution for the level of education variable. What percentage of heads of households have a master's or doctoral degree?
b. Construct a percent frequency distribution for the household income variable. What percentage of households have an income of $50,000 or more?
c. Convert the entries in the crosstabulation into column percentages. Compare the level of education of households with a household income of under $25,000 to the level of education of households with a household income of $100,000 or more. Comment on any other items of interest when reviewing the crosstabulation showing column percentages.

51. Western University has only one women's softball scholarship remaining for the coming year. The final two players that Western is considering are Allison Fealey and Emily Janson. The coaching staff has concluded that the speed and defensive skills are virtually identical for the two players, and that the final decision will be based on which player has the best batting average. Crosstabulations of each player's batting performance in their junior and senior years of high school are as follows:

	Allison Fealey				Emily Janson	
Outcome	Junior	Senior		Outcome	Junior	Senior
Hit	15	75		Hit	70	35
No Hit	25	175		No Hit	130	85
Total At-Bats	40	250		Total At Bats	200	120

A player's batting average is computed by dividing the number of hits a player has by the total number of at-bats. Batting averages are represented as a decimal number with three places after the decimal.

a. Calculate the batting average for each player in her junior year. Then calculate the batting average of each player in her senior year. Using this analysis, which player should be awarded the scholarship? Explain.

b. Combine or aggregate the data for the junior and senior years into one crosstabulation as follows:

	Player	
Outcome	**Fealey**	**Janson**
Hit		
No Hit		
Total At-Bats		

Calculate each player's batting average for the combined two years. Using this analysis, which player should be awarded the scholarship? Explain.

c. Are the recommendations you made in parts (a) and (b) consistent? Explain any apparent inconsistencies.

52. *Fortune* magazine publishes an annual survey of the 100 best companies to work for. The data in the DATAfile named *FortuneBest100* shows the rank, company name, the size of the company, and the percentage job growth for full-time employees for 98 of the *Fortune* 100 companies for which percentage job growth data were available (*Fortune* magazine website, February 25, 2013). The column labeled Rank shows the rank of the company in the Fortune 100 list; the column labeled Size indicates whether the company is a small company (less than 2500 employees), a midsized company (2500 to 10,000 employees), or a large company (more than 10,000 employees); and the column labeled Growth Rate (%) shows the percentage growth rate for full-time employees.

FortuneBest100

a. Construct a crosstabulation with Job Growth (%) as the row variable and Size as the column variable. Use classes starting at −10 and ending at 70 in increments of 10 for Growth Rate (%).

b. Show the frequency distribution for Job Growth (%) and the frequency distribution for Size.

c. Using the crosstabulation constructed in part (a), develop a crosstabulation showing column percentages.

d. Using the crosstabulation constructed in part (a), develop a crosstabulation showing row percentages.

e. Comment on the relationship between the percentage job growth for full-time employees and the size of the company.

53. Table 2.18 shows a portion of the data for a sample of 103 private colleges and universities. The complete data set is contained in the DATAfile named *Colleges*. The data include the name of the college or university, the year the institution was founded, the tuition and fees (not including room and board) for the most recent academic year, and the percentage of full time, first-time bachelor's degree–seeking undergraduate students who obtain their degree in six years or less (*The World Almanac*, 2012)

TABLE 2.18   DATA FOR A SAMPLE OF PRIVATE COLLEGES AND UNIVERSITIES

Colleges

School	Year Founded	Tuition & Fees	% Graduate
American University	1893	$36,697	79.00
Baylor University	1845	$29,754	70.00
Belmont University	1951	$23,680	68.00
.	.	.	.
.	.	.	.
.	.	.	.
Wofford College	1854	$31,710	82.00
Xavier University	1831	$29,970	79.00
Yale University	1701	$38,300	98.00

a. Construct a crosstabulation with Year Founded as the row variable and Tuition & Fees as the column variable. Use classes starting with 1600 and ending with 2000 in increments of 50 for Year Founded. For Tuition & Fees, use classes starting with 1 and ending 45,000 in increments of 5000.

b. Compute the row percentages for the crosstabulation in part (a).

c. What relationship, if any, do you notice between Year Founded and Tuition & Fees?

54. Refer to the data set in Table 2.18.

a. Construct a crosstabulation with Year Founded as the row variable and % Graduate as the column variable. Use classes starting with 1600 and ending with 2000 in increments of 50 for Year Founded. For % Graduate, use classes starting with 35% and ending with 100% in increments of 5%.

b. Compute the row percentages for your crosstabulation in part (a).

c. Comment on any relationship between the variables.

55. Refer to the data set in Table 2.18.

a. Construct a scatter diagram to show the relationship between Year Founded and Tuition & Fees.

b. Comment on any relationship between the variables.

56. Refer to the data set in Table 2.18.

a. Prepare a scatter diagram to show the relationship between Tuition & Fees and % Graduate.

b. Comment on any relationship between the variables.

57. Google has changed its strategy with regard to how much it invests in advertising, and which media it uses to do so. The following table shows Google's marketing budget in millions of dollars for 2008 and 2011 (*The Wall Street Journal,* March 27, 2012).

	2008	2011
Internet	26.0	123.3
Newspaper, etc.	4.0	20.7
Television	0.0	69.3

a. Construct a side-by-side bar chart with year as the variable on the horizontal axis. Comment on any trend in the display.

b. Convert the above table to percentage allocation for each year. Construct a stacked bar chart with year as the variable on the horizontal axis.

c. Is the display in part (a) or part (b) more insightful? Explain.

58. A zoo has categorized its visitors into three categories: member, school, and general. The member category refers to visitors who pay an annual fee to support the zoo. Members receive certain benefits such as discounts on merchandise and trips planned by the zoo. The school category includes faculty and students from day care and elementary and secondary schools; these visitors generally receive a discounted rate. The general category includes all other visitors. The zoo has been concerned about a recent drop in attendance. To help better understand attendance and membership, a zoo staff member has collected the following data:

DATA *file*

Zoo

	Attendance			
Visitor Category	2008	2009	2010	2011
General	153,713	158,704	163,433	169,106
Member	115,523	104,795	98,437	81,217
School	82,885	79,876	81,970	81,290
Total	352,121	343,375	343,840	331,613

a. Construct a bar chart of total attendance over time. Comment on any trend in the data.
b. Construct a side-by-side bar chart showing attendance by visitor category with year as the variable on the horizontal axis.
c. Comment on what is happening to zoo attendance based on the charts from parts (a) and (b).

Case Problem 1   Pelican Stores

Pelican Stores, a division of National Clothing, is a chain of women's apparel stores operating throughout the country. The chain recently ran a promotion in which discount coupons were sent to customers of other National Clothing stores. Data collected for a sample of 100 in-store credit card transactions at Pelican Stores during one day while the promotion was running are contained in the DATAfile named *PelicanStores*. Table 2.19 shows a portion of the data set. The Proprietary Card method of payment refers to charges made using a National Clothing charge card. Customers who made a purchase using a discount coupon are referred to as promotional customers, and customers who made a purchase but did not use a discount coupon are referred to as regular customers. Because the promotional coupons were not sent to regular Pelican Stores customers, management considers the sales made to people presenting the promotional coupons as sales it would not otherwise make. Of course, Pelican also hopes that the promotional customers will continue to shop at its stores.

Most of the variables shown in Table 2.19 are self-explanatory, but two of the variables require some clarification.

Items   The total number of items purchased
Net Sales   The total amount ($) charged to the credit card

Pelican's management would like to use this sample data to learn about its customer base and to evaluate the promotion involving discount coupons.

Managerial Report

Use the tabular and graphical methods of descriptive statistics to help management develop a customer profile and to evaluate the promotional campaign. At a minimum, your report should include the following:

1. Percent frequency distribution for key variables.
2. A bar chart or pie chart showing the number of customer purchases attributable to the method of payment.

TABLE 2.19   DATA FOR A SAMPLE OF 100 CREDIT CARD PURCHASES AT PELICAN STORES

DATA *file*

PelicanStores

Customer	Type of Customer	Items	Net Sales	Method of Payment	Gender	Marital Status	Age
1	Regular	1	39.50	Discover	Male	Married	32
2	Promotional	1	102.40	Proprietary Card	Female	Married	36
3	Regular	1	22.50	Proprietary Card	Female	Married	32
4	Promotional	5	100.40	Proprietary Card	Female	Married	28
5	Regular	2	54.00	MasterCard	Female	Married	34
.	.	.	.		.	.	.
.	.	.	.		.	.	.
.	.	.	.		.	.	.
96	Regular	1	39.50	MasterCard	Female	Married	44
97	Promotional	9	253.00	Proprietary Card	Female	Married	30
98	Promotional	10	287.59	Proprietary Card	Female	Married	52
99	Promotional	2	47.60	Proprietary Card	Female	Married	30
100	Promotional	1	28.44	Proprietary Card	Female	Married	44

3. A crosstabulation of type of customer (regular or promotional) versus net sales. Comment on any similarities or differences present.
4. A scatter diagram to explore the relationship between net sales and customer age.

Case Problem 2   Motion Picture Industry

The motion picture industry is a competitive business. More than 50 studios produce a total of 300 to 400 new motion pictures each year, and the financial success of each motion picture varies considerably. The opening weekend gross sales ($ millions), the total gross sales ($ millions), the number of theaters the movie was shown in, and the number of weeks the motion picture was in release are common variables used to measure the success of a motion picture. Data collected for the top 100 motion pictures produced in 2011 are contained in the DATAfile named *2011Movies* (Box Office Mojo, March 17, 2012). Table 2.20 shows the data for the first 10 motion pictures in this file.

Managerial Report

Use the tabular and graphical methods of descriptive statistics to learn how these variables contribute to the success of a motion picture. Include the following in your report.

1. Tabular and graphical summaries for each of the four variables along with a discussion of what each summary tells us about the motion picture industry.
2. A scatter diagram to explore the relationship between Total Gross Sales and Opening Weekend Gross Sales. Discuss.
3. A scatter diagram to explore the relationship between Total Gross Sales and Number of Theaters. Discuss.
4. A scatter diagram to explore the relationship between Total Gross Sales and Number of Weeks in Release. Discuss.

2011Movies

TABLE 2.20   PERFORMANCE DATA FOR 10 MOTION PICTURES

Motion Picture	Opening Gross Sales ($ millions)	Total Gross Sales ($ millions)	Number of Theaters	Weeks in Release
Harry Potter and the Deathly Hallows Part 2	169.19	381.01	4375	19
Transformers: Dark of the Moon	97.85	352.39	4088	15
The Twilight Saga: Breaking Dawn Part 1	138.12	281.29	4066	14
The Hangover Part II	85.95	254.46	3675	16
Pirates of the Caribbean: On Stranger Tides	90.15	241.07	4164	19
Fast Five	86.20	209.84	3793	15
Mission: Impossible— Ghost Protocol	12.79	208.55	3555	13
Cars 2	66.14	191.45	4115	25
Sherlock Holmes: A Game of Shadows	39.64	186.59	3703	13
Thor	65.72	181.03	3963	16

Case Problem 3   Queen City

Cincinnati, Ohio, also known as the Queen City, has a population of approximately 298,000 and is the third largest city in the state of Ohio. The Cincinnati metropolitan area has a population of about 2.2 million. The city is governed by a mayor and a nine-member city council. The city manager, who is responsible for the day-to-day operation of the city, reports to the mayor and city council. The city manager recently created the Office of Performance and Data Analytics with the goal of improving the efficiency of city operations. One of the first tasks of this new office is to review the previous year's expenditures. The file *QueenCity* contains data on the previous year's expenditures, including the following:

Department   The number of the department incurring the expenditure
Department Description   The name of the department incurring the description
Category   The category of the expenditure
Fund   The fund to which the expenditure was charged
Expenditure   The dollar amount of the expense

QueenCity

Table 2.21 shows the first four entries of the 5427 expenditures for the year. The city manager would like to use this data to better understand how the city's budget is being spent.

Managerial Report

Use tabular and graphical methods of descriptive statistics to help the city manager get a better understanding of how the city is spending its funding. Your report should include the following:

1. Tables and/or graphical displays that show the amount of expenditures by category and percentage of total expenditures by category.
2. A table that shows the amount of expenditures by department and the percentage of total expenditures by department. Combine any department with less than 1% into a category named "Other."
3. A table that shows the amount of expenditures by fund and the percentage of total expenditures by fund. Combine any fund with less than 1% into a category named "Other."

Case Problem 4   Cut-Rate Machining, Inc.

Jon Weideman, first shift foreman for Cut-Rate Machining, Inc., is attempting to decide on a vendor from whom to purchase a drilling machine. He narrows his alternatives to four vendors: The Hole-Maker, Inc. (HM); Shafts & Slips, Inc. (SS); Judge's Jigs (JJ); and

TABLE 2.21   ANNUAL EXPENDITURES FOR QUEEN CITY (FIRST FOUR ENTRIES)

Department	Department Description	Category	Fund	Expenditure
121	Department of Human Resources	Fringe Benefits	050 - GENERAL FUND	$ 7,085.21
121	Department of Human Resources	Fringe Benefits	050 - GENERAL FUND	$102,678.64
121	Department of Human Resources	Fringe Benefits	050 - GENERAL FUND	$ 79,112.85
121	Department of Human Resources	Contractual Services	050 - GENERAL FUND	$ 3,572.50

Drill-for-Bits, Inc. (DB). Each of these vendors is offering machines of similar capabilities at similar prices, so the effectiveness of the machines is the only selection criteria that Mr. Weideman can use. He invites each vendor to ship one machine to his Richmond, Indiana manufacturing facility for a test. He starts all four machines at 8:00 A.M. and lets them warm up for two hours before starting to use any of the machines. Sometime after the warmup period, one of his employees will use each of the shipped machines to drill 3-centimeter-diameter holes in 25-centimeter-thick stainless-steel sheets for two hours. The widths of holes drilled with each machine are then measured and recorded. The results of Mr. Weideman's data collection are shown in Table 2.22.

TABLE 2.22   DATA COLLECTED FOR DRILL-FOR-BITS, INC VENDOR SELECTION

Shift	Time Period	Employee	Vendor	Measured Width (cm)
1	10:00 A.M. – noon	Ms. Ames	HM	3.50
1	10:00 A.M. – noon	Ms. Ames	HM	3.13
1	10:00 A.M. – noon	Ms. Ames	HM	3.39
1	10:00 A.M. – noon	Ms. Ames	HM	3.08
1	10:00 A.M. – noon	Ms. Ames	HM	3.22
1	10:00 A.M. – noon	Ms. Ames	HM	3.45
1	10:00 A.M. – noon	Ms. Ames	HM	3.32
1	10:00 A.M. – noon	Ms. Ames	HM	3.61
1	10:00 A.M. – noon	Ms. Ames	HM	3.10
1	10:00 A.M. – noon	Ms. Ames	HM	3.03
1	10:00 A.M. – noon	Ms. Ames	HM	3.67
1	10:00 A.M. – noon	Ms. Ames	HM	3.59
1	10:00 A.M. – noon	Ms. Ames	HM	3.33
1	10:00 A.M. – noon	Ms. Ames	HM	3.02
1	10:00 A.M. – noon	Ms. Ames	HM	3.55
1	10:00 A.M. – noon	Ms. Ames	HM	3.00
1	noon – 2:00 P.M.	Ms. Ames	SS	2.48
1	noon – 2:00 P.M.	Ms. Ames	SS	2.72
1	noon – 2:00 P.M.	Ms. Ames	SS	2.99
1	noon – 2:00 P.M.	Ms. Ames	SS	2.68
1	noon – 2:00 P.M.	Ms. Ames	SS	2.75
1	noon – 2:00 P.M.	Ms. Ames	SS	2.42
1	noon – 2:00 P.M.	Ms. Ames	SS	2.92
1	noon – 2:00 P.M.	Ms. Ames	SS	2.68
1	noon – 2:00 P.M.	Ms. Ames	SS	2.98
1	noon – 2:00 P.M.	Ms. Ames	SS	2.50
1	noon – 2:00 P.M.	Ms. Ames	SS	2.45
1	noon – 2:00 P.M.	Ms. Ames	SS	2.99
1	noon – 2:00 P.M.	Ms. Ames	SS	2.31
1	noon – 2:00 P.M.	Ms. Ames	SS	2.42

(Continued)

TABLE 2.22   (*CONTINUED*)

Shift	Time Period	Employee	Vendor	Measured Width (cm)
1	noon – 2:00 P.M.	Ms. Ames	SS	2.91
1	noon – 2:00 P.M.	Ms. Ames	SS	2.83
1	2:00 P.M. – 4:00 P.M.	Ms. Ames	JJ	2.66
1	2:00 P.M. – 4:00 P.M.	Ms. Ames	JJ	2.54
1	2:00 P.M. – 4:00 P.M.	Ms. Ames	JJ	2.61
1	2:00 P.M. – 4:00 P.M.	Ms. Ames	JJ	2.57
1	2:00 P.M. – 4:00 P.M.	Ms. Ames	JJ	2.71
1	2:00 P.M. – 4:00 P.M.	Ms. Ames	JJ	2.55
1	2:00 P.M. – 4:00 P.M.	Ms. Ames	JJ	2.59
1	2:00 P.M. – 4:00 P.M.	Ms. Ames	JJ	2.69
1	2:00 P.M. – 4:00 P.M.	Ms. Ames	JJ	2.52
1	2:00 P.M. – 4:00 P.M.	Ms. Ames	JJ	2.57
1	2:00 P.M. – 4:00 P.M.	Ms. Ames	JJ	2.63
1	2:00 P.M. – 4:00 P.M.	Ms. Ames	JJ	2.60
1	2:00 P.M. – 4:00 P.M.	Ms. Ames	JJ	2.58
1	2:00 P.M. – 4:00 P.M.	Ms. Ames	JJ	2.61
1	2:00 P.M. – 4:00 P.M.	Ms. Ames	JJ	2.55
1	2:00 P.M. – 4:00 P.M.	Ms. Ames	JJ	2.62
2	4:00 P.M. – 6:00 P.M.	Mr. Silver	DB	4.22
2	4:00 P.M. – 6:00 P.M.	Mr. Silver	DB	2.68
2	4:00 P.M. – 6:00 P.M.	Mr. Silver	DB	2.45
2	4:00 P.M. – 6:00 P.M.	Mr. Silver	DB	1.84
2	4:00 P.M. – 6:00 P.M.	Mr. Silver	DB	2.11
2	4:00 P.M. – 6:00 P.M.	Mr. Silver	DB	3.95
2	4:00 P.M. – 6:00 P.M.	Mr. Silver	DB	2.46
2	4:00 P.M. – 6:00 P.M.	Mr. Silver	DB	3.79
2	4:00 P.M. – 6:00 P.M.	Mr. Silver	DB	3.91
2	4:00 P.M. – 6:00 P.M.	Mr. Silver	DB	2.22
2	4:00 P.M. – 6:00 P.M.	Mr. Silver	DB	2.42
2	4:00 P.M. – 6:00 P.M.	Mr. Silver	DB	2.09
2	4:00 P.M. – 6:00 P.M.	Mr. Silver	DB	3.33
2	4:00 P.M. – 6:00 P.M.	Mr. Silver	DB	4.07
2	4:00 P.M. – 6:00 P.M.	Mr. Silver	DB	2.54
2	4:00 P.M. – 6:00 P.M.	Mr. Silver	DB	3.96

DATA *file*

CutRate

Based on these results, from which vendor would you suggest Mr. Weideman purchase his new machine?

Managerial Report

Use graphical methods of descriptive statistics to investigate the effectiveness of each vendor. Include the following in your report:

1. Scatter plots of the measured width of each hole (cm).
2. Based on the scatter plots, a discussion of the effectiveness of each vendor and under which conditions (if any) that vendor would be acceptable.
3. A discussion of possible sources of error in the approach taken to assess these vendors.

CHAPTER 3

Descriptive Statistics: Numerical Measures

CONTENTS

STATISTICS *in* PRACTICE

SMALL FRY DESIGN*
SANTA ANA, CALIFORNIA

Founded in 1997, Small Fry Design is a toy and accessory company that designs and imports products for infants. The company's product line includes teddy bears, mobiles, musical toys, rattles, and security blankets and features high-quality soft toy designs with an emphasis on color, texture, and sound. The products are designed in the United States and manufactured in China.

Small Fry Design uses independent representatives to sell the products to infant furnishing retailers, children's accessory and apparel stores, gift shops, upscale department stores, and major catalog companies. Currently, Small Fry Design products are distributed in more than 1000 retail outlets throughout the United States.

Cash flow management is one of the most critical activities in the day-to-day operation of this company. Ensuring sufficient incoming cash to meet both current and ongoing debt obligations can mean the difference between business success and failure. A critical factor in cash flow management is the analysis and control of accounts receivable. By measuring the average age and dollar value of outstanding invoices, management can predict cash availability and monitor changes in the status of accounts receivable. The company set the following goals: The average age for outstanding invoices should not exceed 45 days, and the dollar value of invoices more than 60 days old should not exceed 5% of the dollar value of all accounts receivable.

In a recent summary of accounts receivable status, the following descriptive statistics were provided for the age of outstanding invoices:

Mean	40 days
Median	35 days
Mode	31 days

*The authors are indebted to John A. McCarthy, President of Small Fry Design, for providing this Statistics in Practice.

Small Fry Design uses descriptive statistics to monitor its accounts receivable and incoming cash flow.

Interpretation of these statistics shows that the mean or average age of an invoice is 40 days. The median shows that half of the invoices remain outstanding 35 days or more. The mode of 31 days, the most frequent invoice age, indicates that the most common length of time an invoice is outstanding is 31 days. The statistical summary also showed that only 3% of the dollar value of all accounts receivable was more than 60 days old. Based on the statistical information, management was satisfied that accounts receivable and incoming cash flow were under control.

In this chapter, you will learn how to compute and interpret some of the statistical measures used by Small Fry Design. In addition to the mean, median, and mode, you will learn about other descriptive statistics such as the range, variance, standard deviation, percentiles, and correlation. These numerical measures will assist in the understanding and interpretation of data.

In Chapter 2 we discussed tabular and graphical presentations used to summarize data. In this chapter, we present several numerical measures that provide additional alternatives for summarizing data.

We start by developing numerical summary measures for data sets consisting of a single variable. When a data set contains more than one variable, the same numerical measures can be computed separately for each variable. However, in the two-variable case, we will also develop measures of the relationship between the variables.

Numerical measures of location, dispersion, shape, and association are introduced. If the measures are computed for data from a sample, they are called **sample statistics**. If the measures are computed for data from a population, they are called **population parameters**. In statistical inference, a sample statistic is referred to as the **point estimator** of the corresponding population parameter. In Chapter 7 we will discuss in more detail the process of point estimation.

3.1 Measures of Location

Mean

The mean is sometimes referred to as the arithmetic mean.

Perhaps the most important measure of location is the **mean**, or average value, for a variable. The mean provides a measure of central location for the data. If the data are for a sample, the mean is denoted by $\bar{x}$; if the data are for a population, the mean is denoted by the Greek letter μ.

In statistical formulas, it is customary to denote the value of variable x for the first observation by x_1, the value of variable x for the second observation by x_2, and so on. In general, the value of variable x for the ith observation is denoted by x_i. For a sample with n observations, the formula for the sample mean is as follows.

The sample mean $\bar{x}$ is a sample statistic.

SAMPLE MEAN

$$\bar{x} = \frac{\sum x_i}{n} \tag{3.1}$$

In the preceding formula, the numerator is the sum of the values of the n observations. That is,

$$\sum x_i = x_1 + x_2 + \cdots + x_n$$

The Greek letter $\sum$ is the summation sign.

To illustrate the computation of a sample mean, let us consider the following class size data for a sample of five college classes.

$$46 \quad 54 \quad 42 \quad 46 \quad 32$$

We use the notation x_1, x_2, x_3, x_4, x_5 to represent the number of students in each of the five classes.

$$x_1 = 46 \qquad x_2 = 54 \qquad x_3 = 42 \qquad x_4 = 46 \qquad x_5 = 32$$

Hence, to compute the sample mean, we can write

$$\bar{x} = \frac{\sum x_i}{n} = \frac{x_1 + x_2 + x_3 + x_4 + x_5}{5} = \frac{46 + 54 + 42 + 46 + 32}{5} = 44$$

The sample mean class size is 44 students.

To provide a visual perspective of the mean and to show how it can be influenced by extreme values, consider the dot plot for the class size data shown in Figure 3.1. Treating the horizontal axis used to create the dot plot as a long, narrow board in which each of the dots has the same fixed weight, the mean is the point at which we would place a fulcrum or pivot

FIGURE 3.1   THE MEAN AS THE CENTER OF BALANCE FOR THE DOT PLOT OF THE CLASSROOM SIZE DATA

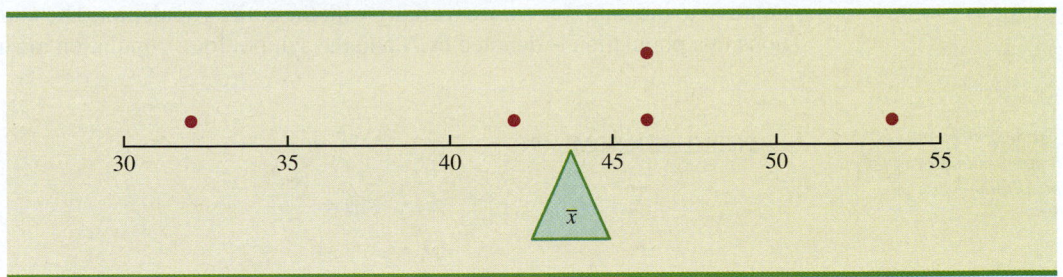

point under the board in order to balance the dot plot. This is the same principle by which a see-saw on a playground works, the only difference being that the see-saw is pivoted in the middle so that as one end goes up, the other end goes down. In the dot plot we are locating the pivot point based upon the location of the dots. Now consider what happens to the balance if we increase the largest value from 54 to 114. We will have to move the fulcrum under the new dot plot in a positive direction in order to reestablish balance. To determine how far we would have to shift the fulcrum, we simply compute the sample mean for the revised class size data.

$$\bar{x} = \frac{\sum x_i}{n} = \frac{x_1 + x_2 + x_3 + x_4 + x_5}{5} = \frac{46 + 114 + 42 + 46 + 32}{5} = \frac{280}{5} = 56$$

Thus, the mean for the revised class size data is 56, an increase of 12 students. In other words, we have to shift the balance point 12 units to the right to establish balance under the new dot plot.

Another illustration of the computation of a sample mean is given in the following situation. Suppose that a college placement office sent a questionnaire to a sample of business school graduates requesting information on monthly starting salaries. Table 3.1 shows the collected data. The mean monthly starting salary for the sample of 12 business college graduates is computed as

$$\bar{x} = \frac{\sum x_i}{n} = \frac{x_1 + x_2 + \cdots + x_{12}}{12}$$

$$= \frac{3{,}850 + 3{,}950 + \cdots + 3{,}880}{12}$$

$$= \frac{47{,}280}{12} = 3940$$

TABLE 3.1   MONTHLY STARTING SALARIES FOR A SAMPLE OF 12 BUSINESS SCHOOL GRADUATES

DATA *file*

StartSalary

Graduate	Monthly Starting Salary ($)	Graduate	Monthly Starting Salary ($)
1	3850	7	3890
2	3950	8	4130
3	4050	9	3940
4	3880	10	4325
5	3755	11	3920
6	3710	12	3880

Equation (3.1) shows how the mean is computed for a sample with n observations. The formula for computing the mean of a population remains the same, but we use different notation to indicate that we are working with the entire population. The number of observations in a population is denoted by N and the symbol for a population mean is μ.

The sample mean $\bar{x}$ is a point estimator of the population mean μ.

POPULATION MEAN

$$\mu = \frac{\sum x_i}{N}$$

(3.2)

Median

The **median** is another measure of central location. The median is the value in the middle when the data are arranged in ascending order (smallest value to largest value). With an odd number of observations, the median is the middle value. An even number of observations has no single middle value. In this case, we follow convention and define the median as the average of the values for the middle two observations. For convenience the definition of the median is restated as follows.

MEDIAN

Arrange the data in ascending order (smallest value to largest value).

(a) For an odd number of observations, the median is the middle value.
(b) For an even number of observations, the median is the average of the two middle values.

Let us apply this definition to compute the median class size for the sample of five college classes. Arranging the data in ascending order provides the following list.

$$32 \quad 42 \quad 46 \quad 46 \quad 54$$

Because $n = 5$ is odd, the median is the middle value. Thus the median class size is 46 students. Even though this data set contains two observations with values of 46, each observation is treated separately when we arrange the data in ascending order.

Suppose we also compute the median starting salary for the 12 business college graduates in Table 3.1. We first arrange the data in ascending order.

3710   3755   3850   3880   3880   3890   3920   3940   3950   4050   4130   4325

Middle Two Values

Because $n = 12$ is even, we identify the middle two values: 3890 and 3920. The median is the average of these values.

$$\text{Median} = \frac{3890 + 3920}{2} = 3905$$

The procedure we used to compute the median depends upon whether there is an odd number of observations or an even number of observations. Let us now describe a more conceptual and visual approach using the monthly starting salary for the 12 business college graduates. As before, we begin by arranging the data in ascending order.

3710   3755   3850   3880   3880   3890   3920   3940   3950   4050   4130   4325

Once the data are in ascending order, we trim pairs of extreme high and low values until no further pairs of values can be trimmed without completely eliminating all the data. For instance after trimming the lowest observation (3710) and the highest observation (4325) we obtain a new data set with 10 observations.

~~3710~~   3755   3850   3880   3880   3890   3920   3940   3950   4050   4130   ~~4325~~

We then trim the next lowest remaining value (3755) and the next highest remaining value (4130) to produce a new data set with eight observations.

~~3710~~   ~~3755~~   3850   3880   3880   3890   3920   3940   3950   4050   ~~4130~~   ~~4325~~

Continuing this process we obtain the following results.

~~3710~~   ~~3755~~   ~~3850~~   3880   3880   3890   3920   3940   3950   ~~4050~~   ~~4130~~   ~~4325~~

~~3710~~   ~~3755~~   ~~3850~~   ~~3880~~   3880   3890   3920   3940   ~~3950~~   ~~4050~~   ~~4130~~   ~~4325~~

~~3710~~   ~~3755~~   ~~3850~~   ~~3880~~   ~~3880~~   3890   3920   ~~3940~~   ~~3950~~   ~~4050~~   ~~4130~~   ~~4325~~

At this point no further trimming is possible without eliminating all the data. So, the median is just the average of the remaining two values. When there is an even number of observations, the trimming process will always result in two remaining values, and the average of these values will be the median. When there is an odd number of observations, the trimming process will always result in one final value, and this value will be the median. Thus, this method works whether the number of observations is odd or even.

The median is the measure of location most often reported for annual income and property value data because a few extremely large incomes or property values can inflate the mean. In such cases, the median is the preferred measure of central location.

Although the mean is the more commonly used measure of central location, in some situations the median is preferred. The mean is influenced by extremely small and large data values. For instance, suppose that the highest paid graduate (see Table 3.1) had a starting salary of $10,000 per month (maybe the individual's family owns the company). If we change the highest monthly starting salary in Table 3.1 from $4325 to $10,000 and recompute the mean, the sample mean changes from $3940 to $4413. The median of $3905, however, is unchanged, because $3890 and $3920 are still the middle two values. With the extremely high starting salary included, the median provides a better measure of central location than the mean. We can generalize to say that whenever a data set contains extreme values, the median is often the preferred measure of central location.

Mode

Another measure of location is the **mode**. The mode is defined as follows.

> MODE
>
> The mode is the value that occurs with greatest frequency.

To illustrate the identification of the mode, consider the sample of five class sizes. The only value that occurs more than once is 46. Because this value, occurring with a frequency of 2, has the greatest frequency, it is the mode. As another illustration, consider the sample of starting salaries for the business school graduates. The only monthly starting salary that occurs more than once is \$3880. Because this value has the greatest frequency, it is the mode.

Situations can arise for which the greatest frequency occurs at two or more different values. In these instances more than one mode exists. If the data contain exactly two modes, we say that the data are *bimodal.* If data contain more than two modes, we say that the data are *multimodal.* In multimodal cases the mode is almost never reported because listing three or more modes would not be particularly helpful in describing a location for the data.

Using Excel to Compute the Mean, Median, and Mode

Excel provides functions for computing the mean, median, and mode. We illustrate the use of these functions by computing the mean, median, and mode for the starting salary data in Table 3.1. Refer to Figure 3.2 as we describe the tasks involved. The formula worksheet is in the background; the value worksheet is in the foreground.

Enter/Access Data: Open the DATAfile named *StartSalary*. The data are in cells B2:B13 and labels are in column A and cell B1.

Enter Functions and Formulas: Excel's AVERAGE function can be used to compute the mean by entering the following formula into cell E2:

=AVERAGE(B2:B13)

Similarly, the formulas =MEDIAN(B2:B13) and =MODE.SNGL(B2:B13) are entered into cells E3 and E4, respectively, to compute the median and the mode.

FIGURE 3.2 EXCEL WORKSHEET USED TO COMPUTE THE MEAN, MEDIAN, AND MODE FOR THE STARTING SALARY DATA

	A	B	C	D	E	F
1	Graduate	Monthly Starting Salary (\$)				
2	1	3850		Mean	=AVERAGE(B2:B13)	
3	2	3950		Median	=MEDIAN(B2:B13)	
4	3	4050		Mode	=MODE.SNGL(B2:B13)	
5	4	3880				
6	5	3755				
7	6	3710				
8	7	3890				
9	8	4130				
10	9	3940				
11	10	4325				
12	11	3920				
13	12	3880				
14						

	A	B	C	D	E	F
1	Graduate	Monthly Starting Salary (\$)				
2	1	3850		Mean	3940	
3	2	3950		Median	3905	
4	3	4050		Mode	3880	
5	4	3880				
6	5	3755				
7	6	3710				
8	7	3890				
9	8	4130				
10	9	3940				
11	10	4325				
12	11	3920				
13	12	3880				
14						

The formulas in cells E2:E4 are displayed in the background worksheet of Figure 3.2 and the values computed using the Excel functions are displayed in the foreground worksheet. Labels were also entered into cell D2:D4 to identify the output. Note that the mean (3940), median (3905), and mode (3880) are the same as we computed earlier.

Weighted Mean

In the formulas for the sample mean and population mean, each x_i is given equal importance or weight. For instance, the formula for the sample mean can be written as follows:

$$\bar{x} = \frac{\sum x_i}{n} = \frac{1}{n}\left(\sum x_i\right) = \frac{1}{n}(x_1 + x_2 + \cdots + x_n) = \frac{1}{n}(x_1) + \frac{1}{n}(x_2) + \cdots + \frac{1}{n}(x_n)$$

This shows that each observation in the sample is given a weight of $1/n$. Although this practice is most common, in some instances the mean is computed by giving each observation a weight that reflects its relative importance. A mean computed in this manner is referred to as a **weighted mean**. The weighted mean is computed as follows:

WEIGHTED MEAN

$$\bar{x} = \frac{\sum w_i x_i}{\sum w_i} \tag{3.3}$$

where

$$w_i = \text{weight for observation } i$$

When the data are from a sample, equation (3.3) provides the weighted sample mean. If the data are from a population, μ replaces $\bar{x}$ and equation (3.3) provides the weighted population mean.

As an example of the need for a weighted mean, consider the following sample of five purchases of a raw material over the past three months.

Purchase	Cost per Pound ($)	Number of Pounds
1	3.00	1200
2	3.40	500
3	2.80	2750
4	2.90	1000
5	3.25	800

Note that the cost per pound varies from $2.80 to $3.40, and the quantity purchased varies from 500 to 2750 pounds. Suppose that a manager wanted to know the mean cost per pound of the raw material. Because the quantities ordered vary, we must use the formula for a weighted mean. The five cost-per-pound data values are $x_1 = 3.00$, $x_2 = 3.40$, $x_3 = 2.80$, $x_4 = 2.90$, and $x_5 = 3.25$. The weighted mean cost per pound is found by weighting each cost by its corresponding quantity. For this example, the weights are $w_1 = 1200$,

$w_2 = 500$, $w_3 = 2750$, $w_4 = 1000$, and $w_5 = 800$. Based on equation (3.3), the weighted mean is calculated as follows:

$$\bar{x} = \frac{1200(3.00) + 500(3.40) + 2750(2.80) + 1000(2.90) + 800(3.25)}{1200 + 500 + 2750 + 1000 + 800}$$

$$= \frac{18,500}{6250} = 2.96$$

Thus, the weighted mean computation shows that the mean cost per pound for the raw material is $2.96. Note that using equation (3.1) rather than the weighted mean formula in equation (3.3) would provide misleading results. In this case, the sample mean of the five cost-per-pound values is $(3.00 + 3.40 + 2.80 + 2.90 + 3.25)/5 = 15.35/5 = \$3.07$, which overstates the actual mean cost per pound purchased.

The choice of weights for a particular weighted mean computation depends upon the application. An example that is well known to college students is the computation of a grade point average (GPA). In this computation, the data values generally used are 4 for an A grade, 3 for a B grade, 2 for a C grade, 1 for a D grade, and 0 for an F grade. The weights are the number of credit hours earned for each grade. Exercise 16 at the end of this section provides an example of this weighted mean computation. In other weighted mean computations, quantities such as pounds, dollars, or volume are frequently used as weights. In any case, when observations vary in importance, the analyst must choose the weight that best reflects the importance of each observation in the determination of the mean.

Geometric Mean

The **geometric mean** is a measure of location that is calculated by finding the *n*th root of the product of *n* values. The general formula for the geometric mean, denoted $\bar{x}_g$, follows.

GEOMETRIC MEAN

$$\bar{x}_g = \sqrt[n]{(x_1)(x_2)\cdots(x_n)} = [(x_1)(x_2)\cdots(x_n)]^{1/n} \qquad \textbf{(3.4)}$$

The geometric mean is often used in analyzing growth rates in financial data. In these types of situations the arithmetic mean or average value will provide misleading results.

To illustrate the use of the geometric mean, consider Table 3.2, which shows the percentage annual returns, or growth rates, for a mutual fund over the past 10 years. Suppose we want to compute how much $100 invested in the fund at the beginning of year 1 would be worth at the end of year 10. Let's start by computing the balance in the fund at the end of year 1. Because the percentage annual return for year 1 was −22.1%, the balance in the fund at the end of year 1 would be

$$\$100 - .221(\$100) = \$100(1 - .221) = \$100(.779) = \$77.90$$

The growth factor for each year is 1 plus .01 times the percentage return. A growth factor less than 1 indicates negative growth, while a growth factor greater than 1 indicates positive growth. The growth factor cannot be less than zero.

Note that .779 is identified as the growth factor for year 1 in Table 3.2. This result shows that we can compute the balance at the end of year 1 by multiplying the value invested in the fund at the beginning of year 1 times the growth factor for year 1.

The balance in the fund at the end of year 1, $77.90, now becomes the beginning balance in year 2. So, with a percentage annual return for year 2 of 28.7%, the balance at the end of year 2 would be

$$\$77.90 + .287(\$77.90) = \$77.90(1 + .287) = \$77.90(1.287) = \$100.2573$$

TABLE 3.2 PERCENTAGE ANNUAL RETURNS AND GROWTH FACTORS FOR THE MUTUAL FUND DATA

Year	Return (%)	Growth Factor
1	−22.1	0.779
2	28.7	1.287
3	10.9	1.109
4	4.9	1.049
5	15.8	1.158
6	5.5	1.055
7	−37.0	0.630
8	26.5	1.265
9	15.1	1.151
10	2.1	1.021

DATA *file*

MutualFund

Note that 1.287 is the growth factor for year 2. And, by substituting $100(.779) for $77.90, we see that the balance in the fund at the end of year 2 is

$$\$100(.779)(1.287) = \$100.2573$$

In other words, the balance at the end of year 2 is just the initial investment at the beginning of year 1 times the product of the first two growth factors. This result can be generalized to show that the balance at the end of year 10 is the initial investment times the product of all 10 growth factors.

$$\$100[(.779)(1.287)(1.109)(1.049)(1.158)(1.055)(.630)(1.265)(1.151)(1.021)] =$$

$$\$100(1.334493) = \$133.4493$$

The nth root can be computed using most calculators or by using the POWER function in Excel. For instance, using Excel, the 10th root of 1.334493 = POWER (1.334493,1/10) or 1.029275.

So, a $100 investment in the fund at the beginning of year 1 would be worth $133.4493 at the end of year 10. Note that the product of the 10 growth factors is 1.334493. Thus, we can compute the balance at the end of year 10 for any amount of money invested at the beginning of year 1 by multiplying the value of the initial investment times 1.334493. For instance, an initial investment of $2500 at the beginning of year 1 would be worth $2500(1.334493) or approximately $3336 at the end of year 10.

But what was the mean percentage annual return or mean rate of growth for this investment over the 10-year period? Let us see how the geometric mean of the 10 growth factors can be used to answer to this question. Because the product of the 10 growth factors is 1.334493, the geometric mean is the 10th root of 1.334493 or

$$\bar{x}_g = \sqrt[10]{1.334493} = 1.029275$$

The geometric mean tells us that annual returns grew at an average annual rate of $(1.029275 - 1)100\%$ or 2.9275%. In other words, with an average annual growth rate of 2.9275%, a $100 investment in the fund at the beginning of year 1 would grow to $100(1.029275)^{10} = \$133.4493$ at the end of 10 years.

It is important to understand that the arithmetic mean of the percentage annual returns does not provide the mean annual growth rate for this investment. The sum of the 10 annual percentage returns in Table 3.2 is 50.4. Thus, the arithmetic mean of the 10 percentage annual returns is 50.4/10 = 5.04%. A broker might try to convince you to invest in this fund by stating that the mean annual percentage return was 5.04%. Such a statement is not only misleading, it is also inaccurate. A mean annual percentage return of 5.04% corresponds to an average growth factor of 1.0504. So, if the average growth factor were really 1.0504, $100 invested in the fund at the beginning of year 1 would have grown to $100(1.0504)^{10} = 163.51 at the end of 10 years. But, using the 10 annual percentage returns in Table 3.2, we showed that an initial $100 investment is worth $133.45 at the end of 10 years. The broker's claim that the mean annual percentage return is 5.04% grossly overstates the true growth for this mutual fund. The problem is that the sample mean is only appropriate for an additive process. For a multiplicative process, such as applications involving growth rates, the geometric mean is the appropriate measure of location.

While the applications of the geometric mean to problems in finance, investments, and banking are particularly common, the geometric mean should be applied any time you want to determine the mean rate of change over several successive periods. Other common applications include changes in populations of species, crop yields, pollution levels, and birth and death rates. Also note that the geometric mean can be applied to changes that occur over any number of successive periods of any length. In addition to annual changes, the geometric mean is often applied to find the mean rate of change over quarters, months, weeks, and even days.

Using Excel to Compute the Geometric Mean

Excel's GEOMEAN function can be used to compute the geometric mean for the mutual fund data in Table 3.2. Refer to Figure 3.3 as we describe the tasks involved. The formula worksheet is in the background; the value worksheet is in the foreground.

Enter/Access Data: Open the DATAfile named *MutualFund*. The data are in cells B2:B11 and labels are in column A and cell B2.

Enter Functions and Formulas: To compute the growth factor for the percentage return in cell B2 (-22.1) we entered the following formula into cell C2:

$$=1+.01*B2$$

To compute the growth factors for the other percentage returns we copied the same formula into cells C3:C11. Excel's GEOMEAN function can now be used to compute the geometric mean for the growth factors in cells C2:C11 by entering the following formula into cell F2:

$$=GEOMEAN(C2:C11)$$

FIGURE 3.3   USING EXCEL TO COMPUTE THE GEOMETRIC MEAN FOR THE MUTUAL FUND DATA

	A	B	C	D	E	F	G
1	Year	Return (%)	Growth Factor				
2	1	-22.1	=1+0.01*B2		Geometric Mean	=GEOMEAN(C2:C11)	
3	2	28.7	=1+0.01*B3				
4	3	10.9	=1+0.01*B4				
5	4	4.9	=1+0.01*B5				
6	5	15.8	=1+0.01*B6				
7	6	5.5	=1+0.01*B7				
8	7	-37	=1+0.01*B8				
9	8	26.5	=1+0.01*B9				
10	9	15.1	=1+0.01*B10				
11	10	2.1	=1+0.01*B11				
12							

	A	B	C	D	E	F	G
1	Year	Return (%)	Growth Factor				
2	1	-22.1	0.779		Geometric Mean	1.029275	
3	2	28.7	1.287				
4	3	10.9	1.109				
5	4	4.9	1.049				
6	5	15.8	1.158				
7	6	5.5	1.055				
8	7	-37	0.63				
9	8	26.5	1.265				
10	9	15.1	1.151				
11	10	2.1	1.021				
12							

The labels Growth Factor and Geometric Mean were entered into cells C1 and E2, respectively, to identify the output. Note that the geometric mean (1.029275) is the same value as we computed earlier.

Percentiles

A **percentile** provides information about how the data are spread over the interval from the smallest value to the largest value. For a data set containing n observations, the **pth percentile** divides the data into two parts: Approximately $p\%$ of the observations are less than the pth percentile, and approximately $(100 - p)\%$ of the observations are greater than the pth percentile.

Colleges and universities frequently report admission test scores in terms of percentiles. For instance, suppose an applicant obtains a score of 630 on the math portion of an admissions test. How this applicant performed in relation to others taking the same test may not be readily apparent. However, if the score of 630 corresponds to the 82nd percentile, we know that approximately that 82% of the applicants scored lower than this individual and approximately 18% of the applicants scored higher than this individual.

To calculate the pth percentile for a data set containing n observations, we must first arrange the data in ascending order (smallest value to largest value). The smallest value is in position 1, the next smallest value is in position 2, and so on. The location of the pth percentile, denoted L_p, is computed using the following equation.

Several procedures can be used to compute the location of the pth percentile using sample data. All provide similar values, especially for large data sets. The procedure we show here is the procedure used by Excel's PERCENTILE.EXC function as well as several other statistical software packages.

LOCATION OF THE pth PERCENTILE

$$L_p = \frac{p}{100}(n + 1) \tag{3.5}$$

To illustrate the computation of the pth percentile, let us compute the 80th percentile for the starting salary data in Table 3.1. We begin by arranging the sample of 12 starting salaries in ascending order.

	3710	3755	3850	3880	3880	3890	3920	3940	3950	4050	4130	4325
Position	1	2	3	4	5	6	7	8	9	10	11	12

The position of each observation in the sorted data is shown directly below its value. For instance, the smallest value (3710) is in position 1, the next smallest value (3755) is in position 2, and so on. Using equation (3.5) with $p = 80$ and $n = 12$, the location of the 80th percentile is

$$L_{80} = \frac{p}{100}(n + 1) = \left(\frac{80}{100}\right)(12 + 1) = 10.4$$

The interpretation of $L_{80} = 10.4$ is that the 80th percentile is 40% of the way between the value in position 10 and the value in position 11. In other words, the 80th percentile is the value in position 10 (4050) plus 0.4 times the difference between the value in position 11 (4130) and the value in position 10 (4050). Thus,

80th percentile $= 4050 + .4(4130 - 4050) = 4050 + .4(80) = 4082$

Let us now compute the 50th percentile for the starting salary data. With $p = 50$ and $n = 12$, the location of the 50th percentile is

$$L_{50} = \frac{p}{100}(n + 1) = \left(\frac{50}{100}\right)(12 + 1) = 6.5$$

With $L_{50} = 6.5$, we see that the 50th percentile is 50% of the way between the value in position 6 (3890) and the value in position 7 (3920). Thus,

50th percentile $= 3890 + .5(3920 - 3890) = 3890 + .5(30) = 3905$

Note that the *50th percentile is also the median*.

Quartiles

Quartiles are just specific percentiles; thus, the steps for computing percentiles can be applied directly in the computation of quartiles.

It is often desirable to divide a data set into four parts, with each part containing approximately one-fourth, or 25%, of the observations. These division points are referred to as the **quartiles** and are defined as follows.

Q_1 = first quartile, or 25th percentile

Q_2 = second quartile, or 50th percentile (also the median)

Q_3 = third quartile, or 75th percentile

Because quartiles are just specific percentiles, the procedure for computing percentiles can be used to compute the quartiles.

To illustrate the computation of the quartiles for a data set consisting of n observations, we will compute the quartiles for the starting salary data in Table 3.1. Previously we showed that the 50th percentile for the starting salary data is 3905; thus, the second quartile (median) is $Q_2 = 3905$. To compute the first and third quartiles we must find the 25th and 75th percentiles. The calculations follow.

For Q_1,

$$L_{25} = \frac{p}{100}(n + 1) = \left(\frac{25}{100}\right)(12 + 1) = 3.25$$

The first quartile, or 25th percentile, is .25 of the way between the value in position 3 (3850) and the value in position 4 (3880). Thus,

$Q_1 = 3850 + .25(3880 - 3850) = 3850 + .25(30) = 3857.5$

For Q_3,

$$L_{75} = \frac{p}{100}(n + 1) = \left(\frac{75}{100}\right)(12 + 1) = 9.75$$

The third quartile, or 75th percentile, is .75 of the way between the value in position 9 (3950) and the value in position 10 (4050). Thus,

$Q_3 = 3950 + .75(4050 - 3950) = 3950 + .75(100) = 4025$

We defined the quartiles as the 25th, 50th, and 75th percentiles. Thus, we computed the quartiles in the same way as percentiles. However, other conventions are sometimes used to compute quartiles, and the actual values reported for quartiles may vary slightly depending on the convention used. Nevertheless, the objective of all procedures for computing quartiles is to divide the data into four equal parts.

Using Excel to Compute Percentiles and Quartiles

Excel provides functions for computing percentiles and quartiles. We will illustrate the use of these functions by showing how to compute the *p*th percentile and the quartiles for the starting salary data in Table 3.1. Refer to Figure 3.4 as we describe the tasks involved. The formula worksheet is in the background; the value worksheet is in the foreground.

Enter/Access Data: Open the DATAfile named *StartSalary*. The data are in cells B2:B13 and labels are in column A and cell B1.

Enter Functions and Formulas: Excel's PERCENTILE.EXC function can be used to compute the *p*th percentile. For the starting salary data the general form of this function is

$$=\text{PERCENTILE.EXC(B2:B13,}p\text{/100)}$$

If we wanted to compute the 80th percentile for the starting salary data we could enter the formula

$$=\text{PERCENTILE.EXC(B2:B13,.8)}$$

into cell E2.

Because the quartiles are just the 25th, 50th, and 75th percentiles, we could compute the quartiles for the starting salary data by using Excel's PERCENTILE.EXC function as described above. But we can also use Excel's QUARTILE.EXC function

FIGURE 3.4 USING EXCEL TO COMPUTE PERCENTILES AND QUARTILES

	A	B	C	D	E	F
1	Graduate	Monthly Starting Salary (S)		Percentile		
2	1	3850		80	=PERCENTILE.EXC(B2:B13,0.8)	
3	2	3950				
4	3	4050		Quartile	Value	
5	4	3880		1	=QUARTILE.EXC($B$2:$B$13,D5)	
6	5	3755		2	=QUARTILE.EXC($B$2:$B$13,D6)	
7	6	3710		3	=QUARTILE.EXC($B$2:$B$13,D7)	
8	7	3890				
9	8	4130				
10	9	3940				
11	10	4325				
12	11	3920				
13	12	3880				
14						

	A	B	C	D	E	F
1	Graduate	Monthly Starting Salary (S)		Percentile		
2	1	3850		80	4082.0	
3	2	3950				
4	3	4050		Quartile	Value	
5	4	3880		1	3857.5	
6	5	3755		2	3905.0	
7	6	3710		3	4025.0	
8	7	3890				
9	8	4130				
10	9	3940				
11	10	4325				
12	11	3920				
13	12	3880				
14						

to compute the quartiles. For the starting salary data, the general form of this function is

$$=\text{QUARTILE.EXC(B2:B13,Quart)}$$

where Quart = 1 for the first quartile, 2 for the second quartile, and 3 for the third quartile. To illustrate the use of this function for computing the quartiles we entered the values 1, 2, and 3 into cells D5:D7 of the worksheet. To compute the first quartile we entered the following function into cell E5:

$$=\text{QUARTILE.EXC(\$B\$2:\$B\$13,D5)}$$

To compute the second and third quartiles we copied the formula in cell E5 into cells E6 and E7. Labels were entered into cells D4 and E4 to identify the output. Note that the three quartiles (3857.5, 3905, and 4025) are the same values as computed previously.

NOTES AND COMMENTS

1. It is better to use the median than the mean as a measure of central location when a data set contains extreme values. Another measure that is sometimes used when extreme values are present is the trimmed mean. The trimmed mean is obtained by deleting a percentage of the smallest and largest values from a data set and then computing the mean of the remaining values. For example, the 5% trimmed mean is obtained by removing the smallest 5% and the largest 5% of the data values and then computing the mean of the remaining values. Using the sample with $n = 12$ starting salaries, $0.05(12) = 0.6$. Rounding this value to 1 indicates that the 5% trimmed mean is obtained by removing the smallest data value and the largest data value and then computing the mean of the remaining 10 values. For the starting salary data, the 5% trimmed mean is 3924.50.

2. Other commonly used percentiles are the quintiles (the 20th, 40th, 60th, and 80th percentiles) and the deciles (the 10th, 20th, 30th, 40th, 50th, 60th, 70th, 80th, and 90th percentiles).

Exercises

Methods

1. Consider a sample with data values of 10, 20, 12, 17, and 16. Compute the mean and median.

2. Consider a sample with data values of 10, 20, 21, 17, 16, and 12. Compute the mean and median.

 SELF*test*

3. Consider the following data and corresponding weights.

x_i	Weight (w_i)
3.2	6
2.0	3
2.5	2
5.0	8

   a. Compute the weighted mean.
   b. Compute the sample mean of the four data values without weighting. Note the difference in the results provided by the two computations.

4. Consider the following data.

Period	Rate of Return (%)
1	−6.0
2	−8.0
3	−4.0
4	2.0
5	5.4

What is the mean growth rate over these five periods?

5. Consider a sample with data values of 27, 25, 20, 15, 30, 34, 28, and 25. Compute the 20th, 25th, 65th, and 75th percentiles.

6. Consider a sample with data values of 53, 55, 70, 58, 64, 57, 53, 69, 57, 68, and 53. Compute the mean, median, and mode.

Applications

7. The average number of minutes Americans commute to work is 27.7 minutes (*Sterling's Best Places*, April 13, 2012). The average commute times in minutes for 48 cities are as follows:

Albuquerque	23.3	Jacksonville	26.2	Phoenix	28.3
Atlanta	28.3	Kansas City	23.4	Pittsburgh	25.0
Austin	24.6	Las Vegas	28.4	Portland	26.4
Baltimore	32.1	Little Rock	20.1	Providence	23.6
Boston	31.7	Los Angeles	32.2	Richmond	23.4
Charlotte	25.8	Louisville	21.4	Sacramento	25.8
Chicago	38.1	Memphis	23.8	Salt Lake City	20.2
Cincinnati	24.9	Miami	30.7	San Antonio	26.1
Cleveland	26.8	Milwaukee	24.8	San Diego	24.8
Columbus	23.4	Minneapolis	23.6	San Francisco	32.6
Dallas	28.5	Nashville	25.3	San Jose	28.5
Denver	28.1	New Orleans	31.7	Seattle	27.3
Detroit	29.3	New York	43.8	St. Louis	26.8
El Paso	24.4	Oklahoma City	22.0	Tucson	24.0
Fresno	23.0	Orlando	27.1	Tulsa	20.1
Indianapolis	24.8	Philadelphia	34.2	Washington, DC	32.8

a. What is the mean commute time for these 48 cities?
b. Compute the median commute time.
c. Compute the mode.
d. Compute the third quartile.

8. *The Wall Street Journal* reported that the median salary for middle-level manager jobs was approximately $85,000 (*The Wall Street Journal*, August 6, 2013). Suppose that an independent study of middle-level managers employed at companies located in Atlanta, Georgia, was conducted to compare the salaries of managers working at firms in Atlanta to the national average. The following data show the salary, in thousands of dollars, for a sample of 15 middle-level managers.

108   83   106   73   53   85   80   63   67   75   124   55   93   118   77

a. Compute the median salary for the sample of 15 middle-level managers. How does the median for this group compare to the median reported by *The Wall Street Journal*?

b. Compute the mean annual salary and discuss how and why it differs from the median computed in part (a).

c. Compute the first and third quartiles.

AdvertisingSpend

9. Which companies spend the most money on advertising? *Business Insider* maintains a list of the top-spending companies. In 2014, Procter & Gamble spent more than any other company, a whopping $5 billion. In second place was Comcast, which spent $3.08 billion (*Business Insider* website, December 2014). The top 12 companies and the amount each spent on advertising in billions of dollars are as follows.

Company	Advertising ($ billions)	Company	Advertising ($ billions)
Procter & Gamble	$5.00	American Express	$2.19
Comcast	3.08	General Motors	2.15
AT&T	2.91	Toyota	2.09
Ford	2.56	Fiat Chrysler	1.97
Verizon	2.44	Walt Disney Company	1.96
L'Oreal	2.34	J.P Morgan	1.88

a. What is the mean amount spent on advertising?

b. What is the median amount spent on advertising?

c. What are the first and third quartiles?

JacketRatings

10. Over a nine-month period, OutdoorGearLab tested hardshell jackets designed for ice climbing, mountaineering, and backpacking. Based on the breathability, durability, versatility, features, mobility, and weight of each jacket, an overall rating ranging from 0 (lowest) to 100 (highest) was assigned to each jacket tested. The following data show the results for 20 top-of-the line jackets (OutdoorGearLab website, February 27, 2013).

42	66	67	71	78	62	61	76	71	67
61	64	61	54	83	63	68	69	81	53

a. Compute the mean, median, and mode.

b. Compute the first and third quartiles.

c. Compute and interpret the 90th percentile.

11. According to the National Education Association (NEA), teachers generally spend more than 40 hours each week working on instructional duties (NEA website, April 2012). The following data show the number of hours worked per week for a sample of 13 high school science teachers and a sample of 11 high school English teachers.

High School Science Teachers: 53 56 54 54 55 58 49 61 54 54 52 53 54

High School English Teachers: 52 47 50 46 47 48 49 46 55 44 47

a. What is the median number of hours worked per week for the sample of 13 high school science teachers?

b. What is the median number of hours worked per week for the sample of 11 high school English teachers?

c. Which group has the highest median number of hours worked per week? What is the difference between the median number of hours worked per week?

BigBangTheory

12. *The Big Bang Theory*, a situation comedy featuring Johnny Galecki, Jim Parsons, and Kaley Cuoco, is one of the most watched programs on network television. The first two episodes for the 2011–2012 season premiered on September 22, 2011; the first episode attracted 14.1 million viewers and the second episode attracted 14.7 million viewers. The

following table shows the number of viewers in millions for the first 21 episodes of the 2011–2012 season (*The Big Bang Theory* website, April 17, 2012).

Air Date	Viewers (millions)	Air Date	Viewers (millions)
September 22, 2011	14.1	January 12, 2012	16.1
September 22, 2011	14.7	January 19, 2012	15.8
September 29, 2011	14.6	January 26, 2012	16.1
October 6, 2011	13.6	February 2, 2012	16.5
October 13, 2011	13.6	February 9, 2012	16.2
October 20, 2011	14.9	February 16, 2012	15.7
October 27, 2011	14.5	February 23, 2012	16.2
November 3, 2011	16.0	March 8, 2012	15.0
November 10, 2011	15.9	March 29, 2012	14.0
November 17, 2011	15.1	April 5, 2012	13.3
December 8, 2011	14.0		

    a.   Compute the minimum and maximum number of viewers.
    b.   Compute the mean, median, and mode.
    c.   Compute the first and third quartiles.
    d.   Has viewership grown or declined over the 2011–2012 season? Discuss.

13.   In automobile mileage and gasoline-consumption testing, 13 automobiles were road tested for 300 miles in both city and highway driving conditions. The following data were recorded for miles-per-gallon performance.

City: 16.2 16.7 15.9 14.4 13.2 15.3 16.8 16.0 16.1 15.3 15.2 15.3 16.2
Highway: 19.4 20.6 18.3 18.6 19.2 17.4 17.2 18.6 19.0 21.1 19.4 18.5 18.7

Use the mean, median, and mode to make a statement about the difference in performance for city and highway driving.

14.   The data contained in the DATAfile named *StateUnemp* show the unemployment rate in March 2011 and the unemployment rate in March 2012 for every state and the District of Columbia (Bureau of Labor Statistics website, April 20, 2012). To compare unemployment rates in March 2011 with unemployment rates in March 2012, compute the first quartile, the median, and the third quartile for the March 2011 unemployment data and the March 2012 unemployment data. What do these statistics suggest about the change in unemployment rates across the states?

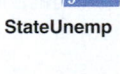

StateUnemp

15.   Martinez Auto Supplies has retail stores located in eight cities in California. The price they charge for a particular product in each city varies because of differing competitive conditions. For instance, the price they charge for a case of a popular brand of motor oil in each city follows. Also shown are the number of cases that Martinez Auto sold last quarter in each city.

City	Price ($)	Sales (cases)
Bakersfield	34.99	501
Los Angeles	38.99	1425
Modesto	36.00	294
Oakland	33.59	882
Sacramento	40.99	715
San Diego	38.59	1088
San Francisco	39.59	1644
San Jose	37.99	819

Compute the average sales price per case for this product during the last quarter.

**SELF***test*

16. The grade point average for college students is based on a weighted mean computation. For most colleges, the grades are given the following data values: A (4), B (3), C (2), D (1), and F (0). After 60 credit hours of course work, a student at State University earned 9 credit hours of A, 15 credit hours of B, 33 credit hours of C, and 3 credit hours of D.
    a. Compute the student's grade point average.
    b. Students at State University must maintain a 2.5 grade point average for their first 60 credit hours of course work in order to be admitted to the business college. Will this student be admitted?

17. The following table shows the total return and the number of funds for four categories of mutual funds.

Type of Fund	Number of Funds	Total Return (%)
Domestic Equity	9191	4.65
International Equity	2621	18.15
Specialty Stock	1419	11.36
Hybrid	2900	6.75

   a. Using the number of funds as weights, compute the weighted average total return for these mutual funds.
   b. Is there any difficulty associated with using the "number of funds" as the weights in computing the weighted average total return in part (a)? Discuss. What else might be used for weights?
   c. Suppose you invested $10,000 in this group of mutual funds and diversified the investment by placing $2000 in Domestic Equity funds, $4000 in International Equity funds, $3000 in Specialty Stock funds, and $1000 in Hybrid funds. What is the expected return on the portfolio?

18. Based on a survey of master's programs in business administration, magazines such as *U.S. News & World Report* rank U.S. business schools. These types of rankings are based in part on surveys of business school deans and corporate recruiters. Each survey respondent is asked to rate the overall academic quality of the master's program on a scale from 1 "marginal" to 5 "outstanding." Use the sample of responses shown below to compute the weighted mean score for the business school deans and the corporate recruiters. Discuss.

Quality Assessment	Business School Deans	Corporate Recruiters
5	44	31
4	66	34
3	60	43
2	10	12
1	0	0

19. Annual revenue for Corning Supplies grew by 5.5% in 2011; 1.1% in 2012; −3.5% in 2013; −1.1% in 2014; and 1.8% in 2015. What is the mean growth annual rate over this period?

20. Suppose that at the beginning of Year 1 you invested $10,000 in the Stivers mutual fund and $5000 in the Trippi mutual fund. The value of each investment at the end of each subsequent year is provided in the table below. Which mutual fund performed better?

Year	Stivers	Trippi
Year 1	11,000	5,600
Year 2	12,000	6,300
Year 3	13,000	6,900
Year 4	14,000	7,600
Year 5	15,000	8,500
Year 6	16,000	9,200
Year 7	17,000	9,900
Year 8	18,000	10,600

21. If an asset declines in value from $5000 to $3500 over nine years, what is the mean annual growth rate in the asset's value over these nine years?

22. The current value of a company is $25 million. If the value of the company six years ago was $10 million, what is the company's mean annual growth rate over the past six years?

3.2 Measures of Variability

In addition to measures of location, it is often desirable to consider measures of variability, or dispersion. For example, suppose that you are a purchasing agent for a large manufacturing firm and that you regularly place orders with two different suppliers. After several months of operation, you find that the mean number of days required to fill orders is 10 days for both of the suppliers. The histograms summarizing the number of working days required to fill orders from the suppliers are shown in Figure 3.5. Although the mean number of days is 10 for both suppliers, do the two suppliers demonstrate the same degree of reliability in terms of making deliveries on schedule? Note the dispersion, or variability, in delivery times indicated by the histograms. Which supplier would you prefer?

The variability in the delivery time creates uncertainty for production scheduling. Methods in this section help measure and understand variability.

For most firms, receiving materials and supplies on schedule is important. The 7- or 8-day deliveries shown for J.C. Clark Distributors might be viewed favorably; however, a

FIGURE 3.5 HISTORICAL DATA SHOWING THE NUMBER OF DAYS REQUIRED TO FILL ORDERS

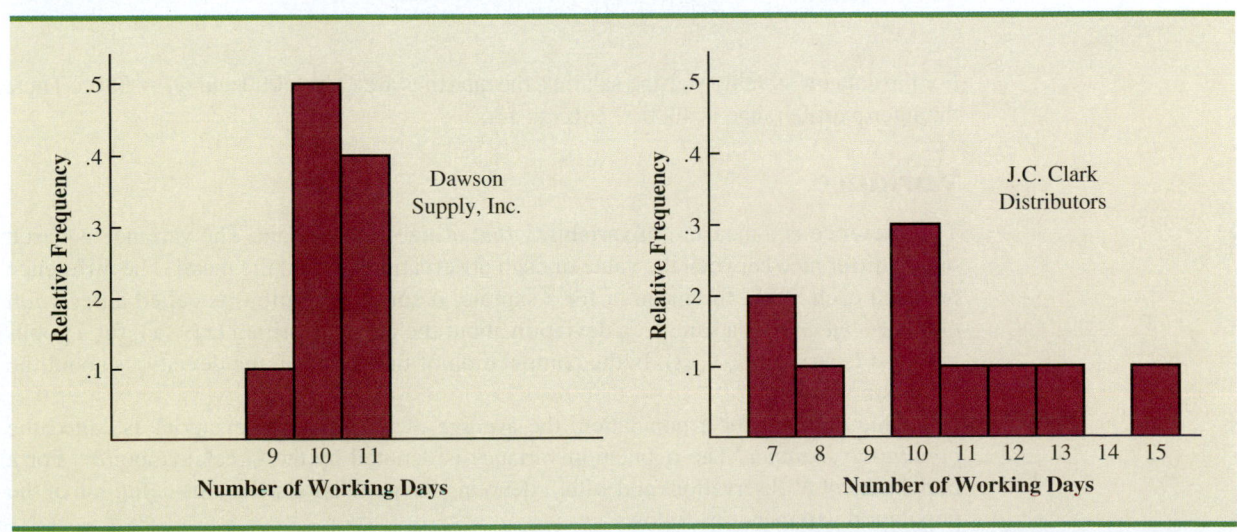

few of the slow 13- to 15-day deliveries could be disastrous in terms of keeping a workforce busy and production on schedule. This example illustrates a situation in which the variability in the delivery times may be an overriding consideration in selecting a supplier. For most purchasing agents, the lower variability shown for Dawson Supply, Inc. would make Dawson the preferred supplier.

We turn now to a discussion of some commonly used measures of variability.

Range

The simplest measure of variability is the **range**.

> **RANGE**
>
> $$\text{Range} = \text{Largest value} - \text{Smallest value}$$

Let us refer to the data on starting salaries for business school graduates in Table 3.1. The largest starting salary is 4325 and the smallest is 3710. The range is $4325 - 3710 = 615$.

Although the range is the easiest of the measures of variability to compute, it is seldom used as the only measure. The reason is that the range is based on only two of the observations and thus is highly influenced by extreme values. Suppose the highest paid graduate received a starting salary of $10,000 per month. In this case, the range would be $10,000 - 3710 = 6290$ rather than 615. This large value for the range would not be especially descriptive of the variability in the data because 11 of the 12 starting salaries are closely grouped between 3710 and 4130.

Interquartile Range

A measure of variability that overcomes the dependency on extreme values is the **interquartile range (IQR)**. This measure of variability is the difference between the third quartile, Q_3, and the first quartile, Q_1. In other words, the interquartile range is the range for the middle 50% of the data.

> **INTERQUARTILE RANGE**
>
> $$\text{IQR} = Q_3 - Q_1 \tag{3.6}$$

For the data on monthly starting salaries, the quartiles are $Q_3 = 4000$ and $Q_1 = 3865$. Thus, the interquartile range is $4000 - 3865 = 135$.

Variance

The **variance** is a measure of variability that utilizes all the data. The variance is based on the difference between the value of each observation (x_i) and the mean. The difference between each x_i and the mean ($\bar{x}$ for a sample, μ for a population) is called a *deviation about the mean*. For a sample, a deviation about the mean is written ($x_i - \bar{x}$); for a population, it is written ($x_i - \mu$). In the computation of the variance, the deviations about the mean are *squared*.

If the data are for a population, the average of the squared deviations is called the *population variance*. The population variance is denoted by the Greek symbol σ^2. For a population of N observations and with μ denoting the population mean, the definition of the population variance is as follows.

POPULATION VARIANCE

$$\sigma^2 = \frac{\sum(x_i - \mu)^2}{N} \tag{3.7}$$

In most statistical applications, the data being analyzed are for a sample. When we compute a sample variance, we are often interested in using it to estimate the population variance σ^2. Although a detailed explanation is beyond the scope of this text, it can be shown that if the sum of the squared deviations about the sample mean is divided by $n - 1$, and not n, the resulting sample variance provides an unbiased estimate of the population variance. For this reason, the *sample variance,* denoted by s^2, is defined as follows.

The sample variance s^2 is a point estimator of the population variance σ^2.

SAMPLE VARIANCE

$$s^2 = \frac{\sum(x_i - \bar{x})^2}{n - 1} \tag{3.8}$$

To illustrate the computation of the sample variance, we will use the data on class size for the sample of five college classes as presented in Section 3.1. A summary of the data, including the computation of the deviations about the mean and the squared deviations about the mean, is shown in Table 3.3. The sum of squared deviations about the mean is $\sum(x_i - \bar{x})^2 = 256$. Hence, with $n - 1 = 4$, the sample variance is

$$s^2 = \frac{\sum(x_i - \bar{x})^2}{n - 1} = \frac{256}{4} = 64$$

Before moving on, let us note that the units associated with the sample variance often cause confusion. Because the values being summed in the variance calculation, $(x_i - \bar{x})^2$, are squared, the units associated with the sample variance are also *squared*. For instance, the sample variance for the class size data is $s^2 = 64$ (students)^2. The squared units associated with variance make it difficult to develop an intuitive understanding and interpretation of the numerical value of the variance. We recommend that you think of the variance as a measure useful in comparing the

The variance is useful in comparing the variability of two or more variables.

TABLE 3.3 COMPUTATION OF DEVIATIONS AND SQUARED DEVIATIONS ABOUT THE MEAN FOR THE CLASS SIZE DATA

Number of Students in Class (x_i)	Mean Class Size $(\bar{x})$	Deviation About the Mean $(x_i - \bar{x})$	Squared Deviation About the Mean $(x_i - \bar{x})^2$
46	44	2	4
54	44	10	100
42	44	−2	4
46	44	2	4
32	44	−12	144
		0	256
		$\sum(x_i - \bar{x})$	$\sum(x_i - \bar{x})^2$

TABLE 3.4   COMPUTATION OF THE SAMPLE VARIANCE FOR THE STARTING SALARY DATA

Monthly Salary (x_i)	Sample Mean $(\bar{x})$	Deviation About the Mean $(x_i - \bar{x})$	Squared Deviation About the Mean $(x_i - \bar{x})^2$
3850	3940	−90	8,100
3950	3940	10	100
4050	3940	110	12,100
3880	3940	−60	3,600
3755	3940	−185	34,225
3710	3940	−230	52,900
3890	3940	−50	2,500
4130	3940	190	36,100
3940	3940	0	0
4325	3940	385	148,225
3920	3940	−20	400
3880	3940	−60	3,600
		0	301,850
		$\sum(x_i - \bar{x})$	$\sum(x_i - \bar{x})^2$

Using equation (3.8),

$$s^2 = \frac{\sum(x_i - \bar{x})^2}{n - 1} = \frac{301,850}{11} = 27,440.91$$

amount of variability for two or more variables. In a comparison of the variables, the one with the largest variance shows the most variability. Further interpretation of the value of the variance may not be necessary.

As another illustration of computing a sample variance, consider the starting salaries listed in Table 3.1 for the 12 business school graduates. In Section 3.1, we showed that the sample mean starting salary was 3940. The computation of the sample variance ($s^2 = 27,440.91$) is shown in Table 3.4.

In Tables 3.3 and 3.4 we show both the sum of the deviations about the mean and the sum of the squared deviations about the mean. For any data set, the sum of the deviations about the mean will *always equal zero*. Note that in Tables 3.3 and 3.4, $\sum(x_i - \bar{x}) = 0$. The positive deviations and negative deviations cancel each other, causing the sum of the deviations about the mean to equal zero.

Standard Deviation

The **standard deviation** is defined to be the positive square root of the variance. Following the notation we adopted for a sample variance and a population variance, we use s to denote the sample standard deviation and σ to denote the population standard deviation. The standard deviation is derived from the variance in the following way.

The sample standard deviation s is a point estimator of the population standard deviation σ.

STANDARD DEVIATION

$$\text{Sample standard deviation} = s = \sqrt{s^2} \tag{3.9}$$

$$\text{Population standard deviation} = \sigma = \sqrt{\sigma^2} \tag{3.10}$$

Recall that the sample variance for the sample of class sizes in five college classes is $s^2 = 64$. Thus, the sample standard deviation is $s = \sqrt{64} = 8$. For the data on starting salaries, the sample standard deviation is $s = \sqrt{27{,}440.91} = 165.65$.

The standard deviation is easier to interpret than the variance because the standard deviation is measured in the same units as the data.

What is gained by converting the variance to its corresponding standard deviation? Recall that the units associated with the variance are squared. For example, the sample variance for the starting salary data of business school graduates is $s^2 = 27{,}440.91$ (dollars)^2. Because the standard deviation is the square root of the variance, the units of the variance, dollars squared, are converted to dollars in the standard deviation. Thus, the standard deviation of the starting salary data is $165.65. In other words, the standard deviation is measured in the same units as the original data. For this reason the standard deviation is more easily compared to the mean and other statistics that are measured in the same units as the original data.

Using Excel to Compute the Sample Variance and Sample Standard Deviation

Excel provides functions for computing the sample variance and sample standard deviation. We illustrate the use of these functions by computing the sample variance and sample standard deviation for the starting salary data in Table 3.1. Refer to Figure 3.6 as we describe the tasks involved. Figure 3.6 is an extension of Figure 3.2, where we showed how to use Excel functions to compute the mean, median, and mode. The formula worksheet is in the background; the value worksheet is in the foreground.

Enter/Access Data: Open the DATAfile named *StartSalary*. The data are in cells B2:B13 and labels appear in column A and cell B1.

Enter Functions and Formulas: Excel's AVERAGE, MEDIAN, and MODE.SNGL functions were entered into cells E2:E4 as described earlier. Excel's VAR.S function can be used to compute the sample variance by entering the following formula into cell E5:

$$=VAR.S(B2:B13)$$

FIGURE 3.6 EXCEL WORKSHEET USED TO COMPUTE THE SAMPLE VARIANCE AND THE SAMPLE STANDARD DEVIATION FOR THE STARTING SALARY DATA

	A	B	C	D	E	F
1	Graduate	Monthly Starting Salary ($)				
2	1	3850		Mean	=AVERAGE(B2:B13)	
3	2	3950		Median	=MEDIAN(B2:B13)	
4	3	4050		Mode	=MODE.SNGL(B2:B13)	
5	4	3880		Variance	=VAR.S(B2:B13)	
6	5	3755		Standard Deviation	=STDEV.S(B2:B13)	
7	6	3710				
8	7	3890				
9	8	4130				
10	9	3940				
11	10	4325				
12	11	3920				
13	12	3880				
14						

	A	B	C	D	E	F
1	Graduate	Monthly Starting Salary ($)				
2	1	3850		Mean	3940	
3	2	3950		Median	3905	
4	3	4050		Mode	3880	
5	4	3880		Variance	27440.91	
6	5	3755		Standard Deviation	165.65	
7	6	3710				
8	7	3890				
9	8	4130				
10	9	3940				
11	10	4325				
12	11	3920				
13	12	3880				
14						

Similarly, the formula =STDEV.S(B2:B13) is entered into cell E6 to compute the sample standard deviation.

The labels in cells D2:D6 identify the output. Note that the sample variance (27440.91) and the sample standard deviation (165.65) are the same as we computed earlier using the definitions.

Coefficient of Variation

The coefficient of variation is a relative measure of variability; it measures the standard deviation relative to the mean.

In some situations we may be interested in a descriptive statistic that indicates how large the standard deviation is relative to the mean. This measure is called the **coefficient of variation** and is usually expressed as a percentage.

> COEFFICIENT OF VARIATION
>
> $$\left(\frac{\text{Standard deviation}}{\text{Mean}} \times 100 \right)\%$$ (3.11)

For the class size data, we found a sample mean of 44 and a sample standard deviation of 8. The coefficient of variation is $[(8/44) \times 100]\% = 18.2\%$. In words, the coefficient of variation tells us that the sample standard deviation is 18.2% of the value of the sample mean. For the starting salary data with a sample mean of 3940 and a sample standard deviation of 165.65, the coefficient of variation, $[(165.65/3940) \times 100]\% = 4.2\%$, tells us the sample standard deviation is only 4.2% of the value of the sample mean. In general, the coefficient of variation is a useful statistic for comparing the variability of variables that have different standard deviations and different means.

Using Excel's Descriptive Statistics Tool

As we have seen, Excel provides statistical functions to compute descriptive statistics for a data set. These functions can be used to compute one statistic at a time (e.g., mean, variance, etc.). Excel also provides a variety of data analysis tools. One of these, called Descriptive Statistics, allows the user to compute a variety of descriptive statistics at once. We will now show how Excel's Descriptive Statistics tool can be used for the starting salary data in Table 3.1. Refer to Figure 3.7 as we describe the tasks involved.

Enter/Access Data: Open the DATAfile named *StartSalary*. The data are in cells B2:B13 and labels appear in column A and in cell B1.

Apply Tools: The following steps describe how to use Excel's Descriptive Statistics tool for these data.

> **Step 1.** Click the **Data** tab on the Ribbon
> **Step 2.** In the **Analysis** group, click **Data Analysis**
> **Step 3.** Choose **Descriptive Statistics** from the list of **Analysis Tools**
> **Step 4.** When the Descriptive Statistics dialog box appears (see Figure 3.7):
> > Enter B1:B13 in the **Input Range** box
> > Select **Grouped By Columns**
> > Select **Labels in First Row**
> > Select **Output Range**
> > Enter D1 in the **Output Range** box (to identify the upper left corner of the section of the worksheet where the descriptive statistics will appear)
> > Select **Summary Statistics**
> > Click **OK**

FIGURE 3.7 DIALOG BOX FOR EXCEL'S DESCRIPTIVE STATISTICS TOOL

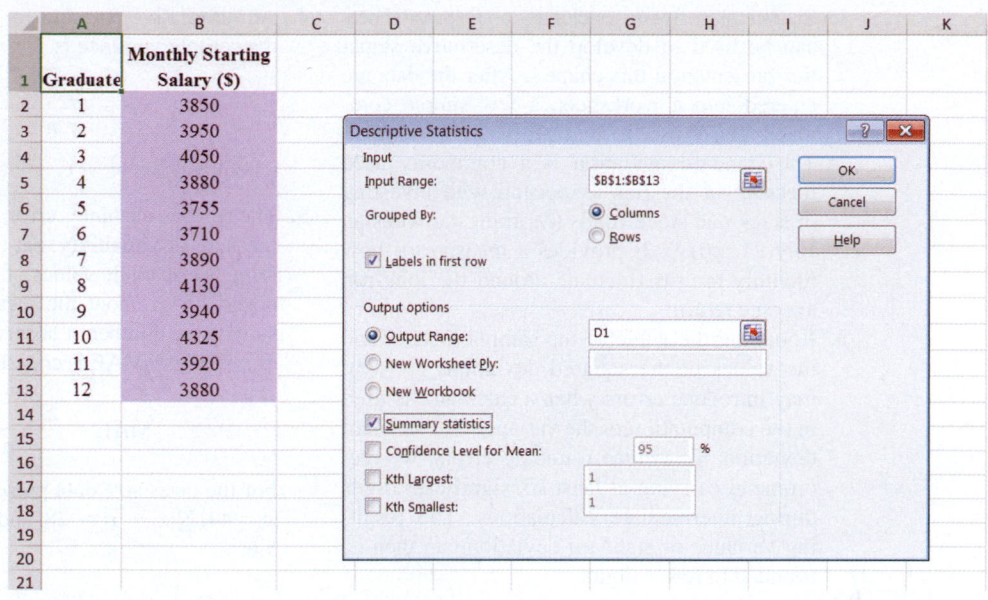

Cells D1:D15 of Figure 3.8 show the descriptive statistics provided by Excel. A gold screen is used to highlight the results. The boldfaced entries are the descriptive statistics that we have already covered. The descriptive statistics that are not boldfaced are either covered subsequently in the text or discussed in more advanced texts.

FIGURE 3.8 DESCRIPTIVE STATISTICS PROVIDED BY EXCEL FOR THE STARTING SALARY DATA

	A	B	C	D	E	F
1	Graduate	Monthly Starting Salary ($)		*Monthly Starting Salary ($)*		
2	1	3850				
3	2	3950		**Mean**	3940	
4	3	4050		Standard Error	47.8199	
5	4	3880		**Median**	3905	
6	5	3755		**Mode**	3880	
7	6	3710		**Standard Deviation**	165.65	
8	7	3890		**Sample Variance**	27440.91	
9	8	4130		Kurtosis	1.72	
10	9	3940		Skewness	1.09	
11	10	4325		**Range**	615	
12	11	3920		**Minimum**	3710	
13	12	3880		**Maximum**	4325	
14				**Sum**	47280	
15				**Count**	12	
16						

NOTES AND COMMENTS

1. Statistical software packages and spreadsheets can be used to develop the descriptive statistics presented in this chapter. After the data are entered into a worksheet, a few simple commands can be used to generate the desired output.

2. The standard deviation is a commonly used measure of the risk associated with investing in stock and stock funds (Morningstar website, July 21, 2012). It provides a measure of how monthly returns fluctuate around the long-run average return.

3. Rounding the value of the sample mean $\bar{x}$ and the values of the squared deviations $(x_i - \bar{x})^2$ may introduce errors when a calculator is used in the computation of the variance and standard deviation. To reduce rounding errors, we recommend carrying at least six significant digits during intermediate calculations. The resulting variance or standard deviation can then be rounded to fewer digits.

4. An alternative formula for the computation of the sample variance is

$$s^2 = \frac{\sum x_i^2 - n\bar{x}^2}{n - 1}$$

where $\sum x_i^2 = x_1^2 + x_2^2 + \cdots + x_n^2$.

5. The mean absolute error (MAE) is another measure of variability that is computed by summing the absolute values of the deviations of the observations about the mean and dividing this sum by the number of observations. For a sample of size n, the MAE is computed as follows:

$$\text{MAE} = \frac{\sum |x_i - \bar{x}|}{n}$$

For the class size data presented in Section 3.1, $\bar{x} = 44$, $\sum|x_i - \bar{x}| = 28$, and the MAE $= 28/5 =$ 5.6.

Exercises

Methods

23. Consider a sample with data values of 10, 20, 12, 17, and 16. Compute the range and interquartile range.

24. Consider a sample with data values of 10, 20, 12, 17, and 16. Compute the variance and standard deviation.

 25. Consider a sample with data values of 27, 25, 20, 15, 30, 34, 28, and 25. Compute the range, interquartile range, variance, and standard deviation.

Applications

 26. Data collected by the Oil Price Information Service from more than 90,000 gasoline and convenience stores throughout the U.S. showed that the average price for a gallon of unleaded gasoline was $3.28 (MSN Auto website, February 2, 2014). The following data show the price per gallon ($) for a sample of 20 gasoline and convenience stores located in San Francisco.

3.59	3.59	4.79	3.56	3.55	3.71	3.65	3.60	3.75	3.56
3.57	3.59	3.55	3.99	4.15	3.66	3.63	3.73	3.61	3.57

a. Use the sample data to estimate the mean price for a gallon of unleaded gasoline in San Francisco.

b. Compute the sample standard deviation.

c. Compare the mean price per gallon for the sample data to the national average price. What conclusions can you draw about the cost living in San Francisco?

27. The results of a search to find the least expensive round-trip flights to Atlanta and Salt Lake City from 14 major U.S. cities are shown in the following table. The departure date was June 20, 2012, and the return date was June 27, 2012.

| | Round-Trip Cost ($) | |
Departure City	Atlanta	Salt Lake City
Cincinnati	340.10	570.10
New York	321.60	354.60
Chicago	291.60	465.60
Denver	339.60	219.60
Los Angeles	359.60	311.60
Seattle	384.60	297.60
Detroit	309.60	471.60
Philadelphia	415.60	618.40
Washington, DC	293.60	513.60
Miami	249.60	523.20
San Francisco	539.60	381.60
Las Vegas	455.60	159.60
Phoenix	359.60	267.60
Dallas	333.90	458.60

Flights

a. Compute the mean price for a round-trip flight into Atlanta and the mean price for a round-trip flight into Salt Lake City. Is Atlanta less expensive to fly into than Salt Lake City? If so, what could explain this difference?

b. Compute the range, variance, and standard deviation for the two samples. What does this information tell you about the prices for flights into these two cities?

28. The Australian Open is the first of the four Grand Slam professional tennis events held each year. Victoria Azarenka beat Maria Sharapova to win the 2012 Australian Open women's title (*Washington Post*, January 27, 2012). During the tournament Ms. Azarenka's serve speed reached 178 kilometers per hour. A list of the 20 Women's Singles serve speed leaders for the 2012 Australian Open is provided below.

AustralianOpen

Player	Serve Speed (km/h)	Player	Serve Speed (km/h)
S. Williams	191	G. Arn	179
S. Lisicki	190	V. Azarenka	178
M. Keys	187	A. Ivanovic	178
L. Hradecka	187	P. Kvitova	178
J. Gajdosova	187	M. Krajicek	178
J. Hampton	181	V. Dushevina	178
B. Mattek-Sands	181	S. Stosur	178
F. Schiavone	179	S. Cirstea	177
P. Parmentier	179	M. Barthel	177
N. Petrova	179	P. Ormaechea	177

a. Compute the mean, variance, and standard deviation for the serve speeds.

b. A similar sample of the 20 Women's Singles serve speed leaders for the 2011 Wimbledon tournament showed a sample mean serve speed of 182.5 kilometers per hour. The variance and standard deviation were 33.3 and 5.77, respectively. Discuss any difference between the serve speeds in the Australian Open and the Wimbledon women's tournaments.

29. The *Los Angeles Times* regularly reports the air quality index for various areas of Southern California. A sample of air quality index values for Pomona provided the following data: 28, 42, 58, 48, 45, 55, 60, 49, and 50.

a. Compute the range and interquartile range.
b. Compute the sample variance and sample standard deviation.
c. A sample of air quality index readings for Anaheim provided a sample mean of 48.5, a sample variance of 136, and a sample standard deviation of 11.66. What comparisons can you make between the air quality in Pomona and that in Anaheim on the basis of these descriptive statistics?

30. The following data were used to construct the histograms of the number of days required to fill orders for Dawson Supply, Inc. and J.C. Clark Distributors (see Figure 3.5).

Dawson Supply Days for Delivery: 11   10   9   10   11   11   10   11   10   10
Clark Distributors Days for Delivery: 8   10   13   7   10   11   10   7   15   12

Use the range and standard deviation to support the previous observation that Dawson Supply provides the more consistent and reliable delivery times.

31. The results of Accounting Principals' latest Workonomix survey indicate the average American worker spends $1092 on coffee annually (*The Consumerist,* January 20, 2012). To determine if there are any differences in coffee expenditures by age group, samples of 10 consumers were selected for three age groups (18–34, 35–44, and 45 and Older). The dollar amount each consumer in the sample spent last year on coffee is provided below.

DATA *file*

Coffee

18–34	35–44	45 and Older
1355	969	1135
115	434	956
1456	1792	400
2045	1500	1374
1621	1277	1244
994	1056	825
1937	1922	763
1200	1350	1192
1567	1586	1305
1390	1415	1510

a. Compute the mean, variance, and standard deviation for the each of these three samples.
b. What observations can be made based on these data?

DATA *file*

Advertising

32. *Advertising Age* annually compiles a list of the 100 companies that spend the most on advertising. Consumer-goods company Procter & Gamble has often topped the list, spending billions of dollars annually (*Advertising Age* website, March 12, 2013). Consider the data found in the DATAfile named *Advertising*. It contains annual advertising expenditures for a sample of 20 companies in the automotive sector and 20 companies in the department store sector.
a. What is the mean advertising spent for each sector?
b. What is the standard deviation for each sector?
c. What is the range of advertising spent for each sector?
d. What is the interquartile range for each sector?
e. Based on this sample and your answers to parts (a) to (d), comment on any differences in the advertising spending in the automotive companies versus the department store companies.

33. Scores turned in by an amateur golfer at the Bonita Fairways Golf Course in Bonita Springs, Florida during 2014 and 2015 are as follows:

2014 Season: 74   78   79   77   75   73   75   77
2015 Season: 71   70   75   77   85   80   71   79

a. Use the mean and standard deviation to evaluate the golfer's performance over the two-year period.

b. What is the primary difference in performance between 2014 and 2015? What improvement, if any, can be seen in the 2015 scores?

34. The following times were recorded by the quarter-mile and mile runners of a university track team (times are in minutes).

Quarter-Mile Times:	.92	.98	1.04	.90	.99
Mile Times:	4.52	4.35	4.60	4.70	4.50

After viewing this sample of running times, one of the coaches commented that the quarter-milers turned in the more consistent times. Use the standard deviation and the coefficient of variation to summarize the variability in the data. Does the use of the coefficient of variation indicate that the coach's statement should be qualified?

Measures of Distribution Shape, Relative Location, and Detecting Outliers

We have described several measures of location and variability for data. In addition, it is often important to have a measure of the shape of a distribution. In Chapter 2 we noted that a histogram provides a graphical display showing the shape of a distribution. An important numerical measure of the shape of a distribution is called **skewness**.

Distribution Shape

Figure 3.9 shows four histograms constructed from relative frequency distributions. The histograms in Panels A and B are moderately skewed. The one in Panel A is skewed to the left; its skewness is −.85. The histogram in Panel B is skewed to the right; its skewness is +.85. The histogram in Panel C is symmetric; its skewness is zero. The histogram in Panel D is highly skewed to the right; its skewness is 1.62. The formula used to compute skewness is somewhat complex.[1] However, the skewness can easily be computed using statistical software. For data skewed to the left, the skewness is negative; for data skewed to the right, the skewness is positive. If the data are symmetric, the skewness is zero.

For a symmetric distribution, the mean and the median are equal. When the data are positively skewed, the mean will usually be greater than the median; when the data are negatively skewed, the mean will usually be less than the median. The data used to construct the histogram in Panel D are customer purchases at a women's apparel store. The mean purchase amount is $77.60 and the median purchase amount is $59.70. The relatively few large purchase amounts tend to increase the mean, whereas the median remains unaffected by the large purchase amounts. The median provides the preferred measure of location when the data are highly skewed.

z-Scores

In addition to measures of location, variability, and shape, we are also interested in the relative location of values within a data set. Measures of relative location help us determine how far a particular value is from the mean.

---

[1]The formula for the skewness of sample data:

$$\text{Skewness} = \frac{n}{(n-1)(n-2)} \sum \left(\frac{x_i - \bar{x}}{s} \right)^3$$

FIGURE 3.9   HISTOGRAMS SHOWING THE SKEWNESS FOR FOUR DISTRIBUTIONS

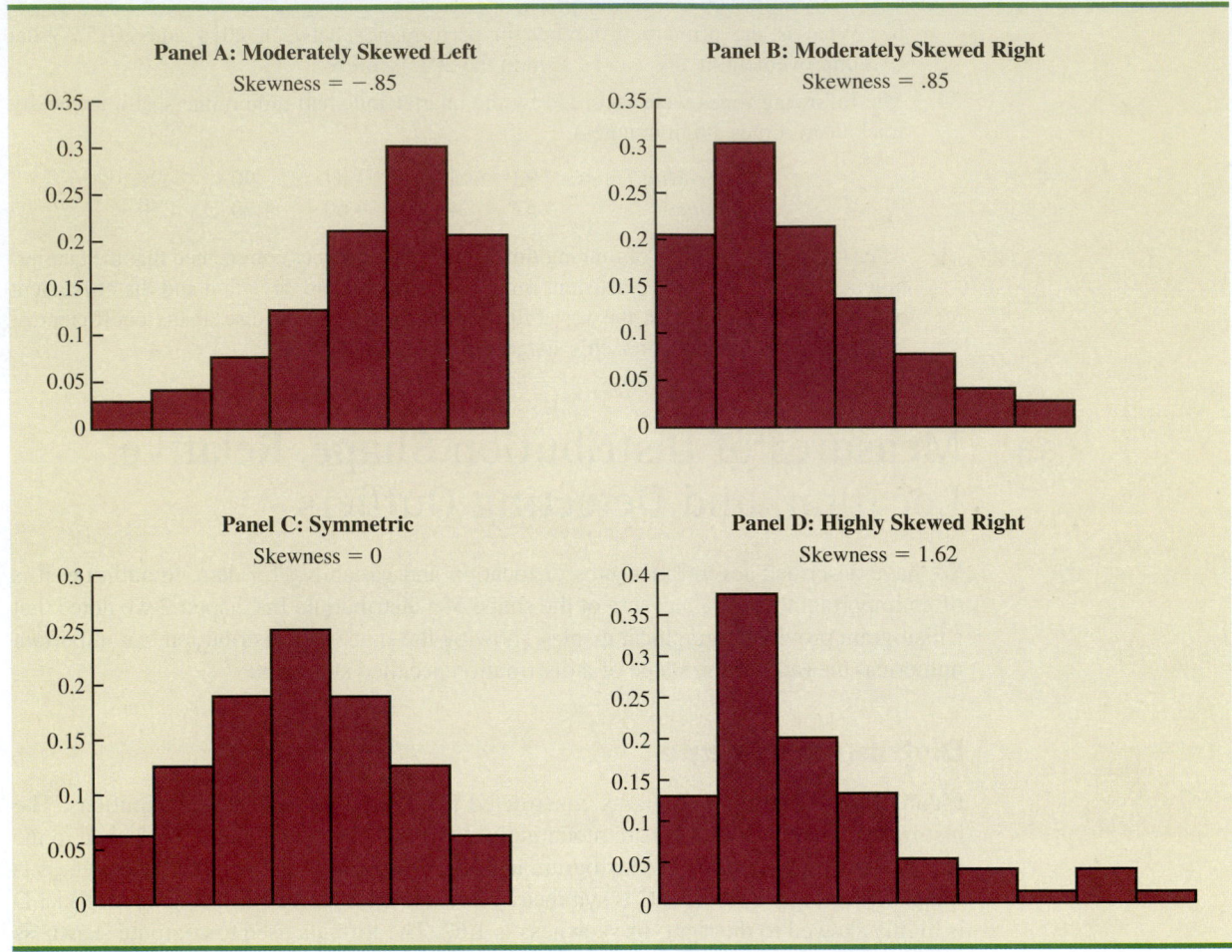

By using both the mean and standard deviation, we can determine the relative location of any observation. Suppose we have a sample of n observations, with the values denoted by $x_1, x_2, \ldots, x_n$. In addition, assume that the sample mean, $\bar{x}$, and the sample standard deviation, s, are already computed. Associated with each value, x_i, is another value called its **z-score**. Equation (3.12) shows how the z-score is computed for each x_i.

z-SCORE

$$z_i = \frac{x_i - \bar{x}}{s} \tag{3.12}$$

where

z_i = the z-score for x_i

$\bar{x}$ = the sample mean

s = the sample standard deviation

TABLE 3.5 z-SCORES FOR THE CLASS SIZE DATA

Number of Students in Class (x_i)	Deviation About the Mean ($x_i - \bar{x}$)	z-Score $\left(\dfrac{x_i - \bar{x}}{s}\right)$
46	2	$2/8 =$ .25
54	10	$10/8 =$ 1.25
42	−2	$-2/8 =$ −.25
46	2	$2/8 =$ .25
32	−12	$-12/8 = -1.50$

The z-score is often called the *standardized value*. The z-score, z_i, can be interpreted as the *number of standard deviations x_i is from the mean $\bar{x}$*. For example, $z_1 = 1.2$ would indicate that x_1 is 1.2 standard deviations greater than the sample mean. Similarly, $z_2 = -.5$ would indicate that x_2 is .5, or 1/2, standard deviation less than the sample mean. A z-score greater than zero occurs for observations with a value greater than the mean, and a z-score less than zero occurs for observations with a value less than the mean. A z-score of zero indicates that the value of the observation is equal to the mean.

The z-score for any observation can be interpreted as a measure of the relative location of the observation in a data set. Thus, observations in two different data sets with the same z-score can be said to have the same relative location in terms of being the same number of standard deviations from the mean.

The process of converting a value for a variable to a z-score is often referred to as a z transformation.

The z-scores for the class size data from Section 3.1 are computed in Table 3.5. Recall the previously computed sample mean, $\bar{x} = 44$, and sample standard deviation, $s = 8$. The z-score of −1.50 for the fifth observation shows it is farthest from the mean; it is 1.50 standard deviations below the mean. Figure 3.10 provides a dot plot of the class size data with a graphical representation of the associated z-scores on the axis below.

FIGURE 3.10 DOT PLOT SHOWING CLASS SIZE DATA AND z-SCORES

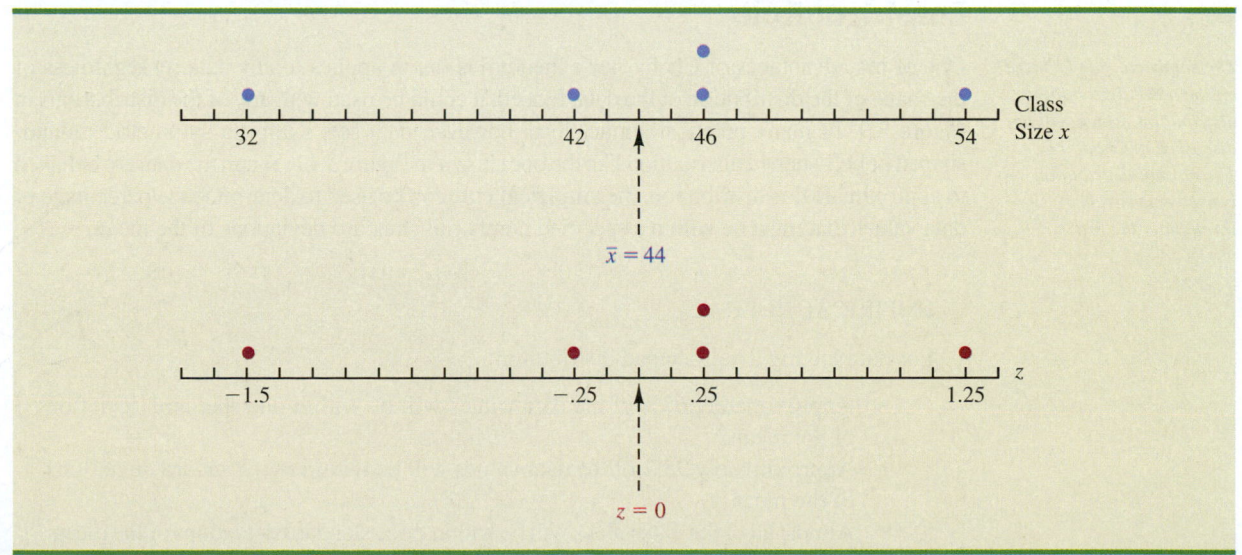

Chebyshev's Theorem

Chebyshev's theorem enables us to make statements about the proportion of data values that must be within a specified number of standard deviations of the mean.

> CHEBYSHEV'S THEOREM
>
> At least $(1 - 1/z^2)$ of the data values must be within z standard deviations of the mean, where z is any value greater than 1.

Some of the implications of this theorem, with $z = 2, 3,$ and 4 standard deviations, follow.

- At least .75, or 75%, of the data values must be within $z = 2$ standard deviations of the mean.
- At least .89, or 89%, of the data values must be within $z = 3$ standard deviations of the mean.
- At least .94, or 94%, of the data values must be within $z = 4$ standard deviations of the mean.

For an example using Chebyshev's theorem, suppose that the midterm test scores for 100 students in a college business statistics course had a mean of 70 and a standard deviation of 5. How many students had test scores between 60 and 80? How many students had test scores between 58 and 82?

For the test scores between 60 and 80, we note that 60 is two standard deviations below the mean and 80 is two standard deviations above the mean. Using Chebyshev's theorem, we see that at least .75, or at least 75%, of the observations must have values within two standard deviations of the mean. Thus, at least 75% of the students must have scored between 60 and 80.

Chebyshev's theorem requires z > 1, but z need not be an integer.

For the test scores between 58 and 82, we see that $(58 - 70)/5 = -2.4$ indicates 58 is 2.4 standard deviations below the mean and that $(82 - 70)/5 = +2.4$ indicates 82 is 2.4 standard deviations above the mean. Applying Chebyshev's theorem with $z = 2.4$, we have

$$\left(1 - \frac{1}{z^2}\right) = \left(1 - \frac{1}{(2.4)^2}\right) = .826$$

At least 82.6% of the students must have test scores between 58 and 82.

Empirical Rule

The empirical rule is based on the normal probability distribution, which will be discussed in Chapter 6. The normal distribution is used extensively throughout the text.

One of the advantages of Chebyshev's theorem is that it applies to any data set regardless of the shape of the distribution of the data. Indeed, it could be used with any of the distributions in Figure 3.9. In many practical applications, however, data sets exhibit a symmetric mound-shaped or bell-shaped distribution like the one shown in Figure 3.11. When the data are believed to approximate this distribution, the **empirical rule** can be used to determine the percentage of data values that must be within a specified number of standard deviations of the mean.

> EMPIRICAL RULE
>
> For data having a bell-shaped distribution:
>
> - Approximately 68% of the data values will be within one standard deviation of the mean.
> - Approximately 95% of the data values will be within two standard deviations of the mean.
> - Almost all of the data values will be within three standard deviations of the mean.

FIGURE 3.11   A SYMMETRIC MOUND-SHAPED OR BELL-SHAPED DISTRIBUTION

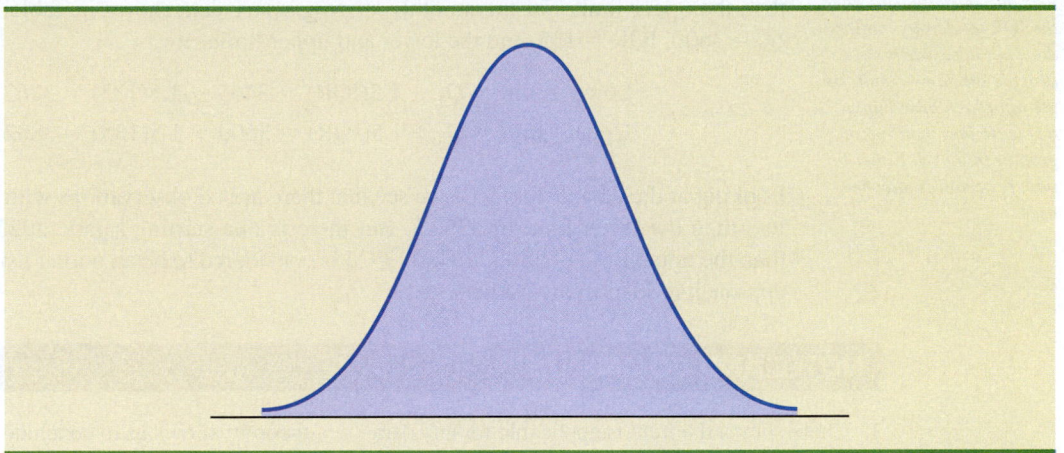

For example, liquid detergent cartons are filled automatically on a production line. Filling weights frequently have a bell-shaped distribution. If the mean filling weight is 16 ounces and the standard deviation is .25 ounces, we can use the empirical rule to draw the following conclusions.

- Approximately 68% of the filled cartons will have weights between 15.75 and 16.25 ounces (within one standard deviation of the mean).
- Approximately 95% of the filled cartons will have weights between 15.50 and 16.50 ounces (within two standard deviations of the mean).
- Almost all filled cartons will have weights between 15.25 and 16.75 ounces (within three standard deviations of the mean).

Detecting Outliers

Sometimes a data set will have one or more observations with unusually large or unusually small values. These extreme values are called **outliers**. Experienced statisticians take steps to identify outliers and then review each one carefully. An outlier may be a data value that has been incorrectly recorded. If so, it can be corrected before further analysis. An outlier may also be from an observation that was incorrectly included in the data set; if so, it can be removed. Finally, an outlier may be an unusual data value that has been recorded correctly and belongs in the data set. In such cases it should remain.

It is a good idea to check for outliers before making decisions based on data analysis. Errors are often made in recording data and entering data into the computer. Outliers should not necessarily be deleted, but their accuracy and appropriateness should be verified.

Standardized values (*z*-scores) can be used to identify outliers. Recall that the empirical rule allows us to conclude that for data with a bell-shaped distribution, almost all the data values will be within three standard deviations of the mean. Hence, in using *z*-scores to identify outliers, we recommend treating any data value with a *z*-score less than −3 or greater than +3 as an outlier. Such data values can then be reviewed for accuracy and to determine whether they belong in the data set.

Refer to the *z*-scores for the class size data in Table 3.5. The *z*-score of −1.50 shows the fifth class size is farthest from the mean. However, this standardized value is well within the −3 to +3 guideline for outliers. Thus, the *z*-scores do not indicate that outliers are present in the class size data.

Another approach to identifying outliers is based upon the values of the first and third quartiles (Q_1 and Q_3) and the interquartile range (IQR). Using this method, we first compute the following lower and upper limits:

$$\text{Lower Limit} = Q_1 - 1.5(\text{IQR})$$
$$\text{Upper Limit} = Q_3 + 1.5(\text{IQR})$$

The approach that uses the first and third quartiles and the IQR to identify outliers does not necessarily provide the same results as the approach based upon a z-score less than −3 or greater than +3. Either or both procedures may be used.

An observation is classified as an outlier if its value is less than the lower limit or greater than the upper limit. For the monthly starting salary data shown in Table 3.1, $Q_1 = 3465$, $Q_3 = 3600$, IQR = 135, and the lower and upper limits are

$$\text{Lower Limit} = Q_1 - 1.5(\text{IQR}) = 3465 - 1.5(135) = 3262.5$$
$$\text{Upper Limit} = Q_3 + 1.5(\text{IQR}) = 3600 + 1.5(135) = 3802.5$$

Looking at the data in Table 3.1 we see that there are no observations with a starting salary less than the lower limit of 3262.5. But there is one starting salary, 3925, that is greater than the upper limit of 3802.5. Thus, 3925 is considered to be an outlier using this alternate approach to identifying outliers.

NOTES AND COMMENTS

1. Chebyshev's theorem is applicable for any data set and can be used to state the minimum number of data values that will be within a certain number of standard deviations of the mean. If the data are known to be approximately bell-shaped, more can be said. For instance, the empirical rule allows us to say that *approximately* 95% of the data values will be within two standard deviations of the mean; Chebyshev's theorem allows us to conclude only that at least 75% of the data values will be in that interval.

2. Before analyzing a data set, statisticians usually make a variety of checks to ensure the validity of data. In a large study it is not uncommon for errors to be made in recording data values or in entering the values into a computer. Identifying outliers is one tool used to check the validity of the data.

Exercises

Methods

35. Consider a sample with data values of 10, 20, 12, 17, and 16. Compute the *z*-score for each of the five observations.

36. Consider a sample with a mean of 500 and a standard deviation of 100. What are the *z*-scores for the following data values: 520, 650, 500, 450, and 280?

 **SELF***test*
37. Consider a sample with a mean of 30 and a standard deviation of 5. Use Chebyshev's theorem to determine the percentage of the data within each of the following ranges:
   a. 20 to 40
   b. 15 to 45
   c. 22 to 38
   d. 18 to 42
   e. 12 to 48

38. Suppose the data have a bell-shaped distribution with a mean of 30 and a standard deviation of 5. Use the empirical rule to determine the percentage of data within each of the following ranges:
   a. 20 to 40
   b. 15 to 45
   c. 25 to 35

Applications

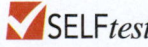 **SELF***test*
39. The results of a national survey showed that on average, adults sleep 6.9 hours per night. Suppose that the standard deviation is 1.2 hours.

a. Use Chebyshev's theorem to calculate the percentage of individuals who sleep between 4.5 and 9.3 hours.

b. Use Chebyshev's theorem to calculate the percentage of individuals who sleep between 3.9 and 9.9 hours.

c. Assume that the number of hours of sleep follows a bell-shaped distribution. Use the empirical rule to calculate the percentage of individuals who sleep between 4.5 and 9.3 hours per day. How does this result compare to the value that you obtained using Chebyshev's theorem in part (a)?

40. The Energy Information Administration reported that the mean retail price per gallon of regular grade gasoline was $3.43 (Energy Information Administration, July 2012). Suppose that the standard deviation was $.10 and that the retail price per gallon has a bell-shaped distribution.

a. What percentage of regular grade gasoline sold for between $3.33 and $3.53 per gallon?

b. What percentage of regular grade gasoline sold for between $3.33 and $3.63 per gallon?

c. What percentage of regular grade gasoline sold for more than $3.63 per gallon?

41. The Graduate Management Admission Test (GMAT) is a standardized exam used by many universities as part of the assessment for admission to graduate study in business. The average GMAT score is 547 (*Magoosh* website, January 5, 2015). Assume that GMAT scores are bell-shaped with a standard deviation of 100.

a. What percentage of GMAT scores are 647 or higher?

b. What percentage of GMAT scores are 747 or higher?

c. What percentage of GMAT scores are between 447 and 547?

d. What percentage of GMAT scores are between 347 and 647?

42. Many families in California are using backyard structures for home offices, art studios, and hobby areas as well as for additional storage. Suppose that the mean price for a customized wooden, shingled backyard structure is $3100. Assume that the standard deviation is $1200.

a. What is the z-score for a backyard structure costing $2300?

b. What is the z-score for a backyard structure costing $4900?

c. Interpret the z-scores in parts (a) and (b). Comment on whether either should be considered an outlier.

d. If the cost for a backyard shed-office combination built in Albany, California is $13,000, should this structure be considered an outlier? Explain.

43. According to a *Los Angeles Times* study of more than 1 million medical dispatches from 2007 to 2012, the 911 response time for medical aid varies dramatically across Los Angeles (*LA Times* website, November 2012). Under national standards adopted by the Los Angeles Fire Department, rescuers are supposed to arrive within six minutes to almost all medical emergencies. But the *Times* analysis found that in affluent hillside communities stretching from Griffith Park to Pacific Palisades, firefighters failed to hit that mark nearly 85% of the time.

The following data show the response times, in minutes, for 10 emergency calls in the Griffith Park neighborhood.

| 11.8 | 10.3 | 10.7 | 10.6 | 11.5 | 8.3 | 10.5 | 10.9 | 10.7 | 11.2 |

Based on this sample of ten response times, compute the descriptive statistics in parts (a) and (b) and then answer the questions in parts (c) and (d):

a. Mean, median, and mode

b. Range and standard deviation

    c. Should the response time of 8.3 minutes be considered an outlier in comparison to the other response times?

    d. Do the response times indicate that the city is meeting the national standards? Should the city consider making changes to its response strategies? Would adding more stations to areas in the city be a practical solution? Discuss.

44. A sample of 10 NCAA college basketball game scores provided the following data.

NCAA

Winning Team	Points	Losing Team	Points	Winning Margin
Arizona	90	Oregon	66	24
Duke	85	Georgetown	66	19
Florida State	75	Wake Forest	70	5
Kansas	78	Colorado	57	21
Kentucky	71	Notre Dame	63	8
Louisville	65	Tennessee	62	3
Oklahoma State	72	Texas	66	6
Purdue	76	Michigan State	70	6
Stanford	77	Southern Cal	67	10
Wisconsin	76	Illinois	56	20

    a. Compute the mean and standard deviation for the points scored by the winning team.

    b. Assume that the points scored by the winning teams for all NCAA games follow a bell-shaped distribution. Using the mean and standard deviation found in part (a), estimate the percentage of all NCAA games in which the winning team scores 84 or more points. Estimate the percentage of NCAA games in which the winning team scores more than 90 points.

    c. Compute the mean and standard deviation for the winning margin. Do the data contain outliers? Explain.

45. *The Wall Street Journal* reported that Walmart Stores Inc. is planning to lay off 2300 employees at its Sam's Club warehouse unit. Approximately half of the layoffs will be hourly employees (*The Wall Street Journal*, January 25–26, 2014). Suppose the following data represent the percentage of hourly employees laid off for 15 Sam's Club stores.

    55   56   44   43   44   56   60   62   57   45   36   38   50   69   65

    a. Compute the mean and median percentage of hourly employees being laid off at these stores.

    b. Compute the first and third quartiles.

    c. Compute the range and interquartile range.

    d. Compute the variance and standard deviation.

    e. Do the data contain any outliers?

    f. Based on the sample data, does it appear that Walmart is meeting its goal for reducing the number of hourly employees?

3.4 Five-Number Summaries and Box Plots

Summary statistics and easy-to-draw graphs based on summary statistics can be used to quickly summarize large quantities of data. In this section we show how five-number summaries and box plots can be developed to identify several characteristics of a data set.

Five-Number Summary

In a **five-number summary**, five numbers are used to summarize the data:

1. Smallest value
2. First quartile (Q_1)
3. Median (Q_2)
4. Third quartile (Q_3)
5. Largest value

To illustrate the development of a five-number summary, we will use the monthly starting salary data in Table 3.1. Arranging the data in ascending order, we obtain the following results.

3710 3755 3850 3880 3880 3890 3920 3940 3950 4050 4130 4325

The smallest value is 3710 and the largest value is 4325. We showed how to compute the quartiles ($Q_1 = 3857.5$; $Q_2 = 3905$; and $Q_3 = 4025$) in Section 3.1. Thus, the five-number summary for the monthly starting salary data is

3710   3857.5   3905   4025   4325

The five-number summary indicates that the starting salaries in the sample are between 3710 and 4325 and that the median or middle value is 3905. The first and third quartiles show that approximately 50% of the starting salaries are between 3857.5 and 4025.

Box Plot

A **box plot** is a graphical display of data based on a five-number summary. A key to the development of a box plot is the computation of the interquartile range, IQR $= Q_3 - Q_1$. Figure 3.12 shows a box plot for the monthly starting salary data. The steps used to construct the box plot follow.

1. A box is drawn with the ends of the box located at the first and third quartiles. For the salary data, $Q_1 = 3857.5$ and $Q_3 = 4025$. This box contains the middle 50% of the data.
2. A horizontal line is drawn in the box at the location of the median (3905 for the salary data). An X indicates the value of the mean (3940 for the salary data).

Box plots provide another way to identify outliers, but they do not necessarily identify the same values as those with a z-score less than −3 or greater than +3. Either or both procedures may be used.

3. By using the interquartile range, IQR $= Q_3 - Q_1$, *limits* are located at 1.5(IQR) below Q_1, and 1.5(IQR) above Q_3. For the salary data, IQR $= Q_3 - Q_1 = 4025 - 3857.5 = 167.5$. Thus, the limits are $3857.5 - 1.5(167.5) = 3606.25$ and $4025 + 1.5(167.5) = 4276.25$. Data outside these limits are considered *outliers*.
4. The vertical lines extending from each end of the box in Figure 3.12 are called *whiskers*. The whiskers are drawn from the ends of the box to the smallest and largest values *inside the limits* computed in step 3. Thus, the whiskers end at salary values of 3710 and 4130.
5. Finally, the location of each outlier is shown with a small dot. In Figure 3.12 we see one outlier, 4325.

In Figure 3.12 we included lines showing the location of the upper and lower limits. These lines were drawn to show how the limits are computed and where they are located. Although the limits are always computed, generally they are not drawn on the box plots.

FIGURE 3.12 BOX PLOT OF THE MONTHLY STARTING SALARY DATA WITH LINES SHOWING THE LOWER AND UPPER LIMITS

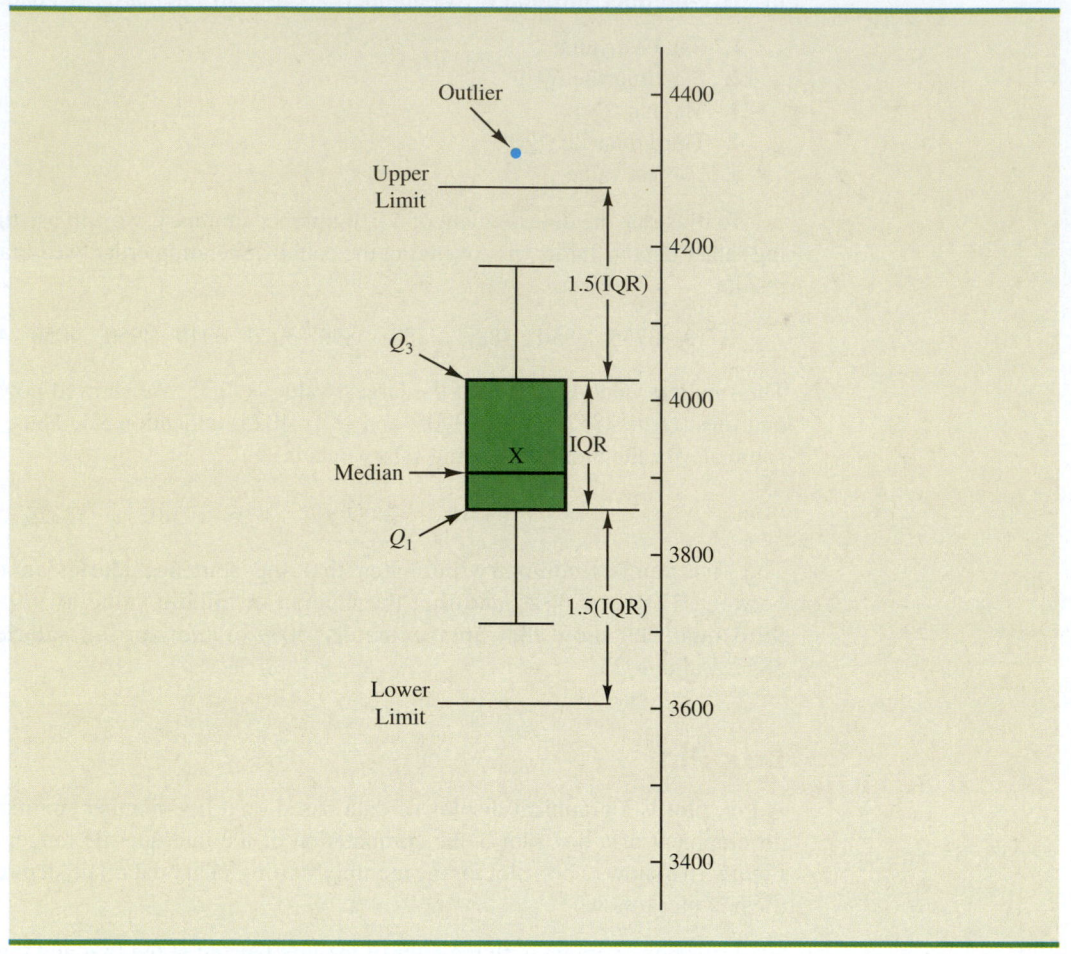

Using Excel to Construct a Box Plot

In Excel, a box plot is referred to as a box and whisker plot.

We can use Excel's Insert Statistic Chart to construct a box plot of the monthly starting salary data as outlined below.

Enter/Access Data: Open the DATAfile named *StartSalary*. The data are in cells B2:B13.

Apply Tools: The following steps describe how to use Excel's Insert Statistic Chart to construct a histogram of the audit time data.

Step 1. Select cells in the data set (B2:B13).
Step 2. Click **Insert** on the Ribbon
Step 3. In the **Charts** group click **Insert Statistic Chart** and then click **Box and Whisker**; the box plot appears in the spreadsheet

Editing Options:

Step 1. Click on **Chart Title** and press the delete key
Step 2. Click on the **1** next to the horizontal axis and press the delete key
Step 3. Click on the **Chart Elements** button ⊞ (located next to the top right corner of the chart)

FIGURE 3.13   BOX PLOT OF THE MONTHLY STARTING SALARY DATA

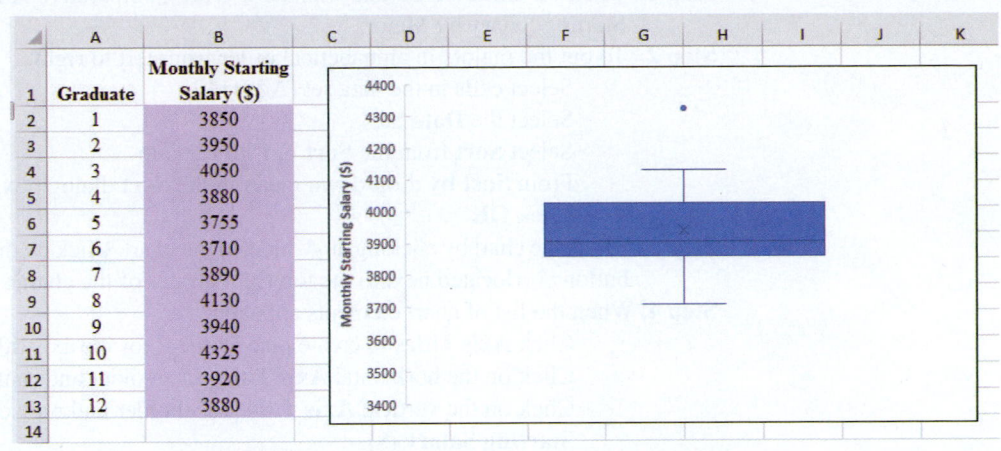

Step 4. When the list of chart elements appears:
> Click **Axis Titles** to create placeholders for the axis titles
> Click on the horizontal **Axis Title** and press the delete key
> Click on the vertical **Axis Title** placeholder and replace it with **Monthly Starting Salary ($)**

Step 5. Click on a horizontal line and press the delete key

Step 6. Click on the verticle axis, right click, select **Format Axis…**

Step 7. In the **Format Axis** pane, select **Tick Marks**, and from the drop-down **Major type** menu, select **Inside**

Figure 3.13 shows the resulting box plot.

Comparative Analysis Using Box Plots

Box plots can also be used to provide a graphical summary of two or more groups and facilitate visual comparisons among the groups. For example, suppose the placement office decided to conduct a follow-up study to compare monthly starting salaries by the graduate's major: accounting, finance, information systems, management, and marketing. The major and starting salary data for a new sample of 111 recent business school graduates are shown in the DATAfile named *MajorSalary*.

MajorSalary

Using Excel to Construct a Comparative Analysis Using Box Plots

We can use Excel's Insert Statistic Chart to construct a comparative box plot of data on the monthly starting salary by major as outlined below.

Enter/Access Data: Open the DATAfile named *MajorSalary*. The data are in cells A2:B112.

Apply Tools: The following steps describe how to use Excel's Insert Statistic Chart to construct box plots of monthly salary by major.

Step 1. Select cells in the data set (A2:B112).

Step 2. Click **Insert** on the Ribbon

Step 3. In the **Charts** group click **Insert Statistic Chart** and then click **Box and Whisker**; the box plot appears in the spreadsheet

Editing Options:

Step 1. Click on **Chart Title** and replace it with Comparative Analysis of Monthly Starting Salary by Major.

Step 2. To put the majors in alphabetical order from left to right:
> Select cells in the data set (A2:B112).
> Select the **Data** tab
> Select **Sort** from the **Sort & Filter** group
> From **Sort by** drop-down menu in the **Sort** dialog box, select **Major**
> Click **OK**

Step 3. Select the chart by clicking anywhere on the chart. Click on the **Chart Elements** button ⊞ (located next to the top right corner of the chart).

Step 4. When the list of chart elements appears:
> Click **Axis Titles** to create placeholders for the axis titles
> Click on the horizontal **Axis Title** placeholder and replace it with **Major**
> Click on the vertical **Axis Title** placeholder and replace it with **Monthly Starting Salary ($)**

Step 5. Click on a horizontal line and press the delete key

Step 6. Click on the horizontal axis, right click, select **Format Axis…**

Step 7. In the **Format Axis** pane, select **Tick Marks**, and from the drop-down **Major type** menu select **Inside**

Figure 3.14 shows the resulting box plot comparative analysis.

What interpretations can you make from the box plots in Figure 3.14? Specifically, we note the following:

- The higher salaries are in accounting; the lower salaries are in management and marketing.
- Based on the medians, accounting and information systems have similar and higher median salaries. Finance is next, with marketing and management showing lower median salaries.
- High salary outliers exist for accounting, finance, and marketing majors.

Perhaps you can see additional interpretations based on these box plots.

FIGURE 3.14 BOX PLOTS OF MONTHLY STARTING SALARY BY MAJOR

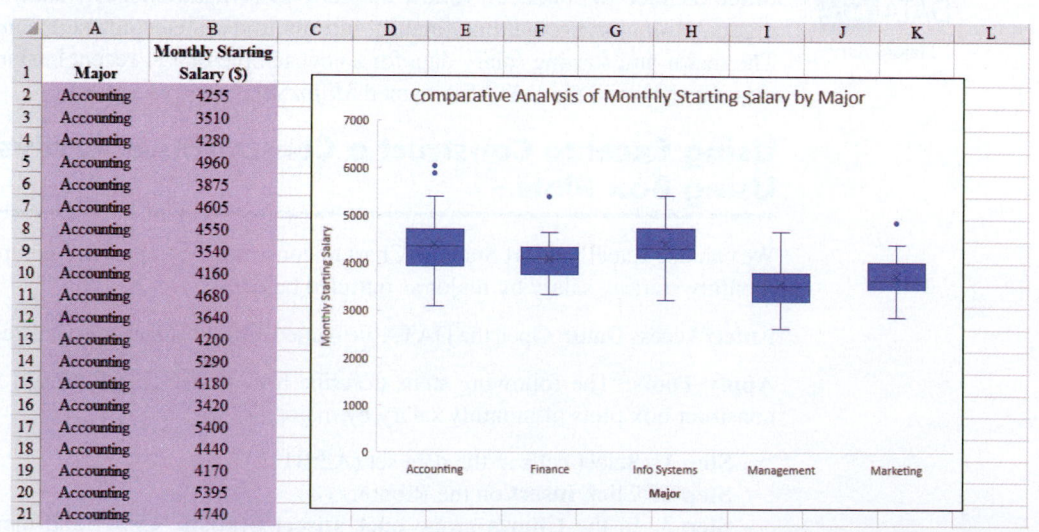

NOTES AND COMMENTS

1. There are several options with Excel's Box and Whisker chart. To invoke these options, right-click on the box part of the chart, select **Format Data Series...**, and the **Format Data Series** pane will appear. This allows you to control what appears in the chart—for example, whether or not to show the mean marker, markers for outliers, and markers for all points. In the case of a comparative chart, you can control the gaps between categories and create a line connecting the means of the different categories.

2. In the **Format Data Series** pane, there are two options for how quartiles are calculated: Inclusive median and Exclusive median. The default is Exclusive median; this option is consistent with the approach discussed in this text. We recommend that you leave this option at its default value of Exclusive median.

Exercises

Methods

46. Consider a sample with data values of 27, 25, 20, 15, 30, 34, 28, and 25. Provide the five-number summary for the data.

47. Show the box plot for the data in exercise 46.

 SELF*test*

48. Show the five-number summary and the box plot for the following data: 5, 15, 18, 10, 8, 12, 16, 10, 6.

49. A data set has a first quartile of 42 and a third quartile of 50. Compute the lower and upper limits for the corresponding box plot. Should a data value of 65 be considered an outlier?

Applications

50. Naples, Florida hosts a half-marathon (13.1-mile race) in January each year. The event attracts top runners from throughout the United States as well as from around the world. In the race results shown below, 22 men and 31 women entered the 19–24 age class. Finish times in minutes are as follows. Times are shown in order of finish.

DATA *file*

Runners

Finish	Men	Women	Finish	Men	Women	Finish	Men	Women
1	65.30	109.03	11	109.05	123.88	21	143.83	136.75
2	66.27	111.22	12	110.23	125.78	22	148.70	138.20
3	66.52	111.65	13	112.90	129.52	23		139.00
4	66.85	111.93	14	113.52	129.87	24		147.18
5	70.87	114.38	15	120.95	130.72	25		147.35
6	87.18	118.33	16	127.98	131.67	26		147.50
7	96.45	121.25	17	128.40	132.03	27		147.75
8	98.52	122.08	18	130.90	133.20	28		153.88
9	100.52	122.48	19	131.80	133.50	29		154.83
10	108.18	122.62	20	138.63	136.57	30		189.27
						31		189.28

a. George Towett of Marietta, Georgia finished in first place for the men and Lauren Wald of Gainesville, Florida finished in first place for the women. Compare the first-place finish times for men and women. If the 53 men and women runners had competed as one group, in what place would Lauren have finished?

b. What is the median time for men and women runners? Compare men and women runners based on their median times.

c. Provide a five-number summary for both the men and the women.

d. Are there outliers in either group?

e. Show the box plots for the two groups. Did men or women have the most variation in finish times? Explain.

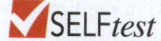

51. Annual sales, in millions of dollars, for 21 pharmaceutical companies follow.

8,408	1,374	1,872	8,879	2,459	11,413
608	14,138	6,452	1,850	2,818	1,356
10,498	7,478	4,019	4,341	739	2,127
3,653	5,794	8,305			

PharmacySales

a. Provide a five-number summary.

b. Compute the lower and upper limits.

c. Do the data contain any outliers?

d. Johnson & Johnson's sales are the largest on the list at $14,138 million. Suppose a data entry error (a transposition) had been made and the sales had been entered as $41,138 million. Would the method of detecting outliers in part (c) identify this problem and allow for correction of the data entry error?

e. Show a box plot.

52. *Consumer Reports* provided overall customer satisfaction scores for AT&T, Sprint, T-Mobile, and Verizon cell phone services in major metropolitan areas throughout the United States. The rating for each service reflects the overall customer satisfaction considering a variety of factors such as cost, connectivity problems, dropped calls, static interference, and customer support. A satisfaction scale from 0 to 100 was used with 0 indicating completely dissatisfied and 100 indicating completely satisfied. The ratings for the four cell phone services in 20 metropolitan areas are as shown.

CellService

Metropolitan Area	AT&T	Sprint	T-Mobile	Verizon
Atlanta	70	66	71	79
Boston	69	64	74	76
Chicago	71	65	70	77
Dallas	75	65	74	78
Denver	71	67	73	77
Detroit	73	65	77	79
Jacksonville	73	64	75	81
Las Vegas	72	68	74	81
Los Angeles	66	65	68	78
Miami	68	69	73	80
Minneapolis	68	66	75	77
Philadelphia	72	66	71	78
Phoenix	68	66	76	81
San Antonio	75	65	75	80
San Diego	69	68	72	79
San Francisco	66	69	73	75
Seattle	68	67	74	77
St. Louis	74	66	74	79
Tampa	73	63	73	79
Washington	72	68	71	76

a.   Consider T-Mobile first. What is the median rating?
b.   Develop a five-number summary for the T-Mobile service.
c.   Are there outliers for T-Mobile? Explain.
d.   Repeat parts (b) and (c) for the other three cell phone services.
e.   Show the box plots for the four cell phone services on one graph. Discuss what a comparison of the box plots tells about the four services. Which service did *Consumer Reports* recommend as being best in terms of overall customer satisfaction?

AdmiredCompanies

53.   *Fortune* magazine's list of the world's most admired companies for 2014 is provided in the data contained in the DATAfile named *AdmiredCompanies* (*Fortune*, March 17, 2014). The data in the column labelled Return shows the one-year total return (%) for the top-ranked 50 companies. For the same time period the S&P average return was 18.4%.
a.   Compute the median return for the top-ranked 50 companies.
b.   What percentage of the top-ranked 50 companies had a one-year return greater than the S&P average return?
c.   Develop the five-number summary for the data.
d.   Are there any outliers?
e.   Develop a box plot for the one-year total return.

BorderCrossings

54.   The Bureau of Transportation Statistics keeps track of all border crossings through ports of entry along the U.S.–Canadian and U.S.–Mexican borders. The data contained in the DATAfile named *BorderCrossings* show the most recently published figures for the number of personal vehicle crossings (rounded to the nearest 1000) at the 50 busiest ports of entry during the month of August (U.S. Department of Transportation website, February 28, 2013).
a.   What are the mean and median number of crossings for these ports of entry?
b.   What are the first and third quartiles?
c.   Provide a five-number summary.
d.   Do the data contain any outliers? Show a box plot.

Measures of Association Between Two Variables

Thus far we have examined numerical methods used to summarize the data for *one variable at a time*. Often a manager or decision maker is interested in the *relationship between two variables*. In this section we present covariance and correlation as descriptive measures of the relationship between two variables.

We begin by reconsidering the application concerning a stereo and sound equipment store in San Francisco as presented in Section 2.4. The store's manager wants to determine the relationship between the number of weekend television commercials shown and the sales at the store during the following week. Sample data with sales expressed in hundreds of dollars are provided in Table 3.6. It shows 10 observations ($n = 10$), one for each week. The scatter diagram in Figure 3.15 shows a positive relationship, with higher sales (y) associated with a greater number of commercials (x). In fact, the scatter diagram suggests that a straight line could be used as an approximation of the relationship. In the following discussion, we introduce **covariance** as a descriptive measure of the linear association between two variables.

TABLE 3.6   SAMPLE DATA FOR THE STEREO AND SOUND EQUIPMENT STORE

DATA *file*

Stereo

Week	Number of Commercials x	Sales ($100s) y
1	2	50
2	5	57
3	1	41
4	3	54
5	4	54
6	1	38
7	5	63
8	3	48
9	4	59
10	2	46

FIGURE 3.15   SCATTER DIAGRAM FOR THE STEREO AND SOUND EQUIPMENT STORE

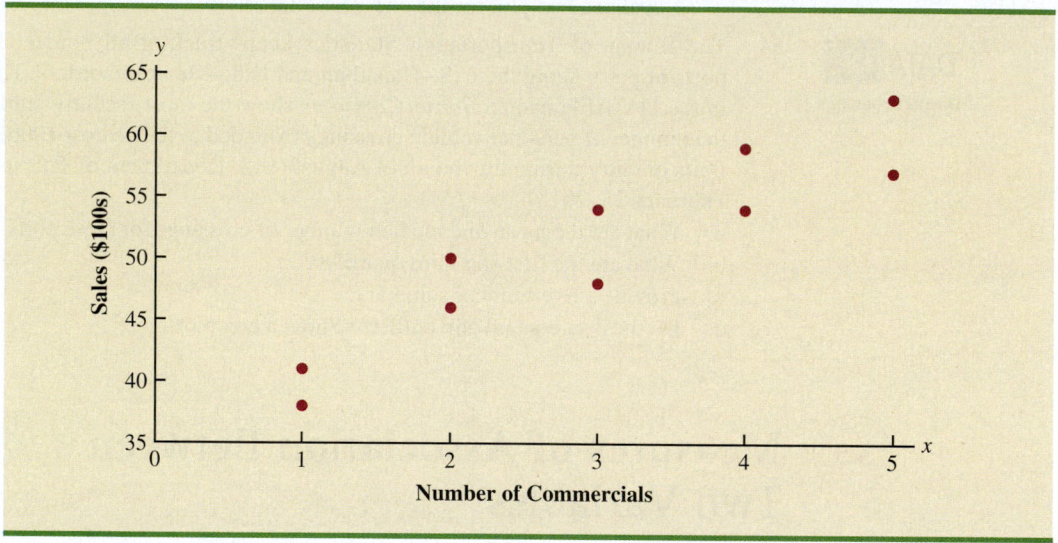

Covariance

For a sample of size n with the observations (x_1, y_1), (x_2, y_2), and so on, the sample covariance is defined as follows:

SAMPLE COVARIANCE

$$s_{xy} = \frac{\sum(x_i - \bar{x})(y_i - \bar{y})}{n - 1} \qquad (3.13)$$

This formula pairs each x_i with a y_i. We then sum the products obtained by multiplying the deviation of each x_i from its sample mean $\bar{x}$ by the deviation of the corresponding y_i from its sample mean $\bar{y}$; this sum is then divided by $n - 1$.

TABLE 3.7 CALCULATIONS FOR THE SAMPLE COVARIANCE

	x_i	y_i	$x_i - \bar{x}$	$y_i - \bar{y}$	$(x_i - \bar{x})(y_i - \bar{y})$
	2	50	−1	−1	1
	5	57	2	6	12
	1	41	−2	−10	20
	3	54	0	3	0
	4	54	1	3	3
	1	38	−2	−13	26
	5	63	2	12	24
	3	48	0	−3	0
	4	59	1	8	8
	2	46	−1	−5	5
Totals	30	510	0	0	99

$$s_{xy} = \frac{\sum(x_i - \bar{x})(y_i - \bar{y})}{n - 1} = \frac{99}{10 - 1} = 11$$

To measure the strength of the linear relationship between the number of commercials x and the sales volume y in the stereo and sound equipment store problem, we use equation (3.13) to compute the sample covariance. The calculations in Table 3.7 show the computation of $\sum(x_i - \bar{x})(y_i - \bar{y})$. Note that $\bar{x} = 30/10 = 3$ and $\bar{y} = 510/10 = 51$. Using equation (3.13), we obtain a sample covariance of

$$s_{xy} = \frac{\sum(x_i - \bar{x})(y_i - \bar{y})}{n - 1} = \frac{99}{9} = 11$$

The formula for computing the covariance of a population of size N is similar to equation (3.13), but we use different notation to indicate that we are working with the entire population.

POPULATION COVARIANCE

$$\sigma_{xy} = \frac{\sum(x_i - \mu_x)(y_i - \mu_y)}{N} \tag{3.14}$$

In equation (3.14) we use the notation μ_x for the population mean of the variable x and μ_y for the population mean of the variable y. The population covariance σ_{xy} is defined for a population of size N.

Interpretation of the Covariance

To aid in the interpretation of the sample covariance, consider Figure 3.16. It is the same as the scatter diagram of Figure 3.15, with a vertical dashed line at $\bar{x} = 3$ and a horizontal dashed line at $\bar{y} = 51$. The lines divide the graph into four quadrants. Points in quadrant I correspond to x_i greater than $\bar{x}$ and y_i greater than $\bar{y}$, points in quadrant II correspond to x_i

FIGURE 3.16   PARTITIONED SCATTER DIAGRAM FOR THE STEREO AND SOUND
EQUIPMENT STORE

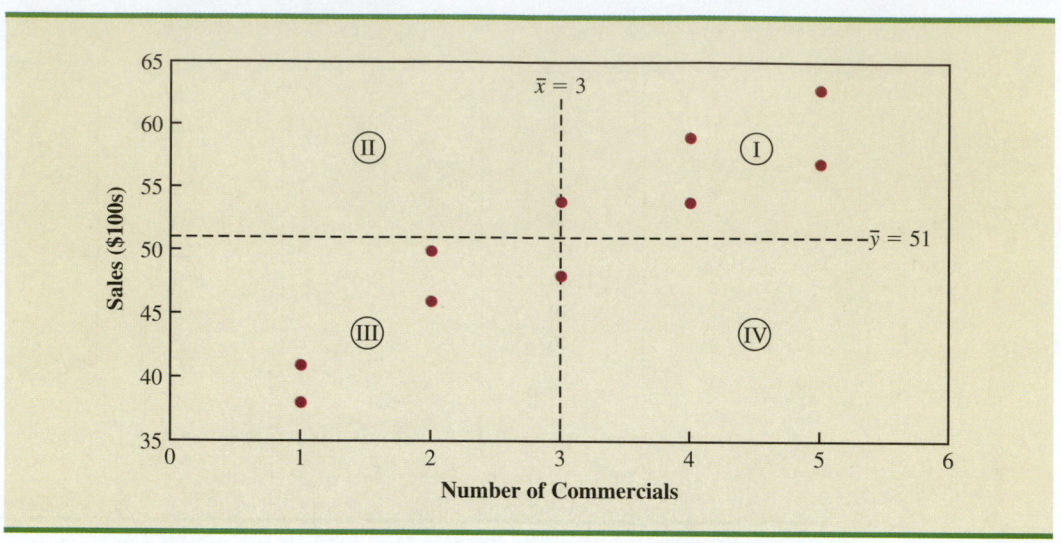

The covariance is a measure of the linear association between two variables.

less than $\bar{x}$ and y_i greater than $\bar{y}$, and so on. Thus, the value of $(x_i - \bar{x})(y_i - \bar{y})$ must be positive for points in quadrant I, negative for points in quadrant II, positive for points in quadrant III, and negative for points in quadrant IV.

If the value of s_{xy} is positive, the points with the greatest influence on s_{xy} must be in quadrants I and III. Hence, a positive value for s_{xy} indicates a positive linear association between x and y; that is, as the value of x increases, the value of y increases. If the value of s_{xy} is negative, however, the points with the greatest influence on s_{xy} are in quadrants II and IV. Hence, a negative value for s_{xy} indicates a negative linear association between x and y; that is, as the value of x increases, the value of y decreases. Finally, if the points are evenly distributed across all four quadrants, the value of s_{xy} will be close to zero, indicating no linear association between x and y. Figure 3.17 shows the values of s_{xy} that can be expected with three different types of scatter diagrams.

Referring again to Figure 3.16, we see that the scatter diagram for the stereo and sound equipment store follows the pattern in the top panel of Figure 3.17. As we should expect, the value of the sample covariance indicates a positive linear relationship with $s_{xy} = 11$.

From the preceding discussion, it might appear that a large positive value for the covariance indicates a strong positive linear relationship and that a large negative value indicates a strong negative linear relationship. However, one problem with using covariance as a measure of the strength of the linear relationship is that the value of the covariance depends on the units of measurement for x and y. For example, suppose we are interested in the relationship between height x and weight y for individuals. Clearly the strength of the relationship should be the same whether we measure height in feet or inches. Measuring the height in inches, however, gives us much larger numerical values for $(x_i - \bar{x})$ than when we measure height in feet. Thus, with height measured in inches, we would obtain a larger value for the numerator $\Sigma(x_i - \bar{x})(y_i - \bar{y})$ in equation (3.13)—and hence a larger covariance—when in fact the relationship does not change. A measure of the relationship between two variables that is not affected by the units of measurement for x and y is the **correlation coefficient**.

FIGURE 3.17   INTERPRETATION OF SAMPLE COVARIANCE

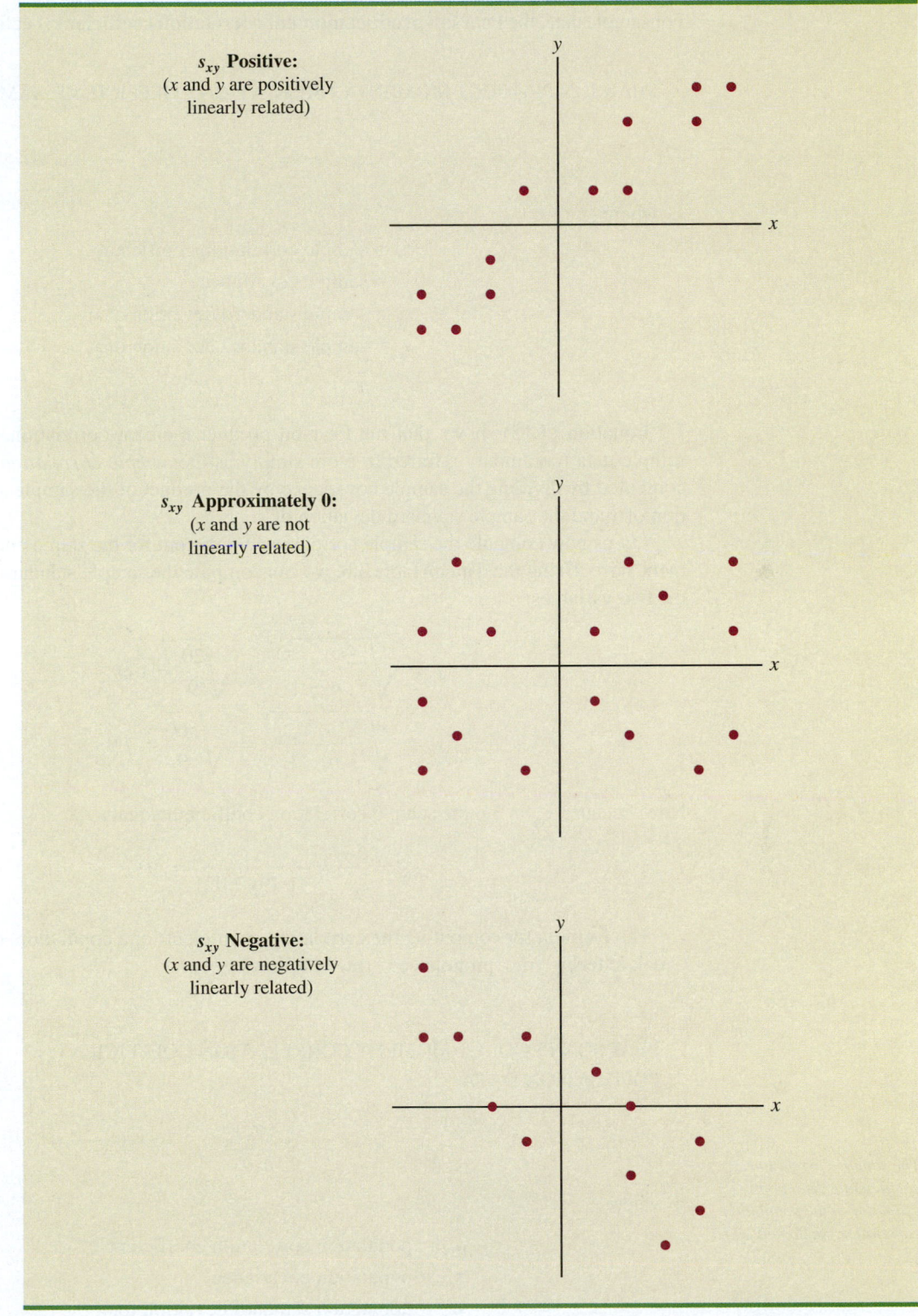

Correlation Coefficient

For sample data, the **Pearson product moment correlation coefficient** is defined as follows.

PEARSON PRODUCT MOMENT CORRELATION COEFFICIENT: SAMPLE DATA

$$r_{xy} = \frac{s_{xy}}{s_x s_y}$$ (3.15)

where

r_{xy} = sample correlation coefficient
s_{xy} = sample covariance
s_x = sample standard deviation of x
s_y = sample standard deviation of y

Equation (3.15) shows that the Pearson product moment correlation coefficient for sample data (commonly referred to more simply as the *sample correlation coefficient*) is computed by dividing the sample covariance by the product of the sample standard deviation of x and the sample standard deviation of y.

Let us now compute the sample correlation coefficient for the stereo and sound equipment store. Using the data in Table 3.6, we can compute the sample standard deviations for the two variables:

$$s_x = \sqrt{\frac{\sum(x_i - \bar{x})^2}{n - 1}} = \sqrt{\frac{20}{9}} = 1.49$$

$$s_y = \sqrt{\frac{\sum(y_i - \bar{y})^2}{n - 1}} = \sqrt{\frac{566}{9}} = 7.93$$

Now, because $s_{xy} = 11$, the sample correlation coefficient equals

$$r_{xy} = \frac{s_{xy}}{s_x s_y} = \frac{11}{(1.49)(7.93)} = .93$$

The formula for computing the correlation coefficient for a population, denoted by the Greek letter ρ_{xy} (rho, pronounced "row"), follows.

The sample correlation coefficient r_{xy} is a point estimator of the population correlation coefficient ρ_{xy}.

PEARSON PRODUCT MOMENT CORRELATION COEFFICIENT:
POPULATION DATA

$$\rho_{xy} = \frac{\sigma_{xy}}{\sigma_x \sigma_y}$$ (3.16)

where

ρ_{xy} = population correlation coefficient
σ_{xy} = population covariance
σ_x = population standard deviation for x
σ_y = population standard deviation for y

The sample correlation coefficient r_{xy} provides an estimate of the population correlation coefficient ρ_{xy}.

Interpretation of the Correlation Coefficient

First let us consider a simple example that illustrates the concept of a perfect positive linear relationship. The scatter diagram in Figure 3.18 depicts the relationship between x and y based on the following sample data.

x_i	y_i
5	10
10	30
15	50

The straight line drawn through each of the three points shows a perfect linear relationship between x and y. In order to apply equation (3.15) to compute the sample correlation we must first compute s_{xy}, s_x, and s_y. Some of the computations are shown in Table 3.8. Using the results in this table, we find

$$s_{xy} = \frac{\sum(x_i - \bar{x})(y_i - \bar{y})}{n - 1} = \frac{200}{2} = 100$$

$$s_x = \sqrt{\frac{\sum(x_i - \bar{x})^2}{n - 1}} = \sqrt{\frac{50}{2}} = 5$$

$$s_y = \sqrt{\frac{\sum(y_i - \bar{y})^2}{n - 1}} = \sqrt{\frac{800}{2}} = 20$$

$$r_{xy} = \frac{s_{xy}}{s_x s_y} = \frac{100}{5(20)} = 1$$

Thus, we see that the value of the sample correlation coefficient is 1.

FIGURE 3.18   SCATTER DIAGRAM DEPICTING A PERFECT POSITIVE LINEAR RELATIONSHIP

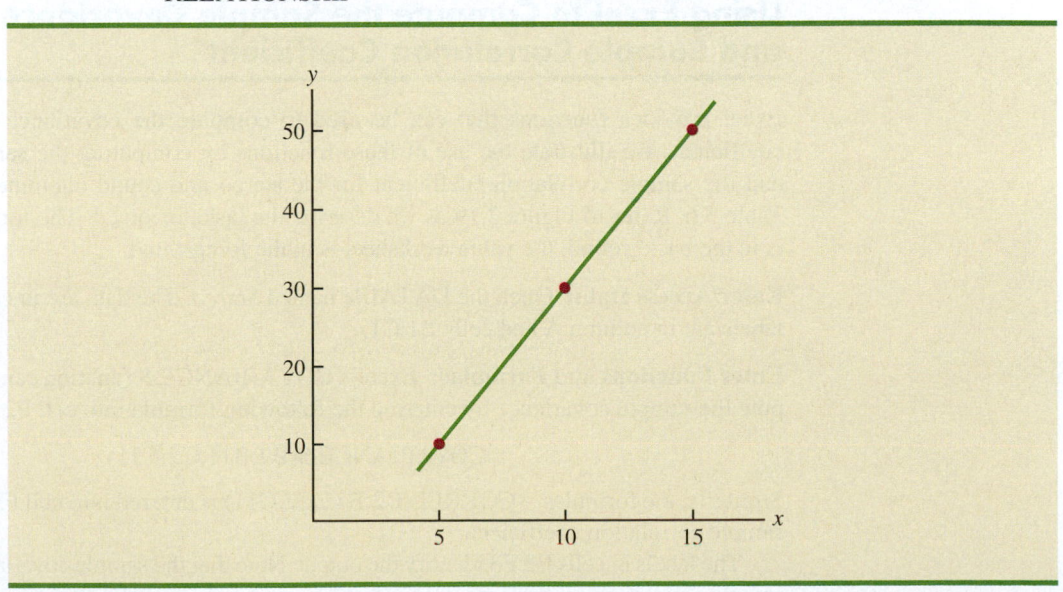

TABLE 3.8   COMPUTATIONS USED IN CALCULATING THE SAMPLE
CORRELATION COEFFICIENT

x_i	y_i	$x_i - \bar{x}$	$(x_i - \bar{x})^2$	$y_i - \bar{y}$	$(y_i - \bar{y})^2$	$(x_i - \bar{x})(y_i - \bar{y})$
5	10	−5	25	−20	400	100
10	30	0	0	0	0	0
15	50	5	25	20	400	100
Totals 30	90	0	50	0	800	200

$$\bar{x} = 10 \quad \bar{y} = 30$$

The correlation coefficient ranges from −1 to +1. Values close to −1 or +1 indicate a strong linear relationship. The closer the correlation is to zero, the weaker the relationship.

In general, it can be shown that if all the points in a data set fall on a positively sloped straight line, the value of the sample correlation coefficient is +1; that is, a sample correlation coefficient of +1 corresponds to a perfect positive linear relationship between x and y. Moreover, if the points in the data set fall on a straight line having negative slope, the value of the sample correlation coefficient is −1; that is, a sample correlation coefficient of −1 corresponds to a perfect negative linear relationship between x and y.

Let us now suppose that a certain data set indicates a positive linear relationship between x and y but that the relationship is not perfect. The value of r_{xy} will be less than 1, indicating that the points in the scatter diagram are not all on a straight line. As the points deviate more and more from a perfect positive linear relationship, the value of r_{xy} becomes smaller and smaller. A value of r_{xy} equal to zero indicates no linear relationship between x and y, and values of r_{xy} near zero indicate a weak linear relationship.

For the data involving the stereo and sound equipment store, $r_{xy} = .93$. Therefore, we conclude that a strong positive linear relationship occurs between the number of commercials and sales. More specifically, an increase in the number of commercials is associated with an increase in sales.

In closing, we note that correlation provides a measure of linear association and not necessarily causation. A high correlation between two variables does not mean that changes in one variable will cause changes in the other variable. For example, we may find that the quality rating and the typical meal price of restaurants are positively correlated. However, simply increasing the meal price at a restaurant will not cause the quality rating to increase.

Using Excel to Compute the Sample Covariance and Sample Correlation Coefficient

Excel provides functions that can be used to compute the covariance and correlation coefficient. We illustrate the use of these functions by computing the sample covariance and the sample correlation coefficient for the stereo and sound equipment store data in Table 3.6. Refer to Figure 3.19 as we describe the tasks involved. The formula worksheet is in the background; the value worksheet is in the foreground.

Enter/Access Data: Open the DATAfile named *Stereo*. The data are in cells B2:C11 and labels are in column A and cells B1:C1.

Enter Functions and Formulas: Excel's COVARIANCE.S function can be used to compute the sample covariance by entering the following formula into cell F2:

$$=COVARIANCE.S(B2:B11,C2:C11)$$

Similarly, the formulas =CORREL(B2:B11,C2:C11) is entered into cell F3 to compute the sample correlation coefficient.

The labels in cells E2:E3 identify the output. Note that the sample covariance (11) and the sample correlation coefficient (.93) are the same as we computed earlier using the definitions.

FIGURE 3.19   USING EXCEL TO COMPUTE THE COVARIANCE AND CORRELATION
COEFFICIENT

	A	B	C	D	E	F	G
1	Week	No. of Commercials	Sales ($100s)				
2	1	2	50		Sample Covariance	=COVARIANCE.S(B2:B11,C2:C11)	
3	2	5	57		Sample Correlation	=CORREL(B2:B11,C2:C11)	
4	3	1	41				
5	4	3	54				
6	5	4	54				
7	6	1	38				
8	7	5	63				
9	8	3	48				
10	9	4	59				
11	10	2	46				
12							

	A	B	C	D	E	F	G
1	Week	No. of Commercials	Sales ($100s)				
2	1	2	50		Sample Covariance		11
3	2	5	57		Sample Correlation		0.93
4	3	1	41				
5	4	3	54				
6	5	4	54				
7	6	1	38				
8	7	5	63				
9	8	3	48				
10	9	4	59				
11	10	2	46				
12							

NOTES AND COMMENTS

1. Because the correlation coefficient measures only the strength of the linear relationship between two quantitative variables, it is possible for the correlation coefficient to be near zero, suggesting no linear relationship, when the relationship between the two variables is nonlinear. For example, the following scatter diagram shows the relationship between the amount spent by a small retail store for environmental control (heating and cooling) and the daily high outside temperature over 100 days.

   The sample correlation coefficient for these data is $r_{xy} = -.007$ and indicates there is no linear relationship between the two variables. However, the scatter diagram provides strong visual evidence of a nonlinear relationship. That is, we can see that as the daily high outside temperature increases, the money spent on environmental control first decreases as less heating is required and then increases as greater cooling is required.

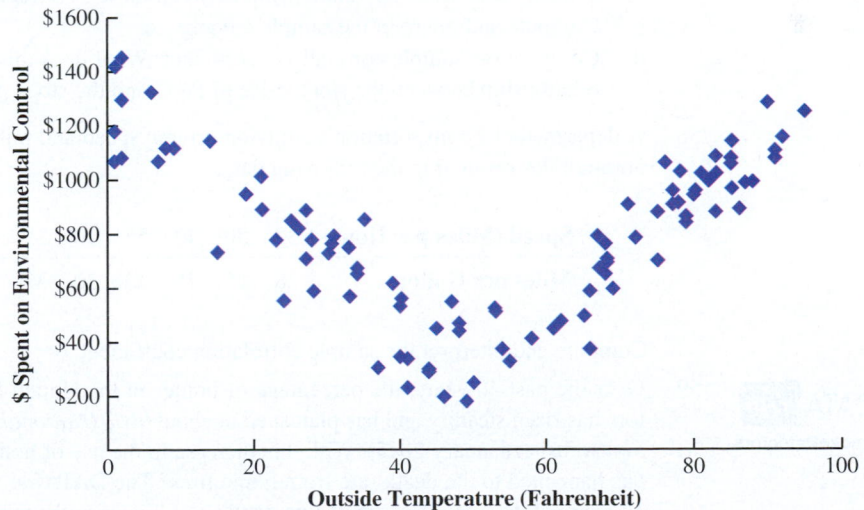

2. While the correlation coefficient is useful in assessing the relationship between two quantitative variables, other measures—such as the Spearman rank-correlation coefficient—can be used to assess a relationship between two variables when at least one of the variables is nominal or ordinal.

Exercises

Methods

55. Five observations taken for two variables follow.

x_i	4	6	11	3	16
y_i	50	50	40	60	30

    a. Develop a scatter diagram with x on the horizontal axis.
    b. What does the scatter diagram developed in part (a) indicate about the relationship between the two variables?
    c. Compute and interpret the sample covariance.
    d. Compute and interpret the sample correlation coefficient.

56. Five observations taken for two variables follow.

x_i	6	11	15	21	27
y_i	6	9	6	17	12

    a. Develop a scatter diagram for these data.
    b. What does the scatter diagram indicate about a relationship between x and y?
    c. Compute and interpret the sample covariance.
    d. Compute and interpret the sample correlation coefficient.

Applications

TwoStocks

57. The DATAfile *TwoStocks* contains adjusted monthly stock prices for technology company Apple, Inc. and consumer-goods company Procter and Gamble (P&G) for the years 2010–2014.
    a. Develop a scatter diagram with P&G's stock price on the vertical axis and the stock price of Apple on the horizontal axis.
    b. What appears to be the relationship between these two stock prices?
    c. Compute and interpret the sample covariance.
    d. Compute the sample correlation coefficient. What does this value indicate about the relationship between the stock price of P&G and the stock price of Apple, Inc.?

58. A department of transportation's study on driving speed and miles per gallon for midsize automobiles resulted in the following data:

Speed (Miles per Hour)	30	50	40	55	30	25	60	25	50	55
Miles per Gallon	28	25	25	23	30	32	21	35	26	25

    Compute and interpret the sample correlation coefficient.

SmokeDetectors

59. Over the past 40 years, the percentage of homes in the United States with smoke detectors has risen steadily and has plateaued at about 96% (*National Fire Protection Association* website, January 2015). With this increase in the use of home smoke detectors, what has happened to the death rate from home fires? The DATAfile *SmokeDetectors* contains 17 years of data on the estimated percentage of homes with smoke detectors and the estimated home fire deaths per million of population.
    a. Do you expect a positive or negative relationship between smoke detector use and deaths from home fires? Why or why not?
    b. Compute and report the correlation coefficient. Is there a positive or negative correlation between smoke detector use and deaths from home fires? Comment.

c. Show a scatter plot of the death rate per million of population and the percentage of homes with smoke detectors.

Russell

60. The Russell 1000 is a stock market index consisting of the largest U.S. companies. The Dow Jones Industrial Average is based on 30 large companies. The DATAfile *Russell* gives the annual percentage returns for each of these stock indexes for the years 1988 to 2012 (1Stock1 website).
    a. Plot these percentage returns using a scatter plot.
    b. Compute the sample mean and standard deviation for each index.
    c. Compute the sample correlation.
    d. Discuss similarities and differences in these two indexes.

BestPrivateColleges

61. A random sample of 30 colleges from Kiplinger's list of the best values in private college provided the data shown in the DATAfile named *BestPrivateColleges* (Kiplinger, October 2013). The variable named Admit Rate (%) shows the percentage of students that applied to the college and were admitted, and the variable named 4-yr Grad. Rate (%) shows the percentage of students that were admitted and graduated in four years.
    a. Develop a scatter diagram with Admit Rate (%) as the independent variable. What does the scatter diagram indicate about the relationship between the two variables?
    b. Compute the sample correlation coefficient. What does the value of the sample correlation coefficient indicate about the relationship between the Admit Rate (%) and the 4-yr Grad. Rate (%)?

3.6   Data Dashboards: Adding Numerical Measures to Improve Effectiveness

In Section 2.5 we provided an introduction to data visualization, a term used to describe the use of graphical displays to summarize and present information about a data set. The goal of data visualization is to communicate key information about the data as effectively and clearly as possible. One of the most widely used data visualization tools is a data dashboard, a set of visual displays that organizes and presents information that is used to monitor the performance of a company or organization in a manner that is easy to read, understand, and interpret. In this section we extend the discussion of data dashboards to show how the addition of numerical measures can improve the overall effectiveness of the display.

The addition of numerical measures, such as the mean and standard deviation of key performance indicators (KPIs), to a data dashboard is critical because numerical measures often provide benchmarks or goals by which KPIs are evaluated. In addition, graphical displays that include numerical measures as components of the display are also frequently included in data dashboards. We must keep in mind that the purpose of a data dashboard is to provide information on the KPIs in a manner that is easy to read, understand, and interpret. Adding numerical measures and graphs that utilize numerical measures can help us accomplish these objectives.

To illustrate the use of numerical measures in a data dashboard, recall the Grogan Oil Company application that we used in Section 2.5 to introduce the concept of a data dashboard. Grogan Oil has offices located in three cities in Texas: Austin (its headquarters), Houston, and Dallas. Grogan's Information Technology (IT) call center, located in the Austin office, handles calls regarding computer-related problems (software, Internet, and e-mail) from employees in the three offices. Figure 3.20 shows the data dashboard that Grogan developed to monitor the performance of the call center. The key components of this dashboard are as follows:

- The stacked bar chart in the upper left corner of the dashboard shows the call volume for each type of problem (software, Internet, or e-mail) over time.

FIGURE 3.20   INITIAL GROGAN OIL INFORMATION TECHNOLOGY CALL CENTER DATA
DASHBOARD

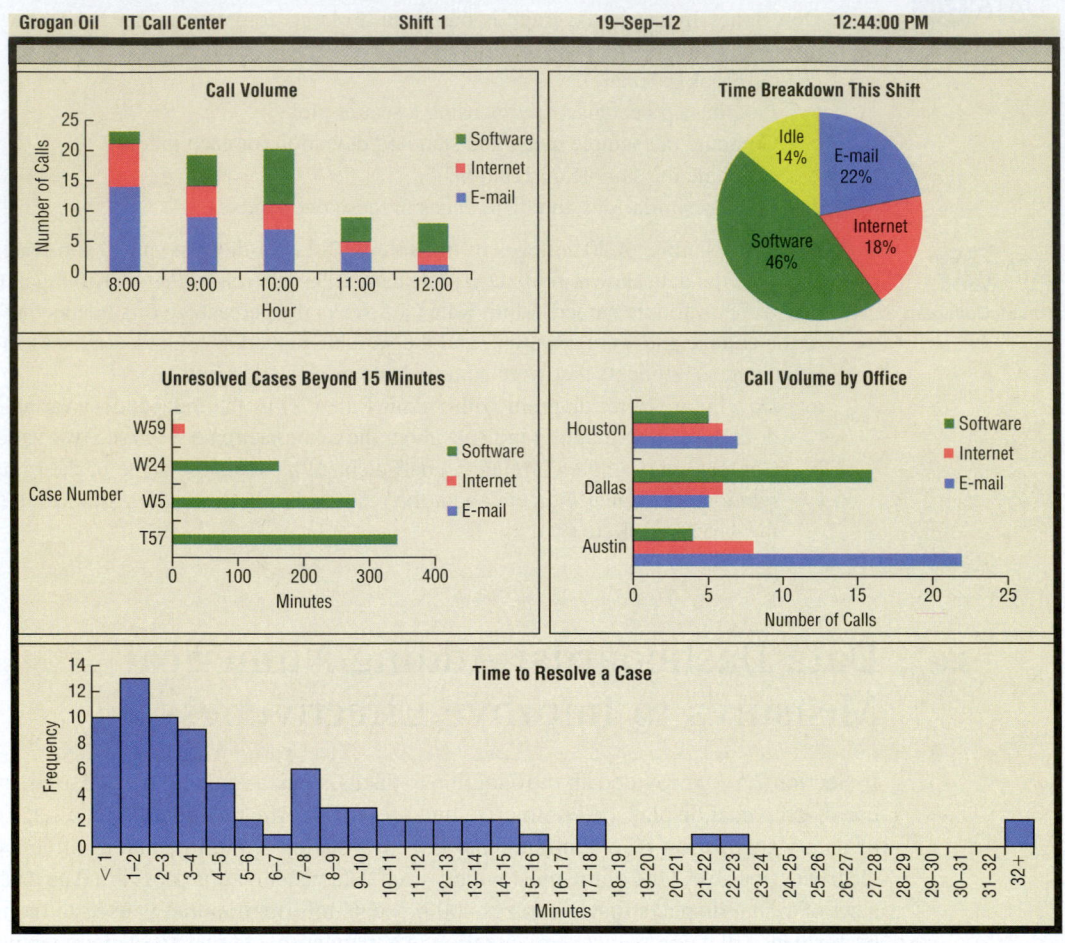

- The pie chart in the upper right corner of the dashboard shows the percentage of time that call center employees spent on each type of problem or not working on a call (idle).
- For each unresolved case that extended beyond 15 minutes, the bar chart shown in the middle left portion of the dashboard shows the length of time that each of these cases has been unresolved.
- The bar chart in the middle right portion of the dashboard shows the call volume by office (Houston, Dallas, Austin) for each type of problem.
- The histogram at the bottom of the dashboard shows the distribution of the time to resolve a case for all resolved cases for the current shift.

In order to gain additional insight into the performance of the call center, Grogan's IT manager has decided to expand the current dashboard by adding box plots for the time required to resolve calls received for each type of problem (e-mail, Internet, and software). In addition, a graph showing the time to resolve individual cases has been added in the lower left portion of the dashboard. Finally, the IT manager added a display of summary statistics for each type of problem and summary statistics for each of the first few hours of the shift. The updated dashboard is shown in Figure 3.21.

FIGURE 3.21   UPDATED GROGAN OIL INFORMATION TECHNOLOGY CALL CENTER DATA DASHBOARD

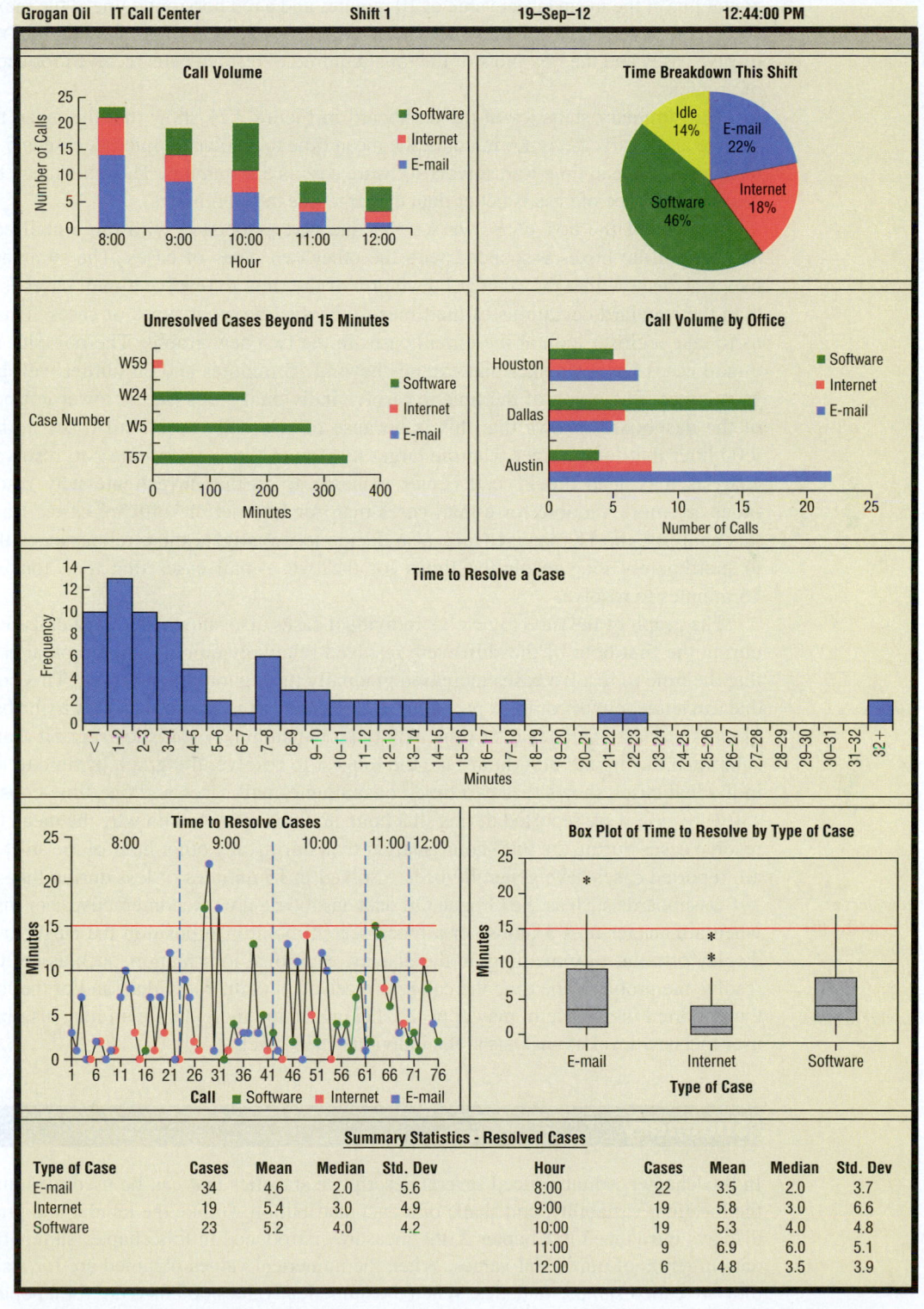

The IT call center has set a target performance level or benchmark of 10 minutes for the mean time to resolve a case. Furthermore, the center has decided it is undesirable for the time to resolve a case to exceed 15 minutes. To reflect these benchmarks, a black horizontal line at the mean target value of 10 minutes and a red horizontal line at the maximum acceptable level of 15 minutes have been added to both the graph showing the time to resolve cases and the box plots of the time required to resolve calls received for each type of problem.

The summary statistics in the dashboard in Figure 3.21 show that the mean time to resolve an e-mail case is 4.6 minutes, the mean time to resolve an Internet case is 5.4 minutes, and the mean time to resolve a software case is 5.2 minutes. Thus, the mean time to resolve each type of case is better than the target mean (10 minutes).

Reviewing the box plots, we see that the box associated with the e-mail cases is *larger* than the boxes associated with the other two types of cases. The summary statistics also show that the standard deviation of the time to resolve e-mail cases is larger than the standard deviations of the times to resolve the other types of cases. This leads us to take a closer look at the e-mail cases in the two new graphs. The box plot for the e-mail cases has a whisker that extends beyond 15 minutes and an outlier well beyond 15 minutes. The graph of the time to resolve individual cases (in the lower left position of the dashboard) shows that this is because of two calls on e-mail cases during the 9:00 hour that took longer than the target maximum time (15 minutes) to resolve. This analysis may lead the IT call center manager to further investigate why resolution times are more variable for e-mail cases than for Internet or software cases. Based on this analysis, the IT manager may also decide to investigate the circumstances that led to inordinately long resolution times for the two e-mail cases that took longer than 15 minutes to resolve.

The graph of the time to resolve individual cases also shows that most calls received during the first hour of the shift were resolved relatively quickly; the graph also shows that the time to resolve cases increased gradually throughout the morning. This could be due to a tendency for complex problems to arise later in the shift or possibly to the backlog of calls that accumulates over time. Although the summary statistics suggest that cases submitted during the 9:00 hour take the longest to resolve, the graph of time to resolve individual cases shows that two time-consuming e-mail cases and one time-consuming software case were reported during that hour, and this may explain why the mean time to resolve cases during the 9:00 hour is larger than during any other hour of the shift. Overall, reported cases have generally been resolved in 15 minutes or less during this shift.

Drilling down *refers to functionality in interactive data dashboards that allows the user to access information and analyses at an increasingly detailed level.*

Dashboards such as the Grogan Oil data dashboard are often interactive. For instance, when a manager uses a mouse or a touch screen monitor to position the cursor over the display or point to something on the display, additional information, such as the time to resolve the problem, the time the call was received, and the individual and/or the location that reported the problem, may appear. Clicking on the individual item may also take the user to a new level of analysis at the individual case level.

Summary

In this chapter we introduced several descriptive statistics that can be used to summarize the location, variability, and shape of a data distribution. Unlike the tabular and graphical displays introduced in Chapter 2, the measures introduced in this chapter summarize the data in terms of numerical values. When the numerical values obtained are for a sample, they are called sample statistics. When the numerical values obtained are for a population, they are called population parameters. Some of the notation used for sample statistics and population parameters follow.

	Sample Statistic	Population Parameter
Mean	$\bar{x}$	μ
Variance	s^2	σ^2
Standard deviation	s	σ
Covariance	s_{xy}	σ_{xy}
Correlation	r_{xy}	ρ_{xy}

In statistical inference, a sample statistic is referred to as a point estimator of the population parameter.

As measures of location, we defined the mean, median, mode, weighted mean, geometric mean, percentiles, and quartiles. Next, we presented the range, interquartile range, variance, standard deviation, and coefficient of variation as measures of variability or dispersion. Our primary measure of the shape of a data distribution was the skewness. Negative values of skewness indicate a data distribution skewed to the left, and positive values of skewness indicate a data distribution skewed to the right. We then described how the mean and standard deviation could be used, applying Chebyshev's theorem and the empirical rule, to provide more information about the distribution of data and to identify outliers.

In Section 3.4 we showed how to develop a five-number summary and a box plot to provide simultaneous information about the location, variability, and shape of the distribution. In Section 3.5 we introduced covariance and the correlation coefficient as measures of association between two variables. In the final section, we showed how adding numerical measures can improve the effectiveness of data dashboards.

The descriptive statistics we discussed can be developed using statistical software packages and spreadsheets.

Glossary

Box plot A graphical summary of data based on a five-number summary.

Chebyshev's theorem A theorem that can be used to make statements about the proportion of data values that must be within a specified number of standard deviations of the mean.

Coefficient of variation A measure of relative variability computed by dividing the standard deviation by the mean and multiplying by 100.

Correlation coefficient A measure of linear association between two variables that takes on values between -1 and $+1$. Values near $+1$ indicate a strong positive linear relationship; values near -1 indicate a strong negative linear relationship; and values near zero indicate the lack of a linear relationship.

Covariance A measure of linear association between two variables. Positive values indicate a positive relationship; negative values indicate a negative relationship.

Empirical rule A rule that can be used to compute the percentage of data values that must be within one, two, and three standard deviations of the mean for data that exhibit a bell-shaped distribution.

Five-number summary A technique that uses five numbers to summarize the data: smallest value, first quartile, median, third quartile, and largest value.

Geometric mean A measure of location that is calculated by finding the nth root of the product of n values.

Interquartile range (IQR) A measure of variability, defined as the difference between the third and first quartiles.

Mean A measure of central location computed by summing the data values and dividing by the number of observations.

Median A measure of central location provided by the value in the middle when the data are arranged in ascending order.

Mode A measure of location, defined as the value that occurs with greatest frequency.

Outlier An unusually small or unusually large data value.

Pearson product moment correlation coefficient A measure of the linear relationship between two variables.

Percentile A value that provides information about how the data are spread over the interval from the smallest to the largest value.

Point estimator A sample statistic, such as $\bar{x}$, s^2, and s, used to estimate the corresponding population parameter.

Population parameter A numerical value used as a summary measure for a population (e.g., the population mean, μ, the population variance, σ^2, and the population standard deviation, σ).

pth percentile For a data set containing n observations, the pth percentile divides the data into two parts: Approximately $p\%$ of the observation are less than the pth percentile and approximately $(100 - p)\%$ of the observations are greater than the pth percentile.

Quartiles The 25th, 50th, and 75th percentiles, referred to as the first quartile, the second quartile (median), and third quartile, respectively. The quartiles can be used to divide a data set into four parts, with each part containing approximately 25% of the data.

Range A measure of variability, defined to be the largest value minus the smallest value.

Sample statistic A numerical value used as a summary measure for a sample (e.g., the sample mean, $\bar{x}$, the sample variance, s^2, and the sample standard deviation, s).

Skewness A measure of the shape of a data distribution. Data skewed to the left result in negative skewness; a symmetric data distribution results in zero skewness; and data skewed to the right result in positive skewness.

Standard deviation A measure of variability computed by taking the positive square root of the variance.

Variance A measure of variability based on the squared deviations of the data values about the mean.

Weighted mean The mean obtained by assigning each observation a weight that reflects its importance.

z-score A value computed by dividing the deviation about the mean $(x_i - \bar{x})$ by the standard deviation s. A z-score is referred to as a standardized value and denotes the number of standard deviations x_i is from the mean.

Key Formulas

Sample Mean

$$\bar{x} = \frac{\sum x_i}{n} \tag{3.1}$$

Population Mean

$$\mu = \frac{\sum x_i}{N} \tag{3.2}$$

Weighted Mean

$$\bar{x} = \frac{\sum w_i x_i}{\sum w_i} \tag{3.3}$$

Geometric Mean

$$\bar{x}_g = \sqrt[n]{(x_1)(x_2)\cdots(x_n)} = [(x_1)(x_2)\cdots(x_n)]^{1/n} \tag{3.4}$$

Location of the *p*th Percentile

$$L_p = \frac{p}{100}(n + 1)$$

(3.5)

Interquartile Range

$$\text{IQR} = Q_3 - Q_1$$

(3.6)

Population Variance

$$\sigma^2 = \frac{\sum(x_i - \mu)^2}{N}$$

(3.7)

Sample Variance

$$s^2 = \frac{\sum(x_i - \bar{x})^2}{n - 1}$$

(3.8)

Standard Deviation

$$\text{Sample standard deviation} = s = \sqrt{s^2}$$

(3.9)

$$\text{Population standard deviation} = \sigma = \sqrt{\sigma^2}$$

(3.10)

Coefficient of Variation

$$\left(\frac{\text{Standard deviation}}{\text{Mean}} \times 100\right)\%$$

(3.11)

z-Score

$$z_i = \frac{x_i - \bar{x}}{s}$$

(3.12)

Sample Covariance

$$s_{xy} = \frac{\sum(x_i - \bar{x})(y_i - \bar{y})}{n - 1}$$

(3.13)

Population Covariance

$$\sigma_{xy} = \frac{\sum(x_i - \mu_x)(y_i - \mu_y)}{N}$$

(3.14)

Pearson Product Moment Correlation Coefficient: Sample Data

$$r_{xy} = \frac{s_{xy}}{s_x s_y}$$

(3.15)

Pearson Product Moment Correlation Coefficient: Population Data

$$\rho_{xy} = \frac{\sigma_{xy}}{\sigma_x \sigma_y}$$

(3.16)

Supplementary Exercises

62. The average number of times Americans dine out in a week fell from 4.0 in 2008 to 3.8 in 2012 (Zagat.com, April 1, 2012). The number of times a sample of 20 families dined out last week provides the following data.

$$\begin{array}{cccccccccc}
6 & 1 & 5 & 3 & 7 & 3 & 0 & 3 & 1 & 3 \\
4 & 1 & 2 & 4 & 1 & 0 & 5 & 6 & 3 & 1
\end{array}$$

   a. Compute the mean and median.
   b. Compute the first and third quartiles.
   c. Compute the range and interquartile range.
   d. Compute the variance and standard deviation.
   e. The skewness measure for these data is 0.34. Comment on the shape of this distribution. Is it the shape you would expect? Why or why not?
   f. Do the data contain outliers?

Coaches

63. *USA Today* reports that NCAA colleges and universities are paying higher salaries to a newly recruited football coach compared to what they paid their previous football coach. (*USA Today*, February 12, 2013). The annual base salaries for the previous head football coach and the new head football coach at 23 schools are given in the DATAfile *Coaches*.
   a. Determine the median annual salary for a previous head football coach and a new head football coach.
   b. Compute the range for salaries for both previous and new head football coaches.
   c. Compute the standard deviation for salaries for both previous and new head football coaches.
   d. Based on your answers to (a) to (c), comment on any differences between the annual base salary a school pays a new head football coach compared to what it paid its previous head football coach.

64. The average waiting time for a patient at an El Paso physician's office is just over 29 minutes, well above the national average of 21 minutes. In fact, El Paso has the longest physician's office waiting times in the United States (*El Paso Times,* January 8, 2012). In order to address the issue of long patient wait times, some physician's offices are using wait tracking systems to notify patients of expected wait times. Patients can adjust their arrival times based on this information and spend less time in waiting rooms. The following data show wait times (minutes) for a sample of patients at offices that do not have an office tracking system and wait times for a sample of patients at offices with an office tracking system.

WaitTracking

Without Wait Tracking System	With Wait Tracking System
24	31
67	11
17	14
20	18
31	12
44	37
12	9
23	13
16	12
37	15

a. What are the mean and median patient wait times for offices with a wait tracking system? What are the mean and median patient wait times for offices without a wait tracking system?
b. What are the variance and standard deviation of patient wait times for offices with a wait tracking system? What are the variance and standard deviation of patient wait times for visits to offices without a wait tracking system?
c. Do offices with a wait tracking system have shorter patient wait times than offices without a wait tracking system? Explain.
d. Considering only offices without a wait tracking system, what is the z-score for the tenth patient in the sample?
e. Considering only offices with a wait tracking system, what is the z-score for the sixth patient in the sample? How does this z-score compare with the z-score you calculated for part (d)?
f. Based on z-scores, do the data for offices without a wait tracking system contain any outliers? Based on z-scores, do the data for offices with a wait tracking system contain any outliers?

Sleep

65. U.S. companies lose $63.2 billion per year from workers with insomnia. Workers lose an average of 7.8 days of productivity per year due to lack of sleep (*Wall Street Journal*, January 23, 2013). The following data show the number of hours of sleep attained during a recent night for a sample of 20 workers.

6	5	10	5	6	9	9	5	9	5
8	7	8	6	9	8	9	6	10	8

a. What is the mean number of hours of sleep for this sample?
b. What is the variance? Standard deviation?

Smartphone

66. A study of smartphone users shows that 68% of smartphone use occurs at home and a user spends an average of 410 minutes per month using a smartphone to interact with other people (*Harvard Business Review*, January–February 2013). Consider the following data indicating the number of minutes in a month spent interacting with others via a smartphone for a sample of 50 smartphone users.

353	458	404	394	416
437	430	369	448	430
431	469	446	387	445
354	468	422	402	360
444	424	441	357	435
461	407	470	413	351
464	374	417	460	352
445	387	468	368	430
384	367	436	390	464
405	372	401	388	367

a. What is the mean number of minutes spent interacting with others for this sample? How does it compare to the mean reported in the study?
b. What is the standard deviation for this sample?
c. Are there any outliers in this sample?

67. Public transportation and the automobile are two methods an employee can use to get to work each day. Samples of travel times recorded for each method are shown. Times are in minutes.

Transportation

Public Transportation:	28	29	32	37	33	25	29	32	41	34
Automobile:		29	31	33	32	34	30	31	32	35	33

a. Compute the sample mean time to get to work for each method.
b. Compute the sample standard deviation for each method.
c. On the basis of your results from parts (a) and (b), which method of transportation should be preferred? Explain.
d. Develop a box plot for each method. Does a comparison of the box plots support your conclusion in part (c)?

68. In 2007 the *New York Times* reported that the median annual household income in the United States was $55,500 (*New York Times* website, August 21, 2013). Answer the following questions based on the following sample of 14 household incomes for 2013 ($1000s).

49.4	52.4	53.4	51.3	52.1	48.7	52.1
52.2	64.5	51.6	46.5	52.9	52.5	51.2

a. What is the median household income for the sample data for 2013?
b. Based on the sample data, estimate the percentage change in the median household income from 2007 to 2013.
c. Compute the first and third quartiles.
d. Provide a five-number summary.
e. Using the *z*-score approach, do the data contain any outliers? Does the approach that uses the values of the first and third quartiles and the interquartile range to detect outliers provide the same results?

69. The data contained in the DATAfile named *FoodIndustry* show the company/chain name, the average sales per store ($1000s), and the food segment industry for 47 restaurant chains (*Quick Service Restaurant Magazine* website, August 2013).

DATA *file*

FoodIndustry

a. What was the mean U.S. sales per store for the 47 restaurant chains?
b. What are the first and third quartiles? What is your interpretation of the quartiles?
c. Show a box plot for the level of sales and discuss if there are any outliers in terms of sales that would skew the results.
d. Develop a frequency distribution showing the average sales per store for each segment. Comment on the results obtained.

70. *Travel + Leisure* magazine presented its annual list of the 500 best hotels in the world. The magazine provides a rating for each hotel along with a brief description that includes the size of the hotel, amenities, and the cost per night for a double room. A sample of 12 of the top-rated hotels in the United States follows.

DATA *file*

Travel

Hotel	Location	Rooms	Cost/Night($)
Boulders Resort & Spa	Phoenix, AZ	220	499
Disney's Wilderness Lodge	Orlando, FL	727	340
Four Seasons Hotel Beverly Hills	Los Angeles, CA	285	585
Four Seasons Hotel	Boston, MA	273	495
Hay-Adams	Washington, DC	145	495
Inn on Biltmore Estate	Asheville, NC	213	279
Loews Ventana Canyon Resort	Phoenix, AZ	398	279
Mauna Lani Bay Hotel	Island of Hawaii	343	455
Montage Laguna Beach	Laguna Beach, CA	250	595
Sofitel Water Tower	Chicago, IL	414	367
St. Regis Monarch Beach	Dana Point, CA	400	675
The Broadmoor	Colorado Springs, CO	700	420

a. What is the mean number of rooms?
b. What is the mean cost per night for a double room?

c. Develop a scatter diagram with the number of rooms on the horizontal axis and the cost per night on the vertical axis. Does there appear to be a relationship between the number of rooms and the cost per night? Discuss.

d. What is the sample correlation coefficient? What does it tell you about the relationship between the number of rooms and the cost per night for a double room? Does this appear reasonable? Discuss.

71. The 32 teams in the National Football League (NFL) are worth, on average, $1.17 billion, 5% more than last year. The following data show the annual revenue ($ millions) and the estimated team value ($ millions) for the 32 NFL teams (*Forbes* website, February 28, 2014).

NFLTeamValue

Team	Revenue ($ millions)	Current Value ($ millions)
Arizona Cardinals	253	961
Atlanta Falcons	252	933
Baltimore Ravens	292	1227
Buffalo Bills	256	870
Carolina Panthers	271	1057
Chicago Bears	298	1252
Cincinnati Bengals	250	924
Cleveland Browns	264	1005
Dallas Cowboys	539	2300
Denver Broncos	283	1161
Detroit Lions	248	900
Green Bay Packers	282	1183
Houston Texans	320	1450
Indianapolis Colts	276	1200
Jacksonville Jaguars	260	840
Kansas City Chiefs	245	1009
Miami Dolphins	268	1074
Minnesota Vikings	234	1007
New England Patriots	408	1800
New Orleans Saints	276	1004
New York Giants	338	1550
New York Jets	321	1380
Oakland Raiders	229	825
Philadelphia Eagles	306	1314
Pittsburgh Steelers	266	1118
San Diego Chargers	250	949
San Francisco 49ers	255	1224
Seattle Seahawks	270	1081
St. Louis Rams	239	875
Tampa Bay Buccaneers	267	1067
Tennessee Titans	270	1055
Washington Redskins	381	1700

a. Develop a scatter diagram with Revenue on the horizontal axis and Value on the vertical axis. Does there appear that there is any relationship between the two variables?

b. What is the sample correlation coefficient? What can you say about the strength of the relationship between Revenue and Value?

72. Does a major league baseball team's record during spring training indicate how the team will play during the regular season? Over the last six years, the correlation coefficient between a team's winning percentage in spring training and its winning percentage in the regular season is .18.

DATA *file*

SpringTraining

Team	Spring Training	Regular Season	Team	Spring Training	Regular Season
Baltimore Orioles	.407	.422	Minnesota Twins	.500	.540
Boston Red Sox	.429	.586	New York Yankees	.577	.549
Chicago White Sox	.417	.546	Oakland A's	.692	.466
Cleveland Indians	.569	.500	Seattle Mariners	.500	.377
Detroit Tigers	.569	.457	Tampa Bay Rays	.731	.599
Kansas City Royals	.533	.463	Texas Rangers	.643	.488
Los Angeles Angels	.724	.617	Toronto Blue Jays	.448	.531

Shown are the winning percentages for the 14 American League teams during a previous season.
a. What is the correlation coefficient between the spring training and the regular season winning percentages?
b. What is your conclusion about a team's record during spring training indicating how the team will play during the regular season? What are some of the reasons why this occurs? Discuss.

73. The days to maturity for a sample of five money market funds are shown here. The dollar amounts invested in the funds are provided. Use the weighted mean to determine the mean number of days to maturity for dollars invested in these five money market funds.

Days to Maturity	Dollar Value ($millions)
20	20
12	30
7	10
5	15
6	10

74. Automobiles traveling on a road with a posted speed limit of 55 miles per hour are checked for speed by a state police radar system. Following is a frequency distribution of speeds.
a. What is the mean speed of the automobiles traveling on this road?
b. Compute the variance and the standard deviation.

Speed (miles per hour)	Frequency
45–49	10
50–54	40
55–59	150
60–64	175
65–69	75
70–74	15
75–79	10
Total	475

75. The Panama Railroad Company was established in 1850 to construct a railroad across the isthmus that would allow fast and easy access between the Atlantic and Pacific Oceans. The following table (*The Big Ditch,* Mauer and Yu, 2011) provides annual returns for Panama Railroad stock from 1853 through 1880.

Year	Return on Panama Railroad Company Stock (%)
1853	−1
1854	−9
1855	19
1856	2
1857	3
1858	36
1859	21
1860	16
1861	−5
1862	43
1863	44
1864	48
1865	7
1866	11
1867	23
1868	20
1869	−11
1870	−51
1871	−42
1872	39
1873	42
1874	12
1875	26
1876	9
1877	−6
1878	25
1879	31
1880	30

PanamaRailroad

a. Create a graph of the annual returns on the stock. The New York Stock Exchange earned an annual average return of 8.4% from 1853 through 1880. Can you tell from the graph if the Panama Railroad Company stock outperformed the New York Stock Exchange?

b. Calculate the mean annual return on Panama Railroad Company stock from 1853 through 1880. Did the stock outperform the New York Stock Exchange over the same period?

Case Problem 1   Pelican Stores

Pelican Stores, a division of National Clothing, is a chain of women's apparel stores operating throughout the country. The chain recently ran a promotion in which discount coupons were sent to customers of other National Clothing stores. Data collected for a sample of 100 in-store credit card transactions at Pelican Stores during one day while the promotion was

TABLE 3.9   SAMPLE OF 100 CREDIT CARD PURCHASES AT PELICAN STORES

PelicanStores

Customer	Type of Customer	Items	Net Sales	Method of Payment	Gender	Marital Status	Age
1	Regular	1	39.50	Discover	Male	Married	32
2	Promotional	1	102.40	Proprietary Card	Female	Married	36
3	Regular	1	22.50	Proprietary Card	Female	Married	32
4	Promotional	5	100.40	Proprietary Card	Female	Married	28
5	Regular	2	54.00	MasterCard	Female	Married	34
6	Regular	1	44.50	MasterCard	Female	Married	44
7	Promotional	2	78.00	Proprietary Card	Female	Married	30
8	Regular	1	22.50	Visa	Female	Married	40
9	Promotional	2	56.52	Proprietary Card	Female	Married	46
10	Regular	1	44.50	Proprietary Card	Female	Married	36
⋮	⋮	⋮	⋮	⋮	⋮	⋮	⋮
96	Regular	1	39.50	MasterCard	Female	Married	44
97	Promotional	9	253.00	Proprietary Card	Female	Married	30
98	Promotional	10	287.59	Proprietary Card	Female	Married	52
99	Promotional	2	47.60	Proprietary Card	Female	Married	30
100	Promotional	1	28.44	Proprietary Card	Female	Married	44

running are contained in the DATAfile named *PelicanStores*. Table 3.9 shows a portion of the data set. The proprietary card method of payment refers to charges made using a National Clothing charge card. Customers who made a purchase using a discount coupon are referred to as promotional customers and customers who made a purchase but did not use a discount coupon are referred to as regular customers. Because the promotional coupons were not sent to regular Pelican Stores customers, management considers the sales made to people presenting the promotional coupons as sales it would not otherwise make. Of course, Pelican also hopes that the promotional customers will continue to shop at its stores.

Most of the variables shown in Table 3.9 are self-explanatory, but two of the variables require some clarification.

Items   The total number of items purchased
Net Sales The total amount ($) charged to the credit card

Pelican's management would like to use this sample data to learn about its customer base and to evaluate the promotion involving discount coupons.

Managerial Report

Use the methods of descriptive statistics presented in this chapter to summarize the data and comment on your findings. At a minimum, your report should include the following:

1. Descriptive statistics on net sales and descriptive statistics on net sales by various classifications of customers.
2. Descriptive statistics concerning the relationship between age and net sales.

Case Problem 2   Motion Picture Industry

The motion picture industry is a competitive business. More than 50 studios produce several hundred new motion pictures each year, and the financial success of the motion pictures varies considerably. The opening weekend gross sales, the total gross sales, the number of

TABLE 3.10   PERFORMANCE DATA FOR 10 MOTION PICTURES

2011Movies

Motion Picture	Opening Gross Sales ($millions)	Total Gross Sales ($millions)	Number of Theaters	Weeks in Release
Harry Potter and the Deathly Hallows Part 2	169.19	381.01	4375	19
Transformers: Dark of the Moon	97.85	352.39	4088	15
The Twilight Saga: Breaking Dawn Part 1	138.12	281.29	4066	14
The Hangover Part II	85.95	254.46	3675	16
Pirates of the Caribbean: On Stranger Tides	90.15	241.07	4164	19
Fast Five	86.20	209.84	3793	15
Mission: Impossible—Ghost Protocol	12.79	208.55	3555	13
Cars 2	66.14	191.45	4115	25
Sherlock Holmes: A Game of Shadows	39.64	186.59	3703	13
Thor	65.72	181.03	3963	16

theaters the movie was shown in, and the number of weeks the motion picture was in release are common variables used to measure the success of a motion picture. Data on the top 100 grossing motion pictures released in 2011 (Box Office Mojo website, March 17, 2012) are contained in the DATAfile named *2011Movies*. Table 3.10 shows the data for the first 10 motion pictures in this file. Note that some movies, such as *War Horse,* were released late in 2011 and continued to run in 2012.

Managerial Report

Use the numerical methods of descriptive statistics presented in this chapter to learn how these variables contribute to the success of a motion picture. Include the following in your report:

1. Descriptive statistics for each of the four variables along with a discussion of what the descriptive statistics tell us about the motion picture industry.
2. What motion pictures, if any, should be considered high-performance outliers? Explain.
3. Descriptive statistics showing the relationship between total gross sales and each of the other variables. Discuss.

Case Problem 3   # Business Schools of Asia–Pacific

Asian

The pursuit of a higher education degree in business is now international. A survey shows that more and more Asians choose the master of business administration (MBA) degree route to corporate success. As a result, the number of applicants for MBA courses at Asia-Pacific schools continues to increase.

Across the region, thousands of Asians show an increasing willingness to temporarily shelve their careers and spend two years in pursuit of a theoretical business qualification. Courses in these schools are notoriously tough and include economics, banking, marketing, behavioral sciences, labor relations, decision making, strategic thinking, business law, and more. The data set in Table 3.11 shows some of the characteristics of the leading Asia-Pacific business schools.

TABLE 3.11 DATA FOR 25 ASIA-PACIFIC BUSINESS SCHOOLS

Business School	Full-Time Enrollment	Students per Faculty	Local Tuition ($)	Foreign Tuition ($)	Age	% Foreign	GMAT	English Test	Work Experience	Starting Salary ($)
Melbourne Business School	200	5	24,420	29,600	28	47	Yes	No	Yes	71,400
University of New South Wales (Sydney)	228	4	19,993	32,582	29	28	Yes	No	Yes	65,200
Indian Institute of Management (Ahmedabad)	392	5	4,300	4,300	22	0	No	No	No	7,100
Chinese University of Hong Kong	90	5	11,140	11,140	29	10	Yes	No	No	31,000
International University of Japan (Niigata)	126	4	33,060	33,060	28	60	Yes	Yes	No	87,000
Asian Institute of Management (Manila)	389	5	7,562	9,000	25	50	Yes	No	Yes	22,800
Indian Institute of Management (Bangalore)	380	5	3,935	16,000	23	1	Yes	No	No	7,500
National University of Singapore	147	6	6,146	7,170	29	51	Yes	Yes	Yes	43,300
Indian Institute of Management (Calcutta)	463	8	2,880	16,000	23	0	No	No	No	7,400
Australian National University (Canberra)	42	2	20,300	20,300	30	80	Yes	Yes	Yes	46,600
Nanyang Technological University (Singapore)	50	5	8,500	8,500	32	20	Yes	No	Yes	49,300
University of Queensland (Brisbane)	138	17	16,000	22,800	32	26	No	No	Yes	49,600
Hong Kong University of Science and Technology	60	2	11,513	11,513	26	37	Yes	No	Yes	34,000
Macquarie Graduate School of Management (Sydney)	12	8	17,172	19,778	34	27	No	No	Yes	60,100
Chulalongkorn University (Bangkok)	200	7	17,355	17,355	25	6	Yes	No	Yes	17,600
Monash Mt. Eliza Business School (Melbourne)	350	13	16,200	22,500	30	30	Yes	Yes	Yes	52,500
Asian Institute of Management (Bangkok)	300	10	18,200	18,200	29	90	No	Yes	Yes	25,000
University of Adelaide	20	19	16,426	23,100	30	10	No	No	Yes	66,000
Massey University (Palmerston North, New Zealand)	30	15	13,106	21,625	37	35	No	Yes	Yes	41,400
Royal Melbourne Institute of Technology Business Graduate School	30	7	13,880	17,765	32	30	No	Yes	Yes	48,900
Jamnalal Bajaj Institute of Management Studies (Mumbai)	240	9	1,000	1,000	24	0	No	No	Yes	7,000
Curtin Institute of Technology (Perth)	98	15	9,475	19,097	29	43	Yes	No	Yes	55,000
Lahore University of Management Sciences	70	14	11,250	26,300	23	2.5	No	No	No	7,500
Universiti Sains Malaysia (Penang)	30	5	2,260	2,260	32	15	No	Yes	Yes	16,000
De La Salle University (Manila)	44	17	3,300	3,600	28	3.5	Yes	No	Yes	13,100

Managerial Report

Use the methods of descriptive statistics to summarize the data in Table 3.11. Discuss your findings.

1. Include a summary for each variable in the data set. Make comments and interpretations based on maximums and minimums, as well as the appropriate means and proportions. What new insights do these descriptive statistics provide concerning Asia-Pacific business schools?
2. Summarize the data to compare the following:
   a. Any difference between local and foreign tuition costs.
   b. Any difference between mean starting salaries for schools requiring and not requiring work experience.
   c. Any difference between starting salaries for schools requiring and not requiring English tests.
3. Do starting salaries appear to be related to tuition?
4. Present any additional graphical and numerical summaries that will be beneficial in communicating the data in Table 3.11 to others.

Case Problem 4   Heavenly Chocolates Website Transactions

Heavenly Chocolates manufactures and sells quality chocolate products at its plant and retail store located in Saratoga Springs, New York. Two years ago the company developed a website and began selling its products over the Internet. Website sales have exceeded the company's expectations, and mangement is now considering stragegies to increase sales even further. To learn more about the website customers, a sample of 50 Heavenly Chocolate transactions was selected from the previous month's sales. Data showing the day of the week each transaction was made, the type of browser the customer used, the time spent on the website, the number of website pages viewed, and the amount spent by each of the 50 customers are contained in the DATAfile named *Shoppers*. A portion of the data is shown in Table 3.12.

TABLE 3.12   A SAMPLE OF 50 HEAVENLY CHOCOLATES WEBSITE
TRANSACTIONS

Shoppers

Customer	Day	Browser	Time (min)	Pages Viewed	Amount Spent ($)
1	Mon	Internet Explorer	12.0	4	54.52
2	Wed	Other	19.5	6	94.90
3	Mon	Internet Explorer	8.5	4	26.68
4	Tue	Firefox	11.4	2	44.73
5	Wed	Internet Explorer	11.3	4	66.27
6	Sat	Firefox	10.5	6	67.80
7	Sun	Internet Explorer	11.4	2	36.04
.	.	.	.	.	.
.	.	.	.	.	.
.	.	.	.	.	.
48	Fri	Internet Explorer	9.7	5	103.15
49	Mon	Other	7.3	6	52.15
50	Fri	Internet Explorer	13.4	3	98.75

Heavenly Chocolates would like to use the sample data to determine if online shoppers who spend more time and view more pages also spend more money during their visit to the website. The company would also like to investigate the effect that the day of the week and the type of browser have on sales.

Managerial Report

Use the methods of descriptive statistics to learn about the customers who visit the Heavenly Chocolates website. Include the following in your report.

1. Graphical and numerical summaries for the length of time the shopper spends on the website, the number of pages viewed, and the mean amount spent per transaction. Discuss what you learn about Heavenly Chocolates' online shoppers from these numerical summaries.
2. Summarize the frequency, the total dollars spent, and the mean amount spent per transaction for each day of week. What observations can you make about Heavenly Chocolates' business based on the day of the week? Discuss.
3. Summarize the frequency, the total dollars spent, and the mean amount spent per transaction for each type of browser. What observations can you make about Heavenly Chocolates' business based on the type of browser? Discuss.
4. Develop a scatter diagram and compute the sample correlation coefficient to explore the relationship between the time spent on the website and the dollar amount spent. Use the horizontal axis for the time spent on the website. Discuss.
5. Develop a scatter diagram and compute the sample correlation coefficient to explore the relationship between the the number of website pages viewed and the amount spent. Use the horizontal axis for the number of website pages viewed. Discuss.
6. Develop a scatter diagram and compute the sample correlation coefficient to explore the relationship between the time spent on the website and the number of pages viewed. Use the horizontal axis to represent the number of pages viewed. Discuss.

Case Problem 5   African Elephant Populations

Although millions of elephants once roamed across Africa, by the mid-1980s elephant populations in African nations had been devastated by poaching. Elephants are important to African ecosystems. In tropical forests, elephants create clearings in the canopy that encourage new tree growth. In savannas, elephants reduce bush cover to create an environment that is favorable to browsing and grazing animals. In addition, the seeds of many plant species depend on passing through an elephant's digestive tract before germination.

The status of the elephant now varies greatly across the continent; in some nations, strong measures have been taken to effectively protect elephant populations, while in other nations the elephant populations remain in danger due to poaching for meat and ivory, loss of habitat, and conflict with humans. Table 3.13 shows elephant populations for several African nations in 1979, 1989, and 2007 (Lemieux and Clarke, "The International Ban on Ivory Sales and Its Effects on Elephant Poaching in Africa," *British Journal of Criminology,* 49(4), 2009).

The David Sheldrick Wildlife Trust was established in 1977 to honor the memory of naturalist David Leslie William Sheldrick, who founded Warden of Tsavo East National Park in Kenya and headed the Planning Unit of the Wildlife Conservation and Management Department in that country. Management of the Sheldrick Trust would like to know what these data indicate about elephant populations in various African countries since 1979.

TABLE 3.13   ELEPHANT POPULATIONS FOR SEVERAL AFRICAN NATIONS IN 1979, 1989, AND 2007

Country	Elephant population		
	1979	**1989**	**2007**
Angola	12,400	12,400	2,530
Botswana	20,000	51,000	175,487
Cameroon	16,200	21,200	15,387
Cen. African Rep.	63,000	19,000	3,334
Chad	15,000	3,100	6,435
Congo	10,800	70,000	22,102
Dem. Rep. of Congo	377,700	85,000	23,714
Gabon	13,400	76,000	70,637
Kenya	65,000	19,000	31,636
Mozambique	54,800	18,600	26,088
Somalia	24,300	6,000	70
Sudan	134,000	4,000	300
Tanzania	316,300	80,000	167,003
Zambia	150,000	41,000	29,231
Zimbabwe	30,000	43,000	99,107

AfricanElephants

Managerial Report

Use methods of descriptive statistics to summarize the data and comment on changes in elephant populations in African nations since 1979. At a minimum your report should include the following.

1. The mean annual change in elephant population for each country in the 10 years from 1979 to 1989, and a discussion of which countries saw the largest changes in elephant population over this 10-year period.
2. The mean annual change in elephant population for each country from 1989 to 2007, and a discussion of which countries saw the largest changes in elephant population over this 18-year period.
3. A comparison of your results from parts 1 and 2, and a discussion of the conclusions you can draw from this comparison.

CHAPTER 4

Introduction to Probability

CONTENTS

STATISTICS *in* PRACTICE

NATIONAL AERONAUTICS AND SPACE ADMINISTRATION*
WASHINGTON, DC

The National Aeronautics and Space Administration (NASA) is the agency of the United States government that is responsible for the U.S. civilian space program and aeronautics and aerospace research. NASA is best known for its manned space exploration; its mission statement is to "pioneer the future in space exploration, scientific discovery and aeronautics research." NASA, with its 18,800 employees, is currently working on the design of a new Space Launch System that will take the astronauts farther into space than ever before and provide the cornerstone for future human space exploration.

Although NASA's primary mission is space exploration, their expertise has been called upon to assist countries and organizations throughout the world. In one such situation, the San José copper and gold mine in Copiapó, Chile, caved in, trapping 33 men more than 2000 feet underground. While it was important to bring the men safely to the surface as quickly as possible, it was imperative that the rescue effort be carefully designed and implemented to save as many miners as possible. The Chilean government asked NASA to provide assistance in developing a rescue method. In response, NASA sent a four-person team consisting of an engineer, two physicians, and a psychologist with expertise in vehicle design and issues of long-term confinement.

The probability of success and failure of various rescue methods was prominent in the thoughts of everyone involved. Since there were no historical data available that applied to this unique rescue situation, NASA scientists developed subjective probability estimates for the success

NASA scientists based probabilities on similar circumstances experienced during space flights.

and failure of various rescue methods based on similar circumstances experienced by astronauts returning from short- and long-term space missions. The probability estimates provided by NASA guided officials in the selection of a rescue method and provided insight as to how the miners would survive the ascent in a rescue cage.

The rescue method designed by the Chilean officials in consultation with the NASA team resulted in the construction of a 13-foot-long, 924-pound steel rescue capsule that would be used to bring up the miners one at a time. All miners were rescued, with the last miner emerging 68 days after the cave-in occurred.

In this chapter you will learn about probability as well as how to compute and interpret probabilities for a variety of situations. In addition to subjective probabilities, you will learn about classical and relative frequency methods for assigning probabilities. The basic relationships of probability, conditional probability, and Bayes' theorem will be covered.

*The authors are indebted to Dr. Michael Duncan and Clinton Cragg at NASA for providing this Statistics in Practice.

Managers often base their decisions on an analysis of uncertainties such as the following:

1. What are the chances that sales will decrease if we increase prices?
2. What is the likelihood a new assembly method will increase productivity?
3. How likely is it that the project will be finished on time?
4. What is the chance that a new investment will be profitable?

Some of the earliest work on probability originated in a series of letters between Pierre de Fermat and Blaise Pascal in the 1650s.

Probability is a numerical measure of the likelihood that an event will occur. Thus, probabilities can be used as measures of the degree of uncertainty associated with the

FIGURE 4.1   PROBABILITY AS A NUMERICAL MEASURE OF THE LIKELIHOOD
OF AN EVENT OCCURRING

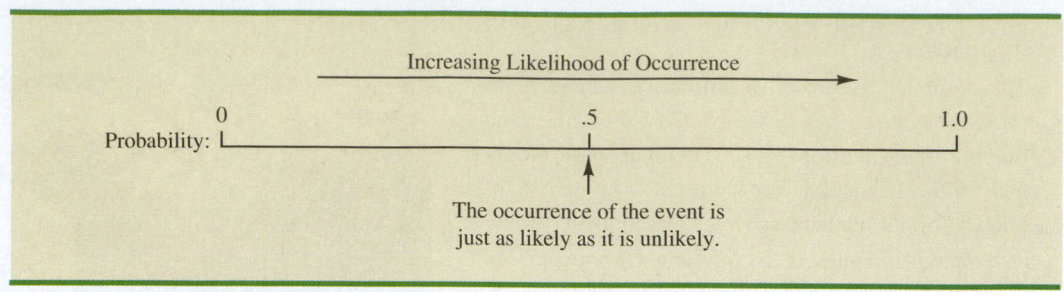

four events previously listed. If probabilities are available, we can determine the likelihood of each event occurring.

Probability values are always assigned on a scale from 0 to 1. A probability near zero indicates an event is unlikely to occur; a probability near 1 indicates an event is almost certain to occur. Other probabilities between 0 and 1 represent degrees of likelihood that an event will occur. For example, if we consider the event "rain tomorrow," we understand that when the weather report indicates "a near-zero probability of rain," it means almost no chance of rain. However, if a .90 probability of rain is reported, we know that rain is likely to occur. A .50 probability indicates that rain is just as likely to occur as not. Figure 4.1 depicts the view of probability as a numerical measure of the likelihood of an event occurring.

 # Experiments, Counting Rules, and Assigning Probabilities

In discussing probability, we define an **experiment** as a process that generates well-defined outcomes. On any single repetition of an experiment, one and only one of the possible experimental outcomes will occur. Several examples of experiments and their associated outcomes follow.

Experiment	Experimental Outcomes
Toss a coin	Head, tail
Select a part for inspection	Defective, nondefective
Conduct a sales call	Purchase, no purchase
Roll a die	1, 2, 3, 4, 5, 6
Play a football game	Win, lose, tie

By specifying all possible experimental outcomes, we identify the **sample space** for an experiment.

SAMPLE SPACE

The sample space for an experiment is the set of all experimental outcomes.

Experimental outcomes are also called sample points.

An experimental outcome is also called a **sample point** to identify it as an element of the sample space.

Consider the first experiment in the preceding table—tossing a coin. The upward face of the coin—a head or a tail—determines the experimental outcomes (sample points). If we let S denote the sample space, we can use the following notation to describe the sample space.

$$S = \{\text{Head, Tail}\}$$

The sample space for the second experiment in the table—selecting a part for inspection—can be described as follows:

$$S = \{\text{Defective, Nondefective}\}$$

Both of these experiments have two experimental outcomes (sample points). However, suppose we consider the fourth experiment listed in the table—rolling a die. The possible experimental outcomes, defined as the number of dots appearing on the upward face of the die, are the six points in the sample space for this experiment.

$$S = \{1, 2, 3, 4, 5, 6\}$$

Counting Rules, Combinations, and Permutations

Being able to identify and count the experimental outcomes is a necessary step in assigning probabilities. We now discuss three useful counting rules.

Multiple-step experiments   The first counting rule applies to **multiple-step experiments**. Consider the experiment of tossing two coins. Let the experimental outcomes be defined in terms of the pattern of heads and tails appearing on the upward faces of the two coins. How many experimental outcomes are possible for this experiment? The experiment of tossing two coins can be thought of as a two-step experiment in which step 1 is the tossing of the first coin and step 2 is the tossing of the second coin. If we use H to denote a head and T to denote a tail, (H, H) indicates the experimental outcome with a head on the first coin and a head on the second coin. Continuing this notation, we can describe the sample space (S) for this coin-tossing experiment as follows:

$$S = \{(H, H), (H, T), (T, H), (T, T)\}$$

Thus, we see that four experimental outcomes are possible. In this case, we can easily list all the experimental outcomes.

The counting rule for multiple-step experiments makes it possible to determine the number of experimental outcomes without listing them.

> **COUNTING RULE FOR MULTIPLE-STEP EXPERIMENTS**
>
> If an experiment can be described as a sequence of k steps with n_1 possible outcomes on the first step, n_2 possible outcomes on the second step, and so on, then the total number of experimental outcomes is given by $(n_1)(n_2)\ldots(n_k)$.

Viewing the experiment of tossing two coins as a sequence of first tossing one coin $(n_1 = 2)$ and then tossing the other coin $(n_2 = 2)$, we can see from the counting rule that $(2)(2) = 4$ distinct experimental outcomes are possible. As shown, they are $S = \{(H, H),$

(H, T), (T, H), (T, T)}. The number of experimental outcomes in an experiment involving tossing six coins is $(2)(2)(2)(2)(2)(2) = 64$.

Without the tree diagram, one might think only three experimental outcomes are possible for two tosses of a coin: 0 heads, 1 head, and 2 heads.

A **tree diagram** is a graphical representation that helps in visualizing a multiple-step experiment. Figure 4.2 shows a tree diagram for the experiment of tossing two coins. The sequence of steps moves from left to right through the tree. Step 1 corresponds to tossing the first coin, and step 2 corresponds to tossing the second coin. For each step, the two possible outcomes are head or tail. Note that for each possible outcome at step 1 two branches correspond to the two possible outcomes at step 2. Each of the points on the right end of the tree corresponds to an experimental outcome. Each path through the tree from the leftmost node to one of the nodes at the right side of the tree corresponds to a unique sequence of outcomes.

Let us now see how the counting rule for multiple-step experiments can be used in the analysis of a capacity expansion project for the Kentucky Power & Light Company (KP&L). KP&L is starting a project designed to increase the generating capacity of one of its plants in northern Kentucky. The project is divided into two sequential stages or steps: stage 1 (design) and stage 2 (construction). Even though each stage will be scheduled and controlled as closely as possible, management cannot predict beforehand the exact time required to complete each stage of the project. An analysis of similar construction projects revealed possible completion times for the design stage of 2, 3, or 4 months and possible completion times for the construction stage of 6, 7, or 8 months. In addition, because of the critical need for additional electrical power, management set a goal of 10 months for the completion of the entire project.

Because this project has three possible completion times for the design stage (step 1) and three possible completion times for the construction stage (step 2), the counting rule for multiple-step experiments can be applied here to determine a total of $(3)(3) = 9$ experimental outcomes. To describe the experimental outcomes, we use a two-number notation; for instance, $(2, 6)$ indicates that the design stage is completed in 2 months and the construction stage is completed in 6 months. This experimental outcome results in a total of $2 + 6 = 8$ months to complete the entire project. Table 4.1 summarizes the nine experimental outcomes for the KP&L problem. The tree diagram in Figure 4.3 shows how the nine outcomes (sample points) occur.

FIGURE 4.2   TREE DIAGRAM FOR THE EXPERIMENT OF TOSSING TWO COINS

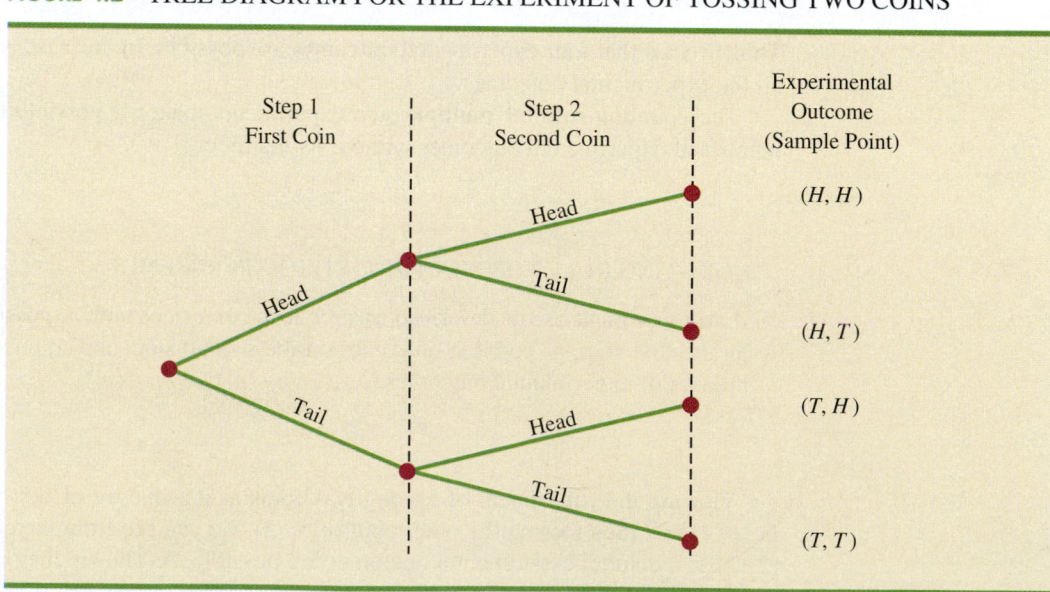

TABLE 4.1 EXPERIMENTAL OUTCOMES (SAMPLE POINTS) FOR THE KP&L PROJECT

Completion Time (months)		Notation for Experimental Outcome	Total Project Completion Time (months)
Stage 1 Design	Stage 2 Construction		
2	6	(2, 6)	8
2	7	(2, 7)	9
2	8	(2, 8)	10
3	6	(3, 6)	9
3	7	(3, 7)	10
3	8	(3, 8)	11
4	6	(4, 6)	10
4	7	(4, 7)	11
4	8	(4, 8)	12

The counting rule and tree diagram help the project manager identify the experimental outcomes and determine the possible project completion times. From the information in Figure 4.3, we see that the project will be completed in 8 to 12 months, with six of the nine experimental outcomes providing the desired completion time of 10 months or less.

FIGURE 4.3 TREE DIAGRAM FOR THE KP&L PROJECT

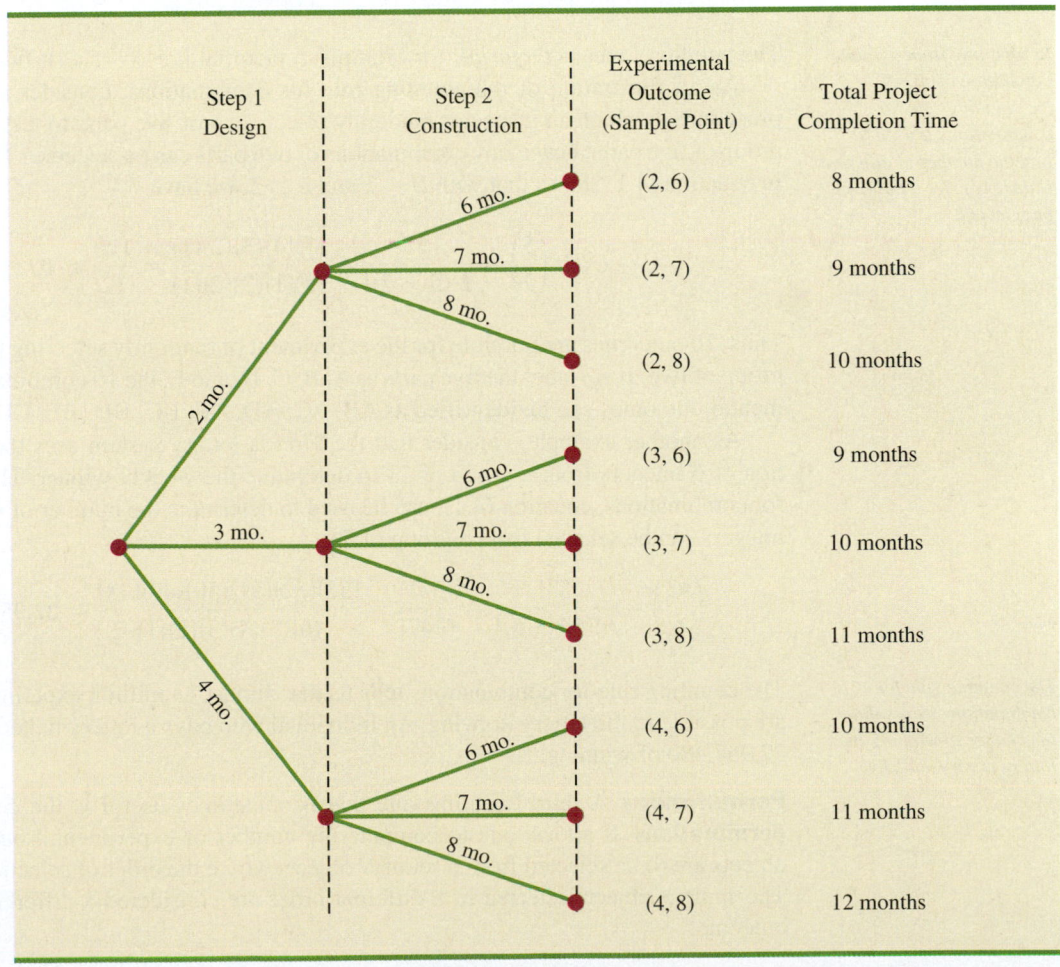

Even though identifying the experimental outcomes may be helpful, we need to consider how probability values can be assigned to the experimental outcomes before making an assessment of the probability that the project will be completed within the desired 10 months.

Combinations A second useful counting rule allows one to count the number of experimental outcomes when the experiment involves selecting n objects from a set of N objects. It is called the counting rule for **combinations**.

COUNTING RULE FOR COMBINATIONS

The number of combinations of N objects taken n at a time is

$$C_n^N = \binom{N}{n} = \frac{N!}{n!(N-n)!} \qquad \textbf{(4.1)}$$

where

$$N! = N(N-1)(N-2) \cdots (2)(1)$$
$$n! = n(n-1)(n-2) \cdots (2)(1)$$

and, by definition,　　　　　　　　　　$0! = 1$

In sampling from a finite population of size N, the counting rule for combinations is used to find the number of different samples of size n that can be selected.

The notation ! means *factorial;* for example, 5 factorial is $5! = (5)(4)(3)(2)(1) = 120$.

As an illustration of the counting rule for combinations, consider a quality control procedure in which an inspector randomly selects two of five parts to test for defects. In a group of five parts, how many combinations of two parts can be selected? The counting rule in equation (4.1) shows that with $N = 5$ and $n = 2$, we have

$$C_2^5 = \binom{5}{2} = \frac{5!}{2!(5-2)!} = \frac{(5)(4)(3)(2)(1)}{(2)(1)(3)(2)(1)} = \frac{120}{12} = 10$$

Thus, 10 outcomes are possible for the experiment of randomly selecting two parts from a group of five. If we label the five parts as A, B, C, D, and E, the 10 combinations or experimental outcomes can be identified as AB, AC, AD, AE, BC, BD, BE, CD, CE, and DE.

As another example, consider that the Florida lottery system uses the random selection of 6 integers from a group of 53 to determine the weekly winner. The counting rule for combinations, equation (4.1), can be used to determine the number of ways 6 different integers can be selected from a group of 53.

$$\binom{53}{6} = \frac{53!}{6!(53-6)!} = \frac{53!}{6!47!} = \frac{(53)(52)(51)(50)(49)(48)}{(6)(5)(4)(3)(2)(1)} = 22{,}957{,}480$$

The counting rule for combinations shows that the chance of winning the lottery is very unlikely.

The counting rule for combinations tells us that almost 23 million experimental outcomes are possible in the lottery drawing. An individual who buys a lottery ticket has 1 chance in 22,957,480 of winning.

Permutations A third counting rule that is sometimes useful is the counting rule for **permutations**. It allows one to compute the number of experimental outcomes when n objects are to be selected from a set of N objects where the order of selection is important. The same n objects selected in a different order are considered a different experimental outcome.

COUNTING RULE FOR PERMUTATIONS

The number of permutations of N objects taken n at a time is given by

$$P_n^N = n!\binom{N}{n} = \frac{N!}{(N-n)!} \tag{4.2}$$

The counting rule for permutations closely relates to the one for combinations; however, an experiment results in more permutations than combinations for the same number of objects because every selection of n objects can be ordered in $n!$ different ways.

As an example, consider again the quality control process in which an inspector selects two of five parts to inspect for defects. How many permutations may be selected? The counting rule in equation (4.2) shows that with $N = 5$ and $n = 2$, we have

$$P_2^5 = \frac{5!}{(5-2)!} = \frac{5!}{3!} = \frac{(5)(4)(3)(2)(1)}{(3)(2)(1)} = \frac{120}{6} = 20$$

Thus, 20 outcomes are possible for the experiment of randomly selecting two parts from a group of five when the order of selection must be taken into account. If we label the parts A, B, C, D, and E, the 20 permutations are AB, BA, AC, CA, AD, DA, AE, EA, BC, CB, BD, DB, BE, EB, CD, DC, CE, EC, DE, and ED.

Assigning Probabilities

Now let us see how probabilities can be assigned to experimental outcomes. The three approaches most frequently used are the classical, relative frequency, and subjective methods. Regardless of the method used, two **basic requirements for assigning probabilities** must be met.

BASIC REQUIREMENTS FOR ASSIGNING PROBABILITIES

1. The probability assigned to each experimental outcome must be between 0 and 1, inclusively. If we let E_i denote the ith experimental outcome and $P(E_i)$ its probability, then this requirement can be written as

$$0 \le P(E_i) \le 1 \text{ for all } i \tag{4.3}$$

2. The sum of the probabilities for all the experimental outcomes must equal 1.0. For n experimental outcomes, this requirement can be written as

$$P(E_1) + P(E_2) + \cdots + P(E_n) = 1 \tag{4.4}$$

The **classical method** of assigning probabilities is appropriate when all the experimental outcomes are equally likely. If n experimental outcomes are possible, a probability of $1/n$ is assigned to each experimental outcome. When using this approach, the two basic requirements for assigning probabilities are automatically satisfied.

For an example, consider the experiment of tossing a fair coin; the two experimental outcomes—head and tail—are equally likely. Because one of the two equally likely outcomes is a head, the probability of observing a head is 1/2, or .50. Similarly, the probability of observing a tail is also 1/2, or .50.

As another example, consider the experiment of rolling a die. It would seem reasonable to conclude that the six possible outcomes are equally likely, and hence each outcome is assigned a probability of 1/6. If $P(1)$ denotes the probability that one dot appears on the upward face of the die, then $P(1) = 1/6$. Similarly, $P(2) = 1/6$, $P(3) = 1/6$, $P(4) = 1/6$, $P(5) = 1/6$, and $P(6) = 1/6$. Note that these probabilities satisfy the two basic requirements of equations (4.3) and (4.4) because each of the probabilities is greater than or equal to zero and they sum to 1.0.

The **relative frequency method** of assigning probabilities is appropriate when data are available to estimate the proportion of the time the experimental outcome will occur if the experiment is repeated a large number of times. As an example, consider a study of waiting times in the X-ray department for a local hospital. A clerk recorded the number of patients waiting for service at 9:00 A.M. on 20 successive days and obtained the following results.

Number Waiting	Number of Days Outcome Occurred
0	2
1	5
2	6
3	4
4	3
	Total 20

These data show that on 2 of the 20 days, zero patients were waiting for service; on 5 of the days, one patient was waiting for service; and so on. Using the relative frequency method, we would assign a probability of 2/20 = .10 to the experimental outcome of zero patients waiting for service, 5/20 = .25 to the experimental outcome of one patient waiting, 6/20 = .30 to two patients waiting, 4/20 = .20 to three patients waiting, and 3/20 = .15 to four patients waiting. As with the classical method, using the relative frequency method automatically satisfies the two basic requirements of equations (4.3) and (4.4).

The **subjective method** of assigning probabilities is most appropriate when one cannot realistically assume that the experimental outcomes are equally likely and when little relevant data are available. When the subjective method is used to assign probabilities to the experimental outcomes, we may use any information available, such as our experience or intuition. After considering all available information, a probability value that expresses our *degree of belief* (on a scale from 0 to 1) that the experimental outcome will occur is specified. Because subjective probability expresses a person's degree of belief, it is personal. Using the subjective method, different people can be expected to assign different probabilities to the same experimental outcome.

The subjective method requires extra care to ensure that the two basic requirements of equations (4.3) and (4.4) are satisfied. Regardless of a person's degree of belief, the probability value assigned to each experimental outcome must be between 0 and 1, inclusive, and the sum of all the probabilities for the experimental outcomes must equal 1.0.

Consider the case in which Tom and Judy Elsbernd make an offer to purchase a house. Two outcomes are possible:

$$E_1 = \text{their offer is accepted}$$
$$E_2 = \text{their offer is rejected}$$

Judy believes that the probability their offer will be accepted is .8; thus, Judy would set $P(E_1) = .8$ and $P(E_2) = .2$. Tom, however, believes that the probability that their offer will be accepted is .6; hence, Tom would set $P(E_1) = .6$ and $P(E_2) = .4$. Note that Tom's probability estimate for E_1 reflects a greater pessimism that their offer will be accepted.

Bayes' theorem (see Section 4.5) provides a means for combining subjectively determined prior probabilities with probabilities obtained by other means to obtain revised, or posterior, probabilities.

Both Judy and Tom assigned probabilities that satisfy the two basic requirements. The fact that their probability estimates are different emphasizes the personal nature of the subjective method.

Even in business situations where either the classical or the relative frequency approach can be applied, managers may want to provide subjective probability estimates. In such cases, the best probability estimates often are obtained by combining the estimates from the classical or relative frequency approach with subjective probability estimates.

Probabilities for the KP&L Project

To perform further analysis on the KP&L project, we must develop probabilities for each of the nine experimental outcomes listed in Table 4.1. On the basis of experience and judgment, management concluded that the experimental outcomes were not equally likely. Hence, the classical method of assigning probabilities could not be used. Management then decided to conduct a study of the completion times for similar projects undertaken by KP&L over the past three years. The results of a study of 40 similar projects are summarized in Table 4.2.

After reviewing the results of the study, management decided to employ the relative frequency method of assigning probabilities. Management could have provided subjective probability estimates but felt that the current project was quite similar to the 40 previous projects. Thus, the relative frequency method was judged best.

In using the data in Table 4.2 to compute probabilities, we note that outcome (2, 6)— stage 1 completed in 2 months and stage 2 completed in 6 months—occurred six times in the 40 projects. We can use the relative frequency method to assign a probability of 6/40 = .15 to this outcome. Similarly, outcome (2, 7) also occurred in six of the 40 projects, providing a 6/40 = .15 probability. Continuing in this manner, we obtain the probability assignments for the sample points of the KP&L project shown in Table 4.3. Note that $P(2, 6)$ represents the probability of the sample point (2, 6), $P(2, 7)$ represents the probability of the sample point (2, 7), and so on.

TABLE 4.2 COMPLETION RESULTS FOR 40 KP&L PROJECTS

Completion Time (months)		Sample Point	Number of Past Projects Having These Completion Times
Stage 1 Design	Stage 2 Construction		
2	6	(2, 6)	6
2	7	(2, 7)	6
2	8	(2, 8)	2
3	6	(3, 6)	4
3	7	(3, 7)	8
3	8	(3, 8)	2
4	6	(4, 6)	2
4	7	(4, 7)	4
4	8	(4, 8)	6
			Total 40

TABLE 4.3   PROBABILITY ASSIGNMENTS FOR THE KP&L PROJECT BASED
ON THE RELATIVE FREQUENCY METHOD

Sample Point	Project Completion Time	Probability of Sample Point
(2, 6)	8 months	$P(2, 6) = 6/40 = .15$
(2, 7)	9 months	$P(2, 7) = 6/40 = .15$
(2, 8)	10 months	$P(2, 8) = 2/40 = .05$
(3, 6)	9 months	$P(3, 6) = 4/40 = .10$
(3, 7)	10 months	$P(3, 7) = 8/40 = .20$
(3, 8)	11 months	$P(3, 8) = 2/40 = .05$
(4, 6)	10 months	$P(4, 6) = 2/40 = .05$
(4, 7)	11 months	$P(4, 7) = 4/40 = .10$
(4, 8)	12 months	$P(4, 8) = 6/40 = .15$
		Total 1.00

NOTES AND COMMENTS

1. In statistics, the notion of an experiment differs somewhat from the notion of an experiment in the physical sciences. In the physical sciences, researchers usually conduct an experiment in a laboratory or a controlled environment in order to learn about cause and effect. In statistical experiments, probability determines outcomes. Even though the experiment is repeated in exactly the same way, an entirely different outcome may occur. Because of this influence of probability on the outcome, the experiments of statistics are sometimes called *random experiments*.

2. When drawing a random sample without replacement from a population of size N, the counting rule for combinations is used to find the number of different samples of size n that can be selected.

Exercises

Methods

1. An experiment has three steps with three outcomes possible for the first step, two outcomes possible for the second step, and four outcomes possible for the third step. How many experimental outcomes exist for the entire experiment?

 2. How many ways can three items be selected from a group of six items? Use the letters A, B, C, D, E, and F to identify the items, and list each of the different combinations of three items.

3. How many permutations of three items can be selected from a group of six? Use the letters A, B, C, D, E, and F to identify the items, and list each of the permutations of items B, D, and F.

4. Consider the experiment of tossing a coin three times.
   a. Develop a tree diagram for the experiment.
   b. List the experimental outcomes.
   c. What is the probability for each experimental outcome?

5. Suppose an experiment has five equally likely outcomes: E_1, E_2, E_3, E_4, E_5. Assign probabilities to each outcome and show that the requirements in equations (4.3) and (4.4) are satisfied. What method did you use?

 6. An experiment with three outcomes has been repeated 50 times, and it was learned that E_1 occurred 20 times, E_2 occurred 13 times, and E_3 occurred 17 times. Assign probabilities to the outcomes. What method did you use?

7.   A decision maker subjectively assigned the following probabilities to the four outcomes of an experiment: $P(E_1) = .10$, $P(E_2) = .15$, $P(E_3) = .40$, and $P(E_4) = .20$. Are these probability assignments valid? Explain.

Applications

8.   In the city of Milford, applications for zoning changes go through a two-step process: a review by the planning commission and a final decision by the city council. At step 1 the planning commission reviews the zoning change request and makes a positive or negative recommendation concerning the change. At step 2 the city council reviews the planning commission's recommendation and then votes to approve or to disapprove the zoning change. Suppose the developer of an apartment complex submits an application for a zoning change. Consider the application process as an experiment.
   a.   How many sample points are there for this experiment? List the sample points.
   b.   Construct a tree diagram for the experiment.

9.   Simple random sampling uses a sample of size n from a population of size N to obtain data that can be used to make inferences about the characteristics of a population. Suppose that, from a population of 50 bank accounts, we want to take a random sample of four accounts in order to learn about the population. How many different random samples of four accounts are possible?

10.   The following table shows the percentage of on-time arrivals, the number of mishandled baggage reports per 1000 passengers, and the number of customer complaints per 1000 passengers for 10 airlines (*Forbes* website, February 2014).

Airline	On-Time Arrivals (%)	Mishandled Baggage per 1000 Passengers	Customer Complaints per 1000 Passengers
Virgin America	83.5	0.87	1.50
JetBlue	79.1	1.88	0.79
AirTran Airways	87.1	1.58	0.91
Delta Air Lines	86.5	2.10	0.73
Alaska Airlines	87.5	2.93	0.51
Frontier Airlines	77.9	2.22	1.05
Southwest Airlines	83.1	3.08	0.25
US Airways	85.9	2.14	1.74
American Airlines	76.9	2.92	1.80
United Airlines	77.4	3.87	4.24

   a.   If you randomly choose a Delta Air Lines flight, what is the probability that this individual flight has an on-time arrival?
   b.   If you randomly choose one of the 10 airlines for a follow-up study on airline quality ratings, what is the probability that you will choose an airline with less than two mishandled baggage reports per 1000 passengers?
   c.   If you randomly choose 1 of the 10 airlines for a follow-up study on airline quality ratings, what is the probability that you will choose an airline with more than one customer complaint per 1000 passengers?
   d.   What is the probability that a randomly selected AirTran Airways flight will not arrive on time?

11.   A Gallup Poll of U.S. adults indicated that Kentucky is the state with the highest percentage of smokers (*Gallup.com*, December 2015). Consider the following example data from

State	Smoker	Non-Smoker
Kentucky	47	176
Indiana	32	134
Ohio	39	182
Total:	118	492

the Tri-State region, an area that comprises northern Kentucky, southeastern Indiana, and southwestern Ohio.

a.   Use the data to compute the probability that an adult in the Tri-State region smokes.

b.   What is the probability of an adult in each state of the Tri-State region being a smoker? Which state in the Tri-State region has the lowest probability of an adult being a smoker?

12.   The Powerball lottery is played twice each week in 31 states, the District of Columbia, and the Virgin Islands. To play Powerball, a participant must purchase a $2 ticket, select five numbers from the digits 1 through 59, and then select a Powerball number from the digits 1 through 35. To determine the winning numbers for each game, lottery officials draw five white balls out a drum of 59 white balls numbered 1 through 59 and one red ball out of a drum of 35 red balls numbered 1 through 35. To win the Powerball jackpot, a participant's numbers must match the numbers on the five white balls in any order and must also match the number on the red Powerball. The numbers 5–16–22–23–29 with a Powerball number of 6 provided the record jackpot of $580 million (Powerball website, November 29, 2012).

a.   How many Powerball lottery outcomes are possible? (*Hint:* Consider this a two-step experiment. Select the five white ball numbers and then select the one red Powerball number.)

b.   What is the probability that a $2 lottery ticket wins the Powerball lottery?

13.   A company that manufactures toothpaste is studying five different package designs. Assuming that one design is just as likely to be selected by a consumer as any other design, what selection probability would you assign to each of the package designs? In an actual experiment, 100 consumers were asked to pick the design they preferred. The following data were obtained. Do the data confirm the belief that one design is just as likely to be selected as another? Explain.

Design	Number of Times Preferred
1	5
2	15
3	30
4	40
5	10

4.2 Events and Their Probabilities

In the introduction to this chapter we used the term *event* much as it would be used in everyday language. Then, in Section 4.1 we introduced the concept of an experiment and its associated experimental outcomes or sample points. Sample points and events provide the foundation for the study of probability. As a result, we must now introduce the formal definition of an **event** as it relates to sample points. Doing so will provide the basis for determining the probability of an event.

EVENT

An event is a collection of sample points.

For an example, let us return to the KP&L project and assume that the project manager is interested in the event that the entire project can be completed in 10 months or less. Referring to Table 4.3, we see that six sample points—(2, 6), (2, 7), (2, 8), (3, 6), (3, 7), and (4, 6)—provide a project completion time of 10 months or less. Let C denote the event that the project is completed in 10 months or less; we write

$$C = \{(2, 6), (2, 7), (2, 8), (3, 6), (3, 7), (4, 6)\}$$

Event C is said to occur if *any one* of these six sample points appears as the experimental outcome.

Other events that might be of interest to KP&L management include the following.

L = The event that the project is completed in *less* than 10 months

M = The event that the project is completed in *more* than 10 months

Using the information in Table 4.3, we see that these events consist of the following sample points.

$$L = \{(2, 6), (2, 7), (3, 6)\}$$
$$M = \{(3, 8), (4, 7), (4, 8)\}$$

A variety of additional events can be defined for the KP&L project, but in each case the event must be identified as a collection of sample points for the experiment.

Given the probabilities of the sample points shown in Table 4.3, we can use the following definition to compute the probability of any event that KP&L management might want to consider.

PROBABILITY OF AN EVENT

The probability of any event is equal to the sum of the probabilities of the sample points in the event.

Using this definition, we calculate the probability of a particular event by adding the probabilities of the sample points (experimental outcomes) that make up the event. We can now compute the probability that the project will take 10 months or less to complete. Because this event is given by $C = \{(2, 6), (2, 7), (2, 8), (3, 6), (3, 7), (4, 6)\}$, the probability of event C, denoted $P(C)$, is given by

$$P(C) = P(2, 6) + P(2, 7) + P(2, 8) + P(3, 6) + P(3, 7) + P(4, 6)$$

Refer to the sample point probabilities in Table 4.3; we have

$$P(C) = .15 + .15 + .05 + .10 + .20 + .05 = .70$$

Similarly, because the event that the project is completed in less than 10 months is given by $L = \{(2, 6), (2, 7), (3, 6)\}$, the probability of this event is given by

$$P(L) = P(2, 6) + P(2, 7) + P(3, 6)$$
$$= .15 + .15 + .10 = .40$$

Finally, for the event that the project is completed in more than 10 months, we have $M = \{(3, 8), (4, 7), (4, 8)\}$ and thus

$$P(M) = P(3, 8) + P(4, 7) + P(4, 8)$$
$$= .05 + .10 + .15 = .30$$

Using these probability results, we can now tell KP&L management that there is a .70 probability that the project will be completed in 10 months or less, a .40 probability that the project will be completed in less than 10 months, and a .30 probability that the project will be completed in more than 10 months. This procedure of computing event probabilities can be repeated for any event of interest to the KP&L management.

Any time that we can identify all the sample points of an experiment and assign probabilities to each, we can compute the probability of an event using the definition. However, in many experiments the large number of sample points makes the identification of the sample points, as well as the determination of their associated probabilities, extremely cumbersome, if not impossible. In the remaining sections of this chapter, we present some basic probability relationships that can be used to compute the probability of an event without knowledge of all the sample point probabilities.

NOTES AND COMMENTS

1. The sample space, S, is an event. Because it contains all the experimental outcomes, it has a probability of 1; that is, $P(S) = 1$.
2. When the classical method is used to assign probabilities, the assumption is that the experimental outcomes are equally likely. In such cases, the probability of an event can be computed by counting the number of experimental outcomes in the event and dividing the result by the total number of experimental outcomes.

Exercises

Methods

14. An experiment has four equally likely outcomes: E_1, E_2, E_3, and E_4.
    a. What is the probability that E_2 occurs?
    b. What is the probability that any two of the outcomes occur (e.g., E_1 or E_3)?
    c. What is the probability that any three of the outcomes occur (e.g., E_1 or E_2 or E_4)?

 15. Consider the experiment of selecting a playing card from a deck of 52 playing cards. Each card corresponds to a sample point with a 1/52 probability.
    a. List the sample points in the event an ace is selected.
    b. List the sample points in the event a club is selected.
    c. List the sample points in the event a face card (jack, queen, or king) is selected.
    d. Find the probabilities associated with each of the events in parts (a), (b), and (c).

16. Consider the experiment of rolling a pair of dice. Suppose that we are interested in the sum of the face values showing on the dice.
    a. How many sample points are possible? (*Hint:* Use the counting rule for multiple-step experiments.)
    b. List the sample points.
    c. What is the probability of obtaining a value of 7?
    d. What is the probability of obtaining a value of 9 or greater?
    e. Because each roll has six possible even values (2, 4, 6, 8, 10, and 12) and only five possible odd values (3, 5, 7, 9, and 11), the dice should show even values more often than odd values. Do you agree with this statement? Explain.
    f. What method did you use to assign the probabilities requested?

Applications

17. Refer to the KP&L sample points and sample point probabilities in Tables 4.2 and 4.3.
    a. The design stage (stage 1) will run over budget if it takes four months to complete. List the sample points in the event the design stage is over budget.
    b. What is the probability that the design stage is over budget?
    c. The construction stage (stage 2) will run over budget if it takes eight months to complete. List the sample points in the event the construction stage is over budget.
    d. What is the probability that the construction stage is over budget?
    e. What is the probability that both stages are over budget?

18. *Fortune* magazine publishes an annual list of the 500 largest companies in the United States. The corporate headquarters for the 500 companies are located in 38 different states The following table shows the eight states with the largest number of Fortune 500 companies (*Money*/CNN website, May 12, 2012).

State	Number of Companies	State	Number of Companies
California	53	Ohio	28
Illinois	32	Pennsylvania	23
New Jersey	21	Texas	52
New York	50	Virginia	24

Suppose one of the 500 companies is selected at random for a follow-up questionnaire.
   a. What is the probability that the company selected has its corporate headquarters in California?
   b. What is the probability that the company selected has its corporate headquarters in California, New York, or Texas?
   c. What is the probability that the company selected has its corporate headquarters in one of the eight states listed above?

19. Do you think global warming will have an impact on you during your lifetime? A CBS News/*New York Times* poll of 1000 adults in the United States asked this question (CBS News website, December 2014). Consider the responses by age groups shown below.

	Age	
Response	**18–29**	**30+**
Yes	134	293
No	131	432
Unsure	2	8

   a. What is the probability that a respondent 18–29 years of age thinks that global warming will not pose a serious threat during his/her lifetime?
   b. What is the probability that a respondent 30+ years of age thinks that global warming will not pose a serious threat during his/her lifetime?
   c. For a randomly selected respondent, what is the probability that a respondent answers yes?
   d. Based on the survey results, does there appear to be a difference between ages 18–29 and 30+ regarding concern over global warming?

20. Junior Achievement USA and the Allstate Foundation surveyed teenagers aged 14 to 18 and asked at what age they think they will become financially independent. The responses of 944 teenagers who answered this survey question are as follows.

Age Financially Independent	Number of Responses
16 to 20	191
21 to 24	467
25 to 27	244
28 or older	42

Consider the experiment of randomly selecting a teenager from the population of teenagers aged 14 to 18.
   a. Compute the probability of being financially independent for each of the four age categories.
   b. What is the probability of being financially independent before the age of 25?
   c. What is the probability of being financially independent after the age of 24?
   d. Do the probabilities suggest that the teenagers may be somewhat unrealistic in their expectations about when they will become financially independent?

21. Data on U.S. work-related fatalities by cause follow (*The World Almanac*, 2012).

Cause of Fatality	Number of Fatalities
Transportation incidents	1795
Assaults and violent acts	837
Contact with objects and equipment	741
Falls	645
Exposure to harmful substances or environments	404
Fires and explosions	113

Assume that a fatality will be randomly chosen from this population.
   a. What is the probability the fatality resulted from a fall?
   b. What is the probability the fatality resulted from a transportation incident?
   c. What cause of fatality is least likely to occur? What is the probability the fatality resulted from this cause?

4.3   Some Basic Relationships of Probability

Complement of an Event

Given an event A, the **complement of A** is defined to be the event consisting of all sample points that are *not* in A. The complement of A is denoted by A^c. Figure 4.4 is a diagram, known as a **Venn diagram**, that illustrates the concept of a complement. The rectangular area represents the sample space for the experiment and as such contains all possible sample points. The circle represents event A and contains only the sample points that belong to A. The shaded region of the rectangle contains all sample points not in event A and is by definition the complement of A.

FIGURE 4.4   COMPLEMENT OF EVENT *A* IS SHADED

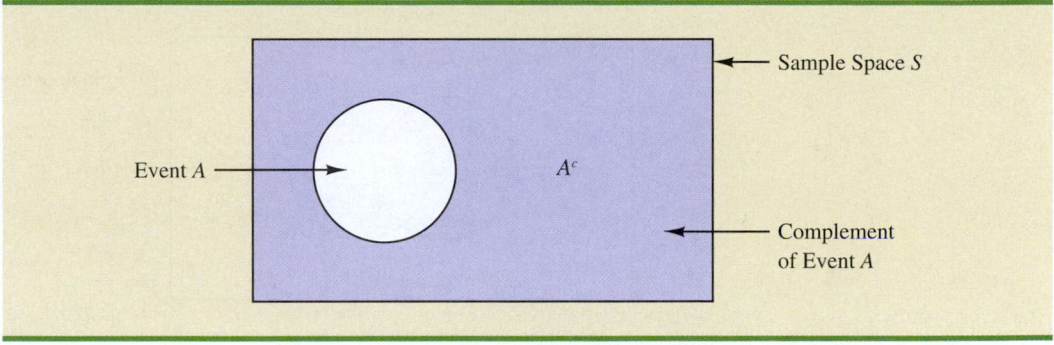

In any probability application, either event *A* or its complement A^c must occur. There-fore, we have

$$P(A) + P(A^c) = 1$$

Solving for $P(A)$, we obtain the following result.

COMPUTING PROBABILITY USING THE COMPLEMENT

$$P(A) = 1 - P(A^c) \qquad\qquad (4.5)$$

Equation (4.5) shows that the probability of an event *A* can be computed easily if the proba-bility of its complement, $P(A^c)$, is known.

As an example, consider the case of a sales manager who, after reviewing sales reports, states that 80% of new customer contacts result in no sale. By allowing *A* to denote the event of a sale and A^c to denote the event of no sale, the manager is stating that $P(A^c) = .80$. Using equation (4.5), we see that

$$P(A) = 1 - P(A^c) = 1 - .80 = .20$$

We can conclude that a new customer contact has a .20 probability of resulting in a sale.

In another example, a purchasing agent states a .90 probability that a supplier will send a shipment that is free of defective parts. Using the complement, we can conclude that there is a $1 - .90 = .10$ probability that the shipment will contain defective parts.

Addition Law

The addition law is helpful when we are interested in knowing the probability that at least one of two events occurs. That is, with events *A* and *B* we are interested in knowing the probability that event *A* or event *B* or both will occur.

Before we present the addition law, we need to discuss two concepts related to the com-bination of events: the *union* of events and the *intersection* of events. Given two events *A* and *B*, the **union of *A* and *B*** is defined as follows.

UNION OF TWO EVENTS

The *union* of *A* and *B* is the event containing *all* sample points belonging to *A or B or both.* The union is denoted by $A \cup B$.

FIGURE 4.5   UNION OF EVENTS *A* AND *B* IS SHADED

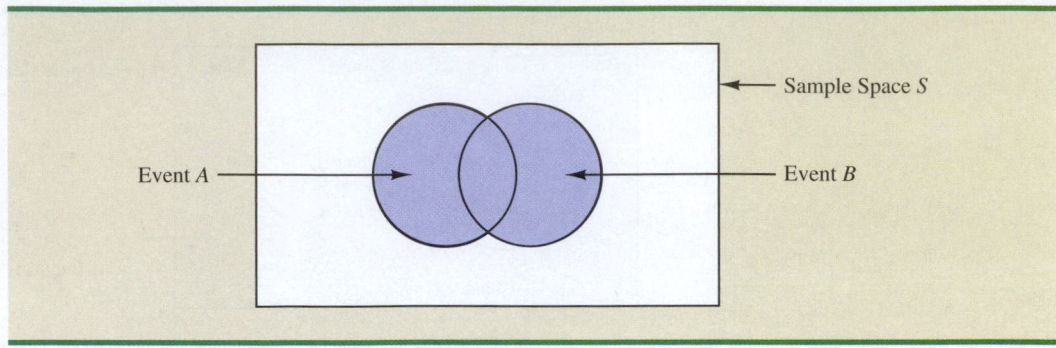

The Venn diagram in Figure 4.5 depicts the union of events *A* and *B*. Note that the two circles contain all the sample points in event *A* as well as all the sample points in event *B*. The fact that the circles overlap indicates that some sample points are contained in both *A* and *B*.

The definition of the **intersection of *A* and *B*** follows.

INTERSECTION OF TWO EVENTS

Given two events *A* and *B*, the *intersection* of *A* and *B* is the event containing the sample points belonging to *both A and B*. The intersection is denoted by $A \cap B$.

The Venn diagram depicting the intersection of events *A* and *B* is shown in Figure 4.6. The area where the two circles overlap is the intersection; it contains the sample points that are in both *A* and *B*.

Let us now continue with a discussion of the addition law. The **addition law** provides a way to compute the probability that event *A* or event *B* or both occur. In other words, the addition law is used to compute the probability of the union of two events. The addition law is written as follows.

ADDITION LAW

$$P(A \cup B) = P(A) + P(B) - P(A \cap B) \tag{4.6}$$

FIGURE 4.6   INTERSECTION OF EVENTS *A* AND *B* IS SHADED

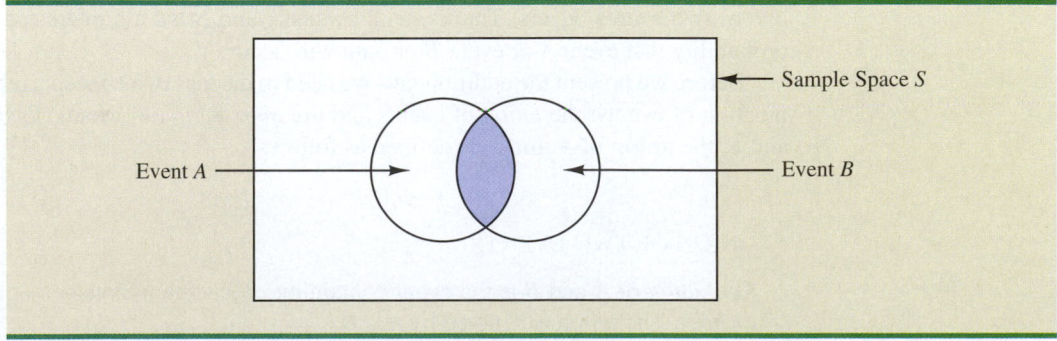

To understand the addition law intuitively, note that the first two terms in the addition law, $P(A) + P(B)$, account for all the sample points in $A \cup B$. However, because the sample points in the intersection $A \cap B$ are in both A and B, when we compute $P(A) + P(B)$, we are in effect counting each of the sample points in $A \cap B$ twice. We correct for this overcounting by subtracting $P(A \cap B)$.

As an example of an application of the addition law, let us consider the case of a small assembly plant with 50 employees. Each worker is expected to complete work assignments on time and in such a way that the assembled product will pass a final inspection. On occasion, some of the workers fail to meet the performance standards by completing work late or assembling a defective product. At the end of a performance evaluation period, the production manager found that 5 of the 50 workers completed work late, 6 of the 50 workers assembled a defective product, and 2 of the 50 workers both completed work late *and* assembled a defective product.

Let

$$L = \text{the event that the work is completed late}$$

$$D = \text{the event that the assembled product is defective}$$

The relative frequency information leads to the following probabilities.

$$P(L) = \frac{5}{50} = .10$$

$$P(D) = \frac{6}{50} = .12$$

$$P(L \cap D) = \frac{2}{50} = .04$$

After reviewing the performance data, the production manager decided to assign a poor performance rating to any employee whose work was either late or defective; thus the event of interest is $L \cup D$. What is the probability that the production manager assigned an employee a poor performance rating?

Note that the probability question is about the union of two events. Specifically, we want to know $P(L \cup D)$. Using equation (4.6), we have

$$P(L \cup D) = P(L) + P(D) - P(L \cap D)$$

Knowing values for the three probabilities on the right side of this expression, we can write

$$P(L \cup D) = .10 + .12 - .04 = .18$$

This calculation tells us that there is a .18 probability that a randomly selected employee received a poor performance rating.

As another example of the addition law, consider a recent study conducted by the personnel manager of a major computer software company. The study showed that 30% of the employees who left the firm within two years did so primarily because they were dissatisfied with their salary, 20% left because they were dissatisfied with their work assignments, and 12% of the former employees indicated dissatisfaction with *both* their salary and their work assignments. What is the probability that an employee who leaves within two years does so because of dissatisfaction with salary, dissatisfaction with the work assignment, or both?

Let

$$S = \text{the event that the employee leaves because of salary}$$
$$W = \text{the event that the employee leaves because of work assignment}$$

We have $P(S) = .30$, $P(W) = .20$, and $P(S \cap W) = .12$. Using equation (4.6), the addition law, we have

$$P(S \cup W) = P(S) + P(W) - P(S \cap W) = .30 + .20 - .12 = .38$$

We find a .38 probability that an employee leaves for salary or work assignment reasons.

Before we conclude our discussion of the addition law, let us consider a special case that arises for **mutually exclusive events**.

MUTUALLY EXCLUSIVE EVENTS

Two events are said to be mutually exclusive if the events have no sample points in common.

Events A and B are mutually exclusive if, when one event occurs, the other cannot occur. Thus, a requirement for A and B to be mutually exclusive is that their intersection must contain no sample points. The Venn diagram depicting two mutually exclusive events A and B is shown in Figure 4.7. In this case $P(A \cap B) = 0$ and the addition law can be written as follows.

ADDITION LAW FOR MUTUALLY EXCLUSIVE EVENTS

$$P(A \cup B) = P(A) + P(B)$$

FIGURE 4.7   MUTUALLY EXCLUSIVE EVENTS

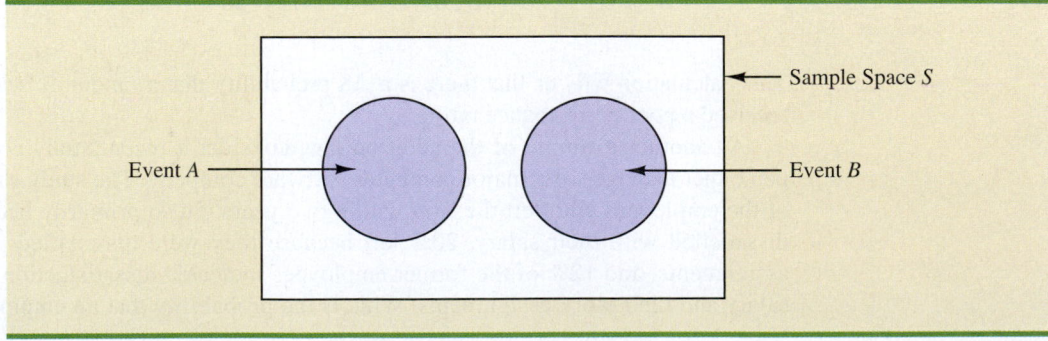

Exercises

Methods

22. Suppose that we have a sample space with five equally likely experimental outcomes: E_1, E_2, E_3, E_4, E_5. Let

$$A = \{E_1, E_2\}$$
$$B = \{E_3, E_4\}$$
$$C = \{E_2, E_3, E_5\}$$

a. Find $P(A)$, $P(B)$, and $P(C)$.
b. Find $P(A \cup B)$. Are A and B mutually exclusive?
c. Find A^c, C^c, $P(A^c)$, and $P(C^c)$.
d. Find $A \cup B^c$ and $P(A \cup B^c)$.
e. Find $P(B \cup C)$.

 SELF*test*

23. Suppose that we have a sample space $S = \{E_1, E_2, E_3, E_4, E_5, E_6, E_7\}$, where $E_1, E_2, \ldots,$ E_7 denote the sample points. The following probability assignments apply: $P(E_1) = .05$, $P(E_2) = .20$, $P(E_3) = .20$, $P(E_4) = .25$, $P(E_5) = .15$, $P(E_6) = .10$, and $P(E_7) = .05$. Let

$$A = \{E_1, E_4, E_6\}$$
$$B = \{E_2, E_4, E_7\}$$
$$C = \{E_2, E_3, E_5, E_7\}$$

a. Find $P(A)$, $P(B)$, and $P(C)$.
b. Find $A \cup B$ and $P(A \cup B)$.
c. Find $A \cap B$ and $P(A \cap B)$.
d. Are events A and C mutually exclusive?
e. Find B^c and $P(B^c)$.

Applications

24. Clarkson University surveyed alumni to learn more about what they think of Clarkson. One part of the survey asked respondents to indicate whether their overall experience at Clarkson fell short of expectations, met expectations, or surpassed expectations. The results showed that 4% of the respondents did not provide a response, 26% said that their experience fell short of expectations, and 65% of the respondents said that their experience met expectations.
    a. If we chose an alumnus at random, what is the probability that the alumnus would say their experience *surpassed* expectations?
    b. If we chose an alumnus at random, what is the probability that the alumnus would say their experience met or surpassed expectations?

25. The Eco Pulse survey from the marketing communications firm Shelton Group asked individuals to indicate things they do that make them feel guilty (*Los Angeles Times*, August 15, 2012). Based on the survey results, there is a .39 probability that a randomly selected person will feel guilty about wasting food and a .27 probability that a randomly selected person will feel guilty about leaving lights on when not in a room. Moreover, there is a .12 probability that a randomly selected person will feel guilty for both of these reasons.
    a. What is the probability that a randomly selected person will feel guilty for either wasting food or leaving lights on when not in a room?
    b. What is the probability that a randomly selected person will not feel guilty for either of these reasons?

26. Information about mutual funds provided by Morningstar Investment Research includes the type of mutual fund (Domestic Equity, International Equity, or Fixed Income) and

the Morningstar rating for the fund. The rating is expressed from 1-star (lowest rating) to 5-star (highest rating). A sample of 25 mutual funds was selected from *Morningstar Funds 500*. The following counts were obtained:

- Sixteen mutual funds were Domestic Equity funds.
- Thirteen mutual funds were rated 3-star or less.
- Seven of the Domestic Equity funds were rated 4-star.
- Two of the Domestic Equity funds were rated 5-star.

Assume that one of these 25 mutual funds will be randomly selected in order to learn more about the mutual fund and its investment strategy.

a. What is the probability of selecting a Domestic Equity fund?
b. What is the probability of selecting a fund with a 4-star or 5-star rating?
c. What is the probability of selecting a fund that is both a Domestic Equity fund *and* a fund with a 4-star or 5-star rating?
d. What is the probability of selecting a fund that is a Domestic Equity fund *or* a fund with a 4-star or 5-star rating?

27. A marketing firm would like to test-market the name of a new energy drink targeted at 18- to 29-year-olds via social media. A study by the Pew Research Center found that 35% of U.S. adults (18 and older) do not use social media (*Pew Research Center* website, October 2015). The percentage of U.S. young adults age 30 and older is 78%. Suppose that the percentage of the U.S. adult population that is either age 18–29 or uses social media is 67.2%.

a. What is the probability that a randomly selected U.S. adult uses social media?
b. What is the probability that a randomly selected U.S. adult is aged 18–29?
c. What is the probability that a randomly selected U.S. adult is 18–29 and a user of social media?

 28. A survey of magazine subscribers showed that 45.8% rented a car during the past 12 months for business reasons, 54% rented a car during the past 12 months for personal reasons, and 30% rented a car during the past 12 months for both business and personal reasons.

a. What is the probability that a subscriber rented a car during the past 12 months for business or personal reasons?
b. What is the probability that a subscriber did not rent a car during the past 12 months for either business or personal reasons?

29. High school seniors with strong academic records apply to the nation's most selective colleges in greater numbers each year. Because the number of slots remains relatively stable, some colleges reject more early applicants. Suppose that for a recent admissions class, an Ivy League college received 2851 applications for early admission. Of this group, it admitted 1033 students early, rejected 854 outright, and deferred 964 to the regular admission pool for further consideration. In the past, this school has admitted 18% of the deferred early admission applicants during the regular admission process. Counting the students admitted early and the students admitted during the regular admission process, the total class size was 2375. Let *E*, *R*, and *D* represent the events that a student who applies for early admission is admitted early, rejected outright, or deferred to the regular admissions pool.

a. Use the data to estimate $P(E)$, $P(R)$, and $P(D)$.
b. Are events *E* and *D* mutually exclusive? Find $P(E \cap D)$.
c. For the 2375 students who were admitted, what is the probability that a randomly selected student was accepted during early admission?
d. Suppose a student applies for early admission. What is the probability that the student will be admitted for early admission or be deferred and later admitted during the regular admission process?

4.4 Conditional Probability

Often, the probability of an event is influenced by whether a related event already occurred. Suppose we have an event A with probability $P(A)$. If we obtain new information and learn that a related event, denoted by B, already occurred, we will want to take advantage of this information by calculating a new probability for event A. This new probability of event A is called a **conditional probability** and is written $P(A \mid B)$. We use the notation | to indicate that we are considering the probability of event A *given* the condition that event B has occurred. Hence, the notation $P(A \mid B)$ reads "the probability of A given B."

As an illustration of the application of conditional probability, consider the situation of the promotion status of male and female officers of a major metropolitan police force in the eastern United States. The police force consists of 1200 officers, 960 men and 240 women. Over the past two years, 324 officers on the police force received promotions. The specific breakdown of promotions for male and female officers is shown in Table 4.4.

After reviewing the promotion record, a committee of female officers raised a discrimination case on the basis that 288 male officers had received promotions, but only 36 female officers had received promotions. The police administration argued that the relatively low number of promotions for female officers was due not to discrimination, but to the fact that relatively few females are members of the police force. Let us show how conditional probability could be used to analyze the discrimination charge.

Let

$$M = \text{event an officer is a man}$$
$$W = \text{event an officer is a woman}$$
$$A = \text{event an officer is promoted}$$
$$A^c = \text{event an officer is not promoted}$$

Dividing the data values in Table 4.4 by the total of 1200 officers enables us to summarize the available information with the following probability values.

$$P(M \cap A) = 288/1200 = .24 \quad \text{probability that a randomly selected officer}$$
$$\text{is a man } and \text{ is promoted}$$

$$P(M \cap A^c) = 672/1200 = .56 \quad \text{probability that a randomly selected officer}$$
$$\text{is a man } and \text{ is not promoted}$$

$$P(W \cap A) = 36/1200 = .03 \quad \text{probability that a randomly selected officer}$$
$$\text{is a woman } and \text{ is promoted}$$

$$P(W \cap A^c) = 204/1200 = .17 \quad \text{probability that a randomly selected officer}$$
$$\text{is a woman } and \text{ is not promoted}$$

Because each of these values gives the probability of the intersection of two events, the probabilities are called **joint probabilities**. Table 4.5, which provides a summary of the probability information for the police officer promotion situation, is referred to as a *joint probability table*.

TABLE 4.4   PROMOTION STATUS OF POLICE OFFICERS OVER THE PAST TWO YEARS

	Men	Women	Total
Promoted	288	36	324
Not Promoted	672	204	876
Total	960	240	1200

TABLE 4.5   JOINT PROBABILITY TABLE FOR PROMOTIONS

Joint probabilities appear in the body of the table.	Men (M)	Women (W)	Total
Promoted (A)	.24	.03	.27
Not Promoted (A^c)	.56	.17	.73
Total	.80	.20	1.00

Marginal probabilities appear in the margins of the table.

The values in the margins of the joint probability table provide the probabilities of each event separately. That is, $P(M) = .80$, $P(W) = .20$, $P(A) = .27$, and $P(A^c) = .73$. These probabilities are referred to as **marginal probabilities** because of their location in the margins of the joint probability table. We note that the marginal probabilities are found by summing the joint probabilities in the corresponding row or column of the joint probability table. For instance, the marginal probability of being promoted is $P(A) = P(M \cap A) + P(W \cap A) = .24 + .03 = .27$. From the marginal probabilities, we see that 80% of the force is male, 20% of the force is female, 27% of all officers received promotions, and 73% were not promoted.

Let us begin the conditional probability analysis by computing the probability that an officer is promoted given that the officer is a man. In conditional probability notation, we are attempting to determine $P(A \mid M)$. To calculate $P(A \mid M)$, we first realize that this notation simply means that we are considering the probability of the event A (promotion) given that the condition designated as event M (the officer is a man) is known to exist. Thus $P(A \mid M)$ tells us that we are now concerned only with the promotion status of the 960 male officers. Because 288 of the 960 male officers received promotions, the probability of being promoted given that the officer is a man is $288/960 = .30$. In other words, given that an officer is a man, that officer had a 30% chance of receiving a promotion over the past two years.

This procedure was easy to apply because the values in Table 4.4 show the number of officers in each category. We now want to demonstrate how conditional probabilities such as $P(A \mid M)$ can be computed directly from related event probabilities rather than the frequency data of Table 4.4.

We have shown that $P(A \mid M) = 288/960 = .30$. Let us now divide both the numerator and denominator of this fraction by 1200, the total number of officers in the study.

$$P(A \mid M) = \frac{288}{960} = \frac{288/1200}{960/1200} = \frac{.24}{.80} = .30$$

We now see that the conditional probability $P(A \mid M)$ can be computed as .24/.80. Refer to the joint probability table (Table 4.5). Note in particular that .24 is the joint probability of A and M; that is, $P(A \cap M) = .24$. Also note that .80 is the marginal probability that a randomly selected officer is a man; that is, $P(M) = .80$. Thus, the conditional probability $P(A \mid M)$ can be computed as the ratio of the joint probability $P(A \cap M)$ to the marginal probability $P(M)$.

$$P(A \mid M) = \frac{P(A \cap M)}{P(M)} = \frac{.24}{.80} = .30$$

The fact that conditional probabilities can be computed as the ratio of a joint probability to a marginal probability provides the following general formula for conditional probability calculations for two events A and B.

CONDITIONAL PROBABILITY

$$P(A \mid B) = \frac{P(A \cap B)}{P(B)} \qquad \text{(4.7)}$$

or

$$P(B \mid A) = \frac{P(A \cap B)}{P(A)} \qquad \text{(4.8)}$$

The Venn diagram in Figure 4.8 is helpful in obtaining an intuitive understanding of conditional probability. The circle on the right shows that event B has occurred; the portion of the circle that overlaps with event A denotes the event $(A \cap B)$. We know that once event B has occurred, the only way that we can also observe event A is for the event $(A \cap B)$ to occur. Thus, the ratio $P(A \cap B)/P(B)$ provides the conditional probability that we will observe event A given that event B has already occurred.

Let us return to the issue of discrimination against the female officers. The marginal probability in row 1 of Table 4.5 shows that the probability of promotion of an officer is $P(A) = .27$ (regardless of whether that officer is male or female). However, the critical issue in the discrimination case involves the two conditional probabilities $P(A \mid M)$ and $P(A \mid W)$. That is, what is the probability of a promotion *given* that the officer is a man, and what is the probability of a promotion *given* that the officer is a woman? If these two probabilities are equal, a discrimination argument has no basis because the chances of a promotion are the same for male and female officers. However, a difference in the two conditional probabilities will support the position that male and female officers are treated differently in promotion decisions.

We already determined that $P(A \mid M) = .30$. Let us now use the probability values in Table 4.5 and the basic relationship of conditional probability in equation (4.7) to compute

FIGURE 4.8   CONDITIONAL PROBABILITY $P(A \mid B) = P(A \cap B)/P(B)$

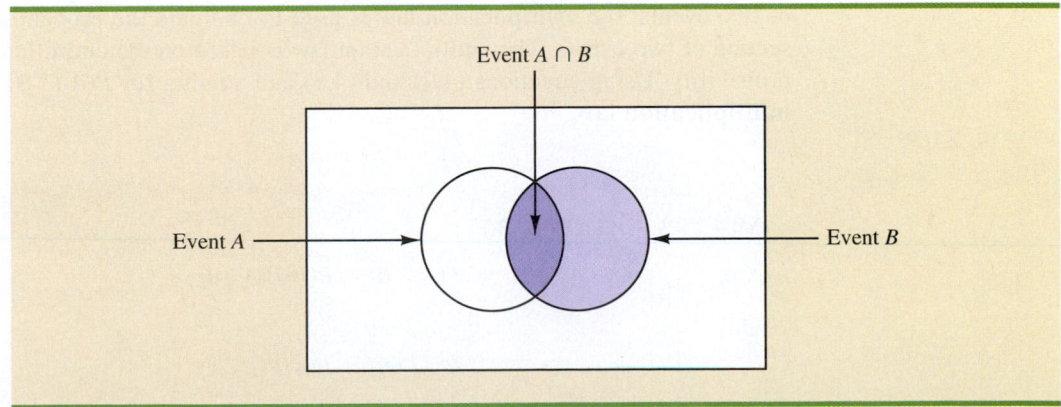

the probability that an officer is promoted given that the officer is a woman; that is, $P(A \mid W)$. Using equation (4.7), with W replacing B, we obtain

$$P(A \mid W) = \frac{P(A \cap W)}{P(W)} = \frac{.03}{.20} = .15$$

What conclusion do you draw? The probability of a promotion given that the officer is a man is .30, twice the .15 probability of a promotion given that the officer is a woman. Although the use of conditional probability does not in itself prove that discrimination exists in this case, the conditional probability values support the argument presented by the female officers.

Independent Events

In the preceding illustration, $P(A) = .27$, $P(A \mid M) = .30$, and $P(A \mid W) = .15$. We see that the probability of a promotion (event A) is affected or influenced by whether the officer is a man or a woman. Particularly, because $P(A \mid M) \neq P(A)$, we would say that events A and M are dependent events. That is, the probability of event A (promotion) is altered or affected by knowing that event M (the officer is a man) exists. Similarly, with $P(A \mid W) \neq P(A)$, we would say that events A and W are dependent events. However, if the probability of event A is not changed by the existence of event M—that is, $P(A \mid M) = P(A)$—we would say that events A and M are **independent events**. This situation leads to the following definition of the independence of two events.

INDEPENDENT EVENTS

Two events A and B are independent if

$$P(A \mid B) = P(A) \qquad\qquad (4.9)$$

or

$$P(B \mid A) = P(B) \qquad\qquad (4.10)$$

Otherwise, the events are dependent.

Multiplication Law

Whereas the addition law of probability is used to compute the probability of a union of two events, the multiplication law is used to compute the probability of the intersection of two events. The multiplication law is based on the definition of conditional probability. Using equations (4.7) and (4.8) and solving for $P(A \cap B)$, we obtain the **multiplication law**.

MULTIPLICATION LAW

$$P(A \cap B) = P(B)P(A \mid B) \qquad\qquad (4.11)$$

or

$$P(A \cap B) = P(A)P(B \mid A) \qquad\qquad (4.12)$$

To illustrate the use of the multiplication law, consider a newspaper circulation department where it is known that 84% of the households in a particular neighborhood subscribe to the daily edition of the paper. If we let D denote the event that a household subscribes to the daily edition, $P(D) = .84$. In addition, it is known that the probability that a household that already holds a daily subscription also subscribes to the Sunday edition (event S) is .75; that is, $P(S \mid D) = .75$. What is the probability that a household subscribes to both the Sunday and daily editions of the newspaper? Using the multiplication law, we compute the desired $P(S \cap D)$ as

$$P(S \cap D) = P(D)P(S \mid D) = .84(.75) = .63$$

We now know that 63% of the households subscribe to both the Sunday and daily editions.

Before concluding this section, let us consider the special case of the multiplication law when the events involved are independent. Recall that events A and B are independent whenever $P(A \mid B) = P(A)$ or $P(B \mid A) = P(B)$. Hence, using equations (4.11) and (4.12) for the special case of independent events, we obtain the following multiplication law.

MULTIPLICATION LAW FOR INDEPENDENT EVENTS

$$P(A \cap B) = P(A)P(B) \qquad\qquad (4.13)$$

To compute the probability of the intersection of two independent events, we simply multiply the corresponding probabilities. Note that the multiplication law for independent events provides another way to determine whether A and B are independent. That is, if $P(A \cap B) = P(A)P(B)$, then A and B are independent; if $P(A \cap B) \neq P(A)P(B)$, then A and B are dependent.

As an application of the multiplication law for independent events, consider the situation of a service station manager who knows from past experience that 80% of the customers use a credit card when they purchase gasoline. What is the probability that the next two customers purchasing gasoline will each use a credit card? If we let

A = the event that the first customer uses a credit card

B = the event that the second customer uses a credit card

then the event of interest is $A \cap B$. Given no other information, we can reasonably assume that A and B are independent events. Thus,

$$P(A \cap B) = P(A)P(B) = (.80)(.80) = .64$$

To summarize this section, we note that our interest in conditional probability is motivated by the fact that events are often related. In such cases, we say the events are dependent and the conditional probability formulas in equations (4.7) and (4.8) must be used to compute the event probabilities. If two events are not related, they are independent; in this case neither event's probability is affected by whether the other event occurred.

NOTE AND COMMENT

Do not confuse the notion of mutually exclusive events with that of independent events. Two events with nonzero probabilities cannot be both mutually exclusive and independent. If one mutually exclusive event is known to occur, the other cannot occur; thus, the probability of the other event occurring is reduced to zero. They are therefore dependent.

Exercises

Methods

30. Suppose that we have two events, A and B, with $P(A) = .50$, $P(B) = .60$, and $P(A \cap B) = .40$.
    a. Find $P(A \mid B)$.
    b. Find $P(B \mid A)$.
    c. Are A and B independent? Why or why not?

31. Assume that we have two events, A and B, that are mutually exclusive. Assume further that we know $P(A) = .30$ and $P(B) = .40$.
    a. What is $P(A \cap B)$?
    b. What is $P(A \mid B)$?
    c. A student in statistics argues that the concepts of mutually exclusive events and independent events are really the same, and that if events are mutually exclusive they must be independent. Do you agree with this statement? Use the probability information in this problem to justify your answer.
    d. What general conclusion would you make about mutually exclusive and independent events given the results of this problem?

Applications

32. Consider the following example survey results of 18- to 34-year-olds in the United States, in response to the question "Are you currently living with your family?":

	Yes	No	Totals
Men	106	141	247
Women	92	161	253
Totals	198	302	500

    a. Develop the joint probability table for these data and use it to answer the following questions.
    b. What are the marginal probabilities?
    c. What is the probability of living with family given you are an 18- to 34-year-old man in the U.S.?
    d. What is the probability of living with family given you are an 18- to 34-year-old woman in the U.S.?
    e. What is the probability of an 18- to 34-year-old in the U.S. living with family?
    f. If, in the U.S., 49.4% of 18- to 34-year-olds are male, do you consider this a good representative sample? Why?

33. Students taking the Graduate Management Admissions Test (GMAT) were asked about their undergraduate major and intent to pursue their MBA as a full-time or part-time student. A summary of their responses follows.

		Undergraduate Major			
		Business	Engineering	Other	Totals
Intended	Full-Time	352	197	251	800
Enrollment	Part-Time	150	161	194	505
Status	Totals	502	358	445	1305

a. Develop a joint probability table for these data.

b. Use the marginal probabilities of undergraduate major (business, engineering, or other) to comment on which undergraduate major produces the most potential MBA students.

c. If a student intends to attend classes full-time in pursuit of an MBA degree, what is the probability that the student was an undergraduate engineering major?

d. If a student was an undergraduate business major, what is the probability that the student intends to attend classes full-time in pursuit of an MBA degree?

e. Let F denote the event that the student intends to attend classes full-time in pursuit of an MBA degree, and let B denote the event that the student was an undergraduate business major. Are events F and B independent? Justify your answer.

34. The Bureau of Transportation Statistics reports on-time performance for airlines at major U.S. airports. JetBlue, United, and US Airways share Terminal C at Boston's Logan Airport. The percentage of on-time flights reported for a sample month were 76.8% for JetBlue, 71.5% for United, and 82.2% for US Airways. Assume that 30% of the flights arriving at Terminal C are JetBlue flights, 32% are United flights, and 38% US Airways flights.

a. Develop a joint probability table with three rows (the airlines) and two columns (on-time and late).

b. An announcement is made that Flight 1382 will be arriving at gate 20 of Terminal C. What is the probability that Flight 1382 will arrive on time?

c. What is the most likely airline for Flight 1382? What is the probability that Flight 1382 is by this airline?

d. Suppose that an announcement is made saying that Flight 1382 will now be arriving late. What is the most likely airline for this flight? What is the probability that Flight 1382 is by this airline?

35. To better understand how husbands and wives feel about their finances, *Money Magazine* conducted a national poll of 1010 married adults age 25 and older with household incomes of $50,000 or more (*Money Magazine* website, December 14, 2014). Consider the following example set of responses to the question, "Who is better at getting deals?"

	Who Is Better?		
Respondent	I Am	My Spouse	We Are Equal
Husband	278	127	102
Wife	290	111	102

a. Develop a joint probability table and use it to answer the following questions.

b. Construct the marginal probabilities for Who Is Better (I Am, My Spouse, We Are Equal). Comment.

c. Given that the respondent is a husband, what is the probability that he feels he is better at getting deals than his wife?

d. Given that the respondent is a wife, what is the probability that she feels she is better at getting deals than her husband?

e. Given a response "My spouse" is better at getting deals, what is the probability that the response came from a husband?

f. Given a response "We are equal," what is the probability that the response came from a husband? What is the probability that the response came from a wife?

36. National Basketball Association player Jamal Crawford of the L.A. Clippers is an excellent free-throw shooter, making 93% of his shots (ESPN website). Assume that, late in a basketball game, Jamal Crawford is fouled and is awarded two shots.

a. What is the probability that he will make both shots?

b. What is the probability that he will make at least one shot?

c.   What is the probability that he will miss both shots?

d.   Late in a basketball game, a team often intentionally fouls an opposing player in order to stop the game clock. The usual strategy is to intentionally foul the other team's worst free-throw shooter. Assume that the Los Angeles Clippers' center makes 58% of his free-throw shots. Calculate the probabilities for the center as shown in parts (a), (b), and (c), and show that intentionally fouling the Los Angeles Clippers' center is a better strategy than intentionally fouling Jamal Crawford. Assume as in parts (a), (b), and (c) that two shots will be awarded.

37.   A joint survey by *Parade* magazine and Yahoo! found that 59% of American workers say that if they could do it all over again, they would choose a different career (*USA Today*, September 24, 2012). The survey also found that 33% of American workers say they plan to retire early and 67% say they plan to wait and retire at age 65 or older. Assume that the following joint probability table applies.

		Retire Early		
		Yes	No	
Career	**Same**	.20	.21	.41
	Different	.13	.46	.59
		.33	.67	

a.   What is the probability a worker would select the same career?

b.   What is the probability a worker who would select the same career plans to retire early?

c.   What is the probability a worker who would select a different career plans to retire early?

d.   What do the conditional probabilities in parts (b) and (c) suggest about the reasons workers say they would select the same career?

38.   The Institute for Higher Education Policy, a Washington, DC–based research firm, studied the payback of student loans for 1.8 million college students who had student loans that began to become due six years prior. The study found that 50% of the student loans were being paid back in a satisfactory fashion, and 50% of the student loans were delinquent. The following joint probability table shows the probabilities of a student's loan status and whether or not the student had received a college degree.

		College Degree		
		Yes	No	
Loan	**Satisfactory**	.26	.24	.50
Status	**Delinquent**	.16	.34	.50
		.42	.58	

a.   What is the probability that a student with a student loan had received a college degree?

b.   What is the probability that a student with a student loan had not received a college degree?

c.   Given the student had received a college degree, what is the probability that the student has a delinquent loan?

d. Given the student had not received a college degree, what is the probability that the student has a delinquent loan?
e. What is the impact of dropping out of college without a degree for students who have a student loan?

4.5 Bayes' Theorem

In the discussion of conditional probability, we indicated that revising probabilities when new information is obtained is an important phase of probability analysis. Often, we begin the analysis with initial or **prior probability** estimates for specific events of interest. Then, from sources such as a sample, a special report, or a product test, we obtain additional information about the events. Given this new information, we update the prior probability values by calculating revised probabilities, referred to as **posterior probabilities. Bayes' theorem** provides a means for making these probability calculations. The steps in this probability revision process are shown in Figure 4.9.

As an application of Bayes' theorem, consider a manufacturing firm that receives shipments of parts from two different suppliers. Let A_1 denote the event that a part is from supplier 1 and A_2 denote the event that a part is from supplier 2. Currently, 65% of the parts purchased by the company are from supplier 1 and the remaining 35% are from supplier 2. Hence, if a part is selected at random, we would assign the prior probabilities $P(A_1) = .65$ and $P(A_2) = .35$.

The quality of the purchased parts varies with the source of supply. Historical data suggest that the quality ratings of the two suppliers are as shown in Table 4.6. If we let G denote the event that a part is good and B denote the event that a part is bad, the information in Table 4.6 provides the following conditional probability values.

$$P(G \mid A_1) = .98 \quad P(B \mid A_1) = .02$$
$$P(G \mid A_2) = .95 \quad P(B \mid A_2) = .05$$

The tree diagram in Figure 4.10 depicts the process of the firm receiving a part from one of the two suppliers and then discovering that the part is good or bad as a two-step experiment. We see that four experimental outcomes are possible; two correspond to the part being good and two correspond to the part being bad.

FIGURE 4.9 PROBABILITY REVISION USING BAYES' THEOREM

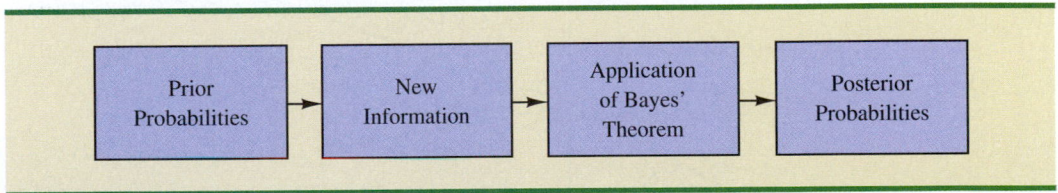

TABLE 4.6 HISTORICAL QUALITY LEVELS OF TWO SUPPLIERS

	Percentage Good Parts	Percentage Bad Parts
Supplier 1	98	2
Supplier 2	95	5

FIGURE 4.10   TREE DIAGRAM FOR TWO-SUPPLIER EXAMPLE

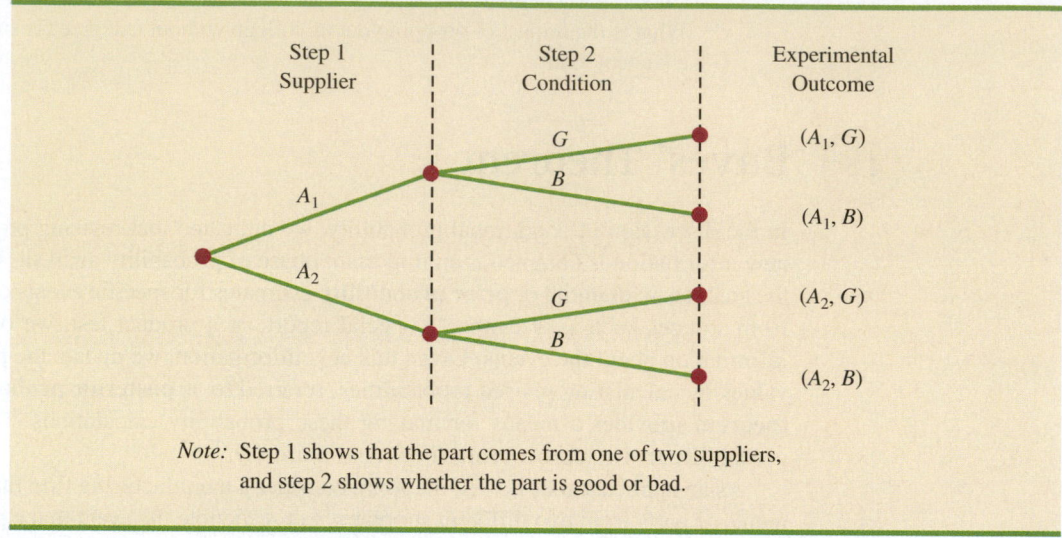

Note: Step 1 shows that the part comes from one of two suppliers,
and step 2 shows whether the part is good or bad.

Each of the experimental outcomes is the intersection of two events, so we can use the multiplication rule to compute the probabilities. For instance,

$$P(A_1, G) = P(A_1 \cap G) = P(A_1)P(G \mid A_1)$$

The process of computing these joint probabilities can be depicted in what is called a probability tree (see Figure 4.11). From left to right through the tree, the probabilities for each branch at step 1 are prior probabilities and the probabilities for each branch at step 2 are conditional probabilities. To find the probabilities of each experimental outcome, we simply multiply the probabilities on the branches leading to the outcome. Each of these joint probabilities is shown in Figure 4.11 along with the known probabilities for each branch.

Suppose now that the parts from the two suppliers are used in the firm's manufacturing process and that a machine breaks down because it attempts to process a bad part. Given

FIGURE 4.11   PROBABILITY TREE FOR TWO-SUPPLIER EXAMPLE

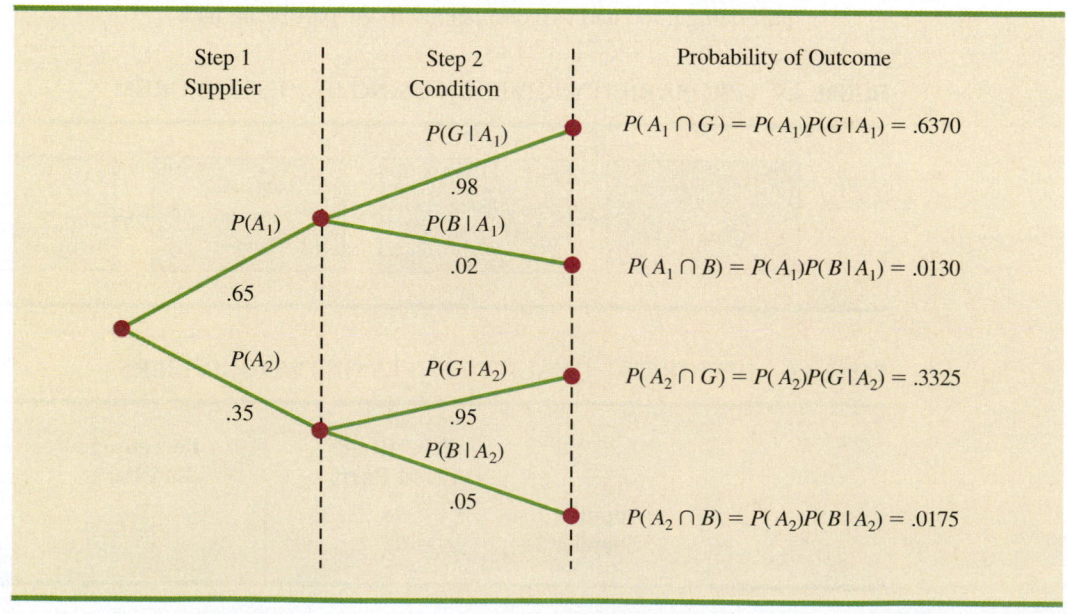

the information that the part is bad, what is the probability that it came from supplier 1 and what is the probability that it came from supplier 2? With the information in the probability tree (Figure 4.11), Bayes' theorem can be used to answer these questions.

Letting B denote the event that the part is bad, we are looking for the posterior probabilities $P(A_1 \mid B)$ and $P(A_2 \mid B)$. From the law of conditional probability, we know that

$$P(A_1 \mid B) = \frac{P(A_1 \cap B)}{P(B)} \qquad \textbf{(4.14)}$$

Referring to the probability tree, we see that

$$P(A_1 \cap B) = P(A_1)P(B \mid A_1) \qquad \textbf{(4.15)}$$

To find $P(B)$, we note that event B can occur in only two ways: $(A_1 \cap B)$ and $(A_2 \cap B)$. Therefore, we have

$$\begin{aligned} P(B) &= P(A_1 \cap B) + P(A_2 \cap B) \\ &= P(A_1)P(B \mid A_1) + P(A_2)P(B \mid A_2) \end{aligned} \qquad \textbf{(4.16)}$$

Substituting from equations (4.15) and (4.16) into equation (4.14) and writing a similar result for $P(A_2 \mid B)$, we obtain Bayes' theorem for the case of two events.

The Reverend Thomas Bayes (1702–1761), a Presbyterian minister, is credited with the original work leading to the version of Bayes' theorem in use today.

BAYES' THEOREM (TWO-EVENT CASE)

$$P(A_1 \mid B) = \frac{P(A_1)P(B \mid A_1)}{P(A_1)P(B \mid A_1) + P(A_2)P(B \mid A_2)} \qquad \textbf{(4.17)}$$

$$P(A_2 \mid B) = \frac{P(A_2)P(B \mid A_2)}{P(A_1)P(B \mid A_1) + P(A_2)P(B \mid A_2)} \qquad \textbf{(4.18)}$$

Using equation (4.17) and the probability values provided in the example, we have

$$P(A_1 \mid B) = \frac{P(A_1)P(B \mid A_1)}{P(A_1)P(B \mid A_1) + P(A_2)P(B \mid A_2)}$$

$$= \frac{(.65)(.02)}{(.65)(.02) + (.35)(.05)} = \frac{.0130}{.0130 + .0175}$$

$$= \frac{.0130}{.0305} = .4262$$

In addition, using equation (4.18), we find $P(A_2 \mid B)$.

$$P(A_2 \mid B) = \frac{(.35)(.05)}{(.65)(.02) + (.35)(.05)}$$

$$= \frac{.0175}{.0130 + .0175} = \frac{.0175}{.0305} = .5738$$

Note that in this application we started with a probability of .65 that a part selected at random was from supplier 1. However, given information that the part is bad, the probability that the part is from supplier 1 drops to .4262. In fact, if the part is bad, there is more than a 50–50 chance that it came from supplier 2; that is, $P(A_2 \mid B) = .5738$.

Bayes' theorem is applicable when the events for which we want to compute posterior probabilities are mutually exclusive and their union is the entire sample space.[1] For the case of n mutually exclusive events $A_1, A_2, \ldots, A_n$, whose union is the entire sample space, Bayes' theorem can be used to compute any posterior probability $P(A_i \mid B)$, as shown here.

BAYES' THEOREM

$$P(A_i \mid B) = \frac{P(A_i)P(B \mid A_i)}{P(A_1)P(B \mid A_1) + P(A_2)P(B \mid A_2) + \cdots + P(A_n)P(B \mid A_n)} \qquad \text{(4.19)}$$

With prior probabilities $P(A_1), P(A_2), \ldots, P(A_n)$ and the appropriate conditional probabilities $P(B \mid A_1), P(B \mid A_2), \ldots, P(B \mid A_n)$, equation (4.19) can be used to compute the posterior probability of the events $A_1, A_2, \ldots, A_n$.

Tabular Approach

A tabular approach is helpful in conducting the Bayes' theorem calculations. Such an approach is shown in Table 4.7 for the parts supplier problem. The computations shown there are done in the following steps.

Step 1. Prepare the following three columns:
   Column 1—The mutually exclusive events A_i for which posterior probabilities are desired
   Column 2—The prior probabilities $P(A_i)$ for the events
   Column 3—The conditional probabilities $P(B \mid A_i)$ of the new information B given each event

Step 2. In column 4, compute the joint probabilities $P(A_i \cap B)$ for each event and the new information B by using the multiplication law. These joint probabilities are found by multiplying the prior probabilities in column 2 by the corresponding conditional probabilities in column 3; that is, $P(A_i \cap B) = P(A_i)P(B \mid A_i)$.

Step 3. Sum the joint probabilities in column 4. The sum is the probability of the new information, $P(B)$. Thus we see in Table 4.7 that there is a .0130 probability that

TABLE 4.7   TABULAR APPROACH TO BAYES' THEOREM CALCULATIONS
FOR THE TWO-SUPPLIER PROBLEM

(1) Events A_i	(2) Prior Probabilities $P(A_i)$	(3) Conditional Probabilities $P(B \mid A_i)$	(4) Joint Probabilities $P(A_i \cap B)$	(5) Posterior Probabilities $P(A_i \mid B)$
A_1	.65	.02	.0130	.0130/.0305 = .4262
A_2	.35	.05	.0175	.0175/.0305 = .5738
	1.00		$P(B) = .0305$	1.0000

---

[1] If the union of events is the entire sample space, the events are said to be collectively exhaustive.

the part came from supplier 1 and is bad and a .0175 probability that the part came from supplier 2 and is bad. Because these are the only two ways in which a bad part can be obtained, the sum .0130 + .0175 shows an overall probability of .0305 of finding a bad part from the combined shipments of the two suppliers.

Step 4. In column 5, compute the posterior probabilities using the basic relationship of conditional probability.

$$P(A_i \mid B) = \frac{P(A_i \cap B)}{P(B)}$$

Note that the joint probabilities $P(A_i \cap B)$ are in column 4 and the probability $P(B)$ is the sum of column 4.

NOTES AND COMMENTS

1. Bayes' theorem is used extensively in decision analysis. The prior probabilities are often subjective estimates provided by a decision maker. Sample information is obtained and posterior probabilities are computed for use in choosing the best decision.

2. An event and its complement are mutually exclusive, and their union is the entire sample space. Thus, Bayes' theorem is always applicable for computing posterior probabilities of an event and its complement.

Exercises

Methods

39. The prior probabilities for events A_1 and A_2 are $P(A_1) = .40$ and $P(A_2) = .60$. It is also known that $P(A_1 \cap A_2) = 0$. Suppose $P(B \mid A_1) = .20$ and $P(B \mid A_2) = .05$.
    a. Are A_1 and A_2 mutually exclusive? Explain.
    b. Compute $P(A_1 \cap B)$ and $P(A_2 \cap B)$.
    c. Compute $P(B)$.
    d. Apply Bayes' theorem to compute $P(A_1 \mid B)$ and $P(A_2 \mid B)$.

40. The prior probabilities for events A_1, A_2, and A_3 are $P(A_1) = .20$, $P(A_2) = .50$, and $P(A_3) = .30$, respectively. The conditional probabilities of event B given A_1, A_2, and A_3 are $P(B \mid A_1) = .50$, $P(B \mid A_2) = .40$, and $P(B \mid A_3) = .30$.
    a. Compute $P(B \cap A_1)$, $P(B \cap A_2)$, and $P(B \cap A_3)$.
    b. Apply Bayes' theorem, equation (4.19), to compute the posterior probability $P(A_2 \mid B)$.
    c. Use the tabular approach to applying Bayes' theorem to compute $P(A_1 \mid B)$, $P(A_2 \mid B)$, and $P(A_3 \mid B)$.

Applications

41. A consulting firm submitted a bid for a large research project. The firm's management initially felt they had a 50–50 chance of getting the project. However, the agency to which the bid was submitted subsequently requested additional information on the bid. Past experience indicates that for 75% of the successful bids and 40% of the unsuccessful bids the agency requested additional information.
    a. What is the prior probability of the bid being successful (that is, prior to the request for additional information)?
    b. What is the conditional probability of a request for additional information given that the bid will ultimately be successful?

c.   Compute the posterior probability that the bid will be successful given a request for additional information.

42. A local bank reviewed its credit card policy with the intention of recalling some of its credit cards. In the past approximately 5% of cardholders defaulted, leaving the bank unable to collect the outstanding balance. Hence, management established a prior probability of .05 that any particular cardholder will default. The bank also found that the probability of missing a monthly payment is .20 for customers who do not default. Of course, the probability of missing a monthly payment for those who default is 1.

a.   Given that a customer missed a monthly payment, compute the posterior probability that the customer will default.

b.   The bank would like to recall its credit card if the probability that a customer will default is greater than .20. Should the bank recall its credit card if the customer misses a monthly payment? Why or why not?

43. In August 2012, tropical storm Isaac formed in the Caribbean and was headed for the Gulf of Mexico. There was an initial probability of .69 that Isaac would become a hurricane by the time it reached the Gulf of Mexico (National Hurricane Center website, August 21, 2012).

a.   What was the probability that Isaac would not become a hurricane but remain a tropical storm when it reached the Gulf of Mexico?

b.   Two days later, the National Hurricane Center projected the path of Isaac would pass directly over Cuba before reaching the Gulf of Mexico. How did passing over Cuba alter the probability that Isaac would become a hurricane by the time it reached the Gulf of Mexico? Using the following probabilities to answer this question. Hurricanes that reach the Gulf of Mexico have a .08 probability of having passed over Cuba. Tropical storms that reach the Gulf of Mexico have a .20 probability of having passed over Cuba.

c.   What happens to the probability of becoming a hurricane when a tropical storm passes over a landmass such as Cuba?

44. ParFore created a website to market golf equipment and golf apparel. Management would like a special pop-up offer to appear for female website visitors and a different special pop-up offer to appear for male website visitors. From a sample of past website visitors, ParFore's management learned that 60% of the visitors are male and 40% are female.

a.   What is the probability that a current visitor to the website is female?

b.   Suppose 30% of ParFore's female visitors previously visited the Dillard's Department Store website and 10% of ParFore's male visitors previously visited the Dillard's Department Store website. If the current visitor to ParFore's website previously visited the Dillard's website, what is the revised probability that the current visitor is female? Should the ParFore's website display the special offer that appeals to female visitors or the special offer that appeals to male visitors?

45. The percentage of adult users of the Internet who use Facebook has increased over time (*Pew Research Internet Project*, 2013). Of adult Internet users age 18–49, 81% use Facebook. Of adult Internet users age 50 and older, 54% use Facebook. Assume that 52% of adult Internet users are age 18–49.

a.   What is the probability that a randomly selected adult user of the Internet is age 50 or older?

b.   Given that an adult Internet user uses Facebook, what is the probability that he/she is age 18–49?

Summary

In this chapter we introduced basic probability concepts and illustrated how probability analysis can be used to provide helpful information for decision making. We described how probability can be interpreted as a numerical measure of the likelihood that an event will occur. In addition, we saw that the probability of an event can be computed either by summing the probabilities of the experimental outcomes (sample points) comprising the event or by using the relationships established by the addition, conditional probability, and multiplication laws of probability. For cases in which additional information is available, we showed how Bayes' theorem can be used to obtain revised or posterior probabilities.

Glossary

Addition law A probability law used to compute the probability of the union of two events. It is $P(A \cap B) = P(A) + P(B) - P(A \cup B)$. For mutually exclusive events, $P(A \cap B) = 0$; in this case the addition law reduces to $P(A \cup B) = P(A) + P(B)$.

Basic requirements for assigning probabilities Two requirements that restrict the manner in which probability assignments can be made: (1) For each experimental outcome E_i we must have $0 \leq P(E_i) \leq 1$; (2) considering all experimental outcomes, we must have $P(E_1) + P(E_2) + \cdots + P(E_n) = 1.0$.

Bayes' theorem A method used to compute posterior probabilities.

Classical method A method of assigning probabilities that is appropriate when all the experimental outcomes are equally likely.

Combination In an experiment we may be interested in determining the number of ways n objects may be selected from among N objects without regard to the *order in which the n objects are selected*. Each selection of n objects is called a combination and the total number of combinations of N objects taken n at a time is $C_n^N = \binom{N}{n} = \dfrac{N!}{n!(N-n)!}$ for $n = 0, 1, 2, \ldots, N$.

Complement of A The event consisting of all sample points that are not in A.

Conditional probability The probability of an event given that another event already occurred. The conditional probability of A given B is $P(A \mid B) = P(A \cap B)/P(B)$.

Event A collection of sample points.

Experiment A process that generates well-defined outcomes.

Independent events Two events A and B where $P(A \mid B) = P(A)$ or $P(B \mid A) = P(B)$; that is, the events have no influence on each other.

Intersection of A and B The event containing the sample points belonging to both A and B. The intersection is denoted $A \cap B$.

Joint probability The probability of two events both occurring; that is, the probability of the intersection of two events.

Marginal probability The values in the margins of a joint probability table that provide the probabilities of each event separately.

Multiple-step experiment An experiment that can be described as a sequence of steps. If a multiple-step experiment has k steps with n_1 possible outcomes on the first step, n_2 possible outcomes on the second step, and so on, the total number of experimental outcomes is given by $(n_1)(n_2) \ldots (n_k)$.

Multiplication law A probability law used to compute the probability of the intersection of two events. It is $P(A \cap B) = P(B)P(A \mid B)$ or $P(A \cap B) = P(A)P(B \mid A)$. For independent events it reduces to $P(A \cap B) = P(A)P(B)$.

Mutually exclusive events Events that have no sample points in common; that is, $A \cap B$ is empty and $P(A \cap B) = 0$.

Permutation In an experiment we may be interested in determining the number of ways n objects may be selected from among N objects when the *order in which the n objects are selected* is important. Each ordering of n objects is called a permutation and the total number of permutations of N objects taken n at a time is $P_n^N = n!\binom{N}{n} = \dfrac{N!}{(N-n)!}$ for $n = 0, 1, 2, \ldots, N$.

Posterior probabilities Revised probabilities of events based on additional information.

Prior probabilities Initial estimates of the probabilities of events.

Probability A numerical measure of the likelihood that an event will occur.

Relative frequency method A method of assigning probabilities that is appropriate when data are available to estimate the proportion of the time the experimental outcome will occur if the experiment is repeated a large number of times.

Sample point An element of the sample space. A sample point represents an experimental outcome.

Sample space The set of all experimental outcomes.

Subjective method A method of assigning probabilities on the basis of judgment.

Tree diagram A graphical representation that helps in visualizing a multiple-step experiment.

Union of *A* and *B* The event containing all sample points belonging to *A* or *B* or both. The union is denoted $A \cup B$.

Venn diagram A graphical representation for showing symbolically the sample space and operations involving events in which the sample space is represented by a rectangle and events are represented as circles within the sample space.

Key Formulas

Counting Rule for Combinations

$$C_n^N = \binom{N}{n} = \frac{N!}{n!(N-n)!} \tag{4.1}$$

Counting Rule for Permutations

$$P_n^N = n!\binom{N}{n} = \frac{N!}{(N-n)!} \tag{4.2}$$

Computing Probability Using the Complement

$$P(A) = 1 - P(A^c) \tag{4.5}$$

Addition Law

$$P(A \cup B) = P(A) + P(B) - P(A \cap B) \tag{4.6}$$

Conditional Probability

$$P(A \mid B) = \frac{P(A \cap B)}{P(B)} \tag{4.7}$$

$$P(B \mid A) = \frac{P(A \cap B)}{P(A)} \tag{4.8}$$

Multiplication Law

$$P(A \cap B) = P(B)P(A \mid B) \tag{4.11}$$
$$P(A \cap B) = P(A)P(B \mid A) \tag{4.12}$$

Multiplication Law for Independent Events

$$P(A \cap B) = P(A)P(B) \tag{4.13}$$

Bayes' Theorem

$$P(A_i \mid B) = \frac{P(A_i)P(B \mid A_i)}{P(A_1)P(B \mid A_1) + P(A_2)P(B \mid A_2) + \cdots + P(A_n)P(B \mid A_n)} \tag{4.19}$$

Supplementary Exercises

46. A *USA Today* survey of adults aged 18 and older conducted by Princess Cruises asked how many days into a vacation it takes until respondents feel truly relaxed. The responses were as follows: 422—a day or less; 181—2 days; 80—3 days; 121—4 or more days; and 201—never feel relaxed.
    a. How many adults participated in the Princess Cruises survey?
    b. What response has the highest probability? What is the probability of this response?
    c. What is the probability a respondent never feels truly relaxed on a vacation?
    d. What is the probability it takes a respondent 2 or more days to feel truly relaxed?

47. A financial manager made two new investments—one in the oil industry and one in municipal bonds. After a one-year period, each of the investments will be classified as either successful or unsuccessful. Consider the making of the two investments as an experiment.
    a. How many sample points exist for this experiment?
    b. Show a tree diagram and list the sample points.
    c. Let O = the event that the oil industry investment is successful and M = the event that the municipal bond investment is successful. List the sample points in O and in M.
    d. List the sample points in the union of the events $(O \cup M)$.
    e. List the sample points in the intersection of the events $(O \cap M)$.
    f. Are events O and M mutually exclusive? Explain.

48. Below are the results of a survey of 1364 individuals who were asked if they use social media and other websites to voice their opinions about television programs.

	Uses Social Media and Other Websites to Voice Opinions About Television Programs	Doesn't Use Social Media and Other Websites to Voice Opinions About Television Programs
Female	395	291
Male	323	355

    a. Show a joint probability table.
    b. What is the probability a respondent is female?
    c. What is the conditional probability a respondent uses social media and other websites to voice opinions about television programs given the respondent is female?

d. Let F denote the event that the respondent is female and A denote the event that the respondent uses social media and other websites to voice opinions about television programs. Are events F and A independent?

49. A study of 31,000 hospital admissions in New York State found that 4% of the admissions led to treatment-caused injuries. One-seventh of these treatment-caused injuries resulted in death, and one-fourth were caused by negligence. Malpractice claims were filed in one out of 7.5 cases involving negligence, and payments were made in one out of every two claims.

a. What is the probability a person admitted to the hospital will suffer a treatment-caused injury due to negligence?

b. What is the probability a person admitted to the hospital will die from a treatment-caused injury?

c. In the case of a negligent treatment-caused injury, what is the probability a malpractice claim will be paid?

50. A telephone survey to determine viewer response to a new television show obtained the following data.

Rating	Frequency
Poor	4
Below average	8
Average	11
Above average	14
Excellent	13

a. What is the probability that a randomly selected viewer will rate the new show as average or better?

b. What is the probability that a randomly selected viewer will rate the new show below average or worse?

51. The U.S. Census Bureau serves as the leading source of quantitative data about the nation's people and economy. The following crosstabulation shows the number of households (1000s) and the household income by the highest level of education for the head of household (U.S. Census Bureau website, 2013). Only households in which the head has a high school diploma or more are included.

Highest Level of Education	Household Income				
	Under $25,000	$25,000 to $49,999	$50,000 to $99,999	$100,000 and Over	Total
High school graduate	9,880	9,970	9,441	3,482	32,773
Bachelor's degree	2,484	4,164	7,666	7,817	22,131
Master's degree	685	1,205	3,019	4,094	9,003
Doctoral degree	79	160	422	1,076	1,737
Total	13,128	15,499	20,548	16,469	65,644

a. Develop a joint probability table.

b. What is the probability of the head of one of these households having a master's degree or more education?

c. What is the probability of a household headed by someone with a high school diploma earning $100,000 or more?

d. What is the probability of one of these households having an income below $25,000?
e. What is the probability of a household headed by someone with a bachelor's degree earning less than $25,000?
f. Is household income independent of educational level?

52. An MBA new matriculants survey provided the following data for 2018 students.

		Applied to More Than One School	
		Yes	No
Age Group	**23 and under**	207	201
	24–26	299	379
	27–30	185	268
	31–35	66	193
	36 and over	51	169

a. For a randomly selected MBA student, prepare a joint probability table for the experiment consisting of observing the student's age and whether the student applied to one or more schools.
b. What is the probability that a randomly selected applicant is 23 or under?
c. What is the probability that a randomly selected applicant is older than 26?
d. What is the probability that a randomly selected applicant applied to more than one school?

53. Refer again to the data from the MBA new matriculants survey in exercise 52.
a. Given that a person applied to more than one school, what is the probability that the person is 24–26 years old?
b. Given that a person is in the 36-and-over age group, what is the probability that the person applied to more than one school?
c. What is the probability that a person is 24–26 years old or applied to more than one school?
d. Suppose a person is known to have applied to only one school. What is the probability that the person is 31 or more years old?
e. Is the number of schools applied to independent of age? Explain.

54. The Pew Internet & American Life project conducted a survey that included several questions about how Internet users feel about search engines and other websites collecting information about them and using this information either to shape search results or target advertising to them. In one question, participants were asked, "If a search engine kept track of what you search for, and then used that information to personalize your future search results, how would you feel about that?" Respondents could indicate either "Would *not* be okay with it because you feel it is an invasion of your privacy" or "Would be *okay* with it, even if it means they are gathering information about you." Joint probabilities of responses and age groups are summarized in the following table.

Age	Not Okay	Okay
18–29	.1485	.0604
30–49	.2273	.0907
50+	.4008	.0723

    a.   What is the probability a respondent will *not be okay* with this practice?

    b.   Given a respondent is 30–49 years old, what is the probability the respondent will *be okay* with this practice?

    c.   Given a respondent is *not okay* with this practice, what is the probability the respondent is 50+ years old?

    d.   Is the attitude about this practice independent of the age of the respondent? Why or why not?

    e.   Do attitudes toward this practice differ for respondents who are 18–29 years old and respondents who are 50+ years old?

55.   A large consumer goods company ran a television advertisement for one of its soap products. On the basis of a survey that was conducted, probabilities were assigned to the following events.

$$B = \text{individual purchased the product}$$

$$S = \text{individual recalls seeing the advertisement}$$

$$B \cap S = \text{individual purchased the product and recalls seeing the advertisement}$$

The probabilities assigned were $P(B) = .20$, $P(S) = .40$, and $P(B \cap S) = .12$.

    a.   What is the probability of an individual's purchasing the product given that the individual recalls seeing the advertisement? Does seeing the advertisement increase the probability that the individual will purchase the product? As a decision maker, would you recommend continuing the advertisement (assuming that the cost is reasonable)?

    b.   Assume that individuals who do not purchase the company's soap product buy from its competitors. What would be your estimate of the company's market share? Would you expect that continuing the advertisement will increase the company's market share? Why or why not?

    c.   The company also tested another advertisement and assigned it values of $P(S) = .30$ and $P(B \cap S) = .10$. What is $P(B \mid S)$ for this other advertisement? Which advertisement seems to have had the bigger effect on customer purchases?

56.   Cooper Realty is a small real estate company located in Albany, New York, specializing primarily in residential listings. They recently became interested in determining the likelihood of one of their listings being sold within a certain number of days. An analysis of company sales of 800 homes in previous years produced the following data.

	Days Listed Until Sold			
	Under 30	**31–90**	**Over 90**	**Total**
Under $150,000	50	40	10	100
$150,000–$199,999	20	150	80	250
$200,000–$250,000	20	280	100	400
Over $250,000	10	30	10	50
Total	100	500	200	800

Initial Asking Price

    a.   If A is defined as the event that a home is listed for more than 90 days before being sold, estimate the probability of A.

    b.   If B is defined as the event that the initial asking price is under $150,000, estimate the probability of B.

    c.   What is the probability of $A \cap B$?

    d.   Assuming that a contract was just signed to list a home with an initial asking price of less than $150,000, what is the probability that the home will take Cooper Realty more than 90 days to sell?

    e.   Are events A and B independent?

57. A company studied the number of lost-time accidents occurring at its Brownsville, Texas plant. Historical records show that 6% of the employees suffered lost-time accidents last year. Management believes that a special safety program will reduce such accidents to 5% during the current year. In addition, it estimates that 15% of employees who had lost-time accidents last year will experience a lost-time accident during the current year.

    a.   What percentage of the employees will experience lost-time accidents in both years?

    b.   What percentage of the employees will suffer at least one lost-time accident over the two-year period?

58. According to the Open Doors Report, 9.5% of all full-time U.S. undergraduate students study abroad. Assume that 60% of the undergraduate students who study abroad are female and that 49% of the undergraduate students who do not study abroad are female.

    a.   Given a female undergraduate student, what is the probability that she studies abroad?

    b.   Given a male undergraduate student, what is the probability that he studies abroad?

    c.   What is the overall percentage of full-time female undergraduate students? What is the overall percentage of full-time male undergraduate students?

59. An oil company purchased an option on land in Alaska. Preliminary geologic studies assigned the following prior probabilities.

$$P(\text{high-quality oil}) = .50$$
$$P(\text{medium-quality oil}) = .20$$
$$P(\text{no oil}) = .30$$

    a.   What is the probability of finding oil?

    b.   After 200 feet of drilling on the first well, a soil test is taken. The probabilities of finding the particular type of soil identified by the test follow.

$$P(\text{soil} \mid \text{high-quality oil}) = .20$$
$$P(\text{soil} \mid \text{medium-quality oil}) = .80$$
$$P(\text{soil} \mid \text{no oil}) = .20$$

How should the firm interpret the soil test? What are the revised probabilities, and what is the new probability of finding oil?

60. A study reported by *Forbes* indicated that the five most common words appearing in spam e-mails are *shipping!, today!, here!, available,* and *fingertips!* Many spam filters separate spam from ham (e-mail not considered to be spam) through application of Bayes' theorem. Suppose that for one e-mail account, 1 in every 10 messages is spam and the proportions of spam messages that have the five most common words in spam e-mail are given below.

shipping!	.051
today!	.045
here!	.034
available	.014
fingertips!	.014

Also suppose that the proportions of ham messages that have these words are

shipping!	.0015
today!	.0022
here!	.0022
available	.0041
fingertips!	.0011

a. If a message includes the word *shipping!,* what is the probability the message is spam? If a message includes the word *shipping!,* what is the probability the message is ham? Should messages that include the word *shipping!* be flagged as spam?

b. If a message includes the word *today!,* what is the probability the message is spam? If a message includes the word *here!,* what is the probability the message is spam? Which of these two words is a stronger indicator that a message is spam? Why?

c. If a message includes the word *available,* what is the probability the message is spam? If a message includes the word *fingertips!,* what is the probability the message is spam? Which of these two words is a stronger indicator that a message is spam? Why?

d. What insights do the results of parts (b) and (c) yield about what enables a spam filter that uses Bayes' theorem to work effectively?

Case Problem 1   Hamilton County Judges

Hamilton County judges try thousands of cases per year. In an overwhelming majority of the cases disposed, the verdict stands as rendered. However, some cases are appealed, and of those appealed, some of the cases are reversed. Kristen DelGuzzi of *The Cincinnati Enquirer* conducted a study of cases handled by Hamilton County judges over a three-year period. Shown in Table 4.8 are the results for 182,908 cases handled (disposed) by 38 judges in Common Pleas Court, Domestic Relations Court, and Municipal Court. Two of the judges (Dinkelacker and Hogan) did not serve in the same court for the entire three-year period.

The purpose of the newspaper's study was to evaluate the performance of the judges. Appeals are often the result of mistakes made by judges, and the newspaper wanted to know which judges were doing a good job and which were making too many mistakes. You are called in to assist in the data analysis. Use your knowledge of probability and conditional probability to help with the ranking of the judges. You also may be able to analyze the likelihood of appeal and reversal for cases handled by different courts.

Managerial Report

Prepare a report with your rankings of the judges. Also, include an analysis of the likelihood of appeal and case reversal in the three courts. At a minimum, your report should include the following:

1. The probability of cases being appealed and reversed in the three different courts.
2. The probability of a case being appealed for each judge.
3. The probability of a case being reversed for each judge.
4. The probability of reversal given an appeal for each judge.
5. Rank the judges within each court. State the criteria you used and provide a rationale for your choice.

TABLE 4.8   TOTAL CASES DISPOSED, APPEALED, AND REVERSED IN HAMILTON COUNTY COURTS

Common Pleas Court

Judge	Total Cases Disposed	Appealed Cases	Reversed Cases
Fred Cartolano	3,037	137	12
Thomas Crush	3,372	119	10
Patrick Dinkelacker	1,258	44	8
Timothy Hogan	1,954	60	7
Robert Kraft	3,138	127	7
William Mathews	2,264	91	18
William Morrissey	3,032	121	22
Norbert Nadel	2,959	131	20
Arthur Ney, Jr.	3,219	125	14
Richard Niehaus	3,353	137	16
Thomas Nurre	3,000	121	6
John O'Connor	2,969	129	12
Robert Ruehlman	3,205	145	18
J. Howard Sundermann	955	60	10
Ann Marie Tracey	3,141	127	13
Ralph Winkler	3,089	88	6
Total	43,945	1762	199

Domestic Relations Court

Judge	Total Cases Disposed	Appealed Cases	Reversed Cases
Penelope Cunningham	2,729	7	1
Patrick Dinkelacker	6,001	19	4
Deborah Gaines	8,799	48	9
Ronald Panioto	12,970	32	3
Total	30,499	106	17

Municipal Court

Judge	Total Cases Disposed	Appealed Cases	Reversed Cases
Mike Allen	6,149	43	4
Nadine Allen	7,812	34	6
Timothy Black	7,954	41	6
David Davis	7,736	43	5
Leslie Isaiah Gaines	5,282	35	13
Karla Grady	5,253	6	0
Deidra Hair	2,532	5	0
Dennis Helmick	7,900	29	5
Timothy Hogan	2,308	13	2
James Patrick Kenney	2,798	6	1
Joseph Luebbers	4,698	25	8
William Mallory	8,277	38	9
Melba Marsh	8,219	34	7
Beth Mattingly	2,971	13	1
Albert Mestemaker	4,975	28	9
Mark Painter	2,239	7	3
Jack Rosen	7,790	41	13
Mark Schweikert	5,403	33	6
David Stockdale	5,371	22	4
John A. West	2,797	4	2
Total	108,464	500	104

DATA *file*

Judge

Case Problem 2   Rob's Market

Rob's Market (RM) is a regional food store chain in the southwest United States. David White, director of Business Intelligence for RM, would like to initiate a study of the purchase behavior of customers who use the RM loyalty card (a card that customers scan at checkout to qualify for discounted prices). The use of the loyalty card allows RM to capture what is known as "point-of-sale" data, that is, a list of products purchased by a given customer as he/she checks out of the market. David feels that better understanding of which products tend to be purchased together could lead to insights for better pricing and display strategies as well as a better understanding of sales and the potential impact of different levels of coupon discounts. This type of analysis is known as *market basket analysis*, as it is a study of what different customers have in their shopping baskets as they check out of the store.

As a prototype study, David wants to investigate customer buying behavior with regard to bread, jelly, and peanut butter. RM's Information Technology (IT) group, at David's request, has provided a data set of purchases by 1000 customers over a one-week period. The data set contains the following variables for each customer:

- Bread – wheat, white, or none
- Jelly – grape, strawberry, or none
- Peanut butter – creamy, natural, or none

The variables appear in the above order from left to right in the data set, where each row is a customer. For example, the first record of the data set is

white   grape   none

which means that customer #1 purchased white bread, grape jelly, and no peanut butter. The second record is

white   strawberry   none

which means that customer #2 purchased white bread, strawberry jelly, and no peanut butter. The sixth record in the data set is

none   none   none

which means that the sixth customer did not purchase bread, jelly, or peanut butter. Other records are interpreted in a similar fashion.

David would like you to do an initial study of the data to get a better understanding of RM customer behavior with regard to these three products.

MarketBasket

Managerial Report

Prepare a report that gives insight into the purchase behavior of customers who use the RM loyalty card. At a minimum your report should include estimates of the following:

1. The probability that a random customer does not purchase any of the three products (bread, jelly, or peanut butter).
2. The probability that a random customer purchases white bread.
3. The probability that a random customer purchases wheat bread.
4. The probability that a random customer purchases grape jelly given that he/she purchases white bread.
5. The probability that a random customer purchases strawberry jelly given that he/she purchases white bread.
6. The probability that a random customer purchases creamy peanut butter given that he/she purchases white bread.

One way to answer these questions is to use pivot tables (discussed in Chapter 2) to obtain absolute frequencies and use the pivot table results to calculate the relevant probabilities.

7. The probability that a random customer purchases natural peanut butter given that he/she purchases white bread.

8. The probability that a random customer purchases creamy peanut butter given that he/she purchases wheat bread.

9. The probability that a random customer purchases natural peanut butter given that he/she purchases wheat bread.

10. The probability that a random customer purchases white bread, grape jelly, and creamy peanut butter.

CHAPTER 5

Discrete Probability Distributions

CONTENTS

STATISTICS IN PRACTICE: CITIBANK

STATISTICS *in* PRACTICE

CITIBANK*
LONG ISLAND CITY, NEW YORK

Citibank, the retail banking division of Citigroup, offers a wide range of financial services including checking and saving accounts, loans and mortgages, insurance, and investment services. It delivers these services through a unique system referred to as Citibanking.

Citibank was one of the first banks in the United States to introduce automatic teller machines (ATMs). Citibank's ATMs, located in Citicard Banking Centers (CBCs), let customers do all of their banking in one place with the touch of a finger, 24 hours a day, 7 days a week. More than 150 different banking functions—from deposits to managing investments—can be performed with ease. Citibank customers use ATMs for 80% of their transactions.

Each Citibank CBC operates as a waiting line system with randomly arriving customers seeking service at one of the ATMs. If all ATMs are busy, the arriving customers wait in line. Periodic CBC capacity studies are used to analyze customer waiting times and to determine whether additional ATMs are needed.

Data collected by Citibank showed that the random customer arrivals followed a probability distribution known as the Poisson distribution. Using the Poisson distribution, Citibank can compute probabilities for the number of customers arriving at a CBC during any time period and make decisions concerning the number of ATMs needed. For example, let x = the number of customers arriving during a one-minute period. Assuming that a particular CBC has a mean arrival rate of two customers per minute, the following table shows the

_____
*The authors are indebted to Ms. Stacey Karter, Citibank, for providing this Statistics in Practice.

Each Citicard Banking Center operates as a waiting line system with randomly arriving customers seeking service at an ATM.

probabilities for the number of customers arriving during a one-minute period.

x	Probability
0	.1353
1	.2707
2	.2707
3	.1804
4	.0902
5 or more	.0527

Discrete probability distributions, such as the one used by Citibank, are the topic of this chapter. In addition to the Poisson distribution, you will learn about the binomial and hypergeometric distributions and how they can be used to provide helpful probability information.

In this chapter we extend the study of probability by introducing the concepts of random variables and probability distributions. Random variables and probability distributions are models for populations of data. The focus of this chapter is on probability distributions for discrete data, that is, discrete probability distributions.

We will introduce two types of discrete probability distributions. The first type is a table with one column for the values of the random variable and a second column for the associated probabilities. We will see that the rules for assigning probabilities to experimental outcomes introduced in Chapter 4 are used to assign probabilities for such a distribution. The second type of discrete probability distribution uses a special mathematical function to compute the probabilities for each value of the random variable. We present three probability distributions of this type that are widely used in practice: the binomial, Poisson, and hypergeometric distributions.

5.1   Random Variables

In Chapter 4 we defined the concept of an experiment and its associated experimental outcomes. A random variable provides a means for describing experimental outcomes using numerical values. Random variables must assume numerical values.

> **RANDOM VARIABLE**
>
> A **random variable** is a numerical description of the outcome of an experiment.

Random variables must assume numerical values.

In effect, a random variable associates a numerical value with each possible experimental outcome. The particular numerical value of the random variable depends on the outcome of the experiment. A random variable can be classified as being either *discrete* or *continuous* depending on the numerical values it assumes.

Discrete Random Variables

A random variable that may assume either a finite number of values or an infinite sequence of values such as $0, 1, 2, \ldots$ is referred to as a **discrete random variable**. For example, consider the experiment of an accountant taking the certified public accountant (CPA) examination. The examination has four parts. We can define a random variable as x = the number of parts of the CPA examination passed. It is a discrete random variable because it may assume the finite number of values 0, 1, 2, 3, or 4.

As another example of a discrete random variable, consider the experiment of cars arriving at a tollbooth. The random variable of interest is x = the number of cars arriving during a one-day period. The possible values for x come from the sequence of integers 0, 1, 2, and so on. Hence, x is a discrete random variable assuming one of the values in this infinite sequence.

Although the outcomes of many experiments can naturally be described by numerical values, others cannot. For example, a survey question might ask an individual to recall the message in a recent television commercial. This experiment would have two possible outcomes: The individual cannot recall the message and the individual can recall the message. We can still describe these experimental outcomes numerically by defining the discrete random variable x as follows: Let $x = 0$ if the individual cannot recall the message and $x = 1$ if the individual can recall the message. The numerical values for this random variable are arbitrary (we could use 5 and 10), but they are acceptable in terms of the definition of a random variable—namely, x is a random variable because it provides a numerical description of the outcome of the experiment.

Table 5.1 provides some additional examples of discrete random variables. Note that in each example the discrete random variable assumes a finite number of values or an infinite sequence of values such as $0, 1, 2, \ldots$. These types of discrete random variables are discussed in detail in this chapter.

Continuous Random Variables

A random variable that may assume any numerical value in an interval or collection of intervals is called a **continuous random variable**. Experimental outcomes based on

TABLE 5.1   EXAMPLES OF DISCRETE RANDOM VARIABLES

Experiment	Random Variable (x)	Possible Values for the Random Variable
Contact five customers	Number of customers who place an order	0, 1, 2, 3, 4, 5
Inspect a shipment of 50 radios	Number of defective radios	0, 1, 2, . . . , 49, 50
Operate a restaurant for one day	Number of customers	0, 1, 2, 3, . . .
Sell an automobile	Gender of the customer	0 if male; 1 if female

measurement scales such as time, weight, distance, and temperature can be described by continuous random variables. For example, consider an experiment of monitoring incoming telephone calls to the claims office of a major insurance company. Suppose the random variable of interest is $x =$ the time between consecutive incoming calls in minutes. This random variable may assume any value in the interval $x \geq 0$. Actually, an infinite number of values are possible for x, including values such as 1.26 minutes, 2.751 minutes, 4.3333 minutes, and so on. As another example, consider a 90-mile section of interstate highway I-75 north of Atlanta, Georgia. For an emergency ambulance service located in Atlanta, we might define the random variable as $x =$ number of miles to the location of the next traffic accident along this section of I-75. In this case, x would be a continuous random variable assuming any value in the interval $0 \leq x \leq 90$. Additional examples of continuous random variables are listed in Table 5.2. Note that each example describes a random variable that may assume any value in an interval of values. Continuous random variables and their probability distributions will be the topic of Chapter 6.

TABLE 5.2   EXAMPLES OF CONTINUOUS RANDOM VARIABLES

Experiment	Random Variable (x)	Possible Values for the Random Variable
Operate a bank	Time between customer arrivals in minutes	$x \geq 0$
Fill a soft drink can (max = 12.1 ounces)	Number of ounces	$0 \leq x \leq 12.1$
Construct a new library	Percentage of project complete after six months	$0 \leq x \leq 100$
Test a new chemical process	Temperature when the desired reaction takes place (min 150° F; max 212° F)	$150 \leq x \leq 212$

NOTE AND COMMENT

One way to determine whether a random variable is discrete or continuous is to think of the values of the random variable as points on a line segment. Choose two points representing values of the random variable. If the entire line segment between the two points also represents possible values for the random variable, then the random variable is continuous.

Exercises

Methods

1. Consider the experiment of tossing a coin twice.
   a. List the experimental outcomes.
   b. Define a random variable that represents the number of heads occurring on the two tosses.
   c. Show what value the random variable would assume for each of the experimental outcomes.
   d. Is this random variable discrete or continuous?

2. Consider the experiment of a worker assembling a product.
   a. Define a random variable that represents the time in minutes required to assemble the product.
   b. What values may the random variable assume?
   c. Is the random variable discrete or continuous?

Applications

3. Three students scheduled interviews for summer employment at the Brookwood Institute. In each case the interview results in either an offer for a position or no offer. Experimental outcomes are defined in terms of the results of the three interviews.
   a. List the experimental outcomes.
   b. Define a random variable that represents the number of offers made. Is the random variable continuous?
   c. Show the value of the random variable for each of the experimental outcomes.

4. In January the U.S. unemployment rate dropped to 8.3% (U.S. Department of Labor website, February 10, 2012). The Census Bureau includes nine states in the Northeast region. Assume that the random variable of interest is the number of Northeastern states with an unemployment rate in January that was less than 8.3%. What values may this random variable assume?

5. To perform a certain type of blood analysis, lab technicians must perform two procedures. The first procedure requires either one or two separate steps, and the second procedure requires one, two, or three steps.
   a. List the experimental outcomes associated with performing the blood analysis.
   b. If the random variable of interest is the total number of steps required to do the complete analysis (both procedures), show what value the random variable will assume for each of the experimental outcomes.

6. Listed is a series of experiments and associated random variables. In each case, identify the values that the random variable can assume and state whether the random variable is discrete or continuous.

Experiment	Random Variable (x)
a. Take a 20-question examination	Number of questions answered correctly
b. Observe cars arriving at a tollbooth for 1 hour	Number of cars arriving at tollbooth
c. Audit 50 tax returns	Number of returns containing errors
d. Observe an employee's work	Number of nonproductive hours in an eight-hour workday
e. Weigh a shipment of goods	Number of pounds

5.2 Developing Discrete Probability Distributions

The **probability distribution** for a random variable describes how probabilities are distributed over the values of the random variable. For a discrete random variable x, a **probability function**, denoted by $f(x)$, provides the probability for each value of the random variable. As such, you might suppose that the classical, subjective, and relative frequency methods of assigning probabilities introduced in Chapter 4 would be useful in developing discrete probability distributions. They are, and in this section we show how. Application of this methodology leads to what we call tabular discrete probability distributions, that is, probability distributions that are presented in a table.

The classical method of assigning probabilities to values of a random variable is applicable when the experimental outcomes generate values of the random variable that are equally likely. For instance, consider the experiment of rolling a die and observing the number on the upward face. It must be one of the numbers 1, 2, 3, 4, 5, or 6, and each of these outcomes is equally likely. Thus, if we let x = number obtained on one roll of a die and $f(x)$ = the probability of x, the probability distribution of x is given in Table 5.3.

The subjective method of assigning probabilities can also lead to a table of values of the random variable together with the associated probabilities. With the subjective method the individual developing the probability distribution uses their best judgment to assign each probability. So, unlike probability distributions developed using the classical method, different people can be expected to obtain different probability distributions.

The relative frequency method of assigning probabilities to values of a random variable is applicable when reasonably large amounts of data are available. We then treat the data as if they were the population and use the relative frequency method to assign probabilities to the experimental outcomes. The use of the relative frequency method to develop discrete probability distributions leads to what is called an **empirical discrete distribution**. With the large amounts of data available today (e.g., scanner data, credit card data), this type of probability distribution is becoming more widely used in practice. Let us illustrate by considering the sale of automobiles at a dealership.

We will use the relative frequency method to develop a probability distribution for the number of cars sold per day at DiCarlo Motors in Saratoga, New York. Over the past 300 days, DiCarlo has experienced 54 days with no automobiles sold, 117 days with one automobile sold, 72 days with two automobiles sold, 42 days with three automobiles sold, 12 days with four automobiles sold, and 3 days with five automobiles sold. Suppose we consider the experiment of observing a day of operations at DiCarlo Motors and define the random variable of interest as x = the number of automobiles sold during a day. Using the relative frequencies to assign probabilities to the values of the random variable x, we can develop the probability distribution for x.

TABLE 5.3 PROBABILITY DISTRIBUTION FOR NUMBER OBTAINED ON ONE ROLL OF A DIE

Number Obtained x	Probability of x $f(x)$
1	1/6
2	1/6
3	1/6
4	1/6
5	1/6
6	1/6

TABLE 5.4 PROBABILITY DISTRIBUTION FOR THE NUMBER OF AUTOMOBILES SOLD DURING A DAY AT DICARLO MOTORS

x	$f(x)$
0	.18
1	.39
2	.24
3	.14
4	.04
5	.01
Total	1.00

In probability function notation, $f(0)$ provides the probability of 0 automobiles sold, $f(1)$ provides the probability of 1 automobile sold, and so on. Because historical data show 54 of 300 days with 0 automobiles sold, we assign the relative frequency 54/300 = .18 to $f(0)$, indicating that the probability of 0 automobiles being sold during a day is .18. Similarly, because 117 of 300 days had 1 automobile sold, we assign the relative frequency 117/300 = .39 to $f(1)$, indicating that the probability of exactly 1 automobile being sold during a day is .39. Continuing in this way for the other values of the random variable, we compute the values for $f(2), f(3), f(4),$ and $f(5)$ as shown in Table 5.4.

A primary advantage of defining a random variable and its probability distribution is that once the probability distribution is known, it is relatively easy to determine the probability of a variety of events that may be of interest to a decision maker. For example, using the probability distribution for DiCarlo Motors as shown in Table 5.4, we see that the most probable number of automobiles sold during a day is 1 with a probability of $f(1) = .39$. In addition, the probability of selling 3 or more automobiles during a day is $f(3) + f(4) + f(5) = .14 + .04 + .01 = .19$. These probabilities, plus others the decision maker may ask about, provide information that can help the decision maker understand the process of selling automobiles at DiCarlo Motors.

In the development of a probability function for any discrete random variable, the following two conditions must be satisfied.

These conditions are the analogs to the two basic requirements for assigning probabilities to experimental outcomes presented in Chapter 4.

> **REQUIRED CONDITIONS FOR A DISCRETE PROBABILITY FUNCTION**
>
> $$f(x \geq 0 \tag{5.1}$$
> $$\sum f(x) = 1 \tag{5.2}$$

Table 5.4 shows that the probabilities for the random variable x satisfy equation (5.1); $f(x)$ is greater than or equal to 0 for all values of x. In addition, because the probabilities sum to 1, equation (5.2) is satisfied. Thus, the DiCarlo Motors probability function is a valid discrete probability function.

We can also show the DiCarlo Motors probability distribution graphically. In Figure 5.1 the values of the random variable x for DiCarlo Motors are shown on the horizontal axis and the probability associated with these values is shown on the vertical axis.

In addition to the probability distributions shown in tables, a formula that gives the probability function, $f(x)$, for every value of x is often used to describe probability

FIGURE 5.1 GRAPHICAL REPRESENTATION OF THE PROBABILITY DISTRIBUTION
FOR THE NUMBER OF AUTOMOBILES SOLD DURING A DAY AT
DICARLO MOTORS

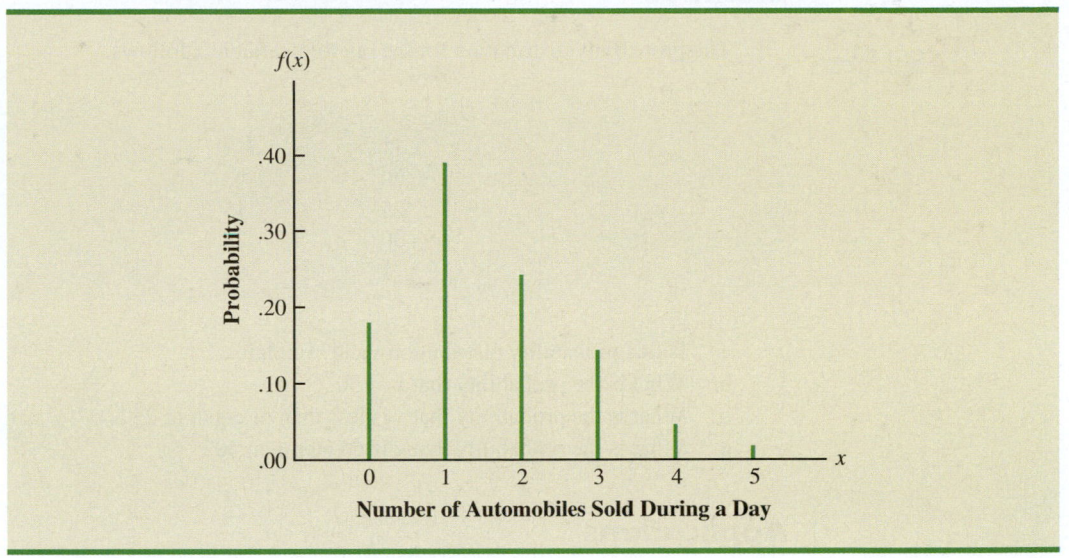

distributions. The simplest example of a discrete probability distribution given by a formula is the **discrete uniform probability distribution**. Its probability function is defined by equation (5.3).

DISCRETE UNIFORM PROBABILITY FUNCTION

$$f(x) = 1/n \qquad \textbf{(5.3)}$$

where

$$n = \text{the number of values the random variable may assume}$$

For example, consider again the experiment of rolling a die. We define the random variable x to be the number of dots on the upward face. For this experiment, $n = 6$ values are possible for the random variable; $x = 1, 2, 3, 4, 5, 6$. We showed earlier how the probability distribution for this experiment can be expressed as a table. Since the probabilities are equally likely, the discrete uniform probability function can also be used. The probability function for this discrete uniform random variable is

$$f(x) = 1/6 \quad x = 1, 2, 3, 4, 5, 6$$

Several widely-used discrete probability distributions are specified by formulas. Three important cases are the binomial, Poisson, and hypergeometric distributions; these distributions are discussed later in the chapter.

Exercises

Methods

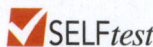

7. The probability distribution for the random variable x follows.

x	$f(x)$
20	.20
25	.15
30	.25
35	.40

a. Is this probability distribution valid? Explain.
b. What is the probability that $x = 30$?
c. What is the probability that x is less than or equal to 25?
d. What is the probability that x is greater than 30?

Applications

8. The following data were collected by counting the number of operating rooms in use at Tampa General Hospital over a 20-day period: On three of the days only one operating room was used, on five of the days two were used, on eight of the days three were used, and on four days all four of the hospital's operating rooms were used.
a. Use the relative frequency approach to construct an empirical discrete probability distribution for the number of operating rooms in use on any given day.
b. Draw a graph of the probability distribution.
c. Show that your probability distribution satisfies the required conditions for a valid discrete probability distribution.

9. Employee retention is a major concern for many companies. A survey of Americans asked how long they have worked for their current employer (Bureau of Labor Statistics website, December 2015). Consider the following example of sample data of 2000 college graduates who graduated five years ago.

Time with Current Employer (years)	Number
1	506
2	390
3	310
4	218
5	576

Let x be the random variable indicating the number of years the respondent has worked for her/his current employer.
a. Use the data to develop an empirical discrete probability distribution for x.
b. Show that your probability distribution satisfies the conditions for a valid discrete probability distribution.
c. What is the probability that a respondent has been at her/his current place of employment for more than 3 years?

10. The percent frequency distributions of job satisfaction scores for a sample of information systems (IS) senior executives and middle managers are as follows. The scores range from a low of 1 (very dissatisfied) to a high of 5 (very satisfied).

Job Satisfaction Score	IS Senior Executives (%)	IS Middle Managers (%)
1	5	4
2	9	10
3	3	12
4	42	46
5	41	28

   a. Develop a probability distribution for the job satisfaction score of a senior executive.
   b. Develop a probability distribution for the job satisfaction score of a middle manager.
   c. What is the probability a senior executive will report a job satisfaction score of 4 or 5?
   d. What is the probability a middle manager is very satisfied?
   e. Compare the overall job satisfaction of senior executives and middle managers.

11. A technician services mailing machines at companies in the Phoenix area. Depending on the type of malfunction, the service call can take 1, 2, 3, or 4 hours. The different types of malfunctions occur at about the same frequency.
   a. Develop a probability distribution for the duration of a service call.
   b. Draw a graph of the probability distribution.
   c. Show that your probability distribution satisfies the conditions required for a discrete probability function.
   d. What is the probability a service call will take 3 hours?
   e. A service call has just come in, but the type of malfunction is unknown. It is 3:00 P.M. and service technicians usually get off at 5:00 P.M. What is the probability the service technician will have to work overtime to fix the machine today?

12. Time Warner Cable provides television and Internet service to millions of customers. Suppose that the management of Time Warner Cable subjectively assesses a probability distribution for the number of new subscribers next year in the state of New York as follows.

x	$f(x)$
100,000	.10
200,000	.20
300,000	.25
400,000	.30
500,000	.10
600,000	.05

   a. Is this probability distribution valid? Explain.
   b. What is the probability Time Warner will obtain more than 400,000 new subscribers?
   c. What is the probability Time Warner will obtain fewer than 200,000 new subscribers?

13. A psychologist determined that the number of sessions required to obtain the trust of a new patient is either 1, 2, or 3. Let x be a random variable indicating the number of sessions required to gain the patient's trust. The following probability function has been proposed.

$$f(x) = \frac{x}{6} \quad \text{for } x = 1, 2, \text{ or } 3$$

a.   Is this probability function valid? Explain.
b.   What is the probability that it takes exactly 2 sessions to gain the patient's trust?
c.   What is the probability that it takes at least 2 sessions to gain the patient's trust?

14.   The following table is a partial probability distribution for the MRA Company's projected profits (x = profit in $1000s) for the first year of operation (the negative value denotes a loss).

x	$f(x)$
−100	.10
0	.20
50	.30
100	.25
150	.10
200	

a.   What is the proper value for $f(200)$? What is your interpretation of this value?
b.   What is the probability that MRA will be profitable?
c.   What is the probability that MRA will make at least $100,000?

5.3   Expected Value and Variance

Expected Value

The **expected value**, or mean, of a random variable is a measure of the central location for the random variable. The formula for the expected value of a discrete random variable x follows.

The expected value is a weighted average of the values of the random variable where the weights are the probabilities.

> **EXPECTED VALUE OF A DISCRETE RANDOM VARIABLE**
>
> $$E(x) = \mu = \sum xf(x) \qquad\qquad \textbf{(5.4)}$$

Both the notations $E(x)$ and μ are used to denote the expected value of a random variable.

The expected value does not have to be a value the random variable can assume.

Equation (5.4) shows that to compute the expected value of a discrete random variable, we must multiply each value of the random variable by the corresponding probability $f(x)$ and then add the resulting products. Using the DiCarlo Motors automobile sales example from Section 5.2, we show the calculation of the expected value for the number of automobiles sold during a day in Table 5.5. The sum of the entries in the $xf(x)$ column shows that the expected value is 1.50 automobiles per day. We therefore know that although sales of 0, 1, 2, 3, 4, or 5 automobiles are possible on any one day, over time DiCarlo can anticipate selling an average of 1.50 automobiles per day. Assuming 30 days of operation during a month, we can use the expected value of 1.50 to forecast average monthly sales of 30(1.50) = 45 automobiles.

Variance

The expected value provides a measure of central tendency for a random variable, but we often also want a measure of variability, or dispersion. Just as we used the variance in Chapter 3 to summarize the variability in data, we now use **variance** to summarize the variability in the values of a random variable. The formula for the variance of a discrete random variable follows.

TABLE 5.5   CALCULATION OF THE EXPECTED VALUE FOR THE NUMBER
OF AUTOMOBILES SOLD DURING A DAY AT DICARLO MOTORS

x	$f(x)$	$xf(x)$
0	.18	$0(.18) =$ .00
1	.39	$1(.39) =$ .39
2	.24	$2(.24) =$ .48
3	.14	$3(.14) =$ .42
4	.04	$4(.04) =$ .16
5	.01	$5(.01) =$ .05
		1.50

$$E(x) = \mu = \sum xf(x)$$

The variance is a weighted average of the squared deviations of a random variable from its mean. The weights are the probabilities.

VARIANCE OF A DISCRETE RANDOM VARIABLE

$$Var(x) = \sigma^2 = \sum (x - \mu)^2 f(x) \tag{5.5}$$

As equation (5.5) shows, an essential part of the variance formula is the deviation, $x - \mu$, which measures how far a particular value of the random variable is from the expected value, or mean, μ. In computing the variance of a random variable, the deviations are squared and then weighted by the corresponding value of the probability function. The sum of these weighted squared deviations for all values of the random variable is referred to as the *variance*. The notations $Var(x)$ and σ^2 are both used to denote the variance of a random variable.

The calculation of the variance for the probability distribution of the number of automobiles sold during a day at DiCarlo Motors is summarized in Table 5.6. We see that the variance is 1.25. The **standard deviation**, σ, is defined as the positive square root of the variance. Thus, the standard deviation for the number of automobiles sold during a day is

$$\sigma = \sqrt{1.25} = 1.118$$

The standard deviation is measured in the same units as the random variable ($\sigma = 1.118$ automobiles) and therefore is often preferred in describing the variability of a random variable. The variance σ^2 is measured in squared units and is thus more difficult to interpret.

TABLE 5.6   CALCULATION OF THE VARIANCE FOR THE NUMBER OF AUTOMOBILES
SOLD DURING A DAY AT DICARLO MOTORS

x	$x - \mu$	$(x - \mu)^2$	$f(x)$	$(x - \mu)^2 f(x)$
0	$0 - 1.50 = -1.50$	2.25	.18	$2.25(.18) =$ .4050
1	$1 - 1.50 = -.50$	.25	.39	$.25(.39) =$ .0975
2	$2 - 1.50 = .50$	.25	.24	$.25(.24) =$ .0600
3	$3 - 1.50 = 1.50$	2.25	.14	$2.25(.14) =$ .3150
4	$4 - 1.50 = 2.50$	6.25	.04	$6.25(.04) =$ .2500
5	$5 - 1.50 = 3.50$	12.25	.01	$12.25(.01) =$ .1225
				1.2500

$$\sigma^2 = \sum (x - \mu)^2 f(x)$$

Using Excel to Compute the Expected Value, Variance, and Standard Deviation

The calculations involved in computing the expected value and variance for a discrete random variable can easily be made in an Excel worksheet. One approach is to enter the formulas necessary to make the calculations in Tables 5.4 and 5.5. An easier way, however, is to make use of Excel's SUMPRODUCT function. In this subsection we show how to use the SUMPRODUCT function to compute the expected value and variance for daily automobile sales at DiCarlo Motors. Refer to Figure 5.2 as we describe the tasks involved. The formula worksheet is in the background; the value worksheet is in the foreground.

Enter/Access Data: The data needed are the values for the random variable and the corresponding probabilities. Labels, values for the random variable, and the corresponding probabilities are entered in cells A1:B7.

Enter Functions and Formulas: The SUMPRODUCT function multiplies each value in one range by the corresponding value in another range and sums the products. To use the SUMPRODUCT function to compute the expected value of daily automobile sales at DiCarlo Motors, we entered the following formula into cell B9:

=SUMPRODUCT(A2:A7,B2:B7)

Note that the first range, A2:A7, contains the values for the random variable, daily automobile sales. The second range, B2:B7, contains the corresponding probabilities. Thus, the SUMPRODUCT function in cell B9 is computing A2*B2 + A3*B3 + A4*B4 + A5*B5 + A6*B6 + A7*B7; hence, it is applying the formula in equation (5.4) to compute the expected value. The result, shown in cell B9 of the value worksheet, is 1.5.

FIGURE 5.2 EXCEL WORKSHEET FOR EXPECTED VALUE, VARIANCE, AND STANDARD DEVIATION

	A	B	C	D
1	Sales	Probability	Sq Dev from Mean	
2	0	0.18	=(A2-$B$9)^2	
3	1	0.39	=(A3-$B$9)^2	
4	2	0.24	=(A4-$B$9)^2	
5	3	0.14	=(A5-$B$9)^2	
6	4	0.04	=(A6-$B$9)^2	
7	5	0.01	=(A7-$B$9)^2	
8				
9	Mean	=SUMPRODUCT(A2:A7,B2:B7)		
10				
11	Variance	=SUMPRODUCT(C2:C7,B2:B7)		
12				
13	Std Deviation	=SQRT(B11)		
14				

	A	B	C	D
1	Sales	Probability	Sq Dev from Mean	
2	0	0.18	2.25	
3	1	0.39	0.25	
4	2	0.24	0.25	
5	3	0.14	2.25	
6	4	0.04	6.25	
7	5	0.01	12.25	
8				
9	Mean	1.5		
10				
11	Variance	1.25		
12				
13	Std Deviation	1.118		
14				

The formulas in cells C2:C7 are used to compute the squared deviations from the expected value or mean of 1.5 (the mean is in cell B9). The results, shown in the value worksheet, are the same as the results shown in Table 5.5. The formula necessary to compute the variance for daily automobile sales was entered into cell B11. It uses the SUMPRODUCT function to multiply each value in the range C2:C7 by each corresponding value in the range B2:B7 and sums the products. The result, shown in the value worksheet, is 1.25. Because the standard deviation is the square root of the variance, we entered the formula =SQRT(B11) into cell B13 to compute the standard deviation for daily automobile sales. The result, shown in the value worksheet, is 1.118.

Exercises

Methods

15. The following table provides a probability distribution for the random variable x.

x	$f(x)$
3	.25
6	.50
9	.25

    a. Compute $E(x)$, the expected value of x.
    b. Compute σ^2, the variance of x.
    c. Compute σ, the standard deviation of x.

SELFtest

16. The following table provides a probability distribution for the random variable y.

y	$f(y)$
2	.20
4	.30
7	.40
8	.10

    a. Compute $E(y)$.
    b. Compute $Var(y)$ and σ.

Applications

17. During the summer of 2014, Coldstream Country Club in Cincinnati, Ohio collected data on 443 rounds of golf played from its white tees. The data for each golfer's score on the twelfth hole are contained in the DATAfile *Coldstream12*.

    a. Construct an empirical discrete probability distribution for the player scores on the twelfth hole.

DATA *file*

Coldstream12

    b. A *par* is the score that a good golfer is expected to get for the hole. For hole number 12, par is four. What is the probability of a player scoring less than or equal to par on hole number 12?
    c. What is the expected score for hole number 12?
    d. What is the variance for hole number 12?
    e. What is the standard deviation for hole number 12?

18. The American Housing Survey reported the following data on the number of times that owner-occupied and renter-occupied units had a water supply stoppage lasting 6 or more hours over a 3-month period.

	Number of Units (1000s)	
Number of Times	Owner Occupied	Renter Occupied
0	439	394
1	1100	760
2	249	221
3	98	92
4 times or more	120	111

a. Define a random variable x = number of times that owner-occupied units had a water supply stoppage lasting 6 or more hours in the past 3 months and develop a probability distribution for the random variable. (Let $x = 4$ represent 4 or more times.)

b. Compute the expected value and variance for x.

c. Define a random variable y = number of times that renter-occupied units had a water supply stoppage lasting 6 or more hours in the past 3 months and develop a probability distribution for the random variable. (Let $y = 4$ represent 4 or more times.)

d. Compute the expected value and variance for y.

e. What observations can you make from a comparison of the number of water supply stoppages reported by owner-occupied units versus renter-occupied units?

19. West Virginia has one of the highest divorce rates in the nation, with an annual rate of approximately 5 divorces per 1000 people (Centers for Disease Control and Prevention website, January 12, 2012). The Marital Counseling Center, Inc. (MCC) thinks that the high divorce rate in the state may require them to hire additional staff. Working with a consultant, the management of MCC has developed the following probability distribution for x = the number of new clients for marriage counseling for the next year.

x	$f(x)$
10	.05
20	.10
30	.10
40	.20
50	.35
60	.20

a. Is this probability distribution valid? Explain.

b. What is the probability MCC will obtain more than 30 new clients?

c. What is the probability MCC will obtain fewer than 20 new clients?

d. Compute the expected value and variance of x.

20. The probability distribution for damage claims paid by the Newton Automobile Insurance Company on collision insurance follows.

Payment ($)	Probability
0	.85
500	.04
1000	.04
3000	.03
5000	.02
8000	.01
10000	.01

a. Use the expected collision payment to determine the collision insurance premium that would enable the company to break even.

b. The insurance company charges an annual rate of $520 for the collision coverage. What is the expected value of the collision policy for a policyholder? (*Hint:* It is the expected payments from the company minus the cost of coverage.) Why does the policyholder purchase a collision policy with this expected value?

21. The following probability distributions of job satisfaction scores for a sample of information systems (IS) senior executives and middle managers range from a low of 1 (very dissatisfied) to a high of 5 (very satisfied).

	Probability	
Job Satisfaction Score	IS Senior Executives	IS Middle Managers
1	.05	.04
2	.09	.10
3	.03	.12
4	.42	.46
5	.41	.28

a. What is the expected value of the job satisfaction score for senior executives?
b. What is the expected value of the job satisfaction score for middle managers?
c. Compute the variance of job satisfaction scores for executives and middle managers.
d. Compute the standard deviation of job satisfaction scores for both probability distributions.
e. Compare the overall job satisfaction of senior executives and middle managers.

22. The demand for a product of Carolina Industries varies greatly from month to month. The probability distribution in the following table, based on the past two years of data, shows the company's monthly demand.

Unit Demand	Probability
300	.20
400	.30
500	.35
600	.15

a. If the company bases monthly orders on the expected value of the monthly demand, what should Carolina's monthly order quantity be for this product?

b. Assume that each unit demanded generates $70 in revenue and that each unit ordered costs $50. How much will the company gain or lose in a month if it places an order based on your answer to part (a) and the actual demand for the item is 300 units?

23. In Gallup's Annual Consumption Habits Poll, telephone interviews were conducted for a random sample of 1014 adults aged 18 and over. One of the questions was, "How many cups of coffee, if any, do you drink on an average day?" The following table shows the results obtained (Gallup website, August 6, 2012).

Number of Cups per Day	Number of Responses
0	365
1	264
2	193
3	91
4 or more	101

Define a random variable x = number of cups of coffee consumed on an average day. Let $x = 4$ represent four or more cups.

a.   Develop a probability distribution for x.
b.   Compute the expected value of x.
c.   Compute the variance of x.
d.   Suppose we are only interested in adults who drink at least one cup of coffee on an average day. For this group, let y = the number of cups of coffee consumed on an average day. Compute the expected value of y and compare it to the expected value of x.

24.   The J. R. Ryland Computer Company is considering a plant expansion to enable the company to begin production of a new computer product. The company's president must determine whether to make the expansion a medium- or large-scale project. Demand for the new product is uncertain, which for planning purposes may be low demand, medium demand, or high demand. The probability estimates for demand are .20, .50, and .30, respectively. Letting x and y indicate the annual profit in thousands of dollars, the firm's planners developed the following profit forecasts for the medium- and large-scale expansion projects.

		Medium-Scale Expansion Profit		Large-Scale Expansion Profit	
		x	$f(x)$	y	$f(y)$
	Low	50	.20	0	.20
Demand	Medium	150	.50	100	.50
	High	200	.30	300	.30

a.   Compute the expected value for the profit associated with the two expansion alternatives. Which decision is preferred for the objective of maximizing the expected profit?
b.   Compute the variance for the profit associated with the two expansion alternatives. Which decision is preferred for the objective of minimizing the risk or uncertainty?

5.4 Bivariate Distributions, Covariance, and Financial Portfolios

A probability distribution involving two random variables is called a **bivariate probability distribution**. In discussing bivariate probability distributions, it is useful to think of a bivariate experiment. Each outcome for a bivariate experiment consists of two values, one for each random variable. For example, consider the bivariate experiment of rolling a pair of dice. The outcome consists of two values, the number obtained with the first die and the number obtained with the second die. As another example, consider the experiment of observing the financial markets for a year and recording the percentage gain for a stock fund and a bond fund. Again, the experimental outcome provides a value for two random variables, the percent gain in the stock fund and the percent gain in the bond fund. When dealing with bivariate probability distributions, we are often interested in the relationship between the random variables. In this section, we introduce bivariate distributions and show how the covariance and correlation coefficient can be used as a measure of linear association between the random variables. We shall also see how bivariate probability distributions can be used to construct and analyze financial portfolios.

A Bivariate Empirical Discrete Probability Distribution

Recall that in Section 5.2 we developed an empirical discrete distribution for daily sales at the DiCarlo Motors automobile dealership in Saratoga, New York. DiCarlo has another

TABLE 5.7 NUMBER OF AUTOMOBILES SOLD AT DICARLO'S SARATOGA AND GENEVA DEALERSHIPS OVER 300 DAYS

Geneva Dealership	Saratoga Dealership						Total
	0	**1**	**2**	**3**	**4**	**5**	
0	21	30	24	9	2	0	86
1	21	36	33	18	2	1	111
2	9	42	9	12	3	2	77
3	3	9	6	3	5	0	26
Total	54	117	72	42	12	3	300

dealership in Geneva, New York. Table 5.7 shows the number of cars sold at each of the dealerships over a 300-day period. The numbers in the bottom row (Labeled Total) are the frequencies we used to develop an empirical probability distribution for daily sales at DiCarlo's Saratoga dealership in Section 5.2. The numbers in the rightmost column (Labeled Total) are the frequencies of daily sales for the Geneva dealership. Entries in the body of the table give the number of days the Geneva dealership had a level of sales indicated by the row, when the Saratoga dealership had the level of sales indicated by the column. For example, the entry of 33 in the Geneva dealership row labeled 1 and the Saratoga column labeled 2 indicates that for 33 days out of the 300, the Geneva dealership sold 1 car and the Saratoga dealership sold 2 cars.

Suppose we consider the bivariate experiment of observing a day of operations at DiCarlo Motors and recording the number of cars sold. Let us define x = number of cars sold at the Geneva dealership and y = the number of cars sold at the Saratoga dealership. We can now divide all of the frequencies in Table 5.7 by the number of observations (300) to develop a bivariate empirical discrete probability distribution for automobile sales at the two DiCarlo dealerships. Table 5.8 shows this bivariate discrete probability distribution. The probabilities in the lower margin provide the marginal distribution for the DiCarlo Motors Saratoga dealership. The probabilities in the right margin provide the marginal distribution for the DiCarlo Motors Geneva dealership.

The probabilities in the body of the table provide the bivariate probability distribution for sales at both dealerships. Bivariate probabilities are often called joint probabilities. We see that the joint probability of selling 0 automobiles at Geneva and 1 automobile at Saratoga on a typical day is $f(0, 1) = .1000$, the joint probability of selling 1 automobile at Geneva and 4 automobiles at Saratoga on a typical day is .0067, and so on. Note that there is one bivariate probability for each experimental outcome. With

TABLE 5.8 BIVARIATE EMPIRICAL DISCRETE PROBABILITY DISTRIBUTION FOR DAILY SALES AT DICARLO DEALERSHIPS IN SARATOGA AND GENEVA, NEW YORK

Geneva Dealership	Saratoga Dealership						Total
	0	**1**	**2**	**3**	**4**	**5**	
0	.0700	.1000	.0800	.0300	.0067	.0000	.2867
1	.0700	.1200	.1100	.0600	.0067	.0033	.3700
2	.0300	.1400	.0300	.0400	.0100	.0067	.2567
3	.0100	.0300	.0200	.0100	.0167	.0000	.0867
Total	.18	.39	.24	.14	.04	.01	1.0000

4 possible values for x and 6 possible values for y, there are 24 experimental outcomes and bivariate probabilities.

Suppose we would like to know the probability distribution for total sales at both DiCarlo dealerships and the expected value and variance of total sales. We can define $s = x + y$ as total sales for DiCarlo Motors. Working with the bivariate probabilities in Table 5.8, we see that $f(s = 0) = .0700, f(s = 1) = .0700 + .1000 = .1700, f(s = 2) = .0300 + .1200 + .0800 = .2300$, and so on. We show the complete probability distribution for $s = x + y$ along with the computation of the expected value and variance in Table 5.9. The expected value is $E(s) = 2.6433$ and the variance is $Var(s) = 2.3895$.

With bivariate probability distributions, we often want to know the relationship between the two random variables. The covariance and/or correlation coefficient are good measures of association between two random variables. We saw in Chapter 3 how to compute the covariance and correlation coefficient for sample data. The formula we will use for computing the covariance between two random variables x and y is given below.

COVARIANCE OF RANDOM VARIABLES x AND y[1]

$$\sigma_{xy} = [Var(x + y) - Var(x) - Var(y)]/2 \tag{5.6}$$

We have already computed $Var(s) = Var(x + y)$ and, in Section 5.2, we computed $Var(y)$. Now we need to compute $Var(x)$ before we can use equation (5.6) to compute the covariance of x and y. Using the probability distribution for x (the right margin of Table 5.8), we compute $E(x)$ and $Var(x)$ in Table 5.10.

We can now use equation (5.6) to compute the covariance of the random variables x and y.

$$\sigma_{xy} = [Var(x + y) - Var(x) - Var(y)]/2 = (2.3895 - .8696 - 1.25)/2 = .1350$$

A covariance of .1350 indicates that daily sales at DiCarlo's two dealerships have a positive relationship. To get a better sense of the strength of the relationship we can compute the

TABLE 5.9   CALCULATION OF THE EXPECTED VALUE AND VARIANCE FOR TOTAL DAILY SALES AT DICARLO MOTORS

s	$f(s)$	$sf(s)$	$s - E(s)$	$(s - E(s))^2$	$(s - E(s))^2 f(s)$
0	.0700	.0000	−2.6433	6.9872	.4891
1	.1700	.1700	−1.6433	2.7005	.4591
2	.2300	.4600	−0.6433	0.4139	.0952
3	.2900	.8700	0.3567	0.1272	.0369
4	.1267	.5067	1.3567	1.8405	.2331
5	.0667	.3333	2.3567	5.5539	.3703
6	.0233	.1400	3.3567	11.2672	.2629
7	.0233	.1633	4.3567	18.9805	.4429
8	.0000	.0000	5.3567	28.6939	.0000
		$E(s) = 2.6433$			$Var(s) = 2.3895$

---

[1]Another formula is often used to compute the covariance of x and y when $Var(x + y)$ is not known. It is $\sigma_{xy} = \sum_{i,j}[x_i - E(x_i)][y_i - E(y_i)]f(x_i, y_j)$.

TABLE 5.10 CALCULATION OF THE EXPECTED VALUE AND VARIANCE OF DAILY AUTOMOBILE SALES AT DICARLO MOTORS' GENEVA DEALERSHIP

x	$f(x)$	$xf(x)$	$x - E(x)$	$[(x - E(x)]^2$	$[x - E(x)]^2 f(x)$
0	.2867	.0000	−1.1435	1.3076	.3749
1	.3700	.3700	−.1435	0.0206	.0076
2	.2567	.5134	.8565	0.8565	.1883
3	.0867	.2601	1.8565	1.8565	.2988
		$E(x) = 1.1435$			$Var(x) = .8696$

correlation coefficient. The correlation coefficient for the two random variables x and y is given by equation (5.7).

CORRELATION BETWEEN RANDOM VARIABLES x AND y

$$\rho_{xy} = \frac{\sigma_{xy}}{\sigma_x \sigma_y} \tag{5.7}$$

From equation (5.7), we see that the correlation coefficient for two random variables is the covariance divided by the product of the standard deviations for the two random variables.

Let us compute the correlation coefficient between daily sales at the two DiCarlo dealerships. First we compute the standard deviations for sales at the Saratoga and Geneva dealerships by taking the square root of the variance.

$$\sigma_x = \sqrt{.8696} = .9325$$

$$\sigma_y = \sqrt{1.25} = 1.1180$$

Now we can compute the correlation coefficient as a measure of the linear association between the two random variables.

$$\rho_{xy} = \frac{\sigma_{xy}}{\sigma_x \sigma_y} = \frac{.1350}{(.9325)(1.1180)} = .1295$$

In Chapter 3 we defined the correlation coefficient as a measure of the linear association between two variables. Values near +1 indicate a strong positive linear relationship; values near −1 indicate a strong negative linear relationship; and values near zero indicate a lack of a linear relationship. This interpretation is also valid for random variables. The correlation coefficient of .1295 indicates there is a weak positive relationship between the random variables representing daily sales at the two DiCarlo dealerships. If the correlation coefficient had equaled zero, we would have concluded that daily sales at the two dealerships were independent.

Financial Applications

Let us now see how what we have learned can be useful in constructing financial portfolios that provide a good balance of risk and return. A financial advisor is considering four possible economic scenarios for the coming year and has developed a probability distribution showing the percent return, x, for investing in a large-cap stock fund and the percent return, y, for investing in a long-term government bond fund given each of the scenarios. The bivariate

TABLE 5.11   PROBABILITY DISTRIBUTION OF PERCENT RETURNS FOR INVESTING IN A LARGE-CAP STOCK FUND, x, AND INVESTING IN A LONG-TERM GOVERNMENT BOND FUND, y

Economic Scenario	Probability $f(x, y)$	Large-Cap Stock Fund (x)	Long-Term Government Bond Fund (y)
Recession	.10	−40	30
Weak growth	.25	5	5
Stable growth	.50	15	4
Strong growth	.15	30	2

probability distribution for x and y is shown in Table 5.11. Table 5.11 is simply a list with a separate row for each experimental outcome (economic scenario). Each row contains the joint probability for the experimental outcome and a value for each random variable. Since there are only 4 joint probabilities, the tabular form used in Table 5.11 is simpler than the one we used for DiCarlo Motors where there were (4)(6) = 24 joint probabilities.

Using the formula in Section 5.3 for computing the expected value of a single random variable, we can compute the expected percent return for investing in the stock fund, $E(x)$, and the expected percent return for investing in the bond fund, $E(y)$.

$$E(x) = .10(-40) + .25(5) + .5(15) + .15(30) = 9.25$$

$$E(y) = .10(30) + .25(5) + .5(4) + .15(2) = 6.55$$

Using this information, we might conclude that investing in the stock fund is a better investment. It has a higher expected return, 9.25%. But financial analysts recommend that investors also consider the risk associated with an investment. The standard deviation of percent return is often used as a measure of risk. To compute the standard deviation, we must first compute the variance. Using the formula in Section 5.3 for computing the variance of a single random variable, we can compute the variance of the percent returns for the stock and bond fund investments.

$$Var(x) = .1(-40 - 9.25)^2 + .25(5 - 9.25)^2 + .50(15 - 9.25)^2 + .15(30 - 9.25)^2 = 328.1875$$

$$Var(y) = .1(30 - 6.55)^2 + .25(5 - 6.55)^2 + .50(4 - 6.55)^2 + .15(2 - 6.55)^2 = 61.9475$$

The standard deviation of the return from an investment in the stock fund is $\sigma_x = \sqrt{328.1875} = 18.1159\%$ and the standard deviation of the return from an investment in the bond fund is $\sigma_y = \sqrt{61.9475} = 7.8707\%$. So, we can conclude that investing in the bond fund is less risky. It has the smaller standard deviation. We have already seen that the stock fund offers a greater expected return, so if we want to choose between investing in either the stock fund or the bond fund it depends on our attitude toward risk and return. An aggressive investor might choose the stock fund because of the higher expected return; a conservative investor might choose the bond fund because of the lower risk. But there are other options. What about the possibility of investing in a portfolio consisting of both an investment in the stock fund and an investment in the bond fund?

Suppose we would like to consider three alternatives: investing solely in the large-cap stock fund, investing solely in the long-term government bond fund, and splitting our funds equally between the stock fund and the bond fund (one-half in each). We have already computed the expected value and standard deviation for investing solely in the stock fund and the bond fund. Let us now evaluate the third alternative: constructing a portfolio by investing equal amounts in the large-cap stock fund and in the long-term government bond fund.

To evaluate this portfolio, we start by computing its expected return. We have previously defined x as the percent return from an investment in the stock fund and y as the percent return from an investment in the bond fund so the percent return for our portfolio is $r = .5x + .5y$. To find the expected return for a portfolio with one-half invested in the stock fund and one-half invested in the bond fund, we want to compute $E(r) = E(.5x + .5y)$. The expression $.5x + .5y$ is called a linear combination of the random variables x and y. Equation (5.8) provides an easy method for computing the expected value of a linear combination of the random variables x and y when we already know $E(x)$ and $E(y)$. In equation (5.8), a represents the coefficient of x and b represents the coefficient of y in the linear combination.

EXPECTED VALUE OF A LINEAR COMBINATION OF RANDOM VARIABLES x AND y

$$E(ax + by) = aE(x) + bE(y) \qquad \textbf{(5.8)}$$

Since we have already computed $E(x) = 9.25$ and $E(y) = 6.55$, we can use equation (5.8) to compute the expected value of our portfolio.

$$E(.5x + .5y) = .5E(x) + .5E(y) = .5(9.25) + .5(6.55) = 7.9$$

We see that the expected return for investing in the portfolio is 7.9%. With $100 invested, we would expect a return of $100(.079) = $7.90; with $1000 invested we would expect a return of $1000(.079) = $79.00; and so on. But what about the risk? As mentioned previously, financial analysts often use the standard deviation as a measure of risk.

Our portfolio is a linear combination of two random variables, so we need to be able to compute the variance and standard deviation of a linear combination of two random variables in order to assess the portfolio risk. When the covariance between two random variables is known, the formula given by equation (5.9) can be used to compute the variance of a linear combination of two random variables.

VARIANCE OF A LINEAR COMBINATION OF TWO RANDOM VARIABLES

$$Var(ax + by) = a^2 Var(x) + b^2 Var(y) + 2ab\sigma_{xy} \qquad \textbf{(5.9)}$$

where σ_{xy} is the covariance of x and y

From equation (5.9), we see that both the variance of each random variable individually and the covariance between the random variables are needed to compute the variance of a linear combination of two random variables and hence the variance of our portfolio.

We computed $Var(x + y) = 119.46$ the same way we did for DiCarlo Motors in the previous subsection.

We have already computed the variance of each random variable individually: $Var(x) = 328.1875$ and $Var(y) = 61.9475$. Also, it can be shown that $Var(x + y) = 119.46$. So, using equation (5.6), the covariance of the random variables x and y is

$$\sigma_{xy} = [Var(x + y) - Var(x) - Var(y)]/2 = [119.46 - 328.1875 - 61.9475]/2 = -135.3375$$

A negative covariance between x and y, such as this, means that when x tends to be above its mean, y tends to be below its mean and vice versa.

We can now use equation (5.9) to compute the variance of return for our portfolio.

$$Var(.5x + .5y) = .5^2(328.1875) + .5^2(61.9475) + 2(.5)(.5)(-135.3375) = 29.865$$

The standard deviation of our portfolio is then given by $\sigma_{.5x + .5y} = \sqrt{29.865} = 5.4650\%$. This is our measure of risk for the portfolio consisting of investing 50% in the stock fund and 50% in the bond fund.

Perhaps we would now like to compare the three investment alternatives: investing solely in the stock fund, investing solely in the bond fund, or creating a portfolio by dividing our investment amount equally between the stock and bond funds. Table 5.12 shows the expected returns, variances, and standard deviations for each of the three alternatives.

Which of these alternatives would you prefer? The expected return is highest for investing 100% in the stock fund, but the risk is also highest. The standard deviation is 18.1159%. Investing 100% in the bond fund has a lower expected return, but a significantly smaller risk. Investing 50% in the stock fund and 50% in the bond fund (the portfolio) has an expected return that is halfway between that of the stock fund alone and the bond fund alone. But note that it has less risk than investing 100% in either of the individual funds. Indeed, it has both a higher return and less risk (smaller standard deviation) than investing solely in the bond fund. So we would say that investing in the portfolio dominates the choice of investing solely in the bond fund.

Whether you would choose to invest in the stock fund or the portfolio depends on your attitude toward risk. The stock fund has a higher expected return. But the portfolio has significantly less risk and also provides a fairly good return. Many would choose it. It is the negative covariance between the stock and bond funds that has caused the portfolio risk to be so much smaller than the risk of investing solely in either of the individual funds.

The portfolio analysis we just performed was for investing 50% in the stock fund and the other 50% in the bond fund. How would you calculate the expected return and the variance for other portfolios? Equations (5.8) and (5.9) can be used to make these calculations easily.

Suppose we wish to create a portfolio by investing 25% in the stock fund and 75% in the bond fund. What are the expected value and variance of this portfolio? The percent return for this portfolio is $r = .25x + .75y$, so we can use equation (5.8) to get the expected value of this portfolio:

$$E(.25x + .75y) = .25E(x) + .75E(y) = .25(9.25) + .75(6.55) = 7.225$$

TABLE 5.12   EXPECTED VALUES, VARIANCES, AND STANDARD DEVIATIONS FOR THREE INVESTMENT ALTERNATIVES

Investment Alternative	Expected Return (%)	Variance of Return	Standard Deviation of Return (%)
100% in Stock Fund	9.25	328.1875	18.1159
100% in Bond Fund	6.55	61.9475	7.8707
Portfolio (50% in Stock fund, 50% in Bond fund)	7.90	29.865	5.4650

Likewise, we may calculate the variance of the portfolio using equation (5.9):

$$Var(.25x + .75y) = (.25)^2 Var(x) + (.75)^2 Var(y) + 2(.25)(.75)\sigma_{xy}$$

$$= .0625(328.1875) + (.5625)(61.9475) + (.375)(-135.3375)$$

$$= 4.6056$$

The standard deviation of the new portfolio is $\sigma_{.25x + .75y} = \sqrt{4.6056} = 2.1461$.

Summary

We have introduced bivariate discrete probability distributions in this section. Since such distributions involve two random variables, we are often interested in a measure of association between the variables. The covariance and the correlation coefficient are the two measures we introduced and showed how to compute. A correlation coefficient near 1 or −1 indicates a strong correlation between the two random variables, and a correlation coefficient near zero indicates a weak correlation between the variables. If two random variables are independent, the covariance and the correlation coefficient will equal zero.

We also showed how to compute the expected value and variance of linear combinations of random variables. From a statistical point of view, financial portfolios are linear combinations of random variables. They are actually a special kind of linear combination called a weighted average. The coefficients are nonnegative and add to 1. The portfolio example we presented showed how to compute the expected value and variance for a portfolio consisting of an investment in a stock fund and a bond fund. The same methodology can be used to compute the expected value and variance of a portfolio consisting of any two financial assets. It is the effect of covariance between the individual random variables on the variance of the portfolio that is the basis for much of the theory of reducing portfolio risk by diversifying across investment alternatives.

NOTES AND COMMENTS

1. Equations (5.8) and (5.9), along with their extensions to three or more random variables, are key building blocks in financial portfolio construction and analysis.

2. Equations (5.8) and (5.9) for computing the expected value and variance of a linear combination of two random variables can be extended to three or more random variables. The extension of equation (5.8) is straightforward; one more term is added for each additional random variable. The extension of equation (5.9) is more complicated because a separate term is needed for the covariance between all pairs of random variables. We leave these extensions to more advanced books.

3. The covariance term of equation (5.9) shows why negatively correlated random variables (investment alternatives) reduce the variance and, hence, the risk of a portfolio.

Exercises

Methods

25. Given below is a bivariate distribution for the random variables x and y.

$f(x, y)$	x	y
.2	50	80
.5	30	50
.3	40	60

a. Compute the expected value and the variance for x and y.
b. Develop a probability distribution for $x + y$.
c. Using the result of part (b), compute $E(x + y)$ and $Var(x + y)$.
d. Compute the covariance and correlation for x and y. Are x and y positively related, negatively related, or unrelated?
e. Is the variance of the sum of x and y bigger than, smaller than, or the same as the sum of the individual variances? Why?

26. A person is interested in constructing a portfolio. Two stocks are being considered. Let x = percent return for an investment in stock 1, and y = percent return for an investment in stock 2. The expected return and variance for stock 1 are $E(x) = 8.45\%$ and $Var(x) = 25$. The expected return and variance for stock 2 are $E(y) = 3.20\%$ and $Var(y) = 1$. The covariance between the returns is $\sigma_{xy} = -3$.
a. What is the standard deviation for an investment in stock 1 and for an investment in stock 2? Using the standard deviation as a measure of risk, which of these stocks is the riskier investment?
b. What is the expected return and standard deviation, in dollars, for a person who invests $500 in stock 1?
c. What is the expected percent return and standard deviation for a person who constructs a portfolio by investing 50% in each stock?
d. What is the expected percent return and standard deviation for a person who constructs a portfolio by investing 70% in stock 1 and 30% in stock 2?
e. Compute the correlation coefficient for x and y and comment on the relationship between the returns for the two stocks.

 27. The Chamber of Commerce in a Canadian city has conducted an evaluation of 300 restaurants in its metropolitan area. Each restaurant received a rating on a 3-point scale on typical meal price (1 least expensive to 3 most expensive) and quality (1 lowest quality to 3 greatest quality). A crosstabulation of the rating data is shown. Forty-two of the restaurants received a rating of 1 on quality and 1 on meal price, 39 of the restaurants received a rating of 1 on quality and 2 on meal price, and so on. Forty-eight of the restaurants received the highest rating of 3 on both quality and meal price.

| | | Meal Price (y) | | |
Quality (x)	1	2	3	Total
1	42	39	3	84
2	33	63	54	150
3	3	15	48	66
Total	78	117	105	300

a. Develop a bivariate probability distribution for quality and meal price of a randomly selected restaurant in this Canadian city. Let x = quality rating and y = meal price.
b. Compute the expected value and variance for quality rating, x.
c. Compute the expected value and variance for meal price, y.
d. The $Var(x + y) = 1.6691$. Compute the covariance of x and y. What can you say about the relationship between quality and meal price? Is this what you would expect?
e. Compute the correlation coefficient between quality and meal price? What is the strength of the relationship? Do you suppose it is likely to find a low-cost restaurant in this city that is also high quality? Why or why not?

28. PortaCom has developed a design for a high-quality portable printer. The two key components of manufacturing cost are direct labor and parts. During a testing period, the

company has developed prototypes and conducted extensive product tests with the new printer. PortaCom's engineers have developed the following bivariate probability distribution for the manufacturing costs. Parts cost (in dollars) per printer is represented by the random variable x and direct labor cost (in dollars) per printer is represented by the random variable y. Management would like to use this probability distribution to estimate manufacturing costs.

Parts (x)	Direct Labor (y)			Total
	43	45	48	
85	0.05	0.2	0.2	0.45
95	0.25	0.2	0.1	0.55
Total	0.30	0.4	0.3	1.00

a. Show the marginal distribution of direct labor cost and compute its expected value, variance, and standard deviation.

b. Show the marginal distribution of parts cost and compute its expected value, variance, and standard deviation.

c. Total manufacturing cost per unit is the sum of direct labor cost and parts cost. Show the probability distribution for total manufacturing cost per unit.

d. Compute the expected value, variance, and standard deviation of total manufacturing cost per unit.

e. Are direct labor and parts costs independent? Why or why not? If you conclude that they are not, what is the relationship between direct labor and parts cost?

f. PortaCom produced 1500 printers for its product introduction. The total manufacturing cost was $198,350. Is that about what you would expect? If it is higher or lower, what do you think may be the reason?

29. J.P. Morgan Asset Management publishes information about financial investments. Over a 10-year period, the expected return for the S&P 500 was 5.04% with a standard deviation of 19.45% and the expected return over that same period for a core bonds fund was 5.78% with a standard deviation of 2.13% (*J.P. Morgan Asset Management, Guide to the Markets*, 1st Quarter, 2012). The publication also reported that the correlation between the S&P 500 and core bonds is $-.32$. You are considering portfolio investments that are composed of an S&P 500 index fund and a core bonds fund.

a. Using the information provided, determine the covariance between the S&P 500 and core bonds.

b. Construct a portfolio that is 50% invested in an S&P 500 index fund and 50% in a core bonds fund. In percentage terms, what are the expected return and standard deviation for such a portfolio?

c. Construct a portfolio that is 20% invested in an S&P 500 index fund and 80% invested in a core bonds fund. In percentage terms, what are the expected return and standard deviation for such a portfolio?

d. Construct a portfolio that is 80% invested in an S&P 500 index fund and 20% invested in a core bonds fund. In percentage terms, what are the expected return and standard deviation for such a portfolio?

e. Which of the portfolios in parts (b), (c), and (d) has the largest expected return? Which has the smallest standard deviation? Which of these portfolios is the best investment alternative?

f. Discuss the advantages and disadvantages of investing in the three portfolios in parts (b), (c), and (d). Would you prefer investing all your money in the S&P 500 index, the core bonds fund, or one of the three portfolios? Why?

30. In addition to the information in exercise 29 on the S&P 500 and core bonds, J.P. Morgan Asset Management reported that the expected return for real estate investment trusts (REITs) was 13.07% with a standard deviation of 23.17% (*J.P. Morgan Asset Management, Guide to the Markets*, 1st Quarter, 2012). The correlation between the S&P 500 and REITs is .74 and the correlation between core bonds and REITs is −.04. You are considering portfolio investments that are composed of an S&P 500 index fund and REITs as well as portfolio investments composed of a core bonds fund and REITs.

    a. Using the information provided here and in exercise 29, determine the covariance between the S&P 500 and REITs and between core bonds and REITs.

    b. Construct a portfolio that is 50% invested in an S&P 500 fund and 50% invested in REITs. In percentage terms, what are the expected return and standard deviation for such a portfolio?

    c. Construct a portfolio that is 50% invested in a core bonds fund and 50% invested in REITs. In percentage terms, what are the expected return and standard deviation for such a portfolio?

    d. Construct a portfolio that is 80% invested in a core bonds fund and 20% invested in REITs. In percentage terms, what are the expected return and standard deviation for such a portfolio?

    e. Which of the portfolios in parts (b), (c), and (d) would you recommend to an aggressive investor? Which would you recommend to a conservative investor? Why?

5.5 Binomial Probability Distribution

The binomial probability distribution is a discrete probability distribution that has many applications. It is associated with a multiple-step experiment that we call the binomial experiment.

A Binomial Experiment

A **binomial experiment** exhibits the following four properties.

> **PROPERTIES OF A BINOMIAL EXPERIMENT**
>
> 1. The experiment consists of a sequence of n identical trials.
> 2. Two outcomes are possible on each trial. We refer to one outcome as a *success* and the other outcome as a *failure*.
> 3. The probability of a success, denoted by p, does not change from trial to trial. Consequently, the probability of a failure, denoted by $1 - p$, does not change from trial to trial.
> 4. The trials are independent.

Jakob Bernoulli (1654–1705), the first of the Bernoulli family of Swiss mathematicians, published a treatise on probability that contained the theory of permutations and combinations, as well as the binomial theorem.

If properties 2, 3, and 4 are present, we say the trials are generated by a Bernoulli process. If, in addition, property 1 is present, we say we have a binomial experiment. Figure 5.3 depicts one possible sequence of successes and failures for a binomial experiment involving eight trials.

In a binomial experiment, our interest is in the *number of successes occurring in the n trials*. If we let x denote the number of successes occurring in the n trials, we see that x can assume the values of 0, 1, 2, 3, . . . , n. Because the number of values is finite, x is a *discrete* random variable. The probability distribution associated with this random variable is called the **binomial probability distribution**. For example, consider the experiment of tossing a

FIGURE 5.3 ONE POSSIBLE SEQUENCE OF SUCCESSES AND FAILURES
FOR AN EIGHT-TRIAL BINOMIAL EXPERIMENT

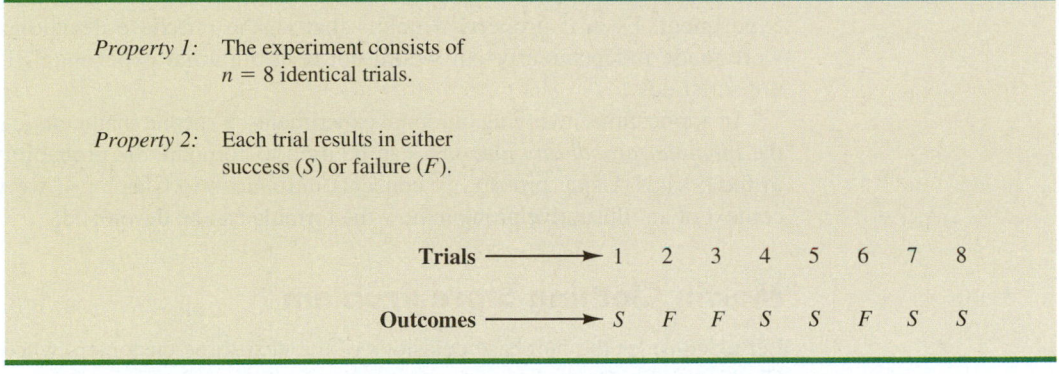

Property 1: The experiment consists of
$n = 8$ identical trials.

Property 2: Each trial results in either
success (S) or failure (F).

Trials ⟶ 1 2 3 4 5 6 7 8

Outcomes ⟶ S F F S S F S S

coin five times and on each toss observing whether the coin lands with a head or a tail on its upward face. Suppose we want to count the number of heads appearing over the five tosses. Does this experiment show the properties of a binomial experiment? What is the random variable of interest? Note that

1. The experiment consists of five identical trials; each trial involves the tossing of one coin.
2. Two outcomes are possible for each trial: a head or a tail. We can designate head a success and tail a failure.
3. The probability of a head and the probability of a tail are the same for each trial, with $p = .5$ and $1 - p = .5$.
4. The trials or tosses are independent because the outcome on any one trial is not affected by what happens on other trials or tosses.

Thus, the properties of a binomial experiment are satisfied. The random variable of interest is $x =$ the number of heads appearing in the five trials. In this case, x can assume the values of 0, 1, 2, 3, 4, or 5.

As another example, consider an insurance salesperson who visits 10 randomly selected families. The outcome associated with each visit is classified as a success if the family purchases an insurance policy and a failure if the family does not. From past experience, the salesperson knows the probability that a randomly selected family will purchase an insurance policy is .10. Checking the properties of a binomial experiment, we observe that

1. The experiment consists of 10 identical trials; each trial involves contacting one family.
2. Two outcomes are possible on each trial: the family purchases a policy (success) or the family does not purchase a policy (failure).
3. The probabilities of a purchase and a nonpurchase are assumed to be the same for each sales call, with $p = .10$ and $1 - p = .90$.
4. The trials are independent because the families are randomly selected.

Because the four assumptions are satisfied, this example is a binomial experiment. The random variable of interest is the number of sales obtained in contacting the 10 families. In this case, x can assume the values of 0, 1, 2, 3, 4, 5, 6, 7, 8, 9, and 10.

Property 3 of the binomial experiment is called the *stationarity assumption* and is sometimes confused with property 4, *independence of trials*. To see how they differ, consider again the case of the salesperson calling on families to sell insurance policies.

If, as the day wore on, the salesperson got tired and lost enthusiasm, the probability of success (selling a policy) might drop to .05, for example, by the tenth call. In such a case, property 3 (stationarity) would not be satisfied, and we would not have a binomial experiment. Even if property 4 held—that is, the purchase decisions of each family were made independently—it would not be a binomial experiment if property 3 was not satisfied.

In applications involving binomial experiments, a special mathematical formula, called the *binomial probability function,* can be used to compute the probability of x successes in the n trials. Using probability concepts introduced in Chapter 4, we will show in the context of an illustrative problem how the formula can be developed.

Martin Clothing Store Problem

Let us consider the purchase decisions of the next three customers who enter the Martin Clothing Store. On the basis of past experience, the store manager estimates the probability that any one customer will make a purchase is .30. What is the probability that two of the next three customers will make a purchase?

Using a tree diagram (Figure 5.4), we can see that the experiment of observing the three customers each making a purchase decision has eight possible outcomes. Using S to denote success (a purchase) and F to denote failure (no purchase), we are interested in experimental outcomes involving two successes in the three trials (purchase decisions). Next, let us verify that the experiment involving the sequence of three purchase decisions

FIGURE 5.4   TREE DIAGRAM FOR THE MARTIN CLOTHING STORE PROBLEM

S = Purchase
F = No purchase
x = Number of customers making a purchase

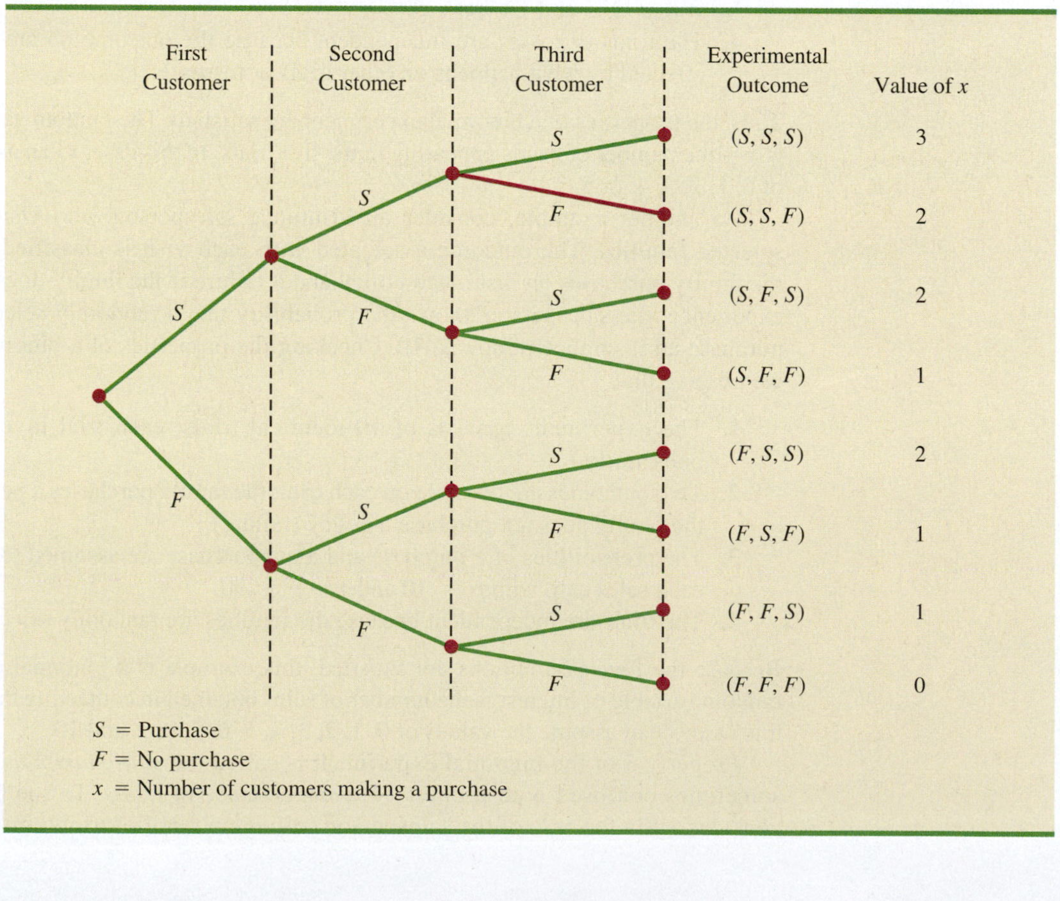

can be viewed as a binomial experiment. Checking the four requirements for a binomial experiment, we note that

1. The experiment can be described as a sequence of three identical trials, one trial for each of the three customers who will enter the store.
2. Two outcomes—the customer makes a purchase (success) or the customer does not make a purchase (failure)—are possible for each trial.
3. The probability that the customer will make a purchase (.30) or will not make a purchase (.70) is assumed to be the same for all customers.
4. The purchase decision of each customer is independent of the decisions of the other customers.

Hence, the properties of a binomial experiment are present.

The number of experimental outcomes resulting in exactly x successes in n trials can be computed using the following formula.[2]

NUMBER OF EXPERIMENTAL OUTCOMES PROVIDING EXACTLY x SUCCESSES IN n TRIALS

$$\binom{n}{x} = \frac{n!}{x!(n-x)!} \qquad (5.10)$$

where

$$n! = n(n-1)(n-2)\cdots(2)(1)$$

and, by definition,

$$0! = 1$$

Now let us return to the Martin Clothing Store experiment involving three customer purchase decisions. Equation (5.10) can be used to determine the number of experimental outcomes involving two purchases; that is, the number of ways of obtaining $x = 2$ successes in the $n = 3$ trials. From equation (5.10) we have

$$\binom{n}{x} = \binom{3}{2} = \frac{3!}{2!(3-2)!} = \frac{(3)(2)(1)}{(2)(1)(1)} = \frac{6}{2} = 3$$

Equation (5.10) shows that three of the experimental outcomes yield two successes. From Figure 5.3 we see that these three outcomes are denoted by (S, S, F), (S, F, S), and (F, S, S).

Using equation (5.10) to determine how many experimental outcomes have three successes (purchases) in the three trials, we obtain

$$\binom{n}{x} = \binom{3}{3} = \frac{3!}{3!(3-3)!} = \frac{3!}{3!0!} = \frac{(3)(2)(1)}{3(2)(1)(1)} = \frac{6}{6} = 1$$

From Figure 5.4 we see that the one experimental outcome with three successes is identified by (S, S, S).

---

[2]This formula, introduced in Chapter 4, determines the number of combinations of n objects selected x at a time. For the binomial experiment, this combinatorial formula provides the number of experimental outcomes (sequences of n trials) resulting in x successes.

We know that equation (5.10) can be used to determine the number of experimental outcomes that result in x successes in n trials. If we are to determine the probability of x successes in n trials, however, we must also know the probability associated with each of these experimental outcomes. Because the trials of a binomial experiment are independent, we can simply multiply the probabilities associated with each trial outcome to find the probability of a particular sequence of successes and failures.

The probability of purchases by the first two customers and no purchase by the third customer, denoted (S, S, F), is given by

$$pp(1 - p)$$

With a .30 probability of a purchase on any one trial, the probability of a purchase on the first two trials and no purchase on the third is given by

$$(.30)(.30)(.70) = (.30)^2(.70) = .063$$

Two other experimental outcomes also result in two successes and one failure. The probabilities for all three experimental outcomes involving two successes follow.

| Trial Outcomes | | | | Probability of |
1st Customer	2nd Customer	3rd Customer	Experimental Outcome	Experimental Outcome
Purchase	Purchase	No purchase	(S, S, F)	$pp(1 - p) = p^2(1 - p)$ $= (.30)^2(.70) = .063$
Purchase	No purchase	Purchase	(S, F, S)	$p(1 - p)p = p^2(1 - p)$ $= (.30)^2(.70) = .063$
No purchase	Purchase	Purchase	(F, S, S)	$(1 - p)pp = p^2(1 - p)$ $= (.30)^2(.70) = .063$

Observe that all three experimental outcomes with two successes have exactly the same probability. This observation holds in general. In any binomial experiment, all sequences of trial outcomes yielding x successes in n trials have the *same probability* of occurrence. The probability of each sequence of trials yielding x successes in n trials follows.

Probability of a particular
sequence of trial outcomes $= p^x(1 - p)^{(n-x)}$ **(5.11)**
with x successes in n trials

For the Martin Clothing Store, this formula shows that any experimental outcome with two successes has a probability of $p^2(1 - p)^{(3-2)} = p^2(1 - p)^1 = (.30)^2(.70)^1 = .063$.

Because equation (5.10) shows the number of outcomes in a binomial experiment with x successes and equation (5.11) gives the probability for each sequence involving x successes, we combine equations (5.10) and (5.11) to obtain the following **binomial probability function**.

BINOMIAL PROBABILITY FUNCTION

$$f(x) = \binom{n}{x} p^x (1-p)^{(n-x)} \tag{5.12}$$

where

$$
\begin{aligned}
x &= \text{the number of successes} \\
p &= \text{the probability of a success on one trial} \\
n &= \text{the number of trials} \\
f(x) &= \text{the probability of } x \text{ successes in } n \text{ trials}
\end{aligned}
$$

$$\binom{n}{x} = \frac{n!}{x!(n-x)!}$$

For the binomial probability distribution, x is a discrete random variable with the probability function $f(x)$ applicable for values of $x = 0, 1, 2, \ldots, n$.

In the Martin Clothing Store example, let us use equation (5.12) to compute the probability that no customer makes a purchase, exactly one customer makes a purchase, exactly two customers make a purchase, and all three customers make a purchase. The calculations are summarized in Table 5.13, which gives the probability distribution of the number of customers making a purchase. Figure 5.5 is a graph of this probability distribution.

The binomial probability function can be applied to *any* binomial experiment. If we are satisfied that a situation demonstrates the properties of a binomial experiment and if we know the values of n and p, we can use equation (5.12) to compute the probability of x successes in the n trials.

If we consider variations of the Martin experiment, such as 10 customers rather than 3 entering the store, the binomial probability function given by equation (5.12) is still applicable. Suppose we have a binomial experiment with $n = 10$, $x = 4$, and $p = .30$. The probability of making exactly four sales to 10 customers entering the store is

$$f(4) = \frac{10!}{4!6!} (.30)^4 (.70)^6 = .2001$$

TABLE 5.13 PROBABILITY DISTRIBUTION FOR THE NUMBER OF CUSTOMERS MAKING A PURCHASE

x	$f(x)$
0	$\dfrac{3!}{0!3!} (.30)^0 (.70)^3 = .343$
1	$\dfrac{3!}{1!2!} (.30)^1 (.70)^2 = .441$
2	$\dfrac{3!}{2!1!} (.30)^2 (.70)^1 = .189$
3	$\dfrac{3!}{3!0!} (.30)^3 (.70)^0 = \dfrac{.027}{1.000}$

FIGURE 5.5   GRAPHICAL REPRESENTATION OF THE PROBABILITY DISTRIBUTION FOR THE NUMBER OF CUSTOMERS MAKING A PURCHASE

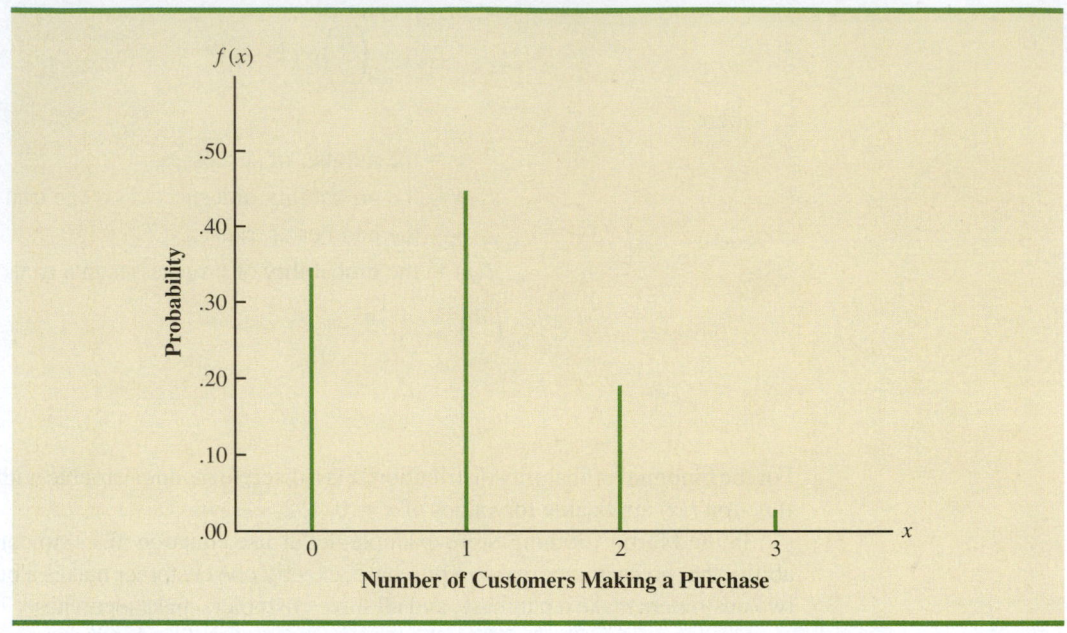

Using Excel to Compute Binomial Probabilities

For many probability functions that can be specified as formulas, Excel provides functions for computing probabilities and cumulative probabilities. In this section, we show how Excel's BINOM.DIST function can be used to compute binomial probabilities and cumulative binomial probabilities. We begin by showing how to compute the binomial probabilities for the Martin Clothing Store example shown in Table 5.13. Refer to Figure 5.6 as we describe the tasks involved. The formula worksheet is in the background; the value worksheet is in the foreground.

FIGURE 5.6   EXCEL WORKSHEET FOR COMPUTING BINOMIAL PROBABILITIES OF NUMBER OF CUSTOMERS MAKING A PURCHASE

	A	B	C	D	E
1			Number of Trials (*n*)	3	
2			Probability of Success (*p*)	0.3	
3					
4		*x*	*f(x)*		
5		0	=BINOM.DIST(B5,$D$1,$D$2,FALSE)		
6		1	=BINOM.DIST(B6,$D$1,$D$2,FALSE)		
7		2	=BINOM.DIST(B7,$D$1,$D$2,FALSE)		
8		3	=BINOM.DIST(B8,$D$1,$D$2,FALSE)		
9					

	A	B	C	D	E
1		Number of Trials (*n*)		3	
2		Probability of Success (*p*)		0.3	
3					
4		*x*	*f(x)*		
5		0	0.343		
6		1	0.441		
7		2	0.189		
8		3	0.027		
9					

Enter/Access Data: In order to compute a binomial probability we must know the number of trials (n), the probability of success (p), and the value of the random variable (x). For the Martin Clothing Store example, the number of trials is 3; this value has been entered into cell D1. The probability of success is .3; this value has been entered into cell D2. Because we want to compute the probability for $x = 0$, 1, 2, and 3, these values were entered into cells B5:B8.

Enter Functions and Formulas: The BINOM.DIST function has four inputs: The first is the value of x, the second is the value of n, the third is the value of p, and the fourth is FALSE or TRUE. We choose FALSE for the fourth input if a probability is desired and TRUE if a cumulative probability is desired. The formula =BINOM.DIST(B5,$D$1,$D$2,FALSE) has been entered into cell C5 to compute the probability of 0 successes in 3 trials. Note in the value worksheet that the probability computed for $f(0)$, .343, is the same as that shown in Table 5.13. The formula in cell C5 is copied to cells C6:C8 to compute the probabilities for $x = 1$, 2, and 3 successes, respectively.

We can also compute cumulative probabilities using Excel's BINOM.DIST function. To illustrate, let us consider the case of 10 customers entering the Martin Clothing Store and compute the probabilities and cumulative probabilities for the number of customers making a purchase. Recall that the cumulative probability for $x = 1$ is the probability of 1 or fewer purchases, the cumulative probability for $x = 2$ is the probability of 2 or fewer purchases, and so on. So, the cumulative probability for $x = 10$ is 1. Refer to Figure 5.7 as we describe the tasks involved in computing these cumulative probabilities. The formula worksheet is in the background; the value worksheet is in the foreground.

Enter/Access Data: We entered the number of trials (10) into cell D1, the probability of success (.3) into cell D2, and the values for the random variable into cells B5:B15.

Enter Functions and Formulas: The binomial probabilities for each value of the random variable are computed in column C and the cumulative probabilities are computed in column D. We entered the formula =BINOM.DIST(B5,$D$1,$D$2,FALSE) into cell C5 to compute the probability of 0 successes in 10 trials. Note that we used FALSE as the

FIGURE 5.7 EXCEL WORKSHEET FOR COMPUTING PROBABILITIES AND CUMULATIVE PROBABILITIES FOR NUMBER OF PURCHASES WITH 10 CUSTOMERS

	A	B	C	D	E
1			Number of Trials (n)	10	
2			Probability of Success (p)	0.3	
3					
4		x	f(x)	Cum Prob	
5		0	=BINOM.DIST(B5,$D$1,$D$2,FALSE)	=BINOM.DIST(B5,$D$1,$D$2,TRUE)	
6		1	=BINOM.DIST(B6,$D$1,$D$2,FALSE)	=BINOM.DIST(B6,$D$1,$D$2,TRUE)	
7		2	=BINOM.DIST(B7,$D$1,$D$2,FALSE)	=BINOM.DIST(B7,$D$1,$D$2,TRUE)	
8		3	=BINOM.DIST(B8,$D$1,$D$2,FALSE)	=BINOM.DIST(B8,$D$1,$D$2,TRUE)	
9		4	=BINOM.DIST(B9,$D$1,$D$2,FALSE)	=BINOM.DIST(B9,$D$1,$D$2,TRUE)	
10		5	=BINOM.DIST(B10,$D$1,$D$2,FALSE)	=BINOM.DIST(B10,$D$1,$D$2,TRUE)	
11		6	=BINOM.DIST(B11,$D$1,$D$2,FALSE)	=BINOM.DIST(B11,$D$1,$D$2,TRUE)	
12		7	=BINOM.DIST(B12,$D$1,$D$2,FALSE)	=BINOM.DIST(B12,$D$1,$D$2,TRUE)	
13		8	=BINOM.DIST(B13,$D$1,$D$2,FALSE)	=BINOM.DIST(B13,$D$1,$D$2,TRUE)	
14		9	=BINOM.DIST(B14,$D$1,$D$2,FALSE)	=BINOM.DIST(B14,$D$1,$D$2,TRUE)	
15		10	=BINOM.DIST(B15,$D$1,$D$2,FALSE)	=BINOM.DIST(B15,$D$1,$D$2,TRUE)	
16					

	A	B	C	D	E
1			Number of Trials (n)	10	
2			Probability of Success (p)	0.3	
3					
4		x	f(x)	Cum Prob	
5		0	0.0282	0.0282	
6		1	0.1211	0.1493	
7		2	0.2335	0.3828	
8		3	0.2668	0.6496	
9		4	0.2001	0.8497	
10		5	0.1029	0.9527	
11		6	0.0368	0.9894	
12		7	0.0090	0.9984	
13		8	0.0014	0.9999	
14		9	0.0001	1.0000	
15		10	0.0000	1.0000	
16					

fourth input in the BINOM.DIST function. The probability (.0282) is shown in cell C5 of the value worksheet. The formula in cell C5 is simply copied to cells C6:C15 to compute the remaining probabilities.

To compute the cumulative probabilities we start by entering the formula =BINOM. DIST(B5,$D$1,$D$2,TRUE) into cell D5. Note that we used TRUE as the fourth input in the BINOM.DIST function. The formula in cell D5 is then copied to cells D6:D15 to compute the remaining cumulative probabilities. In cell D5 of the value worksheet we see that the cumulative probability for $x = 0$ is the same as the probability for $x = 0$. Each of the remaining cumulative probabilities is the sum of the previous cumulative probability and the individual probability in column C. For instance, the cumulative probability for $x = 4$ is given by .6496 + .2001 = .8497. Note also that the cumulative probability for $x = 10$ is 1. The cumulative probability of $x = 9$ is also 1 because the probability of $x = 10$ is zero (to four decimal places of accuracy).

Expected Value and Variance for the Binomial Distribution

In Section 5.3 we provided formulas for computing the expected value and variance of a discrete random variable. In the special case where the random variable has a binomial distribution with a known number of trials n and a known probability of success p, the general formulas for the expected value and variance can be simplified. The results follow.

EXPECTED VALUE AND VARIANCE FOR THE BINOMIAL DISTRIBUTION

$$E(x) = \mu = np \qquad \qquad (5.13)$$

$$Var(x) = \sigma^2 = np(1 - p) \qquad \qquad (5.14)$$

For the Martin Clothing Store problem with three customers, we can use equation (5.13) to compute the expected number of customers who will make a purchase.

$$E(x) = np = 3(.30) = .9$$

Suppose that for the next month the Martin Clothing Store forecasts 1000 customers will enter the store. What is the expected number of customers who will make a purchase? The answer is $\mu = np = (1000)(.3) = 300$. Thus, to increase the expected number of purchases, Martin's must induce more customers to enter the store and/or somehow increase the probability that any individual customer will make a purchase after entering.

For the Martin Clothing Store problem with three customers, we see that the variance and standard deviation for the number of customers who will make a purchase are

$$\sigma^2 = np(1 - p) = 3(.3)(.7) = .63$$
$$\sigma = \sqrt{.63} = .79$$

For the next 1000 customers entering the store, the variance and standard deviation for the number of customers who will make a purchase are

$$\sigma^2 = np(1 - p) = 1000(.3)(.7) = 210$$
$$\sigma = \sqrt{210} = 14.49$$

Exercises

Methods

31. Consider a binomial experiment with two trials and $p = .4$.
    a. Draw a tree diagram for this experiment (see Figure 5.3).
    b. Compute the probability of one success, $f(1)$.
    c. Compute $f(0)$.
    d. Compute $f(2)$.
    e. Compute the probability of at least one success.
    f. Compute the expected value, variance, and standard deviation.

32. Consider a binomial experiment with $n = 10$ and $p = .10$.
    a. Compute $f(0)$.
    b. Compute $f(2)$.
    c. Compute $P(x \leq 2)$.
    d. Compute $P(x \geq 1)$.
    e. Compute $E(x)$.
    f. Compute $Var(x)$ and σ.

33. Consider a binomial experiment with $n = 20$ and $p = .70$.
    a. Compute $f(12)$.
    b. Compute $f(16)$.
    c. Compute $P(x \geq 16)$.
    d. Compute $P(x \leq 15)$.
    e. Compute $E(x)$.
    f. Compute $Var(x)$ and σ.

Applications

34. For its Music 360 survey, Nielsen Co. asked teenagers how they listened to music in the past 12 months. Nearly two-thirds of U.S. teenagers under the age of 18 say they use Google Inc.'s video-sharing site to listen to music and 35% of the teenagers said they use Pandora Media Inc.'s custom online radio service (*The Wall Street Journal*, August 14, 2012). Suppose 10 teenagers are selected randomly to be interviewed about how they listen to music.
    a. Is randomly selecting 10 teenagers and asking whether or not they use Pandora Media Inc.'s online service a binomial experiment?
    b. What is the probability that none of the 10 teenagers uses Pandora Media Inc.'s online radio service?
    c. What is the probability that 4 of the 10 teenagers use Pandora Media Inc.'s online radio service?
    d. What is the probability that at least 2 of the 10 teenagers use Pandora Media Inc.'s online radio service?

35. The Center for Medicare and Medical Services reported that there were 295,000 appeals for hospitalization and other Part A Medicare service. For this group, 40% of first-round appeals were successful (*The Wall Street Journal*, October 22, 2012). Suppose 10 first-round appeals have just been received by a Medicare appeals office.
    a. Compute the probability that none of the appeals will be successful.
    b. Compute the probability that exactly one of the appeals will be successful.
    c. What is the probability that at least two of the appeals will be successful?
    d. What is the probability that more than half of the appeals will be successful?

36. When a new machine is functioning properly, only 3% of the items produced are defective. Assume that we will randomly select two parts produced on the machine and that we are interested in the number of defective parts found.

a. Describe the conditions under which this situation would be a binomial experiment.
b. Draw a tree diagram similar to Figure 5.4 showing this problem as a two-trial experiment.
c. How many experimental outcomes result in exactly one defect being found?
d. Compute the probabilities associated with finding no defects, exactly one defect, and two defects.

37. According to a study by the Pew Research Center, 15% of adults in the United States do not use the Internet (Pew Research Center website, December, 15, 2014). Suppose that 10 adults in the United States are selected randomly.
    a. Is the selection of the 10 adults a binomial experiment? Explain.
    b. What is the probability that none of the adults use the Internet?
    c. What is the probability that 3 of the adults use the Internet?
    d. What is the probability that at least 1 of the adults uses the Internet?

38. Military radar and missile detection systems are designed to warn a country of an enemy attack. A reliability question is whether a detection system will be able to identify an attack and issue a warning. Assume that a particular detection system has a .90 probability of detecting a missile attack. Use the binomial probability distribution to answer the following questions.
    a. What is the probability that a single detection system will detect an attack?
    b. If two detection systems are installed in the same area and operate independently, what is the probability that at least one of the systems will detect the attack?
    c. If three systems are installed, what is the probability that at least one of the systems will detect the attack?
    d. Would you recommend that multiple detection systems be used? Explain.

39. Market-share-analysis company Net Applications monitors and reports on Internet browser usage. According to Net Applications, in the summer of 2014, Google's Chrome browser exceeded a 20% market share for the first time, with a 20.37% share of the browser market (*Forbes* website, December 15, 2014). For a randomly selected group of 20 Internet browser users, answer the following questions.
    a. Compute the probability that exactly 8 of the 20 Internet browser users use Chrome as their Internet browser.
    b. Compute the probability that at least 3 of the 20 Internet browser users use Chrome as their Internet browser.
    c. For the sample of 20 Internet browser users, compute the expected number of Chrome users.
    d. For the sample of 20 Internet browser users, compute the variance and standard deviation for the number of Chrome users.

40. A study conducted by the Pew Research Center showed that 75% of 18- to 34-year-olds living with their parents say they contribute to household expenses. Suppose that a random sample of fifteen 18- to 34-year-olds living with their parents is selected and asked if they contribute to household expenses.
    a. Is the selection of the fifteen 18- to 34-year-olds living with their parents a binomial experiment? Explain.
    b. If the sample shows that none of the fifteen 18- to 34-year-olds living with their parents contributes to household expenses, would you question the results of the Pew Research study? Explain.
    c. What is the probability that at least 10 of the fifteen 18- to 34-year-olds living with their parents contribute to household expenses?

41. A university found that 20% of its students withdraw without completing the introductory statistics course. Assume that 20 students registered for the course.
    a. Compute the probability that 2 or fewer will withdraw.
    b. Compute the probability that exactly 4 will withdraw.
    c. Compute the probability that more than 3 will withdraw.
    d. Compute the expected number of withdrawals.

42. A Gallup Poll showed that 30% of Americans are satisfied with the way things are going in the United States (Gallup website, September 12, 2012). Suppose a sample of 20 Americans is selected as part of a study of the state of the nation.
     a. Compute the probability that exactly 4 of the 20 Americans surveyed are satisfied with the way things are going in the United States.
     b. Compute the probability that at least 2 of the Americans surveyed are satisfied with the way things are going in the United States.
     c. For the sample of 20 Americans, compute the expected number of Americans who are satisfied with the way things are going in the United States.
     d. For the sample of 20 Americans, compute the variance and standard deviation of the number of Americans who are satisfied with the way things are going in the United States.

43. According to a study conducted by the Toronto-based social media analytics firm Sysomos, 71% of all tweets get no reaction. That is, these are tweets that are not replied to or retweeted (Sysomos website, January 5, 2015). Suppose we randomly select 100 tweets.
     a. What is the expected number of these tweets with no reaction?
     b. What are the variance and standard deviation for the number of these tweets with no reaction?

Poisson Probability Distribution

The Poisson probability distribution is often used to model random arrivals in waiting line situations.

In this section, we consider a discrete random variable that is often useful in estimating the number of occurrences over a specified interval of time or space. For example, the random variable of interest might be the number of arrivals at a car wash in one hour, the number of repairs needed in 10 miles of highway, or the number of leaks in 100 miles of pipeline. If the following two properties are satisfied, the number of occurrences is a random variable described by the **Poisson probability distribution**.

PROPERTIES OF A POISSON EXPERIMENT

1. The probability of an occurrence is the same for any two intervals of equal length.
2. The occurrence or nonoccurrence in any interval is independent of the occurrence or nonoccurrence in any other interval.

The **Poisson probability function** is defined by equation (5.15).

Siméon Poisson taught mathematics at the Ecole Polytechnique in Paris from 1802 to 1808. In 1837, he published a work entitled "Researches on the Probability of Criminal and Civil Verdicts," which includes a discussion of what later became known as the Poisson distribution.

POISSON PROBABILITY FUNCTION

$$f(x) = \frac{\mu^x e^{-\mu}}{x!} \qquad (5.15)$$

where

$f(x)$ = the probability of x occurrences in an interval

μ = expected value or mean number of occurrences in an interval

e = 2.71828

For the Poisson probability distribution, x is a discrete random variable indicating the number of occurrences in the interval. Since there is no stated upper limit for the number of occurrences, the probability function $f(x)$ is applicable for values $x = 0, 1, 2, \ldots$ without limit. In practical applications, x will eventually become large enough so that $f(x)$ is approximately zero and the probability of any larger values of x becomes negligible.

An Example Involving Time Intervals

Bell Labs used the Poisson distribution to model the arrival of telephone calls.

Suppose that we are interested in the number of arrivals at the drive-up teller window of a bank during a 15-minute period on weekday mornings. If we can assume that the probability of a car arriving is the same for any two time periods of equal length and that the arrival or nonarrival of a car in any time period is independent of the arrival or nonarrival in any other time period, the Poisson probability function is applicable. Suppose these assumptions are satisfied and an analysis of historical data shows that the average number of cars arriving in a 15-minute period of time is 10; in this case, the following probability function applies.

$$f(x) = \frac{10^x e^{-10}}{x!}$$

The random variable here is x = number of cars arriving in any 15-minute period.

If management wanted to know the probability of exactly five arrivals in 15 minutes, we would set $x = 5$ and thus obtain

$$\text{Probability of exactly} \atop \text{5 arrivals in 15 minutes} = f(5) = \frac{10^5 e^{-10}}{5!} = .0378$$

The probability of five arrivals in 15 minutes was obtained by using a calculator to evaluate the probability function. Excel also provides a function called POISSON.DIST for computing Poisson probabilities and cumulative probabilities. This function is easier to use when numerous probabilities and cumulative probabilities are desired. At the end of this section, we show how to compute these probabilities with Excel.

In the preceding example, the mean of the Poisson distribution is $\mu = 10$ arrivals per 15-minute period. A property of the Poisson distribution is that the mean of the distribution and the variance of the distribution are *equal*. Thus, the variance for the number of arrivals during 15-minute periods is $\sigma^2 = 10$. The standard deviation is $\sigma = \sqrt{10} = 3.16$.

A property of the Poisson distribution is that the mean and variance are equal.

Our illustration involves a 15-minute period, but other time periods can be used. Suppose we want to compute the probability of one arrival in a 3-minute period. Because 10 is the expected number of arrivals in a 15-minute period, we see that $10/15 = 2/3$ is the expected number of arrivals in a 1-minute period and that $(2/3)(3 \text{ minutes}) = 2$ is the expected number of arrivals in a 3-minute period. Thus, the probability of x arrivals in a 3-minute time period with $\mu = 2$ is given by the following Poisson probability function.

$$f(x) = \frac{2^x e^{-2}}{x!}$$

The probability of one arrival in a 3-minute period is calculated as follows:

$$\text{Probability of exactly} \atop \text{1 arrival in 3 minutes} = f(1) = \frac{2^1 e^{-2}}{1!} = .2707$$

Earlier we computed the probability of five arrivals in a 15-minute period; it was .0378. Note that the probability of one arrival in a three-minute period (.2707) is not the same. When computing a Poisson probability for a different time interval, we must first convert the mean arrival rate to the time period of interest and then compute the probability.

An Example Involving Length or Distance Intervals

Let us illustrate an application not involving time intervals in which the Poisson distribution is useful. Suppose we are concerned with the occurrence of major defects in a highway one month after resurfacing. We will assume that the probability of a defect is the same for any two highway intervals of equal length and that the occurrence or nonoccurrence of a defect in any one interval is independent of the occurrence or nonoccurrence of a defect in any other interval. Hence, the Poisson distribution can be applied.

Suppose we learn that major defects one month after resurfacing occur at the average rate of two per mile. Let us find the probability of no major defects in a particular 3-mile section of the highway. Because we are interested in an interval with a length of 3 miles, $\mu = (2 \text{ defects/mile})(3 \text{ miles}) = 6$ represents the expected number of major defects over the 3-mile section of highway. Using equation (5.11), the probability of no major defects is $f(0) = 6^0 e^{-6}/0! = .0025$. Thus, it is unlikely that no major defects will occur in the 3-mile section. In fact, this example indicates a $1 - .0025 = .9975$ probability of at least one major defect in the 3-mile highway section.

Using Excel to Compute Poisson Probabilities

The Excel function for computing Poisson probabilities and cumulative probabilities is called POISSON.DIST. It works in much the same way as the Excel function for computing binomial probabilities. Here we show how to use it to compute Poisson probabilities and cumulative probabilities. To illustrate, we use the example introduced earlier in this section: cars arrive at a bank drive-up teller window at the mean rate of 10 per 15-minute time interval. Refer to Figure 5.8 as we describe the tasks involved.

FIGURE 5.8   EXCEL WORKSHEET FOR COMPUTING POISSON PROBABILITIES

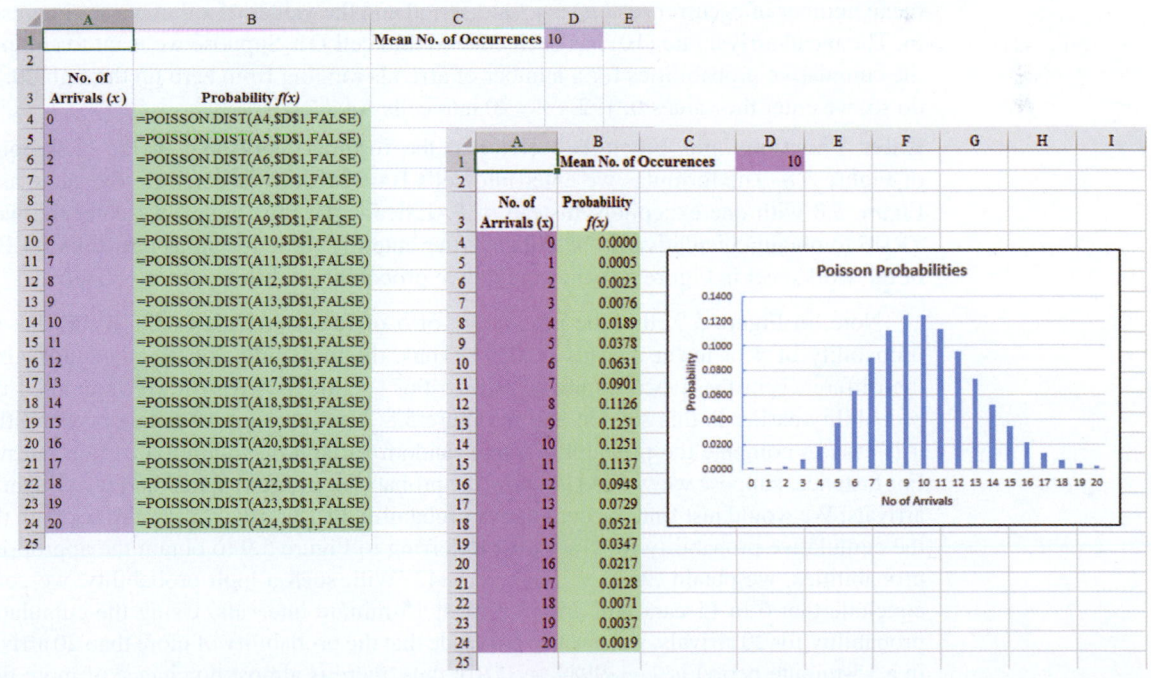

Enter/Access Data: In order to compute a Poisson probability, we must know the mean number of occurrences (μ) per time period and the number of occurrences for which we want to compute the probability (x). For the drive-up teller window example, the occurrences of interest are the arrivals of cars. The mean arrival rate is 10, which has been entered into cell D1. Earlier in this section, we computed the probability of 5 arrivals. But suppose we now want to compute the probability of 0 up through 20 arrivals. To do so, we enter the values 0, 1, 2, . . . , 20 into cells A4:A24.

Enter Functions and Formulas: The POISSON.DIST function has three inputs: The first is the value of x, the second is the value of μ, and the third is FALSE or TRUE. We choose FALSE for the third input if a probability is desired and TRUE if a cumulative probability is desired. The formula =POISSON.DIST(A4,$D$1,FALSE) has been entered into cell B4 to compute the probability of 0 arrivals in a 15-minute period. The value worksheet in the foreground shows that the probability of 0 arrivals is 0.0000. The formula in cell B4 is copied to cells B5:B24 to compute the probabilities for 1 through 20 arrivals. Note, in cell B9 of the value worksheet, that the probability of 5 arrivals is .0378. This result is the same as we calculated earlier in the text.

Notice how easy it was to compute all the probabilities for 0 through 20 arrivals using the POISSON.DIST function. These calculations would take quite a bit of work using a calculator. We have also used Excel's chart tools to develop a graph of the Poisson probability distribution of arrivals. See the value worksheet in Figure 5.8. This chart gives a nice graphical presentation of the probabilities for the various number of arrival possibilities in a 15-minute interval. We can quickly see that the most likely number of arrivals is 9 or 10 and that the probabilities fall off rather smoothly for smaller and larger values.

Let us now see how cumulative probabilities are generated using Excel's POISSON .DIST function. It is really a simple extension of what we have already done. We again use the example of arrivals at a drive-up teller window. Refer to Figure 5.9 as we describe the tasks involved.

Enter/Access Data: To compute cumulative Poisson probabilities we must provide the mean number of occurrences (μ) per time period and the values of x that we are interested in. The mean arrival rate (10) has been entered into cell D1. Suppose we want to compute the cumulative probabilities for a number of arrivals ranging from zero up through 20. To do so, we enter the values 0, 1, 2, . . . , 20 into cells A4:A24.

Enter Functions and Formulas: Refer to the formula worksheet in the background of Figure 5.8. The formulas we enter into cells B4:B24 of Figure 5.9 are the same as in Figure 5.8 with one exception. Instead of FALSE for the third input, we enter the word TRUE to obtain cumulative probabilities. After entering these formulas into cells B4:B24 of the worksheet in Figure 5.9, the cumulative probabilities shown were obtained.

Note, in Figure 5.9, that the probability of 5 or fewer arrivals is .0671 and that the probability of 4 or fewer arrivals is .0293. Thus, the probability of exactly 5 arrivals is the difference in these two numbers: $f(5) = .0671 - .0293 = .0378$. We computed this probability earlier in this section and in Figure 5.8. Using these cumulative probabilities, it is easy to compute the probability that a random variable lies within a certain interval. For instance, suppose we wanted to know the probability of more than 5 and fewer than 16 arrivals. We would just find the cumulative probability of 15 arrivals and subtract from that the cumulative probability for 5 arrivals. Referring to Figure 5.9 to obtain the appropriate probabilities, we obtain $.9513 - .0671 = .8842$. With such a high probability, we could conclude that 6 to 15 cars will arrive in most 15-minute intervals. Using the cumulative probability for 20 arrivals, we can also conclude that the probability of more than 20 arrivals in a 15-minute period is $1 - .9984 = .0016$; thus, there is almost no chance of more than 20 cars arriving.

FIGURE 5.9   EXCEL WORKSHEET FOR COMPUTING CUMULATIVE POISSON PROBABILITIES

	A	B	C	D	E
1			Mean No. of Occurrences	10	
2					
3	No. of Arrivals (x)	Probability f(x)			
4	0	=POISSON.DIST(A4,$D$1,TRUE)			
5	1	=POISSON.DIST(A5,$D$1,TRUE)			
6	2	=POISSON.DIST(A6,$D$1,TRUE)			
7	3	=POISSON.DIST(A7,$D$1,TRUE)			
8	4	=POISSON.DIST(A8,$D$1,TRUE)			
9	5	=POISSON.DIST(A9,$D$1,TRUE)			
10	6	=POISSON.DIST(A10,$D$1,TRUE)			
11	7	=POISSON.DIST(A11,$D$1,TRUE)			
12	8	=POISSON.DIST(A12,$D$1,TRUE)			
13	9	=POISSON.DIST(A13,$D$1,TRUE)			
14	10	=POISSON.DIST(A14,$D$1,TRUE)			
15	11	=POISSON.DIST(A15,$D$1,TRUE)			
16	12	=POISSON.DIST(A16,$D$1,TRUE)			
17	13	=POISSON.DIST(A17,$D$1,TRUE)			
18	14	=POISSON.DIST(A18,$D$1,TRUE)			
19	15	=POISSON.DIST(A19,$D$1,TRUE)			
20	16	=POISSON.DIST(A20,$D$1,TRUE)			
21	17	=POISSON.DIST(A21,$D$1,TRUE)			
22	18	=POISSON.DIST(A22,$D$1,TRUE)			
23	19	=POISSON.DIST(A23,$D$1,TRUE)			
24	20	=POISSON.DIST(A24,$D$1,TRUE)			
25					

	A	B	C	D	E
1		Mean No. of Occurrences		10	
2					
3	No. of Arrivals (x)	Probability f(x)			
4	0	0.0000			
5	1	0.0005			
6	2	0.0028			
7	3	0.0103			
8	4	0.0293			
9	5	0.0671			
10	6	0.1301			
11	7	0.2202			
12	8	0.3328			
13	9	0.4579			
14	10	0.5830			
15	11	0.6968			
16	12	0.7916			
17	13	0.8645			
18	14	0.9165			
19	15	0.9513			
20	16	0.9730			
21	17	0.9857			
22	18	0.9928			
23	19	0.9965			
24	20	0.9984			
25					

Exercises

Methods

44. Consider a Poisson distribution with $\mu = 3$.
  a.   Write the appropriate Poisson probability function.
  b.   Compute $f(2)$.
  c.   Compute $f(1)$.
  d.   Compute $P(x \geq 2)$.

 SELF*test*

45. Consider a Poisson distribution with a mean of two occurrences per time period.
  a.   Write the appropriate Poisson probability function.
  b.   What is the expected number of occurrences in three time periods?
  c.   Write the appropriate Poisson probability function to determine the probability of x occurrences in three time periods.
  d.   Compute the probability of two occurrences in one time period.
  e.   Compute the probability of six occurrences in three time periods.
  f.   Compute the probability of five occurrences in two time periods.

Applications

46. Phone calls arrive at the rate of 48 per hour at the reservation desk for Regional Airways.
  a.   Compute the probability of receiving three calls in a 5-minute interval of time.
  b.   Compute the probability of receiving exactly 10 calls in 15 minutes.

c. Suppose no calls are currently on hold. If the agent takes 5 minutes to complete the current call, how many callers do you expect to be waiting by that time? What is the probability that none will be waiting?

d. If no calls are currently being processed, what is the probability that the agent can take 3 minutes for personal time without being interrupted by a call?

47. During the period of time that a local university takes phone-in registrations, calls come in at the rate of one every two minutes.
   a. What is the expected number of calls in one hour?
   b. What is the probability of three calls in five minutes?
   c. What is the probability of no calls in a five-minute period?

48. In a one-year period, New York City had a total of 11,232 motor vehicle accidents that occurred on Monday through Friday between the hours of 3 P.M. and 6 P.M. (New York State Department of Motor Vehicles website). This corresponds to a mean of 14.4 accidents per hour.
   a. Compute the probability of no accidents in a 15-minute period.
   b. Compute the probability of at least one accident in a 15-minute period.
   c. Compute the probability of four or more accidents in a 15-minute period.

49. Airline passengers arrive randomly and independently at the passenger-screening facility at a major international airport. The mean arrival rate is 10 passengers per minute.
   a. Compute the probability of no arrivals in a one-minute period.
   b. Compute the probability that three or fewer passengers arrive in a one-minute period.
   c. Compute the probability of no arrivals in a 15-second period.
   d. Compute the probability of at least one arrival in a 15-second period.

50. According to the National Oceanic and Atmospheric Administration (NOAA), the state of Colorado averages 18 tornadoes every June (NOAA website, November 8, 2012). (*Note*: There are 30 days in June.)
   a. Compute the mean number of tornadoes per day.
   b. Compute the probability of no tornadoes during a day.
   c. Compute the probability of exactly one tornado during a day.
   d. Compute the probability of more than one tornado during a day.

51. Over 500 million tweets are sent per day (*Digital Marketing Ramblings* website, December 15, 2014). Assume that the number of tweets per hour follows a Poisson distribution and that Bob receives on average 7 tweets during his lunch hour.
   a. What is the probability that Bob receives no tweets during his lunch hour?
   b. What is the probability that Bob receives at least 4 tweets during his lunch hour?
   c. What is the expected number of tweets Bob receives during the first 30 minutes of his lunch hour?
   d. What is the probability that Bob receives no tweets during the first 30 minutes of his lunch hour?

 5.7 # Hypergeometric Probability Distribution

The **hypergeometric probability distribution** is closely related to the binomial distribution. The two probability distributions differ in two key ways. With the hypergeometric distribution, the trials are not independent, and the probability of success changes from trial to trial.

In the usual notation for the hypergeometric distribution, r denotes the number of elements in the population of size N labeled success, and $N - r$ denotes the number of elements in the population labeled failure. The **hypergeometric probability function** is used to compute the probability that in a random selection of n elements, selected without replacement, we obtain x elements labeled success and $n - x$ elements labeled failure. For this outcome to occur, we must obtain x successes from the r successes in the population and $n - x$ failures from the $N - r$ failures. The following hypergeometric probability function provides $f(x)$, the probability of obtaining x successes in n trials.

HYPERGEOMETRIC PROBABILITY FUNCTION

$$f(x) = \frac{\binom{r}{x}\binom{N - r}{n - x}}{\binom{N}{n}} \tag{5.16}$$

where

$x =$ the number of successes

$n =$ the number of trials

$f(x) =$ the probability of x successes in n trials

$N =$ the number of elements in the population

$r =$ the number of elements in the population labeled success

---

Note that $\binom{N}{n}$ represents the number of ways n elements can be selected from a population of size N; $\binom{r}{x}$ represents the number of ways that x successes can be selected from a total of r successes in the population; and $\binom{N - r}{n - x}$ represents the number of ways that $n - x$ failures can be selected from a total of $N - r$ failures in the population.

For the hypergeometric probability distribution, x is a discrete random variable and the probability function $f(x)$ given by equation (5.16) is usually applicable for values of $x = 0, 1, 2, \ldots, n$. However, only values of x where the number of observed successes is *less than or equal* to the number of successes in the population ($x \leq r$) and where the number of observed failures is *less than or equal to* the number of failures in the population ($n - x \leq N - r$) are valid. If these two conditions do not hold for one or more values of x, the corresponding $f(x) = 0$ indicating that the probability of this value of x is zero.

To illustrate the computations involved in using equation (5.16), let us consider the following quality control application. Electric fuses produced by Ontario Electric are packaged in boxes of 12 units each. Suppose an inspector randomly selects 3 of the 12 fuses in a box for testing. If the box contains exactly 5 defective fuses, what is the probability that the inspector will find exactly one of the 3 fuses defective? In this application, $n = 3$ and $N = 12$. With $r = 5$ defective fuses in the box the probability of finding $x = 1$ defective fuse is

$$f(1) = \frac{\binom{5}{1}\binom{7}{2}}{\binom{12}{3}} = \frac{\left(\frac{5!}{1!4!}\right)\left(\frac{7!}{2!5!}\right)}{\left(\frac{12!}{3!9!}\right)} = \frac{(5)(21)}{220} = .4773$$

Now suppose that we wanted to know the probability of finding *at least* 1 defective fuse. The easiest way to answer this question is to first compute the probability that the inspector does not find any defective fuses. The probability of $x = 0$ is

$$f(0) = \frac{\binom{5}{0}\binom{7}{3}}{\binom{12}{3}} = \frac{\left(\frac{5!}{0!5!}\right)\left(\frac{7!}{3!4!}\right)}{\left(\frac{12!}{3!9!}\right)} = \frac{(1)(35)}{220} = .1591$$

With a probability of zero defective fuses $f(0) = .1591$, we conclude that the probability of finding at least 1 defective fuse must be $1 - .1591 = .8409$. Thus, there is a reasonably high probability that the inspector will find at least 1 defective fuse.

The mean and variance of a hypergeometric distribution are as follows.

$$E(x) = \mu = n\left(\frac{r}{N}\right) \tag{5.17}$$

$$Var(x) = \sigma^2 = n\left(\frac{r}{N}\right)\left(1 - \frac{r}{N}\right)\left(\frac{N-n}{N-1}\right) \tag{5.18}$$

In the preceding example $n = 3$, $r = 5$, and $N = 12$. Thus, the mean and variance for the number of defective fuses are

$$\mu = n\left(\frac{r}{N}\right) = 3\left(\frac{5}{12}\right) = 1.25$$

$$\sigma^2 = n\left(\frac{r}{N}\right)\left(1 - \frac{r}{N}\right)\left(\frac{N-n}{N-1}\right) = 3\left(\frac{5}{12}\right)\left(1 - \frac{5}{12}\right)\left(\frac{12-3}{12-1}\right) = .60$$

The standard deviation is $\sigma = \sqrt{.60} = .77$.

Using Excel to Compute Hypergeometric Probabilities

The Excel function for computing hypergeometric probabilities is HYPGEOM.DIST. It has five inputs: the first is the value of x, the second is the value of n, the third is the value of r, the fourth is the value of N, and the fifth is FALSE or TRUE. We choose FALSE if a probability is desired and TRUE if a cumulative probability is desired. This function's usage is similar to that of BINOM.DIST for the binomial distribution and POISSON.DIST for the Poisson distribution, so we dispense with showing a worksheet figure and just explain how to use the function.

Let us reconsider the example of selecting 3 fuses for inspection from a fuse box containing 12 fuses, 5 of which are defective. We want to find the probability that 1 of the 3 fuses selected is defective. In this case, the five inputs are $x = 1$, $n = 3$, $r = 5$, $N = 12$, and FALSE. So, the appropriate formula to place in a cell of an Excel worksheet is =HYPGEOM.DIST(1,3,5,12,FALSE). Placing this formula in a cell of an Excel worksheet provides a hypergeometric probability of .4773.

If we want to know the probability that none of the 3 fuses selected is defective, the five function inputs are $x = 0$, $n = 3$, $r = 5$, $N = 12$, and FALSE. So, using the HYPGEOM. DIST function to compute the probability of randomly selecting 3 fuses without any being defective, we would enter the following formula into an Excel worksheet: =HYPGEOM. DIST(0,3,5,12,FALSE). The probability is .1591.

Cumulative probabilities can be obtained in a similar fashion by using TRUE for the fifth input. For instance, to compute the probability of finding at most 1 defective fuse, the appropriate formula is =HYPGEOM.DIST(1,3,5,12,TRUE). Placing this formula in a cell of an Excel worksheet provides a hypergeometric cumulative probability of .6364.

NOTE AND COMMENT

Consider a hypergeometric distribution with n trials. Let $p = (r/N)$ denote the probability of a success on the first trial. If the population size is large, the term $(N - n)/(N - 1)$ in equation (5.18) approaches 1. As a result, the expected value and variance can be written $E(x) = np$ and $Var(x) = np(1 - p)$. Note that these expressions are the same as the expressions used to compute the expected value and variance of a binomial distribution, as in equations (5.13) and (5.14). When the population size is large, a hypergeometric distribution can be approximated by a binomial distribution with n trials and a probability of success $p = (r/N)$.

Exercises

Methods

52. Suppose $N = 10$ and $r = 3$. Compute the hypergeometric probabilities for the following values of n and x.
    a. $n = 4, x = 1$.
    b. $n = 2, x = 2$.
    c. $n = 2, x = 0$.
    d. $n = 4, x = 2$.
    e. $n = 4, x = 4$.

53. Suppose $N = 15$ and $r = 4$. What is the probability of $x = 3$ for $n = 10$?

Applications

54. A recent survey showed that a majority of Americans plan on doing their holiday shopping online because they don't want to spend money on gas driving from store to store (SOASTA website, October 24, 2012). Suppose we have a group of 10 shoppers; 7 prefer to do their holiday shopping online and 3 prefer to do their holiday shopping in stores. A random sample of 3 of these 10 shoppers is selected for a more in-depth study of how the economy has impacted their shopping behavior.
    a. What is the probability that exactly 2 prefer shopping online?
    b. What is the probability that the majority (either 2 or 3) prefer shopping online?

55. Blackjack, or twenty-one as it is frequently called, is a popular gambling game played in Las Vegas casinos. A player is dealt two cards. Face cards (jacks, queens, and kings) and tens have a point value of 10. Aces have a point value of 1 or 11. A 52-card deck contains 16 cards with a point value of 10 (jacks, queens, kings, and tens) and four aces.
    a. What is the probability that both cards dealt are aces or 10-point cards?
    b. What is the probability that both of the cards are aces?
    c. What is the probability that both of the cards have a point value of 10?
    d. A blackjack is a 10-point card and an ace for a value of 21. Use your answers to parts (a), (b), and (c) to determine the probability that a player is dealt blackjack. (*Hint:* Part (d) is not a hypergeometric problem. Develop your own logical relationship as to how the hypergeometric probabilities from parts (a), (b), and (c) can be combined to answer this question.)

56. Axline Computers manufactures personal computers at two plants, one in Texas and the other in Hawaii. The Texas plant has 40 employees; the Hawaii plant has 20. A random sample of 10 employees is asked to fill out a benefits questionnaire.
    a. What is the probability that none of the employees in the sample work at the plant in Hawaii?
    b. What is the probability that 1 of the employees in the sample works at the plant in Hawaii?
    c. What is the probability that 2 or more of the employees in the sample work at the plant in Hawaii?
    d. What is the probability that 9 of the employees in the sample work at the plant in Texas?

57. The Zagat Restaurant Survey provides food, decor, and service ratings for some of the top restaurants across the United States. For 15 restaurants located in Boston, the average price of a dinner, including one drink and tip, was $48.60. You are leaving on a business trip to Boston and will eat dinner at three of these restaurants. Your company will reimburse you for a maximum of $50 per dinner. Business associates familiar with these restaurants have told you that the meal cost at one-third of these restaurants will exceed $50. Suppose that you randomly select three of these restaurants for dinner.
    a. What is the probability that none of the meals will exceed the cost covered by your company?
    b. What is the probability that one of the meals will exceed the cost covered by your company?
    c. What is the probability that two of the meals will exceed the cost covered by your company?
    d. What is the probability that all three of the meals will exceed the cost covered by your company?

58. Suppose that a shipment of 100 boxes of apples has 8 boxes in which the apples show signs of spoilage. A quality control inspection selects 10 boxes at random, opens these selected boxes, and counts the number of boxes out of 10 in which the apples show signs of spoilage. What is the probability that exactly 2 boxes in the sample show signs of spoilage?

Summary

A random variable provides a numerical description of the outcome of an experiment. The probability distribution for a random variable describes how the probabilities are distributed over the values the random variable can assume. For any discrete random variable x, the probability distribution is defined by a probability function, denoted by $f(x)$, which provides the probability associated with each value of the random variable.

We introduced two types of discrete probability distributions. One type involved providing a list of the values of the random variable and the associated probabilities in a table. We showed how the relative frequency method of assigning probabilities could be used to develop empirical discrete probability distributions of this type. Bivariate empirical distributions were also discussed. With bivariate distributions, interest focuses on the relationship between two random variables. We showed how to compute the covariance and correlation coefficient as measures of such a relationship. We also showed how bivariate distributions involving market returns on financial assets could be used to create financial portfolios.

The second type of discrete probability distribution we discussed involved the use of a mathematical function to provide the probabilities for the random variable. The binomial, Poisson, and hypergeometric distributions discussed were all of this type. The binomial distribution can be used to determine the probability of x successes in n trials whenever the experiment has the following properties:

1. The experiment consists of a sequence of n identical trials.
2. Two outcomes are possible on each trial, one called success and the other failure.
3. The probability of a success p does not change from trial to trial. Consequently, the probability of failure, $1 - p$, does not change from trial to trial.
4. The trials are independent.

When the four properties hold, the binomial probability function can be used to determine the probability of obtaining x successes in n trials. Formulas were also presented for the mean and variance of the binomial distribution.

The Poisson distribution is used when it is desirable to determine the probability of obtaining x occurrences over an interval of time or space. The following assumptions are necessary for the Poisson distribution to be applicable:

1. The probability of an occurrence of the event is the same for any two intervals of equal length.
2. The occurrence or nonoccurrence of the event in any interval is independent of the occurrence or nonoccurrence of the event in any other interval.

A third discrete probability distribution, the hypergeometric, was introduced in Section 5.7. Like the binomial, it is used to compute the probability of x successes in n trials. But, in contrast to the binomial, the probability of success changes from trial to trial.

Glossary

Binomial experiment An experiment having the four properties stated at the beginning of Section 5.5.

Binomial probability distribution A probability distribution showing the probability of x successes in n trials of a binomial experiment.

Binomial probability function The function used to compute binomial probabilities.

Bivariate probability distribution A probability distribution involving two random variables. A discrete bivariate probability distribution provides a probability for each pair of values that may occur for the two random variables.

Continuous random variable A random variable that may assume any numerical value in an interval or collection of intervals.

Discrete random variable A random variable that may assume either a finite number of values or an infinite sequence of values.

Discrete uniform probability distribution A probability distribution for which each possible value of the random variable has the same probability.

Empirical discrete distribution A discrete probability distribution for which the relative frequency method is used to assign the probabilities.

Expected value A measure of the central location, or mean, of a random variable.

Hypergeometric probability distribution A probability distribution showing the probability of x successes in n trials from a population with r successes and $N - r$ failures.

Hypergeometric probability function The function used to compute hypergeometric probabilities.

Poisson probability distribution A probability distribution showing the probability of x occurrences of an event over a specified interval of time or space.

Poisson probability function The function used to compute Poisson probabilities.

Probability distribution A description of how the probabilities are distributed over the values of the random variable.

Probability function A function, denoted by $f(x)$, that provides the probability that x assumes a particular value for a discrete random variable.

Random variable A numerical description of the outcome of an experiment.

Standard deviation The positive square root of the variance.

Variance A measure of the variability, or dispersion, of a random variable.

Key Formulas

Discrete Uniform Probability Function

$$f(x) = 1/n \tag{5.3}$$

Expected Value of a Discrete Random Variable

$$E(x) = \mu = \sum x f(x) \tag{5.4}$$

Variance of a Discrete Random Variable

$$Var(x) = \sigma^2 = \sum (x - \mu)^2 f(x) \tag{5.5}$$

Covariance of Random Variables x and y

$$\sigma_{xy} = [Var(x + y) - Var(x) - Var(y)]/2 \tag{5.6}$$

Correlation between Random Variables x and y

$$\rho_{xy} = \frac{\sigma_{xy}}{\sigma_x \sigma_y} \tag{5.7}$$

Expected Value of a Linear Combination of Random Variables x and y

$$E(ax + by) = aE(x) + bE(y) \tag{5.8}$$

Variance of a Linear Combination of Two Random Variables

$$Var(ax + by) = a^2 Var(x) + b^2 Var(y) + 2ab\sigma_{xy} \tag{5.9}$$

where σ_{xy} is the covariance of x and y

Number of Experimental Outcomes Providing Exactly x Successes in n Trials

$$\binom{n}{x} = \frac{n!}{x!(n - x)!} \tag{5.10}$$

Binomial Probability Function

$$f(x) = \binom{n}{x} p^x (1 - p)^{(n - x)} \tag{5.12}$$

Expected Value for the Binomial Distribution

$$E(x) = \mu = np \tag{5.13}$$

Variance for the Binomial Distribution

$$Var(x) = \sigma^2 = np(1 - p) \tag{5.14}$$

Poisson Probability Function

$$f(x) = \frac{\mu^x e^{-\mu}}{x!} \tag{5.15}$$

Hypergeometric Probability Function

$$f(x) = \frac{\binom{r}{x}\binom{N-r}{n-x}}{\binom{N}{n}} \tag{5.16}$$

Expected Value for the Hypergeometric Distribution

$$E(x) = \mu = n\left(\frac{r}{N}\right) \tag{5.17}$$

Variance for the Hypergeometric Distribution

$$Var(x) = \sigma^2 = n\left(\frac{r}{N}\right)\left(1 - \frac{r}{N}\right)\left(\frac{N-n}{N-1}\right) \tag{5.18}$$

Supplementary Exercises

59. The U.S. Coast Guard (USCG) provides a wide variety of information on boating accidents including the wind condition at the time of the accident. The following table shows the results obtained for 4401 accidents (USCG website, November 8, 2012).

Wind Condition	Percentage of Accidents
None	9.6
Light	57.0
Moderate	23.8
Strong	7.7
Storm	1.9

Let x be a random variable reflecting the known wind condition at the time of each accident. Set $x = 0$ for none, $x = 1$ for light, $x = 2$ for moderate, $x = 3$ for strong, and $x = 4$ for storm.
a. Develop a probability distribution for x.
b. Compute the expected value of x.

     c.   Compute the variance and standard deviation for x.

     d.   Comment on what your results imply about the wind conditions during boating accidents.

60.   The Car Repair Ratings website provides consumer reviews and ratings for garages in the United States and Canada. The time customers wait for service to be completed is one of the categories rated. The following table provides a summary of the wait-time ratings (1 = Slow/Delays; 10 = Quick/On Time) for 40 randomly selected garages located in the province of Ontario, Canada.

Wait-Time Rating	Number of Garages
1	6
2	2
3	3
4	2
5	5
6	2
7	4
8	5
9	5
10	6

     a.   Develop a probability distribution for x = wait-time rating.

     b.   Any garage that receives a wait-time rating of at least 9 is considered to provide outstanding service. If a consumer randomly selects one of the 40 garages for their next car service, what is the probability the garage selected will provide outstanding wait-time service?

     c.   What is the expected value and variance for x?

     d.   Suppose that seven of the 40 garages reviewed were new car dealerships. Of the seven new car dealerships, two were rated as providing outstanding wait-time service. Compare the likelihood of a new car dealership achieving an outstanding wait-time service rating as compared to other types of service providers.

61.   The budgeting process for a midwestern college resulted in expense forecasts for the coming year (in $ millions) of $9, $10, $11, $12, and $13. Because the actual expenses are unknown, the following respective probabilities are assigned: .3, .2, .25, .05, and .2.

     a.   Show the probability distribution for the expense forecast.

     b.   What is the expected value of the expense forecast for the coming year?

     c.   What is the variance of the expense forecast for the coming year?

     d.   If income projections for the year are estimated at $12 million, comment on the financial position of the college.

62.   A bookstore at the Hartsfield-Jackson Airport in Atlanta sells reading materials (paperback books, newspapers, magazines) as well as snacks (peanuts, pretzels, candy, etc.). A point-of-sale terminal collects a variety of information about customer purchases. The following table shows the number of snack items and the number of items of reading material purchased by the most recent 600 customers.

Snacks	Reading Material		
	0	**1**	**2**
0	0	60	18
1	240	90	30
2	120	30	12

a. Using the data in the table construct an empirical discrete bivariate probability distribution for x = number of snack items and y = number of reading materials for a randomly selected customer purchase. What is the probability of a customer purchase consisting of one item of reading materials and two snack items? What is the probability of a customer purchasing one snack item only? Why is the probability $f(x = 0, y = 0) = 0$?

b. Show the marginal probability distribution for the number of snack items purchased. Compute the expected value and variance.

c. What is the expected value and variance for the number of reading materials purchased by a customer?

d. Show the probability distribution for t = total number of items for a randomly selected customer purchase. Compute its expected value and variance.

e. Compute the covariance and correlation coefficient between x and y. What is the relationship, if any, between the number of reading materials and number of snacks purchased?

63. The Knowles/Armitage (KA) group at Merrill Lynch advises clients on how to create a diversified investment portfolio. One of the investment alternatives they make available to clients is the All World Fund composed of global stocks with good dividend yields. One of their clients is interested in a portfolio consisting of investment in the All World Fund and a treasury bond fund. The expected percent return of an investment in the All World Fund is 7.80% with a standard deviation of 18.90%. The expected percent return of an investment in a treasury bond fund is 5.50% and the standard deviation is 4.60%. The covariance of an investment in the All World Fund with an investment in a treasury bond fund is −12.4.

a. Which of the funds would be considered the more risky? Why?

b. If KA recommends that the client invest 75% in the All World Fund and 25% in the treasury bond fund, what is the expected percent return and standard deviation for such a portfolio? What would be the expected return and standard deviation, in dollars, for a client investing $10,000 in such a portfolio?

c. If KA recommends that the client invest 25% in the All World Fund and 75% in the treasury bond fund, what is the expected return and standard deviation for such a portfolio? What would be the expected return and standard deviation, in dollars, for a client investing $10,000 in such a portfolio?

d. Which of the portfolios in parts (b) and (c) would you recommend for an aggressive investor? Which would you recommend for a conservative investor? Why?

64. The Pew Research Center surveyed adults who own/use the following technologies: Internet, smartphone, e-mail, and land-line phone (*USA Today*, March 26, 2014) and asked which of these technologies would be "very hard" to give up. The following responses were obtained: Internet 53%, smartphone 49%, e-mail 36%, and land-line phone 28%.

a. If 20 adult Internet users are surveyed, what is the probability that 3 users will report that it would be very hard to give it up?

b. If 20 adults who own a land-line phone are surveyed, what is the probability that 5 or fewer will report that it would be very hard to give it up?

c. If 2000 owners of smartphones were surveyed, what is the expected number that will report that it would be very hard to give it up?

d. If 2000 users of e-mail were surveyed, what is expected number that will report that it would be very hard to give it up? What is the variance and standard deviation?

65. The following table shows the percentage of individuals in each age group who use an online tax program to prepare their federal income tax return (CompleteTax website, November 9, 2012).

Age	Online Tax Program (%)
18–34	16
35–44	12
45–54	10
55–64	8
65+	2

Suppose a follow-up study consisting of personal interviews is to be conducted to determine the most important factors in selecting a method for filing taxes.

a. How many 18- to 34-year-olds must be sampled to find an expected number of at least 25 who use an online tax program to prepare their federal income tax return?

b. How many 35- to 44-year-olds must be sampled to find an expected number of at least 25 who use an online tax program to prepare their federal income tax return?

c. How many 65+-year-olds must be sampled to find an expected number of at least 25 who use an online tax program to prepare their federal income tax return?

d. If the number of 18- to 34-year-olds sampled is equal to the value identified in part (a), what is the standard deviation of the percentage who use an online tax program?

e. If the number of 35- to 44-year-olds sampled is equal to the value identified in part (b), what is the standard deviation of the percentage who use an online tax program?

66. Many companies use a quality control technique called acceptance sampling to monitor incoming shipments of parts, raw materials, and so on. In the electronics industry, component parts are commonly shipped from suppliers in large lots. Inspection of a sample of n components can be viewed as the n trials of a binomial experiment. The outcome for each component tested (trial) will be that the component is classified as good or defective. Reynolds Electronics accepts a lot from a particular supplier if the defective components in the lot do not exceed 1%. Suppose a random sample of five items from a recent shipment is tested.

a. Assume that 1% of the shipment is defective. Compute the probability that no items in the sample are defective.

b. Assume that 1% of the shipment is defective. Compute the probability that exactly one item in the sample is defective.

c. What is the probability of observing one or more defective items in the sample if 1% of the shipment is defective?

d. Would you feel comfortable accepting the shipment if one item was found to be defective? Why or why not?

67. PBS *News Hour* reported that 39.4% of Americans between the ages of 25 and 64 have at least a two-year college degree (PBS website, December 15, 2014). Assume that 50 Americans between the ages of 25 and 64 are selected randomly.

a. What is the expected number of people with at least a two-year college-degree?

b. What are the variance and standard deviation for the number of people with at least a two-year college degree?

68. Mahoney Custom Home Builders, Inc. of Canyon Lake, Texas asked visitors to their website what is most important when choosing a home builder. Possible responses were quality, price, customer referral, years in business, and special features. Results showed that 23.5% of the respondents chose price as the most important factor (Mahoney Custom Homes website, November 13, 2012). Suppose a sample of 200 potential home buyers in the Canyon Lake area was selected.

a. How many people would you expect to choose price as the most important factor when choosing a home builder?

b.   What is the standard deviation of the number of respondents who would choose price as the most important factor in selecting a home builder?

c.   What is the standard deviation of the number of respondents who do not list price as the most important factor in selecting a home builder?

69.   Cars arrive at a car wash randomly and independently; the probability of an arrival is the same for any two time intervals of equal length. The mean arrival rate is 15 cars per hour. What is the probability that 20 or more cars will arrive during any given hour of operation?

70.   A new automated production process averages 1.5 breakdowns per day. Because of the cost associated with a breakdown, management is concerned about the possibility of having 3 or more breakdowns during a day. Assume that breakdowns occur randomly, that the probability of a breakdown is the same for any two time intervals of equal length, and that breakdowns in one period are independent of breakdowns in other periods. What is the probability of having 3 or more breakdowns during a day?

71.   A regional director responsible for business development in the state of Pennsylvania is concerned about the number of small business failures. If the mean number of small business failures per month is 10, what is the probability that exactly 4 small businesses will fail during a given month? Assume that the probability of a failure is the same for any two months and that the occurrence or nonoccurrence of a failure in any month is independent of failures in any other month.

72.   Customer arrivals at a bank are random and independent; the probability of an arrival in any one-minute period is the same as the probability of an arrival in any other one-minute period. Answer the following questions, assuming a mean arrival rate of 3 customers per minute.

a.   What is the probability of exactly 3 arrivals in a one-minute period?

b.   What is the probability of at least 3 arrivals in a one-minute period?

Case Problem 1   *Go Bananas!*

Great Grasslands Grains, Inc. (GGG) manufactures and sells a wide variety of breakfast cereals. GGG's product development lab recently created a new cereal that consists of rice flakes and banana-flavored marshmallows. The company's marketing research department has tested the new cereal extensively and has found that consumers are enthusiastic about the cereal when 16-ounce boxes contain at least 1.6 ounces and no more than 2.4 ounces of the banana-flavored marshmallows.

As GGG prepares to begin producing and selling 16-ounce boxes of the new cereal, which it has named *Go Bananas!*, management is concerned about the amount of banana-flavored marshmallows. It wants to be careful not to include less than 1.6 ounces or more than 2.4 ounces of banana-flavored marshmallows in each 16-ounce box of *Go Bananas!*. Tina Finkel, VP of Production for GGG, has suggested that the company measure the weight of banana-flavored marshmallows in a random sample of 25 boxes of *Go Bananas!* on a weekly basis. Each week, GGG can count the number of boxes out of the 25 boxes in the sample that contain less than 1.6 ounces or more than 2.4 ounces of banana-flavored marshmallows; if the number of boxes that fail to meet the standard weight of banana-flavored marshmallows is too high, production will be shut down and inspected.

Ms. Finkel and her staff have designed the production process so that only 8% of all 16-ounce boxes of *Go Bananas!* fail to meet the standard weight of banana-flavored marshmallows. After much debate, GGG management has decided to shut down production of *Go Bananas!* if at least five boxes in a weekly sample fail to meet the standard weight of banana-flavored marshmallows.

Managerial Report

Prepare a managerial report that addresses the following issues.

1. Calculate the probability that a weekly sample will result in a shutdown of production if the production process is working properly. Comment on GGG management's policy for deciding when to shut down production of *Go Bananas!*.

2. GGG management wants to shut down production of *Go Bananas!* no more than 1% of the time when the production process is working properly. Suggest the appropriate number of boxes in the weekly sample that must fail to meet the standard weight of banana-flavored marshmallows in order for production to be shut down if this goal is to be achieved.

3. Ms. Finkel has suggested that if given sufficient resources, she could redesign the production process to reduce the percentage of 16-ounce boxes of *Go Bananas!* that fail to meet the standard weight of banana-flavored marshmallows when the process is working properly. To what level must Ms. Finkel reduce the percentage of 16-ounce boxes of *Go Bananas!* that fail to meet the standard weight of banana-flavored marshmallows when the process is working properly in order for her to reduce the probability at least five of the sampled boxes fail to meet the standard to .01 or less?

Case Problem 2   McNeil's Auto Mall

Harriet McNeil, proprietor of McNeil's Auto Mall, believes that it is good business for her automobile dealership to have more customers on the lot than can be served, as she believes this creates an impression that demand for the automobiles on her lot is high. However, she also understands that if there are far more customers on the lot than can be served by her salespeople, her dealership may lose sales to customers who become frustrated and leave without making a purchase.

Ms. McNeil is primarily concerned about the staffing of salespeople on her lot on Saturday mornings (8:00 A.M. to noon), which are the busiest time of the week for McNeil's Auto Mall. On Saturday mornings, an average of 6.8 customers arrive per hour. The customers arrive randomly at a constant rate throughout the morning, and a salesperson spends an average of one hour with a customer. Ms. McNeil's experience has led her to conclude that if there are two more customers on her lot than can be served at any time on a Saturday morning, her automobile dealership achieves the optimal balance of creating an impression of high demand without losing too many customers who become frustrated and leave without making a purchase.

Ms. McNeil now wants to determine how many salespeople she should have on her lot on Saturday mornings in order to achieve her goal of having two more customers on her lot than can be served at any time. She understands that occasionally the number of customers on her lot will exceed the number of salespersons by more than two, and she is willing to accept such an occurrence no more than 10% of the time.

Managerial Report

Ms. McNeil has asked you to determine the number of salespersons she should have on her lot on Saturday mornings in order to satisfy her criteria. In answering Ms. McNeil's question, consider the following three questions:

1. How is the number of customers who arrive on the lot on a Saturday morning distributed?

2. Suppose Ms. McNeil currently uses five salespeople on her lot on Saturday mornings. Using the probability distribution you identified in (1), what is the probability that the number of customers who arrive on her lot will exceed the number of salespersons by more than two? Does her current Saturday morning employment strategy satisfy her stated objective? Why or why not?

3. What is the minimum number of salespeople Ms. McNeil should have on her lot on Saturday mornings to achieve her objective?

Case Problem 3   # Grievance Committee at Tuglar Corporation

Several years ago, management at Tuglar Corporation established a grievance committee composed of employees who volunteered to work toward the amicable resolution of disputes between Tuglar management and its employees. Each year management issues a call for volunteers to serve on the grievance committee, and 10 of the respondents are randomly selected to serve on the committee for the upcoming year.

Employees in the Accounting Department are distressed because no member of their department has served on the Tuglar grievance committee in the past five years. Management has assured its employees in the Accounting Department that the selections have been made randomly, but these assurances have not quelled suspicions that management has intentionally omitted accountants from the committee. The table below summarizes the total number of volunteers and the number of employees from the Accounting Department who have volunteered for the grievance committee in each of the past five years:

	2013	2014	2015	2016	2017
Total Number of Volunteers	29	31	23	26	28
Number of Volunteers from the Accounting Department	1	1	1	2	1

In its defense, management has provided these numbers to the Accounting Department. Given these numbers, is the lack of members of the Accounting Department on the grievance committee for the past five years suspicious (i.e., unlikely)?

Managerial Report

In addressing the issue of whether or not the committee selection process is random, consider the following questions:

1. How is the number of members of the Accounting Department who are selected to serve on the grievance committee distributed?
2. Using the probability distribution you identified in (1), what is the probability for each of these five years that no members of the Accounting Department have been selected to serve?
3. Using the probabilities you identified in (2), what is the probability that no members of the Accounting Department have been selected to serve during the past five years?
4. What is the cause of the lack of Accounting Department representation on the grievance committee over the past five years? What can be done to increase the probability that a member of the Accounting Department will be selected to serve on the grievance committee using the current selection method?

Case Problem 4   # Sagittarius Casino

The Sagittarius Casino's strategy for establishing a competitive advantage over its competitors is to periodically create unique and interesting new games for its customers to play. Sagittarius management feels it is time for the casino to once again introduce a new game to excite its customer base, and Sagittarius's Director of Research and Development, Lou Zerbit, believes he and his staff have developed a new game that will accomplish this goal. The game, which they have named *POSO!* (an acronym for **P**ayouts **O**n **S**elected **O**utcomes), is to be played in the following manner. A player will select two different values from 1, 2, 3, 4, 5, and 6. Two dice are then rolled. If the first number the player selected comes up on at least one of the two dice, the player wins $5.00; if the second number the player selected comes up on both of the dice, the player wins $10.00. If neither of these events occurs, the player wins nothing.

For example, suppose a player fills out the following card for one game of *POSO!*

POSO!	
First Number (select one number from 1, 2, 3, 4, 5, or 6)	Second Number (select a different number from 1, 2, 3, 4, 5, or 6)
4	*2*
If this number comes up on at least one die, *you win $5.00!*	If this number comes up on both dice, *you win $10.00!*

When the two dice are rolled, if at least one die comes up 4 the player will win $5.00, if both dice come up 2 the player will win $10.00, and if any other outcome occurs the player wins nothing.

Managerial Report

Sagittarius management now has three questions about *POSO!* These questions should be addressed in your report.

1. Although they certainly do not want to pay out more than they take in, casinos like to offer games in which players win frequently; casino managers believe this keeps players excited about playing the game. What is the probability a player will win if she or he plays a single game of *POSO!*?
2. What is the expected amount a player will win when playing one game of *POSO!*?
3. Sagittarius managers want to take in more than they pay out on average for a game of *POSO!*. Furthermore, casinos such as Sagittarius are often looking for games that provide their gamers with an opportunity to play for a small bet, and Sagittarius management would like to charge players $2.00 to play one game of *POSO!*. What will be the expected profit earned by Sagittarius Casino on a single play if a player has to pay $2.00 for a single play of *POSO!*? Will Sagittarius Casino expect to earn or lose money on *POSO!* if a player pays $2.00 for a single play? What is the minimum amount Sagittarius Casino can charge a player for a single play of *POSO!* and still expect to earn money?

CHAPTER 6

Continuous Probability Distributions

CONTENTS

STATISTICS IN PRACTICE:
PROCTER & GAMBLE

6.1 UNIFORM PROBABILITY
DISTRIBUTION
Area as a Measure of Probability

6.2 NORMAL PROBABILITY
DISTRIBUTION
Normal Curve
Standard Normal Probability
Distribution
Computing Probabilities for
Any Normal Probability
Distribution
Grear Tire Company Problem
Using Excel to Compute Normal
Probabilities

6.3 EXPONENTIAL PROBABILITY
DISTRIBUTION
Computing Probabilities for the
Exponential Distribution
Relationship Between the
Poisson and Exponential
Distributions
Using Excel to Compute
Exponential Probabilities

PROCTER & GAMBLE*
CINCINNATI, OHIO

Procter & Gamble (P&G) produces and markets such products as detergents, disposable diapers, over-the-counter pharmaceuticals, dentifrices, bar soaps, mouthwashes, and paper towels. Worldwide, it has the leading brand in more categories than any other consumer products company. Since its merger with Gillette, P&G also produces and markets razors, blades, and many other personal care products.

As a leader in the application of statistical methods in decision making, P&G employs people with diverse academic backgrounds: engineering, statistics, operations research, analytics and business. The major quantitative technologies for which these people provide support are probabilistic decision and risk analysis, advanced simulation, quality improvement, and quantitative methods (e.g., linear programming, regression analysis, probability analysis).

The Industrial Chemicals Division of P&G is a major supplier of fatty alcohols derived from natural substances such as coconut oil and from petroleum-based derivatives. The division wanted to know the economic risks and opportunities of expanding its fatty-alcohol production facilities, so it called in P&G's experts in probabilistic decision and risk analysis to help. After structuring and modeling the problem, they determined that the key to profitability was the cost difference between the petroleum- and coconut-based raw materials. Future costs were unknown, but the analysts were able to approximate them with the following continuous random variables.

x = the coconut oil price per pound of fatty alcohol

and

y = the petroleum raw material price per pound of fatty alcohol

Because the key to profitability was the difference between these two random variables, a third random variable, $d = x - y$, was used in the analysis. Experts were interviewed to determine the probability distributions for x and y. In turn, this information was used to develop a probability distribution for the difference in

© John Sommers II/Reuters

Procter & Gamble is a leader in the application of statistical methods in decision making.

prices d. This continuous probability distribution showed a .90 probability that the price difference would be \$.0655 or less and a .50 probability that the price difference would be \$.035 or less. In addition, there was only a .10 probability that the price difference would be \$.0045 or less.[†]

The Industrial Chemicals Division thought that being able to quantify the impact of raw material price differences was key to reaching a consensus. The probabilities obtained were used in a sensitivity analysis of the raw material price difference. The analysis yielded sufficient insight to form the basis for a recommendation to management.

The use of continuous random variables and their probability distributions was helpful to P&G in analyzing the economic risks associated with its fatty-alcohol production. In this chapter, you will gain an understanding of continuous random variables and their probability distributions, including one of the most important probability distributions in statistics, the normal distribution.

---

*The authors are indebted to Joel Kahn of Procter & Gamble for providing this Statistics in Practice.

[†]The price differences stated here have been modified to protect proprietary data.

In the preceding chapter we discussed discrete random variables and their probability distributions. In this chapter we turn to the study of continuous random variables. Specifically, we discuss three continuous probability distributions: the uniform, the normal, and the exponential.

A fundamental difference separates discrete and continuous random variables in terms of how probabilities are computed. For a discrete random variable, the probability function $f(x)$ provides the probability that the random variable assumes a particular value. With continuous random variables, the counterpart of the probability function is the **probability density function**, also denoted by $f(x)$. The difference is that the probability density function does not directly provide probabilities. However, the area under the graph of $f(x)$ corresponding to a given interval does provide the probability that the continuous random variable x assumes a value in that interval. So when we compute probabilities for continuous random variables, we are computing the probability that the random variable assumes any value in an interval.

Because the area under the graph of $f(x)$ at any particular point is zero, one of the implications of the definition of probability for continuous random variables is that the probability of any particular value of the random variable is zero. In Section 6.1 we demonstrate these concepts for a continuous random variable that has a uniform distribution.

Much of the chapter is devoted to describing and showing applications of the normal distribution. The normal distribution is of major importance because of its wide applicability and its extensive use in statistical inference. The chapter closes with a discussion of the exponential distribution. The exponential distribution is useful in applications involving such factors as waiting times and service times.

 # Uniform Probability Distribution

Consider the random variable x representing the flight time of an airplane traveling from Chicago to New York. Suppose the flight time can be any value in the interval from 120 minutes to 140 minutes. Because the random variable x can assume any value in that interval, x is a continuous rather than a discrete random variable. Let us assume that sufficient actual flight data are available to conclude that the probability of a flight time within any 1-minute interval is the same as the probability of a flight time within any other 1-minute interval contained in the larger interval from 120 to 140 minutes. With every 1-minute interval being equally likely, the random variable x is said to have a **uniform probability distribution**. The probability density function, which defines the uniform distribution for the flight-time random variable, is

Whenever the probability is proportional to the length of the interval, the random variable is uniformly distributed.

$$f(x) = \begin{cases} 1/20 & \text{for } 120 \le x \le 140 \\ 0 & \text{elsewhere} \end{cases}$$

Figure 6.1 is a graph of this probability density function. In general, the uniform probability density function for a random variable x is defined by the following formula.

UNIFORM PROBABILITY DENSITY FUNCTION

$$f(x) = \begin{cases} \dfrac{1}{b - a} & \text{for } a \le x \le b \\ 0 & \text{elsewhere} \end{cases} \tag{6.1}$$

For the flight-time random variable, $a = 120$ and $b = 140$.

FIGURE 6.1   UNIFORM PROBABILITY DISTRIBUTION FOR FLIGHT TIME

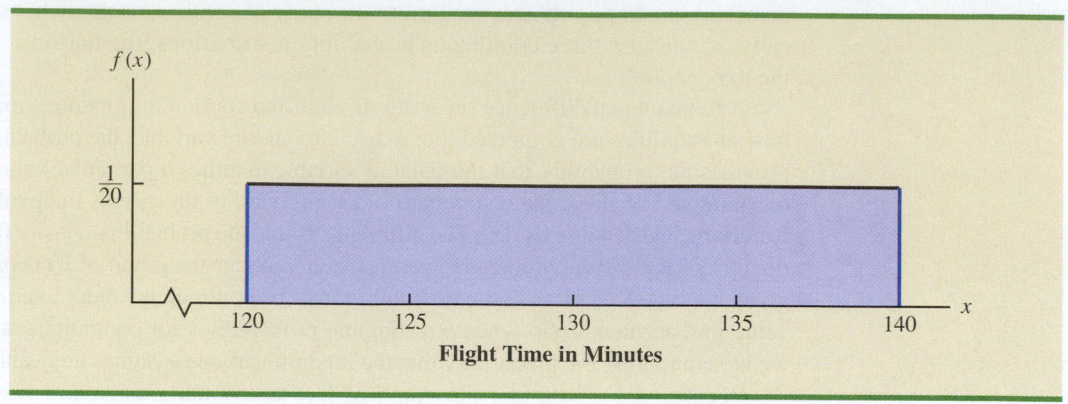

As noted in the introduction, for a continuous random variable, we consider probability only in terms of the likelihood that a random variable assumes a value within a specified interval. In the flight time example, an acceptable probability question is: What is the probability that the flight time is between 120 and 130 minutes? That is, what is $P(120 \leq x \leq 130)$? Because the flight time must be between 120 and 140 minutes and because the probability is described as being uniform over this interval, we feel comfortable saying that $P(120 \leq x \leq 130) = .50$. In the following subsection we show that this probability can be computed as the area under the graph of $f(x)$ from 120 to 130 (see Figure 6.2).

Area as a Measure of Probability

Let us make an observation about the graph in Figure 6.2. Consider the area under the graph of $f(x)$ in the interval from 120 to 130. The area is rectangular, and the area of a rectangle is simply the width multiplied by the height. With the width of the interval equal to $130 - 120 = 10$ and the height equal to the value of the probability density function $f(x) = 1/20$, we have area = width × height = $10(1/20) = 10/20 = .50$.

What observation can you make about the area under the graph of $f(x)$ and probability? They are identical! Indeed, this observation is valid for all continuous random variables.

FIGURE 6.2   AREA PROVIDES PROBABILITY OF A FLIGHT TIME BETWEEN 120 AND 130 MINUTES

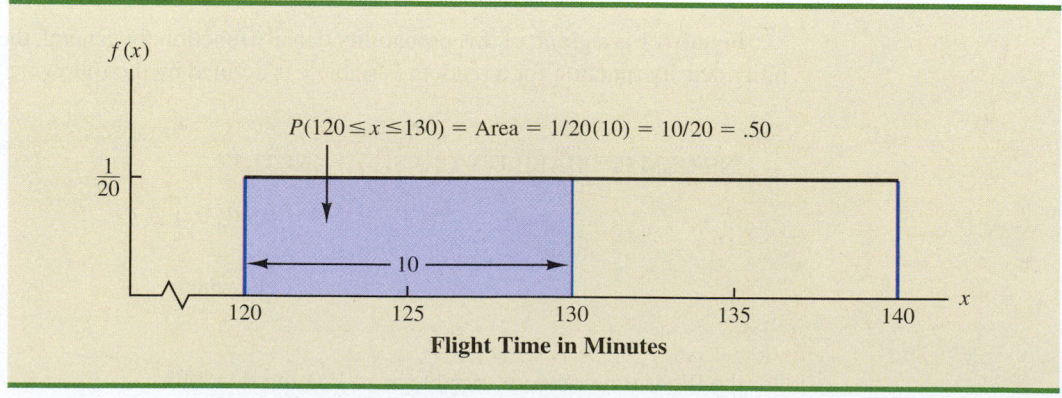

Once a probability density function $f(x)$ is identified, the probability that x takes a value between some lower value x_1 and some higher value x_2 can be found by computing the area under the graph of $f(x)$ over the interval from x_1 to x_2.

Given the uniform distribution for flight time and using the interpretation of area as probability, we can answer any number of probability questions about flight times. For example, what is the probability of a flight time between 128 and 136 minutes? The width of the interval is $136 - 128 = 8$. With the uniform height of $f(x) = 1/20$, we see that $P(128 \leq x \leq 136) = 8(1/20) = .40$.

Note that $P(120 \leq x \leq 140) = 20(1/20) = 1$; that is, the total area under the graph of $f(x)$ is equal to 1. This property holds for all continuous probability distributions and is the analog of the condition that the sum of the probabilities must equal 1 for a discrete probability function. For a continuous probability density function, we must also require that $f(x) \geq 0$ for all values of x. This requirement is the analog of the requirement that $f(x) \geq 0$ for discrete probability functions.

Two major differences stand out between the treatment of continuous random variables and the treatment of their discrete counterparts.

1. We no longer talk about the probability of the random variable assuming a particular value. Instead, we talk about the probability of the random variable assuming a value within some given interval.

To see that the probability of any single point is 0, refer to Figure 6.2 and compute the probability of a single point, say, $x = 125$. $P(x = 125) = P(125 \leq x \leq 125) = 0(1/20) = 0$.

2. The probability of a continuous random variable assuming a value within some given interval from x_1 to x_2 is defined to be the area under the graph of the probability density function between x_1 and x_2. Because a single point is an interval of zero width, this implies that the probability of a continuous random variable assuming any particular value exactly is zero. It also means that the probability of a continuous random variable assuming a value in any interval is the same whether or not the endpoints are included.

The calculation of the expected value and variance for a continuous random variable is analogous to that for a discrete random variable. However, because the computational procedure involves integral calculus, we leave the derivation of the appropriate formulas to more advanced texts.

For the uniform continuous probability distribution introduced in this section, the formulas for the expected value and variance are

$$E(x) = \frac{a + b}{2}$$

$$Var(x) = \frac{(b - a)^2}{12}$$

In these formulas, a is the smallest value and b is the largest value that the random variable may assume.

Applying these formulas to the uniform distribution for flight times from Chicago to New York, we obtain

$$E(x) = \frac{(120 + 140)}{2} = 130$$

$$Var(x) = \frac{(140 - 120)^2}{12} = 33.33$$

The standard deviation of flight times can be found by taking the square root of the variance. Thus, $\sigma = 5.77$ minutes.

NOTE AND COMMENT

To see more clearly why the height of a probability density function is not a probability, think about a random variable with the following uniform probability distribution.

$$f(x) = \begin{cases} 2 & \text{for } 0 \leq x \leq .5 \\ 0 & \text{elsewhere} \end{cases}$$

The height of the probability density function, $f(x)$, is 2 for values of x between 0 and .5. However, we know probabilities can never be greater than 1. Thus, we see that $f(x)$ cannot be interpreted as the probability of x.

Exercises

Methods

 **SELF**test

1. The random variable x is known to be uniformly distributed between 1.0 and 1.5.
    a. Show the graph of the probability density function.
    b. Compute $P(x = 1.25)$.
    c. Compute $P(1.0 \leq x \leq 1.25)$.
    d. Compute $P(1.20 < x < 1.5)$.

2. The random variable x is known to be uniformly distributed between 10 and 20.
    a. Show the graph of the probability density function.
    b. Compute $P(x < 15)$.
    c. Compute $P(12 \leq x \leq 18)$.
    d. Compute $E(x)$.
    e. Compute $Var(x)$.

Applications

3. Delta Airlines quotes a flight time of 2 hours, 5 minutes for its flights from Cincinnati to Tampa. Suppose we believe that actual flight times are uniformly distributed between 2 hours and 2 hours, 20 minutes.
    a. Show the graph of the probability density function for flight time.
    b. What is the probability that the flight will be no more than 5 minutes late?
    c. What is the probability that the flight will be more than 10 minutes late?
    d. What is the expected flight time?

 **SELF**test

4. Most computer languages include a function that can be used to generate random numbers. In Excel, the RAND function can be used to generate random numbers between 0 and 1. If we let x denote a random number generated using RAND, then x is a continuous random variable with the following probability density function.

$$f(x) = \begin{cases} 1 & \text{for } 0 \leq x \leq 1 \\ 0 & \text{elsewhere} \end{cases}$$

    a. Graph the probability density function.
    b. What is the probability of generating a random number between .25 and .75?
    c. What is the probability of generating a random number with a value less than or equal to .30?
    d. What is the probability of generating a random number with a value greater than .60?
    e. Generate 50 random numbers by entering = RAND() into 50 cells of an Excel worksheet.
    f. Compute the mean and standard deviation for the random numbers in part (e).

5. In October 2012, Apple introduced a much smaller variant of the Apple iPad, known as the iPad Mini. Weighing less than 11 ounces, it was about 50% lighter than the standard iPad. Battery tests for the iPad Mini showed a mean life of 10.25 hours (*The Wall Street Journal*, October 31, 2012). Assume that battery life of the iPad Mini is uniformly distributed between 8.5 and 12 hours.

   a. Give a mathematical expression for the probability density function of battery life.
   b. What is the probability that the battery life for an iPad Mini will be 10 hours or less?
   c. What is the probability that the battery life for an iPad Mini will be at least 11 hours?
   d. What is the probability that the battery life for an iPad Mini will be between 9.5 and 11.5 hours?
   e. In a shipment of 100 iPad Minis, how many should have a battery life of at least 9 hours?

6. A Gallup Daily Tracking Survey found that the mean daily discretionary spending by Americans earning over $90,000 per year was $136 per day (*USA Today*, July 30, 2012). The discretionary spending excluded home purchases, vehicle purchases, and regular monthly bills. Let x = the discretionary spending per day and assume that a uniform probability density function applies with $f(x) = .00625$ for $a \leq x \leq b$.

   a. Find the values of a and b for the probability density function.
   b. What is the probability that consumers in this group have daily discretionary spending between $100 and $200?
   c. What is the probability that consumers in this group have daily discretionary spending of $150 or more?
   d. What is the probability that consumers in this group have daily discretionary spending of $80 or less?

7. Suppose we are interested in bidding on a piece of land and we know one other bidder is interested.[1] The seller announced that the highest bid in excess of $10,000 will be accepted. Assume that the competitor's bid x is a random variable that is uniformly distributed between $10,000 and $15,000.

   a. Suppose you bid $12,000. What is the probability that your bid will be accepted?
   b. Suppose you bid $14,000. What is the probability that your bid will be accepted?
   c. What amount should you bid to maximize the probability that you get the property?
   d. Suppose you know someone who is willing to pay you $16,000 for the property. Would you consider bidding less than the amount in part (c)? Why or why not?

Normal Probability Distribution

Abraham de Moivre, a French mathematician, published The Doctrine of Chances *in 1733. He derived the normal distribution.*

The most important probability distribution for describing a continuous random variable is the **normal probability distribution**. The normal distribution has been used in a wide variety of practical applications in which the random variables are heights and weights of people, test scores, scientific measurements, amounts of rainfall, and other similar values. It is also widely used in statistical inference, which is the major topic of the remainder of this book. In such applications, the normal distribution provides a description of the likely results obtained through sampling.

Normal Curve

The form, or shape, of the normal distribution is illustrated by the bell-shaped normal curve in Figure 6.3. The probability density function that defines the bell-shaped curve of the normal distribution follows.

---

[1]This exercise is based on a problem suggested to us by Professor Roger Myerson of Northwestern University.

FIGURE 6.3   BELL-SHAPED CURVE FOR THE NORMAL DISTRIBUTION

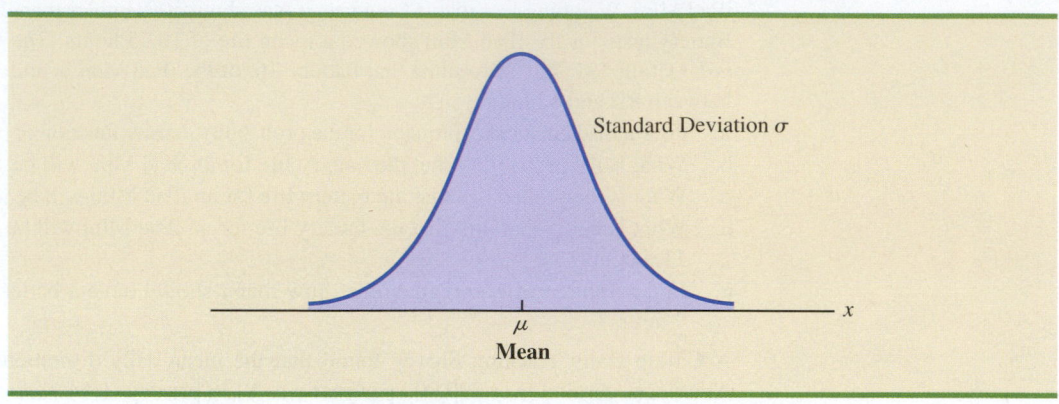

NORMAL PROBABILITY DENSITY FUNCTION

$$f(x) = \frac{1}{\sigma\sqrt{2\pi}} e^{-\frac{1}{2}\left(\frac{x-\mu}{\sigma}\right)^2}$$

(6.2)

where

μ = mean

σ = standard deviation

π = 3.14159

e = 2.71828

We make several observations about the characteristics of the normal distribution.

The normal curve has two parameters, μ and σ. They determine the location and shape of the normal distribution.

1. The entire family of normal distributions is differentiated by two parameters: the mean μ and the standard deviation σ.
2. The highest point on the normal curve is at the mean, which is also the median and mode of the distribution.
3. The mean of the distribution can be any numerical value: negative, zero, or positive. Three normal distributions with the same standard deviation but three different means (-10, 0, and 20) are shown here.

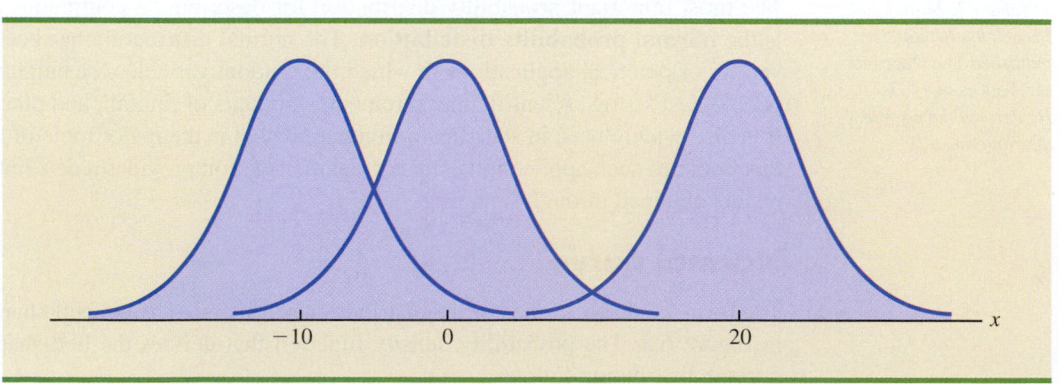

4. The normal distribution is symmetric, with the shape of the normal curve to the left of the mean a mirror image of the shape of the normal curve to the right of the mean.

The tails of the normal curve extend to infinity in both directions and theoretically never touch the horizontal axis. Because it is symmetric, the normal distribution is not skewed; its skewness measure is zero.

5. The standard deviation determines how flat and wide the normal curve is. Larger values of the standard deviation result in wider, flatter curves, showing more variability in the data. Two normal distributions with the same mean but with different standard deviations are shown here.

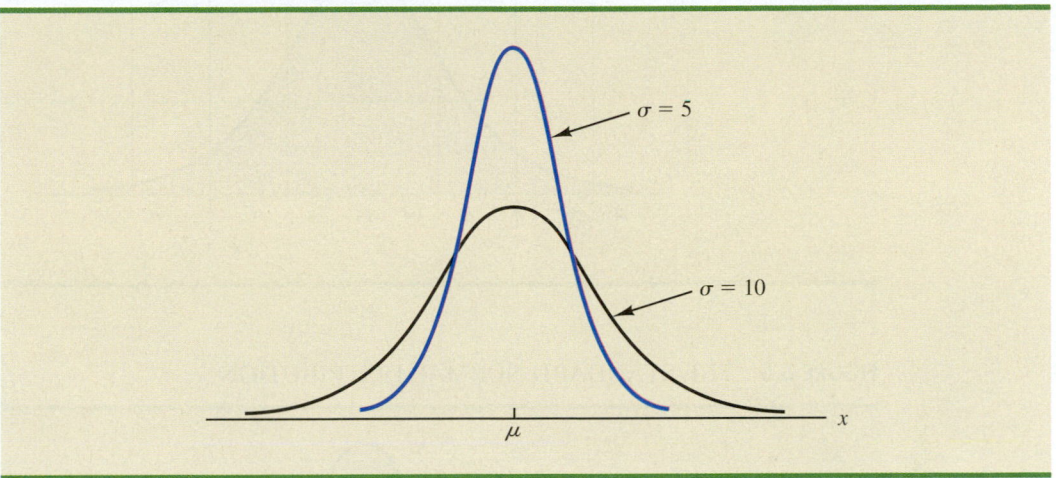

6. Probabilities for the normal random variable are given by areas under the normal curve. The total area under the curve for the normal distribution is 1. Because the distribution is symmetric, the area under the curve to the left of the mean is .50 and the area under the curve to the right of the mean is .50.

7. The percentage of values in some commonly used intervals are
   a. 68.3% of the values of a normal random variable are within plus or minus one standard deviation of its mean;

   These percentages are the basis for the empirical rule introduced in Section 3.3.

   b. 95.4% of the values of a normal random variable are within plus or minus two standard deviations of its mean;
   c. 99.7% of the values of a normal random variable are within plus or minus three standard deviations of its mean.

Figure 6.4 shows properties (a), (b), and (c) graphically.

Standard Normal Probability Distribution

A random variable that has a normal distribution with a mean of zero and a standard deviation of one is said to have a **standard normal probability distribution**. The letter z is commonly used to designate this particular normal random variable. Figure 6.5 is the graph of the standard normal distribution. It has the same general appearance as other normal distributions, but with the special properties of $\mu = 0$ and $\sigma = 1$.

Because $\mu = 0$ and $\sigma = 1$, the formula for the standard normal probability density function is a simpler version of equation (6.2).

STANDARD NORMAL DENSITY FUNCTION

$$f(z) = \frac{1}{\sqrt{2\pi}} e^{-\frac{z^2}{2}}$$

FIGURE 6.4 AREAS UNDER THE CURVE FOR ANY NORMAL DISTRIBUTION

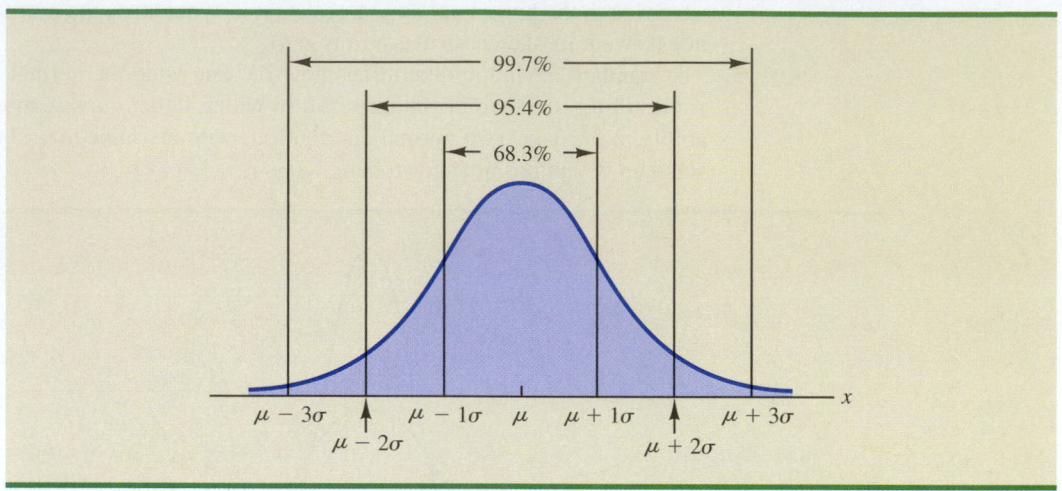

FIGURE 6.5 THE STANDARD NORMAL DISTRIBUTION

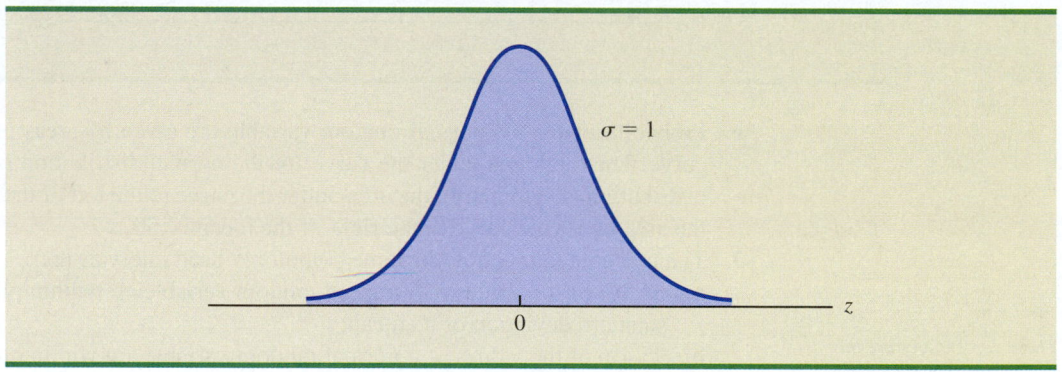

As with other continuous random variables, probability calculations with any normal distribution are made by computing areas under the graph of the probability density function. Thus, to find the probability that a normal random variable is within any specific interval, we must compute the area under the normal curve over that interval.

For the normal probability density function, the height of the normal curve varies and more advanced mathematics is required to compute the areas that represent probability.

For the standard normal distribution, areas under the normal curve have been computed and are available in tables that can be used to compute probabilities. Such a table appears on the two pages inside the front cover of the text. The table on the left-hand page contains areas, or cumulative probabilities, for z values less than or equal to the mean of zero. The table on the right-hand page contains areas, or cumulative probabilities, for z values greater than or equal to the mean of zero.

The three types of probabilities we need to compute include (1) the probability that the standard normal random variable z will be less than or equal to a given value; (2) the probability that z will be between two given values; and (3) the probability that z will be greater than or equal to a given value. To see how the cumulative probability table for the standard normal distribution can be used to compute these three types of probabilities, let us consider some examples.

Because the standard normal random variable is continuous, $P(z \leq 1.00) = P(z < 1.00)$.

We start by showing how to compute the probability that z is less than or equal to 1.00; that is, $P(z \leq 1.00)$. This cumulative probability is the area under the normal curve to the left of $z = 1.00$ in the following graph.

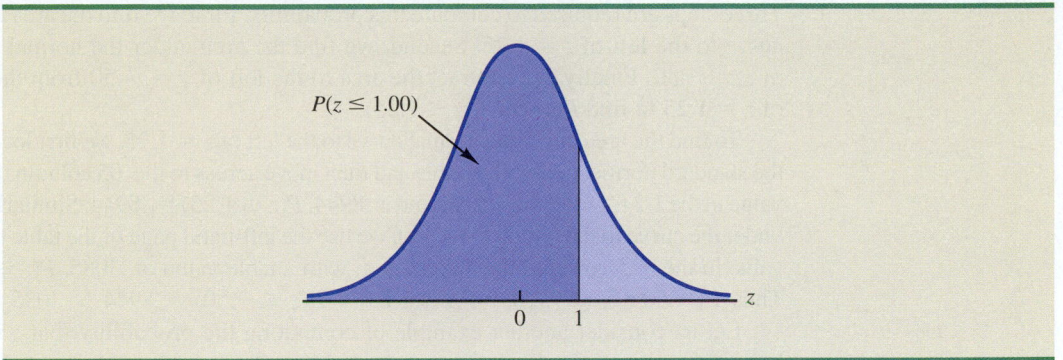

Refer to the right-hand page of the standard normal probability table inside the front cover of the text. The cumulative probability corresponding to $z = 1.00$ is the table value located at the intersection of the row labeled 1.0 and the column labeled .00. First we find 1.0 in the left column of the table and then find .00 in the top row of the table. By looking in the body of the table, we find that the 1.0 row and the .00 column intersect at the value of .8413; thus, $P(z \le 1.00) = .8413$. The following excerpt from the probability table shows these steps.

z	.00	.01	.02
.			
.			
.			
.9	.8159	.8186	.8212
1.0	**.8413**	.8438	.8461
1.1	.8643	.8665	.8686
1.2	.8849	.8869	.8888
.			
.			
.			

$P(z \le 1.00)$

To illustrate the second type of probability calculation, we show how to compute the probability that z is in the interval between $-.50$ and 1.25; that is, $P(-.50 \le z \le 1.25)$. The following graph shows this area, or probability.

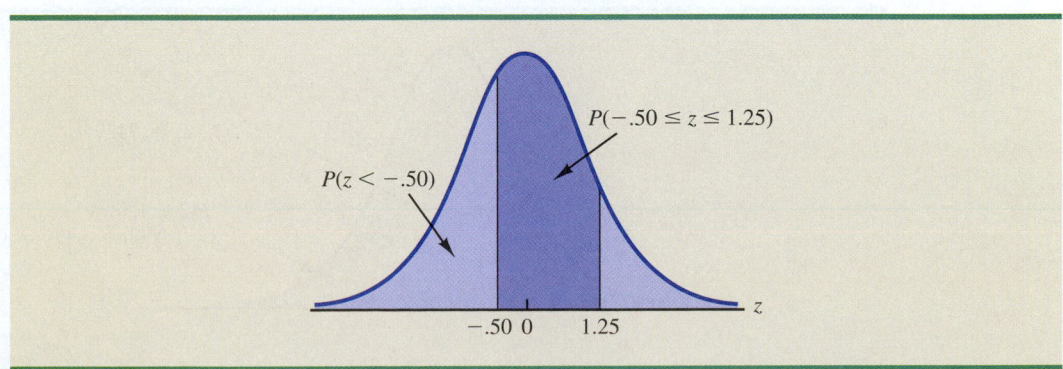

Three steps are required to compute this probability. First, we find the area under the normal curve to the left of $z = 1.25$. Second, we find the area under the normal curve to the left of $z = -.50$. Finally, we subtract the area to the left of $z = -.50$ from the area to the left of $z = 1.25$ to find $P(-.50 \leq z \leq 1.25)$.

To find the area under the normal curve to the left of $z = 1.25$, we first locate the 1.2 row in the standard normal probability table and then move across to the .05 column. Because the table value in the 1.2 row and the .05 column is .8944, $P(z \leq 1.25) = .8944$. Similarly, to find the area under the curve to the left of $z = -.50$, we use the left-hand page of the table to locate the table value in the $-.5$ row and the .00 column; with a table value of .3085, $P(z \leq -.50) = .3085$. Thus, $P(-.50 \leq z \leq 1.25) = P(z \leq 1.25) - P(z \leq -.50) = .8944 - .3085 = .5859$.

Let us consider another example of computing the probability that z is in the interval between two given values. Often it is of interest to compute the probability that a normal random variable assumes a value within a certain number of standard deviations of the mean. Suppose we want to compute the probability that the standard normal random variable is within one standard deviation of the mean; that is, $P(-1.00 \leq z \leq 1.00)$. To compute this probability we must find the area under the curve between -1.00 and 1.00. Earlier we found that $P(z \leq 1.00) = .8413$. Referring again to the table inside the front cover of the book, we find that the area under the curve to the left of $z = -1.00$ is .1587, so $P(z \leq -1.00) = .1587$. Therefore, $P(-1.00 \leq z \leq 1.00) = P(z \leq 1.00) - P(z \leq -1.00) = .8413 - .1587 = .6826$. This probability is shown graphically in the following figure.

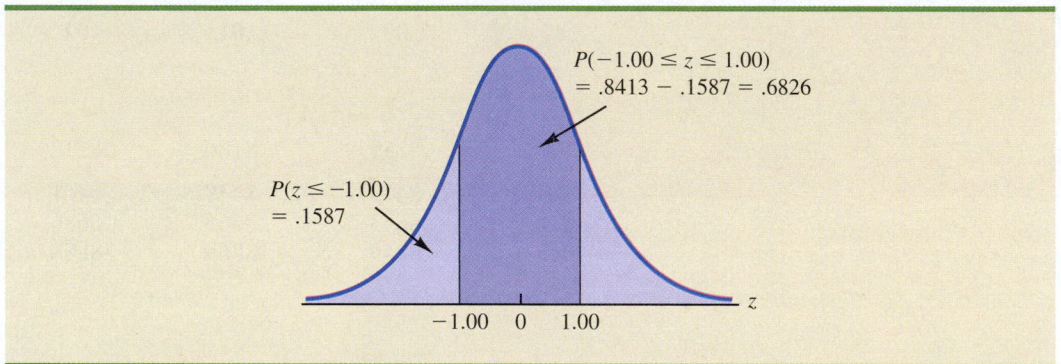

To illustrate how to make the third type of probability computation, suppose we want to compute the probability of obtaining a z value of at least 1.58; that is, $P(z \geq 1.58)$. The value in the $z = 1.5$ row and the .08 column of the cumulative normal table is .9429; thus, $P(z < 1.58) = .9429$. However, because the total area under the normal curve is 1, $P(z \geq 1.58) = 1 - .9429 = .0571$. This probability is shown in the following figure.

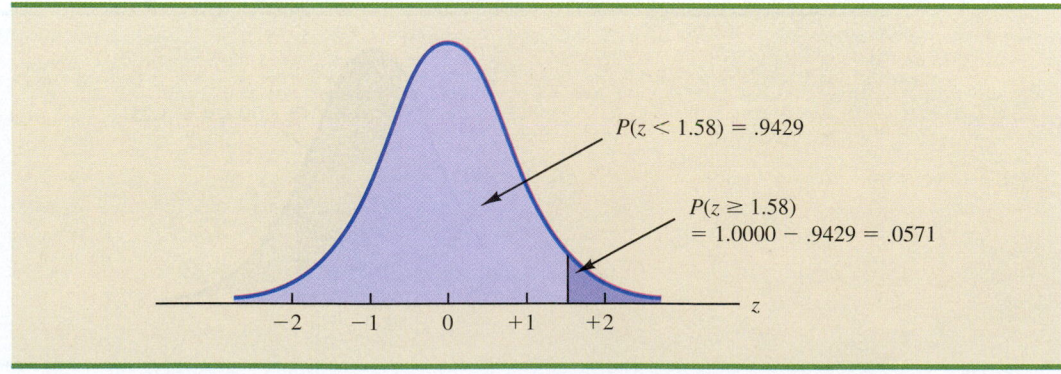

In the preceding illustrations, we showed how to compute probabilities given specified z values. In some situations, we are given a probability and are interested in working backward to find the corresponding z value. Suppose we want to find a z value such that the probability of obtaining a larger z value is .10. The following figure shows this situation graphically.

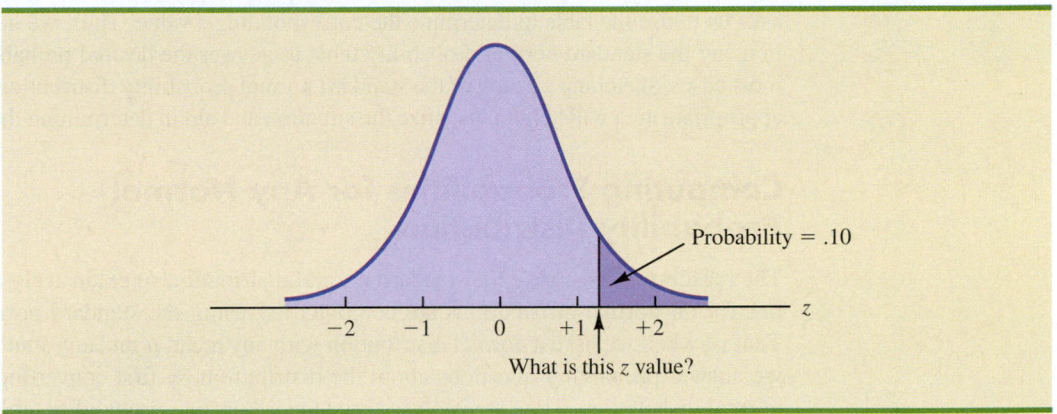

Given a probability, we can use the standard normal table in an inverse fashion to find the corresponding z value.

This problem is the inverse of those in the preceding examples. Previously, we specified the z value of interest and then found the corresponding probability, or area. In this example, we are given the probability, or area, and asked to find the corresponding z value. To do so, we use the standard normal probability table somewhat differently.

Recall that the standard normal probability table gives the area under the curve to the left of a particular z value. We have been given the information that the area in the upper tail of the curve is .10. Hence, the area under the curve to the left of the unknown z value must equal .9000. Scanning the body of the table, we find that .8997 is the cumulative probability value closest to .9000. The section of the table providing this result follows.

z	.06	.07	.08	.09
.				
.				
.				
1.0	.8554	.8577	.8599	.8621
1.1	.8770	.8790	.8810	.8830
1.2	.8962	.8980	.8997	.9015
1.3	.9131	.9147	.9162	.9177
1.4	.9279	.9292	.9306	.9319
.				
.			Cumulative probability value	
.			closest to .9000	

Reading the z value from the leftmost column and the top row of the table, we find that the corresponding z value is 1.28. Thus, an area of approximately .9000 (actually

.8997) will be to the left of $z = 1.28$.[2] In terms of the question originally asked, there is an approximately .10 probability of a z value larger than 1.28.

The examples illustrate that the table of cumulative probabilities for the standard normal probability distribution can be used to find probabilities associated with values of the standard normal random variable z. Two types of questions can be asked. The first type of question specifies a value, or values, for z and asks us to use the table to determine the corresponding areas or probabilities. The second type of question provides an area, or probability, and asks us to use the table to determine the corresponding z value. Thus, we need to be flexible in using the standard normal probability table to answer the desired probability question. In most cases, sketching a graph of the standard normal probability distribution and shading the appropriate area will help to visualize the situation and aid in determining the correct answer.

Computing Probabilities for Any Normal Probability Distribution

The reason for discussing the standard normal distribution so extensively is that probabilities for all normal distributions are computed by using the standard normal distribution. That is, when we have a normal distribution with any mean μ and any standard deviation σ, we answer probability questions about the distribution by first converting to the standard normal distribution. Then we can use the standard normal probability table and the appropriate z values to find the desired probabilities. The formula used to convert any normal random variable x with mean μ and standard deviation σ to the standard normal random variable z follows.

The formula for the standard normal random variable is similar to the formula we introduced in Chapter 3 for computing z-scores for a data set.

> ### CONVERTING TO THE STANDARD NORMAL RANDOM VARIABLE
>
> $$z = \frac{x - \mu}{\sigma} \tag{6.3}$$

A value of x equal to its mean μ results in $z = (\mu - \mu)/\sigma = 0$. Thus, we see that a value of x equal to its mean μ corresponds to $z = 0$. Now suppose that x is one standard deviation above its mean; that is, $x = \mu + \sigma$. Applying equation (6.3), we see that the corresponding z value is $z = [(\mu + \sigma) - \mu]/\sigma = \sigma/\sigma = 1$. Thus, an x value that is one standard deviation above its mean corresponds to $z = 1$. In other words, *we can interpret z as the number of standard deviations that the normal random variable x is from its mean μ.*

To see how this conversion enables us to compute probabilities for any normal distribution, suppose we have a normal distribution with $\mu = 10$ and $\sigma = 2$. What is the probability that the random variable x is between 10 and 14? Using equation (6.3), we see that at $x = 10$, $z = (x - \mu)/\sigma = (10 - 10)/2 = 0$ and that at $x = 14$, $z = (14 - 10)/2 = 4/2 = 2$. Thus, the answer to our question about the probability of x being between 10 and 14 is given by the equivalent probability that z is between 0 and 2 for the standard normal distribution. In other words, the probability that we are seeking is the probability that the random variable x is between its mean and two standard deviations above the mean. Using $z = 2.00$ and the standard normal probability table inside the front cover of the text, we see

---

[2]We could use interpolation in the body of the table to get a better approximation of the z value that corresponds to an area of .9000. Doing so to provide one more decimal place of accuracy would yield a z value of 1.282. However, in most practical situations, sufficient accuracy is obtained simply by using the table value closest to the desired probability.

that $P(z \leq 2) = .9772$. Because $P(z \leq 0) = .5000$, we can compute $P(.00 \leq z \leq 2.00) = P(z \leq 2) - P(z \leq 0) = .9772 - .5000 = .4772$. Hence the probability that x is between 10 and 14 is .4772.

Grear Tire Company Problem

We turn now to an application of the normal probability distribution. Suppose the Grear Tire Company developed a new steel-belted radial tire to be sold through a national chain of discount stores. Because the tire is a new product, Grear's managers believe that the mileage guarantee offered with the tire will be an important factor in the acceptance of the product. Before finalizing the tire mileage guarantee policy, Grear's managers want probability information about the number of miles the tires will last. Let x denote the number of miles the tire lasts.

From actual road tests with the tires, Grear's engineering group estimated that the mean tire mileage is $\mu = 36{,}500$ miles and that the standard deviation is $\sigma = 5000$. In addition, the data collected indicate that a normal distribution is a reasonable assumption. What percentage of the tires can be expected to last more than 40,000 miles? In other words, what is the probability that the tire mileage, x, will exceed 40,000? This question can be answered by finding the area of the darkly shaded region in Figure 6.6.

At $x = 40{,}000$, we have

$$z = \frac{x - \mu}{\sigma} = \frac{40{,}000 - 36{,}500}{5000} = \frac{3500}{5000} = .70$$

Refer now to the bottom of Figure 6.6. We see that a value of $x = 40{,}000$ on the Grear Tire normal distribution corresponds to a value of $z = .70$ on the standard normal distribution. Using the standard normal probability table, we see that the area under the standard normal curve to the left of $z = .70$ is .7580. Thus, $1.000 - .7580 = .2420$ is the probability that z will exceed .70 and hence x will exceed 40,000. We can conclude that about 24.2% of the tires will exceed 40,000 in mileage.

Let us now assume that Grear is considering a guarantee that will provide a discount on replacement tires if the original tires do not provide the guaranteed mileage. What should

FIGURE 6.6   GREAR TIRE COMPANY MILEAGE DISTRIBUTION

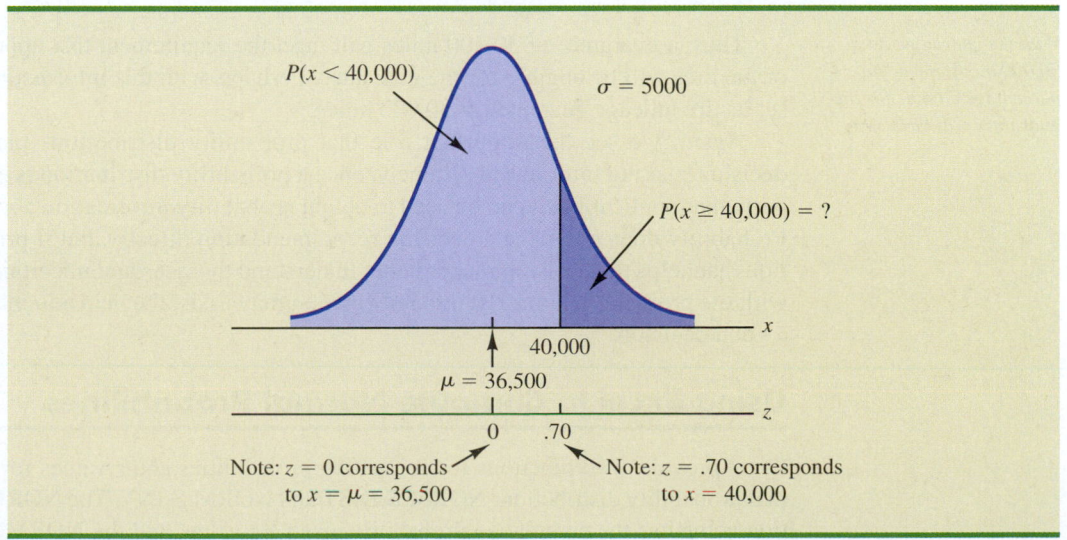

FIGURE 6.7   GREAR'S DISCOUNT GUARANTEE

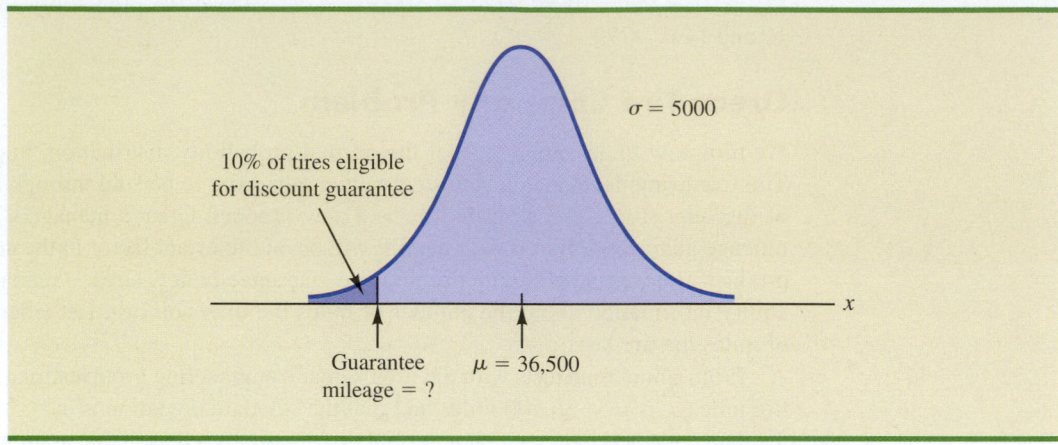

the guaranteed mileage be if Grear wants no more than 10% of the tires to be eligible for the discount guarantee? This question is interpreted graphically in Figure 6.7.

According to Figure 6.7, the area under the curve to the left of the unknown guaranteed mileage must be .10. So, we must first find the z value that cuts off an area of .10 in the left tail of a standard normal distribution. Using the standard normal probability table, we see that $z = -1.28$ cuts off an area of .10 in the lower tail. Hence, $z = -1.28$ is the value of the standard normal random variable corresponding to the desired mileage guarantee on the Grear Tire normal distribution. To find the value of x corresponding to $z = -1.28$, we have

The guaranteed mileage we need to find is 1.28 standard deviations below the mean. Thus, $x = \mu - 1.28\sigma$.

$$z = \frac{x - \mu}{\sigma} = -1.28$$

$$x - \mu = -1.28\sigma$$

$$x = \mu - 1.28\sigma$$

With $\mu = 36{,}500$ and $\sigma = 5000$,

$$x = 36{,}500 - 1.28(5000) = 30{,}100$$

With the guarantee set at 30,000 miles, the actual percentage eligible for the guarantee will be 9.68%.

Thus, a guarantee of 30,100 miles will meet the requirement that approximately 10% of the tires will be eligible for the guarantee. Perhaps, with this information, the firm will set its tire mileage guarantee at 30,000 miles.

Again, we see the important role that probability distributions play in providing decision-making information. Namely, once a probability distribution is established for a particular application, it can be used to obtain probability information about the problem. Probability does not make a decision recommendation directly, but it provides information that helps the decision maker better understand the risks and uncertainties associated with the problem. Ultimately, this information may assist the decision maker in reaching a good decision.

Using Excel to Compute Normal Probabilities

Excel provides two functions for computing probabilities and z values for a standard normal probability distribution: NORM.S.DIST and NORM.S.INV. The NORM.S.DIST function computes the cumulative probability given a z value, and the NORM.S.INV function computes the z value given a cumulative probability. Two similar functions, NORM.DIST and NORM.INV, are available for computing the cumulative probability and the x value for any normal distribution. We begin by showing how to use the NORM.S.DIST and NORM.S.INV functions.

The letter S that appears in the name of the NORM.S.DIST and NORM.S.INV functions reminds us that these functions relate to the standard normal probability distribution.

The NORM.S.DIST function provides the area under the standard normal curve to the left of a given z value; thus, it provides the same cumulative probability we would obtain if we used the standard normal probability table inside the front cover of the text. Using the NORM.S.DIST function is just like having Excel look up cumulative normal probabilities for you. The NORM.S.INV function is the inverse of the NORM.S.DIST function; it takes a cumulative probability as input and provides the z value corresponding to that cumulative probability.

Let's see how both of these functions work by computing the probabilities and z values obtained earlier in this section using the standard normal probability table. Refer to Figure 6.8 as we describe the tasks involved. The formula worksheet is in the background; the value worksheet is in the foreground.

Enter/Access Data: Open a blank worksheet. No data are entered in the worksheet. We will simply enter the appropriate z values and probabilities directly into the formulas as needed.

Enter Functions and Formulas: The NORM.S.DIST function has two inputs: the z value and a value of TRUE or FALSE. For the second input we enter TRUE if a cumulative probability is desired, and we enter FALSE if the height of the standard normal curve is desired. Because we will always be using NORM.S.DIST to compute cumulative probabilities, we always choose TRUE for the second input. To illustrate the use of the NORM.S.DIST function, we compute the four probabilities shown in cells D3:D6 of Figure 6.8.

The probabilities in cells D4, 0.5858, and D5, 0.6827, differ from what we computed earlier due to rounding.

To compute the cumulative probability to the left of a given z value (area in lower tail), we simply evaluate NORM.S.DIST at the z value. For instance, to compute $P(z \leq 1)$ we entered the formula =NORM.S.DIST(1,TRUE) into cell D3. The result, .8413, is the same as obtained using the standard normal probability table.

To compute the probability of z being in an interval we compute the value of NORM.S.DIST at the upper endpoint of the interval and subtract the value of NORM.S.DIST

FIGURE 6.8 EXCEL WORKSHEET FOR COMPUTING PROBABILITIES AND z VALUES FOR THE STANDARD NORMAL DISTRIBUTION

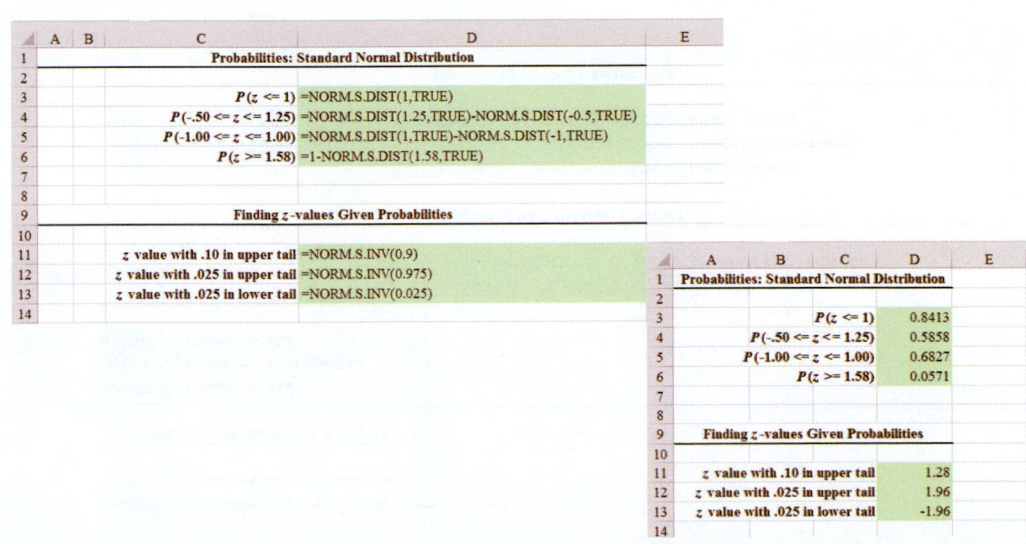

at the lower endpoint of the interval. For instance, to find $P(-.50 \leq z \leq 1.25)$, we entered the formula =NORM.S.DIST(1.25,TRUE)-NORM.S.DIST(-.50,TRUE) into cell D4. The interval probability in cell D5 is computed in a similar fashion.

To compute the probability to the right of a given z value (upper tail area), we must subtract the cumulative probability represented by the area under the curve below the z value (lower tail area) from 1. For example, to compute $P(z \geq 1.58)$ we entered the formula =1-NORM.S.DIST(1.58,TRUE) into cell D6.

To compute the z value for a given cumulative probability (lower tail area), we use the NORM.S.INV function. To find the z value corresponding to an upper tail probability of .10, we note that the corresponding lower tail area is .90 and enter the formula =NORM.S.INV(0.9) into cell D11. Actually, NORM.S.INV(0.9) gives us the z value providing a cumulative probability (lower tail area) of .9. But it is also the z value associated with an upper tail area of .10.

Two other z values are computed in Figure 6.8. These z values will be used extensively in succeeding chapters. To compute the z value corresponding to an upper tail probability of .025, we entered the formula =NORM.S.INV(0.975) into cell D12. To compute the z value corresponding to a lower tail probability of .025, we entered the formula =NORM.S.INV(0.025) into cell D13. We see that $z = 1.96$ corresponds to an upper tail probability of .025, and $z = -1.96$ corresponds to a lower tail probability of .025.

Let us now turn to the Excel functions for computing cumulative probabilities and x values for any normal distribution. The NORM.DIST function provides the area under the normal curve to the left of a given value of the random variable x; thus it provides cumulative probabilities. The NORM.INV function is the inverse of the NORM.DIST function; it takes a cumulative probability as input and provides the value of x corresponding to that cumulative probability. The NORM.DIST and NORM.INV functions do the same thing for any normal distribution that the NORM.S.DIST and NORM.S.INV functions do for the standard normal distribution.

Let's see how both of these functions work by computing probabilities and x values for the Grear Tire Company example introduced earlier in this section. Recall that the lifetime of a Grear tire has a mean of 36,500 miles and a standard deviation of 5000 miles. Refer to Figure 6.9 as we describe the tasks involved. The formula worksheet is in the background; the value worksheet is in the foreground.

FIGURE 6.9 EXCEL WORKSHEET FOR COMPUTING PROBABILITIES AND x VALUES FOR THE NORMAL DISTRIBUTION

	A	B	C	D	E
1			**Probabilities: Normal Distribution**		
2					
3			***P*(*x* <= 20000)**	=NORM.DIST(20000,36500,5000,TRUE)	
4			***P*(20000 <= *x* <= 40000)**	=NORMDIST(40000,36500,5000,TRUE)-NORM.DIST(20000,36500,5000,TRUE)	
5			***P*(*x* >= 40000)**	=1-NORM.DIST(40000,36500,5000,TRUE)	
6					
7			**Finding *x* values Given Probabilities**		
8					
9			***x* value with .10 in lower tail**	=NORM.INV(0.1,36500,5000)	
10			***x* value with .025 in upper tail**	=NORM.INV(0.975,36500,5000)	
11					

	A	B	C	D	E
1	**Probabilities: Normal Distribution**				
2					
3			***P*(*x* <= 20000)**	0.0005	
4			***P*(20000 <= *x* <= 40000)**	0.7576	
5			***P*(*x* >= 40000)**	0.2420	
6					
7	**Finding *x* values Given Probabilities**				
8					
9			***x* value with .10 in lower tail**	30092.24	
10			***x* value with .025 in upper tail**	46299.82	
11					

Enter/Access Data: Open a blank worksheet. No data are entered in the worksheet. We simply enter the appropriate x values and probabilities directly into the formulas as needed.

Enter Functions and Formulas: The NORM.DIST function has four inputs: (1) the x value we want to compute the cumulative probability for, (2) the mean, (3) the standard deviation, and (4) a value of TRUE or FALSE. For the fourth input, we enter TRUE if a cumulative probability is desired, and we enter FALSE if the height of the curve is desired. Because we will always be using NORM.DIST to compute cumulative probabilities, we will always choose TRUE for the fourth input.

To compute the cumulative probability to the left of a given x value (lower tail area), we simply evaluate NORM.DIST at the x value. For instance, to compute the probability that a Grear tire will last 20,000 miles or less, we entered the formula =NORM.DIST(20000,36500,5000,TRUE) into cell D3. The value worksheet shows that this cumulative probability is .0005. So, we can conclude that almost all Grear tires will last at least 20,000 miles.

To compute the probability of x being in an interval we compute the value of NORM.DIST at the upper endpoint of the interval and subtract the value of NORM.DIST at the lower endpoint of the interval. The formula in cell D4 provides the probability that a tire's lifetime is between 20,000 and 40,000 miles, $P(20{,}000 \leq x \leq 40{,}000)$. In the value worksheet, we see that this probability is .7576.

To compute the probability to the right of a given x value (upper tail area), we must subtract the cumulative probability represented by the area under the curve below the x value (lower tail area) from 1. The formula in cell D5 computes the probability that a Grear tire will last for at least 40,000 miles. We see that this probability is .2420.

To compute the x value for a given cumulative probability, we use the NORM.INV function. The NORM.INV function has only three inputs. The first input is the cumulative probability; the second and third inputs are the mean and standard deviation. For instance, to compute the tire mileage corresponding to a lower tail area of .1 for Grear Tire, we enter the formula =NORM.INV(0.1,36500,5000) into cell D9. From the value worksheet, we see that 10% of the Grear tires will last for 30,092.24 miles or less.

To compute the minimum tire mileage for the top 2.5% of Grear tires, we want to find the value of x corresponding to an area of .025 in the upper tail. This calculation is the same as finding the x value that provides a cumulative probability of .975. Thus we entered the formula =NORM.INV(0.975,36500,5000) into cell D10 to compute this tire mileage. From the value worksheet, we see that 2.5% of the Grear tires will last at least 46,299.82 miles.

Exercises

Methods

8. Using Figure 6.4 as a guide, sketch a normal curve for a random variable x that has a mean of $\mu = 100$ and a standard deviation of $\sigma = 10$. Label the horizontal axis with values of 70, 80, 90, 100, 110, 120, and 130.

9. A random variable is normally distributed with a mean of $\mu = 50$ and a standard deviation of $\sigma = 5$.

    a. Sketch a normal curve for the probability density function. Label the horizontal axis with values of 35, 40, 45, 50, 55, 60, and 65. Figure 6.4 shows that the normal curve almost touches the horizontal axis at three standard deviations below and at three standard deviations above the mean (in this case at 35 and 65).

    b. What is the probability that the random variable will assume a value between 45 and 55?

    c. What is the probability that the random variable will assume a value between 40 and 60?

10. Draw a graph for the standard normal distribution. Label the horizontal axis at values of $-3, -2, -1, 0, 1, 2$, and 3. Then compute the following probabilities.
    a. $P(z \le 1.5)$
    b. $P(z \le 1)$
    c. $P(1 \le z \le 1.5)$
    d. $P(0 < z < 2.5)$

11. Given that z is a standard normal random variable, compute the following probabilities.
    a. $P(z \le -1.0)$
    b. $P(z \ge -1)$
    c. $P(z \ge -1.5)$
    d. $P(-2.5 \le z)$
    e. $P(-3 < z \le 0)$

12. Given that z is a standard normal random variable, compute the following probabilities.
    a. $P(0 \le z \le .83)$
    b. $P(-1.57 \le z \le 0)$
    c. $P(z > .44)$
    d. $P(z \ge -.23)$
    e. $P(z < 1.20)$
    f. $P(z \le -.71)$

 13. Given that z is a standard normal random variable, compute the following probabilities.
    a. $P(-1.98 \le z \le .49)$
    b. $P(.52 \le z \le 1.22)$
    c. $P(-1.75 \le z \le -1.04)$

14. Given that z is a standard normal random variable, find z for each situation.
    a. The area to the left of z is .9750.
    b. The area between 0 and z is .4750.
    c. The area to the left of z is .7291.
    d. The area to the right of z is .1314.
    e. The area to the left of z is .6700.
    f. The area to the right of z is .3300.

 15. Given that z is a standard normal random variable, find z for each situation.
    a. The area to the left of z is .2119.
    b. The area between $-z$ and z is .9030.
    c. The area between $-z$ and z is .2052.
    d. The area to the left of z is .9948.
    e. The area to the right of z is .6915.

16. Given that z is a standard normal random variable, find z for each situation.
    a. The area to the right of z is .01.
    b. The area to the right of z is .025.
    c. The area to the right of z is .05.
    d. The area to the right of z is .10.

Applications

17. The mean cost of domestic airfares in the United States rose to an all-time high of $385 per ticket (Bureau of Transportation Statistics website, November 2, 2012). Airfares were based on the total ticket value, which consisted of the price charged by the airlines plus any additional taxes and fees. Assume domestic airfares are normally distributed with a standard deviation of $110.
    a. What is the probability that a domestic airfare is $550 or more?
    b. What is the probability that a domestic airfare is $250 or less?

c. What if the probability that a domestic airfare is between $300 and $500?

d. What is the cost for the highest 3% of domestic airfares?

 **SELF**test

18. The average return for large-cap domestic stock funds over the three years 2009–2011 was 14.4% (*AAII Journal*, February 2012). Assume the three-year returns were normally distributed across funds with a standard deviation of 4.4%.

a. What is the probability an individual large-cap domestic stock fund had a three-year return of at least 20%?

b. What is the probability an individual large-cap domestic stock fund had a three-year return of 10% or less?

c. How big does the return have to be to put a domestic stock fund in the top 10% for the three-year period?

19. Automobile repair costs continue to rise with the average cost now at $367 per repair (*U.S. News & World Report* website, January 5, 2015). Assume that the cost for an automobile repair is normally distributed with a standard deviation of $88. Answer the following questions about the cost of automobile repairs.

a. What is the probability that the cost will be more than $450?

b. What is the probability that the cost will be less than $250?

c. What is the probability that the cost will be between $250 and $450?

d. If the cost for your car repair is in the lower 5% of automobile repair charges, what is your cost?

20. The average price for a gallon of gasoline in the United States is $3.73 and in Russia it is $3.40 (*Bloomberg Businessweek*, March 5–March 11, 2012). Assume these averages are the population means in the two countries and that the probability distributions are normally distributed with a standard deviation of $.25 in the United States and a standard deviation of $.20 in Russia.

a. What is the probability that a randomly selected gas station in the United States charges less than $3.50 per gallon?

b. What percentage of the gas stations in Russia charge less than $3.50 per gallon?

c. What is the probability that a randomly selected gas station in Russia charged more than the mean price in the United States?

21. A person must score in the upper 2% of the population on an IQ test to qualify for membership in Mensa, the international high-IQ society. There are 110,000 Mensa members in 100 countries throughout the world (Mensa International website, January 8, 2013). If IQ scores are normally distributed with a mean of 100 and a standard deviation of 15, what score must a person have to qualify for Mensa?

22. Television viewing reached a new high when the Nielsen Company reported a mean daily viewing time of 8.35 hours per household (*USA Today*, November 11, 2009). Use a normal probability distribution with a standard deviation of 2.5 hours to answer the following questions about daily television viewing per household.

a. What is the probability that a household views television between 5 and 10 hours a day?

b. How many hours of television viewing must a household have in order to be in the top 3% of all television viewing households?

c. What is the probability that a household views television more than 3 hours a day?

23. The time needed to complete a final examination in a particular college course is normally distributed with a mean of 80 minutes and a standard deviation of 10 minutes. Answer the following questions.

a. What is the probability of completing the exam in one hour or less?

b. What is the probability that a student will complete the exam in more than 60 minutes but less than 75 minutes?

c. Assume that the class has 60 students and that the examination period is 90 minutes in length. How many students do you expect will be unable to complete the exam in the allotted time?

24.   The American Automobile Association (AAA) reported that families planning to travel over the Labor Day weekend would spend an average of $749 (*The Associated Press,* August 12, 2012). Assume that the amount spent is normally distributed with a standard deviation of $225.

   a.   What the probability of family expenses for the weekend being less that $400?

   b.   What is the probability of family expenses for the weekend being $800 or more?

   c.   What is the probability that family expenses for the weekend will be between $500 and $1000?

   d.   What would the Labor Day weekend expenses have to be for the 5% of the families with the most expensive travel plans?

25.   New York City is the most expensive city in the United States for lodging. The mean hotel room rate is $204 per night (*USA Today,* April 30, 2012). Assume that room rates are normally distributed with a standard deviation of $55.

   a.   What is the probability that a hotel room costs $225 or more per night?

   b.   What is the probability that a hotel room costs less than $140 per night?

   c.   What is the probability that a hotel room costs between $200 and $300 per night?

   d.   What is the cost of the most expensive 20% of hotel rooms in New York City?

6.3 Exponential Probability Distribution

The **exponential probability distribution** may be used for random variables such as the time between arrivals at a car wash, the time required to load a truck, the distance between major defects in a highway, and so on. The exponential probability density function follows.

EXPONENTIAL PROBABILITY DENSITY FUNCTION

$$f(x) = \frac{1}{\mu} e^{-x/\mu} \qquad \text{for } x \geq 0 \qquad \text{(6.4)}$$

where

μ = expected value or mean

e = 2.71828

As an example of the exponential distribution, suppose that x represents the loading time for a truck at the Schips loading dock and follows such a distribution. If the mean, or average, loading time is 15 minutes ($\mu = 15$), the appropriate probability density function for x is

$$f(x) = \frac{1}{15} e^{-x/15}$$

Figure 6.10 is the graph of this probability density function.

FIGURE 6.10   EXPONENTIAL DISTRIBUTION FOR THE SCHIPS LOADING DOCK EXAMPLE

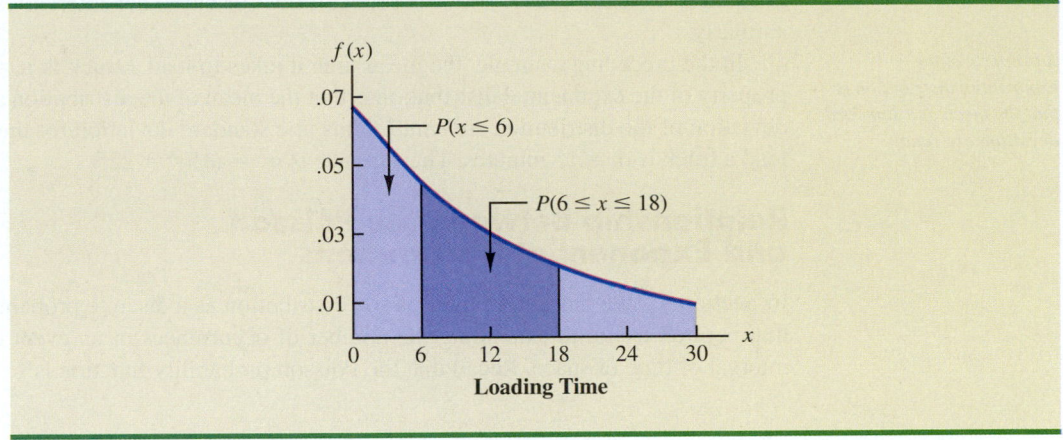

Computing Probabilities for the Exponential Distribution

In waiting line applications, the exponential distribution is often used for service time.

As with any continuous probability distribution, the area under the curve corresponding to an interval provides the probability that the random variable assumes a value in that interval. In the Schips loading dock example, the probability that loading a truck will take 6 minutes or less $P(x \leq 6)$ is defined to be the area under the curve in Figure 6.10 from $x = 0$ to $x = 6$. Similarly, the probability that the loading time will be 18 minutes or less $P(x \leq 18)$ is the area under the curve from $x = 0$ to $x = 18$. Note also that the probability that the loading time will be between 6 minutes and 18 minutes $P(6 \leq x \leq 18)$ is given by the area under the curve from $x = 6$ to $x = 18$.

To compute exponential probabilities such as those just described, we use the following formula. It provides the cumulative probability of obtaining a value for the exponential random variable of less than or equal to some specific value denoted by x_0.

EXPONENTIAL DISTRIBUTION: CUMULATIVE PROBABILITIES

$$P(x \leq x_0) = 1 - e^{-x_0/\mu} \qquad\qquad \textbf{(6.5)}$$

For the Schips loading dock example, $x =$ loading time in minutes and $\mu = 15$ minutes. Using equation (6.5),

$$P(x \leq x_0) = 1 - e^{-x_0/15}$$

Hence, the probability that loading a truck will take 6 minutes or less is

$$P(x \leq 6) = 1 - e^{-6/15} = .3297$$

Using equation (6.5), we calculate the probability of loading a truck in 18 minutes or less.

$$P(x \leq 18) = 1 - e^{-18/15} = .6988$$

Thus, the probability that loading a truck will take between 6 minutes and 18 minutes is equal to .6988 − .3297 = .3691. Probabilities for any other interval can be computed similarly.

A property of the exponential distribution is that the mean and standard deviation are equal.

In the preceding example, the mean time it takes to load a truck is $\mu = 15$ minutes. A property of the exponential distribution is that the mean of the distribution and the standard deviation of the distribution are *equal*. Thus, the standard deviation for the time it takes to load a truck is $\sigma = 15$ minutes. The variance is $\sigma^2 = (15)^2 = 225$.

Relationship Between the Poisson and Exponential Distributions

In Section 5.5 we introduced the Poisson distribution as a discrete probability distribution that is often useful in examining the number of occurrences of an event over a specified interval of time or space. Recall that the Poisson probability function is

$$f(x) = \frac{\mu^x e^{-\mu}}{x!}$$

where

$$\mu = \text{expected value or mean number of}$$
$$\text{occurrences over a specified interval}$$

If arrivals follow a Poisson distribution, the time between arrivals must follow an exponential distribution.

The continuous exponential probability distribution is related to the discrete Poisson distribution. If the Poisson distribution provides an appropriate description of the number of occurrences per interval, the exponential distribution provides a description of the length of the interval between occurrences.

To illustrate this relationship, suppose the number of cars that arrive at a car wash during one hour is described by a Poisson probability distribution with a mean of 10 cars per hour. The Poisson probability function that gives the probability of x arrivals per hour is

$$f(x) = \frac{10^x e^{-10}}{x!}$$

Because the average number of arrivals is 10 cars per hour, the average time between cars arriving is

$$\frac{1 \text{ hour}}{10 \text{ cars}} = .1 \text{ hour/car}$$

Thus, the corresponding exponential distribution that describes the time between the arrivals has a mean of $\mu = .1$ hour per car; as a result, the appropriate exponential probability density function is

$$f(x) = \frac{1}{.1} e^{-x/.1} = 10e^{-10x}$$

Using Excel to Compute Exponential Probabilities

Excel's EXPON.DIST function can be used to compute exponential probabilities. We will illustrate by computing probabilities associated with the time it takes to load a truck at the

FIGURE 6.11   EXCEL WORKSHEET FOR COMPUTING PROBABILITIES FOR THE EXPONENTIAL PROBABILITY DISTRIBUTION

	A	B	C	D	E
1			Probabilities: Exponential Distribution		
2					
3			$P(x <= 18)$	=EXPON.DIST(18,1/15,TRUE)	
4			$P(6 <= x <= 18)$	=EXPON.DIST(18,1/15,TRUE)-EXPON.DIST(6,1/15,TRUE)	
5			$P(x >= 8)$	=1-EXPON.DIST(8,1/15,TRUE)	
6					

	A	B	C	D	E
1	Probabilities: Exponential Distribution				
2					
3			$P(x <= 18)$	0.6988	
4			$P(6 <= x <= 18)$	0.3691	
5			$P(x >= 8)$	0.5866	
6					

Schips loading dock. This example was introduced at the beginning of the section. Refer to Figure 6.11 as we describe the tasks involved. The formula worksheet is in the background; the value worksheet is in the foreground.

Enter/Access Data: Open a blank worksheet. No data are entered in the worksheet. We simply enter the appropriate values for the exponential random variable into the formulas as needed. The random variable is $x =$ loading time.

Enter Functions and Formulas: The EXPON.DIST function has three inputs: The first is the value of x, the second is $1/\mu$, and the third is TRUE or FALSE. We choose TRUE for the third input if a cumulative probability is desired and FALSE if the height of the probability density function is desired. We will always use TRUE because we will be computing cumulative probabilities.

The first probability we compute is the probability that the loading time is 18 minutes or less. For the Schips problem, $1/\mu = 1/15$, so we enter the formula =EXPON.DIST (18,1/15,TRUE) into cell D3 to compute the desired cumulative probability. From the value worksheet, we see that the probability of loading a truck in 18 minutes or less is .6988.

The second probability we compute is the probability that the loading time is between 6 and 18 minutes. To find this probability we first compute the cumulative probability for the upper endpoint of the time interval and subtract the cumulative probability for the lower endpoint of the interval. The formula we have entered into cell D4 calculates this probability. The value worksheet shows that this probability is .3691.

The last probability we calculate is the probability that the loading time is at least 8 minutes. Because the EXPON.DIST function computes only cumulative (lower tail) probabilities, we compute this probability by entering the formula =1-EXPON .DIST(8,1/15,TRUE) into cell D5. The value worksheet shows that the probability of a loading time of 8 minutes or more is .5866.

NOTE AND COMMENT

As we can see in Figure 6.10, the exponential distribution is skewed to the right. Indeed, the skewness measure for the exponential distributions is 2. The exponential distribution gives us a good idea what a skewed distribution looks like.

Exercises

Methods

26. Consider the following exponential probability density function.

$$f(x) = \frac{1}{8} e^{-x/8} \qquad \text{for } x \geq 0$$

   a. Find $P(x \leq 6)$.
   b. Find $P(x \leq 4)$.
   c. Find $P(x \geq 6)$.
   d. Find $P(4 \leq x \leq 6)$.

 27. Consider the following exponential probability density function.

$$f(x) = \frac{1}{3} e^{-x/3} \qquad \text{for } x \geq 0$$

   a. Write the formula for $P(x \leq x_0)$.
   b. Find $P(x \leq 2)$.
   c. Find $P(x \geq 3)$.
   d. Find $P(x \leq 5)$.
   e. Find $P(2 \leq x \leq 5)$.

Applications

28. Battery life between charges for the Motorola Droid Razr Maxx is 20 hours when the primary use is talk time (*The Wall Street Journal*, March 7, 2012). The battery life drops to 7 hours when the phone is primarily used for Internet applications over cellular. Assume that the battery life in both cases follows an exponential distribution.
   a. Show the probability density function for battery life for the Droid Razr Maxx phone when its primary use is talk time.
   b. What is the probability that the battery charge for a randomly selected Droid Razr Maxx phone will last no more than 15 hours when its primary use is talk time?
   c. What is the probability that the battery charge for a randomly selected Droid Razr Maxx phone will last more than 20 hours when its primary use is talk time?
   d. What is the probability that the battery charge for a randomly selected Droid Razr Maxx phone will last no more than 5 hours when its primary use is Internet applications?

 29. The time between arrivals of vehicles at a particular intersection follows an exponential probability distribution with a mean of 12 seconds.
   a. Sketch this exponential probability distribution.
   b. What is the probability that the arrival time between vehicles is 12 seconds or less?
   c. What is the probability that the arrival time between vehicles is 6 seconds or less?
   d. What is the probability of 30 or more seconds between vehicle arrivals?

30. Comcast Corporation is the largest cable television company, the second largest Internet service provider, and the fourth largest telephone service provider in the United States. Generally known for quality and reliable service, the company periodically experiences unexpected service interruptions. On January 14, 2009, such an interruption occurred for the Comcast customers living in southwest Florida. When customers called the Comcast office, a recorded message told them that the company was aware of the service outage and that it was anticipated that service would be restored in two hours. Assume that two hours is the mean time to do the repair and that the repair time has an exponential probability distribution.

a. What is the probability that the cable service will be repaired in one hour or less?
b. What is the probability that the repair will take between one hour and two hours?
c. For a customer who calls the Comcast office at 1:00 P.M., what is the probability that the cable service will not be repaired by 5:00 P.M.?

31. Wendy's restaurant has been recognized for having the fastest average service time among fast food restaurants. In a benchmark study, Wendy's average service time of 2.2 minutes was less than those of Burger King, Chick-fil-A, Krystal, McDonald's, Taco Bell, and Taco John's (*QSR Magazine* website, December 2014). Assume that the service time for Wendy's has an exponential distribution.
a. What is the probability that a service time is less than or equal to one minute?
b. What is the probability that a service time is between 30 seconds and one minute?
c. Suppose a manager of a Wendy's is considering instituting a policy such that if the time it takes to serve you exceeds five minutes, your food is free. What is the probability that you will get your food for free? Comment.

32. The Boston Fire Department receives 911 calls at a mean rate of 1.6 calls per hour (Mass.gov website, November 2012). Suppose the number of calls per hour follows a Poisson probability distribution.
a. What is the mean time between 911 calls to the Boston Fire Department in minutes?
b. Using the mean in part (a), show the probability density function for the time between 911 calls in minutes.
c. What is the probability that there will be less than one hour between 911 calls?
d. What is the probability that there will be 30 minutes or more between 911 calls?
e. What is the probability that there will be more than 5 minutes but less than 20 minutes between 911 calls?

Summary

This chapter extended the discussion of probability distributions to the case of continuous random variables. The major conceptual difference between discrete and continuous probability distributions involves the method of computing probabilities. With discrete distributions, the probability function $f(x)$ provides the probability that the random variable x assumes various values. With continuous distributions, the probability density function $f(x)$ does not provide probability values directly. Instead, probabilities are given by areas under the curve or graph of the probability density function $f(x)$. Because the area under the curve above a single point is zero, we observe that the probability of any particular value is zero for a continuous random variable.

Three continuous probability distributions—the uniform, normal, and exponential distributions—were treated in detail. The normal distribution is used widely in statistical inference and will be used extensively throughout the remainder of the text.

Glossary

Exponential probability distribution A continuous probability distribution that is useful in computing probabilities for the time it takes to complete a task.

Normal probability distribution A continuous probability distribution. Its probability density function is bell shaped and determined by its mean μ and standard deviation σ.

Probability density function A function used to compute probabilities for a continuous random variable. The area under the graph of a probability density function over an interval represents probability.

Standard normal probability distribution A normal distribution with a mean of zero and a standard deviation of one.

Uniform probability distribution A continuous probability distribution for which the probability that the random variable will assume a value in any interval is the same for each interval of equal length.

Key Formulas

Uniform Probability Density Function

$$f(x) = \begin{cases} \dfrac{1}{b-a} & \text{for } a \leq x \leq b \\ \\ 0 & \text{elsewhere} \end{cases} \tag{6.1}$$

Normal Probability Density Function

$$f(x) = \frac{1}{\sigma\sqrt{2\pi}} e^{-\frac{1}{2}\left(\frac{x-\mu}{\sigma}\right)^2} \tag{6.2}$$

Converting to the Standard Normal Random Variable

$$z = \frac{x-\mu}{\sigma} \tag{6.3}$$

Exponential Probability Density Function

$$f(x) = \frac{1}{\mu} e^{-x/\mu} \quad \text{for } x \geq 0 \tag{6.4}$$

Exponential Distribution: Cumulative Probabilities

$$P(x \leq x_0) = 1 - e^{-x_0/\mu} \tag{6.5}$$

Supplementary Exercises

33. A business executive, transferred from Chicago to Atlanta, needs to sell her house in Chicago quickly. The executive's employer has offered to buy the house for $210,000, but the offer expires at the end of the week. The executive does not currently have a better offer but can afford to leave the house on the market for another month. From conversations with her realtor, the executive believes the price she will get by leaving the house on the market for another month is uniformly distributed between $200,000 and $225,000.
    a. If she leaves the house on the market for another month, what is the mathematical expression for the probability density function of the sales price?
    b. If she leaves it on the market for another month, what is the probability that she will get at least $215,000 for the house?

    c.   If she leaves it on the market for another month, what is the probability that she will get less than $210,000?

    d.   Should the executive leave the house on the market for another month? Why or why not?

34. The NCAA estimates that the yearly value of a full athletic scholarship at in-state public universities is $19,000 (*The Wall Street Journal*, March 12, 2012). Assume the scholarship value is normally distributed with a standard deviation of $2100.

    a.   For the 10% of athletic scholarships of least value, how much are they worth?

    b.   What percentage of athletic scholarships are valued at $22,000 or more?

    c.   For the 3% of athletic scholarships that are most valuable, how much are they worth?

35. Motorola used the normal distribution to determine the probability of defects and the number of defects expected in a production process. Assume a production process produces items with a mean weight of 10 ounces. Calculate the probability of a defect and the expected number of defects for a 1000-unit production run in the following situations.

    a.   The process standard deviation is .15, and the process control is set at plus or minus one standard deviation. Units with weights less than 9.85 or greater than 10.15 ounces will be classified as defects.

    b.   Through process design improvements, the process standard deviation can be reduced to .05. Assume the process control remains the same, with weights less than 9.85 or greater than 10.15 ounces being classified as defects.

    c.   What is the advantage of reducing process variation, thereby causing process control limits to be at a greater number of standard deviations from the mean?

36. During early 2012, economic hardship was stretching the limits of France's welfare system. One indicator of the level of hardship was the increase in the number of people bringing items to a Paris pawnbroker. That number had risen to 658 per day (*Bloomberg Businessweek*, March 5–March 11, 2012). Assume the number of people bringing items to the pawnshop per day in 2012 is normally distributed with a mean of 658.

    a.   Suppose you learn that on 3% of the days, 610 or fewer people brought items to the pawnshop. What is the standard deviation of the number of people bringing items to the pawnshop per day?

    b.   On any given day, what is the probability that between 600 and 700 people bring items to the pawnshop?

    c.   How many people bring items to the pawnshop on the busiest 3% of days?

37. The port of South Louisiana, located along 54 miles of the Mississippi River between New Orleans and Baton Rouge, is the largest bulk cargo port in the world. The U.S. Army Corps of Engineers reports that the port handles a mean of 4.5 million tons of cargo per week (*USA Today*, September 25, 2012). Assume that the number of tons of cargo handled per week is normally distributed with a standard deviation of .82 million tons.

    a.   What is the probability that the port handles less than 5 million tons of cargo per week?

    b.   What is the probability that the port handles 3 million or more tons of cargo per week?

    c.   What is the probability that the port handles between 3 million and 4 million tons of cargo per week?

    d.   Assume that 85% of the time the port can handle the weekly cargo volume without extending operating hours. What is the number of tons of cargo per week that will require the port to extend its operating hours?

38. Ward Doering Auto Sales is considering offering a special service contract that will cover the total cost of any service work required on leased vehicles. From experience, the company manager estimates that yearly service costs are approximately normally distributed, with a mean of $150 and a standard deviation of $25.

    a.   If the company offers the service contract to customers for a yearly charge of $200, what is the probability that any one customer's service costs will exceed the contract price of $200?

    b.   What is Ward's expected profit per service contract?

39. The XO Group Inc. conducted a survey of 13,000 brides and grooms married in the United States and found that the average cost of a wedding is $29,858 (XO Group website, January 5, 2015). Assume that the cost of a wedding is normally distributed with a mean of $29,858 and a standard deviation of $5600.
   a.   What is the probability that a wedding costs less than $20,000?
   b.   What is the probability that a wedding costs between $20,000 and $30,000?
   c.   For a wedding to be among the 5% most expensive, how much would it have to cost?

40. Assume that the test scores from a college admissions test are normally distributed, with a mean of 450 and a standard deviation of 100.
   a.   What percentage of the people taking the test score between 400 and 500?
   b.   Suppose someone receives a score of 630. What percentage of the people taking the test score better? What percentage score worse?
   c.   If a particular university will not admit anyone scoring below 480, what percentage of the persons taking the test would be acceptable to the university?

41. According to the National Association of Colleges and Employers, the average starting salary for new college graduates in health sciences is $51,541. The average starting salary for new college graduates in business is $53,901 (National Association of Colleges and Employers website, January 5, 2015). Assume that starting salaries are normally distributed and that the standard deviation for starting salaries for new college graduates in health sciences is $11,000. Assume that the standard deviation for starting salaries for new college graduates in business is $15,000.
   a.   What is the probability that a new college graduate in business will earn a starting salary of at least $65,000?
   b.   What is the probability that a new college graduate in health sciences will earn a starting salary of at least $65,000?
   c.   What is the probability that a new college graduate in health sciences will earn a starting salary less than $40,000?
   d.   How much would a new college graduate in business have to earn in order to have a starting salary higher than 99% of all starting salaries of new college graduates in the health sciences?

42. A machine fills containers with a particular product. The standard deviation of filling weights is known from past data to be .6 ounce. If only 2% of the containers hold less than 18 ounces, what is the mean filling weight for the machine? That is, what must μ equal? Assume the filling weights have a normal distribution.

43. *The American Time Use Study* is a survey of people in the United States regarding the amount of time they spend on various activities in a typical day. On a given day, 22% of American men participate in sports, exercise, or recreation. On days they participated in these activities, men participated on average 1.8 hours in sports, exercise, or recreation (Bureau of Labor Statistics website, December 2015). Suppose that the time spent on sports, exercise, and recreation for men on days of participation is distributed exponentially.
   a.   What is the probability that when a man participates in sports, exercise, or recreation, he does so for less than or equal to 1 hour?
   b.   What is the probability that when a man participates in sports, exercise, or recreation, he does so for more than 2 hours?

44. A website for bed and breakfast inns gets approximately seven visitors per minute. Suppose the number of website visitors per minute follows a Poisson probability distribution.
   a.   What is the mean time between visits to the website?
   b.   Show the exponential probability density function for the time between website visits.
   c.   What is the probability that no one will access the website in a 1-minute period?
   d.   What is the probability that no one will access the website in a 12-second period?

45. Do you dislike waiting in line? Supermarket chain Kroger has used computer simulation and information technology to reduce the average waiting time for customers at 2300 stores. Using a new system called *QueVision*, which allows Kroger to better predict when shoppers will be checking out, the company was able to decrease average customer waiting time to just 26 seconds (*InformationWeek* website and *The Wall Street Journal* website, January 5, 2015).

    a. Assume that Kroger waiting times are exponentially distributed. Show the probability density function of waiting time at Kroger.

    b. What is the probability that a customer will have to wait between 15 and 30 seconds?

    c. What is the probability that a customer will have to wait more than 2 minutes?

46. The time (in minutes) between telephone calls at an insurance claims office has the following exponential probability distribution.

$$f(x) = .50e^{-.50x} \qquad \text{for } x \geq 0$$

    a. What is the mean time between telephone calls?

    b. What is the probability of having 30 seconds or less between telephone calls?

    c. What is the probability of having 1 minute or less between telephone calls?

    d. What is the probability of having 5 or more minutes without a telephone call?

Case Problem 1   Specialty Toys

Specialty Toys, Inc. sells a variety of new and innovative children's toys. Management learned that the preholiday season is the best time to introduce a new toy, because many families use this time to look for new ideas for December holiday gifts. When Specialty discovers a new toy with good market potential, it chooses an October market entry date.

In order to get toys into its stores by October, Specialty places one-time orders with its manufacturers in June or July of each year. Demand for children's toys can be highly volatile. If a new toy catches on, a sense of shortage in the marketplace often increases the demand to high levels and large profits can be realized. However, new toys can also flop, leaving Specialty stuck with high levels of inventory that must be sold at reduced prices. The most important question the company faces is deciding how many units of a new toy should be purchased to meet anticipated sales demand. If too few are purchased, sales will be lost; if too many are purchased, profits will be reduced because of low prices realized in clearance sales.

For the coming season, Specialty plans to introduce a new product called Weather Teddy. This variation of a talking teddy bear is made by a company in Taiwan. When a child presses Teddy's hand, the bear begins to talk. A built-in barometer selects one of five responses that predict the weather conditions. The responses range from "It looks to be a very nice day! Have fun" to "I think it may rain today. Don't forget your umbrella." Tests with the product show that, even though it is not a perfect weather predictor, its predictions are surprisingly good. Several of Specialty's managers claimed Teddy gave predictions of the weather that were as good as those of many local television weather forecasters.

As with other products, Specialty faces the decision of how many Weather Teddy units to order for the coming holiday season. Members of the management team suggested order quantities of 15,000, 18,000, 24,000, or 28,000 units. The wide range of order quantities suggested indicates considerable disagreement concerning the market potential. The product management team asks you for an analysis of the stock-out probabilities for various order quantities, an estimate of the profit potential, and help with making an order quantity recommendation. Specialty expects to sell Weather Teddy for $24 based on a cost of $16 per unit. If inventory remains after the holiday season, Specialty will sell all surplus inventory for $5 per unit. After reviewing the sales history of similar products, Specialty's senior sales forecaster predicted an expected demand of 20,000 units with a .95 probability that demand would be between 10,000 units and 30,000 units.

Managerial Report

Prepare a managerial report that addresses the following issues and recommends an order quantity for the Weather Teddy product.

1. Use the sales forecaster's prediction to describe a normal probability distribution that can be used to approximate the demand distribution. Sketch the distribution and show its mean and standard deviation.
2. Compute the probability of a stock-out for the order quantities suggested by members of the management team.
3. Compute the projected profit for the order quantities suggested by the management team under three scenarios: worst case in which sales = 10,000 units, most likely case in which sales = 20,000 units, and best case in which sales = 30,000 units.
4. One of Specialty's managers felt that the profit potential was so great that the order quantity should have a 70% chance of meeting demand and only a 30% chance of any stock-outs. What quantity would be ordered under this policy, and what is the projected profit under the three sales scenarios?
5. Provide your own recommendation for an order quantity and note the associated profit projections. Provide a rationale for your recommendation.

Case Problem 2   Gebhardt Electronics

Gebhardt Electronics produces a wide variety of transformers that it sells directly to manufacturers of electronics equipment. For one component used in several models of its transformers, Gebhardt uses a 3-foot length of .20 mm diameter solid wire made of pure Oxygen-Free Electronic (OFE) copper. A flaw in the wire reduces its conductivity and increases the likelihood it will break, and this critical component is difficult to reach and repair after a transformer has been constructed. Therefore, Gebhardt wants to use primarily flawless lengths of wire in making this component. The company is willing to accept no more than a 1 in 20 chance that a 3-foot length taken from a spool will be flawless. Gebhardt also occasionally uses smaller pieces of the same wire in the manufacture of other components, so the 3-foot segments to be used for this component are essentially taken randomly from a long spool of .20 mm diameter solid OFE copper wire.

Gebhardt is now considering a new supplier for copper wire. This supplier claims that its spools of .20 mm diameter solid OFE copper wire average 50 inches between flaws. Gebhardt now must determine whether the new supply will be satisfactory if the supplier's claim is valid.

Managerial Report

In making this assessment for Gebhardt Electronics, consider the following three questions:

1. If the new supplier does provide spools of .20 mm solid OFE copper wire that average 50 inches between flaws, how is the length of wire between two consecutive flaws distributed?
2. Using the probability distribution you identified in (1), what is the probability that Gebhardt's criteria will be met (i.e., a 1 in 20 chance that a randomly selected 3-foot segment of wire provided by the new supplier will be flawless)?
3. In inches, what is the minimum mean length between consecutive flaws that would result in satisfaction of Gebhardt's criteria?
4. In inches, what is the minimum mean length between consecutive flaws that would result in a 1 in 100 chance that a randomly selected 3-foot segment of wire provided by the new supplier will be flawless?

CHAPTER 7

Sampling and Sampling Distributions

MEADWESTVACO CORPORATION*
STAMFORD, CONNECTICUT

MeadWestvaco Corporation, a leading producer of packaging, coated and specialty papers, and specialty chemicals, employs more than 17,000 people. It operates worldwide in 30 countries and serves customers located in approximately 100 countries. MeadWestvaco's internal consulting group uses sampling to provide a variety of information that enables the company to obtain significant productivity benefits and remain competitive.

For example, MeadWestvaco maintains large woodland holdings, which supply the trees, or raw material, for many of the company's products. Managers need reliable and accurate information about the timberlands and forests to evaluate the company's ability to meet its future raw material needs. What is the present volume in the forests? What is the past growth of the forests? What is the projected future growth of the forests? With answers to these important questions MeadWestvaco's managers can develop plans for the future, including long-term planting and harvesting schedules for the trees.

How does MeadWestvaco obtain the information it needs about its vast forest holdings? Data collected from sample plots throughout the forests are the basis for learning about the population of trees owned by the company. To identify the sample plots, the timberland holdings are first divided into three sections based on location and types of trees. Using maps and random numbers, MeadWestvaco analysts identify random samples of 1/5- to 1/7-acre plots in each section of the forest. MeadWestvaco foresters collect data from these sample plots to learn about the forest population.

Random sampling of its forest holdings enables MeadWestvaco Corporation to meet future raw material needs.

Foresters throughout the organization participate in the field data collection process. Periodically, two-person teams gather information on each tree in every sample plot. The sample data are entered into the company's continuous forest inventory (CFI) computer system. Reports from the CFI system include a number of frequency distribution summaries containing statistics on types of trees, present forest volume, past forest growth rates, and projected future forest growth and volume. Sampling and the associated statistical summaries of the sample data provide the reports essential for the effective management of MeadWestvaco's forests and timberlands.

In this chapter you will learn about simple random sampling and the sample selection process. In addition, you will learn how statistics such as the sample mean and sample proportion are used to estimate the population mean and population proportion. The important concept of sampling distribution is also introduced.

---

*The authors are indebted to Dr. Edward P. Winkofsky for providing this Statistics in Practice.

In Chapter 1 we presented the following definitions of an element, a population, and a sample.

- An *element* is the entity on which data are collected.
- A *population* is the collection of all the elements of interest.
- A *sample* is a subset of the population.

The reason we select a sample is to collect data to make an inference and answer research questions about a population.

Let us begin by citing two examples in which sampling was used to answer a research question about a population.

1. Members of a political party in Texas were considering supporting a particular candidate for election to the U.S. Senate, and party leaders wanted to estimate the proportion of registered voters in the state favoring the candidate. A sample of 400 registered voters in Texas was selected and 160 of the 400 voters indicated a preference for the candidate. Thus, an estimate of the proportion of the population of registered voters favoring the candidate is 160/400 = .40.

2. A tire manufacturer is considering producing a new tire designed to provide an increase in mileage over the firm's current line of tires. To estimate the mean useful life of the new tires, the manufacturer produced a sample of 120 tires for testing. The test results provided a sample mean of 36,500 miles. Hence, an estimate of the mean useful life for the population of new tires was 36,500 miles.

A sample mean provides an estimate of a population mean, and a sample proportion provides an estimate of a population proportion. With estimates such as these, some estimation error can be expected. This chapter provides the basis for determining how large that error might be.

It is important to realize that sample results provide only *estimates* of the values of the corresponding population characteristics. We do not expect exactly .40, or 40%, of the population of registered voters to favor the candidate, nor do we expect the sample mean of 36,500 miles to exactly equal the mean mileage for the population of all new tires produced. The reason is simply that the sample contains only a portion of the population. Some sampling error is to be expected. With proper sampling methods, the sample results will provide "good" estimates of the population parameters. But how good can we expect the sample results to be? Fortunately, statistical procedures are available for answering this question.

Let us define some of the terms used in sampling. The **sampled population** is the population from which the sample is drawn, and a **frame** is a list of the elements from which the sample will be selected. In the first example, the sampled population is all registered voters in Texas, and the frame is a list of all the registered voters. Because the number of registered voters in Texas is a finite number, the first example is an illustration of sampling from a finite population. In Section 7.2, we discuss how a simple random sample can be selected when sampling from a finite population.

The sampled population for the tire mileage example is more difficult to define because the sample of 120 tires was obtained from a production process at a particular point in time. We can think of the sampled population as the conceptual population of all the tires that could have been made by the production process at that particular point in time. In this sense the sampled population is considered infinite, making it impossible to construct a frame from which to draw the sample. In Section 7.2, we discuss how to select a random sample in such a situation.

In this chapter, we show how simple random sampling can be used to select a sample from a finite population and describe how a random sample can be taken from an infinite population that is generated by an ongoing process. We then show how data obtained from a sample can be used to compute estimates of a population mean, a population standard deviation, and a population proportion. In addition, we introduce the important concept of a sampling distribution. As we will show, knowledge of the appropriate sampling distribution enables us to make statements about how close the sample estimates are to the corresponding population parameters. In section 7.7, we discuss some alternatives to simple random sampling that are often employed in practice. In the last section, we discuss sampling and nonsampling error, and how these relate to large samples.

7.1 The Electronics Associates Sampling Problem

The director of personnel for Electronics Associates, Inc. (EAI), has been assigned the task of developing a profile of the company's 2500 employees. The characteristics to be identified include the mean annual salary for the employees and the proportion of employees having completed the company's management training program.

Using the 2500 employees as the population for this study, we can find the annual salary and the training program status for each individual by referring to the firm's personnel

DATA *file*

EAI

records. The data set containing this information for all 2500 employees in the population is in the DATAfile named *EAI*.

Using the EAI data and the formulas presented in Chapter 3, we compute the population mean and the population standard deviation for the annual salary data.

$$\text{Population mean:} \quad \mu = \$51,800$$
$$\text{Population standard deviation:} \quad \sigma = \$4000$$

The data for the training program status show that 1500 of the 2500 employees completed the training program.

Numerical characteristics of a population are called **parameters**. Letting p denote the proportion of the population that completed the training program, we see that $p = 1500/2500 = .60$. The population mean annual salary ($\mu = \$51,800$), the population standard deviation of annual salary ($\sigma = \$4000$), and the population proportion that completed the training program ($p = .60$) are parameters of the population of EAI employees.

Often the cost of collecting information from a sample is substantially less than from a population, especially when personal interviews must be conducted to collect the information.

Now, suppose that the necessary information on all the EAI employees was not readily available in the company's database. The question we now consider is how the firm's director of personnel can obtain estimates of the population parameters by using a sample of employees rather than all 2500 employees in the population. Suppose that a sample of 30 employees will be used. Clearly, the time and the cost of developing a profile would be substantially less for 30 employees than for the entire population. If the personnel director could be assured that a sample of 30 employees would provide adequate information about the population of 2500 employees, working with a sample would be preferable to working with the entire population. Let us explore the possibility of using a sample for the EAI study by first considering how we can identify a sample of 30 employees.

7.2 Selecting a Sample

In this section we describe how to select a sample. We first describe how to sample from a finite population and then describe how to select a sample from an infinite population.

Sampling from a Finite Population

Other methods of probability sampling are described in Section 7.7.

Statisticians recommend selecting a probability sample when sampling from a finite population because a probability sample allows them to make valid statistical inferences about the population. The simplest type of probability sample is one in which each sample of size n has the same probability of being selected. It is called a simple random sample. A simple random sample of size n from a finite population of size N is defined as follows.

> **SIMPLE RANDOM SAMPLE (FINITE POPULATION)**
>
> A **simple random sample** of size n from a finite population of size N is a sample selected such that each possible sample of size n has the same probability of being selected.

The random numbers generated using Excel's RAND function follow a uniform probability distribution between 0 and 1.

The procedures used to select a simple random sample from a finite population are based upon the use of random numbers. We can use Excel's RAND function to generate a random number between 0 and 1 by entering the formula =RAND() into any cell in a worksheet. The number generated is called a random number because the mathematical procedure used by the RAND function guarantees that every number between 0 and 1 has the same probability of being selected. Let us see how these random numbers can be used to select a simple random sample.

Our procedure for selecting a simple random sample of size n from a population of size N involves two steps.

Step 1. Assign a random number to each element of the population.
Step 2. Select the n elements corresponding to the n smallest random numbers.

Because each set of n elements in the population has the same probability of being assigned the n smallest random numbers, each set of n elements has the same probability of being selected for the sample. If we select the sample using this two-step procedure, every sample of size n has the same probability of being selected; thus, the sample selected satisfies the definition of a simple random sample.

Let us consider an example involving selecting a simple random sample of size $n = 5$ from a population of size $N = 16$. Table 7.1 contains a list of the 16 teams in the 2012 National Baseball League. Suppose we want to select a simple random sample of 5 teams to conduct in-depth interviews about how they manage their minor league franchises.

Step 1 of our simple random sampling procedure requires that we assign a random number to each of the 16 teams in the population. Figure 7.1 shows a worksheet used to generate a random number corresponding to each of the 16 teams in the population. The names of the baseball teams are in column A, and the random numbers generated are in column B. From the formula worksheet in the background we see that the formula =RAND() has been entered into cells B2:B17 to generate the random numbers between 0 and 1. From the value worksheet in the foreground we see that Arizona is assigned the random number .850862, Atlanta has been assigned the random number .706245, and so on.

The second step is to select the five teams corresponding to the five smallest random numbers as our sample. Looking through the random numbers in Figure 7.1, we see that the team corresponding to the smallest random number (.066942) is St. Louis, and that the four teams corresponding to the next four smallest random numbers are Washington, Houston, San Diego, and San Francisco. Thus, these five teams make up the simple random sample.

Searching through the list of random numbers in Figure 7.1 to find the five smallest random numbers is tedious, and it is easy to make mistakes. Excel's Sort procedure simplifies this step. We illustrate by sorting the list of baseball teams in Figure 7.1 to find the five teams corresponding to the five smallest random numbers. Refer to the foreground worksheet in Figure 7.1 as we describe the steps involved.

Step 1. Select any cell in the range B2:B17
Step 2. Click the **Home** tab on the Ribbon
Step 3. In the **Editing** group, click **Sort & Filter**
Step 4. Choose **Sort Smallest to Largest**

TABLE 7.1 2012 NATIONAL BASEBALL LEAGUE TEAMS

Arizona	Milwaukee
Atlanta	New York
Chicago	Philadelphia
Cincinnati	Pittsburgh
Colorado	San Diego
Florida	San Francisco
Houston	St. Louis
Los Angeles	Washington

FIGURE 7.1 WORKSHEET USED TO GENERATE A RANDOM NUMBER CORRESPONDING TO EACH TEAM

DATAfile
National League

	A	B	C
1	**Team**	**Random Numbers**	
2	Arizona	=RAND()	
3	Atlanta	=RAND()	
4	Chicago	=RAND()	
5	Cincinnati	=RAND()	
6	Colorado	=RAND()	
7	Florida	=RAND()	
8	Houston	=RAND()	
9	Los Angeles	=RAND()	
10	Milwaukee	=RAND()	
11	New York	=RAND()	
12	Philadelphia	=RAND()	
13	Pittsburgh	=RAND()	
14	San Diego	=RAND()	
15	San Francisco	=RAND()	
16	St. Louis	=RAND()	
17	Washington	=RAND()	
18			

	A	B	C
1	**Team**	**Random Numbers**	
2	Arizona	0.850862	
3	Atlanta	0.706245	
4	Chicago	0.724789	
5	Cincinnati	0.614784	
6	Colorado	0.553815	
7	Florida	0.857324	
8	Houston	0.179123	
9	Los Angeles	0.525636	
10	Milwaukee	0.471490	
11	New York	0.523103	
12	Philadelphia	0.851552	
13	Pittsburgh	0.806185	
14	San Diego	0.327713	
15	San Francisco	0.374168	
16	St. Louis	0.066942	
17	Washington	0.158452	
18			

After completing these steps we obtain the worksheet shown in Figure 7.2.[1] The teams listed in rows 2–6 are the ones corresponding to the smallest five random numbers; they are our simple random sample. Note that the random numbers shown in Figure 7.2 are in ascending order, and that the teams are not in their original order. For instance, St. Louis is the next to last team listed in Figure 7.1, but it is the first team selected in the simple random sample. Washington, the second team in our sample, is the sixteenth team in the original list, and so on.

The Excel Sort procedure for identifying the employees associated with the 30 smallest random numbers is especially valuable with such a large population.

We now use this simple random sampling procedure to select a simple random sample of 30 EAI employees from the population of 2500 EAI employees. We begin by generating 2500 random numbers, one for each employee in the population. Then we select the 30 employees corresponding to the 30 smallest random numbers as our sample. Refer to Figure 7.3 as we describe the steps involved.

Enter/Access Data: Open the DATAfile named *EAI*. The first three columns of the worksheet in the background show the annual salary data and training program status for the first 30 employees in the population of 2500 EAI employees. (The complete worksheet contains all 2500 employees.)

[1]In order to show the random numbers from Figure 7.1 in ascending order in this worksheet, we turned off the automatic recalculation option prior to sorting for illustrative purposes. If the recalculation option were not turned off, a new set of random numbers would have been generated when the sort was completed. But the same five teams would be selected.

FIGURE 7.2 USING EXCEL'S SORT PROCEDURE TO SELECT THE SIMPLE RANDOM SAMPLE OF FIVE TEAMS

	A	B	C
1	**Team**	**Random Numbers**	
2	St. Louis	0.066942	
3	Washington	0.158452	
4	Houston	0.179123	
5	San Diego	0.327713	
6	San Francisco	0.374168	
7	Milwaukee	0.471490	
8	New York	0.523103	
9	Los Angeles	0.525636	
10	Colorado	0.553815	
11	Cincinnati	0.614784	
12	Atlanta	0.706245	
13	Chicago	0.724789	
14	Pittsburgh	0.806185	
15	Arizona	0.850862	
16	Philadelphia	0.851552	
17	Florida	0.857324	
18			

Enter Functions and Formulas: In the background worksheet, the label **Random Numbers** has been entered into cell D1 and the formula =RAND() has been entered into cells D2:D2501 to generate a random number between 0 and 1 for each of the 2500 EAI employees. The random number generated for the first employee is 0.613872, the random number generated for the second employee is 0.473204, and so on.

Apply Tools: All that remains is to find the employees associated with the 30 smallest random numbers. To do so, we sort the data in columns A through D into ascending order by the random numbers in column D.

Step 1. Select any cell in the range D2:D2501
Step 2. Click the **Home** tab on the Ribbon
Step 3. In the **Editing** group, click **Sort & Filter**
Step 4. Choose **Sort Smallest to Largest**

After completing these steps we obtain the worksheet shown in the foreground of Figure 7.3. The employees listed in rows 2–31 are the ones corresponding to the smallest 30 random numbers that were generated. Hence, this group of 30 employees is a simple random sample. Note that the random numbers shown in the foreground of Figure 7.3 are in ascending order, and that the employees are not in their original order. For instance, employee 812 in the population is associated with the smallest random number and is the first element in the sample, and employee 13 in the population (see row 14 of the background worksheet) has been included as the 22nd observation in the sample (row 23 of the foreground worksheet).

Sampling from an Infinite Population

Sometimes we want to select a sample from a population, but the population is infinitely large or the elements of the population are being generated by an ongoing process for which

FIGURE 7.3 USING EXCEL TO SELECT A SIMPLE RANDOM SAMPLE

	A	B	C	D	E	F	G
1	Manager	Annual Salary	Training Program	Random Numbers			
2	1	55769.50	No	0.613872			
3	2	50823.00	Yes	0.473204			
4	3	48408.20	No	0.549011			
5	4	49787.50	No	0.047482			
6	5	52801.60	Yes	0.531085			
7	6	51767.70	No	0.994296			
8	7	58346.60	Yes	0.189065			
9	8	46670.20	No	0.020714			
10	9	50246.80	Yes	0.647318			
11	10	51255.00	No	0.524341			
12	11	52546.60	No	0.764998			
13	12	49512.50	Yes	0.255244			
14	13	51753.00	Yes	0.010923			
15	14	53547.10	No	0.238003			
16	15	48052.20	No	0.635675			
17	16	44652.50	Yes	0.177294			
18	17	51764.90	Yes	0.415097			
19	18	45187.80	Yes	0.883440			
20	19	49867.50	Yes	0.476824			
21	20	53706.30	Yes	0.101065			
22	21	52039.50	Yes	0.775323			
23	22	52973.60	No	0.011729			
24	23	53372.50	No	0.762026			
25	24	54592.00	Yes	0.066344			
26	25	55738.10	Yes	0.776766			
27	26	52975.10	Yes	0.828493			
28	27	52386.20	Yes	0.841532			
29	28	51051.60	Yes	0.899427			
30	29	52095.60	Yes	0.486284			
31	30	44956.50	No	0.264628			

The formula in cells D2:D2501 is =RAND().

	A	B	C	D	E
1	Manager	Annual Salary	Training Program	Random Numbers	
2	812	49094.30	Yes	0.000193	
3	1411	53263.90	Yes	0.000484	
4	1795	49643.50	Yes	0.002641	
5	2095	49894.90	Yes	0.002763	
6	1235	47621.60	No	0.002940	
7	744	55924.00	Yes	0.002977	
8	470	49092.30	Yes	0.003182	
9	1606	51404.40	Yes	0.003448	
10	1744	50957.70	Yes	0.004203	
11	179	55109.70	Yes	0.005293	
12	1387	45922.60	Yes	0.005709	
13	1782	57268.40	No	0.005729	
14	1006	55688.80	Yes	0.005796	
15	278	51564.70	No	0.005966	
16	1850	56188.20	No	0.006250	
17	844	51766.00	Yes	0.006708	
18	2028	52541.30	No	0.007767	
19	1654	44980.00	Yes	0.008095	
20	444	51932.60	Yes	0.009686	
21	556	52973.00	Yes	0.009711	
22	2449	45120.90	Yes	0.010595	
23	13	51753.00	Yes	0.010923	
24	2187	54391.80	No	0.011364	
25	1633	50164.20	No	0.011603	
26	22	52973.60	No	0.011729	
27	1530	50241.30	No	0.013570	
28	820	52793.90	No	0.013669	
29	1258	50979.40	Yes	0.014042	
30	2349	55860.90	Yes	0.014532	
31	1698	57309.10	No	0.014539	

Note: Rows 32–2501 are not shown.

there is no limit on the number of elements that can be generated. Thus, it is not possible to develop a list of all the elements in the population. This is considered the infinite population case. With an infinite population, we cannot select a simple random sample because we cannot construct a frame consisting of all the elements. In the infinite population case, statisticians recommend selecting what is called a random sample.

RANDOM SAMPLE (INFINITE POPULATION)

A **random sample** of size n from an infinite population is a sample selected such that the following conditions are satisfied.

1. Each element selected comes from the same population.
2. Each element is selected independently.

Care and judgment must be exercised in implementing the selection process for obtaining a random sample from an infinite population. Each case may require a different selection procedure. Let us consider two examples to see what we mean by the conditions: (1) Each element selected comes from the same population and (2) each element is selected independently.

A common quality control application involves a production process where there is no limit on the number of elements that can be produced. The conceptual population we are sampling from is all the elements that could be produced (not just the ones that are produced) by the ongoing production process. Because we cannot develop a list of all the elements that could be produced, the population is considered infinite. To be more specific, let us consider a production line designed to fill boxes of a breakfast cereal with a mean weight of 24 ounces of breakfast cereal per box. Samples of 12 boxes filled by this process are periodically selected by a quality control inspector to determine if the process is operating properly or if, perhaps, a machine malfunction has caused the process to begin underfilling or overfilling the boxes.

With a production operation such as this, the biggest concern in selecting a random sample is to make sure that condition 1 (the sampled elements are selected from the same population) is satisfied. To ensure that this condition is satisfied, the boxes must be selected at approximately the same point in time. This way the inspector avoids the possibility of selecting some boxes when the process is operating properly and other boxes when the process is not operating properly and is underfilling or overfilling the boxes. With a production process such as this, the second condition (each element is selected independently) is satisfied by designing the production process so that each box of cereal is filled independently. With this assumption, the quality control inspector only needs to worry about satisfying the same population condition.

As another example of selecting a random sample from an infinite population, consider the population of customers arriving at a fast-food restaurant. Suppose an employee is asked to select and interview a sample of customers in order to develop a profile of customers who visit the restaurant. The customer arrival process is ongoing and there is no way to obtain a list of all customers in the population. So, for practical purposes, the population for this ongoing process is considered infinite. As long as a sampling procedure is designed so that all the elements in the sample are customers of the restaurant and they are selected independently, a random sample will be obtained. In this case, the employee collecting the sample needs to select the sample from people who come into the restaurant and make a purchase to ensure that the same population condition is satisfied. If, for instance, the employee selected someone for the sample who came into the restaurant just to use the restroom, that person would not be a customer and the same population condition would be violated. So, as long as the interviewer selects the sample from people making a purchase at the restaurant, condition 1 is satisfied. Ensuring that the customers are selected independently can be more difficult.

The purpose of the second condition of the random sample selection procedure (each element is selected independently) is to prevent selection bias. In this case, selection bias would occur if the interviewer were free to select customers for the sample arbitrarily. The interviewer might feel more comfortable selecting customers in a particular age group and might avoid customers in other age groups. Selection bias would also occur if the interviewer selected a group of five customers who entered the restaurant together and asked all of them to participate in the sample. Such a group of customers would be likely to exhibit similar characteristics, which might provide misleading information about the population of customers. Selection bias such as this can be avoided by ensuring that the selection of a particular customer does not influence the selection of any other customer. In other words, the elements (customers) are selected independently.

McDonald's, the fast-food restaurant leader, implemented a random sampling procedure for this situation. The sampling procedure was based on the fact that some customers presented discount coupons. Whenever a customer presented a discount coupon, the next customer served was asked to complete a customer profile questionnaire. Because arriving customers presented discount coupons randomly and independently of other customers, this sampling procedure ensured that customers were selected independently. As a result, the sample satisfied the requirements of a random sample from an infinite population.

Situations involving sampling from an infinite population are usually associated with a process that operates over time. Examples include parts being manufactured on a production line, repeated experimental trials in a laboratory, transactions occurring at a bank, telephone calls arriving at a technical support center, and customers entering a retail store. In each case, the situation may be viewed as a process that generates elements from an infinite population. As long as the sampled elements are selected from the same population and are selected independently, the sample is considered a random sample from an infinite population.

NOTES AND COMMENTS

1. In this section we have been careful to define two types of samples: a simple random sample from a finite population and a random sample from an infinite population. In the remainder of the text, we will generally refer to both of these as either a *random sample* or simply a *sample*. We will not make a distinction of the sample being a "simple" random sample unless it is necessary for the exercise or discussion.

2. Statisticians who specialize in sample surveys from finite populations use sampling methods that provide probability samples. With a probability sample, each possible sample has a known probability of selection and a random process is used to select the elements for the sample. Simple random sampling is one of these methods. In Section 7.7, we describe some other probability sampling methods: stratified random sampling,

   cluster sampling, and systematic sampling. We use the term *simple* in simple random sampling to clarify that this is the probability sampling method that assures each sample of size n has the same probability of being selected.

3. The number of different simple random samples of size n that can be selected from a finite population of size N is

$$\frac{N!}{n!(N - n)!}$$

In this formula, $N!$ and $n!$ are the factorial formulas discussed in Chapter 4. For the EAI problem with $N = 2500$ and $n = 30$, this expression can be used to show that approximately 2.75×10^{69} different simple random samples of 30 EAI employees can be obtained.

Exercises

Methods

 SELF*test*

1. Consider a finite population with five elements labeled A, B, C, D, and E. Ten possible simple random samples of size 2 can be selected.
   a. List the 10 samples beginning with AB, AC, and so on.
   b. Using simple random sampling, what is the probability that each sample of size 2 is selected?

c. Suppose we use Excel's RAND function to assign random numbers to the five elements: A (.7266), B (.0476), C (.2459), D (.0957), E (.9408). List the simple random sample of size 2 that will be selected by using these random numbers.

2. Assume a finite population has 10 elements. Number the elements from 1 to 10 and use the following 10 random numbers to select a sample of size 4.

    .7545 .0936 .0341 .3242 .1449 .9060 .2420 .9773 .5428 .0729

 **SELF**test

3. The 2012 American League consists of 14 baseball teams. Suppose a sample of 5 teams is to be selected to conduct player interviews. The following table lists the 14 teams and the random numbers assigned by Excel's RAND function. Use these random numbers to select a sample of size 5.

 **DATA** *file*
American League

Team	Random Number	Team	Random Number
New York	0.178624	Boston	0.290197
Baltimore	0.578370	Tampa Bay	0.867778
Toronto	0.965807	Minnesota	0.811810
Chicago	0.562178	Cleveland	0.960271
Detroit	0.253574	Kansas City	0.326836
Oakland	0.288287	Anaheim	0.895267
Texas	0.500879	Seattle	0.839071

4. The U.S. Golf Association has instituted a ban on long and belly putters. This has caused a great deal of controversy among both amateur golfers and members of the Professional Golf Association (PGA). Shown below are the names of the top 10 finishers in the recent PGA Tour McGladrey Classic golf tournament.

    1. Tommy Gainey   6. Davis Love III
    2. David Toms   7. Chad Campbell
    3. Jim Furyk   8. Greg Owens
    4. Brendon de Jonge   9. Charles Howell III
    5. D. J. Trahan   10. Arjun Atwal

    Select a simple random sample of 3 of these players to assess their opinions on the use of long and belly putters.

 **DATA** *file*
EAI

5. In this section we used a two-step procedure to select a simple random sample of 30 EAI employees. Use this procedure to select a simple random sample of 50 EAI employees.

6. Indicate which of the following situations involve sampling from a finite population and which involve sampling from an infinite population. In cases where the sampled population is finite, describe how you would construct a frame.
    a. Select a sample of licensed drivers in the state of New York.
    b. Select a sample of boxes of cereal off the production line for the Breakfast Choice Company.
    c. Select a sample of cars crossing the Golden Gate Bridge on a typical weekday.
    d. Select a sample of students in a statistics course at Indiana University.
    e. Select a sample of the orders being processed by a mail-order firm.

 7.3 # Point Estimation

Now that we have described how to select a simple random sample, let us return to the EAI problem. A simple random sample of 30 employees and the corresponding data on annual salary and management training program participation are as shown in Table 7.2. The notation

TABLE 7.2   ANNUAL SALARY AND TRAINING PROGRAM STATUS FOR A SIMPLE RANDOM SAMPLE OF 30 EAI EMPLOYEES

Annual Salary ($)	Management Training Program	Annual Salary ($)	Management Training Program
$x_1 = 49,094.30$	Yes	$x_{16} = 51,766.00$	Yes
$x_2 = 53,263.90$	Yes	$x_{17} = 52,541.30$	No
$x_3 = 49,643.50$	Yes	$x_{18} = 44,980.00$	Yes
$x_4 = 49,894.90$	Yes	$x_{19} = 51,932.60$	Yes
$x_5 = 47,621.60$	No	$x_{20} = 52,973.00$	Yes
$x_6 = 55,924.00$	Yes	$x_{21} = 45,120.90$	Yes
$x_7 = 49,092.30$	Yes	$x_{22} = 51,753.00$	Yes
$x_8 = 51,404.40$	Yes	$x_{23} = 54,391.80$	No
$x_9 = 50,957.70$	Yes	$x_{24} = 50,164.20$	No
$x_{10} = 55,109.70$	Yes	$x_{25} = 52,973.60$	No
$x_{11} = 45,922.60$	Yes	$x_{26} = 50,241.30$	No
$x_{12} = 57,268.40$	No	$x_{27} = 52,793.90$	No
$x_{13} = 55,688.80$	Yes	$x_{28} = 50,979.40$	Yes
$x_{14} = 51,564.70$	No	$x_{29} = 55,860.90$	Yes
$x_{15} = 56,188.20$	No	$x_{30} = 57,309.10$	No

x_1, x_2, and so on is used to denote the annual salary of the first employee in the sample, the annual salary of the second employee in the sample, and so on. Participation in the management training program is indicated by Yes in the management training program column.

To estimate the value of a population parameter, we compute a corresponding characteristic of the sample, referred to as a **sample statistic**. For example, to estimate the population mean μ and the population standard deviation σ for the annual salary of EAI employees, we use the data in Table 7.2 to calculate the corresponding sample statistics: the sample mean and the sample standard deviation s. Using the formulas for a sample mean and a sample standard deviation presented in Chapter 3, the sample mean is

$$\bar{x} = \frac{\sum x_i}{n} = \frac{1,554,420}{30} = \$51,814$$

and the sample standard deviation is

$$s = \sqrt{\frac{\sum(x_i - \bar{x})^2}{n-1}} = \sqrt{\frac{325,009,260}{29}} = \$3348$$

To estimate p, the proportion of employees in the population who completed the management training program, we use the corresponding sample proportion $\bar{p}$. Let x denote the number of employees in the sample who completed the management training program. The data in Table 7.2 show that $x = 19$. Thus, with a sample size of $n = 30$, the sample proportion is

$$\bar{p} = \frac{x}{n} = \frac{19}{30} = .63$$

By making the preceding computations, we perform the statistical procedure called *point estimation*. We refer to the sample mean $\bar{x}$ as the **point estimator** of the population mean μ, the sample standard deviation s as the point estimator of the population standard deviation σ, and the sample proportion $\bar{p}$ as the point estimator of the population proportion p.

TABLE 7.3 SUMMARY OF POINT ESTIMATES OBTAINED FROM A SIMPLE RANDOM SAMPLE OF 30 EAI EMPLOYEES

Population Parameter	Parameter Value	Point Estimator	Point Estimate
μ = Population mean annual salary	$51,800	$\bar{x}$ = Sample mean annual salary	$51,814
σ = Population standard deviation for annual salary	$4000	s = Sample standard deviation for annual salary	$3348
p = Population proportion having completed the management training program	.60	$\bar{p}$ = Sample proportion having completed the management training program	.63

The numerical value obtained for $\bar{x}$, s, or $\bar{p}$ is called the **point estimate**. Thus, for the simple random sample of 30 EAI employees shown in Table 7.2, $51,814 is the point estimate of μ, $3348 is the point estimate of σ, and .63 is the point estimate of p. Table 7.3 summarizes the sample results and compares the point estimates to the actual values of the population parameters.

As is evident from Table 7.3, the point estimates differ somewhat from the corresponding population parameters. This difference is to be expected because a sample, and not a census of the entire population, is being used to develop the point estimates. In the next chapter, we will show how to construct an interval estimate in order to provide information about how close the point estimate is to the population parameter.

Practical Advice

The subject matter of most of the rest of the book is concerned with statistical inference. Point estimation is a form of statistical inference. We use a sample statistic to make an inference about a population parameter. When making inferences about a population based on a sample, it is important to have a close correspondence between the sampled population and the target population. The **target population** is the population we want to make inferences about, while the sampled population is the population from which the sample is actually taken. In this section, we have described the process of drawing a simple random sample from the population of EAI employees and making point estimates of characteristics of that same population. So the sampled population and the target population are identical, which is the desired situation. But in other cases, it is not as easy to obtain a close correspondence between the sampled and target populations.

Consider the case of an amusement park selecting a sample of its customers to learn about characteristics such as age and time spent at the park. Suppose all the sample elements were selected on a day when park attendance was restricted to employees of a large company. Then the sampled population would be composed of employees of that company and members of their families. If the target population we wanted to make inferences about were typical park customers over a typical summer, then we might encounter a significant difference between the sampled population and the target population. In such a case, we would question the validity of the point estimates being made. Park management would be in the best position to know whether a sample taken on a particular day was likely to be representative of the target population.

In summary, whenever a sample is used to make inferences about a population, we should make sure that the study is designed so that the sampled population and the target population are in close agreement. Good judgment is a necessary ingredient of sound statistical practice.

Exercises

Methods

7. The following data are from a simple random sample.

$$5 \quad 8 \quad 10 \quad 7 \quad 10 \quad 14$$

   a. What is the point estimate of the population mean?
   b. What is the point estimate of the population standard deviation?

8. A survey question for a sample of 150 individuals yielded 75 Yes responses, 55 No responses, and 20 No Opinions.
   a. What is the point estimate of the proportion in the population who respond Yes?
   b. What is the point estimate of the proportion in the population who respond No?

Applications

9. A simple random sample of 5 months of sales data provided the following information:

Month:	1	2	3	4	5
Units Sold:	94	100	85	94	92

   a. Develop a point estimate of the population mean number of units sold per month.
   b. Develop a point estimate of the population standard deviation.

Morningstar

10. Morningstar publishes ratings data on 1208 company stocks. A sample of 40 of these stocks is contained in the DATAfile named *Morningstar*. Use the data set to answer the following questions.
    a. Develop a point estimate of the proportion of the stocks that receive Morningstar's highest rating of 5 Stars.
    b. Develop a point estimate of the proportion of the Morningstar stocks that are rated Above Average with respect to business risk.
    c. Develop a point estimate of the proportion of the Morningstar stocks that are rated 2 Stars or less.

11. The National Football League (NFL) polls fans to develop a rating for each football game (NFL website, October 24, 2012). Each game is rated on a scale from 0 (forgettable) to 100 (memorable). The fan ratings for a random sample of 12 games follow.

57	61	86	74	72	73
20	57	80	79	83	74

   a. Develop a point estimate of mean fan rating for the population of NFL games.
   b. Develop a point estimate of the standard deviation for the population of NFL games.

12. A sample of 426 U.S. adults age 50 and older were asked how important a variety of issues were in choosing whom to vote for in the most recent presidential election.
    a. What is the sampled population for this study?
    b. Social Security and Medicare were cited as "very important" by 350 respondents. Estimate the proportion of the population of U.S. adults age 50 and over who believe this issue is very important.
    c. Education was cited as "very important" by 74% of the respondents. Estimate the number of respondents who believe this issue is very important.
    d. Job Growth was cited as "very important" by 354 respondents. Estimate the proportion of U.S. adults age 50 and over who believe job growth is very important.
    e. What is the target population for the inferences being made in parts (b) and (d)? Is it the same as the sampled population you identified in part (a)? Suppose you later learn

that the sample was restricted to members of the AARP. Would you still feel the inferences being made in parts (b) and (d) are valid? Why or why not?

13. One of the questions in the Pew Internet & American Life Project asked adults if they used the Internet, at least occasionally (Pew website, October 23, 2012). The results showed that 454 out of 478 adults aged 18–29 answered Yes; 741 out of 833 adults aged 30–49 answered Yes; 1058 out of 1644 adults aged 50 and over answered Yes.
    a. Develop a point estimate of the proportion of adults aged 18–29 who use the Internet.
    b. Develop a point estimate of the proportion of adults aged 30–49 who use the Internet.
    c. Develop a point estimate of the proportion of adults aged 50 and over who use the Internet.
    d. Comment on any relationship between age and Internet use that seems apparent.
    e. Suppose your target population of interest is that of all adults (18 years of age and over). Develop an estimate of the proportion of that population who use the Internet.

EAI

14. In this section we showed how a simple random sample of 30 EAI employees can be used to develop point estimates of the population mean annual salary, the population standard deviation for annual salary, and the population proportion having completed the management training program.
    a. Use Excel to select a simple random sample of 50 EAI employees.
    b. Develop a point estimate of the mean annual salary.
    c. Develop a point estimate of the population standard deviation for annual salary.
    d. Develop a point estimate of the population proportion having completed the management training program.

7.4 Introduction to Sampling Distributions

In the preceding section we said that the sample mean $\bar{x}$ is the point estimator of the population mean μ, and the sample proportion $\bar{p}$ is the point estimator of the population proportion p. For the simple random sample of 30 EAI employees shown in Table 7.2, the point estimate of μ is $\bar{x} = \$51,814$ and the point estimate of p is $\bar{p} = .63$. Suppose we select another simple random sample of 30 EAI employees and obtain the following point estimates:

$$\text{Sample mean: } \bar{x} = \$52,670$$
$$\text{Sample proportion: } \bar{p} = .70$$

Note that different values of $\bar{x}$ and $\bar{p}$ were obtained. Indeed, a second simple random sample of 30 EAI employees cannot be expected to provide the same point estimates as the first sample.

Now, suppose we repeat the process of selecting a simple random sample of 30 EAI employees over and over again, each time computing the values of $\bar{x}$ and $\bar{p}$. Table 7.4

TABLE 7.4 VALUES OF $\bar{x}$ AND $\bar{p}$ FROM 500 SIMPLE RANDOM SAMPLES OF 30 EAI EMPLOYEES

Sample Number	Sample Mean ($\bar{x}$)	Sample Proportion ($\bar{p}$)
1	51,814	.63
2	52,670	.70
3	51,780	.67
4	51,588	.53
.	.	.
.	.	.
.	.	.
500	51,752	.50

TABLE 7.5   FREQUENCY AND RELATIVE FREQUENCY DISTRIBUTIONS OF $\bar{x}$ FROM 500 SIMPLE RANDOM SAMPLES OF 30 EAI EMPLOYEES

Mean Annual Salary ($)	Frequency	Relative Frequency
49,500.00–49,999.99	2	.004
50,000.00–50,499.99	16	.032
50,500.00–50,999.99	52	.104
51,000.00–51,499.99	101	.202
51,500.00–51,999.99	133	.266
52,000.00–52,499.99	110	.220
52,500.00–52,999.99	54	.108
53,000.00–53,499.99	26	.052
53,500.00–53,999.99	6	.012
Totals 500		1.000

contains a portion of the results obtained for 500 simple random samples, and Table 7.5 shows the frequency and relative frequency distributions for the 500 $\bar{x}$ values. Figure 7.4 shows the relative frequency histogram for the $\bar{x}$ values.

In Chapter 5 we defined a random variable as a numerical description of the outcome of an experiment. If we consider the process of selecting a simple random sample as an experiment, the sample mean $\bar{x}$ is the numerical description of the outcome of the experiment. Thus, the sample mean $\bar{x}$ is a random variable. As a result, just like other random variables, $\bar{x}$ has a mean or expected value, a standard deviation, and a probability distribution.

FIGURE 7.4   RELATIVE FREQUENCY HISTOGRAM OF $\bar{x}$ VALUES FROM 500 SIMPLE RANDOM SAMPLES OF SIZE 30 EACH

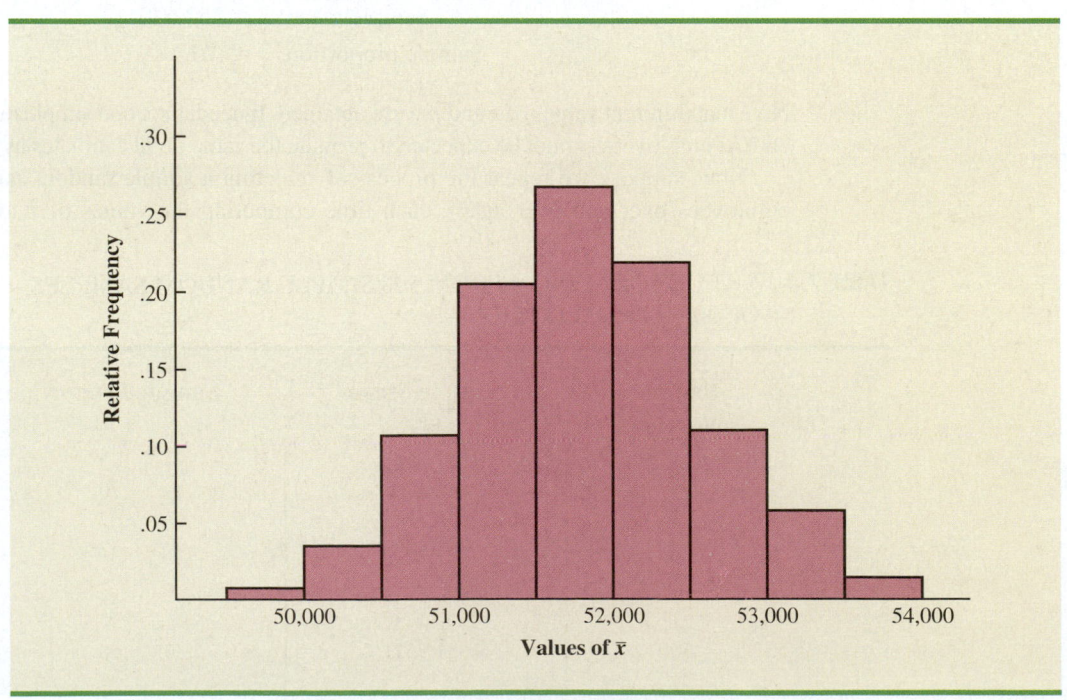

The ability to understand the material in subsequent chapters depends heavily on the ability to understand and use the sampling distributions presented in this chapter.

Because the various possible values of $\bar{x}$ are the result of different simple random samples, the probability distribution of $\bar{x}$ is called the **sampling distribution** of $\bar{x}$. Knowledge of this sampling distribution and its properties will enable us to make probability statements about how close the sample mean $\bar{x}$ is to the population mean μ.

Let us return to Figure 7.4. We would need to enumerate every possible sample of 30 employees and compute each sample mean to completely determine the sampling distribution of $\bar{x}$. However, the histogram of 500 $\bar{x}$ values gives an approximation of this sampling distribution. From the approximation we observe the bell-shaped appearance of the distribution. We note that the largest concentration of the $\bar{x}$ values and the mean of the 500 $\bar{x}$ values is near the population mean $\mu = \$51,800$. We will describe the properties of the sampling distribution of $\bar{x}$ more fully in the next section.

The 500 values of the sample proportion $\bar{p}$ are summarized by the relative frequency histogram in Figure 7.5. As in the case of $\bar{x}$, $\bar{p}$ is a random variable. If every possible sample of size 30 were selected from the population and if a value of $\bar{p}$ were computed for each sample, the resulting probability distribution would be the sampling distribution of $\bar{p}$. The relative frequency histogram of the 500 sample values in Figure 7.5 provides a general idea of the appearance of the sampling distribution of $\bar{p}$.

In practice, we select only one simple random sample from the population. We repeated the sampling process 500 times in this section simply to illustrate that many different samples are possible and that the different samples generate a variety of values for the sample statistics $\bar{x}$ and $\bar{p}$. The probability distribution of any particular sample statistic is called the sampling distribution of the statistic. In Section 7.5 we discuss the

FIGURE 7.5 RELATIVE FREQUENCY HISTOGRAM OF $\bar{p}$ VALUES FROM 500 SIMPLE RANDOM SAMPLES OF SIZE 30 EACH

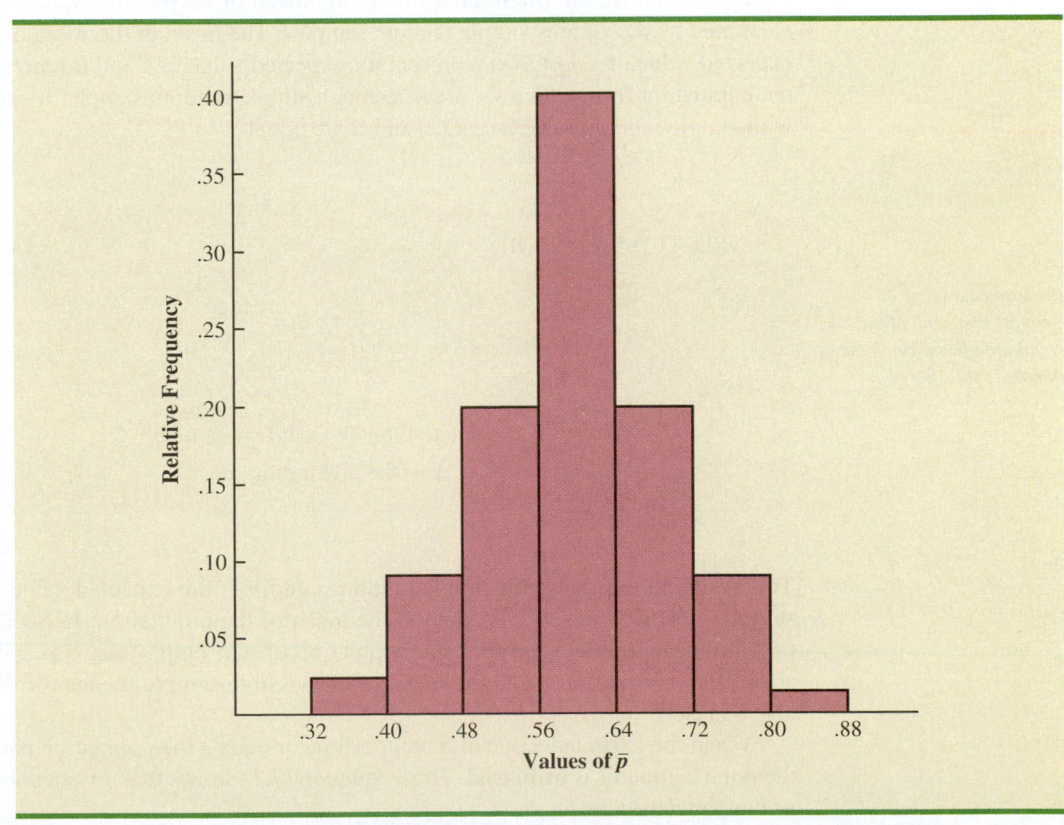

characteristics of the sampling distribution of $\bar{x}$. In Section 7.6 we discuss the characteristics of the sampling distribution of $\bar{p}$.

 ## 7.5 Sampling Distribution of $\bar{x}$

In the previous section we said that the sample mean $\bar{x}$ is a random variable and its probability distribution is called the sampling distribution of $\bar{x}$.

SAMPLING DISTRIBUTION OF $\bar{x}$

The sampling distribution of $\bar{x}$ is the probability distribution of all possible values of the sample mean $\bar{x}$.

This section describes the properties of the sampling distribution of $\bar{x}$. Just as with other probability distributions we studied, the sampling distribution of $\bar{x}$ has an expected value or mean, a standard deviation, and a characteristic shape or form. Let us begin by considering the mean of all possible $\bar{x}$ values, which is referred to as the expected value of $\bar{x}$.

Expected Value of $\bar{x}$

In the EAI sampling problem we saw that different simple random samples result in a variety of values for the sample mean $\bar{x}$. Because many different values of the random variable $\bar{x}$ are possible, we are often interested in the mean of all possible values of $\bar{x}$ that can be generated by the various simple random samples. The mean of the $\bar{x}$ random variable is the expected value of $\bar{x}$. Let $E(\bar{x})$ represent the expected value of $\bar{x}$ and μ represent the mean of the population from which we are selecting a simple random sample. It can be shown that with simple random sampling, $E(\bar{x})$ and μ are equal.

EXPECTED VALUE OF $\bar{x}$

The expected value of $\bar{x}$ equals the mean of the population from which the sample is selected.

$$E(\bar{x}) = \mu \qquad\qquad \textbf{(7.1)}$$

where

$$E(\bar{x}) = \text{the expected value of } \bar{x}$$
$$\mu = \text{the population mean}$$

This result shows that with simple random sampling, the expected value or mean of the sampling distribution of $\bar{x}$ is equal to the mean of the population. In Section 7.1 we saw that the mean annual salary for the population of EAI employees is $\mu = \$51{,}800$. Thus, according to equation (7.1), the mean of all possible sample means for the EAI study is also $51,800.

When the expected value of a point estimator equals the population parameter, we say the point estimator is **unbiased**. Thus, equation (7.1) shows that $\bar{x}$ is an unbiased estimator of the population mean μ.

Standard Deviation of $\bar{x}$

Let us define the standard deviation of the sampling distribution of $\bar{x}$. We will use the following notation.

$$\sigma_{\bar{x}} = \text{the standard deviation of } \bar{x}$$
$$\sigma = \text{the standard deviation of the population}$$
$$n = \text{the sample size}$$
$$N = \text{the population size}$$

It can be shown that the formula for the standard deviation of $\bar{x}$ depends on whether the population is finite or infinite. The two formulas for the standard deviation of $\bar{x}$ follow.

STANDARD DEVIATION OF $\bar{x}$

Finite Population   *Infinite Population*

$$\sigma_{\bar{x}} = \sqrt{\frac{N-n}{N-1}}\left(\frac{\sigma}{\sqrt{n}}\right) \qquad\qquad \sigma_{\bar{x}} = \frac{\sigma}{\sqrt{n}} \qquad\qquad \textbf{(7.2)}$$

In comparing the two formulas in equation (7.2), we see that the factor $\sqrt{(N-n)/(N-1)}$ is required for the finite population case but not for the infinite population case. This factor is commonly referred to as the **finite population correction factor**. In many practical sampling situations, we find that the population involved, although finite, is "large," whereas the sample size is relatively "small." In such cases the finite population correction factor $\sqrt{(N-n)/(N-1)}$ is close to 1. As a result, the difference between the values of the standard deviation of $\bar{x}$ for the finite and infinite population cases becomes negligible. Then, $\sigma_{\bar{x}} = \sigma/\sqrt{n}$ becomes a good approximation to the standard deviation of $\bar{x}$ even though the population is finite. This observation leads to the following general guideline, or rule of thumb, for computing the standard deviation of $\bar{x}$.

USE THE FOLLOWING EXPRESSION TO COMPUTE THE STANDARD DEVIATION OF $\bar{x}$

$$\sigma_{\bar{x}} = \frac{\sigma}{\sqrt{n}} \qquad\qquad \textbf{(7.3)}$$

whenever
1. The population is infinite; or
2. The population is finite *and* the sample size is less than or equal to 5% of the population size; that is, $n/N \leq .05$.

Exercise 17 shows that when $n/N \leq .05$, the finite population correction factor has little effect on the value of $\sigma_{\bar{x}}$.

In cases where $n/N > .05$, the finite population version of formula (7.2) should be used in the computation of $\sigma_{\bar{x}}$. Unless otherwise noted, throughout the text we will assume that the population size is "large," $n/N \leq .05$, and expression (7.3) can be used to compute $\sigma_{\bar{x}}$.

The term standard error *is used throughout statistical inference to refer to the standard deviation of a point estimator.*

To compute $\sigma_{\bar{x}}$, we need to know σ, the standard deviation of the population. To further emphasize the difference between $\sigma_{\bar{x}}$ and σ, we refer to the standard deviation of $\bar{x}$, $\sigma_{\bar{x}}$, as the **standard error** of the mean. In general, the term *standard error* refers to the standard deviation of a point estimator. Later we will see that the value of the standard error of the mean is helpful in determining how far the sample mean may be from the population mean. Let us now return to the EAI example and compute the standard error of the mean associated with simple random samples of 30 EAI employees.

In Section 7.1 we saw that the standard deviation of annual salary for the population of 2500 EAI employees is $\sigma = 4000$. In this case, the population is finite, with $N = 2500$. However, with a sample size of 30, we have $n/N = 30/2500 = .012$. Because the sample size is less than 5% of the population size, we can ignore the finite population correction factor and use equation (7.3) to compute the standard error.

$$\sigma_{\bar{x}} = \frac{\sigma}{\sqrt{n}} = \frac{4000}{\sqrt{30}} = 730.3$$

Form of the Sampling Distribution of $\bar{x}$

The preceding results concerning the expected value and standard deviation for the sampling distribution of $\bar{x}$ are applicable for any population. The final step in identifying the characteristics of the sampling distribution of $\bar{x}$ is to determine the form or shape of the sampling distribution. We will consider two cases: (1) The population has a normal distribution; and (2) the population does not have a normal distribution.

Population has a normal distribution In many situations it is reasonable to assume that the population from which we are selecting a random sample has a normal, or nearly normal, distribution. When the population has a normal distribution, the sampling distribution of $\bar{x}$ is normally distributed for any sample size.

Population does not have a normal distribution When the population from which we are selecting a random sample does not have a normal distribution, the **central limit theorem** is helpful in identifying the shape of the sampling distribution of $\bar{x}$. A statement of the central limit theorem as it applies to the sampling distribution of $\bar{x}$ follows.

CENTRAL LIMIT THEOREM

In selecting random samples of size n from a population, the sampling distribution of the sample mean $\bar{x}$ can be approximated by a *normal distribution* as the sample size becomes large.

Figure 7.6 shows how the central limit theorem works for three different populations; each column refers to one of the populations. The top panel of the figure shows that none of the populations are normally distributed. Population I follows a uniform distribution. Population II is often called the rabbit-eared distribution. It is symmetric, but the more likely values fall in the tails of the distribution. Population III is shaped like the exponential distribution; it is skewed to the right.

The bottom three panels of Figure 7.6 show the shape of the sampling distribution for samples of size $n = 2, n = 5$, and $n = 30$. When the sample size is 2, we see that the shape of each sampling distribution is different from the shape of the corresponding population distribution. For samples of size 5, we see that the shapes of the sampling distributions

FIGURE 7.6   ILLUSTRATION OF THE CENTRAL LIMIT THEOREM
                 FOR THREE POPULATIONS

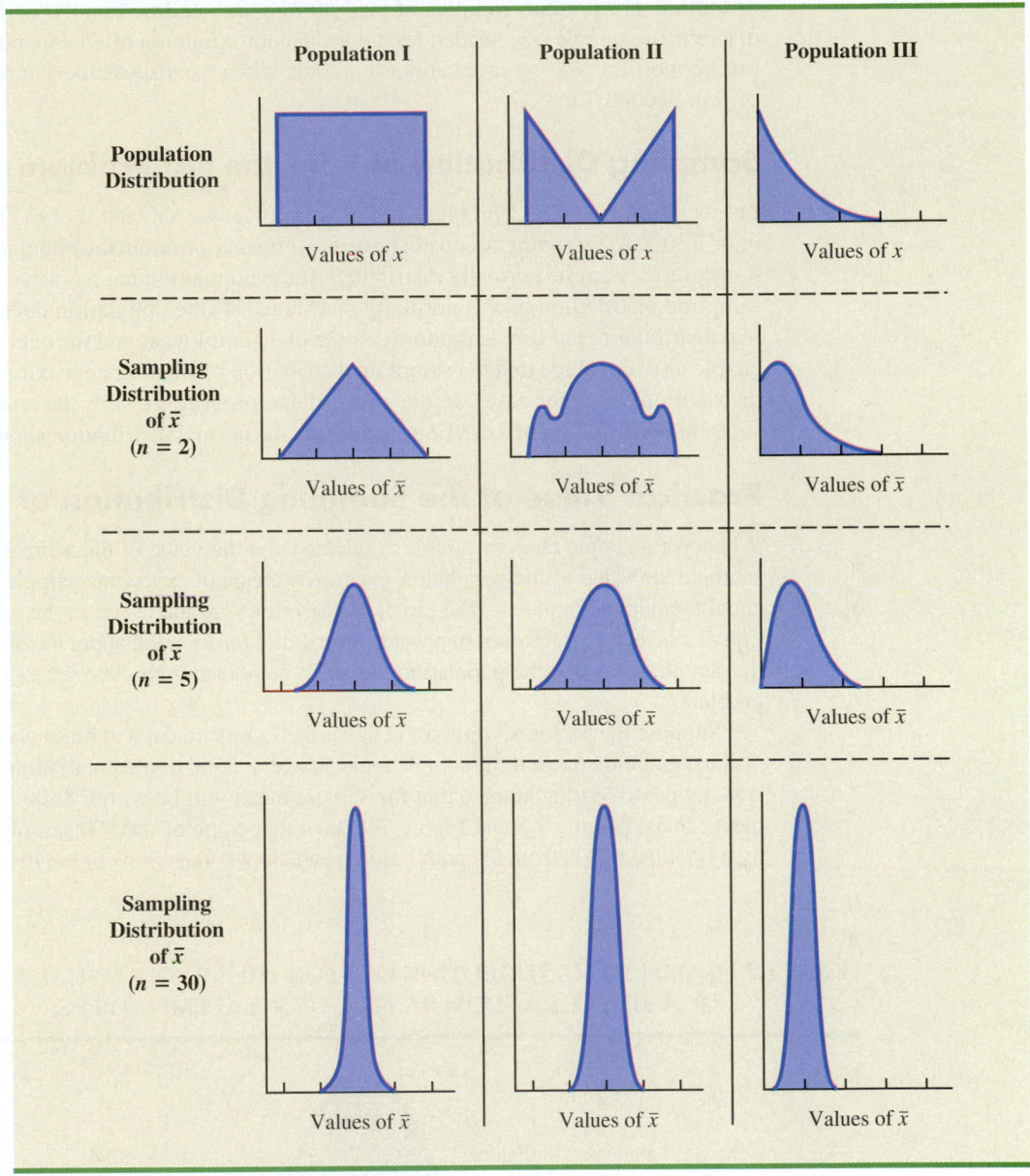

for populations I and II begin to look similar to the shape of a normal distribution. Even though the shape of the sampling distribution for population III begins to look similar to the shape of a normal distribution, some skewness to the right is still present. Finally, for samples of size 30, the shapes of each of the three sampling distributions are approximately normal.

From a practitioner standpoint, we often want to know how large the sample size needs to be before the central limit theorem applies and we can assume that the shape of the sampling distribution is approximately normal. Statistical researchers have investigated this question by studying the sampling distribution of $\bar{x}$ for a variety of populations and a variety of sample sizes. General statistical practice is to assume that, for most applications, the sampling distribution of $\bar{x}$ can be approximated by a normal distribution whenever the sample is size 30 or more. In cases where the population is highly skewed or outliers are present, samples of size 50 may be needed. Finally, if the population is discrete, the sample size needed for a normal approximation often depends on the population proportion. We say more about this issue when we discuss the sampling distribution of $\bar{p}$ in Section 7.6.

Sampling Distribution of $\bar{x}$ for the EAI Problem

Let us return to the EAI problem where we previously showed that $E(\bar{x}) = \$51,800$ and $\sigma_{\bar{x}} = 730.3$. At this point, we do not have any information about the population distribution; it may or may not be normally distributed. If the population has a normal distribution, the sampling distribution of $\bar{x}$ is normally distributed. If the population does not have a normal distribution, the simple random sample of 30 employees and the central limit theorem enable us to conclude that the sampling distribution of $\bar{x}$ can be approximated by a normal distribution. In either case, we are comfortable proceeding with the conclusion that the sampling distribution of $\bar{x}$ can be described by the normal distribution shown in Figure 7.7.

Practical Value of the Sampling Distribution of $\bar{x}$

Whenever a simple random sample is selected and the value of the sample mean is used to estimate the value of the population mean μ, we cannot expect the sample mean to exactly equal the population mean. The practical reason we are interested in the sampling distribution of $\bar{x}$ is that it can be used to provide probability information about the difference between the sample mean and the population mean. To demonstrate this use, let us return to the EAI problem.

Suppose the personnel director believes the sample mean will be an acceptable estimate of the population mean if the sample mean is within $500 of the population mean. However, it is not possible to guarantee that the sample mean will be within $500 of the population mean. Indeed, Table 7.5 and Figure 7.4 show that some of the 500 sample means differed by more than $2000 from the population mean. So we must think of the personnel director's

FIGURE 7.7   SAMPLING DISTRIBUTION OF $\bar{x}$ FOR THE MEAN ANNUAL SALARY
OF A SIMPLE RANDOM SAMPLE OF 30 EAI EMPLOYEES

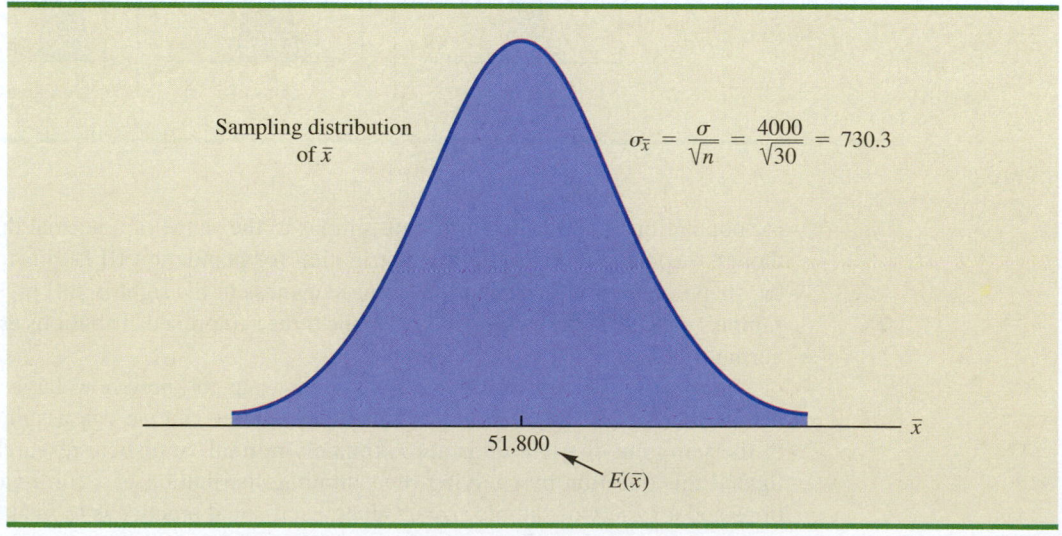

request in probability terms. That is, the personnel director is concerned with the following question: What is the probability that the sample mean computed using a simple random sample of 30 EAI employees will be within $500 of the population mean?

Because we have identified the properties of the sampling distribution of $\bar{x}$ (see Figure 7.7), we will use this distribution to answer the probability question. Refer to the sampling distribution of $\bar{x}$ shown again in Figure 7.8. With a population mean of $51,800, the personnel director wants to know the probability that $\bar{x}$ is between $51,300 and $52,300. This probability is given by the darkly shaded area of the sampling distribution shown in Figure 7.8. Because the sampling distribution is normally distributed, with mean 51,800 and standard error of the mean 730.3, we can use the standard normal probability table to find the area or probability.

We first calculate the z value at the upper endpoint of the interval (52,300) and use the table to find the cumulative probability at that point (left tail area). Then we compute the z value at the lower endpoint of the interval (51,300) and use the table to find the area under the curve to the left of that point (another left tail area). Subtracting the second tail area from the first gives us the desired probability.

At $\bar{x} = 52,300$, we have

$$z = \frac{52,300 - 51,800}{730.30} = .68$$

Referring to the standard normal probability table, we find a cumulative probability (area to the left of $z = .68$) of .7517.

At $\bar{x} = 51,300$, we have

$$z = \frac{51,300 - 51,800}{730.30} = -.68$$

The area under the curve to the left of $z = -.68$ is .2483. Therefore, $P(51,300 \leq \bar{x} \leq 52,300) = P(z \leq .68) - P(z < -.68) = .7517 - .2483 = .5034$.

FIGURE 7.8   PROBABILITY OF A SAMPLE MEAN BEING WITHIN $500
OF THE POPULATION MEAN FOR A SIMPLE RANDOM
SAMPLE OF 30 EAI EMPLOYEES

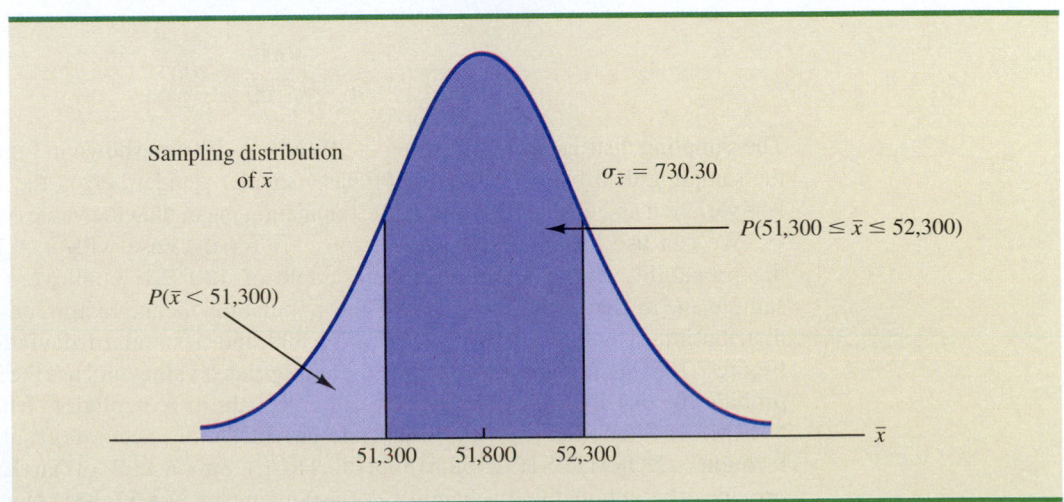

Using Excel's NORM.DIST function is easier and provides more accurate results than using the tables with rounded values for z.

The desired probability can also be computed using Excel's NORM.DIST function. The advantage of using the NORM.DIST function is that we do not have to make a separate computation of the z value. Evaluating the NORM.DIST function at the upper endpoint of the interval provides the cumulative probability at 52,300. Entering the formula =NORM.DIST(52300,51800,730.30,TRUE) into a cell of an Excel worksheet provides .7532 for this cumulative probability. Evaluating the NORM.DIST function at the lower endpoint of the interval provides the area under the curve to the left of 51,300. Entering the formula =NORM.DIST(51300,51800,730.30,TRUE) into a cell of an Excel worksheet provides .2468 for this cumulative probability. The probability of $\bar{x}$ being in the interval from 51,300 to 52,300 is then given by .7532 − .2468 = .5064. We note that this result is slightly different from the probability obtained using the table, because in using the normal table we rounded to two decimal places of accuracy when computing the z value. The result obtained using NORM.DIST is thus more accurate.

The sampling distribution of $\bar{x}$ can be used to provide probability information about how close the sample mean $\bar{x}$ is to the population mean μ.

The preceding computations show that a simple random sample of 30 EAI employees has a .5064 probability of providing a sample mean $\bar{x}$ that is within $500 of the population mean. Thus, there is a $1 - .5064 = .4936$ probability that the sampling error will be more than $500. In other words, a simple random sample of 30 EAI employees has roughly a 50–50 chance of providing a sample mean within the allowable $500. Perhaps a larger sample size should be considered. Let us explore this possibility by considering the relationship between the sample size and the sampling distribution of $\bar{x}$.

Relationship Between the Sample Size and the Sampling Distribution of $\bar{x}$

Suppose that in the EAI sampling problem we select a simple random sample of 100 EAI employees instead of the 30 originally considered. Intuitively, it would seem that with more data provided by the larger sample size, the sample mean based on $n = 100$ should provide a better estimate of the population mean than the sample mean based on $n = 30$. To see how much better, let us consider the relationship between the sample size and the sampling distribution of $\bar{x}$.

First note that $E(\bar{x}) = \mu$ regardless of the sample size. Thus, the mean of all possible values of $\bar{x}$ is equal to the population mean μ regardless of the sample size n. However, note that the standard error of the mean, $\sigma_{\bar{x}} = \sigma/\sqrt{n}$, is related to the square root of the sample size. Whenever the sample size is increased, the standard error of the mean $\sigma_{\bar{x}}$ decreases. With $n = 30$, the standard error of the mean for the EAI problem is 730.3. However, with the increase in the sample size to $n = 100$, the standard error of the mean is decreased to

$$\sigma_{\bar{x}} = \frac{\sigma}{\sqrt{n}} = \frac{4000}{\sqrt{100}} = 400$$

The sampling distributions of $\bar{x}$ with $n = 30$ and $n = 100$ are shown in Figure 7.9. Because the sampling distribution with $n = 100$ has a smaller standard error, the values of $\bar{x}$ have less variation and tend to be closer to the population mean than the values of $\bar{x}$ with $n = 30$.

We can use the sampling distribution of $\bar{x}$ for the case with $n = 100$ to compute the probability that a simple random sample of 100 EAI employees will provide a sample mean that is within $500 of the population mean. In this case the sampling distribution is normal with a mean of 51,800 and a standard deviation of 400 (see Figure 7.10). Again, we could compute the appropriate z values and use the standard normal probability distribution table to make this probability calculation. However, Excel's NORM.DIST function is easier to use and provides more accurate results. Entering the formula =NORM.DIST(52300,51800,400,TRUE) into a cell of an Excel worksheet provides the cumulative probability corresponding to $\bar{x} = 52,300$. The value provided

FIGURE 7.9 A COMPARISON OF THE SAMPLING DISTRIBUTIONS OF $\bar{x}$ FOR SIMPLE RANDOM SAMPLES OF $n = 30$ AND $n = 100$ EAI EMPLOYEES

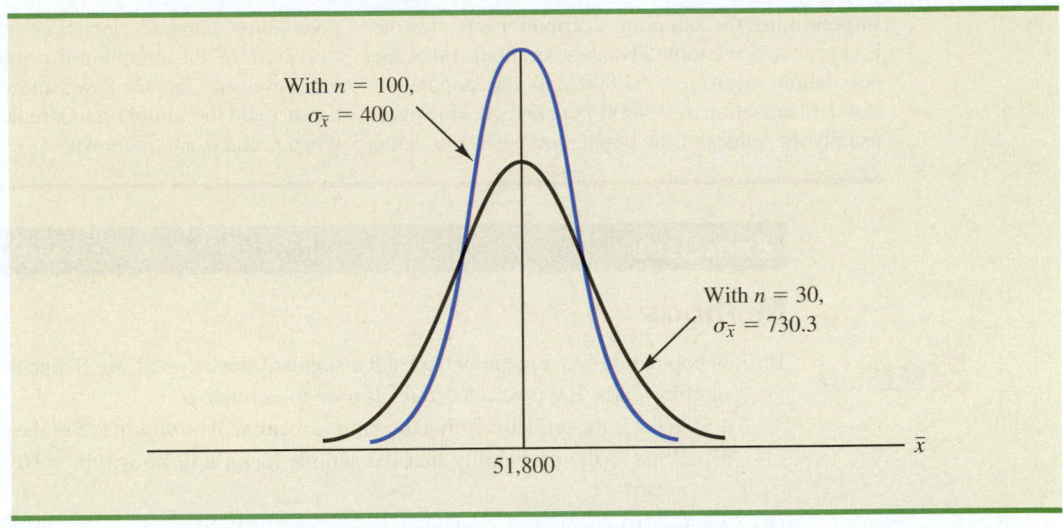

FIGURE 7.10 PROBABILITY OF A SAMPLE MEAN BEING WITHIN $500 OF THE POPULATION MEAN FOR A SIMPLE RANDOM SAMPLE OF 100 EAI EMPLOYEES

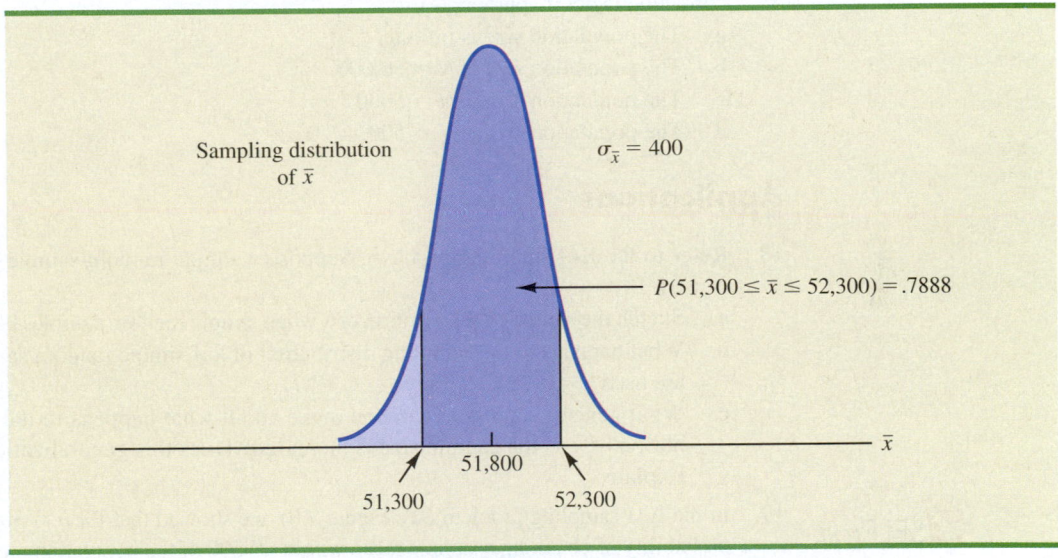

by Excel is .8944. Entering the formula $=$ NORM.DIST (51300,51800,400,TRUE) into a cell of an Excel worksheet provides the cumulative probability corresponding to $\bar{x} = 51{,}300$. The value provided by Excel is .1056. Thus, the probability of $\bar{x}$ being in the interval from 51,300 to 52,300 is given by .8944 $-$ .1056 $=$ .7888. By increasing the sample size from 30 to 100 EAI employees, we increase the probability that the sampling error will be $500 or less; that is, probability of obtaining a sample mean within $500 of the population mean increases from .5064 to .7888.

The important point in this discussion is that as the sample size increases, the standard error of the mean decreases. As a result, a larger sample size will provide a higher probability that the sample mean falls within a specified distance of the population mean.

NOTE AND COMMENT

In presenting the sampling distribution of $\bar{x}$ for the EAI problem, we took advantage of the fact that the population mean $\mu = 51,800$ and the population standard deviation $\sigma = 4000$ were known. However, usually the values of the population mean μ and the population standard deviation σ that are needed to determine the sampling distribution of $\bar{x}$ will be unknown. In Chapter 8 we show how the sample mean $\bar{x}$ and the sample standard deviation s are used when μ and σ are unknown.

Exercises

Methods

15. A population has a mean of 200 and a standard deviation of 50. Suppose a simple random sample of size 100 is selected and $\bar{x}$ is used to estimate μ.
    a. What is the probability that the sample mean will be within ± 5 of the population mean?
    b. What is the probability that the sample mean will be within ± 10 of the population mean?

16. Assume the population standard deviation is $\sigma = 25$. Compute the standard error of the mean, $\sigma_{\bar{x}}$, for sample sizes of 50, 100, 150, and 200. What can you say about the size of the standard error of the mean as the sample size is increased?

17. Suppose a random sample of size 50 is selected from a population with $\sigma = 10$. Find the value of the standard error of the mean in each of the following cases (use the finite population correction factor if appropriate).
    a. The population size is infinite.
    b. The population size is $N = 50,000$.
    c. The population size is $N = 5000$.
    d. The population size is $N = 500$.

Applications

18. Refer to the EAI sampling problem. Suppose a simple random sample of 60 employees is used.
    a. Sketch the sampling distribution of $\bar{x}$ when simple random samples of size 60 are used.
    b. What happens to the sampling distribution of $\bar{x}$ if simple random samples of size 120 are used?
    c. What general statement can you make about what happens to the sampling distribution of $\bar{x}$ as the sample size is increased? Does this generalization seem logical? Explain.

19. In the EAI sampling problem (see Figure 7.8), we showed that for $n = 30$, there was .5064 probability of obtaining a sample mean within $\pm\$500$ of the population mean.
    a. What is the probability that $\bar{x}$ is within $\$500$ of the population mean if a sample of size 60 is used?
    b. Answer part (a) for a sample of size 120.

20. *Barron's* reported that the average number of weeks an individual is unemployed is 17.5 weeks. Assume that for the population of all unemployed individuals the population mean length of unemployment is 17.5 weeks and that the population standard deviation is 4 weeks. Suppose you would like to select a random sample of 50 unemployed individuals for a follow-up study.
    a. Show the sampling distribution of $\bar{x}$, the sample mean average for a sample of 50 unemployed individuals.
    b. What is the probability that a simple random sample of 50 unemployed individuals will provide a sample mean within 1 week of the population mean?

c.   What is the probability that a simple random sample of 50 unemployed individuals will provide a sample mean within 1/2 week of the population mean?

21.   The average full-sized front-loading Energy Star clothes washer uses 15 gallons of water per load (greenbuildingadvisor.com, December 4, 2015). Assume that the population standard deviation for the number of gallons of water used to wash a load by these machines is 3.0.

a.   What is the probability that a random sample of 90 loads washed in a full-sized front-loading Energy Star clothes washer will provide a sample mean gallons of water used that is within one-half gallon of the population mean of 15 gallons?

b.   What is the probability that a random sample of 50 loads washed in a full-sized front-loading Energy Star clothes washer will provide a sample mean gallons of water used that is at least three-quarters of a gallon greater than the population mean of 15 gallons?

c.   What is the probability that a random sample of 75 loads washed in a full-sized front-loading Energy Star clothes washer will provide a sample mean gallons of water used that is no more than one-quarter of a gallon less than the population mean of 15 gallons?

22.   *The Wall Street Journal* reported that 33% of taxpayers with adjusted gross incomes between $30,000 and $60,000 itemized deductions on their federal income tax return. The mean amount of deductions for this population of taxpayers was $16,642. Assume the standard deviation is $\sigma = \$2400$.

a.   What is the probability that a sample of taxpayers from this income group who have itemized deductions will show a sample mean within $200 of the population mean for each of the following sample sizes: 30, 50, 100, and 400?

b.   What is the advantage of a larger sample size when attempting to estimate the population mean?

23.   The Economic Policy Institute periodically issues reports on wages of entry-level workers. The institute reported that entry-level wages for male college graduates were $21.68 per hour and for female college graduates were $18.80 per hour in 2011 (Economic Policy Institute website, March 30, 2012). Assume the standard deviation for male graduates is $2.30, and for female graduates it is $2.05.

a.   What is the probability that a sample of 50 male graduates will provide a sample mean within $.50 of the population mean, $21.68?

b.   What is the probability that a sample of 50 female graduates will provide a sample mean within $.50 of the population mean, $18.80?

c.   In which of the preceding two cases, part (a) or part (b), do we have a higher probability of obtaining a sample estimate within $.50 of the population mean? Why?

d.   What is the probability that a sample of 120 female graduates will provide a sample mean more than $.30 below the population mean?

24.   According to the Current Results website, the state of California has a mean annual rainfall of 22 inches, whereas the state of New York has a mean annual rainfall of 42 inches. Assume that the standard deviation for both states is 4 inches. A sample of 30 years of rainfall for California and a sample of 45 years of rainfall for New York have been taken.

a.   Show the probability distribution of the sample mean annual rainfall for California.

b.   What is the probability that the sample mean is within 1 inch of the population mean for California?

c.   What is the probability that the sample mean is within 1 inch of the population mean for New York?

d.   In which case, part (b) or part (c), is the probability of obtaining a sample mean within 1 inch of the population mean greater? Why?

25. The mean preparation fee H&R Block charged retail customers in 2012 was $183 (*The Wall Street Journal*, March 7, 2012). Use this price as the population mean and assume the population standard deviation of preparation fees is $50.
    a. What is the probability that the mean price for a sample of 30 H&R Block retail customers is within $8 of the population mean?
    b. What is the probability that the mean price for a sample of 50 H&R Block retail customers is within $8 of the population mean?
    c. What is the probability that the mean price for a sample of 100 H&R Block retail customers is within $8 of the population mean?
    d. Which, if any, of the sample sizes in parts (a), (b), and (c) would you recommend to have at least a .95 probability that the sample mean is within $8 of the population mean?

26. To estimate the mean age for a population of 4000 employees, a simple random sample of 40 employees is selected.
    a. Would you use the finite population correction factor in calculating the standard error of the mean? Explain.
    b. If the population standard deviation is $\sigma = 8.2$ years, compute the standard error both with and without the finite population correction factor. What is the rationale for ignoring the finite population correction factor whenever $n/N \leq .05$?
    c. What is the probability that the sample mean age of the employees will be within ± 2 years of the population mean age?

7.6   Sampling Distribution of $\bar{p}$

The sample proportion $\bar{p}$ is the point estimator of the population proportion p. The formula for computing the sample proportion is

$$\bar{p} = \frac{x}{n}$$

where

   x = the number of elements in the sample that possess the characteristic of interest
   n = sample size

As noted in Section 7.4, the sample proportion $\bar{p}$ is a random variable and its probability distribution is called the sampling distribution of $\bar{p}$.

SAMPLING DISTRIBUTION OF $\bar{p}$

The sampling distribution of $\bar{p}$ is the probability distribution of all possible values of the sample proportion $\bar{p}$.

To determine how close the sample proportion $\bar{p}$ is to the population proportion p, we need to understand the properties of the sampling distribution of $\bar{p}$: the expected value of $\bar{p}$, the standard deviation of $\bar{p}$, and the shape or form of the sampling distribution of $\bar{p}$.

Expected Value of $\bar{p}$

The expected value of $\bar{p}$, the mean of all possible values of $\bar{p}$, is equal to the population proportion p.

EXPECTED VALUE OF $\bar{p}$

$$E(\bar{p}) = p \tag{7.4}$$

---

where

$$E(\bar{p}) = \text{the expected value of } \bar{p}$$
$$p = \text{the population proportion}$$

Because $E(\bar{p}) = p$, $\bar{p}$ is an unbiased estimator of p. Recall from Section 7.1 we noted that $p = .60$ for the EAI population, where p is the proportion of the population of employees who participated in the company's management training program. Thus, the expected value of $\bar{p}$ for the EAI sampling problem is .60.

Standard Deviation of $\bar{p}$

Just as we found for the standard deviation of $\bar{x}$, the standard deviation of $\bar{p}$ depends on whether the population is finite or infinite. The two formulas for computing the standard deviation of $\bar{p}$ follow.

STANDARD DEVIATION OF $\bar{p}$

$$\qquad\qquad \textit{Finite Population} \qquad\qquad\qquad \textit{Infinite Population}$$

$$\sigma_{\bar{p}} = \sqrt{\frac{N-n}{N-1}} \sqrt{\frac{p(1-p)}{n}} \qquad\qquad \sigma_{\bar{p}} = \sqrt{\frac{p(1-p)}{n}} \qquad\qquad \textbf{(7.5)}$$

Comparing the two formulas in equation (7.5), we see that the only difference is the use of the finite population correction factor $\sqrt{(N-n)/(N-1)}$.

As was the case with the sample mean $\bar{x}$, the difference between the expressions for the finite population and the infinite population becomes negligible if the size of the finite population is large in comparison to the sample size. We follow the same rule of thumb that we recommended for the sample mean. That is, if the population is finite with $n/N \leq .05$, we will use $\sigma_{\bar{p}} = \sqrt{p(1-p)/n}$. However, if the population is finite with $n/N > .05$, the finite population correction factor should be used. Again, unless specifically noted, throughout the text we will assume that the population size is large in relation to the sample size and thus the finite population correction factor is unnecessary.

In Section 7.5 we used the term *standard error of the mean* to refer to the standard deviation of $\bar{x}$. We stated that in general the term *standard error* refers to the standard deviation of a point estimator. Thus, for proportions we use *standard error of the proportion* to refer to the standard deviation of $\bar{p}$. Let us now return to the EAI example and compute the standard error of the proportion associated with simple random samples of 30 EAI employees.

For the EAI study we know that the population proportion of employees who participated in the management training program is $p = .60$. With $n/N = 30/2500 = .012$, we can ignore the finite population correction factor when we compute the standard error of the proportion. For the simple random sample of 30 employees, $\sigma_{\bar{p}}$ is

$$\sigma_{\bar{p}} = \sqrt{\frac{p(1-p)}{n}} = \sqrt{\frac{.60(1-.60)}{30}} = .0894$$

Form of the Sampling Distribution of $\bar{p}$

Now that we know the mean and standard deviation of the sampling distribution of $\bar{p}$, the final step is to determine the form or shape of the sampling distribution. The sample proportion is $\bar{p} = x/n$. For a simple random sample from a large population, the value of x is a binomial random variable indicating the number of elements in the sample with the characteristic of interest. Because n is a constant, the probability of x/n is the same as the binomial probability of x, which means that the sampling distribution of $\bar{p}$ is also a discrete probability distribution and that the probability for each value of x/n is the same as the probability of x.

Statisticians have shown that a binomial distribution can be approximated by a normal distribution whenever the sample size is large enough to satisfy the following two conditions:

$$np \geq 5 \quad \text{and} \quad n(1 - p) \geq 5$$

Assuming these two conditions are satisfied, the probability distribution of x in the sample proportion, $\bar{p} = x/n$, can be approximated by a normal distribution. And because n is a constant, the sampling distribution of $\bar{p}$ can also be approximated by a normal distribution. This approximation is stated as follows:

> The sampling distribution of $\bar{p}$ can be approximated by a normal distribution whenever $np \geq 5$ and $n(1 - p) \geq 5$.

In practical applications, when an estimate of a population proportion is desired, we find that sample sizes are almost always large enough to permit the use of a normal approximation for the sampling distribution of $\bar{p}$.

Recall that for the EAI sampling problem we know that the population proportion of employees who participated in the training program is $p = .60$. With a simple random sample of size 30, we have $np = 30(.60) = 18$ and $n(1 - p) = 30(.40) = 12$. Thus, the sampling distribution of $\bar{p}$ can be approximated by the normal distribution shown in Figure 7.11.

FIGURE 7.11   SAMPLING DISTRIBUTION OF $\bar{p}$ FOR THE PROPORTION OF EAI EMPLOYEES WHO PARTICIPATED IN THE MANAGEMENT TRAINING PROGRAM

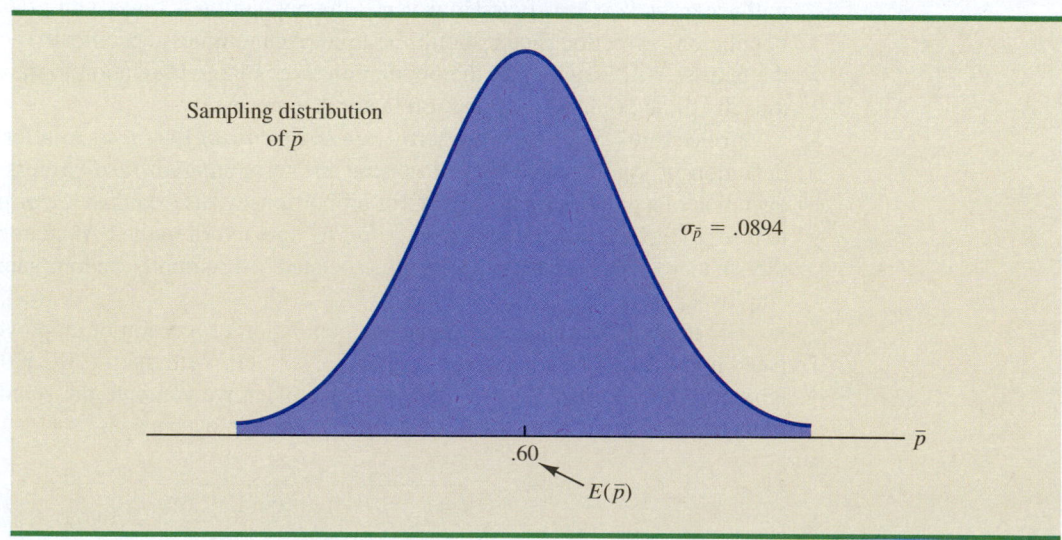

Practical Value of the Sampling Distribution of $\bar{p}$

The practical value of the sampling distribution of $\bar{p}$ is that it can be used to provide probability information about the difference between the sample proportion and the population proportion. For instance, suppose that in the EAI problem the personnel director wants to know the probability of obtaining a value of $\bar{p}$ that is within .05 of the population proportion of EAI employees who participated in the training program. That is, what is the probability of obtaining a sample with a sample proportion $\bar{p}$ between .55 and .65? The darkly shaded area in Figure 7.12 shows this probability. Using the fact that the sampling distribution of $\bar{p}$ can be approximated by a normal probability distribution with a mean of .60 and a standard error of $\sigma_{\bar{p}} = .0894$, we can use Excel's NORM.DIST function to make this calculation. Entering the formula =NORM.DIST(.65,.60,.0894,TRUE) into a cell of an Excel worksheet provides the cumulative probability corresponding to $\bar{p} = .65$. The value calculated by Excel is .7120. Entering the formula =NORM.DIST(.55,.60,.0894,TRUE) into a cell of an Excel worksheet provides the cumulative probability corresponding to $\bar{p} = .55$. The value calculated by Excel is .2880. Thus, the probability of $\bar{p}$ being in the interval from .55 to .65 is given by $.7120 - .2880 = .4240$.

If we consider increasing the sample size to $n = 100$, the standard error of the proportion becomes

$$\sigma_{\bar{p}} = \sqrt{\frac{.60(1 - .60)}{100}} = .0490$$

With a sample size of 100 EAI employees, the probability of the sample proportion having a value within .05 of the population proportion can now be computed. Because the sampling distribution is approximately normal, with mean .60 and standard deviation .0490, we can use Excel's NORM.DIST function to make this calculation. Entering the formula =NORM.DIST(.65,.60,.0490,TRUE) into a cell of an Excel worksheet provides the cumulative probability corresponding to $\bar{p} = .65$. The value calculated by Excel is .8462. Entering the formula =NORM.DIST(.55,.60,.0490,TRUE) into a cell of an Excel worksheet provides the cumulative probability corresponding to $\bar{p} = .55$. The value calculated by Excel is .1538. Thus, the probability of $\bar{p}$ being in the interval from .55 to .65 is given by $.8462 - .1538 = .6924$. Increasing the sample size increases the probability that the sampling error will be less than or equal to .05 by .2684 (from .4240 to .6924).

FIGURE 7.12 PROBABILITY OF OBTAINING $\bar{p}$ BETWEEN .55 AND .65

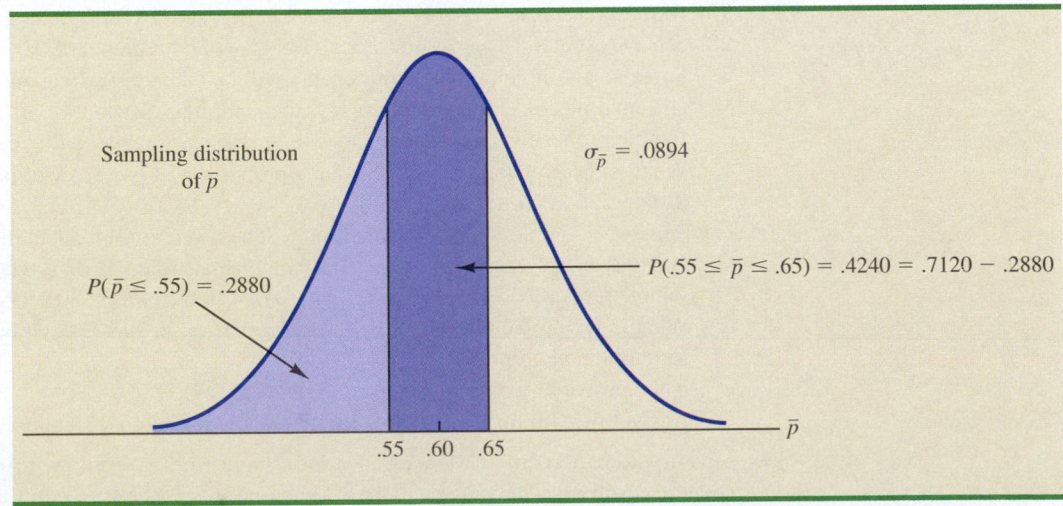

Exercises

Methods

27. A random sample of size 100 is selected from a population with $p = .40$.
    a. What is the expected value of $\bar{p}$?
    b. What is the standard error of $\bar{p}$?
    c. Show the sampling distribution of $\bar{p}$.
    d. What does the sampling distribution of $\bar{p}$ show?

 **SELF**test

28. A population proportion is .40. A random sample of size 200 will be taken and the sample proportion $\bar{p}$ will be used to estimate the population proportion.
    a. What is the probability that the sample proportion will be within $\pm.03$ of the population proportion?
    b. What is the probability that the sample proportion will be within $\pm.05$ of the population proportion?

29. Assume that the population proportion is .55. Compute the standard error of the proportion, $\sigma_{\bar{p}}$, for sample sizes of 100, 200, 500, and 1000. What can you say about the size of the standard error of the proportion as the sample size is increased?

30. The population proportion is .30. What is the probability that a sample proportion will be within $\pm.04$ of the population proportion for each of the following sample sizes?
    a. $n = 100$
    b. $n = 200$
    c. $n = 500$
    d. $n = 1000$
    e. What is the advantage of a larger sample size?

Applications

 **SELF**test

31. The president of Doerman Distributors, Inc. believes that 30% of the firm's orders come from first-time customers. A random sample of 100 orders will be used to estimate the proportion of first-time customers.
    a. Assume that the president is correct and $p = .30$. What is the sampling distribution of $\bar{p}$ for this study?
    b. What is the probability that the sample proportion $\bar{p}$ will be between .20 and .40?
    c. What is the probability that the sample proportion will be between .25 and .35?

32. *The Wall Street Journal* reported that the age at first startup for 55% of entrepreneurs was 29 years or less and the age at first startup for 45% of entrepreneurs was 30 years or more.
    a. Suppose a sample of 200 entrepreneurs will be taken to learn about the most important qualities of entrepreneurs. Show the sampling distribution of $\bar{p}$ where $\bar{p}$ is the sample proportion of entrepreneurs whose first startup was at 29 years of age or less.
    b. What is the probability that the sample proportion in part (a) will be within $\pm.05$ of its population proportion?
    c. Suppose a sample of 200 entrepreneurs will be taken to learn about the most important qualities of entrepreneurs. Show the sampling distribution of $\bar{p}$ where $\bar{p}$ is now the sample proportion of entrepreneurs whose first startup was at 30 years of age or more.
    d. What is the probability that the sample proportion in part (c) will be within $\pm.05$ of its population proportion?
    e. Is the probability different in parts (b) and (d)? Why?
    f. Answer part (b) for a sample of size 400. Is the probability smaller? Why?

33. Seventy two percent of American adults have read a book within the past year (pewresearch.org, December 3, 2014). Assume this is the true population proportion

and that you plan to take a sample survey of 540 American adults to further investigate their behavior.

a. Show the sampling distribution of $\bar{p}$, the proportion of your sample respondents who have read a book in the past year.

b. What is the probability that your survey will provide a sample proportion within $\pm.03$ of the population proportion?

c. What is the probability that your survey will provide a sample proportion within $\pm.015$ of the population proportion?

34. According to *Reader's Digest*, 42% of primary care doctors think their patients receive unnecessary medical care.

a. Suppose a sample of 300 primary care doctors was taken. Show the sampling distribution of the proportion of the doctors who think their patients receive unnecessary medical care.

b. What is the probability that the sample proportion will be within $\pm.03$ of the population proportion?

c. What is the probability that the sample proportion will be within $\pm.05$ of the population proportion?

d. What would be the effect of taking a larger sample on the probabilities in parts (b) and (c)? Why?

35. Thirty-six percent of all Americans drink bottled water more than once a week (Natural Resources Defense Council, December 4, 2015). Suppose you have been hired by the Natural Resources Defense Council to investigate bottled water consumption in St. Paul. You plan to select a sample of St. Paulites to estimate the proportion who drink bottled water more than once a week. Assume the population proportion of St. Paulites who drink bottled water more than once a week is .36, the same as the overall proportion of Americans who drink bottled water more than once a week.

a. Suppose you select a sample of 540 St. Paulites. Show the sampling distribution of $\bar{p}$.

b. Based upon a sample of 540 St. Paulites, what is the probability that the sample proportion will be within .04 of the population proportion?

c. Suppose you select a sample of 200 St. Paulites. Show the sampling distribution of $\bar{p}$.

d. Based upon the smaller sample of only 200 St. Paulites, what is the probability that the sample proportion will be within .04 of the population proportion?

e. As measured by the increase in probability, how much do you gain in precision by taking the larger sample in parts (a) and (b) rather than the smaller sample in parts (c) and (d)?

36. The Grocery Manufacturers of America reported that 76% of consumers read the ingredients listed on a product's label. Assume the population proportion is $p = .76$ and a sample of 400 consumers is selected from the population.

a. Show the sampling distribution of the sample proportion $\bar{p}$, where $\bar{p}$ is the proportion of the sampled consumers who read the ingredients listed on a product's label.

b. What is the probability that the sample proportion will be within $\pm.03$ of the population proportion?

c. Answer part (b) for a sample of 750 consumers.

37. The Food Marketing Institute shows that 17% of households spend more than $100 per week on groceries. Assume the population proportion is $p = .17$ and a simple random sample of 800 households will be selected from the population.

a. Show the sampling distribution of $\bar{p}$, the sample proportion of households spending more than $100 per week on groceries.

b. What is the probability that the sample proportion will be within $\pm.02$ of the population proportion?

c. Answer part (b) for a sample of 1600 households.

Other Sampling Methods

This section provides a brief introduction to survey sampling methods other than simple random sampling.

We described simple random sampling as a procedure for sampling from a finite population and discussed the properties of the sampling distributions of $\bar{x}$ and $\bar{p}$ when simple random sampling is used. Other methods such as stratified random sampling, cluster sampling, and systematic sampling provide advantages over simple random sampling in some of these situations. In this section we briefly introduce these alternative sampling methods.

Stratified Random Sampling

Stratified random sampling works best when the variance among elements in each stratum is relatively small.

In **stratified random sampling**, the elements in the population are first divided into groups called *strata,* such that each element in the population belongs to one and only one stratum. The basis for forming the strata, such as department, location, age, industry type, and so on, is at the discretion of the designer of the sample. However, the best results are obtained when the elements within each stratum are as much alike as possible. Figure 7.13 is a diagram of a population divided into *H* strata.

   After the strata are formed, a simple random sample is taken from each stratum. Formulas are available for combining the results for the individual stratum samples into one estimate of the population parameter of interest. The value of stratified random sampling depends on how homogeneous the elements are within the strata. If elements within strata are alike, the strata will have low variances. Thus relatively small sample sizes can be used to obtain good estimates of the strata characteristics. If strata are homogeneous, the stratified random sampling procedure provides results just as precise as those of simple random sampling by using a smaller total sample size.

Cluster Sampling

Cluster sampling works best when each cluster provides a small-scale representation of the population.

In **cluster sampling**, the elements in the population are first divided into separate groups called *clusters*. Each element of the population belongs to one and only one cluster (see Figure 7.14). A simple random sample of the clusters is then taken. All elements within each sampled cluster form the sample. Cluster sampling tends to provide the best results when the elements within the clusters are not alike. In the ideal case, each cluster is a representative small-scale version of the entire population. The value of cluster sampling depends on how representative each cluster is of the entire population. If all clusters are alike in this regard, sampling a small number of clusters will provide good estimates of the population parameters.

FIGURE 7.13   DIAGRAM FOR STRATIFIED RANDOM SAMPLING

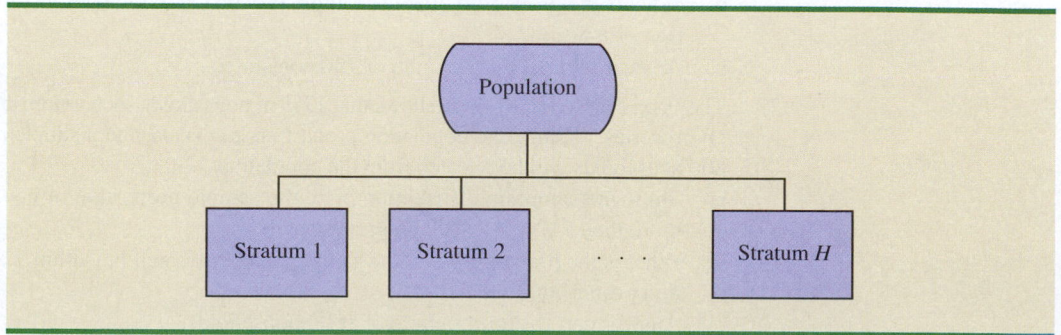

FIGURE 7.14   DIAGRAM FOR CLUSTER SAMPLING

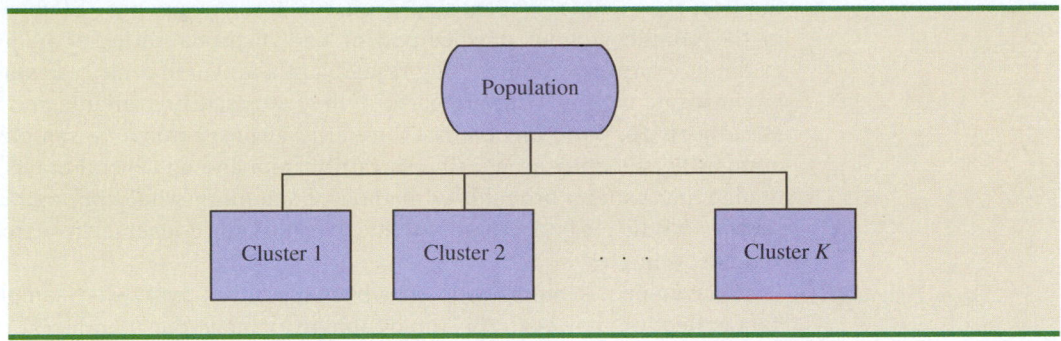

One of the primary applications of cluster sampling is area sampling, where clusters are city blocks or other well-defined areas. Cluster sampling generally requires a larger total sample size than either simple random sampling or stratified random sampling. However, it can result in cost savings because when an interviewer is sent to a sampled cluster (e.g., a city-block location), many sample observations can be obtained in a relatively short time. Hence, a larger sample size may be obtainable with a significantly lower total cost.

Systematic Sampling

In some sampling situations, especially those with large populations, it is time-consuming to select a simple random sample by first finding a random number and then counting or searching through the list of the population until the corresponding element is found. An alternative to simple random sampling is **systematic sampling**. For example, if a sample size of 50 is desired from a population containing 5000 elements, we will sample one element for every $5000/50 = 100$ elements in the population. A systematic sample for this case involves selecting randomly one of the first 100 elements from the population list. Other sample elements are identified by starting with the first sampled element and then selecting every 100th element that follows in the population list. In effect, the sample of 50 is identified by moving systematically through the population and identifying every 100th element after the first randomly selected element. The sample of 50 usually will be easier to identify in this way than it would be if simple random sampling were used. Because the first element selected is a random choice, a systematic sample is usually assumed to have the properties of a simple random sample. This assumption is especially applicable when the list of elements in the population is a random ordering of the elements.

Convenience Sampling

The sampling methods discussed thus far are referred to as *probability sampling* techniques. Elements selected from the population have a known probability of being included in the sample. The advantage of probability sampling is that the sampling distribution of the appropriate sample statistic generally can be identified. Formulas such as the ones for simple random sampling presented in this chapter can be used to determine the properties of the sampling distribution. Then the sampling distribution can be used to make probability statements about the error associated with using the sample results to make inferences about the population.

Convenience sampling is a *nonprobability sampling* technique. As the name implies, the sample is identified primarily by convenience. Elements are included in the sample without prespecified or known probabilities of being selected. For example, a professor conducting research at a university may use student volunteers to constitute a sample simply because they are readily available and will participate as subjects for little or no cost. Similarly, an inspector may sample a shipment of oranges by selecting oranges haphazardly from among several crates. Labeling each orange and using a probability method of sampling would be impractical. Samples such as wildlife captures and volunteer panels for consumer research are also convenience samples.

Convenience samples have the advantage of relatively easy sample selection and data collection; however, it is impossible to evaluate the "goodness" of the sample in terms of its representativeness of the population. A convenience sample may provide good results or it may not; no statistically justified procedure allows a probability analysis and inference about the quality of the sample results. Sometimes researchers apply statistical methods designed for probability samples to a convenience sample, arguing that the convenience sample can be treated as though it were a probability sample. However, this argument cannot be supported, and we should be cautious in interpreting the results of convenience samples that are used to make inferences about populations.

Judgment Sampling

One additional nonprobability sampling technique is **judgment sampling**. In this approach, the person most knowledgeable on the subject of the study selects elements of the population that he or she feels are most representative of the population. Often this method is a relatively easy way of selecting a sample. For example, a reporter may sample two or three senators, judging that those senators reflect the general opinion of all senators. However, the quality of the sample results depends on the judgment of the person selecting the sample. Again, great caution is warranted in drawing conclusions based on judgment samples used to make inferences about populations.

NOTE AND COMMENT

We recommend using probability sampling methods when sampling from finite populations: simple random sampling, stratified random sampling, cluster sampling, or systematic sampling. For these methods, formulas are available for evaluating the "goodness" of the sample results in terms of the closeness of the results to the population parameters being estimated. An evaluation of the goodness cannot be made with convenience or judgment sampling. Thus, great care should be used in interpreting the results based on nonprobability sampling methods.

7.8 Practical Advice: Big Data and Errors in Sampling

The purpose of collecting a sample is to make inferences and answer research questions about a population. Therefore, it is important that the sample look like, or be representative of, the population being investigated. In practice, a sample may fail to be representative of the population of interest because of sampling error and/or nonsampling error.

Sampling Error

Whenever we use a sample to estimate the value of a population parameter, it is highly unlikely that the value of the sample statistic will be equal to the population parameter being estimated. For example, we would not expect the sample mean $\bar{x}$ to be exactly equal to the population mean μ. The difference between the value of the sample statistic and the value of the corresponding population parameter is called the **sampling error**. If repeated independent random samples of the same size are collected from the population of interest using any of the four previously discussed probability sampling methods (simple random sampling, stratified random sampling, cluster sampling, or systematic sampling), on average the samples will be representative of the population.

However, the use of random sampling does not ensure that any single sample will be representative of the population of interest. As discussed in the introduction to this chapter, sampling error is unavoidable when collecting a random sample; it is the risk we must accept when we chose to collect a random sample rather than incur the costs associated with taking a census of the population.

Note that the standard errors of the sampling distributions of the sample mean $\bar{x}$ (shown in formula 7.2) and the sample proportion of $\bar{p}$ (shown in formula 7.5) reflect the potential for sampling error when using sample data to estimate the population mean μ and the population proportion p, respectively. As the sample size increases, the standard errors of these sampling distributions decrease. Because these standard errors reflect the potential for sampling error when using sample data to estimate the population mean μ and the population proportion p, we see that for an extremely large sample there may be little potential for sampling error.

For example, consider the online news service PenningtonDailyTimes.com (PDT). PDT's primary source of revenue is the sale of advertising. Because prospective advertisers are willing to pay a premium to advertise on websites that have long visit times, PDT's management is keenly interested in the amount of time customers spend during their visits to PDT's website. Based on historical data, PDT assumes $\sigma = 20$ seconds for the population standard deviation of the times spent by customers when they visit PDT's website. Table 7.6 shows how the standard error of the sampling distribution of the sample mean time spent by customers when they visit PDT's website decreases as the sample size increases when $\sigma = 20$.

PDT could also collect information from this sample on whether a visitor to its website clicked on any of the ads featured on the website. From its historical data, PDT knows that 50% of visitors to its website clicked on an ad featured on the website. Based upon this data, PDT now assumes a known value of $p = .50$. Table 7.7 shows how the standard error of the sampling distribution of the proportion of the sample that clicked on any of the ads featured on PenningtonDailyTimes.com decreases as the sample size increases when $p = .50$.

The PDT example illustrates the relationship between standard errors and the sample size. We see in Table 7.6 that the standard error of the sample mean decreases as the sample size increases. For a sample of $n = 10$, the standard error of the sample mean is 6.32456; when we increase the sample size to $n = 100,000$, the standard error of the sample mean decreases to 0.06325; and at a sample size of $n = 1,000,000,000$, the standard error of the sample mean decreases to only 0.00063. In Table 7.7 we see that the standard error of the sample proportion also decreases as the sample size increases. For a sample of $n = 10$, the standard error of the sample proportion is .15811; when we increase the sample size to $n = 100,000$, the standard error of the sample proportion decreases to .00158; and at a sample size of $n = 1,000,000,000$, the standard error of the sample mean decreases to only .00002. In both instances, the standard error when $n = 1,000,000,000$ is only *one ten thousandth of the standard error when n = 10!*

A sample of one million or more visitors might seem unrealistic, but keep in mind that amazon.com had over 91 million visitors in March of 2016 (quantcast.com, May 13, 2016).

TABLE 7.6 STANDARD ERROR OF THE SAMPLE MEAN $\bar{x}$ AT VARIOUS SAMPLE SIZES n

Sample Size n	Standard Error $\sigma_{\bar{x}} = \sigma/\sqrt{n}$
10	6.32456
100	2.00000
500	0.89443
1,000	0.63246
10,000	0.20000
100,000	0.06325
1,000,000	0.02000
10,000,000	0.00632
100,000,000	0.00200
1,000,000,000	0.00063

TABLE 7.7 STANDARD ERROR OF THE SAMPLE PROPORTION $\bar{p}$ AT VARIOUS SAMPLE SIZES n

Sample Size n	Standard Error $\sigma_{\bar{p}} = \sqrt{p(1-p)/n}$
10	.15811
100	.05000
500	.02236
1,000	.01581
10,000	.00500
100,000	.00158
1,000,000	.00050
10,000,000	.00016
100,000,000	.00005
1,000,000,000	.00002

Nonsampling Error

The standard error of a sampling distribution decreases as the sample size n increases because a larger sample tends to better represent the population from which it has been drawn. However, this does not mean that we can conclude that an extremely large sample will always provide reliable information about the population of interest; this is because sampling error is not the sole reason a sample may fail to represent the target population. Deviations of the sample from the population that occur for reasons other than random sampling are referred to as **nonsampling errors**. Nonsampling errors are introduced into the sample data systematically and can occur for a variety of reasons.

Nonsampling error can occur in a sample or a census.

For example, the data in the sample may not have been drawn from the population of interest. From whom should PDT collect its data? Should it collect data on current visits to PenningtonDailyTimes.com? Should it attempt to attract new visitors and collect data on these visits? If so, should it measure the time spent at its website by visitors it has attracted from competitors' websites or visitors who do not routinely visit online news sites? The answers depend on PDT's research objectives. Is the company attempting to evaluate its current market, assess the potential of customers it can attract from competitors, or explore the potential of an entirely new market (individuals who do not routinely obtain their news from online news services)? If the research objective and the population from which the sample is to be drawn are not aligned, the data that PDT collects will not help the company accomplish its research objective. This type of error is referred to as a coverage error.

Even when the sample is selected from the appropriate population, nonsampling error can occur when segments of the target population are systematically underrepresented or overrepresented in the sample. This may occur because the study design is flawed or because some segments of the population are either more likely or less likely to respond. Suppose PDT implements a pop-up questionnaire that opens when the visitor leaves PenningtonDailyTimes.com. Visitors to PenningtonDailyTimes.com who have installed pop-up blockers will likely be underrepresented, and visitors to PenningtonDailyTimes.com who have not installed pop-up blockers will likely be overrepresented. If the behavior of PenningtonDailyTimes.com visitors who have installed pop-up blockers differs from the behaviors of PenningtonDailyTimes.com visitors who have not installed pop-up blockers, attempting to draw conclusions from this sample about how all visitors to the PDT website behave may be misleading. This type of error is referred to as a non-response error.

Another potential source of nonsampling error is incorrect measurement of the characteristic of interest. If PDT asks questions that are ambiguous or difficult for respondents to understand, the responses may not accurately reflect how the respondents intended to respond. For example, if PDT asks *Are the news stories on PenningtonDailyTimes.com compelling and accurate?*, respondents may be unsure how to respond. How should a visitor respond if she or he feels the news stories on PenningtonDailyTimes.com are compelling but not accurate? What response is appropriate if the respondent feels the news stories on PenningtonDailyTimes.com are accurate but not compelling? A similar issue can arise if a questions is asked in a biased or leading way. If PDT says, *Many readers find the news stories on PenningtonDailyTimes.com to be compelling and accurate! Do you find the news stories on PenningtonDailyTimes.com to be to be compelling and accurate?*, the qualifying statement PDT makes prior to the actual question will likely result in a bias toward positive responses. Note that incorrect measurement of the characteristic of interest can also occur when respondents provide incorrect answers; this may be due to a respondent's poor recall, unwillingness to respond honestly, or desire to provide an "acceptable" response. This type of error is referred to as a measurement error.

Errors that are introduced by interviewers or during the recording and preparation of the data are other types of nonresponse error. These types of error are referred to as interviewer errors and processing errors, respectively.

Implications of Big Data

Suppose that last year the mean time spent by all visitors to the PDT website was 84 seconds. Further suppose that the mean time has not changed since last year and that PDT now collects a sample of 1,000,000 visitors to its website (recall from chapter 1 that we often refer to very large or complex data sets as big data). With $n = 1,000,000$ and the assumed known value of $\sigma = 20$ seconds for the population standard deviation, the standard error will be $\sigma_{\bar{x}} = \sigma/\sqrt{n} = 20/\sqrt{1,000,000} = 0.02$. Note that because of the very large sample size, the sampling distribution of the sample mean $\bar{x}$ will be normally distributed. PDT can use this information to calculate the probability the sample mean $\bar{x}$ will fall within .15 of the population mean, or within the interval $84 \pm .15$. At $\bar{x} = 83.85$

$$z = \frac{83.85 - 84}{.02} = -7.5$$

and at $\bar{x} = 84.15$,

$$z = \frac{84.15 - 84}{.02} = 7.5$$

Because $P(z \leq -7.5) \approx .0000$ and $P(z \leq 7.5) \approx 1.0000$, the probability the sample mean $\bar{x}$ will fall within 1.5 of the population mean μ is

$$P(-7.5 \leq z \leq 7.5) \approx 1.0000 - .0000 = 1.0000$$

Using Excel we find

NORM.DIST(84.15,84,.02,TRUE) − NORM.DIST(83.85,84,.02,TRUE) = 1.000

Now, suppose that for the new sample of 1,000,000 visitors the sample mean time spent by all visitors to the PDT website is 88 seconds. What could PDT conclude? Its calculations show that the probability the sample mean will be between 83.85 and 84.15 is approximately 1.0000, and yet the mean of PDT's sample is 88. There are three possible reasons that PDT's sample mean differs so substantially from the population mean for last year:

- sampling error
- nonsampling error
- the population mean has changed since last year

Because the sample size is extremely large, the sample should have very little sampling error and so sampling error cannot explain the substantial difference between PDT's sample mean of $\bar{x} = 88$ seconds and the population mean of $\mu = 84$ seconds for last year. Nonsampling error is a possible explanation and should be investigated. If PDT determines that it introduced little or no nonsampling error into its sample data, the only remaining plausible explanation for the substantial difference between PDT's sample mean and the population mean for last year is that the population mean has changed since last year. If the sample was collected properly, it provides evidence of a potentially important change in behavior of visitors to the PDT website that could have tremendous implications for PDT.

No matter how small or large the sample, we must contend with the limitations of sampling whenever we use sample data to learn about a population of interest. Although sampling error decreases as the size of the sample increases, an extremely large sample can indeed suffer from failure to be representative of the population of interest because of nonsampling error. When sampling, care must be taken to ensure that we minimize the introduction of nonsampling error into the data collection process. This can be done by taking the following steps:

- Carefully define the target population before collecting sample data, and subsequently design the data collection procedure so that a probability sample is drawn from this target population.
- Carefully design the data collection process and train the data collectors.
- Pretest the data collection procedure to identify and correct for potential sources of nonsampling error prior to final data collection.
- Use stratified random sampling when population-level information about an important qualitative variable is available to ensure the sample is representative of the population for that qualitative characteristic.
- Use systematic sampling when population-level information about an important quantitative variable is available to ensure the sample is representative of the population for that quantitative characteristic.

Finally, recognize that every random sample (even an extremely large sample) will suffer from some degree of sampling error, and eliminating all potential sources of nonsampling error may be impractical. Understanding these limitations of sampling will enable us to be more realistic when interpreting sample data and using sample data to draw conclusions about the target population. In the next several chapters we will explore statistical methods for dealing with these issues in greater detail.

NOTES AND COMMENTS

1. In the previous section of this chapter, we explained that one reason probability sampling methods are generally preferred over nonprobability sampling methods is that formulas are available for evaluating the "goodness" of the sample results in terms of the closeness of the results to the population parameters being estimated for sample data collected using probability sampling methods. An evaluation of the goodness cannot be made with convenience or judgment sampling. Another reason for the general preference of probability sampling methods over nonprobability sampling methods is that probability sampling methods are less likely than nonprobability sampling methods to introduce nonsampling error. Although nonsampling can occur when either a probability sampling method or a nonprobability sampling method is used, nonprobability sampling methods such as convenience sampling and judgement sampling frequently introduce nonsampling error into the sample data. This is because of the manner in which sample data are collected when using a nonprobability sampling method.

2. Several approaches to statistical inference (interval estimation and hypothesis testing) are introduced in subsequent chapters of this book. These approaches assume nonsampling error has not been introduced into the sample data. The reliability of the results of statistical inference decreases as greater nonsampling error is introduced into the sample data.

Exercises

Applications

38. Martina Levitt, director of marketing for the messaging app Spontanversation, has been assigned the task of profiling users of this app. Assume that individuals who have downloaded Spontanversation use the app an average of 30 times per day with a standard deviation of 6.

    a. What is the sampling distribution of $\bar{x}$ if a random sample of 50 individuals who have downloaded Spontanversation is used?

    b. What is the sampling distribution of $\bar{x}$ if a random sample of 500,000 individuals who have downloaded Spontanversation is used?

    c. What general statement can you make about what happens to the sampling distribution of $\bar{x}$ as the sample size becomes extremely large? Does this generalization seem logical? Explain.

39. Consider the Spontanversation sampling problem for which individuals who have downloaded Spontanversation use the app an average of 30 times per day with a standard deviation of 6.

    a. What is the probability that $\bar{x}$ is within .5 of the population mean if a random sample of 50 individuals who have downloaded Spontanversation is used?

    b. What would you conclude if the mean of the sample collected in part (a) is 30.2?

    c. What is the probability that $\bar{x}$ is within .5 of the population mean if a sample of 500,000 individuals who have downloaded Spontanversation is used?

    d. What would you conclude if the mean of the sample collected in part (c) is 30.2?

40. *The Wall Street Journal* reported that 37% of all entrepreneurs who opened new U.S. businesses in the previous year were female (*The Wall Street Journal*, May 13, 2015).

    a. Suppose a random sample of 300 entrepreneurs who opened new U.S. businesses in the previous year will be taken to learn about which industries are most appealing to entrepreneurs. Show the sampling distribution of $\bar{p}$, where $\bar{p}$ is the sample proportion of entrepreneurs who opened new U.S. businesses in the previous year that are female.

    b. What is the probability that the sample proportion in part (a) will be within $\pm.05$ of its population proportion?

    c. Suppose a random sample of 30,000 entrepreneurs who opened new U.S. businesses in the previous year will be taken to learn about which industries are most appealing to entrepreneurs. Show the sampling distribution of $\bar{p}$ where $\bar{p}$ is the sample proportion of entrepreneurs who opened new U.S. businesses last year that are female.

    d. What is the probability that the sample proportion in part (c) will be within $\pm.05$ of its population proportion?

    e. Is the probability different in parts (b) and (d)? Why?

41. The vice president of sales for Blasterman Cosmetics, Inc. believes that 40% of the company's orders come from customers who are less than 30 years old. A random sample of 10,000 orders will be used to estimate the proportion of customers who are less than 30 years old.

    a. Assume that the vice president of sales is correct and $p = .40$. What is the sampling distribution of $\bar{p}$ for this study?

    b. What is the probability that the sample proportion will be between .37 and .43?

    c. What is the probability that the sample proportion will be between .39 and .41?

    d. What would you conclude if the sample proportion is .36?

Summary

In this chapter we presented the concepts of sampling and sampling distributions. We demonstrated how a simple random sample can be selected from a finite population and how a random sample can be selected from an infinite population. The data collected from such samples can be used to develop point estimates of population parameters. Because different samples provide different values for the point estimators, point estimators such as $\bar{x}$ and $\bar{p}$ are random variables. The probability distribution of such a random variable is called a sampling distribution. In particular, we described in detail the sampling distributions of the sample mean $\bar{x}$ and the sample proportion $\bar{p}$.

In considering the characteristics of the sampling distributions of $\bar{x}$ and $\bar{p}$, we stated that $E(\bar{x}) = \mu$ and $E(\bar{p}) = p$. After developing the standard deviation or standard error formulas for these estimators, we described the conditions necessary for the sampling distributions of $\bar{x}$ and $\bar{p}$ to follow a normal distribution. Other sampling methods including stratified random sampling, cluster sampling, systematic sampling, convenience sampling, and judgment sampling were discussed. Finally, we discussed practical considerations to be made when working with very large samples.

Glossary

Central limit theorem A theorem that enables one to use the normal probability distribution to approximate the sampling distribution of $\bar{x}$ whenever the sample size is large.

Cluster sampling A probability sampling method in which the population is first divided into clusters and then a simple random sample of the clusters is taken.

Convenience sampling A nonprobability method of sampling whereby elements are selected for the sample on the basis of convenience.

Finite population correction factor The term $\sqrt{(N-n)/(N-1)}$ that is used in the formulas for $\sigma_{\bar{x}}$ and $\sigma_{\bar{p}}$ whenever a finite population, rather than an infinite population, is being sampled. The generally accepted rule of thumb is to ignore the finite population correction factor whenever $n/N \leq .05$.

Frame A listing of the elements the sample will be selected from.

Judgment sampling A nonprobability method of sampling whereby elements are selected for the sample based on the judgment of the person doing the study.

Nonsampling error All types of errors other than sampling error, such as coverage error, nonresponse error, measurement error, interviewer error, and processing error.

Parameter A numerical characteristic of a population, such as a population mean μ, a population standard deviation σ, a population proportion p, and so on.

Point estimate The value of a point estimator used in a particular instance as an estimate of a population parameter.

Point estimator The sample statistic, such as $\bar{x}$, s, or $\bar{p}$, that provides the point estimate of the population parameter.

Random sample A random sample from an infinite population is a sample selected such that the following conditions are satisfied: (1) Each element selected comes from the same population; (2) each element is selected independently.

Sample statistic A sample characteristic, such as a sample mean $\bar{x}$, a sample standard deviation s, a sample proportion $\bar{p}$, and so on. The value of the sample statistic is used to estimate the value of the corresponding population parameter.

Sampled population The population from which the sample is taken.

Sampling distribution A probability distribution consisting of all possible values of a sample statistic.

Sampling error The error that occurs because a sample, and not the entire population, is used to estimate a population parameter.

Simple random sample A simple random sample of size n from a finite population of size N is a sample selected such that each possible sample of size n has the same probability of being selected.

Standard error The standard deviation of a point estimator.

Stratified random sampling A probability sampling method in which the population is first divided into strata and a simple random sample is then taken from each stratum.

Systematic sampling A probability sampling method in which we randomly select one of the first k elements and then select every kth element thereafter.

Target population The population for which statistical inferences such as point estimates are made. It is important for the target population to correspond as closely as possible to the sampled population.

Unbiased A property of a point estimator that is present when the expected value of the point estimator is equal to the population parameter it estimates.

Key Formulas

Expected Value of $\bar{x}$

$$E(\bar{x}) = \mu \tag{7.1}$$

Standard Deviation of $\bar{x}$ (Standard Error)

Finite Population *Infinite Population*

$$\sigma_{\bar{x}} = \sqrt{\frac{N-n}{N-1}}\left(\frac{\sigma}{\sqrt{n}}\right) \qquad \sigma_{\bar{x}} = \frac{\sigma}{\sqrt{n}} \tag{7.2}$$

Expected Value of $\bar{p}$

$$E(\bar{p}) = p \tag{7.4}$$

Standard Deviation of $\bar{p}$ (Standard Error)

Finite Population *Infinite Population*

$$\sigma_{\bar{p}} = \sqrt{\frac{N-n}{N-1}}\sqrt{\frac{p(1-p)}{n}} \qquad \sigma_{\bar{p}} = \sqrt{\frac{p(1-p)}{n}} \tag{7.5}$$

Supplementary Exercises

ShadowStocks

42. Jack Lawler, a financial analyst, wants to prepare an article on the Shadow Stock portfolio developed by the American Association of Individual Investors (AAII). A list of the 30 companies in the Shadow Stock portfolio as of March 2014 is contained in the DATAfile named *ShadowStocks* (AAII website, March 27, 2014). Jack would like to select a simple random sample of 5 of these companies for an interview concerning management practices.
    a. In the DATAfile the Shadow Stock companies are listed in column A of an Excel worksheet. In column B we have generated a random number for each of the companies. Use these random numbers to select a simple random sample of 5 of these companies for Jack.

b. Generate a new set of random numbers and use them to select a new simple random sample. Did you select the same companies?

43. The latest available data showed health expenditures were $8086 per person in the United States or 17.6% of gross domestic product (Centers for Medicare & Medicaid Services website, April 1, 2012). Use $8086 as the population mean and suppose a survey research firm will take a sample of 100 people to investigate the nature of their health expenditures. Assume the population standard deviation is $2500.
   a. Show the sampling distribution of the mean amount of health care expenditures for a sample of 100 people.
   b. What is the probability the sample mean will be within ±$200 of the population mean?
   c. What is the probability the sample mean will be greater than $9000? If the survey research firm reports a sample mean greater than $9000, would you question whether the firm followed correct sampling procedures? Why or why not?

44. According to a report in *The Wall Street Journal*, Foot Locker uses sales per square foot as a measure of store productivity. Sales are currently running at an annual rate of $406 per square foot. You have been asked by management to conduct a study of a sample of 64 Foot Locker stores. Assume the standard deviation in annual sales per square foot for the population of all 3400 Foot Locker stores is $80.
   a. Show the sampling distribution of $\bar{x}$, the sample mean annual sales per square foot for a sample of 64 Foot Locker stores.
   b. What is the probability that the sample mean will be within $15 of the population mean?
   c. Suppose you find a sample mean of $380. What is the probability of finding a sample mean of $380 or less? Would you consider such a sample to be an unusually low performing group of stores?

45. Allegiant Airlines charges a mean base fare of $89. In addition, the airline charges for making a reservation on its website, checking bags, and inflight beverages. These additional charges average $39 per passenger (*Bloomberg Businessweek*, October 8–14, 2012). Suppose a random sample of 60 passengers is taken to determine the total cost of their flight on Allegiant Airlines. The population standard deviation of total flight cost is known to be $40.
   a. What is the population mean cost per flight?
   b. What is the probability the sample mean will be within $10 of the population mean cost per flight?
   c. What is the probability the sample mean will be within $5 of the population mean cost per flight?

46. According to *U.S. News & World Report's* publication *America's Best Colleges*, the average cost to attend the University of Southern California (USC) after deducting grants based on need is $27,175. Assume the population standard deviation is $7400. Suppose that a random sample of 60 USC students will be taken from this population.
   a. What is the value of the standard error of the mean?
   b. What is the probability that the sample mean will be more than $27,175?
   c. What is the probability that the sample mean will be within $1000 of the population mean?
   d. How would the probability in part (c) change if the sample size were increased to 100?

47. Three firms carry inventories that differ in size. Firm A's inventory contains 2000 items, firm B's inventory contains 5000 items, and firm C's inventory contains 10,000 items. The population standard deviation for the cost of the items in each firm's inventory is $\sigma = 144$. A statistical consultant recommends that each firm take a sample of 50 items from its inventory to provide statistically valid estimates of the average cost per item. Employees of the small firm state that because it has the smallest population, it should be able to make the estimate from a much smaller sample than that required by the larger firms. However, the consultant

states that to obtain the same standard error and thus the same precision in the sample results, all firms should use the same sample size regardless of population size.

a. Using the finite population correction factor, compute the standard error for each of the three firms given a sample of size 50.

b. What is the probability that for each firm the sample mean $\bar{x}$ will be within ± 25 of the population mean μ?

48. A researcher reports survey results by stating that the standard error of the mean is 20. The population standard deviation is 500.

a. How large was the sample used in this survey?

b. What is the probability that the point estimate was within ± 25 of the population mean?

49. A production process is checked periodically by a quality control inspector. The inspector selects simple random samples of 30 finished products and computes the sample mean product weights $\bar{x}$. If test results over a long period of time show that 5% of the $\bar{x}$ values are over 2.1 pounds and 5% are under 1.9 pounds, what are the mean and the standard deviation for the population of products produced with this process?

50. Fifteen percent of Australians smoke. Reuters reports that by introducing tough laws banning brand labels on cigarette packages, Australia hopes to reduce the percentage of people smoking to 10% by 2018. Answer the following questions based on a sample of 240 Australians.

a. Show the sampling distribution of $\bar{p}$, the proportion of Australians who are smokers.

b. What is the probability the sample proportion will be within $\pm.04$ of the population proportion?

c. What is the probability the sample proportion will be within $\pm.02$ of the population proportion?

51. A market research firm conducts telephone surveys with a 40% historical response rate. What is the probability that in a new sample of 400 telephone numbers, at least 150 individuals will cooperate and respond to the questions? In other words, what is the probability that the sample proportion will be at least $150/400 = .375$?

52. Advertisers contract with Internet service providers and search engines to place ads on websites. They pay a fee based on the number of potential customers who click on their ad. Unfortunately, click fraud—the practice of someone clicking on an ad solely for the purpose of driving up advertising revenue—has become a problem. According to *BusinessWeek*, 40% of advertisers claim they have been a victim of click fraud. Suppose a simple random sample of 380 advertisers will be taken to learn more about how they are affected by this practice.

a. What is the probability that the sample proportion will be within $\pm.04$ of the population proportion experiencing click fraud?

b. What is the probability that the sample proportion will be greater than .45?

53. The proportion of individuals insured by the All-Driver Automobile Insurance Company who received at least one traffic ticket during a five-year period is .15.

a. Show the sampling distribution of $\bar{p}$ if a random sample of 150 insured individuals is used to estimate the proportion having received at least one ticket.

b. What is the probability that the sample proportion will be within $\pm.03$ of the population proportion?

54. Lori Jeffrey is a successful sales representative for a major publisher of college textbooks. Historically, Lori obtains a book adoption on 25% of her sales calls. Viewing her sales calls for one month as a sample of all possible sales calls, assume that a statistical analysis of the data yields a standard error of the proportion of .0625.

a. How large was the sample used in this analysis? That is, how many sales calls did Lori make during the month?

b. Let $\bar{p}$ indicate the sample proportion of book adoptions obtained during the month. Show the sampling distribution of $\bar{p}$.

c. Using the sampling distribution of $\bar{p}$, compute the probability that Lori will obtain book adoptions on 30% or more of her sales calls during a one-month period.

Case Problem 1   Marion Dairies

Last year Marion Dairies decided to enter the yogurt market, and it began cautiously by producing, distributing, and marketing a single flavor – a blueberry-flavored yogurt that it calls Blugurt. The company's initial venture into the yogurt market has been very successful; sales of Blugurt are higher than expected, and consumers' ratings of the product have a mean of 80 and a standard deviation of 25 on a 100-point scale for which 100 is the most favorable score and zero is the least favorable score. Past experience has also shown Marion Dairies that a consumer who rates one of its products with a score greater than 75 on this scale will consider purchasing the product, and a score of 75 or less indicates the consumer will not consider purchasing the product.

Emboldened by the success and popularity of its blueberry-flavored yogurt, Marion Dairies management is now considering the introduction of a second flavor. Marion's marketing department is pressing to extend the product line through the introduction of a strawberry-flavored yogurt that would be called Strawgurt, but senior managers are concerned about whether or not Strawgurt will increase Marion's market share by appealing to potential customers who do not like Blugurt. That is, the goal in offering the new product is to increase Marion's market share rather than cannibalize existing sales of Blugurt. The marketing department has proposed giving tastes of both Blugurt and Strawgurt to a simple random sample of 50 customers and asking each of them to rate the two flavors of yogurt on the 100-point scale. If the mean score given to Blugurt by this sample of consumers is 75 or less, Marion's senior management believes the sample can be used to assess whether Strawgurt will appeal to potential customers who do not like Blugurt.

Managerial Report

Prepare a managerial report that addresses the following issues.

1. Calculate the probability the mean score of Blugurt given by the simple random sample of Marion Dairies customers will be 75 or less.
2. If the Marketing Department increases the sample size to 150, what is the probability the mean score of Blugurt given by the simple random sample of Marion Dairies customers will be 75 or less?
3. Explain to Marion Dairies senior management why the probability that the mean score of Blugurt for a random sample of Marion Dairies customers will be 75 or less is different for samples of 50 and 150 Marion Dairies customers.

CHAPTER 8

Interval Estimation

CONTENTS

STATISTICS *in* PRACTICE

FOOD LION*
SALISBURY, NORTH CAROLINA

© Davis Turner/Bloomberg/Getty Images

Founded in 1957 as Food Town, Food Lion is one of the largest supermarket chains in the United States, with 1100 stores in 10 Southeastern and Mid-Atlantic states. The company sells more than 24,000 different products and offers nationally and regionally advertised brand-name merchandise, as well as a growing number of high-quality private label products manufactured especially for Food Lion. The company maintains its low price leadership and quality assurance through operating efficiencies such as standard store formats, innovative warehouse design, energy-efficient facilities, and data synchronization with suppliers. Food Lion looks to a future of continued innovation, growth, price leadership, and service to its customers.

Being in an inventory-intense business, Food Lion made the decision to adopt the LIFO (last-in, first-out) method of inventory valuation. This method matches current costs against current revenues, which minimizes the effect of radical price changes on profit and loss results. In addition, the LIFO method reduces net income, thereby reducing income taxes during periods of inflation.

Food Lion establishes a LIFO index for each of seven inventory pools: Grocery, Paper/Household, Pet Supplies, Health & Beauty Aids, Dairy, Cigarettes/Tobacco, and Beer/Wine. For example, a LIFO index of 1.008 for the Grocery pool would indicate that the company's grocery inventory value at current costs reflects a 0.8% increase due to inflation over the most recent one-year period.

A LIFO index for each inventory pool requires that the year-end inventory count for each product be valued

at the current year-end cost and at the preceding year-end cost. To avoid excessive time and expense associated with counting the inventory in all 1100 store locations, Food Lion selects a random sample of 50 stores. Year-end physical inventories are taken in each of the sample stores. The current-year and preceding-year costs for each item are then used to construct the required LIFO indexes for each inventory pool.

For a recent year, the sample estimate of the LIFO index for the Health & Beauty Aids inventory pool was 1.015. Using a 95% confidence level, Food Lion computed a margin of error of .006 for the sample estimate. Thus, the interval from 1.009 to 1.021 provided a 95% confidence interval estimate of the population LIFO index. This level of precision was judged to be very good.

In this chapter you will learn how to compute the margin of error associated with sample estimates. You will also learn how to use this information to construct and interpret interval estimates of a population mean and a population proportion.

---

*The authors are indebted to Keith Cunningham, Tax Director, and Bobby Harkey, Staff Tax Accountant, at Food Lion for providing this Statistics in Practice.

In Chapter 7, we stated that a point estimator is a sample statistic used to estimate a population parameter. For instance, the sample mean $\bar{x}$ is a point estimator of the population mean μ and the sample proportion $\bar{p}$ is a point estimator of the population proportion p. Because a point estimator cannot be expected to provide the exact value of the population parameter, an **interval estimate** is often computed by adding and subtracting a value, called the **margin of error**, to the point estimate. The general form of an interval estimate is as follows:

$$\text{Point estimate} \pm \text{Margin of error}$$

The purpose of an interval estimate is to provide information about how close the point estimate, provided by the sample, is to the value of the population parameter.

In this chapter we show how to compute interval estimates of a population mean μ and a population proportion p. The general form of an interval estimate of a population mean is

$$\bar{x} \pm \text{Margin of error}$$

Similarly, the general form of an interval estimate of a population proportion is

$$\bar{p} \pm \text{Margin of error}$$

The sampling distributions of $\bar{x}$ and $\bar{p}$ play key roles in computing these interval estimates.

8.1 Population Mean: σ Known

In order to develop an interval estimate of a population mean, either the population standard deviation σ or the sample standard deviation s must be used to compute the margin of error. In most applications σ is not known, and s is used to compute the margin of error. In some applications, however, large amounts of relevant historical data are available and can be used to estimate the population standard deviation prior to sampling. Also, in quality control applications where a process is assumed to be operating correctly, or "in control," it is appropriate to treat the population standard deviation as known. We refer to such cases as **σ known** cases. In this section we introduce an example in which it is reasonable to treat σ as known and show how to construct an interval estimate for this case.

Each week Lloyd's Department Store selects a simple random sample of 100 customers in order to learn about the amount spent per shopping trip. With x representing the amount spent per shopping trip, the sample mean $\bar{x}$ provides a point estimate of μ, the mean amount spent per shopping trip for the population of all Lloyd's customers. Lloyd's has been using the weekly survey for several years. Based on the historical data, Lloyd's now assumes a known value of $\sigma = \$20$ for the population standard deviation. The historical data also indicate that the population follows a normal distribution.

During the most recent week, Lloyd's surveyed 100 customers ($n = 100$) and obtained a sample mean of $\bar{x} = \$82$. The sample mean amount spent provides a point estimate of the population mean amount spent per shopping trip, μ. In the discussion that follows, we show how to compute the margin of error for this estimate and develop an interval estimate of the population mean.

Margin of Error and the Interval Estimate

In Chapter 7 we showed that the sampling distribution of $\bar{x}$ can be used to compute the probability that $\bar{x}$ will be within a given distance of μ. In the Lloyd's example, the historical data show that the population of amounts spent is normally distributed with a standard deviation of $\sigma = 20$. So, using what we learned in Chapter 7, we can conclude that the sampling distribution of $\bar{x}$ follows a normal distribution with a standard error of $\sigma_{\bar{x}} = \sigma/\sqrt{n} = 20/\sqrt{100} = 2$. This sampling distribution is shown in Figure 8.1.[1] Because the sampling distribution shows how values of $\bar{x}$ are distributed around the population mean μ, the sampling distribution of $\bar{x}$ provides information about the possible differences between $\bar{x}$ and μ.

---

[1]We use the fact that the population of amounts spent has a normal distribution to conclude that the sampling distribution of $\bar{x}$ has a normal distribution. If the population did not have a normal distribution, we could rely on the central limit theorem and the sample size of $n = 100$ to conclude that the sampling distribution of $\bar{x}$ is approximately normal. In either case, the sampling distribution of $\bar{x}$ would appear as shown in Figure 8.1.

FIGURE 8.1   SAMPLING DISTRIBUTION OF THE SAMPLE MEAN AMOUNT
SPENT FROM SIMPLE RANDOM SAMPLES OF 100 CUSTOMERS

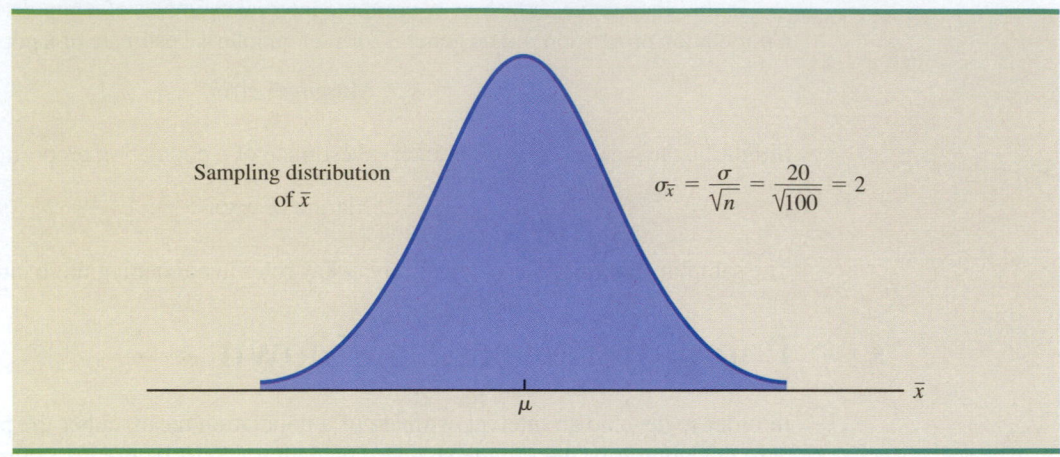

Using the standard normal probability table, we find that 95% of the values of any normally distributed random variable are within ± 1.96 standard deviations of the mean. Thus, when the sampling distribution of $\bar{x}$ is normally distributed, 95% of the $\bar{x}$ values must be within $\pm 1.96\sigma_{\bar{x}}$ of the mean μ. In the Lloyd's example, we know that the sampling distribution of $\bar{x}$ is normally distributed with a standard error of $\sigma_{\bar{x}} = 2$. Because $\pm 1.96\sigma_{\bar{x}} = 1.96(2) = 3.92$, we can conclude that 95% of all $\bar{x}$ values obtained using a sample size of $n = 100$ will be within ± 3.92 of the population mean μ. See Figure 8.2.

In the introduction to this chapter, we said that the general form of an interval estimate of the population mean μ is $\bar{x} \pm$ margin of error. For the Lloyd's example, suppose we set

FIGURE 8.2   SAMPLING DISTRIBUTION OF $\bar{x}$ SHOWING THE LOCATION OF SAMPLE
MEANS THAT ARE WITHIN 3.92 OF μ

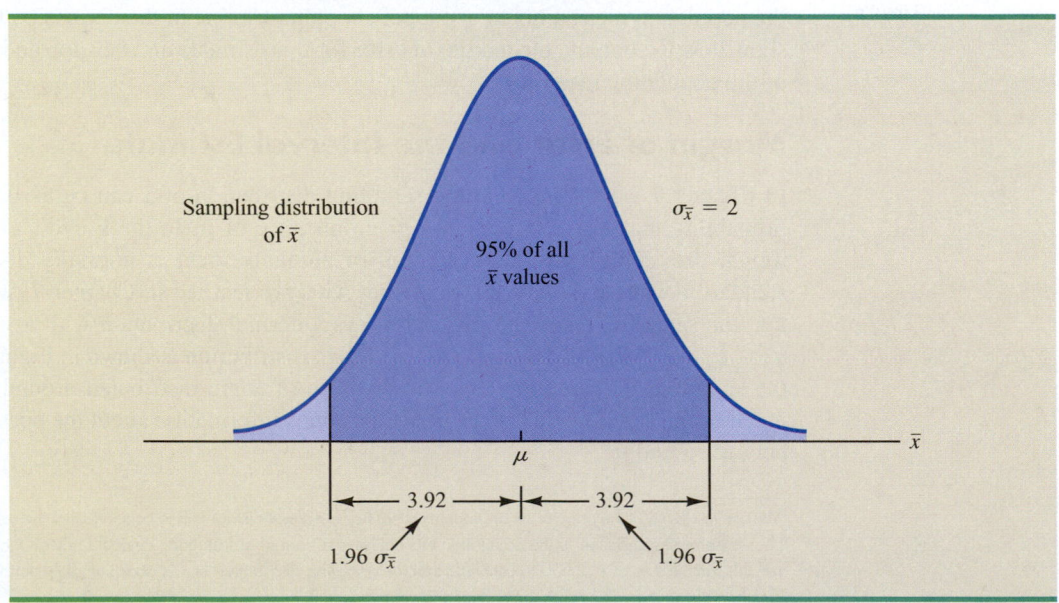

FIGURE 8.3   INTERVALS FORMED FROM SELECTED SAMPLE MEANS
AT LOCATIONS $\bar{x}_1$, $\bar{x}_2$, AND $\bar{x}_3$

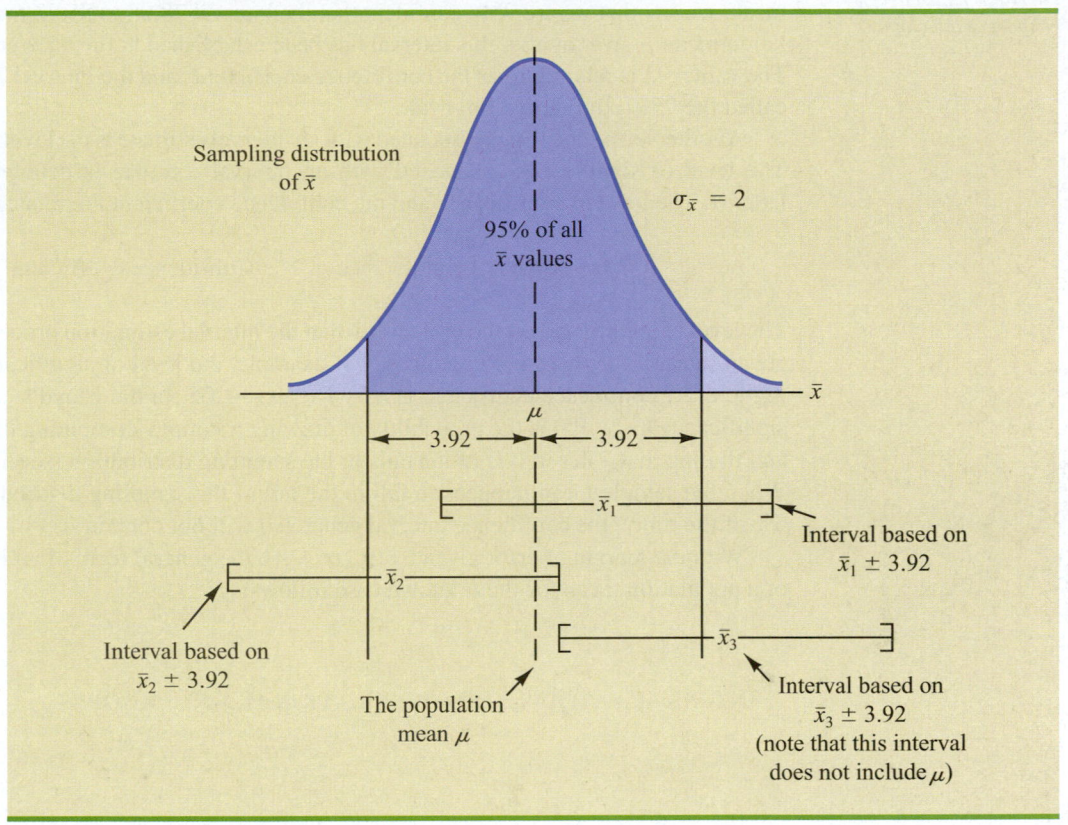

the margin of error equal to 3.92 and compute the interval estimate of μ using $\bar{x} \pm 3.92$.
To provide an interpretation for this interval estimate, let us consider the values of $\bar{x}$ that
could be obtained if we took three *different* simple random samples, each consisting of
100 Lloyd's customers. The first sample mean might turn out to have the value shown as $\bar{x}_1$
in Figure 8.3. In this case, Figure 8.3 shows that the interval formed by subtracting 3.92
from $\bar{x}_1$ and adding 3.92 to $\bar{x}_1$ includes the population mean μ. Now consider what happens
if the second sample mean turns out to have the value shown as $\bar{x}_2$ in Figure 8.3. Although
this sample mean differs from the first sample mean, we see that the interval formed by
subtracting 3.92 from $\bar{x}_2$ and adding 3.92 to $\bar{x}_2$ also includes the population mean μ. However, consider what happens if the third sample mean turns out to have the value shown as
$\bar{x}_3$ in Figure 8.3. In this case, the interval formed by subtracting 3.92 from $\bar{x}_3$ and adding
3.92 to $\bar{x}_3$ does not include the population mean μ. Because $\bar{x}_3$ falls in the upper tail of the
sampling distribution and is farther than 3.92 from μ, subtracting and adding 3.92 to $\bar{x}_3$
forms an interval that does not include μ.

Any sample mean $\bar{x}$ that is within the darkly shaded region of Figure 8.3 will provide
an interval that contains the population mean μ. Because 95% of all possible sample means
are in the darkly shaded region, 95% of all intervals formed by subtracting 3.92 from $\bar{x}$ and
adding 3.92 to $\bar{x}$ will include the population mean μ.

Recall that during the most recent week, the quality assurance team at Lloyd's surveyed
100 customers and obtained a sample mean amount spent of $\bar{x} = 82$. Using $\bar{x} \pm 3.92$ to
construct the interval estimate, we obtain 82 ± 3.92. Thus, the specific interval estimate of

This discussion provides insight as to why the interval is called a 95% confidence interval.

μ based on the data from the most recent week is $82 - 3.92 = 78.08$ to $82 + 3.92 = 85.92$. Because 95% of all the intervals constructed using $\bar{x} \pm 3.92$ will contain the population mean, we say that we are 95% confident that the interval 78.08 to 85.92 includes the population mean μ. We say that this interval has been established at the 95% **confidence level**. The value .95 is referred to as the **confidence coefficient**, and the interval 78.08 to 85.92 is called the 95% **confidence interval**.

Another term sometimes associated with an interval estimate is the **level of significance**. The level of significance associated with an interval estimate is denoted by the Greek letter α. The level of significance and the confidence coefficient are related as follows:

$$\alpha = \text{Level of significance} = 1 - \text{Confidence coefficient}$$

The level of significance is the probability that the interval estimation procedure will generate an interval that does not contain μ. For example, the level of significance corresponding to a .95 confidence coefficient is $\alpha = 1 - .95 = .05$. In the Lloyd's case, the level of significance ($\alpha = .05$) is the probability of drawing a sample, computing the sample mean, and finding that $\bar{x}$ lies in one of the tails of the sampling distribution (see $\bar{x}_3$ in Figure 8.3). When the sample mean happens to fall in the tail of the sampling distribution (and it will 5% of the time), the confidence interval generated will not contain μ.

With the margin of error given by $(z_{\alpha/2}\sigma/\sqrt{n})$, the general form of an interval estimate of a population mean for the σ known case follows.

INTERVAL ESTIMATE OF A POPULATION MEAN: σ KNOWN

$$\bar{x} \pm z_{\alpha/2} \frac{\sigma}{\sqrt{n}} \qquad (8.1)$$

where $(1 - \alpha)$ is the confidence coefficient and $z_{\alpha/2}$ is the z value providing an area of $\alpha/2$ in the upper tail of the standard normal probability distribution.

Let us use expression (8.1) to construct a 95% confidence interval for the Lloyd's example. For a 95% confidence interval, the confidence coefficient is $(1 - \alpha) = .95$ and thus, $\alpha = .05$. Using the standard normal probability table, an area of $\alpha/2 = .05/2 = .025$ in the upper tail provides $z_{.025} = 1.96$. With the Lloyd's sample mean $\bar{x} = 82$, $\sigma = 20$, and a sample size $n = 100$, we obtain

$$82 \pm 1.96 \frac{20}{\sqrt{100}}$$

$$82 \pm 3.92$$

Thus, using expression (8.1), the margin of error is 3.92 and the 95% confidence interval is $82 - 3.92 = 78.08$ to $82 + 3.92 = 85.92$.

Although a 95% confidence level is frequently used, other confidence levels such as 90% and 99% may be considered. Values of $z_{\alpha/2}$ for the most commonly used confidence levels are shown in Table 8.1. Using these values and expression (8.1), the 90% confidence interval for the Lloyd's example is

$$82 \pm 1.645 \frac{20}{\sqrt{100}}$$

$$82 \pm 3.29$$

TABLE 8.1 VALUES OF $z_{\alpha/2}$ FOR THE MOST COMMONLY USED CONFIDENCE LEVELS

Confidence Level	α	$\alpha/2$	$z_{\alpha/2}$
90%	.10	.05	1.645
95%	.05	.025	1.960
99%	.01	.005	2.576

Thus, at 90% confidence, the margin of error is 3.29 and the confidence interval is $82 - 3.29 = 78.71$ to $82 + 3.29 = 85.29$. Similarly, the 99% confidence interval is

$$82 \pm 2.576 \frac{20}{\sqrt{100}}$$

$$82 \pm 5.15$$

Thus, at 99% confidence, the margin of error is 5.15 and the confidence interval is $82 - 5.15 = 76.85$ to $82 + 5.15 = 87.15$.

Comparing the results for the 90%, 95%, and 99% confidence levels, we see that in order to have a higher level of confidence, the margin of error and thus the width of the confidence interval must be larger.

Using Excel

We will use the Lloyd's Department Store data to illustrate how Excel can be used to construct an interval estimate of the population mean for the σ known case. Refer to Figure 8.4 as we describe the tasks involved. The formula worksheet is in the background; the value worksheet appears in the foreground.

Enter/Access Data: Open the DATAfile named *Lloyd's*. A label and the sales data are entered into cells A1:A101.

FIGURE 8.4 EXCEL WORKSHEET: CONSTRUCTING A 95% CONFIDENCE INTERVAL FOR LLOYD'S DEPARTMENT STORE

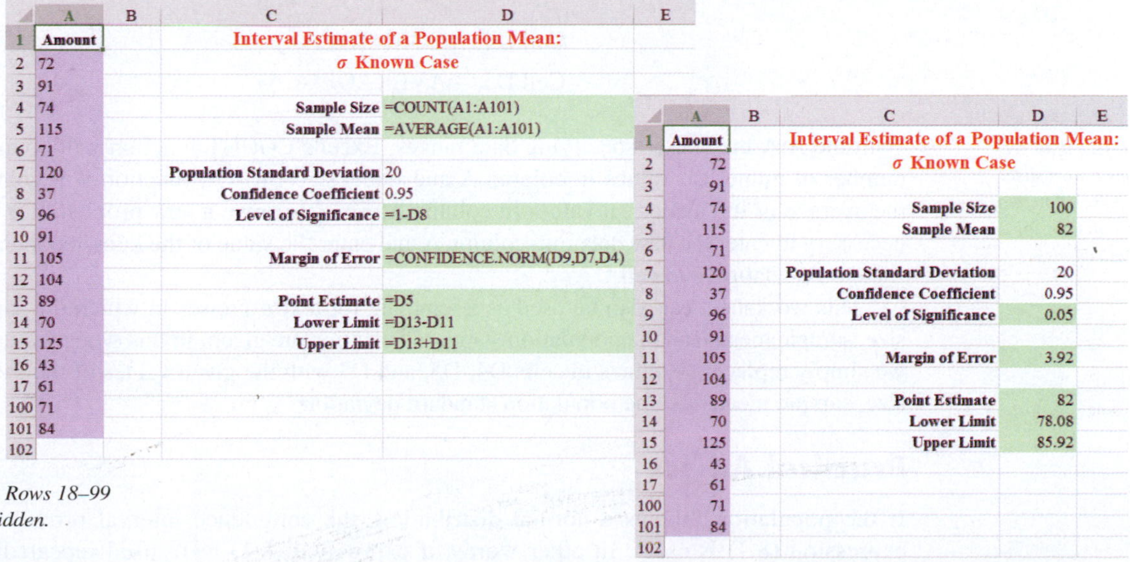

Note: Rows 18–99 are hidden.

Enter Functions and Formulas: The sample size and sample mean are computed in cells D4:D5 using Excel's COUNT and AVERAGE functions, respectively. The value worksheet shows that the sample size is 100 and the sample mean is 82. The value of the known population standard deviation (20) is entered into cell D7 and the desired confidence coefficient (.95) is entered into cell D8. The level of significance is computed in cell D9 by entering the formula =1-D8; the value worksheet shows that the level of significance associated with a confidence coefficient of .95 is .05. The margin of error is computed in cell D11 using Excel's CONFIDENCE.NORM function. The CONFIDENCE.NORM function has three inputs: the level of significance (cell D9); the population standard deviation (cell D7); and the sample size (cell D4). Thus, to compute the margin of error associated with a 95% confidence interval, the following formula is entered into cell D11:

$$=CONFIDENCE.NORM(D9,D7,D4)$$

The resulting value of 3.92 is the margin of error associated with the interval estimate of the population mean amount spent per week.

Cells D13:D15 provide the point estimate and the lower and upper limits for the confidence interval. Because the point estimate is just the sample mean, the formula =D5 is entered into cell D13. To compute the lower limit of the 95% confidence interval, $\bar{x} -$ (margin of error), we enter the formula =D13-D11 into cell D14. To compute the upper limit of the 95% confidence interval, $\bar{x} +$ (margin of error), we enter the formula =D13+D11 into cell D15. The value worksheet shows a lower limit of 78.08 and an upper limit of 85.92. In other words, the 95% confidence interval for the population mean is from 78.08 to 85.92.

A template for other problems To use this worksheet as a template for another problem of this type, we must first enter the new problem data in column A. Then, the cell formulas in cells D4 and D5 must be updated with the new data range and the known population standard deviation must be entered into cell D7. After doing so, the point estimate and a 95% confidence interval will be displayed in cells D13:D15. If a confidence interval with a different confidence coefficient is desired, we simply change the value in cell D8.

We can further simplify the use of Figure 8.4 as a template for other problems by eliminating the need to enter new data ranges in cells D4 and D5. To do so we rewrite the cell formulas as follows:

Cell D4: =COUNT(A:A)

Cell D5: =AVERAGE(A:A)

The Lloyd's data set includes a worksheet entitled Template that uses the A:A method for entering the data ranges.

With the A:A method of specifying data ranges, Excel's COUNT function will count the number of numerical values in column A and Excel's AVERAGE function will compute the average of the numerical values in column A. Thus, to solve a new problem it is only necessary to enter the new data into column A and enter the value of the known population standard deviation into cell D7.

This worksheet can also be used as a template for text exercises in which the sample size, sample mean, and the population standard deviation are given. In this type of situation we simply replace the values in cells D4, D5, and D7 with the given values of the sample size, sample mean, and the population standard deviation.

Practical Advice

If the population follows a normal distribution, the confidence interval provided by expression (8.1) is exact. In other words, if expression (8.1) were used repeatedly to generate 95% confidence intervals, exactly 95% of the intervals generated would contain the population mean. If the population does not follow a normal distribution, the confidence interval provided by expression (8.1) will be approximate. In this case, the quality of the approximation depends on both the distribution of the population and the sample size.

In most applications, a sample size of $n \geq 30$ is adequate when using expression (8.1) to develop an interval estimate of a population mean. If the population is not normally distributed, but is roughly symmetric, sample sizes as small as 15 can be expected to provide good approximate confidence intervals. With smaller sample sizes, expression (8.1) should only be used if the analyst believes, or is willing to assume, that the population distribution is at least approximately normal.

NOTES AND COMMENTS

1. The interval estimation procedure discussed in this section is based on the assumption that the population standard deviation σ is known. By σ known we mean that historical data or other information are available that permit us to obtain a good estimate of the population standard deviation prior to taking the sample that will be used to develop an estimate of the population mean. So technically we don't mean that σ is actually known with certainty. We just mean that we obtained a good estimate of the standard deviation prior to sampling and thus we won't be using the same sample to estimate both the population mean and the population standard deviation.

2. The sample size n appears in the denominator of the interval estimation expression (8.1). Thus, if a particular sample size provides too wide an interval to be of any practical use, we may want to consider increasing the sample size. With n in the denominator, a larger sample size will provide a smaller margin of error, a narrower interval, and greater precision. The procedure for determining the size of a simple random sample necessary to obtain a desired precision is discussed in Section 8.3.

3. When developing a confidence interval for the mean with a sample size that is at least 5% of the population size (that is, $n/N \geq .05$), the finite population correction factor should be used when calculating the standard error of the sampling distribution of $\bar{x}$ when σ is known, i.e., $\sigma_{\bar{x}} = \sqrt{\dfrac{N-n}{N-1}}\left(\dfrac{\sigma}{\sqrt{n}}\right)$.

Exercises

Methods

1. A simple random sample of 40 items resulted in a sample mean of 25. The population standard deviation is $\sigma = 5$.
   a. What is the standard error of the mean, $\sigma_{\bar{x}}$?
   b. At 95% confidence, what is the margin of error?

2. A simple random sample of 50 items from a population with $\sigma = 6$ resulted in a sample mean of 32.
   a. Provide a 90% confidence interval for the population mean.
   b. Provide a 95% confidence interval for the population mean.
   c. Provide a 99% confidence interval for the population mean.

3. A simple random sample of 60 items resulted in a sample mean of 80. The population standard deviation is $\sigma = 15$.
   a. Compute the 95% confidence interval for the population mean.
   b. Assume that the same sample mean was obtained from a sample of 120 items. Provide a 95% confidence interval for the population mean.
   c. What is the effect of a larger sample size on the interval estimate?

4. A 95% confidence interval for a population mean was reported to be 152 to 160. If $\sigma = 15$, what sample size was used in this study?

Applications

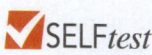

Houston

5. Data were collected on the amount spent by 64 customers for lunch at a major Houston restaurant. These data are contained in the DATAfile named *Houston*. Based upon past studies the population standard deviation is known with $\sigma = \$6$.
   a. At 99% confidence, what is the margin of error?
   b. Develop a 99% confidence interval estimate of the mean amount spent for lunch.

TravelTax

6. In an attempt to assess total daily travel taxes in various cities, the Global Business Travel Association conducted a study of daily travel taxes on lodging, rental car, and meals. The data contained in the DATAfile named *TravelTax* are consistent with the findings of that study for business travel to Chicago. Assume the population standard deviation is known to be $8.50 and develop a 95% confidence interval of the population mean total daily travel taxes for Chicago.

7. The National Fire Protection Association reported that house fires in the United States result in $6.8 billion in losses annually (National Fire Protection Association, September 2015). Suppose a random sample of 50 house fires in San Antonio yields a mean loss of $18,503. If the population standard deviation is $\sigma = \$3300$, what is the margin of error for a 95% confidence interval? What would you recommend if the study required a margin of error of $300 or less?

8. *The Wall Street Journal* reported on several studies that show massage therapy has a variety of health benefits and it is not too expensive. A sample of 10 typical one-hour massage therapy sessions showed an average charge of $59. The population standard deviation for a one-hour session is $\sigma = \$5.50$.
   a. What assumptions about the population should we be willing to make if a margin of error is desired?
   b. Using 95% confidence, what is the margin of error?
   c. Using 99% confidence, what is the margin of error?

TobaccoFires

9. The mean cost to repair the smoke and fire damage that result from home fires of all causes is $11,389 (HomeAdvisor website, December 2014). How does the damage that results from home fires caused by careless use of tobacco compare? The file named *TobaccoFires* provides the cost to repair smoke and fire damage associated with a sample of 55 fires caused by careless use of tobacco products. Using past years' data, the population standard deviation can be assumed known with $\sigma = \$3027$. What is the 95% confidence interval estimate of the mean cost to repair smoke and fire damage that results from home fires caused by careless use of tobacco? How does this compare with the mean cost to repair the smoke and fire damage that result from home fires of all causes?

10. Costs are rising for all kinds of medical care. According to *The Wall Street Journal*, the mean monthly rent at assisted-living facilities was reported to have increased 17% over the last five years to $3486. Assume this cost estimate is based on a sample of 120 facilities and, from past studies, it can be assumed that the population standard deviation is $\sigma = \$650$.
   a. Develop a 90% confidence interval estimate of the population mean monthly rent.
   b. Develop a 95% confidence interval estimate of the population mean monthly rent.
   c. Develop a 99% confidence interval estimate of the population mean monthly rent.
   d. What happens to the width of the confidence interval as the confidence level is increased? Does this seem reasonable? Explain.

8.2 Population Mean: σ Unknown

When developing an interval estimate of a population mean, we usually do not have a good estimate of the population standard deviation either. In these cases, we must use the same sample to estimate both μ and σ. This situation represents the σ **unknown** case. When s is used to estimate σ, the margin of error and the interval estimate for the population mean are based on a probability distribution known as the *t* **distribution**. Although the mathematical development of the *t* distribution is based on the assumption of a normal distribution for the population we are sampling from, research shows that the *t* distribution can be successfully applied in many situations where the population deviates significantly from normal. Later in this section we provide guidelines for using the *t* distribution if the population is not normally distributed.

William Sealy Gosset, writing under the name "Student," is the founder of the t distribution. Gosset, an Oxford graduate in mathematics, worked for the Guinness Brewery in Dublin, Ireland. He developed the t distribution while working on small-scale materials and temperature experiments.

The *t* distribution is a family of similar probability distributions, with a specific *t* distribution depending on a parameter known as the **degrees of freedom**. The *t* distribution with 1 degree of freedom is unique, as is the *t* distribution with 2 degrees of freedom, with 3 degrees of freedom, and so on. As the number of degrees of freedom increases, the difference between the *t* distribution and the standard normal distribution becomes smaller and smaller. Figure 8.5 shows *t* distributions with 10 and 20 degrees of freedom and their relationship to the standard normal probability distribution. Note that a *t* distribution with more degrees of freedom exhibits less variability and more closely resembles the standard normal distribution. Note also that the mean of the *t* distribution is zero.

We place a subscript on *t* to indicate the area in the upper tail of the *t* distribution. For example, just as we used $z_{.025}$ to indicate the *z* value providing a .025 area in the upper tail of a standard normal distribution, we will use $t_{.025}$ to indicate a .025 area in the upper tail of a *t* distribution. In general, we will use the notation $t_{\alpha/2}$ to represent a *t* value with an area of $\alpha/2$ in the upper tail of the *t* distribution. See Figure 8.6.

As the degrees of freedom increase, the t distribution approaches the standard normal distribution.

Table 2 in Appendix B contains a table for the *t* distribution. A portion of this table is shown in Table 8.2. Each row in the table corresponds to a separate *t* distribution with the degrees of freedom shown. For example, for a *t* distribution with 9 degrees of freedom, $t_{.025} = 2.262$. Similarly, for a *t* distribution with 60 degrees of freedom, $t_{.025} = 2.000$. As the degrees of freedom continue to increase, $t_{.025}$ approaches $z_{.025} = 1.96$. In fact, the standard normal distribution *z* values can be found in the infinite degrees of freedom row (labeled ∞) of the *t* distribution table. If the degrees of freedom exceed 100, the infinite degrees of freedom row can be used to approximate the actual *t* value; in other words, for more than 100 degrees of freedom, the standard normal *z* value provides a good approximation to the *t* value.

FIGURE 8.5 COMPARISON OF THE STANDARD NORMAL DISTRIBUTION WITH *t* DISTRIBUTIONS HAVING 10 AND 20 DEGREES OF FREEDOM

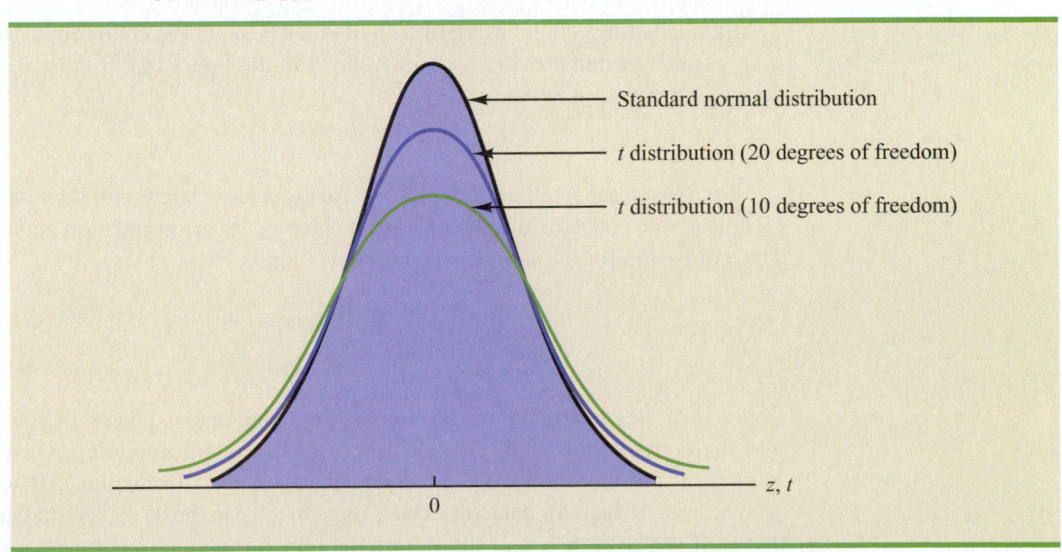

FIGURE 8.6 t DISTRIBUTION WITH $\alpha/2$ AREA OR PROBABILITY IN THE UPPER TAIL

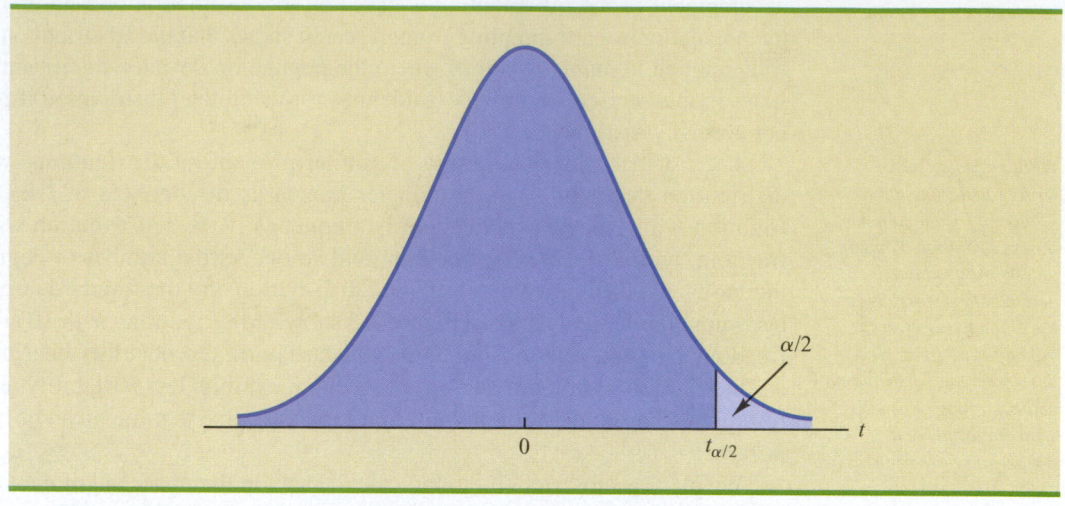

Margin of Error and the Interval Estimate

In Section 8.1 we showed that an interval estimate of a population mean for the σ known case is

$$\bar{x} \pm z_{\alpha/2} \frac{\sigma}{\sqrt{n}}$$

To compute an interval estimate of μ for the σ unknown case, the sample standard deviation s is used to estimate σ, and $z_{\alpha/2}$ is replaced by the t distribution value $t_{\alpha/2}$. The margin of error is then given by $t_{\alpha/2} s/\sqrt{n}$. With this margin of error, the general expression for an interval estimate of a population mean when σ is unknown follows.

INTERVAL ESTIMATE OF A POPULATION MEAN: σ UNKNOWN

$$\bar{x} \pm t_{\alpha/2} \frac{s}{\sqrt{n}} \tag{8.2}$$

where s is the sample standard deviation, $(1 - \alpha)$ is the confidence coefficient, and $t_{\alpha/2}$ is the t value providing an area of $\alpha/2$ in the upper tail of the t distribution with $n - 1$ degrees of freedom.

The reason the number of degrees of freedom associated with the t value in expression (8.2) is $n - 1$ concerns the use of s as an estimate of the population standard deviation σ. The expression for the sample standard deviation is

$$s = \sqrt{\frac{\sum(x_i - \bar{x})^2}{n - 1}}$$

Degrees of freedom refer to the number of independent pieces of information that go into the computation of $\sum(x_i - \bar{x})^2$. The n pieces of information involved in computing $\sum(x_i - \bar{x})^2$ are as follows: $x_1 - \bar{x}, x_2 - \bar{x}, \ldots, x_n - \bar{x}$. In Section 3.2 we indicated that $\sum(x_i - \bar{x}) = 0$ for any data set. Thus, only $n - 1$ of the $x_i - \bar{x}$ values are independent; that is, if we know $n - 1$ of the values, the remaining value can be determined exactly by

TABLE 8.2 SELECTED VALUES FROM THE *t* DISTRIBUTION TABLE*

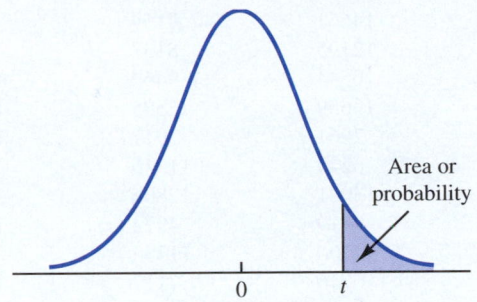

Degrees of Freedom	Area in Upper Tail					
	.20	.10	.05	.025	.01	.005
1	1.376	3.078	6.314	12.706	31.821	63.656
2	1.061	1.886	2.920	4.303	6.965	9.925
3	.978	1.638	2.353	3.182	4.541	5.841
4	.941	1.533	2.132	2.776	3.747	4.604
5	.920	1.476	2.015	2.571	3.365	4.032
6	.906	1.440	1.943	2.447	3.143	3.707
7	.896	1.415	1.895	2.365	2.998	3.499
8	.889	1.397	1.860	2.306	2.896	3.355
9	.883	1.383	1.833	2.262	2.821	3.250
⋮	⋮	⋮	⋮	⋮	⋮	⋮
60	.848	1.296	1.671	2.000	2.390	2.660
61	.848	1.296	1.670	2.000	2.389	2.659
62	.847	1.295	1.670	1.999	2.388	2.657
63	.847	1.295	1.669	1.998	2.387	2.656
64	.847	1.295	1.669	1.998	2.386	2.655
65	.847	1.295	1.669	1.997	2.385	2.654
66	.847	1.295	1.668	1.997	2.384	2.652
67	.847	1.294	1.668	1.996	2.383	2.651
68	.847	1.294	1.668	1.995	2.382	2.650
69	.847	1.294	1.667	1.995	2.382	2.649
⋮	⋮	⋮	⋮	⋮	⋮	⋮
90	.846	1.291	1.662	1.987	2.368	2.632
91	.846	1.291	1.662	1.986	2.368	2.631
92	.846	1.291	1.662	1.986	2.368	2.630
93	.846	1.291	1.661	1.986	2.367	2.630
94	.845	1.291	1.661	1.986	2.367	2.629
95	.845	1.291	1.661	1.985	2.366	2.629
96	.845	1.290	1.661	1.985	2.366	2.628
97	.845	1.290	1.661	1.985	2.365	2.627
98	.845	1.290	1.661	1.984	2.365	2.627
99	.845	1.290	1.660	1.984	2.364	2.626
100	.845	1.290	1.660	1.984	2.364	2.626
∞	.842	1.282	1.645	1.960	2.326	2.576

Note: A more extensive table is provided as Table 2 of Appendix B.

TABLE 8.3   CREDIT CARD BALANCES FOR A SAMPLE OF 70 HOUSEHOLDS

NewBalance

9430	14661	7159	9071	9691	11032
7535	12195	8137	3603	11448	6525
4078	10544	9467	16804	8279	5239
5604	13659	12595	13479	5649	6195
5179	7061	7917	14044	11298	12584
4416	6245	11346	6817	4353	15415
10676	13021	12806	6845	3467	15917
1627	9719	4972	10493	6191	12591
10112	2200	11356	615	12851	9743
6567	10746	7117	13627	5337	10324
13627	12744	9465	12557	8372	
18719	5742	19263	6232	7445	

using the condition that the sum of the $x_i - \bar{x}$ values must be 0. Thus, $n - 1$ is the number of degrees of freedom associated with $\sum(x_i - \bar{x})^2$ and hence the number of degrees of freedom for the t distribution in expression (8.2).

To illustrate the interval estimation procedure for the σ unknown case, we will consider a study designed to estimate the mean credit card debt for the population of U.S. households. A sample of $n = 70$ households provided the credit card balances shown in Table 8.3. For this situation, no previous estimate of the population standard deviation σ is available. Thus, the sample data must be used to estimate both the population mean and the population standard deviation. Using the data in Table 8.3, we compute the sample mean $\bar{x} = \$9312$ and the sample standard deviation $s = \$4007$. With 95% confidence and $n - 1 = 69$ degrees of freedom, Table 8.2 can be used to obtain the appropriate value for $t_{.025}$. We want the t value in the row with 69 degrees of freedom, and the column corresponding to .025 in the upper tail. The value shown is $t_{.025} = 1.995$.

We use expression (8.2) to compute an interval estimate of the population mean credit card balance.

$$9312 \pm 1.995 \frac{4007}{\sqrt{70}}$$

$$9312 \pm 955$$

The point estimate of the population mean is \$9312, the margin of error is \$955, and the 95% confidence interval is $9312 - 955 = \$8357$ to $9312 + 955 = \$10,267$. Thus, we are 95% confident that the mean credit card balance for the population of all households is between \$8357 and \$10,267.

Using Excel

We will use the credit card balances in Table 8.3 to illustrate how Excel can be used to construct an interval estimate of the population mean for the σ unknown case. We start by summarizing the data using Excel's Descriptive Statistics tool described in Chapter 3. Refer to Figure 8.7 as we describe the tasks involved. The formula worksheet is in the background; the value worksheet is in the foreground.

Enter/Access Data: Open the DATAfile named *NewBalance*. A label and the credit card balances are entered into cells A1:A71.

FIGURE 8.7   EXCEL WORKSHEET: 95% CONFIDENCE INTERVAL FOR CREDIT CARD BALANCES

	A	B	C	D	E
1	NewBalance			NewBalance	
2	9430				
3	7535		Mean	9312	
4	4078		Standard Error	478.9281	
5	5604		Median	9466	
6	5179		Mode	13627	
7	4416		Standard Deviation	4007	
8	10676		Sample Variance	16056048	
9	1627		Kurtosis	-0.2960	
10	10112		Skewness	0.1879	
11	6567		Range	18648	
12	13627		Minimum	615	
13	18719		Maximum	19263	
14	14661		Sum	651840	
15	12195		Count	70	
16	10544		Confidence Level(95.0%)	955	
17	13659				
18	7061		Point Estimate	=D3	
19	6245		Lower Limit	=D18-D16	
20	13021		Upper Limit	=D3+D16	
70	9743				
71	10324				
72					

Note: Rows 21–69 are hidden.

	A	B	C	D	E	F
1	NewBalance			NewBalance		
2	9430					
3	7535		Mean	9312	Point Estimate	
4	4078		Standard Error	478.9281		
5	5604		Median	9466		
6	5179		Mode	13627		
7	4416		Standard Deviation	4007		
8	10676		Sample Variance	16056048		
9	1627		Kurtosis	-0.2960		
10	10112		Skewness	0.1879		
11	6567		Range	18648		
12	13627		Minimum	615		
13	18719		Maximum	19263		
14	14661		Sum	651840		
15	12195		Count	70		
16	10544		Confidence Level(95.0%)	955	Margin of Error	
17	13659					
18	7061		Point Estimate	9312		
19	6245		Lower Limit	8357		
20	13021		Upper Limit	10267		
70	9743					
71	10324					
72						

Apply Analysis Tools: The following steps describe how to use Excel's Descriptive Statistics tool for these data:

Step 1. Click the **Data** tab on the Ribbon
Step 2. In the **Analysis** group, click **Data Analysis**
Step 3. Choose **Descriptive Statistics** from the list of Analysis Tools
Step 4. When the Descriptive Statistics dialog box appears:
　　　　Enter A1:A71 in the **Input Range** box
　　　　Select **Grouped By Columns**
　　　　Select **Labels in First Row**
　　　　Select **Output Range:**
　　　　　　Enter C1 in the **Output Range** box
　　　　Select **Summary Statistics**
　　　　Select **Confidence Level for Mean**
　　　　　　Enter 95 in the **Confidence Level for Mean** box
　　　　Click **OK**

The sample mean ($\bar{x}$) is in cell D3. The margin of error, labeled "Confidence Level(95%)," appears in cell D16. The value worksheet shows $\bar{x} = 9312$ and a margin of error equal to 955.

Enter Functions and Formulas: Cells D18:D20 provide the point estimate and the lower and upper limits for the confidence interval. Because the point estimate is just the sample mean, the formula =D3 is entered into cell D18. To compute the lower limit of the 95% confidence interval, $\bar{x} -$ (margin of error), we enter the formula =D18-D16 into cell D19. To compute the upper limit of the 95% confidence interval, $\bar{x} +$ (margin of error), we enter the formula =D18+D16 into cell D20. The value worksheet shows a lower limit of 8357 and an upper limit of 10,267. In other words, the 95% confidence interval for the population mean is from 8357 to 10,267.

Practical Advice

If the population follows a normal distribution, the confidence interval provided by expression (8.2) is exact and can be used for any sample size. If the population does not follow a normal distribution, the confidence interval provided by expression (8.2) will be approximate. In this case, the quality of the approximation depends on both the distribution of the population and the sample size.

Larger sample sizes are needed if the distribution of the population is highly skewed or includes outliers.

In most applications, a sample size of $n \geq 30$ is adequate when using expression (8.2) to develop an interval estimate of a population mean. However, if the population distribution is highly skewed or contains outliers, most statisticians would recommend increasing the sample size to 50 or more. If the population is not normally distributed but is roughly symmetric, sample sizes as small as 15 can be expected to provide good approximate confidence intervals. With smaller sample sizes, expression (8.2) should only be used if the analyst believes, or is willing to assume, that the population distribution is at least approximately normal.

Using a Small Sample

In the following example we develop an interval estimate for a population mean when the sample size is small. As we already noted, an understanding of the distribution of the population becomes a factor in deciding whether the interval estimation procedure provides acceptable results.

Scheer Industries is considering a new computer-assisted program to train maintenance employees to do machine repairs. In order to fully evaluate the program, the director of manufacturing requested an estimate of the population mean time required for maintenance employees to complete the computer-assisted training.

A sample of 20 employees is selected, with each employee in the sample completing the training program. Data on the training time in days for the 20 employees are shown in Table 8.4. A histogram of the sample data appears in Figure 8.8. What can we say about the distribution of the population based on this histogram? First, the sample data do not support the conclusion that the distribution of the population is normal, yet we do not see any evidence of skewness or outliers. Therefore, using the guidelines in the previous subsection, we conclude that an interval estimate based on the t distribution appears acceptable for the sample of 20 employees.

TABLE 8.4   TRAINING TIME IN DAYS FOR A SAMPLE OF 20 SCHEER
INDUSTRIES EMPLOYEES

DATA *file*

Scheer

52	59	54	42
44	50	42	48
55	54	60	55
44	62	62	57
45	46	43	56

FIGURE 8.8 HISTOGRAM OF TRAINING TIMES FOR THE SCHEER INDUSTRIES SAMPLE

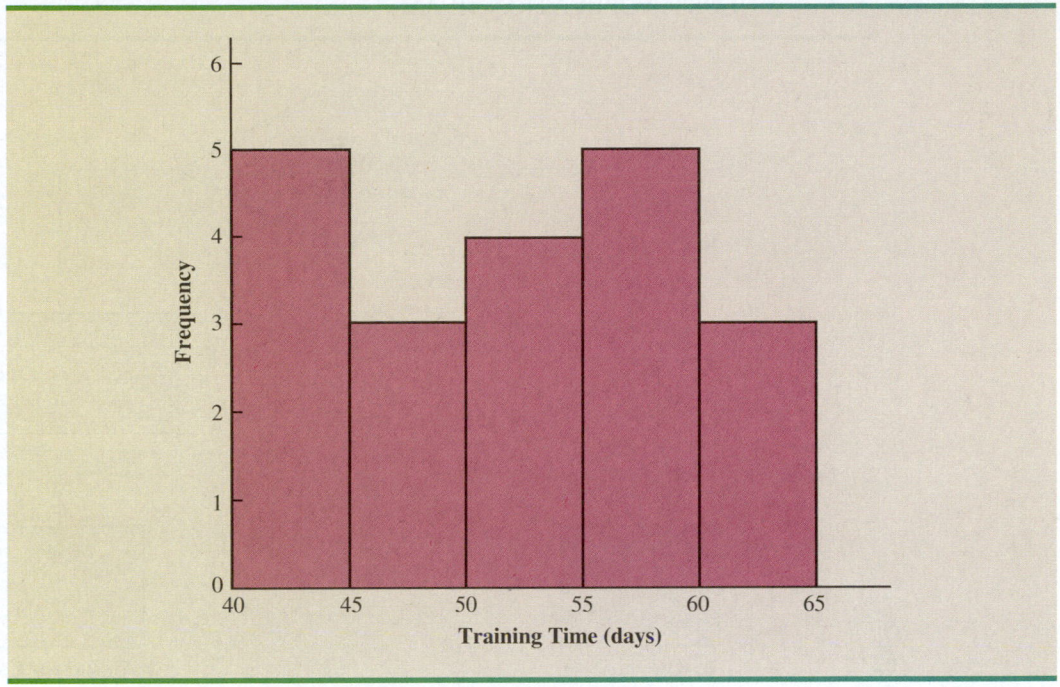

We continue by computing the sample mean and sample standard deviation as follows.

$$\bar{x} = \frac{\sum x_i}{n} = \frac{1030}{20} = 51.5 \text{ days}$$

$$s = \sqrt{\frac{\sum(x_i - \bar{x})^2}{n-1}} = \sqrt{\frac{889}{20-1}} = 6.84 \text{ days}$$

For a 95% confidence interval, we use Table 2 of Appendix B and $n - 1 = 19$ degrees of freedom to obtain $t_{.025} = 2.093$. Expression (8.2) provides the interval estimate of the population mean.

$$51.5 \pm 2.093\left(\frac{6.84}{\sqrt{20}}\right)$$

$$51.5 \pm 3.2$$

The point estimate of the population mean is 51.5 days. The margin of error is 3.2 days and the 95% confidence interval is $51.5 - 3.2 = 48.3$ days to $51.5 + 3.2 = 54.7$ days.

Using a histogram of the sample data to learn about the distribution of a population is not always conclusive, but in many cases it provides the only information available. The histogram, along with judgment on the part of the analyst, can often be used to decide whether expression (8.2) can be used to develop the interval estimate.

Summary of Interval Estimation Procedures

We provided two approaches to developing an interval estimate of a population mean. For the σ known case, σ and the standard normal distribution are used in expression (8.1) to compute the margin of error and to develop the interval estimate. For the σ unknown case, the sample standard deviation s and the t distribution are used in expression (8.2) to compute the margin of error and to develop the interval estimate.

FIGURE 8.9   SUMMARY OF INTERVAL ESTIMATION PROCEDURES
FOR A POPULATION MEAN

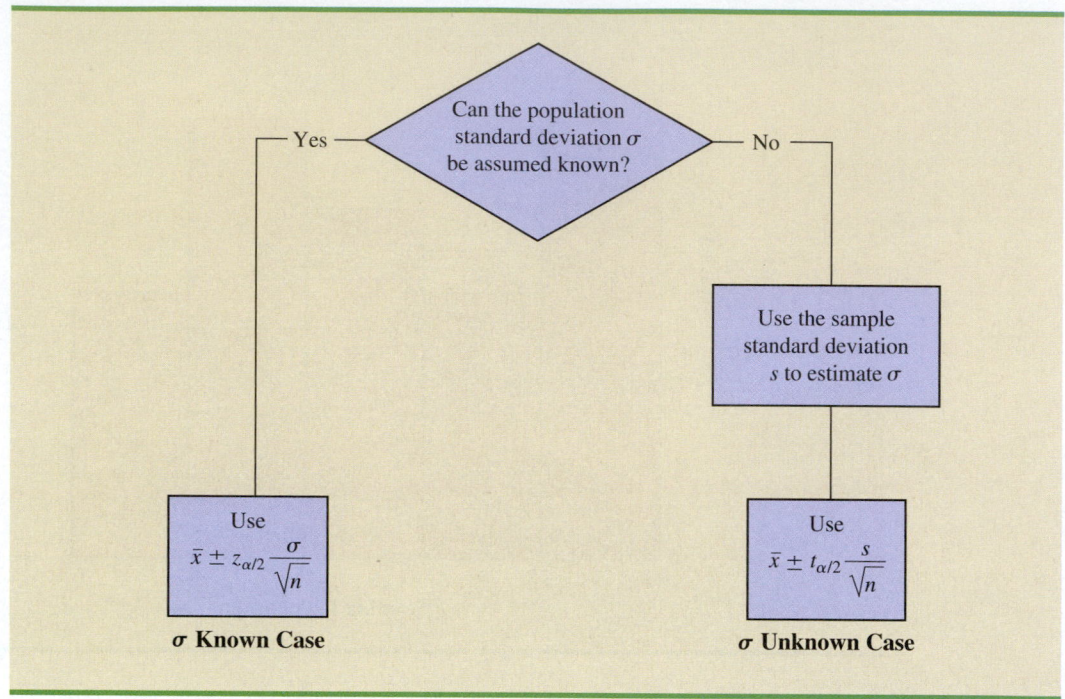

A summary of the interval estimation procedures for the two cases is shown in Figure 8.9. In most applications, a sample size of $n \geq 30$ is adequate. If the population has a normal or approximately normal distribution, however, smaller sample sizes may be used. For the σ unknown case a sample size of $n \geq 50$ is recommended if the population distribution is believed to be highly skewed or has outliers.

NOTES AND COMMENTS

1. When σ is known, the margin of error, $z_{\alpha/2}(\sigma/\sqrt{n})$, is fixed and is the same for all samples of size n. When σ is unknown, the margin of error, $t_{\alpha/2}(s/\sqrt{n})$, varies from sample to sample. This variation occurs because the sample standard deviation s varies depending upon the sample selected. A large value for s provides a larger margin of error, while a small value for s provides a smaller margin of error.

2. What happens to confidence interval estimates when the population is skewed? Consider a population that is skewed to the right with large data values stretching the distribution to the right. When such skewness exists, the sample mean $\bar{x}$ and the sample standard deviation s are positively correlated. Larger values of s tend to be associated with larger values of $\bar{x}$. Thus, when $\bar{x}$ is larger than the population mean, s tends to be larger than σ. This skewness causes the margin of error, $t_{\alpha/2}(s/\sqrt{n})$, to be larger than it would be with σ

known. The confidence interval with the larger margin of error tends to include the population mean μ more often than it would if the true value of σ were used. But when $\bar{x}$ is smaller than the population mean, the correlation between $\bar{x}$ and s causes the margin of error to be small. In this case, the confidence interval with the smaller margin of error tends to miss the population mean more than it would if we knew σ and used it. For this reason, we recommend using larger sample sizes with highly skewed population distributions.

3. When developing a confidence interval for the mean with a sample size that is at least 5% of the population size (that is, $n/N \geq .05$), the finite population correction factor should be used when calculating the standard error of the sampling distribution of $\bar{x}$ when σ is unknown, i.e.,

$$s_{\bar{x}} = \sqrt{\frac{N-n}{N-1}}\left(\frac{s}{\sqrt{n}}\right).$$

Exercises

Methods

11. For a t distribution with 16 degrees of freedom, find the area, or probability, in each region.
    a. To the right of 2.120
    b. To the left of 1.337
    c. To the left of -1.746
    d. To the right of 2.583
    e. Between -2.120 and 2.120
    f. Between -1.746 and 1.746

12. Find the t value(s) for each of the following cases.
    a. Upper tail area of .025 with 12 degrees of freedom
    b. Lower tail area of .05 with 50 degrees of freedom
    c. Upper tail area of .01 with 30 degrees of freedom
    d. Where 90% of the area falls between these two t values with 25 degrees of freedom
    e. Where 95% of the area falls between these two t values with 45 degrees of freedom

 13. The following sample data are from a normal population: 10, 8, 12, 15, 13, 11, 6, 5.
    a. What is the point estimate of the population mean?
    b. What is the point estimate of the population standard deviation?
    c. With 95% confidence, what is the margin of error for the estimation of the population mean?
    d. What is the 95% confidence interval for the population mean?

14. A simple random sample with $n = 54$ provided a sample mean of 22.5 and a sample standard deviation of 4.4.
    a. Develop a 90% confidence interval for the population mean.
    b. Develop a 95% confidence interval for the population mean.
    c. Develop a 99% confidence interval for the population mean.
    d. What happens to the margin of error and the confidence interval as the confidence level is increased?

Applications

 15. Sales personnel for Skillings Distributors submit weekly reports listing the customer contacts made during the week. A sample of 65 weekly reports showed a sample mean of 19.5 customer contacts per week. The sample standard deviation was 5.2. Provide 90% and 95% confidence intervals for the population mean number of weekly customer contacts for the sales personnel.

CorporateBonds 16. A sample of years to maturity and yield for 40 corporate bonds taken from *Barron's* is in the DATAfile named *CorporateBonds*.
    a. What is the sample mean years to maturity for corporate bonds and what is the sample standard deviation?
    b. Develop a 95% confidence interval for the population mean years to maturity.
    c. What is the sample mean yield on corporate bonds and what is the sample standard deviation?
    d. Develop a 95% confidence interval for the population mean yield on corporate bonds.

Miami 17. The International Air Transport Association surveys business travelers to develop quality ratings for transatlantic gateway airports. The maximum possible rating is 10. Suppose a simple random sample of 50 business travelers is selected and each traveler is asked to provide a rating for the Miami International Airport. The ratings obtained from the sample of 50 business travelers follow.

6	4	6	8	7	7	6	3	3	8	10	4	8
7	8	7	5	9	5	8	4	3	8	5	5	4
4	4	8	4	5	6	2	5	9	9	8	4	8
9	9	5	9	7	8	3	10	8	9	6		

Develop a 95% confidence interval estimate of the population mean rating for Miami.

JobSearch

18. Older people often have a hard time finding work. AARP reported on the number of weeks it takes a worker aged 55 plus to find a job. The data on number of weeks spent searching for a job contained in the DATAfile named *JobSearch* are consistent with the AARP findings.

  a. Provide a point estimate of the population mean number of weeks it takes a worker aged 55 plus to find a job.
  b. At 95% confidence, what is the margin of error?
  c. What is the 95% confidence interval estimate of the mean?
  d. Discuss the degree of skewness found in the sample data. What suggestion would you make for a repeat of this study?

HongKongMeals

19. The mean cost of a meal for two in a mid-range restaurant in Tokyo is $40. (Numbeo.com website, December 14, 2014). How do prices for comparable meals in Hong Kong compare? The DATAfile *HongKongMeals* contains the costs for a sample of 42 recent meals for two in Hong Kong mid-range restaurants.

  a. With 95% confidence, what is the margin of error?
  b. What is the 95% confidence interval estimate of the population mean?
  c. How do prices for meals for two in mid-range restaurants in Hong Kong compare to prices for comparable meals in Tokyo restaurants?

AutoInsurance

20. The average annual premium for automobile insurance in the United States is $1503 (Insure.com website, March 6, 2014). The following annual premiums ($) are representative of the website's findings for the state of Michigan.

1905	3112	2312
2725	2545	2981
2677	2525	2627
2600	2370	2857
2962	2545	2675
2184	2529	2115
2332	2442	

Assume the population is approximately normal.

  a. Provide a point estimate of the mean annual automobile insurance premium in Michigan.
  b. Develop a 95% confidence interval for the mean annual automobile insurance premium in Michigan.
  c. Does the 95% confidence interval for the annual automobile insurance premium in Michigan include the national average for the United States? What is your interpretation of the relationship between auto insurance premiums in Michigan and the national average?

TeleHealth

21. Health insurers are beginning to offer telemedicine services online that replace the common office visit. Wellpoint provides a video service that allows subscribers to connect with a physician online and receive prescribed treatments (*Bloomberg Businessweek*, March 4–9, 2014). Wellpoint claims that users of its LiveHealth Online service saved a significant amount of

money on a typical visit. The data shown below ($), for a sample of 20 online doctor visits, are consistent with the savings per visit reported by Wellpoint.

92	34	40
105	83	55
56	49	40
76	48	96
93	74	73
78	93	100
53	82	

Assuming the population is roughly symmetric, construct a 95% confidence interval for the mean savings for a televisit to the doctor as opposed to an office visit.

Guardians

22. Marvel Studio's motion picture *Guardians of the Galaxy* opened over the first two days of the 2014 Labor Day weekend to a record-breaking $94.3 million in ticket sales revenue in North America (*The Hollywood Reporter*, August 3, 2014). The ticket sales revenue in dollars for a sample of 30 theaters is provided in the DATAfile named *Guardians*.
   a. What is the 95% confidence interval estimate for the mean ticket sales revenue per theater? Interpret this result.
   b. Using the movie ticket price of $8.11 per ticket, what is the estimate of the mean number of customers per theater?
   c. The movie was shown in 4080 theaters. Estimate the total number of customers who saw *Guardians of the Galaxy* and the total box office ticket sales for the weekend.

8.3 Determining the Sample Size

If a desired margin of error is selected prior to sampling, the procedures in this section can be used to determine the sample size necessary to satisfy the margin of error requirement.

In providing practical advice in the two preceding sections, we commented on the role of the sample size in providing good approximate confidence intervals when the population is not normally distributed. In this section, we focus on another aspect of the sample size issue. We describe how to choose a sample size large enough to provide a desired margin of error. To understand how this process works, we return to the σ known case presented in Section 8.1. Using expression (8.1), the interval estimate is

$$\bar{x} \pm z_{\alpha/2} \frac{\sigma}{\sqrt{n}}$$

The quantity $z_{\alpha/2}(\sigma/\sqrt{n})$ is the margin of error. Thus, we see that $z_{\alpha/2}$, the population standard deviation σ, and the sample size n combine to determine the margin of error. Once we select a confidence coefficient $1 - \alpha$, $z_{\alpha/2}$ can be determined. Then, if we have a value for σ, we can determine the sample size n needed to provide any desired margin of error. Development of the formula used to compute the required sample size n follows.

Let E = the desired margin of error:

$$E = z_{\alpha/2} \frac{\sigma}{\sqrt{n}}$$

Solving for $\sqrt{n}$, we have

$$\sqrt{n} = \frac{z_{\alpha/2}\sigma}{E}$$

Squaring both sides of this equation, we obtain the following expression for the sample size.

Equation (8.3) can be used to provide a good sample size recommendation. However, judgment on the part of the analyst should be used to determine whether the final sample size should be adjusted upward.

SAMPLE SIZE FOR AN INTERVAL ESTIMATE OF A POPULATION MEAN

$$n = \frac{(z_{\alpha/2})^2 \sigma^2}{E^2} \qquad\qquad (8.3)$$

This sample size provides the desired margin of error at the chosen confidence level.

In equation (8.3), E is the margin of error that the user is willing to accept, and the value of $z_{\alpha/2}$ follows directly from the confidence level to be used in developing the interval estimate. Although user preference must be considered, 95% confidence is the most frequently chosen value ($z_{.025} = 1.96$).

Finally, use of equation (8.3) requires a value for the population standard deviation σ. However, even if σ is unknown, we can use equation (8.3) provided we have a preliminary or *planning value* for σ. In practice, one of the following procedures can be chosen.

A planning value for the population standard deviation σ must be specified before the sample size can be determined. Three methods of obtaining a planning value for σ are discussed here.

1. Use the estimate of the population standard deviation computed from data of previous studies as the planning value for σ.
2. Use a pilot study to select a preliminary sample. The sample standard deviation from the preliminary sample can be used as the planning value for σ.
3. Use judgment or a "best guess" for the value of σ. For example, we might begin by estimating the largest and smallest data values in the population. The difference between the largest and smallest values provides an estimate of the range for the data. Finally, the range divided by 4 is often suggested as a rough approximation of the standard deviation and thus an acceptable planning value for σ.

Let us demonstrate the use of equation (8.3) to determine the sample size by considering the following example. A previous study that investigated the cost of renting automobiles in the United States found a mean cost of approximately $55 per day for renting a midsize automobile. Suppose that the organization that conducted this study would like to conduct a new study in order to estimate the population mean daily rental cost for a midsize automobile in the United States. In designing the new study, the project director specifies that the population mean daily rental cost be estimated with a margin of error of $2 and a 95% level of confidence.

The project director specified a desired margin of error of $E = 2$, and the 95% level of confidence indicates $z_{.025} = 1.96$. Thus, we only need a planning value for the population standard deviation σ in order to compute the required sample size. At this point, an analyst reviewed the sample data from the previous study and found that the sample standard deviation for the daily rental cost was $9.65. Using 9.65 as the planning value for σ, we obtain

Equation (8.3) provides the minimum sample size needed to satisfy the desired margin of error requirement. If the computed sample size is not an integer, rounding up to the next integer value will provide a margin of error slightly smaller than required.

$$n = \frac{(z_{\alpha/2})^2 \sigma^2}{E^2} = \frac{(1.96)^2(9.65)^2}{2^2} = 89.43$$

Thus, the sample size for the new study needs to be at least 89.43 midsize automobile rentals in order to satisfy the project director's $2 margin-of-error requirement. In cases where the computed n is not an integer, we round up to the next integer value; hence, the recommended sample size is 90 midsize automobile rentals.

NOTE AND COMMENT

Equation (8.3) provides the recommended sample size n for an infinite population as well as for a large finite population of size N provided $n/N \le .05$. This is fine for most statistical studies. However, if we have a finite population such that $n/N > .05$, a smaller sample size can be used to obtain the desired margin of error. The smaller sample size, denoted by n', can be computed using the following equation:

$$n' = \frac{n}{(1 + n/N)}$$

For example, suppose that the example presented in this section showing $n = 89.43$ was computed for a population of size $N = 500$. With $n/N = 89.43/500 = .18 > .05$, a smaller sample size can be computed by

$$n' = \frac{n}{1 + n/N} = \frac{89.43}{1 + 89.43/500} = 75.86$$

Thus, for the finite population of $N = 500$, the sample size required to obtain the desired margin of error $E = 2$ would be reduced from 90 to 76.

Exercises

Methods

23. How large a sample should be selected to provide a 95% confidence interval with a margin of error of 10? Assume that the population standard deviation is 40.

24. The range for a set of data is estimated to be 36.
    a. What is the planning value for the population standard deviation?
    b. At 95% confidence, how large a sample would provide a margin of error of 3?
    c. At 95% confidence, how large a sample would provide a margin of error of 2?

Applications

25. Refer to the Scheer Industries example in Section 8.2. Use 6.84 days as a planning value for the population standard deviation.
    a. Assuming 95% confidence, what sample size would be required to obtain a margin of error of 1.5 days?
    b. If the precision statement was made with 90% confidence, what sample size would be required to obtain a margin of error of 2 days?

26. The U.S. Energy Information Administration (US EIA) reported that the average price for a gallon of regular gasoline is $3.94. The US EIA updates its estimates of average gas prices on a weekly basis. Assume the standard deviation is $.25 for the price of a gallon of regular gasoline and recommend the appropriate sample size for the US EIA to use if they wish to report each of the following margins of error at 95% confidence.
    a. The desired margin of error is $.10.
    b. The desired margin of error is $.07.
    c. The desired margin of error is $.05.

27. Annual starting salaries for college graduates with degrees in business administration are generally expected to be between $30,000 and $45,000. Assume that a 95% confidence interval estimate of the population mean annual starting salary is desired.
    a. What is the planning value for the population standard deviation?
    b. How large a sample should be taken if the desired margin of error is $500? $200? $100?
    c. Would you recommend trying to obtain the $100 margin of error? Explain.

28. Many medical professionals believe that eating too much red meat increases the risk of heart disease and cancer (WebMD website, March 12, 2014). Suppose you would like to conduct a survey to determine the yearly consumption of beef by a typical American and want to use 3 pounds as the desired margin of error for a confidence interval estimate of the population mean amount of beef consumed annually. Use 25 pounds as a planning value for the population standard deviation and recommend a sample size for each of the following situations.
    a. A 90% confidence interval is desired for the mean amount of beef consumed.
    b. A 95% confidence interval is desired for the mean amount of beef consumed.
    c. A 99% confidence interval is desired for the mean amount of beef consumed.
    d. When the desired margin of error is set, what happens to the sample size as the confidence level is increased? Would you recommend using a 99% confidence interval in this case? Discuss.

29. Customers arrive at a movie theater at the advertised movie time only to find that they have to sit through several previews and prepreview ads before the movie starts. Many complain that the time devoted to previews is too long (*The Wall Street Journal*, October 12, 2012).

A preliminary sample conducted by *The Wall Street Journal* showed that the standard deviation of the amount of time devoted to previews was 4 minutes. Use that as a planning value for the standard deviation in answering the following questions.

a.   If we want to estimate the population mean time for previews at movie theaters with a margin of error of 75 seconds, what sample size should be used? Assume 95% confidence.

b.   If we want to estimate the population mean time for previews at movie theaters with a margin of error of 1 minute, what sample size should be used? Assume 95% confidence.

30.   Americans eat out very frequently; the average American adult buys a meal or snack from a restaurant 5.8 times a week (The United States Healthful Food Council, December 5, 2015). Assume the standard deviation for the number of meals or snacks American adults buy from restaurants per week is 1.5. Suppose you would like to conduct a survey to develop a 95% confidence interval estimate of the number of meals or snacks American adults buy from restaurants per week. A margin of error of 0.5 is desired. How large a sample should be used for the current survey?

8.4   Population Proportion

In the introduction to this chapter, we said that the general form of an interval estimate of a population proportion p is

$$\bar{p} \pm \text{Margin of error}$$

The sampling distribution of $\bar{p}$ plays a key role in computing the margin of error for this interval estimate.

In Chapter 7 we said that the sampling distribution of $\bar{p}$ can be approximated by a normal distribution whenever $np \geq 5$ and $n(1 - p) \geq 5$. Figure 8.10 shows the normal approximation of the sampling distribution of $\bar{p}$. The mean of the sampling distribution of $\bar{p}$ is the population proportion p, and the standard error of $\bar{p}$ is

$$\sigma_{\bar{p}} = \sqrt{\frac{p(1 - p)}{n}} \tag{8.4}$$

FIGURE 8.10   NORMAL APPROXIMATION OF THE SAMPLING DISTRIBUTION OF $\bar{p}$

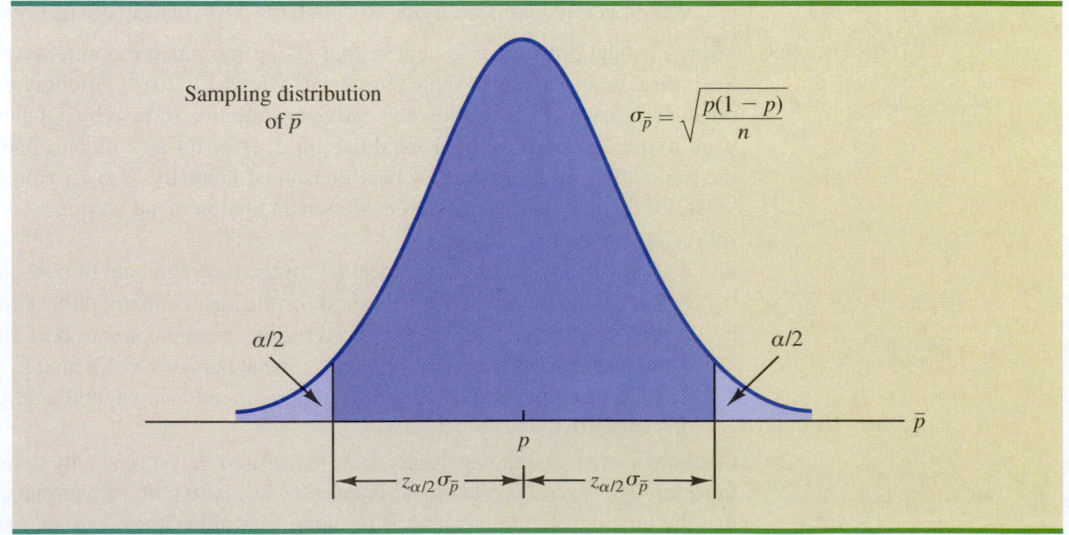

Because the sampling distribution of $\bar{p}$ is normally distributed, if we choose $z_{\alpha/2}\sigma_{\bar{p}}$ as the margin of error in an interval estimate of a population proportion, we know that $100(1 - \alpha)\%$ of the intervals generated will contain the true population proportion. But $\sigma_{\bar{p}}$ cannot be used directly in the computation of the margin of error because p will not be known; p is what we are trying to estimate. So $\bar{p}$ is substituted for p and the margin of error for an interval estimate of a population proportion is given by

$$\text{Margin of error} = z_{\alpha/2}\sqrt{\frac{\bar{p}(1 - \bar{p})}{n}} \qquad \textbf{(8.5)}$$

With this margin of error, the general expression for an interval estimate of a population proportion is as follows.

INTERVAL ESTIMATE OF A POPULATION PROPORTION

When developing confidence intervals for proportions, the quantity $z_{\alpha/2}\sqrt{\bar{p}(1 - \bar{p})/n}$ provides the margin of error.

$$\bar{p} \pm z_{\alpha/2}\sqrt{\frac{\bar{p}(1 - \bar{p})}{n}} \qquad \textbf{(8.6)}$$

where $1 - \alpha$ is the confidence coefficient and $z_{\alpha/2}$ is the z value providing an area of $\alpha/2$ in the upper tail of the standard normal distribution.

DATA *file*

TeeTimes

The following example illustrates the computation of the margin of error and interval estimate for a population proportion. A national survey of 900 women golfers was conducted to learn how women golfers view their treatment at golf courses in the United States. The survey found that 396 of the women golfers were satisfied with the availability of tee times. Thus, the point estimate of the proportion of the population of women golfers who are satisfied with the availability of tee times is $396/900 = .44$. Using expression (8.6) and a 95% confidence level,

$$\bar{p} \pm z_{\alpha/2}\sqrt{\frac{\bar{p}(1 - \bar{p})}{n}}$$

$$.44 \pm 1.96\sqrt{\frac{.44(1 - .44)}{900}}$$

$$.44 \pm .0324$$

Thus, the margin of error is .0324 and the 95% confidence interval estimate of the population proportion is .4076 to .4724. Using percentages, the survey results enable us to state with 95% confidence that between 40.76% and 47.24% of all women golfers are satisfied with the availability of tee times.

Using Excel

Excel can be used to construct an interval estimate of the population proportion of women golfers who are satisfied with the availability of tee times. The responses in the survey were recorded as a Yes or No for each woman surveyed. Refer to Figure 8.11 as we describe the tasks involved in constructing a 95% confidence interval. The formula worksheet is in the background; the value worksheet appears in the foreground.

Enter/Access Data: Open the DATAfile named *TeeTimes*. A label and the Yes/No data for the 900 women golfers are entered into cells A1:A901.

FIGURE 8.11 EXCEL WORKSHEET: 95% CONFIDENCE INTERVAL FOR SURVEY OF WOMEN GOLFERS

DATA *file*

TeeTimes

	A	B	C	D	E
1	Response		Interval Estimate of a Population Proportion		
2	Yes				
3	No		Sample Size	=COUNTA(A2:A901)	
4	Yes		Response of Interest	Yes	
5	Yes		Count for Response	=COUNTIF(A2:A901,D4)	
6	No		Sample Proportion	=D5/D3	
7	No				
8	No		Confidence Coefficient	0.95	
9	Yes		Level of Significance (alpha)	=1-D8	
10	Yes		*z* Value	=NORM.S.INV(1-D9/2)	
11	Yes				
12	No		Standard Error	=SQRT(D6*(1-D6)/D3)	
13	No		Margin of Error	=D10*D12	
14	Yes				
15	No		Point Estimate	=D6	
16	No		Lower Limit	=D15-D13	
17	Yes		Upper Limit	=D15+D13	
18	No				
900	Yes				
901	Yes				
902					

	A	B	C	D	E	F	G
1	Response		Interval Estimate of a Population Proportion				
2	Yes						
3	No		Sample Size	900	Enter Yes as the Response of Interest		
4	Yes		Response of Interest	Yes			
5	Yes		Count for Response	396			
6	No		Sample Proportion	0.44			
7	No						
8	No		Confidence Coefficient	0.95			
9	Yes		Level of Significance	0.05			
10	Yes		*z* Value	1.96			
11	Yes						
12	No		Standard Error	0.0165			
13	No		Margin of Error	0.0324			
14	Yes						
15	No		Point Estimate	0.44			
16	No		Lower Limit	0.4076			
17	Yes		Upper Limit	0.4724			
18	No						
900	Yes						
901	Yes						
902							

Note: Rows 19 to 899 are hidden.

Enter Functions and Formulas: The descriptive statistics we need and the response of interest are provided in cells D3:D6. Because Excel's COUNT function works only with numerical data, we used the COUNTA function in cell D3 to compute the sample size. The response for which we want to develop an interval estimate, Yes or No, is entered into cell D4. Figure 8.11 shows that Yes has been entered into cell D4, indicating that we want to develop an interval estimate of the population proportion of women golfers who are satisfied with the availability of tee times. If we had wanted to develop an interval estimate of the population proportion of women golfers who are not satisfied with the availability of tee times, we would have entered No in cell D4. With Yes entered in cell D4, the COUNTIF function in cell D5 counts the number of Yes responses in the sample. The sample proportion is then computed in cell D6 by dividing the number of Yes responses in cell D5 by the sample size in cell D3.

Cells D8:D10 are used to compute the appropriate z value. The confidence coefficient (0.95) is entered into cell D8 and the level of significance (α) is computed in cell D9 by entering the formula =1-D8. The z value corresponding to an upper tail area of $\alpha/2$ is computed by entering the formula =NORM.S.INV(1-D9/2) into cell D10. The value worksheet shows that $z_{.025} = 1.96$.

Cells D12:D13 provide the estimate of the standard error and the margin of error. In cell D12, we entered the formula =SQRT(D6*(1-D6)/D3) to compute the standard error using the sample proportion and the sample size as inputs. The formula =D10*D12 is entered into cell D13 to compute the margin of error.

Cells D15:D17 provide the point estimate and the lower and upper limits for a confidence interval. The point estimate in cell D15 is the sample proportion. The lower and upper limits in cells D16 and D17 are obtained by subtracting and adding the margin of error to the point estimate. We note that the 95% confidence interval for the proportion of women golfers who are satisfied with the availability of tee times is .4076 to .4724.

A template for other problems The worksheet in Figure 8.11 can be used as a template for developing confidence intervals about a population proportion p. To use this worksheet for another problem of this type, we must first enter the new problem data in column A. The response of interest would then be typed in cell D4 and the ranges for the formulas in cells D3 and D5 would be revised to correspond to the new data. After doing so, the point estimate and a 95% confidence interval will be displayed in cells D15:D17. If a confidence interval with a different confidence coefficient is desired, we simply change the value in cell D8.

Determining the Sample Size

Let us consider the question of how large the sample size should be to obtain an estimate of a population proportion at a specified level of precision. The rationale for the sample size determination in developing interval estimates of p is similar to the rationale used in Section 8.3 to determine the sample size for estimating a population mean.

Previously in this section we said that the margin of error associated with an interval estimate of a population proportion is $z_{\alpha/2}\sqrt{\bar{p}(1-\bar{p})/n}$. The margin of error is based on the value of $z_{\alpha/2}$, the sample proportion $\bar{p}$, and the sample size n. Larger sample sizes provide a smaller margin of error and better precision.

Let E denote the desired margin of error.

$$E = z_{\alpha/2}\sqrt{\frac{\bar{p}(1-\bar{p})}{n}}$$

Solving this equation for n provides a formula for the sample size that will provide a margin of error of size E.

$$n = \frac{(z_{\alpha/2})^2\,\bar{p}(1-\bar{p})}{E^2}$$

Note, however, that we cannot use this formula to compute the sample size that will provide the desired margin of error because $\bar{p}$ will not be known until after we select the sample. What we need, then, is a planning value for $\bar{p}$ that can be used to make the computation. Using p^* to denote the planning value for $\bar{p}$, the following formula can be used to compute the sample size that will provide a margin of error of size E.

SAMPLE SIZE FOR AN INTERVAL ESTIMATE OF A POPULATION PROPORTION

$$n = \frac{(z_{\alpha/2})^2 p^*(1-p^*)}{E^2} \tag{8.7}$$

In practice, the planning value p^* can be chosen by one of the following procedures.

1. Use the sample proportion from a previous sample of the same or similar units.
2. Use a pilot study to select a preliminary sample. The sample proportion from this sample can be used as the planning value, p^*.
3. Use judgment or a "best guess" for the value of p^*.
4. If none of the preceding alternatives applies, use a planning value of $p^* = .50$.

Let us return to the survey of women golfers and assume that the company is interested in conducting a new survey to estimate the current proportion of the population of women golfers who are satisfied with the availability of tee times. How large should the sample be if the survey director wants to estimate the population proportion with a margin of error of .025 at 95% confidence? With $E = .025$ and $z_{\alpha/2} = 1.96$, we need a planning value p^* to answer the sample size question. Using the previous survey result of $\bar{p} = .44$ as the planning value p^*, equation (8.7) shows that

$$n = \frac{(z_{\alpha/2})^2 p^*(1-p^*)}{E^2} = \frac{(1.96)^2(.44)(1-.44)}{(.025)^2} = 1514.5$$

Thus, the sample size must be at least 1514.5 women golfers to satisfy the margin of error requirement. Rounding up to the next integer value indicates that a sample of 1515 women golfers is recommended to satisfy the margin of error requirement.

TABLE 8.5   SOME POSSIBLE VALUES FOR $p^*(1 - p^*)$

p^*	$p^*(1 - p^*)$	
.10	$(.10)(.90) = .09$	
.30	$(.30)(.70) = .21$	
.40	$(.40)(.60) = .24$	
.50	$(.50)(.50) = .25$	← Largest value for $p^*(1 - p^*)$
.60	$(.60)(.40) = .24$	
.70	$(.70)(.30) = .21$	
.90	$(.90)(.10) = .09$	

The fourth alternative suggested for selecting a planning value p^* is to use $p^* = .50$. This value of p^* is frequently used when no other information is available. To understand why, note that the numerator of equation (8.7) shows that the sample size is proportional to the quantity $p^*(1 - p^*)$. A larger value for the quantity $p^*(1 - p^*)$ will result in a larger sample size. Table 8.5 gives some possible values of $p^*(1 - p^*)$. Note that the largest value of $p^*(1 - p^*)$ occurs when $p^* = .50$. Thus, in case of any uncertainty about an appropriate planning value, we know that $p^* = .50$ will provide the largest sample size recommendation. In effect, we play it safe by recommending the largest necessary sample size. If the sample proportion turns out to be different from the .50 planning value, the margin of error will be smaller than anticipated. Thus, in using $p^* = .50$, we guarantee that the sample size will be sufficient to obtain the desired margin of error.

In the survey of women golfers example, a planning value of $p^* = .50$ would have provided the sample size

$$n = \frac{(z_{\alpha/2})^2 p^*(1 - p^*)}{E^2} = \frac{(1.96)^2(.50)(1 - .50)}{(.025)^2} = 1536.6$$

Thus, a slightly larger sample size of 1537 women golfers would be recommended.

NOTES AND COMMENTS

1. The desired margin of error for estimating a population proportion is almost always .10 or less. In national public opinion polls conducted by organizations such as Gallup and Harris, a .03 or .04 margin of error is common. With such margins of error, equation (8.7) will almost always provide a sample size that is large enough to satisfy the requirements of $np \geq 5$ and $n(1 - p) \geq 5$ for using a normal distribution as an approximation for the sampling distribution of $\bar{x}$.

2. When developing a confidence interval for the proportion with a sample size that is at least 5% of the population size (that is, $n/N \geq .05$), the finite population correction factor should be used when calculating the standard error of the sampling distribution of $\bar{p}$, i.e.,

$$s_{\bar{p}} = \sqrt{\frac{N - n}{N - 1}} \sqrt{\frac{\bar{p}(1 - \bar{p})}{n}}.$$

3. Equation (8.7) provides the recommended sample size n for an infinite population as well as for a large finite population of size N provided $n/N < .05$. This is fine for most statistical studies. However, if we have a finite population such that $n/N > .05$, a smaller sample size can be used to obtain the desired margin of error. The smaller sample size denoted by n' can be computed using the following equation.

$$n' = \frac{n}{(1 + n/N)}$$

For example, suppose that the example presented in this section showing $n = 1536.6$ was computed for a population of size $N = 2500$. With $n/N = 1536.6/2500 = .61 > .05$, a smaller sample size can be computed by

$$n' = \frac{n}{(1 + n/N)} = \frac{1536.6}{(1 + 1536.6/2500)} = 951.67$$

Thus, for the finite population of $N = 2500$, the sample size required to obtain the desired margin of error $E = .025$ would be reduced from 1537 to 952.

Exercises

Methods

31. A simple random sample of 400 individuals provides 100 Yes responses.
    a. What is the point estimate of the proportion of the population that would provide Yes responses?
    b. What is your estimate of the standard error of the proportion, $\sigma_{\bar{p}}$?
    c. Compute the 95% confidence interval for the population proportion.

32. A simple random sample of 800 elements generates a sample proportion $\bar{p} = .70$.
    a. Provide a 90% confidence interval for the population proportion.
    b. Provide a 95% confidence interval for the population proportion.

33. In a survey, the planning value for the population proportion is $p^* = .35$. How large a sample should be taken to provide a 95% confidence interval with a margin of error of .05?

34. At 95% confidence, how large a sample should be taken to obtain a margin of error of .03 for the estimation of a population proportion? Assume that past data are not available for developing a planning value for p^*.

Applications

35. The Pew Research Center conducted a survey of 45,535 adults in 40 countries to learn about major concerns for the future (Pew Research Center website, December 5, 2015). The survey results showed that 20,901 of the respondents are very concerned about climate change.
    a. What is the point estimate of the population proportion of adults who are very concerned about climate change?
    b. At 90% confidence, what is the margin of error?
    c. Develop a 90% confidence interval for the population proportion of adults who are very concerned about climate change.
    d. Develop a 95% confidence interval for the population proportion of adults who are very concerned about climate change.

36. According to statistics reported on CNBC, a surprising number of motor vehicles are not covered by insurance. Sample results, consistent with the CNBC report, showed 46 of 200 vehicles were not covered by insurance.
    a. What is the point estimate of the proportion of vehicles not covered by insurance?
    b. Develop a 95% confidence interval for the population proportion.

ChildOutlook

37. One of the questions on a survey of 1000 adults asked if today's children will be better off than their parents (Rasmussen Reports website, October 26, 2012). Representative data are shown in the DATAfile named *ChildOutlook*. A response of Yes indicates that the adult surveyed did think today's children will be better off than their parents. A response of No indicates that the adult surveyed did not think today's children will be better off than their parents. A response of Not Sure was given by 23% of the adults surveyed.
    a. What is the point estimate of the proportion of the population of adults who do think that today's children will be better off than their parents?
    b. At 95% confidence, what is the margin of error?
    c. What is the 95% confidence interval for the proportion of adults who do think that today's children will be better off than their parents?
    d. What is the 95% confidence interval for the proportion of adults who do not think that today's children will be better off than their parents?
    e. Which of the confidence intervals in parts (c) and (d) has the smaller margin of error? Why?

38. According to Thomson Financial, through last month, the majority of companies reporting profits had beaten estimates. A sample of 162 companies showed that 104 beat estimates, 29 matched estimates, and 29 fell short.
    a. What is the point estimate of the proportion that fell short of estimates?
    b. Determine the margin of error and provide a 95% confidence interval for the proportion that beat estimates.
    c. How large a sample is needed if the desired margin of error is .05?

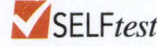 **SELF**test 39. The percentage of Texans not covered by health care insurance in 2015 was 17% (The Henry J. Kaiser Family Foundation website, December 5, 2015). The Texas Health and Human Services Commission (HHSC) has been charged with conducting a sample survey to obtain more current information.
    a. What sample size would you recommend if the HHSC's goal is to estimate the current proportion of Texans without health care insurance with a margin of error of .03? Use a 95% confidence level.
    b. Repeat part (a) using a 99% confidence level.

40. For many years businesses have struggled with the rising cost of health care. But recently, the increases have slowed due to less inflation in health care prices and employees paying for a larger portion of health care benefits. A recent Mercer survey showed that 52% of U.S. employers were likely to require higher employee contributions for health care coverage in the upcoming year. Suppose the survey was based on a sample of 800 companies. Compute the margin of error and a 95% confidence interval for the proportion of companies likely to require higher employee contributions for health care coverage in the upcoming year.

41. Fewer young people are driving. In 1983, 87% of 19-year-olds had a driver's license. Twenty-five years later that percentage had dropped to 75% (University of Michigan Transportation Research Institute website, April 7, 2012). Suppose these results are based on random samples of 1200 19-year-olds in 1983 and 2008.
    a. At 95% confidence, what is the margin of error and the interval estimate of the number of 19-year-old drivers in 1983?
    b. At 95% confidence, what is the margin of error and the interval estimate of the number of 19-year-old drivers in 2008?
    c. Is the margin of error the same in parts (a) and (b)? Why or why not?

42. A poll for the presidential campaign sampled 491 potential voters in June. A primary purpose of the poll was to obtain an estimate of the proportion of potential voters who favored each candidate. Assume a planning value of $p^* = .50$ and a 95% confidence level.
    a. For $p^* = .50$, what was the planned margin of error for the June poll?
    b. Closer to the November election, better precision and smaller margins of error are desired. Assume the following margins of error are requested for surveys to be conducted during the presidential campaign. Compute the recommended sample size for each survey.

Survey	Margin of Error
September	.04
October	.03
Early November	.02
Pre-Election Day	.01

43. The Pew Research Center Internet Project, conducted on the 25th anniversary of the Internet, involved a survey of 857 Internet users (Pew Research Center website, April 1, 2014). It provided a variety of statistics on Internet users. For instance, in 2014, 87% of American adults were Internet users. In 1995 only 14% of American adults used the Internet.

a. The sample survey showed that 90% of respondents said the Internet has been a good thing for them personally. Develop a 95% confidence interval for the proportion of respondents who say the Internet has been a good thing for them personally.

b. The sample survey showed that 67% of Internet users said the Internet has generally strengthened their relationship with family and friends. Develop a 95% confidence interval for the proportion of respondents who say the Internet has strengthened their relationship with family and friends.

c. Fifty-six percent of Internet users have seen an online group come together to help a person or community solve a problem, whereas only 25% have left an online group because of unpleasant interaction. Develop a 95% confidence interval for the proportion of Internet users who say online groups have helped solve a problem.

d. Compare the margin of error for the interval estimates in parts (a), (b), and (c). How is the margin of error related to the sample proporttion?

8.5 Practical Advice: Big Data and Interval Estimation

Confidence intervals are powerful tools for making inferences about population parameters, but the validity of any interval estimate depends on the quality of the data used to develop the interval estimate. No matter how large the sample is, if the sample is not representative of the population of interest, the confidence interval cannot provide useful information about the population parameter of interest. In these circumstances, statistical inference can actually be misleading.

Big Data and the Precision of Confidence Intervals

In section 7.8 we saw that the standard errors of the sampling distributions of the sample mean $\bar{x}$ (shown in formula 7.2) and the sample proportion of $\bar{p}$ (shown in formula 7.5) reflect the potential for sampling error when using sample data to estimate the population mean μ and the population proportion p, respectively. As the standard error of either of these sampling distributions decreases, the potential sampling error also decreases. A review of formulas (8.1), (8.2), and (8.3) shows that confidence intervals narrow and interval estimates become more precise as the standard error decreases. But how rapidly do these interval estimates narrow for a given confidence level? To address this question, let us again consider the PenningtonDailyTimes.com (PDT) example discussed in Section 7.8.

Recall that PDT's primary source of revenue is the sale of advertising, and prospective advertisers are willing to pay a premium to advertise on websites that have long visit times. Suppose PDT's management wants to develop a 95% confidence interval estimate of the mean time spent by customers when they visit PDT's website. Based on historical data, PDT assumes that the standard deviation of the times spent by individual customers is $\sigma = 20$. Table 8.6 shows how the margin of error at the 95% confidence level decreases as the sample size increases when $\sigma = 20$ seconds.

Suppose that in addition to estimating the mean amount of time the population of customers spend during their visits to PDT's website, PDT would like to develop a 95% confidence interval estimate of the proportion of visitors to its website that clicked on any of the ads featured on the website. Table 8.7 shows how the margin of error for a 95% confidence interval estimate of the population proportion decreases as the sample size increases when the sample proportion is $\bar{p} = .50$.

The PDT example illustrates the relationship between the precision of interval estimates and the sample size. We see in Table 8.6 and Table 8.7, that at a given confidence level, the margins of error decrease as the sample size increases. As a result, if the sample mean time spent by customers when they visit PDT's website is 84.5, the 95% confidence interval

TABLE 8.6   MARGIN OF ERROR FOR INTERVAL ESTIMATES OF THE POPULATION MEAN AT THE 95% CONFIDENCE LEVEL FOR VARIOUS SAMPLE SIZES n

Sample Size n	Margin of Error $z_{\alpha/2}\sigma_{\bar{x}}$
100	3.92000
500	1.75308
1,000	1.23961
10,000	0.39200
100,000	0.12396
1,000,000	0.03920
10,000,000	0.01240
100,000,000	0.00392
1,000,000,000	0.00124

TABLE 8.7   MARGIN OF ERROR FOR INTERVAL ESTIMATES OF THE POPULATION PROPORTION AT THE 95% CONFIDENCE LEVEL FOR VARIOUS SAMPLE SIZES n

Sample Size n	Margin of Error $z_{\alpha/2}\sigma_{\bar{p}}$
100	0.09800
500	0.04383
1,000	0.03099
10,000	0.00980
100,000	0.00310
1,000,000	0.00098
10,000,000	0.00031
100,000,000	0.00010
1,000,000,000	0.00003

estimate of the population mean time spent by customers when they visit PDT's website decreases from (80.58, 88.42) for a sample of $n = 100$ to (84.37604, 84.62396) for a sample size of $n = 100,000$ and (84.49876, 84.50124) for a sample size of $n = 1,000,000,000$. Similarly, if the sample proportion of visitors to its website who clicked on an ad featured on the website is .50, the 95% confidence interval estimate of the population proportion of visitors to its website who clicked on an ad featured on the website decreases from (.4020, .5980) for a sample of $n = 100$ to (.4969, .5031) for a sample size of $n = 100,000$ and (.49997, .50003) for a sample size of $n = 1,000,000,000$. In both instances, as the sample size becomes extremely large, the margin of error becomes extremely small and the resulting confidence intervals become extremely narrow and precise.

Implications of Big Data

Last year, the mean time spent by all visitors to PenningtonDailyTimes.com was 84 seconds. Suppose that PDT wants to assess whether the population mean time has changed since last year. PDT now collects a new sample of 1,000,000 visitors to its website and calculates sample mean time spent by these visitors to the PDT website to be $\bar{x} = 84.5$ seconds. The population standard deviation is $\sigma = 20$, so the standard error is $\sigma_x = \sigma/\sqrt{n} = 0.02$. Furthermore, the sample is sufficiently large to ensure that the sampling distribution of the sample mean will be normally distributed. Thus, the 95% confidence interval estimate of the population mean is

$$\bar{x} \pm z_{\alpha/2}\sigma_{\bar{x}}\ 84.5 \pm 1.96(.02) = 84.5 \pm .0392 = (84.4608, 84.5392)$$

What could PDT conclude from these results? Note that the 95% confidence interval estimate of the population mean does not include the value for the mean time for last year (84 seconds), suggesting that the difference between PDT's sample mean for the new sample (84.5 seconds) and the mean from last year (84 seconds) is not likely to be exclusively a consequence of sampling error. Nonsampling error is a possible explanation and should be investigated. If PDT determines that it introduced little or no nonsampling error into its sample data, the only remaining plausible explanation for a difference of this magnitude is that the population mean has changed since last year. However, if PDT concludes that the sample has provided reliable evidence and the population mean has changed since last year, management must still consider the potential impact of the difference between the sample mean and the mean from last year. Will a one-half second difference in time spent by visitors to PenningtonDailyTimes.com have an effect on what PDT can charge for advertising on its site? If so, these results could have tremendous implications for PDT. If not, the fact that the difference is significantly different has no real practical value.

Confidence intervals are extremely useful, but as with any other statistical tool, they are only effective when properly applied. Because interval estimates become increasingly narrow as the sample size increases, extremely large samples will yield extremely precise estimates. However, an interval estimate, no matter how precise, will not accurately reflect the parameter being estimated unless the sample is relatively free of nonsampling error. Therefore, when using interval estimation it is always important to carefully consider whether a random sample of the population of interest has actually been taken. Also, although the data for a large sample may indicate a statistically significant difference, whether or not that differecne is of practical significance must be considered. Ultimately, no business decision should be based exclusively on statistical inference; when executed properly, statistical inference provides evidence that should be considered in combination with information collected from other sources to make the most informed decision possible.

NOTE AND COMMENT

When taking an extremely large sample, it is conceivable that the sample size is at least 5% of the population size; that is, $n/N \geq .05$. Under these conditions it is necessary to use the finite population correction factor when calculating the standard error of the sampling distribution.

Exercises

Applications

FedTaxErrors

44. Suppose a sample of 10001 erroneous Federal income tax returns from last year has been taken and is provided in the DATAfile *FedTaxErrors*. A positive value indicates the taxpayer underpaid and a negative value indicates that the taxpayer overpaid. Also suppose the IRS has established that the standard deviation of errors made on Federal income tax returns is $\sigma = 12,300$.
    a. What is the point estimate for the mean error made on erroneous Federal income tax returns last year?
    b. Using 95% confidence, what is the margin of error?
    c. Using the results from part (a) and part (b), develop the 95% confidence interval estimate of the mean error made on erroneous Federal income tax returns last year.

FedSickHours

45. According to the Census Bureau, 2,475,780 people are employed by the federal government in the United States (U.S. Census Bureau website, May 30, 2016). Suppose that a random sample of 3500 of these federal employees was selected and the number of sick hours each of these employees took last year was collected from an electronic personnel database. The data collected in this survey are provided in the DATAfile named *FedSickHours*. Based on historical data, the population standard deviation can be assumed to be known with $\sigma = 34.5$.
    a. What is the point estimate for the mean number of sick hours taken by federal employees last year?
    b. Using 99% confidence, what is the margin of error?
    c. Using the results from part (a) and part (b), develop the 99% confidence interval estimate of the mean number of sick hours taken by federal employees last year.
    d. If the mean sick hours federal employees took two years ago was 62.2, what would the confidence interval in part (c) lead you to conclude about last year?

46. Internet users were recently asked online to rate their satisfaction with the web browser they use most frequently. Of 102,519 respondents, 65,120 indicated they were very satisfied with the web browser they use most frequently.
    a. What is the point estimate for the proportion of Internet users who are very satisfied with the web browser they use most frequently?

b.   Using 95% confidence, what is the margin of error?

c.   Using the results from part (a) and part (b), develop the 95% confidence interval estimate of the proportion of Internet users who are very satisfied with the web browser they use most frequently.

47.   ABC News reports that 58% of U.S. drivers admit to speeding (ABC News website, May 27, 2016). Suppose that a new satellite technology can instantly measure the speed of any vehicle on a U.S. road and determine whether the vehicle is speeding, and this satellite technology was used to take a sample of 20,000 vehicles at 6:00 P.M. EST on a recent Tuesday afternoon. Of these 20,000 vehicles, 9252 were speeding.

a.   What is the point estimate for the proportion of vehicles on U.S. roads that speed?

b.   Using 99% confidence, what is the margin of error?

c.   Using the results from part (a) and part (b), develop the 99% confidence interval estimate of the proportion of vehicles on U.S. roads that speed.

d.   What the confidence interval in part (c) lead you to conclude about the ABC News report?

Summary

In this chapter we presented methods for developing interval estimates of a population mean and a population proportion. A point estimator may or may not provide a good estimate of a population parameter. The use of an interval estimate provides a measure of the precision of an estimate. Both the interval estimate of the population mean and the population proportion are of the form: point estimate ± margin of error.

We presented interval estimates for a population mean for two cases. In the σ known case, historical data or other information is used to develop an estimate of σ prior to taking a sample. Analysis of new sample data then proceeds based on the assumption that σ is known. In the σ unknown case, the sample data are used to estimate both the population mean and the population standard deviation. The final choice of which interval estimation procedure to use depends upon the analyst's understanding of which method provides the best estimate of σ.

In the σ known case, the interval estimation procedure is based on the assumed value of σ and the use of the standard normal distribution. In the σ unknown case, the interval estimation procedure uses the sample standard deviation s and the t distribution. In both cases the quality of the interval estimates obtained depends on the distribution of the population and the sample size. If the population is normally distributed the interval estimates will be exact in both cases, even for small sample sizes. If the population is not normally distributed, the interval estimates obtained will be approximate. Larger sample sizes will provide better approximations, but the more highly skewed the population is, the larger the sample size needs to be to obtain a good approximation. Practical advice about the sample size necessary to obtain good approximations was included in Sections 8.1 and 8.2. In most cases a sample of size 30 or more will provide good approximate confidence intervals.

The general form of the interval estimate for a population proportion is $\bar{p}$ ± margin of error. In practice the sample sizes used for interval estimates of a population proportion are generally large. Thus, the interval estimation procedure is based on the standard normal distribution.

Often a desired margin of error is specified prior to developing a sampling plan. We showed how to choose a sample size large enough to provide the desired precision. Finally, we discussed practical considerations to be made when working with confidence intervals based on very large samples.

Glossary

Confidence coefficient The confidence level expressed as a decimal value. For example, .95 is the confidence coefficient for a 95% confidence level.

Confidence interval Another name for an interval estimate.

Confidence level The confidence associated with an interval estimate. For example, if an interval estimation procedure provides intervals such that 95% of the intervals formed using the procedure will include the population parameter, the interval estimate is said to be constructed at the 95% confidence level.

Degrees of freedom A parameter of the t distribution. When the t distribution is used in the computation of an interval estimate of a population mean, the appropriate t distribution has $n - 1$ degrees of freedom, where n is the size of the sample.

Interval estimate An estimate of a population parameter that provides an interval believed to contain the value of the parameter. For the interval estimates in this chapter, it has the form: point estimate $\pm$ margin of error.

Level of significance The probability that the interval estimation procedure will generate an interval that does not contain μ.

Margin of error The $\pm$ value added to and subtracted from a point estimate in order to develop an interval estimate of a population parameter.

σ known The case when historical data or other information provide a good value for the population standard deviation prior to taking a sample. The interval estimation procedure uses this known value of σ in computing the margin of error.

σ unknown The more common case when no good basis exists for estimating the population standard deviation prior to taking the sample. The interval estimation procedure uses the sample standard deviation s in computing the margin of error.

t distribution A family of probability distributions that can be used to develop an interval estimate of a population mean whenever the population standard deviation σ is unknown and is estimated by the sample standard deviation s.

Key Formulas

Interval Estimate of a Population Mean: σ Known

$$\bar{x} \pm z_{\alpha/2} \frac{\sigma}{\sqrt{n}} \tag{8.1}$$

Interval Estimate of a Population Mean: σ Unknown

$$\bar{x} \pm t_{\alpha/2} \frac{s}{\sqrt{n}} \tag{8.2}$$

Sample Size for an Interval Estimate of a Population Mean

$$n = \frac{(z_{\alpha/2})^2 \sigma^2}{E^2} \tag{8.3}$$

Interval Estimate of a Population Proportion

$$\bar{p} \pm z_{\alpha/2} \sqrt{\frac{\bar{p}(1 - \bar{p})}{n}} \tag{8.6}$$

Sample Size for an Interval Estimate of a Population Proportion

$$n = \frac{(z_{\alpha/2})^2 p^*(1 - p^*)}{E^2} \tag{8.7}$$

Supplementary Exercises

48. A sample survey of 54 discount brokers showed that the mean price charged for a trade of 100 shares at $50 per share was $33.77. The survey is conducted annually. With the historical data available, assume a known population standard deviation of $15.
     a. Using the sample data, what is the margin of error associated with a 95% confidence interval?
     b. Develop a 95% confidence interval for the mean price charged by discount brokers for a trade of 100 shares at $50 per share.

49. A survey conducted by the American Automobile Association (AAA) showed that a family of four spends an average of $215.60 per day while on vacation. Suppose a sample of 64 families of four vacationing at Niagara Falls resulted in a sample mean of $252.45 per day and a sample standard deviation of $74.50.
     a. Develop a 95% confidence interval estimate of the mean amount spent per day by a family of four visiting Niagara Falls.
     b. Based on the confidence interval from part (a), does it appear that the population mean amount spent per day by families visiting Niagara Falls differs from the mean reported by the American Automobile Association? Explain.

50. The 92 million Americans of age 50 and over control 50 percent of all discretionary income. AARP estimated that the average annual expenditure on restaurants and carryout food was $1873 for individuals in this age group. Suppose this estimate is based on a sample of 80 persons and that the sample standard deviation is $550.
     a. At 95% confidence, what is the margin of error?
     b. What is the 95% confidence interval for the population mean amount spent on restaurants and carryout food?
     c. What is your estimate of the total amount spent by Americans of age 50 and over on restaurants and carryout food?
     d. If the amount spent on restaurants and carryout food is skewed to the right, would you expect the median amount spent to be greater or less than $1873?

51. Russia has recently started a push for stronger smoking regulations much like those in Western countries concerning cigarette advertising, smoking in public places, and so on. The DATAfile named *Russia* contains sample data on smoking habits of Russians that are consistent with those reported by *The Wall Street Journal* (*The Wall Street Journal*, October 16, 2012). Analyze the data using Excel and answer the following questions.
     a. Develop a point estimate and a 95% confidence interval for the proportion of Russians who smoke.
     b. Develop a point estimate and a 95% confidence interval for the mean annual per capita consumption (number of cigarettes) of a Russian.
     c. For those Russians who do smoke, estimate the number of cigarettes smoked per day.

52. The Health Care Cost Institute tracks health care expenditures for beneficiaries under the age of 65 who are covered by employer-sponsored private health insurance. The data contained in the DATAfile named *DrugCost* are consistent with the institute's findings concerning annual prescription costs per employee. Analyze the data using Excel and answer the following questions.
     a. Develop a 90% confidence interval for the annual cost of prescription drugs.
     b. Develop a 90% confidence interval for the amount of out-of-pocket expense per employee.
     c. What is your point estimate of the proportion of employees who incurred no prescription drug costs?
     d. Which, if either, of the confidence intervals in parts (a) and (b) has a larger margin of error? Why?

53. GlobalWebIndex reports that American Internet users spend an average of 1.72 hours per day on social media platforms (SocialTimes website, December 4, 2015). Suppose we collect a

SocialMedia

sample of 75 teenage American Internet users. The data are in the DATAfile named *Social-Media*. These data provide the number of hours respondents spend on a recent day on social media platforms.

a. Use the SocialMedia data set to develop a point estimate of the number of hours that teenage American Internet users spend per day on social media platforms. Compare this to the actual number of hours American Internet users spend per day on social media platforms. Are you surprised?

b. What is the sample standard deviation?

c. Develop a 95% confidence interval for the number of hours that teenage American Internet users spend per day on social media platforms.

54. Mileage tests are conducted for a particular model of automobile. If a 98% confidence interval with a margin of error of 1 mile per gallon is desired, how many automobiles should be used in the test? Assume that preliminary mileage tests indicate the standard deviation is 2.6 miles per gallon.

55. In developing patient appointment schedules, a medical center wants to estimate the mean time that a staff member spends with each patient. How large a sample should be taken if the desired margin of error is two minutes at a 95% level of confidence? How large a sample should be taken for a 99% level of confidence? Use a planning value for the population standard deviation of eight minutes.

56. Annual salary plus bonus data for chief executive officers are presented in an annual pay survey. A preliminary sample showed that the standard deviation is $675 with data provided in thousands of dollars. How many chief executive officers should be in a sample if we want to estimate the population mean annual salary plus bonus with a margin of error of $100,000? (*Note:* The desired margin of error would be $E = 100$ if the data are in thousands of dollars.) Use 95% confidence.

57. The National Center for Education Statistics reported that 47% of college students work to pay for tuition and living expenses. Assume that a sample of 450 college students was used in the study.

a. Provide a 95% confidence interval for the population proportion of college students who work to pay for tuition and living expenses.

b. Provide a 99% confidence interval for the population proportion of college students who work to pay for tuition and living expenses.

c. What happens to the margin of error as the confidence is increased from 95% to 99%?

58. A *USA Today*/CNN/Gallup survey of 369 working parents found 200 who said they spend too little time with their children because of work commitments.

a. What is the point estimate of the proportion of the population of working parents who feel they spend too little time with their children because of work commitments?

b. At 95% confidence, what is the margin of error?

c. What is the 95% confidence interval estimate of the population proportion of working parents who feel they spend too little time with their children because of work commitments?

59. The Pew Research Center has conducted extensive research on the young adult population (Pew Research website, November 6, 2012). One finding was that 93% of adults aged 18 to 29 use the Internet. Another finding was that 21% of those aged 18 to 28 are married. Assume the sample size associated with both findings is 500.

a. Develop a 95% confidence interval for the proportion of adults aged 18 to 29 who use the Internet.

b. Develop a 99% confidence interval for the proportion of adults aged 18 to 28 who are married.

c. In which case, part (a) or part (b), is the margin of error larger? Explain why.

60. A survey of 750 likely voters in Ohio was conducted by the Rasmussen Poll just prior to the general election (Rasmussen Reports website, November 4, 2012). The state of the economy

was thought to be an important determinant of how people would vote. Among other things, the survey found that 165 of the respondents rated the economy as good or excellent and 315 rated the economy as poor.

   a.   Develop a point estimate of the proportion of likely voters in Ohio who rated the economy as good or excellent.

   b.   Construct a 95% confidence interval for the proportion of likely voters in Ohio who rated the economy as good or excellent.

   c.   Construct a 95% confidence interval for the proportion of likely voters in Ohio who rated the economy as poor.

   d.   Which of the confidence intervals in parts (b) and (c) is wider? Why?

61. The *2003 Statistical Abstract of the United States* reported the percentage of people 18 years of age and older who smoke. Suppose that a study designed to collect new data on smokers and nonsmokers uses a preliminary estimate of the proportion who smoke of .30.

   a.   How large a sample should be taken to estimate the proportion of smokers in the population with a margin of error of .02? Use 95% confidence.

   b.   Assume that the study uses your sample size recommendation in part (a) and finds 520 smokers. What is the point estimate of the proportion of smokers in the population?

   c.   What is the 95% confidence interval for the proportion of smokers in the population?

62. A well-known bank credit card firm wishes to estimate the proportion of credit card holders who carry a nonzero balance at the end of the month and incur an interest charge. Assume that the desired margin of error is .03 at 98% confidence.

   a.   How large a sample should be selected if it is anticipated that roughly 70% of the firm's card holders carry a nonzero balance at the end of the month?

   b.   How large a sample should be selected if no planning value for the proportion could be specified?

63. The American Enterprise Institute (AEI) Public Opinion Study found that 86% of Americans are satisfied with their job (AEI website, December 4, 2015). Is this consistent across age groups? A follow-up survey revealed that 72% of Americans age 18–30 are satisfied with their job, 85% of Americans age 31–50 are satisfied with their job, and 93% of Americans age 51–70 are satisfied with their job. Suppose that 200 workers were surveyed in each age group.

   a.   Construct a 95% confidence interval for the proportion of workers in each of these age groups who is satisfied with her or his job. Do these results surprise you? Why or why not?

   b.   Assuming the same sample size will be used in each age group, how large would the sample need to be to ensure that the margin of error is .05 or less for each of the three confidence intervals?

64. Although airline schedules and cost are important factors for business travelers when choosing an airline carrier, a *USA Today* survey found that business travelers list an airline's frequent flyer program as the most important factor. From a sample of $n = 1993$ business travelers who responded to the survey, 618 listed a frequent flyer program as the most important factor.

   a.   What is the point estimate of the proportion of the population of business travelers who believe a frequent flyer program is the most important factor when choosing an airline carrier?

   b.   Develop a 95% confidence interval estimate of the population proportion.

   c.   How large a sample would be required to report the margin of error of .01 at 95% confidence? Would you recommend that *USA Today* attempt to provide this degree of precision? Why or why not?

Case Problem 1   *Young Professional* Magazine

Young Professional magazine was developed for a target audience of recent college graduates who are in their first 10 years in a business/professional career. In its two years of publication, the magazine has been fairly successful. Now the publisher is interested in expanding the magazine's advertising base. Potential advertisers continually ask about the demographics and interests of subscribers to *Young Professional*. To collect this information, the magazine commissioned a survey to develop a profile of its subscribers. The survey results will be used to help the magazine choose articles of interest and provide advertisers with a profile of subscribers. As a new employee of the magazine, you have been asked to help analyze the survey results.

Some of the survey questions follow:

1. What is your age?
2. Are you: Male_____   Female_____
3. Do you plan to make any real estate purchases in the next two years? Yes_____   No_____
4. What is the approximate total value of financial investments, exclusive of your home, owned by you or members of your household?
5. How many stock/bond/mutual fund transactions have you made in the past year?
6. Do you have broadband access to the Internet at home? Yes_____   No_____
7. Please indicate your total household income last year.
8. Do you have children? Yes_____   No_____

Professional

The DATAfile named *Professional* contains the responses to these questions. Table 8.8 shows the portion of the file pertaining to the first five survey respondents.

Managerial Report

Prepare a managerial report summarizing the results of the survey. In addition to statistical summaries, discuss how the magazine might use these results to attract advertisers. You might also comment on how the survey results could be used by the magazine's editors to identify topics that would be of interest to readers. Your report should address the following issues, but do not limit your analysis to just these areas.

1. Develop appropriate descriptive statistics to summarize the data.
2. Develop 95% confidence intervals for the mean age and household income of subscribers.
3. Develop 95% confidence intervals for the proportion of subscribers who have Internet access at home and the proportion of subscribers who have children.
4. Would *Young Professional* be a good advertising outlet for online brokers? Justify your conclusion with statistical data.
5. Would this magazine be a good place to advertise for companies selling educational software and computer games for young children?
6. Comment on the types of articles you believe would be of interest to readers of *Young Professional*.

TABLE 8.8   PARTIAL SURVEY RESULTS FOR *YOUNG PROFESSIONAL* MAGAZINE

Age	Gender	Real Estate Purchases	Value of Investments($)	Number of Transactions	Internet Access	Household Income($)	Children
38	Female	No	12200	4	Yes	75200	Yes
30	Male	No	12400	4	Yes	70300	Yes
41	Female	No	26800	5	Yes	48200	No
28	Female	Yes	19600	6	No	95300	No
31	Female	Yes	15100	5	No	73300	Yes
⋮	⋮	⋮	⋮	⋮	⋮	⋮	⋮

Case Problem 2   Gulf Real Estate Properties

Gulf Real Estate Properties, Inc. is a real estate firm located in southwest Florida. The company, which advertises itself as "expert in the real estate market," monitors condominium sales by collecting data on location, list price, sale price, and number of days it takes to sell each unit. Each condominium is classified as *Gulf View* if it is located directly on the Gulf of Mexico or *No Gulf View* if it is located on the bay or a golf course, near but not on the Gulf. Sample data from the Multiple Listing Service in Naples, Florida, provided sales data for 40 Gulf View condominiums and 18 No Gulf View condominiums.* Prices are in thousands of dollars. The data are shown in Table 8.9.

TABLE 8.9   SALES DATA FOR GULF REAL ESTATE PROPERTIES

GulfProp

Gulf View Condominiums			No Gulf View Condominiums		
List Price	Sale Price	Days to Sell	List Price	Sale Price	Days to Sell
495.0	475.0	130	217.0	217.0	182
379.0	350.0	71	148.0	135.5	338
529.0	519.0	85	186.5	179.0	122
552.5	534.5	95	239.0	230.0	150
334.9	334.9	119	279.0	267.5	169
550.0	505.0	92	215.0	214.0	58
169.9	165.0	197	279.0	259.0	110
210.0	210.0	56	179.9	176.5	130
975.0	945.0	73	149.9	144.9	149
314.0	314.0	126	235.0	230.0	114
315.0	305.0	88	199.8	192.0	120
885.0	800.0	282	210.0	195.0	61
975.0	975.0	100	226.0	212.0	146
469.0	445.0	56	149.9	146.5	137
329.0	305.0	49	160.0	160.0	281
365.0	330.0	48	322.0	292.5	63
332.0	312.0	88	187.5	179.0	48
520.0	495.0	161	247.0	227.0	52
425.0	405.0	149			
675.0	669.0	142			
409.0	400.0	28			
649.0	649.0	29			
319.0	305.0	140			
425.0	410.0	85			
359.0	340.0	107			
469.0	449.0	72			
895.0	875.0	129			
439.0	430.0	160			
435.0	400.0	206			
235.0	227.0	91			
638.0	618.0	100			
629.0	600.0	97			
329.0	309.0	114			
595.0	555.0	45			
339.0	315.0	150			
215.0	200.0	48			
395.0	375.0	135			
449.0	425.0	53			
499.0	465.0	86			
439.0	428.5	158			

*Data based on condominium sales reported in the Naples MLS (Coldwell Banker, June 2000).

Managerial Report

1. Use appropriate descriptive statistics to summarize each of the three variables for the 40 Gulf View condominiums.
2. Use appropriate descriptive statistics to summarize each of the three variables for the 18 No Gulf View condominiums.
3. Compare your summary results. Discuss any specific statistical results that would help a real estate agent understand the condominium market.
4. Develop a 95% confidence interval estimate of the population mean sales price and population mean number of days to sell for Gulf View condominiums. Interpret your results.
5. Develop a 95% confidence interval estimate of the population mean sales price and population mean number of days to sell for No Gulf View condominiums. Interpret your results.
6. Assume the branch manager requested estimates of the mean selling price of Gulf View condominiums with a margin of error of $40,000 and the mean selling price of No Gulf View condominiums with a margin of error of $15,000. Using 95% confidence, how large should the sample sizes be?
7. Gulf Real Estate Properties just signed contracts for two new listings: a Gulf View condominium with a list price of $589,000 and a No Gulf View condominium with a list price of $285,000. What is your estimate of the final selling price and number of days required to sell each of these units?

Case Problem 3   Metropolitan Research, Inc.

Metropolitan Research, Inc., a consumer research organization, conducts surveys designed to evaluate a wide variety of products and services available to consumers. In one particular study, Metropolitan looked at consumer satisfaction with the performance of automobiles produced by a major Detroit manufacturer. A questionnaire sent to owners of one of the manufacturer's full-sized cars revealed several complaints about early transmission problems. To learn more about the transmission failures, Metropolitan used a sample of actual transmission repairs provided by a transmission repair firm in the Detroit area. The following data show the actual number of miles driven for 50 vehicles at the time of transmission failure.

85,092	32,609	59,465	77,437	32,534	64,090	32,464	59,902
39,323	89,641	94,219	116,803	92,857	63,436	65,605	85,861
64,342	61,978	67,998	59,817	101,769	95,774	121,352	69,568
74,276	66,998	40,001	72,069	25,066	77,098	69,922	35,662
74,425	67,202	118,444	53,500	79,294	64,544	86,813	116,269
37,831	89,341	73,341	85,288	138,114	53,402	85,586	82,256
77,539	88,798						

Managerial Report

1. Use appropriate descriptive statistics to summarize the transmission failure data.
2. Develop a 95% confidence interval for the mean number of miles driven until transmission failure for the population of automobiles with transmission failure. Provide a managerial interpretation of the interval estimate.

3. Discuss the implication of your statistical findings in terms of the belief that some owners of the automobiles experienced early transmission failures.
4. How many repair records should be sampled if the research firm wants the population mean number of miles driven until transmission failure to be estimated with a margin of error of 5000 miles? Use 95% confidence.
5. What other information would you like to gather to evaluate the transmission failure problem more fully?

CHAPTER 9

Hypothesis Tests

CONTENTS

STATISTICS *in* PRACTICE

JOHN MORRELL & COMPANY*
CINCINNATI, OHIO

John Morrell & Company, which began in England in 1827, is considered the oldest continuously operating meat manufacturer in the United States. It is a wholly owned and independently managed subsidiary of Smithfield Foods, Smithfield, Virginia. John Morrell & Company offers an extensive product line of processed meats and fresh pork to consumers under 13 regional brands, including John Morrell, E-Z-Cut, Tobin's First Prize, Dinner Bell, Hunter, Kretschmar, Rath, Rodeo, Shenson, Farmers Hickory Brand, Iowa Quality, and Peyton's. Each regional brand enjoys high brand recognition and loyalty among consumers.

Market research at Morrell provides management with up-to-date information on the company's various products and how the products compare with competing brands of similar products. A recent study compared a Beef Pot Roast made by Morrell to similar beef products from two major competitors. In the three-product comparison test, a sample of consumers was used to indicate how the products rated in terms of taste, appearance, aroma, and overall preference.

One research question concerned whether the Beef Pot Roast made by Morrell was the preferred choice of more than 50% of the consumer population. Letting p indicate the population proportion preferring Morrell's product, the hypothesis test for the research question is as follows:

$$H_0: p \leq .50$$
$$H_a: p > .50$$

The null hypothesis H_0 indicates that the preference for Morrell's product is less than or equal to 50%. If the sample data support rejecting H_0 in favor of the alternative hypothesis H_a, Morrell will draw the research conclusion

Hypothesis testing helps John Morrell & Company analyze market research about its products.

that in a three-product comparison, its Beef Pot Roast is preferred by more than 50% of the consumer population.

In an independent taste test study using a sample of 224 consumers in Cincinnati, Milwaukee, and Los Angeles, 150 consumers selected the Beef Pot Roast made by Morrell as the preferred product. Using statistical hypothesis testing procedures, the null hypothesis H_0 was rejected. The study provided statistical evidence supporting H_a and the conclusion that the Morrell product is preferred by more than 50% of the consumer population.

The point estimate of the population proportion was $\bar{p} = 150/224 = .67$. Thus, the sample data provided support for a food magazine advertisement showing that in a three-product taste comparison, Beef Pot Roast made by Morrell was "preferred 2 to 1 over the competition."

In this chapter we will discuss how to formulate hypotheses and how to conduct tests like the one used by Morrell. Through the analysis of sample data, we will be able to determine whether a hypothesis should or should not be rejected.

*The authors are indebted to Marty Butler, Vice President of Marketing, John Morrell, for providing this Statistics in Practice.

In Chapters 7 and 8 we showed how a sample could be used to develop point and interval estimates of population parameters. In this chapter we continue the discussion of statistical inference by showing how hypothesis testing can be used to determine whether a statement about the value of a population parameter should or should not be rejected.

In hypothesis testing we begin by making a tentative assumption about a population parameter. This tentative assumption is called the **null hypothesis** and is denoted by H_0.

We then define another hypothesis, called the **alternative hypothesis**, which is the opposite of what is stated in the null hypothesis. The alternative hypothesis is denoted by H_a. The hypothesis testing procedure uses data from a sample to test the two competing statements indicated by H_0 and H_a.

This chapter shows how hypothesis tests can be conducted about a population mean and a population proportion. We begin by providing examples that illustrate approaches to developing null and alternative hypotheses.

9.1   Developing Null and Alternative Hypotheses

It is not always obvious how the null and alternative hypotheses should be formulated. Care must be taken to structure the hypotheses appropriately so that the hypothesis testing conclusion provides the information the researcher or decision maker wants. The context of the situation is very important in determining how the hypotheses should be stated. All hypothesis testing applications involve collecting a sample and using the sample results to provide evidence for drawing a conclusion. Good questions to consider when formulating the null and alternative hypotheses are, What is the purpose of collecting the sample? What conclusions are we hoping to make?

Learning to formulate hypotheses correctly will take some practice. Expect some initial confusion over the proper choice of the null and alternative hypotheses. The examples in this section are intended to provide guidelines.

In the chapter introduction, we stated that the null hypothesis H_0 is a tentative assumption about a population parameter such as a population mean or a population proportion. The alternative hypothesis H_a is a statement that is the opposite of what is stated in the null hypothesis. In some situations it is easier to identify the alternative hypothesis first and then develop the null hypothesis. In other situations it is easier to identify the null hypothesis first and then develop the alternative hypothesis. We will illustrate these situations in the following examples.

The Alternative Hypothesis as a Research Hypothesis

Many applications of hypothesis testing involve an attempt to gather evidence in support of a research hypothesis. In these situations, it is often best to begin with the alternative hypothesis and make it the conclusion that the researcher hopes to support. Consider a particular automobile that currently attains a fuel efficiency of 24 miles per gallon in city driving. A product research group has developed a new fuel injection system designed to increase the miles-per-gallon rating. The group will run controlled tests with the new fuel injection system looking for statistical support for the conclusion that the new fuel injection system provides more miles per gallon than the current system.

Several new fuel injection units will be manufactured, installed in test automobiles, and subjected to research-controlled driving conditions. The sample mean miles per gallon for these automobiles will be computed and used in a hypothesis test to determine whether it can be concluded that the new system provides more than 24 miles per gallon. In terms of the population mean miles per gallon μ, the research hypothesis $\mu > 24$ becomes the alternative hypothesis. Since the current system provides an average or mean of 24 miles per gallon, we will make the tentative assumption that the new system is not any better than the current system and choose $\mu \leq 24$ as the null hypothesis. The null and alternative hypotheses are:

$$H_0: \mu \leq 24$$
$$H_a: \mu > 24$$

If the sample results lead to the conclusion to reject H_0, the inference can be made that $H_a: \mu > 24$ is true. The researchers have the statistical support to state that the new

The conclusion that the research hypothesis is true is made if the sample data provide sufficient evidence to show that the null hypothesis can be rejected.

fuel injection system increases the mean number of miles per gallon. The production of automobiles with the new fuel injection system should be considered. However, if the sample results lead to the conclusion that H_0 cannot be rejected, the researchers cannot conclude that the new fuel injection system is better than the current system. Production of automobiles with the new fuel injection system on the basis of better gas mileage cannot be justified. Perhaps more research and further testing can be conducted.

Successful companies stay competitive by developing new products, new methods, new systems, and the like that are better than what is currently available. Before adopting something new, it is desirable to conduct research to determine whether there is statistical support for the conclusion that the new approach is indeed better. In such cases, the research hypothesis is stated as the alternative hypothesis. For example, a new teaching method is developed that is believed to be better than the current method. The alternative hypothesis is that the new method is better. The null hypothesis is that the new method is no better than the old method. A new sales force bonus plan is developed in an attempt to increase sales. The alternative hypothesis is that the new bonus plan increases sales. The null hypothesis is that the new bonus plan does not increase sales. A new drug is developed with the goal of lowering blood pressure more than an existing drug. The alternative hypothesis is that the new drug lowers blood pressure more than the existing drug. The null hypothesis is that the new drug does not provide lower blood pressure than the existing drug. In each case, rejection of the null hypothesis H_0 provides statistical support for the research hypothesis. We will see many examples of hypothesis tests in research situations such as these throughout this chapter and in the remainder of the text.

The Null Hypothesis as an Assumption to Be Challenged

Of course, not all hypothesis tests involve research hypotheses. In the following discussion we consider applications of hypothesis testing where we begin with a belief or an assumption that a statement about the value of a population parameter is true. We will then use a hypothesis test to challenge the assumption and determine whether there is statistical evidence to conclude that the assumption is incorrect. In these situations, it is helpful to develop the null hypothesis first. The null hypothesis H_0 expresses the belief or assumption about the value of the population parameter. The alternative hypothesis H_a is that the belief or assumption is incorrect.

As an example, consider the situation of a manufacturer of soft drink products. The label on a soft drink bottle states that it contains 67.6 fluid ounces. We consider the label correct provided the population mean filling volume for the bottles is *at least* 67.6 fluid ounces. Without any reason to believe otherwise, we would give the manufacturer the benefit of the doubt and assume that the statement provided on the label is correct. Thus, in a hypothesis test about the population mean fluid ounces per bottle, we would begin with the assumption that the label is correct and state the null hypothesis as $\mu \geq 67.6$. The challenge to this assumption would imply that the label is incorrect and the bottles are being underfilled. This challenge would be stated as the alternative hypothesis $\mu < 67.6$. Thus, the null and alternative hypotheses are:

$$H_0: \mu \geq 67.6$$
$$H_a: \mu < 67.6$$

A manufacturer's product information is usually assumed to be true and stated as the null hypothesis. The conclusion that the information is incorrect can be made if the null hypothesis is rejected.

A government agency with the responsibility for validating manufacturing labels could select a sample of soft drink bottles, compute the sample mean fluid ounces, and use the sample results to test the preceding hypotheses. If the sample results lead to the conclusion to reject H_0, the inference that $H_a: \mu < 67.6$ is true can be made. With this statistical support, the agency is justified in concluding that the label is incorrect and underfilling of the bottles is occurring. Appropriate action to force the manufacturer to comply with labeling standards would be considered. However, if the sample results indicate H_0 cannot be rejected, the assumption that the manufacturer's labeling is correct cannot be rejected. With this conclusion, no action would be taken.

Let us now consider a variation of the soft drink bottle-filling example by viewing the same situation from the manufacturer's point of view. The bottle-filling operation has been designed to fill soft drink bottles with 67.6 fluid ounces as stated on the label. The company does not want to underfill the containers because that could result in an underfilling complaint from customers or, perhaps, a government agency. However, the company does not want to overfill containers either because putting more soft drink than necessary into the containers would be an unnecessary cost. The company's goal would be to adjust the bottle-filling operation so that the population mean filling weight per bottle is 67.6 fluid ounces as specified on the label.

Although this is the company's goal, from time to time any production process can get out of adjustment. If this occurs in our example, underfilling or overfilling of the soft drink bottles will occur. In either case, the company would like to know about it in order to correct the situation by readjusting the bottle-filling operation to the designed 67.6 fluid ounces. In this hypothesis testing application, we would begin with the assumption that the production process is operating correctly and state the null hypothesis as $\mu = 67.6$ fluid ounces. The alternative hypothesis that challenges this assumption is that $\mu \neq 67.6$, which indicates either overfilling or underfilling is occurring. The null and alternative hypotheses for the manufacturer's hypothesis test are

$$H_0: \mu = 67.6$$
$$H_a: \mu \neq 67.6$$

Suppose that the soft drink manufacturer uses a quality control procedure to periodically select a sample of bottles from the filling operation and computes the sample mean fluid ounces per bottle. If the sample results lead to the conclusion to reject H_0, the inference is made that $H_a: \mu \neq 67.6$, is true. We conclude that the bottles are not being filled properly and the production process should be adjusted to restore the population mean to 67.6 fluid ounces per bottle. However, if the sample results indicate H_0 cannot be rejected, the assumption that the manufacturer's bottle-filling operation is functioning properly cannot be rejected. In this case, no further action would be taken and the production operation would continue to run.

The two preceding forms of the soft drink manufacturing hypothesis test show that the null and alternative hypotheses may vary depending upon the point of view of the researcher or decision maker. To formulate hypotheses correctly it is important to understand the context of the situation and structure the hypotheses to provide the information the researcher or decision maker wants.

Summary of Forms for Null and Alternative Hypotheses

The hypothesis tests in this chapter involve two population parameters: the population mean and the population proportion. Depending on the situation, hypothesis tests about a population parameter may take one of three forms: Two use inequalities in the null hypothesis; the third uses an equality in the null hypothesis. For hypothesis tests involving a population mean, we let μ_0 denote the hypothesized value and we must choose one of the following three forms for the hypothesis test.

The three possible forms of hypotheses H_0 and H_a are shown here. Note that the equality always appears in the null hypothesis H_0.

$$H_0: \mu \geq \mu_0 \qquad H_0: \mu \leq \mu_0 \qquad H_0: \mu = \mu_0$$
$$H_a: \mu < \mu_0 \qquad H_a: \mu > \mu_0 \qquad H_a: \mu \neq \mu_0$$

For reasons that will be clear later, the first two forms are called one-tailed tests. The third form is called a two-tailed test.

In many situations, the choice of H_0 and H_a is not obvious and judgment is necessary to select the proper form. However, as the preceding forms show, the equality part of the expression (either $\geq$, $\leq$, or $=$) *always* appears in the null hypothesis. In selecting the proper form of H_0 and H_a, keep in mind that the alternative hypothesis is often what the test is attempting to establish. Hence, asking whether the user is looking for evidence to support $\mu < \mu_0$, $\mu > \mu_0$, or $\mu \neq \mu_0$ will help determine H_a. The following exercises are designed to provide practice in choosing the proper form for a hypothesis test involving a population mean.

Exercises

1. The manager of the Danvers-Hilton Resort Hotel stated that the mean guest bill for a weekend is $600 or less. A member of the hotel's accounting staff noticed that the total charges for guest bills have been increasing in recent months. The accountant will use a sample of future weekend guest bills to test the manager's claim.
    a. Which form of the hypotheses should be used to test the manager's claim? Explain.

$$H_0: \mu \geq 600 \qquad H_0: \mu \leq 600 \qquad H_0: \mu = 600$$
$$H_a: \mu < 600 \qquad H_a: \mu > 600 \qquad H_a: \mu \neq 600$$

    b. What conclusion is appropriate when H_0 cannot be rejected?
    c. What conclusion is appropriate when H_0 can be rejected?

 2. The manager of an automobile dealership is considering a new bonus plan designed to increase sales volume. Currently, the mean sales volume is 14 automobiles per month. The manager wants to conduct a research study to see whether the new bonus plan increases sales volume. To collect data on the plan, a sample of sales personnel will be allowed to sell under the new bonus plan for a one-month period.
    a. Develop the null and alternative hypotheses most appropriate for this situation.
    b. Comment on the conclusion when H_0 cannot be rejected.
    c. Comment on the conclusion when H_0 can be rejected.

3. A production line operation is designed to fill cartons with laundry detergent to a mean weight of 32 ounces. A sample of cartons is periodically selected and weighed to determine whether underfilling or overfilling is occurring. If the sample data lead to a conclusion of underfilling or overfilling, the production line will be shut down and adjusted to obtain proper filling.
    a. Formulate the null and alternative hypotheses that will help in deciding whether to shut down and adjust the production line.
    b. Comment on the conclusion and the decision when H_0 cannot be rejected.
    c. Comment on the conclusion and the decision when H_0 can be rejected.

4. Because of high production-changeover time and costs, a director of manufacturing must convince management that a proposed manufacturing method reduces costs before the new method can be implemented. The current production method operates with a mean cost of $220 per hour. A research study will measure the cost of the new method over a sample production period.
    a. Develop the null and alternative hypotheses most appropriate for this study.
    b. Comment on the conclusion when H_0 cannot be rejected.
    c. Comment on the conclusion when H_0 can be rejected.

9.2 Type I and Type II Errors

The null and alternative hypotheses are competing statements about the population. Either the null hypothesis H_0 is true or the alternative hypothesis H_a is true, but not both. Ideally the hypothesis testing procedure should lead to the acceptance of H_0 when H_0 is true and the rejection of H_0 when H_a is true. Unfortunately, the correct conclusions are not always possible. Because hypothesis tests are based on sample information, we must allow for the possibility of errors. Table 9.1 illustrates the two kinds of errors that can be made in hypothesis testing.

The first row of Table 9.1 shows what can happen if the conclusion is to accept H_0. If H_0 is true, this conclusion is correct. However, if H_a is true, we make a **Type II error**; that is, we accept H_0 when it is false. The second row of Table 9.1 shows what can happen if the conclusion is to reject H_0. If H_0 is true, we make a **Type I error**; that is, we reject H_0 when it is true. However, if H_a is true, rejecting H_0 is correct.

Recall the hypothesis testing illustration discussed in Section 9.1, in which an automobile product research group developed a new fuel injection system designed to increase the miles-per-gallon rating of a particular automobile. With the current model obtaining an average of 24 miles per gallon, the hypothesis test was formulated as follows.

$$H_0: \mu \leq 24$$
$$H_a: \mu > 24$$

The alternative hypothesis, $H_a: \mu > 24$, indicates that the researchers are looking for sample evidence to support the conclusion that the population mean miles per gallon with the new fuel injection system is greater than 24.

In this application, the Type I error of rejecting H_0 when it is true corresponds to the researchers claiming that the new system improves the miles-per-gallon rating ($\mu > 24$) when in fact the new system is not any better than the current system. In contrast, the Type II error of accepting H_0 when it is false corresponds to the researchers concluding that the new system is not any better than the current system ($\mu \leq 24$) when in fact the new system improves miles-per-gallon performance.

For the miles-per-gallon rating hypothesis test, the null hypothesis is $H_0: \mu \leq 24$. Suppose the null hypothesis is true as an equality; that is, $\mu = 24$. The probability of making a Type I error when the null hypothesis is true as an equality is called the **level of significance**. Thus, for the miles-per-gallon rating hypothesis test, the level of significance is the probability of rejecting $H_0: \mu \leq 24$ when $\mu = 24$. Because of the importance of this concept, we now restate the definition of level of significance.

TABLE 9.1 ERRORS AND CORRECT CONCLUSIONS IN HYPOTHESIS TESTING

		Population Condition	
		H_0 True	H_a True
Conclusion	Accept H_0	Correct Conclusion	Type II Error
	Reject H_0	Type I Error	Correct Conclusion

> LEVEL OF SIGNIFICANCE
>
> The level of significance is the probability of making a Type I error when the null hypothesis is true as an equality.

The Greek symbol α (alpha) is used to denote the level of significance, and common choices for α are .05 and .01.

In practice, the person responsible for the hypothesis test specifies the level of significance. By selecting α, that person is controlling the probability of making a Type I error. If the cost of making a Type I error is high, small values of α are preferred. If the cost of making a Type I error is not too high, larger values of α are typically used. Applications of hypothesis testing that only control for the Type I error are called *significance tests*. Many applications of hypothesis testing are of this type.

Although most applications of hypothesis testing control for the probability of making a Type I error, they do not always control for the probability of making a Type II error. Hence, if we decide to accept H_0, we cannot determine how confident we can be with that decision. Because of the uncertainty associated with making a Type II error when conducting significance tests, statisticians usually recommend that we use the statement "do not reject H_0" instead of "accept H_0." Using the statement "do not reject H_0" carries the recommendation to withhold both judgment and action. In effect, by not directly accepting H_0, the statistician avoids the risk of making a Type II error. Whenever the probability of making a Type II error has not been determined and controlled, we will not make the statement "accept H_0." In such cases, only two conclusions are possible: *do not reject H_0* or *reject H_0*.

If the sample data are consistent with the null hypothesis H_0, we will follow the practice of concluding "do not reject H_0." This conclusion is preferred over "accept H_0," because the conclusion to accept H_0 puts us at risk of making a Type II error.

Although controlling for a Type II error in hypothesis testing is not common, it can be done. More advanced texts describe procedures for determining and controlling the probability of making a Type II error.[1] If proper controls have been established for this error, action based on the "accept H_0" conclusion can be appropriate.

NOTE AND COMMENT

Walter Williams, syndicated columnist and professor of economics at George Mason University, points out that the possibility of making a Type I or a Type II error is always present in decision making (*The Cincinnati Enquirer*, August 14, 2005). He notes that the Food and Drug Administration runs the risk of making these errors in its drug approval process. The FDA must either approve a new drug or not approve it. Thus, the FDA runs the risk of making a Type I error by approving a new drug that is not safe and effective, or making a Type II error by failing to approve a new drug that is safe and effective. Regardless of the decision made, the possibility of making a costly error cannot be eliminated.

Exercises

5. Duke Energy reported that the cost of electricity for an efficient home in a particular neighborhood of Cincinnati, Ohio was $104 per month (*Home Energy Report*, Duke Energy, March 2012). A researcher believes that the cost of electricity for a comparable neighborhood in Chicago, Illinois is higher. A sample of homes in this Chicago neighborhood will be taken

---

[1]See, for example, D. R. Anderson, D. J. Sweeney, and T. A. Williams, *Statistics for Business and Economics*, 13th edition (Cincinnati: Cengage Learning, 2018).

and the sample mean monthly cost of electricity will be used to test the following null and alternative hypotheses.

$$H_0: \mu \le 104$$
$$H_a: \mu > 104$$

   a.   Assume the sample data lead to rejection of the null hypothesis. What would be your conclusion about the cost of electricity in the Chicago neighborhood?

   b.   What is the Type I error in this situation? What are the consequences of making this error?

   c.   What is the Type II error in this situation? What are the consequences of making this error?

6.   The label on a 3-quart container of orange juice states that the orange juice contains an average of 1 gram of fat or less. Answer the following questions for a hypothesis test that could be used to test the claim on the label.

   a.   Develop the appropriate null and alternative hypotheses.

   b.   What is the Type I error in this situation? What are the consequences of making this error?

   c.   What is the Type II error in this situation? What are the consequences of making this error?

7.   Carpetland salespersons average \$8000 per week in sales. Steve Contois, the firm's vice president, proposes a compensation plan with new selling incentives. Steve hopes that the results of a trial selling period will enable him to conclude that the compensation plan increases the average sales per salesperson.

   a.   Develop the appropriate null and alternative hypotheses.

   b.   What is the Type I error in this situation? What are the consequences of making this error?

   c.   What is the Type II error in this situation? What are the consequences of making this error?

8.   Suppose a new production method will be implemented if a hypothesis test supports the conclusion that the new method reduces the mean operating cost per hour.

   a.   State the appropriate null and alternative hypotheses if the mean cost for the current production method is \$220 per hour.

   b.   What is the Type I error in this situation? What are the consequences of making this error?

   c.   What is the Type II error in this situation? What are the consequences of making this error?

Population Mean: σ Known

In Chapter 8, we said that the σ known case corresponds to applications in which historical data and/or other information are available that enable us to obtain a good estimate of the population standard deviation prior to sampling. In such cases the population standard deviation can, for all practical purposes, be considered known. In this section we show how to conduct a hypothesis test about a population mean for the σ known case.

   The methods presented in this section are exact if the sample is selected from a population that is normally distributed. In cases where it is not reasonable to assume the population is normally distributed, these methods are still applicable if the sample size is large enough. We provide some practical advice concerning the population distribution and the sample size at the end of this section.

One-Tailed Test

One-tailed tests about a population mean take one of the following two forms.

          Lower Tail Test   **Upper Tail Test**

           $H_0: \mu \ge \mu_0$ $H_0: \mu \le \mu_0$

           $H_a: \mu < \mu_0$ $H_a: \mu > \mu_0$

Let us consider an example involving a lower tail test.

The Federal Trade Commission (FTC) periodically conducts statistical studies designed to test the claims that manufacturers make about their products. For example, the label on a large can of Hilltop Coffee states that the can contains 3 pounds of coffee. The FTC knows that Hilltop's production process cannot place exactly 3 pounds of coffee in each can, even if the mean filling weight for the population of all cans filled is 3 pounds per can. However, as long as the population mean filling weight is at least 3 pounds per can, the rights of consumers will be protected. Thus, the FTC interprets the label information on a large can of coffee as a claim by Hilltop that the population mean filling weight is at least 3 pounds per can. We will show how the FTC can check Hilltop's claim by conducting a lower tail hypothesis test.

The first step is to develop the null and alternative hypotheses for the test. If the population mean filling weight is at least 3 pounds per can, Hilltop's claim is correct. This establishes the null hypothesis for the test. However, if the population mean weight is less than 3 pounds per can, Hilltop's claim is incorrect. This establishes the alternative hypothesis. With μ denoting the population mean filling weight, the null and alternative hypotheses are as follows:

$$H_0: \mu \geq 3$$
$$H_a: \mu < 3$$

Note that the hypothesized value of the population mean is $\mu_0 = 3$.

If the sample data indicate that H_0 cannot be rejected, the statistical evidence does not support the conclusion that a label violation has occurred. Hence, no action should be taken against Hilltop. However, if the sample data indicate that H_0 can be rejected, we will conclude that the alternative hypothesis, $H_a: \mu < 3$, is true. In this case a conclusion of underfilling and a charge of a label violation against Hilltop would be justified.

Suppose a sample of 36 cans of coffee is selected and the sample mean $\bar{x}$ is computed as an estimate of the population mean μ. If the value of the sample mean $\bar{x}$ is less than 3 pounds, the sample results will cast doubt on the null hypothesis. What we want to know is how much less than 3 pounds must $\bar{x}$ be before we would be willing to declare the difference significant and risk making a Type I error by falsely accusing Hilltop of a label violation. A key factor in addressing this issue is the value the decision maker selects for the level of significance.

As noted in the preceding section, the level of significance, denoted by α, is the probability of making a Type I error by rejecting H_0 when the null hypothesis is true as an equality. The decision maker must specify the level of significance. If the cost of making a Type I error is high, a small value should be chosen for the level of significance. If the cost is not high, a larger value is more appropriate. In the Hilltop Coffee study, the director of the FTC's testing program made the following statement: "If the company is meeting its weight specifications at $\mu = 3$, I do not want to take action against them. But, I am willing to risk a 1% chance of making such an error." From the director's statement, we set the level of significance for the hypothesis test at $\alpha = .01$. Thus, we must design the hypothesis test so that the probability of making a Type I error when $\mu = 3$ is .01.

For the Hilltop Coffee study, by developing the null and alternative hypotheses and specifying the level of significance for the test, we carry out the first two steps required in conducting every hypothesis test. We are now ready to perform the third step of hypothesis testing: collect the sample data and compute the value of what is called a test statistic.

Test statistic For the Hilltop Coffee study, previous FTC tests show that the population standard deviation can be assumed known with a value of $\sigma = .18$. In addition, these tests also show that the population of filling weights can be assumed to have a normal distribution. From the study of sampling distributions in Chapter 7 we know that if the

FIGURE 9.1   SAMPLING DISTRIBUTION OF $\bar{x}$ FOR THE HILLTOP COFFEE STUDY
WHEN THE NULL HYPOTHESIS IS TRUE AS AN EQUALITY ($\mu = 3$)

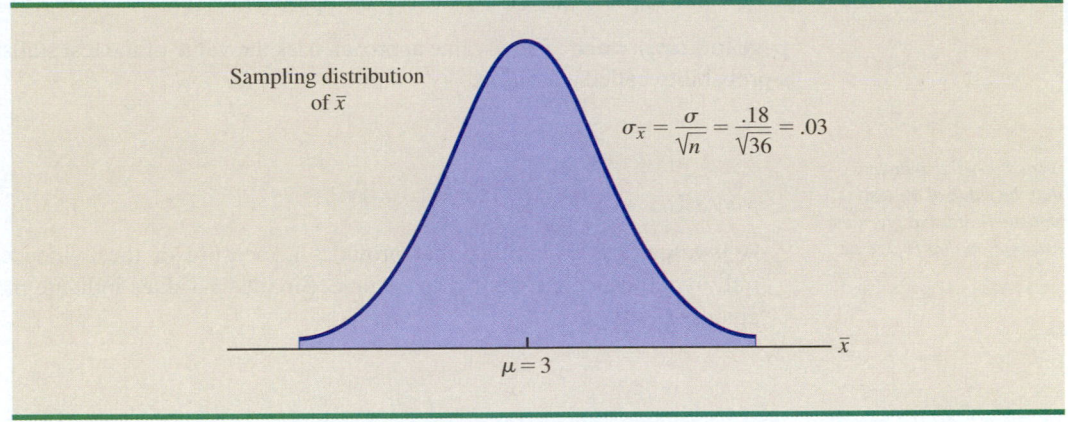

The standard error of $\bar{x}$ is the standard deviation of the sampling distribution of $\bar{x}$.

population from which we are sampling is normally distributed, the sampling distribution of $\bar{x}$ will also be normally distributed. Thus, for the Hilltop Coffee study, the sampling distribution of $\bar{x}$ is normally distributed. With a known value of $\sigma = .18$ and a sample size of $n = 36$, Figure 9.1 shows the sampling distribution of $\bar{x}$ when the null hypothesis is true as an equality, that is, when $\mu = \mu_0 = 3$.[2] Note that the standard error of $\bar{x}$ is given by $\sigma_{\bar{x}} = \sigma/\sqrt{n} = .18/\sqrt{36} = .03$.

Because the sampling distribution of $\bar{x}$ is normally distributed, the sampling distribution of

$$z = \frac{\bar{x} - \mu_0}{\sigma_{\bar{x}}} = \frac{\bar{x} - 3}{.03}$$

is a standard normal distribution. A value of $z = -1$ means that the value of $\bar{x}$ is one standard error below the hypothesized value of the mean, a value of $z = -2$ means that the value of $\bar{x}$ is two standard errors below the hypothesized value of the mean, and so on. We can use the standard normal probability table to find the lower tail probability corresponding to any z value. For instance, the lower tail area at $z = -3.00$ is .0013. Hence, the probability of obtaining a value of z that is three or more standard errors below the mean is .0013. As a result, the probability of obtaining a value of $\bar{x}$ that is 3 or more standard errors below the hypothesized population mean $\mu_0 = 3$ is also .0013. Such a result is unlikely if the null hypothesis is true.

For hypothesis tests about a population mean in the σ known case, we use the standard normal random variable z as a **test statistic** to determine whether $\bar{x}$ deviates from the hypothesized value of μ enough to justify rejecting the null hypothesis. With $\sigma_{\bar{x}} = \sigma/\sqrt{n}$, the test statistic is as follows.

TEST STATISTIC FOR HYPOTHESIS TESTS ABOUT A POPULATION MEAN:
σ KNOWN

$$z = \frac{\bar{x} - \mu_0}{\sigma/\sqrt{n}} \tag{9.1}$$

---

[2]In constructing sampling distributions for hypothesis tests, it is assumed that H_0 is satisfied as an equality.

The key question for a lower tail test is, How small must the test statistic z be before we choose to reject the null hypothesis? Two approaches can be used to answer this question: the p-value approach and the critical value approach.

p-value approach   The p-value approach uses the value of the test statistic z to compute a probability called a **p-value**.

p-VALUE

A p-value is a probability that provides a measure of the evidence against the null hypothesis provided by the sample. Smaller p-values indicate more evidence against H_0.

The p-value is used to determine whether the null hypothesis should be rejected.

Let us see how the p-value is computed and used. The value of the test statistic is used to compute the p-value. The method used depends on whether the test is a lower tail, an upper tail, or a two-tailed test. For a lower tail test, the p-value is the probability of obtaining a value for the test statistic as small as or smaller than that provided by the sample. Thus, to compute the p-value for the lower tail test in the σ known case, we must find, using the standard normal distribution, the probability that z is less than or equal to the value of the test statistic. After computing the p-value, we must then decide whether it is small enough to reject the null hypothesis; as we will show, this decision involves comparing the p-value to the level of significance.

Coffee

Let us now compute the p-value for the Hilltop Coffee lower tail test. Suppose the sample of 36 Hilltop coffee cans provides a sample mean of $\bar{x} = 2.92$ pounds. Is $\bar{x} = 2.92$ small enough to cause us to reject H_0? Because this is a lower tail test, the p-value is the area under the standard normal curve for values of $z \leq$ the value of the test statistic. Using $\bar{x} = 2.92$, $\sigma = .18$, and $n = 36$, we compute the value of the test statistic z.

$$z = \frac{\bar{x} - \mu_0}{\sigma/\sqrt{n}} = \frac{2.92 - 3}{.18/\sqrt{36}} = -2.67$$

Thus, the p-value is the probability that z is less than or equal to -2.67 (the lower tail area corresponding to the value of the test statistic).

Using the standard normal probability table, we find that the lower tail area at $z = -2.67$ is .0038. Figure 9.2 shows that $\bar{x} = 2.92$ corresponds to $z = -2.67$ and a p-value = .0038. This p-value indicates a small probability of obtaining a sample mean of $\bar{x} = 2.92$ (and a test statistic of -2.67) or smaller when sampling from a population with $\mu = 3$. This p-value does not provide much support for the null hypothesis, but is it small enough to cause us to reject H_0? The answer depends upon the level of significance for the test.

As noted previously, the director of the FTC's testing program selected a value of .01 for the level of significance. The selection of $\alpha = .01$ means that the director is willing to tolerate a probability of .01 of rejecting the null hypothesis when it is true as an equality ($\mu_0 = 3$). The sample of 36 coffee cans in the Hilltop Coffee study resulted in a p-value = .0038, which means that the probability of obtaining a value of $\bar{x} = 2.92$ or less when the null hypothesis is true as an equality is .0038. Because .0038 is less than or equal to $\alpha = .01$, we reject H_0. Therefore, we find sufficient statistical evidence to reject the null hypothesis at the .01 level of significance.

FIGURE 9.2 *p*-VALUE FOR THE HILLTOP COFFEE STUDY WHEN $\bar{x} = 2.92$ AND $z = -2.67$

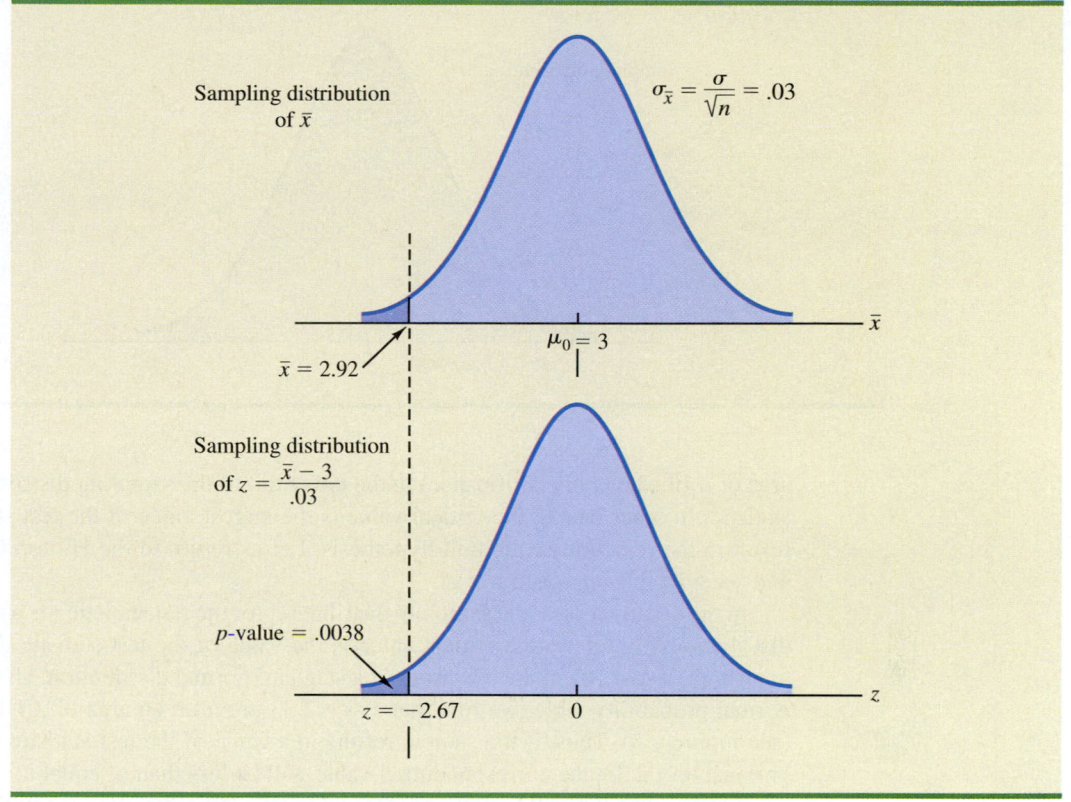

We can now state the general rule for determining whether the null hypothesis can be rejected when using the *p*-value approach. For a level of significance α, the rejection rule using the *p*-value approach is as follows.

> **REJECTION RULE USING *p*-VALUE**
>
> Reject H_0 if *p*-value $\leq \alpha$

In the Hilltop Coffee test, the *p*-value of .0038 resulted in the rejection of the null hypothesis. Although the basis for making the rejection decision involves a comparison of the *p*-value to the level of significance specified by the FTC director, the observed *p*-value of .0038 means that we would reject H_0 for any value of $\alpha \geq .0038$. For this reason, the *p*-value is also called the *observed level of significance.*

Different decision makers may express different opinions concerning the cost of making a Type I error and may choose a different level of significance. By providing the *p*-value as part of the hypothesis testing results, another decision maker can compare the reported *p*-value to his or her own level of significance and possibly make a different decision with respect to rejecting H_0.

Critical value approach The critical value approach requires that we first determine a value for the test statistic called the **critical value**. For a lower tail test, the critical value serves as a benchmark for determining whether the value of the test statistic is small enough to reject the null hypothesis. It is the value of the test statistic that corresponds to an

FIGURE 9.3   CRITICAL VALUE $= -2.33$ FOR THE HILLTOP COFFEE HYPOTHESIS TEST

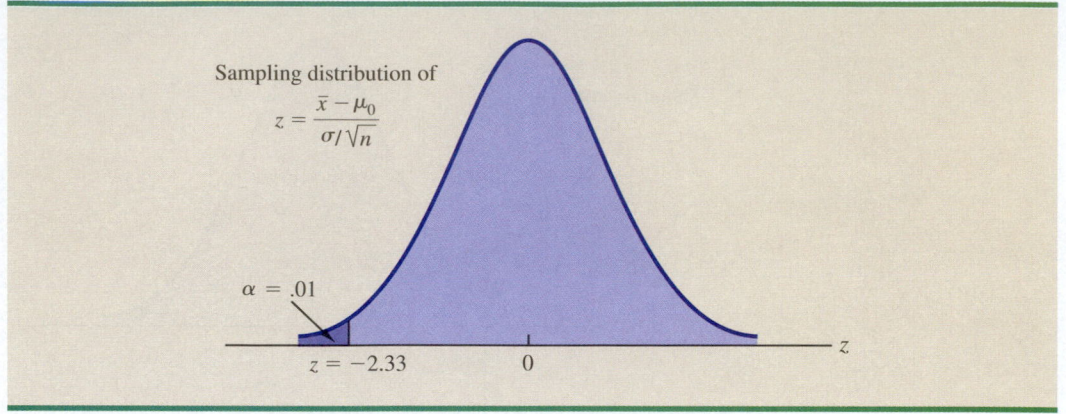

area of α (the level of significance) in the lower tail of the sampling distribution of the test statistic. In other words, the critical value is the largest value of the test statistic that will result in the rejection of the null hypothesis. Let us return to the Hilltop Coffee example and see how this approach works.

In the σ known case, the sampling distribution for the test statistic z is a standard normal distribution. Therefore, the critical value is the value of the test statistic that corresponds to an area of $\alpha = .01$ in the lower tail of a standard normal distribution. Using the standard normal probability table, we find that $z = -2.33$ provides an area of .01 in the lower tail (see Figure 9.3). Thus, if the sample results in a value of the test statistic that is less than or equal to -2.33, the corresponding p-value will be less than or equal to .01; in this case, we should reject the null hypothesis. Hence, for the Hilltop Coffee study the critical value rejection rule for a level of significance of .01 is

$$\text{Reject } H_0 \text{ if } z \leq -2.33$$

In the Hilltop Coffee example, $\bar{x} = 2.92$ and the test statistic is $z = -2.67$. Because $z = -2.67 < -2.33$, we can reject H_0 and conclude that Hilltop Coffee is underfilling cans.

We can generalize the rejection rule for the critical value approach to handle any level of significance. The rejection rule for a lower tail test follows.

REJECTION RULE FOR A LOWER TAIL TEST: CRITICAL VALUE APPROACH

$$\text{Reject } H_0 \text{ if } z \leq -z_\alpha$$

where $-z_\alpha$ is the critical value; that is, the z value that provides an area of α in the lower tail of the standard normal distribution.

Summary   The p-value approach to hypothesis testing and the critical value approach will always lead to the same rejection decision; that is, whenever the p-value is less than or equal to α, the value of the test statistic will be less than or equal to the critical value. The advantage of the p-value approach is that the p-value tells us *how* significant the results are (the observed level of significance). If we use the critical value approach, we only know that the results are significant at the stated level of significance.

At the beginning of this section, we said that one-tailed tests about a population mean take one of the following two forms:

Lower Tail Test	**Upper Tail Test**
$H_0: \mu \geq \mu_0$	$H_0: \mu \leq \mu_0$
$H_a: \mu < \mu_0$	$H_a: \mu > \mu_0$

We used the Hilltop Coffee study to illustrate how to conduct a lower tail test. We can use the same general approach to conduct an upper tail test. The test statistic z is still computed using equation (9.1). But, for an upper tail test, the p-value is the probability of obtaining a value for the test statistic as large as or larger than that provided by the sample. Thus, to compute the p-value for the upper tail test in the σ known case, we must use the standard normal distribution to compute the probability that z is greater than or equal to the value of the test statistic. Using the critical value approach causes us to reject the null hypothesis if the value of the test statistic is greater than or equal to the critical value z_α; in other words, we reject H_0 if $z \geq z_\alpha$.

Let us summarize the steps involved in computing p-values for one-tailed hypothesis tests.

COMPUTATION OF p-VALUES FOR ONE-TAILED TESTS

1. Compute the value of the test statistic using equation (9.1).
2. **Lower tail test:** Using the standard normal distribution, compute the probability that z is less than or equal to the value of the test statistic (area in the lower tail).
3. **Upper tail test:** Using the standard normal distribution, compute the probability that z is greater than or equal to the value of the test statistic (area in the upper tail).

Two-Tailed Test

In hypothesis testing, the general form for a **two-tailed test** about a population mean is as follows:

$$H_0: \mu = \mu_0$$
$$H_a: \mu \neq \mu_0$$

In this subsection we show how to conduct a two-tailed test about a population mean for the σ known case. As an illustration, we consider the hypothesis testing situation facing MaxFlight, Inc.

The U.S. Golf Association (USGA) establishes rules that manufacturers of golf equipment must meet if their products are to be acceptable for use in USGA events. MaxFlight uses a high-technology manufacturing process to produce golf balls with a mean driving distance of 295 yards. Sometimes, however, the process gets out of adjustment and produces golf balls with a mean driving distance different from 295 yards. When the mean distance falls below 295 yards, the company worries about losing sales because the golf balls do not provide as much distance as advertised. When the mean distance passes 295 yards, MaxFlight's golf balls may be rejected by the USGA for exceeding the overall distance standard concerning carry and roll.

MaxFlight's quality control program involves taking periodic samples of 50 golf balls to monitor the manufacturing process. For each sample, a hypothesis test is conducted to determine whether the process has fallen out of adjustment. Let us develop the null and alternative hypotheses. We begin by assuming that the process is functioning correctly; that is, the golf balls being produced have a mean distance of 295 yards. This assumption establishes the null hypothesis. The alternative hypothesis is that the mean distance is not equal to 295 yards. With a hypothesized value of $\mu_0 = 295$, the null and alternative hypotheses for the MaxFlight hypothesis test are as follows:

$$H_0: \mu = 295$$
$$H_a: \mu \neq 295$$

If the sample mean $\bar{x}$ is significantly less than 295 yards or significantly greater than 295 yards, we will reject H_0. In this case, corrective action will be taken to adjust the manufacturing process. On the other hand, if $\bar{x}$ does not deviate from the hypothesized mean $\mu_0 = 295$ by a significant amount, H_0 will not be rejected and no action will be taken to adjust the manufacturing process.

The quality control team selected $\alpha = .05$ as the level of significance for the test. Data from previous tests conducted when the process was known to be in adjustment show that the population standard deviation can be assumed known with a value of $\sigma = 12$. Thus, with a sample size of $n = 50$, the standard error of $\bar{x}$ is

$$\sigma_{\bar{x}} = \frac{\sigma}{\sqrt{n}} = \frac{12}{\sqrt{50}} = 1.7$$

Because the sample size is large, the central limit theorem (see Chapter 7) allows us to conclude that the sampling distribution of $\bar{x}$ can be approximated by a normal distribution. Figure 9.4 shows the sampling distribution of $\bar{x}$ for the MaxFlight hypothesis test with a hypothesized population mean of $\mu_0 = 295$.

DATA *file*

GolfTest

Suppose that a sample of 50 golf balls is selected and that the sample mean is $\bar{x} = 297.6$ yards. This sample mean provides support for the conclusion that the population mean is larger than 295 yards. Is this value of $\bar{x}$ enough larger than 295 to cause us to reject H_0 at the .05 level of significance? In the previous section we described two approaches that can be used to answer this question: the p-value approach and the critical value approach.

p-value approach Recall that the p-value is a probability used to determine whether the null hypothesis should be rejected. For a two-tailed test, values of the test statistic in *either* tail provide evidence against the null hypothesis. For a two-tailed test, the p-value is the probability of obtaining a value for the test statistic *as unlikely as or more unlikely than* that provided by the sample. Let us see how the p-value is computed for the MaxFlight hypothesis test.

FIGURE 9.4   SAMPLING DISTRIBUTION OF $\bar{x}$ FOR THE MAXFLIGHT HYPOTHESIS TEST

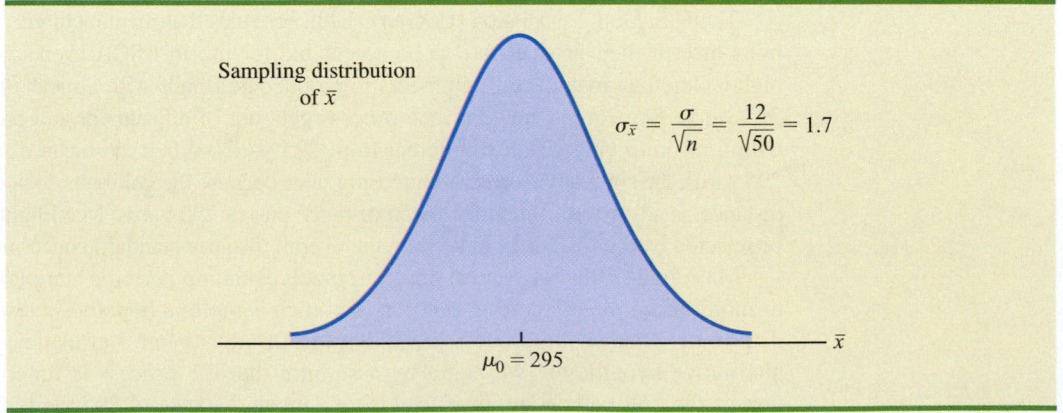

Sampling distribution of $\bar{x}$

$$\sigma_{\bar{x}} = \frac{\sigma}{\sqrt{n}} = \frac{12}{\sqrt{50}} = 1.7$$

$\mu_0 = 295$

FIGURE 9.5 *p*-VALUE FOR THE MAXFLIGHT HYPOTHESIS TEST

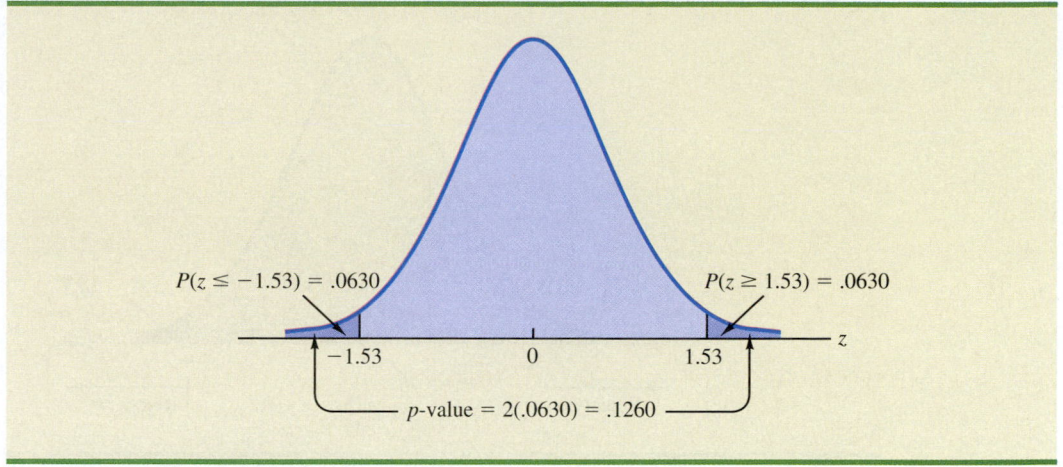

$$P(z \le -1.53) = .0630 \qquad P(z \ge 1.53) = .0630$$

$-1.53 \qquad 0 \qquad 1.53 \qquad z$

p-value = 2(.0630) = .1260

First we compute the value of the test statistic. For the σ known case, the test statistic *z* is a standard normal random variable. Using equation (9.1) with $\bar{x} = 297.6$, the value of the test statistic is

$$z = \frac{\bar{x} - \mu_0}{\sigma/\sqrt{n}} = \frac{297.6 - 295}{12/\sqrt{50}} = 1.53$$

Now to compute the *p*-value we must find the probability of obtaining a value for the test statistic *at least as unlikely as z* = 1.53. Clearly values of $z \ge 1.53$ are *at least as unlikely.* But, because this is a two-tailed test, values of $z \le -1.53$ are also *at least as unlikely as* the value of the test statistic provided by the sample. In Figure 9.5, we see that the two-tailed *p*-value in this case is given by $P(z \le -1.53) + P(z \ge 1.53)$. Because the normal curve is symmetric, we can compute this probability by finding $P(z \ge 1.53)$ and doubling it. The table for the standard normal distribution shows that $P(z < 1.53) = .9370$. Thus, the upper tail area is $P(z \ge 1.53) = 1.0000 - .9370 = .0630$. Doubling this, we find that the *p*-value for the MaxFlight two-tailed hypothesis test is *p*-value = 2(.0630) = .1260.

Next we compare the *p*-value to the level of significance to see whether the null hypothesis should be rejected. With a level of significance of $\alpha = .05$, we do not reject H_0 because the *p*-value = .1260 > .05. Because the null hypothesis is not rejected, no action will be taken to adjust the MaxFlight manufacturing process.

Let us summarize the steps involved in computing *p*-values for two-tailed hypothesis tests.

COMPUTATION OF *p*-VALUES FOR TWO-TAILED TESTS

1. Compute the value of the test statistic using equation (9.1).
2. If the value of the test statistic is in the upper tail, compute the probability that *z* is greater than or equal to the value of the test statistic (the upper tail area). If the value of the test statistic is in the lower tail, compute the probability that *z* is less than or equal to the value of the test statistic (the lower tail area).
3. Double the probability (or tail area) from step 2 to obtain the *p*-value.

Critical value approach Before leaving this section, let us see how the test statistic *z* can be compared to a critical value to make the hypothesis testing decision for a two-tailed test.

FIGURE 9.6 CRITICAL VALUES FOR THE MAXFLIGHT HYPOTHESIS TEST

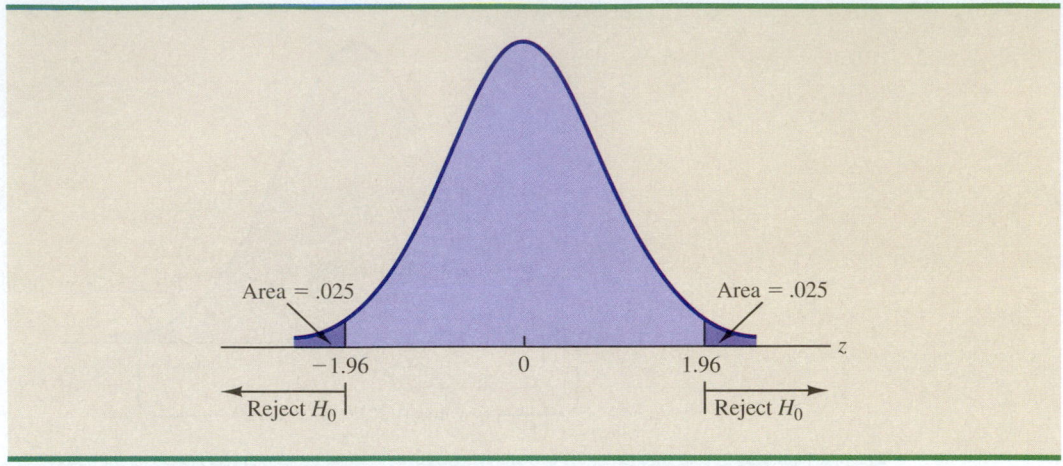

Figure 9.6 shows that the critical values for the test will occur in both the lower and upper tails of the standard normal distribution. With a level of significance of $\alpha = .05$, the area in each tail corresponding to the critical values is $\alpha/2 = .05/2 = .025$. Using the standard normal probability table, we find the critical values for the test statistic are $-z_{.025} = -1.96$ and $z_{.025} = 1.96$. Thus, using the critical value approach, the two-tailed rejection rule is

$$\text{Reject } H_0 \text{ if } z \leq -1.96 \text{ or if } z \geq 1.96$$

Because the value of the test statistic for the MaxFlight study is $z = 1.53$, the statistical evidence will not permit us to reject the null hypothesis at the .05 level of significance.

Using Excel

Excel can be used to conduct one-tailed and two-tailed hypothesis tests about a population mean for the σ known case using the p-value approach. Recall that the method used to compute a p-value depends upon whether the test is lower tail, upper tail, or two-tailed. Therefore, in the Excel procedure we describe we will use the sample results to compute three p-values: p-value (Lower Tail), p-value (Upper Tail), and p-value (Two Tail). The user can then choose α and draw a conclusion using whichever p-value is appropriate for the type of hypothesis test being conducted. We will illustrate using the MaxFlight two-tailed hypothesis test. Refer to Figure 9.7 as we describe the tasks involved. The formula worksheet is in the background; the value worksheet is in the foreground.

Enter/Access Data: Open the DATAfile named *GolfTest*. A label and the distance data for the sample of 50 golf balls are entered into cells A1:A51.

Enter Functions and Formulas: The sample size and sample mean are computed in cells D4 and D5 using Excel's COUNT and AVERAGE functions, respectively. The value worksheet shows that the sample size is 50 and the sample mean is 297.6. The value of the known population standard deviation (12) is entered into cell D7, and the hypothesized value of the population mean (295) is entered into cell D8.

The standard error is obtained in cell D10 by entering the formula =D7/SQRT(D4). The formula =(D5-D8)/D10 entered into cell D11 computes the test statistic z(1.5321). To compute the p-value for a lower tail test, we enter the formula =NORM.S.DIST(D11,TRUE) into cell D13. The p-value for an upper tail test is then computed in cell D14 as 1 minus the

FIGURE 9.7   EXCEL WORKSHEET: HYPOTHESIS TEST FOR THE σ KNOWN CASE

DATA file

GolfTest

	A	B	C	D	E
1	Yards		**Hypothesis Test about a Population Mean:**		
2	303		**σ Known Case**		
3	282				
4	289		Sample Size	=COUNT(A2:A51)	
5	298		Sample Mean	=AVERAGE(A2:A51)	
6	283				
7	317		Population Standard Deviation	12	
8	297		Hypothesized Value	295	
9	308				
10	317		Standard Error	=D7/SQRT(D4)	
11	293		Test Statistic z	=(D5-D8)/D10	
12	284				
13	290		*p*-value (Lower Tail)	=NORM.S.DIST(D11,TRUE)	
14	304		*p*-value (Upper Tail)	=1-D13	
15	290		*p*-value (Two Tail)	=2*(MIN(D13,D14))	
16	311				
50	301				
51	292				
52					

	A	B	C	D	E
1	Yards		**Hypothesis Test about a Population Mean:**		
2	303		**σ Known Case**		
3	282				
4	289		Sample Size	50	
5	298		Sample Mean	297.6	
6	283				
7	317		Population Standard Deviation	12	
8	297		Hypothesized Value	295	
9	308				
10	317		Standard Error	1.6971	
11	293		Test Statistic z	1.5321	
12	284				
13	290		*p*-value (Lower Tail)	0.9372	
14	304		*p*-value (Upper Tail)	0.0628	
15	290		*p*-value (Two Tail)	0.1255	
16	311				
50	301				
51	292				
52					

Note: Rows 17–49 are hidden.

p-value for the lower tail test. Finally, the *p*-value for a two-tailed test is computed in cell D15 as two times the minimum of the two one-tailed *p*-values. The value worksheet shows that *p*-value (Lower Tail) = 0.9372, *p*-value (Upper Tail) = 0.0628, and *p*-value (Two Tail) = 0.1255.

The development of the worksheet is now complete. For the two-tailed MaxFlight problem we cannot reject H_0: $\mu = 295$ using $\alpha = .05$ because the *p*-value (Two Tail) = 0.1255 is greater than α. Thus, the quality control manager has no reason to doubt that the manufacturing process is producing golf balls with a population mean distance of 295 yards.

A template for other problems   The worksheet in Figure 9.7 can be used as a template for conducting any one-tailed and two-tailed hypothesis tests for the σ known case. Just enter the appropriate data in column A, adjust the ranges for the formulas in cells D4 and D5, enter the population standard deviation in cell D7, and enter the hypothesized value in cell D8. The standard error, the test statistic, and the three *p*-values will then appear. Depending on the form of the hypothesis test (lower tail, upper tail, or two-tailed), we can then choose the appropriate *p*-value to make the rejection decision.

We can further simplify the use of Figure 9.7 as a template for other problems by eliminating the need to enter new data ranges in cells D4 and D5. To do so we rewrite the cell formulas as follows:

Cell D4:   =COUNT(A:A)

Cell D5:   =AVERAGE(A:A)

The DATAfile named GolfTest includes a worksheet entitled Template that uses the A:A method for entering the data ranges.

With the A:A method of specifying data ranges, Excel's COUNT function will count the number of numerical values in column A and Excel's AVERAGE function will compute the average of the numerical values in column A. Thus, to solve a new problem it is only necessary to enter the new data in column A, enter the value of the known population standard deviation in cell D7, and enter the hypothesized value of the population mean in cell D8.

The worksheet can also be used as a template for text exercises in which n, $\bar{x}$, and σ are given. Just ignore the data in column A and enter the values for n, $\bar{x}$, and σ into cells D4, D5, and D7, respectively. Then enter the appropriate hypothesized value for the population mean into cell D8. The *p*-values corresponding to lower tail, upper tail, and two-tailed hypothesis tests will then appear in cells D13:D15.

TABLE 9.2   SUMMARY OF HYPOTHESIS TESTS ABOUT A POPULATION MEAN: σ KNOWN CASE

	Lower Tail Test	**Upper Tail Test**	**Two-Tailed Test**
Hypotheses	$H_0: \mu \geq \mu_0$ $H_a: \mu < \mu_0$	$H_0: \mu \leq \mu_0$ $H_a: \mu > \mu_0$	$H_0: \mu = \mu_0$ $H_a: \mu \neq \mu_0$
Test Statistic	$z = \dfrac{\bar{x} - \mu_0}{\sigma/\sqrt{n}}$	$z = \dfrac{\bar{x} - \mu_0}{\sigma/\sqrt{n}}$	$z = \dfrac{\bar{x} - \mu_0}{\sigma/\sqrt{n}}$
Rejection Rule: *p*-**Value Approach**	Reject H_0 if p-value $\leq \alpha$	Reject H_0 if p-value $\leq \alpha$	Reject H_0 if p-value $\leq \alpha$
Rejection Rule: **Critical Value** **Approach**	Reject H_0 if $z \leq -z_\alpha$	Reject H_0 if $z \geq z_\alpha$	Reject H_0 if $z \leq -z_{\alpha/2}$ or if $z \geq z_{\alpha/2}$

Summary and Practical Advice

We presented examples of a lower tail test and a two-tailed test about a population mean. Based upon these examples, we can now summarize the hypothesis testing procedures about a population mean for the σ known case as shown in Table 9.2. Note that μ_0 is the hypothesized value of the population mean.

The hypothesis testing steps followed in the two examples presented in this section are common to every hypothesis test.

STEPS OF HYPOTHESIS TESTING

Step 1. Develop the null and alternative hypotheses.
Step 2. Specify the level of significance.
Step 3. Collect the sample data and compute the value of the test statistic.

p-Value Approach

Step 4. Use the value of the test statistic to compute the *p*-value.
Step 5. Reject H_0 if the *p*-value $\leq \alpha$.
Step 6. Interpret the statistical conclusion in the context of the application.

Critical Value Approach

Step 4. Use the level of significance to determine the critical value and the rejection rule.
Step 5. Use the value of the test statistic and the rejection rule to determine whether to reject H_0.
Step 6. Interpret the statistical conclusion in the context of the application.

Practical advice about the sample size for hypothesis tests is similar to the advice we provided about the sample size for interval estimation in Chapter 8. In most applications, a sample size of $n \geq 30$ is adequate when using the hypothesis testing procedure described in this section. In cases where the sample size is less than 30, the distribution of the population from which we are sampling becomes an important consideration. If the population is normally distributed, the hypothesis testing procedure that we described is exact and can be used for any sample size. If the population is not normally distributed but is at least roughly symmetric, sample sizes as small as 15 can be expected to provide acceptable results.

Relationship Between Interval Estimation and Hypothesis Testing

In Chapter 8 we showed how to develop a confidence interval estimate of a population mean. For the σ known case, the $(1 - \alpha)\%$ confidence interval estimate of a population mean is given by

$$\bar{x} \pm z_{\alpha/2} \frac{\sigma}{\sqrt{n}}$$

In this chapter we showed that a two-tailed hypothesis test about a population mean takes the following form:

$$H_0: \mu = \mu_0$$
$$H_a: \mu \neq \mu_0$$

where μ_0 is the hypothesized value for the population mean.

Suppose that we follow the procedure described in Chapter 8 for constructing a $100(1 - \alpha)\%$ confidence interval for the population mean. We know that $100(1 - \alpha)\%$ of the confidence intervals generated will contain the population mean and $100\alpha\%$ of the confidence intervals generated will not contain the population mean. Thus, if we reject H_0 whenever the confidence interval does not contain μ_0, we will be rejecting the null hypothesis when it is true ($\mu = \mu_0$) with probability α. Recall that the level of significance is the probability of rejecting the null hypothesis when it is true. So constructing a $100(1 - \alpha)\%$ confidence interval and rejecting H_0 whenever the interval does not contain μ_0 is equivalent to conducting a two-tailed hypothesis test with α as the level of significance. The procedure for using a confidence interval to conduct a two-tailed hypothesis test can now be summarized.

> A CONFIDENCE INTERVAL APPROACH TO TESTING A HYPOTHESIS OF THE FORM
>
> $$H_0: \mu = \mu_0$$
> $$H_a: \mu \neq \mu_0$$
>
> 1. Select a simple random sample from the population and use the value of the sample mean $\bar{x}$ to develop the confidence interval for the population mean μ.
>
> $$\bar{x} \pm z_{\alpha/2} \frac{\sigma}{\sqrt{n}}$$
>
> 2. If the confidence interval contains the hypothesized value μ_0, do not reject H_0. Otherwise, reject[3] H_0.

For a two-tailed hypothesis test, the null hypothesis can be rejected if the confidence interval does not include μ_0.

Let us illustrate by conducting the MaxFlight hypothesis test using the confidence interval approach. The MaxFlight hypothesis test takes the following form:

$$H_0: \mu = 295$$
$$H_a: \mu \neq 295$$

---

[3]To be consistent with the rule for rejecting H_0 when the *p*-value $\leq \alpha$, we would also reject H_0 using the confidence interval approach if μ_0 happens to be equal to one of the endpoints of the $100(1 - \alpha)\%$ confidence interval.

To test these hypotheses with a level of significance of $\alpha = .05$, we sampled 50 golf balls and found a sample mean distance of $\bar{x} = 297.6$ yards. Recall that the population standard deviation is $\sigma = 12$. Using these results with $z_{.025} = 1.96$, we find that the 95% confidence interval estimate of the population mean is

$$\bar{x} \pm z_{.025}\frac{\sigma}{\sqrt{n}}$$

$$297.6 \pm 1.96\frac{12}{\sqrt{50}}$$

$$297.6 \pm 3.3$$

or

$$294.3 \text{ to } 300.9$$

This finding enables the quality control manager to conclude with 95% confidence that the mean distance for the population of golf balls is between 294.3 and 300.9 yards. Because the hypothesized value for the population mean, $\mu_0 = 295$, is in this interval, the hypothesis testing conclusion is that the null hypothesis, $H_0: \mu = 295$, cannot be rejected.

Note that this discussion and example pertain to two-tailed hypothesis tests about a population mean. However, the same confidence interval and two-tailed hypothesis testing relationship exists for other population parameters. The relationship can also be extended to one-tailed tests about population parameters. Doing so, however, requires the development of one-sided confidence intervals, which are rarely used in practice.

NOTES AND COMMENTS

1. We have shown how to use p-values. The smaller the p-value the greater the evidence against H_0 and the more the evidence in favor of H_a. Here are some guidelines statisticians suggest for interpreting small p-values.

   - Less than .01—Overwhelming evidence to conclude that H_a is true
   - Between .01 and .05—Strong evidence to conclude that H_a is true
   - Between .05 and .10—Weak evidence to conclude that H_a is true

   - Greater than .10—Insufficient evidence to conclude that H_a is true

2. When testing a hypothesis of the population mean with a sample size that is at least 5% of the population size (that is, $n/N \geq .05$), the finite population correction factor should be used when calculating the standard error of the sampling distribution of $\bar{x}$ when σ is known, that is,

$$\sigma_{\bar{x}} = \sqrt{\frac{N-n}{N-1}}\left(\frac{\sigma}{\sqrt{n}}\right).$$

Exercises

Note to Student: Some of the exercises that follow ask you to use the p-value approach and others ask you to use the critical value approach. Both methods will provide the same hypothesis testing conclusion. We provide exercises with both methods to give you practice using both. In later sections and in following chapters, we will generally emphasize the p-value approach as the preferred method, but you may select either based on personal preference.

Methods

9. Consider the following hypothesis test:

$$H_0: \mu \geq 20$$
$$H_a: \mu < 20$$

A sample of 50 provided a sample mean of 19.4. The population standard deviation is 2.
  a.   Compute the value of the test statistic.
  b.   What is the p-value?
  c.   Using $\alpha = .05$, what is your conclusion?
  d.   What is the rejection rule using the critical value? What is your conclusion?

SELF*test* 10.   Consider the following hypothesis test:

$$H_0: \mu \leq 25$$
$$H_a: \mu > 25$$

A sample of 40 provided a sample mean of 26.4. The population standard deviation is 6.
  a.   Compute the value of the test statistic.
  b.   What is the p-value?
  c.   At $\alpha = .01$, what is your conclusion?
  d.   What is the rejection rule using the critical value? What is your conclusion?

11.   Consider the following hypothesis test:

$$H_0: \mu = 15$$
$$H_a: \mu \neq 15$$

A sample of 50 provided a sample mean of 14.15. The population standard deviation is 3.
  a.   Compute the value of the test statistic.
  b.   What is the p-value?
  c.   At $\alpha = .05$, what is your conclusion?
  d.   What is the rejection rule using the critical value? What is your conclusion?

12.   Consider the following hypothesis test:

$$H_0: \mu \geq 80$$
$$H_a: \mu < 80$$

A sample of 100 is used and the population standard deviation is 12. Compute the p-value and state your conclusion for each of the following sample results. Use $\alpha = .01$.
  a. $\bar{x} = 78.5$
  b. $\bar{x} = 77$
  c. $\bar{x} = 75.5$
  d. $\bar{x} = 81$

13.   Consider the following hypothesis test:

$$H_0: \mu \leq 50$$
$$H_a: \mu > 50$$

A sample of 60 is used and the population standard deviation is 8. Use the critical value approach to state your conclusion for each of the following sample results. Use $\alpha = .05$.
  a. $\bar{x} = 52.5$
  b. $\bar{x} = 51$
  c. $\bar{x} = 51.8$

14.   Consider the following hypothesis test:

$$H_0: \mu = 22$$
$$H_a: \mu \neq 22$$

A sample of 75 is used and the population standard deviation is 10. Compute the *p*-value and state your conclusion for each of the following sample results. Use $\alpha = .01$.

a. $\bar{x} = 23$

b. $\bar{x} = 25.1$

c. $\bar{x} = 20$

Applications

 **SELF***test*

15. Individuals filing federal income tax returns prior to March 31 received an average refund of $1056. Consider the population of "last-minute" filers who mail their tax return during the last five days of the income tax period (typically April 10 to April 15).

   a. A researcher suggests that a reason individuals wait until the last five days is that on average these individuals receive lower refunds than do early filers. Develop appropriate hypotheses such that rejection of H_0 will support the researcher's contention.

   b. For a sample of 400 individuals who filed a tax return between April 10 and 15, the sample mean refund was $910. Based on prior experience, a population standard deviation of $\sigma = \$1600$ may be assumed. What is the *p*-value?

   c. At $\alpha = .05$, what is your conclusion?

   d. Repeat the preceding hypothesis test using the critical value approach.

16. In a study entitled How Undergraduate Students Use Credit Cards, *Sallie Mae* reported that undergraduate students have a mean credit card balance of $3173. This figure was an all-time high and had increased 44% over the previous five years. Assume that a current study is being conducted to determine whether it can be concluded that the mean credit card balance for undergraduate students has continued to increase compared to the April 2009 report. Based on previous studies, use a population standard deviation $\sigma = \$1000$.

   a. State the null and alternative hypotheses.

   b. What is the *p*-value for a sample of 180 undergraduate students with a sample mean credit card balance of $3325?

   c. Using a .05 level of significance, what is your conclusion?

17. The mean hourly wage for employees in goods-producing industries is $24.57 (Bureau of Labor Statistics website, April 12, 2012). Suppose we take a sample of employees from the manufacturing industry to see if the mean hourly wage differs from the reported mean of $24.57 for the goods-producing industries.

   a. State the null and alternative hypotheses we should use to test whether the population mean hourly wage in the manufacturing industry differs from the population mean hourly wage in the goods-producing industries.

   b. Suppose a sample of 30 employees from the manufacturing industry showed a sample mean of $23.89 per hour. Assume a population standard deviation of $2.40 per hour and compute the *p*-value.

   c. With $\alpha = .05$ as the level of significance, what is your conclusion?

   d. Repeat the preceding hypothesis test using the critical value approach.

18. Young millennials, adults aged 18 to 34, are viewed as the future of the restaurant industry. During 2011, this group consumed a mean of 192 restaurant meals per person (NPD Group website, November 7, 2012). Conduct a hypothesis test to determine whether the poor economy has caused a change in the frequency of consuming restaurant meals by young millennials in 2012.

   a. Formulate hypotheses that can be used to determine whether the annual mean number of restaurant meals per person has changed for young millennials in 2012.

   b. Based on a sample, the NPD Group stated that the mean number of restaurant meals consumed by young millennials in 2012 was 182. Assume the sample size was 150 and that, based on past studies, the population standard deviation can be assumed to be $\sigma = 55$. Use the sample results to compute the test statistic and *p*-value for your hypothesis test.

   c. At $\alpha = .05$, what is your conclusion?

19. The Internal Revenue Service (IRS) provides a toll-free help line for taxpayers to call in and get answers to questions as they prepare their tax returns. In recent years, the IRS has been inundated with taxpayer calls and has redesigned its phone service as well as posting answers to frequently asked questions on its website (*The Cincinnati Enquirer*, January 7, 2010). According to a report by a taxpayer advocate, callers using the new system can expect to wait on hold for an unreasonably long time of 12 minutes before being able to talk to an IRS employee. Suppose you select a sample of 50 callers after the new phone service has been implemented; the sample results show a mean waiting time of 10 minutes before an IRS employee comes on line. Based upon data from past years, you decide it is reasonable to assume that the standard deviation of waiting times is 8 minutes. Using your sample results, can you conclude that the actual mean waiting time turned out to be significantly less than the 12-minute claim made by the taxpayer advocate? Use $\alpha = .05$.

20. According to the Hospital Care Cost Institute the annual expenditure for prescription drugs is $838 per person in the Northeast region of the country. A sample of 60 individuals in the Midwest shows a per person annual expenditure for prescription drugs of $745. Use a population standard deviation of $300 to answer the following questions.
    a. Formulate hypotheses for a test to determine whether the sample data support the conclusion that the population annual expenditure for prescription drugs per person is lower in the Midwest than in the Northeast.
    b. What is the value of the test statistic?
    c. What is the *p*-value?
    d. At $\alpha = .01$, what is your conclusion?

Fowle

21. Fowle Marketing Research, Inc. bases charges to a client on the assumption that telephone surveys can be completed in a mean time of 15 minutes or less. If a longer mean survey time is necessary, a premium rate is charged. A sample of 35 surveys provided the survey times shown in the DATAfile named *Fowle*. Based upon past studies, the population standard deviation is assumed known with $\sigma = 4$ minutes. Is the premium rate justified?
    a. Formulate the null and alternative hypotheses for this application.
    b. Compute the value of the test statistic.
    c. What is the *p*-value?
    d. At $\alpha = .01$, what is your conclusion?

22. CCN and ActMedia provided a television channel targeted to individuals waiting in supermarket checkout lines. The channel showed news, short features, and advertisements. The length of the program was based on the assumption that the population mean time a shopper stands in a supermarket checkout line is 8 minutes. A sample of actual waiting times will be used to test this assumption and determine whether actual mean waiting time differs from this standard.
    a. Formulate the hypotheses for this application.
    b. A sample of 120 shoppers showed a sample mean waiting time of 8.4 minutes. Assume a population standard deviation of $\sigma = 3.2$ minutes. What is the *p*-value?
    c. At $\alpha = .05$, what is your conclusion?
    d. Compute a 95% confidence interval for the population mean. Does it support your conclusion?

9.4   Population Mean: *σ* Unknown

In this section we describe how to conduct hypothesis tests about a population mean for the σ unknown case. Because the σ unknown case corresponds to situations in which an estimate of the population standard deviation cannot be developed prior to sampling, the sample must be used to develop an estimate of both μ and σ. Thus, to conduct a hypothesis test about a population mean for the σ unknown case, the sample mean $\bar{x}$ is used as an estimate of μ and the sample standard deviation s is used as an estimate of σ.

The steps of the hypothesis testing procedure for the σ unknown case are the same as those for the σ known case described in Section 9.3. But, with σ unknown, the computation of the test statistic and p-value is a bit different. Recall that for the σ known case, the sampling distribution of the test statistic has a standard normal distribution. For the σ unknown case, however, the sampling distribution of the test statistic follows the t distribution; it has slightly more variability because the sample is used to develop estimates of both μ and σ.

In Section 8.2 we showed that an interval estimate of a population mean for the σ unknown case is based on a probability distribution known as the t distribution. Hypothesis tests about a population mean for the σ unknown case are also based on the t distribution. For the σ unknown case, the test statistic has a t distribution with $n - 1$ degrees of freedom.

> **TEST STATISTIC FOR HYPOTHESIS TESTS ABOUT A POPULATION MEAN: σ UNKNOWN**
>
> $$t = \frac{\bar{x} - \mu_0}{s/\sqrt{n}} \qquad (9.2)$$

In Chapter 8 we said that the t distribution is based on an assumption that the population from which we are sampling has a normal distribution. However, research shows that this assumption can be relaxed considerably when the sample size is large enough. We provide some practical advice concerning the population distribution and sample size at the end of the section.

One-Tailed Test

Let us consider an example of a one-tailed test about a population mean for the σ unknown case. A business travel magazine wants to classify transatlantic gateway airports according to the mean rating for the population of business travelers. A rating scale with a low score of 0 and a high score of 10 will be used, and airports with a population mean rating greater than 7 will be designated as superior service airports. The magazine staff surveyed a sample of 60 business travelers at each airport to obtain the ratings data. The sample for London's Heathrow Airport provided a sample mean rating of $\bar{x} = 7.25$ and a sample standard deviation of $s = 1.052$. Do the data indicate that Heathrow should be designated as a superior service airport?

DATA *file*

AirRating

We want to develop a hypothesis test for which the decision to reject H_0 will lead to the conclusion that the population mean rating for the Heathrow Airport is *greater* than 7. Thus, an upper tail test with H_a: $\mu > 7$ is required. The null and alternative hypotheses for this upper tail test are as follows:

$$H_0\text{: } \mu \le 7$$
$$H_a\text{: } \mu > 7$$

We will use $\alpha = .05$ as the level of significance for the test.

Using equation (9.2) with $\bar{x} = 7.25$, $\mu_0 = 7$, $s = 1.052$, and $n = 60$, the value of the test statistic is

$$t = \frac{\bar{x} - \mu_0}{s/\sqrt{n}} = \frac{7.25 - 7}{1.052/\sqrt{60}} = 1.84$$

The sampling distribution of t has $n - 1 = 60 - 1 = 59$ degrees of freedom. Because the test is an upper tail test, the p-value is $P(t \geq 1.84)$, that is, the upper tail area corresponding to the value of the test statistic.

The t distribution table provided in most textbooks will not contain sufficient detail to determine the exact p-value, such as the p-value corresponding to $t = 1.84$. For instance, using Table 2 in Appendix B, the t distribution with 59 degrees of freedom provides the following information.

Area in Upper Tail	.20	.10	.05	.025	.01	.005
t Value (59 df)	.848	1.296	1.671	2.001	2.391	2.662

$$t = 1.84$$

We see that $t = 1.84$ is between 1.671 and 2.001. Although the table does not provide the exact p-value, the values in the "Area in Upper Tail" row show that the p-value must be less than .05 and greater than .025. With a level of significance of $\alpha = .05$, this placement is all we need to know to make the decision to reject the null hypothesis and conclude that Heathrow should be classified as a superior service airport.

It is cumbersome to use a t table to compute p-values, and only approximate values are obtained. We describe how to compute exact p-values using Excel's T.DIST function in the Using Excel subsection which follows. The exact upper tail p-value for the Heathrow Airport hypothesis test is .0354. With $.0354 < .05$, we reject the null hypothesis and conclude that Heathrow should be classified as a superior service airport.

The decision whether to reject the null hypothesis in the σ unknown case can also be made using the critical value approach. The critical value corresponding to an area of $\alpha = .05$ in the upper tail of a t distribution with 59 degrees of freedom is $t_{.05} = 1.671$. Thus the rejection rule using the critical value approach is to reject H_0 if $t \geq 1.671$. Because $t = 1.84 > 1.671$, H_0 is rejected. Heathrow should be classified as a superior service airport.

Two-Tailed Test

To illustrate how to conduct a two-tailed test about a population mean for the σ unknown case, let us consider the hypothesis testing situation facing Holiday Toys. The company manufactures and distributes its products through more than 1000 retail outlets. In planning production levels for the coming winter season, Holiday must decide how many units of each product to produce prior to knowing the actual demand at the retail level. For this year's most important new toy, Holiday's marketing director is expecting demand to average 40 units per retail outlet. Prior to making the final production decision based upon this estimate, Holiday decided to survey a sample of 25 retailers in order to develop more information about the demand for the new product. Each retailer was provided with information about the features of the new toy along with the cost and the suggested selling price. Then each retailer was asked to specify an anticipated order quantity.

With μ denoting the population mean order quantity per retail outlet, the sample data will be used to conduct the following two-tailed hypothesis test:

$$H_0: \mu = 40$$
$$H_a: \mu \neq 40$$

If H_0 cannot be rejected, Holiday will continue its production planning based on the marketing director's estimate that the population mean order quantity per retail outlet will be $\mu = 40$ units. However, if H_0 is rejected, Holiday will immediately reevaluate its production plan for the product. A two-tailed hypothesis test is used because Holiday wants to reevaluate the production plan if the population mean quantity per retail outlet is less than anticipated or greater than anticipated. Because no historical data are available (it's a new product), the population mean μ and the population standard deviation must both be estimated using $\bar{x}$ and s from the sample data.

DATA *file*

Orders

The sample of 25 retailers provided a mean of $\bar{x} = 37.4$ and a standard deviation of $s = 11.79$ units. Before going ahead with the use of the t distribution, the analyst constructed a histogram of the sample data in order to check on the form of the population distribution. The histogram of the sample data showed no evidence of skewness or any extreme outliers, so the analyst concluded that the use of the t distribution with $n - 1 = 24$ degrees of freedom was appropriate. Using equation (9.2) with $\bar{x} = 37.4$, $\mu_0 = 40$, $s = 11.79$, and $n = 25$, the value of the test statistic is

$$t = \frac{\bar{x} - \mu_0}{s/\sqrt{n}} = \frac{37.4 - 40}{11.79/\sqrt{25}} = -1.10$$

Because we have a two-tailed test, the p-value is two times the area under the curve of the t distribution for $t \leq -1.10$. Using Table 2 in Appendix B, the t distribution table for 24 degrees of freedom provides the following information.

Area in Upper Tail	.20	.10	.05	.025	.01	.005
t-Value (24 df)	.857	1.318	1.711	2.064	2.492	2.797

$t = 1.10$

The t distribution table contains only positive t values (corresponding to areas in the upper tail). Because the t distribution is symmetric, however, the upper tail area for $t = 1.10$ is the same as the lower tail area for $t = -1.10$. We see that $t = 1.10$ is between 0.857 and 1.318. From the "Area in Upper Tail" row, we see that the area in the tail to the right of $t = 1.10$ is between .20 and .10. When we double these amounts, we see that the p-value must be between .40 and .20. With a level of significance of $\alpha = .05$, we now know that the p-value is greater than α. Therefore, H_0 cannot be rejected. Sufficient evidence is not available to conclude that Holiday should change its production plan for the coming season.

In the Using Excel subsection which follows, we show how to compute the exact p-value for this hypothesis test using Excel. The p-value obtained is .2811. With a level of significance of $\alpha = .05$, we cannot reject H_0 because .2811 > .05.

The test statistic can also be compared to the critical value to make the two-tailed hypothesis testing decision. With $\alpha = .05$ and the t distribution with 24 degrees of freedom, $-t_{.025} = -2.064$ and $t_{.025} = 2.064$ are the critical values for the two-tailed test. The rejection rule using the test statistic is

$$\text{Reject } H_0 \text{ if } t \leq -2.064 \text{ or if } t \geq 2.064$$

Based on the test statistic $t = -1.10$, H_0 cannot be rejected. This result indicates that Holiday should continue its production planning for the coming season based on the expectation that $\mu = 40$.

Using Excel

Excel can be used to conduct one-tailed and two-tailed hypothesis tests about a population mean for the σ unknown case. The approach is similar to the procedure used in the σ known case. The sample data and the test statistic (t) are used to compute three p-values: p-value (Lower Tail), p-value (Upper Tail), and p-value (Two Tail). The user can then choose α and

FIGURE 9.8   EXCEL WORKSHEET: HYPOTHESIS TEST FOR THE σ UNKNOWN CASE

DATA *file*

Orders

	A	B	C	D	E
1	Units		**Hypothesis Test about a Population Mean:**		
2	26		**σ Unknown Case**		
3	23				
4	32		Sample Size	=COUNT(A2:A26)	
5	47		Sample Mean	=AVERAGE(A2:A26)	
6	45		Sample Standard Deviation	=STDEV.S(A2:A26)	
7	31				
8	47		Hypothesized Value	40	
9	59				
10	21		Standard Error	=D6/SQRT(D4)	
11	52		Test Statistic t	=(D5-D8)/D10	
12	45		Degrees of Freedom	=D4-1	
13	53				
14	34		p-value (Lower Tail)	=T.DIST(D11,D12,TRUE)	
15	45		p-value (Upper Tail)	=1-D14	
16	39		p-value (Two Tail)	=2*MIN(D14,D15)	
17	52				
25	30				
26	28				
27					

Note: Rows 18–24 are hidden.

	A	B	C	D	E	F
1	Units		**Hypothesis Test about a Population Mean:**			
2	26		**σ Unknown Case**			
3	23					
4	32		Sample Size	25		
5	47		Sample Mean	37.4		
6	45		Sample Standard Deviation	11.79		
7	31					
8	47		Hypothesized Value	40		
9	59					
10	21		Standard Error	2.3580		
11	52		Test Statistic t	-1.1026		
12	45		Degrees of Freedom	24		
13	53					
14	34		p-value (Lower Tail)	0.1406		
15	45		p-value (Upper Tail)	0.8594		
16	39		p-value (Two Tail)	0.2811		
17	52					
25	30					
26	28					
27						

draw a conclusion using whichever p-value is appropriate for the type of hypothesis test being conducted.

Let's start by showing how to use Excel's T.DIST function to compute a lower tail p-value. The T.DIST function has three inputs; its general form is as follows:

$$\text{T.DIST(test statistic, degrees of freedom, cumulative)}$$

For the first input, we enter the value of the test statistic, for the second input we enter the number of degrees of freedom. For the third input, we enter TRUE if we want a cumulative probability and FALSE if we want the height of the curve. When we want to compute a lower tail p-value, we enter TRUE.

Once the lower tail p-value has been computed, it is easy to compute the upper tail and the two-tailed p-values. The upper tail p-value is just 1 minus the lower tail p-value. And the two-tailed p-value is given by two times the smaller of the lower and upper tail p-values.

Let us now construct an Excel worksheet to conduct the two-tailed hypothesis test for the Holiday Toys study. Refer to Figure 9.8 as we describe the tasks involved. The formula worksheet is in the background; the value worksheet is in the foreground.

Enter/Access Data: Open the DATAfile named *Orders*. A label and the order quantity data for the sample of 25 retailers are entered into cells A1:A26.

Enter Functions and Formulas: The sample size, sample mean, and sample standard deviation are computed in cells D4:D6 using Excel's COUNT, AVERAGE, and STDEV.S functions, respectively. The value worksheet shows that the sample size is 25, the sample mean is 37.4, and the sample standard deviation is 11.79. The hypothesized value of the population mean (40) is entered into cell D8.

Using the sample standard deviation as an estimate of the population standard deviation, an estimate of the standard error is obtained in cell D10 by dividing the sample standard deviation in cell D6 by the square root of the sample size in cell D4. The formula =(D5-D8)/D10 entered into cell D11 computes the test statistic $t(-1.1026)$. The degrees of freedom are computed in cell D12 as the sample size in cell D4 minus 1.

To compute the *p*-value for a lower tail test, we enter the following formula into cell D14:

$$=T.DIST(D11,D12,TRUE)$$

The *p*-value for an upper tail test is then computed in cell D15 as 1 minus the *p*-value for the lower tail test. Finally, the *p*-value for a two-tailed test is computed in cell D16 as two times the minimum of the two one-tailed *p*-values. The value worksheet shows that the three *p*-values are *p*-value (Lower Tail) = 0.1406, *p*-value (Upper Tail) = 0.8594, and *p*-value (Two Tail) = 0.2811.

The development of the worksheet is now complete. For the two-tailed Holiday Toys problem we cannot reject H_0: $\mu = 40$ using $\alpha = .05$ because the *p*-value (Two Tail) = 0.2811 is greater than α. This result indicates that Holiday should continue its production planning for the coming season based on the expectation that $\mu = 40$. The worksheet in Figure 9.8 can also be used for any one-tailed hypothesis test involving the *t* distribution. If a lower tail test is required, compare the *p*-value (Lower Tail) with α to make the rejection decision. If an upper tail test is required, compare the *p*-value (Upper Tail) with α to make the rejection decision.

A template for other problems   The worksheet in Figure 9.8 can be used as a template for any hypothesis tests about a population mean for the σ unknown case. Just enter the appropriate data in column A, adjust the ranges for the formulas in cells D4:D6, and enter the hypothesized value in cell D8. The standard error, the test statistic, and the three *p*-values will then appear. Depending on the form of the hypothesis test (lower tail, upper tail, or two-tailed), we can then choose the appropriate *p*-value to make the rejection decision.

We can further simplify the use of Figure 9.8 as a template for other problems by eliminating the need to enter new data ranges in cells D4:D6. To do so we rewrite the cell formulas as follows:

Cell D4: =COUNT(A:A)

Cell D5: =AVERAGE(A:A)

Cell D6: =STDEV(A:A)

The DATAfile named Orders *includes a worksheet entitled* Template *that uses the A:A method for entering the data ranges.*

With the A:A method of specifying data ranges, Excel's COUNT function will count the number of numeric values in column A, Excel's AVERAGE function will compute the average of the numeric values in column A, and Excel's STDEV function will compute the standard deviation of the numeric values in Column A. Thus, to solve a new problem it is only necessary to enter the new data in column A and enter the hypothesized value of the population mean in cell D8.

Summary and Practical Advice

Table 9.3 provides a summary of the hypothesis testing procedures about a population mean for the σ unknown case. The key difference between these procedures and the ones for the σ known case is that *s* is used, instead of σ, in the computation of the test statistic. For this reason, the test statistic follows the *t* distribution.

The applicability of the hypothesis testing procedures of this section is dependent on the distribution of the population being sampled from and the sample size. When the population is normally distributed, the hypothesis tests described in this section provide exact results for any sample size. When the population is not normally distributed, the procedures are approximations. Nonetheless, we find that sample sizes of 30 or greater will provide good results in most cases. If the population is approximately normal, small sample sizes (e.g., $n < 15$) can provide acceptable results. If the population is highly skewed or contains outliers, sample sizes approaching 50 are recommended.

TABLE 9.3 SUMMARY OF HYPOTHESIS TESTS ABOUT A POPULATION MEAN: σ UNKNOWN CASE

	Lower Tail Test	Upper Tail Test	Two-Tailed Test
Hypotheses	$H_0: \mu \geq \mu_0$ $H_a: \mu < \mu_0$	$H_0: \mu \leq \mu_0$ $H_a: \mu > \mu_0$	$H_0: \mu = \mu_0$ $H_a: \mu \neq \mu_0$
Test Statistic	$t = \dfrac{\bar{x} - \mu_0}{s/\sqrt{n}}$	$t = \dfrac{\bar{x} - \mu_0}{s/\sqrt{n}}$	$t = \dfrac{\bar{x} - \mu_0}{s/\sqrt{n}}$
Rejection Rule: p-Value Approach	Reject H_0 if p-value $\leq \alpha$	Reject H_0 if p-value $\leq \alpha$	Reject H_0 if p-value $\leq \alpha$
Rejection Rule: Critical Value Approach	Reject H_0 if $t \leq -t_\alpha$	Reject H_0 if $t \geq t_\alpha$	Reject H_0 if $t \leq -t_{\alpha/2}$ or if $t \geq t_{\alpha/2}$

NOTE AND COMMENT

When testing a hypothesis of the population mean with a sample size that is at least 5% of the population size (that is, $n/N \geq .05$), the finite population correction factor should be used when calculating the standard error of the sampling distribution of $\bar{x}$ when σ is unknown, i.e., $s_{\bar{x}} = \sqrt{\dfrac{N-n}{N-1}}\left(\dfrac{s}{\sqrt{n}}\right)$.

Exercises

Methods

23. Consider the following hypothesis test:

$$H_0: \mu \leq 12$$
$$H_a: \mu > 12$$

A sample of 25 provided a sample mean $\bar{x} = 14$ and a sample standard deviation $s = 4.32$.
a. Compute the value of the test statistic.
b. Use the t distribution table (Table 2 in Appendix B) to compute a range for the p-value.
c. At $\alpha = .05$, what is your conclusion?
d. What is the rejection rule using the critical value? What is your conclusion?

 24. Consider the following hypothesis test:

$$H_0: \mu = 18$$
$$H_a: \mu \neq 18$$

A sample of 48 provided a sample mean $\bar{x} = 17$ and a sample standard deviation $s = 4.5$.
a. Compute the value of the test statistic.
b. Use the t distribution table (Table 2 in Appendix B) to compute a range for the p-value.
c. At $\alpha = .05$, what is your conclusion?
d. What is the rejection rule using the critical value? What is your conclusion?

25. Consider the following hypothesis test:

$$H_0: \mu \geq 45$$
$$H_a: \mu < 45$$

A sample of 36 is used. Identify the p-value and state your conclusion for each of the following sample results. Use $\alpha = .01$.
   a. $\bar{x} = 44$ and $s = 5.2$
   b. $\bar{x} = 43$ and $s = 4.6$
   c. $\bar{x} = 46$ and $s = 5.0$

26. Consider the following hypothesis test:

$$H_0: \mu = 100$$
$$H_a: \mu \neq 100$$

A sample of 65 is used. Identify the p-value and state your conclusion for each of the following sample results. Use $\alpha = .05$.
   a. $\bar{x} = 103$ and $s = 11.5$
   b. $\bar{x} = 96.5$ and $s = 11.0$
   c. $\bar{x} = 102$ and $s = 10.5$

Applications

 27. Which is cheaper: eating out or dining in? The mean cost of a flank steak, broccoli, and rice bought at the grocery store is $13.04 (Money.msn website, November 7, 2012). A sample of 100 neighborhood restaurants showed a mean price of $12.75 and a standard deviation of $2 for a comparable restaurant meal.
   a. Develop appropriate hypotheses for a test to determine whether the sample data support the conclusion that the mean cost of a restaurant meal is less than fixing a comparable meal at home.
   b. Using the sample from the 100 restaurants, what is the p-value?
   c. At $\alpha = .05$, what is your conclusion?
   d. Repeat the preceding hypothesis test using the critical value approach.

28. A shareholders' group, in lodging a protest, claimed that the mean tenure for a chief executive officer (CEO) was at least nine years. A survey of companies reported in *The Wall Street Journal* found a sample mean tenure of $\bar{x} = 7.27$ years for CEOs with a standard deviation of $s = 6.38$ years.
   a. Formulate hypotheses that can be used to challenge the validity of the claim made by the shareholders' group.
   b. Assume 85 companies were included in the sample. What is the p-value for your hypothesis test?
   c. At $\alpha = .01$, what is your conclusion?

 29. The national mean annual salary for a school administrator is $90,000 a year (*The Cincinnati Enquirer*, April 7, 2012). A school official took a sample of 25 school administrators in the state of Ohio to learn about salaries in that state to see if they differed from the national average.
   a. Formulate hypotheses that can be used to determine whether the population mean annual administrator salary in Ohio differs from the national mean of $90,000.
   b. The sample data for 25 Ohio administrators is contained in the DATAfile named *Administrator*. What is the p-value for your hypothesis test in part (a)?
   c. At $\alpha = .05$, can your null hypothesis be rejected? What is your conclusion?
   d. Repeat the preceding hypothesis test using the critical value approach.

ChildCare

30. *Time* reports that the time married men with children spend on child care averages 6.4 hours per week. You belong to a professional group on family practices that would like to do its own study to determine whether the time married men in your area spend on child care per week differs from the reported mean of 6.4 hours per week. A sample of 40 married couples will be used with the data collected showing the hours per week the husband spends on child care. The sample data are contained in the DATAfile named *ChildCare*.

    a.   What are the hypotheses if your group would like to determine whether the population mean number of hours married men are spending in child care differs from the mean reported by *Time* in your area?

    b.   What is the sample mean and the p-value?

    c.   Select your own level of significance. What is your conclusion?

31. The United States ranks ninth in the world in per capita chocolate consumption; the average American eats 9.5 pounds of chocolate annually (*Forbes*, July 22, 2015). Suppose you are curious whether chocolate consumption is higher in Hershey, Pennsylvania, the location of The Hershey Company's corporate headquarters. A sample of 36 individuals from the Hershey area showed a sample mean annual consumption of 10.05 pounds and a standard deviation of $s = 1.5$ pounds. Using $\alpha = .05$, do the sample results support the conclusion that mean annual consumption of chocolate is higher in Hershey than it is throughout the United States?

UsedCars

32. According to the National Automobile Dealers Association, the mean price for used cars is $10,192. A manager of a Kansas City used car dealership reviewed a sample of 50 recent used car sales at the dealership in an attempt to determine whether the population mean price for used cars at this particular dealership differed from the national mean. The prices for the sample of 50 cars are shown in the DATAfile named *UsedCars*.

    a.   Formulate the hypotheses that can be used to determine whether a difference exists in the mean price for used cars at the dealership.

    b.   What is the p-value?

    c.   At $\alpha = .05$, what is your conclusion?

33. The mean annual premium for automobile insurance in the United States is $1503 (Insure .com website, March 6, 2014). Being from Pennsylvania, you believe automobile insurance is cheaper there and wish to develop statistical support for your opinion. A sample of 25 automobile insurance policies from the state of Pennsylvania showed a mean annual premium of $1440 with a standard deviation of $s = \$165$.

    a.   Develop a hypothesis test that can be used to determine whether the mean annual premium in Pennsylvania is lower than the national mean annual premium.

    b.   What is a point estimate of the difference between the mean annual premium in Pennsylvania and the national mean?

    c.   At $\alpha = .05$, test for a significant difference. What is your conclusion?

34. Joan's Nursery specializes in custom-designed landscaping for residential areas. The estimated labor cost associated with a particular landscaping proposal is based on the number of plantings of trees, shrubs, and so on to be used for the project. For cost-estimating purposes, managers use two hours of labor time for the planting of a medium-sized tree. Actual times from a sample of 10 plantings during the past month follow (times in hours).

1.7	1.5	2.6	2.2	2.4	2.3	2.6	3.0	1.4	2.3

With a .05 level of significance, test to see whether the mean tree-planting time differs from two hours.

    a.   State the null and alternative hypotheses.

    b.   Compute the sample mean.

    c.   Compute the sample standard deviation.

    d.   What is the p-value?

    e.   What is your conclusion?

9.5 Population Proportion

In this section we show how to conduct a hypothesis test about a population proportion p. Using p_0 to denote the hypothesized value for the population proportion, the three forms for a hypothesis test about a population proportion are as follows.

$$H_0: p \geq p_0 \qquad H_0: p \leq p_0 \qquad H_0: p = p_0$$
$$H_a: p < p_0 \qquad H_a: p > p_0 \qquad H_a: p \neq p_0$$

The first form is called a lower tail test, the second form is called an upper tail test, and the third form is called a two-tailed test.

Hypothesis tests about a population proportion are based on the difference between the sample proportion $\bar{p}$ and the hypothesized population proportion p_0. The methods used to conduct the hypothesis test are similar to those used for hypothesis tests about a population mean. The only difference is that we use the sample proportion and its standard error to compute the test statistic. The p-value approach or the critical value approach is then used to determine whether the null hypothesis should be rejected.

Let us consider an example involving a situation faced by Pine Creek golf course. Over the past year, 20% of the players at Pine Creek were women. In an effort to increase the proportion of women players, Pine Creek implemented a special promotion designed to attract women golfers. One month after the promotion was implemented, the course manager requested a statistical study to determine whether the proportion of women players at Pine Creek had increased. Because the objective of the study is to determine whether the proportion of women golfers increased, an upper tail test with $H_a: p > .20$ is appropriate. The null and alternative hypotheses for the Pine Creek hypothesis test are as follows:

$$H_0: p \leq .20$$
$$H_a: p > .20$$

If H_0 can be rejected, the test results will give statistical support for the conclusion that the proportion of women golfers increased and the promotion was beneficial. The course manager specified that a level of significance of $\alpha = .05$ be used in carrying out this hypothesis test.

The next step of the hypothesis testing procedure is to select a sample and compute the value of an appropriate test statistic. To show how this step is done for the Pine Creek upper tail test, we begin with a general discussion of how to compute the value of the test statistic for any form of a hypothesis test about a population proportion. The sampling distribution of $\bar{p}$, the point estimator of the population parameter p, is the basis for developing the test statistic.

When the null hypothesis is true as an equality, the expected value of $\bar{p}$ equals the hypothesized value p_0; that is, $E(\bar{p}) = p_0$. The standard error of $\bar{p}$ is given by

$$\sigma_{\bar{p}} = \sqrt{\frac{p_0(1 - p_0)}{n}}$$

In Chapter 7 we said that if $np \geq 5$ and $n(1 - p) \geq 5$, the sampling distribution of $\bar{p}$ can be approximated by a normal distribution.[4] Under these conditions, which usually apply in practice, the quantity

$$z = \frac{\bar{p} - p_0}{\sigma_{\bar{p}}} \qquad\qquad \textbf{(9.3)}$$

---

[4]In most applications involving hypothesis tests of a population proportion, sample sizes are large enough to use the normal approximation. The exact sampling distribution of $\bar{p}$ is discrete, with the probability for each value of $\bar{p}$ given by the binomial distribution. So hypothesis testing is a bit more complicated for small samples when the normal approximation cannot be used.

has a standard normal probability distribution. With $\sigma_{\bar{p}} = \sqrt{p_0(1 - p_0)/n}$, the standard normal random variable z is the test statistic used to conduct hypothesis tests about a population proportion.

> **TEST STATISTIC FOR HYPOTHESIS TESTS ABOUT A POPULATION PROPORTION**
>
> $$z = \frac{\bar{p} - p_0}{\sqrt{\dfrac{p_0(1 - p_0)}{n}}} \qquad (9.4)$$

WomenGolf

We can now compute the test statistic for the Pine Creek hypothesis test. Suppose a random sample of 400 players was selected, and that 100 of the players were women. The proportion of women golfers in the sample is

$$\bar{p} = \frac{100}{400} = .25$$

Using equation (9.4), the value of the test statistic is

$$z = \frac{\bar{p} - p_0}{\sqrt{\dfrac{p_0(1 - p_0)}{n}}} = \frac{.25 - .20}{\sqrt{\dfrac{.20(1 - .20)}{400}}} = \frac{.05}{.02} = 2.50$$

Because the Pine Creek hypothesis test is an upper tail test, the *p*-value is the probability that z is greater than or equal to $z = 2.50$; that is, it is the upper tail area corresponding to $z \geq 2.50$. Using the standard normal probability table, we find that the lower tail area for $z = 2.50$ is .9938. Thus, the *p*-value for the Pine Creek test is $1.0000 - .9938 = .0062$. Figure 9.9 shows this *p*-value calculation.

Recall that the course manager specified a level of significance of $\alpha = .05$. A *p*-value = $.0062 < .05$ gives sufficient statistical evidence to reject H_0 at the .05 level of significance. Thus, the test provides statistical support for the conclusion that the special promotion increased the proportion of women players at the Pine Creek golf course.

The decision whether to reject the null hypothesis can also be made using the critical value approach. The critical value corresponding to an area of .05 in the upper tail of a normal probability distribution is $z_{.05} = 1.645$. Thus, the rejection rule using the critical value approach is to reject H_0 if $z \geq 1.645$. Because $z = 2.50 > 1.645$, H_0 is rejected.

FIGURE 9.9 CALCULATION OF THE *p*-VALUE FOR THE PINE CREEK HYPOTHESIS TEST

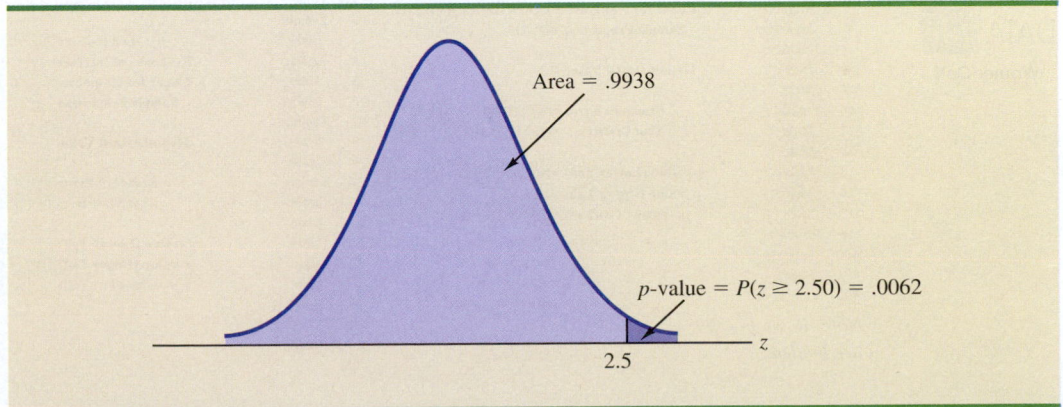

Again, we see that the *p*-value approach and the critical value approach lead to the same hypothesis testing conclusion, but the *p*-value approach provides more information. With a *p*-value $= .0062$, the null hypothesis would be rejected for any level of significance greater than or equal to .0062.

Using Excel

Excel can be used to conduct one-tailed and two-tailed hypothesis tests about a population proportion using the *p*-value approach. The procedure is similar to the approach used with Excel in conducting hypothesis tests about a population mean. The primary difference is that the test statistic is based on the sampling distribution of $\bar{x}$ for hypothesis tests about a population mean and on the sampling distribution of $\bar{p}$ for hypothesis tests about a population proportion. Thus, although different formulas are used to compute the test statistic needed to make the hypothesis testing decision, the computations of the critical value and the *p*-value for the tests are identical.

We will illustrate the procedure by showing how Excel can be used to conduct the upper tail hypothesis test for the Pine Creek golf course study. Refer to Figure 9.10 as we describe the tasks involved. The formula worksheet is in the background; the value worksheet is in the foreground.

Enter/Access Data: Open the DATAfile named *WomenGolf*. A label and the gender of each golfer in the study are entered into cells A1:A401.

Enter Functions and Formulas: The sample size, response count, and sample proportion are calculated in cells D3, D5, and D6. Because the data are not numeric, Excel's COUNTA function, not the COUNT function, is used in cell D3 to determine the sample size. We entered Female in cell D4 to identify the response for which we wish to compute a proportion. The COUNTIF function is then used in cell D5 to determine the number of responses of the type identified in cell D4. The sample proportion is then computed in cell D6 by dividing the response count by the sample size.

The hypothesized value of the population proportion (.20) is entered into cell D8. The standard error is obtained in cell D10 by entering the formula $=$SQRT(D8*(1-D8)/D3). The formula $=$(D6-D8)/D10 entered into cell D11 computes the test statistic *z* (2.50). To compute the *p*-value for a lower tail test, we enter the formula $=$NORM.S.DIST(D11,TRUE)

FIGURE 9.10   EXCEL WORKSHEET: HYPOTHESIS TEST FOR PINE CREEK GOLF COURSE

DATA *file*
WomenGolf

	A	B	C	D	E
1	Golfer		Hypothesis Test about a Population Proportion		
2	Female				
3	Male		Sample Size	=COUNTA(A2:A401)	
4	Female		Response of Interest	Female	
5	Male		Count for Response	=COUNTIF(A2:A401,D4)	
6	Male		Sample Proportion	=D5/D3	
7	Female				
8	Male		Hypothesized Value	0.2	
9	Male				
10	Female		Standard Error	=SQRT(D8*(1-D8)/D3)	
11	Male		Test Statistic *z*	=(D6-D8)/D10	
12	Male				
13	Male		*p*-value (Lower Tail)	=NORM.S.DIST(D11,TRUE)	
14	Male		*p*-value (Upper Tail)	=1-D13	
15	Male		*p*-value (TwoTail)	=2*MIN(D13,D14)	
16	Female				
400	Male				
401	Male				
402					

	A	B	C	D	E	F
1	Golfer		Hypothesis Test about a Population Proportion			
2	Female					
3	Male		Sample Size	400		
4	Female		Response of Interest	Female		
5	Male		Count for Response	100		
6	Male		Sample Proportion	0.25		
7	Female					
8	Male		Hypothesized Value	0.20		
9	Male					
10	Female		Standard Error	0.02		
11	Male		Test Statistic *z*	2.5000		
12	Male					
13	Male		*p*-value (Lower Tail)	0.9938		
14	Male		*p*-value (Upper Tail)	0.0062		
15	Male		*p*-value (TwoTail)	0.0124		
16	Female					
400	Male					
401	Male					
402						

Note: Rows 17–399 are hidden.

TABLE 9.4 SUMMARY OF HYPOTHESIS TESTS ABOUT A POPULATION PROPORTION

	Lower Tail Test	**Upper Tail Test**	**Two-Tailed Test**
Hypotheses	$H_0: p \geq p_0$ $H_a: p < p_0$	$H_0: p \leq p_0$ $H_a: p > p_0$	$H_0: p = p_0$ $H_a: p \neq p_0$
Test Statistic	$z = \dfrac{\bar{p} - p_0}{\sqrt{\dfrac{p_0(1-p_0)}{n}}}$	$z = \dfrac{\bar{p} - p_0}{\sqrt{\dfrac{p_0(1-p_0)}{n}}}$	$z = \dfrac{\bar{p} - p_0}{\sqrt{\dfrac{p_0(1-p_0)}{n}}}$
Rejection Rule: **p-Value Approach**	Reject H_0 if p-value $\leq \alpha$	Reject H_0 if p-value $\leq \alpha$	Reject H_0 if p-value $\leq \alpha$
Rejection Rule: **Critical Value** **Approach**	Reject H_0 if $z \leq -z_\alpha$	Reject H_0 if $z \geq z_\alpha$	Reject H_0 if $z \leq -z_{\alpha/2}$ or if $z \geq z_{\alpha/2}$

into cell D13. The p-value for an upper tail test is then computed in cell D14 as 1 minus the p-value for the lower tail test. Finally, the p-value for a two-tailed test is computed in cell D15 as two times the minimum of the two one-tailed p-values. The value worksheet shows that the three p-values are as follows: p-value (Lower Tail) $= 0.9938$; p-value (Upper Tail) $= 0.0062$; and p-value (Two Tail) $= 0.0124$.

The development of the worksheet is now complete. For the Pine Creek upper tail hypothesis test, we reject the null hypothesis that the population proportion is .20 or less because the p-value (Upper Tail) $= 0.0062$ is less than $\alpha = .05$. Indeed, with this p-value we would reject the null hypothesis for any level of significance of .0062 or greater.

A template for other problems The worksheet in Figure 9.10 can be used as a template for hypothesis tests about a population proportion whenever $np \geq 5$ and $n(1-p) \geq 5$. Just enter the appropriate data in column A, adjust the ranges for the formulas in cells D3 and D5, enter the appropriate response in cell D4, and enter the hypothesized value in cell D8. The standard error, the test statistic, and the three p-values will then appear. Depending on the form of the hypothesis test (lower tail, upper tail, or two-tailed), we can then choose the appropriate p-value to make the rejection decision.

Summary

The procedure used to conduct a hypothesis test about a population proportion is similar to the procedure used to conduct a hypothesis test about a population mean. Although we only illustrated how to conduct a hypothesis test about a population proportion for an upper tail test, similar procedures can be used for lower tail and two-tailed tests. Table 9.4 provides a summary of the hypothesis tests about a population proportion. We assume that $np \geq 5$ and $n(1-p) \geq 5$; thus the normal probability distribution can be used to approximate the sampling distribution of $\bar{p}$.

NOTE AND COMMENT

When testing a hypothesis of the population proportion with a sample size that is at least 5% of the population size (that is, $n/N \geq .05$), the finite population correction factor should be used when calculating the standard error of the sampling distribution of $\bar{p}$, i.e., $s_{\bar{p}} = \sqrt{\dfrac{N-n}{N-1}} \sqrt{\dfrac{p_0(1-p_0)}{n}}$.

Exercises

Methods

35. Consider the following hypothesis test:

$$H_0: p = .20$$
$$H_a: p \neq .20$$

A sample of 400 provided a sample proportion $\bar{p} = .175$.
a. Compute the value of the test statistic.
b. What is the p-value?
c. At $\alpha = .05$, what is your conclusion?
d. What is the rejection rule using the critical value? What is your conclusion?

 36. Consider the following hypothesis test:

$$H_0: p \geq .75$$
$$H_a: p < .75$$

A sample of 300 items was selected. Compute the p-value and state your conclusion for each of the following sample results. Use $\alpha = .05$.
a. $\bar{p} = .68$
b. $\bar{p} = .72$
c. $\bar{p} = .70$
d. $\bar{p} = .77$

Applications

37. The U.S. Bureau of Labor Statistics reports that 11.3% of U.S. workers belong to unions (BLS website, January 2014). Suppose a sample of 400 U.S. workers is collected in 2014 to determine whether union efforts to organize have increased union membership.
a. Formulate the hypotheses that can be used to determine whether union membership increased in 2014.
b. If the sample results show that 52 of the workers belonged to unions, what is the p-value for your hypothesis test?
c. At $\alpha = .05$, what is your conclusion?

 38. A study by *Consumer Reports* showed that 64% of supermarket shoppers believe supermarket brands to be as good as national name brands. To investigate whether this result applies to its own product, the manufacturer of a national name-brand ketchup asked a sample of shoppers whether they believed that supermarket ketchup was as good as the national brand ketchup.
a. Formulate the hypotheses that could be used to determine whether the percentage of supermarket shoppers who believe that the supermarket ketchup was as good as the national brand ketchup differed from 64%.
b. If a sample of 100 shoppers showed 52 stating that the supermarket brand was as good as the national brand, what is the p-value?
c. At $\alpha = .05$, what is your conclusion?
d. Should the national brand ketchup manufacturer be pleased with this conclusion? Explain.

 39. What percentage of the population live in their state of birth? According to the U.S. Census Bureau's American Community Survey, the figure ranges from 25% in Nevada to 78.7% in Louisiana (*AARP Bulletin*, March 2014). The average percentage across all states and the District of Columbia is 57.7%. The data in the DATAfile *Homestate* are consistent with the findings in the American Community Survey. The data represent a random sample of 120 Arkansas residents and for a random sample of 180 Virginia residents.

a. Formulate hypotheses that can be used to determine whether the percentage of stay-at-home residents in the two states differs from the overall average of 57.7%.

b. Estimate the proportion of stay-at-home residents in Arkansas. Does this proportion differ significantly from the mean proportion for all states? Use $\alpha = .05$.

c. Estimate the proportion of stay-at-home residents in Virginia. Does this proportion differ significantly from the mean proportion for all states? Use $\alpha = .05$.

d. Would you expect the proportion of stay-at-home residents to be higher in Virginia than in Arkansas? Support your conclusion with the results obtained in parts (b) and (c).

40. Last year, 46% of business owners gave a holiday gift to their employees. A survey of business owners conducted this year indicated that 35% plan to provide a holiday gift to their employees. Suppose the survey results are based on a sample of 60 business owners.

a. How many business owners in the survey plan to provide a holiday gift to their employees this year?

b. Suppose the business owners in the sample do as they plan. Compute the *p*-value for a hypothesis test that can be used to determine whether the proportion of business owners providing holiday gifts has decreased from last year.

c. Using a .05 level of significance, would you conclude that the proportion of business owners providing gifts has decreased? What is the smallest level of significance for which you could draw such a conclusion?

41. Ten years ago 53% of American families owned stocks or stock funds. Sample data collected by the Investment Company Institute indicate that the percentage is now 46% (*The Wall Street Journal*, October 5, 2012).

a. Develop appropriate hypotheses such that rejection of H_0 will support the conclusion that a smaller proportion of American families own stocks or stock funds in 2012 than 10 years ago.

b. Assume the Investment Company Institute sampled 300 American families to estimate that the percent owning stocks or stock funds was 46% in 2012. What is the *p*-value for your hypothesis test?

c. At $\alpha = .01$, what is your conclusion?

42. According to the University of Nevada Center for Logistics Management, 6% of all merchandise sold in the United States gets returned. A Houston department store sampled 80 items sold in January and found that 12 of the items were returned.

a. Construct a point estimate of the proportion of items returned for the population of sales transactions at the Houston store.

b. Construct a 95% confidence interval for the porportion of returns at the Houston store.

c. Is the proportion of returns at the Houston store significantly different from the returns for the nation as a whole? Provide statistical support for your answer.

Eagle

43. Eagle Outfitters is a chain of stores specializing in outdoor apparel and camping gear. It is considering a promotion that involves mailing discount coupons to all its credit card customers. This promotion will be considered a success if more than 10% of those receiving the coupons use them. Before going national with the promotion, coupons were sent to a sample of 100 credit card customers.

a. Develop hypotheses that can be used to test whether the population proportion of those who will use the coupons is sufficient to go national.

b. The DATAfile named *Eagle* contains the sample data. Develop a point estimate of the population proportion.

c. Use $\alpha = .05$ to conduct your hypothesis test. Should Eagle go national with the promotion?

LawSuit

44. One of the reasons health care costs have been rising rapidly in recent years is the increasing cost of malpractice insurance for physicians. Also, fear of being sued causes doctors to run more precautionary tests (possibly unnecessary) just to make sure they are not guilty of missing something (*Reader's Digest*, October 2012). These precautionary tests also add to health

care costs. Data in the DATAfile named *LawSuit* are consistent with findings in the *Reader's Digest* article and can be used to estimate the proportion of physicians over the age of 55 who have been sued at least once.

a. Formulate hypotheses that can be used to see if these data can support a finding that more than half of physicians over the age of 55 have been sued at least once.

b. Use Excel and the DATAfile named *LawSuit* to compute the sample proportion of physicians over the age of 55 who have been sued at least once. What is the *p*-value for your hypothesis test?

c. At $\alpha = .01$, what is your conclusion?

45. The American Association of Individual Investors conducts a weekly survey of its members to measure the percent who are bullish, bearish, and neutral on the stock market for the next six months. For the week ending November 7, 2012, the survey results showed 38.5% bullish, 21.6% neutral, and 39.9% bearish (AAII website, November 12, 2012). Assume these results are based on a sample of 300 AAII members.

a. Over the long term, the proportion of bullish AAII members is .39. Conduct a hypothesis test at the 5% level of significance to see if the current sample results show that bullish sentiment differs from its long-term average of .39. What are your findings?

b. Over the long term, the proportion of bearish AAII members is .30. Conduct a hypothesis test at the 1% level of significance to see if the current sample results show that bearish sentiment is above its long-term average of .30. What are your findings?

c. Would you feel comfortable extending these results to all investors? Why or why not?

9.6   Practical Advice: Big Data and Hypothesis Testing

Technological advances and improvements in electronic (and often automated) data collection make it easy to collect millions, or even billions, of observations in a relatively short time. In this section, we provide practical advice on using large samples for hypothesis testing. As with any other statistical tool, the validity of a hypothesis test depends on the quality of the data used in the inference process. No matter how large the sample used to test a hypothesis, we are dealing with a sample that has been drawn from a population and we must therefore still contend with the limitations of sampling. If the sample is not representative of the population of interest, a hypothesis test based on the sample data will reveal little or nothing about the population of interest and may actually be misleading.

Big Data and *p*-Values

In section 8.5 we saw that interval estimates of the population mean μ (shown in formulas 8.1 and 8.2) and the population proportion p (shown in formula 8.4) narrow as the sample size increases. This occurs because the standard error of the associated sampling distributions decreases as the sample size increases. For a similar reason, in hypothesis testing the *p*-value associated with a given difference between a point estimate and a hypothesized value of a parameter also decreases as the sample size increases. But how rapidly does the *p*-value associated with a given difference between a point estimate and a hypothesized value of a parameter decreases as the sample size increases?

Let us again consider the online news service PenningtonDailyTimes.com (PDT), discussed in Chapters 7 and 8. Recall that PDT's primary source of revenue is the sale of advertising, and prospective advertisers are willing to pay a premium to advertise on websites that have long visit times. To promote its news service, PDT's management wants to promise potential advertisers that the mean time spent by customers when they visit

PenningtonDailyTimes.com exceeds 84 seconds, so PDT decides to collect sample data and test the null hypothesis H_0: $\mu \leq 84$. From historical data PDT knows that the standard deviation of the times spent by individual customers when they visit PDT's website is $\sigma = 20$. Table 9.5 provides the values of the test statistic z and the p-values for the test of the null hypothesis H_0: $\mu \leq 84$ if the mean for PDT's sample is 84.5 seconds. The p-value for this hypothesis test is essentially 0 for all samples in Table 9.5 that are at least $n = 100,000$.

This relationship also holds for hypothesis tests about the population proportion p; the p-value associated with a given difference between the sample proportion $\bar{p}$ and a hypothesized value of the population proportion p_0 decreases as the sample size increases. In general, the same can be said for for any hypothesis test; the p-value associated with a given difference between a point estimate and a hypothesized value of a parameter decreases as the sample size increases.

Implications of Big Data

Suppose PDT now collects a sample of 1,000,000 visitors to its website and uses these data to test its null hypothesis H_0: $\mu \leq 84$ at the .05 level of significance. Suppose also that the sample mean is 84.5, so the null hypothesis is rejected. As a result, PDT can promise potential advertisers that the mean time spent by individual customers who visit PDT's website exceeds 84 seconds. These results suggest that for this hypothesis test, the difference between the point estimate and the hypothesized value of the parameter being tested is not likely solely a consequence of sampling error. However, the results of any hypothesis test, no matter the sample size, are reliable only if the sample is relatively free of nonsampling error. If nonsampling error is introduced in the data collection process, the likelihood of making a Type I or Type II error may be higher than if the sample data are free of nonsampling error. Therefore, when testing a hypothesis it is always important to think carefully about whether a random sample of the population of interest has actually been taken.

If PDT determines that it has introduced little or no nonsampling error into its sample data, the only remaining plausible explanation for these results is that this null hypothesis is false. At this point PDT and the companies that advertise on PenningtonDailyTimes.com should also consider whether this statistically significant difference is of **practical significance**, i.e., consider the potential ramifications of the difference of .5 seconds between the sample mean time visitors spent at PenningtonDailyTimes.com and the hypothesized mean time.

The answers to this question will help PDT and its advertisers better assess whether this statistically significant difference has meaningful implications for its ensuing business decisions.

TABLE 9.5 VALUES OF THE TEST STATISTIC z AND THE p-VALUES FOR THE TEST OF THE NULL HYPOTHESIS H_0: $\mu \leq 84$ AND SAMPLE MEAN OF 84.5 SECONDS FOR VARIOUS SAMPLE SIZES n

Sample Size n	z	p-value
100	0.25	0.4013
500	0.56	0.2877
1,000	0.79	0.2148
10,000	2.50	0.0062
100,000	7.91	1.29E−15
1,000,000	25.00	3.06E−138
10,000,000	79.06	< 0.00E−200
100,000,000	250.00	< 0.00E−200
1,000,000,000	790.57	< 0.00E−200

Ultimately, no business decision should be based solely on statistical inference. Practical significance should always be considered in conjunction with statistical significance; this is particularly important when the hypothesis test is based on an extremely large sample because the minimum significant differences in such cases can be extremely small. When done properly, statistical inference provides evidence that should be considered in combination with information collected from other sources to make the most informed decision possible.

NOTE AND COMMENT

When taking an extremely large sample, it is still conceivable that the sample size is at least 5% of the population size; that is, $n/N \geq .05$. Under these conditions, it is necessary to use the finite population correction factor when calculating the standard error of the sampling distribution.

EXERCISES

Applications

FedEmail

46. A large department of the Federal Government wants to determine whether the average number of business emails sent and received per business day by its employees differs from the average number of emails sent and received per day by corporate employees. Suppose the department electronically collects information on the number of business emails sent and received on a randomly selected business day over the past year from each of 10,163 randomly selected federal employees. The results are provided in the DATAfile named *FedEmail*. Assuming that the standard deviation of the number of emails sent and received by this department's employees is $\sigma = 25$ and the average number of emails sent and received per day by corporate employees is 101.5, test the department's hypothesis at $\alpha = .01$. Discuss the practical significance of the results.

SocialNetwork

47. CEOs who belong to a popular business-oriented social networking service have an average of 930 connections. Do other members have fewer connections than CEOs? The number of connections for a random sample of 7515 members who are not CEOs is provided in the DATAfile named *SocialNetwork*. Based on historical data, the population standard deviation can be assumed to be known with $\sigma = 250$. Using this sample, test the hypothesis that other members have fewer connections than CEOs at $\alpha = .01$. Discuss the practical significance of the results.

48. The American Potato Growers Association (APGA) would like to test the claim that the proportion of fast food orders this year that includes French fries exceeds the proportion of fast food orders that included French fries last year. Suppose that a random sample of 49,581 electronic receipts for fast food orders placed this year shows that 31,038 included French fries. Assuming that the proportion of fast food orders that included French fries last year is .62, use this information to test APGA's claim at $\alpha = .05$. Discuss the practical significance of the results.

49. According to CNN, 55% of all U.S. smartphone users have used their GPS capability to get directions (CNN.com, May 2016). Suppose a provider of wireless telephone service in Canada wants to know if GPS usage by its customers differs from U.S. smartphone users. The company collects usage records for this year for a random sample of 547,192 of its customers and determines that 302,050 of these customers have used their telephone's GPS capability this year. Use this information to test the Canadian company's claim at $\alpha = .01$. Discuss the practical significance of the results.

Summary

Hypothesis testing is a statistical procedure that uses sample data to determine whether a statement about the value of a population parameter should or should not be rejected. The hypotheses are two competing statements about a population parameter. One statement is called the null hypothesis (H_0), and the other statement is called the alternative hypothesis (H_a). In Section 9.1 we provided guidelines for developing hypotheses for situations frequently encountered in practice.

Whenever historical data or other information provide a basis for assuming that the population standard deviation is known, the hypothesis testing procedure for the population mean is based on the standard normal distribution. Whenever σ is unknown, the sample standard deviation s is used to estimate σ and the hypothesis testing procedure is based on the t distribution. In both cases, the quality of results depends on both the form of the population distribution and the sample size. If the population has a normal distribution, both hypothesis testing procedures are applicable, even with small sample sizes. If the population is not normally distributed, larger sample sizes are needed. General guidelines about the sample size were provided in Sections 9.3 and 9.4. In the case of hypothesis tests about a population proportion, the hypothesis testing procedure uses a test statistic based on the standard normal distribution.

In all cases, the value of the test statistic can be used to compute a p-value for the test. A p-value is a probability used to determine whether the null hypothesis should be rejected. If the p-value is less than or equal to the level of significance α, the null hypothesis can be rejected.

Hypothesis testing conclusions can also be made by comparing the value of the test statistic to a critical value. For lower tail tests, the null hypothesis is rejected if the value of the test statistic is less than or equal to the critical value. For upper tail tests, the null hypothesis is rejected if the value of the test statistic is greater than or equal to the critical value. Two-tailed tests consist of two critical values: one in the lower tail of the sampling distribution and one in the upper tail. In this case, the null hypothesis is rejected if the value of the test statistic is less than or equal to the critical value in the lower tail or greater than or equal to the critical value in the upper tail. Finally, we discussed practical considerations to be made when testing hypotheses with very large samples.

Glossary

Alternative hypothesis The hypothesis concluded to be true if the null hypothesis is rejected.
Critical value A value that is compared with the test statistic to determine whether H_0 should be rejected.
Level of significance The probability of making a Type I error when the null hypothesis is true as an equality.
Minimum significant difference The smallest difference between a point estimate and a hypothesized value of a parameter that will result in rejection a null hypothesis for a given level of significance α.
Null hypothesis The hypothesis tentatively assumed true in the hypothesis testing procedure.
One-tailed test A hypothesis test in which rejection of the null hypothesis occurs for values of the test statistic in one tail of its sampling distribution.
Practical significance The usefulness or meaningfulness to a decision maker of the difference between a point estimate and the hypothesized value of a parameter.
p-value A probability that provides a measure of the evidence against the null hypothesis provided by the sample. Smaller p-values indicate more evidence against H_0. For a lower tail test, the p-value is the probability of obtaining a value for the test statistic as small as

or smaller than that provided by the sample. For an upper tail test, the *p*-value is the probability of obtaining a value for the test statistic as large as or larger than that provided by the sample. For a two-tailed test, the *p*-value is the probability of obtaining a value for the test statistic at least as unlikely as or more unlikely than that provided by the sample.

Test statistic A statistic whose value helps determine whether a null hypothesis should be rejected.

Two-tailed test A hypothesis test in which rejection of the null hypothesis occurs for values of the test statistic in either tail of its sampling distribution.

Type I error The error of rejecting H_0 when it is true.

Type II error The error of accepting H_0 when it is false.

Key Formulas

Test Statistic for Hypothesis Tests About a Population Mean: σ Known

$$z = \frac{\bar{x} - \mu_0}{\sigma/\sqrt{n}} \tag{9.1}$$

Test Statistic for Hypothesis Tests About a Population Mean: σ Unknown

$$t = \frac{\bar{x} - \mu_0}{s/\sqrt{n}} \tag{9.2}$$

Test Statistic for Hypothesis Tests About a Population Proportion

$$z = \frac{\bar{p} - p_0}{\sqrt{\dfrac{p_0(1 - p_0)}{n}}} \tag{9.4}$$

Supplementary Exercises

50. A production line operates with a mean filling weight of 16 ounces per container. Overfilling or underfilling presents a serious problem and when detected requires the operator to shut down the production line to readjust the filling mechanism. From past data, a population standard deviation $\sigma = .8$ ounces is assumed. A quality control inspector selects a sample of 30 items every hour and at that time makes the decision of whether to shut down the line for readjustment. The level of significance is $\alpha = .05$.
    a. State the hypothesis test for this quality control application.
    b. If a sample mean of $\bar{x} = 16.32$ ounces were found, what is the *p*-value? What action would you recommend?
    c. If a sample mean of $\bar{x} = 15.82$ ounces were found, what is the *p*-value? What action would you recommend?
    d. Use the critical value approach. What is the rejection rule for the preceding hypothesis testing procedure? Repeat parts (b) and (c). Do you reach the same conclusion?

51. At Western University the historical mean of scholarship examination scores for freshman applications is 900. A historical population standard deviation $\sigma = 180$ is assumed known. Each year, the assistant dean uses a sample of applications to determine whether the mean examination score for the new freshman applications has changed.
    a. State the hypotheses.
    b. What is the 95% confidence interval estimate of the population mean examination score if a sample of 200 applications provided a sample mean of $\bar{x} = 935$?
    c. Use the confidence interval to conduct a hypothesis test. Using $\alpha = .05$, what is your conclusion?
    d. What is the p-value?

52. Young children in the United States are exposed to an average of 4 hours of background television per day (CNN website, November 13, 2012). Having the television on in the background while children are doing other activities may have adverse consequences on a child's well-being. You have a research hypothesis that children from low-income families are exposed to more than 4 hours of daily background television. In order to test this hypothesis, you have collected a random sample of 60 children from low-income families and found that these children were exposed to a sample mean of 4.5 hours of daily background television.
    a. Develop hypotheses that can be used to test your research hypothesis.
    b. Based on a previous study, you are willing to assume that the population standard deviation is $\sigma = 1.5$ hours. What is the p-value based on your sample of 60 children from low-income families?
    c. Use $\alpha = .01$ as the level of significance. What is your conclusion?

53. The *Wall Street Journal* reported that bachelor's degree recipients with majors in business received average starting salaries of $53,900 in 2012 (*The Wall Street Journal*, March 17, 2014). The results for a sample of 100 business majors receiving a bachelor's degree in 2013 showed a mean starting salary of $55,144 with a sample standard deviation of $5200. Conduct a hypothesis test to determine whether the mean starting salary for business majors in 2013 is greater than the mean starting salary in 2012. Use $\alpha = .01$ as the level of significance.

BritainMarriages

54. Data from the Office for National Statistics show that the mean age at which men in Great Britain get married is 30.8 years (*The Guardian*, February 15, 2013). A news reporter noted that this represents a continuation of the trend of waiting until a later age to wed. A new sample of 47 recently wed British men provided their age at the time of marriage. These data are contained in the DATAfile named *BritainMarriages*. Do these data indicate that the mean age of British men at the time of marriage exceeds the mean age in 2013? Test this hypothesis at $\alpha = .05$. What is your conclusion?

YearsToGrad

55. The mean time to earn a bachelor's degree is 5.8 years (Education Planning Resources website, December 5, 2015). Suppose you would like to determine whether the mean time to earn a bachelor's degree is significantly less for students who attend private universities. Data on the time to earn a bachelor's degree for a random sample of 50 individuals who recently earned their bachelor's degrees from private universities are available in the DATAfile named *YearsToGrad*.
    a. State the hypotheses that should be used to test whether the mean time to earn a bachelor's degree is significantly less for students who attend private universities.
    b. Use the data in the DATAfile named *YearsToGrad* to compute the sample mean, the test statistic, and the p-value.
    c. Use $\alpha = .05$. What is your conclusion?
    d. Repeat the hypothesis test using the critical value approach.

56. The chamber of commerce of a Florida Gulf Coast community advertises that area residential property is available at a mean cost of $125,000 or less per lot. Suppose a sample of 32 properties provided a sample mean of $130,000 per lot and a sample

standard deviation of $12,500. Use a .05 level of significance to test the validity of the advertising claim.

57. In Hamilton County, Ohio, the mean number of days needed to sell a house is 86 days (Cincinnati Multiple Listing Service, April 2012). Data for the sale of 40 houses in a nearby county showed a sample mean of 80 days with a sample standard deviation of 20 days. Conduct a hypothesis test to determine whether the mean number of days until a house is sold is different than the Hamilton County mean of 86 days in the nearby county. Use $\alpha = .05$ for the level of significance, and state your conclusion.

58. Fifty-two percent of Americans report that they generally can sleep during flights (Expedia website, December 6, 2015). Are people who fly frequently more likely to be able to sleep during flights? Suppose we have a random sample of 510 individuals who flew at least 25,000 miles last year and 285 indicated that they were able to sleep during flights.

   a. Conduct a hypothesis test to determine whether the results justify concluding that people who fly frequently are more likely to be able to sleep during flights. Use $\alpha = .05$.

   b. Conduct the same hypothesis test you performed in part (a) at $\alpha = .01$. What is your conclusion?

59. The Bureau of Labor Statistics reports a 6.0% unemployment rate for Americans whose maximum attained level of education is a high school diploma (Bureau of Labor Statistics website, December 5, 2015). Is the unemployment rate significantly different for Americans who have earned their bachelor's degrees? Suppose we have a random sample of 500 Americans whose maximum attained level of education is a bachelor's degree and found 18 who are unemployed. Use these sample results to conduct a hypothesis test to determine whether the unemployment rate for Americans whose maximum attained level of education is a bachelor's degree differs significantly from the unemployment rate for Americans whose maximum attained level of education is a high school diploma.

   a. State the appropriate hypotheses for your significance test.

   b. Use the sample results to compute the test statistic and the p-value.

   c. Using $\alpha = .10$, what is your conclusion?

60. Members of the millennial generation are continuing to be dependent on their parents (either living with or otherwise receiving support from parents) into early adulthood (*The Cincinnati Enquirer*, March 16, 2014). A family research organization has claimed that, in past generations, no more than 30% of individuals aged 18 to 32 continued to be dependent on their parents. Suppose that a sample of 400 individuals aged 18 to 32 showed that 136 of them continue to be dependent on their parents.

   a. Develop hypotheses for a test to determine whether the proportion of millennials continuing to be dependent on their parents is higher than for past generations.

   b. What is your point estimate of the proportion of millennials that are continuing to be dependent on their parents?

   c. What is the p-value provided by the sample data?

   d. What is your hypothesis testing conclusion? Use $\alpha = .05$ as the level of significance.

61. The unemployment rate for 18- to 34-year-olds was reported to be 10.8% (*The Cincinnati Enquirer*, November 6, 2012). Assume that this report was based on a random sample of four hundred 18- to 34-year-olds.

   a. A political campaign manager wants to know if the sample results can be used to conclude that the unemployment rate for 18- to 34-years-olds is significantly higher than the unemployment rate for all adults. According to the Bureau of Labor Statistics, the unemployment rate for all adults was 7.9%. Develop a hypothesis test that can be used to see if the conclusion that the unemployment rate is higher for 18- to 34-year-olds can be supported.

b. Use the sample data collected for the 18- to 34-year-olds to compute the *p*-value for the hypothesis test in part (a). Using $\alpha = .05$, what is your conclusion?

c. Explain to the campaign manager what can be said about the observed level of significance for the hypothesis testing results using the *p*-value.

62. A radio station in Myrtle Beach announced that at least 90% of the hotels and motels would be full for the Memorial Day weekend. The station advised listeners to make reservations in advance if they planned to be in the resort over the weekend. On Saturday night a sample of 58 hotels and motels showed 49 with a no-vacancy sign and 9 with vacancies. What is your reaction to the radio station's claim after seeing the sample evidence? Use $\alpha = .05$ in making the statistical test. What is the *p*-value?

63. In recent years more people have been working past the age of 65. In 2005, 27% of people aged 65–69 worked. A recent report from the Organization for Economic Co-operation and Development (OECD) claimed that the percentage working had increased (*USA Today*, November 16, 2012). The findings reported by the OECD were consistent with taking a sample of 600 people aged 65–69 and finding that 180 of them were working.

a. Develop a point estimate of the proportion of people aged 65–69 who are working.

b. Set up a hypothesis test so that the rejection of H_0 will allow you to conclude that the proportion of people aged 65–69 working has increased from 2005.

c. Conduct your hypothesis test using $\alpha = .05$. What is your conclusion?

Case Problem 1   Quality Associates, Inc.

Quality Associates, Inc., a consulting firm, advises its clients about sampling and statistical procedures that can be used to control their manufacturing processes. In one particular application, a client gave Quality Associates a sample of 800 observations taken during a time in which that client's process was operating satisfactorily. The sample standard deviation for these data was .21; hence, with so much data, the population standard deviation was assumed to be .21. Quality Associates then suggested that random samples of size 30 be taken periodically to monitor the process on an ongoing basis. By analyzing the new samples, the client could quickly learn whether the process was operating satisfactorily. When the process was not operating satisfactorily, corrective action could be taken to eliminate the problem. The design specification indicated the mean for the process should be 12. The hypothesis test suggested by Quality Associates follows.

$$H_0: \mu = 12$$
$$H_a: \mu \neq 12$$

Corrective action will be taken any time H_0 is rejected.

The samples on the following page were collected at hourly intervals during the first day of operation of the new statistical process control procedure. These data are available in the DATAfile named *Quality*.

Managerial Report

1. Conduct a hypothesis test for each sample at the .01 level of significance and determine what action, if any, should be taken. Provide the test statistic and *p*-value for each test.

2. Compute the standard deviation for each of the four samples. Does the assumption of .21 for the population standard deviation appear reasonable?

3. Compute limits for the sample mean $\bar{x}$ around $\mu = 12$ such that, as long as a new sample mean is within those limits, the process will be considered to be operating satisfactorily. If $\bar{x}$ exceeds the upper limit or if $\bar{x}$ is below the lower limit, corrective action will be taken. These limits are referred to as upper and lower control limits for quality control purposes.

4. Discuss the implications of changing the level of significance to a larger value. What mistake or error could increase if the level of significance is increased?

Quality

Sample 1	Sample 2	Sample 3	Sample 4
11.55	11.62	11.91	12.02
11.62	11.69	11.36	12.02
11.52	11.59	11.75	12.05
11.75	11.82	11.95	12.18
11.90	11.97	12.14	12.11
11.64	11.71	11.72	12.07
11.64	11.71	11.72	12.07
11.80	11.87	11.61	12.05
12.03	12.10	11.85	11.64
11.94	12.01	12.16	12.39
11.92	11.99	11.91	11.65
12.13	12.20	12.12	12.11
12.09	12.16	11.61	11.90
11.93	12.00	12.21	12.22
12.21	12.28	11.56	11.88
12.32	12.39	11.95	12.03
11.93	12.00	12.01	12.35
11.85	11.92	12.06	12.09
11.76	11.83	11.76	11.77
12.16	12.23	11.82	12.20
11.77	11.84	12.12	11.79
12.00	12.07	11.60	12.30
12.04	12.11	11.95	12.27
11.98	12.05	11.96	12.29
12.30	12.37	12.22	12.47
12.18	12.25	11.75	12.03
11.97	12.04	11.96	12.17
12.17	12.24	11.95	11.94
11.85	11.92	11.89	11.97
12.30	12.37	11.88	12.23
12.15	12.22	11.93	12.25

Case Problem 2   Ethical Behavior of Business Students at Bayview University

During the global recession of 2008 and 2009, there were many accusations of unethical behavior by Wall Street executives, financial managers, and other corporate officers. At that time, an article appeared that suggested that part of the reason for such unethical business behavior may stem from the fact that cheating has become more prevalent among business students (*Chronicle of Higher Education*, February 10, 2009). The article reported that 56% of business students admitted to cheating at some time during their academic career as compared to 47% of nonbusiness students.

Cheating has been a concern of the dean of the College of Business at Bayview University for several years. Some faculty members in the college believe that cheating is more widespread at Bayview than at other universities, whereas other faculty members think that cheating is not a major problem in the college. To resolve some of these issues, the dean commissioned a study to assess the current ethical behavior of business students at Bayview. As part of this study, an anonymous exit survey was administered to a sample of 90 business students from this year's graduating class. Responses to the following questions were used to obtain data regarding three types of cheating.

During your time at Bayview, did you ever present work copied off the Internet as your own?

Yes _____   No _____

During your time at Bayview, did you ever copy answers off another student's exam?

Yes _____   No _____

During your time at Bayview, did you ever collaborate with other students on projects that were supposed to be completed individually?

Yes _____   No _____

Any student who answered Yes to one or more of these questions was considered to have been involved in some type of cheating. A portion of the data collected follows. The complete data set is in the DATAfile named Bayview.

Bayview

Student	Copied from Internet	Copied on Exam	Collaborated on Individual Project	Gender
1	No	No	No	Female
2	No	No	No	Male
3	Yes	No	Yes	Male
4	Yes	Yes	No	Male
5	No	No	Yes	Male
6	Yes	No	No	Female
.	.	.	.	.
.	.	.	.	.
.	.	.	.	.
88	No	No	No	Male
89	No	Yes	Yes	Male
90	No	No	No	Female

Managerial Report

Prepare a report for the dean of the college that summarizes your assessment of the nature of cheating by business students at Bayview University. Be sure to include the following items in your report.

1. Use descriptive statistics to summarize the data and comment on your findings.
2. Develop 95% confidence intervals for the proportion of all students, the proportion of male students, and the proportion of female students who were involved in some type of cheating.

3. Conduct a hypothesis test to determine whether the proportion of business students at Bayview University who were involved in some type of cheating is less than that of business students at other institutions as reported by the *Chronicle of Higher Education*.

4. Conduct a hypothesis test to determine whether the proportion of business students at Bayview University who were involved in some form of cheating is less than that of nonbusiness students at other institutions as reported by the *Chronicle of Higher Education*.

5. What advice would you give to the dean based upon your analysis of the data?

CHAPTER 10

Inference About Means and Proportions with Two Populations

CONTENTS

U.S. FOOD AND DRUG ADMINISTRATION
WASHINGTON, D.C.

It is the responsibility of the U.S. Food and Drug Administration (FDA), through its Center for Drug Evaluation and Research (CDER), to ensure that drugs are safe and effective. But CDER does not do the actual testing of new drugs itself. It is the responsibility of the company seeking to market a new drug to test it and submit evidence that it is safe and effective. CDER statisticians and scientists then review the evidence submitted.

Companies seeking approval of a new drug conduct extensive statistical studies to support their application. The testing process in the pharmaceutical industry usually consists of three stages: (1) preclinical testing, (2) testing for long-term usage and safety, and (3) clinical efficacy testing. At each successive stage, the chance that a drug will pass the rigorous tests decreases; however, the cost of further testing increases dramatically. Industry surveys indicate that on average the research and development for one new drug costs $250 million and takes 12 years. Hence, it is important to eliminate unsuccessful new drugs in the early stages of the testing process, as well as to identify promising ones for further testing.

Statistics plays a major role in pharmaceutical research, where government regulations are stringent and rigorously enforced. In preclinical testing, a two- or three-population statistical study typically is used to determine whether a new drug should continue to be studied in the long-term usage and safety program. The populations may consist of the new drug, a control, and a standard drug. The preclinical testing process begins when a new drug is sent to the pharmacology group for evaluation of efficacy—the capacity of the drug to produce the desired effects. As part of the process, a statistician is asked to design an experiment that can be used to test the new drug. The design must specify the sample size and the statistical methods of analysis. In a two-population study, one sample is used to obtain data on the efficacy of the new drug (population 1) and a second sample is used to obtain data on the efficacy of a standard drug (population 2). Depending on the intended use, the new and standard drugs are tested in such disciplines

Statistical methods are used to test and develop new drugs.

as neurology, cardiology, and immunology. In most studies, the statistical method involves hypothesis testing for the difference between the means of the new drug population and the standard drug population. If a new drug lacks efficacy or produces undesirable effects in comparison with the standard drug, the new drug is rejected and withdrawn from further testing. Only new drugs that show promising comparisons with the standard drugs are forwarded to the long-term usage and safety testing program.

Further data collection and multipopulation studies are conducted in the long-term usage and safety testing program and in the clinical testing programs. The FDA requires that statistical methods be defined prior to such testing to avoid data-related biases. In addition, to avoid human biases, some of the clinical trials are double or triple blind. That is, neither the subject nor the investigator knows what drug is administered to whom. If the new drug meets all requirements in relation to the standard drug, a new drug application (NDA) is filed with the FDA. The application is rigorously scrutinized by statisticians and scientists at the agency.

In this chapter you will learn how to construct interval estimates and make hypothesis tests about means and proportions with two populations. Techniques will be presented for analyzing independent random samples as well as matched samples.

In Chapters 8 and 9 we showed how to develop interval estimates and conduct hypothesis tests for situations involving a single population mean and a single population proportion. In this chapter we continue our discussion of statistical inference by showing how interval estimates and hypothesis tests can be developed for situations involving two populations when the difference between the two population means or the two population proportions is of prime importance. For example, we may want to develop an interval estimate of the difference between the mean starting salary for a population of men and the mean starting salary for a population of women or conduct a hypothesis test to determine whether any difference is present between the proportion of defective parts in a population of parts produced by supplier A and the proportion of defective parts in a population of parts produced by supplier B. We begin our discussion of statistical inference about two populations by showing how to develop interval estimates and conduct hypothesis tests about the difference between the means of two populations when the standard deviations of the two populations can be assumed known.

10.1 Inferences About the Difference Between Two Population Means: σ_1 and σ_2 Known

Letting μ_1 denote the mean of population 1 and μ_2 denote the mean of population 2, we will focus on inferences about the difference between the means: $\mu_1 - \mu_2$. To make an inference about this difference, we select a random sample of n_1 units from population 1 and a second random sample of n_2 units from population 2. The two samples, taken separately and independently, are referred to as **independent random samples**. In this section, we assume that information is available such that the two population standard deviations, σ_1 and σ_2, can be assumed known prior to collecting the samples. We refer to this situation as the σ_1 and σ_2 known case. In the following example we show how to compute a margin of error and develop an interval estimate of the difference between the two population means when σ_1 and σ_2 are known.

Interval Estimation of $\mu_1 - \mu_2$

HomeStyle sells furniture at two stores in Buffalo, New York: One is in the inner city and the other is in a suburban shopping center. The regional manager noticed that products that sell well in one store do not always sell well in the other. The manager believes this situation may be attributable to differences in customer demographics at the two locations. Customers may differ in age, education, income, and so on. Suppose the manager asks us to investigate the difference between the mean ages of the customers who shop at the two stores.

Let us define population 1 as all customers who shop at the inner-city store and population 2 as all customers who shop at the suburban store.

μ_1 = mean of population 1 (i.e., the mean age of all customers who shop at the inner-city store)

μ_2 = mean of population 2 (i.e., the mean age of all customers who shop at the suburban store)

The difference between the two population means is $\mu_1 - \mu_2$.

To estimate $\mu_1 - \mu_2$, we will select a random sample of n_1 customers from population 1 and a random sample of n_2 customers from population 2. We then compute the two sample means.

$\bar{x}_1$ = sample mean age for the random sample of n_1 inner-city customers
$\bar{x}_2$ = sample mean age for the random sample of n_2 suburban customers

The point estimator of the difference between the two population means is the difference between the two sample means.

POINT ESTIMATOR OF THE DIFFERENCE BETWEEN TWO POPULATION MEANS

$$\bar{x}_1 - \bar{x}_2 \tag{10.1}$$

The standard error of $\bar{x}_1 - \bar{x}_2$ is the standard deviation of the sampling distribution of $\bar{x}_1 - \bar{x}_2$.

Figure 10.1 provides an overview of the process used to estimate the difference between two population means based on two independent random samples.

As with other point estimators, the point estimator $\bar{x}_1 - \bar{x}_2$ has a standard error that describes the variation in the sampling distribution of the estimator. With two independent random samples, the standard error of $\bar{x}_1 - \bar{x}_2$ is as follows.

STANDARD ERROR OF $\bar{x}_1 - \bar{x}_2$

$$\sigma_{\bar{x}_1 - \bar{x}_2} = \sqrt{\frac{\sigma_1^2}{n_1} + \frac{\sigma_2^2}{n_2}} \tag{10.2}$$

If both populations have a normal distribution, or if the sample sizes are large enough that the central limit theorem enables us to conclude that the sampling distributions of $\bar{x}_1$ and $\bar{x}_2$ can be approximated by a normal distribution, the sampling distribution of $\bar{x}_1 - \bar{x}_2$ will have a normal distribution with mean given by $\mu_1 - \mu_2$.

As we showed in Chapter 8, an interval estimate is given by a point estimate ± a margin of error. In the case of estimation of the difference between two population means, an interval estimate will take the following form:

$$\bar{x}_1 - \bar{x}_2 \pm \text{Margin of error}$$

FIGURE 10.1   ESTIMATING THE DIFFERENCE BETWEEN TWO POPULATION MEANS

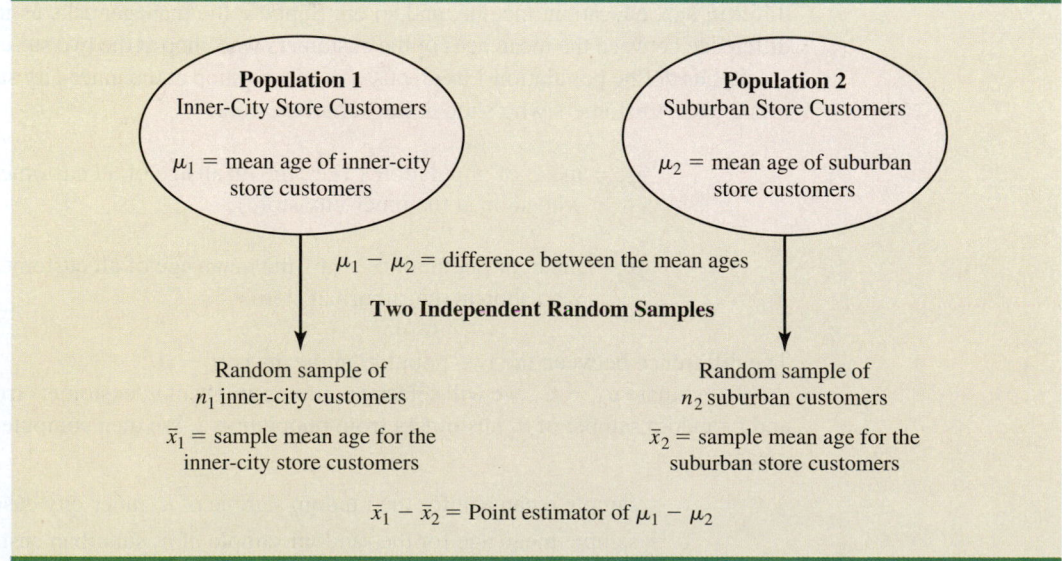

With the sampling distribution of $\bar{x}_1 - \bar{x}_2$ having a normal distribution, we can write the margin of error as follows:

The margin of error is given by multiplying the standard error by $z_{\alpha/2}$.

$$\text{Margin of error} = z_{\alpha/2}\sigma_{\bar{x}_1 - \bar{x}_2} = z_{\alpha/2}\sqrt{\frac{\sigma_1^2}{n_1} + \frac{\sigma_2^2}{n_2}} \tag{10.3}$$

Thus the interval estimate of the difference between two population means is as follows.

> **INTERVAL ESTIMATE OF THE DIFFERENCE BETWEEN TWO POPULATION MEANS: σ_1 AND σ_2 KNOWN**
>
> $$\bar{x}_1 - \bar{x}_2 \pm z_{\alpha/2}\sqrt{\frac{\sigma_1^2}{n_1} + \frac{\sigma_2^2}{n_2}} \tag{10.4}$$
>
> where $1 - \alpha$ is the confidence coefficient.

Let us return to the HomeStyle example. Based on data from previous customer demographic studies, the two population standard deviations are known with $\sigma_1 = 9$ years and $\sigma_2 = 10$ years. The data collected from the two independent random samples of HomeStyle customers provided the following results.

DATA *file*

HomeStyle

	Inner City Store	Suburban Store
Sample Size	$n_1 = 36$	$n_2 = 49$
Sample Mean	$\bar{x}_1 = 40$ years	$\bar{x}_2 = 35$ years

Using expression (10.1), we find that the point estimate of the difference between the mean ages of the two populations is $\bar{x}_1 - \bar{x}_2 = 40 - 35 = 5$ years. Thus, we estimate that the customers at the inner-city store have a mean age five years greater than the mean age of the suburban store customers. We can now use expression (10.4) to compute the margin of error and provide the interval estimate of $\mu_1 - \mu_2$. Using 95% confidence and $z_{\alpha/2} = z_{.025} = 1.96$, we have

$$\bar{x}_1 - \bar{x}_2 \pm z_{\alpha/2}\sqrt{\frac{\sigma_1^2}{n_1} + \frac{\sigma_2^2}{n_2}}$$

$$40 - 35 \pm 1.96\sqrt{\frac{9^2}{36} + \frac{10^2}{49}}$$

$$5 \pm 4.06$$

Thus, the margin of error is 4.06 years and the 95% confidence interval estimate of the difference between the two population means is $5 - 4.06 = .94$ years to $5 + 4.06 = 9.06$ years.

Using Excel to Construct a Confidence Interval

Excel's data analysis tools do not provide a procedure for developing interval estimates involving two population means. However, we can develop an Excel worksheet that can be used as a template to construct interval estimates. We will illustrate by constructing an interval estimate of the difference between the population means in the HomeStyle Furniture Stores study. Refer to Figure 10.2 as we describe the tasks involved. The formula worksheet is in the background; the value worksheet is in the foreground.

FIGURE 10.2 EXCEL WORKSHEET: CONSTRUCTING A 95% CONFIDENCE INTERVAL FOR HOMESTYLE FURNITURE STORES

	A	B	C	D	E	F	G	H
1	Inner City	Suburban		Interval Estimate of Difference in Population Means:				
2	38	29		σ_1 and σ_2 Known Case				
3	46	35						
4	32	39			Inner City	Suburban		
5	23	10		Sample Size	=COUNT(A2:A37)	=COUNT(B2:B50)		
6	39	37		Sample Mean	=AVERAGE(A2:A37)	=AVERAGE(B2:B50)		
7	40	52						
8	35	40		Population Standard Deviation	9	10		
9	35	37		Standard Error	=SQRT(E8^2/E5+F8^2/F5			
10	36	43						
11	41	38		Confidence Coefficient	0.95			
12	32	28		Level of Significance	=1-E11			
13	38	37		*z* Value	=NORM.S.INV(1-E12/2)			
14	44	51		Margin of Error	=E13*E9			
15	50	23						
16	47	25		Point Estimate of Difference	=E6-F6			
17	59	37		Lower Limit	=E16-E14			
18	38	38		Upper Limit	=E16+E14			
36	44	19						
37	62	40						
49		22						
50		47						
51								

	A	B	C	D	E	F	G	H
1	Inner City	Suburban		Interval Estimate of Difference in Population Means:				
2	38	29		σ_1 and σ_2 Known Case				
3	46	35						
4	32	39			Inner City	Suburban		
5	23	10		Sample Size	36	49		
6	39	37		Sample Mean	40	35		
7	40	52						
8	35	40		Population Standard Deviation	9	10		
9	35	37		Standard Error	2.07			
10	36	43						
11	41	38		Confidence Coefficient	0.95			
12	32	28		Level of Significance	0.05			
13	38	37		*z* Value	1.960			
14	44	51		Margin of Error	4.06			
15	50	23						
16	47	25		Point Estimate of Difference	5			
17	59	37		Lower Limit	0.94			
18	38	38		Upper Limit	9.06			
36	44	19						
37	62	40						
49		22						
50		47						
51								

Note: Rows 19–35 and 38–48 are hidden.

Enter/Access Data: Open the DATAfile named *HomeStyle*. Column A contains the age data and a label for the random sample of 36 inner-city customers, and column B contains the age data and a label for the random sample of 49 suburban customers.

Enter Functions and Formulas: The descriptive statistics needed are provided in cells E5:F6. The known population standard deviations are entered into cells E8 and F8. Using the two population standard deviations and the sample sizes, the standard error of the point estimator $\bar{x}_1 - \bar{x}_2$, is computed using equation (10.2) by entering the following formula into cell E9:

$$=\text{SQRT(E8\^{}2/E5+F8\^{}2/F5)}$$

Cells E11:E14 are used to compute the appropriate z value and the margin of error. The confidence coefficient is entered into cell E11 (.95) and the corresponding level of significance ($\alpha = 1 -$ confidence coefficient) is computed in cell E12. In cell E13, we used the NORM.S.INV function to compute the z value needed for the interval estimate. The margin of error is computed in cell E14 by multiplying the z value by the standard error.

In cell E16 the difference in the sample means is used to compute the point estimate of the difference in the two population means. The lower limit of the confidence interval is computed in cell E17 (.94) and the upper limit is computed in cell E18 (9.06); thus, the 95% confidence interval estimate of the difference in the two population means is .94 to 9.06.

A template for other problems This worksheet can be used as a template for developing interval estimates of the difference in population means when the population standard deviations are assumed known. For another problem of this type, we must first enter the new problem data in columns A and B. The data ranges in cells E5:F6 must be modified in order to compute the sample means and sample sizes for the new data. Also, the assumed known population standard deviations must be entered into cells E8 and F8. After doing so, the point estimate and a 95% confidence interval will be displayed in cells E16:E18. If a confidence interval with a different confidence coefficient is desired, we simply change the value in cell E11.

We can further simplify the use of Figure 10.2 as a template for other problems by eliminating the need to enter new data ranges in cells E5:F6. We rewrite the cell formulas as follows:

Cell E5: =COUNT(A:A)

Cell F5: =COUNT(B:B)

Cell E6: =AVERAGE(A:A)

Cell F6: =AVERAGE(B:B)

The DATAfile named HomeStyle includes a worksheet entitled Template that uses the A:A and B:B methods for entering the data ranges.

Using the A:A method of specifying data ranges in cells E5 and E6, Excel's COUNT function will count the number of numerical values in column A and Excel's AVERAGE function will compute the average of the numerical values in column A. Similarly, using the B:B method of specifying data ranges in cells F5 and F6, Excel's COUNT function will count the number of numerical values in column B and Excel's AVERAGE function will compute the average of the numerical values in column B. Thus, to solve a new problem it is only necessary to enter the new data into columns A and B and enter the known population standard deviations in cells E8 and F8.

This worksheet can also be used as a template for text exercises in which the sample sizes, sample means, and population standard deviations are given. In this type of situation, no change in the data is necessary. We simply replace the values in cells E5:F6 and E8:F8 with the given values of the sample sizes, sample means, and population standard deviations. If something other than a 95% confidence interval is desired, the confidence coefficient in cell E11 must also be changed.

Hypothesis Tests About $\mu_1 - \mu_2$

Let us consider hypothesis tests about the difference between two population means. Using D_0 to denote the hypothesized difference between μ_1 and μ_2, the three forms for a hypothesis test are as follows:

$$H_0: \mu_1 - \mu_2 \geq D_0 \qquad H_0: \mu_1 - \mu_2 \leq D_0 \qquad H_0: \mu_1 - \mu_2 = D_0$$
$$H_a: \mu_1 - \mu_2 < D_0 \qquad H_a: \mu_1 - \mu_2 > D_0 \qquad H_a: \mu_1 - \mu_2 \neq D_0$$

In many applications, $D_0 = 0$. Using the two-tailed test as an example, when $D_0 = 0$ the null hypothesis is $H_0: \mu_1 - \mu_2 = 0$. In this case, the null hypothesis is that μ_1 and μ_2 are equal. Rejection of H_0 leads to the conclusion that $H_a: \mu_1 - \mu_2 \neq 0$ is true; that is, μ_1 and μ_2 are not equal.

The steps for conducting hypothesis tests presented in Chapter 9 are applicable here. We must choose a level of significance, compute the value of the test statistic, and find the p-value to determine whether the null hypothesis should be rejected. With two independent random samples, we showed that the point estimator $\bar{x}_1 - \bar{x}_2$ has a standard error $\sigma_{\bar{x}_1 - \bar{x}_2}$ given by expression (10.2) and, when the sample sizes are large enough, the distribution of $\bar{x}_1 - \bar{x}_2$ can be described by a normal distribution. In this case, the test statistic for the difference between two population means when σ_1 and σ_2 are known is as follows.

TEST STATISTIC FOR HYPOTHESIS TESTS ABOUT $\mu_1 - \mu_2$: σ_1 AND σ_2 KNOWN

$$z = \frac{(\bar{x}_1 - \bar{x}_2) - D_0}{\sqrt{\dfrac{\sigma_1^2}{n_1} + \dfrac{\sigma_2^2}{n_2}}} \qquad \text{(10.5)}$$

Let us demonstrate the use of this test statistic in the following hypothesis testing example.

As part of a study to evaluate differences in education quality between two training centers, a standardized examination is given to individuals who are trained at the centers. The difference between the mean examination scores is used to assess quality differences between the centers. The population means for the two centers are as follows.

$$\mu_1 = \text{the mean examination score for the population}$$
of individuals trained at center A

$$\mu_2 = \text{the mean examination score for the population}$$
of individuals trained at center B

We begin with the tentative assumption that no difference exists between the training quality provided at the two centers. Hence, in terms of the mean examination scores, the null hypothesis is that $\mu_1 - \mu_2 = 0$. If sample evidence leads to the rejection of this hypothesis, we will conclude that the mean examination scores differ for the two populations. This conclusion indicates a quality differential between the two centers and suggests that a follow-up study investigating the reason for the differential may be warranted. The null and alternative hypotheses for this two-tailed test are written as follows.

$$H_0: \mu_1 - \mu_2 = 0$$
$$H_a: \mu_1 - \mu_2 \neq 0$$

The standardized examination given previously in a variety of settings always resulted in an examination score standard deviation near 10 points. Thus, we will use this information to assume that the population standard deviations are known with $\sigma_1 = 10$ and $\sigma_2 = 10$. An $\alpha = .05$ level of significance is specified for the study.

ExamScores

Independent random samples of $n_1 = 30$ individuals from training center A and $n_2 = 40$ individuals from training center B are taken. The respective sample means are $\bar{x}_1 = 82$ and $\bar{x}_2 = 78$. Do these data suggest a significant difference between the population means at the two training centers? To help answer this question, we compute the test statistic using equation (10.5).

$$z = \frac{(\bar{x}_1 - \bar{x}_2) - D_0}{\sqrt{\dfrac{\sigma_1^2}{n_1} + \dfrac{\sigma_2^2}{n_2}}} = \frac{(82 - 78) - 0}{\sqrt{\dfrac{10^2}{30} + \dfrac{10^2}{40}}} = 1.66$$

Next let us compute the p-value for this two-tailed test. Because the test statistic z is in the upper tail, we first compute the upper tail area corresponding to $z = 1.66$. Using the standard normal distribution table, the area to the left of $z = 1.66$ is .9515. Thus, the area in the upper tail of the distribution is $1.0000 - .9515 = .0485$. Because this test is a two-tailed test, we must double the tail area: p-value $= 2(.0485) = .0970$. Following the usual rule to reject H_0 if p-value $\leq \alpha$, we see that the p-value of .0970 does not allow us to reject H_0 at the .05 level of significance. The sample results do not provide sufficient evidence to conclude that the training centers differ in quality.

In this chapter we will use the p-value approach to hypothesis testing as described in Chapter 9. However, if you prefer, the test statistic and the critical value rejection rule may be used. With $\alpha = .05$ and $z_{\alpha/2} = z_{.025} = 1.96$, the rejection rule employing the critical value approach would be reject H_0 if $z \leq -1.96$ or if $z \geq 1.96$. With $z = 1.66$, we reach the same do not reject H_0 conclusion.

In the preceding example, we demonstrated a two-tailed hypothesis test about the difference between two population means. Lower tail and upper tail tests can also be considered. These tests use the same test statistic as given in equation (10.5). The procedure for computing the *p*-value and the rejection rules for these one-tailed tests are the same as those presented in Chapter 9.

Using Excel to Conduct a Hypothesis Test

The Excel tool used to conduct the hypothesis test to determine whether there is a significant difference in population means when σ_1 and σ_2 are assumed known is called *z-Test: Two Sample for Means*. We illustrate using the sample data for exam scores at center A and at center B. With an assumed known standard deviation of 10 points at each center, the known variance of exam scores for each of the two populations is equal to $10^2 = 100$. Refer to the Excel worksheets shown in Figure 10.3 and Figure 10.4 as we describe the tasks involved.

Enter/Access Data: Open the DATAfile named *ExamScores*. Column A in Figure 10.3 contains the examination score data and a label for the random sample of 30 individuals trained at center A, and column B contains the examination score data and a label for the random sample of 40 individuals trained at center B.

Apply Tools: The following steps will provide the information needed to conduct the hypothesis test to see whether there is a significant difference in test scores at the two centers.

Step 1. Click the **Data** tab on the Ribbon
Step 2. In the **Analyze** group, click **Data Analysis**
Step 3. Choose **z-Test: Two Sample for Means** from the list of Analysis Tools
Step 4. When the z-Test: Two Sample for Means dialog box appears (Figure 10.3):
  Enter A1:A31 in the **Variable 1 Range** box
  Enter B1:B41 in the **Variable 2 Range** box
  Enter 0 in the **Hypothesized Mean Difference** box

FIGURE 10.3   DIALOG BOX FOR EXCEL'S z-TEST: TWO SAMPLE FOR MEANS TOOL

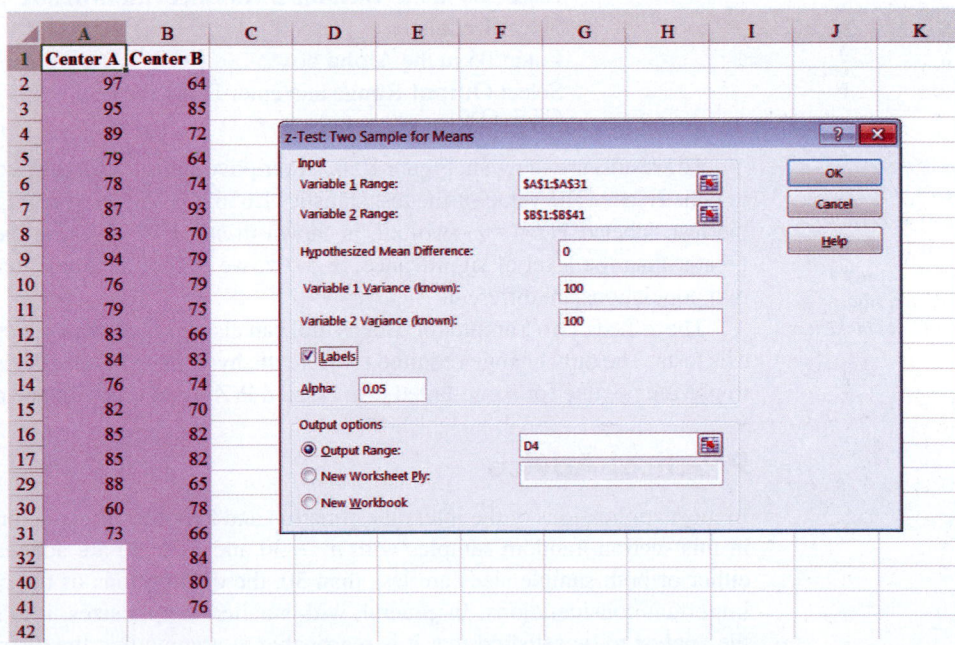

Note: Rows 18–28 and 33–39 are hidden.

FIGURE 10.4   EXCEL RESULTS FOR THE HYPOTHESIS TEST ABOUT EQUALITY
OF EXAM SCORES AT TWO TRAINING CENTERS

	A	B	C	D	E	F	G
1	Center A	Center B					
2	97	64					
3	95	85					
4	89	72		z-Test: Two Sample for Means			
5	79	64					
6	78	74				Center A	Center B
7	87	93		Mean	82	78	
8	83	70		Known Variance	100	100	
9	94	79		Observations	30	40	
10	76	79		Hypothesized Mean Difference	0		
11	79	75		z	1.6562		
12	83	66		P(Z<=z) one-tail	0.0488		
13	84	83		z Critical one-tail	1.6449		
14	76	74		P(Z<=z) two-tail	0.0977		
15	82	70		z Critical two-tail	1.9600		
16	85	82					
17	85	82					
29	88	65					
30	60	78					
31	73	66					
32		84					
40		80					
41		76					
42							

*Note: Rows 18–28
and 33–39 are
hidden.*

Enter 100 in the **Variable 1 Variance (known)** box
Enter 100 in the **Variable 2 Variance (known)** box
Select **Labels**
Enter .05 in the **Alpha** box
Select **Output Range** and enter D4 in the box
Click **OK**

*The value of the test statistic
shown here (1.6562) and
the p-value (.0977) differ
slightly from those shown
previously, because we
rounded the test statistic to
two places (1.66) in the text.*

The results are shown in Figure 10.4. Descriptive statistics for the two samples are shown
in cells E7:F9. The value of the test statistic, 1.6562, is shown in cell E11. The p-value for
the test, labeled P(Z<=z) two-tail, is shown in cell E14. Because the p-value, .0977, is
greater than the level of significance, $\alpha = .05$, we cannot conclude that the means for the
two populations are different.

The z-Test: Two Sample for Means tool can also be used to conduct one-tailed hypothesis tests. The only change required to make the hypothesis testing decision is that we need
to use the p-value for a one-tailed test, labeled P(Z<=z) one-tail (see cell E12).

Practical Advice

In most applications of the interval estimation and hypothesis testing procedures presented
in this section, random samples with $n_1 \geq 30$ and $n_2 \geq 30$ are adequate. In cases where
either or both sample sizes are less than 30, the distributions of the populations become
important considerations. In general, with smaller sample sizes, it is more important for
the analyst to be satisfied that it is reasonable to assume that the distributions of the two
populations are at least approximately normal.

Exercises

Methods

1. The following results come from two independent random samples taken of two populations.

Sample 1	Sample 2
$n_1 = 50$	$n_2 = 35$
$\bar{x}_1 = 13.6$	$\bar{x}_2 = 11.6$
$\sigma_1 = 2.2$	$\sigma_2 = 3.0$

   a. What is the point estimate of the difference between the two population means?
   b. Provide a 90% confidence interval for the difference between the two population means.
   c. Provide a 95% confidence interval for the difference between the two population means.

2. Consider the following hypothesis test.

$$H_0: \mu_1 - \mu_2 \leq 0$$
$$H_a: \mu_1 - \mu_2 > 0$$

The following results are for two independent samples taken from the two populations.

Sample 1	Sample 2
$n_1 = 40$	$n_2 = 50$
$\bar{x}_1 = 25.2$	$\bar{x}_2 = 22.8$
$\sigma_1 = 5.2$	$\sigma_2 = 6.0$

   a. What is the value of the test statistic?
   b. What is the p-value?
   c. With $\alpha = .05$, what is your hypothesis testing conclusion?

3. Consider the following hypothesis test.

$$H_0: \mu_1 - \mu_2 = 0$$
$$H_a: \mu_1 - \mu_2 \neq 0$$

The following results are for two independent samples taken from the two populations.

Sample 1	Sample 2
$n_1 = 80$	$n_2 = 70$
$\bar{x}_1 = 104$	$\bar{x}_2 = 106$
$\sigma_1 = 8.4$	$\sigma_2 = 7.6$

   a. What is the value of the test statistic?
   b. What is the p-value?
   c. With $\alpha = .05$, what is your hypothesis testing conclusion?

Applications

4. *Condé Nast Traveler* conducts an annual survey in which readers rate their favorite cruise ship. All ships are rated on a 100-point scale, with higher values indicating better service. A sample of 37 ships that carry fewer than 500 passengers resulted in an average rating of 85.36, and a sample of 44 ships that carry 500 or more passengers provided an average rating of 81.40. Assume that the population standard deviation is 4.55 for ships that carry fewer than 500 passengers and 3.97 for ships that carry 500 or more passengers.
   a. What is the point estimate of the difference between the population mean rating for ships that carry fewer than 500 passengers and the population mean rating for ships that carry 500 or more passengers?
   b. At 95% confidence, what is the margin of error?
   c. What is a 95% confidence interval estimate of the difference between the population mean ratings for the two sizes of ships?

5. *USA Today* reports that the average expenditure on Valentine's Day is $100.89. Do male and female consumers differ in the amounts they spend? The average expenditure in a sample survey of 40 male consumers was $135.67, and the average expenditure in a sample survey of 30 female consumers was $68.64. Based on past surveys, the standard deviation for male consumers is assumed to be $35, and the standard deviation for female consumers is assumed to be $20.
   a. What is the point estimate of the difference between the population mean expenditure for males and the population mean expenditure for females?
   b. At 99% confidence, what is the margin of error?
   c. Develop a 99% confidence interval for the difference between the two population means.

Hotel

6. Suppose that you are responsible for making arrangements for a business convention and that you have been charged with choosing a city for the convention that has the least expensive hotel rooms. You have narrowed your choices to Atlanta and Houston. The DATAfile named *Hotel* contains samples of prices for rooms in Atlanta and Houston that are consistent with the results reported by Smith Travel Research. Because considerable historical data on the prices of rooms in both cities are available, the population standard deviations for the prices can be assumed to be $20 in Atlanta and $25 in Houston. Based on the sample data, can you conclude that the mean price of a hotel room in Atlanta is lower than one in Houston?

7. *Consumer Reports* uses a survey of readers to obtain customer satisfaction ratings for the nation's largest retailers (*Consumer Reports*, March 2012). Each survey respondent is asked to rate a specified retailer in terms of six factors: quality of products, selection, value, check-out efficiency, service, and store layout. An overall satisfaction score summarizes the rating for each respondent with 100 meaning the respondent is completely satisfied in terms of all six factors. Sample data representative of independent samples of Target and Walmart customers are shown below.

Target	Walmart
$n_1 = 25$	$n_2 = 30$
$\bar{x}_1 = 79$	$\bar{x}_2 = 71$

   a. Formulate the null and alternative hypotheses to test whether there is a difference between the population mean customer satisfaction scores for the two retailers.
   b. Assume that experience with the *Consumer Reports* satisfaction rating scale indicates that a population standard deviation of 12 is a reasonable assumption for both retailers. Conduct the hypothesis test and report the p-value. At a .05 level of significance what is your conclusion?

c.   Which retailer, if either, appears to have the greater customer satisfaction? Provide a 95% confidence interval for the difference between the population mean customer satisfaction scores for the two retailers.

8.   Will improving customer service result in higher stock prices for the companies providing the better service? "When a company's satisfaction score has improved over the prior year's results and is above the national average (75.7), studies show its shares have a good chance of outperforming the broad stock market in the long run." The following satisfaction scores of three companies for the fourth quarters of two previous years were obtained from the American Customer Satisfaction Index. Assume that the scores are based on a poll of 60 customers from each company. Because the polling has been done for several years, the standard deviation can be assumed to equal 6 points in each case.

Company	Year 1 Score	Year 2 Score
Rite Aid	73	76
Expedia	75	77
J.C. Penney	77	78

a.   For Rite Aid, is the increase in the satisfaction score from Year 1 to Year 2 statistically significant? Use $\alpha = .05$. What can you conclude?
b.   Can you conclude that the Year 2 score for Rite Aid is above the national average of 75.7? Use $\alpha = .05$.
c.   For Expedia, is the increase from Year 1 to Year 2 statistically significant? Use $\alpha = .05$.
d.   When conducting a hypothesis test with the values given for the standard deviation, sample size, and α, how large must the increase from Year 1 to Year 2 be for it to be statistically significant?
e.   Use the result of part (d) to state whether the increase for J.C. Penney from Year 1 to Year 2 is statistically significant.

Inferences About the Difference Between Two Population Means: σ_1 and σ_2 Unknown

In this section we extend the discussion of inferences about the difference between two population means to the case when the two population standard deviations, σ_1 and σ_2, are unknown. In this case, we will use the sample standard deviations, s_1 and s_2, to estimate the unknown population standard deviations. When we use the sample standard deviations, the interval estimation and hypothesis testing procedures will be based on the t distribution rather than the standard normal distribution.

Interval Estimation of $\mu_1 - \mu_2$

In the following example we show how to compute a margin of error and develop an interval estimate of the difference between two population means when σ_1 and σ_2 are unknown. Clearwater National Bank is conducting a study designed to identify differences between checking account practices by customers at two of its branch banks. A random sample of 28 checking accounts is selected from the Cherry Grove Branch and an independent random sample of 22 checking accounts is selected from the Beechmont Branch. The current checking account balance is recorded for each of the checking accounts. A summary of the account balances follows:

CheckAcct

	Cherry Grove	**Beechmont**
Sample Size	$n_1 = 28$	$n_2 = 22$
Sample Mean	$\bar{x}_1 = \$1025$	$\bar{x}_2 = \$910$
Sample Standard Deviation	$s_1 = \$150$	$s_2 = \$125$

Clearwater National Bank would like to estimate the difference between the mean checking account balance maintained by the population of Cherry Grove customers and the population of Beechmont customers. Let us develop the margin of error and an interval estimate of the difference between these two population means.

In Section 10.1, we provided the following interval estimate for the case when the population standard deviations, σ_1 and σ_2, are known.

$$\bar{x}_1 - \bar{x}_2 \pm z_{\alpha/2} \sqrt{\frac{\sigma_1^2}{n_1} + \frac{\sigma_2^2}{n_2}}$$

When σ_1 and σ_2 are estimated by s_1 and s_2, the t distribution is used to make inferences about the difference between two population means.

With σ_1 and σ_2 unknown, we will use the sample standard deviations s_1 and s_2 to estimate σ_1 and σ_2 and replace $z_{\alpha/2}$ with $t_{\alpha/2}$. As a result, the interval estimate of the difference between two population means is given by the following expression.

INTERVAL ESTIMATE OF THE DIFFERENCE BETWEEN TWO POPULATION MEANS: σ_1 AND σ_2 UNKNOWN

$$\bar{x}_1 - \bar{x}_2 \pm t_{\alpha/2} \sqrt{\frac{s_1^2}{n_1} + \frac{s_2^2}{n_2}} \tag{10.6}$$

where $1 - \alpha$ is the confidence coefficient.

In this expression, the use of the t distribution is an approximation, but it provides excellent results and is relatively easy to use. The only difficulty that we encounter in using expression (10.6) is determining the appropriate degrees of freedom for $t_{\alpha/2}$. Statistical software packages compute the appropriate degrees of freedom automatically. The formula used is as follows.

DEGREES OF FREEDOM: t DISTRIBUTION WITH TWO INDEPENDENT RANDOM SAMPLES

$$df = \frac{\left(\dfrac{s_1^2}{n_1} + \dfrac{s_2^2}{n_2}\right)^2}{\dfrac{1}{n_1 - 1}\left(\dfrac{s_1^2}{n_1}\right)^2 + \dfrac{1}{n_2 - 1}\left(\dfrac{s_2^2}{n_2}\right)^2} \tag{10.7}$$

Let us return to the Clearwater National Bank example and show how to use expression (10.6) to provide a 95% confidence interval estimate of the difference between the population mean checking account balances at the two branch banks. The sample data show $n_1 = 28$, $\bar{x}_1 = \$1025$, and $s_1 = \$150$ for the Cherry Grove branch, and $n_2 = 22$, $\bar{x}_2 = \$910$, and $s_2 = \$125$ for the Beechmont branch. The calculation for degrees of freedom for $t_{\alpha/2}$ is as follows:

$$df = \frac{\left(\dfrac{s_1^2}{n_1} + \dfrac{s_2^2}{n_2}\right)^2}{\dfrac{1}{n_1 - 1}\left(\dfrac{s_1^2}{n_1}\right)^2 + \dfrac{1}{n_2 - 1}\left(\dfrac{s_2^2}{n_2}\right)^2} = \frac{\left(\dfrac{150^2}{28} + \dfrac{125^2}{22}\right)^2}{\dfrac{1}{28 - 1}\left(\dfrac{150^2}{28}\right)^2 + \dfrac{1}{22 - 1}\left(\dfrac{125^2}{22}\right)^2} = 47.8$$

We round the noninteger degrees of freedom *down* to 47 to provide a larger t value and a more conservative interval estimate. Using the t distribution table with 47 degrees of freedom, we find $t_{.025} = 2.012$. Using expression (10.6), we develop the 95% confidence interval estimate of the difference between the two population means as follows.

$$\bar{x}_1 - \bar{x}_2 \pm t_{.025}\sqrt{\frac{s_1^2}{n_1} + \frac{s_2^2}{n_2}}$$

$$1025 - 910 \pm 2.012\sqrt{\frac{150^2}{28} + \frac{125^2}{22}}$$

$$115 \pm 78$$

The point estimate of the difference between the population mean checking account balances at the two branches is $115. The margin of error is $78, and the 95% confidence interval estimate of the difference between the two population means is $115 - 78 = \$37$ to $115 + 78 = \$193$.

This suggestion should help if you are using equation (10.7) to calculate the degrees of freedom by hand.

The computation of the degrees of freedom (equation (10.7)) is cumbersome if you are doing the calculation by hand, but it is easily implemented with a computer software package. However, note that the expressions s_1^2/n_1 and s_2^2/n_2 appear in both expression (10.6) and equation (10.7). These values only need to be computed once in order to evaluate both (10.6) and (10.7).

Using Excel to Construct a Confidence Interval

Excel's data analysis tools do not provide a procedure for developing interval estimates involving two population means. However, we can develop an Excel worksheet that can be used as a template to construct interval estimates. We will illustrate by constructing an interval estimate of the difference between the population means in the Clearwater National Bank study. Refer to Figure 10.5 as we describe the tasks involved. The formula worksheet is in the background; the value worksheet is in the foreground.

Enter/Access Data: Open the DATAfile named *CheckAcct*. Column A contains the account balances and a label for the random sample of 28 customers at the Cherry Grove Branch, and column B contains the account balances and a label for the random sample of 22 customers at the Beechmont Branch.

Enter Functions and Formulas: The descriptive statistics needed are provided in cells E5:F7. Using the two sample standard deviations and the sample sizes, an estimate of the variance of the point estimator $\bar{x}_1 - \bar{x}_2$ is computed by entering the following formula into cell E9:

$$=E7^2/E5+F7^2/F5$$

An estimate of the standard error is then computed in cell E10 by taking the square root of the variance.

FIGURE 10.5 EXCEL WORKSHEET: CONSTRUCTING A 95% CONFIDENCE INTERVAL FOR CLEARWATER NATIONAL BANK

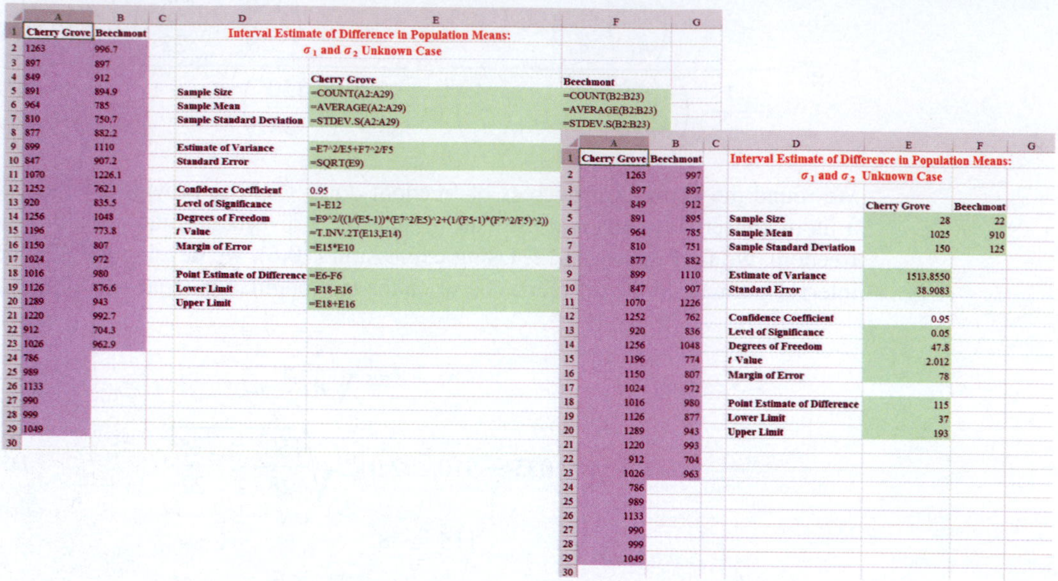

	A	B	C	D	E	F	G
1	Cherry Grove	Beechmont		**Interval Estimate of Difference in Population Means:**			
2	1263	996.7		**σ_1 and σ_2 Unknown Case**			
3	897	897					
4	849	912			**Cherry Grove**	**Beechmont**	
5	891	894.9		**Sample Size**	=COUNT(A2:A29)	=COUNT(B2:B23)	
6	964	785		**Sample Mean**	=AVERAGE(A2:A29)	=AVERAGE(B2:B23)	
7	810	750.7		**Sample Standard Deviation**	=STDEV.S(A2:A29)	=STDEV.S(B2:B23)	
8	877	882.2					
9	899	1110		**Estimate of Variance**	=E7^2/E5+F7^2/F5		
10	847	907.2		**Standard Error**	=SQRT(E9)		
11	1070	1226.1					
12	1252	762.1		**Confidence Coefficient**	0.95		
13	920	835.5		**Level of Significance**	=1-E12		
14	1256	1048		**Degrees of Freedom**	=E9^2/((1/(E5-1))*(E7^2/E5)^2+(1/(F5-1)*(F7^2/F5)^2))		
15	1196	773.8		***t* Value**	=T.INV.2T(E13,E14)		
16	1150	807		**Margin of Error**	=E15*E10		
17	1024	972					
18	1016	980		**Point Estimate of Difference**	=E6-F6		
19	1126	876.6		**Lower Limit**	=E18-E16		
20	1289	943		**Upper Limit**	=E18+E16		
21	1220	992.7					
22	912	704.3					
23	1026	962.9					
24	786						
25	989						
26	1133						
27	990						
28	999						
29	1049						
30							

	A	B	C	D	E	F	G
1	Cherry Grove	Beechmont		**Interval Estimate of Difference in Population Means:**			
2	1263	997		**σ_1 and σ_2 Unknown Case**			
3	897	897					
4	849	912			**Cherry Grove**	**Beechmont**	
5	891	895		**Sample Size**	28	22	
6	964	785		**Sample Mean**	1025	910	
7	810	751		**Sample Standard Deviation**	150	125	
8	877	882					
9	899	1110		**Estimate of Variance**	1513.8550		
10	847	907		**Standard Error**	38.9083		
11	1070	1226					
12	1252	762		**Confidence Coefficient**	0.95		
13	920	836		**Level of Significance**	0.05		
14	1256	1048		**Degrees of Freedom**	47.8		
15	1196	774		***t* Value**	2.012		
16	1150	807		**Margin of Error**	78		
17	1024	972					
18	1016	980		**Point Estimate of Difference**	115		
19	1126	877		**Lower Limit**	37		
20	1289	943		**Upper Limit**	193		
21	1220	993					
22	912	704					
23	1026	963					
24	786						
25	989						
26	1133						
27	990						
28	999						
29	1049						
30							

Cells E12:E16 are used to compute the appropriate t value and the margin of error. The confidence coefficient is entered into cell E12 (.95) and the corresponding level of significance is computed in cell E13 ($\alpha = .05$). In cell E14, we used formula (10.7) to compute the degrees of freedom (47.8). In cell E15, we used the T.INV.2T function to compute the t value needed for the interval estimate. The margin of error is computed in cell E16 by multiplying the t value by the standard error.

In cell E18 the difference in the sample means is used to compute the point estimate of the difference in the two population means (115). The lower limit of the confidence interval is computed in cell E19 (37) and the upper limit is computed in cell E20 (193); thus, the 95% confidence interval estimate of the difference in the two population means is 37 to 193.

A template for other problems This worksheet can be used as a template for developing interval estimates of the difference in population means when the population standard deviations are unknown. For another problem of this type, we must first enter the new problem data in columns A and B. The data ranges in cells E5:F7 must be modified in order to compute the sample means, sample sizes, and sample standard deviations for the new data. After doing so, the point estimate and a 95% confidence interval will be displayed in cells E18:E20. If a confidence interval with a different confidence coefficient is desired, we simply change the value in cell E12.

We can further simplify the use of Figure 10.5 as a template for other problems by eliminating the need to enter new data ranges in cells E5:F7. We rewrite the cell formulas as follows:

Cell E5: =COUNT(A:A)
Cell F5: =COUNT(B:B)
Cell E6: =AVERAGE(A:A)
Cell F6: =AVERAGE(B:B)
Cell E7: =STDEV.S(A:A)
Cell F7: =STDEV.S(B:B)

The DATAfile named CheckAcct includes a worksheet entitled Template that uses the A:A and B:B methods for entering the data ranges.

Using the A:A method of specifying data ranges in cells E5:E7, Excel's COUNT function will count the number of numeric values in column A, Excel's AVERAGE function will compute the average of the numeric values in column A, and Excel's STDEV function will compute the standard deviation of the numeric values in column A. Similarly, using the B:B method of specifying data ranges in cells F5:F7, Excel's COUNT function will count the number of numeric values in column B, Excel's AVERAGE function will compute the average of the numeric values in column B, and Excel's STDEV.S function will compute the standard deviation of the numeric values in column B. Thus, to solve a new problem it is only necessary to enter the new data into columns A and B.

This worksheet can also be used as a template for text exercises in which the sample sizes, sample means, and sample standard deviations are given. In this type of situation, no change in the data is necessary. We simply replace the values in cells E5:F7 with the given values of the sample sizes, sample means, and sample standard deviations. If something other than a 95% confidence interval is desired, the confidence coefficient in cell E12 must also be changed.

Hypothesis Tests About $\mu_1 - \mu_2$

Let us now consider hypothesis tests about the difference between the means of two populations when the population standard deviations σ_1 and σ_2 are unknown. Letting D_0 denote the hypothesized difference between μ_1 and μ_2, Section 10.1 showed that the test statistic used for the case where σ_1 and σ_2 are known is as follows.

$$z = \frac{(\bar{x}_1 - \bar{x}_2) - D_0}{\sqrt{\dfrac{\sigma_1^2}{n_1} + \dfrac{\sigma_2^2}{n_2}}}$$

The test statistic, z, follows the standard normal distribution.

When σ_1 and σ_2 are unknown, we use s_1 as an estimator of σ_1 and s_2 as an estimator of σ_2. Substituting these sample standard deviations for σ_1 and σ_2 provides the following test statistic when σ_1 and σ_2 are unknown.

TEST STATISTIC FOR HYPOTHESIS TESTS ABOUT $\mu_1 - \mu_2$: σ_1 AND σ_2 UNKNOWN

$$t = \frac{(\bar{x}_1 - \bar{x}_2) - D_0}{\sqrt{\dfrac{s_1^2}{n_1} + \dfrac{s_2^2}{n_2}}} \tag{10.8}$$

The degrees of freedom for t are given by equation (10.7).

Let us demonstrate the use of this test statistic in the following hypothesis testing example.

Consider a new computer software package developed to help systems analysts reduce the time required to design, develop, and implement an information system. To evaluate the benefits of the new software package, a random sample of 24 systems analysts is selected. Each analyst is given specifications for a hypothetical information system. Then 12 of the analysts are instructed to produce the information system by using current technology. The other 12 analysts are trained in the use of the new software package and then instructed to use it to produce the information system.

This study involves two populations: a population of systems analysts using the current technology and a population of systems analysts using the new software package. In terms of the time required to complete the information system design project, the population means are as follow.

μ_1 = the mean project completion time for systems analysts using the current technology

μ_2 = the mean project completion time for systems analysts using the new software package

The researcher in charge of the new software evaluation project hopes to show that the new software package will provide a shorter mean project completion time. Thus, the researcher is looking for evidence to conclude that μ_2 is less than μ_1; in this case, the difference between the two population means, $\mu_1 - \mu_2$, will be greater than zero. The research hypothesis $\mu_1 - \mu_2 > 0$ is stated as the alternative hypothesis. Thus, the hypothesis test becomes

$$H_0: \mu_1 - \mu_2 \leq 0$$
$$H_a: \mu_1 - \mu_2 > 0$$

We will use $\alpha = .05$ as the level of significance.

Suppose that the 24 analysts complete the study with the results shown in Table 10.1. Using the test statistic in equation (10.8), we have

$$t = \frac{(\bar{x}_1 - \bar{x}_2) - D_0}{\sqrt{\dfrac{s_1^2}{n_1} + \dfrac{s_2^2}{n_2}}} = \frac{(325 - 286) - 0}{\sqrt{\dfrac{40^2}{12} + \dfrac{44^2}{12}}} = 2.27$$

TABLE 10.1 COMPLETION TIME DATA AND SUMMARY STATISTICS FOR THE SOFTWARE TESTING STUDY

DATA *file*

SoftwareTest

	Current Technology	New Software
	300	274
	280	220
	344	308
	385	336
	372	198
	360	300
	288	315
	321	258
	376	318
	290	310
	301	332
	283	263
Summary Statistics		
Sample size	$n_1 = 12$	$n_2 = 12$
Sample mean	$\bar{x}_1 = 325$ hours	$\bar{x}_2 = 286$ hours
Sample standard deviation	$s_1 = 40$	$s_2 = 44$

Computing the degrees of freedom using equation (10.7), we have

$$
df = \frac{\left(\dfrac{s_1^2}{n_1} + \dfrac{s_2^2}{n_2}\right)^2}{\dfrac{1}{n_1 - 1}\left(\dfrac{s_1^2}{n_1}\right)^2 + \dfrac{1}{n_2 - 1}\left(\dfrac{s_2^2}{n_2}\right)^2} = \frac{\left(\dfrac{40^2}{12} + \dfrac{44^2}{12}\right)^2}{\dfrac{1}{12 - 1}\left(\dfrac{40^2}{12}\right)^2 + \dfrac{1}{12 - 1}\left(\dfrac{44^2}{12}\right)^2} = 21.8
$$

Rounding down, we will use a t distribution with 21 degrees of freedom. This row of the t distribution table is as follows:

Area in Upper Tail	.20	.10	.05	.025	.01	.005
t-Value (21 df)	0.859	1.323	1.721	2.080	2.518	2.831

$t = 2.27$

Using the t distribution table, we can only determine a range for the p-value. Use of Excel (see Figure 10.7) shows the exact p-value = .017.

With an upper tail test, the p-value is the area in the upper tail to the right of $t = 2.27$. From the above results, we see that the p-value is between .025 and .01. Thus, the p-value is less than $\alpha = .05$ and H_0 is rejected. The sample results enable the researcher to conclude that $\mu_1 - \mu_2 > 0$, or $\mu_1 > \mu_2$. Thus, the research study supports the conclusion that the new software package provides a smaller population mean completion time.

Using Excel to Conduct a Hypothesis Test

The Excel tool used to conduct a hypothesis test to determine whether there is a significant difference in population means when the population standard deviations are unknown is called *t-Test: Two-Sample Assuming Unequal Variances*. We illustrate using the sample data for the software evaluation study. Twelve systems analysts developed an information system using current technology, and 12 systems analysts developed an information system using a new software package. A one-tailed hypothesis test is to be conducted to see whether the mean completion time is shorter using the new software package. Refer to the Excel worksheets shown in Figure 10.6 and Figure 10.7 as we describe the tasks involved.

Enter/Access Data: Open the DATAfile named *SoftwareTest*. Column A in Figure 10.6 contains the completion time data and a label for the random sample of 12 individuals using the current technology, and column B contains the completion time data and a label for the random sample of 12 individuals using the new software.

Apply Tools: The following steps will provide the information needed to conduct the hypothesis test to see whether there is a significant difference in favor of the new software.

Step 1. Click the **Data** tab on the Ribbon
Step 2. In the **Analyze** group, click **Data Analysis**
Step 3. Choose **t-Test: Two-Sample Assuming Unequal Variances** from the list of Analysis Tools
Step 4. When the t-Test: Two-Sample Assuming Unequal Variances dialog box appears (Figure 10.6):
   Enter A1:A13 in the **Variable 1 Range** box
   Enter B1:B13 in the **Variable 2 Range** box
   Enter 0 in the **Hypothesized Mean Difference** box
   Select **Labels**
   Enter .05 in the **Alpha** box
   Select **Output Range** and enter D1 in the box
   Click **OK**

FIGURE 10.6 DIALOG BOX FOR EXCEL'S t-TEST: TWO-SAMPLE ASSUMING UNEQUAL VARIANCES TOOL

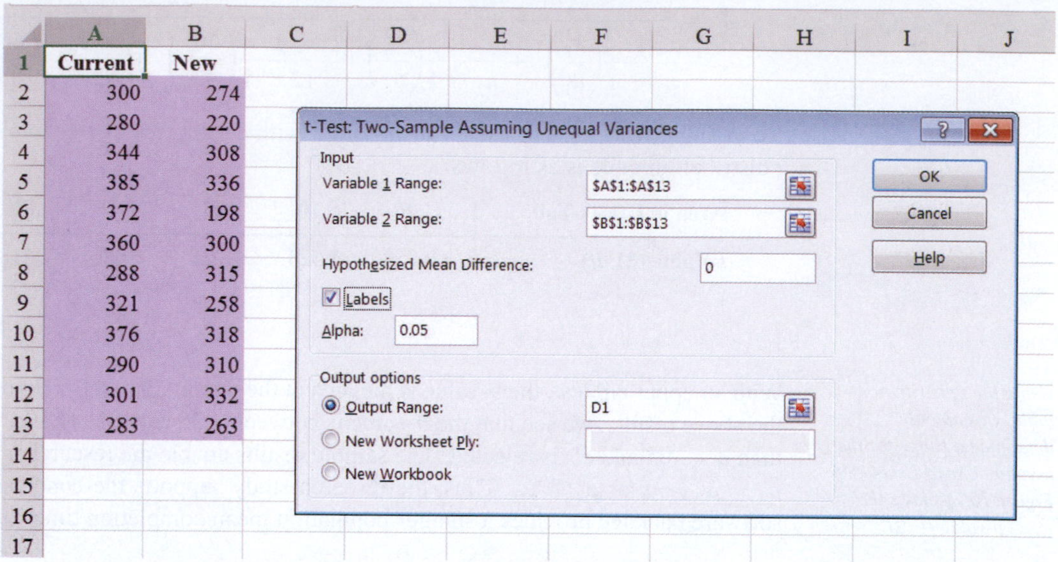

The results are shown in Figure 10.7. Descriptive statistics for the two samples are shown in cells E4:F6. The value of the test statistic, 2.2721, is shown in cell E9. The *p*-value for the test, labeled P(T<=t) one-tail, is shown in cell E10. Because the *p*-value, .0166, is less than the level of significance $\alpha = .05$, we can conclude that the mean completion time for the population using the new software package is smaller.

The t-Test: Two-Sample Assuming Unequal Variances tool can also be used to conduct two-tailed hypothesis tests. The only change required to make the hypothesis testing decision is that we need to use the *p*-value for a two-tailed test, labeled P(T<=t) two-tail (see cell E12).

FIGURE 10.7 EXCEL RESULTS FOR THE HYPOTHESIS TEST ABOUT EQUALITY OF MEAN PROJECT COMPLETION TIMES

	A	B	C	D	E	F	G
1	Current	New		t-Test: Two-Sample Assuming Unequal Variances			
2	300	274					
3	280	220			*Current*	*New*	
4	344	308		Mean	325	286	
5	385	336		Variance	1599.6364	1935.8182	
6	372	198		Observations	12	12	
7	360	300		Hypothesized Mean Difference	0		
8	288	315		df	22		
9	321	258		t Stat	2.2721		
10	376	318		P(T<=t) one-tail	0.0166		
11	290	310		t Critical one-tail	1.7171		
12	301	332		P(T<=t) two-tail	0.0332		
13	283	263		t Critical two-tail	2.0739		
14							

Practical Advice

Whenever possible, equal sample sizes, $n_1 = n_2$, are recommended.

The interval estimation and hypothesis testing procedures presented in this section are robust and can be used with relatively small sample sizes. In most applications, equal or nearly equal sample sizes such that the total sample size $n_1 + n_2$ is at least 20 can be expected to provide very good results even if the populations are not normal. Larger sample sizes are recommended if the distributions of the populations are highly skewed or contain outliers. Smaller sample sizes should only be used if the analyst is satisfied that the distributions of the populations are at least approximately normal.

NOTE AND COMMENT

Another approach used to make inferences about the difference between two population means when σ_1 and σ_2 are unknown is based on the assumption that the two population standard deviations are *equal* ($\sigma_1 = \sigma_2 = \sigma$). Under this assumption, the two sample standard deviations are combined to provide the following *pooled sample variance:*

$$s_p^2 = \frac{(n_1 - 1)s_1^2 + (n_2 - 1)s_2^2}{n_1 + n_2 - 2}$$

The t test statistic becomes

$$t = \frac{(\bar{x}_1 - \bar{x}_2) - D_0}{s_p \sqrt{\dfrac{1}{n_1} + \dfrac{1}{n_2}}}$$

and has $n_1 + n_2 - 2$ degrees of freedom. At this point, the computation of the p-value and the interpretation of the sample results are identical to the procedures discussed earlier in this section.

A difficulty with this procedure is that the assumption that the two population standard deviations are equal is usually difficult to verify. Unequal population standard deviations are frequently encountered. Using the pooled procedure may not provide satisfactory results, especially if the sample sizes n_1 and n_2 are quite different.

The t procedure that we presented in this section does not require the assumption of equal population standard deviations and can be applied whether the population standard deviations are equal or not. It is a more general procedure and is recommended for most applications.

Exercises

Methods

9.   The following results are for independent random samples taken from two populations.

Sample 1	Sample 2
$n_1 = 20$	$n_2 = 30$
$\bar{x}_1 = 22.5$	$\bar{x}_2 = 20.1$
$s_1 = 2.5$	$s_2 = 4.8$

a.   What is the point estimate of the difference between the two population means?
b.   What is the degrees of freedom for the t distribution?
c.   At 95% confidence, what is the margin of error?
d.   What is the 95% confidence interval for the difference between the two population means?

**SELF***test*

10. Consider the following hypothesis test.

$$H_0: \mu_1 - \mu_2 = 0$$
$$H_a: \mu_1 - \mu_2 \neq 0$$

The following results are from independent samples taken from two populations.

Sample 1	Sample 2
$n_1 = 35$	$n_2 = 40$
$\bar{x}_1 = 13.6$	$\bar{x}_2 = 10.1$
$s_1 = 5.2$	$s_2 = 8.5$

a. What is the value of the test statistic?
b. What is the degrees of freedom for the t distribution?
c. What is the p-value?
d. At $\alpha = .05$, what is your conclusion?

11. Consider the following data for two independent random samples taken from two normal populations.

Sample 1	10	7	13	7	9	8
Sample 2	8	7	8	4	6	9

a. Compute the two sample means.
b. Compute the two sample standard deviations.
c. What is the point estimate of the difference between the two population means?
d. What is the 90% confidence interval estimate of the difference between the two population means?

Applications

**SELF***test*

12. The U.S. Department of Transportation provides the number of miles that residents of the 75 largest metropolitan areas travel per day in a car. Suppose that for a random sample of 50 Buffalo residents the mean is 22.5 miles a day and the standard deviation is 8.4 miles a day, and for an independent random sample of 40 Boston residents the mean is 18.6 miles a day and the standard deviation is 7.4 miles a day.
a. What is the point estimate of the difference between the mean number of miles that Buffalo residents travel per day and the mean number of miles that Boston residents travel per day?
b. What is the 95% confidence interval for the difference between the two population means?

CollegeCosts

13. The average annual cost (including tuition, room, board, books, and fees) to attend a public college takes nearly a third of the annual income of a typical family with college-age children (*Money,* April 2012). At private colleges, the average annual cost is equal to about 60% of the typical family's income. The following random samples show the annual cost of attending private and public colleges. Data are in thousands of dollars.

Private Colleges					
52.8	43.2	45.0	33.3	44.0	
30.6	45.8	37.8	50.5	42.0	
Public Colleges					
20.3	22.0	28.2	15.6	24.1	28.5
22.8	25.8	18.5	25.6	14.4	21.8

a.   Compute the sample mean and sample standard deviation for private and public colleges.

b.   What is the point estimate of the difference between the two population means? Interpret this value in terms of the annual cost of attending private and public colleges.

c.   Develop a 95% confidence interval of the difference between the mean annual cost of attending private and pubic colleges.

14.   Are nursing salaries in Tampa, Florida, lower than those in Dallas, Texas? As reported by the *Tampa Tribune*, salary data show staff nurses in Tampa earn less than staff nurses in Dallas. Suppose that in a follow-up study of 40 staff nurses in Tampa and 50 staff nurses in Dallas you obtain the following results.

Tampa	Dallas
$n_1 = 40$	$n_2 = 50$
$\bar{x}_1 = \$56{,}100$	$\bar{x}_2 = \$59{,}400$
$s_1 = \$6000$	$s_2 = \$7000$

a.   Formulate a hypothesis so that, if the null hypothesis is rejected, we can conclude that salaries for staff nurses in Tampa are significantly lower than for those in Dallas. Use $\alpha = .05$.

b.   What is the value of the test statistic?

c.   What is the *p*-value?

d.   What is your conclusion?

IntHotels

15.   Hotel prices worldwide are projected to increase by 3% next year (*Lodging Magazine* website, June 15, 2016), but is there a difference between Europe and the U.S.? Suppose we have projected changes in hotel costs for 47 randomly selected major European cities and 53 randomly selected major U.S. cities. These data are provided in the DATAfile *IntHotels*.

a.   On the basis of the sample results, can we conclude that the mean change in hotels rates in Europe and the U.S. are different? Develop appropriate null and alternative hypotheses.

b.   Use $\alpha = .01$. What is your conclusion?

SATMath

16.   The College Board provided comparisons of Scholastic Aptitude Test (SAT) scores based on the highest level of education attained by the test taker's parents. A research hypothesis was that students whose parents had attained a higher level of education would on average score higher on the SAT. The overall mean SAT math score was 514. SAT math scores for independent samples of students follow. The first sample shows the SAT math test scores for students whose parents are college graduates with a bachelor's degree. The second sample shows the SAT math test scores for students whose parents are high school graduates but do not have a college degree.

Student's Parents			
College Grads		High School Grads	
485	487	442	492
534	533	580	478
650	526	479	425
554	410	486	485
550	515	528	390
572	578	524	535
497	448		
592	469		

a.   Formulate the hypotheses that can be used to determine whether the sample data support the hypothesis that students show a higher population mean math score on the SAT if their parents attained a higher level of education.

b.   What is the point estimate of the difference between the means for the two populations?

c.   Compute the p-value for the hypothesis test.

d.   At $\alpha = .05$, what is your conclusion?

17.   Periodically, Merrill Lynch customers are asked to evaluate Merrill Lynch financial consultants and services. Higher ratings on the client satisfaction survey indicate better service, with 7 the maximum service rating. Independent samples of service ratings for two financial consultants are summarized here. Consultant A has 10 years of experience, whereas consultant B has 1 year of experience. Use $\alpha = .05$ and test to see whether the consultant with more experience has the higher population mean service rating.

Consultant A	Consultant B
$n_1 = 16$	$n_2 = 10$
$\bar{x}_1 = 6.82$	$\bar{x}_2 = 6.25$
$s_1 = .64$	$s_2 = .75$

a.   State the null and alternative hypotheses.

b.   Compute the value of the test statistic.

c.   What is the p-value?

d.   What is your conclusion?

AirDelay

18.   Researchers at Purdue University and Wichita State University found that airlines are doing a better job of getting passengers to their destinations on time. AirTran Airways and Southwest Airlines were among the leaders in on-time arrivals, with both having 88% of their flights arriving on time. But for the 12% of flights that were delayed, how many minutes were these flights late? Sample data showing the number of minutes that delayed flights were late are provided in the DATAfile named *AirDelay*. Data are shown for both airlines.

a.   Formulate the hypotheses that can be used to test for a difference between the population mean minutes late for delayed flights by these two airlines.

b.   What is the sample mean number of minutes late for delayed flights for each of these two airlines?

c.   Using a .05 level of significance, what is the p-value and what is your conclusion?

Inferences About the Difference Between Two Population Means: Matched Samples

Suppose employees at a manufacturing company can use two different methods to perform a production task. To maximize production output, the company wants to identify the method with the smaller population mean completion time. Let μ_1 denote the population mean completion time for production method 1 and μ_2 denote the population mean completion time for production method 2. With no preliminary indication of the preferred production method, we begin by tentatively assuming that the two production methods have the same population mean completion time. Thus, the null hypothesis is $H_0\colon \mu_1 - \mu_2 = 0$. If this hypothesis is rejected, we can conclude that the population mean completion times differ. In this case, the method providing the smaller mean completion time would be recommended. The null and alternative hypotheses are written as follows.

$$H_0: \mu_1 - \mu_2 = 0$$
$$H_a: \mu_1 - \mu_2 \neq 0$$

In choosing the sampling procedure that will be used to collect production time data and test the hypotheses, we consider two alternative designs. One is based on independent samples and the other is based on **matched samples**.

1. *Independent sample design:* A random sample of workers is selected and each worker in the sample uses method 1. A second independent random sample of workers is selected and each worker in this sample uses method 2. The test of the difference between population means is based on the procedures in Section 10.2.
2. *Matched sample design:* One random sample of workers is selected. Each worker first uses one method and then uses the other method. The order of the two methods is assigned randomly to the workers, with some workers performing method 1 first and others performing method 2 first. Each worker provides a pair of data values, one value for method 1 and another value for method 2.

In the matched sample design the two production methods are tested under similar conditions (i.e., with the same workers); hence this design often leads to a smaller sampling error than the independent sample design. The primary reason is that in a matched sample design, variation between workers is eliminated because the same workers are used for both production methods.

Let us demonstrate the analysis of a matched sample design by assuming it is the method used to test the difference between population means for the two production methods. A random sample of six workers is used. The data on completion times for the six workers are given in Table 10.2. Note that each worker provides a pair of data values, one for each production method. Also note that the last column contains the difference in completion times d_i for each worker in the sample.

The key to the analysis of the matched sample design is to realize that we consider only the column of differences. Therefore, we have six data values (.6, −.2, .5, .3, .0, and .6) that will be used to analyze the difference between population means of the two production methods.

TABLE 10.2   TASK COMPLETION TIMES FOR A MATCHED SAMPLE DESIGN

DATA *file*

Matched

Worker	Completion Time for Method 1 (minutes)	Completion Time for Method 2 (minutes)	Difference in Completion Times (d_i)
1	6.0	5.4	.6
2	5.0	5.2	−.2
3	7.0	6.5	.5
4	6.2	5.9	.3
5	6.0	6.0	.0
6	6.4	5.8	.6

Let μ_d = the mean of the *difference* in values for the population of workers. With this notation, the null and alternative hypotheses are rewritten as follows.

$$H_0: \mu_d = 0$$
$$H_a: \mu_d \neq 0$$

Other than the use of the d notation, the formulas for the sample mean and sample standard deviation are the same ones used previously in the text.

If H_0 is rejected, we can conclude that the population mean completion times differ.

The d notation is a reminder that the matched sample provides *difference* data. The sample mean and sample standard deviation for the six difference values in Table 10.2 follow.

$$\bar{d} = \frac{\sum d_i}{n} = \frac{1.8}{6} = .30$$

$$s_d = \sqrt{\frac{\sum(d_i - \bar{d})^2}{n-1}} = \sqrt{\frac{.56}{5}} = .335$$

It is not necessary to make the assumption that the population has a normal distribution if the sample size is large. Sample size guidelines for using the t distribution were presented in Chapters 8 and 9.

With the small sample of $n = 6$ workers, we need to make the assumption that the population of differences has a normal distribution. This assumption is necessary so that we may use the t distribution for hypothesis testing and interval estimation procedures. Based on this assumption, the following test statistic has a t distribution with $n - 1$ degrees of freedom.

> **TEST STATISTIC FOR HYPOTHESIS TESTS INVOLVING MATCHED SAMPLES**
>
> $$t = \frac{\bar{d} - \mu_d}{s_d/\sqrt{n}} \qquad \textbf{(10.9)}$$

Once the difference data are computed, the t distribution procedure for matched samples is the same as the one-population estimation and hypothesis testing procedures described in Chapters 8 and 9.

Let us use equation (10.9) to test the hypotheses $H_0: \mu_d = 0$ and $H_a: \mu_d \neq 0$, using $\alpha = .05$. Substituting the sample results $\bar{d} = .30$, $s_d = .335$, and $n = 6$ into equation (10.9), we compute the value of the test statistic.

$$t = \frac{\bar{d} - \mu_d}{s_d/\sqrt{n}} = \frac{.30 - 0}{.335/\sqrt{6}} = 2.20$$

Now let us compute the *p*-value for this two-tailed test. Because $t = 2.20 > 0$, the test statistic is in the upper tail of the t distribution. With $t = 2.20$, the area in the upper tail to the right of the test statistic can be found by using the t distribution table with degrees of freedom $= n - 1 = 6 - 1 = 5$. Information from the 5 degrees of freedom row of the t distribution table is as follows:

Area in Upper Tail	.20	.10	.05	.025	.01	.005
t-Value (5 *df*)	0.920	1.476	2.015	2.571	3.365	4.032

$$t = 2.20$$

Thus, we see that the area in the upper tail is between .05 and .025. Because this test is a two-tailed test, we double these values to conclude that the *p*-value is between .10 and .05.

This *p*-value is greater than $\alpha = .05$. Thus, the null hypothesis H_0: $\mu_d = 0$ is not rejected. Using Excel and the data in Table 10.2, we find the exact *p*-value = .0795.

In addition we can obtain an interval estimate of the difference between the two population means by using the single population methodology of Chapter 8. At 95% confidence, the calculation follows.

$$\bar{d} \pm t_{.025}\frac{s_d}{\sqrt{n}}$$

$$.3 \pm 2.571\left(\frac{.335}{\sqrt{6}}\right)$$

$$.3 \pm .35$$

Thus, the margin of error is .35 and the 95% confidence interval for the difference between the population means of the two production methods is $-.05$ minutes to .65 minutes.

Using Excel to Conduct a Hypothesis Test

Excel's t-Test: Paired Two Sample for Means tool can be used to conduct a hypothesis test about the difference between the population means when a matched sample design is used. We illustrate by conducting the hypothesis test involving the two production methods. Refer to the Excel worksheets shown in Figure 10.8 and Figure 10.9 as we describe the tasks involved.

Enter/Access Data: Open the DATAfile named *Matched*. Column A in Figure 10.8 is used to identify each of the six workers who participated in the study. Column B contains the completion time data for each worker using method 1, and column C contains the completion time data for each worker using method 2.

Apply Tools: The following steps describe how to use Excel's t-Test: Paired Two Sample for Means tool to conduct the hypothesis test about the difference between the means of the two production methods

FIGURE 10.8 DIALOG BOX FOR EXCEL'S t-TEST: PAIRED TWO SAMPLE FOR MEANS TOOL

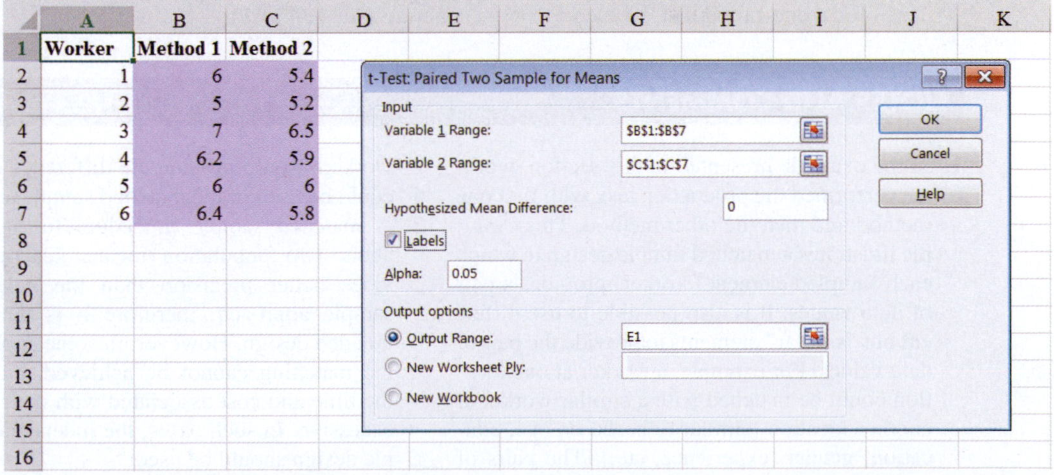

FIGURE 10.9 EXCEL RESULTS FOR THE HYPOTHESIS TEST IN THE MATCHED SAMPLES STUDY

	A	B	C	D	E	F	G	H
1	Worker	Method 1	Method 2		t-Test: Paired Two Sample for Means			
2	1	6	5.4					
3	2	5	5.2			*Method 1*	*Method 2*	
4	3	7	6.5		Mean	6.1	5.8	
5	4	6.2	5.9		Variance	0.428	0.212	
6	5	6	6		Observations	6	6	
7	6	6.4	5.8		Pearson Correlation	0.8764		
8					Hypothesized Mean Difference	0		
9					df	5		
10					t Stat	2.196		
11					P(T<=t) one-tail	0.0398		
12					t Critical one-tail	2.015		
13					P(T<=t) two-tail	0.0795		
14					t Critical two-tail	2.571		
15								

Step 1. Click the **Data** tab on the Ribbon
Step 2. In the **Analyze** group, click **Data Analysis**
Step 3. Choose **t-Test: Paired Two Sample for Means** from the list of Analysis Tools
Step 4. When the t-Test: Paired Two Sample for Means dialog box appears (Figure 10.8):

> Enter B1:B7 in the **Variable 1 Range** box
> Enter C1:C7 in the **Variable 2 Range** box
> Enter 0 in the **Hypothesized Mean Difference** box
> Select **Labels**
> Enter .05 in the **Alpha** box
> Select **Output Range**
> Enter E1 in the **Output Range** box (to identify the upper left corner of the section of the worksheet where the output will appear)
> Click **OK**

The results are shown in cells E1:G14 of the worksheet shown in Figure 10.9. The p-value for the test, labeled P(T<=t) two-tail, is shown in cell F13. Because the p-value, .0795, is greater than the level of significance $\alpha = .05$, we cannot reject the null hypothesis that the mean completion times are equal.

The same procedure can also be used to conduct one-tailed hypothesis tests. The only change required to make the hypothesis testing decision is that we need to use the p-value for a one-tailed test, labeled P(T<=t) one-tail (see cell F11).

NOTES AND COMMENTS

1. In the example presented in this section, workers performed the production task with first one method and then the other method. This example illustrates a matched sample design in which each sampled element (worker) provides a pair of data values. It is also possible to use different but "similar" elements to provide the pair of data values. For example, a worker at one location could be matched with a similar worker at another location (similarity based on age, education, gender, experience, etc.). The pairs of workers would provide the difference data that could be used in the matched sample analysis.

2. A matched sample procedure for inferences about two population means generally provides better precision than the independent sample approach; therefore it is the recommended design. However, in some applications the matching cannot be achieved, or perhaps the time and cost associated with matching are excessive. In such cases, the independent sample design should be used.

Exercises

Methods

19.   Consider the following hypothesis test.

$$H_0: \mu_d \le 0$$
$$H_a: \mu_d > 0$$

The following data are from matched samples taken from two populations.

		Population	
Element		**1**	**2**
1		21	20
2		28	26
3		18	18
4		20	20
5		26	24

   a.   Compute the difference value for each element.
   b.   Compute $\bar{d}$.
   c.   Compute the standard deviation s_d.
   d.   Conduct a hypothesis test using $\alpha = .05$. What is your conclusion?

20.   The following data are from matched samples taken from two populations.

		Population	
Element		**1**	**2**
1		11	8
2		7	8
3		9	6
4		12	7
5		13	10
6		15	15
7		15	14

   a.   Compute the difference value for each element.
   b.   Compute $\bar{d}$.
   c.   Compute the standard deviation s_d.
   d.   What is the point estimate of the difference between the two population means?
   e.   Provide a 95% confidence interval for the difference between the two population means.

Applications

21.   A market research firm used a sample of individuals to rate the purchase potential of a particular product before and after the individuals saw a new television commercial about the
   product. The purchase potential ratings were based on a 0 to 10 scale, with higher values
   indicating a higher purchase potential. The null hypothesis stated that the mean rating "after"
   would be less than or equal to the mean rating "before." Rejection of this hypothesis would
   show that the commercial improved the mean purchase potential rating. Use $\alpha = .05$ and the
   following data to test the hypothesis and comment on the value of the commercial.

| | Purchase Rating | | | | Purchase Rating | |
Individual	After	Before	Individual	After	Before
1	6	5	5	3	5
2	6	4	6	9	8
3	7	7	7	7	5
4	4	3	8	6	6

DATA file

StockPrices

22. The price per share of stock for a sample of 25 companies was recorded at the beginning of 2012 and then again at the end of the first quarter of 2012. How stocks perform during the first quarter is an indicator of what is ahead for the stock market and the economy. Use the sample data in the DATAfile named *StockPrices* to answer the following.

   a. Let d_i denote the change in price per share for company i where $d_i =$ first quarter of 2012 price per share minus the beginning of 2012 price per share. Use the sample mean of these values to estimate the dollar amount a share of stock has changed during the first quarter.

   b. What is the 95% confidence interval estimate of the population mean change in the price per share of stock during the first quarter? Interpret this result.

23. Bank of America's Consumer Spending Survey collected data on annual credit card charges in seven different categories of expenditures: transportation, groceries, dining out, household expenses, home furnishings, apparel, and entertainment. Using data from a sample of 42 credit card accounts, assume that each account was used to identify the annual credit card charges for groceries (population 1) and the annual credit card charges for dining out (population 2). Using the difference data, the sample mean difference was $\bar{d} = \$850$, and the sample standard deviation was $s_d = \$1123$.

   a. Formulate the null and alternative hypotheses to test for no difference between the population mean credit card charges for groceries and the population mean credit card charges for dining out.

   b. Use a .05 level of significance. Can you conclude that the population means differ? What is the p-value?

   c. Which category, groceries or dining out, has a higher population mean annual credit card charge? What is the point estimate of the difference between the population means? What is the 95% confidence interval estimate of the difference between the population means?

DATA file

BusinessTravel

24. The Global Business Travel Association reported the domestic airfare for business travel for the current year and the previous year. Below is a sample of 12 flights with their domestic airfares shown for both years.

Current Year	Previous Year	Current Year	Previous Year
345	315	635	585
526	463	710	650
420	462	605	545
216	206	517	547
285	275	570	508
405	432	610	580

   a. Formulate the hypotheses and test for a significant increase in the mean domestic airfare for business travel for the one-year period. What is the p-value? Using a .05 level of significance, what is your conclusion?

   b. What is the sample mean domestic airfare for business travel for each year?

   c. What is the percentage change in the airfare for the one-year period?

25. The College Board SAT college entrance exam consists of three parts: math, writing, and critical reading (*The World Almanac*, 2012). Sample data showing the math and writing scores for a sample of 12 students who took the SAT follow.

TestScores

Student	Math	Writing	Student	Math	Writing
1	540	474	7	480	430
2	432	380	8	499	459
3	528	463	9	610	615
4	574	612	10	572	541
5	448	420	11	390	335
6	502	526	12	593	613

a. Use a .05 level of significance and test for a difference between the population mean for the math scores and the population mean for the writing scores. What is the *p*-value and what is your conclusion?

b. What is the point estimate of the difference between the mean scores for the two tests? What are the estimates of the population mean scores for the two tests? Which test reports the higher mean score?

26. Scores in the first and fourth (final) rounds for a sample of 20 golfers who competed in PGA tournaments are shown in the following table. Suppose you would like to determine whether the mean score for the first round of a PGA Tour event is significantly different than the mean score for the fourth and final round. Does the pressure of playing in the final round cause scores to go up? Or does the increased player concentration cause scores to come down?

GolfScores

Player	First Round	Final Round	Player	First Round	Final Round
Michael Letzig	70	72	Aron Price	72	72
Scott Verplank	71	72	Charles Howell	72	70
D. A. Points	70	75	Jason Dufner	70	73
Jerry Kelly	72	71	Mike Weir	70	77
Soren Hansen	70	69	Carl Pettersson	68	70
D. J. Trahan	67	67	Bo Van Pelt	68	65
Bubba Watson	71	67	Ernie Els	71	70
Reteif Goosen	68	75	Cameron Beckman	70	68
Jeff Klauk	67	73	Nick Watney	69	68
Kenny Perry	70	69	Tommy Armour III	67	71

a. Use $\alpha = .10$ to test for a statistically significantly difference between the population means for first- and fourth-round scores. What is the *p*-value? What is your conclusion?

b. What is the point estimate of the difference between the two population means? For which round is the population mean score lower?

c. What is the margin of error for a 90% confidence interval estimate for the difference between the population means? Could this confidence interval have been used to test the hypothesis in part (a)? Explain.

27. A manufacturer produces both a deluxe and a standard model of an automatic sander designed for home use. Selling prices obtained from a sample of retail outlets follow.

	Model Price ($)			Model Price ($)	
Retail Outlet	**Deluxe**	**Standard**	**Retail Outlet**	**Deluxe**	**Standard**
1	39	27	5	40	30
2	39	28	6	39	34
3	45	35	7	35	29
4	38	30			

a. The manufacturer's suggested retail prices for the two models show a $10 price differential. Use a .05 level of significance and test that the mean difference between the prices of the two models is $10.

b. What is the 95% confidence interval for the difference between the mean prices of the two models?

Inferences About the Difference Between Two Population Proportions

Letting p_1 denote the proportion for population 1 and p_2 denote the proportion for population 2, we next consider inferences about the difference between the two population proportions: $p_1 - p_2$. To make an inference about this difference, we will select two independent random samples consisting of n_1 units from population 1 and n_2 units from population 2.

Interval Estimation of $p_1 - p_2$

In the following example, we show how to compute a margin of error and develop an interval estimate of the difference between two population proportions.

A tax preparation firm is interested in comparing the quality of work at two of its regional offices. By randomly selecting samples of tax returns prepared at each office and verifying the sample returns' accuracy, the firm will be able to estimate the proportion of erroneous returns prepared at each office. Of particular interest is the difference between these proportions.

$$p_1 = \text{proportion of erroneous returns for population 1 (office 1)}$$
$$p_2 = \text{proportion of erroneous returns for population 2 (office 2)}$$
$$\bar{p}_1 = \text{sample proportion for a random sample from population 1}$$
$$\bar{p}_2 = \text{sample proportion for a random sample from population 2}$$

The difference between the two population proportions is given by $p_1 - p_2$. The point estimator of $p_1 - p_2$ is as follows.

> **POINT ESTIMATOR OF THE DIFFERENCE BETWEEN TWO POPULATION PROPORTIONS**
>
> $$\bar{p}_1 - \bar{p}_2 \tag{10.10}$$

Thus, the point estimator of the difference between two population proportions is the difference between the sample proportions of two independent random samples.

As with other point estimators, the point estimator $\bar{p}_1 - \bar{p}_2$ has a sampling distribution that reflects the possible values of $\bar{p}_1 - \bar{p}_2$ if we repeatedly took two independent random samples. The mean of this sampling distribution is $p_1 - p_2$ and the standard error of $\bar{p}_1 - \bar{p}_2$ is as follows:

STANDARD ERROR OF $\bar{p}_1 - \bar{p}_2$

$$\sigma_{\bar{p}_1 - \bar{p}_2} = \sqrt{\frac{p_1(1 - p_1)}{n_1} + \frac{p_2(1 - p_2)}{n_2}} \qquad \text{(10.11)}$$

Sample sizes involving proportions are usually large enough to use this approximation.

If the sample sizes are large enough that $n_1 p_1$, $n_1(1 - p_1)$, $n_2 p_2$, and $n_2(1 - p_2)$ are all greater than or equal to 5, the sampling distribution of $\bar{p}_1 - \bar{p}_2$ can be approximated by a normal distribution.

As we showed previously, an interval estimate is given by a point estimate $\pm$ a margin of error. In the estimation of the difference between two population proportions, an interval estimate will take the following form:

$$\bar{p}_1 - \bar{p}_2 \pm \text{Margin of error}$$

With the sampling distribution of $\bar{p}_1 - \bar{p}_2$ approximated by a normal distribution, we would like to use $z_{\alpha/2}\sigma_{\bar{p}_1 - \bar{p}_2}$ as the margin of error. However, $\sigma_{\bar{p}_1 - \bar{p}_2}$ given by equation (10.11) cannot be used directly because the two population proportions, p_1 and p_2, are unknown. Using the sample proportion $\bar{p}_1$ to estimate p_1 and the sample proportion $\bar{p}_2$ to estimate p_2, the margin of error is as follows.

$$\text{Margin of error} = z_{\alpha/2} \sqrt{\frac{\bar{p}_1(1 - \bar{p}_1)}{n_1} + \frac{\bar{p}_2(1 - \bar{p}_2)}{n_2}} \qquad \text{(10.12)}$$

The general form of an interval estimate of the difference between two population proportions is as follows.

INTERVAL ESTIMATE OF THE DIFFERENCE BETWEEN TWO POPULATION PROPORTIONS

$$\bar{p}_1 - \bar{p}_2 \pm z_{\alpha/2} \sqrt{\frac{\bar{p}_1(1 - \bar{p}_1)}{n_1} + \frac{\bar{p}_2(1 - \bar{p}_2)}{n_2}} \qquad \text{(10.13)}$$

where $1 - \alpha$ is the confidence coefficient.

Returning to the tax preparation example, we find that independent random samples from the two offices provide the following information.

Office 1	Office 2
$n_1 = 250$	$n_2 = 300$
Number of returns with errors $= 35$	Number of returns with errors $= 27$

TaxPrep

The sample proportions for the two offices follow.

$$\bar{p}_1 = \frac{35}{250} = .14$$

$$\bar{p}_2 = \frac{27}{300} = .09$$

The point estimate of the difference between the proportions of erroneous tax returns for the two populations is $\bar{p}_1 - \bar{p}_2 = .14 - .09 = .05$. Thus, we estimate that office 1 has a .05, or 5%, greater error rate than office 2.

Expression (10.13) can now be used to provide a margin of error and interval estimate of the difference between the two population proportions. Using a 90% confidence interval with $z_{\alpha/2} = z_{.05} = 1.645$, we have

$$\bar{p}_1 - \bar{p}_2 \pm z_{\alpha/2} \sqrt{\frac{\bar{p}_1(1 - \bar{p}_1)}{n_1} + \frac{\bar{p}_2(1 - \bar{p}_2)}{n_2}}$$

$$.14 - .09 \pm 1.645 \sqrt{\frac{.14(1 - .14)}{250} + \frac{.09(1 - .09)}{300}}$$

$$.05 \pm .045$$

Thus, the margin of error is .045, and the 90% confidence interval is .005 to .095.

Using Excel to Construct a Confidence Interval

We can create a worksheet for developing an interval estimate of the difference between population proportions. Let us illustrate by developing an interval estimate of the difference between the proportions of erroneous tax returns at the two offices of the tax preparation firm. Refer to Figure 10.10 as we describe the tasks involved. The formula worksheet is in the background; the value worksheet appears in the foreground.

Enter/Access Data: Open the DATAfile named *TaxPrep*. Columns A and B contain headings and Yes or No data that indicate which of the tax returns from each office contain an error.

Enter Functions and Formulas: The descriptive statistics needed are provided in cells E5:F5 and E7:F8. Note that Excel's COUNTA function is used in cells E5 and F5 to count the number of observations for each of the samples. The value worksheet indicates 250 returns in the sample from office 1 and 300 returns in the sample from office 2. In cells E6 and F6, we type Yes to indicate the response of interest (an erroneous return). Excel's COUNTIF function is used in cells E7 and F7 to count the number of Yes responses from each office. Formulas entered into cells E8 and F8 compute the sample proportions. The confidence coefficient entered into cell E10 (.9) is used to compute the corresponding level of significance ($\alpha = .10$) in cell E11. In cell E12 we use the NORM.S.INV function to compute the z value needed to compute the margin of error for the interval estimate.

In cell E14, a point estimate of $\sigma_{\bar{p}_1 - \bar{p}_2}$, the standard error of the point estimator $\bar{p}_1 - \bar{p}_2$, is computed based on the two sample proportions (E8 and F8) and sample sizes (E5 and F5). The margin of error is then computed in cell E15 by multiplying the z value by the estimate of the standard error.

The point estimate of the difference in the two population proportions is computed in cell E17 as the difference in the sample proportions; the result, shown in the value worksheet, is .05. The lower limit of the confidence interval is computed in cell E18 by subtracting the margin of error from the point estimate. The upper limit is computed in cell E19 by adding

FIGURE 10.10   CONSTRUCTING A 90% CONFIDENCE INTERVAL FOR THE DIFFERENCE
IN THE PROPORTION OF ERRONEOUS TAX RETURNS PREPARED BY TWO OFFICES

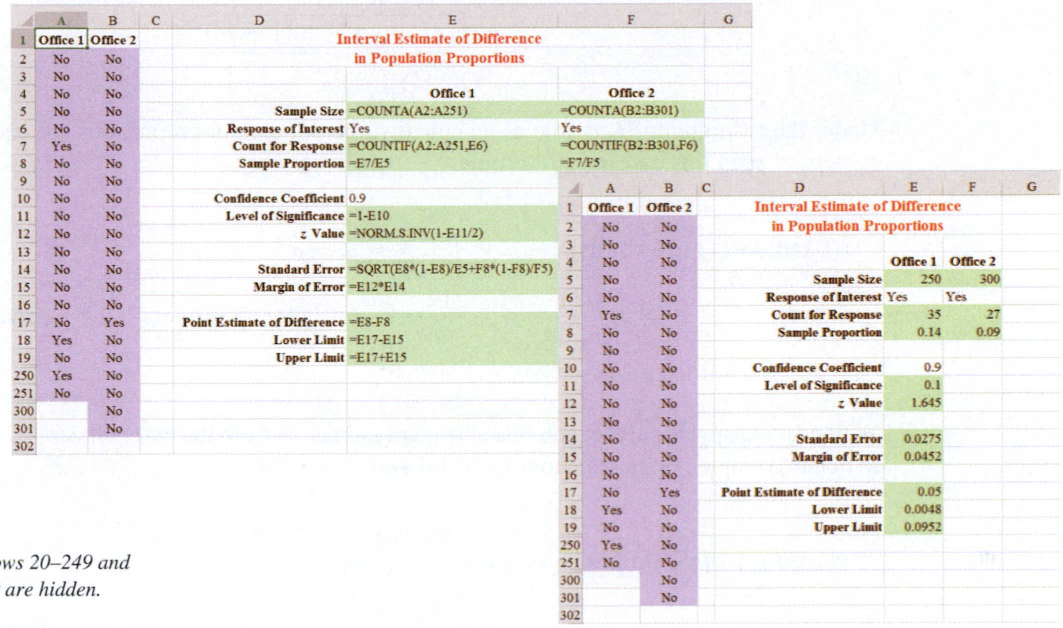

*Note: Rows 20–249 and
252–299 are hidden.*

the margin of error to the point estimate. The value worksheet shows that the 90% confidence interval estimate of the difference in the two population proportions is .0048 to .0952.

A template for other problems   This worksheet can be used as a template for other problems requiring an interval estimate of the difference in population proportions. The new data must be entered in columns A and B. The data ranges in the cells used to compute the sample size (E5:F5) and the cells used to compute a count of the response of interest (E7:F7) must be changed to correctly indicate the location of the new data. The response of interest must be typed into cells E6:F6. The 90% confidence interval for the new data will then appear in cells E17:E19. If an interval estimate with a different confidence coefficient is desired, simply change the entry in cell E10.

This worksheet can also be used as a template for solving text exercises in which the sample data have already been summarized. No change in the data section is necessary. Simply type the values for the given sample sizes in cells E5:F5 and type the given values for the sample proportions in cells E8:F8. The 90% confidence interval will then appear in cells E17:E19. If an interval estimate with a different confidence coefficient is desired, simply change the entry in cell E10.

Hypothesis Tests About $p_1 - p_2$

Let us now consider hypothesis tests about the difference between the proportions of two populations. We focus on tests involving no difference between the two population proportions. In this case, the three forms for a hypothesis test are as follows:

All hypotheses considered use 0 as the difference of interest.

$$H_0: p_1 - p_2 \geq 0 \qquad H_0: p_1 - p_2 \leq 0 \qquad H_0: p_1 - p_2 = 0$$
$$H_a: p_1 - p_2 < 0 \qquad H_a: p_1 - p_2 > 0 \qquad H_a: p_1 - p_2 \neq 0$$

When we assume H_0 is true as an equality, we have $p_1 - p_2 = 0$, which is the same as saying that the population proportions are equal, $p_1 = p_2$.

We will base the test statistic on the sampling distribution of the point estimator $\bar{p}_1 - \bar{p}_2$. In equation (10.11), we showed that the standard error of $\bar{p}_1 - \bar{p}_2$ is given by

$$\sigma_{\bar{p}_1 - \bar{p}_2} = \sqrt{\frac{p_1(1 - p_1)}{n_1} + \frac{p_2(1 - p_2)}{n_2}}$$

Under the assumption H_0 is true as an equality, the population proportions are equal and $p_1 = p_2 = p$. In this case, $\sigma_{\bar{p}_1 - \bar{p}_2}$ becomes

---

STANDARD ERROR OF $\bar{p}_1 - \bar{p}_2$ WHEN $p_1 = p_2 = p$

$$\sigma_{\bar{p}_1 - \bar{p}_2} = \sqrt{\frac{p(1 - p)}{n_1} + \frac{p(1 - p)}{n_2}} = \sqrt{p(1 - p)\left(\frac{1}{n_1} + \frac{1}{n_2}\right)} \quad \textbf{(10.14)}$$

With p unknown, we pool, or combine, the point estimators from the two samples ($\bar{p}_1$ and $\bar{p}_2$) to obtain a single point estimator of p as follows:

POOLED ESTIMATOR OF p WHEN $p_1 = p_2 = p$

$$\bar{p} = \frac{n_1 \bar{p}_1 + n_2 \bar{p}_2}{n_1 + n_2} \quad \textbf{(10.15)}$$

This **pooled estimator of p** is a weighted average of $\bar{p}_1$ and $\bar{p}_2$.

Substituting $\bar{p}$ for p in equation (10.14), we obtain an estimate of the standard error of $\bar{p}_1 - \bar{p}_2$. This estimate of the standard error is used in the test statistic. The general form of the test statistic for hypothesis tests about the difference between two population proportions is the point estimator divided by the estimate of $\sigma_{\bar{p}_1 - \bar{p}_2}$.

TEST STATISTIC FOR HYPOTHESIS TESTS ABOUT $p_1 - p_2$

$$z = \frac{(\bar{p}_1 - \bar{p}_2)}{\sqrt{\bar{p}(1 - \bar{p})\left(\frac{1}{n_1} + \frac{1}{n_2}\right)}} \quad \textbf{(10.16)}$$

This test statistic applies to large sample situations where $n_1 p_1$, $n_1(1 - p_1)$, $n_2 p_2$, and $n_2(1 - p_2)$ are all greater than or equal to 5.

Let us return to the tax preparation firm example and assume that the firm wants to use a hypothesis test to determine whether the error proportions differ between the two offices. A two-tailed test is required. The null and alternative hypotheses are as follows:

$$H_0: p_1 - p_2 = 0$$
$$H_a: p_1 - p_2 \neq 0$$

If H_0 is rejected, the firm can conclude that the error rates at the two offices differ. We will use $\alpha = .10$ as the level of significance.

The sample data previously collected showed $\bar{p}_1 = .14$ for the $n_1 = 250$ returns sampled at office 1 and $\bar{p}_2 = .09$ for the $n_2 = 300$ returns sampled at office 2. We continue by computing the pooled estimate of p.

$$\bar{p} = \frac{n_1\bar{p}_1 + n_2\bar{p}_2}{n_1 + n_2} = \frac{250(.14) + 300(.09)}{250 + 300} = .1127$$

Using this pooled estimate and the difference between the sample proportions, the value of the test statistic is as follows.

$$z = \frac{(\bar{p}_1 - \bar{p}_2)}{\sqrt{\bar{p}(1 - \bar{p})\left(\dfrac{1}{n_1} + \dfrac{1}{n_2}\right)}} = \frac{(.14 - .09)}{\sqrt{.1127(1 - .1127)\left(\dfrac{1}{250} + \dfrac{1}{300}\right)}} = 1.85$$

In computing the p-value for this two-tailed test, we first note that $z = 1.85$ is in the upper tail of the standard normal distribution. Using $z = 1.85$ and the standard normal distribution table, we find the area in the upper tail is $1.0000 - .9678 = .0322$. Doubling this area for a two-tailed test, we find the p-value $= 2(.0322) = .0644$. With the p-value less than $\alpha = .10$, H_0 is rejected at the .10 level of significance. The firm can conclude that the error rates differ between the two offices. This hypothesis testing conclusion is consistent with the earlier interval estimation results that showed the interval estimate of the difference between the population error rates at the two offices to be .005 to .095, with office 1 having the higher error rate.

Using Excel to Conduct a Hypothesis Test

We can create a worksheet for conducting a hypothesis test about the difference between population proportions. Let us illustrate by testing to see whether there is a significant difference between the proportions of erroneous tax returns at the two offices of the tax preparation firm. Refer to Figure 10.11 as we describe the tasks involved. The formula worksheet is in the background; the value worksheet is in the foreground.

Enter/Access Data: Open the DATAfile named *TaxPrep*. Columns A and B contain headings and Yes or No data that indicate which of the tax returns from each office contain an error.

Enter Functions and Formulas: The descriptive statistics needed to perform the hypothesis test are provided in cells E5:F5 and E7:F8. They are the same as the ones used for an interval estimate (see Figure 10.10). The hypothesized value of the difference between the two populations is zero; it is entered into cell E10. In cell E11, the difference in the sample proportions is used to compute a point estimate of the difference in the two population proportions. Using the two sample proportions and sample sizes, a pooled estimate of the population proportion p is computed in cell E13; its value is .1127. Then, in cell E14, an estimate of $\sigma_{\bar{p}_1 - \bar{p}_2}$ is computed using equation (10.14), with the pooled estimate of p and the sample sizes.

The formula =(E11-E10)/E14 entered into cell E15 computes the test statistic z (1.8462). The NORM.S.DIST function is then used to compute the p-value (Lower Tail) and the p-value (Upper Tail) in cells E17 and E18. The p-value (Two Tail) is computed in cell E19 as twice the minimum of the two one-tailed p-values. The value worksheet shows that p-value (Two Tail) $= .0649$. Because the p-value $= .0649$ is less than the level of significance, $\alpha = .10$, we have sufficient evidence to reject the null hypothesis and conclude that the population proportions are not equal.

The p-value here (.0649) differs from the one we found using the cumulative normal probability tables (.0644) due to rounding.

FIGURE 10.11   HYPOTHESIS TEST CONCERNING DIFFERENCE IN PROPORTION OF ERRONEOUS
TAX RETURNS PREPARED BY TWO OFFICES

	A	B	C	D	E	F	G
1	Office 1	Office 2		Hypothesis Test Concerning Difference			
2	No	No		Between Population Proportions			
3	No	No					
4	No	No			Office 1	Office 2	
5	No	No		Sample Size	=COUNTA(A2:A251)	=COUNTA(B2:B301)	
6	No	No		Response of Interest	Yes	Yes	
7	Yes	No		Count for Response	=COUNTIF(A2:A251,E6)	=COUNTIF(B2:B301,F6)	
8	No	No		Sample Proportion	=E7/E5	=F7/F5	
9	No	No					
10	No	No		Hypothesized Value	0		
11	No	No		Point Estimate of Difference	=E8-F8		
12	No	No					
13	No	No		Pooled Estimate of p	=(E5*E8+F5*F8)/(E5+F5)		
14	No	No		Standard Error	=SQRT(E13*(1-E13)*(1/E5+1/F5))		
15	No	No		Test Statistic	=(E11-E10)/E14		
16	No	No					
17	No	Yes		p-value (Lower Tail)	=NORM.S.DIST(E15,TRUE)		
18	Yes	No		p-value (Upper Tail)	=1-NORM.S.DIST(E15,TRUE)		
19	No	No		p-value (Two Tail)	=2*MIN(E17,E18)		
250	Yes	No					
251	No	No					
300		No					
301		No					
302							

	A	B	C	D	E	F	G
1	Office 1	Office 2		Hypothesis Test Concerning Difference			
2	No	No		Between Population Proportions			
3	No	No					
4	No	No			Office 1	Office 2	
5	No	No		Sample Size	250	300	
6	No	No		Response of Interest	Yes	Yes	
7	Yes	No		Count for Response	35	27	
8	No	No		Sample Proportion	0.14	0.09	
9	No	No					
10	No	No		Hypothesized Value	0		
11	No	No		Point Estimate of Difference	0.05		
12	No	No					
13	No	No		Pooled Estimate of p	0.1127		
14	No	No		Standard Error	0.0271		
15	No	No		Test Statistic	1.8462		
16	No	No					
17	No	Yes		p-value (Lower Tail)	0.9676		
18	Yes	No		p-value (Upper Tail)	0.0324		
19	No	No		p-value (Two Tail)	0.0649		
250	Yes	No					
251	No	No					
300		No					
301		No					
302							

*Note: Rows 20–249 and
252–299 are hidden.*

This worksheet can be used as a template for hypothesis testing problems involving differences between population proportions. The new data can be entered into columns A and B. The ranges for the new data and the response of interest need to be revised in cells E5:F7. The remainder of the worksheet will then be updated as needed to conduct the hypothesis test. If a hypothesized difference other than 0 is to be used, the new value must be entered in cell E10.

To use this worksheet for exercises in which the sample statistics are given, just type in the given values for cells E5:F5 and E7:F8. The remainder of the worksheet will then be updated to conduct the hypothesis test. If a hypothesized difference other than 0 is to be used, the new value must be entered in cell E10.

Exercises

Methods

28.   Consider the following results for independent samples taken from two populations.

Sample 1	Sample 2
$n_1 = 400$	$n_2 = 300$
$\bar{p}_1 = .48$	$\bar{p}_2 = .36$

a.   What is the point estimate of the difference between the two population proportions?
b.   Develop a 90% confidence interval for the difference between the two population proportions.
c.   Develop a 95% confidence interval for the difference between the two population proportions.

SELF*test*

29.   Consider the hypothesis test

$$H_0: p_1 - p_2 \le 0$$
$$H_a: p_1 - p_2 > 0$$

The following results are for independent samples taken from the two populations.

Sample 1	Sample 2
$n_1 = 200$	$n_2 = 300$
$\bar{p}_1 = .22$	$\bar{p}_2 = .16$

a.   What is the p-value?
b.   With $\alpha = .05$, what is your hypothesis testing conclusion?

Applications

30.   A *BusinessWeek*/Harris survey asked senior executives at large corporations their opinions about the economic outlook for the future. One question was, "Do you think that there will be an increase in the number of full-time employees at your company over the next 12 months?" In the current survey, 220 of 400 executives answered Yes, while in a previous year survey, 192 of 400 executives had answered Yes. Provide a 95% confidence interval estimate for the difference between the proportions at the two points in time. What is your interpretation of the interval estimate?

31.   *Forbes* reports that women trust recommendations from Pinterest more than recommendations from any other social network platform (*Forbes* website, April 10, 2012). But does trust in Pinterest differ by gender? The following sample data show the number of women and men who stated in a recent sample that they trust recommendations made on Pinterest.

	Women	Men
Sample	150	170
Trust Recommendations Made on Pinterest	117	102

a.   What is the point estimate of the proportion of women who trust recommendations made on Pinterest?
b.   What is the point estimate of the proportion of men who trust recommendations made on Pinterest?
c.   Provide a 95% confidence interval estimate of the difference between the proportion of women and men who trust recommendations made on Pinterest.

32.   Researchers with Oceana, a group dedicated to preserving the ocean ecosystem, reported finding that 33% of fish sold in retail outlets, grocery stores, and sushi bars throughout the United States had been mislabeled (*San Francisco Chronicle* website, February 21, 2013). Does this mislabeling differ for different species of fish? The following data show the number labeled incorrectly for samples of tuna and mahi mahi.

	Tuna	Mahi Mahi
Sample	220	160
Mislabeled	99	56

a. What is the point estimate of the proportion of tuna that is mislabeled?
b. What is the point estimate of the proportion of mahi mahi that is mislabeled?
c. Provide a 95% confidence interval estimate of the difference between the proportions of tuna and mahi mahi that is mislabeled.

33. Minnesota had the highest turnout rate of any state for the 2012 presidential election (United States Election Project website, February 9, 2013). Political analysts wonder if turnout in rural Minnesota was higher than turnout in the urban areas of the state. A sample shows that 663 of 884 registered voters from rural Minnesota voted in the 2012 presidential election, while 414 out of 575 registered voters from urban Minnesota voted.
   a. Formulate the null and alternative hypotheses that can be used to test whether registered voters in rural Minnesota were more likely than registered voters in urban Minnesota to vote in the 2012 presidential election.
   b. What is the proportion of sampled registered voters in rural Minnesota that voted in the 2012 presidential election?
   c. What is the proportion of sampled registered voters in urban Minnesota that voted in the 2012 presidential election?
   d. At $\alpha = .05$, test the political analysts' hypothesis. What is the p-value, and what conclusion do you draw from your results?

34. Oil wells are expensive to drill, and dry wells are a great concern to oil exploration companies. The domestic oil and natural gas producer Aegis Oil, LLC describes on its website how improvements in technologies such as three-dimensional seismic imaging have dramatically reduced the number of dry (nonproducing) wells it and other oil exploration companies drill. The following sample data for wells drilled in 2005 and 2012 show the number of dry wells that were drilled in each year.

	2005	2012
Wells Drilled	119	162
Dry Wells	24	18

   a. Formulate the null and alternative hypotheses that can be used to test whether the wells drilled in 2005 were more likely to be dry than wells drilled in 2012.
   b. What is the point estimate of the proportion of wells drilled in 2005 that were dry?
   c. What is the point estimate of the proportion of wells drilled in 2012 that were dry?
   d. What is the p-value of your hypothesis test? At $\alpha = .05$, what conclusion do you draw from your results?

35. In a test of the quality of two television commercials, each commercial was shown in a separate test area six times over a one-week period. The following week a telephone survey was conducted to identify individuals who had seen the commercials. Those individuals were asked to state the primary message in the commercials. The following results were recorded.

	Commercial A	Commercial B
Number Who Saw Commercial	150	200
Number Who Recalled Message	63	60

a. Use $\alpha = .05$ and test the hypothesis that there is no difference in the recall proportions for the two commercials.

b. Compute a 95% confidence interval for the difference between the recall proportions for the two populations.

36. Winter visitors are extremely important to the economy of Southwest Florida. Hotel occupancy is an often-reported measure of visitor volume and visitor activity (*Naples Daily News,* March 22, 2012). Hotel occupancy data for February in two consecutive years are as follows.

	Current Year	Previous Year
Occupied Rooms	1470	1458
Total Rooms	1750	1800

a. Formulate the hypothesis test that can be used to determine whether there has been an increase in the proportion of rooms occupied over the one-year period.

b. What is the estimated proportion of hotel rooms occupied each year?

c. Using a .05 level of significance, what is your hypothesis test conclusion? What is the *p*-value?

d. What is the 95% confidence interval estimate of the change in occupancy for the one-year period? Do you think area officials would be pleased with the results?

37. The Adecco Workplace Insights Survey sampled men and women workers and asked if they expected to get a raise or promotion this year (*USA Today,* February 16, 2012). Suppose the survey sampled 200 men and 200 women. If 104 of the men replied Yes and 74 of the women replied Yes, are the results statistically significant in that you can conclude a greater proportion of men are expecting to get a raise or a promotion this year?

a. State the hypothesis test in terms of the population proportion of men and the population proportion of women?

b. What is the sample proportion for men? For women?

c. Use a .01 level of significance. What is the *p*-value and what is your conclusion?

Summary

In this chapter we discussed procedures for developing interval estimates and conducting hypothesis tests involving two populations. First, we showed how to make inferences about the difference between two population means when independent random samples are selected. We first considered the case where the population standard deviations σ_1 and σ_2 could be assumed known. The standard normal distribution z was used to develop the interval estimate and served as the test statistic for hypothesis tests. We then considered the case where the population standard deviations were unknown and estimated by the sample standard deviations s_1 and s_2. In this case, the t distribution was used to develop the interval estimate and the t value served as the test statistic for hypothesis tests.

Inferences about the difference between two population means were then discussed for the matched sample design. In the matched sample design each element provides a pair of data values, one from each population. The difference between the paired data values is then used in the statistical analysis. The matched sample design is generally preferred to the independent sample design because the matched sample procedure often improves the precision of the estimate.

Finally, interval estimation and hypothesis testing about the difference between two population proportions were discussed. Statistical procedures for analyzing the difference between two population proportions are similar to the procedures for analyzing the difference between two population means.

We showed how Excel can be used to develop the interval estimates and conduct the hypothesis tests discussed in the chapter. Many of the worksheets can be used as templates to solve problems encountered in practice as well as the exercises and case problems found in the text.

Glossary

Independent random samples Samples selected from two populations in such a way that the elements making up one sample are chosen independently of the elements making up the other sample.

Matched samples Samples in which each data value of one sample is matched with a corresponding data value of the other sample.

Pooled estimator of p An estimator of a population proportion obtained by computing a weighted average of the point estimators obtained from two independent samples.

Key Formulas

Point Estimator of the Difference Between Two Population Means

$$\bar{x}_1 - \bar{x}_2 \tag{10.1}$$

Standard Error of $\bar{x}_1 - \bar{x}_2$

$$\sigma_{\bar{x}_1 - \bar{x}_2} = \sqrt{\frac{\sigma_1^2}{n_1} + \frac{\sigma_2^2}{n_2}} \tag{10.2}$$

Interval Estimate of the Difference Between Two Population Means: σ_1 and σ_2 Known

$$\bar{x}_1 - \bar{x}_2 \pm z_{\alpha/2} \sqrt{\frac{\sigma_1^2}{n_1} + \frac{\sigma_2^2}{n_2}} \tag{10.4}$$

Test Statistic for Hypothesis Tests About $\mu_1 - \mu_2$: σ_1 and σ_1 Known

$$z = \frac{(\bar{x}_1 - \bar{x}_2) - D_0}{\sqrt{\dfrac{\sigma_1^2}{n_1} + \dfrac{\sigma_2^2}{n_2}}} \tag{10.5}$$

Interval Estimate of the Difference Between Two Population Means: σ_1 and σ_2 Unknown

$$\bar{x}_1 - \bar{x}_2 \pm t_{\alpha/2} \sqrt{\frac{s_1^2}{n_1} + \frac{s_2^2}{n_2}} \tag{10.6}$$

Degrees of Freedom: t Distribution with Two Independent Random Samples

$$df = \frac{\left(\dfrac{s_1^2}{n_1} + \dfrac{s_2^2}{n_2}\right)^2}{\dfrac{1}{n_1 - 1}\left(\dfrac{s_1^2}{n_1}\right)^2 + \dfrac{1}{n_2 - 1}\left(\dfrac{s_2^2}{n_2}\right)^2} \tag{10.7}$$

Test Statistic for Hypothesis Tests About $\mu_1 - \mu_2$: σ_1 and σ_2 Unknown

$$t = \frac{(\bar{x}_1 - \bar{x}_2) - D_0}{\sqrt{\dfrac{s_1^2}{n_1} + \dfrac{s_2^2}{n_2}}} \qquad \textbf{(10.8)}$$

Test Statistic for Hypothesis Tests Involving Matched Samples

$$t = \frac{\bar{d} - \mu_d}{s_d/\sqrt{n}} \qquad \textbf{(10.9)}$$

Point Estimator of the Difference Between Two Population Proportions

$$\bar{p}_1 - \bar{p}_2 \qquad \textbf{(10.10)}$$

Standard Error of $\bar{p}_1 - \bar{p}_2$

$$\sigma_{\bar{p}_1 - \bar{p}_2} = \sqrt{\frac{p_1(1 - p_1)}{n_1} + \frac{p_2(1 - p_2)}{n_2}} \qquad \textbf{(10.11)}$$

Interval Estimate of the Difference Between Two Population Proportions

$$\bar{p}_1 - \bar{p}_2 \pm z_{\alpha/2} \sqrt{\frac{\bar{p}_1(1 - \bar{p}_1)}{n_1} + \frac{\bar{p}_2(1 - \bar{p}_2)}{n_2}} \qquad \textbf{(10.13)}$$

Standard Error of $\bar{p}_1 - \bar{p}_2$ When $p_1 = p_2 = p$

$$\sigma_{\bar{p}_1 - \bar{p}_2} = \sqrt{p(1 - p)\left(\frac{1}{n_1} + \frac{1}{n_2}\right)} \qquad \textbf{(10.14)}$$

Pooled Estimator of p When $p_1 = p_2 = p$

$$\bar{p} = \frac{n_1\bar{p}_1 + n_2\bar{p}_2}{n_1 + n_2} \qquad \textbf{(10.15)}$$

Test Statistic for Hypothesis Tests About $p_1 - p_2$

$$z = \frac{(\bar{p}_1 - \bar{p}_2)}{\sqrt{\bar{p}(1 - \bar{p})\left(\dfrac{1}{n_1} + \dfrac{1}{n_2}\right)}} \qquad \textbf{(10.16)}$$

Supplementary Exercises

38. Safegate Foods, Inc., is redesigning the checkout lanes in its supermarkets throughout the country and is considering two designs. Tests on customer checkout times conducted at two stores where the two new systems have been installed result in the following summary of the data.

System A	System B
$n_1 = 120$	$n_2 = 100$
$\bar{x}_1 = 4.1$ minutes	$\bar{x}_2 = 3.4$ minutes
$\sigma_1 = 2.2$ minutes	$\sigma_2 = 1.5$ minutes

Test at the .05 level of significance to determine whether the population mean checkout times of the two systems differ. Which system is preferred?

SUVLease

39. Statista reports that the average monthly lease payment for an automobile is falling in the U.S. (Statista website, June 15, 2016), but does this apply to all classes of automobiles? Suppose you are interested in whether this trend is true for sport utility vehicles (SUVs). The file *SUVLease* contains monthly lease payment data for 33 randomly selected SUVs in 2015 and 46 randomly selected SUVs in 2016.
    a. Provide and interpret a point estimate of the difference between the population mean monthly lease payments for the two years.
    b. Develop a 99% confidence interval estimate of the difference between the mean monthly lease payments in 2015 and 2016.
    c. Would you feel justified in concluding that monthly lease payments have declined from 2015 to 2016? Why or why not?

40. Mutual funds are classified as *load* or *no-load* funds. Load funds require an investor to pay an initial fee based on a percentage of the amount invested in the fund. The no-load funds do not require this initial fee. Some financial advisors argue that the load mutual funds may be worth the extra fee because these funds provide a higher mean rate of return than the no-load mutual funds. A sample of 30 load mutual funds and a sample of 30 no-load mutual funds were selected. Data were collected on the annual return for the funds over a five-year period. The data are contained in the DATAfile named *Mutual*. The data for the first five load and first five no-load mutual funds are as follows.

Mutual

Mutual Funds—Load	Return	Mutual Funds—No-Load	Return
American National Growth	15.51	Amana Income Fund	13.24
Arch Small Cap Equity	14.57	Berger One Hundred	12.13
Bartlett Cap Basic	17.73	Columbia International Stock	12.17
Calvert World International	10.31	Dodge & Cox Balanced	16.06
Colonial Fund A	16.23	Evergreen Fund	17.61

    a. Formulate H_0 and H_a such that rejection of H_0 leads to the conclusion that the load mutual funds have a higher mean annual return over the five-year period.
    b. Use the 60 mutual funds in the DATAfile named *Mutual* to conduct the hypothesis test. What is the *p*-value? At $\alpha = .05$, what is your conclusion?

41. The National Association of Home Builders provided data on the cost of the most popular home remodeling projects. Sample data on cost in thousands of dollars for two types of remodeling projects are as follows.

Kitchen	Master Bedroom	Kitchen	Master Bedroom
25.2	18.0	23.0	17.8
17.4	22.9	19.7	24.6
22.8	26.4	16.9	21.0
21.9	24.8	21.8	
19.7	26.9	23.6	

a. Develop a point estimate of the difference between the population mean remodeling costs for the two types of projects.

b. Develop a 90% confidence interval for the difference between the two population means.

42. In *Born Together—Reared Apart: The Landmark Minnesota Twin Study* (2012), Nancy Segal discusses the efforts of research psychologists at the University of Minnesota to understand similarities and differences between twins by studying sets of twins who were raised separately. Below are critical reading SAT scores for several pairs of identical twins (twins who share all of their genes) and were raised separately, one of whom was raised in a family with no other children (no siblings) and one of whom was raised in a family with other children (with siblings).

DATA *file*

Twins

No Siblings		With Siblings	
Name	**SAT Score**	**Name**	**SAT Score**
Bob	440	Donald	420
Matthew	610	Ronald	540
Shannon	590	Kedriana	630
Tyler	390	Kevin	430
Michelle	410	Erin	460
Darius	430	Michael	490
Wilhelmina	510	Josephine	460
Donna	620	Jasmine	540
Drew	510	Kraig	460
Lucinda	680	Bernadette	650
Barry	580	Larry	450
Julie	610	Jennifer	640
Hannah	510	Diedra	460
Roger	630	Latishia	580
Garrett	570	Bart	490
Roger	630	Kara	640
Nancy	530	Rachel	560
Sam	590	Joey	610
Simon	500	Drew	520
Megan	610	Annie	640

a. What is the mean difference between the critical reading SAT scores for the twins raised with no siblings and the twins raised with siblings?

b. Provide a 90% confidence interval estimate of the mean difference between the critical reading SAT scores for the twins raised with no siblings and the twins raised with siblings.

c. Conduct a hypothesis test of equality of the critical reading SAT scores for the twins raised with no siblings and the twins raised with siblings at $\alpha = .01$. What is your conclusion?

43. Country Financial, a financial services company, uses surveys of adults age 18 and older to determine whether personal financial fitness is changing over time (*USA Today*, April 4, 2012). In February 2012, a sample of 1000 adults showed 410 indicating that their financial security was more than fair. In February 2010, a sample of 900 adults showed 315 indicating that their financial security was more than fair.

a. State the hypotheses that can be used to test for a significant difference between the population proportions for the two years.

b. What is the sample proportion indicating that their financial security was more than fair in 2012? In 2010?

c. Conduct the hypothesis test and compute the *p*-value. At a .05 level of significance, what is your conclusion?

d. What is the 95% confidence interval estimate of the difference between the two population proportions?

44. A large automobile insurance company selected samples of single and married male policyholders and recorded the number who made an insurance claim over the preceding three-year period.

Single Policyholders	Married Policyholders
$n_1 = 400$	$n_2 = 900$
Number making claims = 76	Number making claims = 90

a. Use $\alpha = .05$. Test to determine whether the claim rates differ between single and married male policyholders.

b. Provide a 95% confidence interval for the difference between the proportions for the two populations.

45. Medical tests were conducted to learn about drug-resistant tuberculosis. Of 142 cases tested in New Jersey, 9 were found to be drug-resistant. Of 268 cases tested in Texas, 5 were found to be drug-resistant. Do these data suggest a statistically significant difference between the proportions of drug-resistant cases in the two states? Use a .02 level of significance. What is the *p*-value, and what is your conclusion?

ComputerNews

46. The American Press Institute reports that almost 70% of all American adults use a computer to gain access to news. Suppose you suspect that the proportion of American adults under 30 years old who use a computer to gain access to news exceeds the proportion of Americans at least 30 years old who use a computer to gain access to news. Data in the file *ComputerNews* represent responses to the question "Do you use a computer to gain access to news?" given by random samples of American adults under 30 years old and Americans who are at least 30 years old.

a. Estimate the proportion of American adults under 30 years old who use a computer to gain access to news and the proportion of Americans at least 30 years old who use a computer to gain access to news.

b. Provide a 95% confidence interval for the difference in these proportions.

c. On the basis of your findings, does it appear the proportion of American adults under 30 years old who use a computer to gain access to news exceeds the proportion of Americans who are at least 30 years old that use a computer to gain access to news?

47. For the week ended January 15, 2009, the bullish sentiment of individual investors was 27.6% (*AAII Journal,* February 2009). The bullish sentiment was reported to be 48.7% one week earlier and 39.7% one month earlier. The sentiment measures are based on a poll conducted by the American Assocation of Individual Investors. Assume that each of the bullish sentiment measures was based on a sample size of 240.

a. Develop a 95% confidence interval for the difference between the bullish sentiment measures for the most recent two weeks.

b. Develop hypotheses so that rejection of the null hypothesis will allow us to conclude that the most recent bullish sentiment is weaker than that of one month ago.

c. Conduct a hypotheses test of part (b) using $\alpha = .01$. What is your conclusion?

Case Problem Par, Inc.

Par, Inc., is a major manufacturer of golf equipment. Management believes that Par's market share could be increased with the introduction of a cut-resistant, longer-lasting golf ball. Therefore, the research group at Par has been investigating a new golf ball coating designed to resist cuts and provide a more durable ball. The tests with the coating have been promising.

One of the researchers voiced concern about the effect of the new coating on driving distances. Par would like the new cut-resistant ball to offer driving distances comparable to those of the current-model golf ball. To compare the driving distances for the two balls, 40 balls of both the new and current models were subjected to distance tests. The testing was performed with a mechanical hitting machine so that any difference between the mean distances for the two models could be attributed to a difference in the two models. The results of the tests, with distances measured to the nearest yard, follow. These data are available on the website that accompanies the text.

Golf

Model		Model		Model		Model	
Current	**New**	**Current**	**New**	**Current**	**New**	**Current**	**New**
264	277	270	272	263	274	281	283
261	269	287	259	264	266	274	250
267	263	289	264	284	262	273	253
272	266	280	280	263	271	263	260
258	262	272	274	260	260	275	270
283	251	275	281	283	281	267	263
258	262	265	276	255	250	279	261
266	289	260	269	272	263	274	255
259	286	278	268	266	278	276	263
270	264	275	262	268	264	262	279

Inferences About Population Variances

STATISTICS *in* PRACTICE

U.S. GOVERNMENT ACCOUNTABILITY OFFICE*
WASHINGTON, D.C.

The U.S. Government Accountability Office (GAO) is an independent, nonpolitical audit organization in the legislative branch of the federal government. GAO evaluators determine the effectiveness of current and proposed federal programs. To carry out their duties, evaluators must be proficient in records review, legislative research, and statistical analysis techniques.

In one case, GAO evaluators studied a Department of Interior program established to help clean up the nation's rivers and lakes. As part of this program, federal grants were made to small cities throughout the United States. Congress asked the GAO to determine how effectively the program was operating. To do so, the GAO examined records and visited the sites of several waste treatment plants.

One objective of the GAO audit was to ensure that the effluent (treated sewage) at the plants met certain standards. Among other things, the audits reviewed sample data on the oxygen content, the pH level, and the amount of suspended solids in the effluent. A requirement of the program was that a variety of tests be taken daily at each plant and that the collected data be sent periodically to the state engineering department. The GAO's investigation of the data showed whether various characteristics of the effluent were within acceptable limits.

For example, the mean or average pH level of the effluent was examined carefully. In addition, the variance in the reported pH levels was reviewed. The following hypothesis test was conducted about the variance in pH level for the population of effluent.

$$H_0: \sigma^2 = \sigma_0^2$$
$$H_a: \sigma^2 \neq \sigma_0^2$$

In this test, σ_0^2 is the population variance in pH level expected at a properly functioning plant. In one particular

Effluent at this facility must fall within a statistically determined pH range.

plant, the null hypothesis was rejected. Further analysis showed that this plant had a variance in pH level that was significantly less than normal.

The auditors visited the plant to examine the measuring equipment and to discuss their statistical findings with the plant manager. The auditors found that the measuring equipment was not being used because the operator did not know how to work it. Instead, the operator had been told by an engineer what level of pH was acceptable and had simply recorded similar values without actually conducting the test. The unusually low variance in this plant's data resulted in rejection of H_0. The GAO suspected that other plants might have similar problems and recommended an operator training program to improve the data collection aspect of the pollution control program.

In this chapter you will learn how to conduct statistical inferences about the variances of one and two populations. Two new distributions, the chi-square distribution and the F distribution, will be introduced and used to make interval estimates and hypothesis tests about population variances.

*The authors thank Mr. Art Foreman and Mr. Dale Ledman of the U.S. Government Accountability Office for providing this Statistics in Practice.

In the preceding four chapters we examined methods of statistical inference involving population means and population proportions. In this chapter we expand the discussion to situations involving inferences about population variances. As an example of a case in which a variance can provide important decision-making information, consider the production process of filling containers with a liquid detergent product. The filling mechanism for the process is adjusted so that the mean filling weight is 16 ounces per container.

Although a mean of 16 ounces is desired, the variance of the filling weights is also critical. That is, even with the filling mechanism properly adjusted for the mean of 16 ounces, we cannot expect every container to have exactly 16 ounces. By selecting a sample of containers, we can compute a sample variance for the number of ounces placed in a container. This value will serve as an estimate of the variance for the population of containers being filled by the production process. If the sample variance is modest, the production process will be continued. However, if the sample variance is excessive, overfilling and underfilling may be occurring even though the mean is correct at 16 ounces. In this case, the filling mechanism will be readjusted in an attempt to reduce the filling variance for the containers.

In many manufacturing applications, controlling the process variance is extremely important in maintaining quality.

In the first section we consider inferences about the variance of a single population. Subsequently, we will discuss procedures that can be used to make inferences about the variances of two populations.

11.1 Inferences About a Population Variance

The sample variance

$$s^2 = \frac{\sum(x_i - \bar{x})^2}{n - 1} \qquad \textbf{(11.1)}$$

is the point estimator of the population variance σ^2. In using the sample variance as a basis for making inferences about a population variance, the sampling distribution of the quantity $(n - 1)s^2/\sigma^2$ is helpful. This sampling distribution is described as follows.

The chi-square distribution is based on sampling from a normal population.

> **SAMPLING DISTRIBUTION OF $(n - 1)s^2/\sigma^2$**
>
> Whenever a random sample of size n is selected from a normal population, the sampling distribution of
>
> $$\frac{(n - 1)s^2}{\sigma^2} \qquad \textbf{(11.2)}$$
>
> has a chi-square distribution with $n - 1$ degrees of freedom.

Figure 11.1 shows some possible forms of the sampling distribution of $(n - 1)s^2/\sigma^2$.

Since the sampling distribution of $(n - 1)s^2/\sigma^2$ is known to have a chi-square distribution whenever a random sample of size n is selected from a normal population, we can use the chi-square distribution to develop interval estimates and conduct hypothesis tests about a population variance.

Interval Estimation

To show how the chi-square distribution can be used to develop a confidence interval estimate of a population variance σ^2, suppose that we are interested in estimating the population variance for the production filling process mentioned at the beginning of this chapter. A sample of 20 containers is taken, and the sample variance for the filling quantities is found to be $s^2 = .0025$. However, we know we cannot expect the variance of a sample of 20 containers to provide the exact value of the variance for the population of containers filled by the production process. Hence, our interest will be in developing an interval estimate for the population variance.

FIGURE 11.1   EXAMPLES OF THE SAMPLING DISTRIBUTION OF $(n - 1)s^2/\sigma^2$
(A CHI-SQUARE DISTRIBUTION)

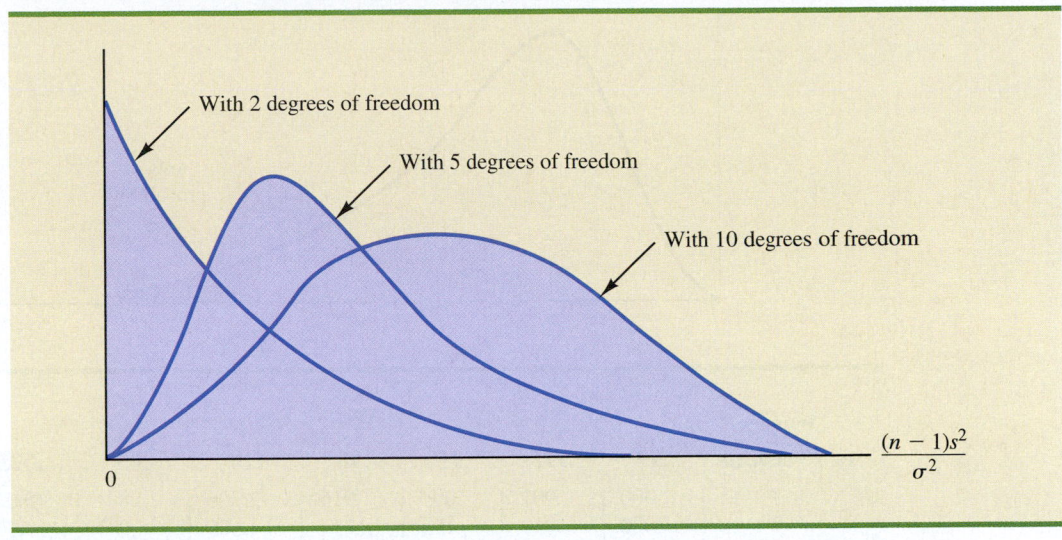

We will use the notation χ^2_α to denote the value for the chi-square distribution that pro-vides an area or probability of α to the *right* of the χ^2_α value. For example, in Figure 11.2 the chi-square distribution with 19 degrees of freedom is shown with $\chi^2_{.025} = 32.852$ indicating that 2.5% of the chi-square values are to the right of 32.852, and $\chi^2_{.975} = 8.907$ indicating that 97.5% of the chi-square values are to the right of 8.907. Tables of areas or probabilities are readily available for the chi-square distribution. Refer to Table 11.1 and verify that these chi-square values with 19 degrees of freedom (19th row of the table) are correct. Table 3 of Appendix B provides a more extensive table of chi-square values.

From the graph in Figure 11.2 we see that .95, or 95%, of the chi-square values are between $\chi^2_{.975}$ and $\chi^2_{.025}$. That is, there is a .95 probability of obtaining a χ^2 value such that

$$\chi^2_{.975} \leq \chi^2 \leq \chi^2_{.025}$$

FIGURE 11.2   A CHI-SQUARE DISTRIBUTION WITH 19 DEGREES OF FREEDOM

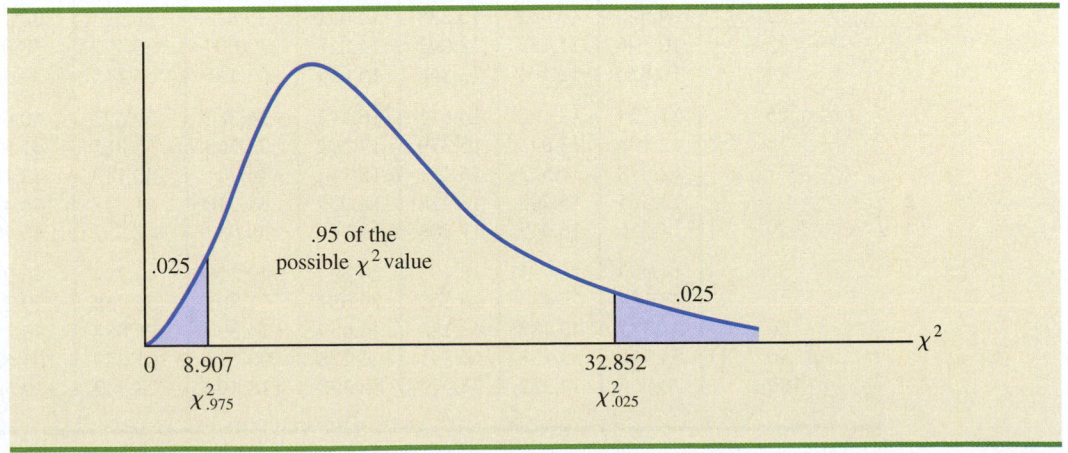

TABLE 11.1 SELECTED VALUES FROM THE CHI-SQUARE DISTRIBUTION TABLE*

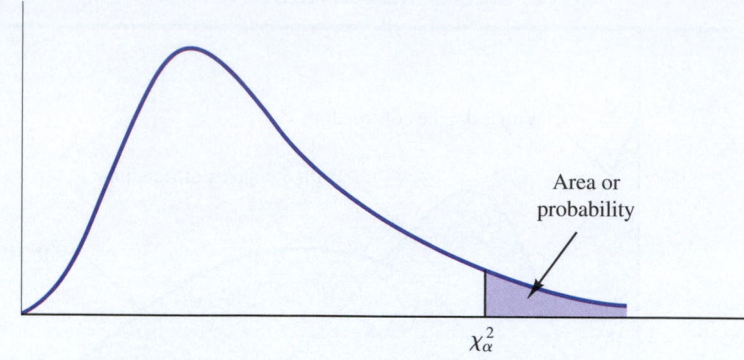

Degrees of Freedom	Area in Upper Tail							
	.99	.975	.95	.90	.10	.05	.025	.01
1	.000	.001	.004	.016	2.706	3.841	5.024	6.635
2	.020	.051	.103	.211	4.605	5.991	7.378	9.210
3	.115	.216	.352	.584	6.251	7.815	9.348	11.345
4	.297	.484	.711	1.064	7.779	9.488	11.143	13.277
5	.554	.831	1.145	1.610	9.236	11.070	12.832	15.086
6	.872	1.237	1.635	2.204	10.645	12.592	14.449	16.812
7	1.239	1.690	2.167	2.833	12.017	14.067	16.013	18.475
8	1.647	2.180	2.733	3.490	13.362	15.507	17.535	20.090
9	2.088	2.700	3.325	4.168	14.684	16.919	19.023	21.666
10	2.558	3.247	3.940	4.865	15.987	18.307	20.483	23.209
11	3.053	3.816	4.575	5.578	17.275	19.675	21.920	24.725
12	3.571	4.404	5.226	6.304	18.549	21.026	23.337	26.217
13	4.107	5.009	5.892	7.041	19.812	22.362	24.736	27.688
14	4.660	5.629	6.571	7.790	21.064	23.685	26.119	29.141
15	5.229	6.262	7.261	8.547	22.307	24.996	27.488	30.578
16	5.812	6.908	7.962	9.312	23.542	26.296	28.845	32.000
17	6.408	7.564	8.672	10.085	24.769	27.587	30.191	33.409
18	7.015	8.231	9.390	10.865	25.989	28.869	31.526	34.805
19	7.633	8.907	10.117	11.651	27.204	30.144	32.852	36.191
20	8.260	9.591	10.851	12.443	28.412	31.410	34.170	37.566
21	8.897	10.283	11.591	13.240	29.615	32.671	35.479	38.932
22	9.542	10.982	12.338	14.041	30.813	33.924	36.781	40.289
23	10.196	11.689	13.091	14.848	32.007	35.172	38.076	41.638
24	10.856	12.401	13.848	15.659	33.196	36.415	39.364	42.980
25	11.524	13.120	14.611	16.473	34.382	37.652	40.646	44.314
26	12.198	13.844	15.379	17.292	35.563	38.885	41.923	45.642
27	12.878	14.573	16.151	18.114	36.741	40.113	43.195	46.963
28	13.565	15.308	16.928	18.939	37.916	41.337	44.461	48.278
29	14.256	16.047	17.708	19.768	39.087	42.557	45.722	49.588
30	14.953	16.791	18.493	20.599	40.256	43.773	46.979	50.892
40	22.164	24.433	26.509	29.051	51.805	55.758	59.342	63.691
60	37.485	40.482	43.188	46.459	74.397	79.082	83.298	88.379
80	53.540	57.153	60.391	64.278	96.578	101.879	106.629	112.329
100	70.065	74.222	77.929	82.358	118.498	124.342	129.561	135.807

*Note: A more extensive table is provided as Table 3 of Appendix B.

We stated in expression (11.2) that $(n - 1)s^2/\sigma^2$ follows a chi-square distribution; therefore we can substitute $(n - 1)s^2/\sigma^2$ for χ^2 and write

$$\chi^2_{.975} \leq \frac{(n - 1)s^2}{\sigma^2} \leq \chi^2_{.025} \tag{11.3}$$

In effect, expression (11.3) provides an interval estimate in that .95, or 95%, of all possible values for $(n - 1)s^2/\sigma^2$ will be in the interval $\chi^2_{.975}$ to $\chi^2_{.025}$. We now need to do some algebraic manipulations with expression (11.3) to develop an interval estimate for the population variance σ^2. Working with the leftmost inequality in expression (11.3), we have

$$\chi^2_{.975} \leq \frac{(n - 1)s^2}{\sigma^2}$$

Thus

$$\sigma^2\chi^2_{.975} \leq (n - 1)s^2$$

or

$$\sigma^2 \leq \frac{(n - 1)s^2}{\chi^2_{.975}} \tag{11.4}$$

Performing similar algebraic manipulations with the rightmost inequality in expression (11.3) gives

$$\frac{(n - 1)s^2}{\chi^2_{.025}} \leq \sigma^2 \tag{11.5}$$

The results of expressions (11.4) and (11.5) can be combined to provide

$$\frac{(n - 1)s^2}{\chi^2_{.025}} \leq \sigma^2 \leq \frac{(n - 1)s^2}{\chi^2_{.975}} \tag{11.6}$$

Because expression (11.3) is true for 95% of the $(n - 1)s^2/\sigma^2$ values, expression (11.6) provides a 95% confidence interval estimate for the population variance σ^2.

    Let us return to the problem of providing an interval estimate for the population variance of filling quantities. Recall that the sample of 20 containers provided a sample variance of $s^2 = .0025$. With a sample size of 20, we have 19 degrees of freedom. As shown in Figure 11.2, we have already determined that $\chi^2_{.975} = 8.907$ and $\chi^2_{.025} = 32.852$. Using these values in expression (11.6) provides the following interval estimate for the population variance.

$$\frac{(19)(.0025)}{32.852} \leq \sigma^2 \leq \frac{(19)(.0025)}{8.907}$$

or

A confidence interval for a population standard deviation can be found by computing the square roots of the lower limit and upper limit of the confidence interval for the population variance.

$$.0014 \leq \sigma^2 \leq .0053$$

Taking the square root of these values provides the following 95% confidence interval for the population standard deviation.

$$.0380 \leq \sigma \leq .0730$$

Thus, we illustrated the process of using the chi-square distribution to establish interval estimates of a population variance and a population standard deviation. Note specifically that because $\chi^2_{.975}$ and $\chi^2_{.025}$ were used, the interval estimate has a .95 confidence coefficient. Extending expression (11.6) to the general case of any confidence coefficient, we have the following interval estimate of a population variance.

INTERVAL ESTIMATE OF A POPULATION VARIANCE

$$\frac{(n-1)s^2}{\chi^2_{\alpha/2}} \leq \sigma^2 \leq \frac{(n-1)s^2}{\chi^2_{(1-\alpha/2)}} \qquad \textbf{(11.7)}$$

where the χ^2 values are based on a chi-square distribution with $n-1$ degrees of freedom and where $1-\alpha$ is the confidence coefficient.

Using Excel to Construct a Confidence Interval

Excel can be used to construct a 95% confidence interval of the population variance for the example involving filling containers with a liquid detergent product. Refer to Figure 11.3 as we describe the tasks involved. The formula worksheet is in the background; the value worksheet is in the foreground.

DATA *file*

Detergent

Enter/Access Data: Open the DATAfile named *Detergent*. Column A shows the number of ounces of detergent for each of the 20 containers.

Enter Functions and Formulas: The descriptive statistics needed are provided in cells D3:D4. Excel's COUNT and VAR.S functions are used to compute the sample size and the sample variance, respectively.

Cells D6:D9 are used to compute the appropriate chi-square values. The confidence coefficient was entered into cell D6 and the level of significance (α) was computed in

FIGURE 11.3   EXCEL WORKSHEET FOR THE LIQUID DETERGENT FILLING PROCESS

	A	B	C	D	E
1	**Ounces**		**Interval Estimate of a Population Variance**		
2	15.92				
3	16.02		Sample Size	=COUNT(A2:A21)	
4	15.99		Variance	=VAR.S(A2:A21)	
5	16.02				
6	15.91		Confidence Coefficient	0.95	
7	15.98		Level of Significance (alpha)	=1-D6	
8	16.06		Chi-Square Value (lower tail)	=CHISQ.INV(D7/2,D3-1)	
9	15.97		Chi-Square Value (upper tail)	=CHISQ.INV.RT(D7/2,D3-1)	
10	15.97				
11	16.07		Point Estimate	=D4	
12	15.94		Lower Limit	=((D3-1)*D4)/D9	
13	15.96		Upper Limit	=((D3-1)*D4)/D8	
14	16.04				
15	16.01				
16	16.07				
17	16.01				
18	15.9				
19	15.96				
20	16				
21	15.99				
22					

	A	B	C	D	E
1	**Ounces**		**Interval Estimate of a Population Variance**		
2	15.92				
3	16.02		Sample Size	20	
4	15.99		Variance	0.0025	
5	16.02				
6	15.91		Confidence Coefficient	0.95	
7	15.98		Level of Significance (alpha)	0.05	
8	16.06		Chi-Square Value (lower tail)	8.9065	
9	15.97		Chi-Square Value (upper tail)	32.8523	
10	15.97				
11	16.07		Point Estimate	0.0025	
12	15.94		Lower Limit	0.0014	
13	15.96		Upper Limit	0.0053	
14	16.04				
15	16.01				
16	16.07				
17	16.01				
18	15.90				
19	15.96				
20	16.00				
21	15.99				
22					

cell D7 by entering the formula =1-D6. Excel's CHISQ.INV function was used to compute the lower tail chi-square value. The form of the CHISQ.INV function is CHISQ.INV(lower tail probability, degrees of freedom). The formula =CHISQ.INV(D7/2,D3-1) was entered into cell D8 to compute the chi-square value in the lower tail. The value worksheet shows that the chi-square value for 19 degrees of freedom is $\chi^2_{.975} = 8.9065$. Then, to compute the chi-square value corresponding to an upper tail probability of .025, the function =CHISQ.INV.RT(D7/2,D3-1) was entered into cell D9. The value worksheet shows that the chi-square value obtained is $\chi^2_{.025} = 32.8523$.

Cells D11:D13 provide the point estimate and the lower and upper limits for the confidence interval. Because the point estimate is just the sample variance, we entered the formula =D4 into cell D11. Inequality (11.7) shows that the lower limit of the 95% confidence interval is

$$\frac{(n-1)s^2}{\chi^2_{\alpha/2}} = \frac{(n-1)s^2}{\chi^2_{.025}}$$

Thus, to compute the lower limit of the 95% confidence interval, the formula =((D3-1)*D4)/D9 was entered into cell D12. Inequality (11.7) also shows that the upper limit of the confidence interval is

$$\frac{(n-1)s^2}{\chi^2_{(1-\alpha/2)}} = \frac{(n-1)s^2}{\chi^2_{.975}}$$

Thus, to compute the upper limit of the 95% confidence interval, the formula =((D3-1)*D4)/D8 was entered into cell D13. The value worksheet shows a lower limit of .0014 and an upper limit of .0053. In other words, the 95% confidence interval estimate of the population variance is from .0014 to .0053.

Hypothesis Testing

Using σ_0^2 to denote the hypothesized value for the population variance, the three forms for a hypothesis test about a population variance are as follows:

$$H_0: \sigma^2 \geq \sigma_0^2 \qquad H_0: \sigma^2 \leq \sigma_0^2 \qquad H_0: \sigma^2 = \sigma_0^2$$
$$H_a: \sigma^2 < \sigma_0^2 \qquad H_a: \sigma^2 > \sigma_0^2 \qquad H_a: \sigma^2 \neq \sigma_0^2$$

These three forms are similar to the three forms that we used to conduct one-tailed and two-tailed hypothesis tests about population means and proportions in Chapters 9 and 10.

The procedure for conducting a hypothesis test about a population variance uses the hypothesized value for the population variance σ_0^2 and the sample variance s^2 to compute the value of a χ^2 test statistic. Assuming that the population has a normal distribution, the test statistic is as follows.

TEST STATISTIC FOR HYPOTHESIS TESTS ABOUT A POPULATION VARIANCE

$$\chi^2 = \frac{(n-1)s^2}{\sigma_0^2} \qquad\qquad \textbf{(11.8)}$$

where χ^2 has a chi-square distribution with $n-1$ degrees of freedom.

After computing the value of the χ^2 test statistic, either the p-value approach or the critical value approach may be used to determine whether the null hypothesis can be rejected.

Let us consider the following example. The St. Louis Metro Bus Company wants to promote an image of reliability by encouraging its drivers to maintain consistent schedules. As a standard policy the company would like arrival times at bus stops to have low variability. In terms of the variance of arrival times, the company standard specifies an arrival time variance of 4 or less when arrival times are measured in minutes. The following hypothesis test is formulated to help the company determine whether the arrival time population variance is excessive.

$$H_0: \sigma^2 \leq 4$$
$$H_a: \sigma^2 > 4$$

In tentatively assuming H_0 is true, we are assuming that the population variance of arrival times is within the company guideline. We reject H_0 if the sample evidence indicates that the population variance exceeds the guideline. In this case, follow-up steps should be taken to reduce the population variance. We conduct the hypothesis test using a level of significance of $\alpha = .05$.

DATA file

BusTimes

Suppose that a random sample of 24 bus arrivals taken at a downtown intersection provides a sample variance of $s^2 = 4.9$. Assuming that the population distribution of arrival times is approximately normal, the value of the test statistic is as follows:

$$\chi^2 = \frac{(n-1)s^2}{\sigma_0^2} = \frac{(24-1)(4.9)}{4} = 28.18$$

The chi-square distribution with $n - 1 = 24 - 1 = 23$ degrees of freedom is shown in Figure 11.4. Because this is an upper tail test, the area under the curve to the right of the test statistic $\chi^2 = 28.18$ is the p-value for the test.

Like the t distribution table, the chi-square distribution table does not contain sufficient detail to enable us to determine the p-value exactly. However, we can use the chi-square distribution table to obtain a range for the p-value. For example, using Table 11.1, we find the following information for a chi-square distribution with 23 degrees of freedom.

Area in Upper Tail	.10	.05	.025	.01
χ^2 **Value (23 df)**	32.007	35.172	38.076	41.638

$\chi^2 = 28.18$

Using Excel, p-value = CHISQ.DIST.RT (28.18,23) = .2091.

Because $\chi^2 = 28.18$ is less than 32.007, the area in the upper tail (the p-value) is greater than .10. With the p-value $> \alpha = .05$, we cannot reject the null hypothesis. The sample does not support the conclusion that the population variance of the arrival times is excessive.

FIGURE 11.4 CHI-SQUARE DISTRIBUTION FOR THE ST. LOUIS METRO BUS EXAMPLE

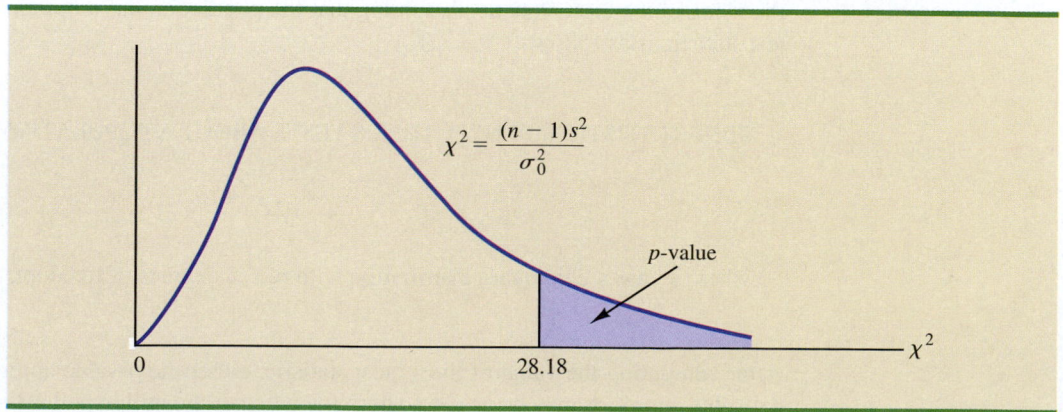

As with other hypothesis testing procedures, the critical value approach can also be used to draw the hypothesis testing conclusion. With $\alpha = .05$, $\chi^2_{.05}$ provides the critical value for the upper tail hypothesis test. Using Table 11.1 and 23 degrees of freedom, $\chi^2_{.05} = 35.172$. Thus, the rejection rule for the bus arrival time example is as follows:

$$\text{Reject } H_0 \text{ if } \chi^2 \geq 35.172$$

Because the value of the test statistic is $\chi^2 = 28.18$, we cannot reject the null hypothesis.

In practice, upper tail tests as presented here are the most frequently encountered tests about a population variance. In situations involving arrival times, production times, filling weights, part dimensions, and so on, low variances are desirable, whereas large variances are unacceptable. With a statement about the maximum allowable population variance, we can test the null hypothesis that the population variance is less than or equal to the maximum allowable value against the alternative hypothesis that the population variance is greater than the maximum allowable value. With this test structure, corrective action will be taken whenever rejection of the null hypothesis indicates the presence of an excessive population variance.

As we saw with population means and proportions, other forms of hypothesis tests can be developed. Let us demonstrate a two-tailed test about a population variance by considering a situation faced by a bureau of motor vehicles. Historically, the variance in test scores for individuals applying for driver's licenses has been $\sigma^2 = 100$. A new examination with new test questions has been developed. Administrators of the bureau of motor vehicles would like the variance in the test scores for the new examination to remain at the historical level. To evaluate the variance in the new examination test scores, the following two-tailed hypothesis test has been proposed.

$$H_0: \sigma^2 = 100$$
$$H_a: \sigma^2 \neq 100$$

Rejection of H_0 will indicate that a change in the variance has occurred and suggest that some questions in the new examination may need revision to make the variance of the new test scores similar to the variance of the old test scores. A sample of 30 applicants for driver's licenses will be given the new version of the examination. We will use a level of significance $\alpha = .05$ to conduct the hypothesis test.

The sample of 30 examination scores provided a sample variance $s^2 = 162$. The value of the chi-square test statistic is as follows:

$$\chi^2 = \frac{(n-1)s^2}{\sigma^2_0} = \frac{(30-1)(162)}{100} = 46.98$$

Now, let us compute the p-value. Using Table 11.1 and $n - 1 = 30 - 1 = 29$ degrees of freedom, we find the following:

Area in Upper Tail	.10	.05	.025	.01
χ^2 **Value (29 *df*)**	39.087	42.557	45.722	49.588

$$\chi^2 = 46.98$$

Using Excel, p-value = 2*CHISQ.DIST.RT (46.98,29) = .0374.

Thus, the value of the test statistic $\chi^2 = 46.98$ provides an area between .025 and .01 in the upper tail of the chi-square distribution. Doubling these values shows that the two-tailed p-value is between .05 and .02. Excel can be used to show that $\chi^2 = 46.98$ provides a

TABLE 11.2 SUMMARY OF HYPOTHESIS TESTS ABOUT A POPULATION VARIANCE

	Lower Tail Test	Upper Tail Test	Two-Tailed Test
Hypotheses	$H_0: \sigma^2 \geq \sigma_0^2$ $H_a: \sigma^2 < \sigma_0^2$	$H_0: \sigma^2 \leq \sigma_0^2$ $H_a: \sigma^2 > \sigma_0^2$	$H_0: \sigma^2 = \sigma_0^2$ $H_a: \sigma^2 \neq \sigma_0^2$
Test Statistic	$\chi^2 = \frac{(n-1)s^2}{\sigma_0^2}$	$\chi^2 = \frac{(n-1)s^2}{\sigma_0^2}$	$\chi^2 = \frac{(n-1)s^2}{\sigma_0^2}$
Rejection Rule: *p*-Value Approach	Reject H_0 if p-value $\leq \alpha$	Reject H_0 if p-value $\leq \alpha$	Reject H_0 if p-value $\leq \alpha$
Rejection Rule: Critical Value Approach	Reject H_0 if $\chi^2 \leq \chi^2_{(1-\alpha)}$	Reject H_0 if $\chi^2 \geq \chi^2_{\alpha}$	Reject H_0 if $\chi^2 \leq \chi^2_{(1-\alpha/2)}$ or if $\chi^2 \geq \chi^2_{\alpha/2}$

p-value $= .0374$. With p-value $\leq \alpha = .05$, we reject H_0 and conclude that the new examination test scores have a population variance different from the historical variance of $\sigma^2 = 100$. A summary of the hypothesis testing procedures for a population variance is shown in Table 11.2.

Using Excel to Conduct a Hypothesis Test

In Chapters 9 and 10 we used Excel to conduct a variety of hypothesis tests. The procedure was general in that, once the test statistic was computed, three p-values were obtained: a p-value (Lower Tail), a p-value (Upper Tail), and a p-value (Two Tail). Then, depending on the form of the hypothesis test, the appropriate p-value was used to make the rejection decision. We will now adapt that approach and use Excel to conduct a hypothesis test about a population variance. The St. Louis Metro Bus example will serve as an illustration. Refer to Figure 11.5 as we describe the tasks involved. The formula worksheet is in the background; the value worksheet is in the foreground.

FIGURE 11.5 HYPOTHESIS TEST FOR VARIANCE IN BUS ARRIVAL TIMES

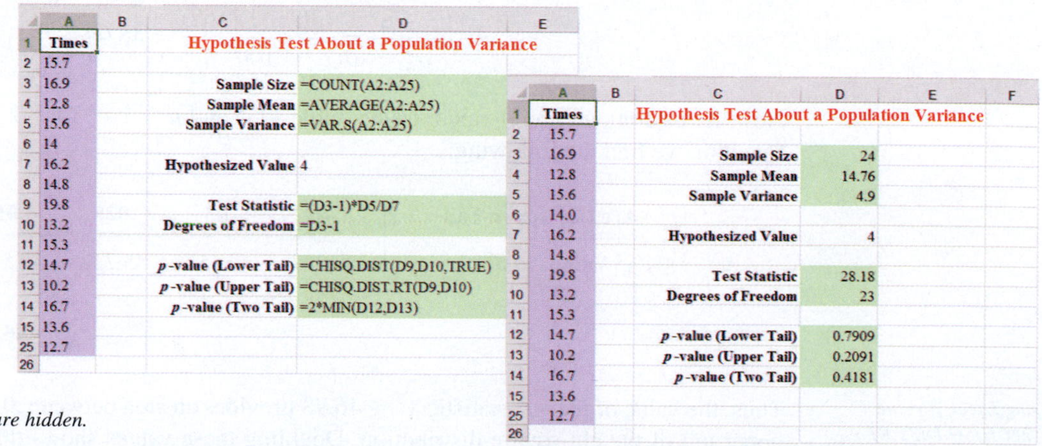

	A	B	C	D	E
1	Times		Hypothesis Test About a Population Variance		
2	15.7				
3	16.9		Sample Size	=COUNT(A2:A25)	
4	12.8		Sample Mean	=AVERAGE(A2:A25)	
5	15.6		Sample Variance	=VAR.S(A2:A25)	
6	14				
7	16.2		Hypothesized Value	4	
8	14.8				
9	19.8		Test Statistic	=(D3-1)*D5/D7	
10	13.2		Degrees of Freedom	=D3-1	
11	15.3				
12	14.7		p-value (Lower Tail)	=CHISQ.DIST(D9,D10,TRUE)	
13	10.2		p-value (Upper Tail)	=CHISQ.DIST.RT(D9,D10)	
14	16.7		p-value (Two Tail)	=2*MIN(D12,D13)	
15	13.6				
25	12.7				
26					

	A	B	C	D	E	F
1	Times		Hypothesis Test About a Population Variance			
2	15.7					
3	16.9		Sample Size	24		
4	12.8		Sample Mean	14.76		
5	15.6		Sample Variance	4.9		
6	14.0					
7	16.2		Hypothesized Value	4		
8	14.8					
9	19.8		Test Statistic	28.18		
10	13.2		Degrees of Freedom	23		
11	15.3					
12	14.7		p-value (Lower Tail)	0.7909		
13	10.2		p-value (Upper Tail)	0.2091		
14	16.7		p-value (Two Tail)	0.4181		
15	13.6					
25	12.7					
26						

Note: Rows 16–24 are hidden.

BusTimes

Enter/Access Data: Open the DATAfile named *BusTimes*. The 24 arrival times in number of minutes past 12:00 noon have been entered into column A.

Enter Functions and Formulas: The descriptive statistics we need are provided in cells D3:D5. Excel's COUNT function has been used to compute the sample size and Excel's AVERAGE and VAR.S functions have been used to compute the sample mean and sample variance. The value worksheet shows $n = 24$, $\bar{x} = 14.76$, and $s^2 = 4.9$.

The hypothesized value of the population variance, $\sigma_0^2 = 4$, was entered into cell D7. The formula =(D3-1)*D5/D7 was entered into cell D9 to compute the χ^2 test statistic (28.18), and the formula =D3-1 was entered into cell D10 to compute the degrees of freedom associated with the test statistic.

The lower and upper tail *p*-values are computed in cells D12 and D13. The CHISQ.DIST function is used to compute the lower tail *p*-value in cell D12. To compute the *p*-value for a one-tailed hypothesis test in which the rejection region is in the lower tail, we entered the formula =CHISQ.DIST(D9,D10,TRUE) into cell D12. The CHISQ.DIST.RT function is used to compute the upper tail *p*-value in cell D13. To compute the *p*-value for a one-tailed hypothesis test in which the rejection region is in the upper tail, we entered the formula =CHISQ.DIST.RT(D9,D10) into cell D13. Finally, to compute the *p*-value for a two-tailed test, we entered the function =2*MIN(D12,D13) into cell D14. The value worksheet shows that *p*-value (Lower Tail) = .7909, *p*-value (Upper Tail) = .2091, and *p*-value (Two Tail) = .4181. The rejection region for the St. Louis Metro Bus example is in the upper tail; thus, the appropriate *p*-value is .2091. At a .05 level of significance, we cannot reject H_0 because .2091 > .05. Hence, the sample variance of $s^2 = 4.9$ is insufficient evidence to conclude that the arrival time variance is not meeting the company standard.

To avoid having to revise the cell ranges for functions in cells D3:D5, the A:A method of specifying cell ranges can be used.

This worksheet can be used as a template for other hypothesis tests about a population variance. Enter the data in column A, revise the ranges for the functions in cells D3:D5 as appropriate for the data, and type the hypothesized value σ_0^2 in cell D7. The *p*-value appropriate for the test can then be selected from cells D12:D14. The worksheet can also be used for exercises in which the sample size, sample variance, and hypothesized value are given. For instance, in the previous subsection we conducted a two-tailed hypothesis test about the variance in scores on a new examination given by the bureau of motor vehicles. The sample size was 30, the sample variance was $s^2 = 162$, and the hypothesized value for the population variance was $\sigma_0^2 = 100$. Using the worksheet in Figure 11.5, we can type 30 into cell D3, 162 into cell D5, and 100 into cell D7. The correct two-tailed *p*-value will then be given in cell D14. Try it. You should get a *p*-value of .0374.

Exercises

Methods

1. Find the following chi-square distribution values from Table 11.1 or Table 3 of Appendix B.
    a. $\chi_{.05}^2$ with $df = 5$
    b. $\chi_{.025}^2$ with $df = 15$
    c. $\chi_{.975}^2$ with $df = 20$
    d. $\chi_{.01}^2$ with $df = 10$
    e. $\chi_{.95}^2$ with $df = 18$

2. A sample of 20 items provides a sample standard deviation of 5.
    a. Compute the 90% confidence interval estimate of the population variance.
    b. Compute the 95% confidence interval estimate of the population variance.
    c. Compute the 95% confidence interval estimate of the population standard deviation.

3. A sample of 16 items provides a sample standard deviation of 9.5. Test the following hypotheses using $\alpha = .05$. What is your conclusion? Use both the p-value approach and the critical value approach.

$$H_0: \sigma^2 \leq 50$$
$$H_a: \sigma^2 > 50$$

Applications

4. The variance in drug weights is critical in the pharmaceutical industry. For a specific drug, with weights measured in grams, a sample of 18 units provided a sample variance of $s^2 = .36$.
    a. Construct a 90% confidence interval estimate of the population variance for the weight of this drug.
    b. Construct a 90% confidence interval estimate of the population standard deviation.

5. John Calipari, head basketball coach for the 2012 national champion University of Kentucky Wildcats, is the highest paid coach in college basketball, with an annual salary of $5.4 million (*USA Today,* March 29, 2012). The following sample shows the head basketball coach's salary for a sample of 10 schools playing NCAA Division I basketball. Salary data are in millions of dollars.

University	Coach's Salary	University	Coach's Salary
Indiana	2.2	Syracuse	1.5
Xavier	.5	Murray State	.2
Texas	2.4	Florida State	1.5
Connecticut	2.7	South Dakota State	.1
West Virginia	2.0	Vermont	.2

a. Use the sample mean for the 10 schools to estimate the population mean annual salary for head basketball coaches at colleges and universities playing NCAA Division I basketball.
b. Use the data to estimate the population standard deviation for the annual salary for head basketball coaches.
c. What is the 95% confidence interval for the population variance?
d. What is the 95% confidence interval for the population standard deviation?

Halloween

6. The *Wall Street Journal* reported that Americans spend nearly $7 billion on Halloween costumes and decorations. Sample data showing the amount, in dollars, that 16 adults spent on a Halloween costume are as follows.

12	69	22	64
33	36	31	44
52	16	13	98
45	32	63	26

a. What is the estimate of the population mean amount adults spend on a Halloween costume?
b. What is the sample standard deviation?
c. Provide a 95% confidence interval estimate of the population standard deviation for the amount adults spend on a Halloween costume?

7. To analyze the risk, or volatility, associated with investing in General Electric common stock, a sample of the eight quarterly percent total returns was identified as shown below (Charles Schwab website, January 2012). The percent total return includes the stock price change plus the dividend payment for the quarter.

    20.0   −20.5   12.2   12.6   10.5   −5.8   −18.7   15.3

    a. What is the value of the sample mean? What is its interpretation?
    b. Compute the sample variance and sample standard deviation as measures of volatility for the quarterly return for General Electric?
    c. Construct a 95% confidence interval for the population variance?
    d. Construct a 95% confidence interval for the population standard deviation?

8. Consider a day when the Dow Jones Industrial Average went up 149.82 points. The following table shows the stock price changes for a sample of 12 companies on that day.

PriceChange

Company	Price Change ($)	Company	Price Change ($)
Aflac	0.81	John.&John.	1.46
Bank of Am.	−0.05	Loews Cp	0.92
Cablevision	0.41	Nokia	0.21
Diageo	1.32	SmpraEngy	0.97
Flour Cp	2.37	Sunoco	0.52
Goodrich	0.3	Tyson Food	0.12

    a. Compute the sample variance for the daily price change.
    b. Compute the sample standard deviation for the price change.
    c. Provide 95% confidence interval estimates of the population variance and the population standard deviation.

9. An automotive part must be machined to close tolerances to be acceptable to customers. Production specifications call for a maximum variance in the lengths of the parts of .0004. Suppose the sample variance for 30 parts turns out to be $s^2 = .0005$. Use $\alpha = .05$ to test whether the population variance specification is being violated.

Costco

10. *Consumer Reports* uses a 100-point customer satisfaction score to rate the nation's major chain stores. Assume that from past experience with the satisfaction rating score, a population standard deviation of $\sigma = 12$ is expected. In 2012, Costco with its 432 warehouses in 40 states was the only chain store to earn an outstanding rating for overall quality. A sample of 15 Costco customer satisfaction scores follows.

95	90	83	75	95
98	80	83	82	93
86	80	94	64	62

    a. What is the sample mean customer satisfaction score for Costco?
    b. What is the sample variance?
    c. What is the sample standard deviation?
    d. Construct a hypothesis test to determine whether the population standard deviation of $\sigma = 12$ should be rejected for Costco. With a .05 level of significance, what is your conclusion?

EconGMAT

11. The variance in GMAT exam scores is 14,660 (the Graduate Management Admission Council's official website of the GMAT, June 17, 2016). A group of economics

professors recently met at a conference to discuss the performance on the GMAT of undergraduate students majoring in economics. Some expected the variability in GMAT scores achieved by undergraduate students majoring in economics to be greater than the variability in GMAT scores of the general population of GMAT test takers. Others took the opposite view. The DATAfile *EconGMAT* contains GMAT scores for 51 randomly selected undergraduate students majoring in economics.

   a. Compute the mean, variance, and standard deviation of the GMAT scores for the 51 randomly selected undergraduate students majoring in economics.

   b. Develop hypotheses to test whether the sample data indicate that the variance in GMAT scores for undergraduate students majoring in economics differs from the general population of GMAT test takers.

   c. Use $\alpha = .05$ to conduct the hypothesis test formulated in part (b). What is your conclusion?

12. A *Fortune* study found that the variance in the number of vehicles owned or leased by subscribers to *Fortune* magazine is .94. Assume a sample of 12 subscribers to another magazine provided the following data on the number of vehicles owned or leased: 2, 1, 2, 0, 3, 2, 2, 1, 2, 1, 0, and 1.

   a. Compute the sample variance in the number of vehicles owned or leased by the 12 subscribers.

   b. Test the hypothesis H_0: $\sigma^2 = .94$ to determine whether the variance in the number of vehicles owned or leased by subscribers of the other magazine differs from $\sigma^2 = .94$ for *Fortune*. At a .05 level of significance, what is your conclusion?

11.2 Inferences About Two Population Variances

In some statistical applications we may want to compare the variances in product quality resulting from two different production processes, the variances in assembly times for two assembly methods, or the variances in temperatures for two heating devices. In making comparisons about the two population variances, we will be using data collected from two independent random samples, one from population 1 and another from population 2. The two sample variances s_1^2 and s_2^2 will be the basis for making inferences about the two population variances σ_1^2 and σ_2^2. Whenever the variances of two normal populations are equal ($\sigma_1^2 = \sigma_2^2$), the sampling distribution of the ratio of the two sample variances s_1^2/s_2^2 is as follows.

SAMPLING DISTRIBUTION OF s_1^2/s_2^2 WHEN $\sigma_1^2 = \sigma_2^2$

Whenever independent random samples of sizes n_1 and n_2 are selected from two normal populations with equal variances, the sampling distribution of

$$\frac{s_1^2}{s_2^2} \tag{11.9}$$

The F distribution is based on sampling from two normal populations.

has an *F* distribution with $n_1 - 1$ degrees of freedom for the numerator and $n_2 - 1$ degrees of freedom for the denominator; s_1^2 is the sample variance for the random sample of n_1 items from population 1, and s_2^2 is the sample variance for the random sample of n_2 items from population 2.

Figure 11.6 is a graph of the *F* distribution with 20 degrees of freedom for both the numerator and denominator. As indicated by this graph, the *F* distribution is not symmetric, and the *F* values can never be negative. The shape of any particular *F* distribution depends on its numerator and denominator degrees of freedom.

FIGURE 11.6   *F* DISTRIBUTION WITH 20 DEGREES OF FREEDOM FOR THE NUMERATOR AND 20 DEGREES OF FREEDOM FOR THE DENOMINATOR

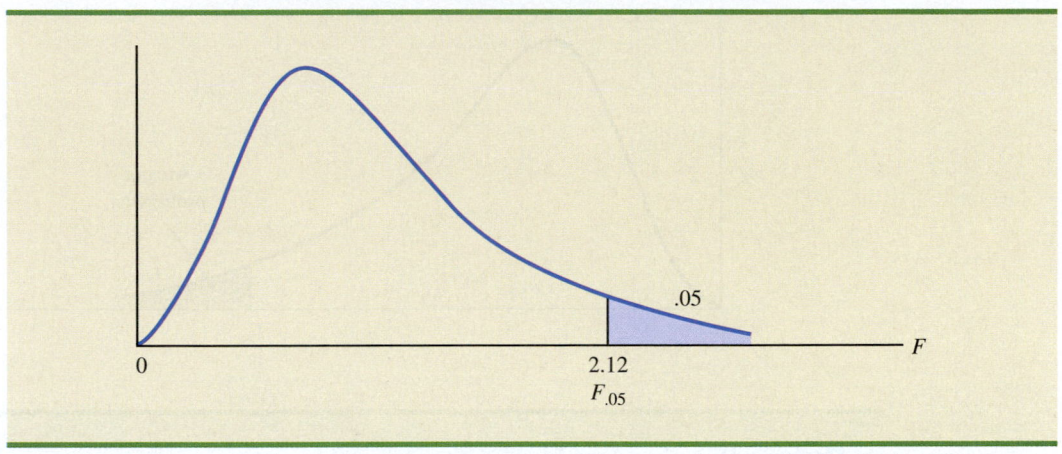

We will use F_α to denote the value of F that provides an area or probability of α in the upper tail of the distribution. For example, as noted in Figure 11.6, $F_{.05}$ denotes the upper tail area of .05 for an F distribution with 20 degrees of freedom for the numerator and 20 degrees of freedom for the denominator. The specific value of $F_{.05}$ can be found by referring to the F distribution table, a portion of which is shown in Table 11.3. Using 20 degrees of freedom for the numerator, 20 degrees of freedom for the denominator, and the row corresponding to an area of .05 in the upper tail, we find $F_{.05} = 2.12$. Note that the table can be used to find F values for upper tail areas of .10, .05, .025, and .01. See Table 4 of Appendix B for a more extensive table for the F distribution.

Let us show how the F distribution can be used to conduct a hypothesis test about the variances of two populations. We begin with a test of the equality of two population variances. The hypotheses are stated as follows.

$$H_0: \sigma_1^2 = \sigma_2^2$$
$$H_a: \sigma_1^2 \neq \sigma_2^2$$

We make the tentative assumption that the population variances are equal. If H_0 is rejected, we will draw the conclusion that the population variances are not equal.

The procedure used to conduct the hypothesis test requires two independent random samples, one from each population. The two sample variances are then computed. We refer to the population providing the *larger* sample variance as population 1. Thus, a sample size of n_1 and a sample variance of s_1^2 correspond to population 1, and a sample size of n_2 and a sample variance of s_2^2 correspond to population 2. Based on the assumption that both populations have a normal distribution, the ratio of sample variances provides the following F test statistic.

TEST STATISTIC FOR HYPOTHESIS TESTS ABOUT POPULATION VARIANCES WITH $\sigma_1^2 = \sigma_2^2$

$$F = \frac{s_1^2}{s_2^2} \qquad (11.10)$$

Denoting the population with the larger sample variance as population 1, the test statistic has an F distribution with $n_1 - 1$ degrees of freedom for the numerator and $n_2 - 1$ degrees of freedom for the denominator.

TABLE 11.3 SELECTED VALUES FROM THE *F* DISTRIBUTION TABLE*

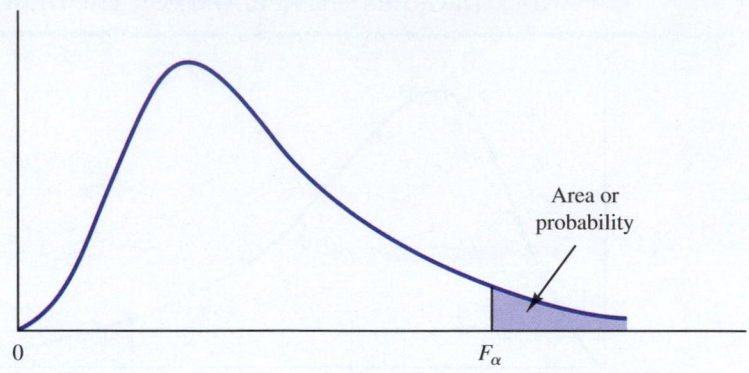

Denominator Degrees of Freedom	Area in Upper Tail	Numerator Degrees of Freedom				
		10	15	20	25	30
10	.10	2.32	2.24	2.20	2.17	2.16
	.05	2.98	2.85	2.77	2.73	2.70
	.025	3.72	3.52	3.42	3.35	3.31
	.01	4.85	4.56	4.41	4.31	4.25
15	.10	2.06	1.97	1.92	1.89	1.87
	.05	2.54	2.40	2.33	2.28	2.25
	.025	3.06	2.86	2.76	2.69	2.64
	.01	3.80	3.52	3.37	3.28	3.21
20	.10	1.94	1.84	1.79	1.76	1.74
	.05	2.35	2.20	2.12	2.07	2.04
	.025	2.77	2.57	2.46	2.40	2.35
	.01	3.37	3.09	2.94	2.84	2.78
25	.10	1.87	1.77	1.72	1.68	1.66
	.05	2.24	2.09	2.01	1.96	1.92
	.025	2.61	2.41	2.30	2.23	2.18
	.01	3.13	2.85	2.70	2.60	2.54
30	.10	1.82	1.72	1.67	1.63	1.61
	.05	2.16	2.01	1.93	1.88	1.84
	.025	2.51	2.31	2.20	2.12	2.07
	.01	2.98	2.70	2.55	2.45	2.39

Note: A more extensive table is provided as Table 4 of Appendix B.

We always denote the population with the larger sample variance as population 1.

Because the *F* test statistic is constructed with the larger sample variance s_1^2 in the numerator, the value of the test statistic will be in the upper tail of the *F* distribution. Therefore, the *F* distribution table as shown in Table 11.3 and in Table 4 of Appendix B need only provide upper tail areas or probabilities. If we did not construct the test statistic in this manner, lower tail areas or probabilities would be needed. In this case, additional calculations or more extensive *F* distribution tables would be required. Let us now consider an example of a hypothesis test about the equality of two population variances.

Dullus County Schools is renewing its school bus service contract for the coming year and must select one of two bus companies, the Milbank Company or the Gulf Park Company. We will use the variance of the arrival or pickup/delivery times as a primary measure of the quality of the bus service. Low variance values indicate the more consistent and higher-quality service. If the variances of arrival times associated with the two services are equal, Dullus School administrators will select the company offering the better financial terms. However, if the sample data on bus arrival times for the two companies indicate a significant difference between the variances, the administrators may want to give special consideration to the company with the better or lower variance service. The appropriate hypotheses follow.

$$H_0: \sigma_1^2 = \sigma_2^2$$
$$H_a: \sigma_1^2 \neq \sigma_2^2$$

If H_0 can be rejected, the conclusion of unequal service quality is appropriate. We will use a level of significance of $\alpha = .10$ to conduct the hypothesis test.

DATA *file*

SchoolBus

A sample of 26 arrival times for the Milbank service provides a sample variance of 48 and a sample of 16 arrival times for the Gulf Park service provides a sample variance of 20. Because the Milbank sample provided the larger sample variance, we will denote Milbank as population 1. Using equation (11.10), we find the value of the test statistic:

$$F = \frac{s_1^2}{s_2^2} = \frac{48}{20} = 2.40$$

The corresponding F distribution has $n_1 - 1 = 26 - 1 = 25$ numerator degrees of freedom and $n_2 - 1 = 16 - 1 = 15$ denominator degrees of freedom.

As with other hypothesis testing procedures, we can use the p-value approach or the critical value approach to obtain the hypothesis testing conclusion. Table 11.3 shows the following areas in the upper tail and corresponding F values for an F distribution with 25 numerator degrees of freedom and 15 denominator degrees of freedom.

Area in Upper Tail	**.10**	**.05**	**.025**	**.01**
F Value ($df_1 = 25, df_2 = 15$)	1.89	2.28	2.69	3.28

$F = 2.40$

Because $F = 2.40$ is between 2.28 and 2.69, the area in the upper tail of the distribution is between .05 and .025. For this two-tailed test, we double the upper tail area, which results in a p-value between .10 and .05. Because we selected $\alpha = .10$ as the level of significance, the p-value $< \alpha = .10$. Thus, the null hypothesis is rejected. This finding leads to the conclusion that the two bus services differ in terms of pickup/delivery time variances. The recommendation is that the Dullus County School administrators give special consideration to the better or lower variance service offered by the Gulf Park Company.

Using Excel, 2*F.DIST.RT = .0812.

We can use Excel to show that the test statistic $F = 2.40$ provides a two-tailed p-value $= .0812$. With $.0812 < \alpha = .10$, the null hypothesis of equal population variances is rejected.

To use the critical value approach to conduct the two-tailed hypothesis test at the $\alpha = .10$ level of significance, we would select critical values with an area of $\alpha/2 = .10/2 = .05$ in each tail of the distribution. Because the value of the test statistic computed using equation (11.10) will always be in the upper tail, we only need to determine the upper tail critical value. From Table 11.3, we see that $F_{.05} = 2.28$. Thus, even though we use a two-tailed test, the rejection rule is stated as follows.

$$\text{Reject } H_0 \text{ if } F \geq 2.28$$

Because the test statistic $F = 2.40$ is greater than 2.28, we reject H_0 and conclude that the two bus services differ in terms of pickup/delivery time variances.

One-tailed tests involving two population variances are also possible. In this case, we use the F distribution to determine whether one population variance is significantly greater than the other. A one-tailed hypothesis test about two population variances will always be formulated as an *upper tail* test:

$$H_0: \sigma_1^2 \leq \sigma_2^2$$
$$H_a: \sigma_1^2 > \sigma_2^2$$

A one-tailed hypothesis test about two population variances can always be formulated as an upper tail test. This approach eliminates the need for lower tail F values.

This form of the hypothesis test always places the p-value and the critical value in the upper tail of the F distribution. As a result, only upper tail F values will be needed, simplifying both the computations and the table for the F distribution.

Let us demonstrate the use of the F distribution to conduct a one-tailed test about the variances of two populations by considering a public opinion survey. Samples of 31 men and 41 women will be used to study attitudes about current political issues. The researcher conducting the study wants to test to see whether the sample data indicate that women show a greater variation in attitude on political issues than men. In the form of the one-tailed hypothesis test given previously, women will be denoted as population 1 and men will be denoted as population 2. The hypothesis test will be stated as follows.

$$H_0: \sigma_{\text{women}}^2 \leq \sigma_{\text{men}}^2$$
$$H_a: \sigma_{\text{women}}^2 > \sigma_{\text{men}}^2$$

A rejection of H_0 gives the researcher the statistical support necessary to conclude that women show a greater variation in attitude on political issues.

With the sample variance for women in the numerator and the sample variance for men in the denominator, the F distribution will have $n_1 - 1 = 41 - 1 = 40$ numerator degrees of freedom and $n_2 - 1 = 31 - 1 = 30$ denominator degrees of freedom. We will use a level of significance $\alpha = .05$ to conduct the hypothesis test. The survey results provide a sample variance of $s_1^2 = 120$ for women and a sample variance of $s_2^2 = 80$ for men. The test statistic is as follows.

$$F = \frac{s_1^2}{s_2^2} = \frac{120}{80} = 1.50$$

Referring to Table 4 in Appendix B, we find that an F distribution with 40 numerator degrees of freedom and 30 denominator degrees of freedom has $F_{.10} = 1.57$. Because the test statistic $F = 1.50$ is less than 1.57, the area in the upper tail must be greater than .10. Thus, we can conclude that the p-value is greater than .10. Excel can be used to show that $F = 1.50$ provides a p-value $= .1256$. Because the p-value $> \alpha = .05$, H_0 cannot be rejected. Hence, the sample results do not support the conclusion that women show greater variation in attitude on political issues than men. Table 11.4 provides a summary of hypothesis tests about two population variances.

Using Excel, p-value = F.DIST.RT(1.5,40,30) = .1256.

Using Excel to Conduct a Hypothesis Test

Excel's F-Test Two-Sample for Variances tool can be used to conduct a hypothesis test comparing the variances of two populations. We illustrate by using Excel to conduct the two-tailed hypothesis test for the Dullus County School Bus study. Refer to the Excel worksheets in Figure 11.7 and in Figure 11.8 as we describe the tasks involved.

TABLE 11.4   SUMMARY OF HYPOTHESIS TESTS ABOUT TWO POPULATION VARIANCES

	Upper Tail Test	**Two-Tailed Test**
Hypotheses	$H_0: \sigma_1^2 \leq \sigma_2^2$ $H_a: \sigma_1^2 > \sigma_2^2$	$H_0: \sigma_1^2 = \sigma_2^2$ $H_a: \sigma_1^2 \neq \sigma_2^2$ Note: Population 1 has the larger sample variance
Test Statistic	$F = \dfrac{s_1^2}{s_2^2}$	$F = \dfrac{s_1^2}{s_2^2}$
Rejection Rule: *p*-Value Approach	Reject H_0 if *p*-value $\leq \alpha$	Reject H_0 if *p*-value $\leq \alpha$
Rejection Rule: Critical Value Approach	Reject H_0 if $F \geq F_\alpha$	Reject H_0 if $F \geq F_{\alpha/2}$

DATA *file*

SchoolBus

Enter/Access Data: Open the DATAfile named *SchoolBus*. Column A contains the sample of 26 arrival times for the Milbank Company and column B contains the sample of 16 arrival times for the Gulf Park Company.

Apply Tools: The following steps describe how to use Excel's F-Test Two-Sample for Variances tool.

Step 1. Click the **Data** tab on the Ribbon
Step 2. In the **Analyze** group, click **Data Analysis**
Step 3. When the Data Analysis dialog box appears:
Choose **F-Test Two-Sample for Variances** from the list of Analysis Tools

FIGURE 11.7   DIALOG BOX FOR F-TEST TWO-SAMPLE FOR VARIANCES

	A	B	C	D	E	F	G	H	I	J
1	**Milbank**	**Gulf Park**								
2	35.9	21.6								
3	29.9	20.5		F-Test Two-Sample for Variances						
4	31.2	23.3		Input						
5	16.2	18.8		Variable 1 Range:		\$A\$1:\$A\$27			OK	
6	19.0	17.2		Variable 2 Range:		\$B\$1:\$B\$17			Cancel	
7	15.9	7.7								
8	18.8	18.6		☑ Labels					Help	
9	22.2	18.7		Alpha:	0.05					
10	19.9	20.4								
11	16.4	22.4		Output options						
16	18.0	27.9		◉ Output Range:		\$D\$1				
17	28.1	20.8		○ New Worksheet Ply:						
18	12.1			○ New Workbook						
26	15.2									
27	28.2									
28										

Note: Rows 12–15 and 19–25 are hidden.

FIGURE 11.8   EXCEL RESULTS FOR HYPOTHESIS TEST COMPARING VARIANCE
IN PICKUP TIMES FOR TWO SCHOOL BUS SERVICES

	A	B	C	D	E	F	G
1	**Milbank**	**Gulf Park**		F-Test Two-Sample for Variances			
2	35.9	21.6					
3	29.9	20.5			*Milbank*	*Gulf Park*	
4	31.2	23.3		Mean	20.2308	20.2438	
5	16.2	18.8		Variance	48.0206	20.0000	
6	19.0	17.2		Observations	26	16	
7	15.9	7.7		df	25	15	
8	18.8	18.6		F	2.4010		
9	22.2	18.7		P(F<=f) one-tail	0.0405		
10	19.9	20.4		F Critical one-tail	2.2797		
11	16.4	22.4					
16	18.0	27.9					
17	28.1	20.8					
18	12.1						
26	15.2						
27	28.2						
28							

Step 4. When the F-Test Two-Sample for Variances dialog box appears (Figure 11.7):
Enter A1:A27 in the **Variable 1 Range** box
Enter B1:B17 in the **Variable 2 Range** box
Select **Labels**
Enter .05 in the **Alpha** box
(*Note:* This Excel procedure uses alpha as the area in the upper tail.)
Select **Output Range** and enter D1 in the box
Click **OK**

The output, P(F<=f) one-tail = .0405, is the one-tail area associated with the test statistic $F = 2.401$. Thus, the two-tailed p-value is 2(.0405) = .081; we reject the null hypothesis at the .10 level of significance. If the hypothesis test had been a one-tail test (with $\alpha = .05$), the one-tail area in cell E9 would provide the p-value directly. We would not need to double it.

NOTE AND COMMENT

Research confirms the fact that the F distribution is sensitive to the assumption of normal populations. The F distribution should not be used unless it is reasonable to assume that both populations are at least approximately normally distributed.

Exercises

Methods

13. Find the following F distribution values from Table 4 of Appendix B.
    a. $F_{.05}$ with degrees of freedom 5 and 10
    b. $F_{.025}$ with degrees of freedom 20 and 15
    c. $F_{.01}$ with degrees of freedom 8 and 12
    d. $F_{.10}$ with degrees of freedom 10 and 20

14. A sample of 16 items from population 1 has a sample variance $s_1^2 = 5.8$ and a sample of 21 items from population 2 has a sample variance $s_2^2 = 2.4$. Test the following hypotheses at the .05 level of significance.

$$H_0: \sigma_1^2 \leq \sigma_2^2$$
$$H_a: \sigma_1^2 > \sigma_2^2$$

   a.   What is your conclusion using the p-value approach?
   b.   Repeat the test using the critical value approach.

15. Consider the following hypothesis test.

$$H_0: \sigma_1^2 = \sigma_2^2$$
$$H_a: \sigma_1^2 \neq \sigma_2^2$$

   a.   What is your conclusion if $n_1 = 21$, $s_1^2 = 8.2$, $n_2 = 26$, and $s_2^2 = 4.0$? Use $\alpha = .05$ and the p-value approach.
   b.   Repeat the test using the critical value approach.

Applications

16. Investors commonly use the standard deviation of the monthly percentage return for a mutual fund as a measure of the risk for the fund; in such cases, a fund that has a larger standard deviation is considered more risky than a fund with a lower standard deviation. The standard deviation for the American Century Equity Growth fund and the standard deviation for the Fidelity Growth Discovery fund were recently reported to be 15.0% and 18.9%, respectively. Assume that each of these standard deviations is based on a sample of 60 months of returns. Do the sample results support the conclusion that the Fidelity fund has a larger population variance than the American Century fund? Which fund is more risky?

17. Most individuals are aware of the fact that the average annual repair cost for an automobile depends on the age of the automobile. A researcher is interested in finding out whether the variance of the annual repair costs also increases with the age of the automobile. A sample of 26 automobiles 4 years old showed a sample standard deviation for annual repair costs of $170 and a sample of 25 automobiles 2 years old showed a sample standard deviation for annual repair costs of $100.
   a.   State the null and alternative versions of the research hypothesis that the variance in annual repair costs is larger for the older automobiles.
   b.   At a .01 level of significance, what is your conclusion? What is the p-value? Discuss the reasonableness of your findings.

18. Data were collected on the top 1000 financial advisers by *Barron's*. Merrill Lynch had 239 people on the list and Morgan Stanley had 121 people on the list. A sample of 16 of the Merrill Lynch advisers and 10 of the Morgan Stanley advisers showed that the advisers managed many very large accounts with a large variance in the total amount of funds managed. The standard deviation of the amount managed by the Merrill Lynch advisers was $s_1 = \$587$ million. The standard deviation of the amount managed by the Morgan Stanley advisers was $s_2 = \$489$ million. Conduct a hypothesis test at $\alpha = .10$ to determine whether there is a significant difference in the population variances for the amounts managed by the two companies. What is your conclusion about the variability in the amount of funds managed by advisers from the two firms?

19. The variance in a production process is an important measure of the quality of the process. A large variance often signals an opportunity for improvement in the process by finding ways to reduce the process variance. Conduct a statistical test to determine whether there is a significant difference between the variances in the bag weights for two machines. Use a .05 level

of significance. What is your conclusion? Which machine, if either, provides the greater opportunity for quality improvements?

Bags

Machine 1	2.95	3.45	3.50	3.75	3.48	3.26	3.33	3.20
	3.16	3.20	3.22	3.38	3.90	3.36	3.25	3.28
	3.20	3.22	2.98	3.45	3.70	3.34	3.18	3.35
	3.12							
Machine 2	3.22	3.30	3.34	3.28	3.29	3.25	3.30	3.27
	3.38	3.34	3.35	3.19	3.35	3.05	3.36	3.28
	3.30	3.28	3.30	3.20	3.16	3.33		

20. On the basis of data provided by a Romac salary survey, the variance in annual salaries for seniors in public accounting firms is approximately 2.1 and the variance in annual salaries for managers in public accounting firms is approximately 11.1. The salary data were provided in thousands of dollars. Assuming that the salary data were based on samples of 25 seniors and 26 managers, test the hypothesis that the population variances in the salaries are equal. At a .05 level of significance, what is your conclusion?

BatteryTime

21. Many smartphones, especially those of the LTE-enabled persuasion, have been criticized for exceptionally poor battery life. Battery life between charges for the Motorola Droid Razr Max averages 20 hours when the primary use is talk time and 7 hours when the primary use is Internet applications (*The Wall Street Journal,* March 7, 2012). Since the mean hours for talk time usage is greater than the mean hours for Internet usage, the question was raised as to whether the variance in hours of usage is also greater when the primary use is talk time. Sample data showing battery hours of use for the two applications follows.

Primary Use: Talking

35.8	22.2	4.0	32.6	8.5	42.5
8.0	3.8	30.0	12.8	10.3	35.5

Primary Use: Internet

14.0	12.5	16.4	1.9	9.9
5.4	1.0	15.2	4.0	4.7

a. Formulate hypotheses about the two population variances that can be used to determine whether the population variance in battery hours of use is greater for the talk time application.

b. What are the standard deviations of battery hours of use for the two samples?

c. Conduct the hypothesis test and compute the p-value. Using a .05 level of significance, what is your conclusion?

22. A research hypothesis is that the variance of stopping distances of automobiles on wet pavement is substantially greater than the variance of stopping distances of automobiles on dry pavement. In the research study, 16 automobiles traveling at the same speeds are tested for stopping distances on wet pavement and then tested for stopping distances on dry pavement. On wet pavement, the standard deviation of stopping distances is 32 feet. On dry pavement, the standard deviation is 16 feet.

a. At a .05 level of significance, do the sample data justify the conclusion that the variance in stopping distances on wet pavement is greater than the variance in stopping distances on dry pavement? What is the p-value?

b. What are the implications of your statistical conclusions in terms of driving safety recommendations?

Summary

In this chapter we presented statistical procedures that can be used to make inferences about population variances. In the process we introduced two new probability distributions: the chi-square distribution and the F distribution. The chi-square distribution can be used as the basis for interval estimation and hypothesis tests about the variance of a normal population.

We illustrated the use of the F distribution in hypothesis tests about the variances of two normal populations. In particular, we showed that with independent random samples of sizes n_1 and n_2 selected from two normal populations with equal variances $\sigma_1^2 = \sigma_2^2$, the sampling distribution of the ratio of the two sample variances s_1^2/s_2^2 has an F distribution with $n_1 - 1$ degrees of freedom for the numerator and $n_2 - 1$ degrees of freedom for the denominator.

Key Formulas

Interval Estimate of a Population Variance

$$\frac{(n-1)s^2}{\chi_{\alpha/2}^2} \le \sigma^2 \le \frac{(n-1)s^2}{\chi_{(1-\alpha/2)}^2} \tag{11.7}$$

Test Statistic for Hypothesis Tests About a Population Variance

$$\chi^2 = \frac{(n-1)s^2}{\sigma_0^2} \tag{11.8}$$

Test Statistic for Hypothesis Tests About Population Variances with $\sigma_1^2 = \sigma_2^2$

$$F = \frac{s_1^2}{s_2^2} \tag{11.10}$$

Supplementary Exercises

23. Because of staffing decisions, managers of the Gibson-Marimont Hotel are interested in the variability in the number of rooms occupied per day during a particular season of the year. A sample of 20 days of operation shows a sample mean of 290 rooms occupied per day and a sample standard deviation of 30 rooms.
    a. What is the point estimate of the population variance?
    b. Provide a 90% confidence interval estimate of the population variance.
    c. Provide a 90% confidence interval estimate of the population standard deviation.

24. Initial public offerings (IPOs) of stocks are on average underpriced. The standard deviation measures the dispersion, or variation, in the underpricing-overpricing indicator. A sample of 13 Canadian IPOs that were subsequently traded on the Toronto Stock Exchange had a standard deviation of 14.95. Develop a 95% confidence interval estimate of the population standard deviation for the underpricing-overpricing indicator.

25. The estimated daily living costs for an executive traveling to various major cities follow. The estimates include a single room at a four-star hotel, beverages, breakfast, taxi fares, and incidental costs.

Travel

City	Daily Living Cost ($)	City	Daily Living Cost ($)
Bangkok	242.87	Mexico City	212.00
Bogotá	260.93	Milan	284.08
Cairo	194.19	Mumbai	139.16
Dublin	260.76	Paris	436.72
Frankfurt	355.36	Rio de Janeiro	240.87
Hong Kong	346.32	Seoul	310.41
Johannesburg	165.37	Tel Aviv	223.73
Lima	250.08	Toronto	181.25
London	326.76	Warsaw	238.20
Madrid	283.56	Washington, D.C.	250.61

    a.   Compute the sample mean.

    b.   Compute the sample standard deviation.

    c.   Compute a 95% confidence interval for the population standard deviation.

26.   Part variability is critical in the manufacturing of ball bearings. Large variances in the size of the ball bearings cause bearing failure and rapid wearout. Production standards call for a maximum variance of .0001 when the bearing sizes are measured in inches. A sample of 15 bearings shows a sample standard deviation of .014 inches.

    a.   Use $\alpha = .10$ to determine whether the sample indicates that the maximum acceptable variance is being exceeded.

    b.   Compute the 90% confidence interval estimate of the variance of the ball bearings in the population.

27.   The filling variance for boxes of cereal is designed to be .02 or less. A sample of 41 boxes of cereal shows a sample standard deviation of .16 ounces. Use $\alpha = .05$ to determine whether the variance in the cereal box fillings is exceeding the design specification.

28.   City Trucking, Inc., claims consistent delivery times for its routine customer deliveries. A sample of 22 truck deliveries shows a sample variance of 1.5. Test to determine whether H_0: $\sigma^2 \le 1$ can be rejected. Use $\alpha = .10$.

29.   A sample of 9 days over the past six months showed that a dentist treated the following numbers of patients: 22, 25, 20, 18, 15, 22, 24, 19, and 26. If the number of patients seen per day is normally distributed, would an analysis of these sample data reject the hypothesis that the variance in the number of patients seen per day is equal to 10? Use a .10 level of significance. What is your conclusion?

30.   A sample standard deviation for the number of passengers taking a particular airline flight is 8. A 95% confidence interval estimate of the population standard deviation is 5.86 passengers to 12.62 passengers.

    a.   Was a sample size of 10 or 15 used in the statistical analysis?

    b.   Suppose the sample standard deviation of $s = 8$ was based on a sample of 25 flights. What change would you expect in the confidence interval for the population standard deviation? Compute a 95% confidence interval estimate of σ with a sample size of 25.

31.   Is there any difference in the variability in golf scores for players on the LPGA Tour (the women's professional golf tour) and players on the PGA Tour (the men's professional golf tour)? A sample of 20 tournament scores from LPGA events showed a standard deviation of 2.4623 strokes, and a sample of 30 tournament scores from PGA events showed a standard deviation of 2.2118 (*Golfweek* website, June 17, 2016). Conduct a hypothesis test for equal population variances to determine whether there is any statistically significant difference in the variability of golf scores for male and female professional golfers. Use $\alpha = .10$. What is your conclusion?

32. The grade point averages of 352 students who completed a college course in financial accounting have a standard deviation of .940. The grade point averages of 73 students who dropped out of the same course have a standard deviation of .797. Do the data indicate a difference between the variances of grade point averages for students who completed a financial accounting course and students who dropped out? Use a .05 level of significance. (*Note:* $F_{.025}$ with 351 and 72 degrees of freedom is 1.466.)

33. The accounting department analyzes the variance of the weekly unit costs reported by two production departments. A sample of 16 cost reports for each of the two departments shows cost variances of 2.3 and 5.4, respectively. Is this sample sufficient to conclude that the two production departments differ in terms of unit cost variance? Use $\alpha = .10$.

34. Two new assembly methods are tested and the variances in assembly times are reported. Use $\alpha = .10$ and test for equality of the two population variances.

	Method A	Method B
Sample Size	$n_1 = 31$	$n_2 = 25$
Sample Variation	$s_1^2 = 25$	$s_2^2 = 12$

Case Problem 1 Air Force Training Program

An Air Force introductory course in electronics uses a personalized system of instruction whereby each student views a videotaped lecture and then is given a programmed instruction text. The students work independently with the text until they have completed the training and passed a test. Of concern is the varying pace at which the students complete this portion of their training program. Some students are able to cover the programmed instruction text relatively quickly, whereas other students work much longer with the text and require additional time to complete the course. The fast students wait until the slow students complete the introductory course before the entire group proceeds together with other aspects of their training.

A proposed alternative system involves use of computer-assisted instruction. In this method, all students view the same videotaped lecture and then each is assigned to a computer terminal for further instruction. The computer guides the student, working independently, through the self-training portion of the course.

To compare the proposed and current methods of instruction, an entering class of 122 students was assigned randomly to one of the two methods. One group of 61 students used the current programmed-text method and the other group of 61 students used the proposed computer-assisted method. The time in hours was recorded for each student in the study. The following data are provided in the DATAfile named *Training*.

DATA *file*
Training

Course Completion Times (hours) for Current Training Method										
76	76	77	74	76	74	74	77	72	78	73
78	75	80	79	72	69	79	72	70	70	81
76	78	72	82	72	73	71	70	77	78	73
79	82	65	77	79	73	76	81	69	75	75
77	79	76	78	76	76	73	77	84	74	74
69	79	66	70	74	72					

Course Completion Times (hours) for Proposed Computer-Assisted Method										
74	75	77	78	74	80	73	73	78	76	76
74	77	69	76	75	72	75	72	76	72	77
73	77	69	77	75	76	74	77	75	78	72
77	78	78	76	75	76	76	75	76	80	77
76	75	73	77	77	77	79	75	75	72	82
76	76	74	72	78	71					

Managerial Report

1. Use appropriate descriptive statistics to summarize the training time data for each method. What similarities or differences do you observe from the sample data?
2. Use the methods of Chapter 10 to comment on any difference between the population means for the two methods. Discuss your findings.
3. Compute the standard deviation and variance for each training method. Conduct a hypothesis test about the equality of population variances for the two training methods. Discuss your findings.
4. What conclusion can you reach about any differences between the two methods? What is your recommendation? Explain.
5. Can you suggest other data or testing that might be desirable before making a final decision on the training program to be used in the future?

Case Problem 2   Meticulous Drill & Reamer

Meticulous Drill & Reamer (MD&R) specializes in drilling and boring precise holes in hard metals (e.g., steel alloys, tungsten carbide, and titanium). The company recently contracted to drill holes with 3-centimeter diameters in large carbon-steel alloy disks, and it will have to purchase a special drill to complete this job. MD&R has eliminated all but two of the drills it has been considering: Davis Drills' T2005 and Worth Industrial Tools' AZ100. These producers have each agreed to allow MD&R to use a T2005 and an AZ100 for one week to determine which drill it will purchase. During the one-week trial, MD&R uses each of these drills to drill 31 holes with a target diameter of 3 centimeters in one large carbon-steel alloy disk, then measures the diameter of each hole and records the results. MD&R's results are provided in the table that follows and are available in the DATAfile named *MeticulousDrills*.

Hole Diameter					
T2005	AZ100	T2005	AZ100	T2005	AZ100
3.06	2.91	3.05	2.97	3.04	3.06
3.04	3.31	3.01	3.05	3.01	3.25
3.13	2.82	2.73	2.95	2.95	2.82
3.01	3.01	3.12	2.92	3.14	3.22
2.95	2.94	3.04	2.71	3.31	2.93
3.02	3.17	3.10	2.77	3.01	3.24
3.02	3.25	3.02	2.73	2.93	2.77
3.12	3.39	2.92	3.18	3.00	2.94
3.00	3.22	3.01	2.95	3.04	3.31
3.04	2.97	3.15	2.86		
3.03	2.93	2.69	3.16		

MeticulousDrills

MD&R wants to consider both the accuracy (closeness of the diameter to 3 centimeters), and the precision (the variance of the diameter) of the holes drilled by the T2005 and the AZ100 when deciding which model to purchase.

Managerial Report

In making this assessment for MD&R, consider the following four questions:

1. Are the holes drilled by the T2005 or the AZ100 more accurate? That is, which model of drill produces holes with a mean diameter closer to 3 centimeters?
2. Are the holes drilled by the T2005 or the AZ100 more precise? That is, which model of drill produces holes with a smaller variance?
3. Conduct a test of the hypothesis that the T2005 and the AZ100 are equally precise (that is, have equal variances) at $a = .05$. Discuss your findings.
4. Which drill do you recommend to MD&R? Why?

CHAPTER 12

Tests of Goodness of Fit, Independence, and Multiple Proportions

CONTENTS

STATISTICS IN PRACTICE:
UNITED WAY

STATISTICS *in* PRACTICE

UNITED WAY*
ROCHESTER, NEW YORK

United Way of Greater Rochester is a nonprofit organization dedicated to improving the quality of life for all people in the seven counties it serves by meeting the community's most important human care needs.

The annual United Way/Red Cross fund-raising campaign funds hundreds of programs offered by more than 200 service providers. These providers meet a wide variety of human needs—physical, mental, and social—and serve people of all ages, backgrounds, and economic means.

The United Way of Greater Rochester decided to conduct a survey to learn more about community perceptions of charities. Focus-group interviews were held with professional, service, and general worker groups to obtain preliminary information on perceptions. The information obtained was then used to help develop the questionnaire for the survey. The questionnaire was pretested, modified, and distributed to 440 individuals.

A variety of descriptive statistics, including frequency distributions and crosstabulations, were provided from the data collected. An important part of the analysis involved the use of chi-square tests of independence. One use of such statistical tests was to determine whether perceptions of administrative expenses were independent of the occupation of the respondent.

The hypotheses for the test of independence were as follows:

H_0: Perception of United Way administrative expenses is independent of the occupation of the respondent.
H_a: Perception of United Way administrative expenses is not independent of the occupation of the respondent.

Two questions in the survey provided categorical data for the statistical test. One question obtained data on perceptions of the percentage of funds going to administrative expenses (up to 10%, 11–20%, and 21% or

United Way programs meet the needs of children as well as adults.

more). The other question asked for the occupation of the respondent.

The test of independence led to rejection of the null hypothesis and to the conclusion that perception of United Way administrative expenses is not independent of the occupation of the respondent. Actual administrative expenses were less than 9%, but 35% of the respondents perceived that administrative expenses were 21% or more. Hence, many respondents had inaccurate perceptions of administrative expenses. In this group, production-line, clerical, sales, and professional-technical employees had the more inaccurate perceptions.

The community perceptions study helped United Way of Rochester develop adjustments to its programs and fund-raising activities. In this chapter, you will learn how tests, such as described here, are conducted.

*The authors are indebted to Dr. Philip R. Tyler, marketing consultant to the United Way, for providing this Statistics in Practice.

In Chapter 11 we showed how the chi-square (χ^2) distribution can be used to compute an interval estimate and conduct hypothesis tests about a population variance. In this chapter we introduce three additional hypothesis tests based on the chi-square distribution. These tests are all based on comparing observed sample results with those that are expected when the null hypothesis is true. The hypothesis testing conclusion is based upon using a chi-square test statistic to determine how "close" the sample results are to the expected results.

All three hypothesis tests are designed for use with categorical data. The goodness of fit test in Section 12.1 is useful when we want to test whether a frequency distribution developed from categorical data is a good fit to a hypothesized probability distribution for the population. In Section 12.2 we show how the chi-square test of independence is used to determine whether two categorical variables sampled from one population are independent. Section 12.3 describes a chi-square test for multiple populations by showing how sample data from three or more populations can be used to determine whether the population proportions are equal.

 ## 12.1   Goodness of Fit Test

The chi-square **goodness of fit test** can be used to determine whether a random variable has a specific probability distribution. In this section we show how to conduct a goodness of fit test for a random variable with a multinomial probability distribution.

Multinomial Probability Distribution

A **multinomial probability distribution** is an extension of the binomial probability distribution to the case where there are three or more categories of outcomes per trial. The category probabilities are the key parameters of the multinomial distribution. For an application of a goodness of fit test to a multinomial probability distribution, consider the market share study being conducted by Scott Marketing Research. Over the past year, market shares for a certain product have stabilized at 30% for company A, 50% for company B, and 20% for company C. Since each customer is classified as buying from one of these companies, we have a multinomial probability distribution with three possible categories of outcomes. The probability for each of the three categories is as follows.

$$p_A = \text{probability a customer purchases the company A product}$$
$$p_B = \text{probability a customer purchases the company B product}$$
$$p_C = \text{probability a customer purchases the company C product}$$

The sum of the probabilities for a multinomial probability distribution equals 1.

Using the historical market shares, we have a multinomial probability distribution with $p_A = .30$, $p_B = .50$, and $p_C = .20$.

Company C plans to introduce a "new and improved" product to replace its current entry in the market. Company C has retained Scott Marketing Research to determine whether the new product will alter or change the market shares for the three companies. Specifically, Scott Marketing Research will introduce a sample of customers to the new company C product and then ask the customers to indicate a preference for the company A product, the company B product, or the new company C product. Based on the sample data, the following hypothesis test can be used to determine whether the new company C product is likely to change the historical market shares for the three companies.

H_0: $p_A = .30$, $p_B = .50$, and $p_C = .20$

H_a: The probabilities are not $p_A = .30$, $p_B = .50$, and $p_C = .20$

The null hypothesis is based on the historical multinomial probability distribution for the market shares. If sample results lead to the rejection of H_0, Scott Marketing Research will have evidence to conclude that the introduction of the new company C product will change the market shares (the category probabilities for the multinomial distribution).

Let us assume that the market research firm has used a consumer panel of 200 customers. Each customer was asked to specify a purchase preference among the three alternatives:

company A's product, company B's product, and company C's new product. The 200 responses are summarized in the following frequency distribution.

Category	Observed Frequency
Company A	48
Company B	98
Company C	54
Total	200

We now can perform a goodness of fit test to determine whether the sample of 200 customer purchase preferences is consistent with the null hypothesis. The goodness of fit test is based on a comparison of observed frequencies from the sample with the expected frequencies under the assumption that the null hypothesis is true. Hence, the next step is to compute expected purchase preferences for the 200 customers under the assumption that H_0: $p_A = .30$, $p_B = .50$, and $p_C = .20$ is true. Doing so provides the following expected frequency distribution.

Category	Expected Frequency
Company A	$200(.30) = 60$
Company B	$200(.50) = 100$
Company C	$200(.20) = 40$
Total	200

Note that the expected frequency for each category is found by multiplying the sample size of 200 by the hypothesized probability for the category.

The goodness of fit test now focuses on the differences between the observed frequencies and the expected frequencies. Whether the differences between the observed and expected frequencies are "large" or "small" is a question answered with the aid of the following chi-square test statistic.

In equation (12.1) the difference between the observed (f_i) and expected (e_i) frequencies is squared; thus, χ^2 will always be positive.

TEST STATISTIC FOR GOODNESS OF FIT

$$\chi^2 = \sum_{i=1}^{k} \frac{(f_i - e_i)^2}{e_i} \tag{12.1}$$

where

f_i = observed frequency for category i
e_i = expected frequency for category i
k = the number of categories

Note: The test statistic has a chi-square distribution with $k - 1$ degrees of freedom provided that the expected frequencies are 5 *or more* for all categories.

TABLE 12.1 COMPUTATION OF THE CHI-SQUARE TEST STATISTIC FOR THE SCOTT MARKETING RESEARCH MARKET SHARE STUDY

Category	Hypothesized Probability	Observed Frequency (f_i)	Expected Frequency (e_i)	Difference $(f_i - e_i)$	Squared Difference $(f_i - e_i)^2$	Squared Difference Divided by Expected Frequency $(f_i - e_i)^2/e_i$
Company A	.30	48	60	−12	144	2.40
Company B	.50	98	100	−2	4	0.04
Company C	.20	54	40	14	196	4.90
Total		200				$\chi^2 = 7.34$

Let us continue with the Scott Marketing Research example and use the sample data to test the hypothesis that the multinomial distribution has the market share probabilities $p_A = .30$, $p_B = .50$, and $p_C = .20$. We will use an $\alpha = .05$ level of significance. We proceed by using the observed and expected frequencies to compute the value of the test statistic. With the expected frequencies all 5 or more, the computation of the chi-square test statistic is shown in Table 12.1. Thus, we have $\chi^2 = 7.34$.

The test for goodness of fit is always a one-tailed test with the rejection occurring in the upper tail of the chi-square distribution.

We will reject the null hypothesis if the differences between the observed and expected frequencies are large. Thus the test of goodness of fit will always be an upper tail test. We can use the upper tail area for the test statistic and the p-value approach to determine whether the null hypothesis can be rejected. With $k - 1 = 3 - 1 = 2$ degrees of freedom, row two of the chi-square distribution Table 3 of Appendix B provides the following:

Area in Upper Tail	.10	.05	.025	.01	.005
χ^2 Value (2 df)	4.605	5.991	7.378	9.210	10.597

$$\chi^2 = 7.34$$

The test statistic $\chi^2 = 7.34$ is between 5.991 and 7.378. Thus, the corresponding upper tail area or p-value must be between .05 and .025. With p-value $\leq .05$, we reject H_0 and conclude that the introduction of the new product by company C will alter the historical market shares. In the Using Excel subsection which follows we will see that the p-value $= .0255$.

Instead of using the p-value, we could use the critical value approach to draw the same conclusion. With $\alpha = .05$ and 2 degrees of freedom, the critical value for the test statistic is $\chi^2_{.05} = 5.991$. The upper tail rejection rule becomes

$$\text{Reject } H_0 \text{ if } \chi^2 \geq 5.991$$

With $7.34 > 5.991$, we reject H_0. The p-value approach and critical value approach provide the same hypothesis testing conclusion.

Now that we have concluded that the introduction of a new company C product will alter the market shares for the three companies, we are interested in knowing more about how the market shares are likely to change. Using the historical market shares and the sample data, we summarize the data as follows:

Company	Historical Market Share (%)	Sample Data Market Share (%)
A	30	48/200 = .24, or 24
B	50	98/200 = .49, or 49
C	20	54/200 = .27, or 27

FIGURE 12.1   BAR CHART OF MARKET SHARES BY COMPANY BEFORE AND AFTER THE NEW PRODUCT FOR COMPANY C

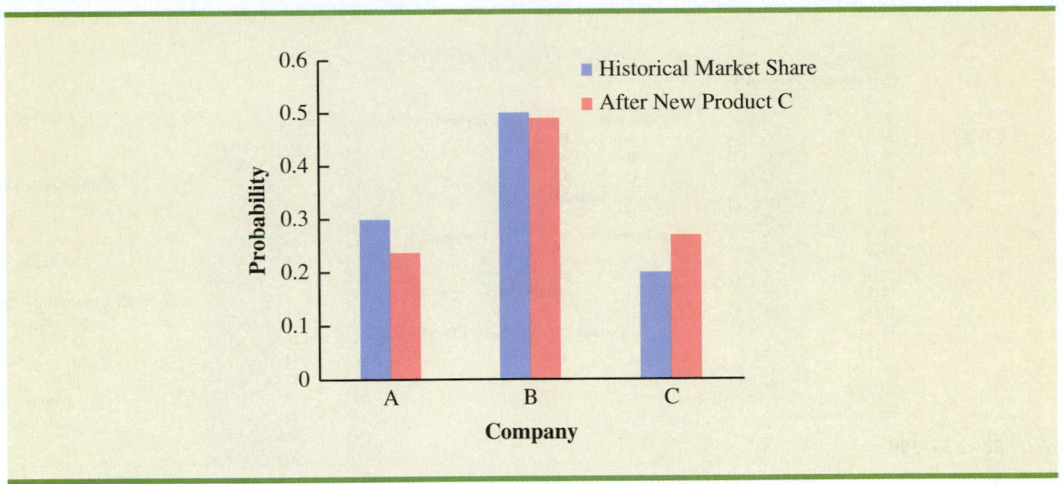

The historical market shares and the sample market shares are compared in the bar chart shown in Figure 12.1. The bar chart shows that the new product will likely increase the market share for company C. Comparisons for the other two companies indicate that company C's gain in market share will hurt company A more than company B.

Let us summarize the steps that can be used to conduct a goodness of fit test for a hypothesized multinomial probability distribution.

MULTINOMIAL PROBABILITY DISTRIBUTION GOODNESS OF FIT TEST

1. State the null and alternative hypotheses.

   H_0: The population follows a multinomial probability distribution with specified probabilities for each of the k categories

   H_a: The population does not follow a multinomial probability distribution with the specified probabilities for each of the k categories

2. Select a random sample and record the observed frequencies f_i for each category.

3. Assume the null hypothesis is true and determine the expected frequency e_i in each category by multiplying the hypothesized category probability by the sample size.

4. If the expected frequency e_i is at least 5 for each category, compute the value of the test statistic.

$$\chi^2 = \sum_{i=1}^{k} \frac{(f_i - e_i)^2}{e_i}$$

5. Rejection rule:

   p-value approach: Reject H_0 if p-value $\leq \alpha$
   Critical value approach: Reject H_0 if $\chi^2 \geq \chi_\alpha^2$

   where α is the level of significance for the test and there are $k - 1$ degrees of freedom.

FIGURE 12.2 EXCEL WORKSHEET FOR THE GOODNESS OF FIT TEST FOR THE SCOTT MARKETING RESEARCH MARKET SHARE STUDY

	A	B	C	D	E	F
1	Customer	Preference				
2	1	B				
3	2	A		Categories	Obs. Frequency	
4	3	C		A	48	
5	4	C		B	98	
6	5	C		C	54	
7	6	A		Total 200		
8	7	A				
9	8	A		Hyp. Probability	Exp. Frequency	
10	9	C		0.3	=D10*$E$7	
11	10	A		0.5	=D11*$E$7	
12	11	C		0.2	=D12*$E$7	
13	12	B				
14	13	C		*p*-value	=CHISQ.TEST(E4:E6,E10:E12)	
15	14	A				
200	199	C				
201	200	C				
202						

	A	B	C	D	E	F
1	Customer	Preference				
2	1	B				
3	2	A		Categories	Obs. Frequency	
4	3	C		A	48	
5	4	C		B	98	
6	5	C		C	54	
7	6	A		Total	200	
8	7	A				
9	8	A		Hyp. Probability	Exp. Frequency	
10	9	C		0.3	60	
11	10	A		0.5	100	
12	11	C		0.2	40	
13	12	B				
14	13	C		*p*-value	0.0255	
15	14	A				
200	199	C				
201	200	C				
202						

Note: Rows 16–199 are hidden.

Using Excel to Conduct a Goodness of Fit Test

Excel can be used to conduct a goodness of fit test for the market share study conducted by Scott Marketing Research. Refer to Figure 12.2 as we describe the tasks involved. The formula worksheet is in the background; the value worksheet is in the foreground.

Research

Enter/Access Data: Open the DATAfile named *Research*. The data are in cells B2:C201 and labels are in column A and cell B1. Values for the hypothesized category probabilities were entered into cells D10:D12.

Apply Tools: Cells D3:E7 shows the results of using Excel's Recommended PivotTable tool (see Section 2.1 for details regarding how to use this tool) to construct a frequency distribution for the purchase preference data.

Enter Functions and Formulas: The Excel formulas in cells E10:E12 were used to compute the expected frequencies for each category by multiplying the hypothesized proportions by the sample size. Once the observed and expected frequencies have been computed, Excel's CHISQ.TEST function can be used to compute the *p*-value for a test of goodness of fit. The inputs to the CHISQ.TEST function are the range of values for the observed and expected frequencies. To compute the *p*-value for this test, we entered the following function into cell E14:

$$=CHISQ.TEST(E4:E6,E10:E12)$$

The value worksheet shows that the resulting *p*-value is .0255. Thus, with $\alpha = .05$, we reject H_0 and conclude that the introduction of the new product by company C will change the current market share structure.

Exercises

Methods

1. Test the following hypotheses for a multinomial probability distribution by using the χ^2 goodness of fit test.

$$H_0: p_A = .40, p_B = .40, \text{ and } p_C = .20$$
$$H_0: \text{The probabilities are not}$$
$$p_A = .40, p_B = .40, \text{ and } p_C = .20$$

A sample of size 200 yielded 60 in category A, 120 in category B, and 20 in category C. Use $\alpha = .01$ and test to see whether the probabilities are as stated in H_0.
a.   Use the p-value approach.
b.   Repeat the test using the critical value approach.

2.   Suppose we have a multinomial population with four categories: A, B, C, and D. The null hypothesis is that the proportion of items is the same in every category. The null hypothesis is

$$H_0: p_A = p_B = p_C = p_D = .25$$

A sample of size 300 yielded the following results.

A: 85   B: 95   C: 50   D: 70

Use $\alpha = .05$ to determine whether H_0 should be rejected. What is the p-value?

Applications

3.   During the first 13 weeks of the television season, the Saturday evening 8:00 P.M. to 9:00 P.M. audience proportions were recorded as ABC 29%, CBS 28%, NBC 25%, and independents 18%. A sample of 300 homes two weeks after a Saturday night schedule revision yielded the following viewing audience data: ABC 95 homes, CBS 70 homes, NBC 89 homes, and independents 46 homes. Test with $\alpha = .05$ to determine whether the viewing audience proportions changed.

4.   Mars, Inc. manufactures M&M's, one of the most popular candy treats in the world. The milk chocolate candies come in a variety of colors including blue, brown, green, orange, red, and yellow (M&M website, March 2012). The overall proportions for the colors are .24 blue, .13 brown, .20 green, .16 orange, .13 red, and .14 yellow. In a sampling study, several bags of M&M milk chocolates were opened and the following color counts were obtained.

Blue	Brown	Green	Orange	Red	Yellow
105	72	89	84	70	80

Use a .05 level of significance and the sample data to test the hypothesis that the overall proportions for the colors are as stated above. What is your conclusion?

5.   The Harris Poll tracks the favorite sport of Americans who follow at least one sport. Results of the poll show that professional football is the favorite sport of 33% of Americans who follow at least one sport, followed by baseball at 15%, men's college football at 10%, auto racing at 6%, men's professional basketball at 5%, and ice hockey at 5%, with other sports at 26% (Harris Poll website, June 22, 2016). Consider a survey in which 344 college undergraduates who follow at least one sport were asked to identify their favorite sport produced the following results:

Professional Football	Baseball	Men's College Football	Auto Racing	Men's Professional Basketball	Ice Hockey	Other Sports
111	39	46	14	6	20	108

Do college undergraduate students differ from the general public with regard to their favorite sports? Use $\alpha = .05$.

6.   The National Highway Traffic Safety Administration reports the percentage of traffic accidents occurring each day of the week. Assume that a sample of 420 accidents provided the following data.

Sunday	Monday	Tuesday	Wednesday	Thursday	Friday	Saturday
66	50	53	47	55	69	80

a.   Conduct a hypothesis test to determine whether the proportion of traffic accidents is the same for each day of the week. What is the *p*-value? Using a .05 level of significance, what is your conclusion?

b.   Compute the percentage of traffic accidents occurring on each day of the week. What day has the highest percentage of traffic accidents? Does this seem reasonable? Discuss.

 ## 12.2 Test of Independence

In this section we show how the chi-square test of independence can be used to determine whether two categorical variables sampled from one population are independent. Like the goodness of fit test, the test of independence is also based on comparing observed and expected frequencies. For this test we take one sample from a single population and record the values for two categorical variables. We then summarize the data by counting the number of responses for each combination of a category for variable 1 and a category for variable 2. The null hypothesis for this test is that the two categorical variables are independent. Thus, the test is referred to as a **test of independence**. We will illustrate this test with the following example.

A beer industry association conducts a survey to determine the preferences of beer drinkers for light, regular, and dark beers. A sample of 200 beer drinkers is taken with each person in the sample asked to indicate a preference for one of the three types of beers: light, regular, or dark. At the end of the survey questionnaire, the respondent is asked to provide information on a variety of demographics including gender: male or female. A research question of interest to the association is whether preference for the three types of beer is independent of the gender of the beer drinker. If the two categorical variables, beer preference and gender, are independent, beer preference does not depend on gender and the preference for light, regular, and dark beer can be expected to be the same for male and female beer drinkers. However, if the test conclusion is that the two categorical variables are not independent, we have evidence that beer preference is associated with or dependent upon the gender of the beer drinker. As a result, we can expect beer preferences to differ for male and female beer drinkers. In this case, a beer manufacturer could use this information to customize its promotions and advertising for the different target markets of male and female beer drinkers.

The hypotheses for this test of independence are as follows:

H_0: Beer preference is independent of gender

H_a: Beer preference is not independent of gender

The two-way table used to summarize the data is also referred to as a contingency table.

The sample data will be summarized in a two-way table with beer preferences of light, regular, and dark as one of the variables and gender of male and female as the other variable. Since an objective of the study is to determine whether there is a difference between the beer preferences for male and female beer drinkers, we consider gender an explanatory variable and follow the usual practice of making the explanatory variable the column variable in the crosstabulation. The beer preference is the categorical response variable and is shown as the row variable. The sample results for the 200 beer drinkers in the study are summarized in Table 12.2.

The sample data are summarized based on the combination of beer preference and gender for the individual respondents. For example, 51 individuals in the study were males who preferred

TABLE 12.2 SAMPLE RESULTS FOR BEER PREFERENCES OF MALE AND FEMALE BEER DRINKERS (OBSERVED FREQUENCIES)

BeerPreference

		Gender		
		Male	**Female**	**Total**
Beer Preference	**Light**	51	39	90
	Regular	56	21	77
	Dark	25	8	33
	Total	132	68	200

light beer, 56 individuals in the study were males who preferred regular beer, and so on. Let us now analyze the data in the table and test for independence of beer preference and gender.

Because we selected a sample of beer drinkers, summarizing the data for each variable separately will provide some insights into the characteristics of the beer drinker population. For the categorical variable gender, 132 of the 200 beer drinkers in the sample are male. Thus, we estimate that $132/200 = .66$, or 66%, of the beer drinker population is male. Similarly we estimate that $68/200 = .34$, or 34%, of the beer drinker population is female. The sample data suggest that male beer drinkers outnumber female beer drinkers approximately 2 to 1. Sample proportions or percentages for the three types of beer are

Prefer Light Beer	$90/200 = .450$, or 45.0%
Prefer Regular Beer	$77/200 = .385$, or 38.5%
Prefer Dark Beer	$33/200 = .165$, or 16.5%

Across all beer drinkers in the sample, light beer is preferred most often and dark beer is preferred least often.

Let us now conduct the chi-square test to determine whether beer preference and gender are independent. The data in Table 12.2 are the observed frequencies for the two categories of gender and the three categories of beer preference.

A table of expected frequencies is developed based on the assumption that gender and beer preference are independent as stated in the null hypothesis. We showed above that for the sample of 200 beer drinkers, the proportions preferring light, regular, and dark beer are .450, .385, and .165, respectively. If the independence assumption is valid, we can conclude that these proportions must be applicable to both male and female beer drinkers. Thus, under the assumption of independence, we would expect that for the 132 male beer drinkers sampled that $.450(132) = 59.40$ would prefer light beer, $.385(132) = 50.82$ would prefer regular beer, and $.165(132) = 21.78$ would prefer dark beer. Application of the same proportions to the female beer drinkers leads to the expected frequencies shown in Table 12.3.

Let us generalize the approach to computing expected frequencies by letting e_{ij} denote the expected frequency in row i and column j of the table of expected frequencies. With this notation, let us reconsider the expected frequency calculation for light beer (row 1) and male beer drinkers (column 1), that is, the expected frequency e_{11}.

Note that 90 is the total number of light beer responses (row 1 total), 132 is the total number of male respondents in the sample (column 1 total), and 200 is the total sample size. Following the logic of the preceding paragraphs, we can compute the expected frequency in row 1 and column 1 as follows:

$$e_{11} = \left(\frac{\text{Row 1 Total}}{\text{Sample Size}} \right) (\text{Column 1 Total}) = \frac{90}{100}(132) = 59.40$$

TABLE 12.3   EXPECTED FREQUENCIES IF BEER PREFERENCE IS INDEPENDENT OF THE GENDER OF THE BEER DRINKER

		Gender		
		Male	**Female**	**Total**
	Light	59.40	30.60	90
Beer Preference	**Regular**	50.82	26.18	77
	Dark	21.78	11.22	33
	Total	132.00	68.00	200

Rewriting this expression slightly we obtain

$$e_{11} = \frac{(\text{Row 1 Total})\,(\text{Column 1 Total})}{\text{Sample Size}} = \frac{(90)(132)}{200} = 59.40$$

Generalizing this expression shows that the following formula can be used to compute the expected frequencies under the assumption that H_0 is true.

$$e_{ij} = \frac{(\text{Row } i \text{ Total})(\text{Column } j \text{ Total})}{\text{Sample Size}} \qquad \textbf{(12.2)}$$

For example, $e_{11} = (90)(132)/200 = 59.40$ is the expected frequency for male beer drinkers who would prefer light beer if beer preference is independent of gender, $e_{12} = (90)(68)/200 = 30.60$, and so on. Show that equation (12.2) can be used to find the other expected frequencies shown in Table 12.3.

Using the table of observed frequencies (Table 12.2) and the table of expected frequencies (Table 12.3), we now wish to compute the chi-square statistic for our test of independence. Since the test of independence involves r rows and c columns, the formula for computing χ^2 involves a double summation.

$$\chi^2 = \sum_i \sum_j \frac{(f_{ij} - e_{ij})^2}{e_{ij}} \qquad \textbf{(12.3)}$$

With r rows and c columns in the table, the chi-square distribution will have $(r - 1)(c - 1)$ degrees of freedom provided the expected frequency is at least 5 for each cell. Thus, in this application we will use a chi-square distribution with $(3 - 1)(2 - 1) = 2$ degrees of freedom. The complete steps to compute the chi-square test statistic are summarized in Table 12.4.

We can use the upper tail area of the chi-square distribution with 2 degrees of freedom and the p-value approach to determine whether the null hypothesis that beer preference is independent of gender can be rejected. Using row two of the chi-square distribution table shown in Table 3 of Appendix B, we have the following:

Area in Upper Tail	**.10**	**.05**	**.025**	**.01**	**.005**
χ^2 **Value (2 df)**	4.605	5.991	7.378	9.210	10.597

$$\chi^2 = 6.45$$

TABLE 12.4 COMPUTATION OF THE CHI-SQUARE TEST STATISTIC FOR THE TEST OF INDEPENDENCE BETWEEN BEER PREFERENCE AND GENDER

Beer Preference	Gender	Observed Frequency f_{ij}	Expected Frequency e_{ij}	Difference $(f_{ij} - e_{ij})$	Squared Difference $(f_{ij} - e_{ij})^2$	Squared Difference Divided by Expected Frequency $(f_{ij} - e_{ij})^2/e_{ij}$
Light	Male	51	59.40	−8.40	70.56	1.19
Light	Female	39	30.60	8.40	70.56	2.31
Regular	Male	56	50.82	5.18	26.83	.53
Regular	Female	21	26.18	−5.18	26.83	1.02
Dark	Male	25	21.78	3.22	10.37	.48
Dark	Female	8	11.22	−3.22	10.37	.92
	Total	200	200.00			$\chi^2 = 6.45$

Thus, we see the upper tail area at $\chi^2 = 6.45$ is between .05 and .025, and so the corresponding upper tail area or p-value must be between .05 and .025. With p-value $\leq .05$, we reject H_0 and conclude that beer preference is not independent of the gender of the beer drinker. Stated another way, the study shows that beer preference can be expected to differ for male and female beer drinkers. In the Using Excel subsection that follows, we will see that the p-value $= .0398$.

Instead of using the p-value, we could use the critical value approach to draw the same conclusion. With $\alpha = .05$ and 2 degrees of freedom, the critical value for the chi-square test statistic is $\chi^2_{.05} = 5.991$. The upper tail rejection region becomes

$$\text{Reject } H_0 \text{ if } \chi^2 \geq 5.991$$

With $6.45 \geq 5.991$, we reject H_0. Again we see that the p-value approach and the critical value approach provide the same conclusion.

While we now have evidence that beer preference and gender are not independent, we will need to gain additional insight from the data to assess the nature of the association between these two variables. One way to do this is to compute the probability of the beer preference responses for males and females separately. These calculations are as follows:

Beer Preference	Male	Female
Light	51/132 = .3864, or 38.64%	39/68 = .5735, or 57.35%
Regular	56/132 = .4242, or 42.42%	21/68 = .3088, or 30.88%
Dark	25/132 = .1894, or 18.94%	8/68 = .1176, or 11.76%

A bar chart showing the beer preference for male and female beer drinkers is shown in Figure 12.3.

What observations can you make about the association between beer preference and gender? For female beer drinkers in the sample, the highest preference is for light beer at 57.35%. For male beer drinkers in the sample, regular beer is most frequently preferred at 42.42%. While female beer drinkers have a higher preference for light beer than males, male beer drinkers have a higher preference for both regular beer and dark beer. Data visualization through bar charts such as shown in Figure 12.3 is helpful in gaining insight as to how two categorical variables are associated.

Before we leave this discussion, we summarize the steps for a test of independence.

FIGURE 12.3 BAR CHART COMPARISON OF BEER PREFERENCE BY GENDER

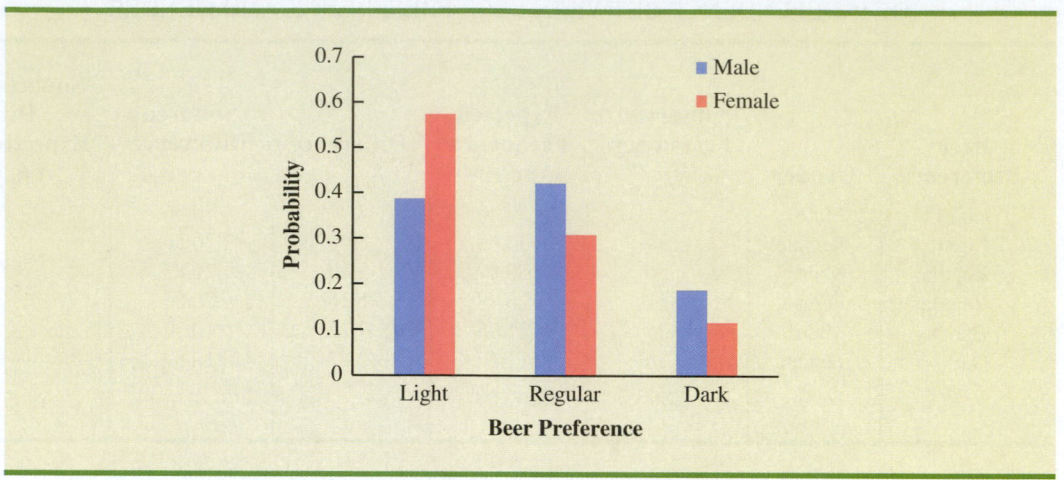

CHI-SQUARE TEST FOR INDEPENDENCE OF TWO CATEGORICAL VARIABLES

1. State the null and alternative hypotheses.

   H_0: The two categorical variables are independent

   H_a: The two categorical variables are not independent

The expected frequencies must all be 5 or more for the chi-square test to be valid.

2. Select a random sample from the population and collect data for both variables for every element in the sample. Record the observed frequencies, f_{ij}, in a table with r rows and c columns.
3. Assume the null hypothesis is true and compute the expected frequencies, e_{ij}
4. If the expected frequency, e_{ij}, is 5 or more for each cell, compute the test statistic:

This chi-square test is a one-tailed test with rejection of H_0 occurring in the upper tail of a chi-square distribution with $(r-1)(c-1)$ degrees of freedom.

$$\chi^2 = \sum_i \sum_j \frac{(f_{ij} - e_{ij})^2}{e_{ij}}$$

5. Rejection rule:

   p-value approach: Reject H_0 if p-value $\leq \alpha$

   Critical value approach: Reject H_0 if $\chi^2 \geq \chi_\alpha^2$

   where the chi-square distribution has $(r-1)(c-1)$ degrees of freedom and α is the level of significance for the test.

Finally, if the null hypothesis of independence is rejected, summarizing the probabilities as shown in the above example will help the analyst determine where the association or dependence exists for the two categorical variables.

Using Excel to Conduct a Test of Independence

Excel can be used to conduct a test of independence for the beer preference example. Refer to Figure 12.4 as we describe the tasks involved. The formula worksheet is in the background; the value worksheet is in the foreground.

FIGURE 12.4 EXCEL WORKSHEET FOR THE BEER PREFERENCE TEST
OF INDEPENDENCE

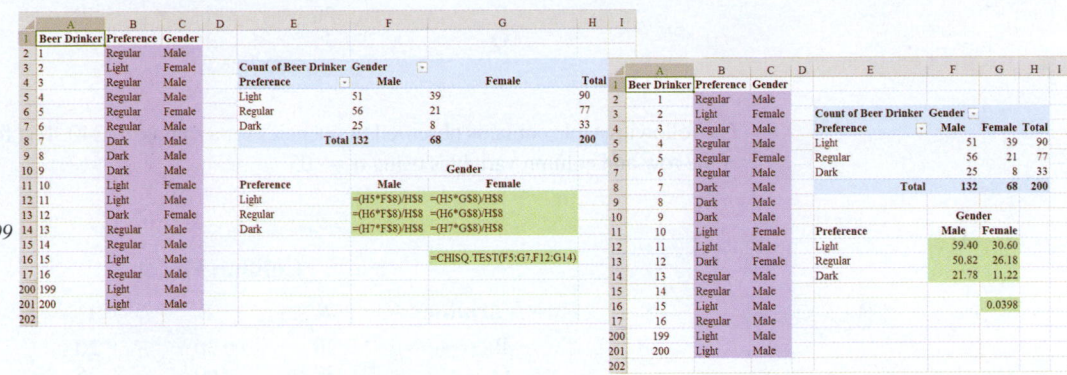

*Note: Rows 18–199
are hidden.*

BeerPreference

Enter/Access Data: Open the DATAfile named *BeerPreference*. The data are in cells
B2:C201 and labels are in column A and cells B1:C1.

Apply Tools: Cells E3:H8 show the contingency table resulting from using Excel's Pivot-
Table tool (see Section 2.4 for details regarding how to use this tool) to construct a two-way
table with beer preferences of light, regular, and dark as one of the variables and gender of
male and female as the other variable.

Enter Functions and Formulas: The Excel formulas in cells F12:G14 were used to compute the expected frequencies for each row and column. Once the observed and expected
frequencies have been computed, Excel's CHISQ.TEST function can be used to compute
the *p*-value for a test of independence. The inputs to the CHISQ.TEST function are the
range of values for the observed and expected frequencies. To compute the *p*-value for this
test of independence, we entered the following function into cell G16:

$$=\text{CHISQ.TEST(F5:G7,F12:G14)}$$

The value worksheet shows that the resulting *p*-value is .0398. Thus, with $\alpha = .05$, we reject
H_0 and conclude that beer preference is not independent of the gender of the beer drinker.

NOTE AND COMMENT

The test statistic for the chi-square tests in this
chapter requires an expected frequency of 5 for
each category. When a category has fewer than

five, it is often appropriate to combine two adjacent
categories to obtain an expected frequency of 5 or
more in each category.

Exercises

Methods

7. The following table contains observed frequencies for a sample of 200. Test for independence
of the row and column variables using $\alpha = .05$.

	Column Variable		
Row Variable	A	B	C
P	20	44	50
Q	30	26	30

8. The following table contains observed frequencies for a sample of 240. Test for independence of the row and column variables using $\alpha = .05$.

	Column Variable		
Row Variable	A	B	C
P	20	30	20
Q	30	60	25
R	10	15	30

 **Applications**

9. A *Bloomberg Businessweek* subscriber study asked, "In the past 12 months, when traveling for business, what type of airline ticket did you purchase most often?" A second question asked if the type of flight was domestic or international travel. Sample data obtained are shown in the following table.

	Type of Flight	
Type of Ticket	Domestic	International
First Class	29	22
Business Class	95	121
Economy Class	518	135

a. Using a .05 level of significance, is the type of ticket purchased independent of the type of flight? What is your conclusion?
b. Discuss any dependence that exists between the type of ticket and type of flight.

WorkforcePlan

10. A Deloitte employment survey asked a sample of human resource executives how their company planned to change its workforce over the next 12 months. A categorical response variable showed three options: The company plans to hire and add to the number of employees, the company plans no change in the number of employees, or the company plans to lay off and reduce the number of employees. Another categorical variable indicated if the company was private or public. Sample data for 180 companies are summarized as follows.

	Company	
Employment Plan	Private	Public
Add Employees	37	32
No Change	19	34
Lay Off Employees	16	42

a.   Conduct a test of independence to determine whether the employment plan for the next 12 months is independent of the type of company. At a .05 level of significance, what is your conclusion?

b.   Discuss any differences in the employment plans for private and public companies over the next 12 months.

11.   Health insurance benefits vary by the size of the company (the Henry J. Kaiser Family Foundation website, June 23, 2016). The sample data below show the number of companies providing health insurance for small, medium, and large companies. For purposes of this study, small companies are companies that have fewer than 100 employees. Medium-sized companies have 100 to 999 employees, and large companies have 1000 or more employees. The questionnaire sent to 225 employees asked whether or not the employee had health insurance and then asked the employee to indicate the size of the company.

	Size of the Company		
Health Insurance	**Small**	**Medium**	**Large**
Yes	36	65	88
No	14	10	12

a.   Conduct a test of independence to determine whether health insurance coverage is independent of the size of the company. What is the p-value? Using a .05 level of significance, what is your conclusion?

b.   A newspaper article indicated employees of small companies are more likely to lack health insurance coverage. Use percentages based on the above data to support this conclusion.

AutoQuality

12.   A J.D. Power and Associates vehicle quality survey asked new owners a variety of questions about their recently purchased automobile. One question asked for the owner's rating of the vehicle using categorical responses of average, outstanding, and exceptional. Another question asked for the owner's education level with the categorical responses some high school, high school graduate, some college, and college graduate. Assume the sample data below are for 500 owners who had recently purchased an automobile.

	Education			
Quality Rating	**Some HS**	**HS Grad**	**Some College**	**College Grad**
Average	35	30	20	60
Outstanding	45	45	50	90
Exceptional	20	25	30	50

a.   Use a .05 level of significance and a test of independence to determine whether a new owner's vehicle quality rating is independent of the owner's education. What is the p-value and what is your conclusion?

b.   Use the overall percentage of average, outstanding, and exceptional ratings to comment on how new owners rate the quality of their recently purchased automobiles.

13.   *The Wall Street Journal* Annual Corporate Perceptions Study surveyed readers and asked how each rated the quality of management and the reputation of the company for over 250 worldwide corporations (*The Wall Street Journal* website, June 23, 2016). Both the quality

of management and the reputation of the company were rated on an excellent, good, and fair categorical scale. Assume the sample data for 200 respondents below applies to this study.

	Reputation of Company		
Quality of Management	Excellent	Good	Fair
Excellent	40	25	5
Good	35	35	10
Fair	25	10	15

a. Use a .05 level of significance and test for independence of the quality of management and the reputation of the company. What is the *p*-value and what is your conclusion?

b. If there is a dependence or association between the two ratings, discuss and use probabilities to justify your answer.

14. As the price of oil rises, there is increased worldwide interest in alternate sources of energy. A *Financial Times*/Harris Poll surveyed people in six countries to assess attitudes toward a variety of alternate forms of energy. The data in the following table are a portion of the poll's findings concerning whether people favor or oppose the building of new nuclear power plants.

	Country					
Response	Great Britain	France	Italy	Spain	Germany	United States
Strongly favor	141	161	298	133	128	204
Favor more than oppose	348	366	309	222	272	326
Oppose more than favor	381	334	219	311	322	316
Strongly oppose	217	215	219	443	389	174

a. How large was the sample in this poll?

b. Conduct a hypothesis test to determine whether people's attitude toward building new nuclear power plants is independent of country. What is your conclusion?

c. Using the percentage of respondents who "strongly favor" and "favor more than oppose," which country has the most favorable attitude toward building new nuclear power plants? Which country has the least favorable attitude?

15. The Carnegie Classification of Institutes of Higher Education categorizes colleges and universities on the basis of their research and degree-granting activities. Universities that grant doctoral degrees are placed into one of three classifications: highest research activity, higher research activity, or moderate research activity. The Carnegie classifications for public and not-for-profit private doctoral degree–granting universities follow.

	Carnegie Classification		
Type of University	Highest Research Activity	Higher Research Activity	Moderate Research Activity
Public	81	76	38
Not-For-Profit Private	34	31	58

Using a .05 level of significance, conduct a test of independence to determine whether Carnegie classification is independent of type of university for universities that grant doctoral degrees. What is the *p*-value and what is your conclusion?

16. On a syndicated television show the two hosts often create the impression that they strongly disagree about which movies are best. Each movie review is categorized as Pro ("thumbs up"), Con ("thumbs down"), or Mixed. The results of 160 movie ratings by the two hosts are shown here.

Host A	Host B		
	Con	**Mixed**	**Pro**
Con	24	8	13
Mixed	8	13	11
Pro	10	9	64

Use a test of independence with a .01 level of significance to analyze the data. What is your conclusion?

Testing for Equality of Three or More Population Proportions

In Section 10.2, we introduced methods of statistical inference for population proportions with two populations where the hypothesis test conclusion was based on the standard normal (z) test statistic. We now show how the chi-square (χ^2) test statistic can be used to make statistical inferences about the equality of population proportions for three or more populations. The methodology is similar to that for the test of independence in Section 12.2 in the sense that we will compare a table of observed frequencies to a table of expected frequencies.

Using the notation

$$p_1 = \text{population proportion for population 1}$$
$$p_2 = \text{population proportion for population 2}$$

and

$$\vdots \qquad\qquad \vdots$$

$$p_k = \text{population proportion for population } k$$

the hypotheses for the equality of population proportions for $k \geq 3$ populations are as follows:

$$H_0: p_1 = p_2 = \cdots = p_k$$

$$H_a: \text{Not all population proportions are equal}$$

If the sample data and the chi-square test computations indicate H_0 cannot be rejected, we cannot detect a difference among the k population proportions. However, if the sample data and the chi-square test computations indicate H_0 can be rejected, we have statistical evidence to conclude that not all k population proportions are equal; that is, one or more population proportions differ from the other population proportions. Further analyses can be conducted to determine which population proportion or proportions are significantly different from others. Let us demonstrate this chi-square test by considering an application.

Organizations such as J.D. Power and Associates use the proportion of owners likely to repurchase a particular automobile as an indication of customer loyalty for the automobile. An automobile with a greater proportion of owners likely to repurchase is considered to

TABLE 12.5   SAMPLE RESULTS OF LIKELY TO REPURCHASE FOR THREE POPULATIONS OF AUTOMOBILE OWNERS (OBSERVED FREQUENCIES)

DATA *file*

AutoLoyalty

| | | **Automobile Owners** | | | |
		Chevrolet Impala	**Ford Fusion**	**Honda Accord**	**Total**
Likely to Repurchase	**Yes**	69	120	123	312
	No	56	80	52	188
	Total	125	200	175	500

have greater customer loyalty. Suppose that in a particular study we want to compare the customer loyalty for three automobiles: Chevrolet Impala, Ford Fusion, and Honda Accord. The current owners of each of the three automobiles form the three populations for the study. The three population proportions of interest are as follows:

p_1 = proportion likely to repurchase for the population of Chevrolet Impala owners

p_2 = proportion likely to repurchase for the population of Ford Fusion owners

p_3 = proportion likely to repurchase for the population of Honda Accord owners

The hypotheses are stated as follows:

$$H_0: p_1 = p_2 = p_3$$

H_a: Not all population proportions are equal

To conduct this hypothesis test we begin by taking a sample of owners from each of the three populations. Thus we will have a sample of Chevrolet Impala owners, a sample of Ford Fusion owners, and a sample of Honda Accord owners. Each sample provides categorical data indicating whether the respondents are likely or not likely to repurchase the automobile. The data for samples of 125 Chevrolet Impala owners, 200 Ford Fusion owners, and 175 Honda Accord owners are summarized in Table 12.5. This table has two rows for the responses Yes and No and three columns, one for each of the populations of automobile owners. The observed frequencies are summarized in the six cells of the table corresponding to each combination of the likely to repurchase responses and the three populations.

In studies such as these, we often use the same sample size for each population. We have chosen different sample sizes in this example to show that the chi-square test is not restricted to equal sample sizes for each of the k populations.

Using Table 12.5, we see that 69 of the 125 Chevrolet Impala owners said they were likely to repurchase a Chevrolet Impala; 120 of the 200 Ford Fusion owners said they were likely to repurchase a Ford Fusion; and 123 of the 175 Honda Accord owners said they were likely to repurchase a Honda Accord. Also, across all three samples, 312 of the 500 owners in the study indicated that they were likely to repurchase their current automobile. The question now is how to analyze the data in Table 12.5 to determine whether the hypothesis $H_0: p_1 = p_2 = p_3$ should be rejected.

The data in Table 12.5 are the *observed frequencies* for each of the six cells that represent the six combinations of the likely to repurchase response and the owner population. If we can determine the *expected frequencies under the assumption H_0 is true*, we can use a chi-square test statistic to determine whether there is a significant difference between the observed and expected frequencies. If a significant difference exists between the observed and expected frequencies, the hypothesis H_0 can be rejected and there is evidence that not all the population proportions are equal.

Expected frequencies for the six cells of the table are based on the following rationale. First, we assume that the null hypothesis of equal population proportions is true. Then we note that the three samples include a total of 500 owners; for this group, 312 owners indicated that they were likely to repurchase their current automobile. Thus, 312/500 = .624 is the overall proportion of owners indicating they are likely to repurchase their current automobile.

If H_0: $p_1 = p_2 = p_3$ is true, .624 would be the best estimate of the proportion responding likely to repurchase for each of the automobile owner populations. So if the assumption of H_0 is true, we would expect .624 of the 125 Chevrolet Impala owners, or .624(125) = 78 owners to indicate they are likely to repurchase the Impala. Using the .624 overall proportion, we would expect .624(200) = 124.8 of the 200 Ford Fusion owners and .624(175) = 109.2 of the Honda Accord owners to respond that they are likely to repurchase their respective model of automobile.

The approach of computing a table of expected frequencies for this test of multiple proportions is essentially the same as we used for expected frequencies in Section 12.2. The following formula can be used to provide the expected frequencies under the assumption that the null hypothesis concerning equality of the population proportions is true.

EXPECTED FREQUENCIES UNDER THE ASSUMPTION H_0 IS TRUE

$$e_{ij} = \frac{(\text{Row } i \text{ Total})(\text{Column } j \text{ Total})}{\text{Sum of Sample Sizes}} \qquad \textbf{(12.4)}$$

Using equation (12.4), we see that the expected frequency of Yes responses (row 1) for Honda Accord owners (column 3) would be e_{13} = (Row 1 Total)(Column 3 Total)/(Sum of Sample Sizes) = (312)(175)/500 = 109.2. Use equation (12.4) to verify the other expected frequencies are as shown in Table 12.6.

The test procedure for comparing the observed frequencies of Table 12.5 with the expected frequencies of Table 12.6 involves the computation of the following chi-square statistic:

CHI-SQUARE TEST STATISTIC

$$\chi^2 = \sum_i \sum_j \frac{(f_{ij} - e_{ij})^2}{e_{ij}} \qquad \textbf{(12.5)}$$

where

f_{ij} = observed frequency for the cell in row i and column j

e_{ij} = expected frequency for the cell in row i and column j under the assumption H_0 is true

Note: In a chi-square test involving the equality of k population proportions, the above test statistic has a chi-square distribution with $k - 1$ degrees of freedom provided the expected frequency is 5 *or more* for each cell.

TABLE 12.6   EXPECTED FREQUENCIES FOR LIKELY TO REPURCHASE FOR THREE POPULATIONS OF AUTOMOBILE OWNERS IF H_0 IS TRUE

		Automobile Owners			
		Chevrolet Impala	**Ford Fusion**	**Honda Accord**	**Total**
Likely to Repurchase	**Yes**	78	124.8	109.2	312
	No	47	75.2	65.8	188
	Total	125	200.0	175.0	500

TABLE 12.7 COMPUTATION OF THE CHI-SQUARE TEST STATISTIC FOR THE TEST OF EQUAL POPULATION PROPORTIONS

Likely to Repurchase?	Automobile Owner	Observed Frequency (f_{ij})	Expected Frequency (e_{ij})	Difference $(f_{ij} - e_{ij})$	Squared Difference $(f_{ij} - e_{ij})^2$	Squared Difference Divided by Expected Frequency $(f_{ij} - e_{ij})^2/e_{ij}$
Yes	Impala	69	78.0	−9.0	81.00	1.04
Yes	Fusion	120	124.8	−4.8	23.04	0.18
Yes	Accord	123	109.2	13.8	190.44	1.74
No	Impala	56	47.0	9.0	81.00	1.72
No	Fusion	80	75.2	4.8	23.04	0.31
No	Accord	52	65.8	−13.8	190.44	2.89
	Total	500	500.0			$\chi^2 = 7.89$

Reviewing the expected frequencies in Table 12.6, we see that the expected frequency is at least five for each cell in the table. We therefore proceed with the computation of the chi-square test statistic. The calculations necessary to compute the value of the test statistic are shown in Table 12.7. In this case, we see that the value of the test statistic is $\chi^2 = 7.89$.

The chi-square test presented in this section is always a one-tailed test with the rejection of H_0 occurring in the upper tail of the chi-square distribution.

We can use the upper tail area of the appropriate chi-square distribution and the p-value approach to determine whether the null hypothesis can be rejected. In the automobile brand loyalty study, the three owner populations indicate that the appropriate chi-square distribution has $k - 1 = 3 - 1 = 2$ degrees of freedom. Using row two of the chi-square distribution table, we have the following:

Area in Upper Tail	.10	.05	.025	.01	.005
χ^2 Value (2 *df*)	4.605	5.991	7.378	9.210	10.597

$$\chi^2 = 7.89$$

We see the upper tail area at $\chi^2 = 7.89$ is between .025 and .01. Thus, the corresponding upper tail area or p-value must be between .025 and .01. With p-value $\leq$ .05, we reject H_0 and conclude that the three population proportions are not all equal and thus there is a difference in brand loyalties among the Chevrolet Impala, Ford Fusion, and Honda Accord owners. In the Using Excel subsection that follows, we will see that the p-value $= .0193$.

Instead of using the p-value, we could use the critical value approach to draw the same conclusion. With $\alpha = .05$ and 2 degrees of freedom, the critical value for the chi-square test statistic is $\chi^2 = 5.991$. The upper tail rejection region becomes

Reject H_0 if $\chi^2 \geq 5.991$

With $7.89 \geq 5.991$, we reject H_0. Thus, the p-value approach and the critical value approach provide the same hypothesis-testing conclusion.

Let us now summarize the general steps that can be used to conduct a chi-square test for the equality of the population proportions for three or more populations.

A CHI-SQUARE TEST FOR THE EQUALITY OF POPULATION
PROPORTIONS FOR $k \geq 3$ POPULATIONS

1. State the null and alternative hypotheses

$$H_0: p_1 = p_2 = \cdots = p_k$$
H_a: Not all population proportions are equal

2. Select a random sample from each of the populations and record the observed frequencies, f_{ij}, in a table with 2 rows and k columns
3. Assume the null hypothesis is true and compute the expected frequencies, e_{ij}
4. If the expected frequency, e_{ij}, is 5 or more for each cell, compute the test statistic:

$$\chi^2 = \sum_i \sum_j \frac{(f_{ij} - e_{ij})^2}{e_{ij}}$$

5. Rejection rule:

p-value approach:	Reject H_0 if p-value $\leq \alpha$
Critical value approach:	Reject H_0 if $\chi^2 \geq \chi_\alpha^2$

where the chi-square distribution has $k - 1$ degrees of freedom and α is the level of significance for the test.

A Multiple Comparison Procedure

We have used a chi-square test to conclude that the population proportions for the three populations of automobile owners are not all equal. Thus, some differences among the population proportions exist and the study indicates that customer loyalties are not all the same for the Chevrolet Impala, Ford Fusion, and Honda Accord owners. To identify where the differences between population proportions exist, we can begin by computing the three sample proportions as follows:

Brand Loyalty Sample Proportions

Chevrolet Impala	$\bar{p}_1 =$	$69/125 = .5520$
Ford Fusion	$\bar{p}_2 =$	$120/200 = .6000$
Honda Accord	$\bar{p}_3 =$	$123/175 = .7029$

Since the chi-square test indicated that not all population proportions are equal, it is reasonable for us to proceed by attempting to determine where differences among the population proportions exist. For this we will rely on a multiple comparison procedure that can be used to conduct statistical tests between all pairs of population proportions. In the following, we discuss a multiple comparison procedure known as the **Marascuilo procedure**. This is a relatively straightforward procedure for making pairwise comparisons of all pairs of population proportions. We will demonstrate the computations required by this multiple comparison test procedure for the automobile customer loyalty study.

We begin by computing the absolute value of the pairwise difference between sample proportions for each pair of populations in the study. In the three-population automobile brand loyalty study we compare populations 1 and 2, populations 1 and 3, and then populations 2 and 3 using the sample proportions as follows:

Chevrolet Impala and Ford Fusion

$$|\bar{p}_1 - \bar{p}_2| = |.5520 - .6000| = .0480$$

Chevrolet Impala and Honda Accord

$$|\bar{p}_1 - \bar{p}_3| = |.5520 - .7029| = .1509$$

Ford Fusion and Honda Accord

$$|\bar{p}_2 - \bar{p}_3| = |.6000 - .7029| = .1029$$

In a second step, we select a level of significance and compute the corresponding critical value for each pairwise comparison using the following expression.

CRITICAL VALUES FOR THE MARASCUILO PAIRWISE COMPARISON PROCEDURE FOR k POPULATION PROPORTIONS

For each pairwise comparison compute a critical value as follows:

$$CV_{ij} = \sqrt{\chi_\alpha^2} \sqrt{\frac{\bar{p}_i(1 - \bar{p}_i)}{n_i} + \frac{\bar{p}_j(1 - \bar{p}_j)}{n_j}} \qquad \textbf{(12.6)}$$

where

χ_α^2 = chi-square with a level of significance α and $k - 1$ degrees of freedom

$\bar{p}_i$ and $\bar{p}_j$ = sample proportions for populations i and j

n_i and n_j = sample sizes for populations i and j

Using the chi-square distribution in Table 3 of Appendix B with $k - 1 = 3 - 1 = 2$ degrees of freedom, and a .05 level of significance, we have $\chi_{.05}^2 = 5.991$. Now using the sample proportions $\bar{p}_1 = .5520$, $\bar{p}_2 = .6000$, and $\bar{p}_3 = .7029$, the critical values for the three pairwise comparison tests are as follows:

Chevrolet Impala and Ford Fusion

$$CV_{12} = \sqrt{5.991} \sqrt{\frac{.5520(1 - .5520)}{125} + \frac{.6000(1 - .6000)}{200}} = .1380$$

Chevrolet Impala and Honda Accord

$$CV_{13} = \sqrt{5.991} \sqrt{\frac{.5520(1 - .5520)}{125} + \frac{.7029(1 - .7029)}{175}} = .1379$$

Ford Fusion and Honda Accord

$$CV_{23} = \sqrt{5.991} \sqrt{\frac{.6000(1 - .6000)}{200} + \frac{.7029(1 - .7029)}{175}} = .1198$$

If the absolute value of any pairwise sample proportion difference $|\bar{p}_i - \bar{p}_j|$ exceeds its corresponding critical value, CV_{ij}, the pairwise difference is significant at the .05 level of significance and we can conclude that the two corresponding population

TABLE 12.8 PAIRWISE COMPARISON TESTS FOR THE AUTOMOBILE BRAND LOYALTY STUDY

Pairwise Comparison	$\lvert \bar{p}_i - \bar{p}_j \rvert$	CV_{ij}	Significant if $\lvert \bar{p}_i - \bar{p}_j \rvert > CV_{ij}$
Chevrolet Impala vs. Ford Fusion	.0480	.1380	Not significant
Chevrolet Impala vs. Honda Accord	.1509	.1379	Significant
Ford Fusion vs. Honda Accord	.1029	.1198	Not significant

An Excel workbook that eases the computational burden of making these pairwise comparison is on the website.

PairwiseComparisons

proportions are different. The final step of the pairwise comparison procedure is summarized in Table 12.8.

The conclusion from the pairwise comparison procedure is that the only significant difference in customer loyalty occurs between the Chevrolet Impala and the Honda Accord. Our sample results indicate that the Honda Accord had a greater population proportion of owners who say they are likely to repurchase the Honda Accord. Thus, we can conclude that the Honda Accord ($\bar{p}_3 = .7029$) has a greater customer loyalty than the Chevrolet Impala ($\bar{p}_1 = .5520$).

The results of the study are inconclusive as to the comparative loyalty of the Ford Fusion. While the Ford Fusion did not show significantly different results when compared to the Chevrolet Impala or Honda Accord, a larger sample may have revealed a significant difference between Ford Fusion and the other two automobiles in terms of customer loyalty. It is not uncommon for a multiple comparison procedure to show significance for some pairwise comparisons and yet not show significance for other pairwise comparisons in the study.

Using Excel to Conduct a Test of Multiple Proportions

The Excel procedure used to test for the equality of three or more population proportions is essentially the same as the Excel procedure used to conduct a test of independence. The CHISQ.TEST function is used with the table of observed frequencies as one input and the table of expected frequencies as the other input. The function output is the p-value for the test. We illustrate using the automobile brand loyalty study. Refer to Figure 12.5 as we describe the tasks involved. The formula worksheet is in the background; the value worksheet is in the foreground.

FIGURE 12.5 EXCEL WORKSHEET FOR THE AUTOMOBILE LOYALTY STUDY

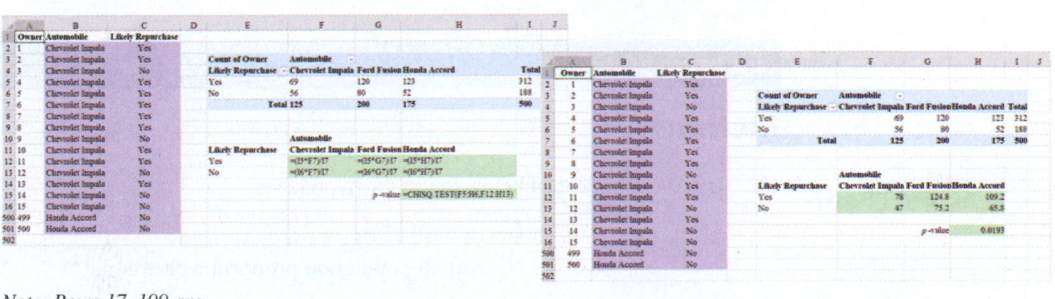

Note: Rows 17–199 are hidden.

Enter/Access Data: Open the DATAfile named *AutoLoyalty*. The data are in cells B2:C501 and labels are in column A and cells B1:C1.

Apply Tools: The observed frequencies have been computed in cells F5:H6 using Excel's PivotTable tool (see Section 2.4 for details regarding how to use this tool).

Enter Functions and Formulas: The Excel formulas in cells F12:H13 were used to compute the expected frequencies for each category. Once the observed and expected frequencies have been computed, Excel's CHISQ.TEST function has been used in cell H15 to compute the p-value for the test. The value worksheet shows that the resulting p-value is .0193. With $\alpha = .05$, we reject the null hypothesis that the three population proportions are equal.

NOTES AND COMMENTS

1. In Chapter 10, we used the standard normal distribution and the z test statistic to conduct hypothesis tests about the proportions of two populations. However, the chi-square test introduced in this section can also be used to conduct the hypothesis test that the proportions of two populations are equal. The results will be the same under both test procedures and the value of the test statistic χ^2 will be equal to the square of the value of the test statistic z. An advantage of the methodology in Chapter 10 is that it can be used for either a one-tailed or a two-tailed hypothesis about the proportions of two populations, whereas the chi-square test in this section can be used only for two-tailed tests. Exercise 22 will give you a chance to use the chi-square test for the hypothesis that the proportions of two populations are equal.

2. Each of the k populations in this section had two response outcomes, Yes or No. In effect, each population had a binomial distribution with parameter p the population proportion of Yes responses. An extension of the chi-square procedure in this section applies when each of the k populations has three or more possible responses. In this case, each

   population is said to have a multinomial distribution. The chi-square calculations for the expected frequencies, e_{ij}, and the test statistic, χ^2, are the same as shown in expressions (12.4) and (12.5). The only difference is that the null hypothesis assumes that the multinomial distribution for the response variable is the same for all populations. With r responses for each of the k populations, the chi-square test statistic has $(r - 1)(k - 1)$ degrees of freedom. Exercise 24 will give you a chance to use the chi-square test to compare three populations with multinomial distributions.

3. The procedure for computing expected frequencies for the test of multiple proportions and for the test of independence in Section 12.2 are the same and both tests employ the same chi-square test statistic. But a key difference is that the test of independence is based on one sample from a single population. The test of multiple proportions is based on k independent samples from k populations. Thus, with the test of multiple proportions we can control the sample size for each of the k population categories. With the test of independence, we control only the overall sample size.

Exercises

Methods

17. Use the sample data below to test the hypotheses

    H_0: $p_1 = p_2 = p_3$

    H_a: Not all population proportions are equal

    where p_i is the population proportion of Yes responses for population i. Using a .05 level of significance, what is the p-value and what is your conclusion?

		Populations	
Response	**1**	**2**	**3**
Yes	150	150	96
No	100	150	104

18. Reconsider the observed frequencies in exercise 17.
    a. Compute the sample proportion for each population.
    b. Use the multiple comparison procedure to determine which population proportions differ significantly. Use a .05 level of significance.

Applications

19. The following sample data represent the number of late and on-time flights for Delta, United, and US Airways (*Bureau of Transportation Statistics,* March 2012).

		Airline	
Flight	**Delta**	**United**	**US Airways**
Late	39	51	56
On Time	261	249	344

a. Formulate the hypotheses for a test that will determine whether the population proportion of late flights is the same for all three airlines.
b. Conduct the hypothesis test with a .05 level of significance. What is the *p*-value and what is your conclusion?
c. Compute the sample proportion of late flights for each airline. What is the overall proportion of late flights for the three airlines?

20. Benson Manufacturing is considering ordering electronic components from three different suppliers. The suppliers may differ in terms of quality in that the proportion or percentage of defective components may differ among the suppliers. To evaluate the proportion of defective components for the suppliers, Benson has requested a sample shipment of 500 components from each supplier. The number of defective components and the number of good components found in each shipment are as follows.

		Supplier	
Component	**A**	**B**	**C**
Defective	15	20	40
Good	485	480	460

a. Formulate the hypotheses that can be used to test for equal proportions of defective components provided by the three suppliers.
b. Using a .05 level of significance, conduct the hypothesis test. What is the *p*-value and what is your conclusion?
c. Conduct a multiple comparison test to determine whether there is an overall best supplier or if one supplier can be eliminated because of poor quality.

21. Kate Sanders, a researcher in the department of biology at IPFW University, studied the effect of agriculture contaminants on the stream fish population in northeastern Indiana (April 2012). Specially designed traps collected samples of fish at each of four stream locations. A research question was, Did the differences in agricultural contaminants found at the four locations alter the proportion of the fish population by gender? Observed frequencies were as follows.

		Stream Locations		
Gender	**A**	**B**	**C**	**D**
Male	49	44	49	39
Female	41	46	36	44

a. Focusing on the proportion of male fish at each location, test the hypothesis that the population proportions are equal for all four locations. Use a .05 level of significance. What is the *p*-value and what is your conclusion?

b. Does it appear that differences in agricultural contaminants found at the four locations altered the fish population by gender?

Exercise 22 shows a chi-square test can be used when the hypothesis is about the equality of two population proportions.

22. A tax preparation firm is interested in comparing the quality of work at two of its regional offices. The observed frequencies showing the number of sampled returns with errors and the number of sampled returns that were correct are as follows.

	Regional Office	
Return	**Office 1**	**Office 2**
Error	35	27
Correct	215	273

a. What are the sample proportions of returns with errors at the two offices?

b. Use the chi-square test procedure to see if there is a significant difference between the population proportion of error rates for the two offices. Test the null hypothesis H_0: $p_1 = p_2$ with a .10 level of significance. What is the *p*-value and what is your conclusion? (*Note*: We generally use the chi-square test of equal proportions when there are three or more populations, but this example shows that the same chi-square test can be used for testing equal proportions with two populations.)

c. In the Section 10.2, a *z* test was used to conduct the above test. Either a χ^2 test statistic or a *z* test statistic may be used to test the hypothesis. However, when we want to make inferences about the proportions for two populations, we generally prefer the *z* test statistic procedure. Refer to the Notes and Comments at the end of this section and comment on why the *z* test statistic provides the user with more options for inferences about the proportions of two populations.

23. Social networking is becoming more and more popular around the world. Pew Research Center used a survey of adults in several countries to determine the percentage of adults who use social networking sites (*USA Today*, February 8, 2012). Assume that the results for surveys in Great Britain, Israel, Russia, and United States are as follows.

	Country			
Use Social Networking Sites	**Great Britain**	**Israel**	**Russia**	**United States**
Yes	344	265	301	500
No	456	235	399	500

a. Conduct a hypothesis test to determine whether the proportion of adults using social networking sites is equal for all four countries. What is the p-value? Using a .05 level of significance, what is your conclusion?

b. What are the sample proportions for each of the four countries? Which country has the largest proportion of adults using social networking sites?

c. Using a .05 level of significance, conduct multiple pairwise comparison tests among the four countries. What is your conclusion?

Exercise 24 shows a chi-square test can also be used for multiple population tests when the categorical response variable has three or more outcomes.

24. A manufacturer is considering purchasing parts from three different suppliers. The parts received from the suppliers are classified as having a minor defect, having a major defect, or being good. Test results from samples of parts received from each of the three suppliers are shown below. Note that any test with these data is no longer a test of proportions for the three supplier populations because the categorical response variable has three outcomes: minor defect, major defect, and good.

	Supplier		
Part Tested	A	B	C
Minor Defect	15	13	21
Major Defect	5	11	5
Good	130	126	124

Using the preceding data, conduct a hypothesis test to determine whether the distribution of defects is the same for the three suppliers. Use the chi-square test calculations as presented in this section with the exception that a table with r rows and c columns results in a chi-square test statistic with $(r - 1)(c - 1)$ degrees of freedom. Using a .05 level of significance, what is the p-value and what is your conclusion?

Summary

In this chapter we have introduced hypothesis tests for the following applications.

1. Goodness of Fit Test. A test designed to determine whether the observed frequency distribution for a sample differs significantly from what we would expect given the hypothesized probabilities for each category.
2. Test of Independence. A test designed to determine whether the table of observed frequencies for a sample involving two categorical variables from the same population differs significantly from what we would expect if the two variables were independent as specified in the null hypothesis.
3. Test of Equality for Three or More Population Proportions. A test designed to determine whether three or more sample proportions differ significantly from what we would expect if the corresponding population proportions were equal as stated in the null hypothesis.

The first two tests are based on a single sample from a single population. The third test is based on independent samples from three or more different populations. All tests use a chi-square (χ^2) test statistic that is based on the differences between observed frequencies from a sample and the frequencies that we would expect if the null hypothesis was true. Large differences between observed and expected frequencies provide a large value for the chi-square test statistic and indicate that the null hypothesis should be rejected; thus, these chi-square tests are upper tailed tests.

Glossary

Goodness of fit test A chi-square test that can be used to test that a probability distribution has a specific historical or theoretical probability distribution. This test was demonstrated for a multinomial probability distribution.

Marascuilo procedure A multiple comparison procedure that can be used to test for a significant difference between pairs of population proportions. This test can be helpful in identifying differences between pairs of population proportions whenever the hypothesis of equal population proportions has been rejected.

Multinomial probability distribution A probability distribution where each outcome belongs to one of three or more categories. The multinomial probability distribution extends the binomial probability distribution from two to three or more outcomes per trial.

Test of independence A chi-square test that can be used to test for the independence of two random variables. If the hypothesis of independence is rejected, it can be concluded that the random variables are associated or dependent.

Key Formulas

Test Statistic for the Goodness of Fit Test

$$\chi^2 = \sum_{i=1}^{k} \frac{(f_i - e_i)^2}{e_i} \tag{12.1}$$

Expected Frequencies: Test of Independence

$$e_{ij} = \frac{(\text{Row } i \text{ Total})(\text{Column } j \text{ Total})}{\text{Sample Size}} \tag{12.2}$$

Chi-Square Test Statistic for Test of Independence and Test for Equality of Three or More Population Proportions

$$\chi^2 = \sum_{i} \sum_{j} \frac{(f_{ij} - e_{ij})^2}{e_{ij}} \tag{12.3 and 12.5}$$

Expected Frequencies: Test for Equality of Three or More Population Proportions

$$e_{ij} = \frac{(\text{Row } i \text{ Total})(\text{Column } j \text{ Total})}{\text{Sum of Sample Sizes}} \tag{12.4}$$

Critical Values for the Marascuilo Pairwise Comparison Procedure

$$CV_{ij} = \sqrt{\chi_\alpha^2} \sqrt{\frac{\bar{p}_i(1 - \bar{p}_i)}{n_i} + \frac{\bar{p}_j(1 - \bar{p}_j)}{n_j}} \tag{12.6}$$

Supplementary Exercises

DATA *file*
BBB

25. In 2011, the industries with the most complaints to the Better Business Bureau were banks, cable and satellite television companies, collection agencies, cellular phone providers, and

new car dealerships (*USA Today*, April 16, 2012). The results for a sample of 200 complaints are contained in the DATAfile named *BBB*.

a. Construct a frequency distribution for the number of complaints by industry.

b. Using $\alpha = .01$, conduct a hypothesis test to determine whether the probability of a complaint is the same for the five industries. What is your conclusion?

c. Drop the industry with the most complaints. Using $\alpha = .05$, conduct a hypothesis test to determine whether the probability of a complaint is the same for the remaining four industries.

26. Bistro 65 is a chain of Italian restaurants with locations in Ohio and Kentucky. The Bistro 65 menu has four categories of entrees: Pasta, Steak & Chops, Seafood, and Other (e.g., pizza, sandwiches, etc.). Historical data for the chain show that the probability a customer will order an entrée from one of the four categories is .4 for Pasta, .1 for Steak & Chops, .2 for Seafood, and .3 for Other. A new Bistro 65 restaurant has just opened in Dayton, Ohio, and the following purchase frequencies have been observed for the first 200 customers.

Category	Frequency
Pasta	70
Steak & Chops	30
Seafood	50
Other	50
Total	200

a. Conduct a hypothesis test to determine whether the order pattern for the new restaurant in Dayton is the same as the historical pattern for the established Bistro 65 restaurants. Use $\alpha = .05$.

b. If the difference in part (a) is significant, prepare a bar chart to show where the differences occur. Comment on any differences observed.

27. Based on sales over a six-month period, the five top-selling compact cars are Chevy Cruze, Ford Focus, Hyundai Elantra, Honda Civic, and Toyota Corolla (*Motor Trend*, November 2, 2011). Based on total sales, the market shares for these five compact cars were Chevy Cruze 24%, Ford Focus 21%, Hyundai Elantra 20%, Honda Civic 18%, and Toyota Corolla 17%. A sample of 400 compact car sales in Chicago showed the following number of vehicles sold.

Chevy Cruze	108
Ford Focus	92
Hyundai Elantra	64
Honda Civic	84
Toyota Corolla	52

Use a goodness of fit test to determine whether the sample data indicate that the market shares for the five compact cars in Chicago are different than the market shares reported by *Motor Trend*. Using a .05 level of significance, what is the *p*-value and what is your conclusion? What market share differences, if any, exist in Chicago?

28. A Pew Research Center survey asked respondents if they would rather live in a place with a slower pace of life or a place with a faster pace of life. The survey also asked the respondent's gender. Consider the following sample data.

	Gender	
Preferred Pace of Life	**Male**	**Female**
Slower	230	218
No Preference	20	24
Faster	90	48

a. Is the preferred pace of life independent of gender? Using a .05 level of significance, what is the *p*-value and what is your conclusion?

b. Discuss any differences between the preferences of men and women.

29. Bara Research Group conducted a survey about church attendance. The survey respondents were asked about their church attendance and asked to indicate their age. Use the sample data to determine whether church attendance is independent of age. Using a .05 level of significance, what is the *p*-value and what is your conclusion? What conclusion can you draw about church attendance as individuals grow older?

	Age			
Church Attendance	**20 to 29**	**30 to 39**	**40 to 49**	**50 to 59**
Yes	31	63	94	72
No	69	87	106	78

Ambulance

30. An ambulance service responds to emergency calls for two counties in Virginia. One county is an urban county and the other is a rural county. A sample of 471 ambulance calls over the past two years showed the county and the day of the week for each emergency call. Data are as follows.

	Day of Week						
County	**Sun**	**Mon**	**Tue**	**Wed**	**Thu**	**Fri**	**Sat**
Urban	61	48	50	55	63	73	43
Rural	7	9	16	13	9	14	10

Test for independence of the county and the day of the week. Using a .05 level of significance, what is the *p*-value and what is your conclusion?

31. In a quality control test of parts manufactured at Dabco Corporation, an engineer sampled parts produced on the first, second, and third shifts. The research study was designed to determine whether the population proportion of good parts was the same for all three shifts. Sample data follow.

	Production Shift		
Quality	**First**	**Second**	**Third**
Good	285	368	176
Defective	15	32	24

a. Using a .05 level of significance, conduct a hypothesis test to determine whether the population proportion of good parts is the same for all three shifts. What is the *p*-value and what is your conclusion?

b.   If the conclusion is that the population proportions are not all equal, use a multiple comparison procedure to determine how the shifts differ in terms of quality. What shift or shifts need to improve the quality of parts produced?

32.   Phoenix Marketing International identified Bridgeport, Connecticut; Los Alamos, New Mexico; Naples, Florida; and Washington, DC, as the four U.S. cities with the highest percentage of millionaires. Data consistent with that study show the following number of millionaires for samples of individuals from each of the four cities.

	City			
Millionaire	**Bridgeport**	**Los Alamos**	**Naples**	**Washington, DC**
Yes	44	35	36	34
No	456	265	364	366

a.   What is the estimate of the percentage of millionaires in each of these cities?
b.   Using a .05 level of significance, test for the equality of the population proportion of millionaires for these four cities. What is the *p*-value and what is your conclusion?

33.   The five most popular art museums in the world are Musée du Louvre, the Metropolitan Museum of Art, British Museum, National Gallery, and Tate Modern (*The Art Newspaper*, April 2012). Which of these five museums would visitors most frequently rate as spectacular? Samples of recent visitors of each of these museums were taken, and the results of these samples follow.

	Musée du Louvre	Metropolitan Museum of Art	British Museum	National Gallery	Tate Modern
Rated Spectacular	113	94	96	78	88
Did Not Rate Spectacular	37	46	64	42	22

a.   Use the sample data to calculate the point estimate of the population proportion of visitors who rated each of these museums as spectacular.
b.   Conduct a hypothesis test to determine if the population proportion of visitors who rated the museum as spectacular is equal for these five museums. Using a .05 level of significance, what is the *p*-value and what is your conclusion?

Case Problem 1   A Bipartisan Agenda for Change

In a study conducted by Zogby International for the *Democrat and Chronicle,* more than 700 New Yorkers were polled to determine whether the New York state government works. Respondents surveyed were asked questions involving pay cuts for state legislators, restrictions on lobbyists, term limits for legislators, and whether state citizens should be able to put matters directly on the state ballot for a vote. The results regarding several proposed reforms had broad support, crossing all demographic and political lines.

Suppose that a follow-up survey of 100 individuals who live in the western region of New York was conducted. The party affiliation (Democrat, Independent, Republican) of each individual surveyed was recorded, as well as their responses to the following three questions.

1.   Should legislative pay be cut for every day the state budget is late?
     Yes _____   No _____
2.   Should there be more restrictions on lobbyists?
     Yes _____   No _____
3.   Should there be term limits requiring that legislators serve a fixed number of years?
     Yes _____   No _____

NYReform

The responses were coded using 1 for a Yes response and 2 for a No response. The complete data set is available in the DATAfile named *NYReform*.

Managerial Report

1. Use descriptive statistics to summarize the data from this study. What are your preliminary conclusions about the independence of the response (Yes or No) and party affiliation for each of the three questions in the survey?
2. With regard to question 1, test for the independence of the response (Yes and No) and party affiliation. Use $\alpha = .05$.
3. With regard to question 2, test for the independence of the response (Yes and No) and party affiliation. Use $\alpha = .05$.
4. With regard to question 3, test for the independence of the response (Yes and No) and party affiliation. Use $\alpha = .05$.
5. Does it appear that there is broad support for change across all political lines? Explain.

Case Problem 2   Fuentes Salty Snacks, Inc.

Six months ago Fuentes Salty Snacks, Inc. added a new flavor to its line of potato chips. The new flavor, candied bacon, was introduced through a nationwide rollout supported by an extensive promotional campaign. Fuentes' management is convinced that quick penetration into grocery stores is a key to the successful introduction of a new salty snack product, and management now wants to determine whether availability of Fuentes' Candied Bacon Potato Chips is consistent in grocery stores across regions of the U.S. Fuentes Marketing department has selected random samples of 40 grocery stores in each of its eight U.S. sales regions:

- New England (Connecticut, Maine, Massachusetts, New Hampshire, Rhode Island, and Vermont)
- Mid-Atlantic (New Jersey, New York, and Pennsylvania)
- Midwest (Illinois, Indiana, Michigan, Ohio, and Wisconsin)
- Great Plains (Iowa, Kansas, Minnesota, Missouri, Nebraska, North Dakota, Oklahoma, and South Dakota)
- South Atlantic (Delaware, Florida, Georgia, Maryland, North Carolina, South Carolina, Virginia, Washington DC, and West Virginia)
- Deep South (Alabama, Arkansas, Kentucky, Louisiana, Mississippi, Tennessee, and Texas)
- Mountain (Arizona, Colorado, Idaho, Montana, Nevada, New Mexico, Utah, and Wyoming)
- Pacific (Alaska, California, Hawaii, Oregon, and Washington)

FuentesChips

The stores in each sample were then contacted, and the manager of each store was asked whether the store currently carries Fuentes' Candied Bacon Potato Chips. The complete data set is available in the DATAfile named *FuentesChips*.

Fuentes' senior management now wants to use these data to assess whether penetration of Fuentes' Candied Bacon Potato Chips in grocery stores is consistent across its eight U.S. sales regions. If penetration of Fuentes' Candied Bacon Potato Chips in grocery stores differs across its eight U.S. sales regions, Fuentes' management would also like to identify sales regions in which penetration of Fuentes' Candied Bacon Potato Chips is lower or higher than expected.

Managerial Report

Prepare a managerial report that addresses the following issues.

1. Use descriptive statistics to summarize the data from Fuentes' study. Based on your descriptive statistics, what are your preliminary conclusions about penetration of

Fuentes' Candied Bacon Potato Chips in grocery stores across its eight U.S. sales regions?

2. Use the data from Fuentes' study to test the hypothesis that the proportion of grocery stores that currently carries Fuentes' Candied Bacon Potato Chips is equal across its eight U.S. sales regions. Use $\alpha = .05$.

3. Do the results of your hypothesis test provide evidence that penetration of Fuentes' Candied Bacon Potato Chips in grocery stores differs across its eight U.S. sales regions? In which sales region(s) is penetration of Fuentes' Candied Bacon Potato Chips lower or higher than expected? Use the Marascuilo pairwise comparison procedure at $\alpha = .05$ to test for differences between regions.

Case Problem 3   Fresno Board Games

Fresno Board Games manufactures and sells several different board games online and through department stores nationwide. Fresno's most popular game, *¡Cabestrillo Cinco!*, is played with 5 six-sided dice. Fresno has purchased dice for this game from Box Cars, Ltd. for twenty-five years, but the company is now considering a move to Big Boss Gaming, Inc. (BBG), a new supplier that has offered to sell dice to Fresno at a substantially lower price. Fresno management is intrigued by the potential savings offered by BBG, but is also concerned about the quality of the dice produced by the new supplier. Fresno has a reputation for high integrity, and its management feels that it is imperative that the dice included with *¡Cabestrillo Cinco!* are fair.

To alleviate concerns about the quality of the dice it produces, BBG allows Fresno's Manager of Product Quality to randomly sample 5 dice from its most recent production run. While being observed by several members of the BBG management team, Fresno's Manager of Product Quality rolls each of these 5 randomly selected dice 500 times and records each outcome. The results for each of these 5 randomly selected dice are available in the DATAfile named *BBG*.

Fresno management now wants to use these data to assess whether any of these 5 six-sided dice is not fair; i.e., does one outcome occur more frequently or less frequently than the other outcomes?

Managerial Report

Prepare a managerial report that addresses the following issues.

1. Use descriptive statistics to summarize the data collected by Fresno's Manager of Product Quality for each of the 5 randomly selected dice. Based on these descriptive statistics, what are your preliminary conclusions about the fairness of the 5 selected dice?

2. Use the data collected by Fresno's Manager of Product Quality to test the hypothesis that the first of the 5 randomly selected dice is fair, i.e., the distribution of outcomes for the first of the 5 randomly selected dice is multinomial with $p_1 = p_2 = p_3 = p_4 = p_5 = p_6 = 1/6$. Repeat this process for each of the other 4 randomly selected dice. Use $\alpha = .01$. Do the results of your hypothesis tests provide evidence that BBG is producing unfair dice?

CHAPTER 13

Experimental Design and Analysis of Variance

CONTENTS

STATISTICS *in* PRACTICE

BURKE MARKETING SERVICES, INC.*
CINCINNATI, OHIO

Burke Marketing Services, Inc., is one of the most experienced market research firms in the industry. Burke writes more proposals, on more projects, every day than any other market research company in the world. Supported by state-of-the-art technology, Burke offers a wide variety of research capabilities, providing answers to nearly any marketing question.

In one study, a firm retained Burke to evaluate potential new versions of a children's dry cereal. To maintain confidentiality, we refer to the cereal manufacturer as the Anon Company. The four key factors that Anon's product developers thought would enhance the taste of the cereal were the following:

1. Ratio of wheat to corn in the cereal flake
2. Type of sweetener: sugar, honey, or artificial
3. Presence or absence of flavor bits with a fruit taste
4. Short or long cooking time

Burke designed an experiment to determine what effects these four factors had on cereal taste. For example, one test cereal was made with a specified ratio of wheat to corn, sugar as the sweetener, flavor bits, and a short cooking time; another test cereal was made with a different ratio of wheat to corn and the other three factors the same, and so on. Groups of children then taste-tested the cereals and stated what they thought about the taste of each.

---

*The authors are indebted to Dr. Ronald Tatham of Burke Marketing Services for providing this Statistics in Practice.

Burke uses taste tests to provide valuable statistical information on what customers want from a product.

Analysis of variance was the statistical method used to study the data obtained from the taste tests. The results of the analysis showed the following:

- The flake composition and sweetener type were highly influential in taste evaluation.
- The flavor bits actually detracted from the taste of the cereal.
- The cooking time had no effect on the taste.

This information helped Anon identify the factors that would lead to the best-tasting cereal.

The experimental design employed by Burke and the subsequent analysis of variance were helpful in making a product design recommendation. In this chapter, we will see how such procedures are carried out.

In Chapter 1 we stated that statistical studies can be classified as either experimental or observational. In an experimental statistical study, an experiment is conducted to generate the data. An experiment begins with identifying a variable of interest. Then one or more other variables, thought to be related, are identified and controlled, and data are collected about how those variables influence the variable of interest.

In an observational study, data are usually obtained through sample surveys and not a controlled experiment. Good design principles are still employed, but the rigorous controls associated with an experimental statistical study are often not possible.

To illustrate the differences between an observational study and an experimental study, consider the product introduction options for a new high-intensity flashlight produced by the High Lumens Flashlight Company (HLFC). The new model, referred to as the HL5, is powered by a rechargeable lithium-ion battery. A large nationwide chain of sporting goods stores has agreed to help HLFC determine the best promotional strategy for the new flashlight. HLFC is considering three promotional strategies: giving each customer who purchases an HL5 a coupon for a 20% discount at checkout; giving each customer who purchases an HL5 a coupon for a free rechargeable battery; and no promotional offer. In order to assess the effect of these three strategies on sales, HLFC randomly selected 60 sporting goods stores to participate in the study. Two options for determining which promotional strategy to use in each of these stores are being considered:

- Allow each store to select any one of the three promotional strategies and then record sales for the thirty-day trial period.
- Randomly assign each of the three promotional strategies to 20 of the 60 stores and then record sales for the thirty-day trial period.

HLFC's first option is an **observational study**, because the 60 stores participating in the study are not each randomly assigned to one of the three promotional strategies. If HLFC employs this option, sales for the thirty-day trial period may be systematically biased by factors other than the promotional strategy that is used at each store. For example, some store managers may have a bias against using the 20% discount at checkout promotion because they have not had great success with such promotions in the past. Other store managers may have a bias against offering a coupon for a free rechargeable battery because of the paperwork involved in processing such offers. HLFC will not be able to determine whether differences in sales can be explained by the effect of the type of promotion used.

HLFC's second option is an **experimental study**, because each of the 60 stores participating in the study is randomly assigned to one of the three promotional strategies. If HLFC uses this option, the likelihood of systematic biases affecting sales is greatly reduced. Therefore, if differences in sales are observed for the three strategies, HLFC will have a much stronger case for concluding that such differences can be explained by the effect of the type of promotion used.

It may be difficult and/or expensive to design and conduct an experimental study for some research questions. And, in some instances, it may be impractical or even impossible. For instance, in a study of the relationship between smoking and lung cancer, the researcher cannot randomly assign a smoking habit to each subject. The researcher is restricted to observing the outcomes for people who already smoke and the outcomes for people who do not already smoke and observing how frequently members of these two groups develop lung cancer. The design of this study prohibits the researcher from drawing a conclusion about whether smoking causes lung cancer; the researcher can only assess whether there is an association between smoking and lung cancer.

An association between two variables is necessary but not sufficient for establishing a causal relationship between the two variables.

In this chapter we introduce three types of experimental designs: a completely randomized design, a randomized block design, and a factorial experiment. For each design we show how a statistical procedure called analysis of variance (ANOVA) can be used to analyze the data available. ANOVA can also be used to analyze the data obtained through an observation a study. For instance, we will see that the ANOVA procedure used for a completely randomized experimental design also works for testing the equality of three or more population means when data are obtained through an observational study. In the following chapters we will see that ANOVA plays a key role in analyzing the results of regression studies involving both experimental and observational data.

Sir Ronald Aylmer Fisher (1890–1962) invented the branch of statistics known as experimental design. In addition to being accomplished in statistics, he was a noted scientist in the field of genetics.

In the first section, we introduce the basic principles of an experimental study and show how they are employed in a completely randomized design. In the second section, we then show how ANOVA can be used to analyze the data from a completely randomized experimental design. In later sections we discuss multiple comparison procedures and two other widely used experimental designs, the randomized block design and the factorial experiment.

An Introduction to Experimental Design and Analysis of Variance

Cause-and-effect relationships can be difficult to establish in observational studies; such relationships are easier to establish in experimental studies.

As an example of an experimental statistical study, let us consider the problem facing Chemitech, Inc. Chemitech developed a new filtration system for municipal water supplies. The components for the new filtration system will be purchased from several suppliers, and Chemitech will assemble the components at its plant in Columbia, South Carolina. The industrial engineering group is responsible for determining the best assembly method for the new filtration system. After considering a variety of possible approaches, the group narrows the alternatives to three: method A, method B, and method C. These methods differ in the sequence of steps used to assemble the system. Managers at Chemitech want to determine which assembly method can produce the greatest number of filtration systems per week.

In the Chemitech experiment, assembly method is the independent variable or **factor**. Because three assembly methods correspond to this factor, we say that three treatments are associated with this experiment; each **treatment** corresponds to one of the three assembly methods. The Chemitech problem is an example of a **single-factor experiment**; it involves one categorical factor (method of assembly). More complex experiments may consist of multiple factors; some factors may be categorical and others may be quantitative.

The three assembly methods or treatments define the three populations of interest for the Chemitech experiment. One population is all Chemitech employees who use assembly method A, another is those who use method B, and the third is those who use method C. Note that for each population the dependent or **response variable** is the number of filtration systems assembled per week, and the primary statistical objective of the experiment is to determine whether the mean number of units produced per week is the same for all three populations (methods).

Randomization is the process of assigning the treatments to the experimental units at random. Prior to the work of Sir R. A. Fisher, treatments were assigned on a systematic or subjective basis.

Suppose a random sample of three employees is selected from all assembly workers at the Chemitech production facility. In experimental design terminology, the three randomly selected workers are the **experimental units**. The experimental design that we will use for the Chemitech problem is called a **completely randomized design**. This type of design requires that each of the three assembly methods or treatments be assigned randomly to one of the experimental units or workers. For example, method A might be randomly assigned to the second worker, method B to the first worker, and method C to the third worker. The concept of *randomization,* as illustrated in this example, is an important principle of all experimental designs.

Note that this experiment would result in only one measurement or number of units assembled for each treatment. To obtain additional data for each assembly method, we must repeat or replicate the basic experimental process. Suppose, for example, that instead of selecting just three workers at random we selected 15 workers and then randomly assigned each of the three treatments to 5 of the workers. Because each method of assembly is assigned to 5 workers, we say that five replicates have been obtained. The process of *replication* is another important principle of experimental design. Figure 13.1 shows the completely randomized design for the Chemitech experiment.

Data Collection

Once we are satisfied with the experimental design, we proceed by collecting and analyzing the data. In the Chemitech case, the employees would be instructed in how to perform the assembly method assigned to them and then would begin assembling the new filtration systems using that method. After this assignment and training, the number of units assembled by each employee during one week is as shown in Table 13.1. The

FIGURE 13.1 COMPLETELY RANDOMIZED DESIGN FOR EVALUATING THE CHEMITECH ASSEMBLY METHOD EXPERIMENT

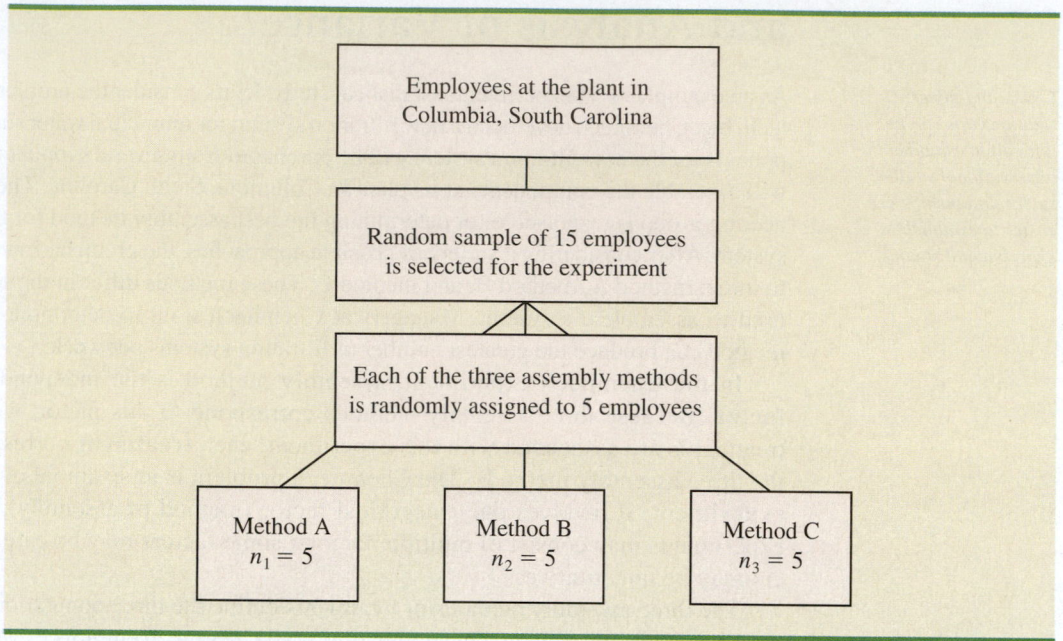

sample means, sample variances, and sample standard deviations for each assembly method are also provided. Thus, the sample mean number of units produced using method A is 62; the sample mean using method B is 66; and the sample mean using method C is 52. From these data, method B appears to result in higher production rates than either of the other methods.

The real issue is whether the three sample means observed are different enough for us to conclude that the means of the populations corresponding to the three methods of assembly are different. To write this question in statistical terms, we introduce the following notation.

μ_1 = mean number of units produced per week using method A

μ_2 = mean number of units produced per week using method B

μ_3 = mean number of units produced per week using method C

TABLE 13.1 NUMBER OF UNITS PRODUCED BY 15 WORKERS

	Method		
	A	**B**	**C**
	58	58	48
	64	69	57
	55	71	59
	66	64	47
	67	68	49
Sample mean	62	66	52
Sample variance	27.5	26.5	31.0
Sample standard deviation	5.244	5.148	5.568

Although we will never know the actual values of μ_1, μ_2, and μ_3, we want to use the sample means to test the following hypotheses.

$$H_0: \mu_1 = \mu_2 = \mu_3$$
$$H_a: \text{Not all population means are equal}$$

If H_0 is rejected, we cannot conclude that all population means are different. Rejecting H_0 means that at least two population means have different values.

As we will demonstrate shortly, analysis of variance (ANOVA) is the statistical procedure used to determine whether the observed differences in the three sample means are large enough to reject H_0.

Assumptions for Analysis of Variance

Three assumptions are required to use analysis of variance.

If the sample sizes are equal, analysis of variance is not sensitive to departures from the assumption of normally distributed populations.

1. **For each population, the response variable is normally distributed.** Implication: In the Chemitech experiment the number of units produced per week (response variable) must be normally distributed for each assembly method.
2. **The variance of the response variable, denoted σ^2, is the same for all of the populations.** Implication: In the Chemitech experiment, the variance of the number of units produced per week must be the same for each assembly method.
3. **The observations must be independent.** Implication: In the Chemitech experiment, the number of units produced per week for each employee must be independent of the number of units produced per week for any other employee.

Analysis of Variance: A Conceptual Overview

If the means for the three populations are equal, we would expect the three sample means to be close together. In fact, the closer the three sample means are to one another, the weaker the evidence we have for the conclusion that the population means differ. Alternatively, the more the sample means differ, the stronger the evidence we have for the conclusion that the population means differ. In other words, if the variability among the sample means is "small," it supports H_0; if the variability among the sample means is "large," it supports H_a.

If the null hypothesis, $H_0: \mu_1 = \mu_2 = \mu_3$, is true, we can use the variability among the sample means to develop an estimate of σ^2. First, note that if the assumptions for analysis of variance are satisfied and the null hypothesis is true, each sample will have come from the same normal distribution with mean μ and variance σ^2. Recall from Chapter 7 that the sampling distribution of the sample mean $\bar{x}$ for a simple random sample of size n from a normal population will be normally distributed with mean μ and variance σ^2/n. Figure 13.2 illustrates such a sampling distribution.

Thus, if the null hypothesis is true, we can think of each of the three sample means, $\bar{x}_1 = 62, \bar{x}_2 = 66$, and $\bar{x}_3 = 52$ from Table 13.1, as values drawn at random from the sampling distribution shown in Figure 13.2. In this case, the mean and variance of the three $\bar{x}$ values can be used to estimate the mean and variance of the sampling distribution. When the sample sizes are equal, as in the Chemitech experiment, the best estimate of the mean of the sampling distribution of $\bar{x}$ is the mean or average of the sample means. In the Chemitech experiment, an estimate of the mean of the sampling distribution of $\bar{x}$ is $(62 + 66 + 52)/3 = 60$. We refer to this estimate as the *overall sample mean*. An estimate of the variance of the sampling distribution of $\bar{x}$, $\sigma_{\bar{x}}^2$ is provided by the variance of the three sample means.

$$s_{\bar{x}}^2 = \frac{(62 - 60)^2 + (66 - 60)^2 + (52 - 60)^2}{3 - 1} = \frac{104}{2} = 52$$

FIGURE 13.2 SAMPLING DISTRIBUTION OF $\bar{x}$ GIVEN H_0 IS TRUE

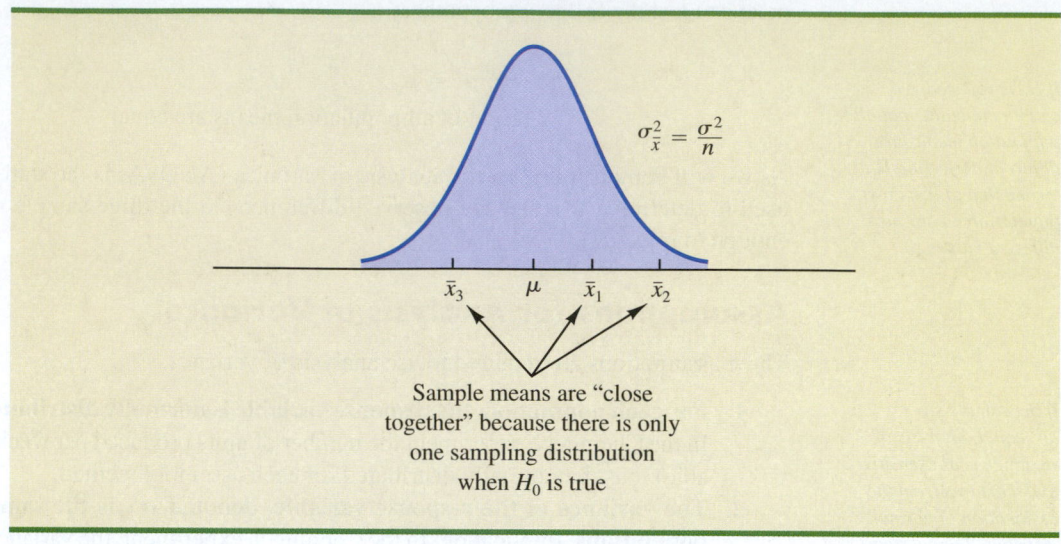

$$\sigma_{\bar{x}}^2 = \frac{\sigma^2}{n}$$

$\bar{x}_3 \quad \mu \quad \bar{x}_1 \quad \bar{x}_2$

Sample means are "close
together" because there is only
one sampling distribution
when H_0 is true

Because $\sigma_{\bar{x}}^2 = \sigma^2/n$, solving for σ^2 gives

$$\sigma^2 = n\sigma_{\bar{x}}^2$$

Hence,

$$\text{Estimate of } \sigma^2 = n \, (\text{Estimate of } \sigma_{\bar{x}}^2) = ns_{\bar{x}}^2 = 5(52) = 260$$

The result, $ns_{\bar{x}}^2 = 260$, is referred to as the *between-treatments* estimate of σ^2.

The between-treatments estimate of σ^2 is based on the assumption that the null hypothesis is true. In this case, each sample comes from the same population, and there is only one sampling distribution of $\bar{x}$. To illustrate what happens when H_0 is false, suppose the population means all differ. Note that because the three samples are from normal populations with different means, they will result in three different sampling distributions. Figure 13.3 shows that in this case, the sample means are not as close together as they were

FIGURE 13.3 SAMPLING DISTRIBUTIONS OF $\bar{x}$ GIVEN H_0 IS FALSE

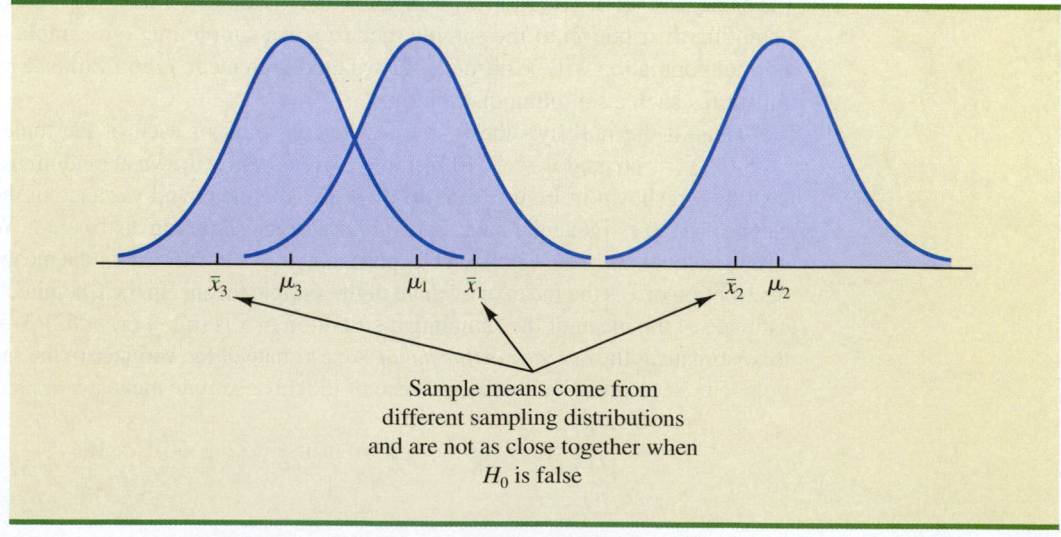

$\bar{x}_3 \quad \mu_3 \qquad \mu_1 \quad \bar{x}_1 \qquad \qquad \bar{x}_2 \quad \mu_2$

Sample means come from
different sampling distributions
and are not as close together when
H_0 is false

when H_0 was true. Thus, $s_{\bar{x}}^2$ will be larger, causing the between-treatments estimate of σ^2 to be larger. In general, when the population means are not equal, the between-treatments estimate will overestimate the population variance σ^2.

The variation within each of the samples also has an effect on the conclusion we reach in analysis of variance. When a random sample is selected from each population, each of the sample variances provides an unbiased estimate of σ^2. Hence, we can combine or pool the individual estimates of σ^2 into one overall estimate. The estimate of σ^2 obtained in this way is called the *pooled* or *within-treatments* estimate of σ^2. Because each sample variance provides an estimate of σ^2 based only on the variation within each sample, the within-treatments estimate of σ^2 is not affected by whether the population means are equal. When the sample sizes are equal, the within-treatments estimate of σ^2 can be obtained by computing the average of the individual sample variances. For the Chemitech experiment we obtain

$$\text{Within-treatments estimate of } \sigma^2 = \frac{27.5 + 26.5 + 31.0}{3} = \frac{85}{3} = 28.33$$

In the Chemitech experiment, the between-treatments estimate of σ^2 (260) is much larger than the within-treatments estimate of σ^2 (28.33). In fact, the ratio of these two estimates is $260/28.33 = 9.18$. Recall, however, that the between-treatments approach provides a good estimate of σ^2 only if the null hypothesis is true; if the null hypothesis is false, the between-treatments approach overestimates σ^2. The within-treatments approach provides a good estimate of σ^2 in either case. Thus, if the null hypothesis is true, the two estimates will be similar and their ratio will be close to 1. If the null hypothesis is false, the between-treatments estimate will be larger than the within-treatments estimate, and their ratio will be large. In the next section we will show how large this ratio must be to reject H_0.

In summary, the logic behind ANOVA is based on the development of two independent estimates of the common population variance σ^2. One estimate of σ^2 is based on the variability among the sample means themselves, and the other estimate of σ^2 is based on the variability of the data within each sample. By comparing these two estimates of σ^2, we will be able to determine whether the population means are equal.

NOTES AND COMMENTS

1. Randomization in experimental design is the analog of probability sampling in an observational study.

2. In many medical experiments, potential bias is eliminated by using a double-blind experimental design. With this design, neither the physician applying the treatment nor the subject knows which treatment is being applied. Many other types of experiments could benefit from this type of design.

3. In this section we provided a conceptual overview of how analysis of variance can be used to test for the equality of k population means for a completely randomized experimental design. We will see that the same procedure can also be used to test for the equality of k population means for an observational or non-experimental study.

4. In Sections 10.1 and 10.2 we presented statistical methods for testing the hypothesis that the means of two populations are equal. ANOVA can also be used to test the hypothesis that the means of two populations are equal. In practice, however, analysis of variance is usually not used except when dealing with three or more population means.

13.2 Analysis of Variance and the Completely Randomized Design

In this section we show how analysis of variance can be used to test for the equality of k population means for a completely randomized design. The general form of the hypotheses tested is

$$H_0: \mu_1 = \mu_2 = \cdots = \mu_k$$
$$H_a: \text{Not all population means are equal}$$

where

$$\mu_j = \text{mean of the } j\text{th population}$$

We assume that a random sample of size n_j has been selected from each of the k populations or treatments. For the resulting sample data, let

$$x_{ij} = \text{value of observation } i \text{ for treatment } j$$
$$n_j = \text{number of observations for treatment } j$$
$$\bar{x}_j = \text{sample mean for treatment } j$$
$$s_j^2 = \text{sample variance for treatment } j$$
$$s_j = \text{sample standard deviation for treatment } j$$

The formulas for the sample mean and sample variance for treatment j are as follow.

$$\bar{x}_j = \frac{\sum_{i=1}^{n_j} x_{ij}}{n_j} \tag{13.1}$$

$$s_j^2 = \frac{\sum_{i=1}^{n_j} (x_{ij} - \bar{x}_j)^2}{n_j - 1} \tag{13.2}$$

The overall sample mean, denoted $\bar{\bar{x}}$, is the sum of all the observations divided by the total number of observations. That is,

$$\bar{\bar{x}} = \frac{\sum_{j=1}^{k} \sum_{i=1}^{n_j} x_{ij}}{n_T} \tag{13.3}$$

where

$$n_T = n_1 + n_2 + \cdots + n_k \tag{13.4}$$

If the size of each sample is n, $n_T = kn$; in this case equation (13.3) reduces to

$$\bar{\bar{x}} = \frac{\sum_{j=1}^{k} \sum_{i=1}^{n_j} x_{ij}}{kn} = \frac{\sum_{j=1}^{k} \sum_{i=1}^{n_j} x_{ij}/n}{k} = \frac{\sum_{j=1}^{k} \bar{x}_j}{k} \tag{13.5}$$

In other words, whenever the sample sizes are the same, the overall sample mean is just the average of the k sample means.

Because each sample in the Chemitech experiment consists of $n = 5$ observations, the overall sample mean can be computed by using equation (13.5). For the data in Table 13.1 we obtained the following result.

$$\bar{\bar{x}} = \frac{62 + 66 + 52}{3} = 60$$

If the null hypothesis is true ($\mu_1 = \mu_2 = \mu_3 = \mu$), the overall sample mean of 60 is the best estimate of the population mean μ.

Between-Treatments Estimate of Population Variance

In the preceding section, we introduced the concept of a between-treatments estimate of σ^2 and showed how to compute it when the sample sizes were equal. This estimate of σ^2 is called the *mean square due to treatments* and is denoted MSTR. The general formula for computing MSTR is

$$MSTR = \frac{\sum_{j=1}^{k} n_j(\bar{x}_j - \bar{\bar{x}})^2}{k - 1} \tag{13.6}$$

The numerator in equation (13.6) is called the *sum of squares due to treatments* and is denoted SSTR. The denominator, $k - 1$, represents the degrees of freedom associated with SSTR. Hence, the mean square due to treatments can be computed using the following formula.

MEAN SQUARE DUE TO TREATMENTS

$$MSTR = \frac{SSTR}{k - 1} \tag{13.7}$$

where

$$SSTR = \sum_{j=1}^{k} n_j(\bar{x}_j - \bar{\bar{x}})^2 \tag{13.8}$$

If H_0 is true, MSTR provides an unbiased estimate of σ^2. However, if the means of the k populations are not equal, MSTR is not an unbiased estimate of σ^2; in fact, in that case, MSTR should overestimate σ^2.

For the Chemitech data in Table 13.1, we obtain the following results.

$$SSTR = \sum_{j=1}^{k} n_j(\bar{x}_j - \bar{\bar{x}})^2 = 5(62 - 60)^2 + 5(66 - 60)^2 + 5(52 - 60)^2 = 520$$

$$MSTR = \frac{SSTR}{k - 1} = \frac{520}{2} = 260$$

Within-Treatments Estimate of Population Variance

Earlier, we introduced the concept of a within-treatments estimate of σ^2 and showed how to compute it when the sample sizes were equal. This estimate of σ^2 is called the *mean square due to error* and is denoted MSE. The general formula for computing MSE is

$$MSE = \frac{\sum_{j=1}^{k}(n_j - 1)s_j^2}{n_T - k} \qquad (13.9)$$

The numerator in equation (13.9) is called the *sum of squares due to error* and is denoted SSE. The denominator of MSE is referred to as the degrees of freedom associated with SSE. Hence, the formula for MSE can also be stated as follows.

MEAN SQUARE DUE TO ERROR

$$MSE = \frac{SSE}{n_T - k} \qquad (13.10)$$

where

$$SSE = \sum_{j=1}^{k}(n_j - 1)s_j^2 \qquad (13.11)$$

Note that MSE is based on the variation within each of the treatments; it is not influenced by whether the null hypothesis is true. Thus, MSE always provides an unbiased estimate of σ^2.

For the Chemitech data in Table 13.1 we obtain the following results.

$$SSE = \sum_{j=1}^{k}(n_j - 1)s_j^2 = (5 - 1)27.5 + (5 - 1)26.5 + (5 - 1)31 = 340$$

$$MSE = \frac{SSE}{n_T - k} = \frac{340}{15 - 3} = \frac{340}{12} = 28.33$$

An introduction to the F distribution and the use of the F distribution table were presented in Section 11.2.

Comparing the Variance Estimates: The F Test

If the null hypothesis is true, MSTR and MSE provide two independent, unbiased estimates of σ^2. Based on the material covered in Chapter 11 we know that for normal populations, the sampling distribution of the ratio of two independent estimates of σ^2 follows an F distribution. Hence, if the null hypothesis is true and the ANOVA assumptions are valid, the sampling distribution of MSTR/MSE is an F distribution with numerator degrees of freedom equal to $k - 1$ and denominator degrees of freedom equal to $n_T - k$. In other words, if the null hypothesis is true, the value of MSTR/MSE should appear to have been selected from this F distribution.

However, if the null hypothesis is false, the value of MSTR/MSE will be inflated because MSTR overestimates σ^2. Hence, we will reject H_0 if the resulting value of MSTR/MSE appears to be too large to have been selected from an F distribution with $k - 1$ numerator degrees of freedom and $n_T - k$ denominator degrees of freedom. Because the decision to reject H_0 is based on the value of MSTR/MSE, the test statistic used to test for the equality of k population means is as follows.

TEST STATISTIC FOR THE EQUALITY OF k POPULATION MEANS

$$F = \frac{\text{MSTR}}{\text{MSE}} \qquad\qquad \textbf{(13.12)}$$

The test statistic follows an F distribution with $k - 1$ degrees of freedom in the numerator and $n_T - k$ degrees of freedom in the denominator.

Let us return to the Chemitech experiment and use a level of significance $\alpha = .05$ to conduct the hypothesis test. The value of the test statistic is

$$F = \frac{\text{MSTR}}{\text{MSE}} = \frac{260}{28.33} = 9.18$$

The numerator degrees of freedom is $k - 1 = 3 - 1 = 2$ and the denominator degrees of freedom is $n_T - k = 15 - 3 = 12$. Because we will only reject the null hypothesis for large values of the test statistic, the p-value is the upper tail area of the F distribution to the right of the test statistic $F = 9.18$. Figure 13.4 shows the sampling distribution of $F = $ MSTR/ MSE, the value of the test statistic, and the upper tail area that is the p-value for the hypothesis test.

From Table 4 of Appendix B we find the following areas in the upper tail of an F distribution with 2 numerator degrees of freedom and 12 denominator degrees of freedom.

Area in Upper Tail	.10	.05	.025	.01
F Value ($df_1 = 2, df_2 = 12$)	2.81	3.89	5.10	6.93

$F = 9.18$

FIGURE 13.4   COMPUTATION OF p-VALUE USING THE SAMPLING DISTRIBUTION OF MSTR/MSE

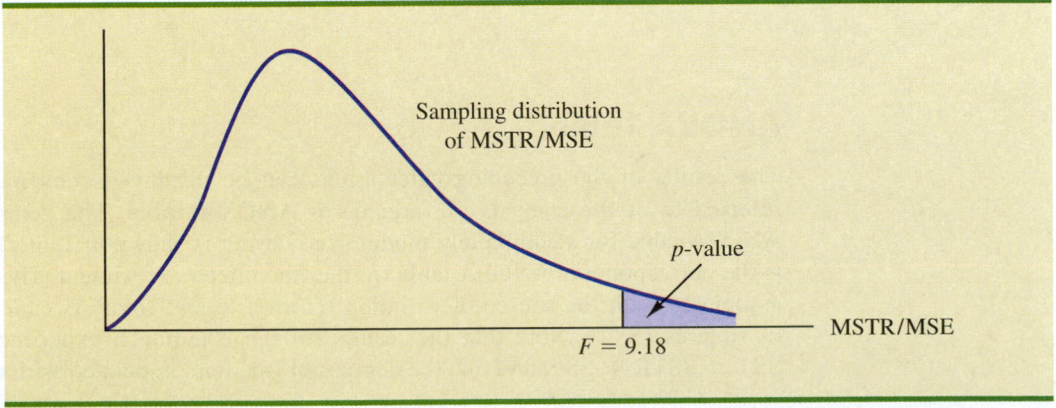

Because $F = 9.18$ is greater than 6.93, the area in the upper tail at $F = 9.18$ is less than .01. Thus, the p-value is less than .01. Excel can be used to show that the p-value is .004. With p-value $\leq \alpha = .05$, H_0 is rejected. The test provides sufficient evidence to conclude that the means of the three populations are not equal. In other words, analysis of variance supports the conclusion that the population mean number of units produced per week for the three assembly methods are not equal.

As with other hypothesis testing procedures, the critical value approach may also be used. With $\alpha = .05$, the critical F value occurs with an area of .05 in the upper tail of an F distribution with 2 and 12 degrees of freedom. From the F distribution table, we find $F_{.05} = 3.89$. Hence, the appropriate upper tail rejection rule for the Chemitech experiment is

$$\text{Reject } H_0 \text{ if } F \geq 3.89$$

With $F = 9.18$, we reject H_0 and conclude that the means of the three populations are not equal. A summary of the overall procedure for testing for the equality of k population means follows.

TEST FOR THE EQUALITY OF k POPULATION MEANS

$$H_0: \mu_1 = \mu_2 = \cdots = \mu_k$$
$$H_a: \text{Not all population means are equal}$$

TEST STATISTIC

$$F = \frac{\text{MSTR}}{\text{MSE}}$$

REJECTION RULE

p-value approach: Reject H_0 if p-value $\leq \alpha$

Critical value approach: Reject H_0 if $F \geq F_\alpha$

where the value of F_α is based on an F distribution with $k - 1$ numerator degrees of freedom and $n_T - k$ denominator degrees of freedom.

ANOVA Table

The results of the preceding calculations can be displayed conveniently in a table referred to as the analysis of variance or **ANOVA table**. The general form of the ANOVA table for a completely randomized design is shown in Table 13.2; Table 13.3 is the corresponding ANOVA table for the Chemitech experiment. The sum of squares associated with the source of variation referred to as "Total" is called the total sum of squares (SST). Note that the results for the Chemitech experiment suggest that SST = SSTR + SSE, and that the degrees of freedom associated with this total sum of

TABLE 13.2   ANOVA TABLE FOR A COMPLETELY RANDOMIZED DESIGN

Source of Variation	Sum of Squares	Degrees of Freedom	Mean Square	F	p-Value
Treatments	SSTR	$k - 1$	$\text{MSTR} = \dfrac{\text{SSTR}}{k - 1}$	$\dfrac{\text{MSTR}}{\text{MSE}}$	
Error	SSE	$n_T - k$	$\text{MSE} = \dfrac{\text{SSE}}{n_T - k}$		
Total	SST	$n_T - 1$			

squares is the sum of the degrees of freedom associated with the sum of squares due to treatments and the sum of squares due to error.

We point out that SST divided by its degrees of freedom $n_T - 1$ is nothing more than the overall sample variance that would be obtained if we treated the entire set of 15 observations as one data set. With the entire data set as one sample, the formula for computing the total sum of squares, SST, is

$$\text{SST} = \sum_{j=1}^{k} \sum_{i=1}^{n_j} (x_{ij} - \bar{\bar{x}})^2 \tag{13.13}$$

It can be shown that the results we observed for the analysis of variance table for the Chemitech experiment also apply to other problems. That is,

$$\text{SST} = \text{SSTR} + \text{SSE} \tag{13.14}$$

Analysis of variance can be thought of as a statistical procedure for partitioning the total sum of squares into separate components.

In other words, SST can be partitioned into two sums of squares: the sum of squares due to treatments and the sum of squares due to error. Note also that the degrees of freedom corresponding to SST, $n_T - 1$, can be partitioned into the degrees of freedom corresponding to SSTR, $k - 1$, and the degrees of freedom corresponding to SSE, $n_T - k$. The analysis of variance can be viewed as the process of **partitioning** the total sum of squares and the degrees of freedom into their corresponding sources: treatments and error. Dividing the sum of squares by the appropriate degrees of freedom provides the variance estimates, the F value, and the p-value used to test the hypothesis of equal population means.

TABLE 13.3   ANALYSIS OF VARIANCE TABLE FOR THE CHEMITECH EXPERIMENT

Source of Variation	Sum of Squares	Degrees of Freedom	Mean Square	F	p-Value
Treatments	520	2	260.00	9.18	.004
Error	340	12	28.33		
Total	860	14			

Using Excel

Excel's Anova: Single Factor tool can be used to conduct a hypothesis test about the difference between the population means for the Chemitech experiment.

Enter/Access Data: Open the DATAfile named *Chemitech*. The data are in cells A2:C6 and labels are in cells A1:C1.

Apply Tools: The following steps describe how to use Excel's Anova: Single Factor tool to test the hypothesis that the mean number of units produced per week is the same for all three methods of assembly.

Step 1. Click the **Data** tab on the Ribbon
Step 2. In the **Analyze** group, click **Data Analysis**
Step 3. Choose **Anova: Single Factor** from the list of Analysis Tools
Step 4. When the Anova: Single Factor dialog box appears (see Figure 13.5):
Enter A1:C6 in the **Input Range** box
Select **Grouped By: Columns**
Select **Labels in First Row**
Enter .05 in the **Alpha** box
Select **Output Range**
Enter A8 in the **Output Range** box (to identify the upper left corner of the section of the worksheet where the output will appear)
Click **OK**

The output, titled *Anova: Single Factor,* appears in cells A8:G22 of the worksheet shown in Figure 13.6. Cells A10:E14 provide a summary of the data. Note that the sample mean and sample variance for each method of assembly are the same as shown in Table 13.1. The ANOVA table, shown in cells A17:G22, is basically the same as the ANOVA table shown in Table 13.2. Excel identifies the treatments source of variation using the label *Between Groups* and the error source of variation using the label *Within Groups*.

FIGURE 13.5 EXCEL'S ANOVA: SINGLE FACTOR TOOL DIALOG BOX FOR THE CHEMITECH EXPERIMENT

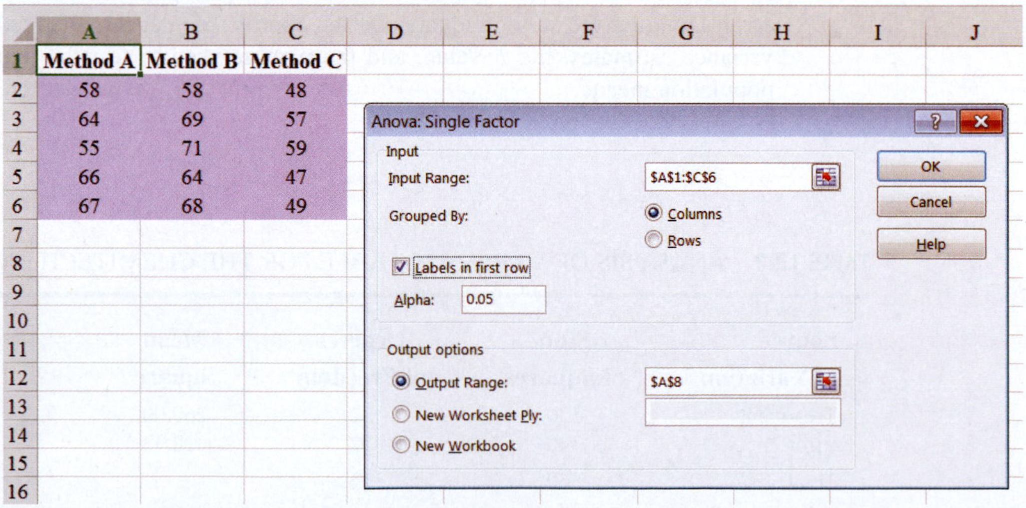

FIGURE 13.6   EXCEL'S ANOVA: SINGLE FACTOR TOOL OUTPUT FOR THE
CHEMITECH EXPERIMENT

	A	B	C	D	E	F	G	H
1	**Method A**	**Method B**	**Method C**					
2	58	58	48					
3	64	69	57					
4	55	71	59					
5	66	64	47					
6	67	68	49					
7								
8	Anova: Single Factor							
9								
10	SUMMARY							
11	*Groups*	*Count*	*Sum*	*Average*	*Variance*			
12	Method A	5	310	62	27.5			
13	Method B	5	330	66	26.5			
14	Method C	5	260	52	31			
15								
16								
17	ANOVA							
18	*Source of Variation*	*SS*	*df*	*MS*	*F*	*P-value*	*F crit*	
19	Between Groups	520	2	260	9.1765	0.0038	3.8853	
20	Within Groups	340	12	28.3333				
21								
22	Total	860	14					
23								

In addition, the Excel output provides the p-value associated with the test as well as the critical F value.

We can use the p-value shown in cell F19, 0.0038, to make the hypothesis testing decision. Thus, at the $\alpha = .05$ level of significance, we reject H_0 because the p-value = $0.0038 < \alpha = .05$. Hence, using the p-value approach we still conclude that the mean number of units produced per week are not the same for the three assembly methods.

Testing for the Equality of k Population Means: An Observational Study

We have shown how analysis of variance can be used to test for the equality of k population means for a completely randomized experimental design. It is important to understand that ANOVA can also be used to test for the equality of three or more population means using data obtained from an observational study. As an example, let us consider the situation at National Computer Products, Inc. (NCP).

NCP manufactures printers and fax machines at plants located in Atlanta, Dallas, and Seattle. To measure how much employees at these plants know about quality management, a random sample of 6 employees was selected from each plant and the employees selected were given a quality awareness examination. The examination

TABLE 13.4   EXAMINATION SCORES FOR 18 EMPLOYEES

NCP

	Plant 1 Atlanta	Plant 2 Dallas	Plant 3 Seattle
	85	71	59
	75	75	64
	82	73	62
	76	74	69
	71	69	75
	85	82	67
Sample mean	79	74	66
Sample variance	34	20	32
Sample standard deviation	5.83	4.47	5.66

scores for these 18 employees are shown in Table 13.4. The sample means, sample variances, and sample standard deviations for each group are also provided. Managers want to use these data to test the hypothesis that the mean examination score is the same for all three plants.

We define population 1 as all employees at the Atlanta plant, population 2 as all employees at the Dallas plant, and population 3 as all employees at the Seattle plant. Let

$$\mu_1 = \text{mean examination score for population 1}$$
$$\mu_2 = \text{mean examination score for population 2}$$
$$\mu_3 = \text{mean examination score for population 3}$$

Although we will never know the actual values of μ_1, μ_2, and μ_3, we want to use the sample results to test the following hypotheses.

$$H_0: \mu_1 = \mu_2 = \mu_3$$
$$H_a: \text{Not all population means are equal}$$

Exercise 8 will ask you to analyze the NCP data using the analysis of variance procedure.

Note that the hypothesis test for the NCP observational study is exactly the same as the hypothesis test for the Chemitech experiment. Indeed, the same analysis of variance methodology we used to analyze the Chemitech experiment can also be used to analyze the data from the NCP observational study.

Even though the same ANOVA methodology is used for the analysis, it is worth noting how the NCP observational statistical study differs from the Chemitech experimental statistical study. The individuals who conducted the NCP study had no control over how the plants were assigned to individual employees. That is, the plants were already in operation and a particular employee worked at one of the three plants. All that NCP could do was to select a random sample of 6 employees from each plant and administer the quality awareness examination. To be classified as an experimental study, NCP would have had to be able to randomly select 18 employees and then assign the plants to each employee in a random fashion.

NOTES AND COMMENTS

1. The overall sample mean can also be computed as a weighted average of the k sample means.

$$\bar{\bar{x}} = \frac{n_1\bar{x}_1 + n_2\bar{x}_2 + \ldots + n_k\bar{x}_k}{n_T}$$

In problems where the sample means are provided, this formula is simpler than equation (13.3) for computing the overall mean.

2. If each sample consists of n observations, equation (13.6) can be written as

$$\text{MSTR} = \frac{n\sum_{j=1}^{k}(\bar{x}_j - \bar{\bar{x}})^2}{k-1} = n\left[\frac{\sum_{j=1}^{k}(\bar{x}_j - \bar{\bar{x}})^2}{k-1}\right]$$

$$= ns_{\bar{x}}^2$$

Note that this result is the same as presented in Section 13.1 when we introduced the concept

of the between-treatments estimate of σ^2. Equation (13.6) is simply a generalization of this result to the unequal sample-size case.

3. If each sample has n observations, $n_T = kn$; thus, $n_T - k = k(n-1)$, and equation (13.9) can be rewritten as

$$\text{MSE} = \frac{\sum_{j=1}^{k}(n-1)s_j^2}{k(n-1)} = \frac{(n-1)\sum_{j=1}^{k}s_j^2}{k(n-1)} = \frac{\sum_{j=1}^{k}s_j^2}{k}$$

In other words, if the sample sizes are the same, MSE is the average of the k sample variances. Note that it is the same result we used in Section 13.1 when we introduced the concept of the within-treatments estimate of σ^2.

Exercises

Methods

1. The following data are from a completely randomized design.

	Treatment		
	A	**B**	**C**
	162	142	126
	142	156	122
	165	124	138
	145	142	140
	148	136	150
	174	152	128
Sample mean	156	142	134
Sample variance	164.4	131.2	110.4

a. Compute the sum of squares between treatments.
b. Compute the mean square between treatments.
c. Compute the sum of squares due to error.
d. Compute the mean square due to error.
e. Set up the ANOVA table for this problem.
f. At the $\alpha = .05$ level of significance, test whether the means for the three treatments are equal.

2. In a completely randomized design, seven experimental units were used for each of the five levels of the factor. Complete the following ANOVA table.

Source of Variation	Sum of Squares	Degrees of Freedom	Mean Square	F	p-Value
Treatments	300				
Error					
Total	460				

3. Refer to exercise 2.
    a.   What hypotheses are implied in this problem?
    b.   At the $\alpha = .05$ level of significance, can we reject the null hypothesis in part (a)? Explain.

4. In an experiment designed to test the output levels of three different treatments, the following results were obtained: SST = 400, SSTR = 150, $n_T = 19$. Set up the ANOVA table and test for any significant difference between the mean output levels of the three treatments. Use $\alpha = .05$.

5. In a completely randomized design, 12 experimental units were used for the first treatment, 15 for the second treatment, and 20 for the third treatment. Complete the following analysis of variance. At a .05 level of significance, is there a significant difference between the treatments?

Source of Variation	Sum of Squares	Degrees of Freedom	Mean Square	F	p-Value
Treatments	1200				
Error					
Total	1800				

6. Develop the analysis of variance computations for the following completely randomized design. At $\alpha = .05$, is there a significant difference between the treatment means?

Exer6

	Treatment		
	A	**B**	**C**
	136	107	92
	120	114	82
	113	125	85
	107	104	101
	131	107	89
	114	109	117
	129	97	110
	102	114	120
		104	98
		89	106
$\bar{x}_j$	119	107	100
s_j^2	146.86	96.44	173.78

Applications

7. Three different methods for assembling a product were proposed by an industrial engineer. To investigate the number of units assembled correctly with each method,

30 employees were randomly selected and randomly assigned to the three proposed methods in such a way that each method was used by 10 workers. The number of units assembled correctly was recorded, and the analysis of variance procedure was applied to the resulting data set. The following results were obtained: SST = 10,800; SSTR = 4560.

    a.   Set up the ANOVA table for this problem.

    b.   Use $\alpha = .05$ to test for any significant difference in the means for the three assembly methods.

8.   Refer to the NCP data in Table 13.4. Set up the ANOVA table and test for any significant difference in the mean examination score for the three plants. Use $\alpha = .05$.

9.   To study the effect of temperature on yield in a chemical process, five batches were produced at each of three temperature levels. The results follow. Construct an analysis of variance table. Use a .05 level of significance to test whether the temperature level has an effect on the mean yield of the process.

Temperature		
50° C	**60° C**	**70° C**
34	30	23
24	31	28
36	34	28
39	23	30
32	27	31

10.   Auditors must make judgments about various aspects of an audit on the basis of their own direct experience, indirect experience, or a combination of the two. In a study, auditors were asked to make judgments about the frequency of errors to be found in an audit. The judgments by the auditors were then compared to the actual results. Suppose the following data were obtained from a similar study; lower scores indicate better judgments.

AudJudg

Direct	Indirect	Combination
17.0	16.6	25.2
18.5	22.2	24.0
15.8	20.5	21.5
18.2	18.3	26.8
20.2	24.2	27.5
16.0	19.8	25.8
13.3	21.2	24.2

Use $\alpha = .05$ to test to see whether the basis for the judgment affects the quality of the judgment. What is your conclusion?

11.   Four different paints are advertised as having the same drying time. To check the manufacturer's claims, five samples were tested for each of the paints. The time in minutes until the paint was dry enough for a second coat to be applied was recorded. The following data were obtained.

At the $\alpha = .05$ level of significance, test to see whether the mean drying time is the same for each type of paint.

Paint

Paint 1	Paint 2	Paint 3	Paint 4
128	144	133	150
137	133	143	142
135	142	137	135
124	146	136	140
141	130	131	153

12. The *Consumer Reports* Restaurant Customer Satisfaction Survey is based upon 148,599 visits to full-service restaurant chains (*Consumer Reports* website). One of the variables in the study is meal price, the average amount paid per person for dinner and drinks, minus the tip. Suppose a reporter for the *Sun Coast Times* thought that it would be of interest to her readers to conduct a similar study for restaurants located on the Grand Strand section in Myrtle Beach, South Carolina. The reporter selected a sample of 8 seafood restaurants, 8 Italian restaurants, and 8 steakhouses. The following data show the meal prices ($) obtained for the 24 restaurants sampled. Use $\alpha = .05$ to test whether there is a significant difference among the mean meal price for the three types of restaurants.

GrandStrand

Italian	Seafood	Steakhouse
$12	$16	$24
13	18	19
15	17	23
17	26	25
18	23	21
20	15	22
17	19	27
24	18	31

13.3 Multiple Comparison Procedures

When we use analysis of variance to test whether the means of k populations are equal, rejection of the null hypothesis allows us to conclude only that the population means are *not all equal*. In some cases we will want to go a step further and determine where the differences among means occur. The purpose of this section is to show how **multiple comparison procedures** can be used to conduct statistical comparisons between pairs of population means.

Fisher's LSD

Suppose that analysis of variance provides statistical evidence to reject the null hypothesis of equal population means. In this case, Fisher's least significant difference (LSD) procedure can be used to determine where the differences occur. To illustrate the use of Fisher's LSD procedure in making pairwise comparisons of population means, recall the Chemitech experiment introduced in Section 13.1. Using analysis of variance, we concluded that the mean number of units produced per week are not the same for the three assembly methods. In this case, the follow-up question is: We believe the assembly methods differ, but where do the differences occur? That is, do the means of populations 1 and 2 differ? Or those of populations 1 and 3? Or those of populations 2 and 3? The following table summarizes Fisher's LSD procedure for comparing pairs of population means.

FISHER'S LSD PROCEDURE

$$H_0: \mu_i = \mu_j$$
$$H_a: \mu_i \neq \mu_j$$

TEST STATISTIC

$$t = \frac{\bar{x}_i - \bar{x}_j}{\sqrt{MSE\left(\frac{1}{n_i} + \frac{1}{n_j}\right)}} \tag{13.16}$$

REJECTION RULE

p-value approach: Reject H_0 if p-value $\leq \alpha$

Critical value approach: Reject H_0 if $t \leq -t_{\alpha/2}$ or $t \geq t_{\alpha/2}$

where the value of $t_{\alpha/2}$ is based on a t distribution with $n_T - k$ degrees of freedom.

Let us now apply this procedure to determine whether there is a significant difference between the means of population 1 (method A) and population 2 (method B) at the $\alpha = .05$ level of significance. Table 13.1 showed that the sample mean is 62 for method A and 66 for method B. Table 13.3 showed that the value of MSE is 28.33; it is the estimate of σ^2 and is based on 12 degrees of freedom. For the Chemitech data the value of the test statistic is

$$t = \frac{62 - 66}{\sqrt{28.33\left(\frac{1}{5} + \frac{1}{5}\right)}} = -1.19$$

Because we have a two-tailed test, the p-value is two times the area under the curve for the t distribution to the left of $t = -1.19$. Using Table 2 in Appendix B, the t distribution table for 12 degrees of freedom provides the following information.

Area in Upper Tail	.20	.10	.05	.025	.01	.005
t **Value (12 df)**	.873	1.356	1.782	2.179	2.681	3.055

$t = 1.19$

The t distribution table only contains positive t values. Because the t distribution is symmetric, however, we can find the area under the curve to the right of $t = 1.19$ and double it to find the p-value corresponding to $t = -1.19$. We see that $t = 1.19$ is between .20 and .10. Doubling these amounts, we see that the p-value must be between .40 and .20. Excel can be used to show that the p-value is .2571. Because the p-value is greater than $\alpha = .05$, we cannot reject the null hypothesis. Hence, we cannot conclude that the population mean number of units produced per week for method A is different from the population mean for method B.

Many practitioners find it easier to determine how large the difference between the sample means must be to reject H_0. In this case the test statistic is $\bar{x}_i - \bar{x}_j$, and the test is conducted by the following procedure.

FISHER'S LSD PROCEDURE BASED ON THE TEST STATISTIC $\bar{x}_i - \bar{x}_j$

$$H_0: \mu_i = \mu_j$$
$$H_a: \mu_i \neq \mu_j$$

TEST STATISTIC

$$\bar{x}_i - \bar{x}_j$$

REJECTION RULE AT A LEVEL OF SIGNIFICANCE α

$$\text{Reject } H_0 \text{ if } |\bar{x}_i - \bar{x}_j| \geq \text{LSD}$$

where

$$\text{LSD} = t_{\alpha/2} \sqrt{\text{MSE}\left(\frac{1}{n_i} + \frac{1}{n_j}\right)} \qquad \textbf{(13.17)}$$

For the Chemitech experiment the value of LSD is

$$\text{LSD} = 2.179 \sqrt{28.33\left(\frac{1}{5} + \frac{1}{5}\right)} = 7.34$$

Note that when the sample sizes are equal, only one value for LSD is computed. In such cases we can simply compare the magnitude of the difference between any two sample means with the value of LSD. For example, the difference between the sample means for population 1 (method A) and population 3 (method C) is $62 - 52 = 10$. This difference is greater than LSD = 7.34, which means we can reject the null hypothesis that the population mean number of units produced per week for method A is equal to the population mean for method C. Similarly, with the difference between the sample means for populations 2 and 3 of $66 - 52 = 14 > 7.34$, we can also reject the hypothesis that the population mean for method B is equal to the population mean for method C. In effect, our conclusion is that methods A and B both differ from method C.

Fisher's LSD can also be used to develop a confidence interval estimate of the difference between the means of two populations. The general procedure follows.

CONFIDENCE INTERVAL ESTIMATE OF THE DIFFERENCE BETWEEN TWO POPULATION MEANS USING FISHER'S LSD PROCEDURE

$$\bar{x}_i - \bar{x}_j \pm \text{LSD} \qquad \textbf{(13.18)}$$

where

$$\text{LSD} = t_{\alpha/2} \sqrt{\text{MSE}\left(\frac{1}{n_i} + \frac{1}{n_j}\right)} \qquad \textbf{(13.19)}$$

and $t_{\alpha/2}$ is based on a t distribution with $n_T - k$ degrees of freedom.

If the confidence interval in expression (13.18) includes the value zero, we cannot reject the hypothesis that the two population means are equal. However, if the confidence interval does not include the value zero, we conclude that there is a difference between the population means. For the Chemitech experiment, recall that LSD = 7.34 (corresponding to $t_{.025} = 2.179$). Thus, a 95% confidence interval estimate of the difference between the means of populations 1 and 2 is $62 - 66 \pm 7.34 = -4 \pm 7.34 = -11.34$ to 3.34; because this interval includes zero, we cannot reject the hypothesis that the two population means are equal.

Type I Error Rates

We began the discussion of Fisher's LSD procedure with the premise that analysis of variance gave us statistical evidence to reject the null hypothesis of equal population means. We showed how Fisher's LSD procedure can be used in such cases to determine where the differences occur. Technically, it is referred to as a *protected* or *restricted* LSD test because it is employed only if we first find a significant *F* value by using analysis of variance. To see why this distinction is important in multiple comparison tests, we need to explain the difference between a *comparisonwise* Type I error rate and an *experimentwise* Type I error rate.

In the Chemitech experiment we used Fisher's LSD procedure to make three pairwise comparisons.

Test 1	Test 2	Test 3
$H_0: \mu_1 = \mu_2$	$H_0: \mu_1 = \mu_3$	$H_0: \mu_2 = \mu_3$
$H_a: \mu_1 \neq \mu_2$	$H_a: \mu_1 \neq \mu_3$	$H_a: \mu_2 \neq \mu_3$

In each case, we used a level of significance of $\alpha = .05$. Therefore, for each test, if the null hypothesis is true, the probability that we will make a Type I error is $\alpha = .05$; hence, the probability that we will not make a Type I error on each test is $1 - .05 = .95$. In discussing multiple comparison procedures we refer to this probability of a Type I error ($\alpha = .05$) as the **comparisonwise Type I error rate**; comparisonwise Type I error rates indicate the level of significance associated with a single pairwise comparison.

Let us now consider a slightly different question. What is the probability that in making three pairwise comparisons, we will commit a Type I error on at least one of the three tests? To answer this question, note that the probability that we will not make a Type I error on any of the three tests is $(.95)(.95)(.95) = .8574$.[1] Therefore, the probability of making at least one Type I error is $1 - .8574 = .1426$. Thus, when we use Fisher's LSD procedure to make all three pairwise comparisons, the Type I error rate associated with this approach is not .05, but actually .1426; we refer to this error rate as the *overall* or **experimentwise Type I error rate**. To avoid confusion, we denote the experimentwise Type I error rate as α_{EW}.

The experimentwise Type I error rate gets larger for problems with more populations. For example, a problem with five populations has 10 possible pairwise comparisons. If we tested all possible pairwise comparisons by using Fisher's LSD with a comparisonwise error rate of $\alpha = .05$, the experimentwise Type I error rate would be $1 - (1 - .05)^{10} = .40$. In such cases, practitioners look to alternatives that provide better control over the experimentwise error rate.

One alternative for controlling the overall experimentwise error rate, referred to as the Bonferroni adjustment, involves using a smaller comparisonwise error rate for each test. For example, if we want to test C pairwise comparisons and want the maximum probability of making

---

[1]The assumption is that the three tests are independent, and hence the joint probability of the three events can be obtained by simply multiplying the individual probabilities. In fact, the three tests are not independent because MSE is used in each test; therefore, the error involved is even greater than that shown.

a Type I error for the overall experiment to be α_{EW}, we simply use a comparisonwise error rate equal to α_{EW}/C. In the Chemitech experiment, if we want to use Fisher's LSD procedure to test all three pairwise comparisons with a maximum experimentwise error rate of $\alpha_{EW} = .05$, we set the comparisonwise error rate to be $\alpha = .05/3 = .017$. For a problem with five populations and 10 possible pairwise comparisons, the Bonferroni adjustment would suggest a comparisonwise error rate of $.05/10 = .005$. Recall from our discussion of hypothesis testing in Chapter 9 that for a fixed sample size, any decrease in the probability of making a Type I error will result in an increase in the probability of making a Type II error, which corresponds to accepting the hypothesis that the two population means are equal when in fact they are not equal. As a result, many practitioners are reluctant to perform individual tests with a low comparisonwise Type I error rate because of the increased risk of making a Type II error.

Several other procedures, such as Tukey's procedure and Duncan's multiple range test, have been developed to help in such situations. However, there is considerable controversy in the statistical community as to which procedure is "best." The truth is that no one procedure is best for all types of problems.

Exercises

Methods

13. The following data are from a completely randomized design.

	Treatment A	Treatment B	Treatment C
	32	44	33
	30	43	36
	30	44	35
	26	46	36
	32	48	40
Sample mean	30	45	36
Sample variance	6.00	4.00	6.50

a. At the $\alpha = .05$ level of significance, can we reject the null hypothesis that the means of the three treatments are equal?
b. Use Fisher's LSD procedure to test whether there is a significant difference between the means for treatments A and B, treatments A and C, and treatments B and C. Use $\alpha = .05$.
c. Use Fisher's LSD procedure to develop a 95% confidence interval estimate of the difference between the means of treatments A and B.

14. The following data are from a completely randomized design. In the following calculations, use $\alpha = .05$.

	Treatment 1	Treatment 2	Treatment 3
	63	82	69
	47	72	54
	54	88	61
	40	66	48
$\bar{x}_j$	51	77	58
s_j^2	96.67	97.34	81.99

a. Use analysis of variance to test for a significant difference among the means of the three treatments.

b. Use Fisher's LSD procedure to determine which means are different.

Applications

15. To test whether the mean time needed to mix a batch of material is the same for machines produced by three manufacturers, the Jacobs Chemical Company obtained the following data on the time (in minutes) needed to mix the material.

	Manufacturer	
1	**2**	**3**
20	28	20
26	26	19
24	31	23
22	27	22

a. Use these data to test whether the population mean times for mixing a batch of material differ for the three manufacturers. Use $\alpha = .05$.

b. At the $\alpha = .05$ level of significance, use Fisher's LSD procedure to test for the equality of the means for manufacturers 1 and 3. What conclusion can you draw after carrying out this test?

16. Refer to exercise 15. Use Fisher's LSD procedure to develop a 95% confidence interval estimate of the difference between the means for manufacturer 1 and manufacturer 2.

17. The following data are from an experiment designed to investigate the perception of corporate ethical values among individuals specializing in marketing (higher scores indicate higher ethical values).

Marketing Managers	Marketing Research	Advertising
6	5	6
5	5	7
4	4	6
5	4	5
6	5	6
4	4	6

a. Use $\alpha = .05$ to test for significant differences in perception among the three groups.

b. At the $\alpha = .05$ level of significance, we can conclude that there are differences in the perceptions for marketing managers, marketing research specialists, and advertising specialists. Use the procedures in this section to determine where the differences occur. Use $\alpha = .05$.

18. To test for any significant difference in the number of hours between breakdowns for four machines, the following data were obtained.

Machine 1	Machine 2	Machine 3	Machine 4
6.4	8.7	11.1	9.9
7.8	7.4	10.3	12.8
5.3	9.4	9.7	12.1
7.4	10.1	10.3	10.8
8.4	9.2	9.2	11.3
7.3	9.8	8.8	11.5

   a. At the $\alpha = .05$ level of significance, what is the difference, if any, in the population mean times among the four machines?

   b. Use Fisher's LSD procedure to test for the equality of the means for machines 2 and 4. Use a .05 level of significance.

19. Refer to exercise 18. Use the Bonferroni adjustment to test for a significant difference between all pairs of means. Assume that a maximum overall experimentwise error rate of .05 is desired.

20. The International League of Triple-A minor league baseball consists of 14 teams organized into three divisions: North, South, and West. The following data show the average attendance for the 14 teams in the International League (The Biz of Baseball website). Also shown are the teams' records; W denotes the number of games won, L denotes the number of games lost, and PCT is the proportion of games played that were won.

DATA file

Triple-A

Team Name	Division	W	L	PCT	Attendance
Buffalo Bisons	North	66	77	.462	8812
Lehigh Valley IronPigs	North	55	89	.382	8479
Pawtucket Red Sox	North	85	58	.594	9097
Rochester Red Wings	North	74	70	.514	6913
Scranton-Wilkes Barre Yankees	North	88	56	.611	7147
Syracuse Chiefs	North	69	73	.486	5765
Charlotte Knights	South	63	78	.447	4526
Durham Bulls	South	74	70	.514	6995
Norfolk Tides	South	64	78	.451	6286
Richmond Braves	South	63	78	.447	4455
Columbus Clippers	West	69	73	.486	7795
Indianapolis Indians	West	68	76	.472	8538
Louisville Bats	West	88	56	.611	9152
Toledo Mud Hens	West	75	69	.521	8234

   a. Use $\alpha = .05$ to test for any difference in the mean attendance for the three divisions.

   b. Use Fisher's LSD procedure to determine where the differences occur. Use $\alpha = .05$.

13.4 Randomized Block Design

Thus far we have considered the completely randomized experimental design. Recall that to test for a difference among treatment means, we computed an F value by using the ratio

$$F = \frac{\text{MSTR}}{\text{MSE}} \qquad \textbf{(13.20)}$$

A completely randomized design is useful when the experimental units are homogeneous. If the experimental units are heterogeneous, **blocking** *is often used to form homogeneous groups.*

   A problem can arise whenever differences due to extraneous factors (ones not considered in the experiment) cause the MSE term in this ratio to become large. In such cases, the F value in equation (13.20) can become small, signaling no difference among treatment means when in fact such a difference exists.

   In this section we present an experimental design known as a **randomized block design**. Its purpose is to control some of the extraneous sources of variation by removing such variation from the MSE term. This design tends to provide a better estimate of the true error variance and leads to a more powerful hypothesis test in terms of the ability to detect differences among treatment means. To illustrate, let us consider a stress study for air traffic controllers.

Air Traffic Controller Stress Test

A study measuring the fatigue and stress of air traffic controllers resulted in proposals for modification and redesign of the controller's workstation. After consideration of several designs for the workstation, three specific alternatives are selected as having the best potential for reducing controller stress. The key question is: To what extent do the three alternatives differ in terms of their effect on controller stress? To answer this question, we need to design an experiment that will provide measurements of air traffic controller stress under each alternative.

Experimental studies in business often involve experimental units that are highly heterogeneous; as a result, randomized block designs are often employed.

In a completely randomized design, a random sample of controllers would be assigned to each workstation alternative. However, controllers are believed to differ substantially in their ability to handle stressful situations. What is high stress to one controller might be only moderate or even low stress to another. Hence, when considering the within-group source of variation (MSE), we must realize that this variation includes both random error and error due to individual controller differences. In fact, managers expected controller variability to be a major contributor to the MSE term.

Blocking in experimental design is similar to stratification in sampling.

One way to separate the effect of the individual differences is to use a randomized block design. Such a design will identify the variability stemming from individual controller differences and remove it from the MSE term. The randomized block design calls for a single sample of controllers. Each controller in the sample is tested with each of the three workstation alternatives. In experimental design terminology, the workstation is the *factor of interest* and the controllers are the *blocks*. The three treatments or populations associated with the workstation factor correspond to the three workstation alternatives. For simplicity, we refer to the workstation alternatives as system A, system B, and system C.

The *randomized* aspect of the randomized block design is the random order in which the treatments (systems) are assigned to the controllers. If every controller were to test the three systems in the same order, any observed difference in systems might be due to the order of the test rather than to true differences in the systems.

To provide the necessary data, the three workstation alternatives were installed at the Cleveland Control Center in Oberlin, Ohio. Six controllers were selected at random and assigned to operate each of the systems. A follow-up interview and a medical examination of each controller participating in the study provided a measure of the stress for each controller on each system. The data are reported in Table 13.5.

Table 13.6 is a summary of the stress data collected. In this table we include column totals (treatments) and row totals (blocks) as well as some sample means that will be helpful in making the sum of squares computations for the ANOVA procedure. Because lower stress values are viewed as better, the sample data seem to favor system B with its mean stress rating of 13. However, the usual question remains: Do the sample results justify the

TABLE 13.5   A RANDOMIZED BLOCK DESIGN FOR THE AIR TRAFFIC CONTROLLER STRESS TEST

DATA *file*

AirTraffic

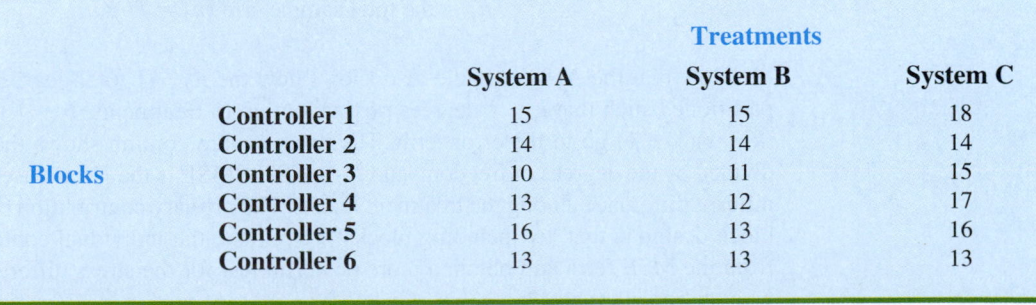

		Treatments	
	System A	System B	System C
Controller 1	15	15	18
Controller 2	14	14	14
Blocks **Controller 3**	10	11	15
Controller 4	13	12	17
Controller 5	16	13	16
Controller 6	13	13	13

TABLE 13.6 SUMMARY OF STRESS DATA FOR THE AIR TRAFFIC CONTROLLER STRESS TEST

		Treatments			Row or Block Totals	Block Means
		System A	System B	System C		
	Controller 1	15	15	18	48	$\bar{x}_{1.} = 48/3 = 16.0$
	Controller 2	14	14	14	42	$\bar{x}_{2.} = 42/3 = 14.0$
Blocks	Controller 3	10	11	15	36	$\bar{x}_{3.} = 36/3 = 12.0$
	Controller 4	13	12	17	42	$\bar{x}_{4.} = 42/3 = 14.0$
	Controller 5	16	13	16	45	$\bar{x}_{5.} = 45/3 = 15.0$
	Controller 6	13	13	13	39	$\bar{x}_{6.} = 39/3 = 13.0$
Column or Treatment Totals		81	78	93	252	$\bar{\bar{x}} = \dfrac{252}{18} = 14.0$
Treatment Means		$\bar{x}_{.1} = \dfrac{81}{6}$ $= 13.5$	$\bar{x}_{.2} = \dfrac{78}{6}$ $= 13.0$	$\bar{x}_{.3} = \dfrac{93}{6}$ $= 15.5$		

conclusion that the population mean stress levels for the three systems differ? That is, are the differences statistically significant? An analysis of variance computation similar to the one performed for the completely randomized design can be used to answer this statistical question.

ANOVA Procedure

The ANOVA procedure for the randomized block design requires us to partition the sum of squares total (SST) into three groups: sum of squares due to treatments (SSTR), sum of squares due to blocks (SSBL), and sum of squares due to error (SSE). The formula for this partitioning follows.

$$SST = SSTR + SSBL + SSE \tag{13.21}$$

This sum of squares partition is summarized in the ANOVA table for the randomized block design as shown in Table 13.7. The notation used in the table is

$$k = \text{the number of treatments}$$
$$b = \text{the number of blocks}$$
$$n_T = \text{the total sample size } (n_T = kb)$$

Note that the ANOVA table also shows how the $n_T - 1$ total degrees of freedom are partitioned such that $k - 1$ degrees of freedom go to treatments, $b - 1$ go to blocks, and $(k - 1)(b - 1)$ go to the error term. The mean square column shows the sum of squares divided by the degrees of freedom, and $F = \text{MSTR/MSE}$ is the F ratio used to test for a significant difference among the treatment means. The primary contribution of the randomized block design is that, by including blocks, we remove the individual controller differences from the MSE term and obtain a more powerful test for the stress differences in the three workstation alternatives.

TABLE 13.7 ANOVA TABLE FOR THE RANDOMIZED BLOCK DESIGN
WITH k TREATMENTS AND b BLOCKS

Source of Variation	Sum of Squares	Degrees of Freedom	Mean Square	F	p-Value
Treatments	SSTR	$k-1$	$MSTR = \dfrac{SSTR}{k-1}$	$\dfrac{MSTR}{MSE}$	
Blocks	SSBL	$b-1$	$MSBL = \dfrac{SSBL}{b-1}$		
Error	SSE	$(k-1)(b-1)$	$MSE = \dfrac{SSE}{(k-1)(b-1)}$		
Total	SST	$n_T - 1$			

Computations and Conclusions

To compute the F statistic needed to test for a difference among treatment means with a randomized block design, we need to compute MSTR and MSE. To calculate these two mean squares, we must first compute SSTR and SSE; in doing so, we will also compute SSBL and SST. To simplify the presentation, we perform the calculations in four steps. In addition to k, b, and n_T as previously defined, the following notation is used.

x_{ij} = value of the observation corresponding to treatment j in block i

$\bar{x}_{\cdot j}$ = sample mean of the jth treatment

$\bar{x}_{i\cdot}$ = sample mean for the ith block

$\bar{\bar{x}}$ = overall sample mean

Step 1. Compute the total sum of squares (SST).

$$SST = \sum_{i=1}^{b}\sum_{j=1}^{k}(x_{ij} - \bar{\bar{x}})^2 \tag{13.22}$$

Step 2. Compute the sum of squares due to treatments (SSTR).

$$SSTR = b\sum_{j=1}^{k}(\bar{x}_{\cdot j} - \bar{\bar{x}})^2 \tag{13.23}$$

Step 3. Compute the sum of squares due to blocks (SSBL).

$$SSBL = k\sum_{i=1}^{b}(\bar{x}_{i\cdot} - \bar{\bar{x}})^2 \tag{13.24}$$

Step 4. Compute the sum of squares due to error (SSE).

$$SSE = SST - SSTR - SSBL \tag{13.25}$$

For the air traffic controller data in Table 13.6, these steps lead to the following sums of squares.

Step 1. $SST = (15 - 14)^2 + (15 - 14)^2 + (18 - 14)^2 + \cdots + (13 - 14)^2 = 70$

Step 2. $SSTR = 6[(13.5 - 14)^2 + (13.0 - 14)^2 + (15.5 - 14)^2] = 21$

Step 3. $SSBL = 3[(16 - 14)^2 + (14 - 14)^2 + (12 - 14)^2 + (14 - 14)^2 + (15 - 14)^2 + (13 - 14)^2] = 30$

Step 4. $SSE = 70 - 21 - 30 = 19$

TABLE 13.8 ANOVA TABLE FOR THE AIR TRAFFIC CONTROLLER STRESS TEST

Source of Variation	Sum of Squares	Degrees of Freedom	Mean Square	F	p-Value
Treatments	21	2	10.5	10.5/1.9 = 5.53	.024
Blocks	30	5	6.0		
Error	19	10	1.9		
Total	70	17			

These sums of squares divided by their degrees of freedom provide the corresponding mean square values shown in Table 13.8.

Let us use a level of significance $\alpha = .05$ to conduct the hypothesis test. The value of the test statistic is

$$F = \frac{\text{MSTR}}{\text{MSE}} = \frac{10.5}{1.9} = 5.53$$

The numerator degrees of freedom is $k - 1 = 3 - 1 = 2$ and the denominator degrees of freedom is $(k - 1)(b - 1) = (3 - 1)(6 - 1) = 10$. Because we will only reject the null hypothesis for large values of the test statistic, the p-value is the area under the F distribution to the right of $F = 5.53$. From Table 4 of Appendix B we find that with the degrees of freedom 2 and 10, $F = 5.53$ is between $F_{.025} = 5.46$ and $F_{.01} = 7.56$. As a result, the area in the upper tail, or the p-value, is between .01 and .025. Alternatively, we can use Excel to show that the p-value for $F = 5.53$ is .024. With p-value $\leq \alpha = .05$, we reject the null hypothesis $H_0: \mu_1 = \mu_2 = \mu_3$ and conclude that the population mean stress levels differ for the three workstation alternatives.

Some general comments can be made about the randomized block design. The experimental design described in this section is a *complete* block design; the word "complete" indicates that each block is subjected to all k treatments. That is, all controllers (blocks) were tested with all three systems (treatments). Experimental designs in which some but not all treatments are applied to each block are referred to as *incomplete* block designs. A discussion of incomplete block designs is beyond the scope of this text.

Because each controller in the air traffic controller stress test was required to use all three systems, this approach guarantees a complete block design. In some cases, however, blocking is carried out with "similar" experimental units in each block. For example, assume that in a pretest of air traffic controllers, the population of controllers was divided into groups ranging from extremely high-stress individuals to extremely low-stress individuals. The blocking could still be accomplished by having three controllers from each of the stress classifications participate in the study. Each block would then consist of three controllers in the same stress group. The randomized aspect of the block design would be the random assignment of the three controllers in each block to the three systems.

Finally, note that the ANOVA table shown in Table 13.7 provides an F value to test for treatment effects but *not* for blocks. The reason is that the experiment was designed to test a single factor—workstation design. The blocking based on individual stress differences was conducted to remove such variation from the MSE term. However, the study was not designed to test specifically for individual differences in stress.

Some analysts compute $F = \text{MSB}/\text{MSE}$ and use that statistic to test for significance of the blocks. Then they use the result as a guide to whether the same type of blocking would be desired in future experiments. However, if individual stress difference is to be a factor in the study, a different experimental design should be used. A test of significance on blocks should not be performed as a basis for a conclusion about a second factor.

Using Excel

Excel's Anova: Two-Factor Without Replication tool can be used to test whether the mean stress levels for air traffic controllers are the same for the three systems.

Enter/Access Data: Open the DATAfile named *AirTraffic*. The data are in cells B2:D7 and labels are in column A and cells B1:D1.

Apply Tools: The following steps describe how to use Excel's Anova: Two-Factor Without Replication tool to test the hypothesis that the mean stress level score is the same for all three systems.

Step 1. Click the **Data** tab on the Ribbon
Step 2. In the **Analyze** group, click **Data Analysis**
Step 3. Choose **Anova: Two-Factor Without Replication** from the list of Analysis Tools
Step 4. When the Anova: Two-Factor Without Replication dialog box appears (see Figure 13.7):
  Enter A1:D7 in the **Input Range** box
  Select **Labels**
  Enter .05 in the **Alpha** box
  Select **Output Range**

FIGURE 13.7 EXCEL'S ANOVA: TWO-FACTOR WITHOUT REPLICATION TOOL DIALOG BOX FOR THE AIR TRAFFIC CONTROLLER STRESS TEST

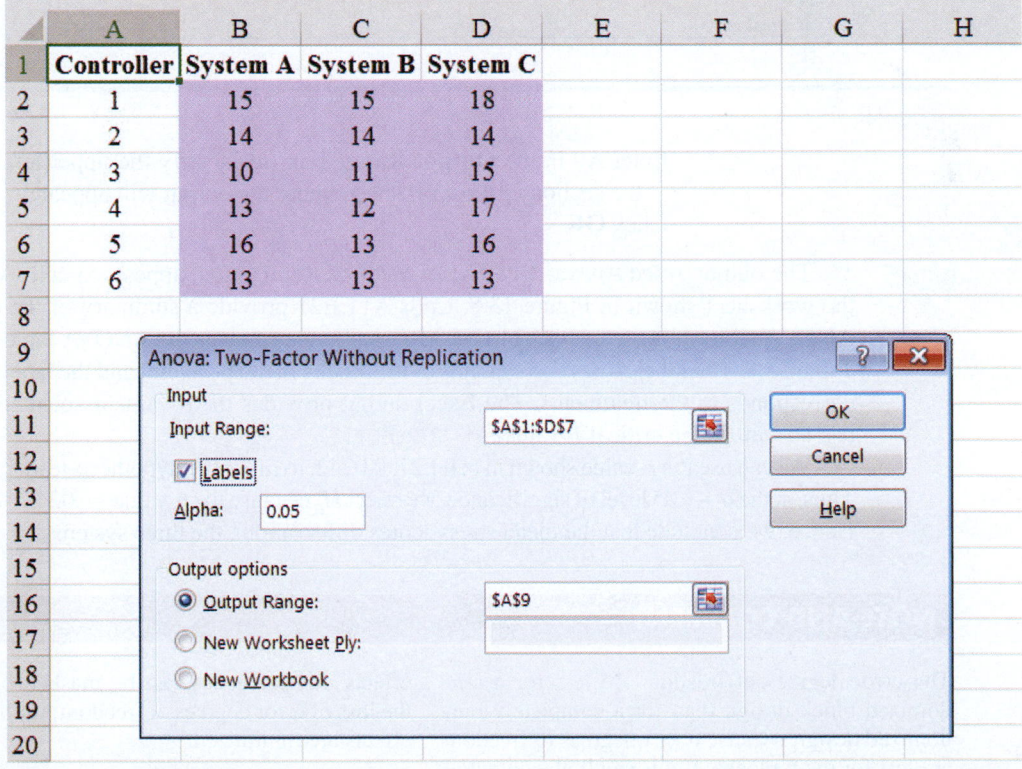

FIGURE 13.8 EXCEL'S ANOVA: TWO-FACTOR WITHOUT REPLICATION TOOL OUTPUT FOR THE AIR TRAFFIC CONTROLLER STRESS TEST

	A	B	C	D	E	F	G	H
1	**Controller**	**System A**	**System B**	**System C**				
2	1	15	15	18				
3	2	14	14	14				
4	3	10	11	15				
5	4	13	12	17				
6	5	16	13	16				
7	6	13	13	13				
8								
9	Anova: Two-Factor Without Replication							
10								
11	*SUMMARY*	*Count*	*Sum*	*Average*	*Variance*			
12	1	3	48	16	3			
13	2	3	42	14	0			
14	3	3	36	12	7			
15	4	3	42	14	7			
16	5	3	45	15	3			
17	6	3	39	13	0			
18								
19	System A	6	81	13.5	4.3			
20	System B	6	78	13	2			
21	System C	6	93	15.5	3.5			
22								
23								
24	ANOVA							
25	*Source of Variation*	*SS*	*df*	*MS*	*F*	*P-value*	*F crit*	
26	Rows	30	5	6	3.1579	0.0574	3.3258	
27	Columns	21	2	10.5	5.5263	0.0242	4.1028	
28	Error	19	10	1.9				
29								
30	Total	70	17					
31								

Enter A9 in the **Output Range** box (to identify the upper left corner of the section of the worksheet where the output will appear)

Click **OK**

The output, titled Anova: Two-Factor Without Replication, appears in cells A9:G30 of the worksheet shown in Figure 13.8. Cells A11:E21 provide a summary of the data. The ANOVA table shown in cells A24:G30 is basically the same as the ANOVA table shown in Table 13.8. The label Rows corresponds to the blocks in the problem, and the label Columns corresponds to the treatments. The Excel output provides the p-value associated with the test as well as the critical F value.

We can use the p-value shown in cell F27, 0.0242, to make the hypothesis testing decision. Thus, at the $\alpha = .05$ level of significance, we reject H_0 because the p-value $= .0242 < \alpha = .05$. Hence, we conclude that the mean stress scores differ among the three systems.

NOTE AND COMMENT

The error degrees of freedom are less for a randomized block design than for a completely randomized design because $b - 1$ degrees of freedom are lost for the b blocks. If n is small, the potential effects due to blocks can be masked because of the loss of error degrees of freedom; for large n, the effects are minimized.

Exercises

Methods

21. Consider the experimental results for the following randomized block design. Make the calculations necessary to set up the analysis of variance table.

		Treatments		
		A	**B**	**C**
	1	10	9	8
	2	12	6	5
Blocks	**3**	18	15	14
	4	20	18	18
	5	8	7	8

Use $\alpha = .05$ to test for any significant differences.

22. The following data were obtained for a randomized block design involving five treatments and three blocks: SST = 430, SSTR = 310, SSBL = 85. Set up the ANOVA table and test for any significant differences. Use $\alpha = .05$.

23. An experiment has been conducted for four treatments with eight blocks. Complete the following analysis of variance table.

Source of Variation	Sum of Squares	Degrees of Freedom	Mean Square	F
Treatments	900			
Blocks	400			
Error				
Total	1800			

Use $\alpha = .05$ to test for any significant differences.

Applications

24. An automobile dealer conducted a test to determine if the time in minutes needed to complete a minor engine tune-up depends on whether a computerized engine analyzer or an electronic analyzer is used. Because tune-up time varies among compact, intermediate, and full-sized cars, the three types of cars were used as blocks in the experiment. The data obtained follow.

		Analyzer	
		Computerized	**Electronic**
	Compact	50	42
Car	**Intermediate**	55	44
	Full-sized	63	46

Use $\alpha = .05$ to test for any significant differences.

25. The price drivers pay for gasoline often varies a great deal across regions throughout the United States. The following data show the price per gallon for regular gasoline for a random sample of gasoline service stations for three major brands of gasoline (Shell, BP, and Marathon) located in 11 metropolitan areas across the upper Midwest region (OhioGasPrices.com website, March 18, 2012).

MidwestGas

Metropolitan Area	Shell	BP	Marathon
Akron, Ohio	3.77	3.83	3.78
Cincinnati, Ohio	3.72	3.83	3.87
Cleveland, Ohio	3.87	3.85	3.89
Columbus, Ohio	3.76	3.77	3.79
Ft. Wayne, Indiana	3.83	3.84	3.87
Indianapolis, Indiana	3.85	3.84	3.87
Lansing, Michigan	3.93	4.04	3.99
Lexington, Kentucky	3.79	3.78	3.79
Louisville, Kentucky	3.78	3.84	3.79
Muncie, Indiana	3.81	3.84	3.86
Toledo, Ohio	3.69	3.83	3.86

Use $\alpha = .05$ to test for any significant difference in the mean price of gasoline for the three brands.

26. The Scholastic Aptitude Test (SAT) contains three parts: critical reading, mathematics, and writing. Each part is scored on an 800-point scale. Information on test scores for the 2009 version of the SAT is available at the College Board website. A sample of SAT scores for six students follows.

SATScores

Student	Critical Reading	Mathematics	Writing
1	526	534	530
2	594	590	586
3	465	464	445
4	561	566	553
5	436	478	430
6	430	458	420

a. Using a .05 level of significance, do students perform differently on the three portions of the SAT?

b. Which portion of the test seems to give the students the most trouble? Explain.

27. A study reported in the *Journal of the American Medical Association* investigated the cardiac demands of heavy snow shoveling. Ten healthy men underwent exercise testing with a treadmill and a cycle ergometer modified for arm cranking. The men then cleared two tracts of heavy, wet snow by using a lightweight plastic snow shovel and an electric snow thrower. Each subject's heart rate, blood pressure, oxygen uptake, and perceived exertion during snow removal were compared with the values obtained during treadmill and arm-crank ergometer testing. Suppose the following table gives the heart rates in beats per minute for each of the 10 subjects.

SnowShoveling

Subject	Treadmill	Arm-Crank Ergometer	Snow Shovel	Snow Thrower
1	177	205	180	98
2	151	177	164	120
3	184	166	167	111
4	161	152	173	122
5	192	142	179	151
6	193	172	205	158
7	164	191	156	117
8	207	170	160	123
9	177	181	175	127
10	174	154	191	109

At the .05 level of significance, test for any significant differences.

Factorial Experiment

The experimental designs we have considered thus far enable us to draw statistical conclusions about one factor. However, in some experiments we want to draw conclusions about more than one variable or factor. A **factorial experiment** is an experimental design that allows simultaneous conclusions about two or more factors. The term *factorial* is used because the experimental conditions include all possible combinations of the factors. For example, for *a* levels of factor A and *b* levels of factor B, the experiment will involve collecting data on *ab* treatment combinations. In this section we will show the analysis for a two-factor factorial experiment. The basic approach can be extended to experiments involving more than two factors.

As an illustration of a two-factor factorial experiment, we will consider a study involving the Graduate Management Admissions Test (GMAT), a standardized test used by graduate schools of business to evaluate an applicant's ability to pursue a graduate program in that field. Scores on the GMAT range from 200 to 800, with higher scores implying higher aptitude.

In an attempt to improve students' performance on the GMAT, a major Texas university is considering offering the following three GMAT preparation programs.

1. A three-hour review session covering the types of questions generally asked on the GMAT.
2. A one-day program covering relevant exam material, along with the taking and grading of a sample exam.
3. An intensive 10-week course involving the identification of each student's weaknesses and the setting up of individualized programs for improvement.

Hence, one factor in this study is the GMAT preparation program, which has three treatments: three-hour review, one-day program, and 10-week course. Before selecting the preparation program to adopt, further study will be conducted to determine how the proposed programs affect GMAT scores.

The GMAT is usually taken by students from three colleges: the College of Business, the College of Engineering, and the College of Arts and Sciences. Therefore, a second factor of interest in the experiment is whether a student's undergraduate college affects the GMAT score. This second factor, undergraduate college, also has three treatments: business, engineering, and arts and sciences. The factorial design for this experiment with three treatments corresponding to factor A, the preparation program, and three treatments corresponding to factor B, the undergraduate college, will have a total of $3 \times 3 = 9$ treatment combinations. These treatment combinations or experimental conditions are summarized in Table 13.9.

Assume that a sample of two students will be selected corresponding to each of the nine treatment combinations shown in Table 13.9: Two business students will take the three-hour review, two will take the one-day program, and two will take the 10-week course. In addition, two engineering students and two arts and sciences students will take each of the three preparation programs. In experimental design terminology, the sample size of two for each

TABLE 13.9   NINE TREATMENT COMBINATIONS FOR THE TWO-FACTOR
GMAT EXPERIMENT

		Factor B: College		
		Business	**Engineering**	**Arts and Sciences**
Factor A:	**Three-hour review**	1	2	3
Preparation	**One-day program**	4	5	6
Program	**10-week course**	7	8	9

TABLE 13.10   GMAT SCORES FOR THE TWO-FACTOR EXPERIMENT

GMATStudy

		Factor B: College		
		Business	Engineering	Arts and Sciences
	Three-hour review	500	540	480
		580	460	400
Factor A: Preparation Program	**One-day program**	460	560	420
		540	620	480
	10-week course	560	600	480
		600	580	410

treatment combination indicates that we have two **replications**. Additional replications and a larger sample size could easily be used, but we elect to minimize the computational aspects for this illustration.

This experimental design requires that 6 students who plan to attend graduate school be randomly selected from *each* of the three undergraduate colleges. Then 2 students from each college should be assigned randomly to each preparation program, resulting in a total of 18 students being used in the study.

Let us assume that the randomly selected students participated in the preparation programs and then took the GMAT. The scores obtained are reported in Table 13.10.

The analysis of variance computations with the data in Table 13.10 will provide answers to the following questions.

- **Main effect (factor A):** Do the preparation programs differ in terms of effect on GMAT scores?
- **Main effect (factor B):** Do the undergraduate colleges differ in terms of effect on GMAT scores?
- **Interaction effect (factors A and B):** Do students in some colleges do better on one type of preparation program whereas others do better on a different type of preparation program?

The term **interaction** refers to a new effect that we can now study because we used a factorial experiment. If the interaction effect has a significant impact on the GMAT scores, we can conclude that the effect of the type of preparation program depends on the undergraduate college.

ANOVA Procedure

The ANOVA procedure for the two-factor factorial experiment requires us to partition the sum of squares total (SST) into four groups: sum of squares for factor A (SSA), sum of squares for factor B (SSB), sum of squares for interaction (SSAB), and sum of squares due to error (SSE). The formula for this partitioning follows.

$$\text{SST} = \text{SSA} + \text{SSB} + \text{SSAB} + \text{SSE} \qquad \textbf{(13.26)}$$

The partitioning of the sum of squares and degrees of freedom is summarized in Table 13.11. The following notation is used.

a = number of levels of factor A

b = number of levels of factor B

r = number of replications

n_T = total number of observations taken in the experiment; $n_T = abr$

TABLE 13.11 ANOVA TABLE FOR THE TWO-FACTOR FACTORIAL EXPERIMENT WITH r REPLICATIONS

Source of Variation	Sum of Squares	Degrees of Freedom	Mean Square	F	p-Value
Factor A	SSA	$a - 1$	$\text{MSA} = \dfrac{\text{SSA}}{a - 1}$	$\dfrac{\text{MSA}}{\text{MSE}}$	
Factor B	SSB	$b - 1$	$\text{MSB} = \dfrac{\text{SSB}}{b - 1}$	$\dfrac{\text{MSB}}{\text{MSE}}$	
Interaction	SSAB	$(a - 1)(b - 1)$	$\text{MSAB} = \dfrac{\text{SSAB}}{(a - 1)(b - 1)}$	$\dfrac{\text{MSAB}}{\text{MSE}}$	
Error	SSE	$ab(r - 1)$	$\text{MSE} = \dfrac{\text{SSE}}{ab(r - 1)}$		
Total	SST	$n_T - 1$			

Computations and Conclusions

To compute the F statistics needed to test for the significance of factor A, factor B, and interaction, we need to compute MSA, MSB, MSAB, and MSE. To calculate these four mean squares, we must first compute SSA, SSB, SSAB, and SSE; in doing so we will also compute SST. To simplify the presentation, we perform the calculations in five steps. In addition to a, b, r, and n_T as previously defined, the following notation is used.

x_{ijk} = observation corresponding to the kth replicate taken from treatment i of factor A and treatment j of factor B

$\bar{x}_{i\cdot}$ = sample mean for the observations in treatment i (factor A)

$\bar{x}_{\cdot j}$ = sample mean for the observations in treatment j (factor B)

$\bar{x}_{ij}$ = sample mean for the observations corresponding to the combination of treatment i (factor A) and treatment j (factor B)

$\bar{\bar{x}}$ = overall sample mean of all n_T observations

Step 1. Compute the total sum of squares.

$$\text{SST} = \sum_{i=1}^{a} \sum_{j=1}^{b} \sum_{k=1}^{r} (x_{ijk} - \bar{\bar{x}})^2 \tag{13.27}$$

Step 2. Compute the sum of squares for factor A.

$$\text{SSA} = br \sum_{i=1}^{a} (\bar{x}_{i\cdot} - \bar{\bar{x}})^2 \tag{13.28}$$

Step 3. Compute the sum of squares for factor B.

$$\text{SSB} = ar \sum_{j=1}^{b} (\bar{x}_{\cdot j} - \bar{\bar{x}})^2 \tag{13.29}$$

Step 4. Compute the sum of squares for interaction.

$$\text{SSAB} = r \sum_{i=1}^{a} \sum_{j=1}^{b} (\bar{x}_{ij} - \bar{x}_{i\cdot} - \bar{x}_{\cdot j} + \bar{\bar{x}})^2 \tag{13.30}$$

Step 5. Compute the sum of squares due to error.

$$\text{SSE} = \text{SST} - \text{SSA} - \text{SSB} - \text{SSAB} \qquad\qquad \textbf{(13.31)}$$

Table 13.12 reports the data collected in the experiment and the various sums that will help us with the sum of squares computations. Using equations (13.27) through (13.31), we calculate the following sums of squares for the GMAT two-factor factorial experiment.

Step 1. $\text{SST} = (500 - 515)^2 + (580 - 515)^2 + (540 - 515)^2 + \cdots +$
$(410 - 515)^2 = 82{,}450$

Step 2. $\text{SSA} = (3)(2)[(493.33 - 515)^2 + (513.33 - 515)^2 +$
$(538.33 - 515)^2] = 6100$

Step 3. $\text{SSB} = (3)(2)[(540 - 515)^2 + (560 - 515)^2 + (445 - 515)^2] = 45{,}300$

Step 4. $\text{SSAB} = 2[(540 - 493.33 - 540 + 515)^2 + (500 - 493.33 -$
$560 + 515)^2 + \cdots + (445 - 538.33 - 445 + 515)^2] = 11{,}200$

Step 5. $\text{SSE} = 82{,}450 - 6100 - 45{,}300 - 11{,}200 = 19{,}850$

These sums of squares divided by their corresponding degrees of freedom provide the following mean square values for testing the two main effects (preparation program and undergraduate college) and interaction effect.

Factor A: $\text{MSA} = \dfrac{\text{SSA}}{a - 1} = \dfrac{6100}{3 - 1} = 3050$

Factor B: $\text{MSB} = \dfrac{\text{SSB}}{b - 1} = \dfrac{45{,}300}{3 - 1} = 22{,}650$

Interaction: $\text{MSAB} = \dfrac{\text{SSAB}}{(a - 1)(b - 1)} = \dfrac{11{,}200}{(3 - 1)(3 - 1)} = 2800$

Error: $\text{MSE} = \dfrac{\text{SSE}}{ab(r - 1)} = \dfrac{19{,}850}{(3)(3)(2 - 1)} = 2205.5556$

Excel's F.DIST.RT function makes it easy to compute the p-value for each F value. For example, for factor A, p-value = F.DIST.RT(1.3829,2,9) = .2994.

Let us use a level of significance of $\alpha = .05$ to conduct the hypothesis tests for the two-factor GMAT study. The F ratio used to test for differences among preparation programs (factor A) is $F = \text{MSA/MSE} = 3050/2205.5556 = 1.3829$. We can use Excel to show that the p-value corresponding to $F = 1.3829$ is .2994. Because the p-value $> \alpha = .05$, we cannot reject the null hypothesis and must conclude that there is no significant difference among the three preparation programs. However, for the undergraduate college (factor B) effect, the p-value corresponding to $F = \text{MSB/MSE} = 22{,}650/2205.5556 = 10.2695$ is .0048. Hence, the analysis of variance results enable us to conclude that the GMAT test scores do differ among the three undergraduate colleges; that is, the three undergraduate colleges do not provide the same preparation for performance on the GMAT. Finally, the interaction F value of $F = \text{MSAB/MSE} = 2800/2205.5556 = 1.2695$ and its corresponding p-value of .3503 mean we cannot identify a significant interaction effect. Therefore, we have no reason to believe that the three preparation programs differ in their ability to prepare students from the different colleges for the GMAT. The ANOVA table shown in Table 13.13 provides a summary of these results for the two-factor GMAT study.

Undergraduate college was found to be a significant factor. Checking the calculations in Table 13.12, we see that the sample means are: business students $\bar{x}_{\cdot 1} = 540$, engineering students $\bar{x}_{\cdot 2} = 560$, and arts and sciences students $\bar{x}_{\cdot 3} = 445$. Tests on individual treatment means can be conducted; yet after reviewing the three sample means, we would anticipate no difference in preparation for business and engineering graduates. However, the arts and

TABLE 13.12   GMAT SUMMARY DATA FOR THE TWO-FACTOR EXPERIMENT

Factor A: Preparation Program	Factor B: College			Row Totals	Factor A Means
	Business	**Engineering**	**Arts and Sciences**		
Three-hour review	500 580 1080 $\bar{x}_{11} = \dfrac{1080}{2} = 540$	540 460 1000 $\bar{x}_{12} = \dfrac{1000}{2} = 500$	480 400 880 $\bar{x}_{13} = \dfrac{880}{2} = 440$	2960	$\bar{x}_{1\cdot} = \dfrac{2960}{6} = 493.33$
One-day program	460 540 1000 $\bar{x}_{21} = \dfrac{1000}{2} = 500$	560 620 1180 $\bar{x}_{22} = \dfrac{1180}{2} = 590$	420 480 900 $\bar{x}_{23} = \dfrac{900}{2} = 450$	3080	$\bar{x}_{2\cdot} = \dfrac{3080}{6} = 513.33$
10-week course	560 600 1160 $\bar{x}_{31} = \dfrac{1160}{2} = 580$	600 580 1180 $\bar{x}_{32} = \dfrac{1180}{2} = 590$	480 410 890 $\bar{x}_{33} = \dfrac{890}{2} = 445$	3230	$\bar{x}_{3\cdot} = \dfrac{3230}{6} = 538.33$
Column Totals	3240	3360	2670	9270	$\bar{\bar{x}} = \dfrac{9270}{18} = 515$
Factor B Means	$\bar{x}_{\cdot 1} = \dfrac{3240}{6} = 540$	$\bar{x}_{\cdot 2} = \dfrac{3360}{6} = 560$	$\bar{x}_{\cdot 3} = \dfrac{2670}{6} = 445$		

Treatment combination totals

Overall total

TABLE 13.13   ANOVA TABLE FOR THE TWO-FACTOR GMAT STUDY

Source of Variation	Sum of Squares	Degrees of Freedom	Mean Square	F	p-Value
Factor A	6,100	2	3,050	$3{,}050/2{,}205.5556 = 1.3829$	.2994
Factor B	45,300	2	22,650	$22{,}650/2{,}205.5556 = 10.2695$	.0048
Interaction	11,200	4	2,800	$2{,}800/2{,}205.5556 = 1.2695$	.3503
Error	19,850	9	2,205.5556		
Total	82,450	17			

sciences students appear to be significantly less prepared for the GMAT than students in the other colleges. Perhaps this observation will lead the university to consider other options for assisting these students in preparing for graduate management admission tests.

Using Excel

Excel's Anova: Two-Factor With Replication tool can be used to analyze the data for the two-factor GMAT experiment. Refer to Figures 13.9 and 13.10 as we describe the tasks involved.

FIGURE 13.9   EXCEL'S ANOVA: TWO-FACTOR WITH REPLICATION TOOL OUTPUT FOR THE GMAT EXPERIMENT

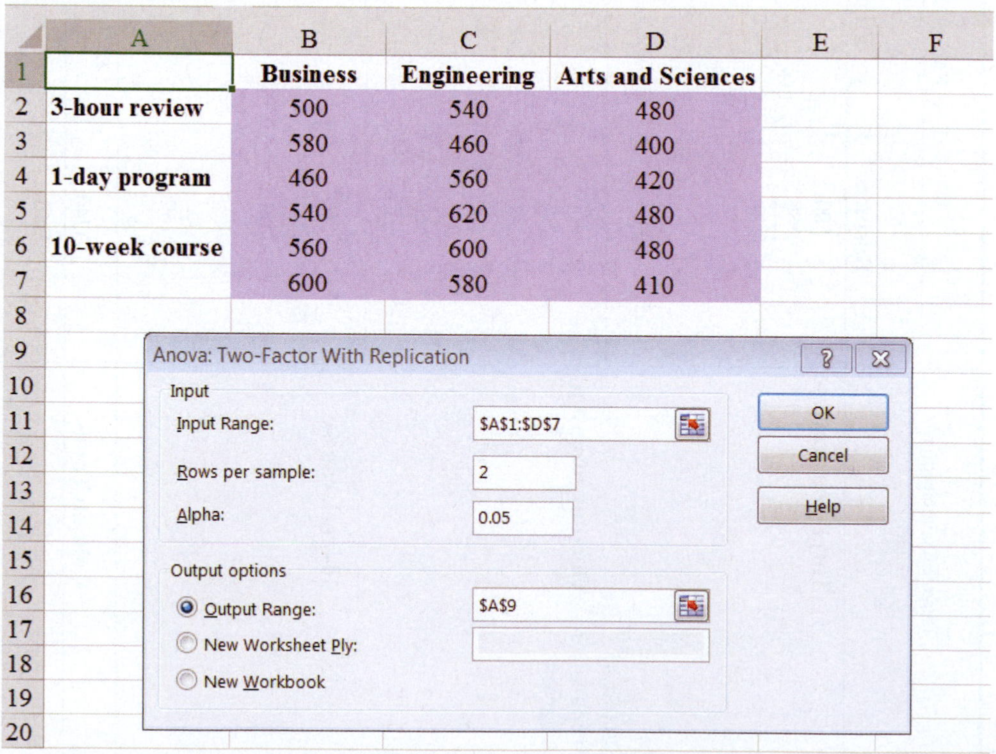

FIGURE 13.10 EXCEL'S ANOVA: TWO-FACTOR WITH REPLICATION TOOL OUTPUT
FOR THE GMAT EXPERIMENT

	A	B	C	D	E	F	G	H
1		**Business**	**Engineering**	**Arts and Sciences**				
2	**3-hour review**	500	540	480				
3		580	460	400				
4	**1-day program**	460	560	420				
5		540	620	480				
6	**10-week course**	560	600	480				
7		600	580	410				
8								
9	Anova: Two-Factor With Replication							
10								
11	SUMMARY	Business	Engineering	Arts and Sciences	Total			
12	*3-hour review*							
13	Count	2	2	2	6			
14	Sum	1080	1000	880	2960			
15	Average	540	500	440	493.3333			
16	Variance	3200	3200	3200	3946.667			
17								
18	*1-day program*							
19	Count	2	2	2	6			
20	Sum	1000	1180	900	3080			
21	Average	500	590	450	513.3333			
22	Variance	3200	1800	1800	5386.667			
23								
24	*10-week course*							
25	Count	2	2	2	6			
26	Sum	1160	1180	890	3230			
27	Average	580	590	445	538.3333			
28	Variance	800	200	2450	5936.667			
29								
30	*Total*							
31	Count	6	6	6				
32	Sum	3240	3360	2670				
33	Average	540	560	445				
34	Variance	2720	3200	1510				
35								
36								
37	ANOVA							
38	*Source of Variation*	*SS*	*df*	*MS*	*F*	*P-value*	*F crit*	
39	Sample	6100	2	3050	1.3829	0.2994	4.2565	
40	Columns	45300	2	22650	10.2695	0.0048	4.2565	
41	Interaction	11200	4	2800	1.2695	0.3503	3.6331	
42	Within	19850	9	2205.5556				
43								
44	Total	82450	17					
45								

Enter/Access Data: Open the DATAfile named *GMATStudy*. The data are in cells B2:D7
and labels are in cells A2, A4, A6, and B1:D1.

Apply Tools: The following steps describe how Excel's Anova: Two-Factor With Replication tool can be used to analyze the data for the two-factor GMAT experiment.

    Step 1. Click the **Data** tab on the Ribbon
    Step 2. In the **Analyze** group, click **Data Analysis**
    Step 3. Choose **Anova: Two-Factor With Replication** from the list of Analysis Tools

Step 4. When the Anova: Two-Factor With Replication dialog box appears (see Figure 13.9),

Enter A1:D7 in the **Input Range** box

Enter 2 in the **Rows per sample** box

Enter .05 in the **Alpha** box

Select **Output Range**

Enter A9 in the Output Range box (to identify the upper left corner of the section of the worksheet where the output will appear)

Click **OK**

The output, titled Anova: Two-Factor With Replication, appears in cells A9:G44 of the worksheet shown in Figure 13.10. Cells A11:E34 provide a summary of the data. The ANOVA table, shown in cells A37:G44, is basically the same as the ANOVA table shown in Table 13.13. The label Sample corresponds to factor A, the label Columns corresponds to factor B, and the label Within corresponds to error. The Excel output provides the p-value associated with each F test as well as the critical F values.

We can use the p-value of .2994 in cell F39 to make the hypothesis testing decision for factor A (Preparation Program). At the $\alpha = .05$ level of significance, we cannot reject H_0 because the p-value $= .2994 > \alpha = .05$. We can make the hypothesis testing decision for factor B (College) by using the p-value of 0.0048 shown in cell F40. At the $\alpha = .05$ level of significance, we reject H_0 because the p-value $= .0048 < \alpha = .05$. Finally, the interaction p-value of 0.3503 in cell F41 means that we cannot identify a significant interaction effect.

Exercises

Methods

 SELF*test*

28. A factorial experiment involving two levels of factor A and three levels of factor B resulted in the following data.

			Factor B	
		Level 1	Level 2	Level 3
Factor A	**Level 1**	135 165	90 66	75 93
	Level 2	125 95	127 105	120 136

Test for any significant main effects and any interaction. Use $\alpha = .05$.

29. The calculations for a factorial experiment involving four levels of factor A, three levels of factor B, and three replications resulted in the following data: SST = 280, SSA = 26, SSB = 23, SSAB = 175. Set up the ANOVA table and test for any significant main effects and any interaction effect. Use $\alpha = .05$.

Applications

30. A mail-order catalog firm designed a factorial experiment to test the effect of the size of a magazine advertisement and the advertisement design on the number of catalog requests received (data in thousands). Three advertising designs and two different size advertisements were considered. The data obtained follow. Use the ANOVA procedure for factorial designs to test for any significant effects due to type of design, size of advertisement, or interaction. Use $\alpha = .05$.

		Size of Advertisement	
		Small	**Large**
	A	8	12
		12	8
Design	**B**	22	26
		14	30
	C	10	18
		18	14

31. An amusement park studied methods for decreasing the waiting time (minutes) for rides by loading and unloading riders more efficiently. Two alternative loading/unloading methods have been proposed. To account for potential differences due to the type of ride and the possible interaction between the method of loading and unloading and the type of ride, a factorial experiment was designed. Use the following data to test for any significant effect due to the loading and unloading method, the type of ride, and interaction. Use $\alpha = .05$.

	Type of Ride		
	Roller Coaster	**Screaming Demon**	**Log Flume**
Method 1	41	52	50
	43	44	46
Method 2	49	50	48
	51	46	44

32. As part of a study designed to compare hybrid and similarly equipped conventional vehicles, *Consumer Reports* tested a variety of classes of hybrid and all-gas model cars and sport utility vehicles (SUVs). The following data show the miles-per-gallon rating *Consumer Reports* obtained for two hybrid small cars, two hybrid midsize cars, two hybrid small SUVs, and two hybrid midsize SUVs; also shown are the miles per gallon obtained for eight similarly equipped conventional models.

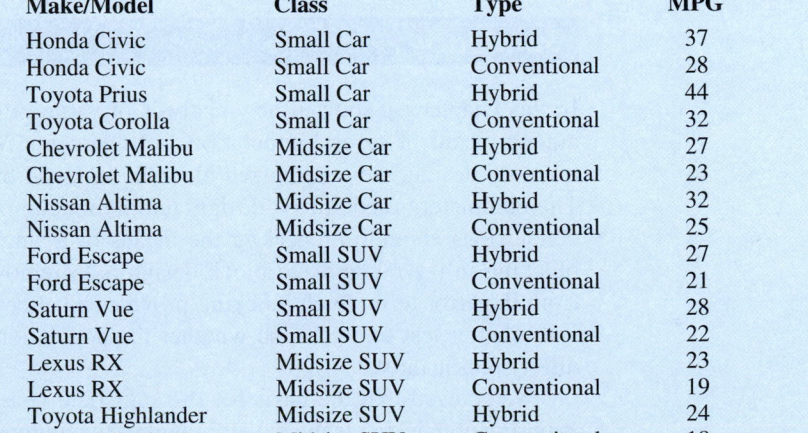

Make/Model	Class	Type	MPG
Honda Civic	Small Car	Hybrid	37
Honda Civic	Small Car	Conventional	28
Toyota Prius	Small Car	Hybrid	44
Toyota Corolla	Small Car	Conventional	32
Chevrolet Malibu	Midsize Car	Hybrid	27
Chevrolet Malibu	Midsize Car	Conventional	23
Nissan Altima	Midsize Car	Hybrid	32
Nissan Altima	Midsize Car	Conventional	25
Ford Escape	Small SUV	Hybrid	27
Ford Escape	Small SUV	Conventional	21
Saturn Vue	Small SUV	Hybrid	28
Saturn Vue	Small SUV	Conventional	22
Lexus RX	Midsize SUV	Hybrid	23
Lexus RX	Midsize SUV	Conventional	19
Toyota Highlander	Midsize SUV	Hybrid	24
Toyota Highlander	Midsize SUV	Conventional	18

At the $\alpha = .05$ level of significance, test for significant effects due to class, type, and interaction.

33. A study reported in *The Accounting Review* examined the separate and joint effects of two levels of time pressure (low and moderate) and three levels of knowledge (naive, declarative, and procedural) on key word selection behavior in tax research. Subjects were given a tax case containing a set of facts, a tax issue, and a key word index consisting of 1336 key words. They were asked to select the key words they believed would refer them to a tax authority relevant to resolving the tax case. Prior to the experiment, a group of tax experts determined that the text contained 19 relevant key words. Subjects in the naive group had little or no declarative or procedural knowledge, subjects in the declarative group had significant declarative knowledge but little or no procedural knowledge, and subjects in the procedural group had significant declarative knowledge and procedural knowledge. Declarative knowledge consists of knowledge of both the applicable tax rules and the technical terms used to describe such rules. Procedural knowledge is knowledge of the rules that guide the tax researcher's search for relevant key words. Subjects in the low time pressure situation were told they had 25 minutes to complete the problem, an amount of time which should be "more than adequate" to complete the case; subjects in the moderate time pressure situation were told they would have "only" 11 minutes to complete the case. Suppose 25 subjects were selected for each of the six treatment combinations and the sample means for each treatment combination are as follows (standard deviations are in parentheses).

		Knowledge		
		Naive	**Declarative**	**Procedural**
	Low	1.13 (1.12)	1.56 (1.33)	2.00 (1.54)
Time Pressure				
	Moderate	0.48 (0.80)	1.68 (1.36)	2.86 (1.80)

Use the ANOVA procedure to test for any significant differences due to time pressure, knowledge, and interaction. Use a .05 level of significance. Assume that the total sum of squares for this experiment is 327.50.

Summary

In this chapter we showed how analysis of variance can be used to test for differences among means of several populations or treatments. We introduced the completely randomized design, the randomized block design, and the two-factor factorial experiment. The completely randomized design and the randomized block design are used to draw conclusions aboutdifferences in the means of a single factor. The primary purpose of blocking in the randomized block design is to remove extraneous sources of variation from the error term. Such blocking provides a better estimate of the true error variance and a better test to determine whether the population or treatment means of the factor differ significantly.

We showed that the basis for the statistical tests used in analysis of variance and experimental design is the development of two independent estimates of the population variance σ^2. In the single-factor case, one estimator is based on the variation between the treatments; this estimator provides an unbiased estimate of σ^2 only if the means $\mu_1, \mu_2, \ldots, \mu_k$ are all equal. A second estimator of σ^2 is based on the variation of the observations within each sample; this estimator will always provide an unbiased estimate of σ^2. By computing the ratio of these two estimators (the F statistic) we developed a rejection rule for determining whether to reject the null hypothesis that the population or treatment means are equal. In all the experimental designs considered, the partitioning of the sum of squares and degrees of freedom into their various sources enabled us to compute the appropriate values for the analysis of variance calculations and tests. We also showed how Fisher's LSD procedure and the Bonferroni adjustment can be used to perform pairwise comparisons to determine which means are different.

Glossary

ANOVA table A table used to summarize the analysis of variance computations and results. It contains columns showing the source of variation, the sum of squares, the degrees of freedom, the mean square, the F value(s), and the p-value(s).

Blocking The process of using the same or similar experimental units for all treatments. The purpose of blocking is to remove a source of variation from the error term and hence provide a more powerful test for a difference in population or treatment means.

Comparisonwise Type I error rate The probability of a Type I error associated with a single pairwise comparison.

Completely randomized design An experimental design in which the treatments are randomly assigned to the experimental units.

Experimental statistical study A study in which the investigator controls the values of one or more variables believed to be related to the outcome of interest, and then measures and records the outcome. The investigator's control over the values of variables believed to be related to the outcome of interest allows for possible conclusions about whether any of the manipulated variables might have a cause-and-effect relationship with the outcome.

Experimental units The objects of interest in the experiment.

Experimentwise Type I error rate The probability of making a Type I error on at least one of several pairwise comparisons.

Factor Another word for the independent variable of interest.

Factorial experiment An experimental design that allows simultaneous conclusions about two or more factors.

Interaction The effect produced when the levels of one factor interact with the levels of another factor in influencing the response variable.

Multiple comparison procedures Statistical procedures that can be used to conduct statistical comparisons between pairs of population means.

Observational study A study in which the investigator observes the outcome of interest and possibly values of one or more variables believed to be related to the outcome without controlling the values of any variables, and then measures and records the outcome. The investigator's lack of control over the values of variables believed to be related to the outcome of interest allows only for possible conclusions about associations between the outcome and the variables.

Partitioning The process of allocating the total sum of squares and degrees of freedom to the various components.

Randomized block design An experimental design employing blocking.

Replications The number of times each experimental condition is repeated in an experiment.

Response variable Another word for the dependent variable of interest.

Single-factor experiment An experiment involving only one factor with k populations or treatments.

Treatments Different levels of a factor.

Key Formulas

Completely Randomized Design

Sample Mean for Treatment j

$$\bar{x}_j = \frac{\sum\limits_{i=1}^{n_j} x_{ij}}{n_j} \tag{13.1}$$

Sample Variance for Treatment j

$$s_j^2 = \frac{\sum\limits_{i=1}^{n_j} (x_{ij} - \bar{x}_j)^2}{n_j - 1} \tag{13.2}$$

Overall Sample Mean

$$\bar{\bar{x}} = \frac{\sum\limits_{j=1}^{k} \sum\limits_{i=1}^{n_j} x_{ij}}{n_T} \tag{13.3}$$

$$n_T = n_1 + n_2 + \cdots + n_k \tag{13.4}$$

Mean Square Due to Treatments

$$\text{MSTR} = \frac{\text{SSTR}}{k - 1} \tag{13.7}$$

Sum of Squares Due to Treatments

$$\text{SSTR} = \sum\limits_{j=1}^{k} n_j (\bar{x}_j - \bar{\bar{x}})^2 \tag{13.8}$$

Mean Square Due to Error

$$\text{MSE} = \frac{\text{SSE}}{n_T - k} \tag{13.10}$$

Sum of Squares Due to Error

$$\text{SSE} = \sum\limits_{j=1}^{k} (n_j - 1) s_j^2 \tag{13.11}$$

Test Statistic for the Equality of k Population Means

$$F = \frac{\text{MSTR}}{\text{MSE}} \tag{13.12}$$

Total Sum of Squares

$$\text{SST} = \sum\limits_{j=1}^{k} \sum\limits_{i=1}^{n_j} (x_{ij} - \bar{\bar{x}})^2 \tag{13.13}$$

Partitioning of Sum of Squares

$$\text{SST} = \text{SSTR} + \text{SSE} \tag{13.14}$$

Multiple Comparison Procedures

Test Statistic for Fisher's LSD Procedure

$$t = \frac{\bar{x}_i - \bar{x}_j}{\sqrt{\text{MSE}\left(\dfrac{1}{n_i} + \dfrac{1}{n_j}\right)}}$$ **(13.16)**

Fisher's LSD

$$\text{LSD} = t_{\alpha/2} \sqrt{\text{MSE}\left(\frac{1}{n_i} + \frac{1}{n_j}\right)}$$ **(13.17)**

Randomized Block Design

Total Sum of Squares

$$\text{SST} = \sum_{i=1}^{b} \sum_{j=1}^{k} (x_{ij} - \bar{\bar{x}})^2$$ **(13.22)**

Sum of Squares Due to Treatments

$$\text{SSTR} = b \sum_{j=1}^{k} (\bar{x}_{\cdot j} - \bar{\bar{x}})^2$$ **(13.23)**

Sum of Squares Due to Blocks

$$\text{SSBL} = k \sum_{i=1}^{b} (\bar{x}_{i\cdot} - \bar{\bar{x}})^2$$ **(13.24)**

Sum of Squares Due to Error

$$\text{SSE} = \text{SST} - \text{SSTR} - \text{SSBL}$$ **(13.25)**

Factorial Experiment

Total Sum of Squares

$$\text{SST} = \sum_{i=1}^{a} \sum_{j=1}^{b} \sum_{k=1}^{r} (x_{ijk} - \bar{\bar{x}})^2$$ **(13.27)**

Sum of Squares for Factor A

$$\text{SSA} = br \sum_{i=1}^{a} (\bar{x}_{i\cdot} - \bar{\bar{x}})^2$$ **(13.28)**

Sum of Squares for Factor B

$$\text{SSB} = ar \sum_{j=1}^{b} (\bar{x}_{\cdot j} - \bar{\bar{x}})^2$$ **(13.29)**

Sum of Squares for Interaction

$$\text{SSAB} = r \sum_{i=1}^{a} \sum_{j=1}^{b} (\bar{x}_{ij} - \bar{x}_{i\cdot} - \bar{x}_{\cdot j} + \bar{\bar{x}})^2$$ **(13.30)**

Sum of Squares for Error

$$\text{SSE} = \text{SST} - \text{SSA} - \text{SSB} - \text{SSAB}$$ **(13.31)**

Supplementary Exercises

34. In a completely randomized experimental design, three brands of paper towels were tested for their ability to absorb water. Equal-size towels were used, with four sections of towels tested per brand. The absorbency rating data follow. At a .05 level of significance, does there appear to be a difference in the ability of the brands to absorb water?

	Brand	
x	*y*	*z*
91	99	83
100	96	88
88	94	89
89	99	76

35. A study reported in the *Journal of Small Business Management* concluded that self-employed individuals do not experience higher job satisfaction than individuals who are not self-employed. In this study, job satisfaction is measured using 18 items, each of which is rated using a Likert-type scale with 1–5 response options ranging from strong agreement to strong disagreement. A higher score on this scale indicates a higher degree of job satisfaction. The sum of the ratings for the 18 items, ranging from 18–90, is used as the measure of job satisfaction. Suppose that this approach was used to measure the job satisfaction for lawyers, physical therapists, cabinetmakers, and systems analysts. The results obtained for a sample of 10 individuals from each profession follow.

DATA *file*

SatisJob

Lawyer	Physical Therapist	Cabinetmaker	Systems Analyst
44	55	54	44
42	78	65	73
74	80	79	71
42	86	69	60
53	60	79	64
50	59	64	66
45	62	59	41
48	52	78	55
64	55	84	76
38	50	60	62

At the $\alpha = .05$ level of significance, test for any difference in the job satisfaction among the four professions.

36. The U.S. Environmental Protection Agency (EPA) monitors levels of pollutants in the air for cities across the country. Ozone pollution levels are measured using a 500-point scale; lower scores indicate little health risk, and higher scores indicate greater health risk. The following data show the peak levels of ozone pollution in four cities (Birmingham, Alabama; Memphis, Tennessee; Little Rock, Arkansas; and Jackson, Mississippi) for 10 dates from last year.

OzoneLevels

	City			
Date	Birmingham AL	Memphis TN	Little Rock AR	Jackson MS
Jan 9	18	20	18	14
Jan 17	23	31	22	30
Jan 18	19	25	22	21
Jan 31	29	36	28	35
Feb 1	27	31	28	24
Feb 6	26	31	31	25
Feb 14	31	24	19	25
Feb 17	31	31	28	28
Feb 20	33	35	35	34
Feb 29	20	42	42	21

Use $\alpha = .05$ to test for any significant difference in the mean peak ozone levels among the four cities.

37. The following data show the percentage of 17- to 24-year-olds who are attending college in several metropolitan statistical areas in four geographic regions of the United States (U.S. Census Bureau website, April 2015).

CollegeRates

Northeast	Midwest	South	West
28.6	36.7	59.9	16.4
39.9	33.4	37.2	33.5
31.9	22.8	28.0	22.3
46.3	43.8	41.1	12.4
32.5	32.1	33.9	43.7
14.9	58.3	18.8	26.8
36.8	31.1	30.3	57.3
36.3	64.0	67.4	14.3
37.7	27.6	32.6	37.0
58.4	55.5	30.0	28.1
60.6	78.8	39.1	17.5
	42.2	29.7	32.3
	74.7	29.8	52.4
	36.5	23.7	51.5
	28.7	34.0	25.4
	60.4	24.5	29.6
	58.2	54.2	27.6
	21.0	31.0	31.5
	28.8	41.9	22.8
	25.5	70.2	34.6
	73.9	22.7	33.0
	36.8	30.7	37.0
	28.4	30.8	33.8
	27.2	21.6	28.7
	31.8	31.5	21.8
	56.8	38.2	
	28.3	40.2	
	33.3	35.4	
	39.4	21.6	
	39.2	35.5	
		26.1	
		32.7	

Use $\alpha = .05$ to test whether the mean percentage of 17- to 24-year-olds who are attending college is the same for the four geographic regions.

38. Three different assembly methods have been proposed for a new product. A completely randomized experimental design was chosen to determine which assembly method results in the greatest number of parts produced per hour, and 30 workers were randomly selected and assigned to use one of the proposed methods. The number of units produced by each worker follows.

DATA file

Assembly

	Method	
A	**B**	**C**
97	93	99
73	100	94
93	93	87
100	55	66
73	77	59
91	91	75
100	85	84
86	73	72
92	90	88
95	83	86

Use these data and test to see whether the mean number of parts produced is the same with each method. Use $\alpha = .05$.

39. In a study conducted to investigate browsing activity by shoppers, each shopper was initially classified as a nonbrowser, light browser, or heavy browser. For each shopper, the study obtained a measure to determine how comfortable the shopper was in a store. Higher scores indicated greater comfort. Suppose the following data were collected.

DATA file

Browsing

Nonbrowser	Light Browser	Heavy Browser
4	5	5
5	6	7
6	5	5
3	4	7
3	7	4
4	4	6
5	6	5
4	5	7

a. Use $\alpha = .05$ to test for differences among comfort levels for the three types of browsers.
b. Use Fisher's LSD procedure to compare the comfort levels of nonbrowsers and light browsers. Use $\alpha = .05$. What is your conclusion?

40. A research firm tests the miles-per-gallon characteristics of three brands of gasoline. Because of different gasoline performance characteristics in different brands of automobiles, five brands of automobiles are selected and treated as blocks in the experiment; that is, each brand of automobile is tested with each type of gasoline. The results of the experiment (in miles per gallon) follow.

		Gasoline Brands		
		I	**II**	**III**
	A	18	21	20
	B	24	26	27
Automobiles	C	30	29	34
	D	22	25	24
	E	20	23	24

a. At $\alpha = .05$, is there a significant difference in the mean miles-per-gallon characteristics of the three brands of gasoline?

b. Analyze the experimental data using the ANOVA procedure for completely randomized designs. Compare your findings with those obtained in part (a). What is the advantage of attempting to remove the block effect?

41. *Jimmy Kimmel Live!* on ABC, *The Tonight Show Starring Jimmy Fallon* on NBC, and *The Late Show with Stephen Colbert* on CBS are three popular late-night talk shows. The following table shows the number of viewers in millions for a 10-week period during the spring for each of these shows (TV by the Numbers website, June 29, 2016).

TalkShows

Week	Jimmy Kimmel Live (ABC)	The Tonight Show Starring Jimmy Fallon (NBC)	The Late Show with Stephen Colbert (CBS)
June 13 – June 17	2.67	3.24	2.27
June 6 – June 10	2.58	3.32	2.05
May 30 – June 3	2.64	2.66	2.08
May 23 – May 27	2.47	3.30	2.07
May 16 – May 20	1.97	3.10	2.31
May 9 – May 16	2.21	3.31	2.45
May 2 – May 6	2.12	3.20	2.57
April 25 – April 29	2.24	3.15	2.45
April 18 – April 22	2.10	2.77	2.56
April 11 – April 15	2.21	3.24	2.16

At the .05 level of significance, test for a difference in the mean number of viewers per week for the three late-night talk shows.

42. Major League Baseball franchises rely on attendance for a large share of their total revenue, and weekend games are particularly important. The following table shows the attendance for the Houston Astros for games played during seven weekend series for the first three months (April, May, and June) of the 2011 season (ESPN website, January 12, 2012).

HoustonAstros

Opponent	Friday	Saturday	Sunday
Florida Marlins	41,042	25,421	22,299
San Diego Padres	23,755	28,100	22,899
Milwaukee Brewers	25,734	26,514	23,908
New York Mets	28,791	31,140	28,406
Arizona Diamondbacks	21,834	31,405	21,882
Atlanta Braves	29,252	32,117	23,765
Tampa Bay Rays	26,682	27,208	23,965

At the .05 level of significance, test whether the mean attendance is the same for these three days. The Houston Astros are considering running a special promotion to increase attendance during one game of each weekend series during the second half of the season. Do these data suggest a particular day on which the Astros should schedule these promotions?

43. A factorial experiment was designed to test for any significant differences in the time needed to perform English to foreign language translations with two computerized language translators. Because the type of language translated was also considered a significant factor, translations were made with both systems for three different languages: Spanish, French, and German. Use the following data for translation time in hours.

	Language		
	Spanish	**French**	**German**
System 1	8	10	12
	12	14	16
System 2	6	14	16
	10	16	22

Test for any significant differences due to language translator, type of language, and interaction. Use $\alpha = .05$.

44. A manufacturing company designed a factorial experiment to determine whether the number of defective parts produced by two machines differed and if the number of defective parts produced also depended on whether the raw material needed by each machine was loaded manually or by an automatic feed system. The following data give the numbers of defective parts produced. Use $\alpha = .05$ to test for any significant effect due to machine, loading system, and interaction.

	Loading System	
	Manual	**Automatic**
Machine 1	30	30
	34	26
Machine 2	20	24
	22	28

Case Problem 1   Wentworth Medical Center

As part of a long-term study of individuals 65 years of age or older, sociologists and physicians at the Wentworth Medical Center in upstate New York investigated the relationship between geographic location and depression. A sample of 60 individuals, all in reasonably good health, was selected; 20 individuals were residents of Florida, 20 were residents of New York, and 20 were residents of North Carolina. Each of the individuals sampled was given a standardized test to measure depression. The data collected follow; higher test scores indicate higher levels of depression. These data are contained in the DATAfile named *Medical1*.

A second part of the study considered the relationship between geographic location and depression for individuals 65 years of age or older who had a chronic health condition such as arthritis, hypertension, and/or heart ailment. A sample of 60 individuals with such conditions was identified. Again, 20 were residents of Florida, 20 were residents of New York, and 20 were residents of North Carolina. The levels of depression recorded for this study follow. These data are contained in the DATAfile named *Medical2*.

Medical1

Medical2

Data from Medical1			Data from Medical2		
Florida	New York	North Carolina	Florida	New York	North Carolina
3	8	10	13	14	10
7	11	7	12	9	12
7	9	3	17	15	15
3	7	5	17	12	18
8	8	11	20	16	12
8	7	8	21	24	14
8	8	4	16	18	17
5	4	3	14	14	8
5	13	7	13	15	14
2	10	8	17	17	16
6	6	8	12	20	18
2	8	7	9	11	17
6	12	3	12	23	19
6	8	9	15	19	15
9	6	8	16	17	13
7	8	12	15	14	14
5	5	6	13	9	11
4	7	3	10	14	12
7	7	8	11	13	13
3	8	11	17	11	11

Managerial Report

1. Use descriptive statistics to summarize the data from the two studies. What are your preliminary observations about the depression scores?
2. Use analysis of variance on both data sets. State the hypotheses being tested in each case. What are your conclusions?
3. Use inferences about individual treatment means where appropriate. What are your conclusions?

Case Problem 2   Compensation for Sales Professionals

Suppose that a local chapter of sales professionals in the greater San Francisco area conducted a survey of its membership to study the relationship, if any, between the years of experience and salary for individuals employed in inside and outside sales positions. On the survey, respondents were asked to specify one of three levels of years of experience: low (1–10 years), medium (11–20 years), and high (21 or more years). A portion of the data obtained follows. The complete data set, consisting of 120 observations, is contained in the DATAfile named *SalesSalary*.

DATA *file*

SalesSalary

Observation	Salary $	Position	Experience
1	53,938	Inside	Medium
2	52,694	Inside	Medium
3	70,515	Outside	Low
4	52,031	Inside	Medium
5	62,283	Outside	Low
6	57,718	Inside	Low
7	79,081	Outside	High
8	48,621	Inside	Low
9	72,835	Outside	High
10	54,768	Inside	Medium
.	.	.	.
.	.	.	.
.	.	.	.
115	58,080	Inside	High
116	78,702	Outside	Medium
117	83,131	Outside	Medium
118	57,788	Inside	High
119	53,070	Inside	Medium
120	60,259	Outside	Low

Managerial Report

1. Use descriptive statistics to summarize the data.
2. Develop a 95% confidence interval estimate of the mean annual salary for all salespersons, regardless of years of experience and type of position.
3. Develop a 95% confidence interval estimate of the mean salary for inside salespersons.
4. Develop a 95% confidence interval estimate of the mean salary for outside salespersons.
5. Use analysis of variance to test for any significant differences due to position. Use a .05 level of significance, and for now, ignore the effect of years of experience.
6. Use analysis of variance to test for any significant differences due to years of experience. Use a .05 level of significance, and for now, ignore the effect of position.
7. At the .05 level of significance test for any significant differences due to position, years of experience, and interaction.

Case Problem 3   ## TourisTopia Travel

DATA *file*

TourisTopia

TourisTopia Travel (Triple T) is an online travel agency that specializes in trips to exotic locations around the world for groups of ten or more travelers. Triple T's marketing manager has been working on a major revision of the homepage of Triple T's website. The content for the homepage has been selected and the only remaining decisions involve the selection of the background color (white, green, or pink) and the type of font (Arial, Calibri, or Tahoma).

Triple T's IT group has designed prototype homepages featuring every combination of these background colors and fonts, and it has implemented computer code that will randomly direct each Triple T website visitor to one of these prototype homepages. For three weeks, the prototype homepage to which each visitor was directed and the amount of time in seconds spent at Triple T's website during each visit were recorded. Ten visitors to each of the prototype homepages were then selected randomly; the complete data set for these visitors is available in the DATAfile named *TourisTopia*.

Triple T wants to use these data to determine if the time spent by visitors to Triple T's website differs by background color or font. It would also like to know if the time spent by visitors to the Triple T website differs by different combinations of background color and font.

Managerial Report

Prepare a managerial report that addresses the following issues.

1. Use descriptive statistics to summarize the data from Triple T's study. Based on descriptive statistics, what are your preliminary conclusions about whether the time spent by visitors to the Triple T website differs by background color or font? What are your preliminary conclusions about whether time spent by visitors to the Triple T website differs by different combinations of background color and font?
2. Has Triple T used an observational study or a controlled experiment? Explain.
3. Use the data from Triple T's study to test the hypothesis that the time spent by visitors to the Triple T website is equal for the three background colors. Include both factors and their interaction in the ANOVA model, and use $\alpha = .05$.
4. Use the data from Triple T's study to test the hypothesis that the time spent by visitors to the Triple T website is equal for the three fonts. Include both factors and their interaction in the ANOVA model, and use $\alpha = .05$.
5. Use the data from Triple T's study to test the hypothesis that time spent by visitors to the Triple T website is equal for the nine combinations of background color and font. Include both factors and their interaction in the ANOVA model, and use $\alpha = .05$.
6. Do the results of your analysis of the data provide evidence that the time spent by visitors to the Triple T website differs by background color, font, or combination of background color and font? What is your recommendation?

CHAPTER 14

Simple Linear Regression

CONTENTS

STATISTICS *in* PRACTICE

ALLIANCE DATA SYSTEMS*
DALLAS, TEXAS

Alliance Data Systems (ADS) provides transaction processing, credit services, and marketing services for clients in the rapidly growing customer relationship management (CRM) industry. ADS clients are concentrated in four industries: retail, petroleum/convenience stores, utilities, and transportation. In 1983, Alliance began offering end-to-end credit processing services to the retail, petroleum, and casual dining industries; today they employ more than 6500 employees who provide services to clients around the world. Operating more than 140,000 point-of-sale terminals in the United States alone, ADS processes in excess of 2.5 billion transactions annually. The company ranks second in the United States in private label credit services by representing 49 private label programs with nearly 72 million cardholders. In 2001, ADS made an initial public offering and is now listed on the New York Stock Exchange.

As one of its marketing services, ADS designs direct mail campaigns and promotions. With its database containing information on the spending habits of more than 100 million consumers, ADS can target those consumers most likely to benefit from a direct mail promotion. The Analytical Development Group uses regression analysis to build models that measure and predict the responsiveness of consumers to direct market campaigns. Some regression models predict the probability of purchase for individuals receiving a promotion, and others predict the amount spent by those consumers making a purchase.

For one particular campaign, a retail store chain wanted to attract new customers. To predict the effect of the campaign, ADS analysts selected a sample from the consumer database, sent the sampled individuals promotional materials, and then collected transaction data on the consumers' response. Sample data were collected on the amount of purchase made by the consumers responding to the campaign, as well as a variety of consumer-specific variables thought to be useful in predicting sales. The consumer-specific variable that contributed most to predicting the amount purchased was the total amount of

Alliance Data Systems analysts discuss use of a regression model to predict sales for a direct marketing campaign.

Courtesy of Alliance Data Systems

credit purchases at related stores over the past 39 months. ADS analysts developed an estimated regression equation relating the amount of purchase to the amount spent at related stores:

$$\hat{y} = 26.7 + 0.00205x$$

where

$\hat{y}$ = amount of purchase

x = amount spent at related stores

Using this equation, we could predict that someone spending \$10,000 over the past 39 months at related stores would spend \$47.20 when responding to the direct mail promotion. In this chapter, you will learn how to develop this type of estimated regression equation.

The final model developed by ADS analysts also included several other variables that increased the predictive power of the preceding equation. Some of these variables included the absence/presence of a bank credit card, estimated income, and the average amount spent per trip at a selected store. In the following chapter, we will learn how such additional variables can be incorporated into a multiple regression model.

---

*The authors are indebted to Philip Clemance, Director of Analytical Development at Alliance Data Systems, for providing this Statistics in Practice.

Managerial decisions often are based on the relationship between two or more variables. For example, after considering the relationship between advertising expenditures and sales, a marketing manager might attempt to predict sales for a given level of advertising expenditures. In another case, a public utility might use the relationship between the daily high temperature and the demand for electricity to predict electricity usage on the basis of next month's anticipated daily high temperatures. Sometimes a manager will rely on intuition to judge how two variables are related. However, if data can be obtained, a statistical procedure called *regression analysis* can be used to develop an equation showing how the variables are related.

The statistical methods used in studying the relationship between two variables were first employed by Sir Francis Galton (1822–1911). Galton was interested in studying the relationship between a father's height and the son's height. Galton's disciple, Karl Pearson (1857–1936), analyzed the relationship between the father's height and the son's height for 1078 pairs of subjects.

In regression terminology, the variable being predicted is called the **dependent variable**. The variable or variables being used to predict the value of the dependent variable are called the **independent variables**. For example, in analyzing the effect of advertising expenditures on sales, a marketing manager's desire to predict sales would suggest making sales the dependent variable. Advertising expenditure would be the independent variable used to help predict sales. In statistical notation, y denotes the dependent variable and x denotes the independent variable.

In this chapter we consider the simplest type of regression analysis involving one independent variable and one dependent variable in which the relationship between the variables is approximated by a straight line. It is called **simple linear regression**. Regression analysis involving two or more independent variables is called multiple regression analysis.

14.1 Simple Linear Regression Model

Armand's Pizza Parlors is a chain of Italian-food restaurants located in a five-state area. Armand's most successful locations are near college campuses. The managers believe that quarterly sales for these restaurants (denoted by y) are related positively to the size of the student population (denoted by x); that is, restaurants near campuses with a large student population tend to generate more sales than those located near campuses with a small student population. Using regression analysis, we can develop an equation showing how the dependent variable y is related to the independent variable x.

Regression Model and Regression Equation

In the Armand's Pizza Parlors example, the population consists of all the Armand's restaurants. For every restaurant in the population, there is a value of x (student population) and a corresponding value of y (quarterly sales). The equation that describes how y is related to x and an error term is called the **regression model**. The regression model used in simple linear regression follows.

> **SIMPLE LINEAR REGRESSION MODEL**
>
> $$y = \beta_0 + \beta_1 x + \epsilon \qquad (14.1)$$

β_0 and β_1 are referred to as the parameters of the model, and ϵ (the Greek letter epsilon) is a random variable referred to as the error term. The error term accounts for the variability in y that cannot be explained by the linear relationship between x and y.

The population of all Armand's restaurants can also be viewed as a collection of subpopulations, one for each distinct value of x. For example, one subpopulation consists of all Armand's restaurants located near college campuses with 8000 students; another subpopulation consists of all Armand's restaurants located near college campuses with 9000 students; and so on. Each subpopulation has a corresponding distribution of y values. Thus, a distribution of y values is associated with restaurants located near campuses with 8000 students; a distribution of y values is associated with restaurants located near campuses with 9000 students; and so on. Each distribution of y values has its own mean or expected value. The equation that describes how the expected value of y, denoted $E(y)$, is related to x is called the **regression equation**. The regression equation for simple linear regression follows.

SIMPLE LINEAR REGRESSION EQUATION

$$E(y) = \beta_0 + \beta_1 x \qquad\qquad (14.2)$$

The graph of the simple linear regression equation is a straight line; β_0 is the y-intercept of the regression line, β_1 is the slope, and $E(y)$ is the mean or expected value of y for a given value of x.

Examples of possible regression lines are shown in Figure 14.1. The regression line in Panel A shows that the mean value of y is related positively to x, with larger values of $E(y)$ associated with larger values of x. The regression line in Panel B shows the mean value of y is related negatively to x, with smaller values of $E(y)$ associated with larger values of x. The regression line in Panel C shows the case in which the mean value of y is not related to x; that is, the mean value of y is the same for every value of x.

Estimated Regression Equation

If the values of the population parameters β_0 and β_1 were known, we could use equation (14.2) to compute the mean value of y for a given value of x. In practice, the parameter values are not known and must be estimated using sample data. Sample statistics (denoted b_0 and b_1) are computed as estimates of the population parameters β_0 and β_1. Substituting

FIGURE 14.1   POSSIBLE REGRESSION LINES IN SIMPLE LINEAR REGRESSION

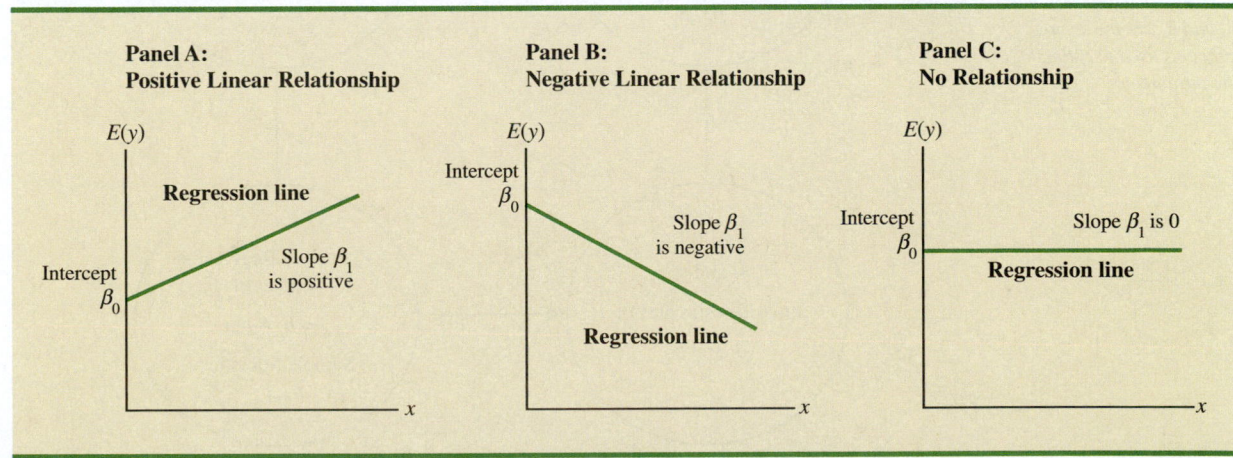

the values of the sample statistics b_0 and b_1 for β_0 and β_1 in the regression equation, we obtain the **estimated regression equation**. The estimated regression equation for simple linear regression follows.

ESTIMATED SIMPLE LINEAR REGRESSION EQUATION

$$\hat{y} = b_0 + b_1 x \qquad\qquad (14.3)$$

Figure 14.2 provides a summary of the estimation process for simple linear regression.

The graph of the estimated simple linear regression equation is called the *estimated regression line*; b_0 is the y-intercept and b_1 is the slope. In the next section, we show how the least squares method can be used to compute the values of b_0 and b_1 in the estimated regression equation.

The value of $\hat{y}$ provides both a point estimate of $E(y)$ for a given value of x and a prediction of an individual value of y for a given value of x.

In general, $\hat{y}$ is the point estimator of $E(y)$, the mean value of y for a given value of x. Thus, to estimate the mean or expected value of quarterly sales for all restaurants located near campuses with 10,000 students, Armand's would substitute the value of 10,000 for x in equation (14.3). In some cases, however, Armand's may be more interested in predicting sales for one particular restaurant. For example, suppose Armand's would like to predict quarterly sales for the restaurant they are considering building near Talbot College, a school with 10,000 students. As it turns out, the best predictor of y for a given value of x is also provided by $\hat{y}$. Thus, to predict quarterly sales for the restaurant located near Talbot College, Armand's would also substitute the value of 10,000 for x in equation (14.3).

FIGURE 14.2   THE ESTIMATION PROCESS IN SIMPLE LINEAR REGRESSION

The estimation of β_0 and β_1 is a statistical process much like the estimation of μ discussed in Chapter 7. β_0 and β_1 are the unknown parameters of interest, and b_0 and b_1 are the sample statistics used to estimate the parameters.

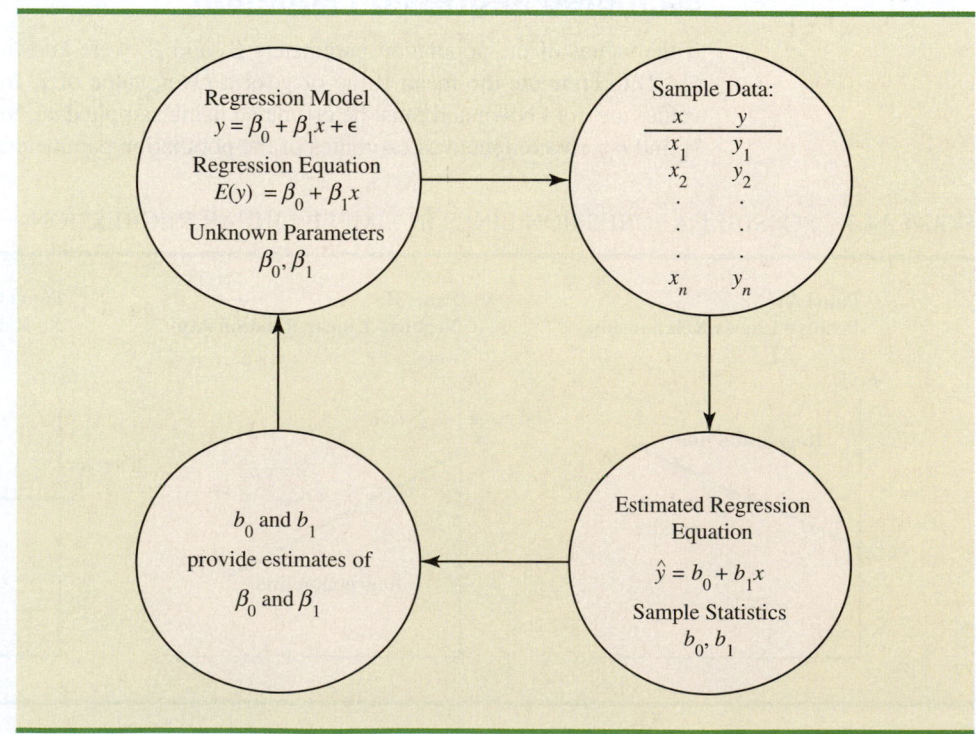

NOTES AND COMMENTS

1. Regression analysis cannot be interpreted as a procedure for establishing a cause-and-effect relationship between variables. It can only indicate how or to what extent variables are associated with each other. Any conclusions about cause and effect must be based upon the judgment of those individuals most knowledgeable about the application.

2. The regression equation in simple linear regression is $E(y) = \beta_0 + \beta_1 x$. More advanced texts in regression analysis often write the regression equation as $E(y|x) = \beta_0 + \beta_1 x$ to emphasize that the regression equation provides the mean value of y for a given value of x.

Least Squares Method

In simple linear regression, each observation consists of two values: one for the independent variable and one for the dependent variable.

The **least squares method** is a procedure for using sample data to find the estimated regression equation. To illustrate the least squares method, suppose data were collected from a sample of 10 Armand's Pizza Parlor restaurants located near college campuses. For the ith observation or restaurant in the sample, x_i is the size of the student population (in thousands) and y_i is the quarterly sales (in thousands of dollars). The values of x_i and y_i for the 10 restaurants in the sample are summarized in Table 14.1. We see that restaurant 1, with $x_1 = 2$ and $y_1 = 58$, is near a campus with 2000 students and has quarterly sales of $58,000. Restaurant 2, with $x_2 = 6$ and $y_2 = 105$, is near a campus with 6000 students and has quarterly sales of $105,000. The largest sales value is for restaurant 10, which is near a campus with 26,000 students and has quarterly sales of $202,000.

   Figure 14.3 is a scatter diagram of the data in Table 14.1. Student population is shown on the horizontal axis and quarterly sales is shown on the vertical axis. **Scatter diagrams** for regression analysis are constructed with the independent variable x on the horizontal axis and the dependent variable y on the vertical axis. The scatter diagram enables us to observe the data graphically and to draw preliminary conclusions about the possible relationship between the variables.

   What preliminary conclusions can be drawn from Figure 14.3? Quarterly sales appear to be higher at campuses with larger student populations. In addition, for these data the relationship between the size of the student population and quarterly sales appears to be approximated by a straight line; indeed, a positive linear relationship is indicated between x

TABLE 14.1   STUDENT POPULATION AND QUARTERLY SALES DATA
FOR 10 ARMAND'S PIZZA PARLORS

DATA *file*

Armand's

Restaurant i	Student Population (1000s) x_i	Quarterly Sales ($1000s) y_i
1	2	58
2	6	105
3	8	88
4	8	118
5	12	117
6	16	137
7	20	157
8	20	169
9	22	149
10	26	202

FIGURE 14.3   SCATTER DIAGRAM OF STUDENT POPULATION AND QUARTERLY
SALES FOR ARMAND'S PIZZA PARLORS

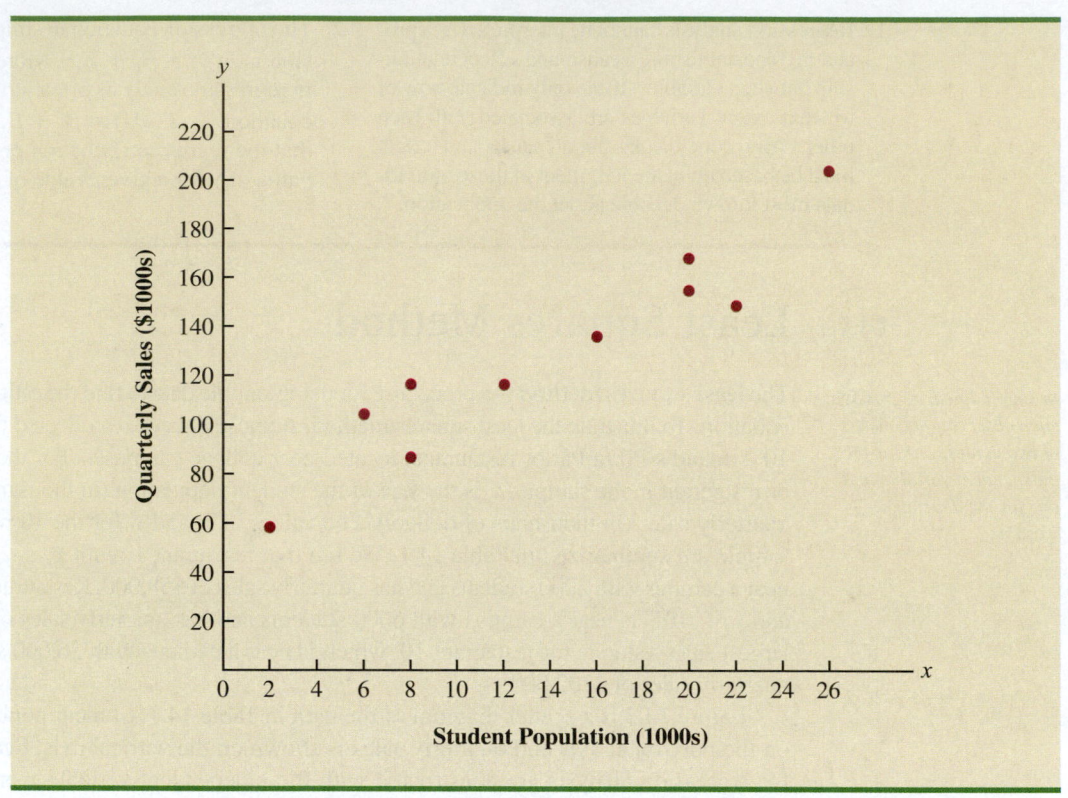

and y. We therefore choose the simple linear regression model to represent the relationship between quarterly sales and student population. Given that choice, our next task is to use the sample data in Table 14.1 to determine the values of b_0 and b_1 in the estimated simple linear regression equation. For the ith restaurant, the estimated regression equation provides

$$\hat{y}_i = b_0 + b_1 x_i \tag{14.4}$$

where

$\hat{y}_i$ = predicted value of quarterly sales ($1000s) for the ith restaurant

b_0 = the y-intercept of the estimated regression line

b_1 = the slope of the estimated regression line

x_i = size of the student population (1000s) for the ith restaurant

With y_i denoting the observed (actual) sales for restaurant i and $\hat{y}_i$ in equation (14.4) representing the predicted value of sales for restaurant i, every restaurant in the sample will have an observed value of sales y_i and a predicted value of sales $\hat{y}_i$. For the estimated regression line to provide a good fit to the data, we want the differences between the observed sales values and the predicted sales values to be small.

The least squares method uses the sample data to provide the values of b_0 and b_1 that minimize the *sum of the squares of the deviations* between the observed values of the dependent variable y_i and the predicted values of the dependent variable $\hat{y}_i$. The criterion for the least squares method is given by expression (14.5).

LEAST SQUARES CRITERION

$$\min \sum(y_i - \hat{y}_i)^2 \qquad \text{(14.5)}$$

where

y_i = observed value of the dependent variable for the ith observation
$\hat{y}_i$ = predicted value of the dependent variable for the ith observation

Differential calculus can be used to show (see Appendix 14.1) that the values of b_0 and b_1 that minimize expression (14.5) can be found by using equations (14.6) and (14.7).

SLOPE AND y-INTERCEPT FOR THE ESTIMATED REGRESSION EQUATION[1]

In computing b_1 with a calculator, carry as many significant digits as possible in the intermediate calculations. We recommend carrying at least four significant digits.

$$b_1 = \frac{\sum(x_i - \bar{x})(y_i - \bar{y})}{\sum(x_i - \bar{x})^2} \qquad \text{(14.6)}$$

$$b_0 = \bar{y} - b_1\bar{x} \qquad \text{(14.7)}$$

where

x_i = value of the independent variable for the ith observation
y_i = value of the dependent variable for the ith observation
$\bar{x}$ = mean value for the independent variable
$\bar{y}$ = mean value for the dependent variable
n = total number of observations

Some of the calculations necessary to develop the least squares estimated regression equation for Armand's Pizza Parlors are shown in Table 14.2. With the sample of 10 restaurants, we have $n = 10$ observations. Because equations (14.6) and (14.7) require $\bar{x}$ and $\bar{y}$ we begin the calculations by computing $\bar{x}$ and $\bar{y}$.

$$\bar{x} = \frac{\sum x_i}{n} = \frac{140}{10} = 14$$

$$\bar{y} = \frac{\sum y_i}{n} = \frac{1300}{10} = 130$$

Using equations (14.6) and (14.7) and the information in Table 14.2, we can compute the slope and intercept of the estimated regression equation for Armand's Pizza Parlors. The calculation of the slope (b_1) proceeds as follows.

---

[1] An alternate formula for b_1 is

$$b_1 = \frac{\sum x_i y_i - (\sum x_i \sum y_i)/n}{\sum x_i^2 - (\sum x_i)^2/n}$$

This form of equation (14.6) is often recommended when using a calculator to compute b_1.

TABLE 14.2 CALCULATIONS FOR THE LEAST SQUARES ESTIMATED REGRESSION EQUATION FOR ARMAND'S PIZZA PARLORS

Restaurant i	x_i	y_i	$x_i - \bar{x}$	$y_i - \bar{y}$	$(x_i - \bar{x})(y_i - \bar{y})$	$(x_i - \bar{x})^2$
1	2	58	−12	−72	864	144
2	6	105	−8	−25	200	64
3	8	88	−6	−42	252	36
4	8	118	−6	−12	72	36
5	12	117	−2	−13	26	4
6	16	137	2	7	14	4
7	20	157	6	27	162	36
8	20	169	6	39	234	36
9	22	149	8	19	152	64
10	26	202	12	72	864	144
Totals	140	1300			2840	568
	Σx_i	Σy_i			$\Sigma(x_i - \bar{x})(y_i - \bar{y})$	$\Sigma(x_i - \bar{x})^2$

$$b_1 = \frac{\Sigma(x_i - \bar{x})(y_i - \bar{y})}{\Sigma(x_i - \bar{x})^2}$$

$$= \frac{2840}{568}$$

$$= 5$$

The calculation of the y-intercept (b_0) follows.

$$b_0 = \bar{y} - b_1\bar{x}$$

$$= 130 - 5(14)$$

$$= 60$$

Thus, the estimated regression equation is

$$\hat{y} = 60 + 5x$$

Figure 14.4 shows the graph of this equation on the scatter diagram.

The slope of the estimated regression equation ($b_1 = 5$) is positive, implying that as student population increases, sales increase. In fact, we can conclude (based on sales measured in $1000s and student population in 1000s) that an increase in the student population of 1000 is associated with an increase of $5000 in expected sales; that is, quarterly sales are expected to increase by $5 per student.

Using the estimated regression equation to make predictions outside the range of the values of the independent variable should be done with caution because outside that range we cannot be sure that the same relationship is valid.

If we believe the least squares estimated regression equation adequately describes the relationship between x and y, it would seem reasonable to use the estimated regression equation to predict the value of y for a given value of x. For example, if we wanted to predict quarterly sales for a restaurant to be located near a campus with 16,000 students, we would compute

$$\hat{y} = 60 + 5(16) = 140$$

Hence, we would predict quarterly sales of $140,000 for this restaurant. In the following sections we will discuss methods for assessing the appropriateness of using the estimated regression equation for estimation and prediction.

FIGURE 14.4   GRAPH OF THE ESTIMATED REGRESSION EQUATION FOR ARMAND'S
PIZZA PARLORS: $\hat{y} = 60 + 5x$

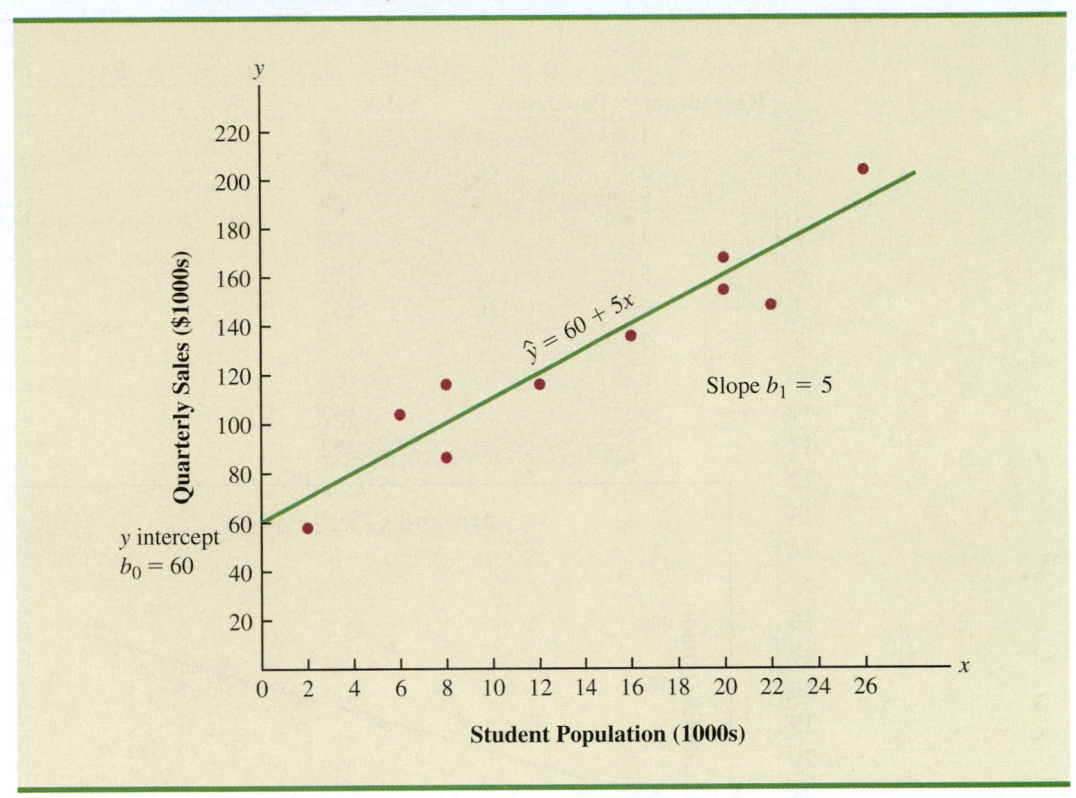

Using Excel to Construct a Scatter Diagram, Display the Estimated Regression Line, and Display the Estimated Regression Equation

We can use Excel to construct a scatter diagram, display the estimated regression line, and display the estimated regression equation for the Armand's Pizza Parlors data appearing in Table 14.1. Refer to Figure 14.5 as we describe the tasks involved.

Enter/Access Data: Open the DATAfile named *Armand's*. The data are in cells B2:C11 and labels appear in column A and cells B1:C1.

Apply Tools: The following steps describe how to construct a scatter diagram from the data in the worksheet.

 Step 1. Select cells B2:C11
 Step 2. Click the **Insert** tab on the Ribbon
 Step 3. In the **Charts** group, click the **Insert Scatter (X,Y) or Bubble Chart**
 Step 4. When the list of scatter diagram subtypes appears:
     Click **Scatter** (the chart in the upper left corner)

Editing Options: You can edit the scatter diagram to add a more descriptive chart title, add axis titles, and display the trendline and estimated regression equation. For instance, suppose you would like to use "Armand's Pizza Parlors" as the chart title and insert "Student Population (1000s)" for the horizontal axis title and "Quarterly Sales ($1000s)" for the vertical axis title.

FIGURE 14.5 SCATTER DIAGRAM, ESTIMATED REGRESSION LINE, AND THE ESTIMATED REGRESSION EQUATION FOR ARMAND'S PIZZA PARLORS

	A	B	C	D	E	F
1	Restaurant	Population	Sales			
2	1	2	58			
3	2	6	105			
4	3	8	88			
5	4	8	118			
6	5	12	117			
7	6	16	137			
8	7	20	157			
9	8	20	169			
10	9	22	149			
11	10	26	202			
12						

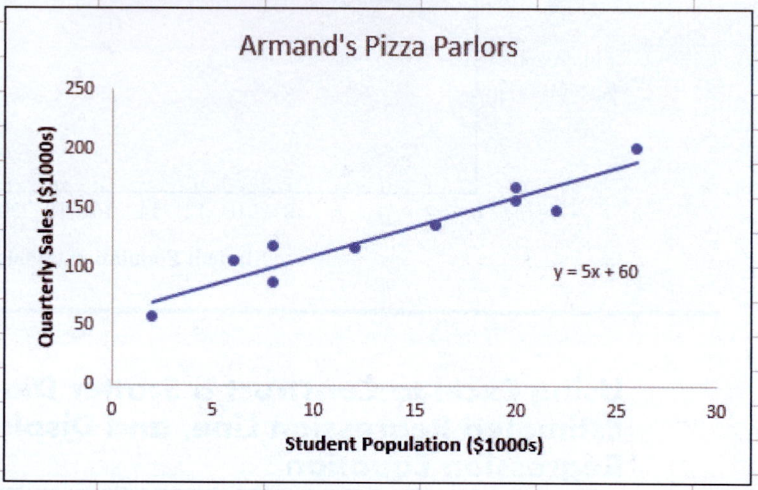

Armand's Pizza Parlors chart: scatter plot with trendline $y = 5x + 60$. Horizontal axis: Student Population ($1000s). Vertical axis: Quarterly Sales ($1000s).

Step 1. Click the **Chart Title** and replace it with **Armand's Pizza Parlors**

Step 2. Click the **Chart Elements** button ⊞ (located next to the top right corner of the chart)

Step 3. When the list of chart elements appears:
>Click **Axis Titles** (creates placeholders for the axis titles)
>Click **Gridlines** (to deselect the Gridlines option)
>Click **Trendline**

Step 4. Click the **Horizontal (Category) Axis Title** and replace it with **Student Population (1000s)**

Step 5. Click the **Vertical (Value) Axis Title** and replace it with **Quarterly Sales ($1000s)**

Step 6. To change the trendline from a dashed line to a solid line, right-click on the trendline and select the **Format Trendline** option

Step 7. When the Format Trendline dialog box appears:
>Scroll down and select **Display Equation on chart**
>Click the **Fill & Line** button ◇
>>In the **Dash type** box, select Solid
>Close the Format Trendline dialog box

The worksheet displayed in Figure 14.5 shows the scatter diagram, the estimated regression line, and the estimated regression equation.

NOTE AND COMMENT

The least squares method provides an estimated regression equation that minimizes the sum of squared deviations between the observed values of the dependent variable y_i and the predicted values of the dependent variable $\hat{y}_i$. This least squares criterion is used to choose the equation that provides the best fit. If some other criterion were used, such as minimizing the sum of the absolute deviations between y_i and $\hat{y}_i$, a different equation would be obtained. In practice, the least squares method is the most widely used.

Exercises

Methods

1. Given are five observations for two variables, x and y.

x_i	1	2	3	4	5
y_i	3	7	5	11	14

   a. Develop a scatter diagram for these data.
   b. What does the scatter diagram developed in part (a) indicate about the relationship between the two variables?
   c. Try to approximate the relationship between x and y by drawing a straight line through the data.
   d. Develop the estimated regression equation by computing the values of b_0 and b_1 using equations (14.6) and (14.7).
   e. Use the estimated regression equation to predict the value of y when $x = 4$.

2. Given are five observations for two variables, x and y.

x_i	3	12	6	20	14
y_i	55	40	55	10	15

   a. Develop a scatter diagram for these data.
   b. What does the scatter diagram developed in part (a) indicate about the relationship between the two variables?
   c. Try to approximate the relationship between x and y by drawing a straight line through the data.
   d. Develop the estimated regression equation by computing the values of b_0 and b_1 using equations (14.6) and (14.7).
   e. Use the estimated regression equation to predict the value of y when $x = 10$.

3. Given are five observations collected in a regression study on two variables.

x_i	2	6	9	13	20
y_i	7	18	9	26	23

   a. Develop a scatter diagram for these data.
   b. Develop the estimated regression equation for these data.
   c. Use the estimated regression equation to predict the value of y when $x = 6$.

Applications

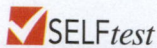

4. The following data give the percentage of women working in five companies in the retail and trade industry. The percentage of management jobs held by women in each company is also shown.

% Working	67	45	73	54	61
% Management	49	21	65	47	33

    a. Develop a scatter diagram for these data with the percentage of women working in the company as the independent variable.
    b. What does the scatter diagram developed in part (a) indicate about the relationship between the two variables?
    c. Try to approximate the relationship between the percentage of women working in the company and the percentage of management jobs held by women in that company.
    d. Develop the estimated regression equation by computing the values of b_0 and b_1.
    e. Predict the percentage of management jobs held by women in a company that has 60% women employees.

5. Brawdy Plastics, Inc., produces plastic seat belt retainers for General Motors at their plant in Buffalo, New York. After final assembly and painting, the parts are placed on a conveyor belt that moves the parts past a final inspection station. How fast the parts move past the final inspection station depends upon the line speed of the conveyor belt (feet per minute). Although faster line speeds are desirable, management is concerned that increasing the line speed too much may not provide enough time for inspectors to identify which parts are actually defective. To test this theory, Brawdy Plastics conducted an experiment in which the same batch of parts, with a known number of defective parts, was inspected using a variety of line speeds. The following data were collected.

Line Speed	Number of Defective Parts Found
20	23
20	21
30	19
30	16
40	15
40	17
50	14
50	11

    a. Develop a scatter diagram with the line speed as the independent variable.
    b. What does the scatter diagram developed in part (a) indicate about the relationship between the two variables?
    c. Use the least squares method to develop the estimated regression equation.
    d. Predict the number of defective parts found for a line speed of 25 feet per minute.

6. The National Football League (NFL) records a variety of performance data for individuals and teams. To investigate the importance of passing on the percentage of games won by a team, the following data show the average number of passing yards per attempt (Yds/Att) and the percentage of games won (WinPct) for a random sample of 10 NFL teams for the 2011 season (NFL website, February 12, 2012).

NFLPassing

Team	Yds/Att	WinPct
Arizona Cardinals	6.5	50
Atlanta Falcons	7.1	63
Carolina Panthers	7.4	38
Chicago Bears	6.4	50
Dallas Cowboys	7.4	50
New England Patriots	8.3	81
Philadelphia Eagles	7.4	50
Seattle Seahawks	6.1	44
St. Louis Rams	5.2	13
Tampa Bay Buccaneers	6.2	25

a. Develop a scatter diagram with the number of passing yards per attempt on the horizontal axis and the percentage of games won on the vertical axis.

b. What does the scatter diagram developed in part (a) indicate about the relationship between the two variables?

c. Develop the estimated regression equation that could be used to predict the percentage of games won given the average number of passing yards per attempt.

d. Provide an interpretation for the slope of the estimated regression equation.

e. For the 2011 season, the average number of passing yards per attempt for the Kansas City Chiefs was 6.2. Use the estimated regression equation developed in part (c) to predict the percentage of games won by the Kansas City Chiefs. (*Note:* For the 2011 season the Kansas City Chiefs' record was 7 wins and 9 losses.) Compare your prediction to the actual percentage of games won by the Kansas City Chiefs.

7. A sales manager collected the following data on annual sales for new customer accounts and the number of years of experience for a sample of 10 salespersons.

Sales

Salesperson	Years of Experience	Annual Sales ($1000s)
1	1	80
2	3	97
3	4	92
4	4	102
5	6	103
6	8	111
7	10	119
8	10	123
9	11	117
10	13	136

a. Develop a scatter diagram for these data with years of experience as the independent variable.

b. Develop an estimated regression equation that can be used to predict annual sales given the years of experience.

c. Use the estimated regression equation to predict annual sales for a salesperson with 9 years of experience.

8. The American Association of Individual Investors (AAII) On-Line Discount Broker Survey polls members on their experiences with discount brokers. As part of the survey, members were asked to rate the quality of the speed of execution with their broker as well as provide an overall satisfaction rating for electronic trades. Possible responses (scores) were no opinion (0), unsatisfied (1), somewhat satisfied (2), satisfied (3), and very satisfied (4). For each broker summary scores were computed by calculating a weighted average of the scores provided by each respondent. A portion of the survey results follow (AAII website, February 7, 2012).

BrokerRatings

Brokerage	Speed	Satisfaction
Scottrade, Inc.	3.4	3.5
Charles Schwab	3.3	3.4
Fidelity Brokerage Services	3.4	3.9
TD Ameritrade	3.6	3.7
E*Trade Financial	3.2	2.9
Vanguard Brokerage Services	3.8	2.8
USAA Brokerage Services	3.8	3.6
Thinkorswim	2.6	2.6
Wells Fargo Investments	2.7	2.3
Interactive Brokers	4.0	4.0
Zecco.com	2.5	2.5

a. Develop a scatter diagram for these data with the speed of execution as the independent variable.

b. What does the scatter diagram developed in part (a) indicate about the relationship between the two variables?

c. Develop the least squares estimated regression equation.

d. Provide an interpretation for the slope of the estimated regression equation.

e. Suppose Zecco.com developed new software to increase their speed of execution rating. If the new software is able to increase their speed of execution rating from the current value of 2.5 to the average speed of execution rating for the other 10 brokerage firms that were surveyed, what value would you predict for the overall satisfaction rating?

9. Companies in the U.S. car rental market vary greatly in terms of the size of the fleet, the number of locations, and annual revenue. In 2011 Hertz had 320,000 cars in service and annual revenue of approximately $4.2 billion. The following data show the number of cars in service (1000s) and the annual revenue ($millions) for six smaller car rental companies (*Auto Rental News* website, August 7, 2012).

Company	Cars (1000s)	Revenue ($millions)
U-Save Auto Rental System, Inc.	11.5	118
Payless Car Rental System, Inc.	10.0	135
ACE Rent A Car	9.0	100
Rent-A-Wreck of America	5.5	37
Triangle Rent-A-Car	4.2	40
Affordable/Sensible	3.3	32

a. Develop a scatter diagram with the number of cars in service as the independent variable.

b. What does the scatter diagram developed in part (a) indicate about the relationship between the two variables?

c. Use the least squares method to develop the estimated regression equation.

d. For every additional car placed in service, estimate how much annual revenue will change.

e. Fox Rent A Car has 11,000 cars in service. Use the estimated regression equation developed in part (c) to predict annual revenue for Fox Rent A Car.

10. For a particular red wine, the following data show the auction price for a 750-milliliter bottle and the age of the wine (WineX website, June 2016).

Age (years)	Price ($)
36	256
20	142
29	212
33	255
41	331
27	173
30	209
45	297
34	237
22	182

DATA *file*

WinePrices

a. Develop a scatter diagram for these data with age as the independent variable.
b. What does the scatter diagram developed in part (a) indicate about the relationship between age and price?
c. Develop the least squares estimated regression equation.
d. Provide an interpretation for the slope of the estimated equation.

11. To help consumers in purchasing a laptop computer, *Consumer Reports* calculates an overall test score for each computer tested based upon rating factors such as ergonomics, portability, performance, display, and battery life. Higher overall scores indicate better test results. The following data show the average retail price and the overall score for ten 13-inch models (*Consumer Reports* website, October 25, 2012).

DATA *file*

Computer

Brand & Model	Price ($)	Overall Score
Samsung Ultrabook NP900X3C-A01US	1250	83
Apple MacBook Air MC965LL/A	1300	83
Apple MacBook Air MD231LL/A	1200	82
HP ENVY 13-2050nr Spectre XT	950	79
Sony VAIO SVS13112FXB	800	77
Acer Aspire S5-391-9880 Ultrabook	1200	74
Apple MacBook Pro MD101LL/A	1200	74
Apple MacBook Pro MD313LL/A	1000	73
Dell Inspiron I13Z-6591SLV	700	67
Samsung NP535U3C-A01US	600	63

a. Develop a scatter diagram with price as the independent variable.
b. What does the scatter diagram developed in part (a) indicate about the relationship between the two variables?
c. Use the least squares method to develop the estimated regression equation.
d. Provide an interpretation of the slope of the estimated regression equation.
e. Another laptop that *Consumer Reports* tested is the Acer Aspire S3-951-6646 Ultrabook; the price for this laptop was $700. Predict the overall score for this laptop using the estimated regression equation developed in part (c).

12. *Yahoo Finance* reported the beta value for Coca-Cola was .82 (*Yahoo Finance* website, June 30, 2016). Betas for individual stocks are determined by simple linear regression. The dependent variable is the total return for the stock, and the independent variable is the total return for the stock market, such as the return of the S&P 500. The slope of this regression equation is referred to as the stock's *beta*. Many financial analysts prefer to measure the risk of a stock by computing the stock's beta value.

For more discussion and practice estimating stock betas, see Case 1 at the end of this chapter.

The data contained in the DATAfile named *CocaCola* show the monthly percentage returns for the S&P 500 and the Coca-Cola Company for August 2015 to May 2016.

CocaCola

Month	S&P 500 % Return	Coca-Cola % Return
August	−3	3
September	8	6
October	0	1
November	−2	1
December	−5	0
January	0	0
February	7	8
March	0	−3
April	2	0
May	−5	−1

a.   Develop a scatter diagram with the S&P % Return as the independent variable.
b.   What does the scatter diagram developed in part (a) indicate about the relationship between the returns of the S&P 500 and those of the Coca-Cola Company?
c.   Develop the least squares estimated regression equation.
d.   Provide an interpretation for the slope of the estimated equation (that is, the beta).
e.   Is your beta estimate close to .82? If not, why might your estimate be different?

13.   A large city hospital conducted a study to investigate the relationship between the number of unauthorized days that employees are absent per year and the distance (miles) between home and work for the employees. A sample of 10 employees was selected and the following data were collected.

Distance to Work (miles)	Number of Days Absent
1	8
3	5
4	8
6	7
8	6
10	3
12	5
14	2
14	4
18	2

a.   Develop a scatter diagram for these data. Does a linear relationship appear reasonable? Explain.
b.   Develop the least squares estimated regression equation that relates the distance to work to the number of days absent.
c.   Predict the number of days absent for an employee that lives 5 miles from the hospital.

14.   Using a global-positioning-system (GPS)-based navigator for your car, you enter a destination and the system will plot a route, give spoken turn-by-turn directions, and show your progress along the route. Today, even budget units include features previously available only on more expensive models. *Consumer Reports* conducted extensive tests of GPS-based navigators and developed an overall rating based on factors such as ease of use, driver information, display, and battery life. The following data show the price and

rating for a sample of 20 GPS units with a 4.3-inch screen that *Consumer Reports* tested (*Consumer Reports* website, April 17, 2012).

Brand and Model	Price ($)	Rating
Garmin Nuvi 3490LMT	400	82
Garmin Nuvi 3450	330	80
Garmin Nuvi 3790T	350	77
Garmin Nuvi 3790LMT	400	77
Garmin Nuvi 3750	250	74
Garmin Nuvi 2475LT	230	74
Garmin Nuvi 2455LT	160	73
Garmin Nuvi 2370LT	270	71
Garmin Nuvi 2360LT	250	71
Garmin Nuvi 2360LMT	220	71
Garmin Nuvi 755T	260	70
Motorola Motonab TN565t	200	68
Motorola Motonab TN555	200	67
Garmin Nuvi 1350T	150	65
Garmin Nuvi 1350LMT	180	65
Garmin Nuvi 2300	160	65
Garmin Nuvi 1350	130	64
Tom Tom VIA 1435T	200	62
Garmin Nuvi 1300	140	62
Garmin Nuvi 1300LM	180	62

DATA *file*

GPS

a.   Develop a scatter diagram with price as the independent variable.
b.   What does the scatter diagram developed in part (a) indicate about the relationship between the two variables?
c.   Use the least squares method to develop the estimated regression equation.
d.   Predict the rating for a GPS system with a 4.3-inch screen that has a price of $200.

14.3

Coefficient of Determination

For the Armand's Pizza Parlors example, we developed the estimated regression equation $\hat{y} = 60 + 5x$ to approximate the linear relationship between the size of the student population x and quarterly sales y. A question now is: How well does the estimated regression equation fit the data? In this section, we show that the **coefficient of determination** provides a measure of the goodness of fit for the estimated regression equation.

For the ith observation, the difference between the observed value of the dependent variable, y_i, and the predicted value of the dependent variable, $\hat{y}_i$, is called the ***i*th residual**. The ith residual represents the error in using $\hat{y}_i$ to estimate y_i. Thus, for the ith observation, the residual is $y_i - \hat{y}_i$. The sum of squares of these residuals or errors is the quantity that is minimized by the least squares method. This quantity, also known as the *sum of squares due to error,* is denoted by SSE.

> **SUM OF SQUARES DUE TO ERROR**
>
> $$SSE = \sum(y_i - \hat{y}_i)^2 \qquad\qquad (14.8)$$

The value of SSE is a measure of the error in using the estimated regression equation to predict the values of the dependent variable in the sample.

TABLE 14.3 CALCULATION OF SSE FOR ARMAND'S PIZZA PARLORS

Restaurant i	x_i = Student Population (1000s)	y_i = Quarterly Sales ($1000s)	Predicted Sales $\hat{y}_i = 60 + 5x_i$	Error $y_i - \hat{y}_i$	Squared Error $(y_i - \hat{y}_i)^2$
1	2	58	70	−12	144
2	6	105	90	15	225
3	8	88	100	−12	144
4	8	118	100	18	324
5	12	117	120	−3	9
6	16	137	140	−3	9
7	20	157	160	−3	9
8	20	169	160	9	81
9	22	149	170	−21	441
10	26	202	190	12	144
					SSE = 1530

In Table 14.3 we show the calculations required to compute the sum of squares due to error for the Armand's Pizza Parlors example. For instance, for restaurant 1 the values of the independent and dependent variables are $x_1 = 2$ and $y_1 = 58$. Using the estimated regression equation, we find that the predicted value of quarterly sales for restaurant 1 is $\hat{y}_1 = 60 + 5(2) = 70$. Thus, the error in using $\hat{y}_1$ to predict y_1 for restaurant 1 is $y_1 - \hat{y}_1 = 58 - 70 = -12$. The squared error, $(-12)^2 = 144$, is shown in the last column of Table 14.3. After computing and squaring the residuals for each restaurant in the sample, we sum them to obtain SSE = 1530. Thus, SSE = 1530 measures the error in using the estimated regression equation $\hat{y} = 60 + 5x$ to predict sales.

Now suppose we are asked to develop an estimate of quarterly sales without knowledge of the size of the student population. Without knowledge of any related variables, we would use the sample mean as an estimate of quarterly sales at any given restaurant. Table 14.2 showed that for the sales data, $\sum y_i = 1300$. Hence, the mean value of quarterly sales for the sample of 10 Armand's restaurants is $\bar{y} = \sum y_i/n = 1300/10 = 130$. In Table 14.4 we

TABLE 14.4 COMPUTATION OF THE TOTAL SUM OF SQUARES FOR ARMAND'S PIZZA PARLORS

Restaurant i	x_i = Student Population (1000s)	y_i = Quarterly Sales ($1000s)	Deviation $y_i - \bar{y}$	Squared Deviation $(y_i - \bar{y})^2$
1	2	58	−72	5184
2	6	105	−25	625
3	8	88	−42	1764
4	8	118	−12	144
5	12	117	−13	169
6	16	137	7	49
7	20	157	27	729
8	20	169	39	1521
9	22	149	19	361
10	26	202	72	5184
				SST = 15,730

show the sum of squared deviations obtained by using the sample mean $\bar{y} = 130$ to predict the value of quarterly sales for each restaurant in the sample. For the ith restaurant in the sample, the difference $y_i - \bar{y}$ provides a measure of the error involved in using $\bar{y}$ to predict sales. The corresponding sum of squares, called the *total sum of squares,* is denoted SST.

TOTAL SUM OF SQUARES

$$SST = \sum(y_i - \bar{y})^2 \qquad\qquad \textbf{(14.9)}$$

With SST = 15,730 and SSE = 1530, the estimated regression line provides a much better fit to the data than the line $y = \bar{y}$.

The sum at the bottom of the last column in Table 14.4 is the total sum of squares for Armand's Pizza Parlors; it is SST = 15,730.

In Figure 14.6 we show the estimated regression line $\hat{y} = 60 + 5x$ and the line corresponding to $\bar{y} = 130$. Note that the points cluster more closely around the estimated regression line than they do about the line $\bar{y} = 130$. For example, for the 10th restaurant in the sample we see that the error is much larger when $\bar{y} = 130$ is used to predict y_{10} than when $\hat{y}_{10} = 60 + 5(26) = 190$ is used. We can think of SST as a measure of how well the observations cluster about the $\bar{y}$ line and SSE as a measure of how well the observations cluster about the $\hat{y}$ line.

FIGURE 14.6   DEVIATIONS ABOUT THE ESTIMATED REGRESSION LINE AND THE LINE $y = \bar{y}$ FOR ARMAND'S PIZZA PARLORS

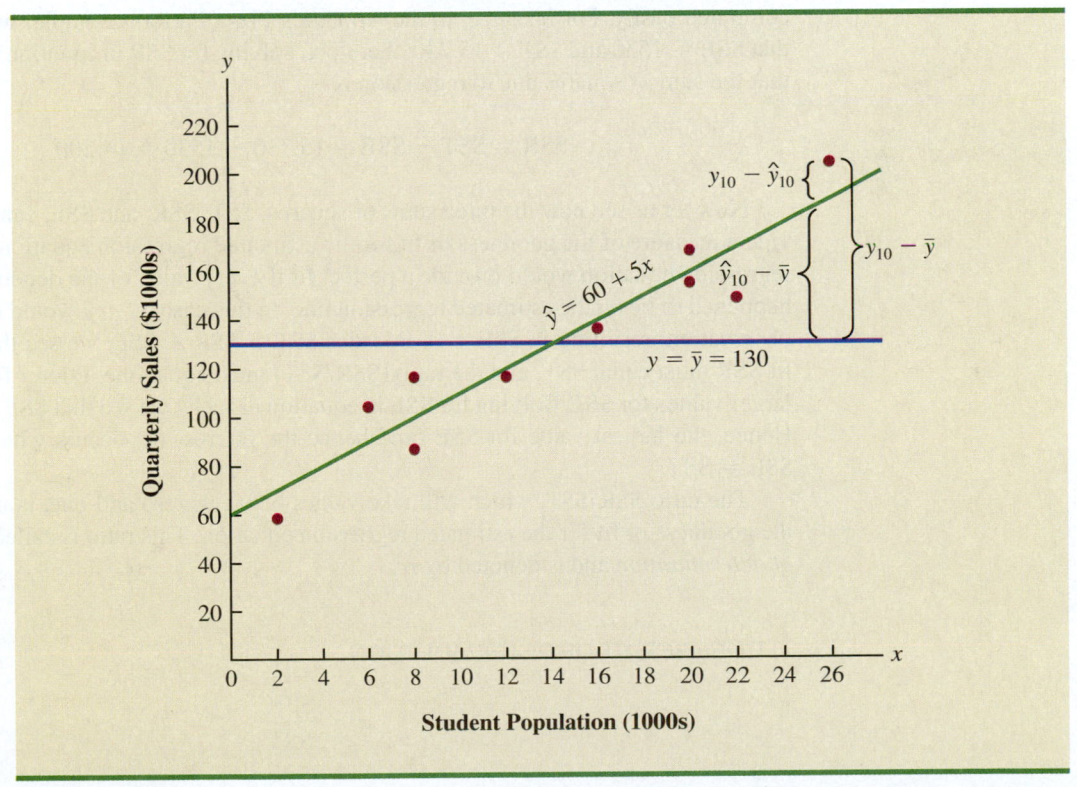

To measure how much the $\hat{y}$ values on the estimated regression line deviate from $\bar{y}$, another sum of squares is computed. This sum of squares, called the *sum of squares due to regression,* is denoted SSR.

SUM OF SQUARES DUE TO REGRESSION

$$SSR = \sum(\hat{y}_i - \bar{y})^2 \tag{14.10}$$

From the preceding discussion, we should expect that SST, SSR, and SSE are related. Indeed, the relationship among these three sums of squares provides one of the most important results in statistics.

RELATIONSHIP AMONG SST, SSR, AND SSE

$$SST = SSR + SSE \tag{14.11}$$

where

SST = total sum of squares
SSR = sum of squares due to regression
SSE = sum of squares due to error

SSR can be thought of as the explained portion of SST, and SSE can be thought of as the unexplained portion of SST.

Equation (14.11) shows that the total sum of squares can be partitioned into two components, the sum of squares due to regression and the sum of squares due to error. Hence, if the values of any two of these sum of squares are known, the third sum of squares can be computed easily. For instance, in the Armand's Pizza Parlors example, we already know that SSE = 1530 and SST = 15,730; therefore, solving for SSR in equation (14.11), we find that the sum of squares due to regression is

$$SSR = SST - SSE = 15{,}730 - 1530 = 14{,}200$$

Now let us see how the three sums of squares, SST, SSR, and SSE, can be used to provide a measure of the goodness of fit for the estimated regression equation. The estimated regression equation would provide a perfect fit if every value of the dependent variable y_i happened to lie on the estimated regression line. In this case, $y_i - \hat{y}_i$ would be zero for each observation, resulting in SSE = 0. Because SST = SSR + SSE, we see that for a perfect fit SSR must equal SST, and the ratio (SSR/SST) must equal one. Poorer fits will result in larger values for SSE. Solving for SSE in equation (14.11), we see that SSE = SST − SSR. Hence, the largest value for SSE (and hence the poorest fit) occurs when SSR = 0 and SSE = SST.

The ratio SSR/SST, which will take values between zero and one, is used to evaluate the goodness of fit for the estimated regression equation. This ratio is called the *coefficient of determination* and is denoted by r^2.

COEFFICIENT OF DETERMINATION

$$r^2 = \frac{SSR}{SST} \tag{14.12}$$

For the Armand's Pizza Parlors example, the value of the coefficient of determination is

$$r^2 = \frac{\text{SSR}}{\text{SST}} = \frac{14{,}200}{15{,}730} = .9027$$

When we express the coefficient of determination as a percentage, r^2 can be interpreted as the percentage of the total sum of squares that can be explained by using the estimated regression equation. For Armand's Pizza Parlors, we can conclude that 90.27% of the total sum of squares can be explained by using the estimated regression equation $\hat{y} = 60 + 5x$ to predict quarterly sales. In other words, 90.27% of the variability in sales can be explained by the linear relationship between the size of the student population and sales. We should be pleased to find such a good fit for the estimated regression equation.

Using Excel to Compute the Coefficient of Determination

In Section 14.2 we showed how Excel can be used to construct a scatter diagram, display the estimated regression line, and compute the estimated regression equation for the Armand's Pizza Parlors data appearing in Table 14.1. We will now describe how to compute the coefficient of determination using the scatter diagram in Figure 14.5.

Step 1. Right-click on the trendline and select the **Format Trendline** option
Step 2. When the Format Trendline dialog box appears:
   Scroll down and select **Display R-squared value on chart**
   Close the Format Trendline dialog box

The worksheet displayed in Figure 14.7 shows the scatter diagram, the estimated regression line, and the estimated regression equation.

Correlation Coefficient

In Chapter 3 we introduced the **correlation coefficient** as a descriptive measure of the strength of linear association between two variables, x and y. Values of the correlation coefficient are always between -1 and $+1$. A value of $+1$ indicates that the two variables x and y are perfectly related in a positive linear sense. That is, all data points are on a straight line that has a positive slope. A value of -1 indicates that x and y are perfectly related in a negative linear sense, with all data points on a straight line that has a negative slope. Values of the correlation coefficient close to zero indicate that x and y are not linearly related.

In Section 3.5 we presented the equation for computing the sample correlation coefficient. If a regression analysis has already been performed and the coefficient of determination r^2 computed, the sample correlation coefficient can be computed as follows.

SAMPLE CORRELATION COEFFICIENT

$$r_{xy} = (\text{sign of } b_1)\sqrt{\text{Coefficient of determination}}$$
$$= (\text{sign of } b_1)\sqrt{r^2} \tag{14.13}$$

where

b_1 = the slope of the estimated regression equation $\hat{y} = b_0 + b_1 x$

FIGURE 14.7 USING EXCEL'S CHART TOOLS TO COMPUTE THE COEFFICIENT OF DETERMINATION FOR ARMAND'S PIZZA PARLORS

	A	B	C	D	E	F
1	Restaurant	Population	Sales			
2	1	2	58			
3	2	6	105			
4	3	8	88			
5	4	8	118			
6	5	12	117			
7	6	16	137			
8	7	20	157			
9	8	20	169			
10	9	22	149			
11	10	26	202			
12						

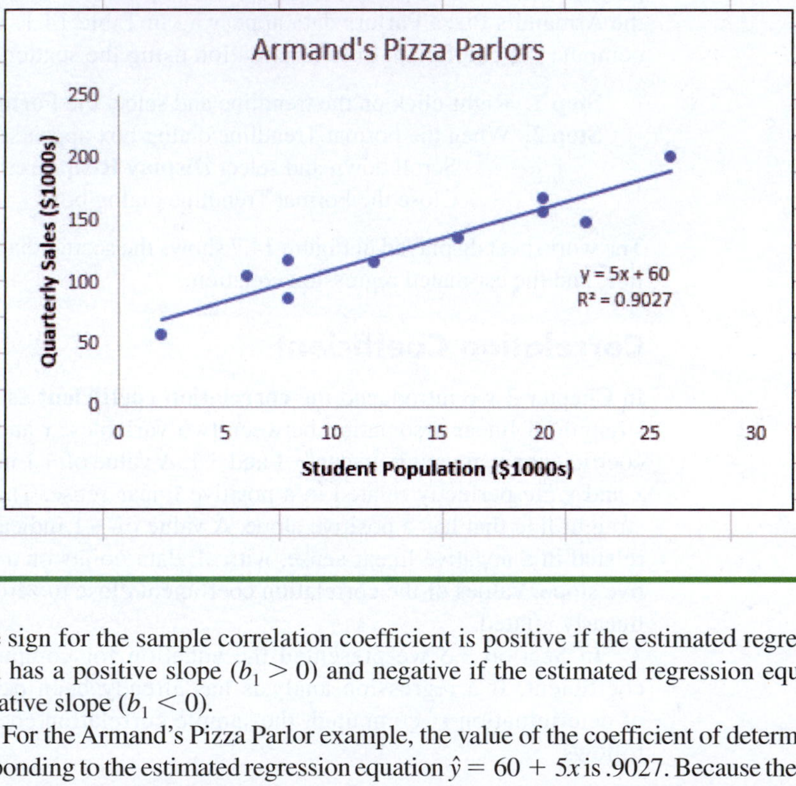

Armand's Pizza Parlors chart, $y = 5x + 60$, $R^2 = 0.9027$

The sign for the sample correlation coefficient is positive if the estimated regression equation has a positive slope ($b_1 > 0$) and negative if the estimated regression equation has a negative slope ($b_1 < 0$).

For the Armand's Pizza Parlor example, the value of the coefficient of determination corresponding to the estimated regression equation $\hat{y} = 60 + 5x$ is .9027. Because the slope of the estimated regression equation is positive, equation (14.13) shows that the sample correlation coefficient is $+\sqrt{.9027} = +.9501$. With a sample correlation coefficient of $r_{xy} = +.9501$, we would conclude that a strong positive linear association exists between x and y.

In the case of a linear relationship between two variables, both the coefficient of determination and the sample correlation coefficient provide measures of the strength of the relationship. The coefficient of determination provides a measure between zero and one, whereas the sample correlation coefficient provides a measure between -1 and $+1$. Although the sample correlation coefficient is restricted to a linear relationship between two variables, the coefficient of determination can be used for nonlinear relationships and for relationships that have two or more independent variables. Thus, the coefficient of determination provides a wider range of applicability.

NOTES AND COMMENTS

1. In developing the least squares estimated regression equation and computing the coefficient of determination, we made no probabilistic assumptions about the error term ϵ, and no statistical tests for significance of the relationship between x and y were conducted. Larger values of r^2 imply that the least squares line provides a better fit to the data; that is, the observations are more closely grouped about the least squares line. But, using only r^2, we can draw no conclusion about whether the relationship between x and y is statistically significant. Such a conclusion must be based on considerations that involve the sample size and the properties of the appropriate sampling distributions of the least squares estimators.

2. As a practical matter, for typical data found in the social sciences, values of r^2 as low as .25 are often considered useful. For data in the physical and life sciences, r^2 values of .60 or greater are often found; in fact, in some cases, r^2 values greater than .90 can be found. In business applications, r^2 values vary greatly, depending on the unique characteristics of each application.

Exercises

Methods

15. The data from exercise 1 follow.

x_i	1	2	3	4	5
y_i	3	7	5	11	14

The estimated regression equation for these data is $\hat{y} = .20 + 2.60x$.
   a. Compute SSE, SST, and SSR using equations (14.8), (14.9), and (14.10).
   b. Compute the coefficient of determination r^2. Comment on the goodness of fit.
   c. Compute the sample correlation coefficient.

16. The data from exercise 2 follow.

x_i	3	12	6	20	14
y_i	55	40	55	10	15

The estimated regression equation for these data is $\hat{y} = 68 - 3x$.
   a. Compute SSE, SST, and SSR.
   b. Compute the coefficient of determination r^2. Comment on the goodness of fit.
   c. Compute the sample correlation coefficient.

17. The data from exercise 3 follow.

x_i	2	6	9	13	20
y_i	7	18	9	26	23

The estimated regression equation for these data is $\hat{y} = 7.6 + .9x$. What percentage of the total sum of squares can be accounted for by the estimated regression equation? What is the value of the sample correlation coefficient?

Applications

18. The following data show the brand, price ($), and the overall score for six stereo headphones that were tested by *Consumer Reports* (*Consumer Reports* website, March 5, 2012). The overall score is based on sound quality and effectiveness of ambient noise reduction. Scores range from 0 (lowest) to 100 (highest). The estimated regression equation for these data is $\hat{y} = 23.194 + .318x$, where x = price ($) and y = overall score.

Brand	Price ($)	Score
Bose	180	76
Skullcandy	150	71
Koss	95	61
Phillips/O'Neill	70	56
Denon	70	40
JVC	35	26

a. Compute SST, SSR, and SSE.
b. Compute the coefficient of determination r^2. Comment on the goodness of fit.
c. What is the value of the sample correlation coefficient?

19. In exercise 7 a sales manager collected the following data on x = annual sales and y = years of experience. The estimated regression equation for these data is $\hat{y} = 80 + 4x$.

DATA *file*

Sales

Salesperson	Years of Experience	Annual Sales ($1000s)
1	1	80
2	3	97
3	4	92
4	4	102
5	6	103
6	8	111
7	10	119
8	10	123
9	11	117
10	13	136

a. Compute SST, SSR, and SSE.
b. Compute the coefficient of determination r^2. Comment on the goodness of fit.
c. What is the value of the sample correlation coefficient?

20. *Bicycling,* the world's leading cycling magazine, reviews hundreds of bicycles throughout the year. Their "Road-Race" category contains reviews of bikes used by riders primarily interested in racing. One of the most important factors in selecting a bike for racing is the weight of the bike. The following data show the weight (pounds) and price ($) for 10 racing bikes reviewed by the magazine (*Bicycling* website, March 8, 2012).

DATA *file*

RacingBicycles

Brand	Weight	Price ($)
FELT F5	17.8	2100
PINARELLO Paris	16.1	6250
ORBEA Orca GDR	14.9	8370
EDDY MERCKX EMX-7	15.9	6200
BH RC1 Ultegra	17.2	4000
BH Ultralight 386	13.1	8600
CERVELO S5 Team	16.2	6000
GIANT TCR Advanced 2	17.1	2580
WILIER TRIESTINA Gran Turismo	17.6	3400
SPECIALIZED S-Works Amira SL4	14.1	8000

a. Use the data to develop an estimated regression equation that could be used to estimate the price for a bike given the weight.

b. Compute r^2. Did the estimated regression equation provide a good fit?
c. Predict the price for a bike that weighs 15 pounds.

21. An important application of regression analysis in accounting is in the estimation of cost. By collecting data on volume and cost and using the least squares method to develop an estimated regression equation relating volume and cost, an accountant can estimate the cost associated with a particular manufacturing volume. Consider the following sample of production volumes and total cost data for a manufacturing operation.

Production Volume (units)	Total Cost ($)
400	4000
450	5000
550	5400
600	5900
700	6400
750	7000

a. Use these data to develop an estimated regression equation that could be used to predict the total cost for a given production volume.
b. What is the variable cost per unit produced?
c. Compute the coefficient of determination. What percentage of the variation in total cost can be explained by production volume?
d. The company's production schedule shows 500 units must be produced next month. Predict the total cost for this operation.

22. Refer to exercise 9 where the following data were used to investigate the relationship between the number of cars in service (1000s) and the annual revenue ($millions) for six smaller car rental companies (*Auto Rental News* website, August 7, 2012).

Company	Cars (1000s)	Revenue ($millions)
U-Save Auto Rental System, Inc.	11.5	118
Payless Car Rental System, Inc.	10.0	135
ACE Rent A Car	9.0	100
Rent-A-Wreck of America	5.5	37
Triangle Rent-A-Car	4.2	40
Affordable/Sensible	3.3	32

With x = cars in service (1000s) and y = annual revenue ($millions), the estimated regression equation is $\hat{y} = -17.005 + 12.966x$. For these data SSE = 1043.03.
a. Compute the coefficient of determination r^2.
b. Did the estimated regression equation provide a good fit? Explain.
c. What is the value of the sample correlation coefficient? Does it reflect a strong or weak relationship between the number of cars in service and the annual revenue?

14.4 Model Assumptions

In conducting a regression analysis, we begin by making an assumption about the appropriate model for the relationship between the dependent and independent variable(s). For the case of simple linear regression, the assumed regression model is

$$y = \beta_0 + \beta_1 x + \epsilon$$

Then the least squares method is used to develop values for b_0 and b_1, the estimates of the model parameters β_0 and β_1, respectively. The resulting estimated regression equation is

$$\hat{y} = b_0 + b_1 x$$

We saw that the value of the coefficient of determination (r^2) is a measure of the goodness of fit of the estimated regression equation. However, even with a large value of r^2, the estimated regression equation should not be used until further analysis of the appropriateness of the assumed model has been conducted. An important step in determining whether the assumed model is appropriate involves testing for the significance of the relationship. The tests of significance in regression analysis are based on the following assumptions about the error term ϵ.

ASSUMPTIONS ABOUT THE ERROR TERM ϵ IN THE REGRESSION MODEL

$$y = \beta_0 + \beta_1 x + \epsilon$$

1. The error term ϵ is a random variable with a mean or expected value of zero; that is, $E(\epsilon) = 0$.
   Implication: β_0 and β_1 are constants, therefore $E(\beta_0) = \beta_0$ and $E(\beta_1) = \beta_1$; thus, for a given value of x, the expected value of y is

$$E(y) = \beta_0 + \beta_1 x \tag{14.14}$$

   As we indicated previously, equation (14.14) is referred to as the regression equation.
2. The variance of ϵ, denoted by σ^2, is the same for all values of x.
   Implication: The variance of y about the regression line equals σ^2 and is the same for all values of x.
3. The values of ϵ are independent.
   Implication: The value of ϵ for a particular value of x is not related to the value of ϵ for any other value of x; thus, the value of y for a particular value of x is not related to the value of y for any other value of x.
4. The error term ϵ is a normally distributed random variable for all values of x.
   Implication: Because y is a linear function of ϵ, y is also a normally distributed random variable for all values of x.

Figure 14.8 illustrates the model assumptions and their implications; note that in this graphical interpretation, the value of $E(y)$ changes according to the specific value of x considered. However, regardless of the x value, the probability distribution of ϵ and hence the probability distributions of y are normally distributed, each with the same variance. The specific value of the error ϵ at any particular point depends on whether the actual value of y is greater than or less than $E(y)$.

At this point, we must keep in mind that we are also making an assumption or hypothesis about the form of the relationship between x and y. That is, we assume that a straight line represented by $\beta_0 + \beta_1 x$ is the basis for the relationship between the variables. We must not lose sight of the fact that some other model, for instance $y = \beta_0 + \beta_1 x^2 + \epsilon$, may turn out to be a better model for the underlying relationship.

FIGURE 14.8   ASSUMPTIONS FOR THE REGRESSION MODEL

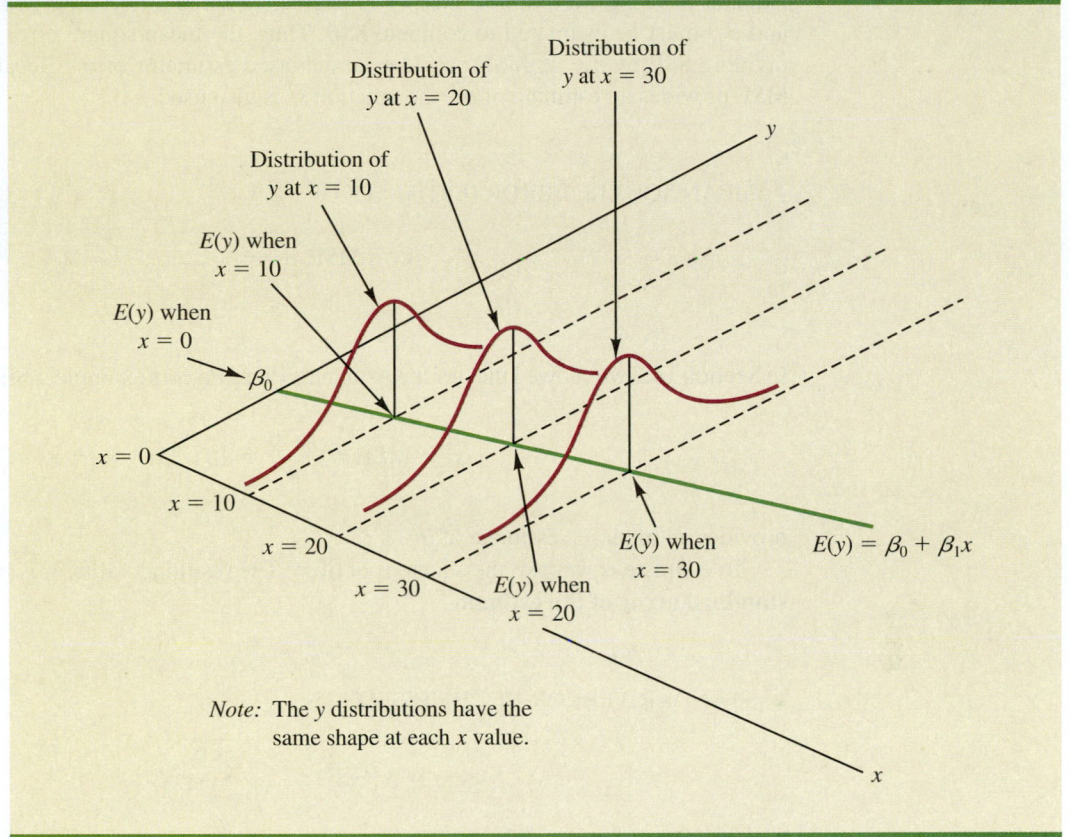

Testing for Significance

In a simple linear regression equation, the mean or expected value of y is a linear function of x: $E(y) = \beta_0 + \beta_1 x$. If the value of β_1 is zero, $E(y) = \beta_0 + (0)x = \beta_0$. In this case, the mean value of y does not depend on the value of x and hence we would conclude that x and y are not linearly related. Alternatively, if the value of β_1 is not equal to zero, we would conclude that the two variables are related. Thus, to test for a significant regression relationship, we must conduct a hypothesis test to determine whether the value of β_1 is zero. Two tests are commonly used. Both require an estimate of σ^2, the variance of ϵ in the regression model.

Estimate of σ^2

From the regression model and its assumptions we can conclude that σ^2, the variance of ϵ, also represents the variance of the y values about the regression line. Recall that the deviations of the y values about the estimated regression line are called residuals. Thus, SSE, the sum of squared residuals, is a measure of the variability of the actual observations about the estimated regression line. The **mean square error (MSE)** provides the estimate of σ^2; it is SSE divided by its degrees of freedom.

With $\hat{y}_i = b_0 + b_1 x_i$, SSE can be written as

$$\text{SSE} = \sum(y_i - \hat{y}_i)^2 = \sum(y_i - b_0 - b_1 x_i)^2$$

Every sum of squares has associated with it a number called its degrees of freedom. Statisticians have shown that SSE has $n - 2$ degrees of freedom because two parameters (β_0 and β_1) must be estimated to compute SSE. Thus, the mean square error is computed by dividing SSE by $n - 2$. MSE provides an unbiased estimator of σ^2. Because the value of MSE provides an estimate of σ^2, the notation s^2 is also used.

MEAN SQUARE ERROR (ESTIMATE OF σ^2)

$$s^2 = \text{MSE} = \frac{\text{SSE}}{n - 2} \tag{14.15}$$

In Section 14.3 we showed that for the Armand's Pizza Parlors example, SSE = 1530; hence,

$$s^2 = \text{MSE} = \frac{1530}{8} = 191.25$$

provides an unbiased estimate of σ^2.

To estimate σ we take the square root of s^2. The resulting value, s, is referred to as the **standard error of the estimate**.

STANDARD ERROR OF THE ESTIMATE

$$s = \sqrt{\text{MSE}} = \sqrt{\frac{\text{SSE}}{n - 2}} \tag{14.16}$$

For the Armand's Pizza Parlors example, $s = \sqrt{\text{MSE}} = \sqrt{191.25} = 13.829$. In the following discussion, we use the standard error of the estimate in the tests for a significant relationship between x and y.

t Test

The simple linear regression model is $y = \beta_0 + \beta_1 x + \epsilon$. If x and y are linearly related, we must have $\beta_1 \neq 0$. The purpose of the t test is to see whether we can conclude that $\beta_1 \neq 0$. We will use the sample data to test the following hypotheses about the parameter β_1.

$$H_0: \beta_1 = 0$$
$$H_a: \beta_1 \neq 0$$

If H_0 is rejected, we will conclude that $\beta_1 \neq 0$ and that a statistically significant relationship exists between the two variables. However, if H_0 cannot be rejected, we will have insufficient evidence to conclude that a significant relationship exists. The properties of the sampling distribution of b_1, the least squares estimator of β_1, provide the basis for the hypothesis test.

First, let us consider what would happen if we used a different random sample for the same regression study. For example, suppose that Armand's Pizza Parlors used the sales records of a different sample of 10 restaurants. A regression analysis of this new sample might result in an estimated regression equation similar to our previous estimated regression equation $\hat{y} = 60 + 5x$. However, it is doubtful that we would obtain exactly the same equation (with an intercept of exactly 60 and a slope of exactly 5). Indeed, b_0 and b_1, the least squares estimators, are sample statistics with their own sampling distributions. The properties of the sampling distribution of b_1 follow.

SAMPLING DISTRIBUTION OF b_1

Expected Value

$$E(b_1) = \beta_1$$

Standard Deviation

$$\sigma_{b_1} = \frac{\sigma}{\sqrt{\sum(x_i - \bar{x})^2}} \qquad (14.17)$$

Distribution Form

Normal

Note that the expected value of b_1 is equal to β_1, so b_1 is an unbiased estimator of β_1.

Because we do not know the value of σ, we develop an estimate of σ_{b_1}, denoted s_{b_1}, by estimating σ with s in equation (14.17). Thus, we obtain the following estimate of σ_{b_1}.

The standard deviation of b_1 is also referred to as the standard error of b_1. Thus, s_{b_1} provides an estimate of the standard error of b_1.

ESTIMATED STANDARD DEVIATION OF b_1

$$s_{b_1} = \frac{s}{\sqrt{\sum(x_i - \bar{x})^2}} \qquad (14.18)$$

For Armand's Pizza Parlors, $s = 13.829$. Hence, using $\sum(x_i - \bar{x})^2 = 568$ as shown in Table 14.2, we have

$$s_{b_1} = \frac{13.829}{\sqrt{568}} = .5803$$

as the estimated standard deviation of b_1.

The t test for a significant relationship is based on the fact that the test statistic

$$\frac{b_1 - \beta_1}{s_{b_1}}$$

follows a t distribution with $n - 2$ degrees of freedom. If the null hypothesis is true, then $\beta_1 = 0$ and $t = b_1/s_{b_1}$.

Let us conduct this test of significance for Armand's Pizza Parlors at the $\alpha = .01$ level of significance. The test statistic is

$$t = \frac{b_1}{s_{b_1}} = \frac{5}{.5803} = 8.62$$

The t distribution table (Table 2 of Appendix B) shows that with $n - 2 = 10 - 2 = 8$ degrees of freedom, $t = 3.355$ provides an area of .005 in the upper tail. Thus, the area in the upper tail of the t distribution corresponding to the test statistic $t = 8.62$ must be less than .005. Because this test is a two-tailed test, we double this value to conclude that the p-value associated with $t = 8.62$ must be less than $2(.005) = .01$. Using Excel, the p-value $= .000$. Because the p-value is less than $\alpha = .01$, we reject H_0 and conclude that β_1 is not equal to zero. This evidence is sufficient to conclude that a significant relationship exists between student population and quarterly sales. A summary of the t test for significance in simple linear regression follows.

---

t TEST FOR SIGNIFICANCE IN SIMPLE LINEAR REGRESSION

$$H_0: \beta_1 = 0$$
$$H_a: \beta_1 \neq 0$$

TEST STATISTIC

$$t = \frac{b_1}{s_{b_1}} \tag{14.19}$$

REJECTION RULE

p-value approach: Reject H_0 if p-value $\leq \alpha$

Critical value approach: Reject H_0 if $t \leq -t_{\alpha/2}$ or if $t \geq t_{\alpha/2}$

where $t_{\alpha/2}$ is based on a t distribution with $n - 2$ degrees of freedom.

Confidence Interval for β_1

The form of a confidence interval for β_1 is as follows:

$$b_1 \pm t_{\alpha/2} s_{b_1}$$

The point estimator is b_1 and the margin of error is $t_{\alpha/2} s_{b_1}$. The confidence coefficient associated with this interval is $1 - \alpha$, and $t_{\alpha/2}$ is the t value providing an area of $\alpha/2$ in the upper tail of a t distribution with $n - 2$ degrees of freedom. For example, suppose that we wanted to develop a 99% confidence interval estimate of β_1 for Armand's Pizza Parlors. From Table 2 of Appendix B we find that the t value corresponding to $\alpha = .01$ and $n - 2 = 10 - 2 = 8$ degrees of freedom is $t_{.005} = 3.355$. Thus, the 99% confidence interval estimate of β_1 is

$$b_1 \pm t_{\alpha/2} s_{b_1} = 5 \pm 3.355(.5803) = 5 \pm 1.95$$

or 3.05 to 6.95.

In using the t test for significance, the hypotheses tested were

$$H_0: \beta_1 = 0$$
$$H_a: \beta_1 \neq 0$$

At the $\alpha = .01$ level of significance, we can use the 99% confidence interval as an alternative for drawing the hypothesis testing conclusion for the Armand's data. Because 0, the hypothesized value of β_1, is not included in the confidence interval (3.05 to 6.95), we can reject H_0 and conclude that a significant statistical relationship exists between the size of the student population and quarterly sales. In general, a confidence interval can be used to test any two-sided hypothesis about β_1. If the hypothesized value of β_1 is contained in the confidence interval, do not reject H_0. Otherwise, reject H_0.

F Test

An *F* test, based on the *F* probability distribution, can also be used to test for significance in regression. With only one independent variable, the *F* test will provide the same conclusion as the *t* test; that is, if the *t* test indicates $\beta_1 \neq 0$ and hence a significant relationship, the *F* test will also indicate a significant relationship. But with more than one independent variable, only the *F* test can be used to test for an overall significant relationship.

The logic behind the use of the *F* test for determining whether the regression relationship is statistically significant is based on the development of two independent estimates of σ^2. We explained how MSE provides an estimate of σ^2. If the null hypothesis $H_0: \beta_1 = 0$ is true, the sum of squares due to regression, SSR, divided by its degrees of freedom provides another independent estimate of σ^2. This estimate is called the *mean square due to regression*, or simply the *mean square regression*, and is denoted MSR. In general,

$$MSR = \frac{SSR}{\text{Regression degrees of freedom}}$$

For the models we consider in this text, the regression degrees of freedom is always equal to the number of independent variables in the model:

$$MSR = \frac{SSR}{\text{Number of independent variables}} \tag{14.20}$$

Because we consider only regression models with one independent variable in this chapter, we have MSR = SSR/1 = SSR. Hence, for Armand's Pizza Parlors, MSR = SSR = 14,200.

If the null hypothesis ($H_0: \beta_1 = 0$) is true, MSR and MSE are two independent estimates of σ^2 and the sampling distribution of MSR/MSE follows an *F* distribution with numerator degrees of freedom equal to 1 and denominator degrees of freedom equal to $n - 2$. Therefore, when $\beta_1 = 0$, the value of MSR/MSE should be close to 1. However, if the null hypothesis is false ($\beta_1 \neq 0$), MSR will overestimate σ^2 and the value of MSR/MSE will be inflated; thus, large values of MSR/MSE lead to the rejection of H_0 and the conclusion that the relationship between x and y is statistically significant.

Let us conduct the *F* test for the Armand's Pizza Parlors example. The test statistic is

$$F = \frac{MSR}{MSE} = \frac{14,200}{191.25} = 74.25$$

The F test and the t test provide identical results for simple linear regression.

The *F* distribution table (Table 4 of Appendix B) shows that with 1 degree of freedom in the numerator and $n - 2 = 10 - 2 = 8$ degrees of freedom in the denominator, $F = 11.26$ provides an area of .01 in the upper tail. Thus, the area in the upper tail of the *F* distribution corresponding to the test statistic $F = 74.25$ must be less than .01. Thus, we conclude that the *p*-value must be less than .01. Using Excel, the *p*-value = .000. Because the *p*-value is less than $\alpha = .01$, we reject H_0 and conclude that a significant relationship exists between the size of the student population and quarterly sales. A summary of the *F* test for significance in simple linear regression follows.

If H_0 is false, MSE still provides an unbiased estimate of σ^2 and MSR overestimates σ^2. If H_0 is true, both MSE and MSR provide unbiased estimates of σ^2; in this case the value of MSR/MSE should be close to 1.

F TEST FOR SIGNIFICANCE IN SIMPLE LINEAR REGRESSION

$$H_0: \beta_1 = 0$$
$$H_a: \beta_1 \neq 0$$

TEST STATISTIC

$$F = \frac{MSR}{MSE} \tag{14.21}$$

REJECTION RULE

p-value approach: Reject H_0 if p-value $\leq \alpha$
Critical value approach: Reject H_0 if $F \geq F_\alpha$

where F_α is based on an F distribution with 1 degree of freedom in the numerator and $n - 2$ degrees of freedom in the denominator.

In Chapter 13 we covered analysis of variance (ANOVA) and showed how an **ANOVA table** could be used to provide a convenient summary of the computational aspects of analysis of variance. A similar ANOVA table can be used to summarize the results of the F test for significance in regression. Table 14.5 is the general form of the ANOVA table for simple linear regression. Table 14.6 is the ANOVA table with the F test computations performed for Armand's Pizza Parlors. Regression, Error, and Total are the labels for the three sources of variation, with SSR, SSE, and SST appearing as the corresponding sum of

TABLE 14.5 GENERAL FORM OF THE ANOVA TABLE FOR SIMPLE LINEAR REGRESSION

In every analysis of variance table the total sum of squares is the sum of the regression sum of squares and the error sum of squares; in addition, the total degrees of freedom is the sum of the regression degrees of freedom and the error degrees of freedom.

Source of Variation	Sum of Squares	Degrees of Freedom	Mean Square	F	p-Value
Regression	SSR	1	$MSR = \dfrac{SSR}{1}$	$F = \dfrac{MSR}{MSE}$	
Error	SSE	$n - 2$	$MSE = \dfrac{SSE}{n - 2}$		
Total	SST	$n - 1$			

TABLE 14.6 ANOVA TABLE FOR THE ARMAND'S PIZZA PARLORS PROBLEM

Source of Variation	Sum of Squares	Degrees of Freedom	Mean Square	F	p-Value
Regression	14,200	1	$\dfrac{14,200}{1} = 14,200$	$\dfrac{14,200}{191.25} = 74.25$	.000
Error	1,530	8	$\dfrac{1530}{8} = 191.25$		
Total	15,730	9			

squares in column 2. The degrees of freedom, 1 for SSR, $n - 2$ for SSE, and $n - 1$ for SST, are shown in column 3. Column 4 contains the values of MSR and MSE, column 5 contains the value of $F = $ MSR/MSE, and column 6 contains the p-value corresponding to the F value in column 5. Almost all computer printouts of regression analysis include an ANOVA table summary of the F test for significance.

Some Cautions About the Interpretation of Significance Tests

Regression analysis, which can be used to identify how variables are associated with one another, cannot be used as evidence of a cause-and-effect relationship.

Rejecting the null hypothesis H_0: $\beta_1 = 0$ and concluding that the relationship between x and y is significant does not enable us to conclude that a cause-and-effect relationship is present between x and y. Concluding a cause-and-effect relationship is warranted only if the analyst can provide some type of theoretical justification that the relationship is in fact causal. In the Armand's Pizza Parlors example, we can conclude that there is a significant relationship between the size of the student population x and quarterly sales y; moreover, the estimated regression equation $\hat{y} = 60 + 5x$ provides the least squares estimate of the relationship. We cannot, however, conclude that changes in student population x *cause* changes in quarterly sales y just because we identified a statistically significant relationship. The appropriateness of such a cause-and-effect conclusion is left to supporting theoretical justification and to good judgment on the part of the analyst. Armand's managers felt that increases in the student population were a likely cause of increased quarterly sales. Thus, the result of the significance test enabled them to conclude that a cause-and-effect relationship was present.

In addition, just because we are able to reject H_0: $\beta_1 = 0$ and demonstrate statistical significance does not enable us to conclude that the relationship between x and y is linear. We can state only that x and y are related and that a linear relationship explains a significant portion of the variability in y over the range of values for x observed in the sample. Figure 14.9 illustrates this situation. The test for significance calls for the rejection of the null hypothesis H_0: $\beta_1 = 0$ and leads to the conclusion that x and y are significantly related, but the figure shows that the actual relationship between x and y is not linear. Although the

FIGURE 14.9   EXAMPLE OF A LINEAR APPROXIMATION OF A NONLINEAR RELATIONSHIP

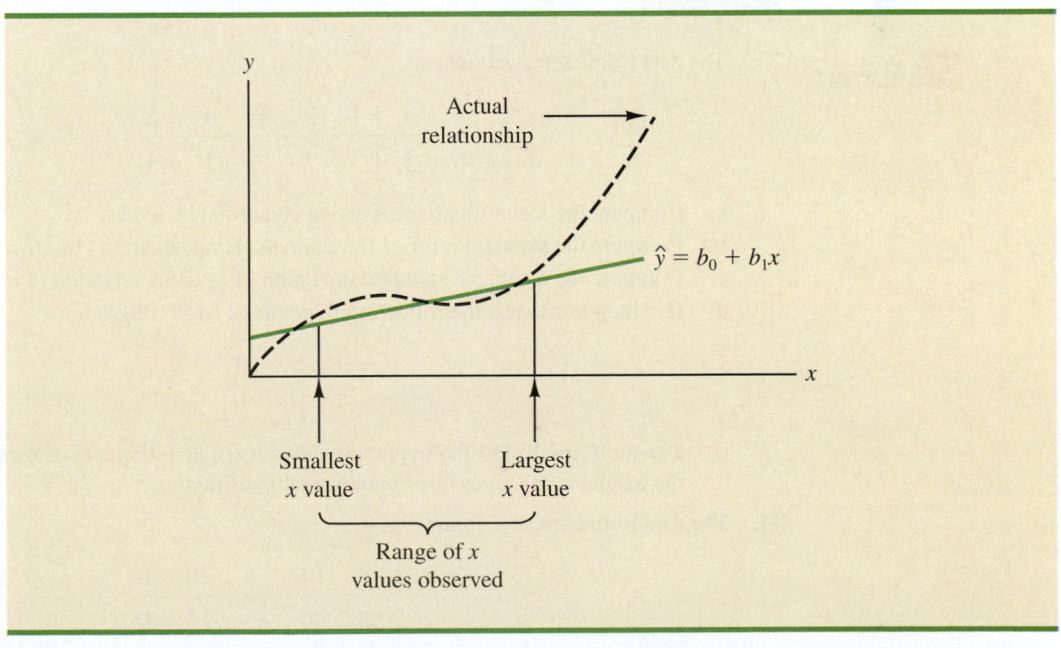

linear approximation provided by $\hat{y} = b_0 + b_1x$ is good over the range of x values observed in the sample, it becomes poor for x values outside that range.

Given a significant relationship, we should feel confident in using the estimated regression equation for predictions corresponding to x values within the range of the x values observed in the sample. For Armand's Pizza Parlors, this range corresponds to values of x between 2 and 26. Unless other reasons indicate that the model is valid beyond this range, predictions outside the range of the independent variable should be made with caution. For Armand's Pizza Parlors, because the regression relationship has been found significant at the .01 level, we should feel confident using it to predict sales for restaurants where the associated student population is between 2000 and 26,000.

NOTES AND COMMENTS

1. The assumptions made about the error term (Section 14.4) are what allow the tests of statistical significance in this section. The properties of the sampling distribution of b_1 and the subsequent t and F tests follow directly from these assumptions.

2. Do not confuse statistical significance with practical significance. With very large sample sizes, statistically significant results can be obtained for small values of b_1; in such cases, one must exercise care in concluding that the relationship has practical significance. We discuss this in more detail in Section 14.10.

3. A test of significance for a linear relationship between x and y can also be performed by using the sample correlation coefficient r_{xy}. With ρ_{xy} denoting the population correlation coefficient, the hypotheses are as follows.

$$H_0: \rho_{xy} = 0$$
$$H_a: \rho_{xy} \neq 0$$

A significant relationship can be concluded if H_0 is rejected. The details of this test are provided in Appendix 14.2. However, the t and F tests presented previously in this section give the same result as the test for significance using the correlation coefficient. Conducting a test for significance using the correlation coefficient therefore is not necessary if a t or F test has already been conducted.

Exercises

Methods

23. The data from exercise 1 follow.

x_i	1	2	3	4	5
y_i	3	7	5	11	14

a. Compute the mean square error using equation (14.15).
b. Compute the standard error of the estimate using equation (14.16).
c. Compute the estimated standard deviation of b_1 using equation (14.18).
d. Use the t test to test the following hypotheses ($\alpha = .05$):

$$H_0: \beta_1 = 0$$
$$H_a: \beta_1 \neq 0$$

e. Use the F test to test the hypotheses in part (d) at a .05 level of significance. Present the results in the analysis of variance table format.

24. The data from exercise 2 follow.

x_i	3	12	6	20	14
y_i	55	40	55	10	15

a. Compute the mean square error using equation (14.15).
b. Compute the standard error of the estimate using equation (14.16).
c. Compute the estimated standard deviation of b_1 using equation (14.18).
d. Use the t test to test the following hypotheses ($\alpha = .05$):

$$H_0: \beta_1 = 0$$
$$H_a: \beta_1 \neq 0$$

e. Use the F test to test the hypotheses in part (d) at a .05 level of significance. Present the results in the analysis of variance table format.

25. The data from exercise 3 follow.

x_i	2	6	9	13	20
y_i	7	18	9	26	23

a. What is the value of the standard error of the estimate?
b. Test for a significant relationship by using the t test. Use $\alpha = .05$.
c. Use the F test to test for a significant relationship. Use $\alpha = .05$. What is your conclusion?

Applications

26. In exercise 18 the data on price ($) and the overall score for six stereo headphones tested by *Consumer Reports* were as follows (*Consumer Reports* website, March 5, 2012).

Brand	Price ($)	Score
Bose	180	76
Skullcandy	150	71
Koss	95	61
Phillips/O'Neill	70	56
Denon	70	40
JVC	35	26

a. Does the t test indicate a significant relationship between price and the overall score? What is your conclusion? Use $\alpha = .05$.
b. Test for a significant relationship using the F test. What is your conclusion? Use $\alpha = .05$.
c. Show the ANOVA table for these data.

27. To identify high-paying jobs for people who do not like stress, the following data were collected showing the average annual salary ($1000s) and the stress tolerance for a variety of occupations (Business Insider website, November 8, 2013).

SalaryStress

Job	Average Annual Salary ($1000s)	Stress Tolerance
Art directors	81	69.0
Astronomers	96	62.0
Audiologists	70	67.5
Dental hygienists	70	71.3
Economists	92	63.3
Engineers	92	69.5
Law teachers	100	62.8
Optometrists	98	65.5
Political scientists	102	60.1
Urban and regional planners	65	69.0

The stress tolerance for each job is rated on a scale from 0 to 100, where a lower rating indicates less stress.

a. Develop a scatter diagram for these data with average annual salary as the independent variable. What does the scatter diagram indicate about the relationship between the two variables?

b. Use these data to develop an estimated regression equation that can be used to predict stress tolerance given the average annual salary.

c. At the .05 level of significance, does there appear to be a significant statistical relationship between the two variables?

d. Would you feel comfortable in predicting the stress tolerance for a different occupation given the average annual salary for the occupation? Explain.

e. Does the relationship between average annual salary and stress tolerance for these data seem reasonable to you? Explain.

BrokerRatings

28. In exercise 8, ratings data on $x =$ the quality of the speed of execution and $y =$ overall satisfaction with electronic trades provided the estimated regression equation $\hat{y} = .2046 + .9077x$ (AAII website, February 7, 2012). At the .05 level of significance, test whether speed of execution and overall satisfaction are related. Show the ANOVA table. What is your conclusion?

29. Refer to exercise 21, where data on production volume and cost were used to develop an estimated regression equation relating production volume and cost for a particular manufacturing operation. Use $\alpha = .05$ to test whether the production volume is significantly related to the total cost. Show the ANOVA table. What is your conclusion?

30. Refer to exercise 9, where the following data were used to investigate the relationship between the number of cars in service (1000s) and the annual revenue ($millions) for six smaller car rental companies (*Auto Rental News* website, August 7, 2012).

Company	Cars (1000s)	Revenue ($millions)
U-Save Auto Rental System, Inc.	11.5	118
Payless Car Rental System, Inc.	10.0	135
ACE Rent A Car	9.0	100
Rent-A-Wreck of America	5.5	37
Triangle Rent-A-Car	4.2	40
Affordable/Sensible	3.3	32

With $x =$ cars in service (1000s) and $y =$ annual revenue ($millions), the estimated regression equation is $\hat{y} = -17.005 + 12.966x$. For these data SSE $= 1043.03$ and SST $= 10,568$. Do these results indicate a significant relationship between the number of cars in service and the annual revenue?

RacingBicycles

31. In exercise 20, data on $x =$ weight (pounds) and $y =$ price ($) for 10 road-racing bikes provided the estimated regression equation $\hat{y} = 28,574 - 1439x$ (*Bicycling* website, March 8, 2012). For these data SSE $= 7,102,922.54$ and SST $= 52,120,800$. Use the F test to determine whether the weight for a bike and the price are related at the .05 level of significance.

14.6 Using the Estimated Regression Equation for Estimation and Prediction

When using the simple linear regression model, we are making an assumption about the relationship between x and y. We then use the least squares method to obtain the estimated simple linear regression equation. If a significant relationship exists between x and y and the coefficient of determination shows that the fit is good, the estimated regression equation should be useful for estimation and prediction.

For the Armand's Pizza Parlors example, the estimated regression equation is $\hat{y} = 60 + 5x$. At the end of Section 14.1 we stated that $\hat{y}$ can be used as a *point estimator* of $E(y)$, the mean or expected value of y for a given value of x, and as a predictor of an individual value of y. For example, suppose Armand's managers want to estimate the mean quarterly sales for *all* restaurants located near college campuses with 10,000 students. Using the estimated regression equation $\hat{y} = 60 + 5x$, we see that for $x = 10$ (10,000 students), $\hat{y} = 60 + 5(10) = 110$. Thus, a *point estimate* of the mean quarterly sales for all restaurant locations near campuses with 10,000 students is $110,000. In this case we are using $\hat{y}$ as the point estimator of the mean value of y when $x = 10$.

We can also use the estimated regression equation to *predict* an individual value of y for a given value of x. For example, to predict quarterly sales for a new restaurant Armand's is considering building near Talbot College, a campus with 10,000 students, we would compute $\hat{y} = 60 + 5(10) = 110$. Hence, we would predict quarterly sales of $110,000 for such a new restaurant. In this case, we are using $\hat{y}$ as the *predictor* of y for a new observation when $x = 10$.

When we are using the estimated regression equation to estimate the mean value of y or to predict an individual value of y, it is clear that the estimate or prediction depends on the given value of x. For this reason, as we discuss in more depth the issues concerning estimation and prediction, the following notation will help clarify matters.

$x^* = $ the given value of the independent variable x

$y^* = $ the random variable denoting the possible values of the dependent variable y when $x = x^*$

$E(y^*) = $ the mean or expected value of the dependent variable y when $x = x^*$

$\hat{y}^* = b_0 + b_1 x^* = $ the point estimator of $E(y^*)$ and the predictor of an individual value of y^* when $x = x^*$

To illustrate the use of this notation, suppose we want to estimate the mean value of quarterly sales for *all* Armand's restaurants located near a campus with 10,000 students. For this case, $x^* = 10$ and $E(y^*)$ denotes the unknown mean value of quarterly sales for all restaurants where $x^* = 10$. Thus, the point estimate of $E(y^*)$ is provided by $\hat{y}^* = 60 + 5(10) = 110$, or $110,000. But, using this notation, $\hat{y}^* = 110$ is also the predictor of quarterly sales for the new restaurant located near Talbot College, a school with 10,000 students.

Interval Estimation

Point estimators and predictors do not provide any information about the precision associated with the estimate and/or prediction. For that we must develop confidence intervals and prediction intervals. A **confidence interval** is an interval estimate of the *mean value of y* for a given value of x. A **prediction interval** is used whenever we want to *predict an individual value of y* for a new observation corresponding to a given value of x. Although the predictor of y for a given value of x is the same as the point estimator of the mean value of y for a given value of x, the interval estimates we obtain for the two cases are different. As we will show, the margin of error is larger for a prediction interval. We begin by showing how to develop an interval estimate of the mean value of y.

Confidence intervals and prediction intervals show the precision of the regression results. Narrower intervals provide a higher degree of precision.

Confidence Interval for the Mean Value of y

In general, we cannot expect $\hat{y}^*$ to equal $E(y^*)$ exactly. If we want to make an inference about how close $\hat{y}^*$ is to the true mean value $E(y^*)$, we will have to estimate the variance of $\hat{y}^*$. The formula for estimating the variance of $\hat{y}^*$, denoted by $s_{\hat{y}^*}^2$, is

$$s_{\hat{y}^*}^2 = s^2 \left[\frac{1}{n} + \frac{(x^* - \bar{x})^2}{\sum(x_i - \bar{x})^2} \right] \tag{14.22}$$

The estimate of the standard deviation of $\hat{y}^*$ is given by the square root of equation (14.22).

$$s_{\hat{y}^*} = s \sqrt{\frac{1}{n} + \frac{(x^* - \bar{x})^2}{\sum(x_i - \bar{x})^2}} \tag{14.23}$$

The computational results for Armand's Pizza Parlors in Section 14.5 provided $s = 13.829$. With $x^* = 10$, $\bar{x} = 14$, and $\sum(x_i - \bar{x})^2 = 568$, we can use equation (14.23) to obtain

$$s_{\hat{y}^*} = 13.829 \sqrt{\frac{1}{10} + \frac{(10 - 14)^2}{568}}$$

$$= 13.829 \sqrt{.1282} = 4.95$$

The general expression for a confidence interval follows.

CONFIDENCE INTERVAL FOR $E(y^*)$

The margin of error associated with this confidence interval is $t_{\alpha/2}s_{\hat{y}^*}$.

$$\hat{y}^* \pm t_{\alpha/2}s_{\hat{y}^*} \tag{14.24}$$

where the confidence coefficient is $1 - \alpha$ and $t_{\alpha/2}$ is based on the t distribution with $n - 2$ degrees of freedom.

Using expression (14.24) to develop a 95% confidence interval of the mean quarterly sales for all Armand's restaurants located near campuses with 10,000 students, we need the value of t for $\alpha/2 = .025$ and $n - 2 = 10 - 2 = 8$ degrees of freedom. Using Table 2 of Appendix B, we have $t_{.025} = 2.306$. Thus, with $\hat{y}^* = 110$ and a margin of error of $t_{\alpha/2}s_{\hat{y}^*} = 2.306(4.95) = 11.415$, the 95% confidence interval estimate is

$$110 \pm 11.415$$

In dollars, the 95% confidence interval for the mean quarterly sales of all restaurants near campuses with 10,000 students is $110,000 \pm 11,415$. Therefore, the 95% confidence interval for the mean quarterly sales when the student population is 10,000 is $98,585 to $121,415.

Note that the estimated standard deviation of $\hat{y}^*$ given by equation (14.23) is smallest when $x^* - \bar{x} = 0$. In this case the estimated standard deviation of $\hat{y}^*$ becomes

$$s_{\hat{y}^*} = s \sqrt{\frac{1}{n} + \frac{(\bar{x} - \bar{x})^2}{\sum(x_i - \bar{x})^2}} = s \sqrt{\frac{1}{n}}$$

This result implies that we can make the best or most precise estimate of the mean value of y whenever $x^* = \bar{x}$. In fact, the further x^* is from $\bar{x}$, the larger $x^* - \bar{x}$ becomes. As a result, the confidence interval for the mean value of y will become wider as x^* deviates more from $\bar{x}$. This pattern is shown graphically in Figure 14.10.

FIGURE 14.10   CONFIDENCE INTERVALS FOR THE MEAN SALES y AT GIVEN VALUES OF STUDENT POPULATION x

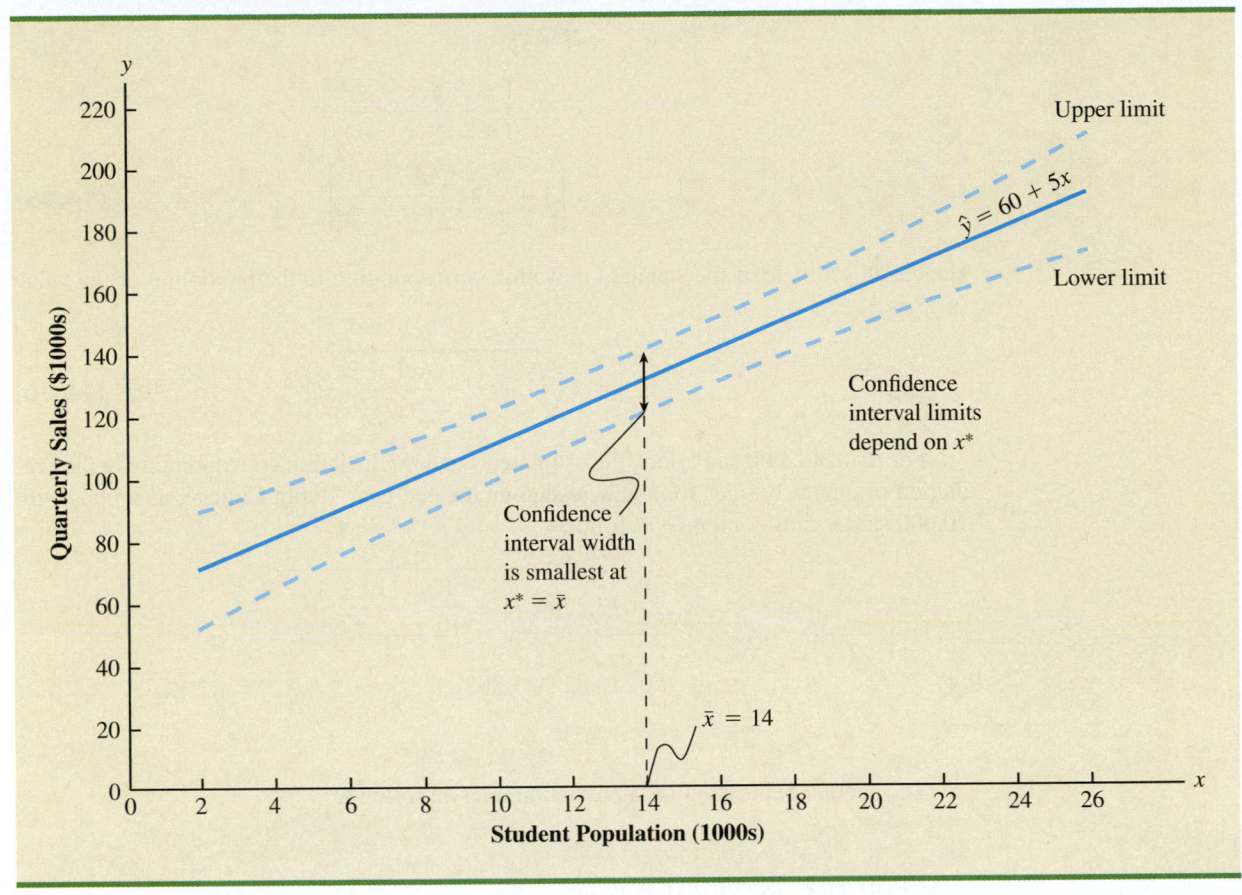

Prediction Interval for an Individual Value of y

Instead of estimating the mean value of quarterly sales for all Armand's restaurants located near campuses with 10,000 students, suppose we want to predict quarterly sales for a new restaurant Armand's is considering building near Talbot College, a campus with 10,000 students. As noted previously, the predictor of y^*, the value of y corresponding to the given x^*, is $\hat{y}^* = b_0 + b_1 x^*$. For the new restaurant located near Talbot College, $x^* = 10$ and the prediction of quarterly sales is $\hat{y}^* = 60 + 5(10) = 110$, or \$110,000. Note that the prediction of quarterly sales for the new Armand's restaurant near Talbot College is the same as the point estimate of the mean sales for all Armand's restaurants located near campuses with 10,000 students.

To develop a prediction interval, let us first determine the variance associated with using $\hat{y}^*$ as a predictor of y when $x = x^*$. This variance is made up of the sum of the following two components.

1. The variance of the y^* values about the mean $E(y^*)$, an estimate of which is given by s^2
2. The variance associated with using $\hat{y}^*$ to estimate $E(y^*)$, an estimate of which is given by $s_{\hat{y}^*}^2$.

The formula for estimating the variance corresponding to the prediction of the value of y when $x = x^*$, denoted s_{pred}^2, is

$$s_{pred}^2 = s^2 + s_{\hat{y}^*}^2$$

$$= s^2 + s^2\left[\frac{1}{n} + \frac{(x^* - \bar{x})^2}{\sum(x_i - \bar{x})^2}\right]$$

$$= s^2\left[1 + \frac{1}{n} + \frac{(x^* - \bar{x})^2}{\sum(x_i - \bar{x})^2}\right] \qquad \textbf{(14.25)}$$

Hence, an estimate of the standard deviation corresponding to the prediction of the value of y^* is

$$s_{pred} = s\sqrt{1 + \frac{1}{n} + \frac{(x^* - \bar{x})^2}{\sum(x_i - \bar{x})^2}} \qquad \textbf{(14.26)}$$

For Armand's Pizza Parlors, the estimated standard deviation corresponding to the prediction of quarterly sales for a new restaurant located near Talbot College, a campus with 10,000 students, is computed as follows.

$$s_{pred} = 13.829\sqrt{1 + \frac{1}{10} + \frac{(10 - 14)^2}{568}}$$

$$= 13.829\sqrt{1.282}$$

$$= 14.69$$

The general expression for a prediction interval follows.

PREDICTION INTERVAL FOR y^*

The margin of error associated with this prediction interval is $t_{\alpha/2}s_{pred}$.

$$\hat{y}^* \pm t_{\alpha/2}s_{pred} \qquad \textbf{(14.27)}$$

where the confidence coefficient is $1 - \alpha$ and $t_{\alpha/2}$ is based on a t distribution with $n - 2$ degrees of freedom.

The 95% prediction interval for quarterly sales for the new Armand's restaurant located near Talbot College can be found using $t_{\alpha/2} = t_{.025} = 2.306$ and $s_{pred} = 14.69$. Thus, with $\hat{y}^* = 110$ and a margin of error of $t_{.025}s_{pred} = 2.306(14.69) = 33.875$, the 95% prediction interval is

$$110 \pm 33.875$$

In dollars, this prediction interval is \$110,000 $\pm$ \$33,875 or \$76,125 to \$143,875. Note that the prediction interval for the new restaurant located near Talbot College, a campus with 10,000 students, is wider than the confidence interval for the mean quarterly sales of all restaurants located near campuses with 10,000 students. The difference reflects the fact that we are able to estimate the mean value of y more precisely than we can predict an individual value of y.

In general, the lines for the confidence interval limits and the prediction interval limits both have curvature.

Confidence intervals and prediction intervals are both more precise when the value of the independent variable x^* is closer to $\bar{x}$. The general shapes of confidence intervals and the wider prediction intervals are shown together in Figure 14.11.

FIGURE 14.11   CONFIDENCE AND PREDICTION INTERVALS FOR SALES y AT GIVEN VALUES
OF STUDENT POPULATION x

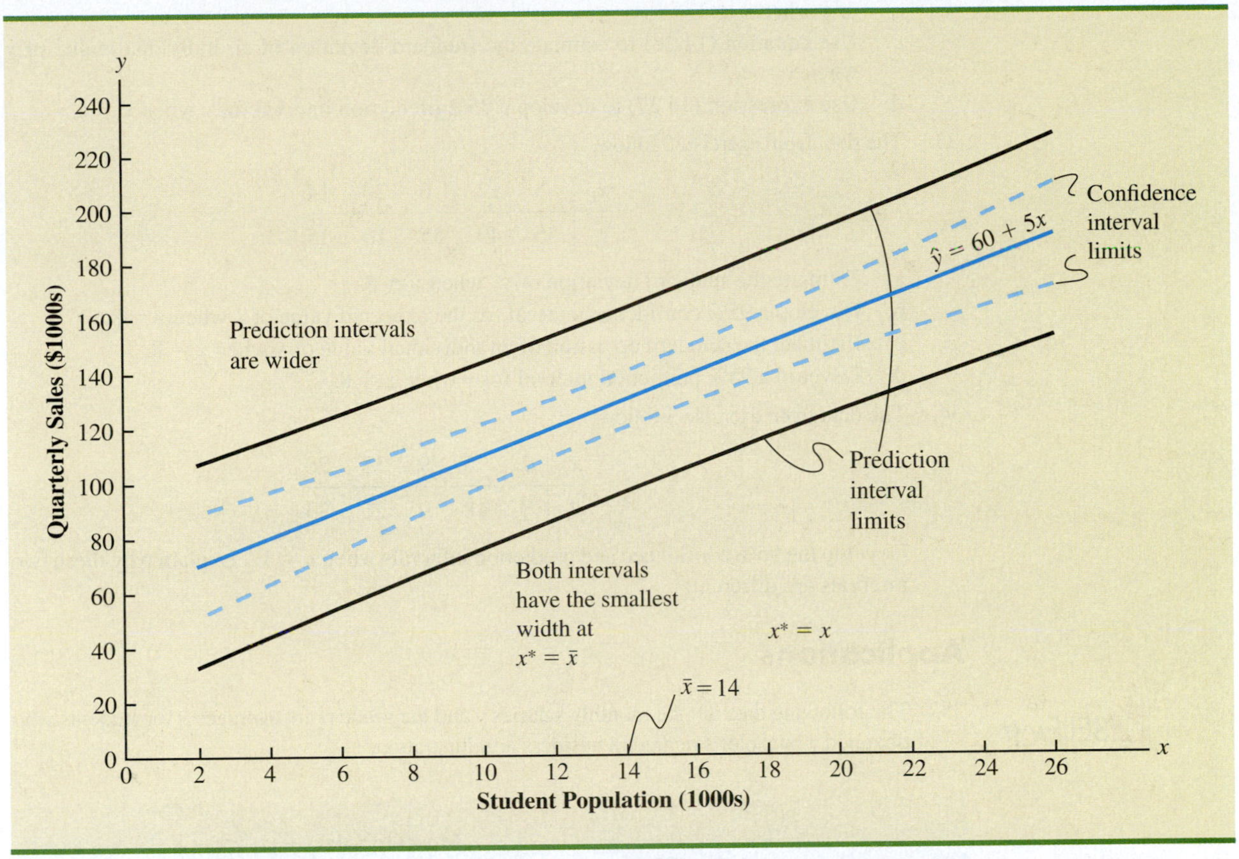

NOTE AND COMMENT

A prediction interval is used to predict the value of the dependent variable y for a *new observation*. As an illustration, we showed how to develop a prediction interval of quarterly sales for a new restaurant that Armand's is considering building near Talbot College, a campus with 10,000 students. The fact that the value of $x = 10$ is not one of the values of student population for the Armand's sample data in Table 14.1 is not meant to imply that prediction intervals cannot be developed for values of x in the

sample data. But, for the 10 restaurants that make up the data in Table 14.1, developing a prediction interval for quarterly sales for *one of these restaurants* does not make any sense because we already know the value of quarterly sales for each of these restaurants. In other words, a prediction interval only has meaning for something new, in this case a new observation corresponding to a particular value of x that may or may not equal one of the values of x in the sample.

Exercises

Methods

SELFtest

32.   The data from exercise 1 follow.

x_i	1	2	3	4	5
y_i	3	7	5	11	14

   a.   Use equation (14.23) to estimate the standard deviation of $\hat{y}^*$ when $x = 4$.

   b.   Use expression (14.24) to develop a 95% confidence interval for the expected value of y when $x = 4$.

   c.   Use equation (14.26) to estimate the standard deviation of an individual value of y when $x = 4$.

   d.   Use expression (14.27) to develop a 95% prediction interval for y when $x = 4$.

33.   The data from exercise 2 follow.

x_i	3	12	6	20	14
y_i	55	40	55	10	15

   a.   Estimate the standard deviation of $\hat{y}^*$ when $x = 8$.

   b.   Develop a 95% confidence interval for the expected value of y when $x = 8$.

   c.   Estimate the standard deviation of an individual value of y when $x = 8$.

   d.   Develop a 95% prediction interval for y when $x = 8$.

34.   The data from exercise 3 follow.

x_i	2	6	9	13	20
y_i	7	18	9	26	23

Develop the 95% confidence and prediction intervals when $x = 12$. Explain why these two intervals are different.

Applications

35.   The following data are the monthly salaries y and the grade point averages x for students who obtained a bachelor's degree in business administration.

GPA	Monthly Salary ($)
2.6	3600
3.4	3900
3.6	4300
3.2	3800
3.5	4200
2.9	3900

The estimated regression equation for these data is $\hat{y} = 2090.5 + 581.1x$ and MSE = 21,284.

   a.   Develop a point estimate of the starting salary for a student with a GPA of 3.0.

   b.   Develop a 95% confidence interval for the mean starting salary for all students with a 3.0 GPA.

   c.   Develop a 95% prediction interval for Ryan Dailey, a student with a GPA of 3.0.

   d.   Discuss the differences in your answers to parts (b) and (c).

36.   In exercise 7, the data on y = annual sales ($1000s) for new customer accounts and x = number of years of experience for a sample of 10 salespersons provided the estimated regression equation $\hat{y} = 80 + 4x$. For these data $\bar{x} = 7$, $\sum(x_i - \bar{x})^2 = 142$, and $s = 4.6098$.

   a.   Develop a 95% confidence interval for the mean annual sales for all salespersons with nine years of experience.

   b.   The company is considering hiring Tom Smart, a salesperson with nine years of experience. Develop a 95% prediction interval of annual sales for Tom Smart.

   c.   Discuss the differences in your answers to parts (a) and (b).

37.   In exercise 5, the following data on $x =$ the number of defective parts found and $y =$ the line speed (feet per minute) for a production process at Brawdy Plastics provided the estimated regression equation $\hat{y} = 27.5 - .3x$.

Line Speed	Number of Defective Parts Found
20	23
20	21
30	19
30	16
40	15
40	17
50	14
50	11

For these data SSE = 16. Develop a 95% confidence interval for the mean number of defective parts for a line speed of 25 feet per minute.

38.   Refer to exercise 21, where data on the production volume x and total cost y for a particular manufacturing operation were used to develop the estimated regression equation $\hat{y} = 1246.67 + 7.6x$.

   a.   The company's production schedule shows that 500 units must be produced next month. Predict the total cost for next month.

   b.   Develop a 99% prediction interval for the total cost for next month.

   c.   If an accounting cost report at the end of next month shows that the actual production cost during the month was $6000, should managers be concerned about incurring such a high total cost for the month? Discuss.

39.   In exercise 12, the following data on $x =$ average daily hotel room rate and $y =$ amount spent on entertainment (*The Wall Street Journal*, August 18, 2011) lead to the estimated regression equation $\hat{y} = 17.49 + 1.0334x$. For these data SSE = 1541.4.

DATA *file*

BusinessTravel

City	Room Rate ($)	Entertainment ($)
Boston	148	161
Denver	96	105
Nashville	91	101
New Orleans	110	142
Phoenix	90	100
San Diego	102	120
San Francisco	136	167
San Jose	90	140
Tampa	82	98

   a.   Predict the amount spent on entertainment for a particular city that has a daily room rate of $89.

   b.   Develop a 95% confidence interval for the mean amount spent on entertainment for all cities that have a daily room rate of $89.

   c.   The average room rate in Chicago is $128. Develop a 95% prediction interval for the amount spent on entertainment in Chicago.

14.7   Excel's Regression Tool

In previous sections of this chapter we have shown how Excel's chart tools can be used for various tasks in a regression analysis. Excel also has a more comprehensive Regression tool. In this section we will illustrate how Excel's Regression tool can be used to perform a complete regression analysis, including statistical tests of significance for the Armand's Pizza Parlors data in Table 14.2.

Using Excel's Regression Tool for the Armand's Pizza Parlors Example

Refer to Figures 14.12 and 14.13 as we describe the tasks involved to use Excel's Regression tool to perform the regression analysis computations for the Armand's data.

Enter/Access Data: Open the DATAfile named *Armand's*. The data are in cells B2:C11 and labels are in Column A and cells B1:C1.

Apply Tools: The following steps describe how to use Excel's Regression tool to perform the regression analysis computations performed in Sections 14.2–14.5.

Step 1. Click the **Data** tab on the Ribbon
Step 2. In the **Analyze** group, click **Data Analysis**
Step 3. Choose **Regression** from the list of Analysis Tools
Step 4. When the Regression dialog box appears (see Figure 14.12):
   Enter C1:C11 in the **Input Y Range** box
   Enter B1:B11 in the **Input X Range** box
   Select **Labels**
   Select **Confidence Level**
   Enter 99 in the **Confidence Level** box
   Select **Output Range**
   Enter A13 in the **Output Range** box (to identify the upper left corner of the section of the worksheet where the output will appear)
   Click **OK**

FIGURE 14.12   REGRESSION TOOL DIALOG BOX FOR THE ARMAND'S PIZZA PARLORS EXAMPLE

FIGURE 14.13   REGRESSION TOOL OUTPUT FOR ARMAND'S PIZZA PARLORS

	A	B	C	D	E	F	G	H	I	J
1	Restaurant	Population	Sales							
2	1	2	58							
3	2	6	105							
4	3	8	88							
5	4	8	118							
6	5	12	117							
7	6	16	137							
8	7	20	157							
9	8	20	169							
10	9	22	149							
11	10	26	202							
12										
13	SUMMARY OUTPUT									
14										
15	*Regression Statistics*									
16	Multiple R	0.9501								
17	R Square	0.9027								
18	Adjusted R Square	0.8906								
19	Standard Error	13.8293								
20	Observations	10								
21										
22	ANOVA									
23		*df*	*SS*	*MS*	*F*	*Significance F*				
24	Regression	1	14200	14200	74.2484	2.55E-05				
25	Residual	8	1530	191.25						
26	Total	9	15730							
27										
28		*Coefficients*	*Standard Error*	*t Stat*	*P-value*	*Lower 95%*	*Upper 95%*	*Lower 99.0%*	*Upper 99.0%*	
29	Intercept	60	9.2260	6.5033	0.0002	38.7247	81.2753	29.0431	90.9569	
30	Population	5	0.5803	8.6167	2.55E-05	3.6619	6.3381	3.0530	6.9470	
31										

The Excel output can be reformatted to improve readability.

The regression output, titled SUMMARY OUTPUT, begins with row 13 in Figure 14.13. Because Excel initially displays the output using standard column widths, many of the row and column labels are unreadable. In several places we have reformatted to improve readability. We have also reformatted cells displaying numerical values to a maximum of four decimal places. Numbers displayed using scientific notation have not been modified. Regression output in future figures will be similarly reformatted to improve readability.

The first section of the summary output, entitled *Regression Statistics,* contains summary statistics such as the coefficient of determination (R Square). The second section of the output, titled ANOVA, contains the analysis of variance table. The last section of the output, which is not titled, contains the estimated regression coefficients and related information. Let us begin our interpretation of the regression output with the information contained in rows 29 and 30.

Interpretation of Estimated Regression Equation Output

Row 29 contains information about the y-intercept of the estimated regression line. Row 30 contains information about the slope of the estimated regression line. The y-intercept of the estimated regression line, $b_0 = 60$, is shown in cell B29, and the slope of the estimated regression line, $b_1 = 5$, is shown in cell B30. The label Intercept in cell A29 and the label Population in cell A30 are used to identify these two values.

In Section 14.5 we showed that the estimated standard deviation of b_1 is $s_{b_1} = .5803$. Cell C30 contains the estimated standard deviation of b_1. As we indicated previously, the standard deviation of b_1 is also referred to as the standard error of b_1. Thus, s_{b_1} provides an estimate of the standard error of b_1. The label Standard Error in cell C28 is Excel's way of indicating that the value in cell C30 is the estimate of the standard error, or standard deviation, of b_1.

In Section 14.5 we stated that the form of the null and alternative hypotheses needed to test for a significant relationship between population and sales are as follows:

$$H_0: \beta_1 = 0$$
$$H_a: \beta_1 \neq 0$$

Recall that the t test for a significant relationship required the computation of the t statistic, $t = b_1/s_{b_1}$. For the Armand's data, the value of t that we computed was $t = 5/.5803 = 8.62$. Note that after rounding, the value in cell D30 is 8.62. The label in cell D28, t Stat, reminds us that cell D30 contains the value of the t test statistic.

t Test   The information in cell E30 provides a means for conducting a test of significance. The value in cell E30 is the p-value associated with the t test for significance. Excel has displayed the p-value using scientific notation. To obtain the decimal equivalent, we move the decimal point 5 places to the left; we obtain a p-value of .0000255. Thus, the p-value associated with the t test for significance is .0000255. Given the level of significance α, the decision of whether to reject H_0 can be made as follows:

$$\text{Reject } H_0 \text{ if } p\text{-value} \leq \alpha$$

Suppose the level of significance is $\alpha = .01$. Because the p-value $= .0000255 < \alpha = .01$, we can reject H_0 and conclude that we have a significant relationship between student population and sales. Because p-values are provided as part of the computer output for regression analysis, the p-value approach is most often used for hypothesis tests in regression analysis.

The information in cells F28:I30 can be used to develop confidence interval estimates of the y-intercept and slope of the estimated regression equation. Excel always provides the lower and upper limits for a 95% confidence interval. Recall that in the Regression dialog box (see Figure 14.12) we selected Confidence Level and entered 99 in the Confidence Level box. As a result, Excel's Regression tool also provides the lower and upper limits for a 99% confidence interval. For instance, the value in cell H30 is the lower limit for the 99% confidence interval estimate of β_1 and the value in cell I30 is the upper limit. Thus, after rounding, the 99% confidence interval estimate of β_1 is 3.05 to 6.95. The values in cells F30 and G30 provide the lower and upper limits for the 95% confidence interval. Thus, the 95% confidence interval is 3.66 to 6.34.

Interpretation of ANOVA Output

Excel refers to the error sum of squares as the residual sum of squares.

The information in cells A22:F26 summarizes the analysis of variance computations for the Armand's data. The three sources of variation are labeled Regression, Residual, and Total. The label *df* in cell B23 stands for degrees of freedom, the label *SS* in cell C23 stands for sum of squares, and the label *MS* in cell D23 stands for mean square. Looking at cells C24:C26, we see that the regression sum of squares is 14200, the residual or error sum of squares is 1530, and the total sum of squares is 15730. The values in cells B24:B26 are the degrees of freedom corresponding to each sum of squares. Thus, the regression sum of squares has 1 degree of freedom, the residual or error sum of squares has 8 degrees of freedom, and the total sum of squares has 9 degrees of freedom. As we discussed previously, the regression degrees of freedom plus the residual degrees of freedom are equal to the total degrees of freedom, and the regression sum of squares plus the residual sum of squares are equal to the total sum of squares.

In Section 14.5 we stated that the mean square error, obtained by dividing the error or residual sum of squares by its degrees of freedom, provides an estimate of σ^2. The value in cell D25, 191.25, is the mean square error for the Armand's regression output. We also stated that the mean square regression is the sum of squares due to regression divided by the regression degrees of freedom. The value in cell D24, 14200, is the mean square regression.

F Test   In Section 14.5 we showed that an F test, based upon the F probability distribution, could also be used to test for significance in regression. The value in cell F24, .0000255, is the p-value associated with the F test for significance. Suppose the level of significance is $\alpha = .01$. Because the p-value $= .0000255 < \alpha = .01$, we can reject H_0 and conclude that we have a significant relationship between student population and sales. Note that it is the same conclusion that we obtained using the p-value approach for the t test for significance. In fact, because the t test for significance is equivalent to the F test for significance in simple linear regression, the p-values provided by both approaches are identical. The label Excel uses to identify the p-value for the F test for significance, shown in cell F23, is *Significance F*. In Chapter 9 we also stated that the p-value is often referred to as the observed level of significance. Thus, the label *Significance F* may be more meaningful if you think of the value in cell F24 as the observed level of significance for the F test.

Interpretation of Regression Statistics Output

The output in cells A15:B20 summarizes the regression statistics. The number of observations in the data set, 10, is shown in cell B20. The coefficient of determination, .9027, appears in cell B17; the corresponding label, R Square, is shown in cell A17. The square root of the coefficient of determination provides the sample correlation coefficient of 0.9501 shown in cell B16. Note that Excel uses the label Multiple R (cell A16) to identify this value. In cell A19, the label Standard Error is used to identify the value of s, the estimate of σ. Cell B19 shows that the value of s is 13.8293. We caution the reader to keep in mind that in the Excel output, the label Standard Error appears in two different places. In the Regression Statistics section of the output the label Standard Error refers to s, the estimate of σ. In the Estimated Regression Equation section of the output, the label Standard Error refers to s_{b_1}, the estimated standard deviation of the sampling distribution of b_1.

Exercises

Applications

40.   The commercial division of a real estate firm conducted a study to determine the extent of the relationship between annual gross rents ($1000s) and the selling price ($1000s) for apartment buildings. Data were collected on several properties sold, and Excel's Regression tool was used to develop an estimated regression equation. A portion of the regression output follows.

a.   How many apartment buildings were in the sample?

ANOVA

	df	SS	MS	F	Significance F
Regression	1	41587.3			
Residual	7				
Total	8	51984.1			

	Coefficients	Standard Error	t Stat	P-value	
Intercept	20.000	3.2213	6.21		
Annual Gross Rents	7.210	1.3626	5.29		

b.   Write the estimated regression equation.

c.   Use the *t* test to determine whether the selling price is related to annual gross rents. Use $\alpha = .05$.

d.   Use the *F* test to determine whether the selling price is related to annual gross rents. Use $\alpha = .05$.

e.   Predict the selling price of an apartment building with gross annual rents of $50,000.

41.   Following is a portion of the regression output for an application relating maintenance expense (dollars per month) to usage (hours per week) for a particular brand of computer terminal.

ANOVA

	df	SS	MS	F	Significance F
Regression	1	1575.76			
Residual	8	349.14			
Total	9	1924.90			

	Coefficients	Standard Error	t Stat	P-value	
Intercept	6.1092	0.9361			
Usage	0.8951	0.149			

a.   Write the estimated regression equation.

b.   Use a *t* test to determine whether monthly maintenance expense is related to usage at the .05 level of significance.

c.   Did the estimated regression equation provide a good fit? Explain.

42.   A regression model relating the number of salespersons at a branch office to annual sales at the office (in thousands of dollars) provided the following regression output.

ANOVA

	df	SS	MS	F	Significance F
Regression		6828.6			
Residual					
Total		9127.4			

	Coefficients	Standard Error	t Stat	P-value	
Intercept	80.0	11.333			
Number of Salespersons	50.0	5.482			

a.   Write the estimated regression equation.

b.   Compute the *F* statistic and test the significance of the relationship at the .05 level of significance.

c.   Compute the *t* statistic and test the significance of the relationship at the .05 level of significance.

d.   Predict the annual sales at the Memphis branch office. This branch employs 12 salespersons.

43.   A 2012 suvey conducted by Idea Works provided data showing the percentage of seats available when customers try to redeem points or miles for free travel. For each airline listed, the column labeled 2011 Percentage shows the percentage of seats available in 2011 and the column labeled 2012 shows the correponding percentage in 2012 (*The Wall Street Journal*, May 17, 2012).

DATA *file*

AirlineSeats

Airline	2011 Percentage	2012 Percentage
AirBerlin	96.4	100.0
Air Canada	82.1	78.6
Air France, KLM	65.0	55.7
AirTran Airways	47.1	87.1
Alaska Airlines	64.3	59.3
American Airlines	62.9	45.7
British Airways	61.4	79.3
Cathay Pacific	66.4	70.7
Delta Air Lines	27.1	27.1
Emirates	35.7	32.9
GOL Airlines (Brazil)	100.0	97.1
Iberia	70.7	63.6
JetBlue	79.3	86.4
Lan (Chile)	75.7	78.6
Lufthansa, Swiss, Austrian	85.0	92.1
Qantas	75.0	78.6
SAS Scandinavian	52.9	57.9
Singapore Airlines	90.7	90.7
Southwest	99.3	100.0
Turkish Airways	49.3	38.6
United Airlines	71.4	87.1
US Airways	25.7	33.6
Virgin Australia	91.4	90.0

a.   Develop a scatter diagram with 2011 Percentage as the independent variable.
b.   What does the scatter diagram developed in part (a) indicate about the relationship between the two variables?
c.   Develop the estimated regression equation.
d.   Test for a significant relationship. Use $\alpha = .05$.
e.   Did the estimated regression equation provide a good fit?

44.   Automobile racing, high-performance driving schools, and driver education programs run by automobile clubs continue to grow in popularity. All these activities require the participant to wear a helmet that is certified by the Snell Memorial Foundation, a not-for-profit organization dedicated to research, education, testing, and development of helmet safety standards. Snell "SA" (Sports Application) rated professional helmets are designed for auto racing and provide extreme impact resistance and high fire protection. One of the key factors in selecting a helmet is weight, since lower weight helmets tend to place less stress on the neck. The following data show the weight and price for 18 SA helmets (SoloRacer website, April 20, 2008).

Helmet	Weight (oz)	Price ($)
Pyrotect Pro Airflow	64	248
Pyrotect Pro Airflow Graphics	64	278
RCi Full Face	64	200
RaceQuip RidgeLine	64	200
HJC AR-10	58	300
HJC Si-12	47	700
HJC HX-10	49	900
Impact Racing Super Sport	59	340
Zamp FSA-1	66	199
Zamp RZ-2	58	299
Zamp RZ-2 Ferrari	58	299
Zamp RZ-3 Sport	52	479
Zamp RZ-3 Sport Painted	52	479
Bell M2	63	369
Bell M4	62	369
Bell M4 Pro	54	559
G Force Pro Force 1	63	250
G Force Pro Force 1 Grafx	63	280

DATA *file*

RaceHelmets

a.   Develop a scatter diagram with weight as the independent variable.
b.   Does there appear to be any relationship between these two variables?
c.   Develop the estimated regression equation that could be used to predict the price given the weight.
d.   Test for the significance of the relationship at the .05 level of significance.
e.   Did the estimated regression equation provide a good fit? Explain.

14.8   Residual Analysis: Validating Model Assumptions

Residual analysis is the primary tool for determining whether the assumed regression model is appropriate.

As we noted previously, the *residual* for observation i is the difference between the observed value of the dependent variable (y_i) and the predicted value of the dependent variable ($\hat{y}_i$).

RESIDUAL FOR OBSERVATION i

$$y_i - \hat{y}_i \qquad\qquad\qquad \textbf{(14.28)}$$

where

y_i is the observed value of the dependent variable
$\hat{y}_i$ is the predicted value of the dependent variable

In other words, the ith residual is the error resulting from using the estimated regression equation to predict the value of the dependent variable. The residuals for the Armand's Pizza Parlors example are computed in Table 14.7. The observed values of the dependent variable are in the second column and the predicted values of the dependent variable, obtained using the estimated regression equation $\hat{y} = 60 + 5x$, are in the third column. An analysis of the corresponding residuals in the fourth column will help determine whether the assumptions made about the regression model are appropriate.

TABLE 14.7   RESIDUALS FOR ARMAND'S PIZZA PARLORS

Student Population x_i	Sales y_i	Predicted Sales $\hat{y}_i = 60 + 5x_i$	Residuals $y_i - \hat{y}_i$
2	58	70	−12
6	105	90	15
8	88	100	−12
8	118	100	18
12	117	120	−3
16	137	140	−3
20	157	160	−3
20	169	160	9
22	149	170	−21
26	202	190	12

Let us now review the regression assumptions for the Armand's Pizza Parlors example. A simple linear regression model was assumed.

$$y = \beta_0 + \beta_1 x + \epsilon \tag{14.29}$$

This model indicates that we assumed quarterly sales (y) to be a linear function of the size of the student population (x) plus an error term ϵ. In Section 14.4 we made the following assumptions about the error term ϵ.

1. $E(\epsilon) = 0$.
2. The variance of ϵ, denoted by σ^2, is the same for all values of x.
3. The values of ϵ are independent.
4. The error term ϵ has a normal distribution.

These assumptions provide the theoretical basis for the t test and the F test used to determine whether the relationship between x and y is significant, and for the confidence and prediction interval estimates presented in Section 14.6. If the assumptions about the error term ϵ appear questionable, the hypothesis tests about the significance of the regression relationship and the interval estimation results may not be valid.

The residuals provide the best information about ϵ; hence an analysis of the residuals is an important step in determining whether the assumptions for ϵ are appropriate. Much of residual analysis is based on an examination of graphical plots. In this section, we discuss the following residual plots.

1. A plot of the residuals against values of the independent variable x
2. A plot of residuals against the predicted values of the dependent variable y
3. A standardized residual plot
4. A normal probability plot

Residual Plot Against x

A **residual plot** against the independent variable x is a graph in which the values of the independent variable are represented by the horizontal axis and the corresponding residual values are represented by the vertical axis. A point is plotted for each residual. The first coordinate for each point is given by the value of x_i and the second coordinate is given by the corresponding value of the residual $y_i - \hat{y}_i$. For a residual plot against x with the Armand's Pizza Parlors data from Table 14.7, the coordinates of the first point are $(2, -12)$, corresponding to $x_1 = 2$ and $y_1 - \hat{y}_1 = -12$; the coordinates of the second point are $(6, 15)$, corresponding to $x_2 = 6$ and $y_2 - \hat{y}_2 = 15$; and so on. Figure 14.15 shows the resulting residual plot.

FIGURE 14.15   PLOT OF THE RESIDUALS AGAINST THE INDEPENDENT VARIABLE x FOR ARMAND'S PIZZA PARLORS

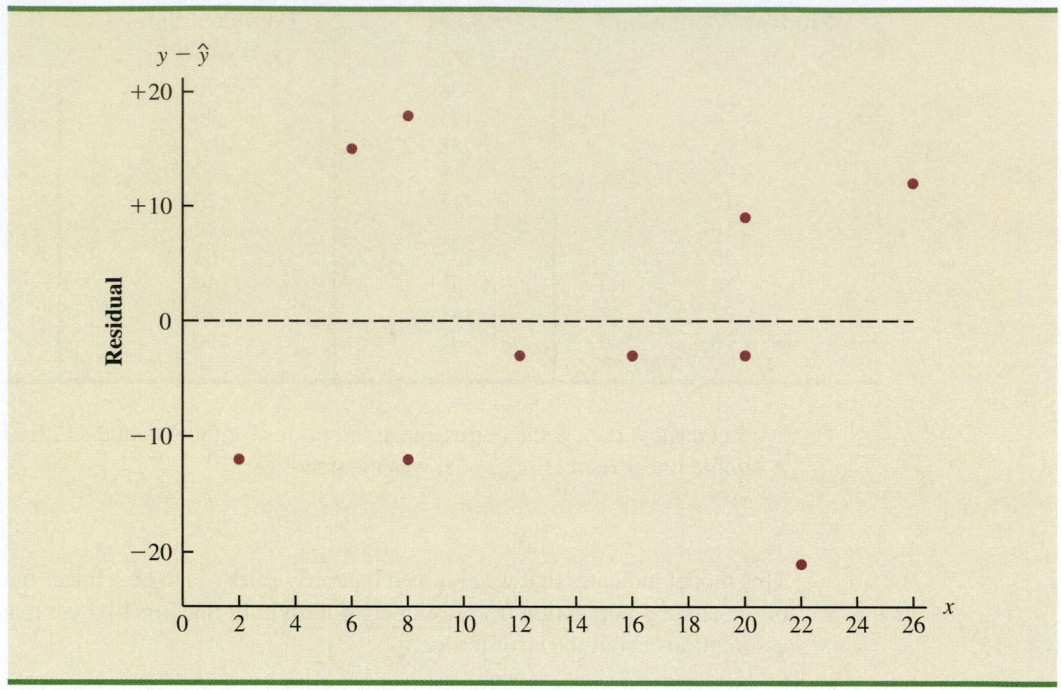

Before interpreting the results for this residual plot, let us consider some general patterns that might be observed in any residual plot. Three examples appear in Figure 14.16. If the assumption that the variance of ϵ is the same for all values of x and the assumed regression model is an adequate representation of the relationship between the variables, the residual plot should give an overall impression of a horizontal band of points such as the one in Panel A of Figure 14.16. However, if the variance of ϵ is not the same for all values of x—for example, if variability about the regression line is greater for larger values of x—a pattern such as the one in Panel B of Figure 14.16 could be observed. In this case, the assumption of a constant variance of ϵ is violated. Another possible residual plot is shown in Panel C. In this case, we would conclude that the assumed regression model is not an adequate representation of the relationship between the variables. A curvilinear regression model or multiple regression model should be considered.

Now let us return to the residual plot for Armand's Pizza Parlors shown in Figure 14.15. The residuals appear to approximate the horizontal pattern in Panel A of Figure 14.16. Hence, we conclude that the residual plot does not provide evidence that the assumptions made for Armand's regression model should be challenged. At this point, we are confident in the conclusion that Armand's simple linear regression model is valid.

Experience and good judgment are always factors in the effective interpretation of residual plots. Seldom does a residual plot conform precisely to one of the patterns in Figure 14.16. Yet analysts who frequently conduct regression studies and frequently review residual plots become adept at understanding the differences between patterns that are reasonable and patterns that indicate the assumptions of the model should be questioned. A residual plot provides one technique to assess the validity of the assumptions for a regression model.

Residual Plot Against $\hat{y}$

Another residual plot represents the predicted value of the dependent variable $\hat{y}$ on the horizontal axis and the residual values on the vertical axis. A point is plotted for each residual.

FIGURE 14.16 RESIDUAL PLOTS FROM THREE REGRESSION STUDIES

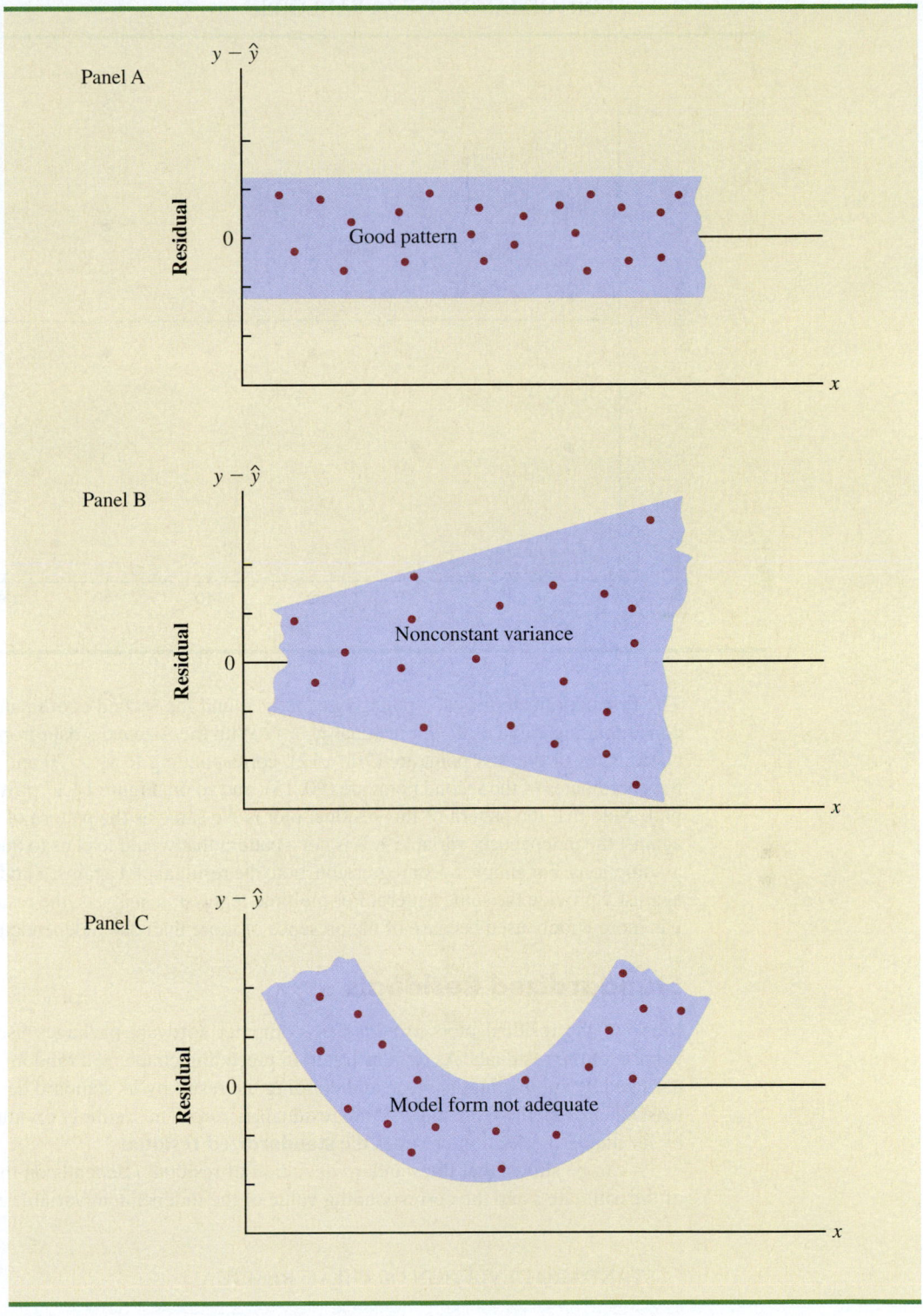

FIGURE 14.17 PLOT OF THE RESIDUALS AGAINST THE PREDICTED VALUES $\hat{y}$
FOR ARMAND'S PIZZA PARLORS

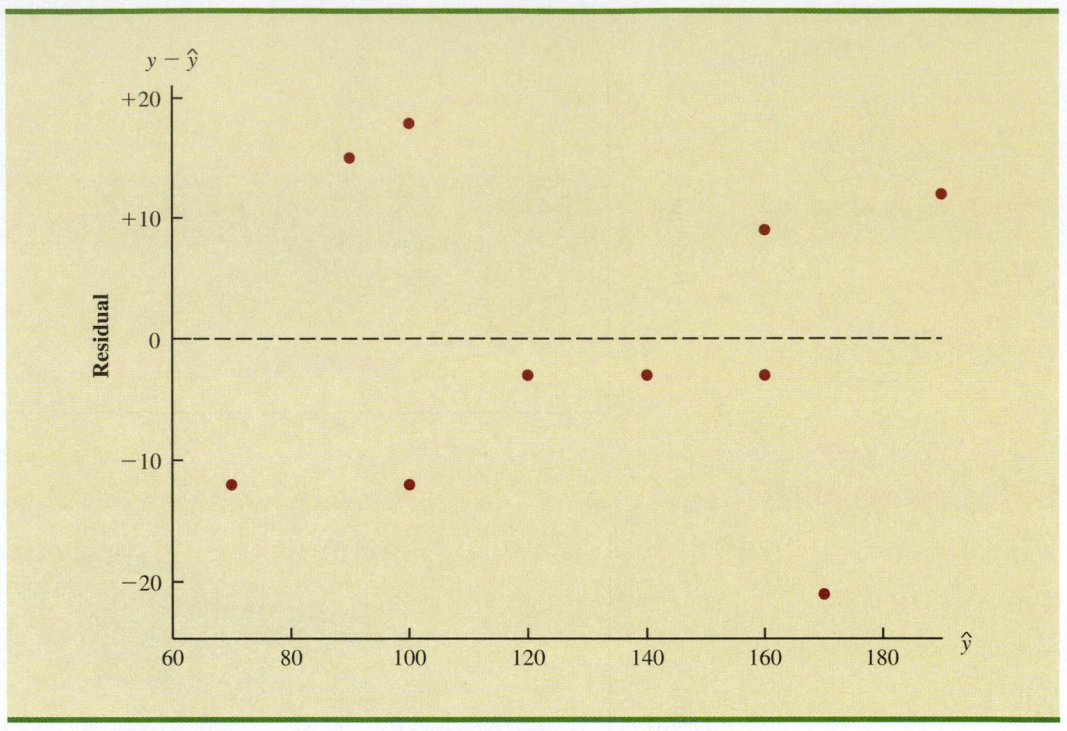

The first coordinate for each point is given by $\hat{y}_i$ and the second coordinate is given by the corresponding value of the ith residual $y_i - \hat{y}_i$. With the Armand's data from Table 14.7, the coordinates of the first point are $(70, -12)$, corresponding to $\hat{y}_1 = 70$ and $y_1 - \hat{y}_1 = -12$; the coordinates of the second point are $(90, 15)$; and so on. Figure 14.17 provides the residual plot. Note that the pattern of this residual plot is the same as the pattern of the residual plot against the independent variable x. It is not a pattern that would lead us to question the model assumptions. For simple linear regression, both the residual plot against x and the residual plot against $\hat{y}$ provide the same pattern. For multiple regression analysis, the residual plot against $\hat{y}$ is more widely used because of the presence of more than one independent variable.

Standardized Residuals

Many of the residual plots provided by computer software packages use a standardized version of the residuals. As demonstrated in preceding chapters, a random variable is standardized by subtracting its mean and dividing the result by its standard deviation. With the least squares method, the mean of the residuals is zero. Thus, simply dividing each residual by its standard deviation provides the **standardized residual**.

It can be shown that the standard deviation of residual i depends on the standard error of the estimate s and the corresponding value of the independent variable x_i.

STANDARD DEVIATION OF THE ith RESIDUAL[2]

$$s_{y_i - \hat{y}_i} = s\sqrt{1 - h_i} \qquad (14.30)$$

---

[2]This equation actually provides an estimate of the standard deviation of the ith residual, because s is used instead of σ.

where

$$s_{y_i - \hat{y}_i} = \text{the standard deviation of residual } i$$

$$s = \text{the standard error of the estimate}$$

$$h_i = \frac{1}{n} + \frac{(x_i - \bar{x})^2}{\sum(x_i - \bar{x})^2} \qquad \textbf{(14.31)}$$

Note that equation (14.30) shows that the standard deviation of the ith residual depends on x_i because of the presence of h_i in the formula.[3] Once the standard deviation of each residual is calculated, we can compute the standardized residual by dividing each residual by its corresponding standard deviation.

STANDARDIZED RESIDUAL FOR OBSERVATION i

$$\frac{y_i - \hat{y}_i}{s_{y_i - \hat{y}_i}} \qquad \textbf{(14.32)}$$

Table 14.8 shows the calculation of the standardized residuals for Armand's Pizza Parlors. Recall that previous calculations showed $s = 13.829$. Figure 14.18 is the plot of the standardized residuals against the independent variable x.

TABLE 14.8 COMPUTATION OF STANDARDIZED RESIDUALS FOR ARMAND'S PIZZA PARLORS

Restaurant i	x_i	$x_i - \bar{x}$	$(x_i - \bar{x})^2$	$\dfrac{(x_i - \bar{x})^2}{\sum(x_i - \bar{x})^2}$	h_i	$s_{y_i - \hat{y}_i}$	$y_i - \hat{y}_i$	Standardized Residual
1	2	−12	144	.2535	.3535	11.1193	−12	−1.0792
2	6	−8	64	.1127	.2127	12.2709	15	1.2224
3	8	−6	36	.0634	.1634	12.6493	−12	−.9487
4	8	−6	36	.0634	.1634	12.6493	18	1.4230
5	12	−2	4	.0070	.1070	13.0682	−3	−.2296
6	16	2	4	.0070	.1070	13.0682	−3	−.2296
7	20	6	36	.0634	.1634	12.6493	−3	−.2372
8	20	6	36	.0634	.1634	12.6493	9	.7115
9	22	8	64	.1127	.2127	12.2709	−21	−1.7114
10	26	12	144	.2535	.3535	11.1193	12	1.0792
		Total	568					

Note: The values of the residuals were computed in Table 14.7.

---

[3] h_i is referred to as the *leverage* of observation i. Leverage will be discussed further when we consider influential observations in Section 14.9.

FIGURE 14.18   PLOT OF THE STANDARDIZED RESIDUALS AGAINST THE
INDEPENDENT VARIABLE x FOR ARMAND'S PIZZA PARLORS

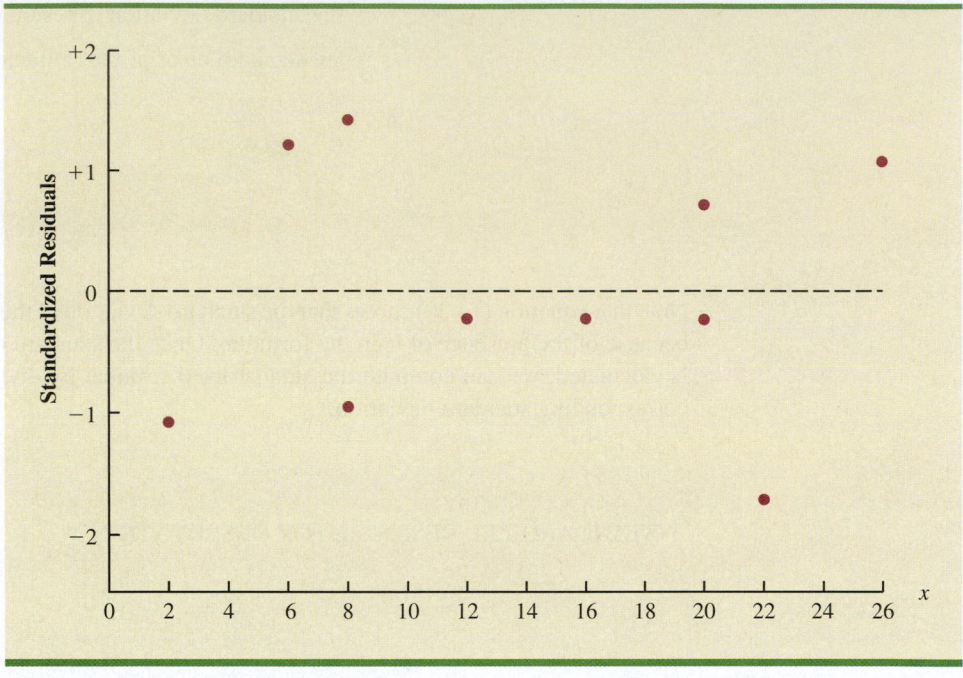

Small departures from normality do not have a great effect on the statistical tests used in regression analysis.

The standardized residual plot can provide insight about the assumption that the error term ϵ has a normal distribution. If this assumption is satisfied, the distribution of the standardized residuals should appear to come from a standard normal probability distribution.[4] Thus, when looking at a standardized residual plot, we should expect to see approximately 95% of the standardized residuals between -2 and $+2$. We see in Figure 14.18 that for the Armand's example all standardized residuals are between -2 and $+2$. Therefore, on the basis of the standardized residuals, this plot gives us no reason to question the assumption that ϵ has a normal distribution.

Because of the effort required to compute the estimated values of $\hat{y}$, the residuals, and the standardized residuals, most statistical packages provide these values as optional regression output. Hence, residual plots can be easily obtained. For large problems computer packages are the only practical means for developing the residual plots discussed in this section.

Using Excel to Construct a Residual Plot

In Section 14.7 we showed how Excel's Regression tool could be used for regression analysis. The Regression tool also provides the capability to obtain a residual plot against the independent variable x and, when used with Excel's chart tools, the Regression tool residual output can also be used to construct a residual plot against $\hat{y}$ as well as an Excel version of a standardized residual plot.

Residual plot against x To obtain a residual plot against x, the steps that we describe in Section 14.7 in order to obtain the regression output are performed with one change.

---

[4]Because s is used instead of σ in equation (14.30), the probability distribution of the standardized residuals is not technically normal. However, in most regression studies, the sample size is large enough that a normal approximation is very good.

FIGURE 14.19   REGRESSION TOOL RESIDUAL OUTPUT FOR THE ARMAND'S PIZZA PARLORS PROBLEM

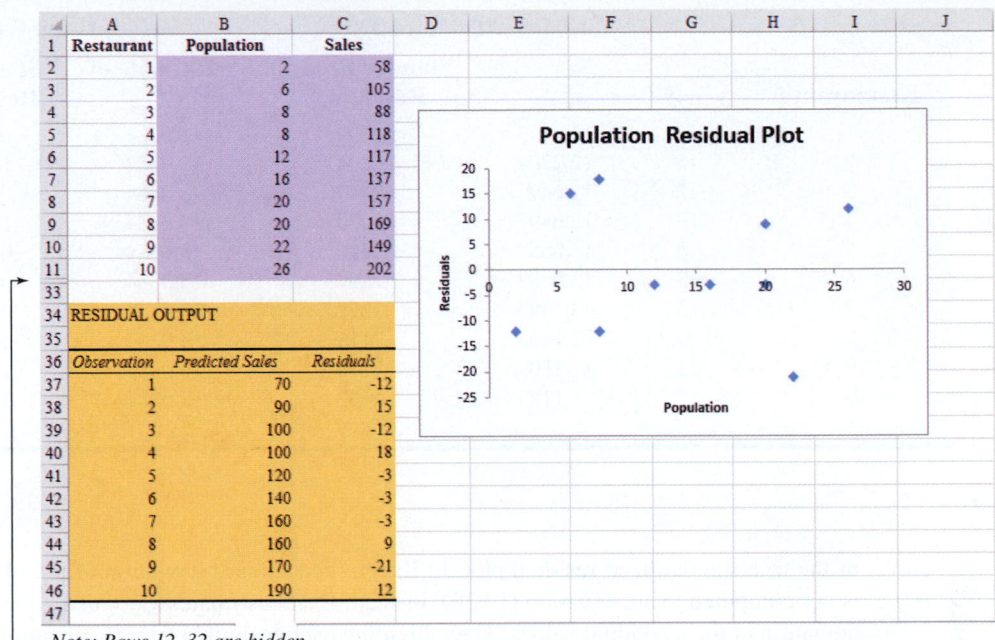

Note: Rows 12–32 are hidden.

When the Regression tool dialog box appears (see Figure 14.13), we must also select the Residual Plots option in the Residual section. The regression output will appear as described previously, and the worksheet will also contain a chart showing a plot of the residuals against the independent variable Population. In addition, a list of predicted values of y and the corresponding residual values are provided below the regression output. Figure 14.19 shows the residual output for the Armand's Pizza Parlors problem; note that rows 12–32, containing the standard Regression tool output, have been hidden to better focus on the residual portion of the output. We see that the shape of this plot is the same as shown previously in Figure 14.15.

Residual plot against $\hat{y}$ Using Excel's chart tools and the residual output provided in Figure 14.19, we can easily construct a residual plot against $\hat{y}$. The following steps describe how to use Excel's chart tools to construct the residual plot using the regression tool output in the worksheet.

> **Step 1.** Select cells B37:C46
> **Step 2.** Click the **Insert** tab on the Ribbon
> **Step 3.** In the **Charts** group, click **Insert Scatter (X, Y) or Bubble Chart**
> **Step 4.** When the list of scatter diagram subtypes appears:
>   Click **Scatter with only Markers** (the chart in the upper left corner)

The resulting chart will look similar to the residual plot shown in Figure 14.17. Adding a chart title, labels for the horizontal and vertical axes, as well as other formatting options can be easily done. Note that except for using different data to construct the chart as well as different labels for the chart output, the steps describing how to use Excel's chart tools to construct a residual plot against $\hat{y}$ are the same as the steps we used to construct a scatter diagram in Section 14.2.

Excel's standardized residual plot   Excel can be used to construct what it calls a standardized residual plot. Excel's standardized residual plot is really an approximation

TABLE 14.9   COMPUTATION OF EXCEL'S STANDARD RESIDUALS

		Values from Table 14.8		Values Using Excel	
Restaurant i	$y_i - \hat{y}$	$s_{y_i - \hat{y}_i}$	Standardized Residual	Estimate of $s_{y_i - \hat{y}_i}$	Standard Residual
1	−12	11.1193	−1.0792	13.0384	−0.9204
2	15	12.2709	1.2224	13.0384	1.1504
3	−12	12.6493	−.9487	13.0384	−0.9204
4	18	12.6493	1.4230	13.0384	1.3805
5	−3	13.0682	−.2296	13.0384	−0.2301
6	−3	13.0682	−.2296	13.0384	−0.2301
7	−3	12.6493	−.2372	13.0384	−0.2301
8	9	12.6493	.7115	13.0384	0.6903
9	−21	12.2709	−1.7114	13.0384	−1.6106
10	12	11.1193	1.0792	13.0384	0.9204

of the true standardized residual plot. In Excel, the standard deviation of the ith residual is not computed using equation (14.30). Instead, Excel estimates $s_{y_i - \hat{y}_i}$ using the standard deviation of the n residual values. Then, dividing each residual by this estimate, Excel obtains what it refers to as a standard residual. The plot of these standard residuals is what you get when you request a plot of the standardized residuals using Excel's Regression tool.

We will illustrate how to construct a standardized residual plot using Excel for the Armand's Pizza Parlors problem. The residuals for the Armand's Pizza Parlors problem are −12, 15, −12, 18, −3, −3, −3, 9, −21, and 12. Using Excel's STDEV.S function, we computed a standard deviation of 13.0384 for these 10 data values. To compute the standard residuals, Excel divides each residual by 13.0384; the results are shown in Table 14.9. Both the standardized residuals, computed in Table 14.8, and Excel's standard residuals are shown. There is not a great deal of difference between Excel's standard residuals and the true standardized residuals. In general, the differences get smaller as the sample size increases. Often we are interested only in identifying the general pattern of the points in a standardized residual plot; in such cases, the small differences between the standardized residuals and Excel's standard residuals will have little effect on the pattern observed. Thus these differences will not influence the conclusions reached when we use the residual plot to validate model assumptions.

The Regression tool and the chart tools can be used to obtain Excel's standardized residual plot. First, the steps that we described in Section 14.7 in order to conduct a regression analysis are performed with one change. When the Regression dialog box appears (see Figure 14.13), we must select the Standardized Residuals option. In addition to the regression output described previously, the output will contain a list of predicted values of y, residuals, and standard residuals, as shown in cells A34:D46 in Figure 14.20.

The Standardized Residuals option does not automatically produce a standardized residual plot. But we can use Excel's chart tools to construct a scatter diagram in which the values of the independent variable are placed on the horizontal axis and the values of the standard residuals are placed on the vertical axis. The procedure that describes how to use Excel's chart tools to construct a standardized residual plot is similar to the steps we showed for using Excel's chart tools to construct a residual plot against $\hat{y}$. Because Excel requires

FIGURE 14.20   STANDARDIZED RESIDUAL PLOT AGAINST THE INDEPENDENT VARIABLE
POPULATION FOR THE ARMAND'S PIZZA PARLORS EXAMPLE

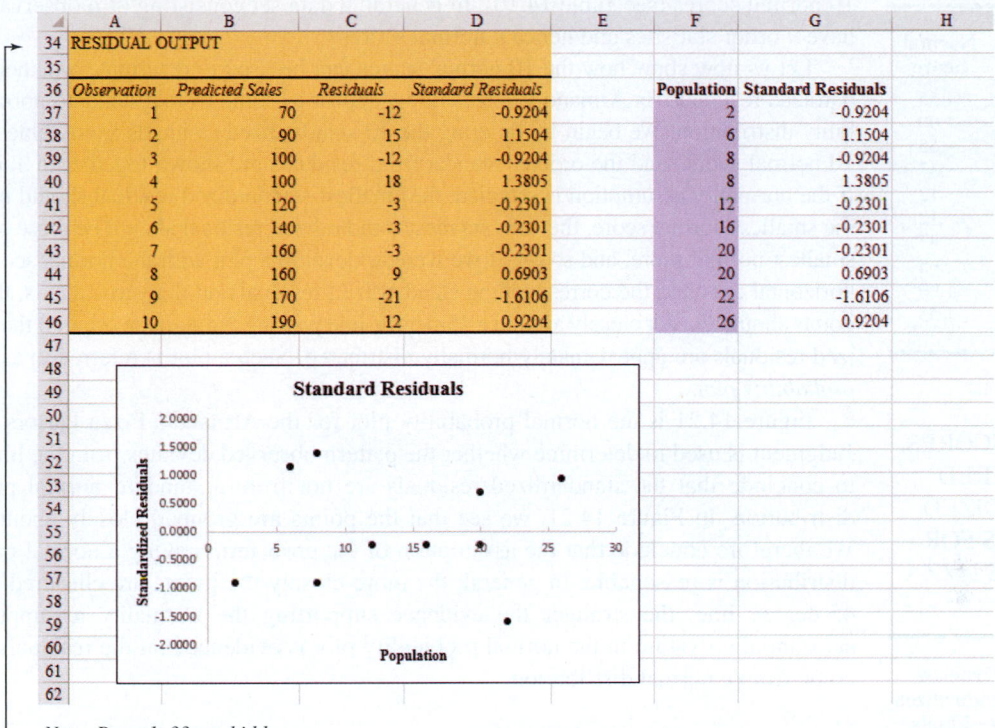

Note: Rows 1–33 are hidden.

that the two variables being plotted be located in adjacent columns of the worksheet, we copied the data and heading for the independent variable Population into cells F36:F46 and the data and heading for the standard residuals into cells G36:G46.

Using the data in cells F36:G46 and Excel's chart tools we obtained the scatter diagram shown in Figure 14.20; this scatter diagram is Excel's version of the standardized residual plot for the Armand's Pizza Parlors example. Comparing Excel's version of the standardized residual plot to the standardized residual plot in Figure 14.17, we see the same pattern evident. All of the standardized residuals in both figures are between −2 and +2, indicating no reason to question the assumption that ϵ has a normal distribution.

Normal Probability Plot

Another approach for determining the validity of the assumption that the error term has a normal distribution is the **normal probability plot**. To show how a normal probability plot is developed, we introduce the concept of *normal scores*.

Suppose 10 values are selected randomly from a normal probability distribution with a mean of zero and a standard deviation of one, and that the sampling process is repeated over and over with the values in each sample of 10 ordered from smallest to largest. For now, let us consider only the smallest value in each sample. The random variable representing the smallest value obtained in repeated sampling is called the first-order statistic.

TABLE 14.10

NORMAL SCORES
FOR $n = 10$

Order Statistic	Normal Score
1	−1.55
2	−1.00
3	−.65
4	−.37
5	−.12
6	.12
7	.37
8	.65
9	1.00
10	1.55

TABLE 14.11

NORMAL SCORES
AND ORDERED
STANDARDIZED
RESIDUALS FOR
ARMAND'S PIZZA
PARLORS

Normal Scores	Ordered Standardized Residuals
−1.55	−1.7114
−1.00	−1.0792
−.65	−.9487
−.37	−.2372
−.12	−.2296
.12	−.2296
.37	.7115
.65	1.0792
1.00	1.2224
1.55	1.4230

Statisticians show that for samples of size 10 from a standard normal probability distribution, the expected value of the first-order statistic is −1.55. This expected value is called a normal score. For the case with a sample of size $n = 10$, there are 10 order statistics and 10 normal scores (see Table 14.10). In general, a data set consisting of n observations will have n order statistics and hence n normal scores.

Let us now show how the 10 normal scores can be used to determine whether the standardized residuals for Armand's Pizza Parlors appear to come from a standard normal probability distribution. We begin by ordering the 10 standardized residuals from Table 14.8. The 10 normal scores and the ordered standardized residuals are shown together in Table 14.11. If the normality assumption is satisfied, the smallest standardized residual should be close to the smallest normal score, the next smallest standardized residual should be close to the next smallest normal score, and so on. If we were to develop a plot with the normal scores on the horizontal axis and the corresponding standardized residuals on the vertical axis, the plotted points should cluster closely around a 45-degree line passing through the origin if the standardized residuals are approximately normally distributed. Such a plot is referred to as a *normal probability plot*.

Figure 14.21 is the normal probability plot for the Armand's Pizza Parlors example. Judgment is used to determine whether the pattern observed deviates from the line enough to conclude that the standardized residuals are not from a standard normal probability distribution. In Figure 14.21, we see that the points are grouped closely about the line. We therefore conclude that the assumption of the error term having a normal probability distribution is reasonable. In general, the more closely the points are clustered about the 45-degree line, the stronger the evidence supporting the normality assumption. Any substantial curvature in the normal probability plot is evidence that the residuals have not come from a normal distribution.

FIGURE 14.21   NORMAL PROBABILITY PLOT FOR ARMAND'S PIZZA PARLORS

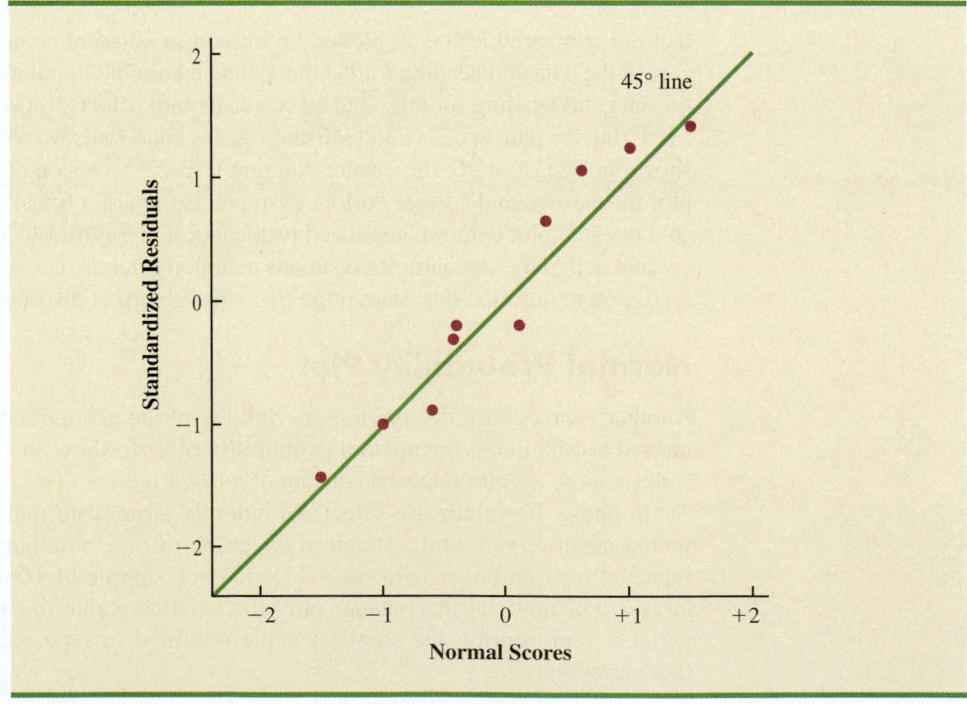

NOTES AND COMMENTS

1. We use residual and normal probability plots to validate the assumptions of a regression model. If our review indicates that one or more assumptions are questionable, a different regression model or a transformation of the data should be considered. The appropriate corrective action when the assumptions are violated must be based on good judgment; recommendations from an experienced statistician can be valuable.

2. Analysis of residuals is the primary method statisticians use to verify that the assumptions associated with a regression model are valid. Even if no violations are found, it does not necessarily follow that the model will yield good predictions. However, if additional statistical tests support the conclusion of significance and the coefficient of determination is large, we should be able to develop good estimates and predictions using the estimated regression equation.

Exercises

Methods

45. Given are data for two variables, x and y.

x_i	6	11	15	18	20
y_i	6	8	12	20	30

a. Develop an estimated regression equation for these data.
b. Compute the residuals.
c. Develop a plot of the residuals against the independent variable x. Do the assumptions about the error terms seem to be satisfied?
d. Compute the standardized residuals.
e. Develop a plot of the standardized residuals against $\hat{y}$. What conclusions can you draw from this plot?

Observation	x_i	y_i	Observation	x_i	y_i
1	2	4	6	7	6
2	3	5	7	7	9
3	4	4	8	8	5
4	5	6	9	9	11
5	7	4			

46. The following data were used in a regression study.
a. Develop an estimated regression equation for these data.
b. Construct a plot of the residuals. Do the assumptions about the error term seem to be satisfied?

Applications

47. Data on advertising expenditures and revenue (in thousands of dollars) for the Four Seasons Restaurant follow.

Advertising Expenditures	Revenue
1	19
2	32
4	44
6	40
10	52
14	53
20	54

a. Let x equal advertising expenditures and y equal revenue. Use the method of least squares to develop a straight line approximation of the relationship between the two variables.

b. Test whether revenue and advertising expenditures are related at a .05 level of significance.

c. Prepare a residual plot of $y - \hat{y}$ versus $\hat{y}$. Use the result from part (a) to obtain the values of $\hat{y}$.

d. What conclusions can you draw from residual analysis? Should this model be used, or should we look for a better one?

48. Refer to exercise 7, where an estimated regression equation relating years of experience and annual sales was developed.

a. Compute the residuals and construct a residual plot for this problem.

b. Do the assumptions about the error terms seem reasonable in light of the residual plot?

CostLiving

49. The DATAfile named *CostLiving* contains the cost of living indexes and the population densities (number of people per square mile) for 61 cities in the United States. The cost of living index measures the cost of living in a particular city relative to the cost of living in New York City. San Francisco has an index of 112.15, meaning that is 12.15% more expensive to live in San Francisco than New York City. Washington DC has an index of 84.64, which means that the cost to live in Washington DC is only 84.64% of what it costs to live in New York City (Numbeo website, July 13, 2016).

a. Develop the estimated regression equation that can be used to predict the cost of living index for a U.S. city, given the city's population density.

b. Construct a residual plot against the independent variable.

c. Review the residual plot constructed in part (b). Do the assumptions of the error term and model form seem reasonable?

Outliers and Influential Observations

In this section we discuss how to identify observations that can be classified as outliers or as being especially influential in determining the estimated regression equation. Some steps that should be taken when such observations are identified are provided.

Detecting Outliers

An **outlier** is a data point (observation) that does not fit the trend shown by the remaining data. Outliers represent observations that are suspect and warrant careful examination. They may represent erroneous data; if so, they should be corrected. They may signal a violation of model assumptions; if so, another model should be considered.

x_i	y_i
1	45
1	55
2	50
3	75
3	40
3	45
4	30
4	35
5	25
6	15

Finally, they may simply be unusual values that have occurred by chance. In this case, they should be retained.

To illustrate the process of detecting outliers, consider the data set in Table 14.12; Figure 14.22 shows the scatter diagram for these data and a portion of the Regression tool output, including the tabular residual output obtained using the Standardized Residuals option. The estimated regression equation is $\hat{y} = 64.95 - 7.330x$ and R Square is .4968; thus, only 49.68% of the variability in the values of y is explained by the estimated regression equation. However, except for observation 4 ($x_4 = 3$, $y_4 = 75$), a pattern suggesting a strong negative linear relationship is apparent. Indeed, given the pattern of the rest of the data, we would have expected y_4 to be much smaller and hence would consider observation 4 to be an outlier. For the case of simple linear regression, one can often detect outliers by simply examining the scatter diagram.

The standardized residuals can also be used to identify outliers. If an observation deviates greatly from the pattern of the rest of the data, the corresponding standardized residual will be large in absolute value. We recommend considering any observation with a standardized residual of less than -2 or greater than $+2$ as an outlier. With normally distributed errors, standardized residuals should be outside these limits approximately 5% of the time. In the residual output section of Figure 14.22 we see that the standard residual value for observation 4 is 2.68; this value suggests we treat observation 4 as an outlier.

FIGURE 14.22   REGRESSION TOOL OUTPUT FOR THE OUTLIER DATA SET

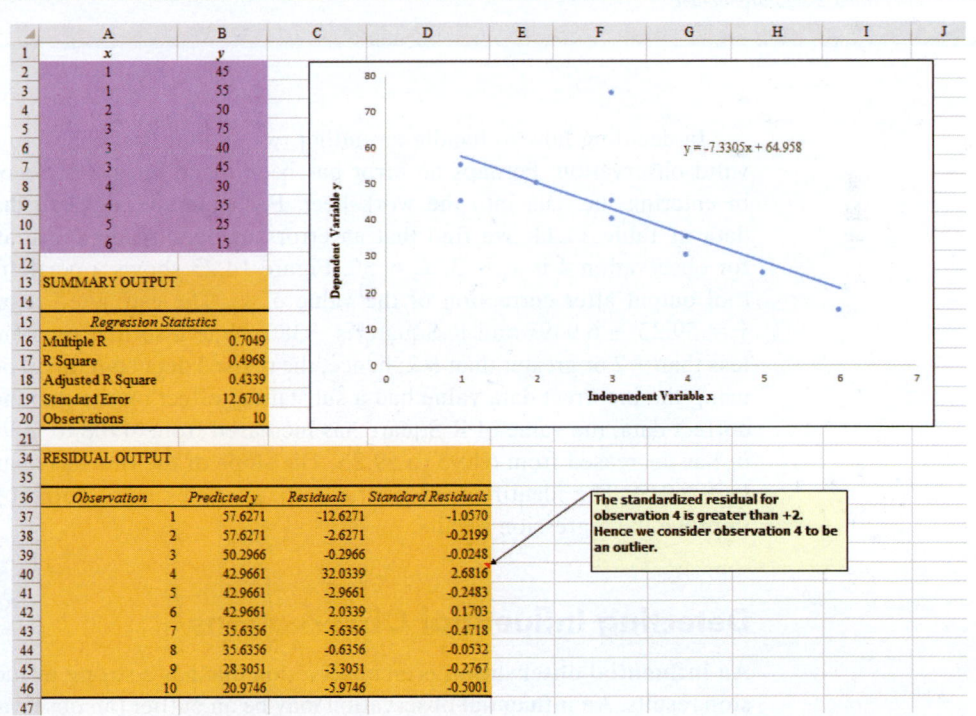

Note: Rows 22–33 are hidden.

FIGURE 14.23   REGRESSION TOOL OUTPUT FOR THE REVISED OUTLIER DATA SET

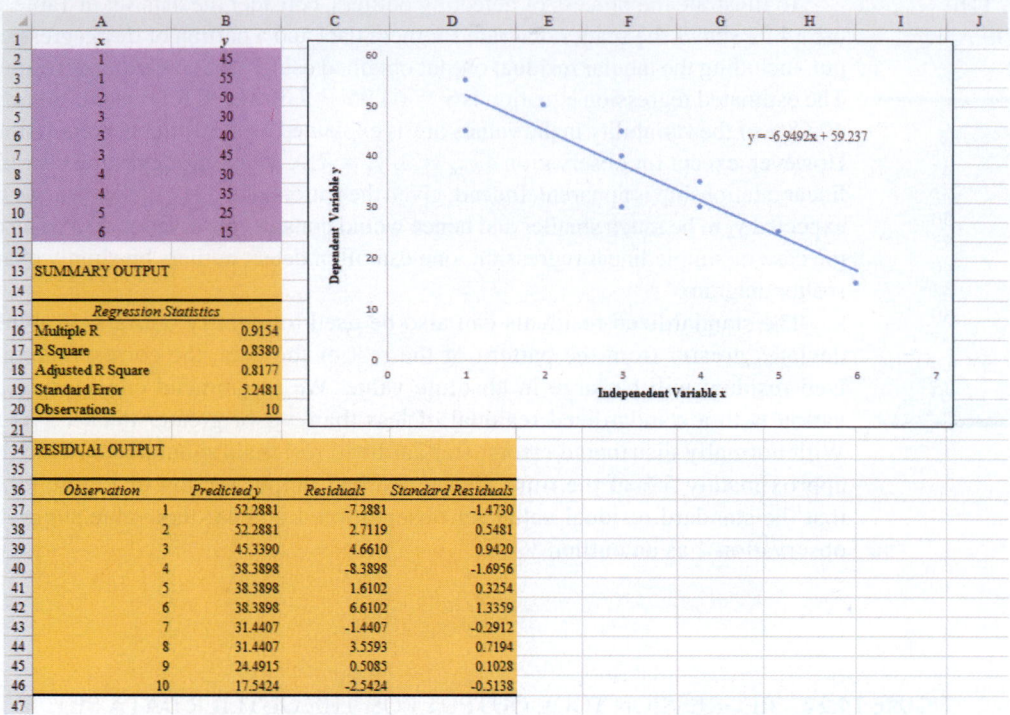

Note: Rows 22–33 are hidden.

In deciding how to handle an outlier, we should first check to see whether it is a valid observation. Perhaps an error has been made in initially recording the data or in entering the data into the worksheet. For example, suppose that in checking the data in Table 14.11, we find that an error has been made and that the correct value for observation 4 is $x_4 = 3$, $y_4 = 30$. Figure 14.23 shows a portion of the Regression tool output after correction of the value of y_4. The estimated regression equation is $\hat{y} = 59.23 - 6.949x$ and R Square is .8380. Note also that no standard residuals are less than -2 or greater than $+2$; hence, the revised data contain no outliers. We see that using the incorrect data value had a substantial effect on the goodness of fit. With the correct data, the value of R Square has increased from .4968 to .8380 and the value of b_0 has decreased from 64.95 to 59.23. The slope of the line has changed from -7.330 to -6.949. The identification of the outlier enables us to correct the data error and improve the regression results.

Detecting Influential Observations

An **influential observation** is an observation that has a strong influence on the regression results. An influential observation may be an outlier (an observation with a y value that deviates substantially from the trend of the remaining data), it may correspond to an x value far from its mean (extreme x value), or it may be caused by a combination of a somewhat off-trend y value and a somewhat extreme x value. Because influential observations may have such a dramatic effect on the estimated regression equation,

TABLE 14.13

DATA SET ILLUSTRATING THE EFFECT OF AN INFLUENTIAL OBSERVATION

x_i	y_i
10	125
10	130
15	120
20	115
20	120
25	110
70	100

they must be examined carefully. First, we should check to make sure no error has been made in collecting or recording the data. If such an error has occurred, it can be corrected and a new estimated regression equation developed. If the observation is valid, we might consider ourselves fortunate to have it. Such a point, if valid, can contribute to a better understanding of the appropriate model and can lead to a better estimated regression equation.

To illustrate the process of detecting influential observations, consider the data set in Table 14.13. The top part of Figure 14.24 shows the scatter diagram for these data and the graph of the corresponding estimated regression equation $\hat{y} = 127.4 - .425x$. The bottom part of Figure 14.24 shows the scatter diagram for the data in Table 14.13 with observation 7 ($x_7 = 70$, $y_7 = 100$) deleted; for these data the estimated regression equation is $\hat{y} = 138.1 - 1.090x$. With observation 7 deleted, the value of b_0 has increased from 127.4 to 138.1. The slope of the line has changed from -0.425 to -1.090. The effect of observation 7 on the regression results is dramatic and is confirmed by looking at the graphs of the two estimated regression equations. Clearly observation 7 is influential.

Observations with extreme values for the independent variables are called **high leverage points**. Observation 7 in the data set shown in Table 14.13 (which we have identified as being influential) is a point with high leverage. The leverage of an observation is determined by how far the value of the independent variable is from its mean value. For the

FIGURE 14.24   SCATTER DIAGRAMS FOR THE DATA SET WITH AN INFLUENTIAL OBSERVATION

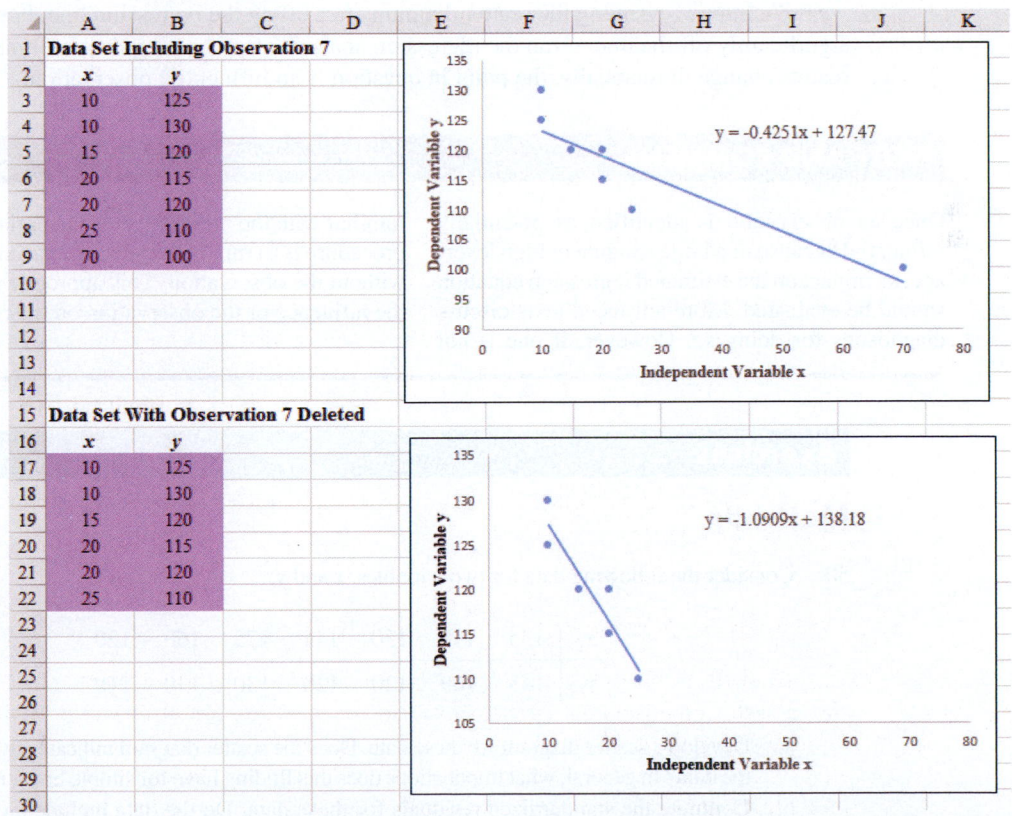

single-independent-variable case, the leverage of the ith observation, denoted h_i, can be computed using equation (14.33).

> **LEVERAGE OF OBSERVATION i**
>
> $$h_i = \frac{1}{n} + \frac{(x_i - \bar{x})^2}{\sum(x_i - \bar{x})^2} \qquad\qquad \textbf{(14.33)}$$

From the formula, it is clear that the farther x_i is from its mean $\bar{x}$, the higher the leverage of observation i. For the data in Table 14.13, the leverage of observation 7 is computed using equation (14.33) as follows:

$$h_i = \frac{1}{n} + \frac{(x_i - \bar{x})^2}{\sum(x_i - \bar{x})^2} = \frac{1}{7} + \frac{(70 - 24.286)^2}{2621.43} = .94$$

For simple linear regression, we consider observations as having high leverage if $h_i > 6/n$; for the data in Table 14.13, $6/n = 6/7 = .86$. Thus, because $h_i = .94 > .86$, observation 7 would be identified as having high leverage. Data points having high leverage are often influential. Influential observations that are caused by an interaction of somewhat large residuals and somewhat high leverage can be difficult to detect. Diagnostic procedures are available that take both into account in determining when an observation is influential. More advanced books on regression analysis discuss the use of such procedures. Excel does not have built-in capabilities for identifying outliers and high leverage points. Thus, we recommend reviewing the scatter diagram after fitting the regression line. For any point significantly off the line, rerun the regression analysis after deleting the observation. If the results change dramatically, the point in question is an influential observation.

NOTE AND COMMENT

Once an observation is identified as potentially influential because of a large residual or high leverage, its impact on the estimated regression equation should be evaluated. More advanced texts discuss diagnostics for doing so. However, if one is not familiar with the more advanced material, a simple procedure is to run the regression analysis with and without the observation. This approach will reveal the influence of the observation on the results.

Exercises

Methods

50. Consider the following data for two variables, x and y.

x_i	135	110	130	145	175	160	120
y_i	145	100	120	120	130	130	110

a. Develop a scatter diagram for these data. Does the scatter diagram indicate any outliers in the data? In general, what implications does this finding have for simple linear regression?

b. Compute the standardized residuals for these data. Do the data include any outliers? Explain.

51. Consider the following data for two variables, x and y.

x_i	4	5	7	8	10	12	12	22
y_i	12	14	16	15	18	20	24	19

a. Develop a scatter diagram for these data. Does the scatter diagram indicate any influential observations? Explain.
b. Compute the standardized residuals for these data. Do the data include any outliers? Explain.
c. Compute the leverage values for these data. Does there appear to be any influential observations in these data? Explain.

Applications

52. Charity Navigator is America's leading independent charity evaluator. The following data show the total expenses ($), the percentage of the total budget spent on administrative expenses, the percentage spent on fundraising, and the percentage spent on program expenses for 10 supersized charities (Charity Navigator website, April 12, 2012). Administrative expenses include overhead, administrative staff and associated costs, and organizational meetings. Fundraising expenses are what a charity spends to raise money, and program expenses are what the charity spends on the programs and services it exists to deliver. The sum of the three percentages does not add to 100% because of rounding.

DATA file

Charities

Charity	Total Expenses ($)	Administrative Expenses (%)	Fundraising Expenses (%)	Program Expenses (%)
American Red Cross	3,354,177,445	3.9	3.8	92.1
World Vision	1,205,887,020	4.0	7.5	88.3
Smithsonian Institution	1,080,995,083	23.5	2.6	73.7
Food For The Poor	1,050,829,851	.7	2.4	96.8
American Cancer Society	1,003,781,897	6.1	22.2	71.6
Volunteers of America	929,158,968	8.6	1.9	89.4
Dana-Farber Cancer Institute	877,321,613	13.1	1.6	85.2
AmeriCares	854,604,824	.4	.7	98.8
ALSAC—St. Jude Children's Research Hospital	829,662,076	9.6	16.9	73.4
City of Hope	736,176,619	13.7	3.0	83.1

a. Develop a scatter diagram with fundraising expenses (%) on the horizontal axis and program expenses (%) on the vertical axis. Looking at the data, do there appear to be any outliers and/or influential observations?
b. Develop an estimated regression equation that could be used to predict program expenses (%) given fundraising expenses (%).
c. Does the value for the slope of the estimated regression equation make sense in the context of this problem situation?
d. Use residual analysis to determine whether any outliers and/or influential observations are present. Briefly summarize your findings and conclusions.

53. Many countries, especially those in Europe, have significant gold holdings. But many of these countries also have massive debts. The following data show the total value of gold holdings in billions of U.S. dollars and the debt as a percentage of the gross domestic product for nine countries (WordPress and Trading Economics websites, February 24, 2012).

GoldHoldings

Country	Gold Value ($ billions)	Debt (% of GDP)
China	63	17.7
France	146	81.7
Germany	203	83.2
Indonesia	33	69.2
Italy	147	119.0
Netherlands	36	63.7
Russia	50	9.9
Switzerland	62	55.0
United States	487	93.2

a. Develop a scatter diagram for the total value of a country's gold holdings ($ billions) as the independent variable.

b. What does the scatter diagram developed in part (a) indicate about the relationship between the two variables? Does there appear to be any outliers and/or influential observations? Explain.

c. Using the entire data set, develop the estimated regression equation that can be used to predict the debt of a country given the total value of its gold holdings.

d. Suppose that after looking at the scatter diagram in part (a) that you were able to visually identify what appears to be an influential observation. Drop this observation from the data set and fit an estimated regression equation to the remaining data. Compare the estimated slope for the new estimated regression equation to the estimated slope obtained in part (c). Does this approach confirm the conclusion you reached in part (d)? Explain.

54. The following data show the annual revenue ($ millions) and the estimated team value ($ millions) for the 30 Major League Baseball teams (*Forbes* website, January 16, 2014).

MLBValues

Team	Revenue ($ millions)	Value ($ millions)
Arizona Diamondbacks	195	584
Atlanta Braves	225	629
Baltimore Orioles	206	618
Boston Red Sox	336	1312
Chicago Cubs	274	1000
Chicago White Sox	216	692
Cincinnati Reds	202	546
Cleveland Indians	186	559
Colorado Rockies	199	537
Detroit Tigers	238	643
Houston Astros	196	626
Kansas City Royals	169	457
Los Angeles Angels of Anaheim	239	718
Los Angeles Dodgers	245	1615
Miami Marlins	195	520
Milwaukee Brewers	201	562
Minnesota Twins	214	578
New York Mets	232	811
New York Yankees	471	2300
Oakland Athletics	173	468
Philadelphia Phillies	279	893

Team	Revenue ($ millions)	Value ($ millions)
Pittsburgh Pirates	178	479
San Diego Padres	189	600
San Francisco Giants	262	786
Seattle Mariners	215	644
St. Louis Cardinals	239	716
Tampa Bay Rays	167	451
Texas Rangers	239	764
Toronto Blue Jays	203	568
Washington Nationals	225	631

a.   Develop a scatter diagram with Revenue on the horizontal axis and Value on the vertical axis. Looking at the scatter diagram, does it appear that there are any outliers and/ or influential observations in the data?

b.   Develop the estimated regression equation that can be used to predict team value given the value of annual revenue.

c.   Use residual analysis to determine whether any outliers and/or influential observations are present. Briefly summarize your findings and conclusions.

14.10 Practical Advice: Big Data and Hypothesis Testing in Simple Linear Regression

In Chapter 7, we observed that the standard errors of the sampling distributions of the sample mean $\bar{x}$ (shown in formula 7.2) and the sample proportion of $\bar{p}$ (shown in formula 7.5) decrease as the sample size increases. In Chapters 8 and 9, we observed that this results in narrower confidence interval estimates for μ and p and smaller p-values for the tests of the hypotheses H_0: $\mu \leq \mu_0$ and H_0: $p \leq p_0$ as the sample size increases. These results extend to simple linear regression. In simple linear regression, as the sample size increases,

- the p-value for the t-test used to determine whether a significant relationship exists between the dependent variable and the independent decreases;
- the confidence interval for the slope parameter associated with the independent variable narrows;
- the confidence interval for the mean value of y narrows;
- the prediction interval for an individual value of y narrows.

Thus, we are more likely to reject the hypothesis that a relationship does not exist between the dependent variable and the independent variable and conclude that a relationship exists as the sample size increases. The interval estimates for the slope parameter associated with the independent variable, the mean value of y, and predicted individual value of y will become more precise as the sample size increases. But this does not necessarily mean that these results become more reliable as the sample size increases.

No matter how large the sample used to estimate the simple linear regression equation, we must be concerned about the potential presence of nonsampling error in the data. It is important to carefully consider whether a random sample of the population of interest has actually been taken. If the data to be used for testing the hypothesis of no relationship between the independent and dependent variable are corrupted by nonsampling error, the likelihood of making a Type I or Type II error may be higher than if the sample data are free of nonsampling error. If the relationship between the independent and dependent variable is statistically significant, it is also important to consider whether the relationship in the simple linear regression equation is of *practical* significance.

Although simple linear regression is an extremely powerful statistical tool, it provides evidence that should be considered only in combination with information collected from other sources to make the most informed decision possible. No business decision should be based exclusively on inference in simple linear regression. Nonsampling error may lead to misleading results, and practical significance should always be considered in conjunction with statistical significance. This is particularly important when a hypothesis test is based on an extremely large sample because *p*-values in such cases can be extremely small. When executed properly, inference based on simple linear regression can be an important component in the business decision-making process.

Summary

In this chapter we showed how regression analysis can be used to determine how a dependent variable y is related to an independent variable x. In simple linear regression, the regression model is $y = \beta_0 + \beta_1 x + \epsilon$. The simple linear regression equation $E(y) = \beta_0 + \beta_1 x$ describes how the mean or expected value of y is related to x. We used sample data and the least squares method to develop the estimated regression equation $\hat{y} = b_0 + b_1 x$. In effect, b_0 and b_1 are the sample statistics used to estimate the unknown model parameters β_0 and β_1.

The coefficient of determination was presented as a measure of the goodness of fit for the estimated regression equation; it can be interpreted as the proportion of the variation in the dependent variable y that can be explained by the estimated regression equation. We reviewed correlation as a descriptive measure of the strength of a linear relationship between two variables.

The assumptions about the regression model and its associated error term ϵ were discussed, and t and F tests, based on those assumptions, were presented as a means for determining whether the relationship between two variables is statistically significant. We showed how to use the estimated regression equation to develop confidence interval estimates of the mean value of y and prediction interval estimates of individual values of y.

The computer solution of regression problems and the use of residual analysis to validate the model assumptions and to identify outliers and influential observations were discussed. In the final section, we discussed the impact of big data on interpreting hypothesis tests in simple linear regression.

Glossary

ANOVA table The analysis of variance table used to summarize the computations associated with the F test for significance.

Coefficient of determination A measure of the goodness of fit of the estimated regression equation. It can be interpreted as the proportion of the variability in the dependent variable y that is explained by the estimated regression equation.

Confidence interval The interval estimate of the mean value of y for a given value of x.

Correlation coefficient A measure of the strength of the linear relationship between two variables (previously discussed in Chapter 3).

Dependent variable The variable that is being predicted or explained. It is denoted by y.

Estimated regression equation The estimate of the regression equation developed from sample data by using the least squares method. For simple linear regression, the estimated regression equation is $\hat{y} = b_0 + b_1 x$.

High leverage points Observations with extreme values for the independent variables.

Independent variable The variable that is doing the predicting or explaining. It is denoted by x.

Influential observation An observation that has a strong influence or effect on the regression results.

ith residual The difference between the observed value of the dependent variable and the value predicted using the estimated regression equation; for the ith observation the ith residual is $y_i - \hat{y}_i$.

Least squares method A procedure used to develop the estimated regression equation. The objective is to minimize $\sum(y_i - \hat{y}_i)^2$.

Mean square error The unbiased estimate of the variance of the error term σ^2. It is denoted by MSE or s^2.

Normal probability plot A graph of the standardized residuals plotted against values of the normal scores. This plot helps determine whether the assumption that the error term has a normal probability distribution appears to be valid.

Outlier A data point or observation that does not fit the trend shown by the remaining data.

Prediction interval The interval estimate of an individual value of y for a given value of x.

Regression equation The equation that describes how the mean or expected value of the dependent variable is related to the independent variable; in simple linear regression, $E(y) = \beta_0 + \beta_1 x$.

Regression model The equation that describes how y is related to x and an error term; in simple linear regression, the regression model is $y = \beta_0 + \beta_1 x + \epsilon$.

Residual analysis The analysis of the residuals used to determine whether the assumptions made about the regression model appear to be valid. Residual analysis is also used to identify outliers and influential observations.

Residual plot Graphical representation of the residuals that can be used to determine whether the assumptions made about the regression model appear to be valid.

Scatter diagram A graph of bivariate data in which the independent variable is on the horizontal axis and the dependent variable is on the vertical axis.

Simple linear regression Regression analysis involving one independent variable and one dependent variable in which the relationship between the variables is approximated by a straight line.

Standard error of the estimate The square root of the mean square error, denoted by s. It is the estimate of σ, the standard deviation of the error term ϵ.

Standardized residual The value obtained by dividing a residual by its standard deviation.

Key Formulas

Simple Linear Regression Model

$$y = \beta_0 + \beta_1 x + \epsilon \tag{14.1}$$

Simple Linear Regression Equation

$$E(y) = \beta_0 + \beta_1 x \tag{14.2}$$

Estimated Simple Linear Regression Equation

$$\hat{y} = b_0 + b_1 x \tag{14.3}$$

Least Squares Criterion

$$\min \sum(y_i - \hat{y}_i)^2 \tag{14.5}$$

Slope and y-Intercept for the Estimated Regression Equation

$$b_1 = \frac{\sum(x_i - \bar{x})(y_i - \bar{y})}{\sum(x_i - \bar{x})^2}$$
(14.6)

$$b_0 = \bar{y} - b_1\bar{x}$$
(14.7)

Sum of Squares Due to Error

$$SSE = \sum(y_i - \hat{y}_i)^2$$
(14.8)

Total Sum of Squares

$$SST = \sum(y_i - \bar{y})^2$$
(14.9)

Sum of Squares Due to Regression

$$SSR = \sum(\hat{y}_i - \bar{y})^2$$
(14.10)

Relationship Among SST, SSR, and SSE

$$SST = SSR + SSE$$
(14.11)

Coefficient of Determination

$$r^2 = \frac{SSR}{SST}$$
(14.12)

Sample Correlation Coefficient

$$r_{xy} = (\text{sign of } b_1)\sqrt{\text{Coefficient of determination}}$$
$$= (\text{sign of } b_1)\sqrt{r^2}$$
(14.13)

Mean Square Error (Estimate of σ^2)

$$s^2 = MSE = \frac{SSE}{n - 2}$$
(14.15)

Standard Error of the Estimate

$$s = \sqrt{MSE} = \sqrt{\frac{SSE}{n - 2}}$$
(14.16)

Standard Deviation of b_1

$$\sigma_{b_1} = \frac{\sigma}{\sqrt{\sum(x_i - \bar{x})^2}}$$
(14.17)

Estimated Standard Deviation of b_1

$$s_{b_1} = \frac{s}{\sqrt{\sum(x_i - \bar{x})^2}}$$
(14.18)

t Test Statistic

$$t = \frac{b_1}{s_{b_1}}$$
(14.19)

Mean Square Regression

$$MSR = \frac{SSR}{Number\ of\ independent\ variables}$$
(14.20)

F Test Statistic

$$F = \frac{MSR}{MSE}$$
(14.21)

Estimated Standard Deviation of $\hat{y}^*$

$$s_{\hat{y}^*} = s\sqrt{\frac{1}{n} + \frac{(x^* - \bar{x})^2}{\sum(x_i - \bar{x})^2}}$$
(14.23)

Confidence Interval for $E(y^*)$

$$\hat{y}^* \pm t_{\alpha/2}s_{\hat{y}^*}$$
(14.24)

Estimated Standard Deviation of an Individual Value

$$s_{pred} = s\sqrt{1 + \frac{1}{n} + \frac{(x^* - \bar{x})^2}{\sum(x_i - \bar{x})^2}}$$
(14.26)

Prediction Interval for y^*

$$\hat{y}^* \pm t_{\alpha/2}s_{pred}$$
(14.27)

Residual for Observation i

$$y_i - \hat{y}_i$$
(14.28)

Standard Deviation of the ith Residual

$$s_{y_i - \hat{y}_i} = s\sqrt{1 - h_i}$$
(14.30)

Standardized Residual for Observation i

$$\frac{y_i - \hat{y}_i}{s_{y_i - \hat{y}_i}}$$
(14.32)

Leverage of Observation i

$$h_i = \frac{1}{n} + \frac{(x_i - \bar{x})^2}{\sum(x_i - \bar{x})^2}$$
(14.33)

Supplementary Exercises

55. The Dow Jones Industrial Average (DJIA) and the Standard & Poor's 500 (S&P 500) indexes are used as measures of overall movement in the stock market. The DJIA is based on the price movements of 30 large companies; the S&P 500 is an index composed of 500 stocks. Some say the S&P 500 is a better measure of stock market performance because it is broader based. The closing price for the DJIA and the S&P 500 for 15 weeks, beginning with January 6, 2012, follow (*Barron's* website, April 17, 2012).

DATA *file*

DJIAS&P500

Date	DJIA	S&P
January 6	12,360	1278
January 13	12,422	1289
January 20	12,720	1315
January 27	12,660	1316
February 3	12,862	1345
February 10	12,801	1343
February 17	12,950	1362
February 24	12,983	1366
March 2	12,978	1370
March 9	12,922	1371
March 16	13,233	1404
March 23	13,081	1397
March 30	13,212	1408
April 5	13,060	1398
April 13	12,850	1370

a. Develop a scatter diagram with DJIA as the independent variable.
b. Develop the estimated regression equation.
c. Test for a significant relationship. Use $\alpha = .05$.
d. Did the estimated regression equation provide a good fit? Explain.
e. Suppose that the closing price for the DJIA is 13,500. Predict the closing price for the S&P 500.
f. Should we be concerned that the DJIA value of 13,500 used to predict the S&P 500 value in part (e) is beyond the range of the data used to develop the estimated regression equation?

56. Is the number of square feet of living space a good predictor of a house's selling price? The following data show the square footage and selling price for 15 houses in Winston Salem, North Carolina (*Zillow.com*, April 5, 2015).

DATA *file*

WSHouses

Size (1000s sq. ft)	Selling Price ($1000s)
1.26	117.5
3.02	299.9
1.99	139.0
0.91	45.6
1.87	129.9
2.63	274.9
2.60	259.9
2.27	177.0

Size (1000s sq. ft)	Selling Price ($1000s)
2.30	175.0
2.08	189.9
1.12	95.0
1.38	82.1
1.80	169.0
1.57	96.5
1.45	114.9

a. Develop a scatter diagram with square feet of living space as the independent variable and selling price as the dependent variable. What does the scatter diagram indicate about the relationship between the size of a house and the selling price?

b. Develop the estimated regression equation that could be used to predict the selling price given the number of square feet of living space.

c. At the .05 level, is there a significant relationship between the two variables?

d. Use the estimated regression equation to predict the selling price of a 2000 square foot house in Winston Salem, North Carolina.

e. Do you believe the estimated regression equation developed in part (b) will provide a good prediction of selling price of a particular house in Winston Salem, North Carolina? Explain.

f. Would you be comfortable using the estimated regression equation developed in part (b) to predict the selling price of a particular house in Seattle, Washington? Why or why not?

57. One of the biggest changes in higher education in recent years has been the growth of online universities. The Online Education Database is an independent organization whose mission is to build a comprehensive list of the top accredited online colleges. The following table shows the retention rate (%) and the graduation rate (%) for 29 online colleges.

DATA *file*

OnlineEdu

Retention Rate (%)	Graduation Rate (%)
7	25
51	25
4	28
29	32
33	33
47	33
63	34
45	36
60	36
62	36
67	36
65	37
78	37
75	38
54	39
45	41

(continued)

Retention Rate (%)	Graduation Rate (%)
38	44
51	45
69	46
60	47
37	48
63	50
73	51
78	52
48	53
95	55
68	56
100	57
100	61

a. Develop a scatter diagram with retention rate as the independent variable. What does the scatter diagram indicate about the relationship between the two variables?
b. Develop the estimated regression equation.
c. Test for a significant relationship. Use $\alpha = .05$.
d. Did the estimated regression equation provide a good fit?

58. Jensen Tire & Auto is in the process of deciding whether to purchase a maintenance contract for its new computer wheel alignment and balancing machine. Managers feel that maintenance expense should be related to usage, and they collected the following information on weekly usage (hours) and annual maintenance expense (in hundreds of dollars).

DATA *file*

Jensen

Weekly Usage (hours)	Annual Maintenance Expense
13	17.0
10	22.0
20	30.0
28	37.0
32	47.0
17	30.5
24	32.5
31	39.0
40	51.5
38	40.0

a. Develop the estimated regression equation that relates annual maintenance expense to weekly usage.
b. Test the significance of the relationship in part (a) at a .05 level of significance.
c. Jensen expects to use the new machine 30 hours per week. Develop a 95% prediction interval for the company's annual maintenance expense.
d. If the maintenance contract costs $3000 per year, would you recommend purchasing it? Why or why not?

59. The regional transit authority for a major metropolitan area wants to determine whether there is any relationship between the age of a bus and the annual maintenance cost. A sample of 10 buses resulted in the following data.

DATA *file*

AgeCost

Age of Bus (years)	Maintenance Cost ($)
1	350
2	370
2	480
2	520
2	590
3	550
4	750
4	800
5	790
5	950

a. Develop the least squares estimated regression equation.
b. Test to see whether the two variables are significantly related with $\alpha = .05$.
c. Did the least squares line provide a good fit to the observed data? Explain.
d. Develop a 95% prediction interval for the maintenance cost for a specific bus that is 4 years old.

60. A marketing professor at Givens College is interested in the relationship between hours spent studying and total points earned in a course. Data collected on 10 students who took the course last quarter follow.

DATA *file*

HoursPts

Hours Spent Studying	Total Points Earned
45	40
30	35
90	75
60	65
105	90
65	50
90	90
80	80
55	45
75	65

a. Develop an estimated regression equation showing how total points earned is related to hours spent studying.
b. Test the significance of the model with $\alpha = .05$.
c. Predict the total points earned by Mark Sweeney. He spent 95 hours studying.
d. Develop a 95% prediction interval for the total points earned by Mark Sweeney.

61. The Toyota Camry is one of the best-selling cars in North America. The cost of a previously owned Camry depends upon many factors, including the model year, mileage, and condition. To investigate the relationship between the car's mileage and the sales price for a 2007 model year Camry, the following data show the mileage and sale price for 19 sales (PriceHub website, February 24, 2012).

DATA *file*

Camry

Miles (1000s)	Price ($1000s)
22	16.2
29	16.0
36	13.8
47	11.5
63	12.5
77	12.9
73	11.2
87	13.0
92	11.8
101	10.8
110	8.3
28	12.5
59	11.1
68	15.0
68	12.2
91	13.0
42	15.6
65	12.7
110	8.3

a. Develop a scatter diagram with the car mileage on the horizontal axis and the price on the vertical axis.

b. What does the scatter diagram developed in part (a) indicate about the relationship between the two variables?

c. Develop the estimated regression equation that could be used to predict the price ($1000s) given the miles (1000s).

d. Test for a significant relationship at the .05 level of significance.

e. Did the estimated regression equation provide a good fit? Explain.

f. Provide an interpretation for the slope of the estimated regression equation.

g. Suppose that you are considering purchasing a previously owned 2007 Camry that has been driven 60,000 miles. Using the estimated regression equation developed in part (c), predict the price for this car. Is this the price you would offer the seller?

Case Problem 1   Measuring Stock Market Risk

One measure of the risk or volatility of an individual stock is the standard deviation of the total return (capital appreciation plus dividends) over several periods of time. Although the standard deviation is easy to compute, it does not take into account the extent to which the price of a given stock varies as a function of a standard market index, such as the S&P 500. As a result, many financial analysts prefer to use another measure of risk referred to as *beta*.

Betas for individual stocks are determined by simple linear regression. The dependent variable is the total return for the stock and the independent variable is the total return for the stock market.* For this case problem we will use the S&P 500 index as the measure of the total return for the stock market, and an estimated regression equation will be developed using monthly data. The beta for the stock is the slope of the estimated regression

DATA *file*

Beta

---

*Various sources use different approaches for computing betas. For instance, some sources subtract the return that could be obtained from a risk-free investment (e.g., T-bills) from the dependent variable and the independent variable before computing the estimated regression equation. Some also use different indexes for the total return of the stock market; for instance, Value Line computes betas using the New York Stock Exchange composite index.

equation (b_1). The data contained in the DATAfile named *Beta* provides the total return (capital appreciation plus dividends) over 36 months for eight widely traded common stocks and the S&P 500.

The value of beta for the stock market will always be 1; thus, stocks that tend to rise and fall with the stock market will also have a beta close to 1. Betas greater than 1 indicate that the stock is more volatile than the market, and betas less than 1 indicate that the stock is less volatile than the market. For instance, if a stock has a beta of 1.4, it is 40% *more* volatile than the market, and if a stock has a beta of .4, it is 60% *less* volatile than the market.

Managerial Report

You have been assigned to analyze the risk characteristics of these stocks. Prepare a report that includes but is not limited to the following items.

   a. Compute descriptive statistics for each stock and the S&P 500. Comment on your results. Which stocks are the most volatile?

   b. Compute the value of beta for each stock. Which of these stocks would you expect to perform best in an up market? Which would you expect to hold their value best in a down market?

   c. Comment on how much of the return for the individual stocks is explained by the market.

Case Problem 2   # U.S. Department of Transportation

As part of a study on transportation safety, the U.S. Department of Transportation collected data on the number of fatal accidents per 1000 licenses and the percentage of licensed drivers under the age of 21 in a sample of 42 cities. Data collected over a one-year period follow. These data are contained in the DATAfile named *Safety*.

Safety

Percent Under 21	Fatal Accidents per 1000 Licenses	Percent Under 21	Fatal Accidents per 1000 Licenses
13	2.962	17	4.100
12	0.708	8	2.190
8	0.885	16	3.623
12	1.652	15	2.623
11	2.091	9	0.835
17	2.627	8	0.820
18	3.830	14	2.890
8	0.368	8	1.267
13	1.142	15	3.224
8	0.645	10	1.014
9	1.028	10	0.493
16	2.801	14	1.443
12	1.405	18	3.614
9	1.433	10	1.926
10	0.039	14	1.643
9	0.338	16	2.943
11	1.849	12	1.913
12	2.246	15	2.814
14	2.855	13	2.634
14	2.352	9	0.926
11	1.294	17	3.256

Managerial Report

1. Develop numerical and graphical summaries of the data.
2. Use regression analysis to investigate the relationship between the number of fatal accidents and the percentage of drivers under the age of 21. Discuss your findings.
3. What conclusion and recommendations can you derive from your analysis?

Case Problem 3 Selecting a Point-and-Shoot Digital Camera

Consumer Reports tested 166 different point-and-shoot digital cameras. Based upon factors such as the number of megapixels, weight (oz.), image quality, and ease of use, they developed an overall score for each camera tested. The overall score ranges from 0 to 100, with higher scores indicating better overall test results. Selecting a camera with many options can be a difficult process, and price is certainly a key issue for most consumers. By spending more, will a consumer really get a superior camera? And, do cameras that have more megapixels, a factor often considered to be a good measure of picture quality, cost more than cameras with fewer megapixels? Table 14.15 shows the brand, average retail

DATA *file*

Cameras

TABLE 14.15   DATA FOR 28 POINT-AND-SHOOT DIGITAL CAMERAS

Observation	Brand	Price ($)	Megapixels	Weight (oz.)	Score
1	Canon	330	10	7	66
2	Canon	200	12	5	66
3	Canon	300	12	7	65
4	Canon	200	10	6	62
5	Canon	180	12	5	62
6	Canon	200	12	7	61
7	Canon	200	14	5	60
8	Canon	130	10	7	60
9	Canon	130	12	5	59
10	Canon	110	16	5	55
11	Canon	90	14	5	52
12	Canon	100	10	6	51
13	Canon	90	12	7	46
14	Nikon	270	16	5	65
15	Nikon	300	16	7	63
16	Nikon	200	14	6	61
17	Nikon	400	14	7	59
18	Nikon	120	14	5	57
19	Nikon	170	16	6	56
20	Nikon	150	12	5	56
21	Nikon	230	14	6	55
22	Nikon	180	12	6	53
23	Nikon	130	12	6	53
24	Nikon	80	12	7	52
25	Nikon	80	14	7	50
26	Nikon	100	12	4	46
27	Nikon	110	12	5	45
28	Nikon	130	14	4	42

price ($), number of megapixels, weight (oz.), and the overall score for 13 Canon and 15 Nikon subcompact cameras tested by *Consumer Reports* (*Consumer Reports* website, February 7, 2012).

Managerial Report

1. Develop numerical summaries of the data.
2. Using overall score as the dependent variable, develop three scatter diagrams, one using price as the independent variable, one using the number of megapixels as the independent variable, and one using weight as the independent variable. Which of the three independent variables appears to be the best predictor of overall score?
3. Using simple linear regression, develop an estimated regression equation that could be used to predict the overall score given the price of the camera.
4. Analyze the data using only the observations for the Canon cameras. Discuss the appropriateness of using simple linear regression and make any recommendations regarding the prediction of overall score using just the price of the camera.

Case Problem 4 # Finding the Best Car Value

When trying to decide what car to buy, real value is not necessarily determined by how much you spend on the initial purchase. Instead, cars that are reliable and don't cost much to own often represent the best values. But, no matter how reliable or inexpensive a car may cost to own, it must also perform well.

To measure value, *Consumer Reports* developed a statistic referred to as a value score. The value score is based upon five-year owner costs, overall road-test scores, and predicted reliability ratings. Five-year owner costs are based on the expenses incurred in the first five years of ownership, including depreciation, fuel, maintenance and repairs, and so on. Using a national average of 12,000 miles per year, an average cost per mile driven is used as the measure of five-year owner costs. Road-test scores are the results of more than 50 tests and evaluations and are based upon a 100-point scale, with higher scores indicating better performance, comfort, convenience, and fuel economy. The highest road-test score obtained in the tests conducted by *Consumer Reports* was a 99 for a Lexus LS 460L. Predicted-reliability ratings (1 = Poor, 2 = Fair, 3 = Good, 4 = Very Good, and 5 = Excellent) are based on data from *Consumer Reports'* Annual Auto Survey.

A car with a value score of 1.0 is considered to be "average-value." A car with a value score of 2.0 is considered to be twice as good a value as a car with a value score of 1.0; a car with a value score of 0.5 is considered half as good as average; and so on. The data for 20 family sedans, including the price ($) of each car tested, follow.

DATA *file*

FamilySedans

Car	Price ($)	Cost/Mile	Road-Test Score	Predicted Reliability	Value Score
Nissan Altima 2.5 S (4-cyl.)	23,970	0.59	91	4	1.75
Kia Optima LX (2.4)	21,885	0.58	81	4	1.73
Subaru Legacy 2.5i Premium	23,830	0.59	83	4	1.73
Ford Fusion Hybrid	32,360	0.63	84	5	1.70
Honda Accord LX-P (4-cyl.)	23,730	0.56	80	4	1.62
Mazda6 i Sport (4-cyl.)	22,035	0.58	73	4	1.60
Hyundai Sonata GLS (2.4)	21,800	0.56	89	3	1.58
Ford Fusion SE (4-cyl.)	23,625	0.57	76	4	1.55

(continued)

Car	Price ($)	Cost/Mile	Road-Test Score	Predicted Reliability	Value Score
Chevrolet Malibu LT (4-cyl.)	24,115	0.57	74	3	1.48
Kia Optima SX (2.0T)	29,050	0.72	84	4	1.43
Ford Fusion SEL (V6)	28,400	0.67	80	4	1.42
Nissan Altima 3.5 SR (V6)	30,335	0.69	93	4	1.42
Hyundai Sonata Limited (2.0T)	28,090	0.66	89	3	1.39
Honda Accord EX-L (V6)	28,695	0.67	90	3	1.36
Mazda6 s Grand Touring (V6)	30,790	0.74	81	4	1.34
Ford Fusion SEL (V6, AWD)	30,055	0.71	75	4	1.32
Subaru Legacy 3.6R Limited	30,094	0.71	88	3	1.29
Chevrolet Malibu LTZ (V6)	28,045	0.67	83	3	1.20
Chrysler 200 Limited (V6)	27,825	0.70	52	5	1.20
Chevrolet Impala LT (3.6)	28,995	0.67	63	3	1.05

Managerial Report

1. Develop numerical summaries of the data.
2. Use regression analysis to develop an estimated regression equation that could be used to predict the value score given the price of the car.
3. Use regression analysis to develop an estimated regression equation that could be used to predict the value score given the five-year owner costs (cost/mile).
4. Use regression analysis to develop an estimated regression equation that could be used to predict the value score given the road-test score.
5. Use regression analysis to develop an estimated regression equation that could be used to predict the value score given the predicted-reliability.
6. What conclusions can you derive from your analysis?

Case Problem 5 # Buckeye Creek Amusement Park

Buckeye Creek Amusement Park is open from the beginning of May to the end of October. Buckeye Creek relies heavily on the sale of season passes. The sale of season passes brings in significant revenue prior to the park opening each season, and season pass holders contribute a substantial portion of the food, beverage, and novelty sales in the park. Greg Ross, director of marketing at Buckeye Creek, has been asked to develop a targeted marketing campaign to increase season pass sales.

BuckeyeCreek

Greg has data for last season that show the number of season pass holders for each zip code within 50 miles of Buckeye Creek. He has also obtained the total population of each zip code from the U.S. Census bureau website. Greg thinks it may be possible to use regression analysis to predict the number of season pass holders in a zip code given the total population of a zip code. If this is possible, he could then conduct a direct mail campaign that would target zip codes that have fewer than the expected number of season pass holders.

Managerial Report

1. Compute descriptive statistics and construct a scatter diagram for the data. Discuss your findings.
2. Using simple linear regression, develop an estimated regression equation that could be used to predict the number of season pass holders in a zip code given the total population of the zip code.

3. Test for a significant relationship at the .05 level of significance.
4. Did the estimated regression equation provide a good fit?
5. Use residual analysis to determine whether the assumed regression model is appropriate.
6. Discuss if/how the estimated regression equation should be used to guide the marketing campaign.
7. What other data might be useful to predict the number of season pass holders in a zip code?

Appendix 14.1 Calculus–Based Derivation of Least Squares Formulas

As mentioned in the chapter, the least squares method is a procedure for determining the values of b_0 and b_1 that minimize the sum of squared residuals. The sum of squared residuals is given by

$$\sum(y_i - \hat{y}_i)^2$$

Substituting $\hat{y}_i = b_0 + b_1 x_i$, we get

$$\sum(y_i - b_0 - b_1 x_i)^2 \tag{14.34}$$

as the expression that must be minimized.

To minimize expression (14.34), we must take the partial derivatives with respect to b_0 and b_1, set them equal to zero, and solve. Doing so, we get

$$\frac{\partial \sum(y_i - b_0 - b_1 x_i)^2}{\partial b_0} = -2\sum(y_i - b_0 - b_1 x_i) = 0 \tag{14.35}$$

$$\frac{\partial \sum(y_i - b_0 - b_1 x_i)^2}{\partial b_1} = -2\sum x_i(y_i - b_0 - b_1 x_i) = 0 \tag{14.36}$$

Dividing equation (14.35) by two and summing each term individually yields

$$-\sum y_i + \sum b_0 + \sum b_1 x_i = 0$$

Bringing $\sum y_i$ to the other side of the equal sign and noting that $\sum b_0 = nb_0$, we obtain

$$nb_0 + (\sum x_i)b_1 = \sum y_i \tag{14.37}$$

Similar algebraic simplification applied to equation (14.36) yields

$$(\sum x_i)b_0 + (\sum x_i^2)b_1 = \sum x_i y_i \tag{14.38}$$

Equations (14.37) and (14.38) are known as the *normal equations*. Solving equation (14.37) for b_0 yields

$$b_0 = \frac{\sum y_i}{n} - b_1 \frac{\sum x_i}{n} \tag{14.39}$$

Using equation (14.39) to substitute for b_0 in equation (14.38) provides

$$\frac{\sum x_i \sum y_i}{n} - \frac{(\sum x_i)^2}{n} b_1 + (\sum x_i^2) b_1 = \sum x_i y_i \qquad \textbf{(14.40)}$$

By rearranging the terms in equation (14.40), we obtain

$$b_1 = \frac{\sum x_i y_i - (\sum x_i \sum y_i)/n}{\sum x_i^2 - (\sum x_i)^2/n} = \frac{\sum (x_i - \bar{x})(y_i - \bar{y})}{\sum (x_i - \bar{x})^2} \qquad \textbf{(14.41)}$$

Because $\bar{y} = \sum y_i/n$ and $\bar{x} = \sum x_i/n$, we can rewrite equation (14.39) as

$$b_0 = \bar{y} - b_1 \bar{x} \qquad \textbf{(14.42)}$$

Equations (14.41) and (14.42) are the formulas (14.6) and (14.7) we used in the chapter to compute the coefficients in the estimated regression equation.

Appendix 14.2 A Test for Significance Using Correlation

Using the sample correlation coefficient r_{xy}, we can determine whether the linear relationship between x and y is significant by testing the following hypotheses about the population correlation coefficient ρ_{xy}.

$$H_0: \rho_{xy} = 0$$
$$H_a: \rho_{xy} \neq 0$$

If H_0 is rejected, we can conclude that the population correlation coefficient is not equal to zero and that the linear relationship between the two variables is significant. This test for significance follows.

A TEST FOR SIGNIFICANCE USING CORRELATION

$$H_0: \rho_{xy} = 0$$
$$H_a: \rho_{xy} \neq 0$$

TEST STATISTIC

$$t = r_{xy} \sqrt{\frac{n-2}{1-r_{xy}^2}} \qquad \textbf{(14.43)}$$

REJECTION RULE

p-value approach:　　　Reject H_0 if p-value $\leq \alpha$

Critical value approach: Reject H_0 if $t \leq -t_{\alpha/2}$ or if $t \geq t_{\alpha/2}$

where $t_{\alpha/2}$ is based on a t distribution with $n - 2$ degrees of freedom.

In Section 14.3, we found that the sample with $n = 10$ provided the sample correlation coefficient for student population and quarterly sales of $r_{xy} = .9501$. The test statistic is

$$t = r_{xy} \sqrt{\frac{n-2}{1 - r_{xy}^2}} = .9501 \sqrt{\frac{10 - 2}{1 - (.9501)^2}} = 8.61$$

The t distribution table shows that with $n - 2 = 10 - 2 = 8$ degrees of freedom, $t = 3.355$ provides an area of .005 in the upper tail. Thus, the area in the upper tail of the t distribution corresponding to the test statistic $t = 8.61$ must be less than .005. Because this test is a two-tailed test, we double this value to conclude that the p-value associated with $t = 8.61$ must be less than $2(.005) = .01$. Using Excel, the p-value $= .000$. Because the p-value is less than $\alpha = .01$, we reject H_0 and conclude that ρ_{xy} is not equal to zero. This evidence is sufficient to conclude that a significant linear relationship exists between student population and quarterly sales.

Note that except for rounding, the test statistic t and the conclusion of a significant relationship are identical to the results obtained in Section 14.5 for the t test conducted using Armand's estimated regression equation $\hat{y} = 60 + 5x$. Performing regression analysis provides the conclusion of a significant relationship between x and y and in addition provides the equation showing how the variables are related. Most analysts therefore use modern computer packages to perform regression analysis and find that using correlation as a test of significance is unnecessary.

CHAPTER 15

Multiple Regression

CONTENTS

STATISTICS *in* PRACTICE

INTERNATIONAL PAPER*
PURCHASE, NEW YORK

International Paper is the world's largest paper and forest products company. The company employs more than 117,000 people in its operations in nearly 50 countries, and exports its products to more than 130 nations. International Paper produces building materials such as lumber and plywood; consumer packaging materials such as disposable cups and containers; industrial packaging materials such as corrugated boxes and shipping containers; and a variety of papers for use in photocopiers, printers, books, and advertising materials.

To make paper products, pulp mills process wood chips and chemicals to produce wood pulp. The wood pulp is then used at a paper mill to produce paper products. In the production of white paper products, the pulp must be bleached to remove any discoloration. A key bleaching agent used in the process is chlorine dioxide, which, because of its combustible nature, is usually produced at a pulp mill facility and then piped in solution form into the bleaching tower of the pulp mill. To improve one of the processes used to produce chlorine dioxide, researchers studied the process's control and efficiency. One aspect of the study looked at the chemical feed rate for chlorine dioxide production.

To produce the chlorine dioxide, four chemicals flow at metered rates into the chlorine dioxide generator. The chlorine dioxide produced in the generator flows to an absorber where chilled water absorbs the chlorine dioxide gas to form a chlorine dioxide solution. The solution is then piped into the paper mill. A key part of controlling the process involves the chemical feed rates. Historically, experienced operators set the chemical feed rates, but this approach led to overcontrol by the operators. Consequently, chemical engineers at the mill requested that a set of control equations, one for

RGB Ventures/SuperStock/Alamy Stock Photo

Multiple regression analysis assisted in the development of a better bleaching process for making white paper products.

each chemical feed, be developed to aid the operators in setting the rates.

Using multiple regression analysis, statistical analysts developed an estimated multiple regression equation for each of the four chemicals used in the process. Each equation related the production of chlorine dioxide to the amount of chemical used and the concentration level of the chlorine dioxide solution. The resulting set of four equations was programmed into a microcomputer at each mill. In the new system, operators enter the concentration of the chlorine dioxide solution and the desired production rate; the computer software then calculates the chemical feed needed to achieve the desired production rate. After the operators began using the control equations, the chlorine dioxide generator efficiency increased, and the number of times the concentrations fell within acceptable ranges increased significantly.

This example shows how multiple regression analysis can be used to develop a better bleaching process for producing white paper products. In this chapter we will show how Excel can be used for such purposes. Most of the concepts introduced in Chapter 14 for simple linear regression can be directly extended to the multiple regression case.

---

*The authors are indebted to Marian Williams and Bill Griggs for providing this Statistics in Practice. This application was originally developed at Champion International Corporation, which became part of International Paper in 2000.

In Chapter 14 we presented simple linear regression and demonstrated its use in developing an estimated regression equation that describes the relationship between two variables. Recall that the variable being predicted or explained is called the dependent variable and the variable being used to predict or explain the dependent variable is called the independent variable. In this chapter we continue our study of regression analysis by considering situations involving two or more independent variables. This subject area, called **multiple regression analysis**, enables us to consider more factors and thus obtain better predictions than are possible with simple linear regression.

15.1   Multiple Regression Model

Multiple regression analysis is the study of how a dependent variable y is related to two or more independent variables. In the general case, we will use p to denote the number of independent variables.

Regression Model and Regression Equation

The concepts of a regression model and a regression equation introduced in the preceding chapter are applicable in the multiple regression case. The equation that describes how the dependent variable y is related to the independent variables $x_1, x_2, \ldots, x_p$ and an error term is called the **multiple regression model**. We begin with the assumption that the multiple regression model takes the following form.

MULTIPLE REGRESSION MODEL

$$y = \beta_0 + \beta_1 x_1 + \beta_2 x_2 + \cdots + \beta_p x_p + \epsilon \qquad \textbf{(15.1)}$$

In the multiple regression model, $\beta_0, \beta_1, \beta_2, \ldots, \beta_p$ are the parameters and the error term ϵ (the Greek letter epsilon) is a random variable. A close examination of this model reveals that y is a linear function of $x_1, x_2, \ldots, x_p$ (the $\beta_0 + \beta_1 x_1 + \beta_2 x_2 + \cdots + \beta_p x_p$ part) plus the error term ϵ. The error term accounts for the variability in y that cannot be explained by the linear effect of the p independent variables.

In Section 15.4 we will discuss the assumptions for the multiple regression model and ϵ. One of the assumptions is that the mean or expected value of ϵ is zero. A consequence of this assumption is that the mean or expected value of y, denoted $E(y)$, is equal to $\beta_0 + \beta_1 x_1 + \beta_2 x_2 + \cdots + \beta_p x_p$. The equation that describes how the mean value of y is related to $x_1, x_2, \ldots, x_p$ is called the **multiple regression equation**.

MULTIPLE REGRESSION EQUATION

$$E(y) = \beta_0 + \beta_1 x_1 + \beta_2 x_2 + \cdots + \beta_p x_p \qquad \textbf{(15.2)}$$

Estimated Multiple Regression Equation

If the values of $\beta_0, \beta_1, \beta_2, \ldots, \beta_p$ were known, equation (15.2) could be used to compute the mean value of y at given values of $x_1, x_2, \ldots, x_p$. Unfortunately, these parameter values will not, in general, be known and must be estimated from sample data. A simple random sample is used to compute sample statistics $b_0, b_1, b_2, \ldots, b_p$ that are used as the point

FIGURE 15.1 THE ESTIMATION PROCESS FOR MULTIPLE REGRESSION

In simple linear regression, b_0 and b_1 were the sample statistics used to estimate the parameters β_0 and β_1. Multiple regression parallels this statistical inference process, with b_0, b_1, b_2, ..., b_p denoting the sample statistics used to estimate the parameters β_0, β_1, β_2, ..., β_p.

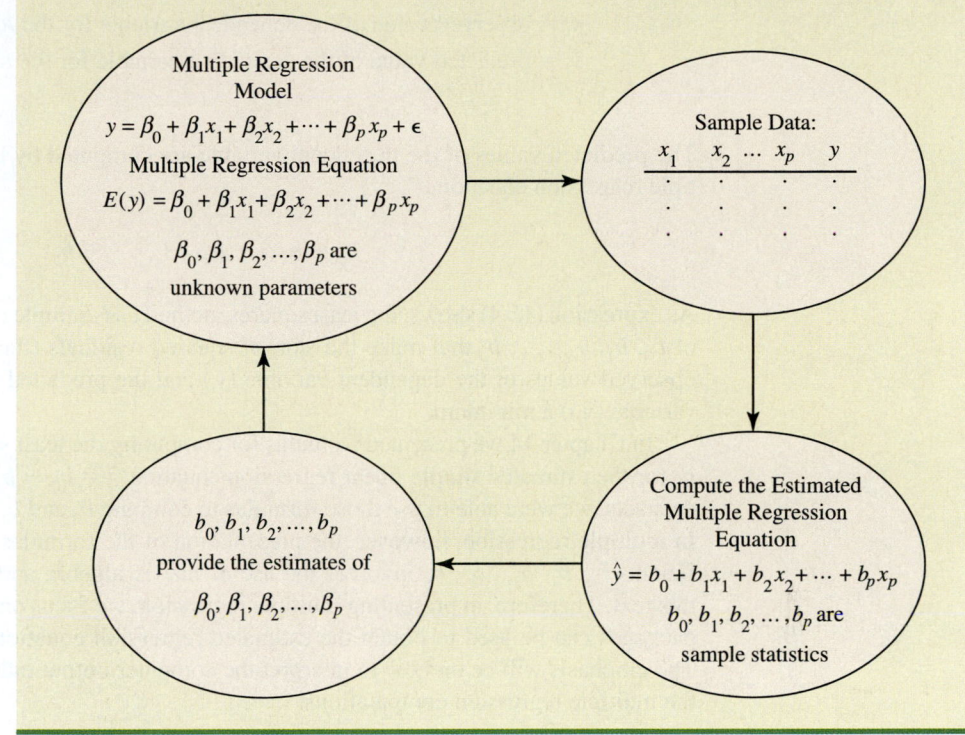

estimators of the parameters $\beta_0, \beta_1, \beta_2, \ldots, \beta_p$. These sample statistics provide the following **estimated multiple regression equation**.

ESTIMATED MULTIPLE REGRESSION EQUATION

$$\hat{y} = b_0 + b_1 x_1 + b_2 x_2 + \cdots + b_p x_p \qquad \textbf{(15.3)}$$

where

$b_0, b_1, b_2, \ldots, b_p$ are the estimates of $\beta_0, \beta_1, \beta_2, \ldots, \beta_p$
$\hat{y}$ = predicted value of the dependent variable

The estimation process for multiple regression is shown in Figure 15.1.

15.2 Least Squares Method

In Chapter 14, we used the **least squares method** to develop the estimated regression equation that best approximated the straight-line relationship between the dependent and independent variables. This same approach is used to develop the estimated multiple regression equation. The least squares criterion is restated as follows.

LEAST SQUARES CRITERION

$$\min \sum (y_i - \hat{y}_i)^2 \qquad \textbf{(15.4)}$$

where

y_i = observed value of the dependent variable for the ith observation

$\hat{y}_i$ = predicted value of the dependent variable for the ith observation

The predicted values of the dependent variable are computed by using the estimated multiple regression equation,

$$\hat{y} = b_0 + b_1 x_1 + b_2 x_2 + \cdots + b_p x_p$$

As expression (15.4) shows, the least squares method uses sample data to provide the values of $b_0, b_1, b_2, \ldots, b_p$ that make the sum of squared residuals (the deviations between the observed values of the dependent variable (y_i) and the predicted values of the dependent variable ($\hat{y}_i$)) a minimum.

In Chapter 14 we presented formulas for computing the least squares estimators b_0 and b_1 for the estimated simple linear regression equation $\hat{y} = b_0 + b_1 x$. With relatively small data sets, we were able to use those formulas to compute b_0 and b_1 by manual calculations. In multiple regression, however, the presentation of the formulas for the regression coefficients $b_0, b_1, b_2, \ldots, b_p$ involves the use of matrix algebra and is beyond the scope of this text. Therefore, in presenting multiple regression, we focus on how computer software packages can be used to obtain the estimated regression equation and other information. The emphasis will be on how to interpret the computer output rather than on how to make the multiple regression computations.

An Example: Butler Trucking Company

As an illustration of multiple regression analysis, we will consider a problem faced by the Butler Trucking Company, an independent trucking company in southern California. A major portion of Butler's business involves deliveries throughout its local area. To develop better work schedules, the managers want to predict the total daily travel time for their drivers.

Initially the managers believed that the total daily travel time would be closely related to the number of miles traveled in making the daily deliveries. A simple random sample of 10 driving assignments provided the data shown in Table 15.1 and the scatter diagram shown in Figure 15.2. After reviewing this scatter diagram, the managers hypothesized that the simple linear regression model $y = \beta_0 + \beta_1 x_1 + \epsilon$ could be used to describe the

TABLE 15.1   PRELIMINARY DATA FOR BUTLER TRUCKING

Butler

Driving Assignment	x_1 = Miles Traveled	y = Travel Time (hours)
1	100	9.3
2	50	4.8
3	100	8.9
4	100	6.5
5	50	4.2
6	80	6.2
7	75	7.4
8	65	6.0
9	90	7.6
10	90	6.1

FIGURE 15.2 SCATTER DIAGRAM OF PRELIMINARY DATA FOR BUTLER TRUCKING

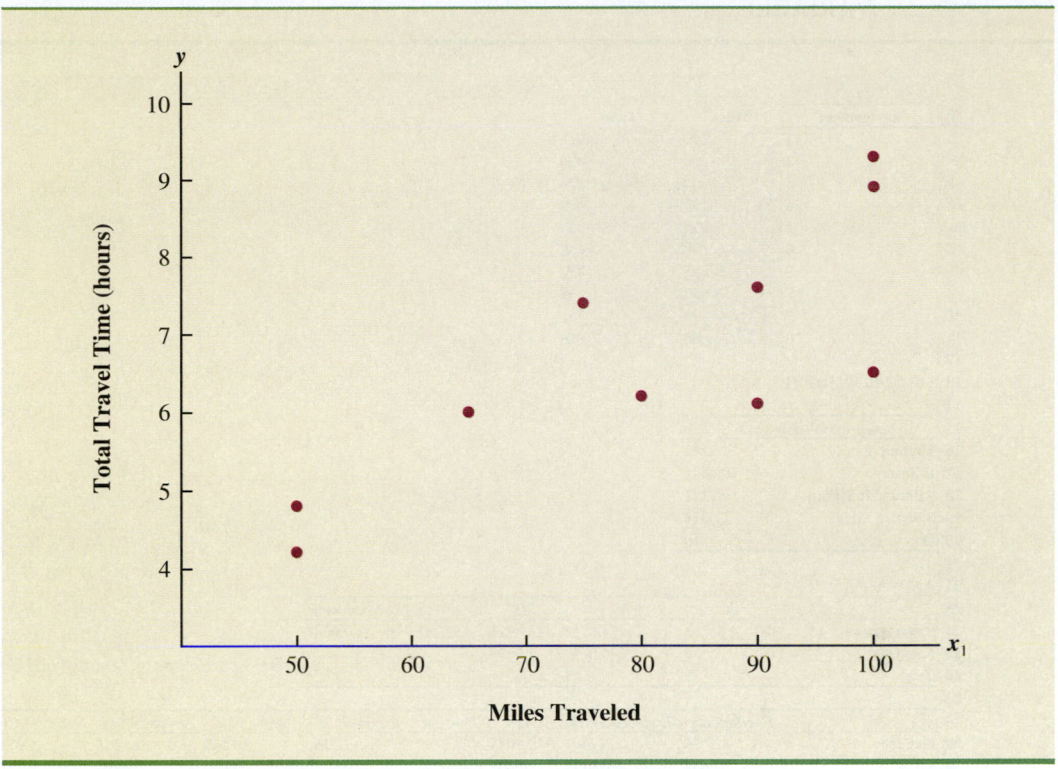

relationship between the total travel time (y) and the number of miles traveled (x_1). To estimate the parameters β_0 and β_1, the least squares method was used to develop the estimated regression equation.

$$\hat{y} = b_0 + b_1 x_1 \tag{15.5}$$

In Figure 15.3, we show the Excel Regression tool output[1] from applying simple linear regression to the data in Table 15.1. The estimated regression equation is

$$\hat{y} = 1.2739 + .0678 x_1$$

At the .05 level of significance, the F value of 15.8146 and its corresponding p-value of .0041 indicate that the relationship is significant; that is, we can reject H_0: $\beta_1 = 0$ because the p-value is less than $\alpha = .05$. Note that the same conclusion is obtained from the t value of 3.9768 and its associated p-value of .0041. Thus, we can conclude that the relationship between the total travel time and the number of miles traveled is significant; longer travel times are associated with more miles traveled. With a coefficient of determination of R Square = .6641, we see that 66.41% of the variability in travel time can be explained by the linear effect of the number of miles traveled. This finding is fairly good, but the managers might want to consider adding a second independent variable to explain some of the remaining variability in the dependent variable.

---

[1]Excel's Regression tool was used to obtain the output. Section 14.7 describes how to use Excel's Regression tool for simple linear regression.

FIGURE 15.3 REGRESSION TOOL OUTPUT FOR BUTLER TRUCKING WITH ONE INDEPENDENT VARIABLE

	A	B	C	D	E	F	G	H	I	J
1	Assignment	Miles	Time							
2	1	100	9.3							
3	2	50	4.8							
4	3	100	8.9							
5	4	100	6.5							
6	5	50	4.2							
7	6	80	6.2							
8	7	75	7.4							
9	8	65	6							
10	9	90	7.6							
11	10	90	6.1							
12										
13	SUMMARY OUTPUT									
14										
15	*Regression Statistics*									
16	Multiple R	0.8149								
17	R Square	0.6641								
18	Adjusted R Square	0.6221								
19	Standard Error	1.0018								
20	Observations	10								
21										
22	ANOVA									
23		*df*	*SS*	*MS*	*F*	*Significance F*				
24	Regression	1	15.8713	15.8713	15.8146	0.0041				
25	Residual	8	8.0287	1.0036						
26	Total	9	23.9							
27										
28		*Coefficients*	*Standard Error*	*t Stat*	*P-value*	*Lower 95%*	*Upper 95%*	*Lower 99.0%*	*Upper 99.0%*	
29	Intercept	1.2739	1.4007	0.9095	0.3897	-1.9562	4.5040	-3.4261	5.9739	
30	Miles	0.0678	0.0171	3.9768	0.0041	0.0285	0.1072	0.0106	0.1251	
31										

In attempting to identify another independent variable, the managers felt that the number of deliveries could also contribute to the total travel time. The Butler Trucking data, with the number of deliveries added, are shown in Table 15.2. To develop the estimated multiple regression equation with both miles traveled (x_1) and number of deliveries (x_2) as independent variables, we will use Excel's Regression tool.

TABLE 15.2 DATA FOR BUTLER TRUCKING WITH MILES TRAVELED (x_1) AND NUMBER OF DELIVERIES (x_2) AS THE INDEPENDENT VARIABLES

Driving Assignment	x_1 = Miles Traveled	x_2 = Number of Deliveries	y = Travel Time (hours)
1	100	4	9.3
2	50	3	4.8
3	100	4	8.9
4	100	2	6.5
5	50	2	4.2
6	80	2	6.2
7	75	3	7.4
8	65	4	6.0
9	90	3	7.6
10	90	2	6.1

Using Excel's Regression Tool to Develop the Estimated Multiple Regression Equation

In Section 14.7 we showed how Excel's Regression tool could be used to determine the estimated regression equation for Armand's Pizza Parlors. We can use the same procedure with minor modifications to develop the estimated multiple regression equation for Butler Trucking. Refer to Figures 15.4 and 15.5 as we describe the tasks involved.

Enter/Access Data: Open the DATAfile named *Butler*. The data are in cells B2:D11 and labels are in column A and cells B1:D1.

Apply Tools: The following steps describe how to use Excel's Regression tool for multiple regression analysis.

Step 1. Click the **DATA** tab on the Ribbon

Step 2. In the **Analyze** group, click **Data Analysis**

Step 3. Choose **Regression** from the list of Analysis Tools

Step 4. When the Regression dialog box appears (see Figure 15.4):

Enter D1:D11 in the **Input Y Range** box

Enter B1:C11 in the **Input X Range** box

Select **Labels**

Select **Confidence Level**

Enter 99 in the **Confidence Level** box

Select **Output Range**

Enter A13 in the **Output Range** box (to identify the upper left corner of the section of the worksheet where the output will appear)

Click **OK**

FIGURE 15.4 REGRESSION TOOL DIALOG BOX FOR THE BUTLER TRUCKING EXAMPLE

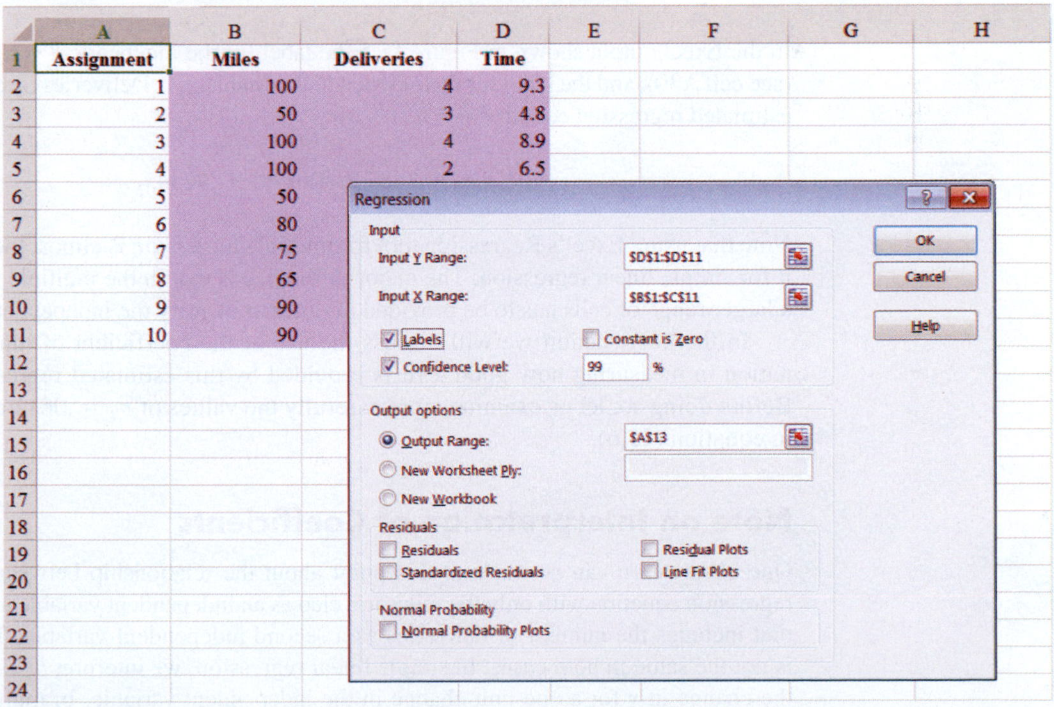

FIGURE 15.5 REGRESSION TOOL OUTPUT FOR BUTLER TRUCKING WITH TWO INDEPENDENT VARIABLES

	A	B	C	D	E	F	G	H	I	J
1	Assignment	Miles	Deliveries	Time						
2	1	100	4	9.3						
3	2	50	3	4.8						
4	3	100	4	8.9						
5	4	100	2	6.5						
6	5	50	2	4.2						
7	6	80	2	6.2						
8	7	75	3	7.4						
9	8	65	4	6						
10	9	90	3	7.6						
11	10	90	2	6.1						
12										
13	SUMMARY OUTPUT									
14										
15	Regression Statistics									
16	Multiple R	0.9507								
17	R Square	0.9038								
18	Adjusted R Square	0.8763								
19	Standard Error	0.5731								
20	Observations	10								
21										
22	ANOVA									
23		df	SS	MS	F	Significance F				
24	Regression	2	21.6006	10.8003	32.8784	0.0003				
25	Residual	7	2.2994	0.3285						
26	Total	9	23.9							
27										
28		Coefficients	Standard Error	t Stat	P-value	Lower 95%	Upper 95%	Lower 99.0%	Upper 99.0%	
29	Intercept	-0.8687	0.9515	-0.9129	0.3916	-3.1188	1.3813	-4.1986	2.4612	
30	Miles	0.0611	0.0099	6.1824	0.0005	0.0378	0.0845	0.0265	0.0957	
31	Deliveries	0.9234	0.2211	4.1763	0.0042	0.4006	1.4463	0.1496	1.6972	
32										

In the Excel output shown in Figure 15.5 the label for the independent variable x_1 is Miles (see cell A30), and the label for the independent variable x_2 is Deliveries (see cell A31). The estimated regression equation is

$$\hat{y} = -.8687 + .0611x_1 + .9234x_2 \tag{15.6}$$

Note that using Excel's Regression tool for multiple regression is almost the same as using it for simple linear regression. The major difference is that in the multiple regression case a larger range of cells has to be provided in order to identify the independent variables.

In the next section we will discuss the use of the coefficient of multiple determination in measuring how good a fit is provided by this estimated regression equation. Before doing so, let us examine more carefully the values of $b_1 = .0611$ and $b_2 = .9234$ in equation (15.6).

Note on Interpretation of Coefficients

One observation can be made at this point about the relationship between the estimated regression equation with only the miles traveled as an independent variable and the equation that includes the number of deliveries as a second independent variable. The value of b_1 is not the same in both cases. In simple linear regression, we interpret b_1 as an estimate of the change in y for a one-unit change in the independent variable. In multiple regression analysis, this interpretation must be modified somewhat. That is, in multiple regression analysis, we interpret each regression coefficient as follows: b_i represents an estimate of the change in y corresponding to a one-unit change in x_i when all other independent variables are held constant. In the Butler Trucking example involving two independent variables, $b_1 = .0611$. Thus, .0611 hours is an estimate of the expected increase in travel time corresponding to an increase of 1 mile in the distance traveled when the number of deliveries is held constant. Similarly, because $b_2 = .9234$, an estimate of the expected increase in travel time corresponding to an increase of one delivery when the number of miles traveled is held constant is .9234 hours.

Exercises

Note to student: The exercises involving data in this and subsequent sections were designed to be solved using a computer software package.

Methods

1. The estimated regression equation for a model involving two independent variables and 10 observations follows.

$$\hat{y} = 29.1270 + .5906x_1 + .4980x_2$$

   a. Interpret b_1 and b_2 in this estimated regression equation.
   b. Predict y when $x_1 = 180$ and $x_2 = 310$.

SELF*test*

2. Consider the following data for a dependent variable y and two independent variables, x_1 and x_2.

DATA *file*
Exer2

x_1	x_2	y
30	12	94
47	10	108
25	17	112
51	16	178
40	5	94
51	19	175
74	7	170
36	12	117
59	13	142
76	16	211

   a. Develop an estimated regression equation relating y to x_1. Predict y if $x_1 = 45$.
   b. Develop an estimated regression equation relating y to x_2. Predict y if $x_2 = 15$.
   c. Develop an estimated regression equation relating y to x_1 and x_2. Predict y if $x_1 = 45$ and $x_2 = 15$.

3. In a regression analysis involving 30 observations, the following estimated regression equation was obtained.

$$\hat{y} = 17.6 + 3.8x_1 - 2.3x_2 + 7.6x_3 + 2.7x_4$$

a. Interpret b_1, b_2, b_3, and b_4 in this estimated regression equation.
b. Predict y when $x_1 = 10$, $x_2 = 5$, $x_3 = 1$, and $x_4 = 2$.

Applications

4. A shoe store developed the following estimated regression equation relating sales to inventory investment and advertising expenditures.

$$\hat{y} = 25 + 10x_1 + 8x_2$$

where

$$x_1 = \text{inventory investment (\$1000s)}$$
$$x_2 = \text{advertising expenditures (\$1000s)}$$
$$y = \text{sales (\$1000s)}$$

a. Predict the sales resulting from a $15,000 investment in inventory and an advertising budget of $10,000.
b. Interpret b_1 and b_2 in this estimated regression equation.

 5. The owner of Showtime Movie Theaters, Inc. would like to predict weekly gross revenue as a function of advertising expenditures. Historical data for a sample of eight weeks follow.

Weekly Gross Revenue ($1000s)	Television Advertising ($1000s)	Newspaper Advertising ($1000s)
96	5.0	1.5
90	2.0	2.0
95	4.0	1.5
92	2.5	2.5
95	3.0	3.3
94	3.5	2.3
94	2.5	4.2
94	3.0	2.5

a. Develop an estimated regression equation with the amount of television advertising as the independent variable.
b. Develop an estimated regression equation with both television advertising and newspaper advertising as the independent variables.
c. Is the estimated regression equation coefficient for television advertising expenditures the same in part (a) and in part (b)? Interpret the coefficient in each case.
d. Predict weekly gross revenue for a week when $3500 is spent on television advertising and $1800 is spent on newspaper advertising?

6. The National Football League (NFL) records a variety of performance data for individuals and teams. To investigate the importance of passing on the percentage of games won by a team, the following data show the conference (Conf), average number

of passing yards per attempt (Yds/Att), the number of interceptions thrown per attempt (Int/Att), and the percentage of games won (Win%) for a random sample of 16 NFL teams for one full season.

NFLPassing

Team	Conf	Yds/Att	Int/Att	Win%
Arizona Cardinals	NFC	6.5	.042	50.0
Atlanta Falcons	NFC	7.1	.022	62.5
Carolina Panthers	NFC	7.4	.033	37.5
Cincinnati Bengals	AFC	6.2	.026	56.3
Detroit Lions	NFC	7.2	.024	62.5
Green Bay Packers	NFC	8.9	.014	93.8
Houstan Texans	AFC	7.5	.019	62.5
Indianapolis Colts	AFC	5.6	.026	12.5
Jacksonville Jaguars	AFC	4.6	.032	31.3
Minnesota Vikings	NFC	5.8	.033	18.8
New England Patriots	AFC	8.3	.020	81.3
New Orleans Saints	NFC	8.1	.021	81.3
Oakland Raiders	AFC	7.6	.044	50.0
San Francisco 49ers	NFC	6.5	.011	81.3
Tennessee Titans	AFC	6.7	.024	56.3
Washington Redskins	NFC	6.4	.041	31.3

a. Develop the estimated regression equation that could be used to predict the percentage of games won given the average number of passing yards per attempt.

b. Develop the estimated regression equation that could be used to predict the percentage of games won given the number of interceptions thrown per attempt.

c. Develop the estimated regression equation that could be used to predict the percentage of games won given the average number of passing yards per attempt and the number of interceptions thrown per attempt.

d. The average number of passing yards per attempt for the Kansas City Chiefs was 6.2 and the number of interceptions thrown per attempt was .036. Use the estimated regression equation developed in part (c) to predict the percentage of games won by the Kansas City Chiefs. (*Note:* For this season the Kansas City Chiefs' record was 7 wins and 9 losses.) Compare your prediction to the actual percentage of games won by the Kansas City Chiefs.

Satisfaction

7. The United States Office of Personnel Management (OPM) manages the civil service of the federal government. Results from its annual Federal Employee Viewpoint Survey (FEVS) are used to measure employee satisfaction on several work aspects, including Job Satisfaction, Pay Satisfaction, Organization Satisfaction, and an overall measure of satisfaction referred to as Global Satisfaction. In each case a 100-point scale with higher values indicating greater satisfaction is used (OPM website, July 6, 2016). Scores for Global Satisfaction, Job Satisfaction, Pay Satisfaction, and Organization Satisfaction for a sample of 65 employees are provided in the DATAfile named *Satisfaction*.

a. Develop the estimated multiple regression equation that can be used to predict the Global Satisfaction score using the Job Satisfaction, Pay Satisfaction, and Organization Satisfaction scores.

b. Predict the overall Global Satisfaction score for an employee with a Job Satisfaction score of 72, a Pay Satisfaction score of 54, and an Organization Satisfaction score of 53.

8. The *Condé Nast Traveler* Gold List provides ratings for the top 20 small cruise ships. The following data shown are the scores each ship received based upon the results from *Condé Nast Traveler*'s annual Readers' Choice Survey. Each score represents the percentage of respondents who rated a ship as excellent or very good on several criteria, including Shore Excursions and Food/Dining. An overall score is also reported and used to rank the ships. The highest ranked ship, the *Seabourn Odyssey,* has an overall score of 94.4, the highest component of which is 97.8 for Food/Dining.

DATA file

Ships

Ship	Overall	Shore Excursions	Food/Dining
Seabourn Odyssey	94.4	90.9	97.8
Seabourn Pride	93.0	84.2	96.7
National Geographic Endeavor	92.9	100.0	88.5
Seabourn Sojourn	91.3	94.8	97.1
Paul Gauguin	90.5	87.9	91.2
Seabourn Legend	90.3	82.1	98.8
Seabourn Spirit	90.2	86.3	92.0
Silver Explorer	89.9	92.6	88.9
Silver Spirit	89.4	85.9	90.8
Seven Seas Navigator	89.2	83.3	90.5
Silver Whisperer	89.2	82.0	88.6
National Geographic Explorer	89.1	93.1	89.7
Silver Cloud	88.7	78.3	91.3
Celebrity Xpedition	87.2	91.7	73.6
Silver Shadow	87.2	75.0	89.7
Silver Wind	86.6	78.1	91.6
SeaDream II	86.2	77.4	90.9
Wind Star	86.1	76.5	91.5
Wind Surf	86.1	72.3	89.3
Wind Spirit	85.2	77.4	91.9

a. Determine an estimated regression equation that can be used to predict the overall score given the score for Shore Excursions.
b. Consider the addition of the independent variable Food/Dining. Develop the estimated regression equation that can be used to predict the overall score given the scores for Shore Excursions and Food/Dining.
c. Predict the overall score for a cruise ship with a Shore Excursions score of 80 and a Food/Dining Score of 90.

9. The Professional Golfers Association (PGA) maintains data on performance and earnings for members of the PGA Tour. For the 2012 season Bubba Watson led all players in total driving distance, with an average of 309.2 yards per drive. Some of the factors thought to influence driving distance are club head speed, ball speed, and launch angle. For the 2012 season Bubba Watson had an average club head speed of 124.69 miles per hour, an average ball speed of 184.98 miles per hour, and an average launch angle of 8.79 degrees. The DATAfile named *PGADrivingDist* contains data on total driving distance and the factors related to driving distance for 190 members of the PGA Tour (PGA Tour website, November 1, 2012). Descriptions for the variables in the data set follow.

DATA file

PGADrivingDist

Club Head Speed: Speed at which the club impacts the ball (mph).
Ball Speed: Peak speed of the golf ball at launch (mph).
Launch Angle: Vertical launch angle of the ball immediately after leaving the club (degrees).
Total Distance: The average number of yards per drive.

a. Develop an estimated regression equation that can be used to predict the average number of yards per drive given the club head speed.

b. Develop an estimated regression equation that can be used to predict the average number of yards per drive given the ball speed.

c. A recommendation has been made to develop an estimated regression equation that uses both club head speed and ball speed to predict the average number of yards per drive. Do you agree with this? Explain.

d. Develop an estimated regression equation that can be used to predict the average number of yards per drive given the ball speed and the launch angle.

e. Suppose a new member of the PGA Tour for 2013 has a ball speed of 170 miles per hour and a launch angle of 11 degrees. Use the estimated regression equation in part (d) to predict the average number of yards per drive for this player.

10. Major League Baseball (MLB) consists of teams that play in the American League and the National League. MLB collects a wide variety of team and player statistics. Some of the statistics often used to evaluate pitching performance are as follows:

ERA: The average number of earned runs given up by the pitcher per nine innings. An earned run is any run that the opponent scores off a particular pitcher except for runs scored as a result of errors.

SO/IP: The average number of strikeouts per inning pitched.

HR/IP: The average number of home runs per inning pitched.

R/IP: The number of runs given up per inning pitched.

The following data show values for these statistics for a random sample of 20 pitchers from the American League for a full season.

MLBPitching

Player	Team	W	L	ERA	SO/IP	HR/IP	R/IP
Verlander, J	DET	24	5	2.40	1.00	.10	.29
Beckett, J	BOS	13	7	2.89	.91	.11	.34
Wilson, C	TEX	16	7	2.94	.92	.07	.40
Sabathia, C	NYY	19	8	3.00	.97	.07	.37
Haren, D	LAA	16	10	3.17	.81	.08	.38
McCarthy, B	OAK	9	9	3.32	.72	.06	.43
Santana, E	LAA	11	12	3.38	.78	.11	.42
Lester, J	BOS	15	9	3.47	.95	.10	.40
Hernandez, F	SEA	14	14	3.47	.95	.08	.42
Buehrle, M	CWS	13	9	3.59	.53	.10	.45
Pineda, M	SEA	9	10	3.74	1.01	.11	.44
Colon, B	NYY	8	10	4.00	.82	.13	.52
Tomlin, J	CLE	12	7	4.25	.54	.15	.48
Pavano, C	MIN	9	13	4.30	.46	.10	.55
Danks, J	CWS	8	12	4.33	.79	.11	.52
Guthrie, J	BAL	9	17	4.33	.63	.13	.54
Lewis, C	TEX	14	10	4.40	.84	.17	.51
Scherzer, M	DET	15	9	4.43	.89	.15	.52
Davis, W	TB	11	10	4.45	.57	.13	.52
Porcello, R	DET	14	9	4.75	.57	.10	.57

a. Develop an estimated regression equation that can be used to predict the average number of runs given up per inning given the average number of strikeouts per inning pitched.

b. Develop an estimated regression equation that can be used to predict the average number of runs given up per inning given the average number of home runs per inning pitched.

c. Develop an estimated regression equation that can be used to predict the average number of runs given up per inning given the average number of strikeouts per inning pitched and the average number of home runs per inning pitched.

d. A. J. Burnett, a pitcher for the New York Yankees, had an average number of strikeouts per inning pitched of .91 and an average number of home runs per inning of .16. Use the estimated regression equation developed in part (c) to predict the average number of runs given up per inning for A. J. Burnett. (*Note:* The actual value for R/IP was .6.)

e. Suppose a suggestion was made to also use the earned run average as another independent variable in part (c). What do you think of this suggestion?

 # 15.3 Multiple Coefficient of Determination

In simple linear regression we showed that the total sum of squares can be partitioned into two components: the sum of squares due to regression and the sum of squares due to error. The same procedure applies to the sum of squares in multiple regression.

> RELATIONSHIP AMONG SST, SSR, AND SSE
>
> $$SST = SSR + SSE \tag{15.7}$$
>
> where
>
> SST = total sum of squares = $\sum(y_i - \bar{y})^2$
> SSR = sum of squares due to regression = $\sum(\hat{y}_i - \bar{y})^2$
> SSE = sum of squares due to error = $\sum(y_i - \hat{y}_i)^2$

Because of the computational difficulty in computing the three sums of squares, we rely on computer packages to determine those values. The analysis of variance part of the Excel output in Figure 15.5 shows the three values for the Butler Trucking problem with two independent variables: $SST = 23.9$, $SSR = 21.6006$, and $SSE = 2.2994$. With only one independent variable (number of miles traveled), the Excel output in Figure 15.3 shows that $SST = 23.9$, $SSR = 15.8713$, and $SSE = 8.0287$. The value of SST is the same in both cases because it does not depend on $\hat{y}$, but SSR increases and SSE decreases when a second independent variable (number of deliveries) is added. The implication is that the estimated multiple regression equation provides a better fit for the observed data.

In Chapter 14 we used the coefficient of determination, $r^2 = SSR/SST$, to measure the goodness of fit for the estimated regression equation. The same concept applies to multiple regression. The term **multiple coefficient of determination** indicates that we are measuring the goodness of fit for the estimated multiple regression equation. The multiple coefficient of determination, denoted R^2, is computed as follows.

In the Excel Regression tool output the label R Square is used to identify the value of R^2.

> MULTIPLE COEFFICIENT OF DETERMINATION
>
> $$R^2 = \frac{SSR}{SST} \tag{15.8}$$

The multiple coefficient of determination can be interpreted as the proportion of the variability in the dependent variable that can be explained by the estimated multiple regression equation. Hence, when multiplied by 100, it can be interpreted as the percentage of the variability in y that can be explained by the estimated regression equation.

In the two-independent-variable Butler Trucking example, with SSR = 21.6006 and SST = 23.9, we have

$$R^2 = \frac{21.6006}{23.9} = .9038$$

Therefore, 90.38% of the variability in travel time y is explained by the estimated multiple regression equation with miles traveled and number of deliveries as the independent variables. In Figure 15.5, we see that the multiple coefficient of determination is also provided by the Excel output; it is denoted by R Square = .9038 (see cell B17).

Adding independent variables causes the prediction errors (residuals) to become smaller, thus reducing the sum of squares due to error, SSE. Because SSR = SST − SSE, when SSE becomes smaller, SSR becomes larger, causing R^2 = SSR/SST to increase.

Figure 15.3 shows that the R Square value for the estimated regression equation with only one independent variable, number of miles traveled (x_1), is .6641. Thus, the percentage of the variability in travel time that is explained by the estimated regression equation increases from 66.41% to 90.38% when number of deliveries is added as a second independent variable. In general, R^2 always increases as independent variables are added to the model.

Many analysts prefer adjusting R^2 for the number of independent variables to avoid overestimating the impact of adding an independent variable on the amount of variability explained by the estimated regression equation. With n denoting the number of observations and p denoting the number of independent variables, the **adjusted multiple coefficient of determination** is computed as follows.

If a variable is added to the model, R^2 becomes larger even if the variable added is not statistically significant. The adjusted multiple coefficient of determination compensates for the number of independent variables in the model.

ADJUSTED MULTIPLE COEFFICIENT OF DETERMINATION

$$R_a^2 = 1 - (1 - R^2)\frac{n - 1}{n - p - 1} \tag{15.9}$$

For the Butler Trucking example with $n = 10$ and $p = 2$, we have

$$R_a^2 = 1 - (1 - .9038)\frac{10 - 1}{10 - 2 - 1} = .8763$$

Thus, after adjusting for the two independent variables, we have an adjusted multiple coefficient of determination of .8763. This value is provided by the Excel output in Figure 15.5 as Adjusted R Square = .8763 (see cell B18).

Exercises

Methods

11. In exercise 1, the following estimated regression equation based on 10 observations was presented.

$$\hat{y} = 29.1270 + .5906x_1 + .4980x_2$$

The values of SST and SSR are 6724.125 and 6216.375, respectively.
   a. Find SSE.
   b. Compute R^2.
   c. Compute R_a^2.
   d. Comment on the goodness of fit.

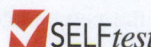

12. In exercise 2, 10 observations were provided for a dependent variable y and two independent variables x_1 and x_2; for these data SST = 15,182.9 and SSR = 14,052.2.
    a. Compute R^2.
    b. Compute R_a^2.
    c. Does the estimated regression equation explain a large amount of the variability in the data? Explain.

13. In exercise 3, the following estimated regression equation based on 30 observations was presented.

$$\hat{y} = 17.6 + 3.8x_1 - 2.3x_2 + 7.6x_3 + 2.7x_4$$

The values of SST and SSR are 1805 and 1760, respectively.
    a. Compute R^2.
    b. Compute R_a^2.
    c. Comment on the goodness of fit.

Applications

14. In exercise 4, the following estimated regression equation relating sales to inventory investment and advertising expenditures was given.

$$\hat{y} = 25 + 10x_1 + 8x_2$$

The data used to develop the model came from a survey of 10 stores; for those data, SST = 16,000 and SSR = 12,000.
    a. For the estimated regression equation given, compute R^2.
    b. Compute R_a^2.
    c. Does the model appear to explain a large amount of variability in the data? Explain.

15. In exercise 5, the owner of Showtime Movie Theaters, Inc. used multiple regression analysis to predict gross revenue (y) as a function of television advertising (x_1) and newspaper advertising (x_2). The estimated regression equation was

$$\hat{y} = 83.2 + 2.29x_1 + 1.30x_2$$

Showtime

The computer solution provided SST = 25.5 and SSR = 23.435.
    a. Compute and interpret R^2 and R_a^2.
    b. When television advertising was the only independent variable, $R^2 = .653$ and $R_a^2 = .595$. Do you prefer the multiple regression results? Explain.

NFLPassing

16. In exercise 6, data were given on the average number of passing yards per attempt (Yds/Att), the number of interceptions thrown per attempt (Int/Att), and the percentage of games won (Win%) for a random sample of 16 National Football League (NFL) teams for one full season.
    a. Did the estimated regression equation that uses only the average number of passing yards per attempt as the independent variable to predict the percentage of games won provide a good fit?
    b. Discuss the benefit of using both the average number of passing yards per attempt and the number of interceptions thrown per attempt to predict the percentage of games won.

PGADrivingDist

17. In part (d) of exercise 9, data contained in the DATAfile named *PGADrivingDist* (PGA Tour website, November 1, 2012) was used to develop an estimated regression equation to predict the average number of yards per drive given the ball speed and the launch angle.
    a. Does the estimated regression equation provide a good fit to the data? Explain.
    b. In part (b) of exercise 9, an estimated regression equation was developed using only ball speed to predict the average number of yards per drive. Compare the fit obtained using just ball speed to the fit obtained using ball speed and the launch angle.

MLBPitching

18. Refer to exercise 10, where Major League Baseball (MLB) pitching statistics were reported for a random sample of 20 pitchers from the American League for one full season.

    a. In part (c) of exercise 10, an estimated regression equation was developed relating the average number of runs given up per inning pitched given the average number of strikeouts per inning pitched and the average number of home runs per inning pitched. What are the values of R^2 and R_a^2?

    b. Does the estimated regression equation provide a good fit to the data? Explain.

    c. Suppose the earned run average (ERA) is used as the dependent variable in part (c) instead of the average number of runs given up per inning pitched. Does the estimated regression equation that uses the ERA provide a good fit to the data? Explain.

15.4   Model Assumptions

In Section 15.1 we introduced the following multiple regression model.

MULTIPLE REGRESSION MODEL

$$y = \beta_0 + \beta_1 x_1 + \beta_2 x_2 + \cdots + \beta_p x_p + \epsilon \qquad \textbf{(15.10)}$$

The assumptions about the error term ϵ in the multiple regression model parallel those for the simple linear regression model.

ASSUMPTIONS ABOUT THE ERROR TERM ϵ IN THE MULTIPLE REGRESSION MODEL $y = \beta_0 + \beta_1 x_1 + \cdots + \beta_p x_p + \epsilon$

1. The error term ϵ is a random variable with mean or expected value of zero; that is, $E(\epsilon) = 0$.
   Implication: For given values of $x_1, x_2, \ldots, x_p$, the expected, or average, value of y is given by

   $$E(y) = \beta_0 + \beta_1 x_1 + \beta_2 x_2 + \cdots + \beta_p x_p \qquad \textbf{(15.11)}$$

   Equation (15.11) is the multiple regression equation we introduced in Section 15.1. In this equation, $E(y)$ represents the average of all possible values of y that might occur for the given values of $x_1, x_2, \ldots, x_p$.

2. The variance of ϵ is denoted by σ^2 and is the same for all values of the independent variables $x_1, x_2, \ldots, x_p$.
   Implication: The variance of y about the regression line equals σ^2 and is the same for all values of $x_1, x_2, \ldots, x_p$.

3. The values of ϵ are independent.
   Implication: The value of ϵ for a particular set of values for the independent variables is not related to the value of ϵ for any other set of values.

4. The error term ϵ is a normally distributed random variable reflecting the deviation between the y value and the expected value of y given by $\beta_0 + \beta_1 x_1 + \beta_2 x_2 + \cdots + \beta_p x_p$.
   Implication: Because $\beta_0, \beta_1, \ldots, \beta_p$ are constants for the given values of $x_1, x_2, \ldots, x_p$, the dependent variable y is also a normally distributed random variable.

FIGURE 15.6   GRAPH OF THE REGRESSION EQUATION FOR MULTIPLE REGRESSION
ANALYSIS WITH TWO INDEPENDENT VARIABLES

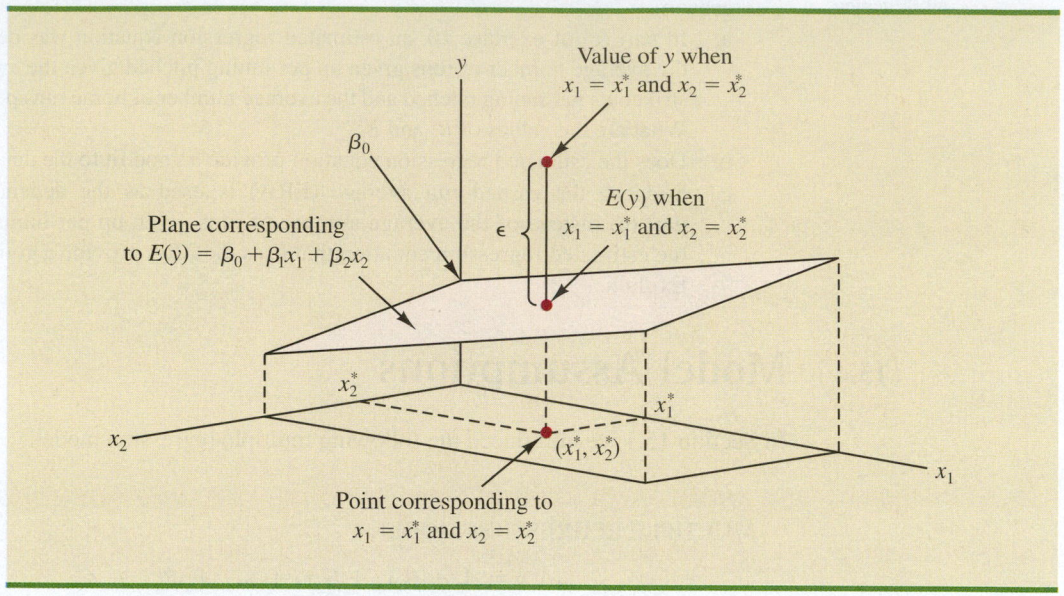

To obtain more insight about the form of the relationship given by equation (15.11),
consider the following two-independent-variable multiple regression equation.

$$E(y) = \beta_0 + \beta_1 x_1 + \beta_2 x_2$$

The graph of this equation is a plane in three-dimensional space. Figure 15.6 provides an
example of such a graph. Note that the value of ϵ shown is the difference between the actual
y value and the expected value of y, $E(y)$, when $x_1 = x_1^*$ and $x_2 = x_2^*$

In regression analysis, the term *response variable* is often used in place of the term
dependent variable. Furthermore, since the multiple regression equation generates a plane
or surface, its graph is called a *response surface*.

15.5 Testing for Significance

In this section we show how to conduct significance tests for a multiple regression relationship. The significance tests we used in simple linear regression were a t test and an
F test. In simple linear regression, both tests provide the same conclusion; that is, if the null
hypothesis is rejected, we conclude that $\beta_1 \neq 0$. In multiple regression, the t test and the
F test have different purposes.

1. The F test is used to determine whether a significant relationship exists between the
   dependent variable and the set of all the independent variables; we will refer to the
   F test as the test for *overall significance*.
2. If the F test shows an overall significance, the t test is used to determine whether
   each of the individual independent variables is significant. A separate t test is conducted for each of the independent variables in the model; we refer to each of these
   t tests as a test for *individual significance*.

In the material that follows, we will explain the F test and the t test and apply each to the
Butler Trucking Company example.

F **Test**

The multiple regression model as defined in Section 15.4 is

$$y = \beta_0 + \beta_1 x_1 + \beta_2 x_2 + \cdots + \beta_p x_p + \epsilon$$

The hypotheses for the *F* test involve the parameters of the multiple regression model.

$$H_0: \beta_1 = \beta_2 = \cdots = \beta_p = 0$$
$$H_a: \text{One or more of the parameters is not equal to zero}$$

If H_0 is rejected, the test gives us sufficient statistical evidence to conclude that one or more of the parameters is not equal to zero and that the overall relationship between *y* and the set of independent variables $x_1, x_2, \ldots, x_p$ is significant. However, if H_0 cannot be rejected, we do not have sufficient evidence to conclude that a significant relationship is present.

Before describing the steps of the *F* test, we need to review the concept of *mean square*. A mean square is a sum of squares divided by its corresponding degrees of freedom. In the multiple regression case, the total sum of squares has $n - 1$ degrees of freedom, the sum of squares due to regression (SSR) has *p* degrees of freedom, and the sum of squares due to error has $n - p - 1$ degrees of freedom. Hence, the mean square due to regression (MSR) is SSR/*p* and the mean square due to error (MSE) is SSE/$(n - p - 1)$.

$$\text{MSR} = \frac{\text{SSR}}{p} \tag{15.12}$$

and

$$\text{MSE} = \frac{\text{SSE}}{n - p - 1} \tag{15.13}$$

As discussed in Chapter 14, MSE provides an unbiased estimate of σ^2, the variance of the error term ϵ. If $H_0: \beta_1 = \beta_2 = \cdots = \beta_p = 0$ is true, MSR also provides an unbiased estimate of σ^2, and the value of MSR/MSE should be close to 1. However, if H_0 is false, MSR overestimates σ^2 and the value of MSR/MSE becomes larger. To determine how large the value of MSR/MSE must be to reject H_0, we make use of the fact that if H_0 is true and the assumptions about the multiple regression model are valid, the sampling distribution of MSR/MSE is an *F* distribution with *p* degrees of freedom in the numerator and $n - p - 1$ in the denominator. A summary of the *F* test for significance in multiple regression follows.

F TEST FOR OVERALL SIGNIFICANCE

$$H_0: \beta_1 = \beta_2 = \cdots = \beta_p = 0$$
$$H_a: \text{One or more of the parameters is not equal to zero}$$

TEST STATISTIC

$$F = \frac{\text{MSR}}{\text{MSE}} \tag{15.14}$$

REJECTION RULE

p-value approach: Reject H_0 if p-value $\leq \alpha$

Critical value approach: Reject H_0 if $F \geq F_\alpha$

where F_α is based on an *F* distribution with *p* degrees of freedom in the numerator and $n - p - 1$ degrees of freedom in the denominator.

FIGURE 15.7   REGRESSION TOOL OUTPUT FOR THE BUTLER TRUCKING EXAMPLE WITH TWO INDEPENDENT VARIABLES

	A	B	C	D	E	F	G	H	I
13	SUMMARY OUTPUT								
14									
15	*Regression Statistics*								
16	Multiple R	0.9507							
17	R Square	0.9038							
18	Adjusted R Square	0.8763							
19	Standard Error	0.5731							
20	Observations	10							
21									
22	ANOVA								
23		*df*	*SS*	*MS*	*F*	*Significance F*			
24	Regression	2	21.6006	10.8003	32.8784	0.0003			
25	Residual	7	2.2994	0.3285					
26	Total	9	23.9						
27									
28		*Coefficients*	*Standard Error*	*t Stat*	*P-value*				
29	Intercept	-0.8687	0.9515	-0.9129	0.3916				
30	Miles	0.0611	0.0099	6.1824	0.0005				
31	Deliveries	0.9234	0.2211	4.1763	0.0042				
32									
33									
34									
35									

> The *Significance F* value in cell F24 is the *p*-value used to test for overall significance.

> The *p*-value in cell E30 is used to test for the individual significance of Miles.

> The *p*-value in cell E31 is used to test for the individual significance of Deliveries.

Note: Rows 1–12 are hidden.

Let us apply the *F* test to the Butler Trucking Company multiple regression problem. With two independent variables, the hypotheses are written as follows.

$$H_0: \beta_1 = \beta_2 = 0$$
$$H_a: \beta_1 \text{ and/or } \beta_2 \text{ is not equal to zero}$$

Figure 15.7 shows a portion of the Excel Regression tool output shown previously in Figure 15.5 with miles traveled (x_1) and number of deliveries (x_2) as the two independent variables. In the analysis of variance part of the output, we see that MSR = 10.8003 and MSE = .3285. Using equation (15.14), we obtain the test statistic.

$$F = \frac{10.8003}{.3285} = 32.9$$

Note that the *F* value in the Excel output is $F = 32.8784$; the value we calculated differs because we used rounded values for MSR and MSE in the calculation. Using $\alpha = .01$, the *p*-value = 0.0003 in cell F24 indicates that we can reject $H_0: \beta_1 = \beta_2 = 0$ because the *p*-value is less than $\alpha = .01$. Alternatively, Table 4 of Appendix B shows that with 2 degrees of freedom in the numerator and 7 degrees of freedom in the denominator, $F_{.01} = 9.55$. With $32.9 > 9.55$, we reject $H_0: \beta_1 = \beta_2 = 0$ and conclude that a significant relationship is present between travel time *y* and the two independent variables, miles traveled and number of deliveries.

The label Significance F in cell F23 is used to identify the p-value in cell F24.

As noted previously, MSE provides an unbiased estimate of σ^2, the variance of the error term ϵ. Thus, the estimate of σ^2 is MSE = .3285. The square root of MSE is the estimate of the standard deviation of the error term. As defined in Section 14.5, this standard deviation is called the standard error of the estimate and is denoted *s*. Hence, we have $s = \sqrt{\text{MSE}} = \sqrt{.3285} = .5731$. Note that the value of the standard error of the estimate appears in cell B19 of Figure 15.7.

TABLE 15.3   GENERAL FORM OF THE ANOVA TABLE FOR MULTIPLE REGRESSION
WITH p INDEPENDENT VARIABLES

Source	Sum of Squares	Degrees of Freedom	Mean Square	F	p-Value
Regression	SSR	p	$\text{MSR} = \dfrac{\text{SSR}}{p}$	$F = \dfrac{\text{MSR}}{\text{MSE}}$	
Error	SSE	$n - p - 1$	$\text{MSE} = \dfrac{\text{SSE}}{n - p - 1}$		
Total	SST	$n - 1$			

Table 15.3 is the general form of the ANOVA table for multiple regression. The value of the F test statistic and its corresponding p-value in the last column can be used to make the hypothesis test conclusion. By reviewing the Excel output for Butler Trucking Company in Figure 15.7, we see that Excel's analysis of variance table contains this information.

t Test

If the F test shows that the multiple regression relationship is significant, a t test can be conducted to determine the significance of each of the individual parameters. The t test for individual significance follows.

---

t TEST FOR INDIVIDUAL SIGNIFICANCE

For any parameter β_i

$$H_0\text{: } \beta_i = 0$$
$$H_a\text{: } \beta_i \neq 0$$

TEST STATISTIC

$$t = \frac{b_i}{s_{b_i}} \tag{15.15}$$

REJECTION RULE

p-value approach: Reject H_0 if p-value $\leq \alpha$

Critical value approach: Reject H_0 if $t \leq -t_{\alpha/2}$ or if $t \geq t_{\alpha/2}$

where $t_{\alpha/2}$ is based on a t distribution with $n - p - 1$ degrees of freedom.

In the test statistic, s_{b_i} is the estimate of the standard deviation of b_i. The value of s_{b_i} will be provided by the computer software package.

Let us conduct the t test for the Butler Trucking regression problem. Refer to the section of Figure 15.7 that shows the Excel output for the t-ratio calculations. Values of b_1, b_2, s_{b_1}, and s_{b_2} are as follows.

$$b_1 = .0611 \quad s_{b_1} = .0099$$
$$b_2 = .9234 \quad s_{b_2} = .2211$$

Using equation (15.15), we obtain the test statistic for the hypotheses involving parameters β_1 and β_2.

$$t = .0611/.0099 = 6.1717$$

$$t = .9234/.2211 = 4.1764$$

The t values in the Regression tool output are 6.1824 and 4.1763. The difference is due to rounding.

Note that both of these t-ratio values and the corresponding p-values are provided by the Excel Regression tool output in Figure 15.7. Using $\alpha = .01$, the p-values of .0005 and .0042 on the Excel output indicate that we can reject $H_0: \beta_1 = 0$ and $H_0: \beta_2 = 0$. Hence, both parameters are statistically significant. Alternatively, Table 2 of Appendix B shows that with $n - p - 1 = 10 - 2 - 1 = 7$ degrees of freedom, $t_{.005} = 3.499$. Because $6.1717 > 3.499$, we reject $H_0: \beta_1 = 0$. Similarly, with $4.1763 > 3.499$, we reject $H_0: \beta_2 = 0$.

Multicollinearity

We use the term *independent variable* in regression analysis to refer to any variable being used to predict or explain the value of the dependent variable. The term does not mean, however, that the independent variables themselves are independent in any statistical sense. On the contrary, most independent variables in a multiple regression problem are correlated to some degree with one another. For example, in the Butler Trucking example involving the two independent variables x_1 (miles traveled) and x_2 (number of deliveries), we could treat the miles traveled as the dependent variable and the number of deliveries as the independent variable to determine whether those two variables are themselves related. We could then compute the sample correlation coefficient $r_{x_1 x_2}$ to determine the extent to which the variables are related. Doing so yields $r_{x_1 x_2} = .16$. Thus, we find some degree of linear association between the two independent variables. In multiple regression analysis, **multicollinearity** refers to the correlation among the independent variables.

To provide a better perspective of the potential problems of multicollinearity, let us consider a modification of the Butler Trucking example. Instead of x_2 being the number of deliveries, let x_2 denote the number of gallons of gasoline consumed. Clearly, x_1 (the miles traveled) and x_2 are related; that is, we know that the number of gallons of gasoline used depends on the number of miles traveled. Hence, we would conclude logically that x_1 and x_2 are highly correlated independent variables.

Assume that we obtain the equation $\hat{y} = b_0 + b_1 x_1 + b_2 x_2$ and find that the F test shows the relationship to be significant. Then suppose we conduct a t test on β_1 to determine whether $\beta_1 \neq 0$, and we cannot reject $H_0: \beta_1 = 0$. Does this result mean that travel time is not related to miles traveled? Not necessarily. What it probably means is that with x_2 already in the model, x_1 does not make a significant contribution to determining the value of y. This interpretation makes sense in our example; if we know the amount of gasoline consumed, we do not gain much additional information useful in predicting y by knowing the miles traveled. Similarly, a t test might lead us to conclude $\beta_2 = 0$ on the grounds that, with x_1 in the model, knowledge of the amount of gasoline consumed does not add much. In addition, if multicollinearity is present the signs and magnitudes of the estimated slope coefficients can be misleading.

A sample correlation coefficient greater than +.7 or less than −.7 for two independent variables is a rule of thumb warning of potential problems with multicollinearity.

To summarize, in t tests for the significance of individual parameters, the difficulty caused by multicollinearity is that it is possible to conclude that none of the individual parameters are significantly different from zero when an F test on the overall multiple regression equation indicates a significant relationship. Furthermore, multicollinearity can cause the estimated slope coefficients to be misleading. These problems are avoided when there is little correlation among the independent variables.

Statisticians have developed several tests for determining whether multicollinearity is high enough to cause problems. According to the rule of thumb test, multicollinearity is a potential problem if the absolute value of the sample correlation coefficient exceeds .7 for any two of the independent variables. The other types of tests are more advanced and beyond the scope of this text.

When the independent variables are highly correlated, it is not possible to determine the separate effect of any particular independent variable on the dependent variable.

If possible, every attempt should be made to avoid including independent variables that are highly correlated. In practice, however, strict adherence to this policy is rarely possible. When decision makers have reason to believe substantial multicollinearity is present, they must realize that separating the effects of the individual independent variables on the dependent variable is difficult.

NOTE AND COMMENT

Ordinarily, multicollinearity does not affect the way in which we perform our regression analysis or interpret the output from a study. However, when multicollinearity is severe—that is, when two or more of the independent variables are highly correlated with one another—we can have difficulty interpreting the results of t tests on the individual parameters. In addition to the type of problem illustrated in this section, severe cases of multicollinearity have been shown to result in least squares estimates that have the wrong sign. That

is, in simulated studies where researchers created the underlying regression model and then applied the least squares technique to develop estimates of β_0, β_1, β_2, and so on, it has been shown that under conditions of high multicollinearity the least squares estimates can have a sign opposite that of the parameter being estimated. For example, β_2 might actually be $+10$ and b_2, its estimate, might turn out to be -2. Thus, little faith can be placed in the individual coefficients if multicollinearity is present to a high degree.

Exercises

Methods

 **SELF*test***

19. In exercise 1, the following estimated regression equation based on 10 observations was presented.

$$\hat{y} = 29.1270 + .5906x_1 + .4980x_2$$

Here SST = 6724.125, SSR = 6216.375, s_{b_1} = .0813, and s_{b_2} = .0567.
    a.   Compute MSR and MSE.
    b.   Compute F and perform the appropriate F test. Use $\alpha = .05$.
    c.   Perform a t test for the significance of β_1. Use $\alpha = .05$.
    d.   Perform a t test for the significance of β_2. Use $\alpha = .05$.

20. Refer to the data presented in exercise 2. The estimated regression equation for these data is

$$\hat{y} = -18.4 + 2.01x_1 + 4.74x_2$$

Here SST = 15,182.9, SSR = 14,052.2, s_{b_1} = .2471, and s_{b_2} = .9484.
    a.   Test for a significant relationship among x_1, x_2, and y. Use $\alpha = .05$.
    b.   Is β_1 significant? Use $\alpha = .05$.
    c.   Is β_2 significant? Use $\alpha = .05$.

21. The following estimated regression equation was developed for a model involving two independent variables.

$$\hat{y} = 40.7 + 8.63x_1 + 2.71x_2$$

After x_2 was dropped from the model, the least squares method was used to obtain an estimated regression equation involving only x_1 as an independent variable.

$$\hat{y} = 42.0 + 9.01x_1$$

    a.   Give an interpretation of the coefficient of x_1 in both models.
    b.   Could multicollinearity explain why the coefficient of x_1 differs in the two models? If so, how?

Applications

22. In exercise 4, the following estimated regression equation relating sales to inventory investment and advertising expenditures was given.

$$\hat{y} = 25 + 10x_1 + 8x_2$$

The data used to develop the model came from a survey of 10 stores; for these data SST = 16,000 and SSR = 12,000.

a. Compute SSE, MSE, and MSR.

b. Use an F test and a .05 level of significance to determine whether there is a relationship among the variables.

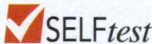 **SELF***test*   23. Refer to exercise 5.

a. Use $\alpha = .01$ to test the hypotheses

$$H_0: \beta_1 = \beta_2 = 0$$
$$H_a: \beta_1 \text{ and/or } \beta_2 \text{ is not equal to zero}$$

for the model $y = \beta_0 + \beta_1 x_1 + \beta_2 x_2 + \epsilon$, where

$$x_1 = \text{television advertising (\$1000s)}$$
$$x_2 = \text{newspaper advertising (\$1000s)}$$

b. Use $\alpha = .05$ to test the significance of β_1. Should x_1 be dropped from the model?

c. Use $\alpha = .05$ to test the significance of β_2. Should x_2 be dropped from the model?

DATA*file*

NFL2011

24. The National Football League (NFL) records a variety of performance data for individuals and teams. A portion of the data showing the average number of passing yards obtained per game on offense (OffPassYds/G), the average number of yards given up per game on defense (DefYds/G), and the precentage of games won (Win%) for one full season follows.

Team	OffPassYds/G	DefYds/G	Win%
Arizona	222.9	355.1	50.0
Atlanta	262.0	333.6	62.5
Baltimore	213.9	288.9	75.0
.	.	.	.
.	.	.	.
.	.	.	.
St. Louis	179.4	358.4	12.5
Tampa Bay	228.1	394.4	25.0
Tennessee	245.2	355.1	56.3
Washington	235.8	339.8	31.3

a. Develop an estimated regression equation that can be used to predict the percentage of games won given the average number of passing yards obtained per game on offense and the average number of yards given up per game on defense.

b. Use the F test to determine the overall significance of the relationship. What is your conclusion at the .05 level of significance?

c. Use the t test to determine the significance of each independent variable. What is your conclusion at the .05 level of significance?

25. The *Condé Nast Traveler* Gold List provides ratings for the top 20 small cruise ships. The following data shown are the scores each ship received based upon the results from *Condé Nast Traveler's* annual Readers' Choice Survey. Each score represents the percentage of respondents who rated a ship as excellent or very good on several

criteria, including Itineraries/Schedule, Shore Excursions, and Food/Dining. An overall score is also reported and used to rank the ships. The highest ranked ship, the *Seabourn Odyssey,* has an overall score of 94.4, the highest component of which is 97.8 for Food/Dining.

DATA file

CruiseShips

Ship	Overall	Itineraries/Schedule	Shore Excursions	Food/Dining
Seabourn Odyssey	94.4	94.6	90.9	97.8
Seabourn Pride	93.0	96.7	84.2	96.7
National Geographic Endeavor	92.9	100.0	100.0	88.5
Seabourn Sojourn	91.3	88.6	94.8	97.1
Paul Gauguin	90.5	95.1	87.9	91.2
Seabourn Legend	90.3	92.5	82.1	98.8
Seabourn Spirit	90.2	96.0	86.3	92.0
Silver Explorer	89.9	92.6	92.6	88.9
Silver Spirit	89.4	94.7	85.9	90.8
Seven Seas Navigator	89.2	90.6	83.3	90.5
Silver Whisperer	89.2	90.9	82.0	88.6
National Geographic Explorer	89.1	93.1	93.1	89.7
Silver Cloud	88.7	92.6	78.3	91.3
Celebrity Xpedition	87.2	93.1	91.7	73.6
Silver Shadow	87.2	91.0	75.0	89.7
Silver Wind	86.6	94.4	78.1	91.6
SeaDream II	86.2	95.5	77.4	90.9
Wind Star	86.1	94.9	76.5	91.5
Wind Surf	86.1	92.1	72.3	89.3
Wind Spirit	85.2	93.5	77.4	91.9

a. Determine the estimated regression equation that can be used to predict the overall score given the scores for Itineraries/Schedule, Shore Excursions, and Food/Dining.

b. Use the *F* test to determine the overall significance of the relationship. What is your conclusion at the .05 level of significance?

c. Use the *t* test to determine the significance of each independent variable. What is your conclusion at the .05 level of significance?

d. Remove any independent variable that is not significant from the estimated regression equation. What is your recommended estimated regression equation?

DATA file

MLBPitching

26. In exercise 10, data showing the values of several pitching statistics for a random sample of 20 pitchers from the American League of Major League Baseball were provided. In part (c) of this exercise an estimated regression equation was developed to predict the average number of runs given up per inning pitched (R/IP) given the average number of strikeouts per inning pitched (SO/IP) and the average number of home runs per inning pitched (HR/IP).

a. Use the *F* test to determine the overall significance of the relationship. What is your conclusion at the .05 level of significance?

b. Use the *t* test to determine the significance of each independent variable. What is your conclusion at the .05 level of significance?

Using the Estimated Regression Equation for Estimation and Prediction

The procedures for estimating the mean value of *y* and predicting an individual value of *y* in multiple regression are similar to those in regression analysis involving one independent variable. First, recall that in Chapter 14 we showed that the estimated regression equation

TABLE 15.4   THE 95% PREDICTION INTERVALS FOR BUTLER TRUCKING

Value of x_1	Value of x_2	Prediction Interval	
		Lower Limit	Upper Limit
50	2	2.414	5.656
50	3	3.368	6.548
50	4	4.157	7.607
100	2	5.500	8.683
100	3	6.520	9.510
100	4	7.362	10.515

$\hat{y} = b_0 + b_1x$ can be used to estimate the mean value of y for a given value of x as well as to predict an individual value of y for a given value of x. In multiple regression we use the same procedure. That is, we substitute the value of $x_1, x_2, \ldots, x_p$ into the estimated regression equation and use the corresponding value of $\hat{y}$ to estimate the mean value of y given $x_1, x_2, \ldots, x_p$ as well as to predict an individual of y given $x_1, x_2, \ldots, x_p$.

To illustrate the procedure in multiple regression, suppose that for the Butler Trucking example we want to use the estimated regression equation involving x_1 (miles traveled) and x_2 (number of deliveries) to develop two interval estimates:

1. A *confidence interval* of the mean travel time for all trucks that travel 100 miles and make two deliveries
2. A *prediction interval* of the travel time for *one specific* truck that travels 100 miles and makes two deliveries

The Excel output in Figure 15.5 showed the estimated regression equation is

$$\hat{y} = -.8687 + .0611x_1 + .9234x_2$$

With $x_1 = 100$ and $x_2 = 2$, we obtain the following value of $\hat{y}$:

$$\hat{y} = -.8687 + .0611(100) + .9234(2) = 7.09$$

Hence a point estimate of the mean travel time for all trucks that travel 100 miles and make two deliveries is approximately 7 hours. And a prediction of the travel time for one specific truck that travels 100 miles and makes two deliveries is also 7 hours.

The formulas required to develop confidence and prediction intervals for multiple regression are beyond the scope of the text. And in multiple regression hand computation is simply not practical. Although Excel's Regression tool does not have an option for computing interval estimates, some software packages do provide confidence and prediction intervals. The interpretation of these intervals is the same as for simple linear regression. Table 15.4 shows the 95% prediction intervals for the Butler Trucking problem for selected values of x_1 and x_2. We see that the prediction interval of the travel time for *one specific* truck that travels 100 miles and makes two deliveries is approximately 5.5 to 8.7 hours.

Exercises

Methods

27.   In exercise 1, the following estimated regression equation based on 10 observations was presented.

$$\hat{y} = 29.1270 + .5906x_1 + .4980x_2$$

a.   Develop a point estimate of the mean value of y when $x_1 = 180$ and $x_2 = 310$.
b.   Predict an individual value of y when $x_1 = 180$ and $x_2 = 310$.

28.   Refer to the data in exercise 2. The estimated regression equation for those data is

$$\hat{y} = -18.4 + 2.01x_1 + 4.74x_2$$

a.   Develop a point estimate of the mean value of y when $x_1 = 45$ and $x_2 = 15$.
b.   Develop a 95% prediction interval for y when $x_1 = 45$ and $x_2 = 15$.

Applications

29.   In exercise 5, the owner of Showtime Movie Theaters, Inc. used multiple regression analysis to predict gross revenue (y) as a function of television advertising (x_1) and newspaper advertising (x_2). The estimated regression equation was

$$\hat{y} = 83.2 + 2.29x_1 + 1.30x_2$$

a.   What is the gross revenue expected for a week when $3500 is spent on television advertising ($x_1 = 3.5$) and $1800 is spent on newspaper advertising ($x_2 = 1.8$)?
b.   Provide a 95% prediction interval for next week's revenue, assuming that the advertising expenditures will be allocated as in part (a).

NFL2011

30.   In exercise 24, an estimated regression equation was developed relating the percentage of games won by a team in the National Football League during a complete season to the average number of passing yards obtained per game on offense and the average number of yards given up per game on defense during the season.
a.   Predict the percentage of games won for a particular team that averages 225 passing yards per game on offense and gives up an average of 300 yards per game on defense.
b.   Develop a 95% prediction interval for the percentage of games won for a particular team that averages 225 passing yards per game on offense and gives up an average of 300 yards per game on defense.

31.   The American Association of Individual Investors (AAII) On-Line Discount Broker Survey polls members on their experiences with electronic trades handled by discount brokers. As part of the survey, members were asked to rate their satisfaction with the trade price and the speed of execution, as well as provide an overall satisfaction rating. Possible responses (scores) were no opinion (0), unsatisfied (1), somewhat satisfied (2), satisfied (3), and very satisfied (4). For each broker, summary scores were computed by computing a weighted average of the scores provided by each respondent. A portion of the survey results follows (AAII website, February 7, 2012).

Broker

Brokerage	Trade Price	Speed of Execution	Satisfaction Electronic Trades
Scottrade, Inc.	3.4	3.4	3.5
Charles Schwab	3.2	3.3	3.4
Fidelity Brokerage Services	3.1	3.4	3.9
TD Ameritrade	2.9	3.6	3.7
E*Trade Financial	2.9	3.2	2.9
(Not listed)	2.5	3.2	2.7
Vanguard Brokerage Services	2.6	3.8	2.8
USAA Brokerage Services	2.4	3.8	3.6
Thinkorswim	2.6	2.6	2.6
Wells Fargo Investments	2.3	2.7	2.3
Interactive Brokers	3.7	4.0	4.0
Zecco.com	2.5	2.5	2.5
Firstrade Securities	3.0	3.0	4.0
Banc of America Investment Services	4.0	1.0	2.0

a. Develop an estimated regression equation using trade price and speed of execution to predict overall satisfaction with the broker.
b. Finger Lakes Investments has developed a new electronic trading system and would like to predict overall customer satisfaction assuming they can provide satisfactory levels of service levels (3) for both trade price and speed of execution. Use the estimated regression equation developed in part (a) to predict overall satisfaction level for Finger Lakes Investments if they can achieve these performance levels.
c. Develop a 95% prediction interval of overall satisfaction for Finger Lakes Investments assuming they achieve service levels of 3 for both trade price and speed of execution.

Categorical Independent Variables

The independent variables may be categorical or quantitative.

Thus far, the examples we have considered involved quantitative independent variables such as student population, distance traveled, and number of deliveries. In many situations, however, we must work with **categorical independent variables** such as gender (male, female), method of payment (cash, credit card, check), and so on. The purpose of this section is to show how categorical variables are handled in regression analysis. To illustrate the use and interpretation of a categorical independent variable, we will consider a problem facing the managers of Johnson Filtration, Inc.

An Example: Johnson Filtration, Inc.

Johnson Filtration, Inc., provides maintenance service for water-filtration systems throughout southern Florida. Customers contact Johnson with requests for maintenance service on their water-filtration systems. To estimate the service time and the service cost, Johnson's managers want to predict the repair time necessary for each maintenance request. Hence, repair time in hours is the dependent variable. Repair time is believed to be related to two factors, the number of months since the last maintenance service and the type of repair problem (mechanical or electrical). Data for a sample of 10 service calls are reported in Table 15.5.

Let y denote the repair time in hours and x_1 denote the number of months since the last maintenance service. The regression model that uses only x_1 to predict y is

$$y = \beta_0 + \beta_1 x_1 + \epsilon$$

TABLE 15.5   DATA FOR THE JOHNSON FILTRATION EXAMPLE

Service Call	Months Since Last Service	Type of Repair	Repair Time in Hours
1	2	electrical	2.9
2	6	mechanical	3.0
3	8	electrical	4.8
4	3	mechanical	1.8
5	2	electrical	2.9
6	7	electrical	4.9
7	9	mechanical	4.2
8	8	mechanical	4.8
9	4	electrical	4.4
10	6	electrical	4.5

FIGURE 15.8 REGRESSION TOOL OUTPUT FOR THE JOHNSON FILTRATION EXAMPLE WITH MONTHS SINCE LAST SERVICE CALL AS THE INDEPENDENT VARIABLE

The Excel Regression tool output appears in a new worksheet because we selected New Worksheet Ply as the Output option in the Regression dialog box.

	A	B	C	D	E	F	G
1	SUMMARY OUTPUT						
2							
3	*Regression Statistics*						
4	Multiple R	0.7309					
5	R Square	0.5342					
6	Adjusted R Square	0.4759					
7	Standard Error	0.7810					
8	Observations	10					
9							
10	ANOVA						
11		*df*	*SS*	*MS*	*F*	*Significance F*	
12	Regression	1	5.5960	5.5960	9.1739	0.0163	
13	Residual	8	4.8800	0.61			
14	Total	9	10.476				
15							
16		*Coefficients*	*Standard Error*	*t Stat*	*P-value*		
17	Intercept	2.1473	0.6050	3.5493	0.0075		
18	Months	0.3041	0.1004	3.0288	0.0163		
19							

Using Excel's Regression tool to develop the estimated regression equation, we obtained the Excel output shown in Figure 15.8. The estimated regression equation is

$$\hat{y} = 2.1473 + .3041x_1 \tag{15.16}$$

At the .05 level of significance, the p-value of .0163 for the t (or F) test indicates that the number of months since the last service is significantly related to repair time. R Square = .5342 indicates that x_1 alone explains 53.42% of the variability in repair time.

To incorporate the type of repair into the regression model, we define the following variable.

$$x_2 = \begin{cases} 0 \text{ if the type of repair is mechanical} \\ 1 \text{ if the type of repair is electrical} \end{cases}$$

In regression analysis x_2 is called a **dummy** or *indicator* **variable**. Using this dummy variable, we can write the multiple regression model as

$$y = \beta_0 + \beta_1 x_1 + \beta_2 x_2 + \epsilon$$

Table 15.6 is the revised data set that includes the values of the dummy variable. Using Excel and the data in Table 15.6, we can develop estimates of the model parameters. The Excel Regression tool output in Figure 15.9 shows that the estimated multiple regression equation is

$$\hat{y} = .9305 + .3876x_1 + 1.2627x_2 \tag{15.17}$$

At the .05 level of significance, the p-value of .0010 associated with the F test ($F = 21.357$) indicates that the regression relationship is significant. The t test part of the printout in

TABLE 15.6   DATA FOR THE JOHNSON FILTRATION EXAMPLE WITH TYPE OF REPAIR
INDICATED BY A DUMMY VARIABLE ($x_2 = 0$ FOR MECHANICAL; $x_2 = 1$
FOR ELECTRICAL)

DATA *file*

Johnson

Customer	Months Since Last Service (x_1)	Type of Repair (x_2)	Repair Time in Hours (y)
1	2	1	2.9
2	6	0	3.0
3	8	1	4.8
4	3	0	1.8
5	2	1	2.9
6	7	1	4.9
7	9	0	4.2
8	8	0	4.8
9	4	1	4.4
10	6	1	4.5

Figure 15.9 shows that both months since last service (p-value = .0004) and type of
repair (p-value = .0051) are statistically significant. In addition, R Square = 0.8952
and Adjusted R Square = 0.8190 indicate that the estimated regression equation does
a good job of explaining the variability in repair times. Thus, equation (15.17) should
prove helpful in predicting the repair time necessary for the various service calls.

FIGURE 15.9   REGRESSION TOOL OUTPUT FOR THE JOHNSON FILTRATION EXAMPLE
WITH MONTHS SINCE LAST SERVICE CALL AND TYPE OF REPAIR
AS THE INDEPENDENT VARIABLES

	A	B	C	D	E	F	G
1	SUMMARY OUTPUT						
2							
3	*Regression Statistics*						
4	Multiple R	0.9269					
5	R Square	0.8592					
6	Adjusted R Square	0.8190					
7	Standard Error	0.4590					
8	Observations	10					
9							
10	ANOVA						
11		*df*	*SS*	*MS*	*F*	*Significance F*	
12	Regression	2	9.0009	4.5005	21.357	0.0010	
13	Residual	7	1.4751	0.2107			
14	Total	9	10.476				
15							
16		*Coefficients*	*Standard Error*	*t Stat*	*P-value*		
17	Intercept	0.9305	0.4670	1.9926	0.0866		
18	Months	0.3876	0.0626	6.1954	0.0004		
19	Type	1.2627	0.3141	4.0197	0.0051		
20							

Interpreting the Parameters

The multiple regression equation for the Johnson Filtration example is

$$E(y) = \beta_0 + \beta_1 x_1 + \beta_2 x_2 \qquad \textbf{(15.18)}$$

To understand how to interpret the parameters β_0, β_1, and β_2 when a categorical variable is present, consider the case when $x_2 = 0$ (mechanical repair). Using $E(y \mid \text{mechanical})$ to denote the mean or expected value of repair time *given* a mechanical repair, we have

$$E(y \mid \text{mechanical}) = \beta_0 + \beta_1 x_1 + \beta_2(0) = \beta_0 + \beta_1 x_1 \qquad \textbf{(15.19)}$$

Similarly, for an electrical repair ($x_2 = 1$), we have

$$E(y \mid \text{electrical}) = \beta_0 + \beta_1 x_1 + \beta_2(1) = \beta_0 + \beta_1 x_1 + \beta_2$$
$$= (\beta_0 + \beta_2) + \beta_1 x_1 \qquad \textbf{(15.20)}$$

Comparing equations (15.19) and (15.20), we see that the mean repair time is a linear function of x_1 for both mechanical and electrical repairs. The slope of both equations is β_1, but the y-intercept differs. The y-intercept is β_0 in equation (15.19) for mechanical repairs and ($\beta_0 + \beta_2$) in equation (15.20) for electrical repairs. The interpretation of β_2 is that it indicates the difference between the mean repair time for an electrical repair and the mean repair time for a mechanical repair.

If β_2 is positive, the mean repair time for an electrical repair will be greater than that for a mechanical repair; if β_2 is negative, the mean repair time for an electrical repair will be less than that for a mechanical repair. Finally, if $\beta_2 = 0$, there is no difference in the mean repair time between electrical and mechanical repairs and the type of repair is not related to the repair time.

Using the estimated multiple regression equation $\hat{y} = .9305 + .3876x_1 + 1.2627x_2$, we see that .9305 is the estimate of β_0, .3876 is the estimate of β_1, and 1.2627 is the estimate of β_2. Thus, when $x_2 = 0$ (mechanical repair)

$$\hat{y} = .9305 + .3876x_1 \qquad \textbf{(15.21)}$$

and when $x_2 = 1$ (electrical repair)

$$\hat{y} = .9305 + .3876x_1 + 1.2627(1)$$
$$= 2.1932 + .3876x_1 \qquad \textbf{(15.22)}$$

In effect, the use of a dummy variable for type of repair provides two estimated regression equations that can be used to predict the repair time, one corresponding to mechanical repairs and one corresponding to electrical repairs. In addition, with $b_2 = 1.2627$, we learn that, on average, electrical repairs require 1.2627 hours longer than mechanical repairs.

Figure 15.10 is the plot of the Johnson data from Table 13.6. Repair time in hours (y) is represented by the vertical axis and months since last service (x_1) is represented by the horizontal axis. A data point for a mechanical repair is indicated by an M and a data point for an electrical repair is indicated by an E. Equations (15.21) and (15.22) are plotted on the graph to show graphically the two equations that can be used to predict the repair time, one corresponding to mechanical repairs and one corresponding to electrical repairs.

FIGURE 15.10   SCATTER DIAGRAM FOR THE JOHNSON FILTRATION REPAIR DATA FROM TABLE 15.6

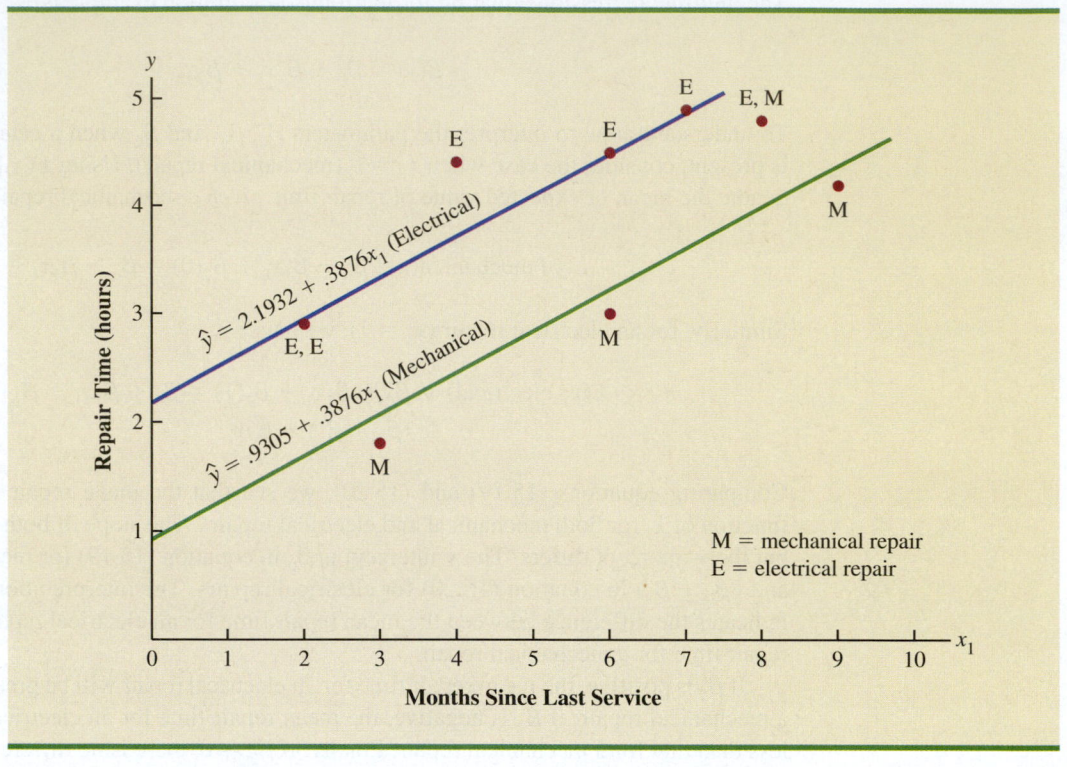

More Complex Categorical Variables

A categorical variable with k levels must be modeled using k − 1 dummy variables. Care must be taken in defining and interpreting the dummy variables.

Because the categorical variable for the Johnson Filtration example had two levels (mechanical and electrical), defining a dummy variable with zero indicating a mechanical repair and one indicating an electrical repair was easy. However, when a categorical variable has more than two levels, care must be taken in both defining and interpreting the dummy variables. As we will show, if a categorical variable has k levels, $k − 1$ dummy variables are required, with each dummy variable being coded as 0 or 1.

For example, suppose a manufacturer of copy machines organized the sales territories for a particular state into three regions: A, B, and C. The managers want to use regression analysis to help predict the number of copiers sold per week. With the number of units sold as the dependent variable, they are considering several independent variables (the number of sales personnel, advertising expenditures, and so on). Suppose the managers believe sales region is also an important factor in predicting the number of copiers sold. Because sales region is a categorical variable with three levels, A, B and C, we will need $3 − 1 = 2$ dummy variables to represent the sales region. Each variable can be coded 0 or 1 as follows.

$$x_1 = \begin{cases} 1 \text{ if sales region B} \\ 0 \text{ otherwise} \end{cases}$$

$$x_2 = \begin{cases} 1 \text{ if sales region C} \\ 0 \text{ otherwise} \end{cases}$$

With this definition, we have the following values of x_1 and x_2.

Region	x_1	x_2
A	0	0
B	1	0
C	0	1

Observations corresponding to region A would be coded $x_1 = 0$, $x_2 = 0$; observations corresponding to region B would be coded $x_1 = 1$, $x_2 = 0$; and observations corresponding to region C would be coded $x_1 = 0$, $x_2 = 1$.

The regression equation relating the expected value of the number of units sold, $E(y)$, to the dummy variables would be written as

$$E(y) = \beta_0 + \beta_1 x_1 + \beta_2 x_2$$

To help us interpret the parameters β_0, β_1, and β_2, consider the following three variations of the regression equation.

$$E(y \mid \text{region A}) = \beta_0 + \beta_1(0) + \beta_2(0) = \beta_0$$
$$E(y \mid \text{region B}) = \beta_0 + \beta_1(1) + \beta_2(0) = \beta_0 + \beta_1$$
$$E(y \mid \text{region C}) = \beta_0 + \beta_1(0) + \beta_2(1) = \beta_0 + \beta_2$$

Thus, β_0 is the mean or expected value of sales for region A; β_1 is the difference between the mean number of units sold in region B and the mean number of units sold in region A; and β_2 is the difference between the mean number of units sold in region C and the mean number of units sold in region A.

Two dummy variables were required because sales region is a categorical variable with three levels. But the assignment of $x_1 = 0$, $x_2 = 0$ to indicate region A, $x_1 = 1$, $x_2 = 0$ to indicate region B, and $x_1 = 0$, $x_2 = 1$ to indicate region C was arbitrary. For example, we could have chosen $x_1 = 1$, $x_2 = 0$ to indicate region A, $x_1 = 0$, $x_2 = 0$ to indicate region B, and $x_1 = 0$, $x_2 = 1$ to indicate region C. In that case, β_1 would have been interpreted as the mean difference between regions A and B and β_2 as the mean difference between regions C and B.

The important point to remember is that when a categorical variable has k levels, $k - 1$ dummy variables are required in the multiple regression analysis. Thus, if the sales region example had a fourth region, labeled D, three dummy variables would be necessary. For example, the three dummy variables can be coded as follows.

$$x_1 = \begin{cases} 1 \text{ if sales region B} \\ 0 \text{ otherwise} \end{cases} \qquad x_2 = \begin{cases} 1 \text{ if sales region C} \\ 0 \text{ otherwise} \end{cases} \qquad x_3 = \begin{cases} 1 \text{ if sales region D} \\ 0 \text{ otherwise} \end{cases}$$

Exercises

Methods

32. Consider a regression study involving a dependent variable y, a quantitative independent variable x_1, and a categorical independent variable with two levels (level 1 and level 2).
    a. Write a multiple regression equation relating x_1 and the categorical variable to y.
    b. What is the expected value of y corresponding to level 1 of the categorical variable?
    c. What is the expected value of y corresponding to level 2 of the categorical variable?
    d. Interpret the parameters in your regression equation.

33. Consider a regression study involving a dependent variable y, a quantitative independent variable x_1, and a categorical independent variable with three possible levels (level 1, level 2, and level 3).
    a. How many dummy variables are required to represent the categorical variable?
    b. Write a multiple regression equation relating x_1 and the categorical variable to y.
    c. Interpret the parameters in your regression equation.

Applications

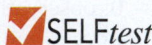 **SELF**test

34. Management proposed the following regression model to predict sales at a fast-food outlet.

$$y = \beta_0 + \beta_1 x_1 + \beta_2 x_2 + \beta_3 x_3 + \epsilon$$

where

$$x_1 = \text{number of competitors within one mile}$$
$$x_2 = \text{population within one mile (1000s)}$$
$$x_3 = \begin{cases} 1 \text{ if drive-up window present} \\ 0 \text{ otherwise} \end{cases}$$
$$y = \text{sales (\$1000s)}$$

The following estimated regression equation was developed after 20 outlets were surveyed.

$$\hat{y} = 10.1 - 4.2x_1 + 6.8x_2 + 15.3x_3$$

   a. What is the expected amount of sales attributable to the drive-up window?
   b. Predict sales for a store with two competitors, a population of 8000 within one mile, and no drive-up window.
   c. Predict sales for a store with one competitor, a population of 3000 within 1 mile, and a drive-up window.

35. Refer to the Johnson Filtration problem introduced in this section. Suppose that in addition to information on the number of months since the machine was serviced and whether a mechanical or an electrical repair was necessary, the managers obtained a list showing which repairperson performed the service. The revised data follow.

 DATA *file*

Repair

Repair Time in Hours	Months Since Last Service	Type of Repair	Repairperson
2.9	2	Electrical	Dave Newton
3.0	6	Mechanical	Dave Newton
4.8	8	Electrical	Bob Jones
1.8	3	Mechanical	Dave Newton
2.9	2	Electrical	Dave Newton
4.9	7	Electrical	Bob Jones
4.2	9	Mechanical	Bob Jones
4.8	8	Mechanical	Bob Jones
4.4	4	Electrical	Bob Jones
4.5	6	Electrical	Dave Newton

   a. Ignore for now the months since the last maintenance service (x_1) and the repairperson who performed the service. Develop the estimated simple linear regression equation to predict the repair time (y) given the type of repair (x_2). Recall that $x_2 = 0$ if the type of repair is mechanical and 1 if the type of repair is electrical.
   b. Does the equation that you developed in part (a) provide a good fit for the observed data? Explain.

    c.   Ignore for now the months since the last maintenance service and the type of repair associated with the machine. Develop the estimated simple linear regression equation to predict the repair time given the repairperson who performed the service. Let $x_3 = 0$ if Bob Jones performed the service and $x_3 = 1$ if Dave Newton performed the service.

    d.   Does the equation that you developed in part (c) provide a good fit for the observed data? Explain.

36.   This problem is an extension of the situation described in exercise 35.

    a.   Develop the estimated regression equation to predict the repair time given the number of months since the last maintenance service, the type of repair, and the repairperson who performed the service.

    b.   At the .05 level of significance, test whether the estimated regression equation developed in part (a) represents a significant relationship between the independent variables and the dependent variable.

    c.   Is the addition of the independent variable x_3, the repairperson who performed the service, statistically significant? Use $\alpha = .05$. What explanation can you give for the results observed?

37.   Best Buy, a nationwide retailer of electronics, computers, and appliances, sells several brands of refrigerators. A random sample of models of full size refrigerators prices sold by Best Buy and the corresponding cubic feet (cu. ft.) and list price follow (Best Buy website, July 26, 2016).

DATA *file*

Refrigerators

Model	Cu. Ft.	List Price
Frigidaire Gallery Custom-Flex Top-Freezer Refrigerator	18.3	$899.99
GE French Door Refrigerator	24.8	$1,599.99
GE Frost-Free Side-by-Side Refrigerator with Thru-the-Door Ice and Water	25.4	$1,599.99
Whirlpool Top-Freezer Refrigerator	19.3	$749.99
GE Frost-Free Top-Freezer Refrigerator	17.5	$599.99
Whirlpool French Door Refrigerator with Thru-the-Ice and Door Water	19.6	$1,619.99
Samsung French Door Refrigerator	25.0	$999.99
Samsung Side-by-Side Refrigerator	24.5	$1,299.99
Whirlpool Side-by-Side Refrigerator with Thru-the-Door Ice and Water	25.4	$1,299.99
Frigidaire Gallery Frost-Free Side-by-Side Refrigerator with Thru-the-Door Ice and Water	26.0	$1,299.99
Frigidaire Side-by-Side Refrigerator with Thru-the-Door Ice and Water	25.6	$1,099.99
Frigidaire Top-Freezer Refrigerator	18.0	$579.99
Whirlpool French Door Refrigerator with Thru-the-Door Ice and Water	25.0	$2,199.99
Whirlpool Top-Freezer Refrigerator	20.5	$849.99
GE Frost-Free Top-Freezer Refrigerator	15.5	$549.99
Samsung 4-Door French Door Refrigerator with Thru-the-Door Ice and Water	28.2	$2,599.99
Samsung Showcase 4-Door French Door Refrigerator	27.8	$2,999.99
Samsung 3-Door French Door Refrigerator with Thru-the-Door Ice and Water	24.6	$2,399.99
Frigidaire Side-by-Side Refrigerator with Thru-the-Door Ice and Water	22.6	$1,099.99
GE Side-by-Side Refrigerator with Thru-the-Door Ice and Water	21.8	$1,499.99
GE Bottom-Freezer Refrigerator	20.9	$1,649.99

a. Develop the estimated simple linear regression equation to show how list price is related to the independent variable cubic feet.

b. At the .05 level of significance, test whether the estimated regression equation developed in part (a) indicates a significant relationship between list price and cubic feet.

c. Develop a dummy variable that will account for whether the refrigerator has the thru-the-door ice and water feature. Code the dummy variable with a value of 1 if the refrigerator has the thru-the-door ice and water feature and with 0 otherwise. Use this dummy variable to develop the estimated multiple regression equation to show how list price is related to cubic feet and the thru-the-door ice and water feature.

d. At $\alpha = .05$, is the thru-the-door ice and water feature a significant factor in the list price of a refrigerator?

38. A 10-year study conducted by the American Heart Association provided data on how age, blood pressure, and smoking relate to the risk of strokes. Assume that the following data are from a portion of this study. Risk is interpreted as the probability (times 100) that the patient will have a stroke over the next 10-year period. For the smoking variable, define a dummy variable with 1 indicating a smoker and 0 indicating a nonsmoker.

DATA *file*

Stroke

Risk	Age	Pressure	Smoker
12	57	152	No
24	67	163	No
13	58	155	No
56	86	177	Yes
28	59	196	No
51	76	189	Yes
18	56	155	Yes
31	78	120	No
37	80	135	Yes
15	78	98	No
22	71	152	No
36	70	173	Yes
15	67	135	Yes
48	77	209	Yes
15	60	199	No
36	82	119	Yes
8	66	166	No
34	80	125	Yes
3	62	117	No
37	59	207	Yes

a. Develop an estimated regression equation that relates risk of a stroke to the person's age, blood pressure, and whether the person is a smoker.

b. Is smoking a significant factor in the risk of a stroke? Explain. Use $\alpha = .05$.

c. What is the probability of a stroke over the next 10 years for Art Speen, a 68-year-old smoker who has blood pressure of 175? What action might the physician recommend for this patient?

15.8 Residual Analysis

In Chapter 14 we showed how a residual plot against the independent variable x can be used to validate the assumptions for a simple linear regression model. Because multiple regression analysis deals with two or more independent variables, we would have to examine a residual plot against each of the independent variables to use this approach. The more

TABLE 15.7   PREDICTED VALUES AND RESIDUALS FOR BUTLER TRUCKING

Miles Traveled (x_1)	Deliveries (x_2)	Travel Time (y)	Predicted Time ($\hat{y}$)	Residual ($y - \hat{y}$)
100	4	9.3	8.9385	0.3615
50	3	4.8	4.9583	−0.1583
100	4	8.9	8.9385	−0.0385
100	2	6.5	7.0916	−0.5916
50	2	4.2	4.0349	0.1651
80	2	6.2	5.8689	0.3311
75	3	7.4	6.4867	0.9133
65	4	6.0	6.7987	−0.7987
90	3	7.6	7.4037	0.1963
90	2	6.1	6.4803	−0.3803

common approach in multiple regression analysis is to develop a residual plot against the predicted values $\hat{y}$.

Residual Plot Against $\hat{y}$

A residual plot against the predicted values $\hat{y}$ represents the predicted value of the dependent variable $\hat{y}$ on the horizontal axis and the residual values on the vertical axis. A point is plotted for each residual. The first coordinate for each point is given by $\hat{y}_i$ and the second coordinate is given by the corresponding value of the ith residual $y_i - \hat{y}_i$. For the Butler Trucking multiple regression example, the estimated regression equation that we developed using Excel (see Figure 15.5) is

$$\hat{y}_i = -.8687 + .0611x_1 + .9234x_2$$

where x_1 = miles traveled and x_2 = number of deliveries. Table 15.7 shows the predicted values and residuals based on this equation. The residual plot against $\hat{y}$ for Butler Trucking is shown in Figure 15.11. The residual plot does not indicate any abnormalities.

FIGURE 15.11   RESIDUAL PLOT AGAINST THE PREDICTED TIME $\hat{y}$
                          FOR BUTLER TRUCKING

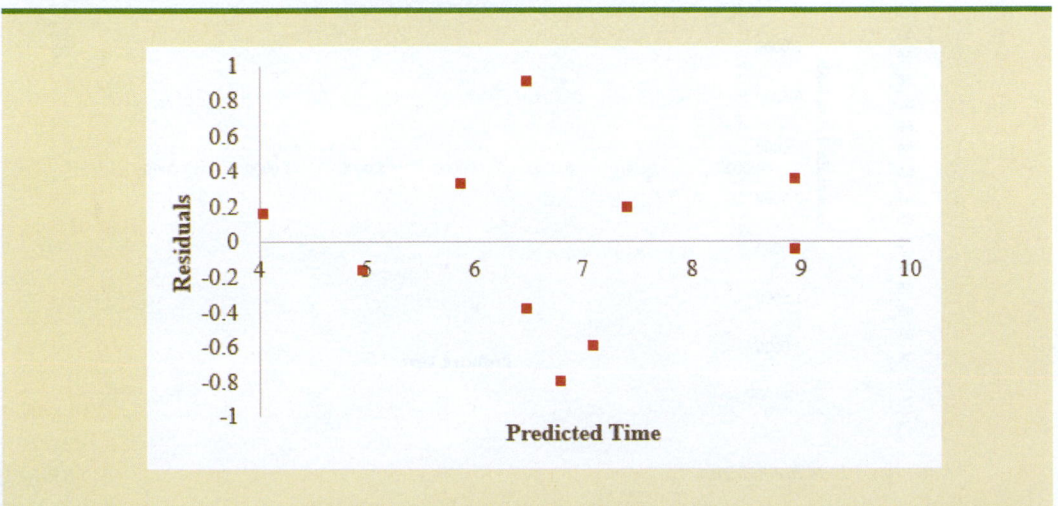

A residual plot against $\hat{y}$ can also be used when performing residual analysis in simple linear regression. In fact, the pattern for a residual plot against $\hat{y}$ in simple linear regression is the same as the pattern of the residual plot against x. Thus, for simple linear regression the residual plot against $\hat{y}$ and the residual plot against x provide the same information. In multiple regression analysis, however, it is preferable to use the residual plot against $\hat{y}$ to determine whether the model's assumptions are satisfied.

Standardized Residual Plot Against $\hat{y}$

In Chapter 14 we pointed out that standardized residuals were frequently used in residual plots. We showed how to construct a standardized residual plot against x and discussed how the standardized residual plot could be used to identify outliers and provide insight about the assumption that the error term ϵ has a normal distribution. Recall that we recommended considering any observation with a standardized residual of less than -2 or greater than $+2$ as an outlier. With normally distributed errors, standardized residuals should be outside these limits approximately 5% of the time.

In multiple regression analysis, the computation of the standardized residuals is too complex to be done by hand. As we showed in Section 14.8, Excel's Regression tool can

FIGURE 15.12 STANDARDIZED RESIDUAL PLOT AGAINST THE PREDICTED VALUES $\hat{y}$ FOR BUTLER TRUCKING

	A	B	C	D	E	F	G	H
37	Observation	Predicted Time	Residuals	Standard Residuals		Predicted Time	Standard Residuals	
38	1	8.9385	0.3615	0.7153		8.9385	0.7153	
39	2	4.9583	-0.1583	-0.3132		4.9583	-0.3132	
40	3	8.9385	-0.0385	-0.0761		8.9385	-0.0761	
41	4	7.0916	-0.5916	-1.1704		7.0916	-1.1704	
42	5	4.0349	0.1651	0.3267		4.0349	0.3267	
43	6	5.8689	0.3311	0.6550		5.8689	0.6550	
44	7	6.4867	0.9133	1.8069		6.4867	1.8069	
45	8	6.7987	-0.7987	-1.5802		6.7987	-1.5802	
46	9	7.4037	0.1963	0.3884		7.4037	0.3884	
47	10	6.4803	-0.3803	-0.7523		6.4803	-0.7523	

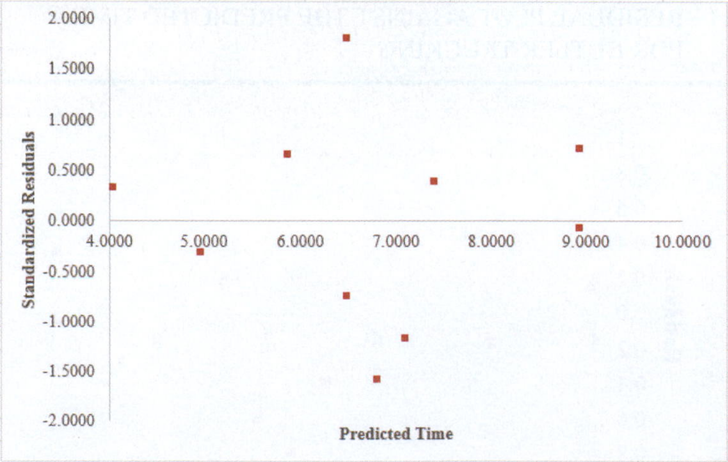

Note: Rows 1–34 are hidden.

be used to compute the standard residuals. In multiple regression analysis we use the same procedure to compute the standard residuals. Instead of developing a standardized residual plot against each of the independent variables, we will construct one standardized residual plot against the predicted values $\hat{y}$.

Figure 15.12 shows the standard residuals and the corresponding standardized residual plot against $\hat{y}$ (Predicted Time) for Butler Trucking developed using Excel's Regression tool and Excel's chart tools. The standardized residual plot does not indicate any abnormalities, and no standard residual is less than -2 or greater than $+2$. Note that the pattern of the standardized residual plot against $\hat{y}$ is the same as the pattern of the residual plot against $\hat{y}$ shown in Figure 15.11. But the standardized residual plot is preferred because it enables us to check for outliers and determine whether the assumption of normality for the regression model is reasonable.

Exercises

Methods

39. Data for two variables, x and y, follow.

x_i	1	2	3	4	5
y_i	3	7	5	11	14

   a. Develop the estimated regression equation for these data.
   b. Plot the residuals against $\hat{y}$. Does the residual plot support the assumptions about ϵ? Explain.
   c. Plot the standardized residuals against $\hat{y}$. Do any outliers appear in these data? Explain.

40. Data for two variables, x and y, follow.

x_i	22	24	26	28	40
y_i	12	21	31	35	70

   a. Develop the estimated regression equation for these data.
   b. Compute the standardized residuals for these data. Can any of these observations be classified as an outlier? Explain.
   c. Develop a standardized residual plot against $\hat{y}$. Does the residual plot support the assumptions about ϵ? Explain.

Applications

41. Exercise 5 gave the following data on weekly gross revenue ($1000s), television advertising expenditures ($1000s), and newspaper advertising expenditures ($1000s) for Showtime Movie Theaters.

DATA *file*

Showtime

Weekly Gross Revenue ($1000s)	Television Advertising ($1000s)	Newspaper Advertising ($1000s)
96	5.0	1.5
90	2.0	2.0
95	4.0	1.5
92	2.5	2.5
95	3.0	3.3
94	3.5	2.3
94	2.5	4.2
94	3.0	2.5

a.   Find an estimated regression equation relating weekly gross revenue to television advertising expenditures and newspaper advertising expenditures.

b.   Plot the standardized residuals against $\hat{y}$. Does the residual plot support the assumptions about ϵ? Explain.

c.   Check for any outliers in these data. What are your conclusions?

42.   The following table reports the price, horsepower, and ¼-mile speed for 16 popular sports and GT cars.

DATA file
Auto2

Sports & GT Car	Price ($1000s)	Curb Weight (lb.)	Horsepower	Speed at ¼ Mile (mph)
Accura Integra Type R	25.035	2577	195	90.7
Accura NSX-T	93.758	3066	290	108.0
BMW Z3 2.8	40.900	2844	189	93.2
Chevrolet Camaro Z28	24.865	3439	305	103.2
Chevrolet Corvette Convertible	50.144	3246	345	102.1
Dodge Viper RT/10	69.742	3319	450	116.2
Ford Mustang GT	23.200	3227	225	91.7
Honda Prelude Type SH	26.382	3042	195	89.7
Mercedes-Benz CLK320	44.988	3240	215	93.0
Mercedes-Benz SLK230	42.762	3025	185	92.3
Mitsubishi 3000GT VR-4	47.518	3737	320	99.0
Nissan 240SX SE	25.066	2862	155	84.6
Pontiac Firebird Trans Am	27.770	3455	305	103.2
Porsche Boxster	45.560	2822	201	93.2
Toyota Supra Turbo	40.989	3505	320	105.0
Volvo C70	41.120	3285	236	97.0

a.   Find the estimated regression equation, which uses price and horsepower to predict ¼-mile speed.

b.   Plot the standardized residuals against $\hat{y}$. Does the residual plot support the assumption about ϵ? Explain.

c.   Check for any outliers. What are your conclusions?

DATA file
2014LPGAStats

43.   The Ladies Professional Golfers Association (LPGA) maintains statistics on performance and earnings for members of the LPGA Tour. Year-end performance statistics for 134 golfers for 2014 appear in the file named *2014LPGAStats* (LPGA website, April 2015). Earnings ($1000s) is the total earnings in thousands of dollars; Scoring Avg. is the scoring average for all events; Greens in Reg. is the percentage of time a player is able to hit the greens in regulation; and Putting Avg. is the average number of putts taken on greens hit in regulation. A green is considered hit in regulation if any part of the ball is touching the putting surface and the difference between par for the hole and the number of strokes taken to hit the green is at least 2.

a.   Develop an estimated regression equation that can be used to predict the scoring average given the percentage of time a player is able to hit the greens in regulation and the average number of putts taken on greens hit in regulation.

b.   Plot the standardized residuals against $\hat{y}$. Does the residual plot support the assumption about ϵ? Explain.

c.   Check for any outliers. What are your conclusions?

d.   Are there any influential observations? Explain.

15.9 Practical Advice: Big Data And Hypothesis Testing In Multiple Regression

In Chapter 14, we observed that in simple linear regression, the p-value for the test of the hypothesis H_0: $\beta_1 = 0$ decreases as the sample size increases. Likewise, for a given level of confidence, the confidence interval for β_1, the confidence interval for the mean value of y, and the prediction interval for an individual value of y each narrows as the sample size increases. These results extend to multiple regression. As the sample size increases:

- the p-value for the F test used to determine whether a significant relationship exists between the dependent variable and the set of all independent variables in the regression model decreases;
- the p-value for each of t-tests used to determine whether a significant relationship exists between the dependent variable and an individual independent variable in the regression model decreases;
- the confidence interval for the slope parameter associated with each individual independent variable narrows;
- the confidence interval for the mean value of y narrows;
- the prediction interval for an individual value of y narrows.

Thus, the interval estimates for the slope parameter associated with each individual independent variable, the mean value of y, and predicted individual value of y will become more precise as the sample size increases. And we are more likely to reject the hypothesis that a relationship does not exist between the dependent variable and the set of all individual independent variables in the model as the sample size increases. And for each individual independent variable, we are more likely to reject the hypothesis that a relationship does not exist between the dependent variable and the individual independent variable as the sample size increases. Even when severe multicollinearity is present, if the sample is sufficiently large, independent variables that are highly correlated may each have a significant relationship with the dependent variable. But this does not necessarily mean that these results become more reliable as the sample size increases.

No matter how large the sample used to estimate the multiple regression model, we must be concerned about the potential presence of nonsampling error in the data. It is important to carefully consider whether a random sample of the population of interest has actually been taken. If nonsampling error is introduced in the data collection process, the likelihood of making a Type I or Type II error on hypothesis tests in multiple regression may be higher than if the sample data are free of nonsampling error. Furthermore, multicollinearity may cause the estimated slope coefficients to be misleading; this problem persists as the size of the sample used to estimate the multiple regression model increases. Finally, it is important to consider whether the statistically significant relationship(s) in the multiple regression model are of practical significance.

Although multiple regression is an extremely powerful statistical tool, no business decision should be based exclusively on hypothesis testing in multiple regression. Nonsampling error may lead to misleading results. If severe multicollinearity is present, we must be cautious in interpreting the estimated slope coefficients. And practical significance should always be considered in conjunction with statistical significance; this is particularly important when a hypothesis test is based on an extremely large sample, because p-values in such cases can be extremely small. When executed properly, hypothesis tests in multiple regression provide evidence that should be considered in combination with information collected from other sources to make the most informed decision possible.

Summary

In this chapter, we introduced multiple regression analysis as an extension of simple linear regression analysis presented in Chapter 14. Multiple regression analysis enables us to understand how a dependent variable is related to two or more independent variables. The regression equation $E(y) = \beta_0 + \beta_1 x_1 + \beta_2 x_2 + \cdots + \beta_p x_p$ shows that the expected value or mean value of the dependent variable y is related to the values of the independent variables $x_1, x_2, \ldots, x_p$. Sample data and the least squares method are used to develop the estimated regression equation $\hat{y} = b_0 + b_1 x_1 + b_2 x_2 + \cdots + b_p x_p$. In effect $b_0, b_1, b_2, \ldots, b_p$ are sample statistics used to estimate the unknown model parameters $\beta_0, \beta_1, \beta_2, \ldots, \beta_p$. Excel output was used throughout the chapter to emphasize the fact that computer software packages are the only realistic means of performing the numerous computations required in multiple regression analysis.

The multiple coefficient of determination was presented as a measure of the goodness of fit of the estimated regression equation. It determines the proportion of the variation of y that can be explained by the estimated regression equation. The adjusted multiple coefficient of determination is a similar measure of goodness of fit that adjusts for the number of independent variables and thus avoids overestimating the impact of adding more independent variables.

An F test and a t test were presented as ways to determine statistically whether the relationship among the variables is significant. The F test is used to determine whether there is a significant overall relationship between the dependent variable and the set of all independent variables. The t test is used to determine whether there is a significant relationship between the dependent variable and an individual independent variable given the other independent variables in the regression model. Correlation among the independent variables, known as multicollinearity, was discussed.

The section on categorical independent variables showed how dummy variables can be used to incorporate categorical data into multiple regression analysis. The section on residual analysis showed how residual analysis can be used to validate the model assumptions and detect outliers. Finally, we discussed the implications of large data sets on the application and interpretation of multiple regression analysis.

Glossary

Adjusted multiple coefficient of determination A measure of the goodness of fit of the estimated multiple regression equation that adjusts for the number of independent variables in the model and thus avoids overestimating the impact of adding more independent variables.

Categorical independent variable An independent variable with categorical data.

Dummy variable A variable used to model the effect of categorical independent variables. A dummy variable may take only the value zero or one.

Estimated multiple regression equation The estimate of the multiple regression equation based on sample data and the least squares method; it is $\hat{y} = b_0 + b_1 x_1 + b_2 x_2 + \cdots + b_p x_p$.

Least squares method The method used to develop the estimated regression equation. It minimizes the sum of squared residuals (the deviations between the observed values of the dependent variable, y_i, and the estimated values of the dependent variable, $\hat{y}_i$).

Multicollinearity The term used to describe the correlation among the independent variables.

Multiple coefficient of determination A measure of the goodness of fit of the estimated multiple regression equation. It can be interpreted as the proportion of the variability in the dependent variable that is explained by the estimated regression equation.

Multiple regression analysis Regression analysis involving two or more independent variables.

Multiple regression equation The mathematical equation relating the expected value or mean value of the dependent variable to the values of the independent variables; that is, $E(y) = \beta_0 + \beta_1 x_1 + \beta_2 x_2 + \cdots + \beta_p x_p$.

Multiple regression model The mathematical equation that describes how the dependent variable y is related to the independent variables $x_1, x_2, \ldots, x_p$ and an error term ϵ.

Key Formulas

Multiple Regression Model

$$y = \beta_0 + \beta_1 x_1 + \beta_2 x_2 + \cdots + \beta_p x_p + \epsilon \tag{15.1}$$

Multiple Regression Equation

$$E(y) = \beta_0 + \beta_1 x_1 + \beta_2 x_2 + \cdots + \beta_p x_p \tag{15.2}$$

Estimated Multiple Regression Equation

$$\hat{y} = b_0 + b_1 x_1 + b_2 x_2 + \cdots + b_p x_p \tag{15.3}$$

Least Squares Criterion

$$\min \Sigma(y_i - \hat{y}_i)^2 \tag{15.4}$$

Relationship Among SST, SSR, and SSE

$$\text{SST} = \text{SSR} + \text{SSE} \tag{15.7}$$

Multiple Coefficient of Determination

$$R^2 = \frac{\text{SSR}}{\text{SST}} \tag{15.8}$$

Adjusted Multiple Coefficient of Determination

$$R_{\text{a}}^2 = 1 - (1 - R^2)\frac{n - 1}{n - p - 1} \tag{15.9}$$

Mean Square Due to Regression

$$\text{MSR} = \frac{\text{SSR}}{p} \tag{15.12}$$

Mean Square Due to Error

$$\text{MSE} = \frac{\text{SSE}}{n - p - 1} \tag{15.13}$$

***F* Test Statistic**

$$F = \frac{\text{MSR}}{\text{MSE}} \tag{15.14}$$

***t* Test Statistic**

$$t = \frac{b_i}{s_{b_i}} \tag{15.15}$$

Supplementary Exercises

44. The admissions officer for Clearwater College developed the following estimated regression equation relating the final college GPA to the student's SAT mathematics score and high-school GPA.

$$\hat{y} = -1.41 + .0235x_1 + .00486x_2$$

where

$$x_1 = \text{high-school grade point average}$$
$$x_2 = \text{SAT mathematics score}$$
$$y = \text{final college grade point average}$$

a. Interpret the coefficients in this estimated regression equation.
b. Predict the final college GPA for a student who has a high-school average of 84 and a score of 540 on the SAT mathematics test.

45. The personnel director for Electronics Associates developed the following estimated regression equation relating an employee's score on a job satisfaction test to his or her length of service and wage rate.

$$\hat{y} = 14.4 - 8.69x_1 + 13.5x_2$$

where

$$x_1 = \text{length of service (years)}$$
$$x_2 = \text{wage rate (dollars)}$$
$$y = \text{job satisfaction test score (higher scores indicate greater job satisfaction)}$$

a. Interpret the coefficients in this estimated regression equation.
b. Predict the job satisfaction test score for an employee who has four years of service and makes $6.50 per hour.

46. A partial computer output from a regression analysis using Excel's Regression tool follows.

▲	A	B	C	D	E	F	G
1	SUMMARY OUTPUT						
2							
3	*Regression Statistics*						
4	Multiple R						
5	R Square	0.923					
6	Adjusted R Square						
7	Standard Error	3.35					
8	Observations						
9							
10	ANOVA						
11		*df*	*SS*	*MS*	*F*	*Significance F*	
12	Regression		1612				
13	Residual	12					
14	Total						
15							
16		*Coefficients*	*Standard Error*	*t Stat*	*P-value*		
17	Intercept	8.103	2.667				
18	X1	7.602	2.105				
19	X2	3.111	0.613				
20							

a. Compute the missing entries in this output.
b. Using $\alpha = .05$, test for overall significance.
c. Use the t test and $\alpha = .05$ to test $H_0: \beta_1 = 0$ and $H_0: \beta_2 = 0$.

47. Recall that in exercise 44, the admissions officer for Clearwater College developed the following estimated regression equation relating final college GPA to the student's SAT mathematics score and high-school GPA.

$$\hat{y} = -1.41 + .0235x_1 + .00486x_2$$

where

$$x_1 = \text{high-school grade point average}$$
$$x_2 = \text{SAT mathematics score}$$
$$y = \text{final college grade point average}$$

A portion of the Excel Regression tool output follows.

	A	B	C	D	E	F	G
1	SUMMARY OUTPUT						
2							
3	*Regression Statistics*						
4	Multiple R						
5	R Square						
6	Adjusted R Square						
7	Standard Error						
8	Observations						
9							
10	ANOVA						
11		*df*	*SS*	*MS*	*F*	*Significance F*	
12	Regression		1.76209				
13	Residual						
14	Total	9	1.88				
15							
16		*Coefficients*	*Standard Error*	*t Stat*	*P-value*		
17	Intercept	-1.4053	0.4848				
18	X1	0.023467	0.0086666				
19	X2	0.00486	0.001077				
20							

a. Complete the missing entries in this output.
b. Using $\alpha = .05$, test for overall significance.
c. Did the estimated regression equation provide a good fit to the data? Explain.
d. Use the t test and $\alpha = .05$ to test $H_0: \beta_1 = 0$ and $H_0: \beta_2 = 0$.

48. Recall that in exercise 45 the personnel director for Electronics Associates developed the following estimated regression equation relating an employee's score on a job satisfaction test to length of service and wage rate.

$$\hat{y} = 14.4 - 8.69x_1 + 13.5x_2$$

where

$$x_1 = \text{length of service (years)}$$
$$x_2 = \text{wage rate (dollars)}$$
$$y = \text{job satisfaction test score (higher scores}$$
$$\text{indicate greater job satisfaction)}$$

A portion of the Excel Regression tool output follows.

	A	B	C	D	E	F	G
1	SUMMARY OUTPUT						
2							
3	*Regression Statistics*						
4	Multiple R						
5	R Square						
6	Adjusted R Square						
7	Standard Error	3.773					
8	Observations						
9							
10	ANOVA						
11		*df*	*SS*	*MS*	*F*	*Significance F*	
12	Regression						
13	Residual		77.17				
14	Total		720				
15							
16		*Coefficients*	*Standard Error*	*t Stat*	*P-value*		
17	Intercept	14.4	8.191				
18	X1	-8.69	1.555				
19	X2	13.517	2.085				
20							

a. Complete the missing entries in this output.
b. Using $\alpha = .05$, test for overall significance.
c. Did the estimated regression equation provide a good fit to the data? Explain.
d. Use the t test and $\alpha = .05$ to test H_0: $\beta_1 = 0$ and H_0: $\beta_2 = 0$.

49. *Fortune* magazine publishes an annual list of the 100 best companies to work for. The data in the DATAfile named *FortuneBest* shows a portion of the data for a random sample of 30 of the companies that made the top 100 list for 2012 (*Fortune,* February 6, 2012). The column labeled Rank shows the rank of the company in the Fortune 100 list; the column labeled Size indicates whether the company is a small, midsize, or large company; the column labeled Salaried ($1000s) shows the average annual salary for salaried employees rounded to the nearest $1000; and the column labeled Hourly ($1000s) shows the average annual salary for hourly employees rounded to the nearest $1000. *Fortune* defines large companies as having more than 10,000 employees, midsize companies as having between 2500 and 10,000 employees, and small companies as having fewer than 2500 employees.

Rank	Company	Size	Salaried ($1000s)	Hourly ($1000s)
4	Wegmans Food Markets	Large	56	29
6	NetApp	Midsize	143	76
7	Camden Property Trust	Small	71	37
8	Recreational Equipment (REI)	Large	103	28
10	Quicken Loans	Midsize	78	54
11	Zappos.com	Midsize	48	25
12	Mercedes-Benz USA	Small	118	50
20	USAA	Large	96	47
22	The Container Store	Midsize	71	45
25	Ultimate Software	Small	166	56

FortuneBest

Rank	Company	Size	Salaried ($1000s)	Hourly ($1000s)
37	Plante Moran	Small	73	45
42	Baptist Health South Florida	Large	126	80
50	World Wide Technology	Small	129	31
53	Methodist Hospital	Large	100	83
58	Perkins Coie	Small	189	63
60	American Express	Large	114	35
64	TDIndustries	Small	93	47
66	QuikTrip	Large	69	44
72	EOG Resources	Small	189	81
75	FactSet Research Systems	Small	103	51
80	Stryker	Large	71	43
81	SRC	Small	84	33
84	Booz Allen Hamilton	Large	105	77
91	CarMax	Large	57	34
93	GoDaddy.com	Midsize	105	71
94	KPMG	Large	79	59
95	Navy Federal Credit Union	Midsize	77	39
97	Schweitzer Engineering Labs	Small	99	28
99	Darden Restaurants	Large	57	24
100	Intercontinental Hotels Group	Large	63	26

a. Use these data to develop an estimated regression equation that could be used to predict the average annual salary for salaried employees given the average annual salary for hourly employees.

b. Use $\alpha = .05$ to test for overall significance.

c. To incorporate the effect of size, a categorical variable with three levels, we used two dummy variables: Size-Midsize and Size-Small. The value of Size-Midsize = 1 if the company is a midsize company and 0 otherwise. And the value of Size-Small = 1 if the company is a small company and 0 otherwise. Develop an estimated regression equation that could be used to predict the average annual salary for salaried employees given the average annual salary for hourly employees and the size of the company.

d. For the estimated regression equation developed in part (c), use the *t* test to determine the significance of the independent variables. Use $\alpha = .05$.

e. Based upon your findings in part (d), develop an estimated regression equation that can be used to predict the average annual salary for salaried employees given the average annual salary for hourly employees and the size of the company.

FuelEcon

50. The Department of Energy and the U.S. Environmental Protection Agency provides fuel efficiency data for cars and trucks. The DATAfile named *FuelEcon* provides a portion of the data for 309 cars. The column labeled Manufacturer shows the name of the company that manufactured the car; the column labeled Displacement shows the engine's displacement in liters; the column labeled Fuel shows the required or recommended type of fuel (regular or premium gasoline); the column labeled Drive identifies the type of drive (F for front wheel, R for rear wheel, and A for all wheel); and the column labeled Hwy MPG shows the fuel efficiency rating for highway driving in terms of miles per gallon.

a. Develop an estimated regression equation that can be used to predict the fuel efficiency for highway driving given the engine's displacement. Test for significance using $\alpha = .05$.

b. Consider the addition of the dummy variable FuelPremium, where the value of FuelPremium is 1 if the required or recommended type of fuel is premium gasoline and 0 if the type of fuel is regular gasoline. Develop the estimated regression equation that can be used to predict the fuel efficiency for highway driving given the engine's displacement and the dummy variable FuelPremium.

c. Use $\alpha = .05$ to determine whether the dummy variable added in part (b) is significant.

d. Consider the addition of the dummy variables FrontWheel and RearWheel. The value of FrontWheel is 1 if the car has front wheel drive and 0 otherwise; the value of RearWheel is 1 if the car has rear wheel drive and 0 otherwise. Thus, for a car that has all-wheel drive, the value of FrontWheel and the value of RearWheel is 0. Develop the estimated regression equation that can be used to predict the fuel efficiency for highway driving given the engine's displacement, the dummy variable FuelPremium, and the dummy variables FrontWheel and RearWheel.

e. For the estimated regression equation developed in part (d), test for overall significance and individual significance using $\alpha = .05$.

51. The Tire Rack, an online distributor of tires and wheels, conducts extensive testing to provide customers with products that are right for their vehicle, driving style, and driving conditions. In addition, The Tire Rack maintains an independent consumer survey to help drivers help each other by sharing their long-term tire experiences (The Tire Rack website, August 1, 2016). The following data show survey ratings (1 to 10 scale with 10 the highest rating) for 18 high-performance all-season tires. The variable Tread Wear rates quickness of wear based on the driver's expectations, the variable Dry Traction rates the grip of a tire on a dry road, the variable Steering rates the tire's steering responsiveness, and the variable Buy Again rates the driver's desire to purchase the same tire again.

DATA *file*

AllSeasonTires

Tire	Tread Wear	Dry Traction	Steering	Buy Again?
Sumitomo HTR A/S P02	8.6	9.0	8.5	8.0
Goodyear Eagle Sport All-Season	8.5	9.3	8.8	7.5
Michelin Pilot Sport A/S 3	7.3	9.2	8.9	7.2
Kumho Ecsta PA31	7.2	8.4	7.9	6.4
Firestone Firehawk Wide Oval AS	7.4	7.6	7.1	5.8
BFGoodrich g-Force Super Sport A/S	7.1	8.7	8.3	6.5
Yokohama AVID ENVigor	6.4	8.7	8.4	5.8
Goodyear Eagle RS-A2	6.6	8.4	7.9	5.4
Hankook Ventus V2 concept2	7.1	8.0	7.9	5.2
Firestone Firehawk GT	6.1	8.2	7.9	4.4
Firestone FR740	5.1	7.8	7.5	3.2
Dunlop SP Sport 7000 A/S	5.0	7.6	7.0	3.0
Goodyear Eagle RS-A	5.6	7.4	7.0	3.6
Bridgestone Potenza RE92A	5.7	7.1	6.5	2.6
Yokohama ADVAN A83A	4.4	8.0	7.6	1.0
Bridgestone Potenza RE92	5.4	6.9	6.3	2.5
Firestone Firehawk GTA-03	3.8	7.9	6.9	2.0

a. Develop an estimated simple linear regression equation that can be used to predict the Buy Again rating given the Tread Wear rating. At the .01 level of significance, test for a significant relationship. Does this estimated regression equation provide a good fit to the data? Explain.

b. Develop an estimated multiple regression equation that can be used to predict the Buy Again rating given the Tread Wear rating and the Dry Traction rating. Is the addition of the Dry Traction independent variable significant at $\alpha = .01$? Explain.

c. Develop an estimated multiple regression equation that can be used to predict the Buy Again rating given the Tread Wear rating, the Dry Traction rating, and the Steering rating. Is the addition of the Steering independent variable significant at $\alpha = .01$? Explain.

52. The National Basketball Association (NBA) records a variety of statistics for each team. Five of these statistics are the percentage of games won (Win%), the percentage of field goals made (FG%), the percentage of three-point shots made (3P%), the percentage of free throws made (FT%), the average number of offensive rebounds per game (RBOff), and the average number of defensive rebounds per game (RBDef). The data contained in the DATAfile named *NBAStats* show the values of these statistics for the 30 teams in the NBA for one full season. A portion of the data follows.

NBAStats

Team	Win%	FG%	3P%	FT%	RBOff	RBDef
Atlanta	60.6	45.4	37.0	74.0	9.9	31.3
Boston	59.1	46.0	36.7	77.8	7.7	31.1
.	.	.	.	.	.	.
.	.	.	.	.	.	.
.	.	.	.	.	.	.
Toronto	34.8	44.0	34.0	77.0	10.6	31.4
Utah	54.5	45.6	32.3	75.4	13.0	31.1
Washington	30.3	44.1	32.0	72.7	11.7	29.9

a. Develop an estimated regression equation that can be used to predict the percentage of games won given the percentage of field goals made. At the .05 level of significance, test for a significant relationship.

b. Provide an interpretation for the slope of the estimated regression equation developed in part (a).

c. Develop an estimated regression equation that can be used to predict the percentage of games won given the percentage of field goals made, the percentage of three-point shots made, the percentage of free throws made, the average number of offensive rebounds per game, and the average number of defensive rebounds per game (RBDef).

d. For the estimated regression equation developed in part (c), remove any independent variables that are not significant at the .05 level of significance and develop a new estimated regression equation using the remaining independent variables.

e. Assuming the estimated regression equation developed in part (d) can be used for the 2012–2013 season, predict the percentage of games won for a team with the following values for the four independent variables: FG% = 45, 3P% = 35, RBOff = 12, and RBDef = 30.

Case Problem 1   Consumer Research, Inc.

Consumer Research, Inc., is an independent agency that conducts research on consumer attitudes and behaviors for a variety of firms. In one study, a client asked for an investigation of consumer characteristics that can be used to predict the amount charged by credit card users. Data were collected on annual income, household size, and annual credit card charges for a sample of 50 consumers. The following data are contained in the DATAfile named *Consumer*.

Income ($1000s)	Household Size	Amount Charged ($)	Income ($1000s)	Household Size	Amount Charged ($)
54	3	4016	54	6	5573
30	2	3159	30	1	2583
32	4	5100	48	2	3866
50	5	4742	34	5	3586
31	2	1864	67	4	5037
55	2	4070	50	2	3605
37	1	2731	67	5	5345
40	2	3348	55	6	5370
66	4	4764	52	2	3890
51	3	4110	62	3	4705
25	3	4208	64	2	4157
48	4	4219	22	3	3579
27	1	2477	29	4	3890
33	2	2514	39	2	2972
65	3	4214	35	1	3121
63	4	4965	39	4	4183
42	6	4412	54	3	3730
21	2	2448	23	6	4127
44	1	2995	27	2	2921
37	5	4171	26	7	4603
62	6	5678	61	2	4273
21	3	3623	30	2	3067
55	7	5301	22	4	3074
42	2	3020	46	5	4820
41	7	4828	66	4	5149

DATA *file*

Consumer

Managerial Report

1. Use methods of descriptive statistics to summarize the data. Comment on the findings.
2. Develop estimated regression equations, first using annual income as the independent variable and then using household size as the independent variable. Which variable is the better predictor of annual credit card charges? Discuss your findings.
3. Develop an estimated regression equation with annual income and household size as the independent variables. Discuss your findings.
4. What is the predicted annual credit card charge for a three-person household with an annual income of $40,000?
5. Discuss the need for other independent variables that could be added to the model. What additional variables might be helpful?

Case Problem 2 Predicting Winnings for NASCAR Drivers

Matt Kenseth won the 2012 Daytona 500, the most important race of the NASCAR season. His win was no surprise because for the 2011 season he finished fourth in the point standings with 2330 points, behind Tony Stewart (2403 points), Carl Edwards (2403 points), and Kevin Harvick (2345 points). In 2011 he earned $6,183,580 by winning three Poles (fastest driver in qualifying), winning three races, finishing in the top five 12 times, and finishing in the top ten 20 times. NASCAR's point system in 2011 allocated 43 points to the driver who finished first, 42 points to the driver who finished second, and so on down to 1 point for the driver who finished in the 43rd position. In addition any driver who led a lap received 1 bonus point, the driver who led the most laps received an additional bonus point, and the race winner was awarded 3 bonus points. But the maximum number of points a driver could earn in any race was 48. Table 15.8 shows data for the 2011 season for the top 35 drivers (NASCAR website, February 28, 2011).

Managerial Report

1. Suppose you wanted to predict Winnings ($) using only the number of poles won (Poles), the number of wins (Wins), the number of top five finishes (Top 5), or the number of top ten finishes (Top 10). Which of these four variables provides the best single predictor of winnings?

TABLE 15.8   NASCAR RESULTS FOR THE 2011 SEASON

DATA *file*

NASCAR

Driver	Points	Poles	Wins	Top 5	Top 10	Winnings ($)
Tony Stewart	2403	1	5	9	19	6,529,870
Carl Edwards	2403	3	1	19	26	8,485,990
Kevin Harvick	2345	0	4	9	19	6,197,140
Matt Kenseth	2330	3	3	12	20	6,183,580
Brad Keselowski	2319	1	3	10	14	5,087,740
Jimmie Johnson	2304	0	2	14	21	6,296,360
Dale Earnhardt Jr.	2290	1	0	4	12	4,163,690
Jeff Gordon	2287	1	3	13	18	5,912,830
Denny Hamlin	2284	0	1	5	14	5,401,190
Ryan Newman	2284	3	1	9	17	5,303,020
Kurt Busch	2262	3	2	8	16	5,936,470
Kyle Busch	2246	1	4	14	18	6,161,020
Clint Bowyer	1047	0	1	4	16	5,633,950
Kasey Kahne	1041	2	1	8	15	4,775,160
A. J. Allmendinger	1013	0	0	1	10	4,825,560
Greg Biffle	997	3	0	3	10	4,318,050
Paul Menard	947	0	1	4	8	3,853,690
Martin Truex Jr.	937	1	0	3	12	3,955,560
Marcos Ambrose	936	0	1	5	12	4,750,390
Jeff Burton	935	0	0	2	5	3,807,780
Juan Montoya	932	2	0	2	8	5,020,780
Mark Martin	930	2	0	2	10	3,830,910
David Ragan	906	2	1	4	8	4,203,660
Joey Logano	902	2	0	4	6	3,856,010
Brian Vickers	846	0	0	3	7	4,301,880
Regan Smith	820	0	1	2	5	4,579,860
Jamie McMurray	795	1	0	2	4	4,794,770
David Reutimann	757	1	0	1	3	4,374,770
Bobby Labonte	670	0	0	1	2	4,505,650
David Gilliland	572	0	0	1	2	3,878,390
Casey Mears	541	0	0	0	0	2,838,320
Dave Blaney	508	0	0	1	1	3,229,210
Andy Lally	398	0	0	0	0	2,868,220
Robby Gordon	268	0	0	0	0	2,271,890
J. J. Yeley	192	0	0	0	0	2,559,500

2. Develop an estimated regression equation that can be used to predict Winnings ($) given the number of poles won (Poles), the number of wins (Wins), the number of top five finishes (Top 5), and the number of top ten (Top 10) finishes. Test for individual significance and discuss your findings and conclusions.

3. Create two new independent variables: Top 2–5 and Top 6–10. Top 2–5 represents the number of times the driver finished between second and fifth place and Top 6–10 represents the number of times the driver finished between sixth and tenth place. Develop an estimated regression equation that can be used to predict Winnings ($) using Poles, Wins, Top 2–5, and Top 6–10. Test for individual significance and discuss your findings and conclusions.

4. Based upon the results of your analysis, what estimated regression equation would you recommend using to predict Winnings ($)? Provide an interpretation of the estimated regression coefficients for this equation.

Case Problem 3   # Finding the Best Car Value

When trying to decide what car to buy, real value is not necessarily determined by how much you spend on the initial purchase. Instead, cars that are reliable and don't cost much to own often represent the best values. But no matter how reliable or inexpensive a car may be to own, it must also perform well.

To measure value, *Consumer Reports* developed a statistic referred to as a value score. The value score is based upon five-year owner costs, overall road-test scores, and predicted-reliability ratings. Five-year owner costs are based upon the expenses incurred in the first five years of ownership, including depreciation, fuel, maintenance and repairs, and so on. Using a national average of 12,000 miles per year, an average cost per mile driven is used as the measure of five-year owner costs. Road-test scores are the results of more than 50 tests and evaluations and are based on a 100-point scale, with higher scores indicating better performance, comfort, convenience, and fuel economy. The highest road-test score obtained in the tests conducted by *Consumer Reports* was a 99 for a Lexus LS 460L. Predicted-reliability ratings (1 = Poor, 2 = Fair, 3 = Good, 4 = Very Good, and 5 = Excellent) are based upon data from *Consumer Reports*' Annual Auto Survey.

CarValues

A car with a value score of 1.0 is considered to be an "average-value" car. A car with a value score of 2.0 is considered to be twice as good a value as a car with a value score of 1.0; a car with a value score of 0.5 is considered half as good as average; and so on. The data for three sizes of cars (13 small sedans, 20 family sedans, and 21 upscale sedans), including the price ($) of each car tested, are contained in the DATAfile named *CarValues* (*Consumer Reports* website, April 18, 2012). To incorporate the effect of size of car, a categorical variable with three values (small sedan, family sedan, and upscale sedan), use the following dummy variables:

$$\text{Family-Sedan} = \begin{cases} 1 \text{ if the car is a Family Sedan} \\ 0 \text{ otherwise} \end{cases}$$

$$\text{Upscale-Sedan} = \begin{cases} 1 \text{ if the car is an Upscale Sedan} \\ 0 \text{ otherwise} \end{cases}$$

Managerial Report

1. Treating Cost/Mile as the dependent variable, develop an estimated regression with Family-Sedan and Upscale-Sedan as the independent variables. Discuss your findings.

2. Treating Value Score as the dependent variable, develop an estimated regression equation using Cost/Mile, Road-Test Score, Predicted Reliability, Family-Sedan, and Upscale-Sedan as the independent variables.
3. Delete any independent variables that are not significant from the estimated regression equation developed in part 2 using a .05 level of significance. After deleting any independent variables that are not significant, develop a new estimated regression equation.
4. Suppose someone claims that "smaller cars provide better values than larger cars." For the data in this case, the Small Sedans represent the smallest type of car and the Upscale Sedans represent the largest type of car. Does your analysis support this claim?
5. Use regression analysis to develop an estimated regression equation that could be used to predict the value score given the value of the Road-Test Score.
6. Use regression analysis to develop an estimated regression equation that could be used to predict the value score given the Predicted Reliability.
7. What conclusions can you derive from your analysis?

APPENDIXES

Appendix A: References and Bibliography

General

Freedman, D., R. Pisani, and R. Purves. *Statistics*, 4th ed. W. W. Norton, 2007.

Hogg, R. V., and E. A. Tanis. *Probability and Statistical Inference*, 8th ed. Prentice Hall, 2009.

McKean, J. W., R. V. Hogg, and A. T. Craig. *Introduction to Mathematical Statistics*, 7th ed. Prentice Hall, 2012.

Miller, I., and M. Miller. *John E. Freund's Mathematical Statistics*, 7th ed. Pearson, 2003.

Moore, D. S., G. P. McCabe, and B. Craig. *Introduction to the Practice of Statistics*, 7th ed. Freeman, 2010.

Wackerly, D. D., W. Mendenhall, and R. L. Scheaffer. *Mathematical Statistics with Applications*, 7th ed. Cengage Learning, 2007.

Experimental Design

Cochran, W. G., and G. M. Cox. *Experimental Designs*, 2nd ed. Wiley, 1992.

Hicks, C. R., and K. V. Turner. *Fundamental Concepts in the Design of Experiments*, 5th ed. Oxford University Press, 1999.

Montgomery, D. C. *Design and Analysis of Experiments*, 8th ed. Wiley, 2012.

Winer, B. J., K. M. Michels, and D. R. Brown. *Statistical Principles in Experimental Design*, 3rd ed. McGraw-Hill, 1991.

Wu, C. F. Jeff, and M. Hamada. *Experiments: Planning, Analysis, and Optimization*, 2nd ed. Wiley, 2009.

Time Series and Forecasting

Bowerman, B. L., and R. T. O'Connell. *Forecasting and Time Series: An Applied Approach*, 3rd ed. Brooks/Cole, 2000.

Box, G. E. P., G. M. Jenkins, and G. C. Reinsel. *Time Series Analysis: Forecasting and Control*, 4th ed. Wiley, 2008.

Makridakis, S. G., S. C. Wheelwright, and R. J. Hyndman. *Forecasting Methods and Applications*, 3rd ed. Wiley, 1997.

Wilson, J. H., B. Keating, and John Galt Solutions, Inc. *Business Forecasting with Accompanying Excel-Based Forecast X^{TM}*, 5th ed. McGraw-Hill/Irwin, 2007.

Nonparametric Methods

Conover, W. J. *Practical Nonparametric Statistics*, 3rd ed. Wiley, 1999.

Gibbons, J. D., and S. Chakraborti. *Nonparametric Statistical Inference*, 5th ed. CRC Press, 2010.

Higgins, J. J. *Introduction to Modern Nonparametric Statistics*. Thomson-Brooks/Cole, 2004.

Hollander, M., and D. A. Wolfe. *Non-Parametric Statistical Methods*, 2nd ed. Wiley, 1999.

Probability

Hogg, R. V., and E. A. Tanis. *Probability and Statistical Inference*, 8th ed. Prentice Hall, 2009.

Ross, S. M. *Introduction to Probability Models*, 10th ed. Academic Press, 2009.

Wackerly, D. D., W. Mendenhall, and R. L. Scheaffer. *Mathematical Statistics with Applications*, 7th ed. Cengage Learning, 2007.

Quality Control

DeFeo, J. A., and J. M. Juran, *Juran's Quality Handbook*, 6th ed. McGraw-Hill, 2010.

Evans, J. R., and W. M. Lindsay. *The Management and Control of Quality*, 6th ed. South-Western, 2006.

Montgomery, D. C. *Introduction to Statistical Quality Control*, 6th ed. Wiley, 2008.

Regression Analysis

Chatterjee, S., and A. S. Hadi. *Regression Analysis by Example*, 4th ed. Wiley, 2006.

Draper, N. R., and H. Smith. *Applied Regression Analysis*, 3rd ed. Wiley, 1998.

Graybill, F. A., and H. K. Iyer. *Regression Analysis: Concepts and Applications*. Wadsworth, 1994.

Kleinbaum, D. G., L. L. Kupper, and K. E. Muller. *Applied Regression Analysis and Multivariate Methods*, 4th ed. Cengage Learning, 2007.

Neter, J., W. Wasserman, M. H. Kutner, and C. Nashtsheim. *Applied Linear Statistical Models*, 5th ed. McGraw-Hill, 2004.

Mendenhall, M., T. Sincich, and T. R. Dye. *A Second Course in Statistics: Regression Analysis*, 7th ed. Prentice Hall, 2011.

Decision Analysis

Clemen, R. T., and T. Reilly. *Making Hard Decisions with Decision Tools*. Cengage Learning, 2004.

Goodwin, P., and G. Wright. *Decision Analysis for Management Judgment*, 4th ed. Wiley, 2010.

Pratt, J. W., H. Raiffa, and R. Schlaifer. *Introduction to Statistical Decision Theory*. MIT Press, 1995.

Sampling

Cochran, W. G. *Sampling Techniques,* 3rd ed. Wiley, 1977.

Hansen, M. H., W. N. Hurwitz, W. G. Madow, and M. N. Hanson. *Sample Survey Methods and Theory.* Wiley, 1993.

Kish, L. *Survey Sampling.* Wiley, 2008.

Levy, P. S., and S. Lemeshow. *Sampling of Populations: Methods and Applications,* 4th ed. Wiley, 2009.

Scheaffer, R. L., W. Mendenhall, and L. Ott. *Elementary Survey Sampling,* 7th ed. Duxbury Press, 2011.

Data Visualization

Cleveland, W. S. *Visualizing Data.* Hobart Press, 1993.

Cleveland, W. S. *The Elements of Graphing Data,* 2nd ed. Hobart Press, 1994.

Few, S. *Show Me the Numbers: Designing Tables and Graphs to Enlighten.* Analytics Press, 2004.

Few, S. *Information Dashboard Design: The Effective Visual Communication of Data.* O'Reilly Media, 2006.

Few, S. *Now You See It: Simple Visualization Techniques for Quantitative Analysis.* Analytics Press, 2009.

Fry, B. *Visualizing Data: Exploring and Explaining Data with the Processing Environment.* O'Reilly Media, 2008.

Robbins, N. B. *Creating More Effective Graphs.* Wiley, 2004.

Telea, A. C. *Data Visualization Principles and Practice.* A. K. Peters Ltd., 2008.

Tufte, E. R. *Envisioning Information.* Graphics Press, 1990.

Tufte, E. R. *The Visual Display of Quantitative Information,* 2nd ed. Graphics Press, 1990.

Tufte, E. R. *Visual Explanations: Images and Quantities, Evidence and Narrative.* Graphics Press, 1997.

Tufte, E. R. *Visual and Statistical Thinking: Displays of Evidence for Making Decisions.* Graphics Press, 1997.

Tufte, E. R. *Beautiful Evidence.* Graphics Press, 2006.

Wong, D. M. *The Wall Street Journal Guide to Information Graphics.* W. W. Norton & Company, 2010.

Young, F. W., P. M. Valero-Mora, and M. Friendly. *Visual Statistics: Seeing Data with Dynamic Interactive Graphics.* Wiley, 2006.

Appendix B: Tables

TABLE 1   CUMULATIVE PROBABILITIES FOR THE STANDARD NORMAL
DISTRIBUTION

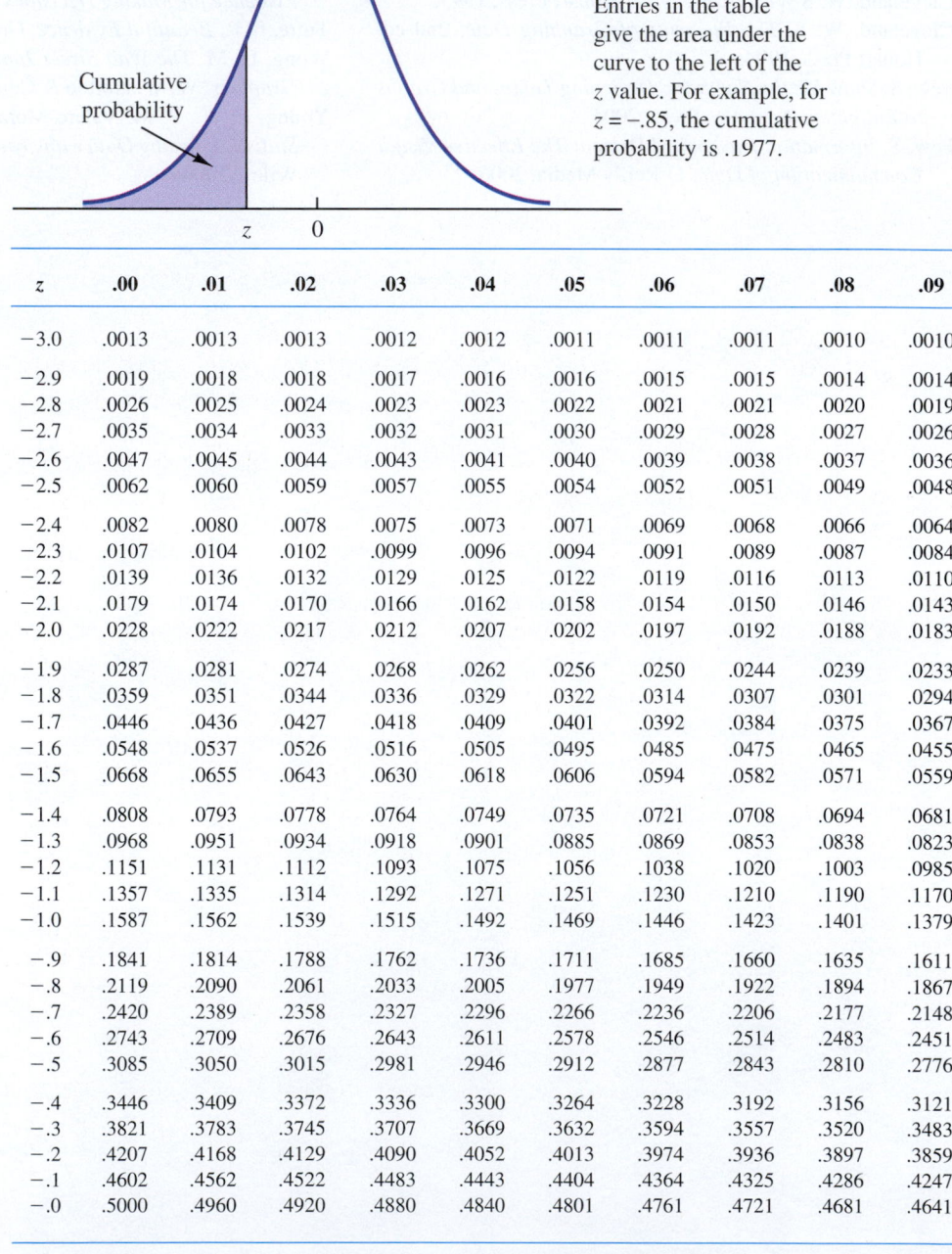

Entries in the table
give the area under the
curve to the left of the
z value. For example, for
z = −.85, the cumulative
probability is .1977.

z	.00	.01	.02	.03	.04	.05	.06	.07	.08	.09
−3.0	.0013	.0013	.0013	.0012	.0012	.0011	.0011	.0011	.0010	.0010
−2.9	.0019	.0018	.0018	.0017	.0016	.0016	.0015	.0015	.0014	.0014
−2.8	.0026	.0025	.0024	.0023	.0023	.0022	.0021	.0021	.0020	.0019
−2.7	.0035	.0034	.0033	.0032	.0031	.0030	.0029	.0028	.0027	.0026
−2.6	.0047	.0045	.0044	.0043	.0041	.0040	.0039	.0038	.0037	.0036
−2.5	.0062	.0060	.0059	.0057	.0055	.0054	.0052	.0051	.0049	.0048
−2.4	.0082	.0080	.0078	.0075	.0073	.0071	.0069	.0068	.0066	.0064
−2.3	.0107	.0104	.0102	.0099	.0096	.0094	.0091	.0089	.0087	.0084
−2.2	.0139	.0136	.0132	.0129	.0125	.0122	.0119	.0116	.0113	.0110
−2.1	.0179	.0174	.0170	.0166	.0162	.0158	.0154	.0150	.0146	.0143
−2.0	.0228	.0222	.0217	.0212	.0207	.0202	.0197	.0192	.0188	.0183
−1.9	.0287	.0281	.0274	.0268	.0262	.0256	.0250	.0244	.0239	.0233
−1.8	.0359	.0351	.0344	.0336	.0329	.0322	.0314	.0307	.0301	.0294
−1.7	.0446	.0436	.0427	.0418	.0409	.0401	.0392	.0384	.0375	.0367
−1.6	.0548	.0537	.0526	.0516	.0505	.0495	.0485	.0475	.0465	.0455
−1.5	.0668	.0655	.0643	.0630	.0618	.0606	.0594	.0582	.0571	.0559
−1.4	.0808	.0793	.0778	.0764	.0749	.0735	.0721	.0708	.0694	.0681
−1.3	.0968	.0951	.0934	.0918	.0901	.0885	.0869	.0853	.0838	.0823
−1.2	.1151	.1131	.1112	.1093	.1075	.1056	.1038	.1020	.1003	.0985
−1.1	.1357	.1335	.1314	.1292	.1271	.1251	.1230	.1210	.1190	.1170
−1.0	.1587	.1562	.1539	.1515	.1492	.1469	.1446	.1423	.1401	.1379
−.9	.1841	.1814	.1788	.1762	.1736	.1711	.1685	.1660	.1635	.1611
−.8	.2119	.2090	.2061	.2033	.2005	.1977	.1949	.1922	.1894	.1867
−.7	.2420	.2389	.2358	.2327	.2296	.2266	.2236	.2206	.2177	.2148
−.6	.2743	.2709	.2676	.2643	.2611	.2578	.2546	.2514	.2483	.2451
−.5	.3085	.3050	.3015	.2981	.2946	.2912	.2877	.2843	.2810	.2776
−.4	.3446	.3409	.3372	.3336	.3300	.3264	.3228	.3192	.3156	.3121
−.3	.3821	.3783	.3745	.3707	.3669	.3632	.3594	.3557	.3520	.3483
−.2	.4207	.4168	.4129	.4090	.4052	.4013	.3974	.3936	.3897	.3859
−.1	.4602	.4562	.4522	.4483	.4443	.4404	.4364	.4325	.4286	.4247
−.0	.5000	.4960	.4920	.4880	.4840	.4801	.4761	.4721	.4681	.4641

TABLE 1   CUMULATIVE PROBABILITIES FOR THE STANDARD NORMAL DISTRIBUTION (*Continued*)

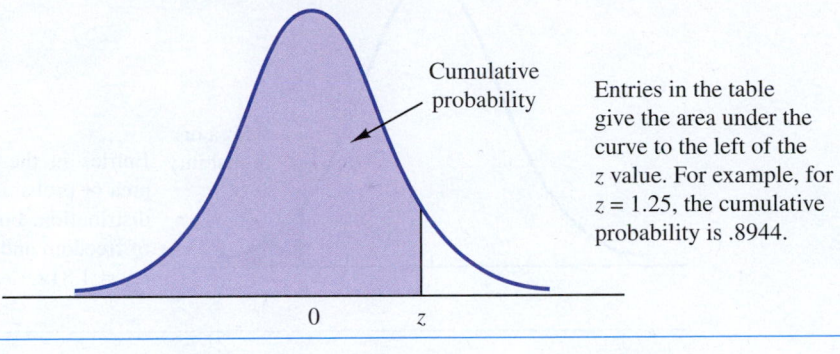

Cumulative probability

Entries in the table give the area under the curve to the left of the z value. For example, for z = 1.25, the cumulative probability is .8944.

z	.00	.01	.02	.03	.04	.05	.06	.07	.08	.09
.0	.5000	.5040	.5080	.5120	.5160	.5199	.5239	.5279	.5319	.5359
.1	.5398	.5438	.5478	.5517	.5557	.5596	.5636	.5675	.5714	.5753
.2	.5793	.5832	.5871	.5910	.5948	.5987	.6026	.6064	.6103	.6141
.3	.6179	.6217	.6255	.6293	.6331	.6368	.6406	.6443	.6480	.6517
.4	.6554	.6591	.6628	.6664	.6700	.6736	.6772	.6808	.6844	.6879
.5	.6915	.6950	.6985	.7019	.7054	.7088	.7123	.7157	.7190	.7224
.6	.7257	.7291	.7324	.7357	.7389	.7422	.7454	.7486	.7517	.7549
.7	.7580	.7611	.7642	.7673	.7704	.7734	.7764	.7794	.7823	.7852
.8	.7881	.7910	.7939	.7967	.7995	.8023	.8051	.8078	.8106	.8133
.9	.8159	.8186	.8212	.8238	.8264	.8289	.8315	.8340	.8365	.8389
1.0	.8413	.8438	.8461	.8485	.8508	.8531	.8554	.8577	.8599	.8621
1.1	.8643	.8665	.8686	.8708	.8729	.8749	.8770	.8790	.8810	.8830
1.2	.8849	.8869	.8888	.8907	.8925	.8944	.8962	.8980	.8997	.9015
1.3	.9032	.9049	.9066	.9082	.9099	.9115	.9131	.9147	.9162	.9177
1.4	.9192	.9207	.9222	.9236	.9251	.9265	.9279	.9292	.9306	.9319
1.5	.9332	.9345	.9357	.9370	.9382	.9394	.9406	.9418	.9429	.9441
1.6	.9452	.9463	.9474	.9484	.9495	.9505	.9515	.9525	.9535	.9545
1.7	.9554	.9564	.9573	.9582	.9591	.9599	.9608	.9616	.9625	.9633
1.8	.9641	.9649	.9656	.9664	.9671	.9678	.9686	.9693	.9699	.9706
1.9	.9713	.9719	.9726	.9732	.9738	.9744	.9750	.9756	.9761	.9767
2.0	.9772	.9778	.9783	.9788	.9793	.9798	.9803	.9808	.9812	.9817
2.1	.9821	.9826	.9830	.9834	.9838	.9842	.9846	.9850	.9854	.9857
2.2	.9861	.9864	.9868	.9871	.9875	.9878	.9881	.9884	.9887	.9890
2.3	.9893	.9896	.9898	.9901	.9904	.9906	.9909	.9911	.9913	.9916
2.4	.9918	.9920	.9922	.9925	.9927	.9929	.9931	.9932	.9934	.9936
2.5	.9938	.9940	.9941	.9943	.9945	.9946	.9948	.9949	.9951	.9952
2.6	.9953	.9955	.9956	.9957	.9959	.9960	.9961	.9962	.9963	.9964
2.7	.9965	.9966	.9967	.9968	.9969	.9970	.9971	.9972	.9973	.9974
2.8	.9974	.9975	.9976	.9977	.9977	.9978	.9979	.9979	.9980	.9981
2.9	.9981	.9982	.9982	.9983	.9984	.9984	.9985	.9985	.9986	.9986
3.0	.9987	.9987	.9987	.9988	.9988	.9989	.9989	.9989	.9990	.9990

TABLE 2   *t* DISTRIBUTION

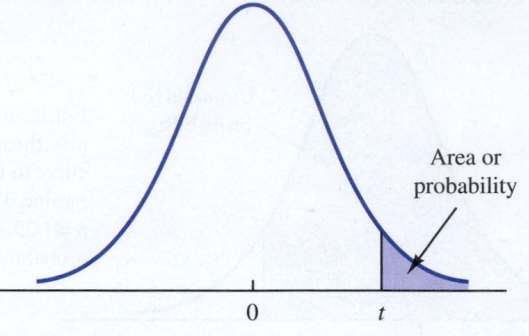

Area or probability

Entries in the table give *t* values for an area or probability in the upper tail of the *t* distribution. For example, with 10 degrees of freedom and a .05 area in the upper tail, $t_{.05} = 1.812$.

Degrees of Freedom	Area in Upper Tail					
	.20	.10	.05	.025	.01	.005
1	1.376	3.078	6.314	12.706	31.821	63.656
2	1.061	1.886	2.920	4.303	6.965	9.925
3	.978	1.638	2.353	3.182	4.541	5.841
4	.941	1.533	2.132	2.776	3.747	4.604
5	.920	1.476	2.015	2.571	3.365	4.032
6	.906	1.440	1.943	2.447	3.143	3.707
7	.896	1.415	1.895	2.365	2.998	3.499
8	.889	1.397	1.860	2.306	2.896	3.355
9	.883	1.383	1.833	2.262	2.821	3.250
10	.879	1.372	1.812	2.228	2.764	3.169
11	.876	1.363	1.796	2.201	2.718	3.106
12	.873	1.356	1.782	2.179	2.681	3.055
13	.870	1.350	1.771	2.160	2.650	3.012
14	.868	1.345	1.761	2.145	2.624	2.977
15	.866	1.341	1.753	2.131	2.602	2.947
16	.865	1.337	1.746	2.120	2.583	2.921
17	.863	1.333	1.740	2.110	2.567	2.898
18	.862	1.330	1.734	2.101	2.552	2.878
19	.861	1.328	1.729	2.093	2.539	2.861
20	.860	1.325	1.725	2.086	2.528	2.845
21	.859	1.323	1.721	2.080	2.518	2.831
22	.858	1.321	1.717	2.074	2.508	2.819
23	.858	1.319	1.714	2.069	2.500	2.807
24	.857	1.318	1.711	2.064	2.492	2.797
25	.856	1.316	1.708	2.060	2.485	2.787
26	.856	1.315	1.706	2.056	2.479	2.779
27	.855	1.314	1.703	2.052	2.473	2.771
28	.855	1.313	1.701	2.048	2.467	2.763
29	.854	1.311	1.699	2.045	2.462	2.756
30	.854	1.310	1.697	2.042	2.457	2.750
31	.853	1.309	1.696	2.040	2.453	2.744
32	.853	1.309	1.694	2.037	2.449	2.738
33	.853	1.308	1.692	2.035	2.445	2.733
34	.852	1.307	1.691	2.032	2.441	2.728

TABLE 2   *t* DISTRIBUTION (*Continued*)

Degrees of Freedom	Area in Upper Tail					
	.20	**.10**	**.05**	**.025**	**.01**	**.005**
35	.852	1.306	1.690	2.030	2.438	2.724
36	.852	1.306	1.688	2.028	2.434	2.719
37	.851	1.305	1.687	2.026	2.431	2.715
38	.851	1.304	1.686	2.024	2.429	2.712
39	.851	1.304	1.685	2.023	2.426	2.708
40	.851	1.303	1.684	2.021	2.423	2.704
41	.850	1.303	1.683	2.020	2.421	2.701
42	.850	1.302	1.682	2.018	2.418	2.698
43	.850	1.302	1.681	2.017	2.416	2.695
44	.850	1.301	1.680	2.015	2.414	2.692
45	.850	1.301	1.679	2.014	2.412	2.690
46	.850	1.300	1.679	2.013	2.410	2.687
47	.849	1.300	1.678	2.012	2.408	2.685
48	.849	1.299	1.677	2.011	2.407	2.682
49	.849	1.299	1.677	2.010	2.405	2.680
50	.849	1.299	1.676	2.009	2.403	2.678
51	.849	1.298	1.675	2.008	2.402	2.676
52	.849	1.298	1.675	2.007	2.400	2.674
53	.848	1.298	1.674	2.006	2.399	2.672
54	.848	1.297	1.674	2.005	2.397	2.670
55	.848	1.297	1.673	2.004	2.396	2.668
56	.848	1.297	1.673	2.003	2.395	2.667
57	.848	1.297	1.672	2.002	2.394	2.665
58	.848	1.296	1.672	2.002	2.392	2.663
59	.848	1.296	1.671	2.001	2.391	2.662
60	.848	1.296	1.671	2.000	2.390	2.660
61	.848	1.296	1.670	2.000	2.389	2.659
62	.847	1.295	1.670	1.999	2.388	2.657
63	.847	1.295	1.669	1.998	2.387	2.656
64	.847	1.295	1.669	1.998	2.386	2.655
65	.847	1.295	1.669	1.997	2.385	2.654
66	.847	1.295	1.668	1.997	2.384	2.652
67	.847	1.294	1.668	1.996	2.383	2.651
68	.847	1.294	1.668	1.995	2.382	2.650
69	.847	1.294	1.667	1.995	2.382	2.649
70	.847	1.294	1.667	1.994	2.381	2.648
71	.847	1.294	1.667	1.994	2.380	2.647
72	.847	1.293	1.666	1.993	2.379	2.646
73	.847	1.293	1.666	1.993	2.379	2.645
74	.847	1.293	1.666	1.993	2.378	2.644
75	.846	1.293	1.665	1.992	2.377	2.643
76	.846	1.293	1.665	1.992	2.376	2.642
77	.846	1.293	1.665	1.991	2.376	2.641
78	.846	1.292	1.665	1.991	2.375	2.640
79	.846	1.292	1.664	1.990	2.374	2.639

TABLE 2   *t* DISTRIBUTION (*Continued*)

Degrees of Freedom	Area in Upper Tail					
	.20	.10	.05	.025	.01	.005
80	.846	1.292	1.664	1.990	2.374	2.639
81	.846	1.292	1.664	1.990	2.373	2.638
82	.846	1.292	1.664	1.989	2.373	2.637
83	.846	1.292	1.663	1.989	2.372	2.636
84	.846	1.292	1.663	1.989	2.372	2.636
85	.846	1.292	1.663	1.988	2.371	2.635
86	.846	1.291	1.663	1.988	2.370	2.634
87	.846	1.291	1.663	1.988	2.370	2.634
88	.846	1.291	1.662	1.987	2.369	2.633
89	.846	1.291	1.662	1.987	2.369	2.632
90	.846	1.291	1.662	1.987	2.368	2.632
91	.846	1.291	1.662	1.986	2.368	2.631
92	.846	1.291	1.662	1.986	2.368	2.630
93	.846	1.291	1.661	1.986	2.367	2.630
94	.845	1.291	1.661	1.986	2.367	2.629
95	.845	1.291	1.661	1.985	2.366	2.629
96	.845	1.290	1.661	1.985	2.366	2.628
97	.845	1.290	1.661	1.985	2.365	2.627
98	.845	1.290	1.661	1.984	2.365	2.627
99	.845	1.290	1.660	1.984	2.364	2.626
100	.845	1.290	1.660	1.984	2.364	2.626
∞	.842	1.282	1.645	1.960	2.326	2.576

TABLE 3 CHI-SQUARE DISTRIBUTION

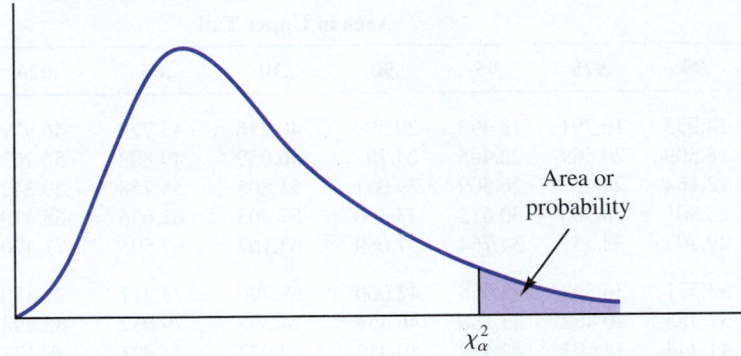

Area or probability

χ_α^2

Entries in the table give χ_α^2 values, where α is the area or probability in the upper tail of the chi-square distribution. For example, with 10 degrees of freedom and a .01 area in the upper tail, $\chi_{.01}^2 = 23.209$.

Degrees of Freedom	Area in Upper Tail									
	.995	.99	.975	.95	.90	.10	.05	.025	.01	.005
1	.000	.000	.001	.004	.016	2.706	3.841	5.024	6.635	7.879
2	.010	.020	.051	.103	.211	4.605	5.991	7.378	9.210	10.597
3	.072	.115	.216	.352	.584	6.251	7.815	9.348	11.345	12.838
4	.207	.297	.484	.711	1.064	7.779	9.488	11.143	13.277	14.860
5	.412	.554	.831	1.145	1.610	9.236	11.070	12.832	15.086	16.750
6	.676	.872	1.237	1.635	2.204	10.645	12.592	14.449	16.812	18.548
7	.989	1.239	1.690	2.167	2.833	12.017	14.067	16.013	18.475	20.278
8	1.344	1.647	2.180	2.733	3.490	13.362	15.507	17.535	20.090	21.955
9	1.735	2.088	2.700	3.325	4.168	14.684	16.919	19.023	21.666	23.589
10	2.156	2.558	3.247	3.940	4.865	15.987	18.307	20.483	23.209	25.188
11	2.603	3.053	3.816	4.575	5.578	17.275	19.675	21.920	24.725	26.757
12	3.074	3.571	4.404	5.226	6.304	18.549	21.026	23.337	26.217	28.300
13	3.565	4.107	5.009	5.892	7.041	19.812	22.362	24.736	27.688	29.819
14	4.075	4.660	5.629	6.571	7.790	21.064	23.685	26.119	29.141	31.319
15	4.601	5.229	6.262	7.261	8.547	22.307	24.996	27.488	30.578	32.801
16	5.142	5.812	6.908	7.962	9.312	23.542	26.296	28.845	32.000	34.267
17	5.697	6.408	7.564	8.672	10.085	24.769	27.587	30.191	33.409	35.718
18	6.265	7.015	8.231	9.390	10.865	25.989	28.869	31.526	34.805	37.156
19	6.844	7.633	8.907	10.117	11.651	27.204	30.144	32.852	36.191	38.582
20	7.434	8.260	9.591	10.851	12.443	28.412	31.410	34.170	37.566	39.997
21	8.034	8.897	10.283	11.591	13.240	29.615	32.671	35.479	38.932	41.401
22	8.643	9.542	10.982	12.338	14.041	30.813	33.924	36.781	40.289	42.796
23	9.260	10.196	11.689	13.091	14.848	32.007	35.172	38.076	41.638	44.181
24	9.886	10.856	12.401	13.848	15.659	33.196	36.415	39.364	42.980	45.558
25	10.520	11.524	13.120	14.611	16.473	34.382	37.652	40.646	44.314	46.928
26	11.160	12.198	13.844	15.379	17.292	35.563	38.885	41.923	45.642	48.290
27	11.808	12.878	14.573	16.151	18.114	36.741	40.113	43.195	46.963	49.645
28	12.461	13.565	15.308	16.928	18.939	37.916	41.337	44.461	48.278	50.994
29	13.121	14.256	16.047	17.708	19.768	39.087	42.557	45.722	49.588	52.335

TABLE 3   CHI-SQUARE DISTRIBUTION (*Continued*)

Degrees of Freedom	Area in Upper Tail									
	.995	.99	.975	.95	.90	.10	.05	.025	.01	.005
30	13.787	14.953	16.791	18.493	20.599	40.256	43.773	46.979	50.892	53.672
35	17.192	18.509	20.569	22.465	24.797	46.059	49.802	53.203	57.342	60.275
40	20.707	22.164	24.433	26.509	29.051	51.805	55.758	59.342	63.691	66.766
45	24.311	25.901	28.366	30.612	33.350	57.505	61.656	65.410	69.957	73.166
50	27.991	29.707	32.357	34.764	37.689	63.167	67.505	71.420	76.154	79.490
55	31.735	33.571	36.398	38.958	42.060	68.796	73.311	77.380	82.292	85.749
60	35.534	37.485	40.482	43.188	46.459	74.397	79.082	83.298	88.379	91.952
65	39.383	41.444	44.603	47.450	50.883	79.973	84.821	89.177	94.422	98.105
70	43.275	45.442	48.758	51.739	55.329	85.527	90.531	95.023	100.425	104.215
75	47.206	49.475	52.942	56.054	59.795	91.061	96.217	100.839	106.393	110.285
80	51.172	53.540	57.153	60.391	64.278	96.578	101.879	106.629	112.329	116.321
85	55.170	57.634	61.389	64.749	68.777	102.079	107.522	112.393	118.236	122.324
90	59.196	61.754	65.647	69.126	73.291	107.565	113.145	118.136	124.116	128.299
95	63.250	65.898	69.925	73.520	77.818	113.038	118.752	123.858	129.973	134.247
100	67.328	70.065	74.222	77.929	82.358	118.498	124.342	129.561	135.807	140.170

TABLE 4 F DISTRIBUTION

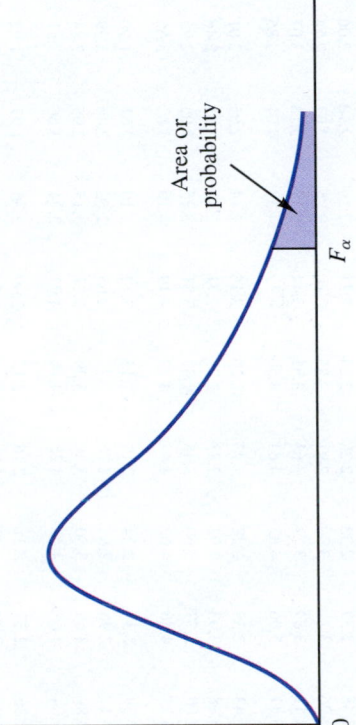

Area or probability

F_α

Entries in the table give F_α values, where α is the area or probability in the upper tail of the F distribution. For example, with 4 numerator degrees of freedom, 8 denominator degrees of freedom, and a .05 area in the upper tail, $F_{.05} = 3.84$.

Denominator Degrees of Freedom	Area in Upper Tail	1	2	3	4	5	6	7	8	9	10	15	20	25	30	40	60	100	100
												Numerator Degrees of Freedom							
1	.10	39.86	49.50	53.59	55.83	57.24	58.20	58.91	59.44	59.86	60.19	61.22	61.74	62.05	62.26	62.53	62.79	63.01	63.30
	.05	161.45	199.50	215.71	224.58	230.16	233.99	236.77	238.88	240.54	241.88	245.95	248.02	249.26	250.10	251.14	252.20	253.04	254.19
	.025	647.79	799.48	864.15	899.60	921.83	937.11	948.20	956.64	963.28	968.63	984.87	993.08	998.09	1001.40	1005.60	1009.79	1013.16	1017.76
	.01	4052.18	4999.34	5403.53	5624.26	5763.96	5858.95	5928.33	5980.95	6022.40	6055.93	6156.97	6208.66	6239.86	6260.35	6286.43	6312.97	6333.92	6362.80
2	.10	8.53	9.00	9.16	9.24	9.29	9.33	9.35	9.37	9.38	9.39	9.42	9.44	9.45	9.46	9.47	9.47	9.48	9.49
	.05	18.51	19.00	19.16	19.25	19.30	19.33	19.35	19.37	19.38	19.40	19.43	19.45	19.46	19.46	19.47	19.48	19.49	19.49
	.025	38.51	39.00	39.17	39.25	39.30	39.33	39.36	39.37	39.39	39.40	39.43	39.45	39.46	39.46	39.47	39.48	39.49	39.50
	.01	98.50	99.00	99.16	99.25	99.30	99.33	99.36	99.38	99.39	99.40	99.43	99.45	99.46	99.47	99.48	99.48	99.49	99.50
3	.10	5.54	5.46	5.39	5.34	5.31	5.28	5.27	5.25	5.24	5.23	5.20	5.18	5.17	5.17	5.16	5.15	5.14	5.13
	.05	10.13	9.55	9.28	9.12	9.01	8.94	8.89	8.85	8.81	8.79	8.70	8.66	8.63	8.62	8.59	8.57	8.55	8.53
	.025	17.44	16.04	15.44	15.10	14.88	14.73	14.62	14.54	14.47	14.42	14.25	14.17	14.12	14.08	14.04	13.99	13.96	13.91
	.01	34.12	30.82	29.46	28.71	28.24	27.91	27.67	27.49	27.34	27.23	26.87	26.69	26.58	26.50	26.41	26.32	26.24	26.14
4	.10	4.54	4.32	4.19	4.11	4.05	4.01	3.98	3.95	3.94	3.92	3.87	3.84	3.83	3.82	3.80	3.79	3.78	3.76
	.05	7.71	6.94	6.59	6.39	6.26	6.16	6.09	6.04	6.00	5.96	5.86	5.80	5.77	5.75	5.72	5.69	5.66	5.63
	.025	12.22	10.65	9.98	9.60	9.36	9.20	9.07	8.98	8.90	8.84	8.66	8.56	8.50	8.46	8.41	8.36	8.32	8.26
	.01	21.20	18.00	16.69	15.98	15.52	15.21	14.98	14.80	14.66	14.55	14.20	14.02	13.91	13.84	13.75	13.65	13.58	13.47
5	.10	4.06	3.78	3.62	3.52	3.45	3.40	3.37	3.34	3.32	3.30	3.24	3.21	3.19	3.17	3.16	3.14	3.13	3.11
	.05	6.61.	5.79	5.41	5.19	5.05	4.95	4.88	4.82	4.77	4.74	4.62	4.56	4.52	4.50	4.46	4.43	4.41	4.37
	.025	10.01	8.43	7.76	7.39	7.15	6.98	6.85	6.76	6.68	6.62	6.43	6.33	6.27	6.23	6.18	6.12	6.08	6.02
	.01	16.26	13.27	12.06	11.39	10.97	10.67	10.46	10.29	10.16	10.05	9.72	9.55	9.45	9.38	9.29	9.20	9.13	9.03

TABLE 4 *F* DISTRIBUTION (*Continued*)

Denominator Degrees of Freedom	Area in Upper Tail	\multicolumn{18}{c}{Numerator Degrees of Freedom}																	
		1	2	3	4	5	6	7	8	9	10	15	20	25	30	40	60	100	1000
6	.10	3.78	3.46	3.29	3.18	3.11	3.05	3.01	2.98	2.96	2.94	2.87	2.84	2.81	2.80	2.78	2.76	2.75	2.72
	.05	5.99	5.14	4.76	4.53	4.39	4.28	4.21	4.15	4.10	4.06	3.94	3.87	3.83	3.81	3.77	3.74	3.71	3.67
	.025	8.81	7.26	6.60	6.23	5.99	5.82	5.70	5.60	5.52	5.46	5.27	5.17	5.11	5.07	5.01	4.96	4.92	4.86
	.01	13.75	10.92	9.78	9.15	8.75	8.47	8.26	8.10	7.98	7.87	7.56	7.40	7.30	7.23	7.14	7.06	6.99	6.89
7	.10	3.59	3.26	3.07	2.96	2.88	2.83	2.78	2.75	2.72	2.70	2.63	2.59	2.57	2.56	2.54	2.51	2.50	2.47
	.05	5.59	4.74	4.35	4.12	3.97	3.87	3.79	3.73	3.68	3.64	3.51	3.44	3.40	3.38	3.34	3.30	3.27	3.23
	.025	8.07	6.54	5.89	5.52	5.29	5.12	4.99	4.90	4.82	4.76	4.57	4.47	4.40	4.36	4.31	4.25	4.21	4.15
	.01	12.25	9.55	8.45	7.85	7.46	7.19	6.99	6.84	6.72	6.62	6.31	6.16	6.06	5.99	5.91	5.82	5.75	5.66
8	.10	3.46	3.11	2.92	2.81	2.73	2.67	2.62	2.59	2.56	2.54	2.46	2.42	2.40	2.38	2.36	2.34	2.32	2.30
	.05	5.32	4.46	4.07	3.84	3.69	3.58	3.50	3.44	3.39	3.35	3.22	3.15	3.11	3.08	3.04	3.01	2.97	2.93
	.025	7.57	6.06	5.42	5.05	4.82	4.65	4.53	4.43	4.36	4.30	4.10	4.00	3.94	3.89	3.84	3.78	3.74	3.68
	.01	11.26	8.65	7.59	7.01	6.63	6.37	6.18	6.03	5.91	5.81	5.52	5.36	5.26	5.20	5.12	5.03	4.96	4.87
9	.10	3.36	3.01	2.81	2.69	2.61	2.55	2.51	2.47	2.44	2.42	2.34	2.30	2.27	2.25	2.23	2.21	2.19	2.16
	.05	5.12	4.26	3.86	3.63	3.48	3.37	3.29	3.23	3.18	3.14	3.01	2.94	2.89	2.86	2.83	2.79	2.76	2.71
	.025	7.21	5.71	5.08	4.72	4.48	4.32	4.20	4.10	4.03	3.96	3.77	3.67	3.60	3.56	3.51	3.45	3.40	3.34
	.01	10.56	8.02	6.99	6.42	6.06	5.80	5.61	5.47	5.35	5.26	4.96	4.81	4.71	4.65	4.57	4.48	4.41	4.32
10	.10	3.29	2.92	2.73	2.61	2.52	2.46	2.41	2.38	2.35	2.32	2.24	2.20	2.17	2.16	2.13	2.11	2.09	2.06
	.05	4.96	4.10	3.71	3.48	3.33	3.22	3.14	3.07	3.02	2.98	2.85	2.77	2.73	2.70	2.66	2.62	2.59	2.54
	.025	6.94	5.46	4.83	4.47	4.24	4.07	3.95	3.85	3.78	3.72	3.52	3.42	3.35	3.31	3.26	3.20	3.15	3.09
	.01	10.04	7.56	6.55	5.99	5.64	5.39	5.20	5.06	4.94	4.85	4.56	4.41	4.31	4.25	4.17	4.08	4.01	3.92
11	.10	3.23	2.86	2.66	2.54	2.45	2.39	2.34	2.30	2.27	2.25	2.17	2.12	2.10	2.08	2.05	2.03	2.01	1.98
	.05	4.84	3.98	3.59	3.36	3.20	3.09	3.01	2.95	2.90	2.85	2.72	2.65	2.60	2.57	2.53	2.49	2.46	2.41
	.025	6.72	5.26	4.63	4.28	4.04	3.88	3.76	3.66	3.59	3.53	3.33	3.23	3.16	3.12	3.06	3.00	2.96	2.89
	.01	9.65	7.21	6.22	5.67	5.32	5.07	4.89	4.74	4.63	4.54	4.25	4.10	4.01	3.94	3.86	3.78	3.71	3.61
12	.10	3.18	2.81	2.61	2.48	2.39	2.33	2.28	2.24	2.21	2.19	2.10	2.06	2.03	2.01	1.99	1.96	1.94	1.91
	.05	4.75	3.89	3.49	3.26	3.11	3.00	2.91	2.85	2.80	2.75	2.62	2.54	2.50	2.47	2.43	2.38	2.35	2.30
	.025	6.55	5.10	4.47	4.12	3.89	3.73	3.61	3.51	3.44	3.37	3.18	3.07	3.01	2.96	2.91	2.85	2.80	2.73
	.01	9.33	6.93	5.95	5.41	5.06	4.82	4.64	4.50	4.39	4.30	4.01	3.86	3.76	3.70	3.62	3.54	3.47	3.37
13	.10	3.14	2.76	2.56	2.43	2.35	2.28	2.23	2.20	2.16	2.14	2.05	2.01	1.98	1.96	1.93	1.90	1.88	1.85
	.05	4.67	3.81	3.41	3.18	3.03	2.92	2.83	2.77	2.71	2.67	2.53	2.46	2.41	2.38	2.34	2.30	2.26	2.21
	.025	6.41	4.97	4.35	4.00	3.77	3.60	3.48	3.39	3.31	3.25	3.05	2.95	2.88	2.84	2.78	2.72	2.67	2.60
	.01	9.07	6.70	5.74	5.21	4.86	4.62	4.44	4.30	4.19	4.10	3.82	3.66	3.57	3.51	3.43	3.34	3.27	3.18
14	.10	3.10	2.73	2.52	2.39	2.31	2.24	2.19	2.15	2.12	2.10	2.01	1.96	1.93	1.91	1.89	1.86	1.83	1.80
	.05	4.60	3.74	3.34	3.11	2.96	2.85	2.76	2.70	2.65	2.60	2.46	2.39	2.34	2.31	2.27	2.22	2.19	2.14
	.025	6.30	4.86	4.24	3.89	3.66	3.50	3.38	3.29	3.21	3.15	2.95	2.84	2.78	2.73	2.67	2.61	2.56	2.50
	.01	8.86	6.51	5.56	5.04	4.69	4.46	4.28	4.14	4.03	3.94	3.66	3.51	3.41	3.35	3.27	3.18	3.11	3.02
15	.10	3.07	2.70	2.49	2.36	2.27	2.21	2.16	2.12	2.09	2.06	1.97	1.92	1.89	1.87	1.85	1.82	1.79	1.76
	.05	4.54	3.68	3.29	3.06	2.90	2.79	2.71	2.64	2.59	2.54	2.40	2.33	2.28	2.25	2.20	2.16	2.12	2.07
	.025	6.20	4.77	4.15	3.80	3.58	3.41	3.29	3.20	3.12	3.06	2.86	2.76	2.69	2.64	2.59	2.52	2.47	2.40
	.01	8.68	6.36	5.42	4.89	4.56	4.32	4.14	4.00	3.89	3.80	3.52	3.37	3.28	3.21	3.13	3.05	2.98	2.88

Numerator Degrees of Freedom

Denominator Degrees of Freedom	Area in Upper Tail	1	2	3	4	5	6	7	8	9	10	15	20	25	30	40	60	100	1000
16	.10	3.05	2.67	2.46	2.33	2.24	2.18	2.13	2.09	2.06	2.03	1.94	1.89	1.86	1.84	1.81	1.78	1.76	1.72
	.05	4.49	3.63	3.24	3.01	2.85	2.74	2.66	2.59	2.54	2.49	2.35	2.28	2.23	2.19	2.15	2.11	2.07	2.02
	.025	6.12	4.69	4.08	3.73	3.50	3.34	3.22	3.12	3.05	2.99	2.79	2.68	2.61	2.57	2.51	2.45	2.40	2.32
	.01	8.53	6.23	5.29	4.77	4.44	4.20	4.03	3.89	3.78	3.69	3.41	3.26	3.16	3.10	3.02	2.93	2.86	2.76
17	.10	3.03	2.64	2.44	2.31	2.22	2.15	2.10	2.06	2.03	2.00	1.91	1.86	1.83	1.81	1.78	1.75	1.73	1.69
	.05	4.45	3.59	3.20	2.96	2.81	2.70	2.61	2.55	2.49	2.45	2.31	2.23	2.18	2.15	2.10	2.06	2.02	1.97
	.025	6.04	4.62	4.01	3.66	3.44	3.28	3.16	3.06	2.98	2.92	2.72	2.62	2.55	2.50	2.44	2.38	2.33	2.26
	.01	8.40	6.11	5.19	4.67	4.34	4.10	3.93	3.79	3.68	3.59	3.31	3.16	3.07	3.00	2.92	2.83	2.76	2.66
18	.10	3.01	2.62	2.42	2.29	2.20	2.13	2.08	2.04	2.00	1.98	1.89	1.84	1.80	1.78	1.75	1.72	1.70	1.66
	.05	4.41	3.55	3.16	2.93	2.77	2.66	2.58	2.51	2.46	2.41	2.27	2.19	2.14	2.11	2.06	2.02	1.98	1.92
	.025	5.98	4.56	3.95	3.61	3.38	3.22	3.10	3.01	2.93	2.87	2.67	2.56	2.49	2.44	2.38	2.32	2.27	2.20
	.01	8.29	6.01	5.09	4.58	4.25	4.01	3.84	3.71	3.60	3.51	3.23	3.08	2.98	2.92	2.84	2.75	2.68	2.58
19	.10	2.99	2.61	2.40	2.27	2.18	2.11	2.06	2.02	1.98	1.96	1.86	1.81	1.78	1.76	1.73	1.70	1.67	1.64
	.05	4.38	3.52	3.13	2.90	2.74	2.63	2.54	2.48	2.42	2.38	2.23	2.16	2.11	2.07	2.03	1.98	1.94	1.88
	.025	5.92	4.51	3.90	3.56	3.33	3.17	3.05	2.96	2.88	2.82	2.62	2.51	2.44	2.39	2.33	2.27	2.22	2.14
	.01	8.18	5.93	5.01	4.50	4.17	3.94	3.77	3.63	3.52	3.43	3.15	3.00	2.91	2.84	2.76	2.67	2.60	2.50
20	.10	2.97	2.59	2.38	2.25	2.16	2.09	2.04	2.00	1.96	1.94	1.84	1.79	1.76	1.74	1.71	1.68	1.65	1.61
	.05	4.35	3.49	3.10	2.87	2.71	2.60	2.51	2.45	2.39	2.35	2.20	2.12	2.07	2.04	1.99	1.95	1.91	1.85
	.025	5.87	4.46	3.86	3.51	3.29	3.13	3.01	2.91	2.84	2.77	2.57	2.46	2.40	2.35	2.29	2.22	2.17	2.09
	.01	8.10	5.85	4.94	4.43	4.10	3.87	3.70	3.56	3.46	3.37	3.09	2.94	2.84	2.78	2.69	2.61	2.54	2.43
21	.10	2.96	2.57	2.36	2.23	2.14	2.08	2.02	1.98	1.95	1.92	1.83	1.78	1.74	1.72	1.69	1.66	1.63	1.59
	.05	4.32	3.47	3.07	2.84	2.68	2.57	2.49	2.42	2.37	2.32	2.18	2.10	2.05	2.01	1.96	1.92	1.88	1.82
	.025	5.83	4.42	3.82	3.48	3.25	3.09	2.97	2.87	2.80	2.73	2.53	2.42	2.36	2.31	2.25	2.18	2.13	2.05
	.01	8.02	5.78	4.87	4.37	4.04	3.81	3.64	3.51	3.40	3.31	3.03	2.88	2.79	2.72	2.64	2.55	2.48	2.37
22	.10	2.95	2.56	2.35	2.22	2.13	2.06	2.01	1.97	1.93	1.90	1.81	1.76	1.73	1.70	1.67	1.64	1.61	1.57
	.05	4.30	3.44	3.05	2.82	2.66	2.55	2.46	2.40	2.34	2.30	2.15	2.07	2.02	1.98	1.94	1.89	1.85	1.79
	.025	5.79	4.38	3.78	3.44	3.22	3.05	2.93	2.84	2.76	2.70	2.50	2.39	2.32	2.27	2.21	2.14	2.09	2.01
	.01	7.95	5.72	4.82	4.31	3.99	3.76	3.59	3.45	3.35	3.26	2.98	2.83	2.73	2.67	2.58	2.50	2.42	2.32
23	.10	2.94	2.55	2.34	2.21	2.11	2.05	1.99	1.95	1.92	1.89	1.80	1.74	1.71	1.69	1.66	1.62	1.59	1.55
	.05	4.28	3.42	3.03	2.80	2.64	2.53	2.44	2.37	2.32	2.27	2.13	2.05	2.00	1.96	1.91	1.86	1.82	1.76
	.025	5.75	4.35	3.75	3.41	3.18	3.02	2.90	2.81	2.73	2.67	2.47	2.36	2.29	2.24	2.18	2.11	2.06	1.98
	.01	7.88	5.66	4.76	4.26	3.94	3.71	3.54	3.41	3.30	3.21	2.93	2.78	2.69	2.62	2.54	2.45	2.37	2.27
24	.10	2.93	2.54	2.33	2.19	2.10	2.04	1.98	1.94	1.91	1.88	1.78	1.73	1.70	1.67	1.64	1.61	1.58	1.54
	.05	4.26	3.40	3.01	2.78	2.62	2.51	2.42	2.36	2.30	2.25	2.11	2.03	1.97	1.94	1.89	1.84	1.80	1.74
	.025	5.72	4.32	3.72	3.38	3.15	2.99	2.87	2.78	2.70	2.64	2.44	2.33	2.26	2.21	2.15	2.08	2.02	1.94
	.01	7.82	5.61	4.72	4.22	3.90	3.67	3.50	3.36	3.26	3.17	2.89	2.74	2.64	2.58	2.49	2.40	2.33	2.22

TABLE 4 F DISTRIBUTION (*Continued*)

Denominator Degrees of Freedom	Area in Upper Tail	Numerator Degrees of Freedom																	
		1	2	3	4	5	6	7	8	9	10	15	20	25	30	40	60	100	1000
25	.10	2.92	2.53	2.32	2.18	2.09	2.02	1.97	1.93	1.89	1.87	1.77	1.72	1.68	1.66	1.63	1.59	1.56	1.52
	.05	4.24	3.39	2.99	2.76	2.60	2.49	2.40	2.34	2.28	2.24	2.09	2.01	1.96	1.92	1.87	1.82	1.78	1.72
	.025	5.69	4.29	3.69	3.35	3.13	2.97	2.85	2.75	2.68	2.61	2.41	2.30	2.23	2.18	2.12	2.05	2.00	1.91
	.01	7.77	5.57	4.68	4.18	3.85	3.63	3.46	3.32	3.22	3.13	2.85	2.70	2.60	2.54	2.45	2.36	2.29	2.18
26	.10	2.91	2.52	2.31	2.17	2.08	2.01	1.96	1.92	1.88	1.86	1.76	1.71	1.67	1.65	1.61	1.58	1.55	1.51
	.05	4.23	3.37	2.98	2.74	2.59	2.47	2.39	2.32	2.27	2.22	2.07	1.99	1.94	1.90	1.85	1.80	1.76	1.70
	.025	5.66	4.27	3.67	3.33	3.10	2.94	2.82	2.73	2.65	2.59	2.39	2.28	2.21	2.16	2.09	2.03	1.97	1.89
	.01	7.72	5.53	4.64	4.14	3.82	3.59	3.42	3.29	3.18	3.09	2.81	2.66	2.57	2.50	2.42	2.33	2.25	2.14
27	.10	2.90	2.51	2.30	2.17	2.07	2.00	1.95	1.91	1.87	1.85	1.75	1.70	1.66	1.64	1.60	1.57	1.54	1.50
	.05	4.21	3.35	2.96	2.73	2.57	2.46	2.37	2.31	2.25	2.20	2.06	1.97	1.92	1.88	1.84	1.79	1.74	1.68
	.025	5.63	4.24	3.65	3.31	3.08	2.92	2.80	2.71	2.63	2.57	2.36	2.25	2.18	2.13	2.07	2.00	1.94	1.86
	.01	7.68	5.49	4.60	4.11	3.78	3.56	3.39	3.26	3.15	3.06	2.78	2.63	2.54	2.47	2.38	2.29	2.22	2.11
28	.10	2.89	2.50	2.29	2.16	2.06	2.00	1.94	1.90	1.87	1.84	1.74	1.69	1.65	1.63	1.59	1.56	1.53	1.48
	.05	4.20	3.34	2.95	2.71	2.56	2.45	2.36	2.29	2.24	2.19	2.04	1.96	1.91	1.87	1.82	1.77	1.73	1.66
	.025	5.61	4.22	3.63	3.29	3.06	2.90	2.78	2.69	2.61	2.55	2.34	2.23	2.16	2.11	2.05	1.98	1.92	1.84
	.01	7.64	5.45	4.57	4.07	3.75	3.53	3.36	3.23	3.12	3.03	2.75	2.60	2.51	2.44	2.35	2.26	2.19	2.08
29	.10	2.89	2.50	2.28	2.15	2.06	1.99	1.93	1.89	1.86	1.83	1.73	1.68	1.64	1.62	1.58	1.55	1.52	1.47
	.05	4.18	3.33	2.93	2.70	2.55	2.43	2.35	2.28	2.22	2.18	2.03	1.94	1.89	1.85	1.81	1.75	1.71	1.65
	.025	5.59	4.20	3.61	3.27	3.04	2.88	2.76	2.67	2.59	2.53	2.32	2.21	2.14	2.09	2.03	1.96	1.90	1.82
	.01	7.60	5.42	4.54	4.04	3.73	3.50	3.33	3.20	3.09	3.00	2.73	2.57	2.48	2.41	2.33	2.23	2.16	2.05
30	.10	2.88	2.49	2.28	2.14	2.05	1.98	1.93	1.88	1.85	1.82	1.72	1.67	1.63	1.61	1.57	1.54	1.51	1.46
	.05	4.17	3.32	2.92	2.69	2.53	2.42	2.33	2.27	2.21	2.16	2.01	1.93	1.88	1.84	1.79	1.74	1.70	1.63
	.025	5.57	4.18	3.59	3.25	3.03	2.87	2.75	2.65	2.57	2.51	2.31	2.20	2.12	2.07	2.01	1.94	1.88	1.80
	.01	7.56	5.39	4.51	4.02	3.70	3.47	3.30	3.17	3.07	2.98	2.70	2.55	2.45	2.39	2.30	2.21	2.13	2.02
40	.10	2.84	2.44	2.23	2.09	2.00	1.93	1.87	1.83	1.79	1.76	1.66	1.61	1.57	1.54	1.51	1.47	1.43	1.38
	.05	4.08	3.23	2.84	2.61	2.45	2.34	2.25	2.18	2.12	2.08	1.92	1.84	1.78	1.74	1.69	1.64	1.59	1.52
	.025	5.42	4.05	3.46	3.13	2.90	2.74	2.62	2.53	2.45	2.39	2.18	2.07	1.99	1.94	1.88	1.80	1.74	1.65
	.01	7.31	5.18	4.31	3.83	3.51	3.29	3.12	2.99	2.89	2.80	2.52	2.37	2.27	2.20	2.11	2.02	1.94	1.82
60	.10	2.79	2.39	2.18	2.04	1.95	1.87	1.82	1.77	1.74	1.71	1.60	1.54	1.50	1.48	1.44	1.40	1.36	1.30
	.05	4.00	3.15	2.76	2.53	2.37	2.25	2.17	2.10	2.04	1.99	1.84	1.75	1.69	1.65	1.59	1.53	1.48	1.40
	.025	5.29	3.93	3.34	3.01	2.79	2.63	2.51	2.41	2.33	2.27	2.06	1.94	1.87	1.82	1.74	1.67	1.60	1.49
	.01	7.08	4.98	4.13	3.65	3.34	3.12	2.95	2.82	2.72	2.63	2.35	2.20	2.10	2.03	1.94	1.84	1.75	1.62
100	.10	2.76	2.36	2.14	2.00	1.91	1.83	1.78	1.73	1.69	1.66	1.56	1.49	1.45	1.42	1.38	1.34	1.29	1.22
	.05	3.94	3.09	2.70	2.46	2.31	2.19	2.10	2.03	1.97	1.93	1.77	1.68	1.62	1.57	1.52	1.45	1.39	1.30
	.025	5.18	3.83	3.25	2.92	2.70	2.54	2.42	2.32	2.24	2.18	1.97	1.85	1.77	1.71	1.64	1.56	1.48	1.36
	.01	6.90	4.82	3.98	3.51	3.21	2.99	2.82	2.69	2.59	2.50	2.22	2.07	1.97	1.89	1.80	1.69	1.60	1.45
1000	.10	2.71	2.31	2.09	1.95	1.85	1.78	1.72	1.68	1.64	1.61	1.49	1.43	1.38	1.35	1.30	1.25	1.20	1.08
	.05	3.85	3.00	2.61	2.38	2.22	2.11	2.02	1.95	1.89	1.84	1.68	1.58	1.52	1.47	1.41	1.33	1.26	1.11
	.025	5.04	3.70	3.13	2.80	2.58	2.42	2.30	2.20	2.13	2.06	1.85	1.72	1.64	1.58	1.50	1.41	1.32	1.13
	.01	6.66	4.63	3.80	3.34	3.04	2.82	2.66	2.53	2.43	2.34	2.06	1.90	1.79	1.72	1.61	1.50	1.38	1.16

Appendix C: Summation Notation

Summation

Definition

$$\sum_{i=1}^{n} x_i = x_1 + x_2 + \cdots + x_n \tag{C.1}$$

Example for $x_1 = 5$, $x_2 = 8$, $x_3 = 14$:

$$\sum_{i=1}^{3} x_i = x_1 + x_2 + x_3$$
$$= 5 + 8 + 14$$
$$= 27$$

Result 1

For a constant c:

$$\sum_{i=1}^{n} c = \underbrace{(c + c + \cdots + c)}_{n \text{ times}} = nc \tag{C.2}$$

Example for $c = 5$, $n = 10$:

$$\sum_{i=1}^{10} 5 = 10(5) = 50$$

Example for $c = \bar{x}$:

$$\sum_{i=1}^{n} \bar{x} = n\bar{x}$$

Result 2

$$\sum_{i=1}^{n} cx_i = cx_1 + cx_2 + \cdots + cx_n$$
$$= c(x_1 + x_2 + \cdots + x_n) = c\sum_{i=1}^{n} x_i \tag{C.3}$$

Example for $x_1 = 5$, $x_2 = 8$, $x_3 = 14$, $c = 2$:

$$\sum_{i=1}^{3} 2x_i = 2\sum_{i=1}^{3} x_i = 2(27) = 54$$

Result 3

$$\sum_{i=1}^{n} (ax_i + by_i) = a\sum_{i=1}^{n} x_i + b\sum_{i=1}^{n} y_i \tag{C.4}$$

Example for $x_1 = 5$, $x_2 = 8$, $x_3 = 14$, $a = 2$, $y_1 = 7$, $y_2 = 3$, $y_3 = 8$, $b = 4$:

$$\sum_{i=1}^{3} (2x_i + 4y_i) = 2 \sum_{i=1}^{3} x_i + 4 \sum_{i=1}^{3} y_i$$

$$= 2(27) + 4(18)$$
$$= 54 + 72$$
$$= 126$$

Double Summations

Consider the following data involving the variable x_{ij}, where i is the subscript denoting the row position and j is the subscript denoting the column position:

		Column		
		1	**2**	**3**
Row	**1**	$x_{11} = 10$	$x_{12} = 8$	$x_{13} = 6$
	2	$x_{21} = 7$	$x_{22} = 4$	$x_{23} = 12$

Definition

$$\sum_{i=1}^{n} \sum_{j=1}^{m} x_{ij} = (x_{11} + x_{12} + \cdots + x_{1m}) + (x_{21} + x_{22} + \cdots + x_{2m})$$
$$+ (x_{31} + x_{32} + \cdots + x_{3m}) + \cdots + (x_{n1} + x_{n2} + \cdots + x_{nm}) \qquad \textbf{(C.5)}$$

Example:

$$\sum_{i=1}^{2} \sum_{j=1}^{3} x_{ij} = x_{11} + x_{12} + x_{13} + x_{21} + x_{22} + x_{23}$$
$$= 10 + 8 + 6 + 7 + 4 + 12$$
$$= 47$$

Definition

$$\sum_{i=1}^{n} x_{ij} = x_{1j} + x_{2j} + \cdots + x_{nj} \qquad \textbf{(C.6)}$$

Example:

$$\sum_{i=1}^{2} x_{i2} = x_{12} + x_{22}$$
$$= 8 + 4$$
$$= 12$$

Shorthand Notation

Sometimes when a summation is for all values of the subscript, we use the following shorthand notations:

$$\sum_{i=1}^{n} x_i = \sum x_i \qquad \textbf{(C.7)}$$

$$\sum_{i=1}^{n} \sum_{j=1}^{m} x_{ij} = \sum \sum x_{ij} \qquad \textbf{(C.8)}$$

$$\sum_{i=1}^{n} x_{ij} = \sum_{i} x_{ij} \qquad \textbf{(C.9)}$$

Completely worked-out solutions can be accessed by students and instructors online two ways:

1. Those with Mindtap access, Appendix D can be found within the Course Materials folder, linking to the free companion site
2. Appendix D can also be accessed at **www.cengagebrain.com** by creating an account to access the free materials that accompany your purchased product

Appendix E: Microsoft Excel 2016 and Tools for Statistical Analysis

Microsoft Excel 2016, part of the Microsoft Office 2016 system, is a spreadsheet program that can be used to organize and analyze data, perform complex calculations, and create a wide variety of graphical displays. We assume that readers are familiar with basic Excel operations such as selecting cells, entering formulas, copying, and so on. But we do not assume readers are familiar with Excel 2016 or the use of Excel for statistical analysis.

The purpose of this appendix is twofold. First, we provide an overview of Excel 2016 and discuss the basic operations needed to work with Excel 2016 workbooks and worksheets. Second, we provide an overview of the tools that are available for conducting statistical analysis with Excel. These include Excel functions and formulas which allow users to conduct their own analyses and add-ins that provide more comprehensive analysis tools.

Excel's Data Analysis add-in, included with the basic Excel system, is a valuable tool for conducting statistical analysis. In the last section of this appendix we provide instruction for installing the Data Analysis add-in. Other add-ins have been developed by outside suppliers to supplement the basic statistical capabilities provided by Excel.

Overview of Microsoft Excel 2016

When using Excel for statistical analysis, data is displayed in workbooks, each of which contains a series of worksheets that typically include the original data as well as any resulting analysis, including charts. Figure E.1 shows the layout of a blank workbook created each time Excel is opened. The workbook is named Book1, and contains one worksheet named Sheet1. Excel highlights the worksheet currently displayed (Sheet1) by setting the name on the worksheet tab in bold. Note that cell A1 is initially selected.

A workbook is a file containing one or more worksheets.

The wide bar located across the top of the workbook is referred to as the Ribbon. Tabs, located at the top of the Ribbon, provide quick access to groups of related commands. There are eight tabs shown on the workbook in Figure E.1: File; Home; Insert; Page Layout; Formulas; Data; Review; and View. Each tab contains a series of groups of related commands. Note that the Home tab is selected when Excel is opened. Figure E.2 displays the groups available when the Home tab is selected. Under the Home tab there are seven groups: Clipboard; Font; Alignment; Number; Styles; Cells; and Editing. Commands are arranged within each group. For example, to change selected text to boldface, click the Home tab and click the Bold B button in the Font group.

Figure E.3 illustrates the location of the Quick Access Toolbar and the Formula Bar. The Quick Access Toolbar allows you to quickly access workbook options. To add or remove features on the Quick Access Toolbar, click the Customize Quick Access Toolbar button ⤵ at the end of the Quick Access Toolbar.

The Formula Bar (see Figure E.3) contains a Name box, the Insert Function button *fx*, and a Formula box. In Figure E.3, "A1" appears in the name box because cell A1 is selected. You can select any other cell in the worksheet by using the mouse to move the cursor to another cell and clicking or by typing the new cell location in the Name box. The Formula box is used to display the formula in the currently selected cell. For instance, if you enter $=A1+A2$ into cell A3, whenever you select cell A3 the formula $=A1+A2$ will be shown in the Formula box. This feature makes it very easy to see and edit a formula in

FIGURE E.1   BLANK WORKBOOK CREATED WHEN EXCEL IS OPENED

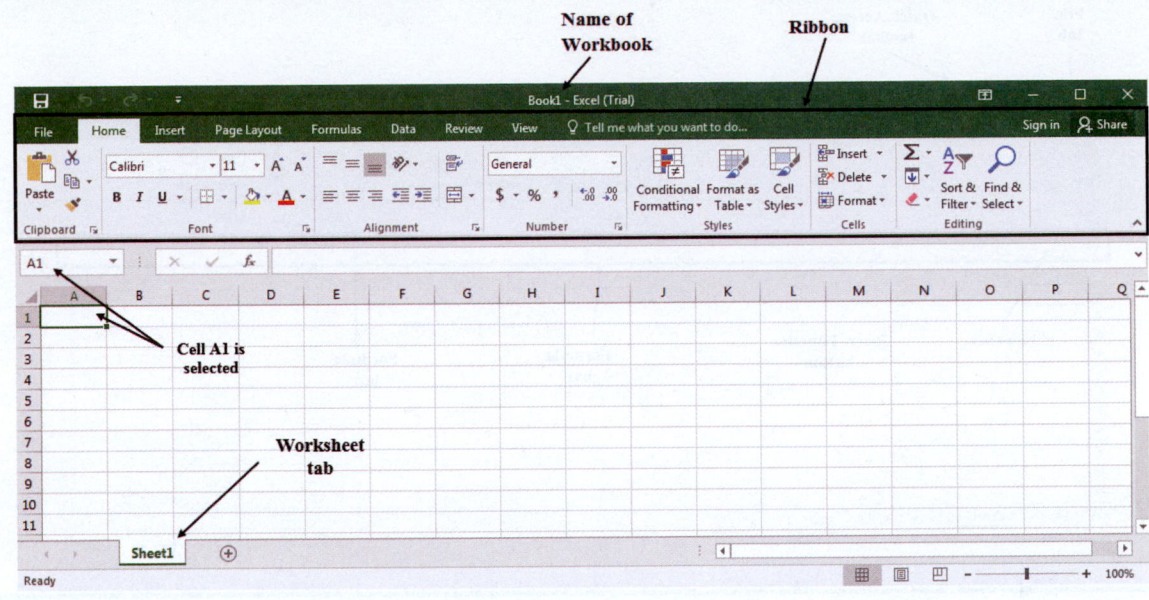

a particular cell. The Insert Function button allows you to quickly access all the functions available in Excel. Later we show how to find and use a particular function.

Basic Workbook Operations

Figure E.4 illustrates the worksheet options that can be performed after right-clicking on a worksheet tab. For instance, to change the name of the current worksheet from "Sheet1" to "Data," right-click the worksheet tab named "Sheet1" and select the Rename option.

FIGURE E.2   PORTION OF THE HOME TAB

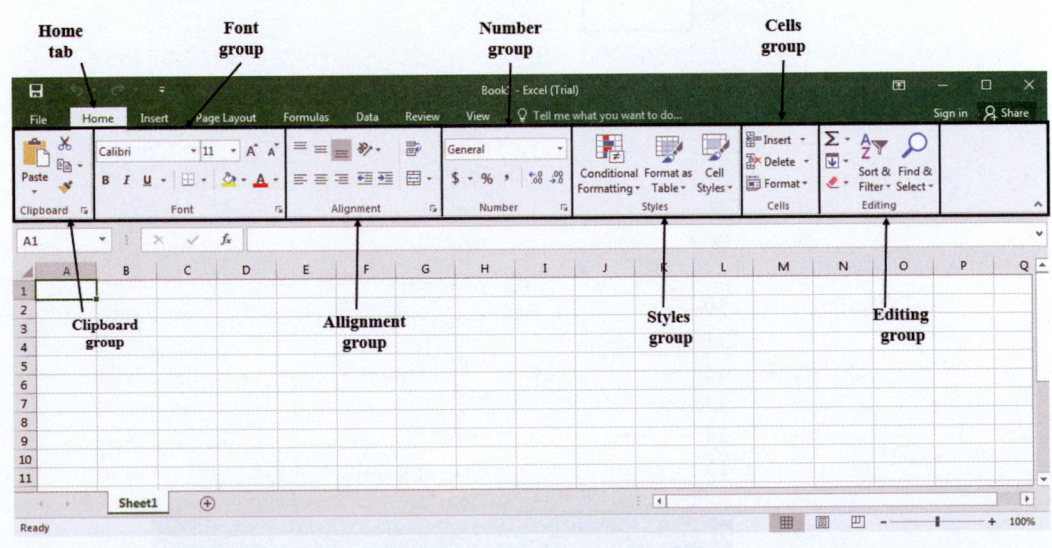

FIGURE E.3   EXCEL 2016 QUICK ACCESS TOOLBAR AND FORMULA BAR

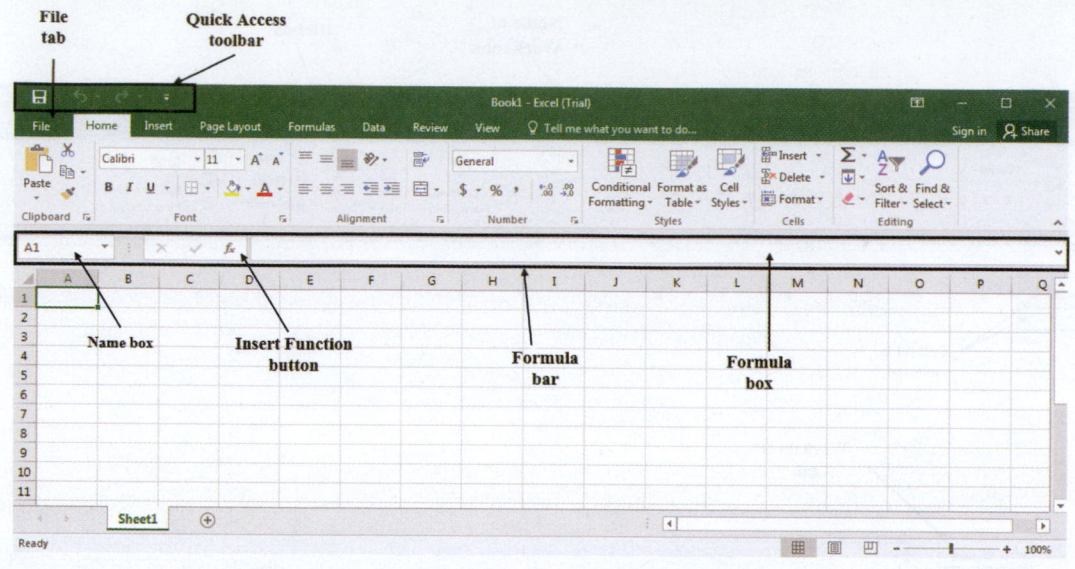

The current worksheet name (Sheet1) will be highlighted. Then, simply type the new name (Data) and press the Enter key to rename the worksheet.

Suppose that you wanted to create a copy of "Sheet1." After right-clicking the tab named "Sheet1," select the Move or Copy option. When the Move or Copy dialog box appears, select Create a Copy and click OK. The name of the copied worksheet will appear as "Sheet1 (2)." You can then rename it, if desired.

FIGURE E.4   WORKSHEET OPTIONS OBTAINED AFTER RIGHT-CLICKING
ON A WORKSHEET TAB

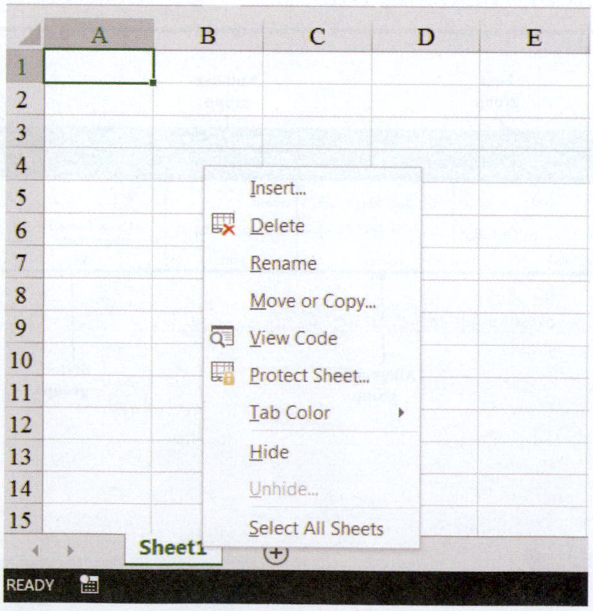

To add a new worksheet to the workbook, right-click any worksheet tab and select the Insert option; when the Insert dialog box appears, select Worksheet and click OK. An additional blank worksheet will appear in the workbook. You can also insert a new worksheet by clicking the New sheet button ⊞ that appears to the right of the last worksheet tab displayed. Worksheets can be deleted by right-clicking the worksheet tab and choosing Delete. Worksheets can also be moved to other workbooks or a different position in the current workbook by using the Move or Copy option.

Creating, Saving, and Opening Files

Data can be entered into an Excel worksheet by manually entering the data into the worksheet or by opening another workbook that already contains the data. As an illustration of manually entering, saving, and opening a file we will use the example from Chapter 2 involving data for a sample of 50 soft drink purchases. The original data are shown in Table E.1.

Suppose we want to enter the data for the sample of 50 soft drink purchases into Sheet1 of the new workbook. First we enter the label "Brand Purchased" into cell A1; then we enter the data for the 50 soft drink purchases into cells A2:A51. As a reminder that this worksheet contains the data, we will change the name of the worksheet from "Sheet1" to "Data" using the procedure described previously. Figure E.5 shows the data worksheet that we just developed.

Before doing any analysis with these data, we recommend that you first save the file; this will prevent you from having to reenter the data in case something happens that causes Excel to close. To save the file as an Excel 2016 workbook using the filename SoftDrink we perform the following steps:

Step 1: Click the **File** tab
Step 2: Click **Save** in the list of options
Step 3: When the **Save As** window appears:
        Select **This PC**
        Select Browse
        Select the location where you want to save the file
        Type the filename **SoftDrink** in the **File name** box
        Click **Save**

TABLE E.1 DATA FROM A SAMPLE OF 50 SOFT DRINK PURCHASES

Coca-Cola	Sprite	Pepsi
Diet Coke	Coca-Cola	Coca-Cola
Pepsi	Diet Coke	Coca-Cola
Diet Coke	Coca-Cola	Coca-Cola
Coca-Cola	Diet Coke	Pepsi
Coca-Cola	Coca-Cola	Dr. Pepper
Dr. Pepper	Sprite	Coca-Cola
Diet Coke	Pepsi	Diet Coke
Pepsi	Coca-Cola	Pepsi
Pepsi	Coca-Cola	Pepsi
Coca-Cola	Coca-Cola	Pepsi
Dr. Pepper	Pepsi	Pepsi
Sprite	Coca-Cola	Coca-Cola
Coca-Cola	Sprite	Dr. Pepper
Diet Coke	Dr. Pepper	Pepsi
Coca-Cola	Pepsi	Sprite
Coca-Cola	Diet Coke	

FIGURE E.5   WORKSHEET CONTAINING THE SOFT DRINK DATA

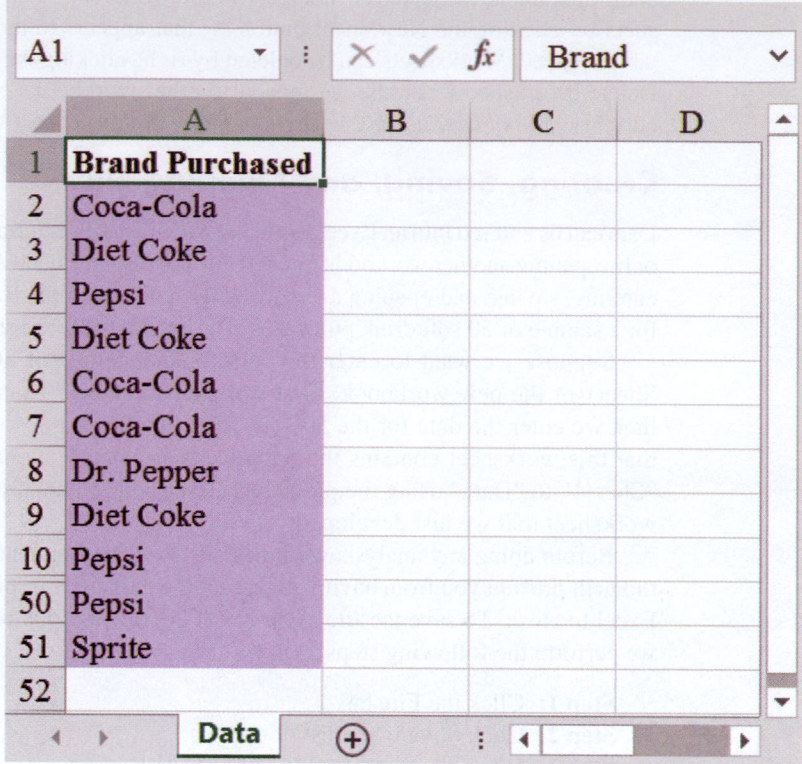

Note: Rows 11–49 are hidden.

Excel's Save command is designed to save the file as an Excel 2016 workbook. As you work with the file to do statistical analysis you should follow the practice of periodically saving the file so you will not lose any statistical analysis you may have performed. Simply click the File tab and select Save in the list of options.

Keyboard shortcut: To save the file, press CTRL+S.

Sometimes you may want to create a copy of an existing file. For instance, suppose you would like to save the soft drink data and any resulting statistical analysis in a new file named "SoftDrink Analysis." The following steps show how to create a copy of the SoftDrink workbook and analysis with the new filename, "SoftDrink Analysis."

Step 1: Click the **File** tab
Step 2: Click **Save As**
Step 3: When the Save As window appears:
　　　　　Select **This PC**
　　　　　Select **Browse**
　　　　　Select the location where you want to save the file
　　　　　Type the filename **SoftDrink Analysis** in the **File name** box
　　　　　Click **Save**

Once the workbook has been saved, you can continue to work with the data to perform whatever type of statistical analysis is appropriate. When you are finished working with the file simply click the File tab and then click close in the list of options. To access the SoftDrink Analysis file at another point in time you can open the file by performing the following steps after launching Excel:

Step 1: Click the **File** tab
Step 2: Click **Open Other Workbooks**
Step 3: When the Open window appears:
> Select **This PC**
> Select **Browse**
> Select the location where you previously saved the file
> Enter the filename **SoftDrink Analysis** in the **File name** box
> Click **Open**

The procedures we showed for saving or opening a workbook begin by clicking the File tab to access the Save and Open commands. Once you have used Excel for a while you will probably find it more convenient to add these commands to the Quick Access Toolbar.

Using Excel Functions

Excel 2016 provides a wealth of functions for data management and statistical analysis. If we know what function is needed, and how to use it, we can simply enter the function into the appropriate worksheet cell. However, if we are not sure what functions are available to accomplish a task, or are not sure how to use a particular function, Excel can provide assistance. Many new functions for statistical analysis have been added with Excel 2016. To illustrate we will use the SoftDrink Analysis workbook created in the previous subsection.

Finding the Right Excel Function

To identify the functions available in Excel, select the cell where you want to insert the function; we have selected cell D2. Click the **Formulas** tab on the Ribbon and then click the **Insert Function** button in the **Function Library** group. Alternatively, click the *fx* button on the formula bar. Either approach provides the **Insert Function** dialog box shown in Figure E.6.

The **Search for a function** box at the top of the Insert Function dialog box enables us to type a brief description of what we want to do. After doing so and clicking **Go**, Excel will search for and display, in the **Select a function** box, the functions that may accomplish our task. In many situations, however, we may want to browse through an entire category of functions to see what is available. For this task, the **Or select a category** box is helpful. It contains a drop-down list of several categories of functions provided by Excel. Figure E.6 shows that we selected the **Statistical** category. As a result, Excel's statistical functions appear in alphabetic order in the Select a function box. We see the AVEDEV function listed first, followed by the AVERAGE function, and so on.

The AVEDEV function is highlighted in Figure E.6, indicating it is the function currently selected. The proper syntax for the function and a brief description of the function appear below the Select a function box. We can scroll through the list in the Select a function box to display the syntax and a brief description for each of the statistical functions that are available. For instance, scrolling down farther, we select the COUNTIF function as shown in Figure E.7. Note that COUNTIF is now highlighted, and that immediately below the Select a function box we see **COUNTIF(range,criteria)**, which indicates that the COUNTIF function contains two inputs, range and criteria. In addition, we see that the description of the COUNTIF function is "Counts the number of cells within a range that meet the given condition."

FIGURE E.6   INSERT FUNCTION DIALOG BOX

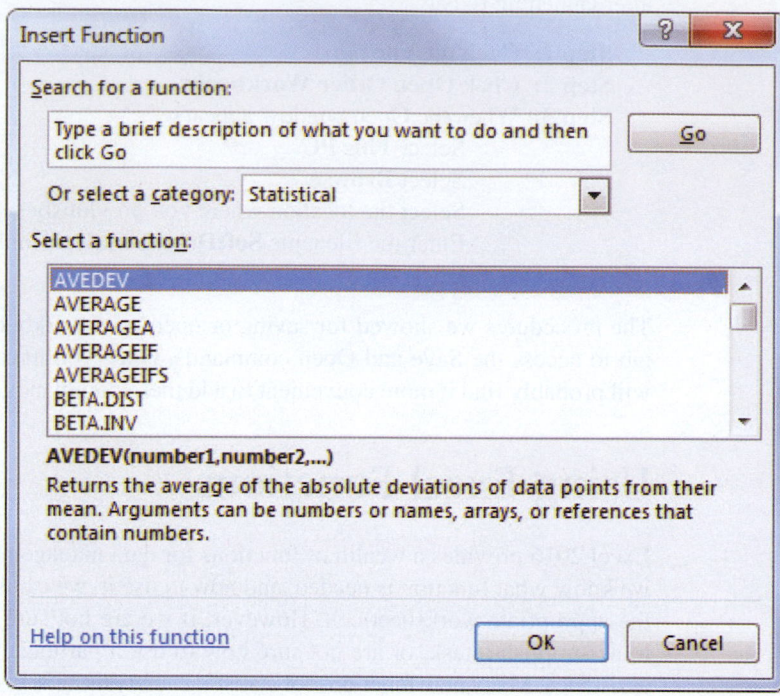

FIGURE E.7   DESCRIPTION OF THE COUNTIF FUNCTION IN THE INSERT FUNCTION
DIALOG BOX

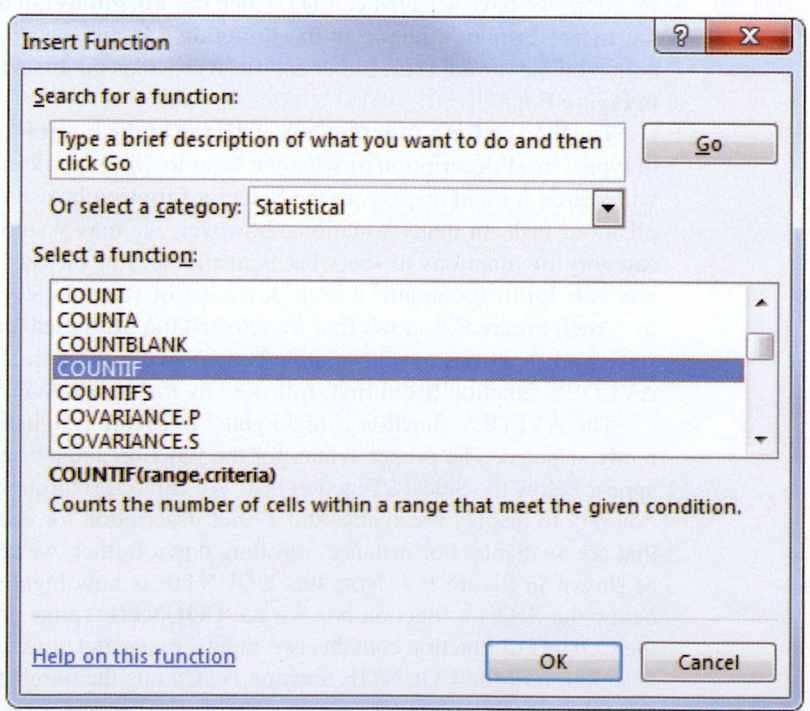

FIGURE E.8   FUNCTION ARGUMENTS DIALOG BOX FOR THE COUNTIF FUNCTION

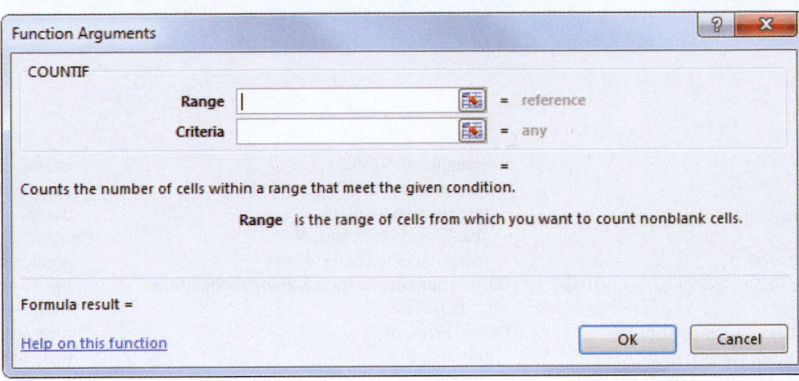

If the function selected (highlighted) is the one we want to use, we click **OK**; the **Function Arguments** dialog box then appears. The Function Arguments dialog box for the COUNTIF function is shown in Figure E.8. This dialog box assists in creating the appropriate arguments (inputs) for the function selected. When finished entering the arguments, we click OK; Excel then inserts the function into a worksheet cell.

Using Excel Add-Ins

Excel's Data Analysis Add-In

Excel's Data Analysis add-in, included with the basic Excel package, is a valuable tool for conducting statistical analysis. Before you can use the Data Analysis add-in it must be installed. To see if the Data Analysis add-in has already been installed, click the Data tab on the Ribbon. In the Analyze group you should see the Data Analysis command. If you do not have an Analyze group and/or the Data Analysis command does not appear in the Analysis group, you will need to install the Data Analysis add-in. The steps needed to install the Data Analysis add-in are as follows:

Step 1. Click the **File** tab
Step 2. Click **Options**
Step 3. When the Excel Options dialog box appears:
  Select **Add-Ins** from the list of options (on the pane on the left)
  In the **Manage** box, select **Excel Add-Ins**
  Click **Go**
Step 4. When the Add-Ins dialog box appears:
  Select **Analysis ToolPak**
  Click **OK**

Index

Essentials of Modern Business Statistics 7e DATAfiles